REX
GERMANORUM,

POPULOS
SCLAVORUM

D1611479

Ivo Vukcevich

REX GERMANORUM, POPULOS SCLAVORUM

AN INQUIRY INTO THE ORIGIN & EARLY HISTORY OF THE SERBS/SLAVS OF SARMATIA, GERMANIA & ILLYRIA

With maps, illustrations, tombstone inscriptions, Indo-Iranian/Serb-Slav glossary, and extended bibliography
(over 2000 entries)

UNIVERSITY CENTER PRESS

Publisher's Cataloging-in-Publication
(Provided by Quality Books, Inc.)

Vukcevich, Ivo.
  Rex Germanorum, populos sclavorum : an inquiry
into the origin & early history of the Serbs/Slavs of
Sarmatia, Germania & Illyria : with maps, illustrations,
tombstone inscriptions, Indo-Iranian/Serb-Slav glossary,
and extended bibliography (over 2000 entries) / Ivo
Vukcevich. – 1st ed.
  p. cm.
  Includes bibliographical references.
  LCCN: 2001116836
  ISBN: 09709319-6-4

  1. Ethnology—Slavic countries. 2. Slavs—History.
3. Slavs—Germany—History. 4. Serbs—History.
5. Slavic countries—History. 6. Slavic languages—
History. I. Title.

DJK27.V85 2001   305.891'8
                           QB101-200488

To the Memory
of my Father and Grandfather

**MIHAILO IVOV VUKCEVICH
IVO DJUROV VUKCEVICH**

*Cetiri su prosla vijeka
i godina nesto vise,
od kako se nasi stari
u Gluhi Do doselise.*

*Ta kitica bjese mala:
sedam brata i rodjaka,
pa se stvori divna ceta
sokolova i junaka.*

CONTENTS

LIST OF ILLUSTRATIONS

LIST OF TOMBSTONE INSCRIPTIONS (MEDIEVAL BOSNIA)

ABBREVIATIONS

The following abbreviations are used in the text, endnotes, and bibliography.

AgO———*Archiv fur Geschichte von Oberfranken*

AiB———*Ausgrabungen In Berlin*

AgT———*Archaologie aus Geschicht-Wissenschaft*

AhL———*Archiv des Vereins fur die Geschichte des Herzogtums Lauenburg*

AiS———*Annales Instituti Slavici*

AnP———*Anzeiger fur Slavische Philologie*

AnT———*Soviet Anthropology and Archaeology*

ApH———*Acta Poloniae Historica*

ArB———*Arbeits und Forschungsberichte zur Sachsiscen Bodendenkmalpflege*

ArC———*Archiv fur Slawische Philologie*

ArP———*Archeologia Polona*

AuF———*Ausgrabungen und Funde*

AuS———*Aus Ur- und Fruhgeschichte*

BaL———*Baltische Studien*

BaM———*Bericht des Historischen Vereins fur die Pflege der Geschichte des ehemaligen Furstbistmus zu Bamberg*

BaP———*Balcanica Posnaniensia*

BeR———*Bericht uber den V. Internationalen Kongress fur Vor- und Fruhgeschichte Hamburg (1958), 1961; Berichte uber den II. Internationalen Kongress fur Slawische Archaologie, 1970.*

BnF———*Beitrage zur Namenforschung*

BuF———*Beitrage zur Ur- und Fruhgeschichte*

ByS———*Byzantinoslavica*

ByV———*Der Bayerische Vorgeschichtsfreund*

ByZ———*Byzantinische Zeitschrift*

BzY———*Byzantion*

CcH———*Ceskoslovensky Casopis Historicky*

CeR———*Cercetari De Linguistica*

CmM———*Casopis Matice Moravske*

CmS———*Casopis Macicy Serbskeje*

CyM———*Cyrillomethodianum*

DaW———*Dawna Kultura*

DiE———*Die Heimat*

DsF	Deutsche-Slawische Forschungen
DwS	Die Welt Der Slaven
EaZ	Ethnographisch Archaologische Zeitschrift
FbP	.Forschungen zur brandenburgischen und preussischen Geschichte
FgB	Fuldaer Geschichtsblatter
FoG	Forschungen zur osteuropaischen Geschichte
FrA	Jahrbuch fur Frankisch Landesforschung
FuF	Forschungen und Forschritte
GgC	Geschicte und Gegenwart des Bezirkes Cottbus
GlA	Glas Serbska Akademija Nauka
GsJ	Griefswald-Stralsunder Jahrbuch
GsL	Germania Slavica
HaR	Zeitschrift des Harzvereins fur Geschichte und Altertumskunde
HmB	Heimatblatter
HmK	Heimatklender
HtB	Heimatbuch
HtZ	Historische Zeitschrift
HuN	Acta Archeologica Academiae Scientarum Hungaricae
HuS	Harvard Ukrainian Studies
InD	The Journal of Indo-European Studies
JbG	Jahrbuch fur die Geshichte Mittle- und Ostdeutschlands
JbK	Jahrbuch fur Kultur und Geschichte der Slaven
JbM	Jahrbuch fur Bodendenkmalpflege Mecklenburg
JbP	Jarbuch fur Heimatkunde des Kreises Plon/Holstein
JbR	Jahrbuch fur Brandenburgische Landesgeschichte
JeZ	Jezyk Polski
JgO	Jahrbucher fur Geschichte Osteuropas
JhR	Jahrbuch des Museums Hohenlllleuben-Reichenfels
JiS	Jahresschrift des Instituts fur sorbische Volksforschung
JmV	Jahresschrift fur mitteldeutsche Vorgeschichte
JuZ	Juznoslovenski Filolog
KoR	Archaologisches Korrespondenzblatt
KwA	Kwartalnik Historyczny
LbH	Lauenburgische Heimat
LgP	Lingua Polski
LpA	Lingua Posnaniensis
LsK	Lubecker Schriften zur Archaologie und Kulturgeschichte
MaG	Neues Lausitzisches Magazin
MaK	Makedonski Jazik
MaR	Markische Heimat
MaT	Materialy zachodnio-pomorske
MbU	Mitteilungen des Bezirks-fachausschusses Ur- und Fruhgeschichte Neubrandenburg.

MdF————*Mitteldeutsche Forschungen*

MgA————*Jahrbucher und Jahresberichte des Vereins fur Mecklenburgische Geschichte und Altertumskunde*

MiT————*Jahressschritte fur Mitteldeutsch*

MvH————*Mittellungen des Vereins fur Erdkunde Halle*

MzB————*Munchner Zeitschrift fur Balkankunde*

NaM————*Namenkundliche Informationen*

NdV————*Nachrichtenblatt fur deutsche Vorzeit*

NeU————*Neues Archiv Fur Sachsische Geschichte*

NiE————*Niederlausitzer Mitteilungen*

NiS————*Niederlausitzer Studien*

NnU————*Nachrichten aus Niedersachsens Urgeschichte*

NuE————*Neue Ausgrabungen und Forschungen*

OnO————*Onomastica*

OnJ————*Onomastica Jugoslavica*

OnP————*Onomastoloski Prilozi*

OsG————*Onomastica Slavogermanica*

OsP————*Oxford Slavonic Papers*

PaM————*Pamietnik Slowianski*

PdZ————*Przeglad Zachodni*

PjB————*Pommersche Jahrbucher*

PoL————*Archaeologia Polski*

PoM————*Unser Pommer*

PrA————*Serbska Pratyka*

PrG————*Przeglad Archeologiczny*

PrZ————*Przeglad Historycany*

PzD————*Przeglad Zachodni*

PzT————*Praehistorische Zeitschrift*

RaP————*Rapports due IIIe Congres International d'Archeologie SlaveBratislava, 1979*

RaT————*Rathenower Heimat Kalender*

ReV————*Revue des Etudes Slaves*

RiC————*Richerche Slavistische*

RoC————*Rocznik Slawistyczny*

RoH————*Roczniki Historiczny*

RoP————*Rozpravy*

RoT————*Rocnik Orientalistyczny*

RuD————*Rudolfstadter Heimathefte*

SaC————*Niedersachsisches Jahrbuch Fur Landesgeschichte*

SaN————*Srbska Akademija Nauka*

SlA————*Slavia Antiqua*

SlG————*Slavica Gandensia*

SlO————*Slavia Occidentalis*

SlV———*Slovenska Archeologia*

SoV———*Sovetskoe Slavjanovedene*

SpL———*Spisy Instituta za Serbski Ludospyt*

SsS———*Slownik Starzytnosci Slowianskich*

StF———*Slavistische Forschungen*

StO———*Studia Onomastica*

StU———*Studia Slavica Academicae Scientarum Hungarica*

SuD———*Sudost-Forschungen*

UrP———*Unser Pommerland*

VbL———*Veroffentlichungen des Brandenburgischen Landesmuseums fur Ur- and Fruhgeschichte 27, 1993.*

VeD———*Slavjanovvedenie*

VjZ———*Voprosy Iazykoznaniia*

VmU———*Veroffentlichungen des Museums fur Ur- und Fruhgeschichte Potsdam*

VoP———*Voprosy Slavianskogo Iazykoznaniia*

VoR———*Nachrichtenblatt fur deutsche Vorzeit*

VpS———*Vznik Z Pocatky Slovanu*

VuK———*Naucni Sastanak Slavista u Vukove Dane*

WiA———*Wiadmosci Archeologiczne*

WiS———*Wissenschaftliche Zetischrifte der Karl Marx-Universitat Leipzig*

WsJ———*Wiener Slavistisches Jahrbuch*

WzH———*Wissenschaftliche Zeitschrift der Humboldt-Universitat Berlin*

WuL———*Wissenschaftliche Zeitschrift der M. Luther-Universitat, Halle-Wittenberg.*

WzJ———*Wissenschaftliche Zeitschrift der Friedrich Schiller-Universitat Jena*

ZaC———*Przeglad Zachodnio-Pomorskie*

ZfO———*Zeitschrift fur Ortsnamenforschung*

ZjA———*Zbornik Historijskog Instituta Jugoslovenske Akademije*

ZgO———*Zgodovinski Casopis*

ZoG———*Zeitschrift fur Osteuropaische Geschichte*

ZoS———*Zeitschrift fur Ostforschung*

ZoW———*Z Otchlani Wiekow*

ZrO———*Studia Zrodlowznawcze*

ZsH———*Zeitschrift der Gesellschaft fur Schleswig-Holsteinische Geschichte*

ZsP———*Zeitschrift fur Slavische Philologie*

ZtA———*Zeitschrift fur Archaologie*

ZtB———*Zeitschrift fur bayerische Landesgeschichte*

ZtG———*Zeitschrift fur Geschichtswissenschaft*

ZtL———*Zeitschrift des Vereins fur thuringische Geschichte und Altertumskunde.*

ZtM———*Zeitschrift fur Archaologie des Mittelalters*

ZtT———*Zeitschrift fur Thuringische Geschichte*

ZtS———*Zeitschrift fur Slawistik*

ZtV———*Zeitschrift des Vereins fur thuringische Geschichte*

A FEW WORDS ABOUT THIS BOOK

This book is not an original work. It is not based on new historical sources. It is not based on new interpretations of old historical sources. From beginning to end it is based on the research of others, on the analysis and commentary of outstanding European scholars.

This book is not and does not pretend to be a definitive work. To the contrary, it is spadework, to use a splendid and appropriate German term. In many instances—e.g. Indo-Iranian roots of Slavic civilization; etymology of the Serb ethnonym; prehistoric *Urheimat* of the Serbs-Slavs; time, place, and circumstances of major migrations and settlements—the spadework barely scratches the surface. More than anything else, it is intended to be a readable, user friendly introduction to the subject and, in spite of its limitations, a useful if wavering baseline for further study.

The chapters are short, outline in form, with step-by-step sentence/paragraphs and subheadings. The extensive bibliography serves several purposes. One, to identify sources of information. Two, to give the reader an idea of the scope, depth, and quality of research on the subject. Three, to suggest the many important and substantive ways the subject relates to the prehistory and early history of Europe. Four, by identifying the major research topics and issues, to stimulate interest, and encourage further research. As to the absence of language/linguistic marks, I defer to J.P. Mallory: **A certain graphic simplicity for linguistic forms is necessitated because too many diacritical marks, necessary though they may be for the proper articulation and analysis of the forms, have a way of terrifying a general reader. Those linguists who will immediately know what is missing will, I am sure, restore the vowel lengths, accents, and other necessary diacritics** *(In Search of Indo-Europeans, 1989).*

ACKNOWLEDGMENTS

Given the nature of this work, its thoroughly derivative character, its reliance on German historical scholarship in particular, the general and special acknowledgments are less a polite and dutiful formality and more an important and necessary recognition of the many scholars who are in very important ways coauthors in fact if not in form. The author owes more than he can say to generations of German historians, of countless inquiries into the early history and settlement of *Germania* that include not only singular and invaluable information on the early social, political, and cultural history of the Slavs, but also generous recognition of their positive role in the formation of the German nation and Germany's history and civilization.

———— • ————

Ernst Eichler
Joachim Herrmann
Heinrich Kunstmann

The German connection is especially strong in the case of the *Serbs/Wends*. Medieval *Germania* sources and German scholars have contributed immensely important information relating to the earliest recorded settlements and history of the *Serbs/ Wends* in Pomerania, Prussia, Mecklenburg, Schleswig-Holstein, Hanover Wendland,

Saxony, Thuringia, Franconia, Bavaria, and Bohemia.

In more recent times, special acknowledgments are in order for E. Eichler, J. Herrmann, and H. Kunstmann. Thanks to old school dedication, integrity, and command of the positive record and historical context, Eichler and Herrmann have raised the level of academic inquiry to its highest moral-intellectual standards and established new boundaries and guidelines for legitimate discussion of the subject. H. Kunstmann deserves special commendation for his informed, insightful, and explorative inquiries into the time, place, and circumstance of the origin not only of *Germanis'a Serbs/Wends*, but also the origin of the Slavs of neighboring and distant lands.

Indeed, the individual and collective contributions are so deep and broad, so rich in archaeological, historical, and onomastic fact and commentary, a thorough review of the scholarship of Eichler, Herrmann, and Kunstmann may very well be a necessary first step in any serious inquiry into the origin and early history of the Serbs/Slavs.

———————— • ————————

This study, as it relates to the *Germania* Serbs, and the Western Slavs generally, would be impossible without the immense contributions of generations of Czech, Slovak, and Polish scholars, from J. Dobrovsky, W. Ketrzynski, J. Kollar, J. Lelewel, F. Palacki, J. Rozwadowski, W. Surowiecki to Z. Golab, L. Havlik, W. Hensel, G. Labuda, T. Lehr-Splawinski, T. Lewicki, H. Lowmianski, L. Moszynski, L.Niederle, J. Otrebski, L. H. Popowska-Taborska, J. Strzelczyk, T.Wasilewski, J. Widajewicz, and many others.

Mention must also be made that this study, as it relates to the origin, history, and institutions of the *Illyria* Serbs, and the South Slavs generally, owes a special debt to, among many others, such pioneers as V. Bogisic, V. Jagic, J. Jirecek, V. Karadzic, V. Klaic, I. Kukuljevic-Sakcinski, S. Ljubic, F. Miklosic, N. Nodilo, P. Safarik, F. Racki, P. Rovinski, F. Sisic, and T. Smiciklas. Numerous Yugoslav scholars also deserve mention, including: N. Banasevic, F. Barisic, I. Bozic, M. Budimir, S. Cirkovic, V. Corovic, J. Cvijic, M. Dinic, B. Ferjancic, J. Ferluga, M.S. Filipovic, B. Grafenauer, P. Ivic, P. Mijovic, S. Mijuskovic, S. Novakovic, G. Ostrogorski, N. Radojicic, R. Samardzic, P. Skok, G. Skrivanic, D. Srejovic, S. Stanojevic, L. Stojanovic, J. Vukmanovic, and N. Zupanic. R. Novakovic's recent studies relating to the origin and early history of the Serbs are inexhaustible sources of information and invaluable guides to European literature on the subject.

———————— • ————————

Special acknowledgements are also in order for the incomparable energy and immense scholarship of Marija Gimbutas, who singlehandedly transformed our understanding of European prehistory and Old European Civilization.

I. SERBS ARE SVARS ARE SERBS?

For more than several centuries questions relating to the origin and meaning of the ethnonyms **Slav** and **Serb** (also *Sarb/Sarbski, Ser/Serski, Sur/Surski*) have attracted the attention of outstanding scholars and generated a rich body of literature on the subject in Continental Europe. In more recent times, the subject has been rather overwhelmed and somewhat degraded by research relating to Indo-European origins.

Regarding this moment, J.P. Mallory, the author of the best English-language survey of Indo-European scholarship, writes:

> **The quest for the origins of the Indo-European has all the fascination of an electric light in the open air on a summer night: it tends to attract every species of scholar or would-be savant who can take pen to hand. It also shows a remarkable ability to mesmerize even scholars of outstanding ability to wander far beyond the realm of reasonable speculation to provide yet another example of academic lunacy. It is sobering to recall that one of the greatest prehistorians of this century, V. Gordon Childe, dismissed his own researches into Indo-European origins as among the most childish things he wrote** *(In Search of Indo-Europeans, 1989).*

Indeed, Childe's attempt to impose a *Pax Nordica* of sorts on European prehistory by tracing the origin of the Indo-Europeans to a Nordic/North European cradle is certainly one of his more childish moments. Childe writes: **Having then agreed that the original Aryan belonged essentially to the Nordic race ... it remains to localize the cradle land ... At the present moment the Scandinavian theory is the most attractive, having been expounded with a wealth of detail and a complete mastery of the archaeological data by such profound students as Kossina, Schliz and Schuchardt** *(V. Gordon Childe, The Aryans, 1987).*

Relatively recent efforts to resolve the issues from a purely linguistic/etymological perspective—in terms of theoretical linguistic constructs (Proto-Slavic, Proto-Indo-European reconstructions) coupled with **ethereal theorizing based on guesswork about the etymologies of miscellaneous place names and allusions in heterogeneous sources to ethnonyms**—have sometimes added new levels of insight and understanding, but almost always new levels of speculation, complexity, and learned eccentricity *(H.G. Lunt, The Rus' Primary Chronicle, HuS 19, 1995).* While the linguistic/etymological theories have a certain contemporary primacy in the entirely theoretical Proto-Indo-European context, in the case of the historical ethnonym **Serb,** the interdisciplinary method, analytical frameworks with the highest integration of historical, textual, onomastic, and linguistic evidence, is better suited to the problem and provides a relatively firm and suggestive empirical basis for further research.

For such reasons, given the established Indo-Iranian dimensions of Proto-Slavic civilization, the established historical, textual, onomastic, and linguistic facts of the matter, this section focuses on mythological-religious **Proto-Slav/Serb** links with Indo-Iranian based languages and civilizations. Without guilt or remorse, therefore, we begin with a highly speculative, exploratory review of some of the historical-linguistic evidence that appears to relate the ethnonyms **Sarb/Surb/Srb** to **Svar**, an ancient, cardinal Indo-Iranian word connoting heaven, sky, sun, light, and fire, to cognates connoting creation, universe, all, everything:

—To Svar as in Isvara, 'supreme lord and originator'; Isvara, 'immanent deity'; Svar, 'heaven'; Svar-gapat, 'lord and creator of heaven and earth'; Svarga, 'lord Indra's Heaven'; Svargadvara, 'gates of heaven'; Svargakama, 'desire for heaven'; Svargaloka, 'world of heaven'; Svarupa, 'nature,' 'essence'; Svarupa-jnana, 'divine knowledge.'

—To Svar as in Sur-ya, the most concrete of the solar deities: from Sur-ya, 'the orb of the sun,' 'the face of the great Agni,' 'the eye of Mitra and [S]Varuna,' 'the lord of eyes', 'the farseeing, all-seeing god who beholds all beings and the good and bad deeds of mortals.'

Also: Ardhanarisvara, 'androgynous godhead'; Atmesvara, 'lord of the soul'; Govsesvara, 'lord of the cows and bulls'; Mahesvara, 'maternal goddess'; Padapesvara, 'lord of trees'; Paramesvara, 'highest lord'; Sarevesvara, 'supreme lordship'; [S]Varuna, 'supreme god of early Vedism, creator of the three worlds, heaven, earth and air'; Vasisvarana, 'sacred fire'; Visvarupadarshana, 'supreme principle'; Visesvara, 'lord of the universe'; Yogisvara, 'supreme saint.'

SURS, SARBS

It should be noted that there is in historical fact a certain precedent for a **Sur**-based **Sarb** ethnonym in Indo-Iranian history. Regarding the origin of one of the great tribes of Afghanistan, a leading authority writes: **The Vais are the Surs (Surajbansi) or Surya (Suryavansi), the 'solar race of Hindustan' and the Sarbs (Sarbanri) or Sarabs (Sarabani) in the Afghan classification of tribes.** Similarly, a major division of the Ismail Afghan tribal complex is called the **Surs** and a minor division the **Sarbs** or **Sarbis** (H.W. Bellew, An Inquiry into the Ethnography of Afghanistan, 1891).

SARVAS, SARBS

Moreover, from a strictly linguistic/etymological perspective, O.N. Trubacev, one of the foremost Linguists/Slavists of the modern era, believes it is possible to derive the **Serb** ethnonym from Old Indo-European **sarva** connoting all, everything, everyone. Since Trubacev's (theoretical) Old Indo-European **sarva** is related to (factual) Indo-Iranian **svar**, Old Indo-European **sarva** appears to be either a roundabout way of deriving **Serb** from **Svar** or a giant etymological step in that direction.

———————— • ————————

EUROPEAN HISTORY

The notion that the Serb ethnonym is derived from *Svar* has deep roots in European historical scholarship. Medieval German documents record that some Serb tribes settled in Germania were called *Svars.* Naming the ancient Serb tribe that settled along the Mulde near Leisnig, citing local sources, a 16ᵗʰ century German historian mentions the *Svars:* **Svarini oder Svardones oder Svordi.**[1] In the same period, another German historian and commentator on Tacitus's Germania, E. Stella, is certain that: **Tacitus's Svars or Svarines are not only Serbs, but Serbs who retained their ancient and original name.**[2]

SVARTOV, TRAVA RIVERS

More concrete evidence of the ancient and original name in Germania is found in place names, hydronyms, and toponyms derived from Svar. Medieval sources, for example, locate Lubeck at the confluence of the Svartov and Trava rivers. Also: Svartava, northeast of Sorby and Sorbino, southeast of Perun; Svartebok, near Ratmir, Crnobog, and Drazevo; Svartava River, near Klecov, Goleska, and Penica; Svartav, near Lubici and Radkov; Svartov, northwest of Svetla Strana; Lake Svartica, northeast of Babica, Dobra, Draze, and Rogolin; Zuarina grad, northeast of Zverin, modern Schwerin.[3]

SVAR, SVAROG

It was well-known to medieval German chroniclers that the Serbs were **Svars** in a primal, religious sense—the people of **Svar, Svaroh, Svarog, Svarozic,** the Supreme God, Lord and Creator, the God of the Shining Sky, who reigns supreme over Heaven and Earth, the Lord and Master of the Universe.[4]

BOG SVAROG

It is important to note that the letter and spirit of the Serb-Slavic word for god, *bog,* as in *bog* Svar or Svarog, as well as its material cognates (*bogat,* rich; *bogatstvo,* wealth) are also derived from the Indo-Iranian tradition.[5]

BHAGA, BAGA

The Sanskrit root is bhaj, to share, distribute. Thus bhaga (Iranian baga): 'the celestial dispenser of good fortune and prosperity'; baga, 'he who distributes good things'; bhaga, 'god of good fortune'; bhagesa, 'lord of happiness'; bhagwan, 'supreme god who created other gods and made them bearers of light'; bhagyam, 'fortune'; saubhagy, 'good luck'; subhaga, 'blessed'; bhoga, 'delight'; upabhoga, 'enjoyment'. Also the 'divine one' as in *Bhagavad Gita* (*Song of the Divine One*); Bhagavan, 'the noble, holy, exalted, and sublime one'; Savita Bhaga, 'the sun god'.

BOGISLAV

In medieval Germania *bog/bozh* is a common element of Slavic personal (Bogislav, Bogolub), family (Bogovici, Bozkovici, Bozov), and Germania place names (Bogumil, later Bomsdrof; Bozetin, later Bozetindorf; Bozici, later Positz). Also Bogumysl, now Bademeusel, and Myslbog, now Meuselwitz.

REGEM EORUM BOZ NOMINE

It is a matter of record that Bog as Bozh is a favored name of early Slavic rulers. In the early 4th century, for example, Bozh is recorded as the ruler of the mighty Antes (***regem eorum Boz nomine***). Several centuries later, a *tsar Bozh* is said to rule over the Antes lands.

THE ALL POWERFUL ONE

Helmold of Bosau, a Saxon cleric who lived in the region of Lubeck around 1170, was an especially keen if not impartial observer of the pagan Slavs. Helmold's *Chronica Slavorum* offers a rather clear and precise statement of ***Svarog's*** supremacy and relation to other gods in the Slavic pantheon: **Svarog was the one god in the heavens ruling over all others. They hold that the all powerful one looks after heavenly matters only; that the others, discharging the duties assigned to them in obedience to him, proceeded from his blood; and that one excels the other in the measure that he is nearer to the god of gods.**

THE SLAV DELPHI

In Bishop Thietmar's chronicle *(Chronicon)* there is a first hand account of ***Svarog's*** temple at **urbs Radogost** in *pago Riedierun,* the great sanctuary of the Slavs, the Slav Delphi: **The triangular, three-gated citadel of Radegast is situated in the Redarii district. The fortress stands in the middle of a great forest regarded by the natives as sacrosanct. Two of the gates are open to all. The third and smallest, to the east, faces a path leading to a neighboring lake of most gloomy aspect. The citadel contains but a single shrine, a wooden structure built upon a foundation of the horns of various animals. Its walls are decorated on the outside, so far as can be seen, with a number of finely carved images of gods and goddesses. Inside the shrine stands a number of man-made idols, each with its incised name, in full armour, terrifying to view. The tallest is called Svarozich and is much feared and revered by the heathens. Their standards are also kept there, only to be removed in case of war and then by foot-soldiers exclusively. Every district in the country has a temple of its own, worshiped by the infidels, but the citadel just mentioned is the most important. The tribesmen take leave of it when they march to war and offer it suitable gifts ... if they return victorious.**[6]

An eminent modern authority on the period, J.W. Thompson, writes of the temple's immense authority throughout Germania: **Upon its wall hung the colored banners of every Slavonic tribe between the Erzgebirge and the Baltic, and the trophies of victorious wars. The priests of Retra cast omens before every campaign. With them lay the final determination of war and peace** *(Feudal Germany, 1928).*[7]

ENDNOTES

[1] E. Brotuff, Chronica von den Salz-Bornen und Erbauung der Stadt Hall an der Sala in Sachsen gelegen, 1554.

[2] E. Stella, De rebus ac populis orae inter Albim et Salam Germaniae flumina, in Erasmus Stella und dessen non erst ans Licht tretende Commentarii, 1773.

[3] Some scholars see a possible connection between Svar and Old Slavic roots relating to matter, being, creator, and creation, namely the modern Serb words *tvorac, tvoriti, tvorivo, stvor, stvorac, stvoriti* (J. Otrebski, Slav. Svarog, DwS

16, 1971). Also: P.J. Safarik, O Svarhovi, bohu pohanskych Slovanu, Casopis 18, 1844. V. Shaian, Naivysche svitlo; studia pro Svaroga i Khorsa, 1969. J. Knebel, Na sledach swjatnicow Swarozica a Svjatowita, PrA, 1969. A. Baiburin, K vostochnoslavianskim danny o Svaroge, Slavica Hierosolymitana 5-6, 1981.

[4] There is mounting archaeological evidence that the God of the Shining Sky was the original god of all Indo-Europeans. According to M. Gimbutas, the Indo-European and their religious beliefs entered Europe in the second half of the 4th millenium B.C. **The new religion was oriented toward the rotating sun and other sky phenomena such as thunder and lightning. Their sky gods shone as 'bright as the sky.'** Thus **the most frequently recorded symbols of the Indo-European religion are the solar groups: the radiating sun, the circle on either side of the radiating sun, the double and spiral pendants, and the breast plate (a semicircle of multiple concentric lines) ... To the specialist in comparative Indo-European mythology, such combinations of symbols will certainly recall the image of the God of the Shining Sky, who bestows progeny and promotes vegetation. This deity is known in various Indo-European groups from early historic records and is still extant in folklore ... This god is associated with morning and daylight, and with the spring, summer, autumn, and winter sun. His powers are transmitted by his weapon; by his animals, the stag and horse; by the shining vehicle in which he travels. As protector of vegetation he is associated with his pair of oxen and with plowing** (The Civilization of the Goddess, 1991).

[5] Regarding the 'essentially dualistic, even polytheistic' religion of the ancient and modern Germania Serbs, Professor G.C. Engerrand writes: **Dualism is everywhere ... When the Wendish peasant calls bread "God's bread" (Boze Khleb) and wheat "God's wheat" (Boze Zito) ... When he refers to the sun, lightning, the storm, the wind, etc., as God's he bows to God's power** (The So-Called Wends Of Germany And Their Colonies In Texas And In Australia, 1934). The following are some of the many 'divine' cognates of the Serb *bog: bogoljubje* (love of God); *bogomolje* (place of worship); *Bogorodica* (mother of God); *bogoslovje* (theology); *bogostovan* (pious); *bogoveran* (faithful to God). Also: *bozanski* (Godlike); *bozanstvo* (God; *bozji* (divine).

[6] The earliest German sources correctly identify Svarozic as the chief god of the Redari at Radigost. In a 1008 letter to Emperor Henry II, for example, St. Bruno, the Apostle of Prussia, identifies Svarozic as the god of gods at Radigost: ***quomodo convenirunt Zuarisiz diabolus et dux sanctorum.*** Later sources tend to confuse god with city and identify Svarozic as Radigost. Helmold, for example, sometimes refers to Svarozic as Radigost: ***quo barbari conto prefigentes in titulum victorie Deo suo Radigasto immolaverunt; Radigast deus terra Obotritorum.*** K.A. Jenc, Rhetra a Radegast, Luzican 1, 1864. L. Niederle, Arkona, Rhethra, Redigast, Slavia 2, 1923-24. W. Karbe, Arkona-Rethra-Vineta, ZtS 2, 1925. T. Witkowski, Der Name der Redarier und ihres zentralen Heiligtums, ZtS 13, 1968.

[7] The following sources offer interesting information on the pagan beliefs of the Slavs of Germania and Sarmatia: two 11th century sources: Thietmar of Merseburg's Chronicon and Adam of Bremen's Gesta Hammaburgensis); Three mid-12th century biographies of Otto of Bamberg (1060-1139), the Apostle of Pomerania; Helmold of Bosau (1120-1170), Chronica Slavorum; Olfa Thordarson (1212-1259), Knylingasaga; Saxo Grammaticus (1150-1204), Gesta Danorum. Of course, the eyewitness accounts of Christian observers and commentators, it is important to note, are distorted by a strong Christian bias, not to mention a deadly, crusading hostility. Indeed, Christian accounts should always be read with an old Latin maxim in mind: ***Pietas obtenditur, Aurum quaeritur*** (Religion is the pretext, Gold is the object).

2. JAROVID, SVETIVID, TRIGLAV

var, the supreme god, was known by other names. Some of these names were related to an essential activity or function. Thus the war god *Jar* or *Jarovid,* cognates of *Svar,* recorded by German chroniclers in the 12th century: **Deum suum Gerovitum; Cuisudam idoli Geroviti nomine celebritatem agebat; Gerovito, qui deus milicie eorum fuit; In Hologosta civitate ... deo suo Gerovito dicitur.**[1]

VOLIGOST

Soon after entering the town of Voligost, Otto, the Apostle of Pomerania, entered a great temple dedicated to *Jarovid,* where, Herbord writes: **There was hanging on the wall a shield of great size and of marvelous workmanship, covered with sheets of gold, which no human might touch, because in it was something sacrosanct and which betokened their pagan religion, so that it would never be moved out of its place save only in time of war. For, as we afterwards found, it was dedicated to their god Gerovit, who in Latin is called Mars, and the people were confident of success in every battle in which it went before them.**

HAVELBERG

There is good evidence that *Jarovid* was alive and well in the early 12thcentury and that there were temples dedicated to *Jarovid* throughout the lands of the Slavs, including Havelburg on the Havel River. To Otto's great distress, Havelburg had been **so completely ruined by the incursions of the heathen that there remained in it hardly anyone who bore the Christian name. On the very day of his [Otto's] arrival flags were placed around the town, which was engaged in celebrating a festival in honour of an idol called Gerovit. When the man of God perceived this, he was pricked to the heart on account of the great delusion of its people and refused to enter the walls of the town.**

CHRISTIAN SYMPATHY

It is interesting that Thietmar of Merseburg's account of a pagan Slav assault on Christian missionary stations at Havelberg and Brandenburg in the very late 10th century suggests a noticeable degree of Christian sympathy for such attacks on Christian sanctuaries and images. **The revolt started with the murder of garrison troops at Havelberg and the destruction of the episcopal see. The days after the attack a group of Slavic rebels assaulted Brandenburg's diocese ... The priests were taken prisoners ... All of the church treasures were stolen, and blood covered the grounds. Where Christ and his disciple, Saint Peter, once stood, cults of diabolical superstitions were established; a sad change, which not only pagans but also some Christians welcomed.**

JAROMIR, JARINA GRAD

Medieval sources reveal numerous personal and family names derived from *Jar* in Germania (e.g. Jarobud, Jarognev, Jarosin, Jaromir, Jaroslav). Medieval sources also reveal numerous place names, including fortified settlements, derived from *Jar* in Germania east and west of the Elbe: Jargolin; Jarichovo grad; Jarina grad; Jarisin; Jarkovici; Jarkovo; Jarkun grad; Jarognev; Jarochol grad; Jarochov; Jarom; Jaromir; Jaromirici;

Jaronici; Jaroslav; Jarosin; Jarosov; Jarovec; Jarovici.[2]

SVAR, JAR, ZAR

From **Svar/Jar** the Serb words *jar*, as in *jarko sunce* or radiant sun, and *jarost*, connoting intense, scorching, torrid heat, fire. Also the words *zar, zarenje, zariti, zarki, zarkost*, connoting heat, warmth, brightness, glowing, red-hot fire. Like *jar*, *zar* is also the root of numerous place names recorded in medieval Germania (e.g. Zar, Zargom, Zarchom, Zarice, Zarkim, Zarnovica, Zarov, Zary, Zarno).

SVAR, SVETI VID

Other names relate to *Svar's* supreme attributes. Thus **Svar** is **Sveti Vid,** the **lord of eyes, the far-seeing, all-seeing god, who beholds all beings and the good and bad deeds of mortals.** Saxo Grammaticus' *Gesta Danorum* is an important source of detailed information on the legendary **Sveti Vid** (**Zvantevit**) cult centre at Arkona on the Baltic island of Rugen.[3] A Danish monk, Saxo, took part in a crusading expedition against the pagan Slavs of Rugen in 1168 and witnessed the destruction of **Sveti Vid's** temple. **In the temple stood an enormous statue, taller than any human form, with four heads and necks, which lent it a somewhat terrifying appearance. Two looked ahead, and two behind, one faced the right, and another the left. The moustache was shaven, and the hair cut in deliberate imitation of the style usually affected by the Rani [Rugenites]. In its right hand it held a horn, fashioned in a variety of precious metals ... The left hand was supported against its side as if the arm were bent. The robe fell to the calves, which were of a different wood, and at the knee was a joint that you would fail to see unless you looked very closely. The feet were at ground level, for the pedestal was buried in the earth. To one side you could see the bit, saddle, and various insignia; a sword of extraordinary size increased the wonder of it all, and the admirable work on sheath and hilt enhanced the intrinsic value of the silver.**

OMNI NATIONE SCLAVORUM

The **Sveti Vid** cult's pan-Slav character is noted by Helmold in the following words: *Zvantevit deus terre Rugianorum inter omnia numina Sclavorum primataum obtinuerit; et fecit prudci simuachrum illud antiquissimum Zvantevith, quod colebaturt ab omni natione Sclavorum.*

SVETOVID, SVETOVIT

In his excellent survey of the abundant empirical evidence relating to the scope and depth of **Sveti Vid's** influence on South Slavic religious civilization (e.g. **Svetovid, Svetovit**), P. Simunovic also finds evidence of a significant medieval political moment— the names of medieval Slavic rulers.[4] **Iako se primanjem krscanstva kult slavenskog bozanstva Svetovit upleo u kult sv. Vida, ostavivsi name pokoje onomasticke i folklorne preztike, ne moze se zanijekati i ne uzeti i obzir u tvorbi nekih od navedenih imena slavenski imenski korijen vit-/-vit. kojji je u imenu bozanstva Svetovit(b), u imenu kneza posavske Hrvatske Ljudevita (817-825), u davno potvrdenim imenima: Dragovit, Trebevit, Dobrovit (11. st.), Vitomir (9 st.), Vitogoj (10. st.), Vitina (10. st.), u kojima vit- /-vit znaci "dominus", "potens", "mogucnik", kako su to vec davno istrazili istaknuti slavenski onomasticari. Sventovit je, dakle,** "gospodar svjetla", Ljudevit je "vladar ljudi". Korijen vit-/vit- u takvim dvodjelnim imenima pretezito sadrzava prvotno slavensko, a ne kasnije, latinsko leksicko znacenje koje ju u imenu sv. Vita/Vida. Ko kao sto se u puckim predodzbama slavenski poganski, sventovitski kult nerazmrsivo spleo s krscanskim, vidovskim kultom, tako se to zbilo i s oblicima imena Vit/Vid u koje se neprepoznatljivo stopili leksicki i onomasticki sadrzaj.

SVAR, TRIGLAV

The same essential attributes are found in *Svar* as *Triglav,* the three-headed all-seeing and all-knowing god of the past, present, and future: *Triglav, deus summo paganorum, Trigelaus dicatus,* the supreme lord and originator of all on, below, and above the earth *(K.A. Jenc, Priboh Triglav, Luzican 1, 1854).* As late as the mid-12th century great temples dedicated to *Triglav* were active in the Havelburg-Berlin-Brandenburg region and the Stettin-Volin region in western Pomerania: *Trigla Slavis triceps est Stetinensium olim ac Brandenburgensium aliorumque locorum idolum.*

IN CIVITAS ANTIQUISSIMA ET NOBILISSIMA

German chroniclers, namely Ebbo and Herbord, give the following facts and details about *Triglav's* temple in ancient and noble Stetin, in *civitas antiquissima et nobilissima in terra Pomeranorum: Stetin, vero amplissima civitas et maior Julin [Volin] tres montes ambitu suo conclusos habebat, quorum medius, qui et alcior, summo paganorum deo Trigelawo dicatus, tricapitum habebat simulacrum, quod aurea cidari oculos et labia contegebat, asserentibus idolorum sacerdotibus ideo summum deum tria habere capita, quoniam tria procuraret regna, id est coeli, ter-rae et inferni, et faciem cidari operiri pro eo quod peccata hominum, quasi non videns et tacens, dissimularet (Ebbo); Erat autem [in civitate Stetinensi] ibi simulacrum triceps, quod in uno corpore tria capite habens Triglaus vocabatur; quod solum accipiens, ipsa capitella sibi cohaerentia, corpore comminuto, secum inde quasi pro trophaeo asportavit, et postea Romam pro agrumento conversionis transimit (Herbord).*

PERSONIFICATION OF THE SKY

The noted Russian scholar A. N. Afanasiev sums up *Svarog* in the following terms: **Svarog, as a personification of the sky, sometimes lighted by the sun's rays, sometimes covered with clouds, and brilliant with lightning, was considered to be the father of the sun and of fire. In the shadows of the clouds he would kindle the lightning's flame and thus he appeared as the creator of celestial fire. As for terres-trial fire, it was a divine gift brought to Earth in the form of lightning. Hence it will be understood why the Slavs worshiped Fire as a son of Svarog.**[5]

IMPARTING LIFE TO THE SUN

Regarding *Svarog's* relation to the Slav solar cult, Afanasiev writes: **Afterwards, splitting the clouds with flashing arrows, Svarog would cause the sun to appear, or in the metaphorical language of antiquity, he would light the torch of the sun which had been extinguished by demons of the shadows. This poetic conception was also applied to the morning sun emerging from the veils of night. With the sunrise and the renewal of its flame the idea of its rebirth was connected.**

HIGHER TRUTH

Even today, it should be noted, some would go so far as to say that then and now a solar cult represents a higher truth. On this point, Lloyd M. Graham writes: **A sun is a cosmic crucible in which that cross called matter is made, in other words, a transmuter of cosmic energy—a fact known thousands of years ago and reduced to myth: 'Prometheus was the first to transmute atoms fit for human clay.' Prometheus, who stole fire from heaven and brought it down to Earth, is but a solar fire personified. Here the fire is imprisoned in matter. This is 'Prometheus Bound.' When released by radiation it is 'Prometheus Unbound' ... All this the ancients knew and left to the world in what we call the 'Ancient Wisdom'** (L. M. Graham, Deceptions and Myths of the Bible, 1975).

NOT THE WORD OF GOD

According to this view, the Judaeo-Christian theology is nothing more than a garbled perversion of ancient wisdom and cosmic truths: **The Bible is not 'the word of God,' but stolen from pagan sources. Its Eden, Adam, and Eve were taken from the Babylonian accounts; its Flood or Deluge is but an epitome of some four hundred flood accounts; its Ark and Ararat have their equivalents in a a score of Deluge myths; even the names of Noah's sons are copies; so also Isaac's sacrifice, Solomon's judgment, and Samson's pillar act; Moses is fashioned after the Syrian Mises; its laws after Hammurabi's code. Its Messiah is derived from the Egyptian Mahdi, Savior, certain verses are verbatim copies of Egyptian scriptures. Between Jesus and the Egyptian Horus, Gerald Massey found 137 similarities, and those between Christ and Krishna run into the hundreds.**

By confusing the laws of nature, the Creation process, with the will of God, Graham believes, the Judaeo-Christian theology confuses Hell with Heaven. Thus he writes: **God wills it! God wills it! is the cry of every mass murderer on record.**

ENDNOTES

[1] P.S. Efimenko, O Iarile, iazycheskom bozhevstve russkikh slavian, 1969. M. Rudnicki, Bostwa lechickie: Jarovit, Nyja, Swietowit, Trzglow, JeZ 50, 1970.

[2] K. Jenc, Priboh Swjatowit a jeho rozimanje w lece 1168, Luciczan 3, 1860. T. Reyman, Posag Swiatowida, ZoW 8, 1933. G. Vernadsky, Svantevit, dieu les slaves Baltiques, Annuaire 7, 1933-34. P. Kurinnyi, Sviatovit, Vyzolnyi shliakh 6, 1954. E. Dyggve, Der slawische Viermastenbau auf Ruegen, beobachtungen aus dem Swantewittempel des Saxo-Grammaticus, Germania 37, 1959. H. Berelkamp, Badania grodu Swiatowita, ZoW 37, 1971. J. Rosen-Przeworska, Sur la genese de "Swiatowid" deite slave a quater visages, ArP 13, 1972. S. Bukowski, Swiatynia-Swiatowida-jak mogla wygladac, ZoW 40, 1974. H. Mueller, Vor 1000 Jahren: Tieropfer fuer den Slawengott Swantewit, Urania 9, 1975. J. Filipowiak, Swiatowit z Wolina, ZoW 41, 1975.

[3] A. Haas, Slawische Kultstaeten aud den Inseln Ruegen, Pommersche Jb 19; Arkona in Jahre 1146, 1925. W. Krabe, Arkona-Rehtra-Vineta, ZtS 2, 1925. K. Schuchhardt, Arkona, Rethra, Vineta, 1926. A.G. Krueger, Rethra und Arkona, die slawistischen Heiligtuemer in Deutschland, Germanien 9, 1936. J. Knebel, Arkona. Poslednja pohanska swatnica zapadnych Slowjanow znici so pred 800 letiami, PrA 1970. J. Osieglowski, Wyspa slowianskich bogov, 1971. J. Herrmann, Arkona auf Ruegen, ZtA 8, 1974. L. Ellis, Reinterpretations of the West Slavic cult site in Arkona, InD 6, 1978.

[4] P. Simunovic, Osobono Ime Vid, MaK XL-XLI, 1989-90 (**Osobno ime Vid rasprostranjeno je na cjelokupnom slavenskom prostoru. Posluzilo je motiviom mnogobrojnom antroponimijskih i toponimijskih likova. Ime Vid smatram i prezitkom kulta slavenskog bozanstva Sventovita, koji se po slavenskom pokrstavanju stopio s kultom svetoga Vida. Izvedenica toga imena nalzi se i u makedonskom prezimenu — Vidoeski**). With regard to an important solar folkloric Vid- moment he writes: **Nadojamo jos kako se na Vidovdan posvecuju izvori prije sunca, te se umiva vodom u koju je bacena biljka vidocica. Tada se okrecu suncu i govore: "Vide, Vidovdane, sto ocima vidio, to rukama stvorio!"** It is perhaps more than medieval politics or coincidence that Sveti Vid/Vit as St. Vitus is the patron saint of Bohemia, that Prague's cathedral church is dedicated to Sveti Vid ('Svetago Vita'), that it is the church of national record: **i vlozi Bog v srdce sozda chram svetago Vita ne zle mysle; i poslav slugi prinese telo brato sovego Veceslava iz Boleslavle grada k slavnoumu grade Praze ... i polozisa i v crkvi svetago Vita** (The First Life of St. Wenceslas).

[5] A.N. Afanasev, Poeticeskija vozzrenija slavjan na prirodu. Opyt sravnitelnago izucenija slavjanskich predanij i verovanij v svjai z mifisceskihm skazanijami drugich rodstvennych narodow, I-III, 1865-69. A. Bruckner, Mitologja slowianska, 1918. F. Ledic, Mitologia slavena, I-II, 1969-70. B. Gediga, Sladami religi praslowian, 1976. A. Gieysztor, Mitologia Slowian, 1982. F. Kmietowicz, Slavic Mythical Beliefs, 1982. L. Moszynski, Die vorchristliche Religion der Slaven im Lichte der slavischen Sprachwissenschaft, 1992. B.Z. Rybakov, Mify Drevnikh Slavian, 1993. A.S. Famintsyn, Bozhestva drevnikh slavian, 1995. N.I. Tolstoi, Iazyk i narodnaia kultura: ocherki po slavianskoi mifologii i ethnolingvistike, 1995.

Pagan Temple (Gross Raden)

3. CELE NASE POHANSKE
BAGESLOVI INDICKE GEST: PURAN/PERUN

Access to ancient Sanskrit texts in early 19th century Europe shed new light on the origin and character of ancient Slavic mythology. Successive studies appeared to reveal deeper and broader connections with ancient India and Iran, so much so that it was hard to escape the idea that ancient Slavic civilization shared a common ancestry with ancient Indo-Iranian civilization. Thus the dramatic conclusion reached by J. Kollar (1798-1852), the great Slovak poet, scholar, and Slavist, in an essay on commonalities and parallels in Indian and Slavic mythology *(Srovnalost Indice a Slavske Mythologie)*: Cele nase pohanske bageslovi indice gest (Our entire pagan religious mythology is Indic in origin and character).[1]

In the Vedic system, the various gods are not separate entities, but merely aspects of the supreme lord and creator, manifestations of the immanent deity.

INDRA

Lord Indra, a name perhaps related to proto-Slav *jendru* or *jedru* (strong), was an immensely popular manifestation. Some scholars find traces of **Perun** in Indra's predecessor, [S]Varun, an earlier Indo-Iranian sky-god of rain and storm and protector of oaths.[2] From his role as God of war and storms, the cognomens Puran-dara (destroyer of cities); Paran-ya (thunderbolt), and mighty Indra (thousand-testicled Indra or sahasramuska), the main subject of early Vedic hymns.[3]

ASPECTS OF THE SUPREME LORD AND CREATOR

The same is true of the pagan Slav system. Here, too, the gods are aspects of the Supreme Lord and Creator; they are manifestations of the universal causality. Here, too, lord **Perun,** the god of war and storms, is a popular and powerful manifestation of the Slav god of gods, **Svarog.**[4] Thus it is not surprising that in a mid-6th century work, commenting on the religion of the Slavs, Procopius identifies **Svarog** in terms of **Perun's** attributes: **They in fact regard one god, the creator of lightning, as the lord and master of the universe; they sacrifice oxen and other animals to him** *(De Bellis Gothico).*[5]

PRIMARY CHRONICLE

Later sources affirm **Perun's** central position in the pagan Slav hierarchy. **Perun** is a prominent figure in the most ancient Russian chronicle, best known as the *Nacalnaja Letopis* or *Primary Chronicle*. According to the *Chronicle,* **Perun** is the primary guarantor of treaties between Kievan Russia and Byzantium in the 10th century.

GRAND PRINCE OLEG

Following the religion of Grand Prince Oleg (879-912) and the Russes, **Perun** is the guarantor of a 907 peace treaty with Byzantium: **Thus the Emperors Leo and**

Alexander made peace with Oleg and agreed to pay tribute, and they took the oath among themselves by kissing the cross, but let Oleg and his men-at-arms take the oath, according to the Rus law: they swore by their arms, and by Perun, their God and Volos, the cattle god and established peace. Furthermore they swore by their arms not in the German manner, but taking their weapons off and putting them at the feet of the idol, in accordance with their own custom.

VOLOS

In order to understand why *Volos, the god of cattle* (the Serbian *vo* and *vol* are ancient and modern Slavic words for cattle), is mentioned as a guarantor of oaths in this and other treaties, once again one must turn to Indo-Iranian mythology.[6] It is only natural that cowherds and cattle or *go* play an important role in the Vedic order, in a community of herders and stockbreeders. Thus Govrsesvara, lord of cattle; Mount Govardhana, where cattle graze and multiply; Goloka, above the world of gods and Brahmans, the world of cattle, the highest region, beyond which there is no region. In Zoroastrian mythology, Vohu Manu is the good spirit's first born. Vohu is the god of cattle, the sacrificial animals. His world equivalent is the cow, bull, ox. What is more important, Vohu is the shepherd of mankind. In opposition to Ako Manu, the evil spirit, Vohu guides the people to good thinking and righteous behavior and keeps the records of men's deeds, words, and thoughts.

GRAND PRINCE IGOR, GRAND PRINCESS OLGA

Following a 945 peace treaty with Byzantium, Grand Prince Igor (913-945) and his men went to a hill in Kiev: **Where there was a statue of Perun. There they laid down their arms and swore to keep the treaty.**[7] It is said that Grand Princess Olga's (945-964) warriors swore by their arms and invoked the name of *Perun.*

GRAND PRINCE SVYATOSLAV

In a 972 treaty with Byzantium, Grand Prince Svyatoslav (964-972) bound himself and his subjects to uphold the conditions of the treaty in the following words: **I, Svyatoslav, Russian Prince ... wish to have peace and abiding friendship with all the great Greek emperors inspired by God, and with all your people; and so do all the Rus subject to me ... Never will I attack your land, or gather an army, or guide a foreign people against those subject to the Greek Government. If we do not observe this ... may we be accursed by the god in whom we believe, by Perun, and Volos the god of flocks, may we become yellow as gold, and perish by our own weapons.**

VLADIMIR VELIKI

Vladimir Veliki (980-1015), later, *Svyatoy Vladimir*, Apostle of Russia, lived most of his life as a pagan, and ruled in the name of *Perun* until his baptism in 988: **Vladimir then began to reign alone in Kiev. And he set up idols on the hill outside the castle courtyard. A wooden Perun with a head of silver and whiskers of gold ... The people sacrificed to them calling them gods ... They desecrated the earth with their offerings, and the land of Rus and that hill were defiled with blood.**

NOVGOROD

Perun was also supreme in the great city of Novgorod: **Vladimir then put his uncle Dobrynia in Novgorod. And when Dobrynia arrived at Novgorod he raised an idol to Perun on the banks of the river Volkhov; and the people of Novgorod offered sacrifices to it as if to God himself.**

PERIN HILL

Twentieth century excavations have uncovered a number of pagan sanctuaries in the lands of the Western and Eastern Slavs. One of the more interesting and revealing sites is the sanctuary dedicated to *Perun* near Novgorod Veliki. V.V. Sedov writes: **The Perin hill magnificently dominates the northern low-lying and woodless banks of the Ilmen lake. The principle sanctuary was raised above the surrounding area ... in the form of a regular circle ... Here [in the center of the circle] stood a wooden statue of Perun ... In front of the idol there was an altar, a circle made of cobble stones. The ditch surrounding the cult was not a simple ring, but a thin rim in the form of a huge flower with eight petals ... During pagan festivals a ritual bonfire was lit on the bottom of each ditch projection ... and an eternal flame burnt in the eastern projection facing the Volkhov river. The layout of the sanctuary is likely to be a geometric representation of one of the flowers devoted to Perun. The pagan Slavs are known to be fond of devoting flowering plants to Perun. The ditch, which surrounded the site with the idol, was of a ritual significance like those of barrow ditches** (*V.V. Sedov, Pagan sanctuaries and idols of the Eastern Slavs, SIG 7-8, 1980-81*).

IN GERMANIA

In medieval German sources there are numerous, albeit rather muddled, references to *Perun*. Helmold, for example, refers to:

- *Prove* (*Prove deus Aldenburg; Prove deus Aldenburgensis terre*)
- *Puruvit* (*in Garz, tria idola ... et Puruvit nominabantur*)
- *Porenuti* (*Quo succiso, Porenuti templum appetitur*)

PERUN

More certain and concrete references to *Perun* in Germania are found in language and place names. As late as the 17th century the native Slavs of Hanover called Thursday *Perundan.* In northeastern Germania, on the coast, near Stralsund, one finds *Perun,* north of Zalikov, *Mokosa,* and *Devin,* place names that resonate with strong and vivid pagan sounds and rhythms. Further west, another *Perun* is recorded near Dargun Grad, southeast of Svetina Grad and Slavomir Grad (*H. Skalova, Mistopisna Mapa uzemi Obodricu a Luticu, VpS 3, 1960*).

T. Witkowski notes that *Perun* is the original name of Prohn (Perun, 1240), a small village near Stralsund, and Pronstorf (Perun/Perone (1199), near Segeberg, and perhaps Pirna (Perne, 1233; Pyrne, 1239), near Dresden (*T. Witkowski, Mythologisch motivierte altpolabische Ortsnamen, ZtS 15, 1970*).

ENDNOTES

[1] J. Kollar, Slawa bohyne, 1839. For an early and excellent introduction to such 'commonalities' and 'parallels' read: I. J. Hanusch, Die Wissenschaft des Slawischen Mythus, 1842; Bajesloveny kalendar slovansky, cili pozustatky pohansko-svatecnych obraduv slovanskych, 1860. J. Rozwadowski, Stosunkileksykalne miedzy jezykami slowianskiemi i iranskiemi, Rocznik Orientalistyczny 1, 1914-1915. A.A. Zalizniak, Problemy slaviano-iranskikh iazykovykh otnoshenii drevneishego perioda, VoP 6, 1962. U. Dukova, Zur Frage des iranischen Einflusses auf die slawische mythologische Lexik, ZtS 24, 1979.

[2] For a recent discussion of ways in which Perun and other members of the pagan Slav pantheon are traced to [S]Varun: O.N. Trubacev, Uberlegungen zu vorchristlichen Religion der Slaven im Lichte der slavischen Sprachwissenschaft, ZtS 54, 1994.

[3] *Muski* is the Serb word for masculine, manly; *muz* for husband; *muzevan*, for brave, manly. In medieval Russia the muzhi were local notables who were active in matters of war and peace (B. Grekov, Kiev Rus, 1959). In 911 Grand Prince Oleg sent his **muzhi to conlude peace and draw up a treaty between Rus and the Greeks.** Decades later, in 944, **Igor sent his muzhi to Roman, and Roman called together his boyars and dignitaries.** Evidence of the deep roots of this institution is found in the fact that the *muzhi* played a similar role in Russian entities organized on a tribal basis. In one embassy, for example, it is recorded that **the Drevlyane sent to Olga their best muzhi, numbering twenty, in a boat**; in another embassy, **the Drevlyane chose their best muzhi who ruled the land of the Drevlyane and sent them after her.** In turn, Olga tells the Drevlyane, **send me noble muzhi.**

[4] N.S. Derzhavin, Perun v iazykovych i folklornykh perzhivaniiakh u slavian, Iazyk i Literatura 3, 1929. J. Machnik, Na sladach kultur Peruna, DaW 2, 1955. I. Ivanov, K etimologii baltiiskogo i slavianskogo nazvami boga groma, VoP 3, 1958. V.P. Darkevich, Topor kak simvol Peruna v drevnerusskom iazykchestve, Sovetskaia arkheologiia 5, 1961. T. Witkowski, Perun und Mokos in altpolabischen Ortsnamen, OnO 16, 1971. H. Schuster-Sewc, Zur Frage der sudeslawischen perunika-Namen, FiL 30, 1973. M. Gimbutas, Perkunas/Perun, the thunder god of the Balts and the Slavs, InD 1, 1973. A. Gieysztor, Sprawca piorunow w mitologii slowianskiej (Ars Historica Poznan, 1976). G.I. Ivakin, Sviaschennyi dub Peruna (Drevnosti srednego Podneprov'ia, 1981). V.V. Martinov, Svyatogor Bilinaya ipostac Peruna, Philologia slavica, 1993.

[5] Archaeological and linguistic evidence suggest that in the religion of the ancient Indo-Europeans, the Shining God of the Sky was closely followed by **the Thunder God, the hunter and warrior ... The axe is connected with the Thunder God; the club, bow, quiver, and arrows are also his ... This god is best preserved in all Indo-European mythologies** (M. Gimbutas, The Civilization of the Goddess, 1991).

[6] J. Jirecek, O slovanskem bohu Velesu, Casopis, 49, 1875. A. Fischer, Kult Welesa u Slowian in Narodopisna spolecnost ceskoslovanska, 1927. W. Szafranski, Slady kultu bozka Welesa u plemion wczesno-polskich, PoL 3, 1959. V. Zivancevic, Volos, Veles slavianskoe bozhevsto teriomorfnogo proikhozhdeniia, 7th International Congress of Anthropological and Ethnographical Sciences, 1964. R. Jakobson, The Slavic God Veles and his Indo-European cognates, Studi linguistici V. Pisani, 1969. N.A. Baskakov, Mifologischeskie i epicheskie imena sobstvennye v "Slove o polku igoreve" (I etimologii Veles i Boian), Vostochnaia filologia 3, 1972.

[7] B.A. Rybakov, Paganism in Medieval Rus, Social Science 6, 1975.

4. PURAN, PERUN, SVETI ILIA

In one way or another *Perun—Perun* as *Perun* or *Perun* in the guise of St. Elia or St. Ilia the Thunderer, who roared through the skies in a fiery war chariot—survived the Christian era *(L.P. Leger, Peroun et les Saint Elie, Etudes de mythologie slave, 1895-97; Slovenska Mitologija, 1904).*

That *Perun* as *Perun* was alive and well in the first centuries of the Christian era is a matter of well-documented record. When Grand Prince Igor and his men laid down their weapons, shields, and gold ornaments and took oath before *Perun,* native and foreign Christians took an oath in *Perun's* Christian sanctuary, the Church of St. Ilia (St. Elias). A 12th century Christian source reports that the Slavs: **Forgot God and believed in that which God created for our use; and they called all this by the names of gods: the sun, moon, earth and water ... the gods Veles [Volos], Perun ... and even to this day remain in a guilty state of dark unenlightenment.**

ISTRIA, MONTENEGRO

Throughout the Dinaric highlands, from Istria in the northwest to Montenegro in the southeast, one finds *Perun* in settings that sometimes vibrate with ancient Slavic cults: in toponyms, especially prominent heights (e.g. Mt. Perun, in eastern Istria; Mt. Perun, in Poljica, east of Split in central Dalmatia; Mts. Perun in central and eastern Bosnia); hydronyms (e.g. Perunisa spring, near Smiljan in Lika); flora (e.g. the iris Perunika, also called Bogisa); place names (e.g. Perun, near Ston, Peljesac peninsula; Perunica, near Kotor in Montenegro). In one recorded instance, a toponym refers to *Perun's* former fortress or stronghold: In the year 1405, Bosnia's Ban Tvrtko II Tvrtkovic's (1404-1409) grant to a deserving subject includes the **village of Drevnik, with Perun, also known as Perun Gradina (ruins of Perun's fortress).** Also the personal and family names Perun, Perunovic, Perunicic in Montenegro: e.g. the Perunovic brastvo/brotherhood of Perunovic in Raicevici, Katun County, Old Montenegro; the Perunovic brastvo/brotherhood of Drenovistica, Pjesivac County, Old Montgenegro. *(M. Filipovic, Tragovi Perunova kulta kod Juznih Slovene, Glasnik 3, 1948; Jos tragovima Perunova kulta kod juznih Slovena, Glasnik 9, 1954).*[1]

IN THE SERB LANDS

Of course, the *Perun/Sv. Ilia cult* had its deepest roots, strength, and vitality in the core Serb lands. Along the ancient religious frontier, the pagan highlands above early Christian enclaves in *Primorska* Serbia on the Adriatic coast, one finds great evidence of pagan adaptation and Christian accomodation.

ILINO BRDO

Here one finds numerous heights with such names as Ilino Brdo, Ilina Glavica, Ilina Gora, Ilin Vrh and others, including, Mount Sv. Ilija towering above the village of Bogdasic on the rugged Vrmac peninsula in the Bay of Kotor. Ilina Voda, Ilina Glavica, Ilina Gora, Ilina Dubrava, Ilina Kamenica, Ilin Vrh, Ilino Brdo are some of the Ilin toponyms and hydronyms recorded in the province of Boka in the early 20th century *(S. Nakicenovic, Boka, Antropogeografska Studija, 1913).* The same or similar toponyms and hydronyms are found in relative abundance throughout Montenegro: Ilina Brdo, near Gradac, Ljesan County; Ilinsko Zdrijelo and Ilinsko Strana, near Kosijeri, Katun County; Ilino Brdo, near Bukovac, Piva County.

MRKOJEVICI

There are fewer more dramatic and telling examples of adaptation and accomodation than those found in the immediate path of Christian expansion radiating from the coastal city of Bar. In the foothills and rugged highlands above Bar, one finds the *Mrkojevici,* an ancient fraternal community or *pleme* with the deepest roots in the Serb past, in the first Serb state, medieval Duklja.[2] The following profile is from a standard reference work: **M, pleme u crnogorskom primorju, izmedju planine Rumike, Mozure i mora. Broji oko pet stotina domova. Zemljiste je nagnuto od Rumije k mora, klima je primorska, radja razno voce. Od maslina cijede ulje na domacim mlinovima. Od gornjih sela ispod Rumije znatniji su Mali i Velji Mikulici. Ostala se spustaju s jedne i druge strane planinskog vijenca Lisinja do Mozure i mora. Od donjih sela glavno je Velje Selo. M. se kao pleme izmedju Bara i Ulcinja spominju 1409. Staro sjediste plemena bili su Mikulici, odakle se ovo pleme razvilo i spustilo k moru. Kasnije je sjediste i zborno mjesto postalo Velje Selo, najvece u M. Od starine su M imali kao glavnog starjesinu plemena barjaktara. Bili su nekada pravoslavni Srbi, pa su od prije dvjesta godina poceli mijenjati vjeru, a od prije sto godina svi su primili Islam. Cestu su na njihovom zemljistu tragovi starih crkava. Pored nesto doseljenika iz raznih strana, glavna masa stanovike je stara. To su stari M koje je prijelaz u Islam ocuvao. U pravoslavnom brastvu Androvica u Veljim Mikulicima cuva se krst, za koji vjeruju da je bio u rukama zetskog kneza Jovana Vladimira, kad je poginuo u Prespi. O Trojcinu dana iznose M. i Krajinjani sve tri vjere taj krst na Rumiju uz veliku i poboznu svecanost** (*S. Stanojevic, Enciklopedija Srba, Hrvata i Slovenaca*).[3]

RADOMIR

In its center, Velje Selu, on a commanding height, Radomir, one finds the Cathedral Church of Sv. Ilia, where, from the most ancient times, the *Mrkojevic* gathered each year on St. Ilia's Day or Ilindan to discuss and resolve community affairs.

VOJNA DRUZHINA

In the mid-15th century the *Mrkojevic vojna druzhina* (military fraternity) enters into an alliance with Venice and thereafter plays an important role in Venice's defense of Bar and Ulcinj on land and Venice's maritime dominance in the eastern Adriatic. Venetian registers offer important documentary evidence relating to the number and vitality of the *Mrkojevic* contribution to the anti-Ottoman wars in the 17th century. With several exceptions all the *Mrkojevics,* generally recorded as *Markovici* in Latin/Venetian sources (***nobilissimus et frequentissimus est pagus Marcovichiorum***) have typical Serb names (*G. Stanojevic, Jedan platni spisak mornara i oficira mletackih naoruzanih barke iz 1626 godine, Istorijski Zapisi XX, 1976*).

ANDRIJA IVOV, VUKO NIKOV

The several exceptions to the rule appear to be early converts to Islam, namely Osman Ivanov, Deli Murat and Zafir Ilin, who served together with their Chrstian brothers-in-blood if not in faith.

Andrija Ivov	Ostoja Ratkov
Djuro Perov	Pero Boskov
[Sargente] Ivo	Pero Djurov
Ivo Dabov	Pero Marov
Ivo Markov	Pero Milov
Ivo Perov	Pero Nikov
Ivo Vulev	Petar Markov
Luka Nikov	Rado Ilin
Markisha Perov	Stefan Ivov
Milo Mladenov	Stijepo
Milosh Milankov	Vuko Ivov
Nikisha Djurov	Vuko Nikov
Nikola Vukov	

DEMOCRACY

As is always the case in western alliances with Montenegrin communities, the Venetians are stunned by their thoroughly democratic character. In the case of the *Mrkojevic,* for example, the Venetians soon learn that every adult male appears to have a title and function meriting recognition and payment. Ultimately, nearly one-third of the *Mrkojevic* demand and receive certain privileges and exemptions from Venetian authorities.

ISLAM

When Christianity vanished, after the *Mrkojevic* adopted Islam, Sv. Ilia remained the *pleme's* vital center, the indomitable guardian of ancient traditions and values.[4] Likewise, Ilindan assemblies remained real and symbolic guarantors of communal unity and solidarity. In a true and authentic expression of ancient values and loyalties, soon after the Cathedral's severe damage by an earthquake in 1979, the Moslem *Mrkojevic* at home and abroad began raising funds for its restoration.

NEW ORDER

The *Mrkojevic* are proud of the fact that during World War II, though the New Order's occupying forces, following standard imperial policies, did everything in their power and more to incite a confessional war in the region, to place Orthodox, Moslem, and Catholic Serbs at each other's throats, there was not a single instance of religous conflict. Ramo Dapcevic captures this *Mrkojevic* moment in the following words: **Ovdje se nije desilo da je brat brata ubio, musliman pravoslavnoga, ili pravloslavni musliman, izmedju vjera da je nesto bilo. Nikako. Nego, kao jedna dusa. Ne mozes razlikovati nista. Naroda je povezan, vrlo dobar. Iako su tri vjerispovijesti, nidje se nije pojavilo da prezire pravoslavni muslimana, ili musliman pravoslavnog ili katolika, no ka'da su od jedne majke. I u ratu se pomagalo, ne samo u ovome kraju, nego sve do Boke Kotorske. Dolazili su odjen da uzimaju hljeba i zita. Ovi narod, ko go je ima, da' je. Neko je proda. Ali odavde niko nije izasa gladan** *(Susreti, January-Feburary, 1990).*

ILINO BRDO, ILINDAN

Several miles north of Bar, in the rugged heights along the coast, one finds Mount

Ilia or Ilino Brdo. On its summit, there is a small chapel dedicated to Sv. Ilia. It is here, on this vigilant height, from times immemorial, on Ilindan, Serbs from the core lands of medieval Duklja, from Crmnica, Papratna, and Krajina, Serbs of all confessions and faiths, Orthodox, Roman Catholic, and Moslem, gathered to honor and celebrate *Sv. Ilia the Thunderer.*[5]

ENDNOTES

[1] P.Z. Petrovic, O Perunova kulta kod juznih Slovena, Glasnik 1-2, 1952. N. Zic, O Perunovu kultu u Istri, Historijski Zbornik 6, 1954. T. Wasilewski, O sladach kultu poganskiego w toponomastyce slowianskiej Istrii, OnO 6, 1958.

[2] The following are the main Mrkojevici villages and lineages cited by A. Jovicevic, Crnogorsko Primorje i Krajina, 1922, an early and reliable source on the subject. 1. Velje Mikulici (Androvic, Markicic, Marljukic, Perazic, Pericic, Perocovic, Pekovic, Sekulic, Ujkasevic,Zagora). 2. Male Mikulici (Marucic, Morstanovic, Mujic). 3. Dobro Voda (Boskovic, Dabovic, Vukovic, Djurovic, Ivanovic, Kolomerovic, Lisice, Nikocevic, Pavlovic, Raskete, Ivanovic, Likovic, Rackovic, Vuckovic, Vukovic). 4. Pecurica (Abazovic, Barjamovic, Becirovic, Djudic). 5. Ravan (Durakovic, Golub, Mujovic, Popovic, Radovic). 6. Komina (Markic, Zudjeli). 7. Grdovic (Andric, Brkanovic, Kodic, Lekovic, Mackic, Nikicic, Seferovic). 8. Velje Selo (Barjaktarovic, Bozovic, Kolovic, Kurtovic, Lunje, Muslovic, Oruccvic, Petricevic, Popovic, Radovic, Spahije). 9. Dabezic (Bojic, Dapcevic, Kalezic, Markezic, Omeragovic, Pekovic, Senalovic, Vulic). 10. Vukici (Vukici). 11. Pelinkovic (Fazlic, Jelezovic, Pecurica, Raicic). 12. Maloj Gorani (Andric, Biledzi, Brajkovic, Dabec, Duricic, Kovac, Vucic). 13. Veljoj Gorani (Bolevic, Djurovic, Isakovic, Kordic, Nikezic, Skure, Sulic, Vucic). 14. Kunje (Duske, Ivackovic, Karastani, Petovic, Poluski, Vuckovic).

[3] For centuries the Mrkojevic were the guardians of a wooden cross said to be St. Vladimir's cross, after Vladimir, medieval Duklja's prince, ruler and saint. Each year, on Saint's Day, a religious procession carried Vladimir's cross to the top of Mount Rumija where commemorative ceremonies were followed by by communal meals, followed by heroic games and songs (junacke igre i pjesme). True to ancient values, for centuries the Mrkojevic were famed for their hospitality, for never permitting a traveller to pass hungry through their territory. Two of the better sources of information on this general area are: A. Jovicevic, Crnogorsko primorje i Krajina, Naselja 11, 1922; P. Radusinovic, Skadarsko jezero i njegov obodni pojas, 1964.

[4] Up to the mid-18th century there was only a single mosque in the Mrkojevic *pleme* and Christians were an overwhelming majority. Following the Pozarevac Peace (1760), Ottoman retrenchment called for the rapid Islamization of strategic borderlands. By the end of the century, the Mrkojevic community was entirely Moslem. J. Vukmanovic, Etnicki procesi i sastav danasnjeg stanovistva u Starom Baru, 1970; Proces islamiziranja i etnicke diferencije Mrkojevica, 1971.

[5] Up to the first decades of the 20th century, in the Slavic lands, on St. Ilia day or Ilindan, one could still find areas where a bull was sacrificed and prepared for a communal feast on a nearby summit. Perun's divine kin, Volos, also survived the Christian era, reappearing as St. Vlas (Blaise), the guardian of flocks. In the former Yugoslav lands, churches dedicated to St. Vlas are often found on the edge of actual or former pasture lands. On March 11th St. Vlas day, a traditional prayer is addressed to St. Vlas: **Give us good luck, so that our heifers shall be sleek and our oxen fat.** In Bulgaria: J.A. Voracek, Pohanske obeti u Bulharu, Slovansky sbornik 2, 1883; Perunova slavnost v Rhodopach, Slovansky sbornik 5, 1886. A. Kaloianov, Bulgarski mitove, 1979.

5. WHERE PERUN WAS STILL WORSHIPPED

There is interesting evidence that **Perun** was alive and well in Bosnia as late as the mid-20th century.

JASENOVAC

While incarcerated at the notorious Jasenovac death camp (June-December 1942), the noted Croat Marxist, Trotskyite, and neo-Ustashi writer and ideologist, Ante Ciliga personally witnessed the liquidation of tens of thousands of Serbs. He estimates the rate of liquidation during his stay at 5,000 per week—mainly Serbs from western Bosnia.

SOVIET PRISONS

After serving some five years in Soviet prisons and camps (at Leningrad, Chelyabinsk, Verkne-Uralsk, Irkutsk, and Krasnoyarsk), Ciliga is a world class authority on prisons and camps. Regarding this experience, Ciliga writes: **Those who have not undergone the prisons, the concentration camps and Soviet exile, where more than five million galley-slaves are kept, those who do not know the greatest forced-labour camps history has known, where men die like flies, are beaten like dogs and work like slaves, they can have no idea of what Soviet Russia and Stalin's classless society are. If I had not been there myself, if I had not seen it with my own eyes, I would not have credited such things possible in our day or in the country of the October revolution** *(A. Ciliga, The Russian Enigma, 1940)*. Soon after his arrival, it was immediately clear to Ciliga that nothing in his past had or could prepare him for Jasenovac.

ORIGINAL SLAVS

At Jasenovac, Ciliga greatly admired the physical and moral attributes of the Bosnian Serbs. Physically, he writes, they were pure-blooded Slavic thoroughbreds: **Tall, fair and sturdy highlanders, true descendants of the original Slav invaders and settlers, untainted by darker Mediterranean and Balkan elements.** *(A. Ciliga, Sam Kroz Europu U Ratu, 1978)*.

DIGNITY, HONOR, COURAGE

Morally, Ciliga writes, the Bosnian Serbs were equally impressive. Indeed, if trial and tribulation are true measures of humanity, the Serbs were without peers: **The Serbs were men who always faced the most horrific death imaginable with unbelievable dignity, honor, and courage.**

SERB CHILDREN

Ciliga was especially moved and troubled by the fate of the Serb children: **Who were all fair and blond.**

Indeed, Ciliga writes: **All the Serb children were healthy, robust, and bright. All were beautiful. It was a joy to see them.**

LIVING DEAD

In less than a week after their arrival, however, after seeing the liquidation pits, the children were transformed into the living dead. Ciliga writes: **Their faces withered,** their eyes darkened, and their hair fell out. Ten days later all but sixteen were dead.

LAST SIXTEEN EXECUTED
Several days later, Ciliga writes: **The last sixteen were executed, except for one hidden by inmates.**

MILIVOJE
The one survivor, Milivoje Milosevic, from the village of Brda, near Bosanska Dubica, was saved thanks to the efforts and courage of a Croat inmate, Dr. Nikola Nikolic, who hid the youngest in the camp clinic and later found other means to keep him alive.

FACING THE SUN
In Ciliga's mind, the Bosnian Serbs recalled the ancient Slavs in their religious values: **Early each morning, standing like statues, facing the sun, they would say their prayers. I don't know if this sun worship was a matter of Orthodox practice or pagan traditions. The Serbs had such uncommon and archaic Slav names. They seemed to come from a land where Perun was still worshiped.**

NEW ORDER *CIVITAS DEI*
Following an exhaustive interview and questioning by a three-man team of leading Ustashi ideologues: Professor Alexander Seitz, a ***brilliant*** Roman Catholic theologian who considers National Socialism a lay path to and model for a New Order *Civitas Dei*; Ivo Bogdan, head of Ministry of Propaganda, Tijas Mortigi, editor-in chief of *Spremnost*, the quasi-official organ of the Roman Catholic Clericalist establishment. Ciliga was released from Jasenovac in December 1942 on condition that, under close clerical supervision, he use his experience and talent to vigorously defend the New Order in Croatia and Europe.[1]

THE PERUN / VEDA HOAX
There is also a rather humorous connection of Bosnia to Perun. In the mid-19th century, friar Stefan I. Verkovic (1821-1893), a *Srbo-Horvata* from a village near Gradac in Bosnia, left the Franciscan Order, and began a relentless pursuit of fame and glory. Some years later, Verkovic published his magnum opus, *Veda Slovena* (1874-1881), a two-volume collection of folk songs and related materials from the most remote and isolated villages in the Rhodope Mountains. Based entirely on the research of his assistant, a certain J. Ekonomov, a self-styled authority on Macedonian-Bulgarian folklore, *Veda Slovena* not only confirmed the *Vedic* roots of pagan Slavic mythology, but demonstrated that the *Veda*, that Perun and others, were alive and well in the Rhodopes. There was only one problem. It was all a gigantic hoax.

6. DAZHBOG, KHORS, STRIBOG, SIMAR'GL AND MOKOS

According to Procopius, the pagan Slavs worshiped many spirits and made offerings to all, and they made vows and predictions at their sacrifices. A number of recorded primary spirits appear to have Indo-Iranian roots. Namely, *Dazhbog, Khors, Stribog, Simarg'l* and *Mokos.*

PRIMARY CHRONICLE

In addition to *Perun,* the highest god, and *Volos,* god of animals, the *Rus Primary Chronicle* (hereafter *Primary Chronicle*) for 980 refers to the gods *Dazhbog, Khors, Stribog, Simar'gl,* and *Mokosh.* The great 12th century Russian epic, *Slovo O Polku Igorevye, Igorya, Sina Svyatoslavya, Vnuka Olegova (The Tale of the Host of Igor, Igor, the Son of Svyatoslav, Grandson of Oleg)* in addition to *Volos/Veles* (**veshei Bojane, Velesove vnuche**), also mentions Dazhbog (**pogibaset zhizn Dazhd-Bozha vnuka**), Stribog (**Se vjetri, Stribozi vnuci, vyut sa morya strelami na hrabriya pulk Igorevi**), Great [K]Hhors (**velikomu Hrsovi vlkom put prerikase**) and Troyan (**risca ve troup Troyaniu cres polya na gori; na zemlyiu Troyaniu**).[1] A 12th century apocrypha detailing the activities and miracles of the blessed virgin also mentions *Perun, Veles, Khors,* and *Troyan (Hozhednie Bogoroditsi Po Mukam).*

DAZHBOG

An early Slavic translation of the first universal Byzantine chronicle, an eighteen-book world history *(Chronographia)* by John Malalas (490-578), identifies *Dazhbog* as the son of *Svarog:* **Below Svarog, his son, the Sun, called Dazhbog ruled**.

DATBHAGA

In all ways, in name and role, the Slavic *Dazhbog,* the giving god (the Sanskrit equivalent is Datbhaga) is consistent with the Indo-Iranian tradition, with *Svar* as Dhata or Dhatabhaga, the creator of all things, with *Svarog* as *Dazhbog,* the solar source and distributor of wealth, health, and good fortune *(V. Jagic, Zum Dazdbog, ArC 8, 1895; E. Dickenmann, Serbokroatische Dabog, ZsP 20, 1950).*

SUN WORSHIPERS

It is not surprising therefore that numerous authoritative sources identify the ancient Slavs as Sun worshipers. The great 10th century Muslim historian, geographer, and cartographer, al-Mas'udi (896-956), the *Herodotus of the Arabs,* for example, records that the Slavs had temples with special architectural arrangements, with an opening in the dome for observing the sunrise *(Muruj adh-dhabab wa ma'adin al-jawahir).*[2] Certain that the course of the Sun determined human affairs, the high priests prophesied future events by coordinating its course with precious stones and magic signs carved in stone inside the temple. It is a matter of record that solar reverence did not end with death. Wanting the dead to face the sunrise, the pagan Slavs buried their dead with the head in the west, feet in the east.

SORABOS, CULTUM SOLIS

A number of German historians are certain that the place name Juterbog is derived from the Serb words *jutro* or morning and *bog* or god, from pagan rituals celebrating the morning sun: **Sorabos advenas eitam cultum Solis ... quem sua lingua Jutre vocant, addito nomine Bog seu Boch, quod apud omnes Slavos Deum significant.**

SOLOTA BAB

In some instances onomastic links with a pagan past have been obscured by time and change. Who would suspect, for example, that the name *Auschwitz* is derived from *Woszwieczich*, a name denoting a place of solar celebrations: **derivatur Auscheweitus a Sorabica voca Woszwieczicz = illuminare, de quyo sibie persuadebant vitam ab eo servari.** Some speculate that Bamberg (*Bamberga—primum vocata fuit Bamberg h.e. mons Babae*), *mons Babae*, as well as many other Germania place names with the prefix bab- (e.g. Babin/1585, near Finsterwalde; Babizna/1378, near Dresden; Babic/1392, near Grimma; Babo/1458, near Cottbus; *mons Babe*/1223, later Papenberge, near Spandau), were sites of pagan rituals relating to *Solota Bab.*

JUTROBOGI APPELLATUR

In an early and outstanding study of the Serbs, A. Frencel writes: **Slavi Sorabique fulgidam auroram sic interpretati sunt, quai esset numen praestantissimum, quod mortalibus in dies bene vellet, cupererque, quodque tenebras discuteret et diem largiertur, aptum tempus operibus agendis conficiendisque. Visa itaque Dea, a qua temperies et su dum coelum discussis fulminibus, tonitruis, fulguribus, ventorumque turbidinibus: illum idolum, quod Soraborum persuasione primam diei facem accendret Jutrebobus seu Jutrobogi appellatur** (A. Frencel, *Commentarius Philologico-Historicus de Diis Soraborum Aliorumque Slavorum, 1719*).

SOLAR IMPULSE

That the solar impulse continued well into the Christian era is confirmed by many sources. The Grand Duke of Kiev, Vladimir Monomakh (1052-1125), in his testament, instructs his sons to praise the Lord first, and then the rising sun in the morning. Another sign of past times is found in *The Book of Deep Wisdom* or *Glubinnaia Kniga,* a work popular in the late medieval period. In it Prince Vladimir has two basic questions to King David: **How did the White Light originate? How did the Sun originate?** King David answers: **The White Light springs from God's heart; the Sun, from God's face.**

SUNS ARE THE CREATORS

Parenthetically, L.M. Graham writes: **Suns are the creators of the worlds, not gods. This the Ancients knew and it became the basis of their sun worship. Today we think of this as pagan ignorance of "the one true God," but alas, the ignorance is ours, not theirs. The story is told of a Christian bishop who said to a Parsee: "So you are one of those peculiar fellows who worship the sun." "Yes," said the Parsee, "and so would you if you had ever seen it." No, the bishop had never seen it mentally and so he worshiped a mythical Creator instead of the real one. And I'm sure he thought his form of worship vastly superior to the peculiar fellow's** (*Deceptions and Myths of the Bible, 1975*).

AND THE BRIGHT SUN

When the daughter of a Balkan Serb was getting married, writes F. Kmietowicz, it was customary for her father to instruct her in the same way as the Grand Duke of Kiev did his son: **To Pray to the righteous God and the bright sun in the east every morning** *(F. Kmietowicz, Slavic Mythical Beliefs, 1982).* The same author writes that it was long the custom in Slavic lands: **That when travellers and people in the field saw the rising sun, they stopped traveling or working, and standing upright they took off their hats, bowing to the sun, they made crosses.** Solar reverence was especially strong and enduring among the Christian Serbs of Germania, where **it was the custom, upon entering a church, to turn around and greet the rising sun; it was forbidden to point out the sun with the finger because, it was said, it could prick God's eye.**

HORS

The pagan Slav Sun god ***Hors*** is a cognate of Vedic *svar,* Old Persian, *hvar* as in *hvar khsaeta* (glorious sun god with chariot and swift steeds), later Persian *horsid* (undying, shining sun). It it interesting and perhaps coincidental that in ancient Egyptian religion, the sky god *Hor* or *Har,* in the form of a falcon, whose outstretched wings filled the heavens, whose eyes were the sun and the moon, was the god of gods. The First Dynasty, the unifiers of Egypt, were *Hor* worshipers. From that time, with occasional interruptions, every pharaoh was believed to be a human manifestation of Hor, and every pharaoh's first name was *Hor.* Coincidentally, ***orao*** is the Serbo-Croat word for eagle. Some scholars believe that the Croat ethnikon, ***Horvat*** or ***Hrvat,*** like that of the kindred Serbs, is also derived from *svar* from *hvar* from *hor.*

HORS, HRSOJEVIC

One finds the given name of *Hors* or *Hrs* recorded in registers of late medieval Balkan Serb communities (e.g. the Hrs-Hrsojevic lineage of Zalaza-Njeguse, Katun county, in mid-16th century Old Montenegro).

SIMURGH, ZAL

The *Primary Chronicle's* **Simarg'l** is **Simurgh,** the radiant bird-god of good omen, a creature of the Indo-Iranic pantheon where he is found with the very same name. While the *Shah-Nameh* depicts ***Simurgh*** as a noble vulture, the 'radiant bird' is generally depicted as a composite creature made up of elements borrowed from the peacock, the lion, the griffin, and the dog. Under the influence of Indo-Iranian dynasts, the Hurrians gave the name *Simigi* to a sun god who appears in various mythological compositions *(V. Pisani, Smarigla, Chorsa-Dazboga, For Roman Jakobson, 1956. B.A. Rybakov, Rusali and the god Simargl-Pereplut, AnT 6, 1968).*

SHAH-NAMEH

Zal is the sad, touching subject of a Persian epic poem *Shah-Nameh* (*Book of the Kings*). Zal was born with pure white hair, and his frightened father, the noble Sam, governor of Hindustan, left the infant to his fate on a distant mountain. Hearing the infant's cries, the noble vulture ***Simurgh*** takes Zal to his nest and raises him. Remorseful and heartbroken, Sam searches for Zal, finds him in early manhood, confesses his crime, and is forgiven by Zal, who begets the glorious and invincible Rustem.

ZAL, ZALITI, ZALOST

In Serb, *zal* as in *zaliti, zalost,* and *zaljenje* is the root of words connoting regret, sorrow, grief, and mourning. In Germania east and west of the Elbe one finds many place names derived from the prefix zal (e.g. Zal, Zalany, Zale, Zalica, Zalici, Zalikov, Zalim, Zalkov, Zaloslavici, Zalogosc, Zalosici, Zalosov, Zalotin, Zalov). Also Zalbogy Grad, a name that radiates the most robust pagan images.

STRIYA, STRIBOG

The Slavic *Stribog,* a god of wind, storm, and gales, appears to be related to Iranic *Ti-Striya,* also *Stribaga (S. Pierchegger, Zum altrussichen Gotternamen Stribog, ZsP 24, 1947; M. Vei, K etimologii drevnerusskogo Stribog, VoP 7, 1985; L. Crepajac, Zum Slav. Stribog, DwS 12, 1967; R. Schmidt, Zur angeblich iranischen Herkunft des altrussischen Gotternamens Stribog, DwS 16, 1971).*

STRIBAGA

Stribaga is an aide to the great warrior/wind god, *Vat,* from which the Serb word for wind, *vet* or *vetar* is derived. *Vat* was the first god to receive sacrifices, and Ahura Mazda himself leads the list of offerants. In his struggle against demonic forces, *Ti-Striya* often appears in the form of a white horse. In the Christian era *Stribog* became the basis for *Striga,* a demonic force. In Serb, stri- as in *strijela* and *strijeljati* is the root of words connoting arrow, shaft, thunderclap, thunderbolt, shoot, and fire. In Germania one finds several place names apparently derived from the root stri (e.g. Stryje and Stryje Grad on the island of Rugen; the Strigus river as in *super fluxio Strigucz sita*). Also, perhaps such place names as Langer-Striegis, formerly Striguz, near Freiberg; Nieder-Striegis, formerly Striguz, near Dobeln; Striegnitz, formerly Striganuitz, near Lommatzsch.

MALKOS, MOKOS

Mokos is *Malkos,* an Iranian deity associated with torrential rains and floods. The pagan Slav *Mokosh,* a cognate of Serb *mokro* (the root word for wet, damp, moisture), dispenses the water that gives life, the moist earth that sustains life. *(T. Witkowski, Perun und Mokos in altpolabischen Ortsnamen, OnO 16, 1971; M. Filipovic, Zur Gottheit Mokos bei den Sudslaven, DwS 6, 1961).*[3] Some evidence of *Mokos'* exalted status in the Russian pantheon of pagan gods is found in the anonymous *Life of Vladimir.* According to this source, *Mokos* alone survived Vladimir's first assault on the pagan gods of Kiev: **Vladimir ... having come to Kiev, destroyed all of his gods, Perun, Xors; again his god was Mokos, and then he destroyed all the gods and drowned them in the Dnieiper.**

MOKOSIC, MOKOSICA

In Germania, *Mokos* is believed to be the root of a number of place names, including Mokos, Mokosic, now Mobschatz, near Dresden; Mokosin, now Moxa, near Saalfeld. Also such modern place names as Megsch, Moggast, Motzo and Mockau *(E. Eichler, Probleme namenkundlicher Etymologie in slawischen Ortsnamen zum Gotternamen Mokos im Altsorbischen, OsG 17, 1988).*

In early medieval times Franconia was an important center of a *Mokos* cult *(H. Jakob, Moggast vulgo Mokos—Kultort der slavischen Gottin Mokos auf dem Frankischen Jura, AgO 61, 1981).* Regarding the *Mokos* cult in this area, E. Eichler writes: **Sichere Belegungen fur die Verehrung heidnischer Gotter bein den Main- und Rednitzwenden besitzen wir nicht; der Gottername Mokos kann mit einiger Sicherheit aus due Toponymie erchlossen werden** *(E. Eichler, Zum Gotternamen Mokos im Altsorbischen, SlG 12, 1986).*

T. Witkowski finds traces of **Mokos** in the names of several villages in northern Germany, including Muuks (Mukus, 1310), not far fom the village of Perun, modern Prohn, and Motzow (Mukzowe, 1161), north of Brandenburg *(T. Witkowski, Mythologische motivierte altpolabische Ortsname, ZtS 15, 1970).*

M. Filipovic identifies a number of Jugoslav toponyms and place names that appear to be derived from **Mokos.** Namely, Mokosica, near Dubrovnik; Mukusina, in Popovo; Mukosa, near Mostar; Mukosa, near Rama; Mokos, in Prekmurje; Mokos, near Zagreb; Mukos, near Prilep, not far from Mt. Perunika *(M. Filipovic, Zur Gottheit Mokos bein den Sudslaven, DwS 6, 1961).* On the islands off the north Croatian coast, *mokos* is a term for a meadow or field still under water several or more days after the last rainfall.

ENDNOTES

[1] N. Veletskaia, Iazycheskaia simvolika slavianskikh arkhaicheskikh ritualov, 1978. H. Kunstmann, Bojan und Trojan. Einige dunkle Stellen de Igorliedes in neuer Sicht, DwS 35, 1990.

[2] With considerable disdain, al-Mas'udi refers to traditional Arab geographies, frequently titled *Kitab al-masalik wa'l-mamalik* or *Books of Routes and Kingdoms,* little more than bare and barren descriptions of routes connecting provinces and towns with an exact indication of distances, a science fit only for "couriers and letter-carriers."

[3] V.D. Zalozetskii, Dazh'dbog, Khors, Lada, Mokosh, Svetovit, Prikarpatskaia Rus, 1911. A.A. Zalizniak, Slaviano-iranskie skozhdeniia v mifologicheskoi i religiozno etnicheskoi oblasti, VoP 6, 1962.

Simurgh, Simarg'l

7. VED

Ved, the Sanskrit word for knowledge/wisdom, is perfectly preserved in Old and Modern Slavic words relating to consciousness, knowledge, understanding, science. Ved, for example, is the root of the following Czech words: *veda* (science); *vedec* (scientist, scholar); *veded* (know); *vedomost* (consciousness); *vedomost* (knowledge).

VESCHT

Ved is also the root of Slavic words connoting sage, seer, wizard, sorcerer, oracle (e.g. Russian, *vescht*, Polish *viezda*, Serb, *vedar*, *vest*, *vestac*), while *Vedma* is a Slavic word for witch. It is thus fitting that *The Tale of the Host of Igor's* prophetic minstrel is called *veschi* (**Tomu veschi Bojanei prvoye pripevku**).

DEVAS, DIV

The *Tale's* omen-screeching bird called *div* (**Div klicet vrhu dreva, velit poslusati zemli neznaem**) also has Indo-Iranian roots *(I.J. Hanus, Deva, zlatovlasa bohyne poganskych Slovanuv, 1860)*. In opposition to the Vedic *devas*, who were divine spirits of the good, the Iranian *div* stands in opposition to the gods, an evil and demonic force. In Serb, *div (e.g. divlji, divljina,* and *divovski)* has similar connotations, namely a wild, savage, and colossal force or condition. In the pagan Slavic tradition the *div* takes several forms. One is *div:* in ominous moments, as in the *Tale*, the *div* often appears as an omen-screeching bird or bird-like creature. Another is *divozena*: a forest-dwelling demonic, superhuman wild woman. In Germania some Slavic place names with the prefix div- and dev- probably have cultic origins (e.g. Devcin, later Dautzschen, near Prettin; Devin, later Dewin, near Halle; Devica, later Dewitz, near Taucha; Divici, later Diwiche on the Saale).

SIVA

In the Hindu tradition, *Siva* is the dark god of cosmic destruction and recreation. There is a single and certain reference to a **Siva** cult in Germania. Helmold records **Siva** as the god of the Elbe Slavs or Polabians: **Siwa dea Polaborum.** That the Polabian **Siva** is derived from the Hindu *Siva* is suggested by siva's dark connotations in Slavic languages. In Serb, for example, *siv* connotes grey, greyish, overcast, to turn grey, ashen (*siv, sivo sivkast, posivjeti*). The same is true of several other words for dark colors. The Sanskrit *tamas* or dark is the Serb *tam, tamno*; the Sanskrit *krsna* or black is the Serb *crna*.

YAM

More important circumstantial evidence of the religious connection between the Hindu *Siva* and the Polabian **Siva** is found in other linguistic connections relating to destruction and creation. For example, the Sanskrit notion of *Yam,* the underground world where the luminous soul of the dead continued to exist, and *Nivrti,* escape from the rotating wheel of rebirth, are manifestly the sources of the Serb *yama*, connoting pit, cavity, underground, and *vrtit*, connoting rotation, twirl. More than a few place names with the root yam- are recorded in Germania. Among others, he place names are Jama, Jamnica, Jamno (e.g. Jama, modern Jahmo, near Zahna; Jamnica, now Jamlitz, near Lieberose; Jamlica, modern Jamlitz, near Spremberg; Jamno, modern Jahmen, near Weisswasser).

PAC, PAK

Similarly, the Sanskrit root *pac,* connoting heat, fire, boiling, is the Serb root *pak* as in *pakao* (hell, inferno), *paklen* (hellish), *pakost* (malice, wickedness), *pec* (oven), *peci* (bake), and *pecen* (burned). It is more likely than not that such Slavic place names as Pak, Pakov, and Paklov recorded in Germania had religious connotations.

DUH, BHUH

In Hindu mythology *Bhuh* is one of three original breaths by which Earth was created, and *bhutani* is the Sanskrit word for spirits. In Serb, *dhu* is the root of words connoting spirits, soul, blowing, breathing (*dhu, dhuhovi, dhuvati*). Saxo's account of pagan Slav ceremonies at Arkona records a ritual reference to the notion of original and sacred breath in the following terms. In a temple dedicated to **Svar** as **Svantevit,** Saxo writes: **He [the priest] took care not to breathe out inside the temple and each time he had to take a breath or breathe out he ran outside so as not to defile the idol with mortal breath.** Numerous place names in Germania appear to be derived from Slavic words for breath, spirit, soul (e.g. Duchov, Duchorov, Dusici, Dusin, Dusino, Duskov, Dusnica). Also Dusny, near Barby; Dusnica, near Jessen; Dusov, near Wittenberg; Dusov, near Schwerin.

BUD, BHUD

The same parallels are found in derivative words. For example, the Sanskrit root *bhud* as in *bhudyati* (awake, conscious, alert), *bhudyate* (awakes, recognizes, understands), thus Buddha, the Enlightened, is the Serb root *bud* as in *budan, budit, buditi, budnost.* As in all lands of Slavic settlement, many place names in Germania are derived from the root bud: Bud, Budic, Budici, Budisko Grad, Budisovo Grad, Budlikov, Budoradz, Budzin and numerous Budims. Also Buda, near Grossenhain; Budchov, near Guben; Budigost, near Leipzig; Budisin, near Dresden; Budsin, near Lubben; Budsko, near Bernburg.

JIV, ZIV

Linguistic parallels are also found in words relating to mortality and life. Sanskrit *Jiv* (one who lives in the body; a mortal being) is the pagan Slav *Ziv,* which is the modern Serb *Ziv* connoting living, alive, lively; Sanskrit *Jivati* ('to live') is the Serb *Ziviti* ('to live'); Sanskrit *Jivana* ('life') is the Serb *Zivot* ('life') *(I. J. Hanus, O bohyni Zive, Casopis 6, 1865).* In one of the Iranian-based mystical Gnostic systems, Abathur, otherwise called *B'hag Ziva,* is an **Uthra, or a divine being of the rank of angel. Born and living within the World of Light, the Uthras ... are of varying ranks and of varying goodness and badness.** In this system, *B'hag Ziva* is an Uthra of the first and highest rank. By contemplation of his own image, **B'hag Ziva brought forth the divine being called Ptah-il-Uthra. The image he contemplated was that of himself reflected off black water. B'hag Ziva ordered his son to create a world in imitation of the heavenly world** *(R. Carlyton, A Guide to the Gods, 1982).*

MRITA, MRTVO

Likewise, at the other end of the spectrum, the Sanskrit *Mrita* (dead) and *Mrityu* (death) is the Serb *Mrtvo* (dead) and *Smert* (death).

8. DENEN DER INDEN

From the earliest times, the warrior, or **rataestar** (Sanskrit, *he who stands in a chariot*) played an important role in Indo-Iranian society. The cultic celebrations of the warrior class (**rathesta**) were the most solemn and impressive and at the same time the most secular and political. There is evidence of similar cultic celebrations in Slavic Germania. To begin with, the Indo-Iranian root *rat* is the Slavic word for war (e.g. the Serb **rat,** war; **ratnik,** warrior; **ratoboran,** militant; **ratovati,** to wage war. Also, the militant personal names *Ratibor, Ratimir,* and *Ratic:* the place names *Ratibor, Ratiborici, Ratimirici,* and *Ratenovic.*

ROYAL CITY OF RATA

It is perhaps more than coincidence that **rat** is the root of one of Germania's leading Slavic nations-provinces, **terra Ratari,** and that the royal city of **Rata** (Rethra) was long the political-religious center of Slavic Germania, the site of the Slavic Delphi, the great temple dedicated to **Svar,** of cultic celebrations featuring the war banners of Germania's Slavic nations. In the royal city of **Rata** great war councils were held. It was here that monks in disguise, spying on a **concilium Paganorum**, were caught and executed in the year 1050 *(T. Witkowski, Der Name der Redarier und ihres zentralen Heiligtums, ZtS 13, 1968. R. Schmidt, Rethra. Das Heiligtum der Lutizen als Heiden-Metropole, FsT W. Schlesinger II, 1974. H. Kunstmann, Zweit Beitrage zu Geschichte der Ostseeslaven. 1. Der Name der Abodriten. 2. Rethra, dier Redarier und Arkona, DwS 26, 1981).*

ASVAMEDHA

The rathestha *asvamedha,* or horse sacrifice, was the king of rites and rite of kings. A symbol of the sun and the universe ('From the substance of the Sun, O Gods, you fashioned this steed'), the immolation and cremation of the sacred horse marked the investiture of a sovereign and endowed him with divine authority and power. Representing the sun, the heart of the universe, the all-seeing and far-seeing eye of the gods, the divine horse had a similar role in pagan Slav rituals and ceremonies.[1]

WHITE HORSE

The oracular horses kept in Slavic sanctuaries in Germania and Pomerania served for divination by stepping over spears. At Arkona on Rugen, the oracular horse was white *(J. Herrmann, Die Pferde von Arkona, Beitrage zur Ur- und Fruhgeschichte, 1982).* We know from Saxo Grammaticus certain basic facts about the horse and ceremony at Rugen. **They foretold the future with the aid of this horse in the following way. When they had decided to wage war on some land, the priests laid three rows of spears in front of the temple. In each row there were two spears in the shape of a cross, with the spearheads buried in the ground, and the rows were equidistant from one another. In the course of preparations for the expedition, the priest offered up a solemn prayer, then brought the horse from the antichamber of the temple, holding it by the halter, and if entering one of these rows, the horse put the right foot first, instead of his left, that was regarded as a good omen for war; if, on the other hand, although it might only happen once, he put his left foot first instead of the right, they abandoned their plan to invade the foreign land.**

SVANTEVIT

The divine horse also played an active and heroic role. At times, Saxo writes, horse and god were one in defense of the faith: **According to the beliefs of the Rani, Svantevit went to war riding this horse against enemies of his faith, and this was proved by the fact that although the horse was shut up all night in the stable, in the morning it often appeared out of breath and spattered with mud, as if it had a long way to travel on returning from some expedtion.**

BLACK HORSE

At Stetin the oracular horse was black. The following details are from Ebbo's biography of Otto, Apostle of Pomerania: **Now the people possessed a horse of great size which was plump and dark coloured and very spirited. It did no work throughout the year and was regarded as being so holy that no one was worthy to ride it. It had also as its attentive guardian one of the four priests who were attached to the temples. Whenever the people contemplated setting out on any expedition by land to attack their enemies, or in order to secure booty, they were accustomed to forecast the result in this way. Nine spears were placed on the ground and separated from one another by the space of a cubit. When the horse had been made ready and was bridled, the priest, who was in charge of it, led the horse three times backwards and forwards across the spears that were lying on the ground. If the horse crossed without knocking its feet or disturbing the spears, they regarded this as an omen of success and proceeded on their expedition without anxiety, but if the result were otherwise they remained inactive.**

VESCHII KON

The prophetic role of the horse in divination ceremonies of the Slavs is confirmed by a wide variety of sources, including Slavic mythology. In Russian mythology, for example, the prophetic horse is well-preserved as the *veschii kon* or prophetic horse *(Z. Rajewski, Kon w wierzwniach u Slowian dzcesnosredniowiecznych, WiA 29, 1975).*

DER INDEN

According to the historical record, the funeral ceremonies of Germania Serb warriors, or *ratnici* (the Serb/Slav word for war is *rat*, for warrior, sing. *ratnik*, pl. *ratnici*), attending the death of a king or prince, resonated with images from the *Rig Veda* and *Avesta*. In Germania Serb ceremonies, lord and horses (sacrificed horses), were cremated and buried together and, in the words of a *Rig Veda* prayer, dispatched to the abode supreme, to the place of their Father and Mother, to a warm welcome among the Gods. Observing the funeral customs of the pagan Serbs of Germania, intrepid horsemen, fierce warriors, feared by one and all, al-Mas'udi found them similar to the customs of the Hindus *(T. Lewicki, al-Mas'udi, SsS 3, 1967).* J. Marquart's German translation reads: **Der bereiets gennanten Serben verbrennen sich selbst, wenn ihnen der Konig oder Hauptling stirbt, sowie dessen Pferde. Sie befolgen dabel Gebrauch, ahnlich denen der Inden** *(J. Marquart, Osteuropaische und Ostastische Streifzuge. Ethnographische und Historiographische-Topographische Studien zur Geschichte des 9. und 10. Jh, 1903).*

HORSE, HORSEMANSHIP

There is strong evidence that similar burial ceremonies were common through out Germania and neighboring Sarmatia. A late 9th century Scandinavian source, for example, depicts the pagan Baltic Slavs as fierce horsemen who favored mare's milk and prized swift horses, whose burial ceremonies featured both horse and horsemanship: **The dead man's treasures were divided into shares, according to their number and value. The richest portion was laid down on the ground about a mile from the dead man's home, and all the other portions at points between the first one and the home, each one nearer the house. All the men who owned the swiftest horses rode from a five or six miles distant in a race to pick up these treasures, and the prizes fell to those who reached them first. Finally the cremation of the dead man, clothed in his best and girded with weapons, was solemnly fulfilled.**

WITH THEIR HORSES

Documentary evidence that in some remote areas *asvamedha*-like ceremonies continued into the 13th century is found in a 1218 treaty with the Teutonic Knights: **Whereby several Slavic tribes agreed to abandon the pagan custom of cremating and burying the dead with their horses.**

SVARGORIC

The role of fire in pagan Slav religious ceremonies also has strong Indo-Iranian overtones. An ancient work of uncertain origin and date *(Unknown Admirer of Christ)* states that **the pagan Slavs also address prayers to Fire, calling him Svargoric** (burning *Svar*). According to an important source of information on affairs in medieval Russia, the *Hypatian Chronicle (Ipat'evskaia Letopis),* the same was long true for Christian Slavs. As late as the 14th century, for example, we are told churchmen censured the common people for praying to fire, calling it ***Svarozic***. In *Hudud al-alam*, a work meant to contain all data known until then on the countries and kingdoms of the world, **all that could be learned from books or from the words of learned men, except all the particulars of the world may be known to none, save God,** a Persian geographer writes that **all Slavs prayed to fire.** In Chapter 43, 'Discourse on the Slav Country', one reads: **All Slavs are fire worshipers** *(V. Minorsky, Hudud al-alam. The Regions of the World. A Persian Geography 372 A.D. Translated and explained by V. Minorsky, 1980).*

CREMATION

Diverse sources agree that the Slavs cremated their dead. The *Primary Chronicle* offers a brief account of the funeral ceremony circa 850: **Whenever a death occurred, a feast was held over the corpse, and then a great pyre was constructed, on which the deceased was laid and burned. After the bones were collected, they were placed in a small urn and set upon a post by the roadside, even as the Vyatichians do to this day.** *Hudud al-Alam* adds several important facts to the matter: **They [Slavs] burn the dead. When a man dies, his wife, if she loves him, kills herself.**

SUTTEE

A more informative and interesting step-by-step account, with the strongest Indic-Hindu overtones, including suttee, was recorded in 922 by a well informed Arab traveler, Ahmed Ibn Fadlan: **When a Slav nobleman died, for ten days his body was laid provisionally in a grave, where he was left until his shroud was prepared for him. His property was divided into three parts: one third was given to the family,** another served to defray the funeral expenses, and the remainder was spent on the intoxicating drinks that were served at the funeral banquet. On the day appointed for the final obsequies, a boat was taken out of the water, and round it were placed pieces of wood shaped to the form of human beings. Then the corpse was removed from the provisional grave and, being clad with a costly garment, was seated in a boat on a richly ornamented armchair, around which were arranged weapons of the deceased, together with intoxicating beverages; not only bread and fruit, but also flesh of killed animals ... were put into the boat. One of his wives who had voluntarily agreed to be burned together with her dead husband was led to the boat by an old woman called *the Angel of Death,* and was stabbed at the side of the corpse; whereupon the wood piled upon it had been consumed, the ashes were collected and scattered over the cairn; and a banquet, lasting four days and nights without interruption, closed the ceremony.

ARAB-ISLAMIC WRITERS

One finds the same notion in the diverse works of other Arab-Islamic writers. A native of Marw, an ancient city that dominated the rich oasis region along the Murghab river on the northeastern fringes of Persia, al-Marwazi, a late 10th early 11th century geographer and man of letters, writes: **The Slavs burn their dead for they worship fire** *(Taba'i al-hayawan).* The Spanish-Arabic historian and geographer Ibn Sa'id al-Maghribi (1213-74) writes about the immense Slav lands where **it is said that they still adhere to the Madjus religion and worship fire** *(Kitabl al-Mughrib fi hula' l-maghrib).* Originally an ancient Iranian priestly caste, in Islamic sources the term *madjus* is primarily for Zoroastrians, and secondarily for all fire worshippers. In his scientific and geographic encyclopaedia, al-Watwat (1234-1318) states that **the Slavs believe in the Madjus religion and burn their dead in fire** *(Mabahidj al-fikar wa-manahidj al-ibar).*

ROYAL TOMBS

It is a matter of record that the tombs of Slav notables compare well with those of other ancient civilizations. Past and recent excavations of royal tombs confirm the presence of horses. Accordingly, in a mid-10th century tomb uncovered by recent excavations, one finds members of a royal family, horses and weapons, placed in a timber mortuary house, equipped with everything believed to be necessary for the afterlife. With regards to the relative material-aesthetic merit, the foremost authority on ancient and prehistoric Europe, M. Gimbutas, writes: **Slavic royal tombs are as eloquent as other Indo-European royal tombs, be they Hittite, Phrygian, Thracian, Greek, or Germanic** *(M. Gimbutas, The Slavs, 1971).*

ENDNOTES

[1] **Comparative Indo-European mythological research indicates the unquestionably prime role of the horse (particularly the white horse) as a sacred and sacrificial animal, the incarnation of divine power of the God of the Shining Sky ... Excavations of graves dating from 4400 - 4300 also uncover the custom of suttee or sacrifice of the female consort or wife** (*M. Gimbutas, The Language of the Goddess, 1991*).

9. INDO-IRANIAN LINGUISTIC ROOTS

A number of eminent archaeologists and linguists suspect that the steppe above, along, and between the northern shores of the Black and Caspian seas, centered in the area between the Volga, Don, and Ural Rivers, is the *vagina gentium* of the Proto-Indo-Europeans.

PROTO-INDO-EUROPEAN

Proto-Indo-European probably evolved out of the languages spoken by hunter-fishing communities in the Pontic-Caspian region, writes J.P. Mallory, in terms that represent a general consensus of archaeological and linguistic consensus on the subject. **It is impossible to select which languages and what areas, though a linguistic continuum from the Dnieper east to the Volga would be possible. Settlement would have been confined primarily to the major river valleys and their tributaries, and this may have resulted in considerable linguistic ramification. But the introduction of the stockbreeding, and the domestication of the horse, permitted the exploration of the open steppe ... During this period to which we notionally assign Proto-Indo-European (4500-2500), most of the Pontic-Caspian served as a vast interaction sphere** *(J.P. Mallory, In Search of the Indo-Europeans, 1989).*

EXPANSION

According to Mallory, the archaeological evidence suggests a Proto-Indo-European expansion eastward across the steppe and forest-steppe of western Siberia beginning in the late fourth millennium. The archaeological and linguistic evidence suggests that in the third millennium B.C. Indo-Iranian languages evolved in an area between the Volga and Kazakhstan. Mallory writes: **Out of this staging area there was a gradual shift southwards ... By the second millennium, Indo-Aryan was spoken by tribes south of the Caspian, and probably also in Afghanistan-north Pakistan from whence it ultimately pressed southwards into the Indus Valley. Concurrent with these developments, Iranian was evolving on the steppe and was then subsequently carried south into present-day Iran and Afghanistan, while the steppe itself was largely left to Eastern Iranian-speaking tribes.**

GENETIC EVIDENCE

The above theory appears to be consistent with the small body of genetic evidence on the subject. **But, in my view,** writes an eminent geneticist, **there is strong support given by the archaeological similarities and, presumably, ties between the western and eastern cultures north of the Caucasus which gave rise to the expansions of pastoral nomads, and the well-known ties between Indo-Iranian, and at least some European languages, could be most easily explained if they all descended from a single group of languages spoken around 5500-6000 years ago, in the Volga-Don area, and if such people spread their genes and languages both westward to central Europe and to the southeast as far as Iran and India** *(L. Luca Cavalli-Sforza, Genetic Evidence Supporting Marija Gimbutas' Work on the Origin of the Indo-European People, From the Realm of Ancestors: An Anthology in Honor of Marija Gimbutas, 1994).*

PROTO-SLAVS, PROTO-INDO-IRANIANS/ARYANS

According to Mallory, the 5th to the 10th centuries A.D. are regarded as both the primary time of Slavic expansion and also the terminal period of Proto- or Common Slavic—the collapse of Common Slavic and its fission into the different modern Slavic languages. Linguistic evidence, Mallory believes, indicates that before the collapse of Common Slavic, the Slavs had been subjected to strong linguistic influences from Iranian-Sarmatian speaking peoples.

TRUBACEV

One of the foremost modern authorities on the ethnogenesis of the Proto-Slavs, the eminent Russian linguist O.N. Trubacev, has different and interesting views on the end of Common Slavic and the beginning of Slav-Iranian ties. Slavic-Iranian relations, he writes, **took place on the eastern periphery of Slavdom, where a symbiosis of Slavs and Iranians began by the first centuries A.D. They also entailed a deep penetration of Iranian tribes into the Slavic areas, which has ... demonstrated the existence of Early Slavic dialects a long time before the period at which the Slavic philology of the 1950s and 1960s believed they existed ... Scythian raids into the area of the Lusatian culture have been known to archaeologists for a long time ... Slavic-Iranian relations probably began mainly about the middle of the first millennium B.C. They have considerably affected Slavic anthroponymy which was in the developing stage at this time, separating itself from the appellative vocabulary; in any case, if there were inherited proto-Indo-European bi-component anthroponymic compounds in Slavic, their lexical (and grammatical) development was influenced by Iranian at that time** *(Linguistics and Ethnogenesis of the Slavs: The Ancient Slavs as Evidenced by Etymology and Onomastics, InD 13, 1985).*

ABAEV

Perhaps the most recent theory on the subject deserves the greatest consideration. V. I. Abaev's pioneering reconstructions of ancient Scythian vocabulary give an entirely different orientation and direction to the question of the origin and character of Slavic-Iranian ties *(Osetinskii iazyk i folklor, 1949).* According to Abaev, Scythian had many old common isoglosses with Balto-Slavic, Germanic, and Italo-Celtic not shared by other Iranian languages, isoglosses that suggest that the Scythian branch of the Iranian languages was autochthonous in Eastern Europe. Abaev writes: **Everything falls into place once we admit that the Iranian element was present in southern Russia at least from the beginning of the second millennium B.C. Then the process that brought about the formation of Scythian-European isoglosses can be sketched in the following way. After the Iranian ethno-linguistic community in Southeastern Europe dissolved, one part of the tribes that had formed it moved south and east, to Media, Parthia, Persia, and Central Asia. Another part, the ancestors of the future Scythian tribes, remained in Europe and in the course of many centuries developed in contact with the peoples of the Central and Eastern European area ... It was in this period that the identity of Scythian within the Iranian language group was determined and numerous Scythian-European isoglosses originated ...The special Scythian-Slavic isoglosses far exceed in number and weight the special ties of Scythian with any other European language or language group** *(V. J. Abaev, Skifo-evropejskie izoglossy Na styke vostoka i zapada, 1965).*

VIVID PARALLELS

The linguistic evidence is impressive. A casual comparison of the language of the ancient/modern Slavs with that of the ancient Indo-Iranians immediately reveals vivid parallels in letter, sound, and meaning. Such parallels are all the more extraordinary when one considers several important facts. The Indo-Iranian basis for comparison, the Sanskrit of the *Rig Veda* and the Iranian of the *Avesta*, are less than ideal base lines. The *Rig Veda*, the oldest known Veda, and the *Avesta*, fragments of ancient sacred writings preserved by the *Zartoshti* or Zoroastrians, were transmitted orally for centuries before they were written down, filtered, and modified by a thousand years or more of history. Though the *Rig Veda's* origins are traced to the 15th century B.C. and earlier, it was written down in one of many Indic dialects no earlier than the 3rd century B.C., when two alphabets appear in Asokan inscriptions. The oldest Iranian language, Avestan, the language of the *Avesta*, was committed to writing at a much later date, the 4th century A.D., with a spelling that tended to obscure the original form of the language.

LOST LANGUAGES, DIALECTS

Many ancient Indo-Iranian and related Indo-European languages are lost or unknown except for isolated fragments. This is the case with the bordering Indo-European languages of Anatolia, the northern Caucasus, and Near East. Some surviving words are intriguing (e.g. Hittite god *Peruas*, Kassite sun god *Surias*, Hittite lord, *Ishan*). Surviving Indo-Iranian languages and dialects remain insufficiently investigated for links with old and modern Slav languages. There is reason to believe that there is linguistic gold in the more remote hills. In the high mountains and remote valleys of the Hindu Kush, for example, *Parun* is the Kafiri God of War; in Afghanistan, his Pushtu name is *Perun*.

9A. INDO-IRANIAN / SERB-SLAV GLOSSARY

Our primary Slav basis for comparison, modern Serb, is separated from the Indo-Iranian model, by several thousand years of history and development, by a great loss of vocabulary, especially in terms of basic social-religious institutions and values. With regard to the pace of linguistic change, it is important to note that by 200 B.C. or earlier, the common language of the migrating Aryans had evolved into two separate and different languages, Indo-Iranian and Indo-Aryan. In some important instances, the words have not only different but opposite meanings. For example, the Indic-Sanskrit word for god, *deva*, is now the Iranian-Avestan word for demon, *daeva*. Nonetheless, in letter, sound and meaning many Indo-Iranian words appear to share roots with old and modern Slav words. Nowhere are the parallels more numerous and profound, the sounds and rhythms more obvious, than in modern Serb. Even the most cursory reading of the *Rig Veda, Avesta,* and later texts and commentaries suggest the following parallels, some perhaps more apparent than real. In the following comparative series, unless otherwise indicated, the first word is a modern Serb equivalent of the Sanskrit word that follows, mainly *Rig Veda* Sanskrit. In some instances, the first or alternative word is an Old Russian (OR), Old Slavic (OS), Russian (R), Czech (CZ) or Polish (PO) equivalent, the second word an Iranian (Iran.) equivalent, mainly *Avestan* Iranian, or a related language as indicated (e.g. Ossetian, Alanic, Pashtu, Tajik).[1]

UNIVERSE
Magla—Megha (cloud)
Mesec—Masa (moon)
Nebo—Nabhas (sky)
Oblak—Abhra (cloud)
Sunca—Surya (sun)
Svet—Visva (world, universe)
Svet—Svita (wholeness)
Vetar—Vata (God of wind)
Zem, Zemlya—Jma (earth)

COSMIC/PRIMARY TRUTH
Istina—Nahista (righteousness)
Istina—Asha Vahista (spirit of 'Supreme Righteousness')

COSMIC/PRIMARY LAW
Rota/OS—Rita (the original cosmic law)
Rota/OS—Vrata (vow, pledge)

COSMIC/PRIMARY JUSTICE
Pravda—Ir/Para-dhata (primary law)

SOUL, SPIRIT
Duh, Dusha—Bhuh ('one of three original breaths by which earth was created').
Duhovi—Bhu-tani (spirits)
Duvati—Dham (to blow)

RELIGION
Bog—Bhaga (God)
Bogdan—Bhagadena (gift of God)
Bogopochitaniya/R—Bhagapujan (Worship of God)
Bogosluzenye—Bhagasusrusha (Service of God)
Blago—Bhalla (blessing)
Bogomater—Bhagamatri (Mother of God)
Boguhval—Ir/Bhagahvarna (Thanks)
Bozevstvo—Bhagatva (godliness)
Boze moi!—Bhaga me! (My God!)
Chist—So-chista (pure)
Diva, Divozena—Ir/Daeva (demonic force)
Hram—Asrama
Hram—Ir/Fsarema (temple, hermitage)
Pocitanije/R—Pujan (worship)
Sluh, Slush—Ir/Sraosh (Originally the genius of hearing, later, Ahura Mazda's 'all-hearing ear which listens to the cries of men wronged on earth by evil spirits')
Spasitelj, Spasti—Svasti (saviour)
Spasitelj, Spasti—Ir/Saoshyant (Savior. In Persian mythology the one who will come to renew all life at the end of time)
Sreca—Sradah (faith)
Strava/OS—Svadah (food offered to dead)
Vera—Ir/Var (the choice between good and evil)
Zal—Ir/Zal (as in Zal, 'the infant left to die on a remote mountain by a sorrowful father')

FATE, FORTUNE, FAME
Gadat—Gadati (to tell fortune)
Sudba—Sukha (fate)
Slava—Sravas (fame, glory)
Slava—Ir/Sravah (fame, glory)
Slava—Sloka (fame)
Sreca—Sreyas (good fortune)

LIFE, DEATH
Kut-ya—Kut (mysterious, invisible)
Mora/OS - Mara (dead)
Mrtvo—Mrita (dead)
Smert—Mrityu (death)
Ziv—Jiv (one who lives in the body; a mortal being)
Ziviti—Jivati (to live)
Zivot—Jivana (Life)

LIGHT, DARK
Crno—Krsna (black)
Crunu /OS - Krsna (blac)
Siv—Siva ('dark God of cosmic destruction')
Siv, Siva, Sivast—Syavas (dark)
Svet—Svita (brightness, wholeness)
Svetli—Sveta (white, bright)
Svetit—Svetate (to shine)
Tamno—Tamas (dark)
Tamno—Tamas (darkness)
Svetleti—Svetah (shine)

HEAVEN, UNDERWORLD
Rai—Rayi (paradise)
Pakao—Pac-at (heat, fire, cook)
Yama—Yam ('the underground world where the luminous soul of the dead continue to exist')

MAN, WOMAN, PEOPLE
Narod—Nar (male)
Narod—Narya (manly)
Narod—Ir/Mard (man)
Narod—Ir/Mardom (people)
Zena—Ir/Zen (woman)

BODY
Cherep/R—Karpara (skull)
Desnica—Daksina (right hand)
Griva—Griva (neck, mane)
Grlo—Gala (throat)
Jetra—Jakrt (liver)
Jezik—Jihva (tongue)
Kosti—Asthi (bone)
Krv—Krav-is (raw, bloody)
Krv—Kravya (blood)
Kvar—Khory (sick)

Mokra—Mutra (urine)
Nagoi—Nagna (nude)
Nokat—Nakha (nail)
Obrva—Bhru (eyebrow)
Peta—Pushtu/panta (heel)
Prsi—Ir/Paeraesi (chest, breast)
Srca—Ir/Zrd; Hrda (heart)
Telo—Tanu (body)
Telo—Ir/Tanus (body)
Usi—Ir/Usni (ears)
Usta—Osta (lips)
Usta—Ir/Aosta
Vlas—Valcas (hair)
Vlas—Ir/Varasu (hair)
Zdravlje—Sudrovy (health)

BRAIN
Mozak—Ir/Mazga (brain)

HEALTH, SICKNESS
Hrom—Srama (lame)
Jedro—Indra (mighty)
Kvar—Kharva (damaged, mutilated)
Khvor—Jvara (fever, illness)
Musko—Muska ('manly' as in 'Thousand testicled Indra or Sahasramuska')
Rana—Vrana (wound)
Snaga—Snavan (sinew, muscle, strength)
Xira—Ir/Xara (wound)
Yad—Vyadi (illness, disease)
Zaraz—Ir/Maraz (disease, infection)
Zdrav—Druva, vazdvar (strong, firm)
Zdrav—Ir/Duruva (health)

RELATIONS
Brat—Bhrata (brother)
Brat—Ir/Brata
Ded—Hindi/Dad (great-grandfather)
Deta—Dhita (child)
Dever—Devar (husband's brother)
Dushti/OS—Duhitri (daughter)
Mati—Matri (mother)
Sestra—Svasri (sister)
Sin—Sunu (son)
Sirocad, OS/Siru—Syeta (orphan)
Sirocad—Ir/Sae (orphan)
Smerd—Ir/Merd (man)
Snaha—Snusa (daughter-in-law)
Svadba—Vah (marry)
Svadba—Vadhu (bride)
Svekar—Svasura (father-in-law)
Svekrva—Srasru (mother-in-law)
Udova—Vidava (widow)
Yetrva, Yetri/OS—Yatyar (sister-in-law)
Zena—Ir/Zen (woman)

Zena—Jani (wife)
Zeniti—Janiyati (to marry)
Zet—Jamatri (son-in-law)

FRIEND
Prijat—Prija (pleasant)
Prijat—Prijas (beloved, dear)
Prijat—Prijati (care for)
Prijat—Prijazni (goodness, kindness)
Prijat—Prinjati (pleases)

CONSCIOUSNESS
Budit—Budhyati (to be awake, conscious, alert)
Budan, Buditi—Bhudyate (awakes, recognizes, understands)
Spavati—Svapiti (sleep)

TO BE
Biti—Bhavati (to be)
Sam—Samam (one self)
Svoj—Sva (one's own)
Svoj—Svajam (for oneself)
Svoj—Sva (one's own)

TO BE FREE, FREEDOM
Sloboda, Svoboda—Svadharma (according to one's own values, self-rule, self-government)

TO KNOW
Mislit—Manute (to think)
Mnit/R—Manute (to think)
Mudar—Medhir (wise, sage)
Prichati—Prichati (to ask)
Pitati—Prichati (to ask)
Um, Uman—Ir/Man (to think)
Vedat/R—Ved (to know)
Vedniye/R—Vedana (knowing)
Voprisit/R—Vipricchati (to question)
Zna—Jna (to know)
Zna—Janati (he knows)
Zna—Ir/Zana (he knows)
Znanje—Jnana (knowledge)

TO TALK, SPEAK, WRITE
Bolto-vnya/R—Bolta (talk)
Boltat/R—Bolati (to speak, chatter)
Govoriti—Gavate (to repeat)
Govor—Garo (songs of praise)
Govoriti—Ir/Gerente (praise, celebrate)
Napisati—Ir/Nipaistanaiy (to write)
Napisao sam—Ir/Niyapisam (I wrote down)
Pricati—Prchati (to ask, to converse)
Rec—Rac (compose)
Reciti—Radhyati (speaks)
Slovo—Sloka (call)

Slovo—Ir/Sravo (word)
Zoviti—Hvayati
Zoviti—Ir/Zbajati (calls)

SOCIAL-POLITICAL TERMS

Bolyar, Bolye, Bolij/OS—Balam (greater)
Drz, Drzava—Drh (to hold together, support, sustain)
Go—Gopa (shepherd, guardian)
Gospodar—Ir/Gospandar (he who owns a flock)
Grad, Gard/OS, Gorod/R—Grha, Ghara (house)
Grad—Grama (village)
Grad—Ngara (city)
Kesa—Kosa (treasury)
Mir—Mihr, Mithra (Some believe that mir is the Slavic equivalent of mihr, that the Mithra the Ruler is the root of old Slavic princely names ending in -mir (e.g. Vladimir, Jaromir)
Mocan—Mahan (powerful, mighty)
Narod—Nar (male)
Narod—Narya (manly)
Narod—Ir/Mardom (people)
Posed—Sad (dwell, settle)
Pravda—Dharma (law, cosmic law, from root Drh, 'to bind, to hold together')
Pravda—Ir/Prahlada (bearer of truth, who rules with justice and wisdom)
Prvak—Purva (elder)
Prvomeshtanin—Parameshtin (who stands in first place)
Sabor—Saba (council)
Savez, Soyuz/R—Samyoga (union)
Slobodu, Svobodu/OS—Sva-dha (self-law, self-rule, self-governing)
Smerd—Mrdhan (head)
Smerd—Ir/Mard (man)
Smerd—Ir/Mardom (people)
Socha/OS—Sakha (plow)
Stan—Stha (to stand)
Stan—Sthana (place, country, state)
Sud—Samdha (law, agreement)
Taty/OS—Tayu (thief)
Ves/OS—Vis (village, settlement)
Vijece—Ir/Vaeta (court)
Vlada—Vah (lead, govern)
Vlada—Ir/Prahlada (bearer of truth, who rules with justice and wisdom)
Vlast—Ir/Flaith (power, authority)
Vod, Ved/CZ—Vah (to lead)
Vrhovni, Vrhovnik—Vr (top, summit)
Vrstan, Vrsni—Vrsan (strong)
Zivotari—Jivitara (resident)
Zupan—Gopa, Gopaya (shepherd, guardian)
Zupan—Sthapati (governor)
Zupan—Ir/Chupan (shepherd, guardian)
Zupan—Ir/Zan-pait (from Zan-tu, tribe, tribal chief)
Zupan—Ir/Vispaitis (chief, clan chief)
Zupan—Armenian/Isxan (prince)
Zupan—Hittite/Ishan (lord)

WAR

Bit—Bhid (to break)
Borba—Bhara (fight)
Grabiti—Grabhati (to seize, loot)
Harati—Harati (steal, plunder)
Hrabar—Ir/Kharadur (firm, resolute)
Hrabar—Ir/Kundavar (hero, brave, leader)
Osvojiti—Svajati (swells, increases)
Patriti/WS—Patray (guard)
Rana—Vrana (wound)
Rat, Ratnik—Ratha (warrior)
Rat, Ratnik—Ir/Rataestar (warrior, literally 'he who stands in a chariot')
Satriti/WS—Ir/Xsatraya (command)
Tuci—Tudati (strike, push)
Upad—Upabda (trampling on)
Udri—Yudh (to fight)
Udri—Ir/Indi (strike)
Yunak—Yuvan (young man)
Yunak—Yudma (fighter)

NATURE

Beryoz/R—Bhurya (birch)
Brez—Bhurya (birch), Tajik/Burz
Cara/WS—Cara (field)
Charna/WS—Ossetic/Xwar (grain, barley)
Dolina—Droni (valley)
Drvo—Daru (wood, tree)
Gora—Giri (mountain)
Gora—Ir/Gairis (mountain)
Gora—Afghan/Gor or Ghor (e.g. Ghor, mountain district of northwestern Afghanistan; the ruling Ghazni Afghans of the **Sur** tribe of Ghor; Gorich, mountaineers 'commonly called Gorchani', a subdivision of the Lund tribe).
Hvost/WS—Ossetic/Xwasae (weed, hay)
Kamen—Asman (stone)
Okmen/OS—Asman (stone)
Pesak—Pansu (sand)
Pust, Pusta, Pustinja—Ir/Pust (highlands, barren mountains)
Sneg—Snih (snow)
Tlo—Ossetian/Tillaeg (crop)
Trava—Trina (grass)
Ugalj—Angara (coal)
Zlat—Ir/Zaran (gold)
Zrna—Pushtu/Zania (grain)

WATER, FIRE

Oganj—Agni (fire)
Topao—Tapo (hot)
Topiti—Tapati (to heat)

Toplota—Tapa (warmth, heat)
Vatra—Atra (fire)
Voda—Uda (water)
Vodopad—Udapata (waterfall)
Zar—Svar (heat, fire, sun, sky)
Zar—Ir/Azar (heat, fire, sun, sky)
Zara—Jvala (burning, heat)
Zima—Hima (snow)
Zima—Ir/Zima (cold weather)

TIME
Din/OS—Dina (day)
Dnevni—Dainiki (daily)
Jutro—Jutara (morning)
Noc—Nakta (night)
Mesec—Masa (month)
Sada—Sadyas (today)
Svetlost—Svetana (dawn)
Vreme—Vaya (time, duration)

SEASONS
Vesna/OS—Vasanta (spring)
Zima—Hima (winter)

ANIMALS
Az, Azdaja—Azi (three-headed dragon or snake)
Bik—Vrisha (bull)
Bobr—Babhra (beaver)
Gnezda—Nida (nest)
Go, Govedo—Go (cow)
Gunja—Ir/Gauna (hair)
Jelen—Harina (deer)
Koza—Aja (goat)
Medved—Madh-uvad (honey eater)
Mish—Mush (mouse)
Nosorog—Nasaringa (rhinoceros)
Ovce—Avi (sheep)
Pero—Parnam (feather)
Pero—Ir/Paran (feather)
Prasa—Sakian/Parsa (pig)
Rog—Sringa (horn)
Sokol—Sakuna (large bird, falcon)
Stena—Ossetian/Staen (male dog)
Veverica—Ir/ Varvarah (squirrel)
Vidra/R—Ir/Udra (otter)
Zivotina—Jivatnu (animal)
Vo—Go (cow, cattle)
Vran—Varnas (black)
Vuk—Vrka (wolf)
Bojise Vuka—Bhayate Vrkat (he fears the wolf)
Vulna—Ossetian/Ulaen (wool)
Vulna—Ir/Varam (wool)

NUMERALS
Dva—Dvi (two)
Oba—Ubha (both)

Dvoika/R—Dvika (couple)
Dvoit/R—Dviyati (to double)
Tri—Tri (three)
Ceteri—Catura (four)
Pet—Panca (five)
Shest—Shash (six)
Deset—Dasa (ten)
Dvanaest—Dvadasa (twelve)
Trideset—Trinsat (thirty)
Sto—Satam (hundred)
Dvesta—Dvisatam (two hundred)

WHO, WHAT, WHEN, HOW
Kada—Kada (when)
Kako—Katham (how)
Ko—Ka (who)
Kuda—Kutra (where)
Kuda—Ir/Kuda (where)
Kada—Kada (when)
Nekada—Ekada (at one time)
Tada—Tada (then)
Uvek—Ir/Yave (forever)

OURS, YOURS
Nas—Nas (ours)

BOTH, SEVERAL, ALL
Neki—Aneka (several)
Oba—Ubha (both)
Sva—Visva (all)

ALWAYS, NEVER
Nikada—Nakada (never)
Svagda—Sada (always)

THIS, THAT
Ono—Ir/Ana (that)
Ovu—Ir/Ava (this)
Radi—Ir/Radiy (because of this)

THAT WAY, NO WAY
Nikako—Nkatham (in no way)
Tako—Thata (in that way)

YOUNG, OLD
Star—Sthaviras (old)
Star—Jara (old age)
Yunost—Yuvan (young man)

LOVE, HATE
Lubav—Lubh, Lubhyati (desire, covet)
Mrzan—Mrdhas (hate, contempt)

FEARFUL, QUIVER
Boyazan—Bhayanna (fearful)

Tresati—Trasati (to shake, quiver)

FRIGHT
Strah—Trasa (fright)
Strasiti—Trasati (to frighten)
Strasno—Trasaniya (frightening)
Tresati—Trasati (to frighten)

TIMID, BOLD
Boyazljiv—Bhayalu (timid)
Drzak—Drsaj (bold)

LIE, CHEAT
Lagati—Slagate (boast)
Varati—Dhvaras (deceiving)

SIT, STAND, FALL
Nispadat/R—Nipatati (to fall down)
Padati—Patati (to fall)
Sedet—Sidati (to sit)
Stati—Stha (to stand)

GO, RUN, RUSH
Bezat—Vetai (to run)
Idi—Ir/Idi (go)
Juriti—Junati (to rush)

SWIM, RIDE
Plivat—Plavati (to swim)
Yahati—Yati (he rides)

REAL PROPERTY
Imanje—Jmaniya (relating to earth)

HOUSE
Dvornik—Dvarika (doorkeeper)
Dom—Dama (house)
Sala—Sala (hall)
Dim—Dhuma (smoke)
Dvor—Dvar (door)
Dvor— Pers/Duvaraya maiy (my door)
Kot, Kotac/WS—Ir/Kata (room, space)
Mesto—Pushtu/Mesta (dwelling place)
Vrata, Vrt—Vrtis (enclosure)
Xata/OS—Xatan (house, room)

FOOD
Hrana—Ahara (food)
Meso—Mansa (flesh, meat)
Med—Madhu (honey)
Med—Ir/Mad
Plod—Phala (fruit)

BREW, BOIL, COOK, BAKE
Hmel/WS—Ir/Haoma (divine brew)

Pec—Pacati (to cook, bake)
Peci—Pacati (cooks)
Pekar—Paktri (baker)
Varen—Svar (heat, fire)

EAT, DRINK
Jesti—Asnati (to eat)
Zhevat/R—Carvati (to chew)
Piti—Pibati (to drink)

BREAK, BREAK WIND
Bit, Razbit—Bhid (to break)
Perditi—Parditi (breaks wind)

PLEASANT, UNPLEASANT
Prijati—Prija (pleasant)
Prijate—Prinyati (pleases)
Neprijatno—Neprijazni (evil)

REWARD, PUNISH
Dar/OS— Daru (gift)
Hvala—Phala (reward)
Mzda/R—Midha (reward)
Vesat—Vishati (to hang)

LIGHT, HEAVY
Lako—Laghu (light)
Breme—Bharma (load)

FULL, EMPTY
Puniti—Purnati (to fill)
Puno—Purna (full)
Puno—Ir/Paru
Tusti/OS—Tuccha (empty)

HIGH, LOW, MIDDLE
Vrh—Varshman (high, top)
Niz—Nisa (low)
Medju—Madhya (middle)

LOUD, QUIET
Krichati—Krosati (cry, scream)
Tih, Tisina—Tusnim (quiet, silence)
Tih, Tisina—Ir/Tusnis (silence)
Voskliknuti/R—Vikrosati (cry, shout)

THIN, NARROW, WIDE
Strana, Storna/OS—Stirna (wide, widen)
Tanko—Tanukas (thin, slender)
Usko, Azuku/OS—Amhu (narrow)

TAKE, GIVE, RETURN
Brati—Bharati (take)
Dati—Dati (to give)
Izbrat—Avarati (select, pick)

Vratiti—Vartati (return)

MISCELLANEOUS

Bogat—Bhagaka (rich)
Bogastvo—Bhagatva (wealth)
Cupati—Chupti (to touch, feel by hand)
Dar—Dana (gift)
Derati—Daryati (to tear apart)
Dira/R—Dari (opening, hole)
Dojit—Duhati (to milk)
Drz—Drh (to hold)
Dubina—Gambana (depth)
Dugo—Dirgha (long)
Dugo—Ir/Dargan
Durnoi/R—Dur (bad)
Girya/R—Guru (weight)
Glotat/R—Gilati (to swallow)
Gluboki/R—Gambhira (deep)
Hoteti—Ir/Hayta (intent)
Hvatiti—Ir/Xvay (swaying motion)
Idi—Eti (to go)
Igrati—Ejati (in vigorous motion)
Igrati—Divjati (play)
Kidat—Ir/Kandan (cut)
Kubok/R—Kumbhaka (goblet)
Krinati/OR—Krinati (buy)
Kroit/R—Krit (cut)
Krn—Krnah (small)
Kucha/R—Guccha (heap)
Lepiti—Lipati (to stick)
Lizati—Lihati (lick)
Mera—Manam (measure)
Mesati—Misra (mix)
Mesati—Misrayati (to mix)
Mrdati—Mardati (to grind)
Naglo—Nagna (nude)
Nizak—Nica (low)
Nositi—Nayati (to carry)

Opak—Apaka (wicked)
Opasno—Pasyati (pay heed)
Ostri—Asri (sharp edge)
Paziti—Pasyati (pay heed)
Pena—Phena (foam)
Pered/R—Puras (before)
Pred—Puras (before)
Protiv—Prati (against)
Prsnuti—Prusnati (sprinkle)
Put—Pantha
Put—Ir/Panta (path)
Raditi—Radhyati (works)
Rana—Avradanta (tender)
Slatko—Svad (sweet)
Slusati—Srinoti (listen, hear)
Stati—Tisthati (stand up)
Stoj—Stha (stop)
Susi—Susati (dry up)
Sushit—Sushyati (to dry)
Svadjati—Vadvi (dispute)
Taty/OS—Tayu (thief)
Tesati—Taksati (to hew)
Tyanut/R—Tanoti (to stretch)
Unutar—Antara (within)
Ustati—Tisthati (rise)
Vezat—Vayati (to knit)
Vesti—Ir/Vazaiti (move)
Voziti—Vahati (to transport)
Vratiti—Vartayati (to return)
Vrtit—Vartayati (to rotate, twirl)
Vrtit—Nivrti (to escape from the rotating wheel of rebirth, to cease all activity)
Zevati—Jambhati (to yawn)
Zvati—Havate (calls)
Zvati—Ir/Zavaiti (call)
Zvoniti—Dhvanati (rings)
Zvonok/R—Dhvanaka (bell)

ENDNOTES

[1] J. Rozwadowski, Stosunki leksykalne miedzy jezykami slowianskiemi i iranskiemi, RoT 1, 1914-15. A. Kalmykov, Iranians and Slavs in South Russia, Journal of the American Oriental Society XLV, 1925. A. Meillet, Le Vocabulaire Slave et Le Vocabulaire Indo-Iranien, ReV VI, 1926. H. Arntz, Sprachliche Beziehungen zwischen Arisch und Balto-slavisch, 1933. J. Harmatta, Studies in the Language of the Iranian Tribes in South Russia, 1952; J. Harmatta, Studies in the History and Language of the Sarmatians, 1970. E. Benveniste, Une correlation slavo-iranienne, FsT M. Wasmer, 1956; Les relations lexicales slavo-iranniennes, To Honor R. Jakobson, 1967. K. Treimer, Skythisch, Iranisch, Urslavisch, Ethnogenetische Erwagungen, WsJ 6, 1957-58; Skythisch-slavische Parallelen, WsJ 14, 1967-68. V. Georgiev, Balto-slavjanski, germanski i indo-iranski, Slavjanskaja Filologija I, 1958; Praslavjanski i indoevropejski, Slavjanskaja Filologija III, 1963; Introduction to the history of the Indo-European Languages, 1981. A.A. Zalizniak, Problemy slaviano-iranskikh iazykovykh otnoshenii drevneishego perioda, VoP 6, 1962. V.V. Ivanov, Obshcheindoevropeiskaja, praslavanskaja i antoliiskaja jazykovye sistemy, 1965. O.N. Trubacev, Iz slavjano-iranskih leksiceskih otnosenij, Etimologija, 1965; Lingvisticeskaja periferija drevnejsego slavjanstva. Indoarijcy w Severnom Pricernomorje, VjZ 6, 1977. V. Pisani, Baltico, Slavo, Iranico, RiC 15, 1967.

10. ETHNONYM SERB:
ALTERNATIVE LINGUISTIC THEORIES

In a recent study, H. Popowska-Taborska (hereafter HPT) presents a singularly informed, insightful, lucid, and comprehensive review of a number of alternative theories relating to the origin and meaning of the Serb ethnonym proposed by authoritative and leading Slavists on a strictly linguistic/etymological basis *(Wczesne Dzieje Slowian w swietle ich Jezyka—The Early History of the Slavs in Light of Their Language, 1993)*.

TWO SCHOOLS

HPT begins her review by identifying the two main schools of thought: **On the whole, scholars are divided into advocates of a native Slavic origin of the name, and those who view its genesis on a wider, Indo-European language plane.**

NATIVE SLAVIC ORIGIN

The Polish *pasierb* is often a key name and starting point in native Slav origin advocacies. HPT writes: **The former most often point to the Polish name pasierb (also widespread in Ukrainian, Belorussian, and Russian dialects). The root -sierb- derived from this appellation denotes, according to some who associate the name with the Ukrainian pryserbytyja, 'to join with, to side with someone—he who has joined with the clan, the tribe, i.e. ally'; according to others, it is connected with the root *srb-, *srb- contained in the Slavic verb *srbati, denoting the sucking or drawing of fluids through the mouth—he who has sucked the same mother's milk, i.e. a person of the same family or tribal community.**

SOCIAL TERM

One finds the same idea well stated in slightly different terms by a noted Russian linguist not included in HPT's review, namely G. Ilinskij, who explains that the ethnonym Serb was originally a social rather than an ethnic term: **But the South Slavic people, which is the primary bearer of this name, has preserved in its way of life the institution of the zadruga which, as is well known, represents only one of the many types of family union in general. And if this is so, then it is natural to suggest that Sьrbь originally meant 'member of the zadruga,' 'zadrugar', collectively Sьrbьja (compare Upper Lusatian, Serbja 'Serbs') –'the sum of people living in a zadruga way of life', and Pa-sьrbьja –'a person not fully legally entered into membership in the zadruga.' In this way we come to the less than surprising conclusion that Sьrbь was initially not so much a 'national' notion as a 'social' one. The ethnic meaning of this name came about afterward when, in the consciousness of its carriers, and also in the eyes of fellow tribe members, the zadruga way of life preserved by the first members became a distinctive characteristic of their nationality. In other words, this means that Serb is 'zadrugar, ' a 'zadruga member' (za drugar) 'par excellence'** *(G. Ilinskij, K etymologii imeni serb, JuZ XII, 1933)*.

PROTO-INDO-EUROPEAN *kerH

Next, HPT introduces a new etymology proposed by Z. Golab, an always interesting and important contributor to the discussion. **A new etymology was proposed** by Z. Golab, who derived the Proto-Slavic appellative preserved in the Polish pasierb and in the Ukrainian pryserbytysja from the Proto-Indo-European *kerH 'to grow' with the suffix -bho and ascribes to it the primary meaning 'affiliate, member of the clan.'

*SIRBU, *KER(H)-

In a 1982 article, Golab states his case in greater detail *(About the Connection Between Kinship Terms and Some Ethnica in Slavic: The Case of *Srbi and Slovene).* **Proto-Slavic sirbu 'member of a kinship group (extended family or kin)' can be retrieved from *pa-sirbu 'stepson' attested by Polish pasierb, East Slavic paserb and by the Ukrainian denominal verb pryserbytysja 'to join somebody's company' (the primary meaning undoubtedly was 'to be adopted'). The ethnikon Srbi 'Serbians' and Serbja 'Lusatian Serbs' is obviously identical with this social term ... These phonetic facts, somehow neglected in the previous etymologies of the ethnikon Srbi and of the noun -sirbu, are crucial for the reconstruction of the Indo-European source of our word: they clearly point out that we must start from an Indo-European root with laryngeal, something like *CerH-. A root which formally and semantically qualifies as the source of Proto-Slavic *sirbu is Indo-European *ker(h)- 'grow'… Thus, nothing seems to prohibit the derivation of PSL *siru from PIE *krH-bho- with the basic meaning 'adolescent, stripling … In view of the above *sirbu (IE *krhbhos) would mean primarily 'one who has grown (in the kin), kinsman—'a natural, regular member of the kin' i.e. 'born wih the same parent as others', whereas *pa-sirbu, with its prefix of depreciation, would mean 'adopted, irregular member of a kin'— 'stepson' (c.f. the same formal and semantic relationship in Russ. Syn: pasynok).** Parenthetically, *pastorak* is the Serbo-Croat word for stepson, *pastorka*, stepdaughter, *pastorce*, stepchild, *pastorcad*, stepchildren, *pasanac*, brother-in-law.

WIDER INDO-EUROPEAN PLANE

Turning to advocates of a wider Indo-European language plane, HPT writes: **O.N. Trubacev perceives the genesis of the name on a wider Indo-European plane, deriving the Slavic ethnonym from the Indo-European *servo- 'the whole, every.' Trubacev suggests a semantic analogue in the Germanic ethnonym Aleman 'all men.' K. Moszynski attributes the Slavic root *Srb- to the Indo-European *servo- 'to carefully protect'. S. Rospond derives the name from the Proto-Indo-European base *serv- 'to flow' (*ser-bh-), noting that in the Indo-European, especially central Satem languages fluvial and tribal names were formed from this base.**

FORTUITOUS CONCORDANCE

HPT continues her review with an important and key point: advocates of a Slavic genesis believe that the name Serb in Asia and elsewhere is more often a matter of coincidence than confirmation. HPT writes: **Advocates of the Slavic genesis of the name in the element Serb- and in similar elements appearing in the onomastics of different countries of the world of antiquity (i.e. the Serbs mentioned by Ptolemy among the tribes between the Caucasus and the Volga in Asiatic Sarmatia) see a fortuitous concordance.**

SEMANTIC PROBLEMS

HPT continues by noting certain semantic problems relating to a Slavic genesis. HPT writes: **The lack of accepted solutions on Slavic grounds is rooted primarily in the semantic sphere of the word. Assignment of the primary meaning 'ally' arises from the direct connection with the Ukrainian pryserbytsja, 'to join with, to side with someone'. However, there is evidence to suggest that the Ukrainian form is a secondary one on Slavic terrain, and that its present form arises from sound and semantic confusion of the root *srb- (*srb-) and *sebr-. For the meaning of the Ukrainian pryserbytsyja is the meaning of the earlier Slavic root *sebr-, widespread in the names of comrades and kinsmen. Confusion of the continuants *srb- (*srb) with this root does not seem impossible (especially the distinction in the clusters -rb and -br- could easily be missed).**

*SEBRU

At this point mention should also be made of Golab's ideas on Proto-Slavic *sebru. In the article cited above, Golab writes: **There is, however, another Proto-Slavic term which should be discussed in this connection: *sebru; it is attested by Old Russian sjabru 'neighbor, a member of the same community', Russian dialect sjaber, Gen. sjabra 'neighbor, companion; partner etc; Old Serbian sebri 'participant, companion, partner'; Serbo-Croatian sebar, Gen. sebra 'farmer' (in Dubrovnik); Slovenian srebar, Gen. srebra 'peasant'; borrowed from the Slavic: Alb. (Tosk) sember 'partner, co-owner of cattle'; Modern Greek ... partner; Hungarian cimbora 'companion, friend'; Romanian simbra f. 'society, community'. According to Trubacev, who derives this word from *sem-ro, i.e. from the basis of fsem-lja 'family', the primary meaning of *sebru was 'member of a "co-habitation" group'; thus this meaning would carry the oldest, primary Indo-European semantics of *koimo- = *semo- as 'lair, camp', earlier than the meaning 'extended family' attested for semlja. I do not think that such a distinction is necessary. If the etymology of *sebru as derived from *sem-ro (or rather from an earlier *soim-ro- or *sim-ro-) is correct, then we are dealing here with a really very old Indo-European term, namely: "koim-ro" or *kim-ro-, representing two apophonic grades of the root** (On the subject of Slavic sebar and Lithuanian sebras: J. Kalima, Slav. *sebr 'Nachbar, Kamerad' und balt. *sebras, ZsP 17, 1941).

YUGOSLAV SCHOLARSHIP

Two distinguished Yugoslav scholars, Petar Skok (1881-1956) and Milan Budimir (1891-1976), who individually and collaboratively added greatly to our knowledge of the early history and Slavic settlement of the Yugoslav lands, give the following information on serb/sebar/srebar. P. Skok offers a brief review of linguistic/etymological scholarship on the subject *(Etimologijski rjecnik hrvatskoga ili srpskoga jezika, I-IV, 1971-73).*[1] **Sebar, gen. -bra, Starosrbski sebьr ... (14. i 15. v.) = slov. seber = sreber, starocrkvenoslovenski sebrЪ = sember "rusticus, kmet, u 14. i 15. v. stanovnici Srbije, stanovnici Srbije osim plemica i pripadnika klera", f (nepravilno) prema prezimenu u Dubrovniku. Bogusa kci Mathase Sebrica. Nalazi se jos u ruskom sjabrЪ "susjed". Prema Vuku govori se u Dubrovniku tezak ... Pridjev na -ov sebrov (Dusanov zakonik); na -ski sebarski. Apstrakt isto tako: sebrost = sebroca (Stulic) = sebarstvo (1520) "villainie, prostotat". Deminiutiv na -ic sebric. Na -**

njak sebrnjak (ogulinski kotar) "drug u oranju kroz cijelo lheto" jedina je potvrda iz danasnjeg narodnog govora. Varijanta s umetnutim m Sember m (Vuk) "covjek iz Semberije (dio zvornicke nahije)", s pridjevom semberski. Upor. u brodskom kotaru brijeg Sember ... Ne postoji jedinstvena etimologija. U lit. i lot. posudeno iz ruskog jezika. Rus. sjabrь = sjaber, gen. sjabra kao i posudjenica arb. sember, rum. simbra, madz cimbora dokazuju da je e u sebar nastao iz palatlnog nazala e ... Prema Joklu potjece od istocno-germ. *sem-bar "Jalbzinsmann", stp Budmani s pravom otklanja. Prema Sobolevskom, Vaillantu i Mladenovicu stoji u vezi s rus. sem'ja "obijelj", to. haims "village" ... <Ind-European *koim-ro. Prema Uhlenbecku i Schulzu u srodstva je sa germ. Sippe < sibja, sanskrit sabha "Versammlung der Dorfgemeinde" ... Prema J. M. Rozwadowskom identicna je s imenom naroda Cimbri itd, a prema Budimiru bila bi pelasticka *(M. Budimir, Dva drustvena termina dubrovacka. 1. Lada, II. Sebar, Anali Historijskog instituta u Dubrovniku, IV-V, 1956).* M. Budimir, the leading Yugoslav authority on the ethnonym Serb, places the subject in its proper context when he notes that most of the names of the Slavic nations remain without convincing etymologies, that the interpretation of the names is questionable in most instances. Budimir's own words on the subject are by far the most informed and provocative in a positive sense. However, Budimir's immense contributions are set in the highly technical and complex philological-linguistic terms that tend to place the subject beyond the reach and critical judgment of all but professional linguists. Selective excerpts from one of Budimir's key articles on the subject *(O starim pomenima srpskog imena, Glas, SAN CCXXXVI, 1959)* are the basis of an attempt to capture the thrust and direction of his stimulating thoughts on the subject, with minimal references to high-powered linguistic-etymological dynamics, in a note (***M. Budimir**) at the end of the chapter.[2]

H. BRUCKNER

Next, HPT calls our attention to an interesting and related hypothesis proposed by the eminent Polish scholar, H. Bruckner: **Worthy of a second look in this context is the hypothesis of Bruckner, who links the Polish pasierba and the Slavic ethnonyms with the root contained in the Slavic verbs designating the sucking or drawing of fluids through the mouth. The fact of the existence of the Slavic appellative *srbь is confirmed by the Czech place name Mlekosrby, etymologically entirely transparent, in which the second member in Czech is homonymous with the ethnonym of interest to us. The name of the Slavic ethnonym Serbs is also connected almost certainly with its original meaning 'to suck, to lap'. Undoubtedly this ethnonym originally referred to those who sucked the milk of the same mother, and thus became the term for family kinship, which was secondarily expanded to the tribal community. In accordance with this etymology the appellative preserved as a relic, *pa-srbь, would signify 'the one who did not suck the milk of the same mother, i.e. the child of another mother'. At what moment *srbь (*srbь) from the appellative denoting 'relative' or 'countryman' transformed itself into a personal name is of course difficult to ascertain. However, if we establish that it was, at the outset, an everyday Slavic name, far-reaching conclusions on the wanderings and migrations of the representatives of this same tribal community cannot be drawn from the fact of its recurrence in different parts of Slavdom. This statement does not negate the possibility of the existence of a genetic connection between, for example, the Southern and Northern Serbs, yet from the mere conver-**

gence of ethnic names one should not draw conclusions about this connection. For, if names with the element *srb- (*srb-) could once belong to the stock of Slavic appellatives, the possibility arose of the independent emergence of these names in different parts of Slavdom.

MLEKOSRBY

Mlekosrby's recorded history is profiled in Profous' register of Czech place names: Mlekosrby, near Chlumce; Jan de Mlekosirb/1343; Sdenco Luawecz de Mlekosirb/1373; Siestak de Mlekosrb/1375; w Mlekosrbiech/1429; Vanek Rezek z Mlekosrb/1454; zamek Chlumecz ... Nepolysy, Wliko srby, Kosycze ... Mlykosrbech/1548; zpraviti zamkem a mestem Chlumczem ... Nepolysy, Mlikosrby/1559; Mlikosrby ves/1654 *(A. Profous, J. Svoboda, Mistni jmena v Cechach, 1957).* Two other place names with the prefix mleko- are recorded in Proufous' register. **Mlekojedy**, near Brandys: in villa Mlekoged/1235; super villa Mlekoged/1390; z Mlekoje/1534; Mylkogedy/1654. Perhaps of greater interest is the prefix with an ethnic qualifier, **Nemecke Mlekojedy**, near Litomerice: Mlekovicz/1369; in Mlecovid/1374; Mlekowid/1408; Mlekogedy/1623; Mlikogedi/1787; Mlikoged/1833.

SRKAT, STREBAT, SRB

Although there does not appear to be any supportive ethnographic or folkloric material, the same source derives -srby from the Czech words **srkati** and **strebati**, from Proto-Slav and Slavic roots **srb** (sipping, sucking) in purely etymological terms: **Jm. Ml. = ves mlekosrbu, to jest lidi, kteri mleko srbi n. srbaji, v. srbiti, srbati (otud strebati, srovnej sorbeo) = srkaje piti, 'schlurfen', srbiti mleko, to jest jisti, Milch essen, staroslovenski sr'bati 'sorbere'** *(F. Miklosic, Etymologisches Worterbuch der slavischen Sprachen, 1886).* Standard Czech etymological dictionaries add the following information. **Srkati:** slovensky srkat; osrkat vzllykati, vzdychati, zachvivati se, postv. osrk vzlyk; zasrkat zachveti se, zavzdychati. Sem i slovenski cmrket, smerkat srkati. Polski sarkac, slovinsky srbocharvatsky srkati, bulharsky sarkam. Zvukomalebne: vzeslo ze srs priponovym k. **Strebati:** csl. srъbati, starocesky strebati z praslovansky *sъrb-, starorusky *serb-, v cesky t vkl). Rusky serbat, Polski sarbac, Slovinsky srbati, Praslovansky *sъrb- dochov. v mist. jm. Mleko-srby. Srk, srkanje, srkati, srknuti are Serbo-Croat words for sipping, licking, lapping, drinking slowly; Sisasti, suck, suckle; Dojiti, nursing, feeding a baby; Lizati, for lick, lap *(J. Holub, F. Kopecny, Etymologicky slovnik jazyka ceskeho, 1952; V. Machek, Etymologicky Slovnik Jazyka Ceskkeho a Slovenskeho, 1957).*

H. SCHUSTER-SEWC

One of Germany's foremost linguists and authorities on Serb/Slavic languages and dialects, H. Schuster-Sewc, finds substantial merit in Bruckner's theory.[3] He writes: **The root *srb- which is found in the words Srb(in) and Serb we can agree is easy to recognize in such onomatopoetic words such as the Slovenian srbati, Old Church Slavic srbrati, Bulgarian srbam, Russian serbat, Ukrainian serbaty, White Russian serbac, Polish sarbac, serbac amd sierbac, siorbac 'srkati'. In other Slavic languages we also have the form with the apophonic root -er- (*serbati), compare with Slovenian srebati, Upper Luzica srebac, Lower Luzica srjebas, Old Russian serbati; Czech strebati and Slovak strebati. In opposition, Russian serbat: Polish sarbac at the same time tell us that the root *sib)r- can appear in two variants, one withs the** frontal palatal *rbr, the other, with the back nonpalatal *rbr. Moreover, Schuster-Sewc writes, Buckner's hypothesis is consistent with the historical-social record. **The notion that in the first instance Srb(in)/Serb connotes 'brother by mother's milk, brothers nursed by the same breasts' makes good sense in terms of the matriarchal order believed to prevail in early Indo-European society, on kinship and community based on maternal lineage.**

SEREV, SEVERЬ

Next, HPT deals with a contending interpretation relating to the East Slavic Sever. HPT writes: **The attempts presented above to explain the names of the Slavs and Serbs directly upon Slavic linguistic grounds collide, however, with the interpretation accepted by some scholars of the East Slavic name SeverЬ, having to do with the peoples situated at the basin of the Desna, Sejm and Sula rivers, and also with the interpretation of the terms Severi, Severci, appearing in the Balkans. Indeed, K. Moszynski sees in the East Slavic SeverЬ, Severa, Severjane and earlier form *Serev - (< —*Serv), which was contaminated under the influence of the term severЬ 'north' and linked with the Slavic ethnonym Serb, yet is is difficult not to perceive the unmistakable connection between the East Slavic and South Slavic names, and thus a convincing interpretation must be based on premises that embrace both these Slavic groups. Z. Golab proposes such an interpretation, viewing the etymology of the Slavic ethnonyms Slovene, SЬrbi // SЬrbi and SeverЬ on Indo-European grounds. Deriving the Slavic Sev(-er) from the Proto-Indo-European k*oiuo-*,*keiuo, the Slavic *Svob-en-* (secondarily *Sloven-*) from the Proto-Indo-European *suoho-* and the Slavic SЬrb-, SЬrb- from the Proto-Indo-European *ker-bho, Golab ascribes the same original meaning 'kinsman, member of the clan' to all of these Proto-Indo-European roots, a meaning further supported by numerous examples drawn from other Indo-European languages. In his opinion, this meaning lay at the foundation of the Proto-Indo-European system of ethnic names at a time when the mobility of individual ethnic units didn't allow for self-identification by reference to concrete territories.**

Continuing the course of reasoning of Z. Golab, HPT writes: **We ought to consider that all these names serving as appellatives with the meaning 'relative, member of the clan' on Proto-Indo-European grounds were already functioning on Slavic grounds as ethnonyms without perception of this original meaning by its speakers. In this formulation, the fact of the recurrence of the Slavic names formed from the roots *Sever- *Sloven, *SЬrb-, SЬrb- in North- and South- Slavdom must have for the scholar another significance: Since they were already concrete names, and not appellatives, from their recurrence in different spheres of Slavdom one can draw conclusions about the wanderings and migrations of the Slavic tribes—and these very suggestions are contained in the further deliberations of Z. Golab. So, once again it has been shown how strongly the methods adopted by scholars for determining the etymology of particular ethnonyms bear upon extra-linguistic conclusions.**

KIMRO, KIMBRO, SEBRB, SBRBI

In a recent article on the subject, Golab states his case in the following terms:

But in connection with the proposed etymology of Severь, etc., one cannot avoid quoting a striking parallel with a similar derivative in -ro- from a stem mentioned already as a close cognate of the underlying PIE *keiuo-: I mean here Slav. *sebr 'companion' (primarily 'a member of the same community') ... Trubacev ... has already derived *sebrь correctly from the same basic stem as semьja (PIE *koim-ija); he hesistated, however, about whether one should reconstruct as underlying PIE *koim-ro or *kimro-. I think that the latter possibility is better justified ... But the parallelism with Sever (i.e. PIE *koiuero-) does not stop here. My contention is that the Germanic ethnikon Kimroi (Ptolemy), Cimbri (Pliny), continued as Old Danish Himber-, New Danish Himmer-land, and the ancient North Pontic ethnikon Kimeroi, Kimeriot belong here too. They represent PIE *kimьro- (=PSL *sebrь) besides kimero-, and the primary meaning was members (mates) of *koimo- i.e. of extended-family dwelling (camp) ... The above etymology of Sever- reconstructing as the primary meaning of this ethnikon the concept of 'kinsmen' finds its well substantiated position within PSL ethnonymy together with two other ethnica namely: Sьrbi, meaning also 'kinsmen' (more specifically 'natural descendants of a clan', cf. North.Slav. *pa-sьrbь 'stepson'), and Slovene through "folketymology" from *Slovene//*Svobene, meaning 'affines' ... It seems not accidental that these three ethnica belong to the oldest layer of Slav. ethnonymy and can be traced in the Slavic North as well as in the Slavic South. And it is also quite interesting that we observe them first of all on the outskirts of the Slavic world: the Danubian Slovene of the 6th century, the Novgorod Slovene of the 9th century, the historical Slovenci, Slovaci and the Pomeranian Slowincy; then the Lusatian Serbja (plur.) and the Balkan Srbi, and ultimately the Danubian Severi//*Sever and the Old Kievan Sever, etc *(Z. Golab, Old Bulgarian Severb and Old Russian Severjane, WsJ 30, 1984).*

INDO-IRANIAN

In the next and final step, HPT deals with theories that relate the ethnonyms Serb and Croat to one another and to Indo-Iranian language roots. **Theories also exist that genetically identify the ethnonyms of the Serbs and Croats with one another. So, for example, J. Nalepa sees a Celticized form of the name Sorb (Serb) in the name of the Croats, while K. Moszynski considers the form *xarv- a Scythian analogue of *serv (<*serb-). Likewise, Trubacev perceives a convergence of the roots in both these names, linking the Iranian form *xarv- with its non-Iranian form *servo- and attributing the latter to the Old Indo-European sarva 'the whole, every' (i.e. the semantic analogy with the Germanic ethnonym Alemanen—literally: 'all people.'**

K. MOSZYNSKI

In *Pierwotny zasiag jezyka praslowianskiego* (1957), Moszynski affirms the Iranian origin of **Svarog**. There is one more connection joining the religious-ritual vocabulary of the Aryans and the Slavs. In this case, however, we are already dealing with a clear borrowing by the Slavs from the Aryans. I mean here the only theonym (except for the name of Perun), which can with great probability be considered Proto-Slavic, namely *Svarog. If one trusts the *Hypatian* chronicle completely, then one can assume that the Slavs (at least the Northern Slavs) worshiped under the name of Svarog a fire deity or a solar deity, who in the course of time embodied in himself both the deified great "celestial fire" (i.e., the sun) and the usual terrestial fire. The word *Svarog was formed by means of the suffix -ogo-, which as we will soon see is of foreign, Scythian origin. But the root svar- also has correspondences in Aryan: Sogdian sparoy- 'shine, gleam,' Avestan hvara 'sun, light, sky,' Old Indian suvar, svar idem, Svarita. As the etymology of these Aryan words indicates, the phoneme r continues here the Indo-European l, which is regularly preserved by the Slavs in their original words; hence the correct conclusion is that the name *Svarog is rather of Iranian, specifically Scythian origin...The root vocalism of the the word...can easily be explained, for example, by the influence of the words *svariti (se), *svarb, *svara, which is very common among the Slavs (especially in the area of beliefs; I myself recorded from a Polesie fisherman on Lake Kniaz: 'Boh svarycsa,' pronounced about thunder; similarly the Polish peasants used to say 'Bog sie swarzy').

Z. GOLAB

Golab believes Moszynski's etymology is in error. He writes: **From a primary Indo-European *su- we must regularly have hv- in Iranian (xv- in Sogdian). So there is insufficient ground to derived Proto-Slavic Svarog from Iranian. If we accept a hypothetical Aryan *svar-arka- 'sunny, shining' (?), i.e., Iranian *hvaraka- or Middle Iranian *hvaraga-, then we would expect Proto-Slavic *xvorog-, but the form we actually have, Svarog, cannot be in any way connected with the posited Iranian model. The whole Iranian etymology of this theonym is void of any linguistic (historical-comparative) background and should be rejected.**

SVARB

The old Slavic etymology deriving Svarog from svarb (*e.g. Old Church Slavic svar 'fight'), Golab writes, **whose basic meaning in most Slavic languages seems to be 'quarrel,' does not satisfy us either from the semantic standpoint: Svarog is not a war-god.**

SVARA

Instead, Golab proposes another etymology: **I would derive this theonym by means of the Slavic suffix rog from the Iranian *svara- 'strong-, powerful — hero, lord.' The Iranian word is posited on the basis of copious Indo-European material: Old Indian savira 'stark, machtig,' sura- kraftig, usually 'Held,' svatra- gedeihlich, kraftig'; Avestan sura- stark, gewaltig.**

AT PRESENT

In her summary, HPT writes: **At present were are not in position to determine unequivocally the location of early Slav homelands either in the light of hydronyms, or through the analysis of Slavic ethnonyms or botanical and zoological terminology, or on the basis of contemporary lexical divisions. We do know that the real Slavs ... appear on the historical stage in the 6th century A.D., where the reconstruction of the early Slavic phonetic and morphological system points to the extreme uniformity of the Proto-Slavic language. On the basis of various data, one can thus maintain that the phonetic differentiation of the Slavic language occurred in the second half of the first millenium A.D., when the Slavs suddenly began to expand ... Pre-and post-war researches have proposed whole range of**

solutions to the difficult problem of Slavic ethnogenesis. The author of this work refrains from providing more detailed conclusions because she claims, on one hand, none of the existing theories is convincing, and, on the other, she is of the opinion that on the basis of the linguistic facts it is impossible to carry out a full reconstruction on the prehistory of the Slavs.

*M. BUDIMIR

Fasmer je protiv veze izmedju grupe serb paserb i grupe seber sebru: die Versuch pas-sirbu weiter mit sebru "freier Bauer" zu verbinden, uberzeugen nicht." Ali ukrstavanje ovih leksickih grupa, koje svakako nisu istog porekla, sasvim je razumljiv s prostog razloga sto se radi o bliskim drustvenim terminima sa gotovo istovetnim znacenjem.

Vaznija je okolnost sto se lit. sebras "sused" ne moze naprosto smatrati pozajmljenim slov. sjabr seber, koje je svakako sekundarnog postanja ... I geografija ovog sekundarnog seber ... ne govori u prilog identifikacije lit. sebras sa ruskim dubletima sjab(e)r i seber. Najzad i finsko seura "drustvo" i eston. sober "prijatelj" ... nedvosmisleno pokazuju da je lit. sebras stara idioglotska pojava. Ostaje prema tome da za sve ove slov. sinonime sirbu pasirbu priserbiti sja sjarbru, prisjabriti sja, pored prisebriti sja i seber, ali odvojeno od lit. sebras, treba traziti zajednicko poreklo.

Taj zajednicki arhetip ovog vaznog drustveno-politickog termina morao je glasiti u protoslovenskoj epose simbra sa kojim se ne moze preko proste metateze likvidskog formativa upostaviti veza s ne manje starim terminom sirba "saveznik, saplemenik, rodjak"... Drugim recima, protoslov. simbra moze se povezati sa sirba na taj nacin sto cemo poci od leksemkog minmuma simb- sa nazalnik infiksom i njegovog derivata pomocu sufiksalnog –go ... Na osnovu tih koradikalnih derivata, cija je semanticka jezgra moze odretiti izrazima "stegnuti, zdruziti, spojiti"... mogu se kao varijante leksemskog minimuma odretiti oblici saip- simb-. Tako bi se moglo uspesno odbraniti prespostavljeno zajednickog zancenje za simbra i sirba "verbundeter", kako kaze Fasmer, ili "suveznik", kako kaze Vuk za zemljoradnike koji zajednicki obradjuju njivu.

Zna se da kimerski Indoevropljani krecu prema jugoistok pocetkom 8. v. st. e. iz oblasti tripolske civilizacije i da su u tu oblast smesta Rostocev protoslovenska plemena. Aristofana zan jos nesto za odelo tih plemena severno od donjeg dunava, kako to pokazuje izraz kaunaka (kuna), pa nije bez osnova prepostavka da u imenu kimbero imamo trakizirano slov. sim-(e)go, jer ti starobalkanski Indoevropljani inicijalni sibilant razvijaju u pravcu guturala.

 Tako bismo morali zakluciti da su u protoslovenskom postojala dva koradikalna oblika, simba i simbra. Ovaj drugi se sacuvao nepromenjen, a prvi je putem diferencijacije dao sirba, tj. u kontaktu s labijalnom nasal je disimilovan u likvidu -g- ... Sve ovo znaci da sa fonetske strane ne moze biti ozbiljnijeg prigovora povezivanju grupa simbra sirba paserb priserbiti sebra prisjabriti i prisebriti, dok semanticka strana, koja pro pravilu u pogledu funkcije preteze, pruza dovoljno jak razlog za takvo vezivanje.

Prema izlozenome Plinijevi Serbi ... i Ptolomejevi Serboi javljaju se upravo u onim oblastima koje su istocno od kimeriskog Bospora, a u te oblasti stigla su kimeriska plemena iz prostora tripoljske civilizacije u kojoj Porfirogenitovi obavestaci znaju za srpske Slovene. Taj podatak potvrdjuje i geomorfoloski termin prag za dnjeparsksе katarakte. To be znacilo da se srpsko ime pominje znatno ranije no sto je to slucaj sa imenima ostalih slovenskih plemena, pa i sa samim imenon Sloveninu. Njegovo prvobitno znacenje "suveznik, drug" sacuvano je i dan danas u novogrc. sempros i arb. sember, odakle po svoj prilici potice i naziv Semberije.

To znaci ime Sigina, ili zapravo Sibina, i po njima pozvanog oruzja, glasilo je u kolektivu si(m) bu- i simb-en/r-. Za pve heterokliticne osnove pokazao je davno J. Smit u svojoj cuvenoj raspravi o obrazovanju plurala kod indoevropskih imenica srednjeg roda da pripadaju najstarijem sloju nominalnih obrazovanja ... Ali nas u ovaj mah vise interesuje morfoloski i semanticki arhetip tih termina kao sto su sibones sibyna simbune i sigunna odnosno sigunos, jer se iza tih termina krije drustveno-politickih termin simbra "sebar" i simbu "zajednica."... Stoga se moze s dovoljno razloga ostati pri shvatanju J. Rozvadovskog i zdruziti imena Abioi Gabioi Sapai Kaprontai Sabini Sabelli Samnites s imenom karpatsko-podunavskih Kimbera, Sibina, cija je metalurgija, isto kao i tracka i kimeriska, bila u vezi s mocnom anadolskom obradom metala.

Ludo bi bilo s nase strane da sva navedena balkanska i italska imena plemena naprosto identifikujemo sa sebrima i Sibinima ... Ovde se radi sam o tobe da se pronadju i objasne klasicni tragovi i stariji pomeni srpskog imena, koliko je to moguce na osnovnu antickih podataka i istoriske fonetike. Kako je znacenje tog imena siroko "saveznik, srodnik", sasvim je prirodno da se ono javlja i van najstarijeg teritorija karpatsko-podunavskih Kimbera i Kimerijaca.

Kod starijih oblika imena Simbra i Sirba, da se posluzimo protoslovenskim rekonstrukcijama, situacija je nesto kompikovanija ... Ali ime boga Hermesa kod indoevropskih Pelasta glasi Imbros. Kako je ... ovo bozanstvo pre svega vodilo brigu oko sitne stoke koju je trebalo pratiti na pasi i cuvati da se ne rastura, prirodno je da takva funkcija ucini od njega ne samo putnika i posrednika, nego u prvom redu sabiraca. Stocarstvo primitivnih indoevropskih plemena dugo je sacuvalo prvobitnih karakter takvih bozanstva u Podunavlju i u prostoru izmedju Karpata i Ponta ... Ako je Herodot pouzdano obavesten o trackoj gospodi i sustinskoj prirodi boga Hermesa, postaju razumljivi pomenuti tracki etnici Sapai, Abioi, Gabioi i Kaprontai, a pre svega osnovni element u Hesihijevu derivatu zibunthides m koji je u pogledu vokalizma najblizi slovenskom terminu sebar i imenima Sibina i Sigina.

Kako se Hermovo kultsko ime Imbros ... i prema njegovim funkcijama i prema propisima istoriske fonetike ocigledno poklapa i sa protoslov. simbra i Aristofanovim kimbero-, povezivanje tih imena ne nailazi na nikakve teskoce, pa se stoga i sa realne i sa formalne strane prosto namece.

ANATOLIA

According to Budimir, possible evidence in favor of an Anatolian connection is found in the fact that the Slav words for gold (*zlato*) and silver (*srebro*) are not related to either German or Baltic forms. The two deviations, he believes, suggest an early and independent Slav connection with Anatolian metallurgy, a contact hinted at by other linguistic terms: e.g. the Slav (*tulmacu*) and Mitanni (*talami*) words for interpreter.

ENDNOTES

[1] P. Skok, Nasa pomorska i ribarska terminologija na Jadaranu, 1935; Dolazak Slovena na Mediteran, 1935; Slavenstvo i romanstvo na jadranskim otocima, 1950. With M. Budimir, Balkanska sudbina, 1936; Balkan i Balkanci, 1937.

[2] Budimir's article includes a brief Latin summary: DE NOMINIS SERBICI VESTIGIIS CLASSICIS (Argumentum): Nomen Serbicum Sirbu eiusque compositum paserb "cosanguineus" una cum appellatione sebar (ex antiquiore simbro), "consociatus", cum Mercuri Pelastici ephitheto Imbros et cum Sigynnis Danuvianis coniungitur. Propter forman sibuna, quae idem valet atque siguna, nomen Sigynnarum ex antiquiore i sibyna, collatis lithuanicis dubnas ex dugnas, deducitur. Nomen collectivum si(m)bu "affines, necessarii" praeter numerum collectivun heteroclyticum sibmen/ros, qui in slav. simbra sirba paserb extat, derivato Hesychiano zibu-nth-ides ... confirmatur. Eiusdem stirpis saip-/simb- "unio, consocio", lat. prosapia, illyr, Sabus, Sabelli Sabini Samnium, thrac. Sapai Abioi Gabioi, et fortasse Kaprontai, esse videntur.

[3] H. Schuster-Sewc, Jazyk luzickih Serbov i jego mesto v sem'je slavjanskich jazykov, VoP 2, 1976. Postoje Li Jezike Veze Izmedju Srpskohrvatskog i Srprskoluzickih Jezika, VuK 6, 1976. Dva Zapazanja O Srpskohrvatskoj Etimologiji (Srbin, Jug, Jugovich), VuK 13, 1983. Razmisljanja O Etimologiji Juznoslovenskog Narodnog Imena "Hrvat", VuK 17, 1987.

PART II

1. BETWEEN THE VOLGA, THE CAUCASUS, AND THE SEA OF AZOV

One finds interesting and substantial support in ancient sources and modern scholarship for an Indo-Iranian origin of the Serbs. More specifically, for a general theory that traces the Proto-Serbs to the 'Scythian-Sarmatian' lands bordering on the Caucasus mountains, the Sea of Azov, and the Caspian Sea.

URHEIMAT

In the mid-19th century, L. Quandt, one of Germany's foremost authorities on Germania's Slavs, especially the Baltic Slavs, was also interested in the time and place of their origin, in the primeval, original homeland of Germania's Slavs. His views on the matter can be best summed up in the following words: **The northern Caucasus is the *Urheimat* of the ancient Slavs, that is, the Serbs who are Sarmatians who are Slavs who are Serbs who were known by many different names** (*L. Quandt, Die Liutizen und Obodriten, BaL 22, 1868*).

PLINY'S SERBI

The first encylopaedia, Pliny the Elder's *Historia Naturalis*, compiled in the first century A.D., locates the Serbs or *Serbi* near the Cimmerio: ***A Cimmerio accolunt Maeotici, Vali, Serbi, Serrei, Gnissi.***

CIMMERIO

Cimmerio takes its name from the Cimmerians, an ancient people living north of the Caucasus and the Sea of Azov, who were driven by the Scythians out of southern Russia into Asia Minor, the Balkans, and the Caucasus **Scythia still retains traces of the Cimmerians,** Herodotus writes, **there are Cimmerian castles, and a tract called Cimmeria and a Cimmerian Bosphorus. It appears likewise that the Cimmerians, when they fled into Asia to escape the Scyths, made a settlement in the peninsula where the Greek city of Sinope was afterwards built** (*V.V. Ivanov, Obschindoevropeiskaja praslavanskaja i anatoliiskaja jazykovye sistemy, 1965. J.R. Mellart, Prehistory of Anatolia and its Relations with the Balkans, L`ethnogenese des peuples balkaniques, 1971. M.I.Artamanov, Kimmeriicy i skify, 1974. A.I. Terenozhkin, Kimmeriicy, 1976*).

CIMMERIAN SERBI ?

There are several other apparent and intriguing references to *Serbi* in a Cimmeria/Crimea/Asia Minor context in Pliny and other sources. Opposite Sinope, near where the Don River enters the Black Sea, Pliny locates **Cimmerium, formerly known as Serberion:** *Ultiomoque in ostio Cimmerium, quod antea Serberion vocabantur.* Near Chersonesus in the Crimea (Chersonesus Taurica), Pliny locates **Sarbacon.**[1] Other sources attest to the fact that northwestern Anatolia, **Sirbis** was another name for the river Ksanthos (also Skamandros, Scamander) that emptied into the Hellespont near Troy. The exact location of *Serbonis Lacus* or Serbonian Lake is uncertain. The best opinion places it southeast of Trojan **Sirbis** and due south of **Cimmerion Serberion** and **Crimean**

Sarbacon somewhere between the Isthmus of Suez, the Mediterranean, and the Nile Delta.

QUAESTIO DE NEURIS CIMMERISQUE

As was noted in Chapter 10, the linguistic-etymological, archaeological, and textual evidence relating to the origin and character of Serb/Balkan ethnic, ethnonymic, and linguistic ties with Cimmeria and Cimmerians, is the specific subject of two pioneering and groundbreaking articles by the eminent Yugoslav linguist M. Budimir *(Protosloveni i Staroanadolski Indoevropljani, 1952; Quaestio De Neuris Cimmerisque, 1952).*

MARYA, MARIANI

One of the more interesting and significant connections relates to a Proto-Indo-European term with Anatolian-Caucasian roots—*mari, mariani, maryani,* an Indo-European military aristocracy that dominated the Mittani, an essentially non-Indo-European people centered in an area between the Euphrates and Tigris rivers. In fact, of course, the term can be traced to the Vedic *marya* or warrior. Budimir and others note that 9th century Byzantine sources refer to the ruler of the Serb principality of Neretvania/Pagania as **Dux Marianorum.** Furthermore, they note, that in the same area, in the Neretva River hinterland, one finds a singular number of places *(trzna)* where knightly skills were once practiced and tournaments were held. Budimir writes: **Da su i kod najstarijih Slovena postojali ratnici kao posebna klasa, vidi se po terminu -trzan—trzni, trzna — trzne i trzno — trzna "odredjeni prostor za ratnicke igre i sastanke" … V. Skaric kaze izricno da je trzan "seosko igriste, sredselo". On pri tom istice da se upravo u srednjoj Bosni, gde je narocito dokumentovano i postojanje i znacenje ovog termina, najvise muslimansko stanovnistvo interesovalo za sportske i viteske utamice. Stoga nije nikakvo cudo sto se neretljanski Sloveni, tako reci odmah po svom dolasku, posvetili ratovanju i osvajanju na Jadranu** *(M. Budimir, Mariani, OnJ 5, 1975).*

URHEIMAT, MIGRATIONS

Further evidence of Cimmerio/Cimmerian links to a Serb/Slav *Urheimat* and migrations is found in one of the more interesting and pioneering works in recent years *(G. Holzer, Entlehungen aus einer bischer unbekannten indeogermanischen Sprache im Urslavischen und Urbaltischen, 1989).* According to Holzer, though the surviving linguistic evidence is scarce, it is nonetheless sufficient to suggest that the largely unknown language of the Cimmerians is a link in the Indo-European chain generally and a vital link in the proto-Slavic and proto-Baltic language chain specifically. In an informed, insightful and interesting review of Holzer, A. Loma writes: **Sve u svemu, moj sud je da ni jedna Holcerova etimologija sama za sebe, niti pak odredjen broj njih u svom zbiru ne pruzaju dokaz o postojanju tematskog sloja pozajmljenica u praslovenskom i prabaltskom. No i nedokazana tematska hipoteza moze se pokazati korisnom ako naucnim pregaocima, uklucujuci i svoga tvorca, da podsticaj za dalja istrazivanja neresenih problema iz proslosti Praslovena i drugih indoevropskih naroda na istoku Evrope. Od Georga Holcera slavistika i indoevropska komparativna lingvistika mogu i u buducnosti ocekivati znacajne doprinose i ideje** *(A. Loma, Pozajmljenice iz Nepoznatog Jezika u Praslovenskom, JuZ XLVI, 1990).*

CAUCASUS, SEA OF AZOV

N. Zupanic's analysis of Pliny's text in the light of other classical sources leads him to to place the **Serbi** between the northwestern edge of the Caucasus range and the Sea of Azov *(Maeotis lacus)*. **Kao rezultat naseg proucavanja Plinijevih Srba i njihovih suseda mozemo postaviti konstataciju, da su u I stolecu posle Hr. ili mozda i pre Serbi i Serrei ziveli izmedju severozapadnog grebena Kavkaza (Corax) i Azovskog mora, u susedstvu Ziga (Zinha) Konapsena, Tata i Vala** *(N. Zupanic, Srbi Plinija i Ptolemeja. Pitanje prve pojave Srba na svetskoj pozornici sa historijskog geografskog i etnologsko stanovista, Zbornik Radova Posvecen Jovanu Cvijicu, 1924; Izvor Srbov, Ljubjanski zvon XLX, 1925; Prvi nosioci etnickih imen Serb, Hrvat, Ceh i Ant, Etnolog II, 1928; Srbi, porijeklo i ime, Narodna Enciklopedia SHS IV, 1929).*

VOLGA, DON, KUBAN

More specifically, Zupanic's places the Serbs not along the Cimmerium coast *(Ora ipsa Bospori utrimque ex Asia atque Europae curvatur in Maeotim, oppida in aditu Hermonasa, dein Cepoe Milesiorum, mox Stratoclia et Phanagoria ac paene desertum Apaturos ultumoque in ostio Cimmerium, quod antea Chimerion vocabatur)*, but in the interior, occupying a large area between the Volga, Don, and Kuban rivers, the Sea of Azov, and the northwest edge of the Caucasus:[2] **Pre mozemo kazati, da su Meocani sedli na celoj spomenutoj obali, do su se ostala plemena u njihovoj pozadini vrstala prema unutrasnjosti uz liniju Kubana, do njegove gornjeg toka, gde smo konstatovali Zige (Zinhe, Zihe). Posto na Vale dolazi donji tok Kubana, treba Srbe i Sereje traziti na srednjem Kubanu.**

SERS, CERS, SYRS, SERRS

It should also be noted that Pliny's text places the **Seraci/Sers** immediately after the **Cercetae Sers**, that Mela's text places the **Syraces/Sers** near and after the **Serri/Sers**. In this general area Strabo (63 B.C.-A.D. 21) places the **Sibins**, to be read **Srbin**, according to W. Ketryzinski *(Die Lygier, 1868)* and others.

SERRI-SERS, SERBI

Zupanic's analysis of Pliny *(Achaei, Mardi, Cercetae, post eos Seraci, Cephalotomi, in intimo eo tractu Pityus oppidum opulentissimum ab Heniochi direptum est)* and other classical texts, mainly Pomponius Mela, leads him to place the **Serri/Sers** *(Malanchlaeni, Serri, Syraces, Colici, Coraxi, Phthirophagi, Heniochi, Achaei Cercetici, et iam in confinio Maeotidis Sindones)* next to the **Serbi** along the middle course of the Kuban River.

SIRACHI, SERACI, SIRACENI

According to Zupanic, the key to identifying nations in the Caucasus is the root and not the various prefixes and suffixes, especially plural suffixes. We see, writes Zupanic, **that nominal plural suffixes (especialy bi- and ni- have been used by the Caucasian peoples … and therefore various name forms have been used for each people. This rule applied to the Serbs gives us the forms Ser + bi = Serbi and Ser + ni = Serni. Without exception the root is Ser. The form Ser + i = Seri might have been given them by their Indo-European neighbors and even earlier by certain Caucasian tribes which also formed the plural by adding the suffix –i** *(R. Novakovic, On the hitherto unused information on the origin of the Serbs, BaP IV, 1989)*. Zupanic, therefore, has no doubt that the **Serri** and others, namely the **Sirachi, Seraci,** and **Siraceni,** are also Serbs.[3]

PTOLEMY'S SERBOI

A century later, Ptolemy's *Geographia* also locates the Serbs or **Serboi** in Sarmatia. Ptolemy identifies the **Serboi** as one of thirteen tribes between the Ceraunian Mountains (the northeastern foothills of the Caucasus) and the river Ra (Volga): ***Inter Ceraunios autem montes et Rha Fluvium Orinei et Vali et Serboi.*** According to Zupanic and others, Ptolemy's text places the Orinei, Vali and **Serboi** in Asian Sarmatia, in a broad area between the Don and Volga rivers, between the Black and Caspian seas south of the northern edge of the Caucasus range: **Srbi bi dakle prema Ptolemejevoj podeli Eurazije, morali sa svojim susedima Orinejima i Valima sedeti u Azijskoj Sarmatiji, koja se u glavnom prostirala izmedju Dona i Volga, izmedju Crnog i Kaspijskog mora sve do grebena Kavkaskih planina na jugu … Orinejce na jugu, u blizini istocnog Kavkaza, Srbe na Volgi, i to na njenom donjem toku a Vale u sredini.**

MIGRATION

On a more tenuous note, Zupanic speculates there is evidence in Ptolemy and other texts that in the post-Pliny period some Kuban Serbs migrated south to a strategic area in the central Caucasus, one that placed them in control of vital military and commercial roadways: **Verovatno su Srbi dosli iz oblasti Kubana na jug starim vojnickim i trgovackim drumom koji vodi od Kimerijskos Bospora preko Surube, Koruzje, Ebriape, Serake i dalje preko prelaza Darjal (istocno od Kasbeka) i Kavkaskih vrata (*portae Caucasicae*) u Iberiju (Gruziju). Tu se se kod juznog izlaza kavkaskog bedema zaustavili, imajuci u ruci najvazni strategijski kljuc.** This area, namely northern Iberia/Georgia, Zupanic believes, is a source of later Serb migrations and settlments in Europe: **Treba Srbe traziti severno od Vala, otprilike u oblasti centralnog Kavkaza, tako da su oni uglavnom imali svoju postojbinu u severnoj Iberij … Sliv reke Argave, koja utice kod grada Mzehet u Kuru, valjda je bio u glavnom domovina Iberski Srba.**[4] Zupanic locates the Vali on the Ljasva River, which, he notes, is also the name of a river in Bosnia.

MELA'S SERACHI / SERBS

With regard to the location of the Serbs, Zupanic notes an obvious and certain consistency in classical sources. In his three-volume geographical survey of the inhabited world *(De Chorographia),* for example, Mela locates the **Serachi/Sers** in the Kuban River region, between the Sea of Azov and the Don River—in essentially the same area as Pliny's Serbs and Ptolemy's **Seraki/Serbs.** Pliny, like Mela, locates them south of the Jaksamati. On this point Zupanic writes: **Bez sumnje su Sirakeni istovetni sa Melinim Sirachima, jer ih Ptolemej postavlja nize Jaksamata.** In his authoritative and comprehensive study, R. Novakovic notes that in Mela's discussion of Scythia, he records the Serbs as **Sers** in the same general area as Pliny's and Ptolemy's Serbs and, centuries later, Jordan's **Seren/Serbs** and **Spali/Serbs** *(Ime Srbi Kroz Vreme i Prostor, 1994).*

SARBACUM

Zupanic and other scholars find traces of the Serb ethnikon in Pliny's text in such place names as: **Sarbacum** (*Sarmatiae Europae Situs*); **Sarbanissa** (*Locus Ponti Polemoniaci*); **Sorba** (*Hircaniae Situs*); **Suruba** (*Sarmatiae Asiaticae Situs*). A noted Russian authority on ancient Sarmatia, V. Borisov, locates **Suruba** on a lower bend of the Kuban River alongside an ancient road that ran from the Cimmerian Bosphorus to Iberia

VOLGA, CAUCASUS, SEA OF AZOV

In his brilliant study, *Constantine Porphyrogenitus and his World,* (1973), A. Toynbee concurs with ancient sources, namely Pliny and Ptolemy, which locate the ancient Serbs **between the Volga, the Caucasus, and the Sea of Azov.** In this area, Toynbee speculates: **The name 'Serb' may perhaps also be detected in the name 'Shirman,' by which Arab geographers called the north-eastern country known to Hellenic geographers as 'Albania.'**

ARCHON-PRINCE OF THE SARBAN

F. Dvornik sees possible evidence of a Serb-Caucasian connection in other times and circumstances, in Constantine VII Porphyrogenitus's mid-10th century *Book of Ceremonies.* He writes: **In describing how the princes of the Caucasian region should be addressed in Byzantine diplomatic correspondence ... he mentions the Archon-Prince of the Sarban, who are located between between Alania and Tsanaria** *(Early Slavic Civilization, 1954).* If, Dvornik continues, we could identify the *Sarban* with the *Serbs,* then we could assume that some of the Serbs were driven by the Huns toward the Caucasus, **where they continued to live under their own princes recognizing a kind of Byzantine protectorate.**

THE 'LAB' CONNECTION

In his study, *O Porijeklu Ilira (1992),* G. Vukcevic presents broad and deep interdisciplinary evidence in support of the thesis that Illyria proper *(Illyri proprie dicti)* was settled by tribes originating in the Caucasus region. He believes the evidence is especially strong in the case of the *'Dinaric type'* centered in the Dinaric highlands opposite the Adriatic Sea. In the case of the Illyrian *Labs* or *Labeati,* a large and prominent tribe occupying the shores of *Lacus Labeates,* modern Lake Skadar, he finds evidence that also relates the *Labs* to the *Serbs* to the *Caucasus.* Noting the history of Serb association with waterways named *Lab* in Caucasia, Germania, and Illyria, Vukcevic states the connection in appropriately cautious terms: **Pleme Labeati je zivjelo oko Skadarskog jezera *(Lacus Labeates)* ... Osnova tog imena je 'lab' sto asocira na ime vise rijeka. Lab imamo na sjevernom Kavkazu, to je lijeva pritoka Kubanja, zatim u Saksoniji slovenska Laba, njemacka Elbe i Lab u Srbiji ... Interesantno je napomenuti da se svuda gdje se pojavljuje r. Lab javljaju kroz istoriju Srbi (Serbi). Na sjevernom Kavkazu, po Pliniju Starijem ... Serbi u dolini Laba. Izmedju Sale i Labe u ranom srednjem vijeku visekratno se u franackim izvorima pominu Srbi, pod raznim imena.**

SAKALIBA

It is interesting that in the Persian-Islamic historical tradition one finds vague references to an early Slav presence in the Caucasus. One source mentions **a pass of the Khazars and Slavs** *(Sakaliba)* in connection with the activities of a Persian dynast that ruled in the last years of the 5th century. In the first years of the 8th century, an Islamic man of letters, al-Akhtal, refers to a **community of reddish Slavs** *(Sakaliba)* in one of his poems. Various sources indicate that the Slavs played an important role in Khazar affairs. According to one Arab historian, Ibn Fadlan, some of the Slav nations were **in**

obedience to the king of the Khazars. Another Arab historian, al-Bakri identifies the Khazars as **one of the northern peoples who speaks Slavic**. Some evidence of their number and status is found in the fact that Slavic was one of the languages spoken at the Khazar court and in the army. In fact, the Khazars adopted *zakon*, a Slavic word connoting law, law code, and *voidvoda*, a Slavic word connoting military command, key administrative-legal and political-military terms. Describing the Khazar inauguration of Magyar *voivoda* Almos, Byzantine Emperor Constantine writes, **that it followed the customs and *zakonon* of the Khazars.** Following a victorious campaign against the Khazars in 737, Caliph Marwan is reported to have settled some 20,000 Slav prisoners in the Khaketia region of Georgia, and established Slav colonies along the border with Byzantium in Cilicia, northern Syria, and the Upper Euprhates.

In the mid-9th century, Georgian mountaineers appeal to an unnamed ruler of the Slavs for aid against caliphal forces. According to Ibn al-Fakih, an early 10th century author of a geography, the Caucasus is connected to the land of the Slavs *(Sakaliba)* and **in it there is also a tribe of the Sakaliba** *(Kitab al-Buldan)*. Intriguing evidence of significant numbers of Slavs north and east of the Caucasus in found in Gardizi's account of Kirghiz origins. According to Gardizi, a mid-11th century Perian historian, the leader of the Kirghiz **was from the Slav lands.** Having killed a Byzantine envoy, he was forced to flee to the Khazar/Khirgiz lands, where other Slavs later joined him. This is why, Gardizi writes, **the features and traits of the Slavs are found among the Khighiz, such as reddishness of hair and whiteness of skin.**

ENDNOTES

[1] Chersonesus is an ancient city in the Crimea founded by Milesians. Chersonesus Taurica is the Crimean peninsula between the Black Sea and the Sea of Azov.

[2] The Kuban River rises in the Greater Caucasus, on the western slope of Mt. Elbruz, flows north in a wide arc. One arm, the Kuban proper, enters the Seza of Azov in a swampy, lagoon-filled delta mouth at Temryuk. The Old Kuban arm, a slow meandering steppe stream in its lower reaches, drains the Kuban Steppe, enters the Black Sea at Kiziltash.

[3] Zupanic notes that the Sirachi occupied an area between the Don and Kuban rivers, that the king of the Sirachi was called Zorsines, who enters the historical record in association with Mithridates the Great (120-63 B.C.), King of Pontus.

[4] Iberia is an ancient name for the eastern half of Georgia (a triangular region on the east coast of Black Sea surrounded by the Caucasus range) and Albania (an ancient and medieval state in southeastern Caucasia, located between the Caucasus Mountains on the north, the Kura River on the south, the Caspian Sea on the east. Zupanic locates the Vali on the Ljasva River, which, he notes, is also the name of a river in Bosnia.

2. IN ANCIENT TIMES ALL SLAVS WERE CALLED SERBS?

In his mid-16th century history of the Goths, Jordanes locates the **Spals** (*Spali*) in an area between the Black, Azov, and Caspian seas: **This part of the Goths, which is said to have crossed the river and entered with Filimir into the country of Oium, came into possession of the desired land, and there they soon came upon the race of the Spali, joined battle with them and won the victory** (*De Origine Actibusque Getarum*).

In the same general area Jordanes' Byzantine contemporary, Procopius of Caesarea places the **Spors** (*Spori*), a large and powerful Slav nation: **Sklawenowie i Antowie kiedys mieli nawet jedna nazwe—zwano ich Sporami—jak sadze dlatego, ze zamieszkuja w rozproszeniu, oddaleni od siebie** (*De Bellis*). Centuries earlier, Pliny locates the **Spals** in this same area (*Tanaian vero transisse Satharcheo Herticleos, Spondolicos, Synthietas, Anasos, Issos, Cataeetas, Tagoras, Caronos, Neripos Agandaeos, Mendaraeos, Satharcheos, Spalaeos*). He also mentions the *Pals* (*Ibi Napaei interisse dicuntura a Palaeis*), which may be another name for the **Spals**. In this same general area, Mela locates the **Spals** recorded as **Spalei** (*A.A. Shamatov, Spoli, Spoli-iskonyie sosedi slavjan, Zhivaja Starina 20, 1911. G. Vernadsky, The Spali of Jordanis and the Spori, Byzantion 13, 1938*).

SPORS ARE SERBS

Important historians, including Josip Dobrovsky (1753-1829), the father of scientific Slavistics, renowned for his objectivity and his insistence on **the bare unvarnished truth whether or not it was in accord with national myths,** are certain that the **Spali, Spalei** and **Spori** are **Serbs: Porovname-li vypovedi, dvou nejhodnovernejsich svekuv o Slovanech 6ho veku, Jornanda a Prokopia, shledame jistotne, za Vindi a Spori (Srbi), jsou hlavni jmena jednoho a tehoz kmene. Vinidove Jornandovi jsou Sporove (Srbove) Prokopiovi a naopak** (*J. Dobrovsky, Uber den Ursprund des Namens Tschech, Tschechen, Geschichte der Bohmen, 1782*).

ALL SLAVS WERE CALLED SPORI

Compelling evidence that the **Spors** and **Spalei** are foreign cognates of the native Serb name is found in Procopius's words that: **In ancient times all Slavs were called Spori.** According to the exhaustive research of 19th and early 20th century historians, Procopius's words—**in ancient times all Slavs were called Spori**—are a clear reference to the Serbs and only Serbs.

VLASTNE STARE JMENO

On this point Safarik writes: **Dame-li tak smysine a pruvodne domnence, zeby v pokazene form Spori u Prokopia vlastne stare jmeno kmene slovanskeho Srbi tkvelo, za pravdu, jakoz pak za dulezitymi pricinami jinak uciniti nemuzeme, tof jiz tim samym nova, prostrana a bezpecnas cesta k vyskooumani pojiti Slovanuv a starobylych sidel jejich nam se otevre. Mamet zajiste dvoji pranarodu tohoto jmeno pred rukama cizozemske, t. Vinidi cilic Vendi, a domaci, t. Srbi: procez potrebi jest jen vsecka svedectvi hodnovernych spisovateluv davnovekosti o narodech dvojim timto jmenem vyznacenych pilne pohledavati, shledana rozsudne oceniti, ocenena pak oustrojne sporadati, a tim samym prvotni sidla Slovanuv a** stare dejiny jejich z mraku nepameti a nevedomosti na jasne svetlo historicke nazornosti pred ocima nasima vystoupi. Oumysl nas a obrany k dosazeni jeho zpusob toho ovsem vymaha, abyehom prede vsim vsecho to, cokoli v nejstarsich pramenech a pamatkach dejeslovi evropejskeho o techto, od nas za neprostredne predky dnesnich Slovanuv uznanych, Vindech a Srbich roztrousene sa nachazi, co nejpilneji do hromady sebrali, a ocidene z prachu vetchosti i dle vnitrniho zavazi ocenene v souhlasny celek spojili, jisti jsouce, za tudyz nabudeme zakladu pevneho pro soustavu starozitnosti slovanskych.

PROKOPIOSA ZAWIERA

H. Popowska-Taborska sums up the view of such eminent Slavists as Dobrovsky, Anton and Safarik in the following terms: **Z etnonimen Serbowie laczyc sie zwyklo zanotowana przez Prokopia z Cezarei w De bello Gothico nazwe Spori, ktora jednakze Prokopio eytmologizowal odmiennie, wykorzystujac gre slow Spori i grecki Sporami: Takze i imie mieli z dawien dawno jedno Sklawinowie i Antowie; jednych i drugich bowiem zwano dawniej Sporami, sadze, za diatego, poniewaz rozproszeni, z dala od siebie zamieszkuja swoj kraj. J. Dobrowski, K. G. Anton, P. Szafarzyk przyjmowali juz, ze relajca Prokopiosa zawiera znieksztalcona nazwe Serbow** *(Wczesne Dzieje Slowian, 1993).*

GREATEST SCRIBBLERS

They are also certain that the names *Spali, Spalei* and *Spori* are consistent with the problems inherent in Greek-Latin transliterations of the Srb/Serb name, especially names with three successive consonants. Greek historians and commentators, Safarik and others note, routinely treated native names in a cavalier manner. In fact, in their accounts of 'barbarian' nations, especially distant ones, the Greeks were the *greatest scribblers*, writes Strabo (63 B.C.-A.D.42), one of the first *scientific geographers*. In his 17-volume study *Geographica*, Strabo writes, the same or worse was often true of Roman imitators who were seldom able or inclined to correct the accounts of their Greek mentors.

SPORS ARE SRBS ARE SPORS

In support of the thesis that *Spals/Spors* are *Srbs,* the following points were made by leading late 18th, 19th, and early 20th century German, Austrian, French, Czech, Slovak, Polish, Hungarian, Romanian, and Croatian historians and Slavists: 1) Procopius' Spors is an obvious corruption of Srbs, the ancient and native name of all the Slavs; 2) Once mentioned, the so-called Spals and Spors disappear from the historical record; 3) If one compares the two most authoritative account of the Slavs in the 6th century, namely Jordan and Procopius, it is both clear and certain that the names Wends and Spors-Srbs are two common names for the one and same people; 4) We can state with certainty that the names Wends and Spors-Srbs are two names for one people. Jordan's Winds are Procopius's Spors/Srbs are Jordan's Winds. Thus the two names for an ancient people, one foreign, Winds or Wends, one native—Srb.

ORIGINAL, PRIMEVAL, NATIVE AND COMMON NAME

As the following brief statements indicate, all the above are absolutely certain that the ancient Slavs—the Wends, Antes, and Sklavini—were first known as Serbs: 1)

Serb was the original, primeval, native and common name of all Slavs; 2) Early Greek-Roman historians know nothing of the name Slav, they speak only of the Wends or Serbs; 3) In the beginning the Slavs called themselves by their native name, Serbs, while foreigners, especially Germans, called them Wends, or Winds; 4) According to the research of the greatest scholars on the subject, in ancient times all Slavs were called Serbs; 5) Serb was the name of all the Slav nations long before the name Slav or Ante appeared; 6) Serb was once the name of all the Slavs, who were also called Wends, Winds and Veneds by their western neighbors; 7) Over time the original name Serb was lost, the name Ante vanished in the 6th century B.C., and from the 6th century forward the name Slavi, Slavini appears in chronicles. When the modern Slavs were a single nation they were called Sarbaci, Sorabi, Sorbi, Srbi. It is still not clear when the ancient Serbs broke into different Slavic peoples; 8) Judging by the fact that the ancient Serbs occupied an immense area, that there were a number of separate Serb states, united only by language, the breakup of the Serbs may have started several thousand years before the birth of Christ; 9) This name [Serb] has the deepest historical roots. We come across it in its original, true, native form in Pliny (79 A.D.) and Ptolemy (175 A.D.) where one finds the name between the Volga, Maeotis, and Don rivers. This information alone gives us some idea how widely distributed the name Serb was even at that time. It absolutely confirms the words of later historians and commentators; 10) As a historical people the Slavs enter the historical record under two different names; one, a native name, Srb, appears in some sources, the other, Veneti, in more sources. Before too long the native name as a collective name, as a name for an immense national entity, will be replaced, as will Veneti, by Slav; 11) In ancient times all Slavs were called Wends or Serbs. I cannot say whether one name preceded the other, or whether both appeared at the same time. More likely than not, at the same time, one name, Serb, was used by the natives (*Domaci starobylich Slovanuv jmeno Srbove*), the other, Wend, by foreigners.

ELBE SERBS, DANUBE SERBS

It is safe to say that all the above agree that it not a coincidence that the Serbs of Germania and Illyria share a common name: 1) The common Serb name of the Illyrian Serbs and the Lusatian Serbs originated in ancient times when all the modern Slav nations were called Serbs, when they spoke a common language, which, step by step, over great space and time, devolved into twelve distinct languages; 2) The identical name of the Luzica [Lusatia] Serbs and the Balkan Serbs is not coincidental. They originate in ancient times when all Slavs were known as Serbs; 3) Though the national name Serb was once widely distributed, today it is carried by only two Slavic nations: Serbs on the Elbe and Serbs on the Danube; 4) Serb, the name which once was the common name of all Slavs, is today carried only by the natives of the two Luzicas and the Jugoslav Serbs. The Serbs of the two Luzicas are called Sorbs so as to distinguish them from the southern Serbs. J. Dobrovsky perhaps best sums up the consensus on the subject in the following terms: **Die Aehnilichkeit der Namens der lausitzer Sorben oder Serben und der illyrischen Serben ist nicht zufallig, sondem stammt aus uralten Zeiten her. Unter diesem Namen waren beide Ordnungen der slawischen Volker, ehe noch der ellgemeine Name Slawen aufgehommen, ehedem begriffen.**

3. IN LESS ANCIENT TIMES:
VENEDI, ANTES, SKLAVINI

In less ancient times, of course, the Serbs/Slavs were known by other names—***Venedi, Antes,*** and ***Sklavini.***[1] The name *Enetoi*, possibly a Greek form of ***Venedi,*** has deep roots in ancient Greek sources. An 8th century B.C. source, Homer's *Iliad*, places the *Enetoi* in Paflagonia (Asia Minor). Herodotus (484-425B.C.) locates the *Enetoi* on the Adriatic: *Enetoi kad en to Adria*. In one of his works, the Greek dramatist Euripiides (480-406 B.C.) refers to *Eneta*, a settlement in either Epirus or Asia Minor. Century's later, Strabo (63 B.C.-A.D. 21) mentions an *Enetoi* on the Adriatic.

VENETI

The name ***Veneti*** also has an impressive historical record. The Roman statesman, soldier and writer, Cato (234-149 B.C.) mentions the ***Veneti.*** In the early 1st century A.D., Pliny locates the ***Venedi*** on the Vistula: **It is said that Pomerania is inhabited as far as the Vistula River by the Sarmatian Venedi, Sciri, Hirri.**

At roughly the same time, Mela locates the ***Indi*** (***Vindi/Vendi***) alongside the ***Ser Serbs*** in Scythia. In early 2nd century A.D., Tacitus places the ***Venedi*** east of the Germans ('*their plundering forays take them over all the wooded and mountainous highlands between the Peucini [Carpathians] and the Fenni' [eastern Russia]*). Ptolemy (A.D. 100-178) places the ***Venedae*** among the Sarmatian tribes on the Baltic Sea: Large nations inhabit Sarmatia: **the Venedae along the whole Venedae Bay.** In the *Tabular Peutigneriana*, a 3rd century A.D. source, in a list of peoples dwelling beyond the boundaries of the Roman Empire, one finds several references to the ***Venedi:*** the ***Venadi Sarmatae*** and the ***Lugiones Sarmatae*** north of Dacia, the ***Venadi*** near the Danube delta.[2]

IMMENSA SPATIA, NATIO POPULOSA

In Jordanes' mid-6th century condensed version of a work of the same title written in the first half of the 6th century by Magnus Aurelius Cassidorius, a learned Roman, the numerous ***Venethi,*** centered on the Vistula, occupy a boundless area: *ab ortu Vistulae fluminis per immensa spatia Winidarum natio populosa consedit.*[3]

ANTES

Pliny places the ***Antes*** between the Sea of Azov and the Caspian. Ptolemy places them in the Crimea and at the mouth of the Don. Other sources place the ***Antes*** at the head of a powerful Slav confederation centered in the area of the Don, Donets, and middle Dnieper.[4] Jordanes locates the mighty ***Antes,*** **the bravest of these peoples, on the curve of the sea of Pontus, spread from the Danaster to the Danaper, rivers that are many days journey apart.**

BOZH, KING OF THE ANTES

According to Jordanes, the ***Antes*** were defeated by the Goths in the Dnieper region in 375, after which *Bozh*, king of the ***Antes,*** his son, and seventy chieftains were executed: ***Vinitharius in Antorum fines moviet procinctum, eosque dum adgreditur prima congressione superatus, deinde fortiter egit regemque eorum Boz nomine cum*** *filiis suit et LXX primatibus in exemplum terroris adfixit, ut dediticiis metum cadaveras pendentium germinarent.*

ANTABI, ANTHABI

An 8th century account of the *Antes* affairs in the year 400 records them as *Antabi, Anthabi* and refers to wars with Langobards crossing their lands: *Egressi ... Langobardi de Mauringa, applicueruntin Golanda, ubi aliquanto tempore commorati, dicuntur post haec Anthaib et Banthaib, pari modo et Vurgundhabi, per annos aliquod possidisse; Et moverunt se exhinde Langobardi, et venerunt in Golaidam, et postea possiderunt aldonus Anthaib et Bainaib seu et Burgundaib; Langobardi porcedurnt in provinciam Anthap, et inde in terram Bathaib* (Pauli Diaconia, Historia Langobardum, c.786).

ANTES, INFINITI

Impressed with their great number, Procopius *Antes* are *populi Antarum infiniti.* Following a defeat at the hands of the Lombards, Procopius writes, the Germanic Heruls were given free passage through Slavs lands, including *Antes* lands in Danubia-Carpathia, in the early 6th century.

BYZANTINE HISTORIANS

The *Antes* in action and war in the Balkans, Carpathia, Danubia, and lands further east are often mentioned in 5th and 6th century Byzantine historians and official sources: Agathias' *On the Reign of Justinian* covers the period 552-558; Theophylactus Simocattes' eight-volume history of the Emperor Maurice (582-602); the *Strategion of Maurice*, an early 7th century Byzantine military handbook, particularly the section titled 'On the habits and tactics of each of the foreign peoples'; *Paschal's Chronicle*, a work covering the period up to 629, especially the reigns of emperors Phokas and Heraclius. During the rule of Imperator Caesar Christi Justinian I (527-565) the *Antes* hold a prominent place in the list of barbarian adversaries/auxiliaries: *Alamanicus, Gotthicus, Francicus, Germanicus, **Anticus,** Alanicus, Vandalicus, etc.* In the year 530, Byzantine authorities appoint **Chilbudius,** an *Antes* chieftain and ally, Supreme Commander on the Danube. Fifteen years later **Justinian offers the Antes a considerable sum of money, lands on the northern bank of the lower Danube, and the status of imperial foederati, on condition that they guard the river against the Bulgars** (D. Obolensky, *The Byzantine Commonwealth, 1971*).

ANTES, AVARS

In the rapidly changing frontier world of friend and foe, less than two decades later, *Antes* invaders come into conflict with Avars serving as imperial *foederati* on the Danube. According to 7th century historian Theophylaktos Simocatta, in 602 the *Antes* allied themselves with Emperor Maurice against the Avars. In response, the Avar *khagan* dispatched an army under the command of Aspich to exterminate the *Antes.* However, the fearful Avars deserted before battle could take place. A nation of uncertain origin, the Avars were not always Avars. According to Byzantine sources, in some instances **they were Slavs called Avars** (F. Barisic, *"Monemvasijska Hronika" o doeseljavanju Avaro-Slovena na Peloponez 587 godine, Godisnjak Centra za balkanoloska ispitivanja I, 1965-66. A. Avenarius, Die Awaren in Europa, 1974. Z. Cilinska, Slovania a Avarski kaganat, 1992. J. Kovacevic, Avarski kaganat, 1977. W. Pohl, Die Awarenkriege Karls des Grossen, 788-803, 1988. B. Zasterova, Les Avares et les Slaves dans la Tactique de Muarice, 1971. O. Pritsak, The Slavs and the Avars,*

Settimane di studio del Centro Italiano di Studii sul Alto Medievo 30, 1982. L.A. Tyskiewicz, Problem zaleznosci slowian od awarow u VI-VII wieku, BaP IV, 1989).

FROM THE IONIAN GULF

Regarding the Justinian and post-Justinian period, Procopius writes: **Illyricum and all of Thrace, that is, from the Ionian Gulf to the suburbs of Constantinople, including Greece and the Chersonese were overrun by the Huns, Sclavini and Antes, almost every year, from the time when Justinian took over the Roman Empire; and intolerable things they did to the inhabitants.** So proud of occasional victories over the *Antes,* Justinian's successor, Justin II (562-578), assumed the title *Anticus.*

AS LONG AS THERE ARE SWORDS AND WARS

Often noted for their martial spirit, in the 6th century, the Bessarabian *Antes* responded to an Avar demand for tribute in the following terms: **No one can challenge our power. We are the ones who take the lands of others ... And so it will be as long as there are swords and wars in the world.** Unmistakably Slavic names of *Antes* kings and chieftains, including several with the suffix -gost, are recorded in diverse sources: *Ardagost, Bozh, Chilbud, Dobrogost, Kelagost, Mezimir, Prigost.* By the mid-7th century the name *Antes* loses its place in written sources in favor of the generic *Sklaveni.*

ANTI, ENTI, INDI, VINDI

It is obvious to some scholars that the *Venedi* and *Antes* are one and the same; the so-called *Anti, Enti, Indi, Vindi, Vendi* are different names for Slavs, the differences more a matter of time, place and language than anything else.

SKLAVINI

In a list of nomadic Scythian tribes between the Volga and Ural mountains, Ptolemy locates the *Soubenoi.* In a list of sedentary tribes between the Baltic Sea and the Black Sea, Ptolemy locates the *Stavani.* If K. Moszynski is right, if *Soubenoi* is actually a corruption of *Sloveni/Slovenoi,* then it is the first time the name *Sloveni* appears in the historical record. Safarik and others, however, read *Soubenoi* not as *Slovenoi,* but as *Svoibenoi,* as 'the free, independent Slavs,' and *Stavani* as *Stani,* connoting a Slav nation, land, settlement.[5]

WILD, FREE, WITHOUT RULERS

The Slavs as *Sklavini* definitely enter the historical record as Danubian *Sklavini* in the *Dialogues of Pseudo-Caesar*, a 5th century compilation based partly on 4th century sources: **The Sklavenoi ... are wild, free, and without rulers ... They hail one another by howling like wolves.** According to the author, the *Sklavenoi* are in every way the exact opposiite of a neighboring non-Slavic nation: **The Fisonians who avoid conflict and readily submit to all in their path.**

WOLVES

Though he fails to mention the Danubians who howl like wolves, O.N. Trubacev finds a Serb-Wolf connection by other means. Namely, by connecting Herodotus' account of the *Neuroi* ('*The Scythians and the Hellenes inhabiting Scythia tell us that once in a year each of the Neuroi becomes a wolf for some days and again becomes what he was*) with the Serb/Balkan belief in *vukodlaks* (werewolves) with the fact that **the vlk, 'wolf', completely absent from the anthroponymy of most of the Slavic languages, is often found in the personal names of South Slavs: Vukobrat, Vukoman, Vukomil, Vukomir, Vukosav, Vukovoj, Bjelovuk, Dobrovuk, Milovuk** *(O.N. Trubacev, Linguistics and Ethnogenesis of the Slavs: The Ancient Slavs as Evidenced by Etymology and Onomastics, InD 13, 1985).*

VUKSA, VUCIC, VUKOTA, VUKIC

In fact, of course, in the some Serb lands, in Montenegro, for example, *Vuk* often seems to be an element of every other personal or family name. A late 15th century register of adult males in several clans settled in the he *Banjani* and *Piva* counties of northwestern Montenegro, for example, reveals a high percentage of names derived from the root *vuk-*. In the following series, the son's name is followed by the father's name: Vuksa, Radic; Vucic, Radosal; Radic, Vukota; Vukic, Grubac; Vukca, Baldun; Radic, Vukic; Knez Vukcic, Bratum; Vukosav, Vrbic; Vukic, Vladko; Vuksa, Vitoja; Vukman, Vulin; Ratko, Vukasin; Vukosav, Milan; Vukosav, Obrad; Radosav, Vukman; Vukasin, Vuk; Vukac, Obrad; Vukac, Milosh; Vukota, Stanimil; Vukac, Pribislav; Vukota, Dabiziv; Radosav, Vukan; Kovac, Vukota; Vukosav, Vukic; Radivoj, Vuksa; Ivan, Vuksa; Radica, Vukic; Vukas, Bratul; Vukosav, Radac; Vucin, Stoje; Vukas, Radasin.

ABODE OF THE SLAVENI

In the next century, Procopius locates the *Sklavenoi* on the lower Danube. According to Jordanes, **the abode of the Sclaveni extends from the city of Noviodunum and the lake called Mursianus to the Danster, and northward as far as the Vistula.** Never one to flatter enemies of the Goths, Jordanes claims that **they have swamps and forests for their cities.**

SCLAVINI OR ANTES

Though divided into many tribes with different names (**Quorum nomina liecet nunce per varias familias et loca mutentur**), Jordanes writes, the *Veneti* mainly call themselves *Sclavini* or *Antes: principaliter Sclavini et Antes nominatur.*

ONE IN BLOOD AND LANGUAGE

Differences in name and place notwithstanding, Jordanes writes: **All, Veneti, Antes and Sclavi, are one in blood and language.**

DO NOT DIFFER IN APPEARANCE

Familiar with both *Antes* and *Sklavini* who served as mercenaries in Byzantine armies, Procopius, an adviser to the great Byzantine commander Belisarius, is unable to distinguish one from the other: **The Sklavini and Antes do not differ in appearance. All of them are tall and strong, their skin and hair neither very light or dark, but all are ruddy of face.**

ENDNOTES

[1] For a solid discussion of the Wends, Antes and Sklavini from a mid-19th century perspective, read 'Prvotni jmena Slovanu, Vidnove a Srbove' and 'Nejstarsi svedectvi o Vindech' in Safarik's Sebrany Spisy I (1862) and Zpravy o 'Vindech, Antech, Slovanech' in Sebrany Spisy II (1862). Also: V. Georgiev, Veneti, Anti, Sklaveni i tredelnieto na slavjanskite ezici, Slavisticen sbornik, 1968. G. Schramm, Venedi, Antes, Sclaveni, Sclavi. Fruhe Sammelgbezeiichungen fur slawische Stamme und ihr geschichtlicher Hintergrund, JgO 43, 1995.

[2] The Tabular Peutigneriana refers to a map in the form of along narrow strip of parchment, more than 21 feet long, copied from a lost original believed to originate in the third century AD. The name stems from an early 16th century scholar named K. Peutinger, who acquired the map in 1509.

[3] For an interesting attempt to explain the origin and primary meaning of the ethnikon, Veneti/Venedi: Z. Golab, Veneti-Venedi-The Oldest Name of the Slavs, InD 3, 1975. Also: J. Perwolf, Polen, Ljachen, Wenden, Arch. Slav. Phi 4, 1880. M. Rudnicki, Denominacjja ethniczna Veneti, SlO 9, 1930. J. Kozlowski, Wendowie w zrodlach historycznych i w swietle karografii prehistorycznej, 1937. M. Rudnicki, Sur la methode d'etudier la toponymie et l'anthroponymie (L'etymologie du noma de la Vistule et de la denomination Veneti), SlO 27, 1938. T. Lehr-Splawinski, O pierwotnych Wenetach ((nter Arma, 1946). F. Bujak, Wendowie na wschodnich brzegach Baltyku, 1948. K. Tymnieniecki, Wentowie, nazwa i rzeczy-wistosc historyczna, SlA 1, 1948. A. Dostal, Venetove, Antove, Slavia XIX, 1949-50. E. Schwarz, Die Urheimat der Veneter, FuF 27, 1953. 0.T. Milewski, Nazwy z obszaru Polski poderjzane o pochodzenie wenetyskie lub ilirjskie, SlA 11, 1964. T. Sulimirski, Die Veneti-Vendae und deren Vehalktnis zu den Slawen Berichte II, 1973. V. Georgiev, Veneti, anti, sklaveni i tridelnieto na slavjanskite ezici (Slavisticen sbornik, 1968). T. Sulimirski, Die Veneti-Venedae und deren Verhalnis zu den Slawen, BeR 2, 1973. G. Labuda, Udzial Wenetow w etnogenezie Slowian (Etnogeneza i topogeneza Slowian, 1980).

[4] N. Zupanic, lzvor in ime Antov, Ethnolog VII, 1934; Boz, rex Antorum, Glasnik 4, 1961. G. Vernadsky, Goten und Anten in Sudrussland, SuD 3, 1938. B.A. Rybakov, Anty i Kievskaia Rus, Vestnik drenei istorii 1, 1939. P.N. Tretiakov, Anti i Rus, Sovet. Etno., 4, 1947. M.J. Brajcevski, Antskij period v istorii vostocych slavjan, Archeologija 7, 1952. M. Budimir, Antai antes anti anticus. Zbornik radova Vizantoloskog instituta, VIII, 1964. V.V. Sedov, Anti, Problemi sovetski arheologii, 1978.

[5] For an interesting discussion of the origin and primary meaning of the ethnikon, Sklavini-Slav: J.P. Maher, The Ethnonym of the Slavs—Common Slavic *Slovene, InD 2, 1974. **The ancient theory championed by Dobrovsky and Safarik,** Maher writes, **that the prehistoric Slavs named themselves the 'the intelligibly speaking' is the only explanation borne out by correct interpretation of the Greek, Slavic and IE data and corroborated by ethnography ... The slovo etymology is the only theory that stands up under linguistic analysis ... In the light of global naming practices of mankind the etymology of *slovene as 'the intelligibly speaking' is unimpugnable ... their self-given name in their own language means 'clear speech' or 'clear words.'**

4. SCYTHS, SARMATS

Scythia is one of the more fluid and elusive terms in the works of ancient geographers. At different times it refers to lesser and greater regions stretching from southeastern Europe in the west to Central Asia in the east. In Europe the geographical term Scythia is associated with two regions, namely the Black Sea Steppe, where the principal Scythic kingdom developed, and, later, *Scythia Minor,* a Roman province comprising the lands immediately south of the mouths of the Danube.

THE SCYTHIAN LOOK

Contemporaneous Greek artisans depict the Scythians as a nation of usually bearded men, who wear their hair long, flowing, swept back from the forehead, with perhaps rather Slavic faces, characterized by heavy browbridges, deep-set eyes, and pronounced noses. Recent excavations of Scythian grave sites offers interesting physical anthropological information. It indicates that, Renate Rollet writes: **in European Scythia, including the Caucasus regions, the Scythians were Europids without any Mongol characteristics** *(Die Welt der Skythen, 1980).* The excavations also indicate that in stature the ancient Scythians resemble the highland Serbs, centered in Montenegro. Rolle writes: **The Scythians were relatively tall. The tallness is particularly noticeable in warrior burials and those of men of the upper social stratum ... They are often over 6 ft (1.80m) in height, sometimes over 6 ft 3 in (1.90m), and have occasionally been been known to exceed 6 ft 6 in. (2m.) ... This phenomenon can be observed all the way to the eastern extremity of the Scythian world.**

TALLEST PEOPLE IN EUROPE

It is perhaps significant that the same is true and truer of the Montenegrin Serbs. The dean of American physical anthropologists, Harvard's Carleton S. Coon, writes: **The Montenegrins who are the tallest people in Europe, live on a barren limestone mountain upland ... They are probably the heaviest as well as the tallest people in Europe ... Although their legs are long, their trunks are correspondingly high ... The Montenegrins' mean shoulder breath is 39cm., and their chests are correspondingly large. The relative span of 101 is extremely low, indicating that their arms are short in proportion to either leg or trunk length. The hands and feet are, as is to be expected, usually of great size. These huge mountaineers are not as a rule slender, leptosome people; they are often thickset, and are large all over.**

AN ALMOST PERFECT EMBODIMENT

One finds the same observations in the accounts of English and other European observers. In one typical instance, a seasoned English traveler writes: **I have never, in all my wanderings throughout the world, met a better fellow than the Montenegrin ... The men of the Tsernagora are justly famous for their good looks and splendid physiques. They are a race of giants, and a man of average height in England would be regarded here as something akin to a dwarf. But notwithsthanding his formidable frame and stature the Montenegrin is graceful in all his movements** *(H. De Windt, Through Savage Europe, 1913).* Another English observer, an officer of the Consular Service, states the case in more succinct terms: **The Montenegrin race presents an**

almost perfect embodiment of all that is admirable in physique *(A.G. Hulme-Beaman, Twenty Years in the Near East, 1898).*

SCYTHARUM, PATRIA SCLAVINORUM

The belief that the Slavs originated in Scythia finds clear expression in a number of early medieval works, including a 7th century cosmography known as the *Ravennatis Anonymil Cosmographia*: **Scythia (Scytharum) is the ancestral land (Scytharum est patria) of the Slavs (Sclavinooum exorta est prosapia).**

SCYTHS

Similarly, medieval and post-medieval annals, chronicles, and histories will sometimes refer to Slavs not as Slavs, but as ***Scyths* or *Scythians.*** One of the more interesting and specific variations on the Scythian theme is found in a 17th century inquiry into the origins of Hungary wherein the author cites the *Scythian **Budins*** *(Origines Hungaricae Seu, Liber, Qui Vera Nationis Hungaricae Origo et Antiquistas, 1692).* Tracing the origin of Hungary's Slavs, F. Otrokosci writes that: **Some are from Old Scythia, some are Veneds from the Baltic, but most are Budins, from the Budins who originated in the Don region of Scythia.**

OLD SCYTHIA

Herodotus gives the borders of Scythia and Old Scythia in the following terms: **Before you come to Scythia, on the seacoast lies Thrace. The land here makes a sweep, and then Scythia begins, the Ister falling into the sea at this point with its mouth facing the east. Starting from the Ister I shall now describe the measurements of the seashore of Scythia. Immediately after the Ister is crossed, Old Scythia begins, and continues as far as the city called Carcinitis.**

BUDINI

Herodotus locates the ***Budini,* a large and powerful nation; they all have blue eyes and red hair**, north of the Sauromatae. The ***Budini,*** he writes: **are the original people of the country, and are nomads. Their country is thickly planted with trees of all manners and kinds. In the very woodiest part is a broad deep lake, surrounded by marshy ground with reeds growing on it.**

PROTO-SLAVS

A number of eminent scholars have little doubt that the ***Budins*** are a Proto-Slav people (e.g. Safarik, Niederle, Lehr-Splawinski, Moszynski, Golab).[1] In most instances, the name ***Budin*** is traced to the Slavic root *bud-* and *the large and powerful nation* is centered in the Middle Desna and Sejm basins, which belong to the forest zone. L. Niederle writes: **I do not hesitate to locate the seats of the Herodotian Budini in the west, in the vicinity of the Neuroi, and to put them in central Kievan Russia between the Dnieper and Don, approximately on Desna and Sejm ... and on the basis of the explicit statement by Herodotus that the Budini are a people different from the Scythians ... and on the basis of their physical type and ultimately because of the meaning and form of their ethnic name I do not hesitate to pronounce them to be a big Slavic tribe belonging to the eastern branch, thus a part of the later Great Russian (velkorusky) stock which obviously already in a very old period occupied the Desna basin having given the river its Slavic name, and** which naturally at the Herodotian time could penetrate along the Sejm as far as **Upper Don** *(L. Niederle, Slovanske starozitnosti, I, 1902).*

NEURI

They also believe that the ***Budin's*** neighbors, the ***Neuri***, are a related Proto-Slav people. Regarding their location, Herodotus writes: **As for the inland boundaries of Scythia, if we start from the Ister, we find it enclosed by the following tribes, first the Agathyrsi, next the Neuri.**

VOLYNIA

Golab's interpretation of Herodotus places the ***Neuri*** in historical Volynia, extending east to the Middle Dnieper and west to the Upper Dniester. According to Herodotus, serpents forced the ***Neuri,*** whose **customs are like the Scythians**, to leave their original home and take refuge with the ***Budini.*** Evidence in favor of a Proto-Slavic identification is found in several areas, including the name's Slavic root (from the Proto-Slavic root *ner-* connoting live, force) and related hydronyms and toponyms (Nur, Nurec, Nuzec and *ziemia Nuska* on the border of Poland and the Ukraine). Indeed, Golab's examination of the textual, linguistic, and onomastic evidence allows him to make the following statement: **So we would consider Neuroi (late PSL *Nervi) to be the oldest attested endogenous Slavic ethnicon used by a large Proto-Slavic tribe concentrated in the 6th-7th centuries B.C. along the northwestern frontier of Scythia, which correponds roughly to the historical East Slavic province of Volynia** *(Z. Golab, The Oldest Ethnica Referring to the Slavs: Neuroi and Budini in Herodotus's Description of Scythia, OnO 19, 1974).*

GREAT SERB NATION

A 10th century Byzantine source locates one part of the Serb nation, the *Black Serbs,* in Scythia: **The great Serb nation, which is divided into two parts, the White Serbs or independent Serbs, and the Black Serbs or dependent Serbs.**

SERBS: SCYTHARUS GENTES

Medieval German sources sometimes refer to Germania's Serbs as: **Scythae or Scytharus gentes**. *The Wends and Their Migration from Scythia to German Lands* is the title of a chapter in a mid-16th century German chronicle compiled by E. Brotuff. The chronicle records the settlement of the salt mines near Halle by **Wends called Serbs who migrated to Germania from Scythia** *(Chronica von den Salz-Bornen und Erbauung der Stadt Hall an der Sala in Sachsen gelegen, 1554).*

SARMATIA

As the *Sarmats* overwhelmed their fraternal rivals ***(Porro Scytharum, Sarmatarumque gens una et eadens ab origine)*** around the middle of the 2nd century B.C., *Sarmatia* succeeded *Scythia* as a more popular name for the 'barbarian' lands beyond Roman-Byzantine Europe's eastern frontier.

WHEN ONE CROSSES THE TANAIS

Regarding the original homeland of the *Sarmatians*, Herodotus writes, **when one crosses the Tanais, one is no longer in Scythia; the first region on crossing is that of the Sauromatae, who, beginning at the upper end of the Palus Maeotis**

[Sea of Azov], stretch northward a distance of fifteen days journey. Polybius locates *Sarmatia* in the Ponto-Caspian steppe *(Historia)*. Ptolemy's *Sarmatia* is an immense area bounded by the Vistula and Volga rivers and the Baltic and Black seas *(Geographike Hyphegesis)*. Pomponius Mela gives *Sarmatia* a European orientation, namely the lands east of the Elbe and north of the Danube *(De Situ Orbis)*.

SARMATS

Similarly, *Sarmat* or *Sarmatae* (also *Sarabatiae, Sauromatae, Syrmatae,* and *Sermende* among others) succeeds *Scyth* or *Scythae* more often than not as a learned archaism for the Slavs (e.g. *Sarmatae Sclavi*). Pliny, Tacitus and Ptolemy refer to the Slavs on the Vendic/Baltic Sea and the Vistula River as Sarmats. Ptolemy, for example, writes: ***Habitant Sarmatiam gentes maximae Venedae propter totum Venedicum sinum; Minores autem gentes Sarmatiam incolunt iuxta Visutalam infra Venedas Gythones.*** Mela locates *Sarmatia* east of Germania: ***Germani ad Sarmatas porriguntur.*** Precisely where *Germania* ends and *Sarmatia* begins, however, was a matter of some confusion. In *De Origine et Situ Germanorum* (A.D. 98), a somewhat garbled description of the various tribes west of the Rhine and north of the Danube, believed to be based largely on out-of-date material, Tacitus is not sure whether some nations were *Germans* or *Sarmats*. **Here Suebia ends. I am not sure whether the tribes of the Peucini, Veneti should be assigned to the Teutons or to the Sarmatians ... The Venedi have adopted many Sarmatian habits; for their plundering takes them over all the wooded and mountainous highlands that lie between the Peucini and the Fenni. Nevertheless, they are one the whole to be classed as Germans; for they have settled homes, carry shields, and are fond of traveling—and travelling as—on foot, differing in all these respects from the Sarmatians.**

SUEBI

It is important to note that the ***Suebi,*** who occupy Germania's heartland, are also a problem of sorts for Tacitus. The ***Suebi,*** Tacitus writes, **do not constitute a single nation. They occupy more than half Germany, and are divided into a number of separate tribes under different names, though all are called by the generic name Suebi.** In the early 1820s, D. Popp was one of the first German historians to identify Tacitus' ***Suebi*** with the Slavs.

NOT ALL SARMATIANS

At the same time it was clear to ancient and modern historians that *Sarmat* and *Sarmatia*[4] referred to an immense area inhabited by numerous and different nations, Slavs and others. In the succinct words of one scholar: **All Slavs are Sarmatians, but all Sarmatians are not Slavs.**

SCLAVI SARMATI

Accordingly, medieval German sources often refer to Slavic Germania as *Sarmatarum* and the native Slavs as *Sarmates* or *Sclavi Sarmati*. In the 16th century one often finds *Sarmatia* in the titles of Polish Kings: ***Invictissimum dominum Sigismundeum, regem Polonie, magnum ducem Lituanie, Russie, Prussie, Sarmatieque Europee dominum et et heredum; Regnum Sarmatiae; Rex Sarmatiae Europee invictissimus; Sarmacie Totius Rex; Sarmatiae Poloniaeque Rex; Sarmatiae Regis;***

Sarmatica respublica, Sarmatae populus *(E. Potkowski, Sarmatissmus als politische ideologie der jagellonischen Dynasties, Zeitschrift fur Ostmitteleuropae Forschung 44, 1995).*

SLOVO APUD SARMATAS

That *Sarmats* were *Slavs* were *Sarmats* was the premise of numerous medieval and later commentaries on the history and language of the Slavs. In a mid-16th century history of Bohemia, the learned Bishop of Olomouc, John Skala of Dubravka (*Johannes Dubravius*), derives the name **Sloven** (Slav) from the *Sarmat* word **Slovo** which, he explains, has the same meaning as *Verbum* in Latin: ***Id enim Slowo apud Sarmatas, quod verbum apud Lationos personat. Quoniam igitur omnes Sarmatarum nationes late jam tunc, longeque per Regna et Provincia sparsae unum nomen eumdemque sermonem, atque eadem propemodum verba sonarant, se uno etiam cognomine Slovanos appellabant. Ab ipsa praeterea gloria, quae apud ilos Slava dicitur, Slavitni dicti*** *(Historiae Regni Boiemiae, 1552).*

SLAWISCHEN VOLKSTAMM

On the basis of historical documents and textual analysis, in the 19th century most historians and Slavists of note read *Sarmat* as *Slav*. Quandt, for example, writes that *Sarmat* is another name for *Slav:* **Der Name bezeichnet den Slawischen Volkstamm.**

OLDEST RETRIEVABLE HABITAT

In the second half of the 20th century linguistic analysis tends to generally confirm the prehistoric 'Sarmat' roots of Slavdom. The following words, for example, follow Z. Golab's examination of a number of Slavic words with the initial x-: **First of all, the problem of the prehistorical ethno-linguistic contacts between the Slavs (Proto-Slavs) and the Pontic Iranians (Scythians and Sarmatians) reappears as an important problem. Such a number of loanwords concerning such different semantic spheres cannot be accidental: it must be interpreted as a result of a prolonged period of very close inter-ethnic relations, especially because among the words discussed there are such for which we should a phonemic 'Iranization' rather than simple borrowing. Briefly, we should 'rehabilitate' the idea of close relations between the Proto-Slav and the Scythians or Scytho-Sarmatians ... Another conclusion which can be drawn from the above lexical facts concerns the location of the oldest 'retrievable' habitat of the Slavs in the period of their close contacts with the Pontic Iranians** *(Z. Golab, The Initial X- in Common Slavic: A Contribution to Prehistorical Slavic-Iranian Contacts, American Contributions to the VII International Congress of Slavists, 1973).*

ENDNOTES

[1] In Sebrany Spisy, I (1862), sub-section *Slovanske narody u Herdota*, Safarik discusses the linguistic, onomastic and textual evidence in favor of a Proto-Slav interpretation of the Budini and the 'Neuri cili Nuri.' M.I. Artmanov, Venedi, Neuri i Budini v slavjanskom etnogeneze, Vestnik Leningradskogo Universiteta 2, 1946. M. Plezie, Neurowie w swietle hisotriografii starozytnej, PdZ 8, 1952. K. Tymniecki, Neurowie—Weneci, PaM 5, 1957. O.N. Trubacev, Staraja Skifija Gerodota i slavjane, AzY 6, 1977. B.A. Rybakov, Gerodotova Skifija, 1979.

5. SLAVS ARE SARMATS ARE SERBS?

The notion that the *Sarmats* were *Slavs* was originally based in large part on the premise that the *Sarmats* were *Serbs,* that the names *Sarmat* and *Serb* share a common root. Thus medieval texts sometimes identify *Sarmatia* as *Sarabatije,* as land of the *Serbs/Sorabs/Sarabs: Sarabatie propie currentes vel sibi viventes Zirbi.*

SARMATAE SIRBI

Bishop Salomon's early 10th century dictionary-encyclopedia, *Mater Verborum* informs readers that the *Sarmats* were once called *Serbs: Sarmatae ... Sirbi tum dicti a serendo id est quasi sirbintiu.* Vecerad, an early 12th century commentator on the Czech edition of *Mater Verborum* equates the *Sarmats* and *Serbs* in the following terms: *Sarmatae populi Zirbi, 1102*

ANTIQUISSIMUM NOMEN SARMATIS

An early 16th century chronicle, *Chronicon Carionis,* originally compiled by J. Carion (1499-1537), a noted German mathematician, astronomer, and historian, first printed in 1532, relates the *Sarmatians* to the *Serbs* in the following ways: **The name Serb is derived from the names Sorab and Sarmat** *(a Sorabos et Sarmatis trahere);* **Sorab is the oldest form of Sarmat:** *(Ex nomine exitimo factum esse nomen Sorabi, paucis literis mutatis; Soraborum antiquissimum nomen a Sarmatis retinuerunt).* The same source asserts that *Sarmat* is the original name of all *Serbs,* of northern and southern *Serbs: Sarmatarum appelationem, cum quae eodem est Soraborum Borealibus, qui supra Pontum et Maeotidem habitarunt.*

SRBLI ILLYRIORUM

In his mid-16th century study Chalcondyles notes the historical and linguistic factors that demonstrate beyond doubt that the *Serbs/Srbli* of *Illyria/Illyriorum* originate in *Sarmatia:* **From the Danubian lands on the the edge of Europe, from Sarmatia.**

SARMATARUM, SORABI, SERBLI

In the 18th and 19th centuries some scholars remained certain that the name *Serb* is derived from *Sarmat,* that over time the name *Sarmat* evolved and survived as *Sorab* and *Serb: Obscurantum tame paulatim et Sarmatarum nomen invenimus ita quidem ut soli Sorabi et Serbli id conservasse existimentur.* In his discussion of the original name of the Slavs (*'Prvotna jmena Slovanu'*) in *Sebrany Spisy II* (1863), P. Safarik makes it clear that: (1) *Wend* and *Sarmat* are other and later names for *Serb* **(Vindove a Sarmati = Srbove)**; (2) that *Sarmat* is another name for *Serb* **(O Sarmatech = Srbech).**

SERBISCHER ABKUNFT

Other scholars, noting that early geographers and commentators routinely abused and misused the name *Sarmat,* are certain that it was often used as a name for the *Serbs:* **Den alten und vielfach missgebrauchten Namen der Sarmaten ... fur alle Zweige serbischer Abkunft.**

JAZYGES

In the 18th, 19th, and early 20th centuries some scholars were certain that the **Sarmats-are-Serbs** thesis was especially strong in the case of the ***Sarmatian Jazyges.*** According to Karl Anton von Gottlob, an 18th century German historian, philologist, and author of an encyclopedic history of the Serbs, the early history of the Serbs is obscured by a generic name for the nations of European and Asian ***Sarmatia,*** the so-called ***Sarmatians,*** a fictitious name for many very different nations including the Serbs, the so-called ***Sarmatians,*** who, according to Herodotus, spoke a corrupt ***Scythian*** language *(Erste Linien Eines Versuches uber der Alten Slawen Ursprung, 1783-89).* In support of the ***Jazgye*** thesis, Gottlob and others make the following basic points: 1. In ancient times **Serb** was the original, native and common name of all the Slavs; 2. Later, the **Serbs** were known by two names: ***Serb*** and ***Jazyge,*** recorded as ***Sarmatian Jazyge*** (e.g. Strabon's ***Jaziges Sarmatae***); 3. In the pre-Christian period elements of the ***Jazyges*** left the **Serb-Jazyge** homeland in the Volga basin, migrated westward, occupied parts of Russia, Podolia, Moldavia, and Dacia and challenged the Romans in Danubia-Pannonia; 4. In the 1st century A.D., perhaps earlier, perhaps under pressure from the Huns, the **Serbs** left ***Sarmatia*** and began settling in Europe; 5. In *Germania* the **Serbs** are called **Wends,** in *Danubia* the **Serbs** are called ***Jazyges***; 6. Beginning with the 6th century the ***Jazyge Serbs*** of *Danubia* are called **Slovens** by the Greeks and others; 7. Both names, ***Jazyge*** and ***Sloven***; ***Jazyge*** from ***Jazyk***, **Sloven** from **Slovo**, are derived from Old Slavic words connoting letter, word, speech, language; 8. All Slavs can be traced to the **Serb** or ***Jazyge*** branches of the great **Serb** trunk. According to Gottlob, vital evidence in favor of the ***Jazyge Serb*** thesis is found in the historical record, in the numerous recorded Slavic hydronyms, toponyms, and towns (e.g. Ptolemy's **Serbitium** in *Pannonia Inferior*) suggesting an early **Serb** presence in Danubia 'coincidental' in time and place with that of the so-called ***Sarmatian Jazyge.***

BABA, BUKA

Mid-5th century sources identify two ***Jazyge*** rulers with Slavic sounding names, namely ***Baba*** and ***Buka*** at the head of the ***Sarmatian Jazyges*** on the Danube near modern Belgrade: *Quorum exitio Suavorum ... freti auxilio Sarmatarum, qui cum Beuca et Babai regibus suis auxiliari ei advenissent (469); Theodoricus ex sattelitibus et ex populo patris elegit sibi pene sex milia viroum, cum quibus patre inscio, permenso Danubio, Sarmatarum regem incurrit, equmque interemit, familiamque ac censum depredans, ad genitorem suum cum victoria redit. Singindunum dehinc civitatem, quam idem Sarmatae possidebant, invadens, non Romanis sed suae subdidit ditioni (470); Theodericus adolescens annorum 18, transito Danubio, super Sarmatas irruit, et regem eorum Babaz perimit, et cum bellicis manubiis victor at patrem redit (470).*

SLAVS CALLED JAZYGES

In *Commentario Historica de Veribus Incois Hungariae Cis-Danuabianae a Morav Amne at Tibiscum* (1767), J. Severini, an early authority on the history of Hungary and Danubia, writes that *Slavs* from the Oder, first called **Sarmats,** then **Wends,** then **Slavs,** and **Slavs** called ***Jazyges,*** with whom they shared a common language and institutions, settled the lands along and between the Tisa and Danube rivers. Zupanic does not identify the ***Jazyges*** as **Slavs.** However, Zupanic suspects that in some instances the name ***Jazyges*** includes **Slavs** called **Serbs.** In the case of the ***Jazgyes*** who settled in the plains between the Danube and Tisa shortly after Christ's birth, for example, Zupanic believes that *Serbs* are included.

SERBS, BULGARS, JASYGES

It is interesting that a 16th century source records the *Jasyges* as one of the nations that made up Hungary's peasantry: **Saxons, Germans, Bohemians, Slavs, Wallachs, Ruthenes, Serbs, Bulgars, Jasyges, Cumans.**

6. SERS, SCIRS, SRBUL

Given Toynbee's and other theories of Slav settlement in southeastern Europe, one thousand years before the birth of Christ, it is not surprising that diverse historical sources present evidence of possible Serb settlement in Danubia and Pannonia in the first centuries of the Christian era.

SERETE, SERBINUM

According to Zupanic, evidence that **Serbs from Sarmatia or Dacia** settled along the Drava and Sava rivers in Panonnia in the first century of the Christian era or earlier is found in both Pliny and Ptolemy. Namely, Pliny's **Serete**, a nation located on the Drava River, and Ptolemy's **Serbitium**, a town on the Sava River in *Pannonia Inferior*.

MONTES SERRORUM

In his multi-volume *Rerum gestarum libri*, Ammianus Marcellanus (A.D. 330-395), Rome's last major historian, refers to a section of the Transylvanian Alps as **montes Serrorum** or the *Serr/Serb Mountains*.[1] Zupanic believes that the **montes Serrorum** can be traced to early Serb settlements in Dacia: **Since we have shown that Serri is the same as Serb, the montes Serrorum mentioned by Marcellinus confirms the presence of Serbs in the southern Carpathians, one of their stations on their move to the heart of Europe ... Of course, It is quite possible that the Serbs were in the southern Carpathians before Marcellinus's time. It is possible that Serb elements, together with Jazyges, moved in as early as the first century B.C.**[2]

EMPEROR LICINIUS

A later mid-12th century work, Joannes Zonaras' *Historical Epitome*, believed to based on earlier sources, notably the complete text of Dio Cassius' *Romaika* and several lost Byzantine historians, relates the **montes Serrorum** to Emperor Valerius Licinianus Licinius (308-324), Roman co-ruler from 308-324, and brother-in-law—married to half-sister Constantia in 313—of Emperor Constantine the Great (307-337). After 313 Licinius was as supreme in the East as Constantine in the West. A deterioration in relations between the two emperors led to open warfare in the Balkans in 614, where Licinius sought the support of pagans. Following defeat by Constantine's forces in 324, Licinius sought support in the *Serr Mountains*. In the same year he was captured and exiled to Thessalonica, where he was executed the following year.

LIKINIJ SRBINY BITI RODOM

An intriguing and as yet unaccountable early 4th century Serb connection is found in medieval Serb church manuscripts that, on the basis of 'authentic sources' (*istinih spisatelja*) refer to Licinius's **Serb** ancestry: **Glagoljut istini spisatelji jako Likinij Srbiny biti rodom ... Sija videv sin jego Bela Uros uze ot sestri carevi Konstatije; Tsarstvujusci Likinijy ... severnim i zapadnim stranama Srbin jest. Sze glagocistivij Konstantin prisvajajet k sebe Likinija i vdaet jem sestry svojy Konstantijy v zenu; Likinije sze Srbin be; I carstvuje v njem imase bolarina nekojego Srbina, imenom Likinije; Sze Likinije bese dlamatinski gospodin rodom Srbin; bese si Likinije Dalmatinski gospodin rodom Srbin. Rodi od Konstantije sina ot negoze pokolenom mi mnozi izidose, daze i do Beloga Urosa** *(R. Novakovic, Karpatski i Likijski Srbi,*

1997).

DAGON, DAGONIA

An even more intriguing early Serb connection with early Danubia/Dacia is found in one of the manuscripts, the *Karlovacki Rodoslov (Karlovac Genealogy)*. According to this source, at the time of Emperor Licinius: **All Serbs worshiped Dagon. From Dagon the Dagonians and Dacians received their names; from Ser, all the Serbs.** It goes on to say that: **Among many others, he [Licinius] persecuted the saints and martyrs Jermil and Stratonik, who were in Dagonia, near the Istar [Danube].**

ASIA MINOR, MIDDLE EAST

Some scholars believe that the reference to *Dagon,* a great Semitic god, suggests an early and substantial Balkan-Danubian connection with Asia Minor and the Middle East *(R. Novakovic, Jos o poreklu Serba — I sva Srbska idolu sluzase Dagonu, 1992).* The eminent German Slavist H. Kunstmann believes that the Dagon cult in Danubia can be traced to Roman Emperor Trajan (98-117 A.D.), to the forced resettlement of subject peoples originating in Asia Minor in Dacia. Later, he believes, in the Christian era, *Dagon* was a generic term for pagans, for pagan Slavs in Dacia, for pagan Serbs who later settled in Poland, where Kunstmann finds traces of *Dagon* (*Dagome-iudex-Regeste*) in late 10th century Polish sources, including the name and titles of the house of Piast's Mieszko I, Poland's first ruler *(H. Kunstmann, Uber de Herkunft der Polen von Balkan, DwS, 29, 1984).*[3] With regard to the Serb-Polish *Dagon Connection,* Kunstmann writes: **Freilich, im Laufe der Jahrhunderte hat sich die Bedeutung Dagons ganz erheblich geandert, namlich ins diametrale Gegenteil, was besagt, dass der Name Dagon zum nomen dei falsi, zur Bezeichnung heidnischer Kulte, der Heiden schlechthin wurde. Dass die Verwendung des Namens Dagon zur Bezeichnung von Heiden sogar nch 1503 unter Balkanslaven ublich gewesen zu sein scheint, lasst sich belegen und beweisen. Eine Urhunde aus Karlovac, in der kurz uber die Geschichte der serbischen "Zaren" berichtet wird, sagt folgendes: I vsa Srbska idolu sluzase Dagonu, otsud i Dagoni i Daky imenujut se. Damit wird nun nicht nur erstmals der Landername Srpska belegt, sondern auch, was im gegebenen Zusammenhang wichtiger ist, dass es zum Namen Dagon offenbar ebenfalls den Plural Dagoni gegeben hat, und zwar im Sinne von Heiden.**

Doch werden in der betreffenden Urkunde unter diesen heidnischen Dagoni ganz konkret die Daci oder Dacier verstanden. Gegen Ende heisst es in der Urkunde ausserdem este si v Dagaoni bliz Istra, was sogar erkennen lasst, dass die ehemalige romische Provinz Dacia, das Land Dacien, im Slavischen einmal Dagon geheissen und wohl die Bedeutung von Heidenland gehabt zu haben scheint. Wenn die Urkunde von 1503 unter diesen heidnischen Dagoni "dacische" Serben versteht, dann spiegelt sich darin auch ein Stuck Siedlungsgeschichte von den Daciern zu den Slaven wider. Die nich zu verkennende lautliche Ubereinstimmung der ersten Silben Dag -oni//Dac -i had die volksetymologische Synonymie fraglos gefordert. Die in den drei Hanschriften der Dagome-iudex-Regest benutzte Form Dagone, also mit -e im Auslaut, ist eindeutig ein Reflex des Slavischen, das namlich Dagon mit Halbvokal verwendet.

Parenthetically, **the fish**, L. M. Graham writes, **is a universal savior symbol ...** The Hindus represented the first Avatar of Vishnu as half fish, half man—Pisces-Aquarius; and our Christ is called by the the Piscean Avatar. In the Talmud the Messiah is called Dag, the fish. The Phoenician and Philistian Dagon, the Chaldean Oannes, and the Greek Phoibos were all fish men. The Greek word for fish ichthus is made up of the initials of the five Greek words Iesous (Ch)ristos, (Th)eou Uios Soter—Jesus Christ the son of God, Savior.

DANUBIA. PANNONIA

As mentioned earlier, in the *Dialogues of Pseudo-Caesar*, an early 5th century compilation based partly on 4th century sources, the Danubian Slavs are recorded as ***Sklavenoi***. A better known and often cited source on mid-5th century Danubia is Priscus of Priam, a Byzantine official and historian. A member of an embassy sent to Attila's camp in Pannonia by the Eastern emperor Theodosius II, Priscus is a perceptive, reliable and rare source of information on this tumultous period. In his account, Priscus mentions several nations that appear to have Slavic sounding names. In 434, Priscus writes: **They [Huns] hastened to Scythia ... Soon they crossed they huge [Maeotic] swamp and ... overwhelmed the Alipurzi, the Alcidzuri, the Itimari, the Tuncassi, and the Boisci who bordered on the shore of Scythia.**

BOISKI SERBS ?

In 432 or 433, Priscus writes: **a Hunnish ruler ... intending to go to war with the Amilzouri, Itimari, Tonosours, Boiski and other races dwelling on the Danube and who had taken refuge in a Roman alliance.** Some scholars suspect that some of the nations so-named are Slavs, perhaps Serbs, namely the *Al-mizuri*, **Milcani** Serbs; the Tono-sursi, **Surs**-Serbs; the Iti-mari, **Moravi** Serbs; the Boiski, **Boiski** Serbs, Emperor Constantine VII's **Boiki** Serbs.

STRAVA

Priscus' account of his visit to Attila's camp in Pannonia also reveals strongs Slavic traces in the personal names, food, drink, and customs of the Huns and their Scythian allies: millet/*proso*; honey/*medos*; funeral feast/*strava*). Especially striking is the Slavic funeral ceremony or *Strava* following Attila's death in 454: **After he had been mourned with such lamentations they celebrated a 'Strava' as they call it, over his tomb with great revelry, coupling opposite extremes of feeling in turn among themselves.**

A SLAVIC TRIBE

C.D. Gordon's authoritative translation and commentary on 5th century Greek historians gives important information on **the Sciri or Scyri, a Slavic tribe, once part of the Hunnish empire** (*The Age of Attila, 1960*). We learn that: 1) **The Sciri, who had settled in Lower Moesia on the Danube,** were a power in Pannonia **where they were in more or less constant conflict with the Goths**; 2) the Sciri played an important role in the **Western armies commanded by Ricimer [appointed commander of imperial armies by emperor Avitus] and his successors**; 3) the **Sciri formed an important part of Odovacar's army in his final conquest of Italy**; 4) Odovacar, the first barbarian king of Italy, either **sprang from the race of Thuringi on his father's side and the Sciri on his mother's side**, according to one account, or **he was of the nation of the**

Scyri, according to another.

SARMATIAN SCIRI

In fact, Pliny suggested the ethnic character of the **Sciri** several centuries earlier **(Pomerania is inhabited as far as the Vistula River by the Sarmatian Venedi, Sciri, Hirri).** While Pliny's text does not identify the **Sciri** as Serbs, evidence in support of that notion is found in the fact that in the general area inhabited by the Sarmatian **Sciri**, in prehistoric Pomerania and Poland west of the Vistula, one finds overwhelming onomastic evidence of Serb settlement.

SCYTHIAN AND GERMAN NATIONS

With regard to this period, to the role of Slavs in Gothic armies, it is important to keep in mind that history and archaeology indicate that the Goths generally, and the Ostrogoths or East Goths, east of the Dniester River, particularly, had significant Slavic components. Referring to an early Gothic ruler, Cassidorius' *Origo Gothica* states that Ermanaric ruled **over all Scythian and German nations.** In this regard it is important to keep in mind that by the mid-4th century, the Ostrogoths, who dominated the Pontic area, were ethnically and culturally transformed by local elements. In fact, recent excavations indicate that Germanic elements were never preponderant, that 'Scythian' Slavs formed an important part of the Ostrogothic kingdom. The 'Scythization' of the Ostrogoths is discussed at length in a recent work by the German historian H. Wolfram *(History of the Goths, 1988).* Linguistic evidence of early and close Slav-German association in military affairs is found in the Old Slav *pluk,* troops in battle formation, in Slavic derivatives *pluk, pulk, puk* connoting regiment, people en masse, and Gothic-German equivalents, namely *fulk, folc, folk;* in such Slavic combination personal names/titles as *Svetopolk,* commander of a strong troop.

MODERN SCHOLARSHIP

In different ways and degrees authoritative modern scholarship offers support for Gottlob's general thesis in terms of early ***Sarmatian-Slav-Serb*** settlement in Danubia-Pannonia. The broad, deep, exhaustive, and thorough research of L. Niederle *(Slovanske Starozitnosti, 1902-1919),* one of the pillars of modern Slavistics, suspects that the Slavs were already in Central Europe at the end of the second millennium, alongside the Germans in the north, alongside the Thracians in the Carpathians, with the Iranians and Caucasians in the Black Sea area, with the Balts along the Baltic Sea, where they lived together in a Baltio-Slavic union. All available evidence, Niederle writes, places the Slavs in southern Hungary, Transylvania, and the Danube in the first centuries of our era, an area settled by the Sarmatian ***Jazgyes*** in the first century A.D.

SIRMIUM, SERDICA, VRBAS

Citing cities along the Danube basin, like *Sirumium* (**Srem**) and *Serdica* (***Srediste***), apparent Latinizations for descriptive Slavonic place names, Toynbee suspects a strong Slavonic presence in the area during the Roman period. F. Dvornik, following Safarik, finds hard, conspicuous evidence of early Slavic settlement in the existence of such prototypical Slavic place names as ***Vuka, Vrbas*** and ***Vucica*** in Danubian Pannonia, modern Slavonia and Banat, areas of ***Sarmatian*** settlment, from the 2nd century onward *(Early Slavic Civilization, 1956; The Making of Central and Eastern Europe, 1974).*

LIMIG-ANTES, ARDAGAR-ANTES

In the early 300s the Sarmatians are recorded as *Limigantes* and *Ardagarantes*. It appears obvious to the noted historian G. Vernadsky, that the *Jazyge*-Sarmatian *Limigantes* are *Limig-Antes* are Antes are Slavs, that the *Ardagantes* are *Ardagar-Antes* are Antes are Slavs *(The Origins of Russia, 1959)*. When civil war broke out about A.D. 332, the defeated *Acarag-Antes* took refuge in Roman territory and were given land in Pannonia or present-day Serb Voivodina. In the war with Rome that followed, the *Limig-Antes* fought well and bravely *(with invincible stubborness, not a single man asked for pardon*, records Ammianus). Defeated in 358, forced to retreat beyond the Tisza River, the *Limig-Antes* remained a force to be reckoned with until the arrival of the Huns circa A.D. 430.

LINGUISTIC RECORD

The linguistic record also points in the direction of early Slavic settlement in Danubia. In *Vanished Civilizations (1963)*, T. Sulimirski, a noted authority on the Sarmatians *(The Sarmatians, 1970)*, makes the following supporting points: 1) The study of the toponomy of Romania shows that the Slavs adopted unromanized Dacian place names in the Roman province of Dacia or Latin names and transmitted them to the Romanians; 2) In the sphere of social and political life, the oldest Romanian terminology shows that Latin terms were translated or replaced by Slavic words; 3) The Slavic element came into Romanian during the common Romanian period and before the division of the language into its four main dialects; 4) The phonetic structure of Romanian words of Slavic origin often reveals their great antiquity; 5) The study of the Slavic names of the Tisa and other rivers of the Hungarian Plain also confirm the theory that the Slavs were on the southern side of the Carpathians well before the sixth century A.D.

SRBUL

Interesting contemporary evidence that the early Slavs in Danubia were called Serbs is found in that fact that centuries after the Serbs disappeared and the Bulgars appeared, the natives of Wallachia and Moldavia still refer to their southern neighbors along the Danube as **Serbs** or **Srbul**. According to Budimir, in addition to other factors, clear evidence of an ancient Serb/Slav element n Danubia and Dacia is also found in the Romanian system of counting from ten upward as well as other linguistic substratums.

ENDNOTES

[1] Ammianus' work is written in extreme detail and its general accuracy has never been challenged. Originally in thirty-one books covering the years 96-378, the extant narrative begins with the events of 353, the year he joined the army and served on Rome's eastern frontier.

[2] In 'Juzne kulture i narodi prema luzickoj kulturi, Praslovenima i Slovenima', a paper presented at the International Congress of Slavic Archaeolog, Warsaw, 1965 (Miedzynanrodowy kongres archeologii slowianskiej, 1968), V. Trbuhovic presents evidence in support of his thesis that in the first century B.C. the Slavs resisted the Romans in Danubia, that some remained, others migrated north and east.

[3] For a Polish interpretation of Dagome iudex: P. Bogdanowicz, Geneza aktu dyplomatycznego zwanego Dagime iudex, RoH 25,1959.

7. ET ALIO NOMINA SORABI DICTI: WENDS, VANDALS

As the following selections indicate, one often finds the statement in early and modern scholarship that Wend in one form or another (e.g. *Guinid* as in *Sarmatoru id est Guinedorum*) is a German name for Slavs called Serbs: 1) **Wend (Wenden) is a German name for the Sorben;** 2) **The Serbs are Wends and the Wends are Serbs;** 3) **The land between the Saale and Elbe were settled by Slavs, Wends who are also called Serbs;** 4) **Winden sind also Serben, und das land Winden ist Srbien;** 5) **The so-called Sarmatians or Wends of Germany and Poland are Serbs.**

VENEDIS SLAVIS, SORABI

One of the earliest German sources refers to the *Venedi Slavs* also called *Serbs: A Venedis Slavis qui et alio nomina Sorabi dicti* (Chronicle of Fredgarius, 642). According to the *Chronicon Carionis* compiled by J. Carion (1499-1537): 1) **Most Sarmats were Wends (Sarmaturum gentem maximam Henetos esse);** 2) **Sarmat and Henet are one and the same name and another name for the Serbs.** *Lingua Heneta* or *Windische sprache* is said to be the common language of the Slavs. According to *Chronicon Saxoniae*, a German chronicle compiled in 1625, the Slavs on Saxony's borders are *Heneti Sorabi* who in different times and places are also known as *Heneti, Wendi, Slavi* and *Vandali:* **The lands east of the Elbe were settled by the Heneti, who the Germans call Wendi, the Italians, Slavi, and even Vandali by some writers.**

VENEDORUM NATIONE

As the title of a 17th century study of the Serbs of Germania and Bohemia indicates the Serbs are *Venedorum Natione* are *Populi Venedicti* are **Wends** are **Serbs:** *Disputatio Historica de Serbis, Venedorum Natione Vulgo Dicti Die Wenden.*

VANDALS, VANDALIA

As the following series indicates, medieval sources sometimes refer to Germania's Slavs and neighboring Slavs as *Vandals/Wandals,* their lands, *Vandalia/Wandalia: 1) Ab oriente Wandalorum gens ferocissima habitat; 2) Contra Wandelicos auxiliantibus; 3) De Sclavia. Sclavia est pars Mesia, multas continens regiones. Nam Sclavi sunt Bohemi, Poloni, Metani, Vandali, Rutheni; 4) In Wandalos; 5) In regionem Wandalorum; 6) Inter Saxoniam et Vandaliam est Albus. Est autem Vandalia terra, cujus gentes Slavi dicuntur; 7) Lingua Rutenorum et Polonorum et Boemorum et Sclavanorum eadem est cum lingua Wandalorum; 8) Sclavorum in regionem Wandalorum; 9) Wandalos, quos nunc appellant Guenedos.* The notion that at one time Germania's Slavs or *Winuli* were called *Vandals* has deep roots in early German sources. In the late 11th century Adam of Bremen writes: *Sclavania igitur, amplissima Germaniae provintia, a Winulis incolitur, qui olim dict sunt Wandali.* One century later, Adam's successor, Helmold, writes: **Where Poland ends one comes into a most extensive Slavic province, that of the people who of old were called Vandali, but now Winithi or Winuli.** Regarding the identity and location of the *Winuthi* or *Winuli*, Helmold writes: **The other river, the Oder, tending toward the north, passes through the territory of the Winuli peoples, dividing the Pomeranians from the Wilzi. At** its mouth, where its waters swell those of the Baltic Sea, there one stood Jumen [Wolin] ... Then, beyond the sluggish current of the Oder and the territory peopled by several Pomeranian tribes, there lies toward the west the country of the Winuli, of those namely, who are called Tholenzi and Redarii.

WANDALO PATRE POLONORUM

In medieval Polish sources one finds the notion that *Wandals* take their name from *Wandalus*, the father, progenitor of the Polish nation, of the Polish or Lechtic nation: *Necno autem quatuor filios genuit, cuius primogenitus Wandalus, a quo Wandalitae, qui Poloni nunc dicuntur, orti sunt. Hic ex nomine suo fluvium, qui nunc Wysla vulgariter nuncupatur, Wandalum censuit appellari, nam et mons, de quo oritur dictus fluvius Wanda ab eiusdem nomine vocitatur; Ipsa denique Wanda a Wandalo, Wandalorum id est Polonorum sive Lechitarum progenitoe, de quo supra diximus nomen accepit; vel potest dici Wanda a Wandalo scilicet flumine Wisla eo, quod eius regni centrum extiterit.* The same sources trace the origin of all Slavic nations to the sons of *Wandalus: Habuit [Wandalus] quoque multos filios, qui generationibus suis ultra quartam partem Europae per regiones et regna semen suum multiplicando possederunt, videlicet: total Russiam ad orientem, Poloniam maximam terrarum et matrem, Pomeraniam, Seleuciam, Cassubiam, Sarbiam quae nunc Saxonia dicitur, Bohemiam, Moraviam, Stiriam, Carinthiam et Sclavoniam: quae nunc Dalmacia dicitur; Chrowatiam, Pannoniam, quae nunc Ungaria dicitur, Bulgariam et alias quam plures, quarum multitudo propter prolixitatem subticetur.*

ALBERT KRANZ

An early authority on Saxony, A. Kranz (1450-1517), author of two important historical treatises, *Vandalia* (1519) and *Saxonia* (1520), is certain that **Vandals** are **Wends** are **Slavs** who are divided into many nations, Poles, Bohemians and many others. A decade later one finds the same notion in D. Chytraei's *Vandalia* (1591). Kranz, Chytraei and other scholars know that the original *Vandals* were a Germanic nation, who first appear in 406 when they crossed the Rhine, invaded Gaul and Spain, established a kingom in North Africa, and sacked Rome in 455. They believe that at some early point in time Slavic peoples settled alongside the Germanic *Vandals,* and that later, after the latter had departed, the Slavs occupied their lands and came to be known as *Vandals.*

GERMAN-SLAV VANDALS

Carrying the *longtime German-Slav neighbors and friends* notion several steps forward, some German writers believe that the Slavic **Vandals** or **Wends** represent the union of *Vandal* oldtimers left behind and Slavic newcomers in former Vandal lands. On this point, M.B. Latimi writes: **Als haben sich die Witzer Wuder und andere Slaven aus Sarmatien Wandalen so heuffig in diese Lender und Stette gemachlich eingedrungen, und mit dem Wandalen vereinbaret und befreudent, dass daruber die alte Teutsche Sprache corrumpiret, und die Wendische Zunge mit eingwurzeit, vermischet und gemein worden is** *(Wiasmariensis megapolitani genealochronicon, 1610).*

EIN WENDE

In a less speculative spirit a German historian writes in 1508 that Sarmatians, Vandals and Slavs are Wends: *Sarmatha et Vandalus et Sclavus* = **ein Wende.** According to another historian of the same period, Slav is a popular name for **Vandal: *Vandali, quos vulgus Sclavos appelant.*** One finds the same notion in the title of an article by a German authority on the subject in the early 20th century: **Wandalen = Wenden** (L. Steinberger, *Wandalen = Wenden, AnP 37, 1915*).

WEND/VANDAL AUS SCYTIA

In the mid-16th century, N. Volrab, a native of Budusin, informs his readers that the ***Wends,*** who originated in ***Scythia*** (***die Wend aus Scythia***) are also known as ***Vandals*** and Slavs *(Chronica von den Antiquiteten des Keiserlichen Striftes der Romische Burg und Stadt Marseburg, 1556)*. In the same period one of Basel's leading scholars, S. Munster (1448-1552), says the same thing in different words: **Vandalen wo man jetzt Wenden nennt** *(Cosmographia Universalis)*.

VANDALS, VENEDS, SARMATS, SCYTHS

Regarding the conquest and settlement of Germania, C.S. Schurzfleisch writes: ***Vandalis Venedi, Venedis Sarmatae, Germanis Schythae successerunt ... Invadunt Vandalorum ditiones Venedi*** *(Origines Pomeranicae, 1673)*.

VANDALOS SORABORUM NOMEN

According to an early 17th century history of Meissen, the ***Vandals*** who founded Meissen were ***Serbs***, actually ***Sorabs***, a name derived from ***Serb*** as in Ptolemy's ***Sarmatian Serbs: Vandalos peculiare Soraborum nomen habuisse ... cuius derivatio a Serbis ... quorum Ptolemaeus meminit sub sarmaticis populis in Asia*** (R. Reinerius, De Misenorum origine, rebus, gestis, mutationibus, variis dominatibus, et adventu in Germaniam)

NUMEROUS, POWERFUL

The Vandals are prominent in M. Orbini's 1602 account of the origin of the Slavs. The ***Vandals,*** Orbini writes, were one of the more numerous and powerful Slav nations, who occupied a great area from the Baltic in the north to the Mediterranean in the south. According to Orbini, the Moscovites, Russians, Poles, Bohemians, Dalmatians, Istrians, Croats and Rasians are some of the modern nations descended from the ***Vandals.***

LEXICON VANDALICUM

In the 17th and 18th centuries it is not uncommon for German Serb scholars to refer to the Serbs as Vandals in the title and text of studies, lexicons, and grammars: ***Didascalia seu Orthographia Vandalica; Enchiridion Vandalicum; Lexicon Vandalicum; Linguae Vandalicae ad dialectum districtus Cotbusiani; Orthographia Vandalica; Principia linguae wendicae quam aliqui wandalicum vocant; Rudimenta Grammaticae Sorabo-Vandalicae Idiomatis Budissinatis; Versio Vandalica Praestandi homagii fidelitatio.*** Thus the full name of *Societatis Jablanoviaae*, a Leipzig based association promoting scholarly research and publication of Slavic studies, originating in the 18th century, included the following ethnonymic elements: ***Acta Societatis Jablanoviaae de Slavis Venedis, Antis, Vilzis, Sorabis aliquid de Vandalis et Henetis.***

8. QUOD TANTUM EST REGNUM

Throughout history, from the medieval to the modern, historians originating in diverse geographical-national circumstances, in diverse intellectual-cultural traditions and perspectives, acting on the basis of similar and different sources, some known, some unknown, have reached the same or similar conclusions, namely that the Serbs are an ancient people, the ancestors of all or most Slavic peoples.

QUOD TANTUM EST REGNUM

According to an important 9th century source, the Bavarian Geographer's *Descriptio Civitatum ad Septentrionalem* (hereafter *Descriptio Civitatum*), all Slavs originate in the immense lands of a great Serb dominion: **Zeriuani, quod tantum est regnum, ut ex eo cunctae gentes Sclavorum exortae sint et originem, sicut affirmant, ducant.** *(A realm so great that from it, as their tradition relates, all the nations of the Slavs are sprung and trace their origin).*

TOTIUS ORBIA ANTIQUISSIMAM EX MAXIMAM

Some six centuries later one finds the same notion in another important and authoritative source, namely Laonicus Chalcondyles' mid-15th century magnum opus, *Historiarum Demonstrationes*. A cautious, solid and reliable historian, Chalcondyles is certain that the Serbs are the one of the greatest nations in the whole world in terms of age and number: ***Serblos autem gentem esse totius orbis antiquissimam et maximam, compertum habeo.***

SERBICA

Certain Serb facts on the ground in the length and breadth of Greece itself were perhaps a factor in a Byzantine Greek historian's estimation of the age and size of the Serb nation. According to Byzantine sources, a Serb principality was established in Thessaly, centered at ***Serbica,*** not far from Mount Olympus, in the 7th century. Diverse sources document a ***Serbia*** or ***Serbica,*** a settlement and stronghold of immense strategic import near the gorge that interrupts the mountain wall of Vermion and Olympus, through which the Bistrica River fights its way to the Aegean Coast. Later medieval Greek sources describe ***Serbia*** as a well-fortified polis divided into three sections, the akra, where the archon lived, and the upper and lower sections inhabited by the politia *(N. Zupanic, The Serb Settlement in the Macedonian Town of Srbiste in the VIIth century and the Ethnological and Sociological Moment in the Report of Constantinus Porphyrogenitus concerning the Advent of Serbs and Croats, Etnolog 1, 1926-27; P. Skok, Konstantinova Serbia u Grckoj, Glas SkA CLXXXI, 1938; B. Ferjancic, Vizantijski i srpski Ser u XIV stolecu, 1994).*

SIRBANOS

A 1454-55 Ottoman document records a number of Christian timar holders with Serb-sounding names in Thessaly: ***Dobros, Miroslavis, Bogdanos, Bogranos, Sirbanos, Rados*** *(N. Belcideanu, Timariotes chretiens in Thessalie, SuD 42, 1983).* Another Ottoman document of the same period reveals a royal Serb presence in the person of Mara Brankovic, daughter of Serbian Despot Djurach Brankovic, widow of Sultan Murad II, and stepmother of Sultan Mehmed II. This source indicates that she was granted extensive ownership of lands in the area of Serres, including two villages with Serb sounding names,

Jezovo and **Mravinci/Muravnica**, situated south of Lake Takhinos *(B. Ferjancic, Tesalija u XIII i XIV veku, 1974).* Later Ottoman documents indicate that Mara granted both villages to the monasteries of Hilandar and St. Paul on Mount Athos in 1466. Excavations in **Jezovo**, now Daphni, have uncovered architectural remains associated with Mara, including a structure known as the *Tower of Mara (M. Ursinius, An Ottoman Census Register for the Area of Serres, SuD 45, 1986).*

THRACE, EPIRUS

The *Serb* ethnikon is also found near Kirk Kilise in Turkish Thrace; near Trikalla in the Trikalla-Karditsa district of Greek Thrace, where the distinguished German historian, M. Vasmer, found 122 Slav place names *(Die Slaven in Griechenland, 1941).* Also near Yanina in the district of Epirus where Vasmer found no less than 334 Slav place names. Also on the rugged Chalcidic Peninsula, on the middle prong of *Longos* (derived from a Slav word for *woodland*), near the isthmus of *Provlakos* (a slightly Graecized word for *isthmus*). In fact, a 10th century document from this area, a testimonial signed by several Slav witnesses, is considered to be the oldest dated *glagolithic* monument *(G. Soulis, On the Slavic Settlement in Hierissos in the Tenth Century, Byzantion 23, 1953).*

SERBISTA, ZERVOKHORIA

In W.M. Leake's late 18th century account of his travels in northern Greece, one finds a number of *Serb-Zerv* place names: *Zervokhia,* one of two rivers of Mt. Pelium; the villages of *Servula,* near Vostitza; *Serp,* also *Serbista,* near Serres; *Zervokhori,* near Negrita. On the territory of the Khimara ('the whole of the ancient Acroceraunian ridge … the towns of Nivitza, Lukovo, Pikernes'), *Serb* appears in the name and ancestry of one one of the leading clans, the *Zervati,* **who take their name from Zerva, a village of the district of Arta. There were three brothers of that village, one of whom turned Turk; another settled at Lefka at Corfu, where there is now a family of Zervates; the third migrated to Suli** *(W.M. Leake, Travels in Northern Greece, 1967).*

PELOPONNESUS

The *Serb* ethnikon is found in greatest numbers in the Peloponnesus. In the district of Argolis, near the isthmus of Corinth, a neck of land connecting the Peloponnesus to the rest of Greece; in the district of Ellis on the west coast of the Peloponnesus. Near Herata, in central Arcadia, an area rich in Slav place names; near Tryphylia in the southwestern district of Messenia. At several places in the rugged southeastern district of Laconia (Sparta), an area that includes the Mani and the high and rugged Taygetos range (D.J. Georgacas, The Medieval Names Melingi and Ezeritae of Slavic Groups in the Peloponnesus, BzT 43, 1950). In his study of Slavic names in Messenian Mani, P. Malingoudis identifies a number of *Serb*-sounding toponyms common to both *Germanian* and *Illyrian Serb* lands, including, among others: **Bolesin, Cernov, Devica, Dubrava, Godine, Golina, Gora, Gostim, Kamenik, Laz, Les, Ljuta, Luka, Malotin, Mokrina, Nizina, Okci, Ostrovo, Plavina, Polica, Prosek, Radesin, Raztok, Rov, Senovica, Slavota, Vrba, Zadel** *(P. Malingoudis, Studien zu den slavischen Ortsnamen Griechenlands, 1981).*

STRATEGIC LOCATIONS

It is interesting and perhaps significant that a number of better-known Serb settlements in Graecia were established at highly strategic points: near Mt. Olympus; the

Chalcidic Peninsula; the isthmus of Corinth; near Mt. Taygetus in Laconia-Sparta. According to Zupanic, this was certainly true of the Serb settlement near Mt. Olympus. Impressed with the obvious military character of Serb settlement, he writes: **It seems to me that the first Srbisce must have a warrior camp. The Serbs came south as an organized army ... The settlement of Srbsice suggests that it served as a military base and as an organizing point for newcomers.**

ANCIENT GRAECIA

There is some evidence that Slav settlement can be traced as far back as the beginnings of ancient Greece. No less an authority than Toynbee notes that some geographical names of that period have **a distinctly Slavonic filter.** Indeed, he suspects that **the ancient Paiones may actually have been a Slavonic speaking people.** Regarding the time of Slavic settlement, Toynbee writes: **Slavs were probably part of the Thracian and Illyrian Volkerwanderung into southeastern Europe from 1,700 to 1,800 years before the massive Volkerwanderung of the Slavs in the 6th and 7th centuries of the Christian era.** In the year 581, John of Ephesis gives the following account of the massive Slav Volkerwanderung in the late 6th century: **An accursed people called Slavonians overran the whole of Greece ... captured the cities and overran numerous strongholds ... reduced the people to slavery, made themselves the masters of the whole and settled in it by means of force and dwelt in it as though it had been their own ... The Slavonians live at ease in the lands and dwell in it as far and wide as God permits them.** Four years later, he writes: **they [Slavonians] live in peace in the Roman territories, free from anxiety and fear ... And they have grown rich in gold and silver and herds of horses and arms, and have learned to fight better than the Romans.**[1]

ENDNOTES

[1] M. Vasmer, Die Slaven in Grieschenland, 1941. P. Charanis, Nicephorus I, the Saviour of Greece from the Slavs, Byzantina-Metabyzantina 1, 1946; On the Question of the Slavonic Settlements in Greece during the Middle Ages, ByS 10, 1949; The Chronicle of Monemvasia and the Question of the Slavonic Settlements in Greece, Dumbarton Oaks Papers 5, 1950; On the Slavic Settlements in the Peloponnesus, ByZ 46, 1953; On the Slavic Settlement in the Peloponnesus, Studies on the Demography of the Byzantine Empire, 1972. J. Werner, Slavische Bronzefiguren aus Nordgriechenland, 1953. P. Lemerle, Invasions et migrations dans les Balkans depuis la fin de l'epoque romaine jusqu au VIIIe siecle, Revue Historique 211, 1954. F. Dolger, Ein Fall slavischer Einsiedlung im Hinterland von Thessalonike im 10. Jhd., Sitzungsber Bayer. Akad. Philo-Hist, 1957. C. Hopf, Die Slaveneinfalle in Griechenland, 1962. P. Malingoudis, La penetration des Slaves dans la peninsule balkanique et la Grece continentale, Revue des Etudes Sud-East Europeenes 1, 1963; Studien zu den slavischen Ortsnamen Griechenlands I, Slavische Flurnamen aus der messenischen Mani, 1981; Toponymy and history: Observations concerning the Slavonic toponymy of the Peloponnese, CyM 7, 1983; Zur fruhslawischen Sozialgeschichte im Spiegel der Toponymie, Etudes Balkanique 21, 1985; Fruhe slawischen Elemente im Namengut Griechenlands, Die Volker Sudosteuropas im 6. bis 8. Jh, 1987. J. Schropfer, Slavisches in Ortsnamen der Peloponnes, besonders der Argolis, Orbis Scriptus, 1966. M.S.F. Hood, An Aspect of the Slav Invasons of Greece in the Early Byzantine Period, Sbornik Narodniho Muzea v Praze, Rada A, Historie XX, 1966. J. Karayannopulos, Zur Frage der Slavenansiedlungen auf dem Peloponnes, RevEtSudEstEur 9, 1971. J. Koder, Zur Frage der slavischen Siedlungsgebiete im mittelalterlichen Griechenland, ByZ 71, 1978. W. Weithmann, Die slavische Bevolkerung auf der grieschischen Halbinsel. Ein Beitrag zur historischen Ethnographie, 1978; Strukturkontinuitat und Diskontinuiat auf der Griechischen Halbinsem im Gefolge der slavischen Landnahme, MzB 2, 1979; Anthropologisches Fundgut zur Einwanderung der Slaven im Griechenland. Eine Materialzusammenstellung, Homo 36, 1985. P.A. Yannopoulos, La Penetration Slave en Argolide, Bulletin de correspondance hellenique 6, 1980. A.A. Beleckij, Slavjanska toponimija Greceii, Perspektivy ravitija slavjansko onomastiki, 1980. S. Vryonis, The Evolution of Slavic Society and the Slavic Invasions of Greece, Hesperia 50, 1981. H. Birnbaum, Noch einmal zu den slavischen Milingen auf der Peloponnes, FsT H. Brauer, 1986. Z. Golab, Jazikot na Prvite Sloveni vo Grcija i istorijata na makedonskiot jazik, MaK XL-XLI, 1989-90.

9. SUPERLATIVISCHE

Commenting on the superlative characterizations of the Serbs in the accounts of important sources and reliable historians, H. Kunstmann writes: **Besonders aufschlussreich ist die sub 2 zitierte Bemerkung uber die Zeruiani, deren "Land so gross ist, dass alles slavischen Stamme von ihnen abstammen und ihren Ursprung haben". Dieser Satz ist, wie schon gesagt einmalig und kann sich auf keinen anderen Stamm als die Serben beziehen. Derartige "superlativische" Merkmale werden den Serben von verschiedenen mittelalterlichen Schriftstellern nachgesagt. Bekannt ist beispielsweise der Ausspruch des byzantinischen Historikers Laonikos Chalkondyles, der noch im 15. Jhd. in seiner die Zeit von 1298-1463 beschreibenden ... von den Serben sagt, dass sie "der alteste und grosste Stamm des ganzem Erdenkreises" seien ... Chalkondyles meint damit naturlich die Serben auf dem Balkan: der ebenfalls die Grosse des Serbenstammes akzentuierende Satz des GB [Geographus Bavarus] bezieht sich hingegen auf die mitteldeutschen Sorben. Das aber lasst den Schluss zu, dass der ruhmvolle Leumund der Balkanserben schon vor 850 von Slaven ubertragen worden ist. Hochst aufschlussreich an der Laudatio des GB ist ausserdem die Behauptung, "alle slavischen Stamme" stammten von den Serben ab, worin sich m.E. eine deutliche Anspielung auf die balkanische Herkunft der mitteldeutschen Slaven ausdruckt**
(H. Kunstmann, Beitrage zur Geschichte der Besiedlung Nord- und Mitteldeutschlands mit Balkanslaven, 1987).

MEZI NIMI SRBOVE

Another source cited by Kunstmann and others confirming the great age, primacy, and range of the ancient Serbs is an early 14th century Czech source, *Dalemil's Chronicle (Staroceska Kronika: Tak Recenheho Dalimila)* where the first chapter ('Ot Babylonske veze a o sedmidcat jazycich') traces the Serbs back to the biblical origin of time, the Tower of Babel, and forward to Greek and Roman lands as far west as Rome: **Mezi nimi Srbove, Tu kdez bydle Rekove, podle more se usadichu, az do Rima rozplodichu.**

ANTIQUITY

It is interesting that one finds consistent reference to the Serbs as an ancient and glorious nation in South Slavic sources. An early historian of ancient and medieval Slav lands, and the first to write for a Western audience *(Il Regno Degli Slavi, 1601)*, Orbini, a native of Dubrovnik, traces the Serbs to times before the Tower of Babel. Orbini believes that the Serbs settled the Balkan lands—to the borders of Rome—in two waves: a first wave originating in Asia Minor; a second and later wave originating in northern Europe some 1400 years before the birth of Christ.

LYUBIDRAG, KING OF THE SERBS

Orbini summarizes Slav wars with Germans and Danes as *Serb* wars with Germans and Danes: **Charles the Great waged many bitter wars, in which died Lyubidrag, King of the Serbs, along with thirty thousand Frank warriors. After negotiating peace with Charles the Great, the Serbs, led by King Drasko, invaded Denmark. In 934, they war with Henry I; in 957, with Otto I; in 1029 with Conrad II; in 1105, with Friedrich.**

GUNDULIC

Dubrovnik's greatest bard, Ivan Gundulic (1589-1638), an early champion of South Slav liberation, finds inspiration in the ancient and glorious Serbs, namely the person and figure of the Serbs' greatest king, Alexander the Great, Gundulic's *Lesandra Srbljanina*. According to F.P. Magoun Jr., Gundulic's *Lesandr the Serb* is less a matter of poetic license and more a matter of a notion that has deep roots in Balkan epic poetry *(Stojan Novakovic on the So-Called 'Serbian Alexander,' Byzantion 26, 1942-43)*. **Od Lesandra Srbljanina; Od svjeh cara, cara slavna; Alesandro to svedoci; Kral veliki svega svita** (Accordingly, in them is still kept; What was written in song long ago; of Lesandr the Serb; A glorious emperor above all emperors).

RITTER

Paul Ritter von Vrendorf (1652-1713), an *Illyrian* historian of German ancestry, also stresses the antiquity of the Serbs. In his magnum opus, Ritter traces Serb settlement on the Adriatic to pre-Roman times. On page 36, for example, Ritter refers to a war between the Serbs and Romans in 35 B.C. *(Kronika iliti Szpomenik Vszega Szvieta Vikov, 1696)*.

ROBERT, PELZEL, HOWORTH

Further evidence of the perceived antiquity and greatness of the ancient Serbs is found in the consistent tendency of diverse historians, independently of one another, to trace the origin of one or more or all the Slav nations to the ancient Serbs. In the mid-19th century, a noted French Slavicist, C. Robert, following a comprehensive, systematic and insightful examination of the historical record, concludes that the ancient Serbs are manifestly the ancestors of all Slavs, that all Slavs are Serbs in terms of origin: **Le plus ancient des peuples slaves ... L'unite de la race slave sous le nome general de Serbes** *(Le Monde Slave, Son Passe, Son Etat Present et Son Avenir, 1852)*. In *Geschichte der Bohmen, von der Bohmen, von den Altesten bis auf die Neuesten Zeiten (1817)*, for example, the learned F.M. Pelzel's analysis of historical sources leads him to conclude that: **The Czechs were Serbs before they were Czechs.** The following century a noted British historian-anthropologist reaches the same conclusion with regards to the Croats. Independent of Dalimil's statement centuries earlier (**W srbskem gazyku gest zeme, Gz Charvati gest gme** or 'in the Serb lands, there is a Croatia'), at the end of his essay, 'The Spread of the Slavs, Part I, The Croats', the learned H.H. Howorth reminds his readers: **But we must never forget that in origin and in race they [Croats] belong to the great Servian stock** *(The Journal of the Anthropological Institute of Great Britain and Ireland, VII, 1878)*.

KRIZANIC, SERBLJANIN

It is interesting that Juraj Krizanic (1617-1683), the eminent Croat scholar and Roman Catholic missionary, determined advocate of *Union*, actually Orthodox Slav submission to the Church of Rome, of *Roman Catholic Pan-Slavism*, actually a united Slavdom serving Rome's exclusive interests (e.g. a great and grand war against the German heretics), identifies himself at the Russian court not as a Croat, but as a Serb, as *Jurij Bilish the Serb:* **Jurij Bilish Serbljanin**, 1659).

Considered to be something of an opportunistic deceiver by his peers in Croatia, able to say one thing one day, the exact opposite the next day if it suited his interests,

Krizanic's Serb identity may be nothing more than a ruse to gain the trust and confidence of others. On the other hand, there may be something to it. In fact, Krizanic's ancestors were not natives of Croatia, but the Una River region near the ancient town-county of **Srb.** In correspondence with Latin colleagues, Krizanic will often use the Serb letter and language to illustrate the beauty of the Illyrian language; Krizanic will refer to Illyrian heroic poetry as Serbian (**Sarbsk**i) poetry, as verse in the Serbian style (**mode et styli Sarbiaci**). A man of many contradictions, in one instance, Krizanic admits that one rarely hears the native Illyrian language spoken well in Croatia proper. In another instance, for similar reasons, Krizanic denies the Slovenians or 'Kranjci' admission to the Illyrian community of nations. According to Krizanic, once Illyrians, the Slovenians were now Germans: **Takvi su Kranjci, jer kranjska zemlja nije ilirska nego Noricka ili Njemacka ... Ondje se upotrebljava samo njemacki jezik u sudstvu, proprovijedima, skolama i svim javnim poslovima tako da se ondje ne moze vidjeti ni pisma pisana slavenski. Ilirski je narod nekoc tamo posredstvom rata nahrupio, ali je od Njemaca starosjedilaca bio ponovno protjeran ili potlacen. Odatle proizlazi da je medju seljacima i to ne medju svima ostala neka slika ilirskog jezika, ali toliko iskvarenog da je mi Iliri bez tumaca ne mozemo razumeti. Polovica je naime jezika njemacka.**

1. WHITE SERBS

In terms of conventional sources, there is no record of proto-Polish civilization, of Poland's social and political foundations, in the centuries prior to the formation of the medieval Polish state in the 10th century. Poland enters the historical record in the mid-10th century with several very brief references to King Mieszko (963-992). One to **King Misaca, under whose rule the Slavs were living**, a second to Mieszko, **king of the north.**

ONOMASTIC EVIDENCE

Nonetheless there is overwhelming onomastic evidence that the Serbs occupied much of the territory of prehistoric Poland and played a seminal role in the early stages of *Corona Regnum Poloniae.*

BIALI SERBOWIE

In a mid-20th century study, the distinguished Polish historian, T. Lewicki identifies numerous place names with the Serb ethnikon in core and perimeter Polish lands *(T. Lewicki, Konstantego Pofirogenety i Biali Serbowe w polnocnje Polsce, RoH 22, 1956).* What is most significant is the fact that the greatest concentrations of the more than thirty-six ethnonymic Serb place names cited are found in the geographic center of the proto-Polish nation.[1] More precisely, place names at and near Gniezno, the center of *Vielkopolska* or Great Poland, and Poznan, the first capitals of the Polish state and the seats of the first Polish metropolis and bishopric. An Old Slavic word, *gniezno* connotes nest, cradle, heart, core, nucleus. Recent evidence of Gniezno's primacy in Poland's historical-national consciousness is found in the words of Pope John Paul at Gniezno in 1979: **Here I greet with veneration the nest of the Piast, the origin of the history of the motherland.**

ORIGIN OF THE MOTHERLAND

In this historic area, bound by the Warta river in the west, the Notec river in the north, and Lake Goplo in the east, with large fortifications at Kurswica, Gniezno, and Poznan, and smaller fortifications at Klecko, Ostros, Lednicki, Giez, Lad, and Trzemesno, in this *nest of the Piast*, this *origin of the history of the motherland*, one finds a great number of ethnonymic Serbs. In fact, in this area Serb place names are found in greater number than anywhere at anytime in Europe.

Sarbia	**Sarbin**
Sarbia	**Sarbina**
Sarbia	**Sarbino**
Sarbia	**Sarbice**
Sarbino	**Sarbicko**
Sarbinovo	**Sarbka**
Sarbinovo	**Sarbka**
Sarbinovo	**Sarbskie Huby**
Sarbinovka	

MALOPOLSKA

The Serbs also appear to be the dominant Slavic element in a secondary center of Polish nationhood. Professor Lewicki finds a concentration of politically strategic Serb place names in *Malopolska* or Little Poland. In the lands of the ancient *Vislanie,* from the river Vis, Visla, Vistula, centered at Vislica, one of the oldest Polish cities, the seat of legendary Prince Vislav, one finds **Szarbia, Szarbia,** and **Szarbkov.** North of Vislica, between the ancient towns of Malogoszcz and Sandomierz, one finds **Sarbin** and **Szarbsko.**

MAZOVIA

East of *Vielkopolska,* the Serb ethnikon is well represented in the former Duchy of Mazovia (united with Poland in 1526) where one finds the Serb ethnikon in both place names and surnames. North of **Szarb,** for example, **Sarbievo** is the birthplace of the great poet and classicist Maciej Kazimierz **Sarbiewski** (1595-1649).

POMERANIA

In language, culture, and geography Pomerania was an integral part of Baltic Slavic civilization west of the Oder River. In government and politics it had strong ties with the powerful *Veletian/Lutician* federation. The same factors that tied the western Pomeranians to the Baltic Slavs separated them from the Polish Slavs. Centered on maritime city-states, the seafaring Pomeranians were far more advanced in industry, trade, commerce, and culture. Some German historians are certain that Pomerania is an original and integral Serb land.[2] One historian refers to **Pomerania as a primary Sorbenland or Surpe-Sorbenland.** Another German historian writes that **the entire Baltic coast to the Vistula, with the interior, was settled by Serb-Wends.** Here too, of course, evidence of Serb occupation and settlement is found in such place names as **Sarbia, Sarbinovo,** and **Sarbsko.** Some measure of the importance and intensity of seafaring trade in Pomerania is found in the fact that in the early 12th century Bishop Otto's missionary activities were sometimes thwarted by the fact that in one town after another, the natives were more at sea than at home: **Thence we came to Colobrega, which is situated, on the border of the sea. As nearly all its citizens were sailors after the manner of traders to the outer islands to do business, those who were found at home said that they could not adopt no new course in the absence of their fellow-citizens, and on this ground they withstood the preaching of the gospel for some time** *(C.H. Robinson, The Life of Otto Apostle of Pomerania 1060-1139, 1920).*

CONVERSION

In fact, fear of their rivals in the northwest, the *Veletian-Pomeranian* alliance, may have changed the course of Polish history *(Z. Wojciehowsk, Poczatki Chrzescijanstwa w Polsce na tle Stosunkov Niemiecko-Wieeckich, Zycie ii Mysli 3/4, 1950).* It appears that severe defeats at the hands of Veletian-Pomeranian forces in 963 **forced Mieszko to look for help against the warlike pagans,** convert to Christianity, and seek the assistance of Christian Bohemia and other members of *Christiana respublica.* Later, the *crusading* impulse that followed conversion will change the course of Polish history in another important way. Christian sources record and celebrate Duke Boleslav's III attacks on Pomerania in 1121 when **he ravaged the country west of the River Oder with fire and sword and announced his intention of converting all the inhabitants to the Christian faith, or of destroying**

them, in the event of their refusing to be converted. Polish knights will also take an active role in serial crusades against pagans in Prussia and Lithuania. To their credit, however, Polish authorities were the first or among the first (e.g. the indictment of the Teutonic Order by Paul Vladimir, a Polish ambassador at the church council in 1415) to rebel against the plunder and slaughter of innocent and peaceful unbelievers who refused to bow to the Holy Roman Empire, to accept Papal servitude.

ZIEMIA KASZUBSKA

In Eastern Pomerania, the **Kaszubs** (*gens Slavonica, Caussbitae dicuntur*) of **Ziemia Kaszubska,** a distinct historic, linguistic, and cultural Pomeranian entity, one finds traces of a Serb past in the Polish present *(H. Kunstmann, Woher die Kaschube ihren Namen haben, DwS 29, 1984).* In a region called **Kaszubow Slowinskich,** one finds a modern town and lake with the Serb ethnonym, namely **Sarbske** and **Sarbske jezero**, immediately west of the better-known town and lake of Leba and Lebsko *(F. Tetzner, Die Slowinzen und Lebaskashcuben, 1899. L. Zablocki, O Slowincach i Kaszubach nadlebskich, Jantar 3, 1947).*

SILESIA

In early German sources one finds reference to Serbs in Silesia: **Sirvi, welch in Schlesien wohneten.** Early and later German sources often identify Silesia as an important junction in the Serb settlement of **Serbska Luzica** or Lusatia. There is evidence of Serb settlement in several place- names (e.g. **Sarbino, Serby**) and a Serb province or **Surbiensis provincia** cited in the mid-10th century *Silesian Annals (Annales Silesiae).* It is interesting that in this area the *Silesian Annals* also record a stubborn resistance to the Latin rite and the defiant use of the *Slav-Heneti* language in church services: **Slavicae seu henetae linguae usum ... in sacris eccleaisasticis ... inibuit ac latin lingua concipi liturgiam precesaque jussit.** Several mountains in Silesia, Mts. Sobotka and Radunia, were long *notorious* centers of pagan rituals. Referring to Mt. Sobotka, Bishop Thietmar writes in the early 11th century: **It was the object of great veneration on the part of all the people because of its size and purpose, for iniquitous mysteries were celebrated there.** The following century finds Sileisia's Bishop of Wroclaw engaged in search-and-destroy missions against pagan cult centers where wooden images of old gods were kept. In the 19th century the pagan past was alive and well in such folk sayings as the one cited by J. Kollar: **Kto na nasu Sobotku neprigdze; ro roka ho glava bolec budze** *(H. Cehak-Holubowicza, Olimp Slaska in Szkice z dziejow Slaska, 1955; Kamienne konstrukcje kultowe pod szczytem na polnocnym sotku gory Slez, Swiatowit 23, 1960).*

ENDNOTES

[1] S. Kozierowski, Atlas nazw Geograficznych Slowianszczyzny Zachodnie, 1934; Badania nazw topograficznych starej Wielkopolski, 1939. W. Taszycki, Najdawniesze polski imiona osobowe, RoP 3, 1925.

[2] L. Quandt, Zur Urgeschichte der Pomoranen, BaL 22, 1868. S. Kozierowski, Nazwy rzeczne w Lechji przybaltyckiej i w przyleglych czesciah Slowianszczyzny polnocno-zachodniej, SlO 9, 1930. R. Kiersnowski, Plemiona Pomorz Zachodniego w swietle naj starsch zrodel pisanych, SlA 3, 1951-2. J. Dowiat, Ekspansja Pomorza zachodniego na ziemie wielecko-obodrzyckie w drugiej polowie XII wieku, PrZ 59, 1959. L. Leciejewicz, Poczatiki nadmorskich miast na Pomorzu Zachodnim, 1962. W. Losinski, Osadnictwo plemienne Pomorza (VI-X wiek), 1982.

Serbs/Sarbs/Sarbias in Poland

2. WHITE SERBIA

Some historians believe that prehistoric Poland's history is in part the history of *White Serbia.* It is a matter of record that the Serb ethnonym was as common east of the Oder as it was in the *White Serb* heartland west of the Oder. East of the Oder,[1] opposite **Serbska Blota** (Serb Marsh) and **Serbska Hola** (Serb Heath) in **Serbska Luzica** (Serb Lusatia), one finds the place names **Zorbenov**, **Sarbinovo**, **Serbov** and **Sarby**.

BORDERS

In his 10th century magnum opus, al-Mas`udi writes: the Bobr, Elbe and Saale rivers mark the borders of *White Serbia (Muruj ahd-dhahab wa ma'adin al jawahir).* One of the more authoritative modern studies, J. Marquart's outlines *White Serbia's* borders in similar terms: from the Bobr in the east, across the Elbe, to the Saale in the west *(Osteuropaische Streifzuege, 1903).* At its height, most historians tend to place *White Serbia's* eastern borders deeper into later Polish territory. Gebhardt, for example, places Silesia and western Poland up to the Vistula within *White Serbia's* 8th century borders *(L. A. Gebhardt, Geschichte aller Wendische-Slawischen Staaten, 1790).* In *Herkunft der Baltischen Wenden (1872)* Quandt extends *White Serbia's* borders in the east to include *White Serb* concentrations at Opole, Poznan, Kaliscz and Gniezno.[2] Noting the location of the *Surpe Serbs* recorded by Alfred the Great (871-899), Quandt is certain that the Serbs of Germania, *Vielkopolska* and Opole/Silesia are one people: **The Surpe are one and the same as the Opolini and the people who live in Poznan, Kaliscz and Gniezno.** It is interesting and should be noted that in recent time, viewing the facts of the matter from an entirely different perspective, H. Kunstmann traces Opolin and Polin to Balkan Slav roots *(Wer waren die Opolini des Geographus Bavarus Bavarus, und woher kommt das Ethnonym Polonia?).*

TO THE BUG

Safarik and other noted Slavists are certain that at one time *White Serbia's* borders reached the Bug and beyond. Some scholars are certain that the ancient *Buzhani* were originally Serbs. For example, the noted historian G. Krek writes: **In ancient times on the Bug were the Buzhani, a Slavic tribe, who were once called Serbs.** A large and powerful tribe comprising some 231 *cities* in the mid-9th century *(Busani habent civitates CCXXXI),* occupying the borderlands separating Poland from White Rus, Red Rus and Kiev Rus, the *Buzhani* ('buzhane, zane sedosha po Bugu'), later, the *Volyni* or Volynians ('poslezhe zhe velynane') occupied a large stretch of the river Bug. On *Buzhian* territory, on the west bank of the Bug, was a region known as *Czervia.* Authoritative German and Polish historians, J. Marquart and J. Otrebski among others, suspect that the *Czervs* of *Czervia* were *Serbs.* The well-known cities of *Czervia* ('ziemia Grodov Czervienskich'), centered at Czervien, included Czervien, near Czermno on the Huczwa, and the historic cities of Chelm and Volyn. It is perhaps interesting and coincidental that one of the lesser-known cities had the highly uncommon name of Sutieska or Sutjeska as in Sutjeska on the border of Bosnia and Montenegro.

BOIKI

Evidence in favor of this general area as an ancient Serb homeland and point of departure for Serbs moving westwards is found in a primary Byzantine source, namely Emperor Constantine Porphyrogenitus's *De Administrando Imperio.* Regarding the origin of the Balkan Serbs, where the Serbs *originally dwelt,* Constantine writes: **The Serbs are descended from the unbaptized Serbs, also called *White,* who lived beyond Turkey [Hungary] in a place called by them Boiki, where the neighbor is Francia** *(N. Zupanic, Bela Srbija, Narodna starina 1, 1922).*

GALICIA

Noting that Byzantine sources are often in error in matters beyond their immediate scope in time and space, some of the early Slav specialists, Safarik, Surowiecki, and other outstanding scholars, including the great Czech scholar Dobrovsky and the Croat F. Racki, are certain that Constantine's statement is in error regarding the location of *Boiki.* They believe that Constantine confused the *derivative* Serbs of Bohemian *Boiki* with the *original* Serbs of Galician *Boiki,* the *Boiki* district of eastern Galicia, a territory believed to be an ancient and direct link between the Eastern and Southern Slavs.

BOIKI HIGHLANDERS

In modern times *Boiki* refers to a distinct Slavic community, Ukrainian highlanders who differ from their Slavic neighbors (e.g. Lemkos/Rusnaks, Hutsuls) in language, dress, architecture, and customs, and who have preserved many ancient customs and rituals that disappeared in other parts of Galicia and Ukraine. The *Boiki* region includes the High Beskid, the eastern part of the Middle Beskid, the Middle Carpathians, and the Carpathian Depression. In this area one finds the small towns of Borinia, Borislav, Dolina, Drogobich, Medenica, Nizhni Vorota, Stari Sambor, Stri, and Volove.

DUKLA

It is interesting and perhaps coincidental that in the Eastern Beskids, in the Lemko region, the *Boiki* border an area with the uncommon name of *Dukla,* centered near the town of *Dukla,* just north of the strategic *Dukla Pass* on the Polish-Czechoslovak border. *Dukla* or *Duklja,* of course, is also the highly uncommon name of a Serb nation that gave its name to the first Serb state, the *Dukljani* of medieval *Duklja* *(J. Udolph, Zu Deutung und Verbreitung des Namens Dukla, BnF 23, 1988; H. Kunstmann, Der Dukla-Name und sein Weg von Montenegro uber die Karpaten nach Nordwestrussland, DwS 33, 1988).*

ENDNOTES

[1] In addition to the several Serb dialects spoken east of the Oder, there are other interesting linguistic continuities (e.g. M. Gruchmanova, Luzycko-Wielkopolska Izomorfa Nom.- Acc.-Voc. Pl. Dny, Z Polskich Studiow Slawistycznych 5, 1978.

[2] Opole refers to the early medieval Duchy of Opole in Silesia, centered at Opole on the Oder River, said to have twenty cities in the mid-9th century *(Opolini, civitates XX).* The name Opol is is Slavic word for a territorial community. Today Opol is the name of a city and county in southwestern Poland. W. Holubowicz, Opolu w wiekach X-XII, 1956. H. Borek, Opolszyzna w swietle nazw miejscowych, 1972.

3. FROM THE UNBAPTIZED SERBS
WHO DWELL ON THE RIVER VISLA

Impressive evidence that some of the Balkan Serbs originated in Poland is found in *De Administrando Imperio*. In his treatise, Emperor Constantine Pophyrogenitus informs us that in **Zahumlja**, a principality in coastal Serbia: **The family of the patrician Mihailo Visevich, son of Viseta, prince of the Zahumlyans, came from the unbaptized Serbs who dwell on the river Visla and are called Litziki.**

LITZIKI

Most historians tend to agree with 319th century Polish historiography that the name *Litziki* is derived from *lug*, an Old Slav word for moor, marshland, pasture, woodland, and wasteland. Thus *Lugizi, Ligizi, Litziki* and other variations are parallel archaic names for the *Polanie*, a name derived from an Old Slav word with similar connotations. According to L. Niederle, however, it is more likely that *Litziki* is a generic name for Poles, derived from one of the better known and westernmost Polish tribes/nations, the *Licicaviki* as in: ***Sclavi qui dicuntur Licicaviki* and *longius degentes barbari ... Licicaviki***, bordering with Serb lands west of the Oder *(J. Widajewicz, Licicaviki Widukina, SlO 6, 1927. G. Labuda, Licicaviki, SsS 3, 1967).*

VIS, VISLA, VISEVIC, VISEVO

The patronymic **Visevich** certainly suggests a *Vis/Visla/Vislani* origin for the house of Visevich. In several place names in medieval **Zahumlja** one finds toponymic evidence in favor of a Vislanian origin of other Serb lineages: e.g. *Viseva zupa* or county; *Viseva*, a local name for the upper Neretva *(T. Wasilewski, Administraja bizantynska na ziemiach slowianskich i jej polityka wobec Slowian w XI-XII w, KwA 70, 1973; Wislanska dynastia ijej zachlumskie panstwo w IX-X w, PaM 15, 1965).*

CIVITATES OMNES ROMANOOS

Anti-Byzantine and pro-Bulgarian in orientation, a close ally of the very learned and powerul ruler of Bulgaria and champion of Slavdom, Tsar Simeon (893-927), seated at Preslav, **Mihailo Visevich** was a force in affairs beyond the borders of **Zahumlja: In the year 925 Pope John X invites Mihailo (*Michaele exellentissimo duce Chulmorum*), along with Tomislav of Croatia, to take part in the resolution of church affairs in Croatia-Dalmatia.**

An inscription found at Ston suggests that **Mihailo** considered himself the supreme authority in the affairs of Byzantine towns along the Dalmatian coast:

MIHAELVS FORTITER SVPER REGO PACIFICO
CIVITATES OMNES ROMANOOS.

REX SCLAVORUM CIVITATEM SIPONTUM

Mihailo was also a force to be reckoned with on the opposite shore of the Adriatic, on the Apulian spur of the Italian boot. Crossing the Adriatic, in 926 **Mihailo** conquered Byzantine Siponto, opening the way for greater Serb settlement in the Gargano peninsula. ***Comprendit Michael rex Sclavorum civitatem Sipontum.***

SERBS CONTRA SERBS

Decade's later Serb settlements in southern Italy will lead to *Serbs* originating in Illyria by way of Poland(?), fighting against invading *Serbs* originating in Germania's *White Serbia.* In the year 981, *Serb* forces recruited in southeastern Italy, reinforced by some 40,000 *Serb* mercenaries under the command of **Vukasin (*40,000 pagani condotti dal loro re Bullicassinus*),** take an active role in the defense of Calabria against the forces of Emperor Otto of Germany, including *Serb* forces from Germania's *White Serbia* and *Serb* knights serving in Otto's personal bodyguard.

ZUPAN GLUBISA

It appears that in some instances the Serbs survived as an independent national-political community as late as the mid-11th century: **When Serb zupans (e.g. zupan Andreas, zupan Glubisa) are found at the head of a number of communities in the Gargano area (e.g. Devia, Varano) where natives with Serb personal names are recorded (e.g. Drago, Radovit).** In this general area one finds numerous references to Slavic settlements in family names (e.g. *Scavone, Schiavone, Cito, Pribo, Pissichio, Stano*), in village names (e.g. *Castellucium de Slavis, Lesin, Peschici, Schiavi*), and toponyms (e.g. *rione degli Schiavonia, Monte Schiavoni, Ponte degli Schiavoni, Schiauni, Ponte Schiavo, Piano Schiavi*).[1]

SRBLYI, POLES

One moment in the second half of the 14th century makes it very clear that the Bosnian Serbs believed that the Serbs and Poles were one people, who, sharing a common ancestry, had an obligation to assist one another in times of trouble, in this instance, the Turkish threat.

KRAL SERBLEM

In 1440, Stevan Tvrtko II (1440-43), King of Bosnia and all the Serbs **(MILOSTYU BOZHNOM MI GOSPODIN KRAL SERBLEM)** asserting a common ancestry, language and interest, sought assistance from the newly elected Slavic king of Hungary, the Pole Vladislav Varnecik (1440-1444).

ISTI PRADJEDOVI

The letter and spirit of this early *Pan-Slav* moment are a matter of historical record. Contemporaneous Hungarian sources offer a clear statement of the thesis advanced by Stevan Tvrkto's emissaries to Vladislav's court at Budim, namely the common ancestry of the Poles and Serbs (*Srblyi*). A Croat translation of the Latin original reads as follows: **Dodje i od kralja bosanskoga sjajne poslanstvo odlicnih muzeva. Ovi su izpricavsi porietlo svoga plemena izticali, da su Bosnjakom isti pradjedovi bili, koji i Poljakom, te da im je zajednicki jezik, koji govore; i da se radi te rek bi srodnosti jezika i porietla njihov kralj zivo raduje, sto je Vladislav—kako se pronio glas—sretan u svojih podhvatih. Mongo su nadalje izticali priliku, kako bi se radi srodnosti i susjedstva mogli, dapace i morali ujedinjenom snagom i savjetom medju sobom pomagati proti uzasnomu zulumu turskomu, koji im prieti. Osim toga zatrazise, da se ugovor i prijateljstvo, koje su svi dotadanji kraljevi najvecom svetoscu postivali i cuvali, medju Bosnom i Ugarskom ili sklopi ili obnovi. Poslanikom bi milostivo odgovoreno: da je pravo, sto se uspjeh i i napredak Vladislavov njihovu** kralju svidja, toli radi onoga srodstva jezika i porietla, koje spominju, koli radi toga, sto je jednim i drugim malo ne jednako do toga, da se sto prije sva Ugarska umiri te krjepkimi silami proti zajednickomu dusmaninu vojna povede. Zatim im zahvalise, sto je njihov kralj sam obrekao, da ce u zgodan cas pomagati Ugarskoj proti Turkom i zborom i tvorom, pa ih obodrise, neka bi kralj do kraja uztrajao u toj namisli. Napokon bje ugovor medju kraljevi i kraljevinami utvrdjen (V. Klaic, Povijest Bosna: Do Propoasti Kraljevstva, 1882).

MORE TURKISH THAN THE TURKS

In fact, of course, then and later, the Polish moment in Bosnia's affairs are far from fraternal. Polish knights take part in serial crusades against the good Christians of Bosnia. Centuries later, Poles serving in Ottoman and Austrian occupation armies and administrations are notorious for their hostility to the native population. An 1877 incident recorded in Pristina perhaps captures the letter and spirit of the Polish moment: **The books at Prishtina were from Belgrade, but as they seemed only to have chitankas adapted for the youngest children, we asked if they had not some histories of Serbia. The master looked furtively around, and then said that he had some, but dared not to use them openly. "Why not?"** *"Because the officers of the Turkish regiments frequently come and loll about in our school, and the cavalry officers are often Hungarians, Cossacks or Poles, and can read the Slavic books."* **"But these dry histories contain nothing revolutionary, and surely the officers who are your fellow Christians would not wish to calumniate you."** *"The rest would not, but the Poles are more Turkish than the Turks themselves. One day a Polish officer looked over the shoulder of one of the children, and called out: 'Halla, master! What do I see here? These books come from the principality [Serbia], and here is something about the history of Serbia. If I catch you at this again, I shall report you to the authorities'. I trembled from head to foot and knew not what I would say or do; but luckily there was also present a Cossack, a deserter from the Russian service, a good man who always befriended us; he got the Pole out of the room, and said to him in displeasure that they were not sent to Prishtina to meddle with the Serb school* (G. Muir Mackenzie, A. P. Irby, The Slavonic Provinces of Turkey in Europe, 1877).

THE BLACK POPE

In World War II, it should be noted, Moslem leaders placed the blame for the crusading war and genocide against the Serbs and the chaos in Bosnia squarely on the shoulders of the Austro-Polish 'Black Pope,' Wladimir Ledochowski, Superior General of the Jesuits, who, perhaps inspired by *deranged* visions of a *divine* Polish mission, appears to have supported a Roman Catholic crusade against *schismatics* in eastern and southeastern Europe.

ENDNOTES

[1] M. Resetar, Die serbokoratischen Kolonien Suditaliens, 1911. G. Reichenkron, Serbokroatisches aus Suditalien, ZsP, 12, 1934. G. Rohlfs, Ignote colonie slave sulle coste del Gargano, CeR 3, 1958. M. Hraste, Nepoznate slavenske kolonije na obalama Gargana, Kolo Matice hrvatske, 1963. G. Rohlfs, Slavische Kolonisation in Suditalien, SuD 29, 1970.

4. NO NATION IN THE WORLD

Though we know very little about the natives of Poland's interior, diverse foreign sources offer a clear picture of the appearance, character, industry, commerce, and civilization of the Slavs on Ptolemy's **Sea of the Slavs, on *Sclavorum maritimas regiones*, of the Serb Wends who settled the entire Baltic coast to the Vistula.**

NO NATION IN THE WORLD

A notorious 10th century Jewish slave-trader from Andalusia, Ibrahim ibn Jakub, a well-travelled, experienced, hard-headed, and bottom-line connoisseur of human flesh and talent, found the Baltic Slavs an especially robust, bold, and enterprising people. **I saw none of better physique than the Slavs; they were as tall as palms, red cheeked and handsome. If it were not for their disunion ... no nation in the world could hope to rival them in power. They inhabit lands rich in resources and foodstuffs. They practice agriculture and the manufacture of many useful objects, surpassing all other northern peoples in these activities.** *(J. Widajewicz, Studia na relacja o Slowianach Ibrahim ibn Jakuba, 1949. T. Lewicki, Zrodla arabskie do dziejow slowianszczyzny, 1956-58).*

PO MORE

Foreign and archaelogical sources substantiate and document the early primacy of the Baltic Slavs in the formation of urban centers of industry and commerce. With regard to ancient Wolin or ***civitas Sclavorum Wolin*** or ***magna civitas Wolin***, Helmold writes: **At one time it was truly the largest of all the cities of Europe.** Wolin was also truly one of the richest cities of Europe: **And there Slavs lived in it and a mixed population of other peoples, Greeks and barbarians ... Rich in the wares of all nations, Wolin lacked nothing that was either charming or rare.**

EXCAVATIONS

Recent excavations reveal a large trading and manufacturing centre, with numerous agrarian satellite settlements and cemeteries, writes G. P. Fehring: **Manufacture is evidenced through the shipyards and the huge volume of waste products of iron, horn, and precious metal working; there are hints of iron smelting, gold smithing and the production of jewellery. Trade is witnessed by weights and scales and the presence of imports like soapstone, coins from Hedeby, Scandinavian jewellery, glass and semi-precious beads, fragments of glass vessels, and Chinese silk. The subdivided, thickly settled core settlement with its market and heathen cult centre ... had suburbs attached to it in the north and south, suburbs that were characterized by artisanal production in one and by fishing in the other** *(The Archaeology of Medieval Germany, 1991).*

PRE-CHRISTIAN CIVILIZATION

The great cities of the Baltic were long vital centers of pre-Christian Slavic civilization and, in the words of fierce and uncompromsing Christian adversaries, the sites of **temples of great size, beauty and marvellous design, shrines of marvellous workmanship, sheltering images of great size, marvellously sculptured, and covered with most beautiful designs.**

TOLERANCE

The pagan Slav cities were renowned for their tolerance. In Wolin, Helmold writes, **alien Saxons also received the right to live there on equal terms with others, provided they did not openly profess the Christian faith.** In times of trouble, Christian princes could find peace and comfort in pagan Wolin. Following a bloody dynastic conflict with son Svein (the Forked Beard, 985-1014), the defeated and wounded Christian king Harald boards a ship and escapes **to the most renowned city of the Slavs, where he was kindly received.** Time after time even divinely ruthless and mindless missionaries concede that in the pagan Slavic lands, *in the kingdom of the devil*, they were received with **so much humility and hospitality.**

ASYLUM

It appears that the traditional system of law provided for a strict system of asylum for one and all. In Duke Vratislav's dominion: **In each of his cities the Duke had a stronghold and a court with rooms in it and the law provided that if anyone had fled to this he should be secure from any enemy who might follow, and should remain there safe and unharmed.**

REASONED, KNOWING TOLERANCE

While it was standard for Christian missionaries to demonize the pagan Slavs in the most hateful and murderous terms, to call their pagan adversaries cruel barbarians, wicked savages, and evil beasts, to incite Christian 'crusaders' to murder, mayhem, and genocide against all *who with unbridled neck spurned the yoke of humility,* all the evidence indicates that the Slavs, when and where possible, in spite of the greatest provocations, as the case of Bishop Berhnard illustrates, responded with reason, with a knowing and civilized tolerance.

THE GLORY OF MARTYRDOM

Determined to *obtain the glory of martyrdom*, to trick the pagans to *murder* God's servant and incite a great crusade against the *pagan barbarians,* the thoroughly mad and evil Bishop Bernhard challenged the good citizens of Volin as follows: **If you do not believe my words, believe my works. Set fire to some house that has collapsed through old age and is not of use to anyone, and throw me into the midst: if, when the house has been consumed by flames, I shall come out from the fire uninjured, that know that I have sent by Him to whose rule fire and every created thing is subject, and whom all the elements serve.** Seeing through the evil plot, instead of violence, the good people responded with reason and humanity. The 'pagan' priests and elders of the people, when they heard this, conferred together and said: **This is a foolish and desperate person who ... seeks death and goes of his own accord to meet it. We are beset by villainy, which seeks to exact vengeance because he has been rejected by us, and to involve us in his own destruction. For if one house is set on fire, the destruction of the whole city must follow. We ought therefore to take care and not to listen to one who is of unsound mind ... If then we desire to consider our own interest, we shall do this man no injury but expel him from our territory and, having placed him on board a ship, make him cross the sea to some other land.**

5. NEC MALIGNUM NEC FRAUDLENTUM

Alll sources agree that the ancient Slavs were an honorable and decent people. Though fierce in battle, Procopius writes, the Slavs were far from an evil or treacherous people: *Ingenium ipsis nec malignum nec fraudlentum.*

HOSPITALITY, HUMANITY

In the second half of the 6th century, a time when Slavic tribes were attacking Thessalonica and settling in Macedonia and Greece, one of the most outstanding Byzantine rulers, Emperor Maurice (582-602), pays tribute to their great hospitality to strangers and humanity to captives. Maurice also notes that the women were virtuous, an attribute confirmed by Christian observers in medieval Germania.

HONORABLE, KINDLIER

The noble character, honor, and decency of the Baltic Slavs is a matter of record. Helmold writes: **As far as morals and hospitality were concerned, a more honorable and kindlier folk could not be found.**

INEXPERTI SUNT

According to contemporaneous sources, the Baltic Slavs (*Sclavorum Maritimas Regiones*) were not up to par in terms of deception and fraud: *anto vero fides et societas est inter eos, ut futorum et fraduium penitus inexerpeti sunt.* Even the most aggressive and intolerant crusader types concede that the Baltic Slavs were not up to Christian standards in terms of deception, fraud, and theft: **So great are the trust and confidence which prevail amongst the people that they possess no boxes or locked cases. We never saw there a lock or key and they were themselves astonished to see our pack saddles and our locked cases. Their clothes, their money and all their precious things they store in cases and large jars, which merely covered over, as they fear no fraud and have never had experience of such** (*Vita S. Ottonis*).

IN THE MANNER OF THE SLAVONIANS

According to all sources, the greatest sin of the Slavs appears to have been a certain deeply ingrained *rusticity*. Speaking of the Danish archbishop, one of Otto's biographers writes: **He was a good and honest man and loved to hear of things that were good: he was also learned and devout, though externally he possessed the rustic manner of the Slavonians. For it was the case with all the men of that country that, whilst living in prosperity and wealth, they seemed harsh, unclutivated and rustic.**

PERVASIVE HUMANITY

It appears that a certain and pervasive tolerant humanity was one of the more evil and offensive components of Slavonian *rusticity*, a sinful condition that Otto, among others, attempted to rectify: **The bishop noticed on one occasion some boys playing in an open space ... The man of God stopped and addressing in a kindly voice those around him inquired if any of them had received baptism. They looked one upon another and began to put forward those of them who had been baptized. The** bishop then called them aside and asked them whether it was their desire to preserve the faith of their baptism. When they strongly asserted that they desired to keep it the bishop said: If you desire to be Christians and to keep the faith in which you have been baptized, you ought not to admit to your games those boys who have not been baptized and who do not believe. Accordingly, as the bishop suggested, like joined with like, and the boys who had been baptized began to repel and show their dislike for those who had not been baptized and refused to let them join in their games.

CHRISTIAN POLITIK

Indeed, all the evidence indicates that Slav resistance to Christianity was not so much a resistance to Christian theology as it was to Christian *politik*. A contemporaneous Christian commentator summed up the essential nature of the struggle, pagan freedom contra Christian servitude, in in the following words: **A struggle for freedom and escape from the direst servitude.** Regarding the political-economic moment in the mid-11th century, Widukind of Corvey writes: **Many days thus passed, one side fighting with varying fortunes for glory and imperial expansion, the other for freedom. The Slavs preferred war to peace, valuing dear liberty above comfort.**

THIEVES, ROBBERS

On another level it was a conflict between opposing social-moral orders. Thus the following words of a defender of the old order in Pomerania, a wealthy land that was said to possess no poor people or beggars: **What have we to do with you? We will not abandon the laws of our fathers, and are content with the religion that we possess. Amongst the Christians there are thieves and robbers, and those who have been deprived of their feet and eyes; all sorts of crimes and penalties are found amongst them and one Christian curses another Christian. Let such a religion be far from us.**

IN WAR

Though honorable, hospitable, kindly, and industrious in peace, in war the Slavs were more than a match for German and Scandinavian neighbors. It is a matter of medieval record that the Slavs were **bolder and more ferocious than the Franks.** In the case of the Galicians, al-Mas'udi writes: **One man of the Galicians can withstand a number of Franks.** Indeed, Arab sources suggest a ratio of one to ten: (*at the time of King Mieszko I*) **Poland was supported by an army of 3,000 armoured men, 100 of whom are equal to 1,000 of others.** In the early 12th century, German sources missionaries characterized the Pomeranians as a free, independent, and unconquerable non-Christian nation: **The Pomeranian people being skilled fighters both by land and sea and being used to live by loot and spoils, and owing to their natural fierceness, having never been conquered, were far removed from Christian faith and refinement.** The same sources add the following details: **Moreover the horses of this country are large and strong and each individual soldier fights without a shield bearer and carries his own pack and shield, performing his military tasks with great agility and energy.**

MORE PLAY THAN WAR

With regard to the Scandinavians, to fierce Vikings, the medieval record is abundantly clear that the fiercest Vikings were no match for the Baltic Slavs. In fact, so much so that war against the Danes was considered more play than war.

PRISONERS

According to a 7th century Byzantine source, the Slavs were noted for their relatively humane treatment of prisoners: **Slavs do not reduce their prisoners to the same type of slavery as other people do. They do not keep them for an indefinite period of time and are given the following choices: They can go back home, provided they pay a ransom, or remain slaves until they are freed and are friends again.**

DUKE MISLAV

Following his conversion, Duke Mislav of Uznoim was asked if he had taken anything by violence from anyone. He answered: **I have done violence to no one, but I have in my possession many captives who are under great obligation to me. Otto, the man of God, said: 'Inquire whether any of them are Christians.' When he had inquired he found that many who came from the country of the Danes were Christians. These he placed, at once, before our blessed father, after he had completely absolved them from their debts.** Later, it was only with great difficulty that the 'man of God' gained freedom for the son of a noble Danish chief who owed Duke Mislav five hundred marks. Of course, it goes without saying that horrific, predatory, genocidal Christian crimes against Duke Mislav, against his people, against all other pagans, were never mentioned by either the 'man of God' or his followers, and never considered a matter for discussion in any manner, shape or form.

Uznoim, Volin

PART IV

1. DANUBIA

I t is very important to note that in opposition to an *Asian* or *Indo-Iranian Urheimat* thesis, a number of leading scholars, past and present, believe that *Danubia* is either a primary or secondary *Urheimat* of the Slavs.

BESIDE THE DANUBE

In fact, the Danubian thesis has the deepest and broadest roots in medieval sources, beginning with the *Primary Chronicle.* According to the *Chronicle,* after the Lord *confused the tongues* and divided the people into seventy-two races, among them *the Slavic race* derived from the line of *Japeth*: **Over a long period the Slavs settled beside the Danube, where the Hungarian and Bulgarian lands now lie. From among these Slavs, parties scattered throughout the country and were known by appropriate names, according to the places where they settled. Thus some came and settled by the river Morava, and were named Moravians, while others were called Czechs. Among these same Slavs are included the White Croats, the Serbs, and the Carinthians. When the Volokhs attacked the Danubian Slavs and did them violence, those Slavs went and settled on the Vistula and obtained the name of Lekhs. Of these same Lekhs some were called Polyanians, some Lutichians, some Mazovians, and still others Pomorians. Certain Slavs settled also on the Dnieper, and were likewise called Polyanians. Still others were named Derevlians, because they lived in the forests. Some also lived between Pripet and the Dvina, and were known as Dregovichians. Other tribes resided along the Dvina and were called Polotians on account of a small stream called the Polota, which flows into the Dvina. It is from this same stream that they were named Polotians. The Slavs also dwelt about Lake Il'men, and were known by their characteristic name. The built a city which they called Desna, the Sem, and the Sula, and were called Severians. Thus the Slavic race was divided, and its language was known as Slavic.**

MATER ET ORIGO OMNIUM SLAVONICARUM NACIONUM

A later Polish variation on the Danubia thesis places the origin of the Slavs in Pannonia, an area south and west of the Danube, near the Christian heartland and the missions of Saints Cyril and Methodius: ***Scribitur enim in vetustissimis codicibus quod Pannonia sit mater et origo omnium Slavonicarum nacionum, Pan enim iuxta Grecam et Slavorum interpretacionem dicitur totem habens. Et iuxta hoc dicitur Pan in Slavonico maior dominus, licet alio nomine iuxta diversitatem linwarum Slavonicarum dicatur Gospodzyn, Xandz autem maior est quam Pan veluti princeps et superior Rex*** (*Chronicae Poloniae maioris*).

One finds the same idea in the 15th century Polish historian, Jan Dlugoscz: **Tedy potomek synow Jafeta, prarodzie wszystkich Slowian, wyszedlszy ze stepu Sennar ... przekroczyl rzeke Hister, ktora teraz nazywamy Dunaj ... z synami, powinowatymi i krewnymi swymi osiadl napierw w Pannonii, najpierwszej i najstraszej Slowian siedzibied, kolebce ich i zywicicelce, ktora obecnie** (*Annales Seu Chronicae Inclyti Regni Poloniae*).[1]

LES PROVINCES DANUBIENNES

In France, C. Robert stated the Danubian thesis in the most absolute terms. In spite of the often highly political and self-serving efforts of some scholars to place the origin of the Slavs beyond the borders of Europe, Robert writes, the historical facts and logic speak otherwise—the Danube is their ancestral homeland: **Les provinces danubiennes en sont au contraire l'axe et le noyau ... Les premieres trainees de la race slave ont resplendi sur le grand fleuve ... de cette race geante ... L'artere la plus vitale du cors slave, le Danube, n'est donc qu'un fleuve slavon** *(Le Monde Slave, 1852).*

O.N. TRUBACEV

O.N. Trubacev, perhaps the modern era's leading authority on Proto-Slavistics, brilliantly represents the Danubian thesis. In one of his first studies on the subject, juxtaposing relevant lexical material relating to early Slavic-Baltic, Slavic-Italic, and Slavic-Germanic language contacts in a number of fields, Trubacev finds that the number of Slavic-Baltic lexical parallels is the smallest compared to those between Slavic and Italic and Slavic and Germanic, the latter amount being the greatest. This evidence, Trubacev writes, is a clear indication of an early orientation of the ancient Slavs towards Central Europe, prior to establishing closer ties with the Balts *(Remeslennaja terminologija v slavjanskih jazykah. Etimologija i opyt gruppovoj rekonstrukcii, 1966).*[2]

RECONQUISTA

In an important 1985 article Trubacev begins his discussion of the Slavs and the Danube by asking: **What has triggered the invasions of the Slavs in the 6ᵗʰ into the Danubian territories and farther to the south?** The answer, Trubacev believes, is, in part, perhaps a matter of historical memory: **A union with the Avars? The weakness of Rome and Constantinople? Or were they prompted by the persistent traditions about an ancient stay on the Danube? Perhaps then this famous Danubian-Balkanic migration of the Slavs would prove to be a Reconquista that ran somewhat out of control owing to favorable circumstances and to the eagerness of the Slavs ... What else, if not a memory of the old stay on the Danube, appears, for example, in the old songs about the Danube among the Eastern Slavs who, it should be remembered, never lived on the Danube (i.e., the Middle Danube) during their written history and never took part in the Balkanic invasions of the Early Middle Ages** *(O.N. Trubacev, Linguistics and Ethnogenesis of the Slavs: The Ancient Slavs as Evidenced by Etymology and Onomastics, InD 13, 1985).*

VOLCAE, VOLOKHS

From the middle of the first millennium B.C. onwards, Trubacev writes**, a critical situation developed for the Slavs and the other tribes in the Danubian plain in connection with the expansion of the Celts.** It seems that the *Primary Chronicle's* reference to the so-called Volokhs *('When the Volokhs attacked the Danubian Slavs, and did them violence')* is actually a reference to the Celts, the Volcae-Tectosagi, who, **after leaving Gaul and moving toward the East along the southern borders of the then Germanic area, became known under a Germanic name (Germanic *walhoz < Gaulish Volcae).** According to Trubacev, the Celtic expansion into Bohemia, Moravia, and Pannonia took place no later than the fourth to the third centuries B.C. **From then on began the contact of the Slavs with the Volokhs as they were called in the Rus-**

sian Primary Chronicle ... **Beside the cultural influence of the Celts under the conditions of a peaceful symbiosis, military pressure could not be avoided; as a result, a considerable part of the Slavs was compelled to move to the North.** Trubacev believes that the centum elements in the Common Slavic vocabulary tend to support his views on the time and place of Slav-Celtic contact.[3]

PROTO-INDO-EUROPEANS

The localization of the Ancient Slavs is related to the localization of the Proto-Indo-Europeans, **where they came from long before Common Slavic emerged, and whether they came at all from far away.** All attempts to trace the original homeland of the Proto-Indo-Europeans to Asia fail to explain the build-up of the Old European hydronomy, to explain the compact Proto-Indo-European onomastic evidence in Central Europe on the one hand, and the relative absence of Proto-Indo-European onomastic evidence in either Asia Minor or Asia Magna on the other. What is especially striking, Trubacev writes, is the fact that **the Old European hydronomy is not directly motivated by any specific language, and we can assume the latter only indirectly on the basis of the Old European hydronomy itself, which indicates ... the greater antiquity of Old European hydronomy than of the obviously secondary Indo-European hydronomy of Anatolia.**

BALKANIA, DANUBIA

According to Trubacev, the established linguistic-onomastic facts of the matter encourage one to reconsider the Danubian theory, Danubia as the original homeland of the Proto-Slavs. **If we assume a close interrelation and a considerable coincidence of the area of the Old European waternames and of the properly Proto-Indo-European population area, it will be appropriate to lend an ear to the opinion of those scholars who for a long time focused attention on the Danube region, e.g., a diffusion from the Danubian zone as early as the Neolithic Age, as stated by anthropologists, Balkanic-Danubian influences, discovered by archaeologists, and the spreading from here into the North Pontic region of cereal, stock-breeding and metals in the 5th-6th millennia B.C.** In his main work on the subject, *Etnogenez i kultura drevnejskich Slavjan. Lingvisticeski issledovanija (1991)*, and subsequent articles, Trubacev presents a powerful linguistic, onomastic and inter-disciplinary case for a Danubian *Urheimat (Etnogenez i kultura drevneiskih slavjan, 1993; SCLAVANIA na Maine v merovingskyu i karolingskyu epohu, 1995; Drevnieslavjane na Dunae, 1997; Prodolzenie razbiskanii o drevnih slavjanah na Dunae, 1998).*

SOUTHEASTERN EUROPE

The eminent Russian linguist and historian I. M. Diakonov has little doubt that the Proto-Indo-European languages orignated in southeastern Europe: **I think that the Balkan-Carpathian area was the homeland of the speakers of Indo-European languages. It has been demonstrated that domesticated animals and agriculture appeared there in the 6th-5th millennia B.C.E., coming from Asia Minor. It is possible that Asia Minor (the area of the Catal-Huyuk culture) was the original homeland of the local population of farmers and cattle-breeders. But the spread of the historical Indo-European languages occurred from the Balkan-Carpathian region, not from the Near East and Asia Minor** *(I. M. Diakonov, On the Original Home of the*

Speakers of Indo-European, InD 13, 1985).

LEPENSKI VIR

By the Balkan-Carpathian area Diakonov means the area between the Balkans and the Carpathians, centered in Danubia. He writes: **I am almost sure that the Indo-European original homeland was located somewhere between the Balkans and the Carpathians.** Diakonov believes it is not unreasonable to assume that Danubia, **near the Iron Gates of the Danube**, was the center area of Common Indo-European. Near the Iron Gates of the Danube is obviously a reference to **Lepenski Vir**, a site on the Danube near Djerdap in eastern Yugoslavia, believed to represent early and critical steps in the evolution of Old European civilization *(D. Srejovic, The Roots of the Lepenski Vir Culture, Archeologia Jugoslavica 10, 1969; Europe's First Monumental Sculpture: New Discoveries at Lepenski Vir, 1972).* In Neolithic times, Diakonov writes: **climatic and ecological conditions were very favorable ... Agriculture developed somewhat later later there then in Asia Minor, and then the breeding of horned cattle, horses and pigs began to play an ever growing role. A homogeneous zone of highly developed neolithic and, later, eneolithic cultures ("Danube" cultures according to Gordon Childe) was created there, and this region could also become a center of population spread as a result of population growth.** At the same time, Diakonov believes that the linguistic-onomastic evidence as well as circumstantial evidence, including and especially that relating to migration patterns, runs counter to both the theory of a primary homeland of European dialects of Indo-European in Asia Minor and the theory of a secondary original homeland in the Black Sea and Trans-Volga regions.

OLD EUROPEAN CIVILIZATION

The Danubian thesis is in different ways both affirmed and refuted by archaeological evidence flowing from the discovery of an Old European civilization centered in Danubian Southeast Europe, the birthplace and heartland of European civilization. According to M. Gimbutas, the indigenous cultures of Old Europe began their development with the transition to agriculture during the 7th millennium B.C. in Southeast Europe and approached their florescence in that area toward the end of the 5th millennium B.C.: **The inhabitants of this region developed a much more complex social organization than their western and northern neighbours, forming settlements which often amounted to small townships, inevitably involving craft specializations and the creation of religious and governmental institutions. They independently discovered the possiblity of utilizing copper and gold for ornaments and tools, and even appear to have evolved a rudimentary script** *(M. Gimbutas, The Goddesses and Gods of Old Europe, 1982).*

VINCA SCRIPT

There is growing evidence that the Old European script, developed some two thousand years earlier than other known scripts, also called the ***Vinca script*** (from the Vinca site, near Belgrade, a distinct cultural entity centered in Morava, Danube, and Tisza basins of Yugoslavia, eastern Hungary, northwestern Bulgaria, and western Romania), survived throughout the Aegean and Mediterranean world, and influenced the development of linear scripts in Crete and Cyprus and archaic versions of Greek alphabetic writing *(S.M.M. Winn, Pre-Writing in Southeastern Europe: The Sign System of the Vinca Culture c. 4000*

BC, 1981). According to H. Haarman: **The historical relationship between Cretan linear writing and the Old European script is apparent in the abundance of sign parallels. About half of the repertory of Linear A signs (more than sixty individual signs) has parallels in the Old European repertory ... The Old European layer of iconic material becomes even more visible in Cypriot Syllabic if the basic constituent element of the sign forms are taken into consideration ... This kind of experimenting with writing that we see in the [Old Europe] pre-Greek era, and its transfer to the world of the ancient Greeks, evolved without any significant influence from outside Europe. Early literacy in Europe ranges among the few original experiments with writing as a civilizational pattern in human history, and it is the oldest known so far** *(H. Haarmann, Writing in the Ancient Mediterranean: The Old European Legacy, From the Realm of the Ancestors, 1997)*.

INDO-EUROPEAN?

While Gimbutas' extraordinary energy and scholarship clearly and irrefutably establish southeastern Europe, the Balkan-Danubia area, as the absolute center of Old European civilization, at the same time, she is certain that it was not Proto-Indo-European in origin or character. According to Gimbutas, the Proto-Indo-Europeans were not its creators, but its destroyers. More precisely, Gimbutas writes, Old European civilization was destroyed by invasions of Proto-Indo-European peoples originating in the Volga steppe region of south Russia and the North Pontic area. The invasions took place in three major waves. The first wave entered the territory west of the Black Sea c. 4400-4300 B.C. from the Volga steppe region. A second wave moved into southeast Europe during the mid-4th millennium B.C. from the North Pontic area between the Lower Dniester and the Caucasus Mountains. A third wave from the Volga steppe entered the Balkano-Danubian area soon after 3000 B.C.

OLD EUROPEAN HYDRONOMY

In opposition, Trubacev and others raise the Old European hydronomy barrier. The new or reformulated theories, Trubacev writes: **about a Near Eastern original homeland of the Indo-Europeans or a secondary, North Pontic, European original homeland of the Indo-Europeans of Europe who would have arrived here a very long time ago, allegedly as a result of a west to east migration around the Caspian Sea, does not satisfy us because it does not explain the most important thing: the building-up of the Old European hydronomy ... We find the compact Indo-European onomastic area only in Europe, and the diagnostic value of this fact for the problem of the localization of the Proto-Indo-Europeans can hardly be overestimated. It cannot be down-played by attempting to discover pre-Indo-European elements within the Indo-European layer ... It cannot be discredited, on the other hand, through the naive attempts to discover 'das letze Indogermanisch' in the 'Northwestblock' on the Lower Rhine.**

CARPATHIA

In certainly one of the more ambitious and exhaustive works in the modern period *(Studien zu slavischen Gewassernamen und Gewasserbezeichnungen. Ein Beitrag zu Frage nach der Urheimat der Slaven, 1979)*, J. Udolph's methodology, a massive study of common Slavic nouns referring to waterways, to streams, rivers, ponds, lakes, swamps, and the derivation of hydronyms (some 640 pages and 199 maps), leads him to place the Slav *Urheimat* in Carpathia north of the Danube.

ZAKOPANE, BUKOWINA

More precisely, Udolph places the Slav *Urheimat* between Zakopane in the west and Bukowina in the east: **Ursprungliches Kerngebiet der slavischen Siedlung war mit grosser Wahrscheinlichkeit der Nordhang der Karpaten, Namenhaufungen sind vor allem and den Punkten zu beobachten, wo Gewasser aus den Karpatens austreten, besonders auffallig im San-Gebiet und bei den Zuflussen des Dnestr aus sudlicher Richtung ... Die Namenhaufungen erlauben es dennoch im Masse, die ursprungliche Ausdehnung der urslavischen Sielungen zu bestimmen: das slavische Kerngebiet umfasst im west-ostlicher Richtung etwa 300 Km., im nord-sudlicher— bedingt durch die geologische schwankende Struktur des Karptaenvorlands—einen Streifen von etwa 50 bis 150 km. Schon fruh wurden jedoch auch die Karpaten selbst, die Sudhange (vor allem der Karpato-Ukraine) und die nordliche Mittelslovakei von Slaven besiedelt, so dass eine Trennung in ursprungliche und spatere Siedlungsraume nich in jedem Fall mit letzter Sicherheit getroffen werden kann.**

OLD EUROPE HEARTLAND?

There are certain immediate and obvious problems with Udolph's theory. If one accepts an early presence of Proto-Slavs in southeastern Europe, there is simply no fact, reason or circumstance to believe that Carpathia, especially the extremely narrow straits and limited resources of the Zakopane-Bukowina complex, rather than Danubia, the Old Europe heartland, would be a primary place of settlement.

TRUBACEV

Trubacev finds fault with Udolph's method and logic, especially the notion that the cumulative area of waternames with genuine Slavic forms is ipso facto the original homeland of the Slavs. According to Trubacev, the facts of the matter are otherwise: **The accumulation of homogeneous Slavic names is more characteristic of colonization zones—not of the point of departure of migrations; the latter seldom present a clear picture, nor are they a sudden outburst.** Another contrary factor that Udolph fails to account for, Trubacev writes, is the relative negativeness of toponymy (*'if there is wood everywhere, then names like Wood don't mean anything'*). Finally, Trubacev finds Udolph's attempt to extinguish the Danube in Russian historical memory by repeating the rather silly notion that the ***Dunaj*** in Russian oral poetry refer not to the Danube but to the Dnieper, a bit much and rather self-serving.

DOUNAV

Another interesting fact attesting to the Danube in *historical memory* is its use as a personal name in Slavic lands near and far. M. Grkovic, for example, finds the personal name ***Dunav*** recorded in an early 14th century Serbian document relating to the founding of St. Stefan Monastery on Kosovo: **Mile, Vojin, Bratoslav ... Milan. Bogdan, *Dounav*.** The personal name ***Dounav*** is also recorded in early Czech, Polish (e.g. ***Dunaj*** de Boyanica/1416), and Russian sources (e.g. ***Dunai***, voevoda Vladimiro-Volinskii/1281). The South Slavic ***Dunav***, furthermore, suggests an adaption of the

Latin **Danuvius** by way of the Celts in the Proto-Slav period *(Prilog Proucavanju Praslovenske Antroponimije—Licno ime Dunav, OnP, VI, 1985).*

With regards to the Danube thesis, Grkovic writes: **S obzirom na to da se u narodnom stvaralastvu i mitologiji govori o Dunavu od granica juznih Slovena u severnoj Grckoj pa do severnih Slovena na Onjeskom jezuru, moze se osnovano prepostaviti da je Dunav unet u slovensko duhovno bice u davno vreme kada je jos postojala jaka povezanost slovenskih plemena. Sve su ovo dovoljno jaki dokazi da je licno ime Dunav/Dunai bilo poznato u praslovenskoj zajednici i pripadalo opsteslovenskom antroponimijskom fondu. Pored mnogobrojnih i ovo moze biti vazan podatak za potkrepljenje hipoteze da slovenske migracije nisu isle samo od Dunava na jugu, na Balkan, nego i od Dunava ka severu.** According to Z. Golab, Udolph's Carpathian thesis is more a matter of misinformation than anything else: **But anybody with some knowledge of the history of the colonization of the Carpathian region is simply surprised by Udolph's conclusion: the concentration of the whole Proto-Slavic ethnos at the foothills of the Northern Carpathians around the birth of Christ seems to be demographically impossible. We know that the Carpathians were colonized relatively late, except for some wide and easily accessible valleys ... We must also remember that the sub-Carpathian regions were well forested and their soil is rather poor, so they could not attract early settlers** *(Z. Golab, Primary Habitat of the Slavs. The Origins of the Slavs. A Linguist's View, 1992).* Regarding the Carpathians, Golab continues: **If anything, they were rather refuge areas, which is quite typical of mountain and sub-mountain regions. And I think that from quite early prehistorical times the Carpathians and their foothills played just that role: they attracted and concentrated various Proto-Slavic tribes which at times of demographic upheaval tried to withdraw to these relatively less accessible peripheries of the Proto-Slavic habitat. This fact explains the concentration in the sub-Carpathian region of the hydronyms derived from Proto-Slavic appellative as defined above** ['common names occurring in all three branches of the Slavic languages']. Moreover, Golab writes, the relative concentration of Slavic hydronyms in the Carpathians can be explained by the simple fact that the network of streams and rivers is usually much more dense in the mountains and foothills than in wide, open plains.

ENDNOTES

[1] L.V. Kurkina, Nekotorye voprosy formirovanija juznych slavjan v svjazi s pannonskoj teoriej E. Kopitara, VoP 3, 1981. J. Udolph, Kamen die Slaven aus Pannonien, Studia nad etnogeneze Slowian i kultura wszesnosredniowieczne, 1987.

[2] A scathing critique of the Danubian theory and methodology of O.N. Trubacev generally and the Primary Chronicle specifically is found in: H.G. Lunt, What the Rus' Primary Chronicle Tells Us about the Origin of the Slavs and of Slavic Writing, HuS XIX, 1995. As with all medieval sources based on biblical models and clumsy interpolations, Lunt outlines the obvious and less obvious reasons why the Primary Chronicle is something less than a credible source as it relates to Slavic settlement, migrations and related matters.

[3] In his discussion of etymology of the name *Volchov* as in the northen Russian river *Volchov [der Name des Flusses Volchov, der dem Ilmen-see entspringt)*, an Ilmen See tributary, Kunstmann writes: Die somit nicht grundlos

vermutete Ubertragung der Wortes *Volch* "Romane" an den Ilmensee lasst sich noch anders begrunden. Zunachst is ganz allgemein an die bedeutende Rolle der *Volochove, Vlasi, Wolosi* "Walchen" auf dem Balkan zu erinnern. Ihr Name taucht in der Literatur zwar erst im 11. Jhd. auf, doch muss ihre Beruhrung mit den Slaven schon erheblich fruher stattgefunden haben. Der ethnische Inhalt von urslav. **volch* war bei den Slaven schon bald der von m*Vlachus, generatim homo Romanae originis*, also *Romanus*, Mensch der alten romischen Siedlungen. Das Gros der Wlachen sass in Thessalien, das daher einiger Zeit *Vlahia* oder sogar *Megal Vlahia* hiess. Wlachen sassen aber auch im Epirus, in der Vlahia, und auch noch weiter nordlich, am oberen Drin, bei Skopje, in der Umgebung von Pec und Pristina, am Lim und namentlich in Bergen bei Dubrovnik und Kotor. Der Anteil der romanischen Bevolkerung, der Wlachen, muss im Raum *Ragusa-Dubrovnik* seit alters besonders gross gewesen sein, das zeigt sich an der gut belegten Tatsache, dass *vlach* sogar zum Synonym fur den Bewohner von Ragusa-Dubrovnik wurde. Eine Urkunde des Gross-Zupans Stjepan (1215-9), sagt: *I da ne jemlje Srblin vlacha bez suda*, was lateinisch besagt*: et ut Sclavus non apprehendat Raguseum sine iudicio.* Der Usus *Vlach = Raguseus* ist zwar erst fur das Hoch-und Spatmittelalter haufig belegt, doch durfte er ohne Frage weit zuruckreichen, wahrscheinlich bis in die Anfange der romanisch-slavischen Kontakte bei *Ragusa (Woher die Russen ihren Namen haben, DwS 31, 1986).*

Vinca Sign-System/Script

2. ILLYRIA, DALMATIA

In opposition to a northeast-southwest Slav invasion/settlement thesis, a contrary position has evolved in German historical scholarship—that the Slavs of Germany, Poland, and bordering lands originated in Serb lands between the Danube and the Adriatic, namely the former Roman provinces of Illyria and Dalmatia.[1]

THE ILLYRIA / DALMATIA THESIS

In terms of the Serb-Wend settlement of Germania, the Illyria/Dalmatia thesis has deep roots in German historical scholarship, dating from C. Schottgen and G. Keysig in the early 18th century to H. Kunstmann in the late 20th century.

ORIGINATED IN SARMATIA

Schottgen and Kreysig find no fault with the notion that Germania's Serb-Wends originated in Sarmatia, in an area between the Volga, the Caucasus, and the Sea of Azov. However, they find fault with the favored notion that the Serb-Wends entered Germania from the north and east. They absolutely reject the views of such writers as T. Segerus: **What, I ask, is more obvious and certain than that the Serbs from Misin/ Meissen established the kingdoms of Slavonia and Serbia in Illyria?** *(T. Segerus, De Slavis et Lecho, 1725).*

FROM THE SOUTH

In fact, they write, the evidence is clear that the exact opposite is true: (1) the Serb-Wends did not enter Germania from the north *by way of Prussia and Pomerania*; (2) the Serb-Wends entered Germania from the south, from Illyria, *by way of Moravia and Czechia*; (3) the Serb-Wends of Germania did not establish Serb kingdoms in Illyria; (4) the Illyrian Serbs migrated to, settled in, and established the Serb-Wend kingdoms of medieval Germania *(C. Schottgen, G. Kreysig, Diplomatische und Curieuse Nachlehre der Historie von Ober-Sachsen und antgrentzenden landern, 1730).* The many onomastic, linguistic, and cultural parallels between the original Illyrian Serb lands and the derivative Germania Serb-Wend lands, they write, are simply too great to have it any other way.

H. KUNSTMANN

One of the foremost exponents of this thesis in modern times is the renowned German Slavist, H. Kunstmann. His broad, deep, and exhaustive research has led him to suspect that (1) the Slavs of Czechoslovakia, Germany, Poland, Russia and neighboring lands originated in the Balkans, mainly Illyria/Dalmatia; that (2) the ethnonyms, ruling dynasties, place names, hydronyms and toponyms in West Slav and East Slav lands often can be traced to Slavic and slavicized roots in Illyria and bordering lands.

Over several decades, in a series of always interesting and often provacative articles, Kunstmann has tirelessly advanced the onomastic, linguistic, textual, and other evidence in support of his thesis. While his views, in the order of suggestive and explorative inquiries, have not gained general acceptance, Kunstmann is not a minority of one. In fact, his views have varying degrees of general and specific support at the highest levels of historical and linguistic scholarship.

ANCIENT CENTER OF CIVILIZATION IN EUROPE

Even the most learned, authoritative, and compelling advocates of a Near East origin of Indo-Europeans, V.V. Ivanov and T.V. Gamkrelidze, make certain concessions to the Danubia thesis *(The Migration of Tribes Speaking the Indo-European Dialects from their Original Homeland in the Middle East to their Historical Habitations in Eurasia, InD 13, 1985)*. They admit (1) that the Balkan area was the most ancient center of civilization in Europe; and (2) that the picture of the original Proto-Indo-European landscape derived from the linguistic reconstruction of the proto-language rules out Central and Eastern Europe, excepting southeastern Europe.

ONE OF SEVERAL POSSIBLE SOLUTIONS

In response to Diakonov's critique, they go so far as to write: **Actually, Diakonov's alternative, the Balkano-Carpathian hypothesis, is merely one of several possible solutions within our hypothesis on the original homeland. We reconstruct a wider area—from the Balkans to Iran and southern Turkmenia—as the expanse within which the Indo-European original homeland might have been located in a definite territory** *(T.V. Gamkrelidze, V.V. Ivanov, The Problem of the Original Homeland of the Speakers of Indo-European Languages in Response to I.M. Diakonov's Article, InD 13, 1985)*.

ORIGINATED IN DANUBIA-PANNONIA

The following are some of the supportive points found in the works of distinguished linguists, historians and Slavists: (1) The Slavs originated in Danubia-Pannonia; (2) Not all Slavs migrated northward from the Danube, some remained (thus the dense Slavic population and Slavic toponymy, the antiquity of Slavic waternames in pre-Hungarian Pannonia-Danubia), others migrated south; (3) The Balkan South Slavs originated in Pannonia-Danubia; (4) The Eastern Slavs originated in the south; (5) Place names and ethnonyms with apparent Balkan roots are found throughout Slavdom (e.g. *Daksa,* an island in the Adriatic, *Doksy,* in Czechoslovakia; *Dukla,* a mountain pass in the Carpathians, *Duklja,* in Montenegro; *Licicaviki,* a Slavic tribe in western Poland, **Liccavici* in Illyria).

With regard to Germania, it should be noted that one of the greatest names in modern German Slavistics, J. Herrmann, concedes a possible connection between the great numbers of Serbs recorded in middle Danubia and along the Byzantine frontier in the 6th century and Serb settlements in Germania: **Es ist ... warscheinlich, dass aus dem Stamm der Serben/Sorben, der am Ende des 6 Jh. im mitteleren Donaugebiet an den Grenzen von Byzanz stand und der sich mit dan Awaren auseinanderzusetzen hatte, ein Teil ausschied und nordwarts wanderte** *(J. Herrmann, Die Slawen in Deutschland: Geschichte und Kultur der slawischen Stamme westlich von Oder und Niesse vom 6. bis 12. Jahrhundert, 1985)*.

ENDNOTES

[1] All attempts to trace **Albania** and **Albanian** roots to ancient **Illyria** and **Illyrians** run contary to the first and last words of authoritative scholarship. On this subject, V. I. Georgiev, for example, perhaps the single greatest authority on ancient Balkan linguistics and onomastics, writes: **But many linguists and historians ... have put forward very important considerations indicating that the Albanians cannot be autochthonic in present-day Albania; that their original home was the eastern part of Mysia Superior, or approximately Dardania and Dacia Mediterranea, i.e., the northern central region of the Balkan peninsula, and part of Dacia. However, since it**

has become clear that Daco-Mysian and Thracian represent two different IE languages, the problem of the origin of the Albanian language and the Albanians themselves appears in a new light. The most important facts and considerations for determining the original habitat of the Albanians are the following: (a) The Illyrian toponyms known from antiquity, e.g. Skhoder from the ancient Scodra (Livius), Tomor from Tomaros (Strabo, Pliny, etc.), have not been directly inherited in Albanian: the contemporary form of these names do not correspond to the phonological laws of Albanian. The same also applies to the ancient toponyms of Latin origin in this region. (b) The most ancient loanwords from Latin in Albanian have the phonetic form of Eastern Balkan Latin, i.e., of proto-Rumanian, and not of Western Balkan Latin, i.e., of Old Dalmatian Latin. Albanian therefore, did not take its borrowings from Vulgar Latin as spoken in Illyria. (c) The Adriatic coast was not part of the original homeland of the Albanians because the maritime terminology of Albanian is not their own but borrowed from different languages. (d) Another indication against local Albanian origin is the insignificant number of ancient Greek loanwords in Albanian. If the earliest habitat of the Albanians had been Albania itself, the Albanian language would have to have many more ancient Greek loanwords. (e) Another indication against local Albanian origin is the insignificant number of ancient Greek loanwords in Albanian. If the earliest habitat of the Albanians had been Albania itself, the Albanian language would have to have many more ancient Greek loanwords. (f) The *Urheimat* of the Albanians must have been near that of the proto-Rumanians. The oldest Latin elements in Albanian come from proto-Rumanian, i.e., Eastern Balkan Latin, and not from Dalmatian, i.e., Western Balkan Latin that was spoken in Illyria ... The agreement in the treatment of Latin words in Rumanian and in Albanian shows that Albanian developed from the 4th to the 6th century where proto-Rumanian was taking shape. (g) Rumanian possesses about a hundred words which have their correspondence only in Albanian. The form of these Rumanian words is so peculiar that they cannot be explained as borrowings from Albanian. This reflects the Dacian substratum in Rumanian, whereas the Albanian correspondences are inherited from Daco-Mysian (V. I. Georgiev, The Earliest Ethnological Situation of the Balkan Peninsula as Evidenced by Linguistic and Onomastic Data, Aspects of the Balkans: Continuity and Change, 1972).

Illyria, Dalmatia

3. REGNUM SLAVORUM

Before we briefly review Kunstmann's articles on the subject, in order to better understand Kunstmann's references to Serb lands south of the Danube, to historic Serb lands in Illyria/Dalmatia, a brief review of the historical record is necessary.

1. DE ADMINISTRANDO IMPERIO

Compiled by Emperor Constantine Pophyrogenitus VII (905-959), *De Administrando Imperio* is an authoritative source of political, geographic, and demographic information about Serb states in maritime and interior Dalmatia.

MARITIME SERBIA

Four Serb states are located in maritime Serbia/Dalmatia: **Pagania, Zachlumia, Terbounia-Kanali, and Dioclea/Duklja.**

MARITIME STATES

Regarding the Serb antecedents and borders of the maritime states, Constantine gives the following information.

PAGANI

These same Pagani are descended from the unbaptized Serbs ... The Pagani are so called because they did not accept baptism when all the Serbs were baptized ... From the river Orontius (Neretva) begins Pagania and stretches as far as the river Zentina (Cetina) ... Also they possess these islands: the large island of Kourka or Kiker (Korcula); another large island, Meleta or Malozeatai (Mljet); another large island, Phara (Hvar); another large island, Bratzis (Brac).[1]

ZACHLUMI

The Zachlumi are Serbs ... They were called Zachlumi from a so-called mount Chlumo, and indeed in the tongue of the Slavs 'Zachlumi' means 'behind the mountain' ... From Ragusa begins the domain of the Zachlumi amd stretches along as far as the river Orontius; and on the side of the coast it is neighbor to the Pagani, but on the side of the mountain country it is neighbor to the Croats on the north and to Serbia at the front.

TERBOUNITES, KANALITES

The country of the Terbounites and the Kanalites is one. The country of Kanali is subordinate to Terbounia. The inhabitants are descended from the unbaptized Serbs ... The princes of Terbounia have always been at the command of the prince of Serbia ... From the city of Decatera (Kotor) begins the domain of Terbounia and stretches along as far as Ragusa and on the side of the mountain country it is neighbor to Serbia.

DIOCLEA

Dioclea gets its name from the city in the country that the emperor Diocletian founded, but now it is a deserted city, though still called Dioclea. Dioclea is neighbor to the forts of Dyrrachium (Serb Drac) ... and comes up as far as Decatera, and on the side of the mountain country it is neighbor to Serbia. In the country of Dioclea are the large and inhabited cities of Gradetai, Nougrade, Lontodokla.

SERBIA-BOSNIA

One Serb state is located in interior Serbia/Dalmatia: Serbia-Bosnia: **Baptized Serbia with its inhabited cities of Destinikon, Tzernabouskei, Medyretous, Dresneik, Lenik, Salines (Soli/Tuzla); and in the territory of Bosnia, Katera and Desnik ... For the country of Serbia is at the front of all the rest of the countries, but on the north is neighbor to Croatia, and on the south Bulgaria.**[2]

2. PRESBYTERIA DIOCLEATIS REGNUM SLAVORUM

Presbyteria Diocleatis Regnum Slavorum, better known as *Ljetopis Popa Dukljanina (The Chronicle of Reverend Dukljanin)*, a late 12th century chronicle is the earliest native source of early medieval history.

EX SCLAVONICA LITTERA

According to *Reverend Dukljanin*, actually an anonymous Roman Catholic priest from Bar, the Chronicle is a compilation of historic facts that were a matter of common knowledge, translated from the original Slavic into the Latin *(ex sclavonica littera verteram in Latinam)*. In spite of the fact that some parts are obviously more legend than fact (e.g. the arrival of the father of the nation), that some parts are colored by certain cycles common to medieval chronicles (e.g. the conversion of the nation to Christianity; the role of the Church in the organization of the kingdom, in the coronation of kings), it remains an invaluable source of information. More than once, modern critics have been forced to take a step or two back. In the past, for example, editors routinely dismissed a reference to *Templana*, said to be an area settled by Oistrolo, the father of the nation, as a matter of legend or imagination. Recent scholarship, however, has revealed that the area around Skadar, a capital city, was at one time known as *Teplana* or *Templana*, and known as such as late as the mid-18th century. In an August 25, 1736, report to Rome, for example, Bishop Antonio Vladagni writes: **I popoli de Scuttari come Teplana, che consiste in case Cattoliche.**

ALL OF DALMATIA

The ancient Slavs, pagan and barbarian, led by **Oistrolo**, Dukljanin writes, **conquered all of Dalmatia, including the coast and the highlands.** Settling in Duklja, **Oistrolo** establishes the house of Oistrolovic, a line that will rule without interruption into the mid-12th century.

KINGDOM OF DUKLJA-DALMATIA

On the coast, the kingdom runs from **Vinodol** in the north to **Drac** in the south, inland, from the **Sava** and **Danube** rivers in the north to the **Adriatic** in the south.

DUKLJA

Duklja is the absolute center of the kingdom. From Duklja, the house of **Oistrolovic** will send brothers, sons, and kin to govern the constituent provinces.

LAKE SKADAR

Duklja itself is centered in the territory surrounding Lake Skadar, anchored at Duklja, Skadar, and Bar, with strong fortification on its flanks at Koplik and Oblik, with favored residences, monasteries and churches on thin strips of land running along both sides of Mt. Rumija.

HEARTLAND

In this heartland national assemblies are held, kings are crowned, royal residences are established, and royal families are buried (e.g. Church of St. Andrew, Papratna; Church of St. George, Bar; Church of St. Mary, Duklja; Church of St. Mary, Krajina; Church of St. Sergius, Bojana).

CHRISTIANITY

With the advice of St. Cyril, King Svetopelek (*rex stanctissimus*) brings Christianity to the Slavs of Dalmatia. At a great national assembly held on the plain of Dalma, Svetopelek establishes two archbishoprics in Dalmatia: one in Solin, the other in Duklja.

ARCHBISHOPRIC OF SOLIN

The archbishopric of Solin includes the bishoprics of Split, Trogir, Skradin, Zadar, Nin, Rab, Osor, Krk and Epidaur.

ARCHBISHOPRIC OF DUKLJA

The archbishopric of Duklja includes the bishoprics of Bar, Budva, Kotor, Ulcinj, Svac, Skadar, Drivast, Pulat, Serbia, Bosnia, Travunia, and Zahumlja.

PRIMORJE, ZAGORJE

In a manner consistent with ancient boundaries and notions, Svetopelek also reorganizes his kingdom. In the first instance, he divides the kingdom into two basic parts: **Primorje or Maritime Dalmatia and Serbia or Zagorje/Interior Dalmatia. Primorje includes lands crossed by rivers flowing into the Adriatic, Zagorje, lands crossed by rivers flowing into the Danube.**

PRIMORJE

Primorje is made up of two parts: **Lower Dalmatia (*Dalmatia inferior*), from Vinodol to Omis, and Upper Dalmatia (*Dalmatia superior*), from Omis to Drac.**

ZAGORJE

Zagorje is also made up of two parts: **Bosnia, from the Drina west to the Pinna mountains, and Raska, from the Drina east to the Lab and Sitnica rivers.**

DUBROVNIK

Dubrovnik is a new city in **Primorje.** It was founded by Pavlimir, grandson of exiled king Radoslav of Duklja. Returning to Dalmatia, Pavlimir lands near Gruz and Ombla, where, his ranks swelled by loyalists from Travunia and Hum, he establishes a fortified settlement. The mainland was settled by Serbs and called Dubrovnik, from the Serb words *dub* (oak) and *dubrava* (oak grove).

ANNALES RAGUSINI ANONYMI

Three hundred years later, the first Dubrovnik chronicle, *Annales Ragusini Anonymi*, restates Dukljanin's account of the origin of Dubrovnik. The same is true of the first serious history of Dubrovnik, *Commentaries* by L. Crijevic (1459-1521). Indeed, Crijevic acknowledges Dukljanin as his primary source (*sequens in primis Diocleatem auctorem*). In fact, Crijevic's words on the founding of Dubrovnik are a restatement of Dukljanin's account: The city's founding by Pavlimir, called Belo, a nephew of King Ratislav, who Crijevic tells us, establishes the city's civil and ecclesiastic foundations, organizes a senate to govern, with equal representation for its Slav founders and Roman refugees from Epidaurus, and, with Rome's approval, creates the See of Dubrovnik and appoints its first archbishop.

RAGUSA

Roman refugees from Epidaurus were given a rocky, seaward ridge to settle, actually an island divided from the mainland by a marshy channel. This part was called Lausion, from *lau,* the Greek word for precipice, then Rausion, Rausa, Ragusium and, finally, Ragusa. In the second half of the 12th century the channel was filled in to form the physically unified city of Ragusa-Dubrovnik. In this context, the term *Roman* refers to the Latin- and Greek-speaking population originating in the Byzantine administration of the coastal cities and towns of Dalmatia. In its first centuries the city's territory was limited to a narrow belt along its mainland walls, a thin coastal strip in Gruz, and several offshore islands. From this microscopic space, the city expands by way of grants from and sales by neighboring Serb rulers (e.g. Rijeka, Zaton, Poljica, Zrnovica, Sumeta, Rijeka Dubrovacka, the islands of Mjljet, Lastovo, Sipan, the Peljesac peninsula (including Ston), Slansko Primorje, Konavli). ***Radoslavus of Duklja*** is one of the earliest donors to the Benedictine monastery on the offshore island of Lokum. ***Branislav,*** a contender for the crown of Duklja, and his brothers ***Gradislav*** and ***Predislav*** are buried there. In the 11th century, ***Branislav's*** nemesis, ***King Bodin of Duklja,*** builds a fortress at Prijeki, the city's oldest district, where, later, his vassal, ***Stephanus dux Bossiane,*** builds the Church of St. Nicholas.

3. ILLYRIA SACRUM

Illyria Sacrum is a massive eight-volume history of the Church in Illyria prepared in the 18th and 19th centuries by three Italian Jesuits, Filipo Riceputi, Daniele Farlati and Jacobo Coleti. Following service as Venetian army chaplain in Dalmatia, Riceputi saw the need for a history of the Church in the lands of ancient Illyria. Returning to Rome in 1720, he submitted an outline draft to the Church: *Prospectus Illyrici sacri suisu historiam describendian typisque mandamum suscipit P. Fi. Riceputi.* With the encouragement and support of Pope Clement XI and his successors, Riceputi's project was soon a work in progress. *Illyria Sacrum* is based on some 300 volumes of raw source materials collected over a twenty-year period. The first seven volumes were published under the name of one of the Jesuit scholars, Farlati, who edited the first five volumes. The first volume was published in 1751 and the eighth in 1819. The first two volumes cover the early history of the Church in Dalmatia. Volumes three and four are a history of the bishopric of Split and its suffragan; volume five, the bishopric of Zadar and its suffragan; volume six, the bishopric of Dubrovnik and its suffragans; volume seven, the bishoprics of Duklja, Bar and Drac; volume eight, a history of the Church in

Serbia and Bulgaria.

TWO SERBIAS

Historically speaking, Farlati writes, **there are two Serbias.**

PRIMORJE

One Serbia is Primorje or Maritime Serbia.

SERBLIAE MARITMAE

Maritime Serbia is also called Upper Dalmatia: *Superioris Dalmatiae, idest Serbliae maritmae.*

SERBLIA MEDITERANEA

On occasion Farlati uses the term Mediterranean Serbia *(Serblia mediteranea)* for Maritime Serbia *(Serblia mediteranea; tum mediterraneos ... tum maritimo, qui Dalmatiam superioris incolebant).*

NERETVA, ZAHUMLJA, TRAVUNIA, DUKLJA

Beginning at the Cetina River *(Serblia pars Dalmatiae cisalpinae orientalis ad Zentina fere initum duciti),* **Maritime Serbia is made up of Neretvania, Zahumlja, Travunia-Konavlja, and Duklja.**

PRIMORDIJA

In royal titles, Farlati notes, **Maritime Serbia is sometimes called *Primordija*, the national and political heartland of the Serbs.**

In the 15th century one finds Primordija in the title of King Stefan Tomash (1443-61): *Nos Stephanus Thomas Dei gratia Rasciae, Serviae, Bosnensium sive Illyriocorum, Primordiae, Dalmatiae.* Also in the title of his son and successor, King Stefan Tomashevich (1461-63): *In nominae et individua Trinitatis Stepphanus Thomassevich Dei Gratia Rassia, Srviae, Bosnensium, sue Illyriocorum, Primordiae, seu Maritmae, partiumque Dalmatiae.*

HI OMNES SERBLI ERANT

Neretvans, Zahumljans, Travunians-Konavlians, Dukljans, all are Serbs: *Hi omnes Serbli erant.*

NERETVANS: GENS SERBICA

The fierce Serbs of Neretva *(gens Serbica ferox immitis)*, Farlati writes, were at the head of the Serb march to statehood *(Haec erat una e quatorzupaniis, e quibus regnum Serbliae maritimae constabat).*

PATERNUM SERBLIAE REGNUM

From Neretva power passes to Zahumlja *(gens Serblorum)* to Travunia-Trebinje *(suamque et regni Serbliani sedem in eadem urbe constituit),* where Pavlmir begins his recovery of the kingdom *(ut avitum regnum recuperaret)* to Duklja, the historic center of the Serb kingdom *(paternum Serbliae regnum),* where a Serb Church is established with jurisdiction over **Bar, Budva, Kotor, Ulcinj, Svac, Skadar, Drivast,**

Pulat, Serbia, Bosnia, Travunia and Zahumlja/Neretvania.

KRAJINA

Following Zahumlja's annexation of Neretva, the coastal land between the Centina and Neretva rivers is called Krajina, *quae olim ad regnum Serbliae pertinebat.*

DUKEDOM OF ST. SAVA, HERCEGOVINA

Later, Farlati writes, **that part of Maritime Serbia, which from the Cetina runs eastward, including Uppper Dalmatia, is called the Dukedom of St. Sava or Hercegovina.**

ZAGORJE

The other Serbia is Zagorje or Interior Serbia. **Zagorje is made up of two parts, Bosnia and Rascia/Raska *(partes Serbliae).***

BOSNIA

Bosnia *(pars Serbliae)*, Farlati writes, **like Raska, is a Serb land, an original and integral part of Zagorja or Interior Serbia.**

SERBIA, RASCIA

Some, Farlati writes, **consider the names Serbia and Rascia (Raska) to be one and the same. This is not true. Rascia cannot be equated with Serbia, nor Serbia with Rascia. Rascia is only one part of Serbia *(pars Serbliae).*** This confusion, Farlati explains, is probably due to the fact that the Rascian liturgy is used in both Serbia and Rascia.

4. SERBIA-BOSNIA

Throughout history there has never been any doubt or question about Bosnia's national-political status. The historical record is clear and consistent from beginning to end: **Bosnia is an original and integral part of Serbia.**

JOHN KINNAMOS

A mid-12th century Byzantine historian, John Kinnamos, served as secretary to the long reigning Emperor Manuel I Comnenus (1143-1180). A brilliant and gifted writer, with a special interest in military matters, Kinnamos is most admired for his objectivity, scrupulousness and straightforward account of political-military affairs. In his account of Emperor Manuel's campaign against Rascia in 1150, Kinnamos writes: **The Drina river separates Bosnia from the rest of Serbia. Bosnia is not subordinate to the archzupan of the Serbs and the people there have their own ways and administration** *(Chronikai).* Some four or five years later, in his account of a Byzantine-Hungarian battle near Branicevo, Kinnamos writes: **On learning that Boric, exarch of the Serb land of Bosnia, was an ally of the Hungarians ... the Emperor gathered his bravest troops and sent them against Boric.**

BATTAGLIA BOSNESI E GRAN TURCO

That Bosnia and Serbia were one and the same, that Bosnians were Serbs and Serbs were Bosnians, is perhaps confirmed in the most absolute and delightful terms by a Dubrovnik source, an important source of record for Serb affairs, for the battle of Kosovo: *1389. Adi 15 giurgno, in giorno di Santo Vito, e fo martedi, fu battaglia tra Bosnesi e Gran Turco, li quali Bosnesi furono Despot Lazar Re di Bosna, et Vuch Brankovich, et Vlatcho Vuchovich Voivoda; et fu gran ocisione tanto de Turchi, quanto de Bosnesi, et pochi tornono in suo paese. Et Zar Murat e amazato et Re de Bosna; et la vittoria non se ha dato, ne a Turchi, ne a Bosnesi, perche fur gran ocisione. Et fur le le battaglio in Kosovo polje* (Annales ragusini Anonymi).

GIOVANI LUCIO (IVAN LUCIC)

Giovani Lucio/Ivan Lucic (1604-79), a native of Trogir, born to an old and noble Italo-Dalmatian family, after extensive studies at home and abroad (e.g. humanities at Rome, law at Padua), returned to Trogir in 1625 where he dedicated himself to document and record for posterity the history of Trogir, Dalmatia, and Croatia. Lucio's magnum opus, *De Regno Dalmatiae et Croatiae Libri Rex (1655)*, the first modern history of Dalmatia and Croatia, was based on an exhaustive, thorough, and critical examination of Dalmatian, Croatian, Italian, and Vatican sources, of public, private, civil and ecclesiastic archives and papers no longer available. Since he found no basis for equivocation in fact, commentary or opinion in his research, Lucio has no difficulty of any sort in placing Bosnia in its proper national-political context. In Chapter III, *Dei Rei de Bosnia e di cio ch'essi tentarono in Dalmazia e in Croazia*, Lucio's first words are: **Serbia is divided into two parts by the Drina River. Bosnia is that part that occupies one side of the Drina River:** *Serbia divisa in due porzione dal fiume Drino. Bosnia e la porzione al di qua del Drino o della Drina.*

THAT PART OF SERBIA

One finds precisely the same information in Hungarian sources. J. Thuroczy, a 15th century Hungarian chronicler, clearly identifies Bosnia as part of Serbia and sheds light on the origin of Hungary's claims to Bosnia: **In 1133, Bela the Blind married Jelena, the daughter of Uros I. From his father-in-law, Uros, Bela received as dowry that part of Serbia which the Greeks (Byzantines) call Bosnia and the Ugri (Hungarians) call Rama. Thereafter the kings of Hungary have always laid claim to Bosnia and for this reason have fought many wars with the Serbs.** In fact of course, *Rama* is not Bosnia, but only a *zupa* in Bosnia that takes its name from the *Rama River,* a right-bank Neretva River tributary, centered at *grad Prozor*. After 1137, *King of Rama* is often found in the titles of Hungarian kings and seldom in the titles of Bosnian rulers.

PALATIN OF HUNGARY, BAN OF CROATIA

Owing to Bela the Blind's disability, royal power was actually in the hands of Queen Jelena, sister of Uros I's son and successor, Uros II, and, what is more important, her brother, Belosh, the very able and energetic Palatin of Hungary and Ban of Croatia. Belosh's influence in Hungary's affairs continued under Bela's minor son and Uros II's nephew, Geza II (1141-1162).

TERRITORIAL DOWRIES

The Hungarians, too, it should be noted, were also generous in the matter of territorial dowries. In one instance, for example, the marriage of Katarina, daughter of King Stefan V of Hungary, to Stefan Dragutin, son of King Stefan Uros I of Serbia

(1243-75), the new bride's teritorial dowry included Macva, Srem and a good part of Slavonia. Soon after this union, Stefan Dragutin was crowned *velikog i strasnog* King of Serbia (1276-82). In another instance, two years after his resignation in favor of his brother Milutin, Stefan Dragutin's father-in-law granted him an appanage that included northern Bosnia and the border districts of Usora and Soli.

SLAVI SERVI, BOSNI

In J.T. Szaszky's *Cospectus introductionis, in notitam Regni Hungariae, geographicam, Historicam, politicam et chronographicam (1759)*, Serbia is Bosnia and Rascia, Serbs are Bosnians and Rascians: ***Slavi Servi, Bosnii, et Slavi Servi, Rasciani.***

ENDNOTES

[1] In another work, *De Ceremonis*, Constantine refers to Pagania as 'Moravia.' In other sources of that period Pagania is sometimes referred to as Maronia or Moravia, the natives, Mariyani or Moryani, the commander of the Maronia fleet as *iudex Marianorum*.

[2] In his study of the Slavs (De Originibus Slavicis, 1745), Joan Christofori de Jordan, one of the founders of Slavistics in Germania, believes that early German sources, namely Einhard ((e.g. ***Sorabos, quae natio magnam Dalmatiae partem obtinere dicitur***), offer important information as to Serbia-Bosnia's western borders. According to Christofori, all the historical evidence strongly suggests that Serbi-Bosnia's western border ran along the Una and Sava rivers, centered at **Srb**, an ancient stronhold on the Una River. For the latest authoritative word on Serbia-Bosnia's 'original' borders and the location of the 'inhabited cities' cited by Constantine: S.M. Cirkovic, "Naseljeni gradovi" Konstantina Porfirogenita i najstarija teritorijalna organizacija, Zbornik Radova Bizantoloski Institut 37, 1998.

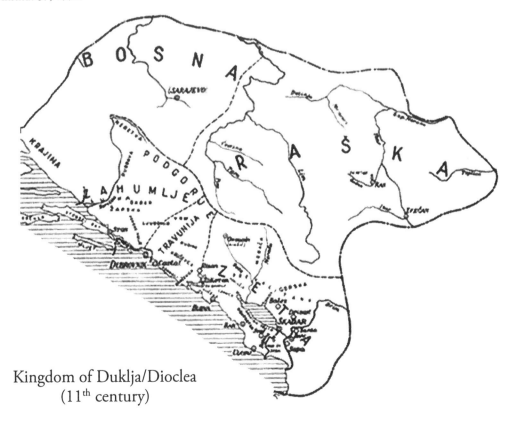

Kingdom of Duklja/Dioclea
(11th century)

4. KAMEN DIE WESTSLAVISCHEN DALEMINCI AUS DALMATIEN?

The following review of Kunstmann's articles is intended only to identify the subject and suggest the general nature and thrust of his explorative inquiries. It goes without saying that in many instances, a serious discussion of the issues and questions raised (e.g. Kunstmann's reference to and undertanding of *Primordia*) requires and deserves nothing less than a monograph of considerable weight and length.[1]

DALEMINCI

In *Kamen die westslavischen Daleminci aus Dalmatien?*, Kunstmann traces Germania's Serbs called Dalminci/Glomaci *(Sclavi, qui vocantur Dalmatii)* to Illyria's Serbs, to Duklya/Dalmatia, to Dlamoc and Glamoc (1983).

Dass ebenfalls altsorbisches Glomac aus dem Landschaftsnamen *Dalmatia* enstanden sein kann, hat eigentlich schon E. Schwarz uberzeugend gezeigt. Mit vollem Recht hat Schwarz aber auch altsorbisches Glomac, das noch heute in dem Namen der Stadt *Lommatzsch* enthalten ist, mit dem dalmatinischen ON Glamoc in Verbindung gebracht, was besagt, dass beide Toponyme Vertretungen fur Dalmatia sind, ohne dass dabei einem unbekanten alteuropaischen Volk die Rolle des tertium comparationis zugewiesen werden muss.

Die im Titel dieses Beitrages aufgeworfene Frage ist damit wohl uberzeugend beantwortet. Der Stammesname der Daleminci ist nun, nachdem die griechische Herkunft des Abodriten-Ethnonyms erkannt wurde, der zweite Hinweis darauf, dass die slavische Besiedlung Nord-west- und Mitteldeutschlands—jedenfalls zum Teil—vom Balkan her, aus dem Suden, nicht aus dem Osten erfolgte.

ZIRZIPANI

In *Mecklenburgs Zirzipanen und der Name der Peene* Germania's Serbs/Sers on the Peene River or Scircipene are traced to Balkan Serb lands (1984).

Die Stadt *Siris* oder *Sirra*, auch *Seres*, *Serra* oder *Serrhai* heisst heute Serra und liegt an der Sudwestecke der Piringebirges, etwa zehn Kilometer nordostlich der unteren Struma ... Viel spater lieteten die Serben ihren Stammesnamen volksetymologisch vom ON *Siris* bzw. *Seres* ab: zu 1503 heisst es *otъ Sera ze srъblje*. Im Slavischen wurde der name der Stadt zu *Serezъ* und *Seresъ*, in gekurzter Form auch zu *Serъ* oder *Serъ*. Dabei setzt das Slavische nicht die antike Form Sir-, sondern die jungere, auf vulgarlateinischem Lautwandel von *i > e* beruhende Version Ser- fort ... Man hat den Namen der mecklenburgischen *Zirzipanen* wohl als *Siri-Paiones* aufzulosen und darunter soviel wie *Paonen aus Siris* zu verstehen. Es wird somit nicht eigentlich das alte Kompositum *Sirto-paiones* verwendent, sondern der ON *Siris* dem Ethnonym *Paion(es)* vorangestellt ... Die dem mecklenburgischen Stammesnamen *Zirzipanen* zugrundeliegende Bedeutung *Siris-Paiones = Paonen aus Siris* ist insofern erstaunlich prazise und unmissverstandlich, sie lasst keine geographische Verwechslung aufkommen.

DULEBI, GLOPEANI

In *Nestors Dulebi und die Glopeani des Geographus Bavarus*, the Dulebi and Glopeani are traced to Slav settlements in Thessaly (1984).

Fur den Beginn des 7. Jahrhunderts glaubt man annehmen zu durfen, dass der Slavenstamm der *Vajunici* das Land Vagenetia in Epirus bewohnte. Moglicherweise siedelten hier auch die slavischen Velegezyci. Beide Stamme werden auch von den—in Fragen der slavischen Invasion vielleicht ubertreibenden—*Miracula Sancti Demetrii* (von 615?) gennant, was naturlich nicht besagt, dass beide Ethnika nicht schon vordem in Thessalien sesshaft waren. Auch wenn es bislang keine stichhaltigen Argumente dafur gibt, dass die Ethnonyme *Vajunici* und *Velegezyci* wirklich slavische Stamme bezeichnen—hinter den unslavisch wirkenden Namen konnen sich freilich auch 'Adaptionen' verbergen—so fehlt es doch fur das fragliche Gebiet nicht an einigen wenigen, sicher slavischen Ortsnamen. Es sind dies namentlich die im Bereich der alteren Haupstadt Dolopiens, zu lokalisierenden Orte *Karditsa* und *Dravitsa*, letzterer in Kreis Karditsa gelegen. Westthessalisches *Karditsa*, Mittelpunkt des gleichnamigen Kreises, geht auf slav. gordьcь `Festung, Burg' zuruck, wahrend Dravitsa nordwestlich des Xynias-Sees vom slav. Wort fur `Kornelkirsche', bulg. dren, skr. drijen, abgeleitet wird. Damit ist unser Wissen uber die slavische Besiedlung des fraglichen Gebietes im wesentlichen auch schon erschopft ... Statt dessen sei nun eine vollig neue Uberlegung zur Diskussion gestellt. Nach meiner Ansicht ist Glopeani eine Sekundar-Ubernahme des griech. Stammesnamens Dolopes.[2]

Es sind dies namentlich die im Bereich der alteren Haupstadt Dolopiens, zu lokalisierenden Orte Karditsa und Dravitsa, letzterer in Kreis Karditsa gelegen. Westthessalisches Karditsa, Mittelpunkt des gleichnamigen Kreises, geht auf slav. gordbcb 'Festung, Burg; zuruck, wahrend Dravitsa nordwestlich des Xynnias-See vom slav. Wort fur 'Kornelkirsche', bulg. [Bulgarian] dren, skr. [Serbo-Croat] drijen, abgeleitet wird.

DEREVLJANI, POLOCANI, VOLYNJANI

In *Die Namen der ostslavischen Derevljane, Polocane und Volynjane*, the ethnonyms are traced to Duklja (1985). The *Derevljane*, for example, to a Duklja borderland in the northwest; the *Polocane* to a borderland in the southeast, to Duklja's *Pilot/Polat* to Stefan Nemanya's *Polatum*. In the 11th century, during the reign of rex Bodin (**filii nostri Bodini, regis Sclavorum gloriosissimi**), Polat is recorded as one of the bishoprics of the Church of Duklja: ***Dioclensem ecclleaism seu Antivarensem et Catrainensem, Dulcinensem, Suuacinensem, Scordinensem, Drivatensem, Polatensem, Serbiensem, Bosniensem, Tribuniensem.***

Dass die *Dervani* das Gacko polje an der hercegovinisch-montenegrinischen Grenze bewohnten...Einen guten Dienst bei der Lokalisierung kann der illyrische ON *Anderva* leisten, da er gewissermassen ein Oppositum zu *Derva* darstellt—vgl. Idg. *ana "in Richtung auf, entlang" –und soviel wie "gegenuber Derva" bedeutet. *Anderva, Anderba*, auch *Andarba*, schon zur Romerzeit unter diesen Namen bekannt, ist identisch mit dem heutigen *Niksic* in Montenegro. *Anderba*, also im sudlichen Teil von Dalmatien gelegen, war Kastell an der strategisch wichtigen Strasse von Narona nach Scodra ... Die Herkunft des Namens der *Polocane* lasst sich noch anders erklaren. Moglicherweise verbirgt sich dahinter ein alter historisch-geographischer Begriff der Serben, was also abermals auf den Balkan verweist...Urkunden bestatigte Diozese...*des episcopus Polatensis*, die in den serbischen Urkunden des Mittealters als *Pilot*...Erst 1180 wird *Polatum* von Stefan Nemanja dem serbischen Staat einverleibt, bei dem es bis zur Turkenherrschaft verbleibt ... Den altrussischen Ethnomymen Derevljane, Polocane und Volynjane entsprechen, wie gezeigt, die Namen der dalmatinischen Dervanoi, der praevalitanischen Polati und das neuepirotische Toponym Valon(a). Auf Grund der bisherigen Untersuchungen gewinnt man den Eindruck, dass die Slaven bis zu ihrer Landnahme auf dem Balkan im 6.-7. Jhd. keine autochthonen Stammesnamen gehabt haben.

SLOVENI

In *Wie die Slovene an den Ilmensee kamen*, the 'Sloveni' *(Sloveni ze sedosa okolo ezera Ilmerja, isdelasa grad i narekosa i Novgorod)* are traced to Duklja, to *Labeatis terra (lacum Labeatum, Labeatis palus)*, to Skadarsko Balta/Blato as in *Miroslavus ... navigansque per Baltam* .

Es ist weder zu beweisen noch auszuschliessen, dass russ. Ilmen mit dem Namen des montegrinisch-serbischen Flusses Lim zusammenhangt, doch ist zu beachten, dass der Lim rund 45 km nordostlich des Skutarisees entspringt, seinen Ursprung also auf dem Gebiet der ehemaligen illyrischen Labeates hat. Wahrscheinlich warer fur den Ilmensee von Anfang an zwei Bezeichnungen in Gebrauch: *Ilmen* und *Ilmer* ... Der Russische Flussname [Lovat] ist die nur geringfugig veranderte Wiedergrabe des illyrischen Stammesnamen der *Labeates, Labeatae,* auch *Lebeatae* oder *Libeate. Lovat* bzw. *Lovot* entstand aus *Labeat-* durch Lautweschel von *a > o* in beiden Siben sowie Betazismus *b > v*; der e-Laut der 2. Sible wurde verschliffen ... Das am Skutarisee gelegene Stammesgebiet der Labeaten heisst bei Polybios *Labeatis* ... Zentrum der illyrischen Labeaten war *Skodra*, lat. *Scodra*, alb. *Shkoder*, ital. *Skutari*, serb. *Skьdьr*, das zugleich Sitz des illyrischen Konigreiches bis zu dessen Fall eben im Jahr 168 v. Chr. war. Durch die diokletianische Reform wurde *Scodra* dann Haupstadt der Provinz *Praevalitana* und im 4. Jh. Bischolsitz, der ein letztes Mal zu 602 erwahnt wird, was gewiss mit dem grossen Awaren-Slaven-Sturm auf Dalmatien zu tun hat. Der Name *Scodra* taucht spater als Ortsname *Scheuder* in Mitteldeutschland auf, wohin ihn fraglos Slaven verfrachtet haben ... Bemerkenswert ist nun allerdings, dass der Skutarisee, der *Labeatis palus* in spaterer Zeit noch einen weiteren Namen hatte, namlich *Balta*. Um 1180 heisst es beim Presbyter von Dioclea: *Miroslavus ... navigansque per Baltam*. Wie alt die Bezeichnung *Balta* fur den Skutarisee ist. lasst sich wohl kaum mehr prazise sagen, doch darf angenommen werden, dass Balta der einheimische, regionalbarbarische Name auf illyrisch *balta* zuruck und ist sowohl mit dalmat. Balta als auch slav. *blato*, "Sumpf, Kot" (ur)verwandt ... Es uberrascht nun freilich, dass der alte Name der in den Ilmensee mundenten *Lovat* ... *Volota* war, was ohne Frage die genaue Entsprechung von *Balta* ist: Durch Betzismus im Anlautskonsonanten und Lautwandel *a > o* sowie polnoglasie ist aus illyrischem

122

(?) *Balta* ein slavisches *Volota* geworden. Die *Lovat* hiess also nicht *Boloto*, was zu erwarten ware, lage ein slav. *blato* zugrunden, auch ist *Volota* feminin, nicht neutral ... Wie sind diese Slovenen an den Ilmensee gekommen? Man hat bereits richtig erkannt, dass "die slavische Besiedlung des osteuropaischen Raumes zu verschiedenen Zeiten, etappenweise und aus verschiedenen Richtungen erfolgte. Die Hydronyme Lovat, Polist, Konduja-vielleicht auch Selon-legen slavische Zuwanderung aus den ehemaligen romischen Provinzen Dalmatia, Praevalitania und Epirus Nova nahe.

HUCULS

In *Woher die Huzulen ihren Namen haben*, the ethnonym Huzul/Hucul/H-ucul is traced to ancient Hesperioi, to the Ozolians of Lokria (1986).

CRACOWIA, WAWEL

In *Der Wawel und die Sage von der Grundung Krakaus* Polish 'Wawel' and 'Krakow' as in *castrum , quod suo nomine Cracowia est appellatum, quod antea Wawel nomen habebat* are traced to Duklja/Dalmatia (1986). In the case of Wawel, for example, Kunstmann reads Wawel as Vamvel as Bambel as Bambalo as Dyrachium (Serb Drac, Alb. Durres) in Dalmae: **Item ab eodem loco Dalmae usque Bambalonam civitatem, quae nunc dicitur Dyrachium.**

RUS

In *Wohrer die Russen ihren Namen haben*, the ethnonym Rus as in *Ruskaja zemlja* is traced to coastal Duklja/Dalmatia (1986).

Wie sich zeigt, tragt eine Reihe von Flussen des Ilmensee-Bassins Namen, die eindeutung balkanischer Provenienz sind, so in erster Linie das Hydronyms *Lovat*, das zusammen mit seinem alteren Namen *Volota* ein schlussiger Beweis dafur ist, dass hier die antike Bezeichnung fur den Skutarisee vorgelegen hat. *Rusa (Staraja Russa)* liegt an der *Polist*, hinter welchem Namen sich wiederum der epirotische ON *Palaeste* verbirgt. Moglicherweise hangt der Name des Ilmensee-Zuflusses *Selon* mit dem dalmatinischen Hydronym *Salon* zusammen, under der Novogoroder Bachname *Konduja* hat wohl weniger mit dem Finnischen zu tun, sondern spiegelt den illyrischen (?) oder thrakischen (?) Landschaftsnamen *Candavia* wider ... Vor diesem Hintergrund kann es nicht mehr uberraschen, wenn auch die Namen *Rusa* und *Rus* weder aus dem Finnischen noch dem Skandinavischen, sondern eben vom Balkan kommen ... Der Russen-Name fugt sich, wie man sieht, vortrefflich in die Reihe derjenigen slavischen Stammesnamen, die nicht autochthonen Ursprungs sind, sondern als fremde Ethnonyme, Toponyme u.a. aus verschiedenen Balkanregionen ubernommen wurden. Die inzwischen stattliche Reiche solcher Ubernahmen reicht von den westslavischen Abodriten, Daleminci, Zirzipani, Kaschuben und Poljane (Polen) biz zu den ostslavischen Derevljane, Volynjane und Huzulen. Mit dem Schlussel zur Fruhgeschichte der Russen erschliessen sich freilich auch andere Einsichten: Wenn namlich die Rusen ihren Namen von Ragusa—die Volynjane von Valona, die Poljane von Apollonia suf. –haben, dann lasst sich die sog. Urheimat der Slaven wohl nicht langer am galizischen Nordrand der Karpaten vermuten. Hier ist selbst die alteuropaische Hydronomie machtlos.

Obwohl die Konturen der slavischen Wanderbewegungen immer deutlicher werden, durfte es vermutlich lange dauern, bis sich die neue Erkenntnis von der Herkunft des Russen-Namens durchsetzen wird. Als hemmend wird sich dabei nicht allein die alte normannistische Rotsi-These erweisen, auch emotionale Reaktionen werden das Ihre dazu tun. Falls es aber vermessen anmutet, den Namen des grossen Russland mit dem der kleinen Adria-Insel-Ragusa in Verbindung zu bringen, dann sie an die 'bescheidenen' Anfange auch anderer grosser Lander erinnert, zum Bespiel daran, dass der Doppelkontinent Amerika seinen Namen dem italienischen Seefahrer Amerigo Vespucci verdankt.

PREMYSLIDS

In *Waren die ersten Premyslides Balkanslaven?*, the Czech house of Premysl is traced to the Serbs, to Balkan Serbs by way of textual analysis (e.g. *Blazanaja Ljudmila bese ot zemle serbskyja, kneze serbskago dosti*), to Dragomira (e.g. *ex provincia Sclavorum paganorum, que Ztodor dicitur*), onomastics (e.g. numerous place names in Bohemia derived from the ethnonym Serb), and other linguistic and historical evidence (1987).

Als Spitzennahnen der Premysliden-Dynastie gelten dux *Borivoj* und seine Gattin *Ludmila*, die spatere Heilige. Wahrend die tschechische Stammeszugehorigkeit Borivojs gesichert oder jedenfalls unangefochten zu sein scheint, gibt die Ludmilas Ratsel auf. Die aksl. Prolog-Legende von der hl. Ludmila: *Blazenaja Ljudmila bese ot zemle serbskyja, kneze serbskago dosti.*

Ratselhaft freilich ist und bleibt, was "*serbisches Land*" und "*serbischer Furst*" in der Prolog-Legende besagen. Wegen der geographischen Nahen zu den Sorben hat man sich im allgemeinen darauf verstandigt, dass Ludmila *sorbischer* Abstammung gewesen sei, ja man ging sogar einen Schritt weiter und unterstellte das Vorhandensein von Sroben in Nord-bohmen, was heute jedoch mit Recht in Frage gestellt wird. Nicht bestreiten lasst sich allerdings, dass der Name der Sorben und Serben identisch ist, comes Slavibor daher sowohl sorbischer als auch serbischer Herkunft sien konnte. Bedenkt man weiter, dass Slaven, die sich Serben nannten, vom Balkan nach Mitteldeutschland gewandert waren und hier zu Sorben wurden, dann konnte es sehr wohl sein, dass Ludmilas Vater noch jener Generation angehorte, in deren Erinnerung die ethnische Identitat von Serben und Sorben noch lebendig war. Auch fallt ins Auge, dass Slavibors Psov sich an jener Stelle Nordbohmens befindet, von wo aus, den archaologischen Funden zufolge, das Elbe-Saale-Gebiet uber das Elbetal mit Slaven, das heisst mit Serben/Sorben besiedelt worden ist. Im Blich auf den Verlauf der slavischen Sud-Nord-Migration liesse sich das Gebiet um Psov-Melnik vielleicht sogar als serbisch-sorbischer Zwischen-Siedelplatz verstehen, an dem ein Teil der slavischen Zuwanderer aus dem Suden sesshaft wurde, wahrend andere Teile in Richtung Sachsen weiterzogen.

CZECHIA

In *Der Oberpfalzisch Pfreimd, cech Primda*, the names [German] 'Pfreimd' and [Czech] 'Primda' are traced to Dalmatia to Primorska Serbia or Primordia, to Namen der kleinen Adria-Insel Primordia (1988).

Moglicherweise war es gerade die Insel-lage, die den Namen der kleinen Adria-Insel *Primordia* bzw. *Premuda* auf die vermutlich schon im Fruhmittelalter enstandene erste Wehrsiedlung an der Mundung Der Pfreimd in die Naab ubertragen liess. Als Ubertraget kommen freilich nur Slaven in Frage, das legt allein der Verlauf der slavischen Migration vom Balkan nach Norden nahe. Auch ist die ursprungliche Lautung von Pfreimd, also *Primodia/Premuda* im Slavischen, eben in czech. *Primda* besser erhalten geblieben als im Deutschen, wo es zu einer Verschiebung des Anlauts gekommen ist … So gesehen ist der Name des naheliegenden Ortes *Perschen*, zu dessen Urpfarei Pfreimd biz 1216 gehorte, spater entstanden, da dieser warhscheinlich auf **Berzjane* "Leute am Ufer (der Naab)" zuruckgeht und somit der mundartlichen Medienverschiebung b > p unterlag. Die Ubernahme dieses Ortsnamens ins Bairische lasst sich mit Schwarz schon vor 770 ansetzen. Pfreimd, dessen Name also nicht vom Fluss, sondern von einer auf einer Insel entstandenen Wehranlage herzuruhren scheint, bestatigt zusammen mit Perschen, dass die sog. *Nabawinida*, also die Naabwenden zu den fruhesten slavischen Siedlern in der Oberpfalz zu zahrend sind. Der sehr wahrscheinlich auf lateinischem Sprachmaterial basierende Name Pfreimd lasst auch darauf schliessen, dass die Nabawinida oder Teile von ihnen aus einer romanischen Gegen des Balkans an die Naab gekommen waren.

SLOVAKIA

In *Die Slovakischen Hydronyme Nitra, Cetinka, Zitava und Ipel' - Zeugen der slavischen Sud-Nord-Wanderung*, a number of Slovakia's hydronyms are traced to Duklja/Dalmatia's Neretva, to the Neretva, Cetina, Zeta, and Ibar rivers (1988).

So wie der dalmatinische Flussname *Neretva* bei entsprechendem slovakischen Niederschlag vom Balkan nach Polen wanderte, gelangte auch das dalmatinische Hydronym *Cetina* nach Polen, wiederum einen Reflex auf slovakischem Gebiet hinterlassend, denn es steht ausser Frage, dass sowohol die slovakische *Cetinka* als auch die polnische *Cetynia, Cetyn,* ein Zufluss des westlichen Bug, ihre Namen dem balkanischen Prototyp *Cetina* verdanken. Wie im Fall der *Neretva* hat man auch den Namen der dalmatisnichen *Cetina* fur Ubertragung des polnischen Gewassernamens gehalten. Doch schon Schramm hielt es fur wahrscheinlicher, "dass es beide sudsla. FIN—zu einem unbekannten Datum un auf unbekannten Wegen—bis nach Polen verschlug." Schramms grundsatzlich richtiger Vermutung ist hinzuzufugen, dass die Wege, auf denen es diese Namen nach Polen verschlug, immer deutlicher werden.

DUKLJA, DUKLA PASS

In *Der Dukla-Name und sein weg von Montenegro uber die Karpaten nach nordwestrussland*, the Dukla-Pass in Carpathia and toponyms and hydronyms in Poland, Russia and Lithuania are traced to ancient Doclea, medieval Duklja, modern Montenegro and Ras or Raska-Serbia (1989).[3]

In der Provinz Praevalitana, unmittelbar ostlich des Gebietes von Kotor befanden sich die Sitze der Illyrischen Docleatae mit ihrem Vorort Doclea. Das Toponym Doclea ist mit Slavan in die Karpaten gewandert, was der noch heute

Dukla genannte Pass bestatigt. Doch scheint dieser name noch wieter nach Norden bis in die baltisch-nordwestrussischen Gebiete im Neman-Bassin ubertragen worden zu sein, was zahlreiche Bildungen wie Dukeli, lett. Dukuli, Dukulevo, Dukulava, vielleicht aber auch solche ohne [l] wie Duki, Dukiski zu bestatigen scheinen ... Luftlinie rund 60 km nordlich des Dukla-Passes liegt am Wislok die Wojewodschaftsstadt Rzeszow, deren Namen wahren der Jahre 1346-1358 auch als Rzassow notiert wird ... Damit sind wir beim prominenten Namen der mittelalterlichen serbischen Haupstadt Ras an der Raska, nordostlich vom heutigen Novi Pazar im Sandzak, angelangt ... Zentrum einer altserbischen Reichsbildung, die sich Raska oder Ras\ska (zemlja) nannte. Um 1235 lautete der serbische Konigstitel Kral\ vsech\ raskich\ zemlb. Die lat. und ital. Bezeichnungen fur den Landschaftsnamen sind Rasaa, Seruia seu Rasia oder Rascia, Raxia.

SLOVAKIA

In *Slovakische Ortsnamen aus Thessalien: Presov, Levoca, Spis*, a number of Slovakia's *landnahmes* are traced to Thessaly, to **zur slavischen Invasion Thessaliens**, to the 581/582 invasion by ***populus maledictus Sclavinorum*** (1989).

Vor diesem historischen Hintergrund kann es eigentlich kaum mehr uberraschen, winn sich die Bekanntschaft der Slaven mit Thessalien nicht nur in slovakischen Ort-s und Gewassernamen niederschlug, sondern auch bei anderen Slaven, ja selbst in Nordwestrussland nachweisen lasst. Ein Nachbarstamm der Thessaler, die *Doloper* oder *Dolopes* im Land *Dolopia*, der im allgemeinen die Schicksale Thessaliens teilte, hat mit hoher Wahrscheinlichkeit zu jener Bezeichnung der slavischen *Dulebi* gefuhrt, die Historiker und Linguisten immer wieder zu Uberlegungen herausfordert. *Sklavos*, der Name einer von Slaven uberfallenen Insel vor der thessalischen Kuste, hat sich in den bekannten ON Stettin, poln. *Szczecin*, verwandelt ... Wie eine in Kurze erscheinende Studie zeigen wird, finden sich thessalische geographische Begriffe aber auch in mehreren altpreussischen Landschaftsbezeichnungen. Die hier aufgezeigten slovakischen Reminiszenzen aus Thessalien sind insofern ein nich unbedeutendes Glied in der Rekonstruktion der fruhmittelalterlichen slavischen Migrationsablaufe.

LITHUANIA, PRUSSIA

In *Zur frage nach der Herkunft der Balten. Kaunas-Pomesanien-Pogesanien-Schalauen*, a number of Lithuanian and Prussian names are traced to the Balkans, in several instances to Praevalitania-Duklja-Montenegro (1990).

Baltische Entsprechungen haben ferner mehrere Namen aus der Provinz Praevalitana, voran das antike *Catarum, Catera, Cathara*, das heutige serbokroat. Kotor, ital. *Cattaro*, das unweit westlich der Sitze des alten Docleaten-Stammes lag. Der Name ist in Bosnien dreimal belegt *Dekatera* lasst an eine vulgarlat...Bildung *Cotera* denken, aus der im Slavischen *koter->*kotbr->*kotr-* werden konnte. Letzteres ist die Basis, auf der sowohl die sudslavische Form als auch der westrussische Gewassername *Kotra* entstehen konnte. Zu *Kotra*, einem re. Nbfl. des Neman im Kreis Lida (Wilna), gehoren die *Kotrovskie*-Sumpfe sowie der ON *Kotry* (Pruzansk) und die litauischen Hydronyme *Katra* (Bez. Alytus) bzw.

Katare (Bez. Siauliai). Weder *Katra* noch *Katare* lassen sich aus dem Baltischen erklaren, beide zahlen aber zur altesten Schicht der baltischen Toponymie. In der Provinz Praevalitana, umittelbar ostlich des Gebietes von Kotor befanden sich die Sitze der illyrischen *Docleatae* mit ihrem Vorort *Doclea*. Das Toponym *Doclea* ist mit Slaven in die Karpaten gewandert, was der noch heute *Dukla* genannte Pass bestatigt. Doch sheint dieser Name noch weiter nach Norden bis in die baltisch-nordwestrussischen Gebiete im Neman-Bassin ubertragen worden zu sein, was zahlreiche Bildungen wie *Dukeli*, lett. *Dukuli, Dukulevo, Dukulevo, Dukulava*, vielleicht aber auch solche ohne wie [*l*] *Dukiu, Dukiski* zu bestatigen scheinen.

MOSKVA

In *Der Russisches fluss-Resp Stadtname Moskva und sein hydronymisches Umfeld. Onomastisches zur Fruhgeschichte der Slaven im Raum Moskau*, the name Moskva (*grad Moskvu, na usti ze Neglinnoj, vyse reki Jauzy, 1156*) is traced to the Balkans, to Moesia/Illyria (1991).

Der Fluss- und Stadtname *Moskva*, dies darf als gesichert gelten, kann unmoglich finnougrisch sein, da, wie geziegt, die Wortsippe eindeutig auch fur das Westslavische nachzuweisen ist. Gewiss ist ausserdem, dass Moskva nich auf *Mosky* zuruckgeht, sondem ein hybrides, aus griechischen und slavischen Bauteilen zusammengesetztes theriophores Hydronym ist. Semantisch entspricht es dem von Ptolemaios genannten *Moschios potamos*, dessen Identitat zwar ungeklart ist, der in jedem Fall aber auf den Balkan, vermutlich auf die Provinz Moesia superior oder Illyricum verweist ... Bei aller Vorsicht lasst sich nun immerhin sagen, dass der grossere Teil der besprochenen Hydronyme jedenfalls vor oder um 800 ins Slavische ubernommen worden sein durfte, was naturlich in keiner Weise einen exakten Schluss auf dass zeitliche Einsetzen der slavischen Besiedlung des Moskauer Raumes zulasst, da Rezeption des Lehngutes und Sesshaftwerden seiner Rezipienten nicht unbedingt synchron erfolgt zu sein brauchen. Bei den beachtlichen geographischen Entfernungen ist wohl eher an grossere zeitliche, vielleicht sogar generative Intervalle zu denken. Die in der gelehrten Welt noch dominierende Ansicht, der Raum Moskau sei spat von Slaven besiedelt worden, ist im Kern wohl zu revidieren.

KIEV

In *Onomastische beitrage zur Vorgeschichte der Rus. 1. Thessalisches in Nordwesrussland. 2. Wie sich der Name Kiev erklart*, a number of names in Northwest Russia and the name 'Kiev', *die Mutter der russischen Stadte*, are traced to the Balkans (1992).

Dass die hybride Bildung **Ky-j-ev(b)* / **Ki-j-ev(b)* nicht auf die Stadt am Denepr beschrankt blieb, sondern auch zur Bezeichnung anderer slavischer Siedlungen—Trunte errechnet, wie gesagt, uber 100 Onn dieses Typs—Verwendung fand, ist bei einer so verbreiten Naturerscheinung wie einer 'Hohle' oder 'Grube' nur zu verstandlich. Die Haufigkeit des offenbar gemeinslavischen Namens spricht zugleich naturlich gegen die Vermutung, die Stadt *Kiev* konne diesen ihren Namen griechischen Handlern verdanken. Doch lasst sich nicht bestreiten, dass es fur

Kiev kaum eine treffendere Bezeichnung als eben 'Hohenort' gegen konnte. Das erklart allein schon das zwischen 1055 und 1060 in Kiev entstandene Hohlenkloster, der *Pecerskij monastyr* auch *Pecerskaja lavra* genannt, der Mittelpunkt des politischen, kirchlichen und kulturellen Lebens der Kiever Rus, der eben aus jenen Hohlen hervorgegangen ist, die der Dnepr an seinen Ufern entstehen liess.

POLAND: BALKAN ROOTS

In addition to the above articles and information relating to the origin of West and East Slav ethnonyms, *landnahmes*, toponyms and hydronyms (e.g. Illyria's Buzani are Germania's Buzani (between the Zuireani and Sittici) and Polish/Russian Buzani as in *Busani habent civitates CCXXXI* and *Buzane, zane sedosa po Bugu*; Illyria's Sermium/ Srem is Germania/Anhalt's Serimunt is Poland's Srem; Balkan Velun/Veluni are Pomerania's Wolin/Wolini), a number of articles specifically relate to Poland.

KASCHUBIA

In *Woher die Kaschuben ihren Namen haben*, the Kaschubs (*gens slavonica, quae Cassubitate dicuntur*) Balkan roots are examined (1985). **Mit dem Namen der ehemals im Land der Molossi ansassigen Kassopaier [Kassiope] werder slavische Kleinstamme oder Sippenverbande wahrend ihres Vordringens auf die Balkanhalbininsel gemacht haben. Gerade fur die hier in Frage kommende westliche Landschaft im Epeiros hat man seit langem auffallend dicthe Slavensiedlungen erkennen konnen ... Die Beobachtung nach welcher der Name der Kaschuben im Einklang steht mid dem altepirotischen Ethnonym der Kassopaier, fugt sich vortrefflich in das "neue" Bild von der Herkunft der Polen.**

MAZOVIA

In *Die Landschaftsnamen Masowien und Masuren*, Mazovia's Balkan roots are traced: Illyria's Mas/Maz/Mazaei as in Massarus Mons, later Mt. Mosor, above Split, is King Alfred's Maega land *(Be nordan Horifti is Maega land)* is Poland's Mazur/Mazuria/ Mazovia/Mazowsze; Illyria/Mazaei's hydronyms Cetina, Neretva, Sana are Poland's hydronyms Cetynia, Neretwa, and Sanna (1985). **Auf der Wurzel *maz- "gross" beruht ebenfalls der illyrische-dalmatinische Bergname Massarus mons bzw Massarum bei Split. Dieser Name setzt sich aus maz- und dem zur Bildung von Bergnamen ofter gebrauchten illyrischen Suffix -ar(o) zussamen. Der Bergname hat im Serbokroatischen Mosor ergeben, ein Toponym, das zur Bezeichnung von Hochlandschaften (planine) oder Ortsnamen, aber auch anthroponymisch verwendent wird.**

VELKOPOLSKA

In *Vom Balkan zur Ostsee*, for example, citing established archaeological and historical facts, Kunstmann cites the Serb ethnikon in Poland, especially Great Poland: **Ein weiterer Teil der Serben nahm seinen Wohnsitz anscheinend in Grosspolen. Dort findet sich eine grossere Anzahl von Ortsnamen vom Typ Sarbia** *(Beitrage, 1987)*.

GNIEZNO, WARTA

In *Gniezno und Warta*, the etymological roots of historic Polish toponyms and hydronyms are traced to the Balkans (1987).

LACH, LECH, LENDIZI

In *Der alte Polenname Lach, Lech und Lendizi*, seminal Polish ethnonyms are traced to Balkan Slavs (1987).

Noch deutlicher konnen die von der Forschung teils erkannten, teils vermuteten Zusammenhange zwischen ost- und westslavischen Lachen kaum bestatigt werden. And der polnischen Ethnogenese waren demzufolge neben aus Apollonia also auch slavische Vlachen und, wie kunftige Arbeiten warhscheinlich machen, verschiedene andere Balkanslaven beteiligt.

GOPLO SEE

In *Polens Goplo-See und die Schiffart*, the etymological roots of Poland's Goplo-See (*Et quoniam lacus Goplo adeo universali Polonorum consensu grandis et famosus est*) are traced to the Balkans (1989).

GACKO

In *Poln. Gdansk, russ. Gdov, kroat. Gacka und Verwandtes*, a number of Polish and Russian *landnahmes* are traced to the Balkans (1991).

UBER DIE HERKUNFT DER POLEN VOM BALKAN

Poland's Serb and Balkan roots are the subject of two impotant articles.[4] One in German, *Uber die Herkunft der Polen vom Balkan (1984)*, the other, a later Polish language version of the same article (*W Sprawie Rrodowodu Mieszka (1988).*[5] The following excerpts should give the reader considerable insight into Kunstmann's scholarship, method and style.

DACKICH SERBOW

With regard to the Serb-Balkan roots of Poland's rulers, as noted earlier, Kunstmann traces the 'Dagome' in the late 10th century Polish *Dagome-iudex-Regeste* to the pagan Serbs of Danubian Dacia: **Pod okresleniem poganskich Dagoni rozumie "dackich" Serbow.**

IUDEX

Kunstmann traces the title *iudex* in *Dagome-iudex-Regeste* to the Balkans in the following terms. **Es ist wohl etwas "eigentumlich, dass Mieszko als `Richter' (iudex)" erscheint, doch ist auch seit einiger Zeit bekannt, dass iudex sowohl in Rom als auch in Byzanz (archon) entweder einen Dignitar mit Amtsauftrag oder aber einen selbstandigen Herrscher bezeichnen kann ... In byzantinisch-griech. Quellen wird fur slavische Stammesfuhrer bisweilen auch der Titel archon gebraucht, so etwa in Bulgarien oder Serbien. Gelegentlich wird griech. archon durch lat. iudex ersetzt, "was gewiss in Dalmatien" der Fall gewesen sin soll. Im allgemeinen bezeichnet iudex somit den Vertreter einer lokalen Herrschaft mit byzantinischem Einfluss; entsprechend bezeichnete iudex bei den Balkanslaven den Stammesfursten oder Zupan. Fur vorliegende Untersuchung ergibt sich eindeutig, dass der Mieszko zugedachte Titel iudex wiederum einen balkanischen Akzent setzt. Dies wird noch deutlicher, sobald die Losung des Ratsels Dagome gegeben ist.**

MIESZKO, MOESIA

In the same two articles Kunstmann attempts to trace the royal Polish name Mieszko to Balkan Moesia (*ktorej pozniejszym centrum bylo Viminacium dzis Kostolac*). **Es ist gelungen, das uralte Geheimnis des strittigen polnischen Dynastennamens zu luften. Wie sich zeigt, is Mieszko sensu stricto kein Name, sondern eine Herkunftsbezeichnung, die einen entscheidenden Hinweis auf die Herkunft wenn nicht unmittelbar des Tragers, so doch seiner Vorfahren enthalt. Die altesten und haufigsten Vairanten des poln. Herrschernamens, also Misaco, Miseco, Misico, Mysico usf. sind adjkektivische Ableitungen vom Namen eines grossen Stammes der Balkanhalbinsel. Es ist der Stamm der Moesi, Moeses, Mysi, deren Name mit dem Landschafts- oder Provinznamen Mesia, Moesia, Mysia, zusammenangt. Zu Mesia, Moesia, Mysia gibt es zahlreiche und gut belegte Adjektive, von denen hier nur diejenigen vorgefurhrt werden, die die Enstehung des polnischen Dynastennamens erkennen lassen. Zu Mesia, der Parallelform von Moesia, sind u.a. die Adjektive Mesacus und Mesiacus belegt: natione Mesacus, legione Mesiaca. Besondere Aufmerksamkeit verdienen die von Mysia, Misia u.a. abgeleiteten Adjektive Misacus und Misiacus insofern, als sie vollig identisch sind mit der Form Misaco des polnischen Herrschernamens: Misacus; his quiescet bone memoriae Pista de numero Misacorum; memoriae Apollinaris de numero Misiacorum candidatus ... ex civitate Tracia. Dem polnischen Dynastennamen ebenso nahe kommen aber auch die adjektivischen Ableitungen von Mysia, und zwar die Formen Mysiacus.**

MOESIA, BOSNIA

Taking his analysis one step forward, Kunstmann relates the name Moesia to Bosnia. **Vor diesem historischen Hintergrund wird es unmoglich, eindeutig festzustellen, ob Mieszkos "Stammbaum" seine Wurzeln in der Moesia prima oder secunda hatte. Im ubrigen scheint sich der Begriff Mesia, Mysia in spaterer Zeit sogar auf die Landschaft Bosnien ubertragen zu haben. Das Land Bosnien, die Bosona, wird erstmals durch Konstantinos Porphyrogennetos, also fur die Mitte des 10 Jhds. erwahnt. Zue dieser Zeit war Bosnien im Rahmen des serbischen Reiches auf das Tal des gleichnamigen Flusses beschrankt. Bei der Schilderung der Ermordung Pribislavs, eines Sohnes Tolimirs von Dioclea, sagt die von Marko Marulic besorgte lateinische Ubersetzung der kroatischen Redaktion der Dukljanin-Chronik: Pribislavus ... a Mysis, qui nun Bosnenses apellantur, interficitur. Daraus geht eindeutig hervor, dass die Bewohner der Bosona auch Mysi, also Mysier genannt wurden. Die Frage, seit wann die Bosnenses auch Mysi hiessen—in der lat. Version und Orbrinis ital. Ubersetzung ist nur von magnates Bosnae bzw. baroni die Bosna—solte von fachkundiger Seite prazisiert werden.**

(A)POLINI, OPOLINI, POLONIA

In his discussion of the ethnonym Pole (Polani, Polanin, Poljanin) Kunstmann finds it interesting that the important mid-9th century source, *Descriptio civitatum ad septenitrionalem plagam Danubii,* records the Opols (*Opolini, civitates XX*), but not the Poles or Poland, sometimes cited as Polonia (e.g. *Polonia, Poloniam Sclavoniae*) in 11th century chronicles. This simple fact leads to informed and interesting speculation that links Polonia to Silesian Opolini to Balkan Appolonia (Slavic Poljani, Albanian Pojani).

SREM, BNIN, POZNAN

In another section, Kunstmann traces three historic Polish toponyms, Srem, Bnin, and Poznan, and the Polish hydronym Drawa, to Pannonia-Danubia. **Den grosspolnischen Toponymen Srem, Bnin und Poznan scheinen demnach die pannonischen Ortsnamen Sirmium, Bononia und Paznan gegenuberzustehen. Sie sind sich sowohl in der Polonia Maior als auch in der Pannonia inferior geographisch nahe ... Die Herkunft polnischer Teilverbande aus Pannonien, das sei an den Schluss gestellt, wird durch ein Beispiel aus der Hydronomie weiter verdeutlicht. Es ist der Name der polnischen Drawa mit ihren Nebenformen und Ableitungen wie den ONn Drawiny, Drawno, der Drawska Puszcza, Drawska Rownina, dem See Drawsko im Drawskie Pojezierze, der Stadt Drawsko Pomorskie usw. Dem polnischen Hydronym Drawa entspricht exakt der sudslavische Flussname Drava, der ehedem die Grenze zwischen der Pannonia Prima und der Savia bildete. Der Name Drava ist ohne Zweifel vorslavisch, sehr wahrscheinlich sogar vorromisch und vermutlich zu Beginn der romischen Landnahme—wenn nicht noch fruher—aus dem Regionalbarbarischen ubernommen worden. Eine Erklarung aus dem Slavischen scheidet sowohl fur die sudslavische Drava als auch die polnische Drawa aus; ein Transfer aus dem Suden scheint auch in diesem Fall die plausibelste Erklarung zu sein.**

ENDNOTES

[1] For a critical review of Kunstmann's theories from a Croatian perspective: R. Katicic, Kunstmannovi lingvisticki dokazi o seobi Slavena s juga na sjever, Starohrvatska prosvjeta 21, 1991.

[2] **Glopeani of Posen/Poznan province: Statt dessen sei nun eine vollig neue Uberlegung zur Diskussion gestellt. Nach meiner Ansicht ist Glopeani eine Sekundar-Ubernahme des griech. Stammersnamens Dolopes. Vor Begrundlung diese Meinung hoch ein Wort zur Bildung des Wortes Glopeani.**

[3] R. Radunovic, O etimologijii toponyma Duklja, OnJ 9, 1982. J. Udolph, Zur Deutung un Verbreitung des Namens Dukla, BnF 23, 1988.

[4] H. Kunstmann, Uber die Herkunft der Polen vom Balkan, DwS, 1984

[5] H. Kunstmann, W Sprawie Rodowodu Mieszka, SlA 31, 1988.

PART V

1. MIROSLAV(A), VOJISLAV(A)

In order to better understand and appreciate the strength and persistence of the notion in past and present German historical scholarship that Germania's Serbs originated in Illyria, in this section, beginning with the names of rulers and notables, we review some of the basic and conspicuous social parallels that underline this view.

GERMANIA, BOSNIA

The names of Slavic rulers and notables recorded in early medieval Germania are often the very same or similar to the names of Serb rulers and notables recorded in historic Serb lands between the Danube and the Adriatic, in medieval Bosnia. In many ways Bosnia was the vital center of the Serb medieval experience. This is especially true in literary matters, in the development of Serb religious literature and the perfection of the Serb language and letter. Succcessive literary-graphic masterpieces in the Serb language and letter follow one after another.

BOSNIAN GOSPELS

In the mid-13th century we have the *Bosnian Gospels*, a work inspired by and similar to *Miroslav's Gospel*. In the 14th century we have several well known masterpieces: *Divos' Gospel (Divosevo Evandjelje)*, the *Mostar Gospel* or *Manojlo's Gospel (Mostarsko-Manojlovo Evandjelje)* and *Kopitar's Gospel (Kopitarova Evandjelja)*, and *Bato's Gospel (Batovo Evandjelje)*. In the very early 15th century we have: *Nikolj's Gospel (Nikoljsko Evandjelje)*, *Hval's Collection (Hvalov Zbornik)*, and Tvrtko Pripkovic's *Four Gospels (Cetvorojevandjelje Tvrtko Pripkovica)*, followed by *Radosav's Apocalypse (Radosavljeva Apokolipsa)* and the *Cajnic Gospel (Cajnicko Jevandjelje)*. In the late 14th and early 15th centuries: *Danicic's Gospel (Danicicevo Evandjelje)*, *Sreckovic's Gospel (Sreckovicevo Evandjelje)*, *Nikolj's Gospel (Nikoljsko Evandjelje)*, and the *Venetian Collection (Mletacki Zbornik)*.

MOST PURE AND BEAUTIFUL FORM

According to Marin Temperica, a native of Dubrovnik, 16th century Jesuit scholar and authority on the Serbian language: **The Serbian language spoken in Bosnia is the Serbian language in its most pure and beautiful form. Srbsko pismo** was long the language and letter of native Roman Catholic chronicles, correspondence and records. It is clear from medieval and later sources, that in Bosnia, where **cirilsko pismo znaju i pastiri citati i pisati,** where Roman Catholic texts were published in *littera et idioma serviano*, there was strong resistance to the Latin letter. In a mid-19th century essay entitled *Hercegovci*, Friar Grga Martic (1822-1905), the most learned and respected Franciscan of his time, noting that the Catholics and Orthodox of Hercegovina are Serbs and only Serbs, and that **Srpski** is the one and only language of Hercegovina **(Jezik Hercegovacki je narecje naseg srbskog jezika),** calls for a Serbian language purged of foreign words and affectations:

PRODJIMO SE KOJEKAKVI MJESANJA, NEGO SERBLJI SRBIMA SRBSKI SRBSTUJMO.

ANCIENT, NATIVE NAMES

In Bosnia, centuries after Christianization, ancient and native Serb names remained the rule and Christian names the exception. The many names common to Germania and Bosnia are preserved in inscriptions carved in the unique tombstones or 'stecaks' centered in medieval Neretva/Zahumlya/Hum and Bosnia (modern Bosnia-Hercegovina). All the materials in this section (e.g. graphics, transcriptions) originated in the works of several outstanding Yugoslav authorities on the subject: *S. Beslagic: Kupres, 1954; Stecci na Blidinju, 1957; Boljuni, Starinar SAN XII, 1961; Kalinovik, 1962; Popovo, 1966; Stecci centralne Bosne, 1966; Stecci i Njihova Umjetnost, 1971; Nekropola drobnjacke vlastele u Poscenju, Zbornik Narodnog muzeja u Beograda VIII, 1975. Stecci-Kultura i Umjetnost, 1982. V. Bogicevic, Pismenost u Bosni i Hercegovini, 1975. V. Corovic, Prilog proucavanja nacina sahranjivanja i podizanja nadgrobnih spomenika u nasim krajevima u srednjem veku, 1956. M. Vego, Ljubuski, 1954; Zbornik srednjovejkovnih natpisa BiH, 1-IV, 1962-1970. G. Tomovic, Morfologija cirilickih natpisa na Balkanu, 1974.*

INSCRIPTIONS, EPITAPHS

Regarding the form and character of the tombstone inscriptions/epitaphs, B. Suvajdzic writes: **However, it must be pointed out that in these epitaphs the stress is put exactly on those segments of life of a deceased that make up a pattern of an epic biography of a hero in our folk epics: heroism, bravery, faithful service to the master, national creed, heroic death. Particular stress is put on the relationship of the deceased towards the collective and life which continues even after his death. The main function of those epigraphs is identical to the sociocultural position of epic poetry in the past: preservation of names and heroic deeds of prominent ancestors in the memory of grateful descendants** *(B. Suvajdzic, Natpisi na stecima kao vid epske (auto)biografije, VuK 27, 1998).*

EPIC SPIRIT

The following epitaphs of Vojvoda Radoslav Pavlovich and his unnamed aide are perfect illustrations of the heroic epic spirit. **Ja, vojvoda Pavlovich Radoslav, gospodar i knez ove zemlje, ovde lezim u ovom grobu. Dok zivljah, turske me car ne moga niti kojim junastvom niti kakvim darovima pa ni ratom, ni teskom silom, na zemlji mojoj pobediti, a jos manje misljah da se od vere odmetnem. Hvalim i slavim Boga sto vazda odolevah i sto zemlju moju ostavljam u veri hriscanskoj ... Vojvoda Pavlovichu, gospodaru moj, tebe lubljah za zivota svoga; vernom sluzbom sluzih tvoju glavu a sad evo lezim mrtav pod nogama tvojim, jer hocu i u zemlji da sam ti veran sluga. Toga si ti vredan, slavni i junacki kneze, jer mac je tvoj oborio po nekog Turcina za veru hriscansku.**

MIROSLAVA, VOJISLAVA

Two of the more regal names recorded in Germania, for example, Miroslava and Vojislava, immediately recall two of the more illustrious figures from the first pages of medieval Serb history *(G.C.F. Lisch, Das Kloster alt-Doberan zu Althof und Woizlava, des Obodriten-*

Konigs Pribislav Gemahlin, JbM 2, 1837. K. Myslinski, Wojslawa, SsS 6, 1977. T. Lalik, Wojslav, SsS 6, 1966).

MIROSLAV

The name Miroslav is found in one of the earliest inscriptions in the Serb language and letter. Namely, a dedication to the Church of St. Damian and Cosme near Blagaj, founded by Zupan Miroslav (***chlmensis zupanus*, 1171-1197)**, in honor of his brother, the great and glorious Zupan Nemanya: **Va ime otsa i sina i svetago duha. Ja zupan Miroslav zidah crkve svetago Kozme i Damjana u svojih sela u dni velijega zupana slavanago Nemanje.**

† ВЬ ИМЕ ОЧА И СНА И СВЕТ АГО ДОУХА Ѣ Ж ОУ
ПАНЬ МИРОСЛАВЬ ЗИДАХЬ Ц РЬКВЬ СВЕТАГ
О КОЗМЕ И ДАМИѢНА ОУ СВОИХЬ СЕЛѢХЬ ОУ Д
НИ ВЕЛИЕГА ЖОУПАНА СЛ АВЬНАГО НЕМАНЕ

MIROSLAVJEVA EVANDJELJA

More important, *velikoslavnomu* Knez/Zupan Miroslav is the patron of the first literary work in the Serb language and letter: *Miroslavjeva Evandjelja* or *Miroslav's Gospel*. A true masterpiece in every sense of the word, its 360 pages in color and gold include 296 exquisite miniatures. The Gospel's superb illuminations in gold are the work of scribe/artisan **dijak Gligorije (Az grjesni Gligorije dijak nedostoini naresti se dijak zastavih sie evangelie zlatom knezju velikoslavnomu Miroslavy sinu Zavidiny).**

АЗЬ ГРѢШНИ ГЛИГОРИЕ ДИѦКЬ НЕДОСТОИНИ НАРЕЩИ СЕ
ДИѦКЬ ЗАСТАВИХЬ СИЕ ЕВАНГЕЛИЕ ЗЛАТОМЬ КНЕЗЮ
ВЕЛИКОСЛАВНОМОУ МИРОСЛАВОУ СЫ НОУ ЗАВИДИНОУ.

VOJVODA MASNA

A later tombstone inscription identifies Miroslav and Radoslav as the sons of *Vojevoda Masna:* **Va ime otsa i sina i svetago duha. A se dvor vojevode Masna i njegoviju sinova Radoslava i Miroslava. Se pisa rab bozhi i svetago Dimitrija u dni gospodina kralja ugarskoga Lojsa i gospodina bana bosanskoga Tvrtka. Tko bi to potres, da je proklet otsem i sinom i svetim duhom.**

† ВА ИМЕ ѠЧА И СНА И С
ТАГО ДХА А СЕ ДВОРЬ ВОЕ
ВОДЕ МАСНА И НЕГОВИ
Ю СНОУ РАДОСЛАВА И М
РОСЛАВА СЕ ПИСА РАБЬ
БЖИ И СТАГО ДМИТ
РИѢ ОУ ДНИ ГДНА КРАЛ
А ОУГАРЬСКОГА ЛОИ
ША И ГНА БАНА БОСАНЬ
СКОГА ТВРЬТКА ТКО
БИ ТО ПОТРЬЛЬ ДА Е
ПРОКЛЕТЬ ѠЧМЬ И С
НОМЬ И СТИМЬ ДХОМ
Ь

VOJISLAVA

The name Vojislava is found in another early and important inscription in the Serb language and letter: the dedication of the Church of St. Michael, founded by medieval Bosnia's greatest ruler, Ban Kulin (1180-1204 and his wife Vojislava: **Siju crk ban Kulin zida...Kucevsko Zagorije i nad na nu gromadu u Podgorje Sljecpcist. I postavi svoj obraz nad pragom. Bog daj banu Kulinu zdravlje i banici Voyislavi** (The renowned Croat historian, V. Jagic is certain that the written record predates Ban Kulin: **Da nije moguce vjerovati, da ne bi bili u Bosni, Zahumlju, Diokliciji itd, da vec davno prije Kulina bana poceli pisati cirilicom i narodnijem jezikom srpskijem**).

СИⰭ ЧРІСВЪ БⰀNЪ КОⰟⰎ-
НNЪ ⰈNⰀⰄ ЄГ ⰄⰀ ПⰎ
ѢNН КОⰟVЄВЪСКО ⰈⰀГО-
РНЄ Н NⰀⰄЄ NⰀ NОⰟ
ГРО МⰀⰄОⰟ

ОⰟ ПОⰄЪГОРѢ СⰎѢПН-
НⱂЪ Н ПОСТⰀВН СВОН
ОБРОⰈЪ NⰀⰄЪ
ПРⰀГОМЪ БⰠ ⰄⰀН БⰀN-
ОⰟ КОⰟⰎНNⰟ ⰈⰄРⰀВНЄ
Н БⰀNН ВОНСⰎⰀВН

Tombstones,
Medieval Bosnia

135

2. PRIBISLAV

Pribislav and related names are among the more common personal names recorded in medieval Germania (e.g. Pribislav *ksiaze Polabian i Wagrov*; Pribislav, *ksiase Obdryzycki*, Pribislav, *ksiaze Stodoran*). Centuries later, the same names are among the more common personal and family names recorded in medieval Serb lands.

PRIBIC, PRIBIL, PRIBILSA

As the following series illustrates, Pribislav and related names (e.g. Pribic, Pribil, Pribilsa, Pribin, Pribisav) are inscribed on a number of tombstones of Bosnia-Hercegovina notables.

VUKAN AND PRIBICEVIC

The tombstone informs us that it was inscribed by nephews Vukan and Pribicevic: **A se pisa Vukan i Pribicevic na svojem stricu.**

Ⰰ ЄС ПИСⰰ ВⰌІСⰰⰐ Н ПРИБⰂЄƏНⰱ
Ⰴ ⰇⰆⰋ СВОЄМЬ С . РⱑЧН

PRIBIL

The inscription informs us that the tombstone was placed by Vuk and the brothers Ljuban, Medos, and Pribil: **I postavi bilig sin mu Vuk i brati njegova Ljuban i Medos i Pribil. Tko se pisanije sije pogubiti, prokleta bogom i sinom.**

Н ПО СТⰀƏН БⰕⰎⰕГЬ СН СНⰐⰱ
ОⰱⰎІСЬ Н БРⰀТНⰕ NЄГОƏ Ⰰ
ⰎⰛБⰕNⰱ Н МЄⰄОⱎⰱ Н
ПРИБ НⰎⰱ . . . ТЫꙆО ⰂЄ
ПНСⰀNНЄ СНЄ ПОГⰛБНТН ПРО
ꙆⰎЄТЬ БОГОМⰱ Н СНNОМⰱ

PRIBIL BELOPCEVJANIN

Stoisav Milosevic's tombstone informs us that it was placed by Pribil Belopcevljanin: **A se lezi Stoisav Milosevic na svoi zemlji na plemenitoj, koga mnogo ludi znase. A se cini Pribil Belopceljanin, a pisa Divin sin negov.**

† Ⰰ СЕ ⰎЄЖН СТОНСⰀꙂЬ МНⰎОⱎЄƏНⰱ NⰀ ЄꙂОН ꙂЕМⰎН

NⰀ ПⰎЄМЄNНТОН ꙆОГⰀ МNОГО ⰎⰛⰄН ꙀNⰀⱎЄ

Ⰰ СЕ ⰂНNН ПРИБNⰎⰱ БⰕⰎОПⰂЄⰎⰀⰍНNⰱ

Ⰰ ПНСⰀ ⰄНꙂⰱNⰱ СNⰱ ЄГОⰂⰱ

136

PRIBIL TUPKOVIC

Dragoje Tupkovic's tombstone was placed by his sons, Milobrat and Pribil: **A se lezi Dragoje junotic Tupkovic, plemeniti Svibnicanin, a postavista bilig sina Milobrat i Pribil. A tko ce si bilig pogubiti, pogubi ga bog.**

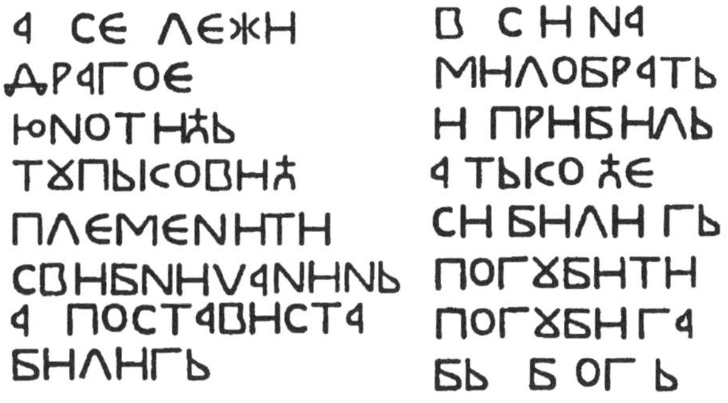

```
Ⰴ СЄ ЛЄЖН          В С Н Nⴷ
ⴷРⴷГОЄ             МНЛОБРⴷТЬ
ЮNОТНⴽ             Н ПРНБНЛЬ
ТⴞПЫⱄОВНⴽ          ⴷ ТЫⱄО ⴽЄ
ПЛЄМЄNНТН          СН БНЛН ГЬ
СВНБННⱱⴷNНNЬ       ПОГⴞБНТН
ⴷ ПОСТⴷВНСТⴷ       ПОГⴞБНГⴷ
БНЛНГЬ             БЬ БОГ Ь
```

PRIBILO

Here lies my son, Pribilo: **Ase lezi sin moi Pribilo ... i negov.**

```
ⴷСЄ ЛЄЖН СНNБ
МОН ПРНБНЛО
Н NЄГОВЬ.
```

PRIBILOVIC, DOBRILO

Dobrilo's tombstone informs us he was buried alongside his nephew Ljubeto: **Se lezi Dobrilo Pribilovic sa sinovcem s Ljubetom, a pisa Obrad Krajkovic.**

```
† СЄ ЛЄЖН
ⴷОБРНЛО ПРНБНЛОВНⴽ
СНNОВЧЄМЬ ш ЛⴞБЄТОМЬ
ⴷ ПНСⴷ ѠБРⴷ� ІⱄРⴷНⱄОВНⴽ
```

PRIBILOVIC, RADOVAN

According to Radovan's tombstone, he died at the hands of Milko Bozinic: **Va ime bozije se lezi Radovan Pribilovic na svojoj zemlji na plemenitoj na Ricici. Bih z bratom se razmenio ... i ubi me Milko Bozihnic i sa svojom bratijom, a brata mi isikose i ucinise vrhu mene krv nezajmitu. Neka zna ko je moj mili.**

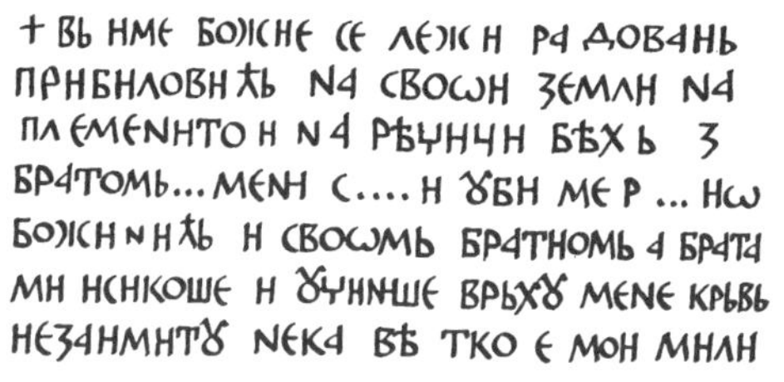

```
† Вь НМЄ БОЖСНЄ СЄ ЛЄЖ Н Рⴷ ⴷОВⴷNЬ
ПРНБНЛОВНⴽ Nⴷ СВОѠН ЗЄМЛН Nⴷ
ПЛ ЄМЄNНТО Н Nⴷ РⴽⱱНⱱН Бⴽⱱⴞ Ь З
БРⴷТОМЬ...МЄN С....Н ⴞБН МЄ Р ... Нⱳ
БОЖСН Н Нⴽ Н СВОѠМЬ БРⴷТНОМЬ ⴷ БРⴷТⴷ
МН НСНКОШЄ Н ⴞⱱНNШЄ ВРЬХⴞ МЄNЄ КРЬВЬ
NЄЗⴷНМНТⴞ NЄКⴷ Вⴽ ТКО Є МОН МНЛН
```

137

PRIBISAV

Vukac Vucinic's tombstone informs us that it was cut and inscribed by scribe/smith Pribisav: **A se lezi Vukac Vucinic na plemenitoj ... Vidi se zlamenije, ctioce pomenite, a vas bog blagoslovio, a sijece kovac-dijak Pribisav.**

† Ⰰ ⰔⰅ ⰎⰅⰜⰉ ⰁⰣⰊⰉⰞⰜⰟ ⰁⰣⰞ Ⰻ ⰜⰐⰋⰶ

Ⱀⰰ ⰐⰎⰅⰏⰅⰐⰊⰕⰑⰉ

ⰁⰐⰬⰉ ⰔⰅ ⰈⰎⰰⰜⰏⰅⰐⰉⰉ ⰛⰕⰉⰑ ⰛⰅ

ⰕⰅ ⰰ ⰁⰰⰔⰟ Ⰱ Ⱁ ⰃⰟ ⰁⰎⰰⰳⰑⰔⰎⰑ ⰁⰐⰉ

ⰰ ⰔⰟⰛⰅ ⰉⰉⰑⰁⰰⰛⰟ — ⰀⰐⰉⰛⰟ

ⰐⰒⰐⰁⰐⰔⰰⰛⰟ

PRIBISAVA

Veoka's tombstone informs us that she was the daughter of Pribisava Kosac, thus the issue of one of the leading families of medieval Hum/Hercegovina (scribe, Vukasin): **Ase lezi Veoka Krstijasinov, kci Pribisava Kosac. A pisa Vukasin.**

ⰰⰔⰅ ⰎⰅⰜⰉ ⰃⰑⰔⰒⰑⱑ Ⰳ

ⰅⰑⰉⰛⰰ ⰉⰛⰐⱑⰔⰕⰐⱑⰐⰐⰛⰑⰏ

ⰉⰶⰐ ⰐⰒⰐⰁⰐⰔⰰⰁⰰ ⰉⰛⰑⰔⰰⰛⰅ

ⰰ ⰒⰐⰔⰰ ⰁⰣⰉⰛⰰ ⰞⰐⰐ

[POPE] PRIBISLAV

Radisav's tombstone informs us that it was inscribed by Pope Pribislav: **Se lezi ovo Radisav Kotmjeric na svojej zemlyi na plemenitoi. Pisa pop Pribislav.**

† ⰔⰅ ⰎⰅⰜⰉ ⰑⰁⰑ

Ⱃ ⰰⰦⰐⰔ ⰰⰁⰟ

ⰉⰛⰑ ⰕⰟⰏⱑⰒⰐⰛⰟ

Ⱀⰰ ⰔⰁⰑⰣⰅⰐ

ⰈⰅⰏⰎⰐ Ⱀⰰ

ⰐⰎⰅⰏⰅⰐⰊⰕⰑⰉ

Ⱀ ⰐⰔⰰ ⰐⰑⰒⰟ

ⰐⰒⰐⰁⰐⰔⰎⰰⰁⰟ

PRIBISLAV PETOJIVIC

Pribislav's tombstone informs us that he was in the service of Ban Tvrtko: **A se lezi dobri Pribislav Petojivic na svoj zemlji na plemenitoj. Sluzih banu Tvrtku, gospodino verno. Na tom pogiboh. Pisa Bratoja.**

ᐊᒐᏆᏔᏔᏔᏔᏔ ᐁᏆᐱᏔᏆᏔ ᏔᏔᏆᏔᏆᏔᐁᏔᏔᏔ ᏔᏆᏔᏆᏔᏔᏔᏔᏆᏔ
Ꮤᐁ ᏔᏔᏔᏔ ᏔᏔᏆᏔᏔ Ꮤᐁ ᏔᏔᏔᏔᏔᏔᏔᏔᏔᏔ
ᏔᏔᏆᏘᏔᏔᏆ ᏔᐁᏔᏔ ᏔᏆᏔᏆᐁᏔᏆᏔ ᏔᐁᏔᏆ ᏆᏔᏆᏆᏔᏔ
Ꮤᐁ ᏔᏔᏆᏆ ᏔᏔᏆᏔᏆᏔᏆᏆ ᏔᏔᐁ ᏆᏔᏔᏔᏆᏔ

PRIBIL DABIZIVOVIC, VUKASIN PRIBICEVIC

The following series of Prib-/Pribislav personal and family names were recorded in Neretva, Zahumlya, Hum (Hercegovina) in the 13th, 14th, and 15th centuries.

PERSONAL NAMES

Pribelja Vranicic
Pribil Dabizivovic
Pribil Krajkovic
Pribil Mandjusic
Pribil Miokusovic
Pribil Veljkovic
Pbibilo Pavlovic
Priboje Drazimiric
Priboje Drazojevic

Priboje Krancic
Priboje Radovcic
Pribota Tvrdojevic
Pribisav Kovacevic
Pribisav Milovcic
Pribisav Nenadic
Pribisav Strelac
Pribislav Grupsic
Pribislav Kocic

FAMILY NAMES

Pribicevic, Vukasin
Pribilic, Stjepan
Pribilovic, Lilat
Pribilovic, Ljubeta
Pribilovic, Petar
Pribilovic, Radac
Pribilovic, Radosav
Pribilovic, Rakovac
Pribilovic, Stojmir

Pribinovic, Velimir
Pribisalic, Milorad
Pribisalic, Radasin
Pribisalic, Radic
Pribisalic, Radin
Pribisalic, Radisa
Pribisalic, Vukic
Pribisic, Hlapac
Pribojevic, Miilos

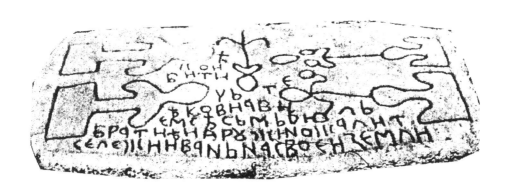

Tombstone, Medieval Bosnia

3. KNEZ RADOSLAV, KNEZ VUK

Diverse sources indicate that **Knez** and **Zupan** were two of the more common titles of Slavic rulers and notables in medieval Germania. Centuries later, the very same titles are recorded in medieval Adriatic-Balkan Serb lands. In the following series, the names and titles of the Serb **Knezes** are found inscribed on tombstones in medieval Bosnia-Hercegovina.

KNEZ BATIC

Knez Batic Mirkovic's tombstone informs us that he was in the service of King Tvrtko, *knez Bosanski*: **Va ime oca i sine i svetoga duha amin. Se lezi knez Batic na svoi zemlji na plemenitoj, milostiju boziom i slavnoga gospodina kralja Tvrtka knez Bosanski. Na Visokom se pobolih, na Dubokume me dni dojde. Si bilig postavi gospoja Vukava s mojimi dobrim, i zivu me vjerno sluzase i mrtvu mi posluzi.**

```
✝ ВА НМЄ ѠЧА Н СНNА Н СВЄТГ ДХА АМNЬ
СЄ ЛЄЖН КNЄЗЬ БАТНЬ
NА СВО  ЗЄМЛН NА ПЛЄМЄNНТОН
МНЛОСТНЮ БЖNОМЬН СЛАВNОГ А
ГNАNА КРАЛА ТВРЬТКА КNЄ ЗЬ БОСАNЬСКН
NА ВНСОКОМЬ СЄ ПОБОЛНХЬ

NА ДУБОКХМЄ МЄДNЬ ДОНДЄ
СН БНЛНГЬ ПОСТАВН ГОСПОѢ ВХКАВА
С МОНМН ДОБРНМН ЖНВХ МН
ВѢРNО СЛХЖАШЄ НМРТВХ МНПОСЛХЖН
```

KNEZ MIRKO RADIVOJEVIC

Knez Mirko's tombsone informs us that it was inscribed by Radonja Markovic. **A pise Radonja Markovic knez Mirko Radivojevic na svoje. Na crto.**

```
А ПНШЄ
РАДОNА МАРКОВНЧ
КNЄЗА МНРА РАДВНЧ
NА СВОЄ Н ЧРАТО
```

KNEZ OBRAD

The inscription informs us that Knez Obrad's son, Vuk, was buried alongside his sister, Jela: **A se lezi Vuk sina Kneza Obrada sa sestrom Jelom, i pokamenova ga mati Ana. Klet i proklet tko ce kreti u me.**

ꙗ СЕ ЛЕЖН
ВꙐІСЬ СНNЬ
ІСNЕꙌꙗ ОБРꙗДꙗ
СЕСТРОМЬ ЕЛОМЬ
Н ПОІСꙗМЕNОВꙗ Гꙗ

KNEZ PAVAO KOMLENOVIC

Knez Pavao's tombstone informs us that he was active in the time of *vojevode Sandal*: **A se lezi knez Pavao Komlenovic na svoj plemenitoj na Prozracu u dni vojevode Sandalj.**

† ꙗ СЕ ЛЕЖН
ІСNЕꙌ ПꙗВꙗѡ ІСОМЛѢNОВНѢЬ
Nꙗ СВОН ПЛЕМЕNНТОN
Nꙗ ПРОꙌРꙗVVꙊ Ꙋ
ДNН ВОЕВОДЕ СꙗNДꙗЛЬ

KNEZ PAVLE

Vlatko Vladjevic's tombstone refers to a Knez Pavle: **Va ime otsa i sina i svetoga duha a se lezi VlatkoVladjevic koji ne moljase nijednoga cloveka bilo kakvog, a obide mnogo zemlje a doma pogibe, a za njim ne osta ni sin ni brat. A na nju usice kami njegova vojvoda Miotos. Sluzi boziom pomocio i kneza Pavla moloscu koji ukopa, Vlatka, pomenu boga.**

† Вꙗ НМЕ ѡТVꙗ Н
СНNꙗ Н СВЕТ ꙗГО ДХꙗ
ꙗ СЕ ЛЕЖН
ВЛꙗТІСО ВЛꙗ ЖЕ ВН
ІСОН NЕ МОЛꙗШЕ
Н ЕДNОГꙗ VЛОВ Е ІСꙗ
ТꙗІСМОРНꙗ ꙗѡБНДЕ МNО-
ГО ꙌЕМЛЕ ꙗ ДОМꙗ ПО-
ГНБЕ ꙗ Ꙍ

ꙗ NНМЬ NЕ ОСТꙗ NН СН-
NЬ NН БРꙗТЬ
ЕNЬ Nꙗ ꙊСНVЕ ІСꙗМН NЕГОВꙗ
ВОЕВОДꙗ МНѡТОШЬ
СЛꙊЖН БОЖNОМЬ ПОМ ѻꙖО
Н ІСNЕꙌꙗ ПꙗВЛꙗ МНЛОСТОꙗ
ІСОН ꙊІСОПꙗ ВЛꙗТІСꙗ ПО-
МЕNꙊ Б О Гꙗ

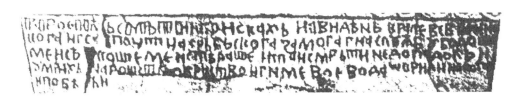

Tombstone, Medieval Bosnia

KNEZ POKRAJAC OLIVEROVIC

Knez Pokrajac's tombstone informs us that he died in the service of Voivoda Sandalj. **V dni gospodina vojvode Sandalja a sej lezi knez Pokrajac Oliveroric, bratjo i vlastele, ja Pokrajac gospodinu momu sluga, sto mogoh v pravadai toliko hotih, u mom domi bog mi rodili, ja mogah gospodina moga i druga moga u postenije primiti i u tom mom dobri dodje smrt, u vreme zivota, dom moj ozalostih.**

† Ꙏь ΛNΗ ГꙆNꙆ   ΤΟΛΗΚΟ ΧΟΧь
ꙎΟЄ ꙎΟ ꙆЄ СꙆNꙆꙆ   Χ ΜΟΜь ꙆΟΜΗ
ѢΛꙆ Ꙇ СЄΗ ΛЄ   ꙠΟГь ΜΗ ΠΟꙆΗ
ЖΗ ΙΚΝЄꙀь ΠΟΙΚ   ΛΗ Ѣ ΜΟГꙆΧь ГNꙆ
РꙆѢ҄ь ꙍΛΗꙎЄ   ΜΟГꙆ Η ꙆΡꙍꙆ ΜΟ
РΟꙎΗ҄ь ꙠΡꙆ   ГꙆ Χ ΠΟΥΤЄΝΗ ΠΡΗ
ΤΗꙍ Η ꙎΛꙆСΤ   ѢΤΗ Η Χ ΤΟΜь ΜΟ
ЄΛЄ Ѣ ΠΟΙΦꙆѢΥ   Μь ꙆΟꙠΡΗ ꙆΟГЄ
ь ГΝΧ ΜΟΜΧ   СΜΡьΤь Χ ꙎΡЄΜЄ ЖΗ
СΛΧГꙆ ѱΟ ΜΟΧ   ꙎΟΤꙆ ꙆΟΜь ΜΟѢ ꙍ
ь Ꙏь ΠΡꙆꙎꙆꙆΗ   ЖꙆΛΟСΤΗΧь

KNEZ PRIJAN

Here lies Knez Prijan: **Se lezi knez Prijan.**

СЄ ΛЄЖΗ ΙΚΝЄꙀь
ΠΡΗ Ꙇ N

KNEZ RADIC

The inscription on Knez Radic's tombstone is brief and to the point: **A sije pociva knez Radic, smerni rab Bozi, titor hrama sego.**

Ꙇ СΗЄ ΠΟΥΗꙎꙆ ΙΚΝЄꙀ РꙆꙆΗΥ
СΜЄΡΝΗ РꙆꙠ ꙠΟЖΗ
ΤΗΤΟΡ ΧΡꙆΜꙆ СЄГΟ

KNEZ RADISA ZLOUSIC

Knez Radisa's tombstone informs us that it was placed by his son, the valiant Tomo Radisa Zlousic: **A se lezi knez Radisa Zlousic. A se pise kami Vukovic za junaka Tomovu Radisi Zlousic.**

```
† Ⰰ СЄ ΛЄЖН
ІСΝЄꙐЬ РⰀ‍ΝШⰀ ꙐΛОⰧШНꙖ
Ⰰ СЄ ПНШЄ ІСⰀМН
ВⰧІСОВНꙖЬ ꙐⰀ ꙖⰧΝⰀІСⰀ
ТⰧМОВⰧ РЬⰀΝШН
ꙐΛОⰧШНꙖЬ
```

KNEZ RADIVOJ VLATKOVIC

Knez Radivoj's tombstone informs us that he was the most valiant man in Dubrava: **A sej lezi knez Radivoj Vlatkovic. U toj vrime njabolji muz u Dubravah bih ... Sej sece Grubac kovac.**

```
† Ⰰ СЄН ΛЄЖН ІСΝЄꙐ Ь
РⰀ‍ΝВОН ВΛⰀТІСОВНꙖЬ
Ⱗ ТОН ВРНМⱔ ΝⰀНБОΛН
МⰧЖЬ Ⱗ ⰀⰧБРⰀВⰀХЬ БНХЬ
Ⰰ ВⰧРЄБ ΛⰀВЬ СЄН СⱔVЄ
ГⱃⰧБⰀVЬ ІСОВⰀVЬ
```

KNEZ RADOJA

Knez Radoja's tombstone informs us that it was placed by his son, Knez Radic: **Se zlamenije kneza Radoja, velikoga kneza Bosanskoga. A postavi njega sin njegov knez Radic, z boziom pomocju i svojih verna a s inom nijednom pomociju nego sam on.**

```
СЄ ꙐⰀΛМЄΝНЄ ІСΝЄꙐⰀ РⰀⰄОⱕ
ВЄΛНІСОГⰀ ІСΝЄꙐⰀ БОСⰀΝСІСОГⰀ
Ⰰ ПОСТⰀВН Є ГⰀ СНΝЬ ΝЄГОВЬ
ІСΝЄꙐЬ РⰀⰄΝVЬ Ꙑ БОЖНОМЬ
ПОМОꙖⰓ Н СВОНХЬ ВⱔРΝⱔХЬ
Ⰰ С НΝОМЬ ΝНЄⰄ Ν ОМЬ
НΝОМЬ ПОМОꙖⰓ ΝЄГО СⰀМЬ ОΝЬ
```

KNEZ RADOJA ZEMLIC

Here lies Knez Radoja Zemlic: **A se lezi knez Radoje Zemlic.**

† 4 СЕ ЛЕЖН ІСΝЕЗЬ
РⱯⰄО Є ⰀⰈЕТⰎΝⰙЬ

KNEZ RADOSLAV SIRINIC

Here lies Knez Radoslav Sirinic: **V ime boga se lezi rabi bozi knez Radoslav Sirinic.**

† ВЬ НМЄ Б͞Ⱝ
СЄ ЛЕЖН РⰀБЬ БОЖН
ІСΝЕЗЬ РⰀⰄОСЛⰀⰂЬ ШНРНΝНUЬ

KNEZ STANKO

The tombstone's inscription refers to a Knez Stanko and several other notables. **Sie lezi Stjepan ban Bosanski i brat mu Bogdan i Dragisa i Knez Bakula i Knez Stanko i Tvrtko s druzinom.**

СНЄ ЛЕЖН СТⰎПⰀΝЬ БⰀΝⰎ БОСⰀΝⰎ
Н Н БРⰀТЬ МUХ БОГⰄⰀЬ Н ⰄРⰀГНШⰀ
ІСΝЕЗЬ БⰀΙСUХЛⰀ Н ІСΝЕЗ СТⰀΝⰎІС
Н ТⰂРⰎТІСО С ⰄРUХЖΝ О М Ь

KNEZ STIPKA

Here lies Bogcin, son of Knez Stipka: **A se lezi Bogcin Kneza Stipka Ugarcica sin na svojoj zemlji na plemenitoj. Druzino, zalite me. Mlad si sega svita otidoh, a jedan bih u majke. A se pisa Ugarak.**

† 4 СЄ ЛЕЖН

ВОГUHNⰎ

ІⰎΝЕЗⰀ СТНПІСⰀ

Х ГⰀРⰎⰂ]НⰜⰀ

СНΝⰎ
NⰀ СⰎВОⰛОН
ЗЕМНⰂ

NⰀ
ПЛЕМЕНИТОН

144

KNEZ TVRDISAV BRSNIC

The inscription informs us that Knez Tvrdisav was a man of honor and valor: **Si bilig kneza Trdisvava Brsnic, posten vitez ovdi jadan dojde.**

† СН БЛГЬ
ІСΝЄꝀ4 ВНΤЄꝀ
ΤВРЬ4ΗС4В4
БРСНN⁜

KNEZ VLADISLAV

Knez Vladislav's tombstone informs us that he is the son of Zupan Nikola and nephew of Ban Stjepan: **A se lezi knez Vladislav, zupana Nikola sin, bana Stepana netijak, lezi na svoj zemlji na plemenito, a pisa Pomocan.**

† 4 СЄ ЛЄЖН
ІСΝЄꝀЬ ВЛ44НСЛ4ВЬ
ЖꙊΠ4Ν4 ΝΗІСОЛЄ СΗΝЬ
Б4Ν4 СΤⲎΠ4Ν4 ΝЄΤΗ
4 ЛЄЖН Ν4 СВОН ꝀЄМЛ
Н Ν4 ΠЛЄМЄΤО
4 ΠΗ.С4 ΠОМОⱰ4ΝЬ

KNEZ VUK

The inscription informs us that Knez Vuk's tombstone was placed by Mihal: **Va ime boga dobroga se zida Mihal svome gospodina kneza Vuka.**

† В4 Н МЄ
Б ОГ 4 ДОБРОГ4
ꝀΗД4 МН Х4ЛЬ
СВОМꙊ
Г ОСΠО Д Н NꙊ
ІСΝЄꝀꙊ
ВꙊІСꙊ

4. ZUPAN GRD, ZUPAN PRIBILSA

In the following series, the names and titles of Serb **Zupans** are found inscribed on tombstones in medieval Bosnia-Hercegovina.

ZUPAN GRD

Zupan Grd Trebinski's tombstone informs us that he was governor of Trebinje: **zupan Grd trebinski.**

ОЪ ДНН КNЄЗД ВЕЛНЕГД МІХОІЛД ОЪМРЬ ЖОΧПДNЬ ГРЬДЬ ТР
ЪБЬІNСІСІН Н ОЪ ТО ЛЪТО ЗІДД ЕМОΧ РДКОΧ БРДТ ЖОΧПДNЬ
РДДОМНРЬ С СNЬМН ЕГОВЪМН І ЖЕNД ЕМОΧ ТОДРД МОНСТРЬ
НМЕNЕМЬ БРДЪ NЬ БОЖН ГN ДДН ЗДРДОНЕ.

ZUPAN JUROJE

This inscription informs us that the faithful Zupan Juroje was killed in action. **A se lezi zupan Juroje koino pogibe na posteno sluzbe za sv. dana ipoblizi ga knez.**

† Д СЕ ЛЕЖН ЖΧПДNЬ ЮРОЕ

КОНNО ПОГБЕБЕ NД ПОΥТЕ

NО СЛΧЖБН ЗД СВ ГДNД

Д ПОБНЛНЖ ГД КNЕЗЬ

ZUPAN KRILE

Ban Kulin's dedication refers to a Zupan Krile: **pisars Desivoj and Radonja and krscanin Desin Ratnicevic: pisah Krile zupan**

Н БДNН
ПНСДХЬ КРНЛЕ ЖΧПДNЬ
ДЗЪ ПНСДХЪ ДЕСНВОН
Р . . Д . . . Б
Н ДЗЪ ПНСДХЬ
СЕ ПНСД РДДОХNД КРЬ-
ТНЪNNЬ
ДЕСЪNЬ РДТЬNУЕВНЖ Д
ПНСД Χ ДЬNН БДNД

146

ZUPAN KRNJE

This tombstone refers to a Zupan Krnje: **A imenem zupan Krnje.**

ПРѢСТАВН СЕ РАБЬ БЖН ꙦЕОРГНѢ
NА ВЕVЕРНЕ Х̄Ѻ̄А АNЕ Ꙇ
НМЕNЕМЬ ЖꙊПАNЬ КРЬNѢ

ZUPAN MEDULIN

Zupan Medulin's tombstone informs us that in spite of his title and status, he lived and died in reduced circumstances: **A se lezi zupan Medulin. Nikada mnogo ne imah, a nikada nista nesta a dijelih.**

† Ꙇ СЕ ЛЕЖН
ЖꙊПАNЬ МЕАꙊЛНNЬ
МNОГО NЕ НМАХЬ Ꙇ
NНКАДА NНψа NЕСТА
Ꙇ АѢХЬ

ZUPAN NIKOLA

Gospoja Katalina's tombstone informs us that she is the wife of Zupan Nikola, that the stone was placed by their sons Vladislav and Bogisa: **A se lezi gospoja Katalina s svojim gospodinom zupanom Nikolom koji sluzase Kotromenevic tasta i slavanago bana Stepana ... Postavi na nju Vladislav i Bogisa brat mu da.**

† Ꙇ СЕ ЛЕЖН ГОС ПОѢ КАТАЛѢNА
СЬ СВОНМ Ь ГОСПОАНNОМЬ
ЖꙊПАNОМЬ NНКОЛОМЬ

ZUPAN OZRIN KOPIJEVIC

Zupan Ozrin Kopijevic's tombstone refers to the Bosnian Kingdom (*kraljevstva bosanskoga* and the Serb nobility/rulers (*gospostva srbskoga*). **Va ime bozije a se lezi Ozrin Kopijevic, zupan kneza Pavla. Se pisa dijak Milosalic. Barojevic, smrt ne poiskah naviden od kraljestva bosanskoga i gospostva srbskoga za moga gospodina sluzbu. Bodose me i sjekose me i oderase, i tu smrti ne dopadoh, i umrih na rostvo Hristovo, i gospodin me vojevoda okrili i ukopa.**

ВА НМЄ БОЖНЄ Ѧ СЄ ЛЄЖН
ОЗРНNЬ ІСОПНЄВНѦЬ
ЖꙊПѦNЬ ІСNЄЗѦ ПѦВЛѦ
СЄ ПНСѦ ѦНѢѦІСѦЬ МНЛОСѦНѦЬ
ІСРѦЛЄВЧ Т ВѦ БОСѦNСІСОГѦ
Н ГОСПОЧ Т ВѦ СРБСІСОГѦ
ЗѦ МОГѦ Г ОСПОѦН NѦ СЛꙊЖБꙊ
БОѦОШЄ МЄ Н СѢІСОШЄ МЄ Н ОѦЄРѦШЄ
Н ТꙊН СМРЬТН NЄ ѦОПѦѦОХЬ Н ХМРЬХЬ
NѦ РОШ С ТВО ХРНС ТОВО Н Г ОСПОѦН N
МЄ ВО ЄВОѦѦ ꙍІСРНЛН Н ꙊІСОПѦ
Н ПОБѢ ЛѢ ЖН

ZUPAN PRIBILSA

Zupan Pribilsa's tombstone informs us that he was active during the reign of King Vladislav [of Hungary]: **Va dni prvonago kralja Vladislav prstavi serab bozi od Grodmila poriklom zupan Pribilsa a po bozijoj milosti na dedina niju.**

† ВѦЬ ѦНН
ПРЬВОВѢРNѦГО
ІСРѦЛѦ ВЛѦѦНСЛѦ
ВѦ ПРѢСТѦВН
СЄ РѦБЬ
НЛѦ ПОРН·СЬЛОМЬ
ЖꙊПѦNЬ
ПРНБНЛШЬ Ѧ
ПО БЖН
МНЛОСТН N

ZUPAN RADOMIR

Zupan Grd's tombstone informs us that it was placed by his brother, Zupan Radomir: **brat zupan Radomir.**

БРѦТ ЖОꙊПѦNЬ РѦѦОМНРЬ
С СNЬМН ЄГОВѢМН І ЖЄNѦ
ЄМОꙊ ТВѦРѦ МОНСТРЬ

ZUPANICA RUDA

This partial inscription refers to the wife of the zupan of Ruda, the 'zupanica' of Ruda.

 4 С4
ЖУП4NHЧ4 РХ4Н
ПРН ТЕШІСН Д4N
ІСТО Д4 СН ЗNД4ДШЕ

ZUPAN VRATKO

The inscription informs us that the deceased was the wife of Zupan Vratko, daughter of Zupan Miltjen Drazivojevic, that the stone was placed by her son Dabiziv: **V ime otca i sina i svetaog duha se lezi raba bozija Polihranija a zovom mirskim gosposja Radaca, zupana Nenca Cihoric Kucnica, a nevesta zupana Vratka i sluge Dabiziva i tepcije Stipka, a kci zupana Miltjena Drazivojevicha a kazancu Sanku sestra a postavi s bjeleg ne sin Dabiziv s bozijom pomosciju sam svojim ljudmi v dni gospodina krala Tvrtka.**

+ ВЬ НМЄ ШЧ҃Д Н С҃ИД Н С҃Т҃ГО Д҃ХД СЄ
ЛЄЖН РАБД Б҃ЖНД ПОЛНХРАNНД Д
ЗОВОМЬ МНРЬСКНМЬ ГОСПОД РАДАЧА
ЖОУПАNД NЄNЬЧД УНХОРНД КОУЬNНЧД
Д NЄВѢСТД ЖОУПАNД ВРАТЬКД Н СЛУГЄ
ДДБНЖНВД Н ТЄПЬУНЄ СТНПЬКД Д К҃БН
ЖОУПАNД МНЛЬТѢNД ДРАЖНВОЄВНКД
Д КАЗNЬЧУ СЬNЬКУ СЄСТРД Д ПОСТДВН
СЬ БѢЛЄГЬ NЄ С҃NЬ ДДБНЖНВЬ СЬ Б҃ЖНШМЬ
ПОМОЦНЮ САМЬ СВОНМЬ ЛЮДЬМН Д ВЬ
ДNН Г҃NД КРАЛД ТВРЬТІКД

5. KNEZ, ZUPAN, VLASTELIN, VOJVODA, KRAL SRBLEM

The following are the names of the greater number of *Knezes, Zupans, Vlastelins* (vlastele nasega plemena), Vojvodas, Bans, Krals (**Kralj sviyu Serba**), and other notables of Bosnia-Hercegovina recorded in medieval sources.

KNEZ CRNOMIR • KNEZ PRIBISLAV VUKOTIC

Crnomir
Gojko Dragosalic
Grgur Milatovic
Ivan Santic
Ivan Vukovic
Ivanis Gojsic
Ivko Simovic
Marko Dragisic
Mirko Mirkovic
Mirko Radojevic

Misljen Zemljic
Obrad Hladomiric
Ostoje Borovinic
Pavle Dinjicic
Pavle Kostanjic
Pavle Radinovic
Pavle Radisic
Pribislav Pohvalic
Pribislav Vukotic
Priboj Mistovic

KNEZ RADOJE VLADIMIRIC • KNEZ ZARKO VLATKOVIC

Radoje Vladimiric
Radoje Dragosalic
Radoje Radosalic
Rados Radosalic
Stanoje Jelascic
Stepan Ostojic
Toljen Nemanjic
Trisa Banovic
Tvrtko Kovacevic
Tvrtko Mihailovic
Vladislav Nikolic
Vladja Bijelica
Vlatko Pohvalic
Vojslav Vojvodic

Vuk Nimicic
Vuk Rogatic
Vuk Sandalj
Vuk Vucic
Vuk Vukoslavic
Vukac Vardic
Vukac Sandalj
Vukac Vukotic
Vukasin Milatovic
Vukasin Vladimiric
Vukasin Zlatonosic
Vukic Vlatkovic
Vukota Pribinic
Zarko Vlatkovic

ZUPAN ANDRIJA NEMANJIC • ZUPAN NEBOJSA • ZUPAN TVRDISLAV

Andrija Nemanyic
Bogdan Nemanyic
Bozicko Brlic
Bijelak Sankovic
Branko Pribinic
Dobromisl Pribinic
Dragisa Dinicic
Grubisa
Ivan Pribilovic

Ivan Trebotic
Ljuboje Dobretkovic
Nebojsa
Novak Ivanic
Rado Radosalic
Radoslav Nemanjic
Toljen Nemanjic
Tvrdislav
Tvrtko

VLASTELIN BOGDAN RADONJIC • VLASTELIN OSTOJE POZNANOVIC

Bogdan Radonjic
Bogdan Prvoslavic
Bozidar Vukcic
Bratoj Radonjic
Bratroslav Vukovic
Budisav Gojsalic
Dobrovit Radoncic
Dragisa Dinjicic
Gojak Vragogermac
Gojsav Vojsalic

Herak Vladisalic
Hrelja Rastimiric
Hrelja Stepkovic
Ivan Pribilovic
Ljubis Bodancic-Ljubibratic
Milos Vuksic
Milutin Hrelyic
Obrad Ivanovic
Ostoje Brajanovic
Ostoje Poznanovic

VLASTELIN PETAR VUKCIC • VLASTELIN VUKOSAV KOBILJACIC

Petar Vukcic
Petar Vukicevic
Pribin Zloselic
Pribislav Milobratic
Pridislav Vukmiric
Prodan Pobrenovic
Prvoslav Prodanic
Radoje Ljubisic
Raodje Srdjevic

Radosav Hlapenovic
Radoslav Bogdanic
Ratko Misanovic
Stanisa Srdjevic
Voislav Mrkovic
Vuk Vucicevic
Vukic Vukasovic
Vukosav Kobiljacic

VOJVODA IVANIS VLATKOVIC • VELIKI VOJVODA BOSANSKI RADOSLAV PAVLOVIC • VOJVODA VUKMIR ZLATONOSIC

Djurac Radivojevic
Ivanis Dragisic
Ivanis Vlatkovic
Kovac Dinjicic
Masan Bubanic
Pavle Klesic
Petar Hrabren
Petar Kovacevic
Purce Dabisic
Radic Sankovic
Radoj Hrabren
Radoj Miloradovic
Radosav Hrabren
(Veliki Vojvoda Bosanski)

Radosav Pavlovic
Sandalj Hranic-Kosac
Tvrtko Ivanic
Tvrtko Kovacevic
Tvrtko Stancic
Vladislav Klesic
Vlatko Tvrtkovic
Vlatko Usorski
Vlatko Vukovic-Kosac
Vojko Bilosevic
Vukasin Sankovic
Vukic Hrabren
Vukmir Zlatonosic

The following are some of the names of notables in the service of rulers and lords of medieval Bosnia-Hercegovina.

BOGDAN MILOSEVIC • DOBROMISL POBRATOVIC • VOYISLAV KOVACEVIC

Balsa Vladisalic
Bogcin Stanislavic
Bogcin Stoisalic

Bogdan Milosevic
Bogisa Hvalovic
Bozicko Medosevic

Bozidar Petrovic	Nikola Pribinovic
Budislav Gojsalic	Ostoje Pribilovic
Dobromisl Pobratovic	Radivoj Hodivojevic
Gojko Medosevic	Radivoj Popratovic
Hrebeljan Dabisic	Radivoj Priljubovic
Milac Bozickovic	Stjepan Miloradovic
Milos Dobrosalic	Tvrdisa Miruskovic
Miluta Radovanic	Voyislav Radosevic

VELIKI BAN BOSANSKI

Throughout recorded history, from the first inscriptions, charters, treaties, and other documents, Bosnia's rulers, in the most simple, direct, straightforward, and unequivocal terms identified themselves and their people as Serbs and only Serbs (**Srblyin, Srblyi, Srblyima**). Successive royal charters regulating Bosnia's trade relations with Dubrovnik identify the Bosnians as Serbs.

In the *golden era* of Bosnia's history, *the good old days of Ban Kulin* (**Od Kulina Bana i dobriyeh dana**), for example, an 1189 charter identifies the Bosnians as Serbs. In the next century successive charters issued by Ban Matei Ninoslav (**ban Matej Ninoslav, po milosti bozijoj veliki ban bosanski**) identify the Bosnians as Serbs. The same is true of a 1245 charter issued in the name of Ban Matei, his brothers (**bratnov**), and nobles (**bolyarimi**). A century later, Ban Stefan Kotromanovic instructs his staff to send four copies of an agreement to Dubrovnik, two in Latin and two in Serbian: **dvije Latinsci a dvije Srpskije**.

KRALJ SVIYU SERBA

As rightful heir to the lands of his ancestors (**zemlyah roditel i praroditel nasih**), Bosnia's Tvrtko (1353-1391) was crowned king of Serbs in 1377 (**nasledovati prestol mojih prarodietl, gospode srbske**). In a 1378 charter regulating relations with Dubrovnik there are repeated references to Serbdom, to **moyih preroditel, gospoda srbska, to srbsku zemlyu, to prestol roditel mojih, to kralju srbljem, to srbske zemlye.**

In this and other acts and correspondence Stefan Tvrtko makes it clear to one and all in standard Serb language and letter that he is the natural and legitimate heir to the Serb crown of his forefathers, that he is *King of all Serbs* (**Kralj sviyu Serba**).

PO MILOSTI GOSPODA BOGA KRAL SRBLEM

Stefan Tvrtko's successors were always first and foremost king of the Serbs or **kral srblem**.

- King Stefan Dabisa (1391-95) was **po milosti gospoda boga kral srblem.**

- King Stefan Ostoja (1398-1404) was **po milosti gospoda boga blagoverni kral srblyem.**

- King Stefan Tvrtko II Tvrtkovic (1404-09) was **po milosti gospoda boga**

moega kral srblem.

• King Stefan Ostojic (1418-21) was **po milosti bozhastva kral srblem.**

———————— • ————————

In his second reign, King Stefan Tvrtko II Tvrtkovic (1421-43) remained **milostyu bozhnom mi gospodin kral serblem.**

• King Stefan Tomash Ostojic (1443-61) was **milostyu bozhim ... kral srblem.**

• His son and successor, King Stefan Tomashevic (1461-63) was **milostyu bozhim mi gospodin Stefan Tomashevic kral srblem.**

Tombstone, Medieval Bosnia

6. DABIZIV, MIOGOST, RADIBRAT, RADOGOST, SLAVOGOST, SRBISIN

The following personal and family names are also found inscribed on medieval tombs in Bosnia-Hercegovina (Neretva/Zahumlya/Hum). It is interesting that centuries after Christianization, Christian personal/family names (e.g. *Marko, Mihal, Pavao, Pavle, Petar, Stjepan*) are few and far between.

Instead, one finds a great preponderance of traditional Serb names and a greater number of archaic Slavic names: e.g. ***Dabiziv, Miogost, Radibrat, Radogost, Slavogost, Zivogost*** (M. Dinic, Humsko-trebinjska vlastela, 1967; A. Peco, Iz Hercegovacke Onomastike Predturskog Period, JuZ 1, 1987).

BOZICKO BANOVIC • POZNAN BOGDANIC • VUKOBRAT DJURDJEVIC

Banovic, Bozicko	Borovicic, Bresko
Banovic, Trtisa	Bozickovic, Dobrilo
Batricevic, Vuk	Braikovic, Bratmijo
Bielic, Vlac	Brankovic, Vlatko
Bilic, Radojica	Bratnovic, Zagor
Bogacic, Bolasin	Brativojevic, Ratko
Bogcinic, Radoje	Bratosalic, Bozicko
Bogosalic, Hotin	Crnicic, Milan
Bogdanic, Poznan	Crpovic, Vukosav
Boljunovic, Bogavac	Djurdjevic, Vukobrat

STANA DJURENOVIC • RADOSAV HERAKOVIC • VUKOSAVA LUPCIC

Djurenovic, Stana	Hrabren, Radoje
Dobrosinovic, Vukasin	Hrabren, Radosav
Dorlosevic, Dragic	Ivkovic, Grubac
Dragisic, Cvijetko	Jurisalic, Radomir
Drascic, Radivoj	Kablovic, Milutin
Draznic, Trivko	Komlinovic, Ivanis
Dubcevic, Vuksa	Krilic, Mileta
Ducic, Radosav	Krivousic, Radivoj
Golobovic, Veseoko	Kucmanic, Vukosav
Herakovic, Radosav	Lupcic, Vukosava

DABIZIV MARKOVIC • MILOBRAT MRCIC • IVAN PAVLOVIC

Markovic, Dabiziv	Milosevic, Viganj
Markovic, Vuk	Mitrovic, Vuksa
Markovic, Drasko	Mrcic, Milobrat
Marojevic, Milutin	Mrksic, Radoje
Marojevic, Vladisava	Mrsinic, Mirisava
Miletic, Dragilo	Novakovic, Dragoilo
Miloradovic, Petar	Novakovic, Vukasin
Miloradovic, Stjepan	Obradovic, Ivko

Obradovic, Radoje
Opodinvoic, Stojan

Ostojic, Ostoja
Pavlovic, Ivan

VESELICA PEROVIC • SRBISIN PRIMILOVIC • STAPAN TVRDANOVIC

Perovic, Veselica
Petrovic, Marko
Petrovic, Vukac
Picevic, Vukac
Primilovic, Milisav
Primilovic, Srbisin
Prpcinic, Milata
Puksic, Djuren
Radic, Milan
Radicevic, Radosav
Radojevic, Brajo

Radonic, Pavko
Radojevic, Radic
Radonic, Vukac
Radosalic, Radic
Radosalic, Stepko
Radovanovic, Miluta
Rakojevic, Radovan
Ratkovic, Radonja
Semirovic, Batric
Trkovic, Radoje
Tvrdanovic, Stapan

PRIRAD TVRDJENOVIC • RADIVOJ VLATKOVIC • DOBRIS VUKICEVIC

Tvrdjenovic, Prirad
Ucukalo, Gavro
Utolovic, Stojan
Verkovic, Branko
Veselinovic, Mihal
Vidojevic, Dragisc
Vladisalic, Radic
Vladisalic, Vladja
Vladjevic, Vukobrat
Vlasnic, Dobrovoj

Vlatkovic, Radivoj
Vucic, Radic
Vucic, Kurjak
Vucinic, Vukac
Vukanovic, Radovac
Vukcic, Bozidar
Vukcic, Radivoj
Vukcic, Vukic
Vukicevic, Blagoj
Vukicevic, Dobris

HUMKO VUKICEVIC • RADIC VUKMANOVIC • PAVAO ZUPANOVIC

Vukicevic, Humko
Vukicevic, Ivan
Vukicevic, Radosav
Vukmanovic, Radic
Vukmir, Milko

Vukotic, Vlatko
Vukovic, Rado
Vukovic, Vukca
Vuksanovic, Ljubo
Zupanovic, Pavao

NERETVA / HUM / ZAHUMLYA

The following series of personal-family names were recorded in Neretva/Zahumlya/Hum (Hercegovina) in the 13th, 14th, and 15th centuries.

VUCHINA BANOVIC • VUCHINA BRATILJEVIC • MIROSLAV DOBROMIROVIC

Banovic, Vuchina
Beckovic, Milac
Bielakovic, Djuro
Bogacevic, Vukoslav
Bogdancic, Ljubisa
Bogdanovic, Ljuben
Bogmilovic, Ljupko

Bjelanovic, Dabiziv
Brajanovic, Djurac
Braticevic, Cvijetko
Bratiljevic, Vucihna
Budisalic, Radivoj
Budisalic, Zivko
Dabisinovic, Radoje

155

Dabizivovic, Pavko
Dobrenovic, Milos
Dobric, Radoslav

Dobricijevic, Dobrilo
Dobrkovic, Radisa
Dobromirovic, Miroslav

GOJAK DOBROSALIC • BOGIC GOJNIC • VUKIC KOVACEVIC

Dobrosalic, Gojak
Dobrosalic, Vidak
Dobrovojevic, Radojko
Dobruskovic, Vitomir
Dragulinovic, Bozidar
Drazojevic, Zarko
Dubravcic, Vlatko
Gojakovic, Ugljesa
Gojkovic, Branilo
Gojnic, Bogic

Gorkovic, Brajan
Gradisalic, Radic
Grubicevic, Mirko
Jovanovic, Djero
Junakovic, Dabiziv
Klobucaric, Vukic
Kobiljacic, Vojislav
Komlenovic, Vlatko
Kosijer, Radovan
Kovacevic, Vukic

BOGDAN LJUBISIC • MILETA MILJANIC • VUKOTA MILUTONIC

Ljubisic, Bogdan
Marinjcic, Vuksa
Martic, Vratislav
Maslovic, Milogost
Medojevic, Tvrtko
Medvedovic, Ljubenko
Miladinovic, Radoja
Milatovic, Vukasin
Milicevic, Ostoja
Milisic, Gojko

Miljanic, Mileta
Miljanic, Radonja
Miljenovic, Vukinir
Milkovic, Dejan
Milobratic, Radic
Milogostic, Stanislav
Milosevic, Obrad
Milosevic, Radovac
Milovanovic, Radac
Milutonic, Vukota

DJURADJ MIRKOVIC • VUKOBRAT OSTOJIC • VUKDRAG RADICEVIC

Mirkovic, Djuradj
Mirosalic, Bogasin
Mrdejovic, Vukota
Novakovic, Bozidar
Obradovic, Vukasin
Orlovic, Gojslav
Ostojcic, Vukan
Ostojic, Radasin
Ostojic, Vukac
Ostojic, Vukobrat

Petanovic, Gojislav
Popovic, Dobroslav
Popovic, Krasoje
Preljubovic, Stan
Prvanovic, Radosav
Radasinovic, Matko
Radetic, Budisav
Radetic, Dobrun
Radicevic, Cvijetko
Radicevic, Vukdrag

RADONJA RADIBRATOVIC • OSTOJE RADOSALIC • BOGIC SLADENOVIC

Radibratovic, Radonja
Radilovic, Dobrivoje
Radisic, Mileta
Radisic, Vukasin
Radmilovic, Vukota
Radobratic, Radin

Radojevic, Prvoslav
Radojkovic, Djuradj
Radonjic, Vuk
Radosalic, Bogdan
Radosalic, Ostoje
Radosalic, Stojsav

Radovcic, Radibrat
Radovcic, Vladoje
Radulinovic, Obrad
Radusnovic, Utjesen

Ratkovic, Medo
Ratkovic, Milutin
Ratkovic, Stojko
Sladenovic, Bogic

NOVAK SLAVOGOSTIC • VUK VLADISALIC • PRIPKA ZORANOVIC

Slavogostic, Novak
Smilovic, Milisa
Stanjevic, Radivoj
Stankovic, Divac
Stojakovic, Dobrosav
Stojislavic, Dobrasin
Tihosalic, Gojak
Tvrdisalic, Mihoc
Vekojevic, Obren
Vladimirovic, Poznan
Vladisalic, Vuk
Vlatkovic, Vuksa
Vojnovic, Radivoj

Vojtanovic, Vukac
Vucihna, Radic
Vucinic, Mihailo
Vukcic, Radivoj
Vukicevic, Blagoje
Vukmanovic, Radic
Vukosalic, Vladimir
Vukosaljic, Dobroslav
Vukotic, Vukac
Zarkovic, Dobrota
Zarkovic, Radivoj
Zoranovic, Pripka

FEMALE PERSONAL NAMES

Cvijeta Pribojeva
Dobrila Dobrijevic
Gojisava Baosic
Jelena Vardic
Jelusa Stanisalic
Jerina Ivkovic
Jerina Vukocamic
Ljubica Vlatkovic
Mara Kalimanic
Milica Borovinic
Milica Simrakovic

Ninoslava Purcic
Radna Bogunovic
Radosava Radojevic
Radosava Vukcic
Stana Nikolic
Stanislava Nikolic
Stojsava Kopijevic
Vladislava Tezalovic
Vladna Brlica
Vukica Kalimanic

The following are some of the Bosnia-Hercegovina place names associated with the above personal and family names.

BISTRICA • BLATO • BUKOVICA

Babajaca
Banovici
Berisalici
Bijela Rudine
Bilece
Biograd
Bistrica
Bjelosalici
Bjelosavljevici
Blagaj

Blagajgrad
Blatnica
Blato
Bobovac
Boganovici
Bojici
Borac
Borovac
Bratac
Brateljevici

Brezna
Brloznik
Brod
Budimir
Bukovica
Capljina
Cernica
Crkvina
Crnac
Dabrica

DOBRUN • DOLJANI • DREZNICA

Dabru Polju
Divovici
Djedici
Dobrak
Dobromani
Dobrun
Doljani
Donje Bare
Donja Dreznica
Donja Presjenica

Dracevo
Dragicina
Dreznica
Dub
Dubostica
Dvorska
Gacko
Glamoc
Glavaticevo
Glasinac

Gorani
Gorazde
Gorica
Gorna Lukavica
Gornje Selo
Gornji
Dragaljevac
Grab
Grabovac

GRADAC • KAMEN, KLJUC

Gradac
Gradina
Gvozno
Gradnici
Hum
Humac
Humsko
Jablanica
Jabuka
Jasena

Kalinovik
Kamenica
Kamensko
Kijevci
Klobuk
Kljuc
Knespolje
Knezak
Knezina
Kobilja

Kokorina
Konjica
Konjsko
Kosor
Krusevo
Krvavo Polje
Kukavica
Kutine
Lastva
Ledinac

LUG • MEDJEDJA • MOKRI DOL

Lipa
Lipik
Lipovica
Lisicici
Livno
Loznica
Ljubjenica
Ljubinja
Ljubomir
Ljubuski

Ljusici
Ljuti Dol
Lug
Luka
Lukavica
Malesici
Medjedja
Medjurjecje
Miljanovici
Mokri Dol

Mokro
Most
Nekuk
Nevesinje
Novo Selo
Obalj
Oblja
Obod
Olovo

OSTROZAC • PONIKVE • PRESJEKA

Ostrozac
Ostruznica
Panik
Plana
Pobrdica
Podbrezje
Podgradac
Podgradinje
Podhum
Podubovac

Podvelez
Polica
Poljica
Ponikve
Praca
Prapratnica
Precani
Premilovo
Presjeka
Pribic

Priboj
Pridol
Pridvornica
Prilep
Priluka
Radmilja
Radisevina
Radmilovici
Raska Gora
Ravno

ROGATICA • STUDENCI • TREBINJE

Rogatica
Rudo
Seljani
Slatina
Sokol
Slivlje
Slivno
Snijeznica
Sopotnica
Srpski Sopotnik

Stanovi
Staribrod
Staro Selo
Staro Slano
Stojkovici
Stolac
Studenci
Stup
Svitava
Sumnjaci

Toplica
Trebijovi
Trebimlja
Trebinje
Treskavica
Trgovista
Trijebanj
Trn
Trnovica
Trnjacka

VISEGRAD • ZAGVOZD • ZBORNA GOMILA

Tvrdos
Velicani
Velika Gareva
Vidotina
Visegrad
Visocica
Vojkovici
Vojnici
Vranja Dubrava
Vranjevo Selo

Vrazici
Vrbica
Vrhovina
Vrhpolje
Zaborani
Zagorje
Zaselak
Zagvozd
Zalom
Zavala

Zborna Gomila
Zitomislici
Zivaljevici
Zivanja
Zlo Selo
Zvornik
Zupca
Zupci

DONJA LJUBOGOSTA • VELIKA DALJEGOSTA

The following are some of the place names with either the archaic Slavic prefix gost- or suffix -gost.

Cagost
Donja Ljubogosta
Gornja Ljubogosta
Goscanica
Gostilj

Gostovici
Mala Gostilja
Otigosce
Slavogostici
Ugosce

Velika Daljegosta
Vogosca
Zivogosce
Zgosca

Tombstones,
Medieval Bosnia

PART VI

1. SLAVIA

The thesis that the Slavs entered Germania from Poland in the 2ⁿᵈ century A.D. finds its most authoritative and comprehensive exposition in the research of a distinguished 19ᵗʰ century German historian and archaeologist, Reinhard Pallman.

In his 1865 magnum opus, *Die Geschichte der Volkerwanderung von der Gothenbekengrund bis zum tode Alarichs*, Pallman relates the advance of the Slavs with the retreat of the Goths, which, in turn, triggered the great migration of nations in the late second century. The Slav-based Volkerwanderung thesis, Pallman insists, is the only one consistent with the historical record and is confirmed by extensive archaeological evidence.

SLAVIA

Most scholars agree that the political borders of medieval *Slavia* ran along lines roughly corresponding with the borders of the former German Democratic Republic or East Germany (the districts of Rostock, Schwerin, Neubrandenburg, Berlin, Potsdam, Frankfurt, Magdeburg, Cottbus, Halle, Leipzig, Dresden, Erfurt, Gera, Chemnitz/ Karl Marx Stadt, and Suhl).

UNIVERSA SLAVIA

Medieval documents often refer to the this area as:

AD REGEM SLAVORUM

- *Ad regem Slavorum*
- *De Sclavia*
- *De Sclavania*
- *In partibus Sclavorum*
- *In patria Sclavorum*
- *In Regione Sclavorum*
- *In Slavis*
- *In Slavonico*
- *In Slavonicum*
- *Regio Slavorum*
- *Regio i Terra Slavorum*
- *Regnum Slavorum*
- *Sclavania*
- *Sclavanicas Terram*
- *Sclavanorum*
- *Sclavia*
- *Sclaviam*
- *Sclavinia*

TERRA SLAVORUM, UNIVERSA SLAVIA

- *Sclavinia occidentales*
- *Sclavinorum*
- *Sclavinium*
- *Sclavonia*
- *Sclavanum*
- *Slavenlande*
- *Slavia*
- *Slaviam*
- *Slavie*
- *Slavinorum regione*
- *Slavorum regione*
- *Terra Slavie*
- *Terra Slavinica*
- *Terra Slavorum*
- *Terram Slawie*
- *Universa Slavia*
- *Universae Slavorum*
- *Universa Terra Slavorum*

INNUMERABILES SCLAVOS

Medieval documents often refer to Germania's innumerable Slavs, to Slavs in great and greater numbers:

- *Cum Saxonibus et innumerabiles Sclavis*
- *Immensam Sclavorum multitudinem*
- *Innumerabiles Sclavos*
- *Magnam Sclavorum multitudinem*
- *Multamiliia paganorum*
- *Multiudo, Multitudines and Multitudinibus Sclavorum*
- *Populosissima natio*
- *Sclavania igitur, amplissima Germaniae provintia*

GENS SLAVONICA

Medieval documents are filled with references to *gens Slavonica*.

GENTEM SLAVORUM, SLAVORUM NACIONES

- *De Genere Sclavorum*
- *Gens Slavonica*
- *Gentem Slavorum*
- *Gentem Sclavenorum*
- *Gentesque Slavinorum*
- *Natio Sclavorum*
- *Omne Natione Slavorum*
- *Omnes Sclavani*
- *Omne Slavorum Genus*
- *Populi Sclavorum*
- *Slavicas Gentis*
- *Slavorum Gente*
- *Slavinorum Generationibus*
- *Slavinorum Gentes*
- *Slavorum Gentis*
- *Slavorum Naciones*
- *Slavorum Nationibus*
- *Slavorum Populi*
- *Slavorum Populus*
- *Universae Slavorum Naciones*

TERRA ET DE GENERE SCLAVORUM

There are numerous references to the Slav language, books, laws, customs, and institutions in the Slav lands (*in Terra et de genere Sclavorum*):

- *Homines Slavice Lingue*
- *Idioma Sclavonicaum*
- *Idioma Slavice Lingwe*
- *In Slavonica Lingua Canonica Horas Et Missasanica*
- *Ius Slavicum*
- *Leges Et Consuetudines Sclavicae Gentis*
- *Libros Sclavonicae Linguae*
- *Lingua Sclavanicam*
- *Lingua Sclavanique*
- *Lingua Sclavorum*
- *Lingua Slavicae*
- *Linguam Slavicam*
- *Sermone In Slavonicum Transtulit Idioma*
- *Sermone Sclavonicam In Linguam Transtulit*
- *Slavica Lingua*
- *Slavonica scripserat verba*

- *Slavonici milites ... unum equum, cum quo serviat domino*

SLAVORUM NACIONES

Medieval documents record **Slavia's** nations (*natio Sclavorum, omni natione Slavorum*) in the following typical terms:

DOXANI SLAVI, SCLAVOS QUI DICUNTUR LUSIKI

- *Doxani Slavi*
- *Rani gens Slavorum*
- *Sclavi autem Glomaci appellant*
- *Sclavi cognomento Winidi*
- *Sclavi Liutewizi*
- *Sclavi qui vocantur Dalmati et Behemii atque Sorabi*
- *Sclavi, qui vocantur Linones*
- *Sclavi, qui vocantur Siusli*
- *Sclavi quidam Lini cognomine dicti*
- *Sclavi Pomerani*
- *Sclavi Rugiacenses*
- *Sclavis qui dicuntur Vulini*
- *Sclavos, qui dicuntur Lusiki*

SCLAVOS QUI DICUNTUR WILTI • SORABOS SCLAVOS

- *Sclavos, qui dicuntur Wilti*
- *Sclavos, quos nos Vionudos dicimus*
- *Sclavos Milkianos*
- *Sclavi Wilzi ... id est sua locutione Veletabi dicuntur*
- *Sclavorum qui vocantur Abodriti*
- *Sclavorum nationibus Zerezepani*
- *Sclavorum rebellione Stoderaniam, que Hevellun dicitur*
- *Sclavos qui nominatur Bethenzr*
- *Sclavos qui nominatur Lana*
- *Sclavos Milkianos*
- *Sclavos, qui dicuntur Hevelli*
- *Sclavos, qui dicuntur Wilti*
- *Sclavos, qui Vucrani vocantur*
- *Sorabi Sclavos*
- *Sorabos Sclavos*

PROVINCIIS SCLAVORUM

The following are typical ethnonymic references to **Slavia's** *pagos, provincias, regioni,* and *terras*:

- *Gente Slavorum, in pago Dargun*
- *In pago lingua sclavorum zitice nominato*
- *In partibus Sclavonie ... in pago Dalminze vel Zlomeka*
- *In partibus Sclavonie ... in pago Nikiki vel Mezumorka*
- *In partibus Sclavonie ... in pago Scitici*
- *In partibus Slavonie ... in pago Havellon*

- *In Slaviam, Rugian vocitatam Theutonicus*
- *Ruiana, a Slavis autem Rana dicitur*
- *Inter Sclavos ... in pago Serimuntilante*
- *Provinciis Sclavorum ... Tolensani*
- *Provinciis Sclavorum Receni*
- *Provintia Sclavorum qui vocantur Riaderi*
- *Provintia Sclavorum Nizizi nominata*
- *Regioni Slaviae Waghere*
- *Slavorum et Vuinidon in pago Salagouue*
- *Terra Sclavinicam Siuseli nuncupatam*
- *Terra Sclavorum qui dicuntur Sorabi*

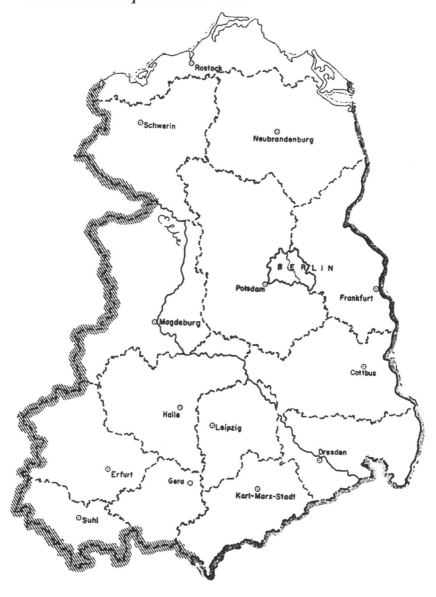

East Germany/Medieval Slavia

2. MILIDUCH, REX SUPERBUS, QUI REGNABAT SURBIS

Medieval German documents refer to *Slavia's* rulers as:

- *Domines Slavie*
- *Duces Slavorum*
- *Primores Slavorum*
- *Primores ac Reguli Sclavorum*
- *Princeps Slavorum*
- *Principes et Duces Sclavorum*
- *Principes et Duces et Primores Sclavorum*
- *Priores et Duces Sclavorum*
- *Reges Slavorum*
- *Reges Sclavaniorum*
- *Regulis et nobilitate Sclavorum*
- *Seniores Slavorum*
- *Satrapas Sclavorum*

RATIBOR, DUX SLAVORUM

Medieval documents abound with references to rulers with such integral Slav names as:

ANADRAG, GODOLIUB

Anadrag *(Princeps Slavorum)*
Barnimir *(dux Slavorum)*
Billug (Fursten der Abodriten)
Bogolub (Fursten der Stodorani)
Bolilut (Fursten der Hevelli)
Budivoj (Fursten der Abodriten)
Cedrag *(Ceadragus, rex Abodritorum)*
Chocimir *(princeps urbis Sirsipani)*
Dalm *(Duc Sclavicus Dalm corpulentus)*
Dervanus *(dux gente Subriorum)*
Dobemysl *(rex Abodritorum)*
Dobromir *(venerabili seniore Dobremiro)*
Dragovit *(rex Slavorum)*
Drasko *(Drosucus rex Abodritorum)*
Gnevos *(princips Winulorum)*
Godoliub *(Godelaibum alium ducem)*
Gnevomir (de Possaric)

GOSTIMYSL, RATIBOR

Gostimysl *(regem Slavorum Gestimulum)*
Jaksa (Knez Jaxa von Kopenick)
Jaromir *(Jaromanus die gracia princeps Ruianorum)*

Knez Jaksa of Berlin/Kopenick

Prince Pribislav of Branibor/Brandenburg

Prince Jaromir of Rugen

Kruto (obtinuitque dominium in universa terra Slavorum)
Liubo (Liubi regis Wilzorum)
Lubomir (Fursten der Abodriten)
Melito (Konig der Serben)
Miliduch (rex superbus, qui regnabat Surbis)
Milogost (Wilzenfursten Milegast)
Mstivoj (dux Slavanicus)
Nakon (Fursten der Abodriten)
Niklot (Fursten der Abodriten)
Pribignev (Sclavorum satrapas)
Pribina (Fursten der Mahrer)
Priznislav (Priznolawo quodam Sclavo duc)
Ratibor (princeps Pomoranie)

RATIBOR, ZISTIBOR

Ratibor (illustris princeps, dux Slavorum)
Semela (regem oerum nomine Semela)
Stoinev (Stoineffo barbaroum rege)
Svantepolk (Suantepolcus dei gracia dux Pomoranie)
Svemysl (Furst der Pomoranen)
Sventipolk (Fursten der Kessiner)
Svetipolk (Fursten der Abodriten)
Svetibor (Fursten der Abodriten)
Tugumir (dominus eorum ... dictus Tugumir)
Tunglo (unus de Soraborum primoribus)
Visan (regis Wizzien, regem Abodridtorum)
Vulk (Fursten, *Balsamorum regio*)
Wallucus (dux Winodorum)
Witzan (rex Abodritorum)
Wyrgeorn (rex Winidorum)
Ysmir (Ysmarum, regem Sclavorum)
Zelibor (Fursten der Wagrier)
Zistibor (Sorabi duce eius Zistiboro nomine)

BOGISLAV, DUX SLAVORUM UNIVERSIS

Throughout **Slavia,** in the north, south, east, and west one finds a high proportion of names with the ethnonym **Slav** as a prefix or suffix among the rulers.

BOGISLAV, PRIBISLAV

Bogislav (Bugislav dei gratia Dux Slavorum universis)
Bolislav (Fursten der Abodriten)
Borislav (Burislaf, Wendenfurst)
Czimislav (Konig der Colodici)
Dobeslav (de Wittow)
Grin/Grinislav (princips Adodritorum)
Jaroslav (dominus Jarozlaus)
Mislav (Fursten der Gutzkow)

Mislav *(Mizlaus, princeps Uznomie)*
Mstislav *(Mistizlaum seniorem)*
Pribislav (Fursten von Brandenberg)
Pribislav (Fursten der Abodriten)

PRISLAV, VRTISLAV

Prislav (Fursten von Mecklenburg)
Priznoslav *(Priznolawo quodam Sclavo duce)*
Rastislav *(reges Abodritorum)*
Slavibor *(Zlawboris comitis)*
Slavomir *(Abodritorum rex)*
Stojslav III *(de Putbus)*
Sulislav *(de Cavitz)*
Teslav (Fursten von Rugen)
Vartislav *(dux Pomeranie)*
Ventislav (Fursten der Heveller)
Vislav *(Wizeslavs die gracia Rivianorum dominus)*
Vratislav *(Warizslavs de gracia dux Slavorum)*
Vrtislav (Fursten von Mecklenburg)

WISLAV, WARTISLAV, BOGISLAV

Two great houses of the north, the Wislavs (I-III) of Rugen, the Wartislavs (I-X) and Bogislavs (I-XIV) of Pomerania were no doubt responsible for the spread of such names among the upper classes in non-Slavic Baltic lands. Thus the personal/family name Bogislav in Prussia and elsewhere: Ernst Bogislav van Segebaden Saxony; Gustav Bogislav van Segebaden; Tetze Slaweke van dem Rosengarden; Slavkovitz de Stangenberg.

Vartislav II *(dux Pomeranie)*
Vartislav III *(dux de Demmin)*
Vartislav IV *(dux de Voligost)*
Vartislav IX *(dux de Voligost)*
Vartislav X *(dux Voligost)*
Bogislav II *(dux de Stetin)*
Bogislav IV *(dux de Voligost/Wolgast)*
Bogislav IX *(dux de Stolpe)*
Bogislav X *(dux Pomeranie)*

MIROSLAVA, SLAVORUM DUCISSA

The ethnonym Slav is often featured in the names of prominent princesses and duchesses:

Bogislava   **Pribislava**
Dobroslava   **Slavinia**
Grimislava   **Svetoslava**
Miroslava   **Voyislava**
                       Zvinislava

3. ZEMI LUZICKYCH SRBU, KDE VLADL SLAVIBOR

Some measure of the high status of the rulers of *Germania/Slavia's* principalities, dukedoms, and kingdoms is found in diverse sources.

REX NAKON

In the mid-10th century, circa 965, for example, Ibrahim ibn Jaqub, an oft-cited authority on the Slavic lands of Europe, numbers **rex Nakon,** *Fursten der Abodriten,* one of the most important Slavic rulers, along with the rulers of Poland, Bohemia, and Bulgaria. **To the west the land of Nakon borders on Saxony and some of the Danes. The land has so many horses that they are exported. They [Abodrites] have complete sets of arms, that is coats of armour, helmets and swords ... Nakon's capital is called Wiligrad which means the great city.**

WILIGRAD (VELGRAD)

Excavations confirm Wiligrad's medieval status. Regarding its relative size, J. Herrmann writes: **Wiligrad was indeed one of the largest Slav defensive structures on the whole Baltic coast; its wall, made of earth and stone and timber-framed, was more than 10 meters high and 12 meters thick, and the area enclosed was about 15,000 square meters. Only the fort of the Polish rulers further south at Gniezno was of comparable size** *(J. Herrmann, The Northern Slavs, The Northern World, 1980).*

ALLIANCES

More important are the following political-military alliances, via marriage, with the great dynasties of Bohemia, Poland, Denmark, and Sweden.

Bohemia

Circa 894, St. **Ludmila,** martyr, patroness of Bohemia (860-921), a native of **Serbska Luzica (ze zeme srbske; zemi Luzickych Srbu, kde vladl Slavibor),** daughter of duke Slavibor *(srbskeho knizete dcera; filiam Zlauboris, comitis ex provincia Sclavorum),* married **Borivoi I,** the first Christian duke of Bohemia. Baptized at Velehrad by St. Methodius, she and her husband struggle to introduce Slavonic priests, Slavonic liturgical texts and Graeco-Slavonic civilization into Bohemia.

Bohemia

A 906 marriage of *Princess Dragomira,* sister of Duke Tugumir, 'Konig der Heveller,' with *Vratislav I* **(be ze knez velik slavoju v Cecha zivyi imenem Vorotislav i zena ego Dorogomir rodista ze syna perven'ca i jako krstitsta i narekosa ime emu Veceslav),** allies *Slavia/Haveland* with the founding and ruling Premysl dynasty of Bohemia. The long and brilliant rule of Dragomira's son, Boleslav I (929-967) established Bohemia as a power in Central and Eastern Europe *(G. Labuda, Drahomira, SsS 1,1961. H.Ludat, Branibor, havolanska dynaties a Premyslovci, CcH 17, 1969).*

Germania

In his excellent 981 study, *Slaven an Havel und Spree. Studien zur Geschichte des Hevellisch-Luzischen Furstentums,* the noted German historian, L. Dralle, notes that at the time of Dragomira's marriage to Vratislav of Bohemia, there was another marriage of equal or greater status, namely the marriage of a member of the Hevellic dynasty to young **Otto** of Germany, a union that was followed by a period of coexistence that came to an end when the Liudofingians acquired the German crown.

Poland

A 963 marriage, that of **Dobrava**, Dragomira's granddaughter, with **Mieszko** (962-992), not only allies Bohemia with the founding and ruling Piast dynasty of Poland, but the conversion of Mieszko and Poland under Bohemian auspices changes the course of Polish history.

Poland

A 963 marriage, that of **Princess Emnildis**, daughter of *rex Dobromir*, with Mieszko's son, **Boleslav the Brave**/Chobry (992-1025), Poland's first king, allies **Slavia/ White Serbia** with one of the periods' most able statesmen *(T. Wasilewski, L'origine d'Emnilda troisieme femme de Boleslav le Vaillant et la genese da la souverainete polonaise sur la Moravie, ApH 61, 1990).* A gifted commander, in support of his son-in-law, Prince Sviatopolk, Boleslav led a successful expedition to Kiev. With Boleslav's assistance, Erik of Sweden was able to defeat Denmark and gain supremacy in Scandinavia.

Denmark

A 967 marriage, that of **Princess Tovi**, daughter of Duke Mstivoj, with **Harald I Bluetooth**, King of Denmark (945-986), the first of the Jelling dynasty who, in the words inscribed on a huge runic stone, won all of Denmark and Norway and converted the Danes to Christianity, and allied **Slavia/Abodritorum** with the greatest power in Scandinavia *(G. Labuda, Harald Gormson, SsS 2, 1964).* A runic stone found in Jutland bears the inscription: **Tovi, Mistivoi's daughter, wife of Harald the Good, Gorm's son, had this memorial made for her mother.**

Denmark

Norse sagas record the marriage of Harald Bluetooth's son, **Svein I** Forkbeard, King of Denmark (986-1014), founder of an Anglo-Danish kingdom, with **Gunhild**, daughter of Wendenfurst Burislav. The historical record only speaks of Svein's marriage with **Piast Princess Svetoslava.**

Sweden

A 1000 marriage, that of **Princess Estred**, daughter of Duke Mstidrag (**filiam Sclavorum Estred nomine de Obodritis**), with **Olaf Skotokonung**, the first Christian King of Sweden (995-1022), son of Eric the Victorious (975-995) and Svetoslava, daughter of Piast Mieszko and Premyslid Dobrava, allies **Slavia/Abodritorum** with Sweden *(G. Labuda, Olaf Skotkonnumg, SsS 3, 1967).*

Sweden

In the same year or so, a second marriage, Edmund, son of King Olaf, grandson of Svein and Sviatoslava, with Princess Edla, **Slavischen Furstentochter Edla**, daughter of the Duke of Wendland, allies **Wendland** with Sweden.

Denmark

Early 11th century sources record Abodrite **Duke Uto/Pribignev's** marriage to a

Danish woman, the mother of his son and successor, Duke Gottschalk (*materno genere Danus*).

Denmark

A 1010 marriage of ***Wrytegor, rex Winidorum,*** with the sister of Canute I the Great, one of Denmark's greatest rulers, after 1015, King of all England, allies ***Winidorum*** with the mighty ruler of Denmark, Norway and England.

Denmark

A 1053 marriage, that of Duke ***Gottschalk,*** son of Budivoj, with ***Sigrid,*** sister of Denmark's Svein II Estridson (1042-1074), nephew of Canute the Great, allies ***Slavia-Abodritorum*** with Denmark.

Christendom

As late as the 12th century neighboring kings, who were Christian, found it in their best interest to pay honor to a pagan Slav god. **And this idol [Svarog as Svetivid at Arkona on Rugen], to which all Slavs paid such heed was also visited by neighbouring kings, Christian kings, like the Danish Sven, who brought gifts** (Saxo).

SCANDINAVIA

That such alliances with *Slavia* could have and had important consequences for Scandinavia's domestic and foreign affairs is demonstrated by several episodes. In the late 11th century, after defeat by his son, Harald I fled to safety in *Slavia.* **Severely wounded, Harald himself fled from the battle, boarded a ship and escaped to Jumne, the most renowned city of the Slavs. There he was kindly received, contrary to his expectations, for the people were barbarians** (Helmold).

SVEIN I

In the mid-12th century, King Svein of the Danes, forced from the throne, fled to safety to Starigard/Oldenburg in *Slavia.* After Svein's alliance with the Saxons failed to recover the throne: **Adopting another course and plan, [Svein] decided to go over to the Slavs ... He went over to Niclot, the prince of the Abodrites. The duke ordered the Slavs in Oldenburg and in the land of the Abodrites to help Svein** (*Helmold*). Thanks to Slav help in men and ships, in the tri-partite division of the Danish kingdom that followed, the greater part, Scania, esteemed as superior in men and arms, went to Svein.

ENGLAND

Suffice to say at this point that the 11th century finds *Slavia's* Slavs side by side with Danes at Canterbury and other battlefields and victories that lead to England's conquest in 1015. Regarding a later Slav moment in the first half of the 11th century, Udo/Pribignev's brave and warlike son, prince Gottschalk, Helmold writes: **Went to the king of the Danes, Cnut, and remained with him many days and years, winning for himself glory by his valour in various warlike deeds in Normany and in England. Wherefore, also, was he honored with the hand of the king's daughter.**

GERMANIA, SCANDINAVIA

In the later medieval period it was common for the leading Slav families of the north, of *regios Obodritorum, Luticiorum, Rugianorum, and Pomeranorum,* to intermarry with leading German, Danish, and Scandinavian families. In fact, the intermarriage was of such scope that few princely families of the north were without varying degrees of blood ties with *Slavia.* Some insight into this factor is found in the marital bonds that tie the ruling families of Rugen, Pomerania, and Denmark together, a terribly complex moment reduced to considerable order and clarity in articles by H. Hannes *(Auf den Spuren des Griefengeschlechtes in Danemark. Denkmaler Erzahlen von den vergindungen der Pommerschen und der Danischen Dynastie, Bal 74, 1987)* and U. Schell *(Uber die Herren de Ruya und ihr Verhaltnis zum rugischen Furstenhause sowie uber andere Adelsfamilein in Rugen und Pommern, Bal 73, 1987).*

Slavo Del Illiryco   Slavo Del Mar Germanica

IL
REGNO
DE GLI SLAVI
HOGGI CORROTTAMENTE
DETTI SCHIAVONI.
HISTORIA
DI DON MAVRO ORBINI RAVSEO
ABBATE MELITENSE.

Nella quale si vede l'Origine quasi di tutti i Popoli, che furono della Lingua SLAVA, con molte, & varie guerre, che fecero in Europa, Asia, & Africa; il progresso dell'Imperio loro, l'antico culto, & il tempo della loro conuertione al Christianesimo.

E in particolare veggonsi i successi de' RA, che anticamente dominarono in DALMATIA, CROATIA, BOSNA, SERVIA, RASSA, & BVLGARIA.

IN PESARO,
Appresso Girolamo Concordia. Con licenza de' Superiori.
M DCI

4. REX GERMANORUM, POPULOS SCLAVORUM

Given the Slavic character of central and eastern Germany, it is not surprising that German and foreign documents sometimes refer to German kings as *kings of the Slavs, kings of Slavorum.*

844. *Ludewicus rex* is **Hlodowicus rex Germanorum, populos Sclavorum.**
851. **Ludouicus rex Sclauos.**
861. **Hlodowici regis Germaniae filius, cum Resticio Winidorum.**

LAND OF THE SLAVS

One finds the same notion in diverse Arab sources. In the mid-9th century, for example, Muhammed Khuwarzimi, an important Arab mathematician, astronomer, and geographer, refers to Germany as the land of the Slavs:

Gharmaniya, which is the land of the Sakaliba *(Surut al-Ard).*

KING OF THE SLAVS

Fluent in the language of the Slavs, Emperor Otto I's identification with his Slav subjects was so strong that contemporary Arab sources sometimes refer to him in the words of Cordoban chroniclers:

Otto I, King of the Slavs.

REX SLAVORUM

The *Chronicon S. Michaelis Luneburgensis* (1127) refers to Heinrich (1106-25) as *rex Slavorum:*

> **Occisus est etiam Henricus rex Slavorum, cuius corpus delatum Luneburg septultumque in ecclesia sancti Michaelis.**

DANORUM SLAVORUMQUE REX

In the 13th century, Danish rulers dominated northern Germany's **Slavia** (*civibus Lubisensibus, Wismeeridenbus, Roztokiensibus, Stralessundis, Gripeswaldis, Sthetynensibus ceterisque civibus,* **ac allis universis per slaviam constitutis**). Danish rulers titled themselves Kings of Denmark and **Slavia (Danorum Sclavorumque rex)** and laid claim to **omnes terras inter Eidram et Albiam fluvios sitas ad imperium pertinentes, videlicet a descensu Eidre in mare usque ad aquam Leuoldesowe et ab eadem aqua usque ad mare, terras Burwini et omnes terra Slavie pret Rugiam et terras ei attinentes imperio dimittere debet.**

- *Waldemarus Dei gratia Danorum Slavorumque Rex, 1230*
- *Critoforus, dei gracia Danorum Slavorumque rex, 1232*
- *Margaretha dei gracia Danorum Sclavorumque regina, 1264*
- *Ericus dei gracia Danorum Slavorumque rex, 1280*
- *Ericus [Erich Menved] dei gracia danorum sclavorumque rex, 1287*
- *Agnes dei gracia danorum sclavorumque regina, 1287*

5. CIVITAT SRBICI

Medieval documents abound with ethnonymic references to *Slavia's* great towns and cities (*metropolis Sclavorum and civitas Slavorum*).

- Jena *(in Sclavico Jene)*
- Leipzig *(Usque Liptzk Slavorum Civitatem Pervenit)*
- Lubeck *(Civitatem Sclavorum, Quae Dicitur Liubicen)*
- Mecklenburg *(Miklenburg, Civitas Slavorum)*
- Rethra *(Metropolis Sclavorum Rethre)*
- Starigrad/Oldenburg *(Aldenburg, Slavica Lingua Starigard)*
- Wolin *(Civitas Slavorum Jumne)*

GARDARIKI

The Scandinavians called the land of the eastern Slavs the *land of forts* or *Gardarike*. The term was even more fitting for *Slavia,* where castle-towns were the focal points of settlement and of economic, social, religious, and cultural life, with several thousand found in the area between the Oder and Elbe.

CIVITATES

The areas of settlement around the forts varied in size from six to twenty or more villages and were known as *civitates* in Latin.

CIVITAT BELA GORA

The following *civitates* with quintessential Slav names are from the Serb heartland between the Neisse and Saale rivers, hereafter referred to as *White Serbia* (original name, followed by Latin citation and date).

BARBOGI, DOBLIN

Barbogi (*Sclavi Ad Barbogi Civitatem*, 964)
Bela Gora (*Civitate Quae Dicitur Belegora*, 983)
Budusin (*Civitas Budusin*, 1002)
Bukov (*Civitas Buchoe*, 946)
Bukovnici (*Civitas Buchownici,* 965)
Businc (*Civitas Businc*, 1015)
Chorin (*Civitatem Corin nominatam*, 983)
Chutic (*Civitat Chut*, 1004)
Cuski (*Civitas Cuskiburg*, 993)
Doblin (*Civitas Dobelin*, 1350)

DOBRA GORA, GVOZDEC

Dobra Gora (*Civitas Dobrogora*, 973)
Dobri Lug (*Qui Dobraluh Dicitur*, 1005)
Domici (*Civitas Dommitz*, 992)
Drezdane (*in Civitate Nostra Dresden*, 1216; Drazdan, 1432; Drazden, 1448)
Dreze: (*Civitas Driezele*, 1011)
Glomaci (*Civitas Lomacz*, 1286)

Gostovici (***Civitas Goztuissi***, 1004)
Grabov (***Civitas Grabaw***, 946)
Grodic (***Civitas Grothisti***, 1004)
Gvozdec (***Citivas et Castellum Gozcoburch***, 979)

HUM, LUBOCHIN

Hum (***Civitas Holm***, 961; Stephanus de Chulme, 1222)
Ilov (***Civitas Ilburg***, 961)
Izgorjelc (***Civitat nostra Gorlicz***, 1322)
Kamenc (***Civitas Kamenz***, 1248)
Kamenica (***Civitate Kemnitz***, 1254)
Komoran (***Civitat Gumbere***, 965)
Lipsk (***Usque Liptzk Slavorum Civitatem Pervenit***, 1193)
Loponec (***Loponoh Civitas***, 961)
Luban (***Civitas Luban***, 1268)
Lubochin (***Civitas Liubochili***, 1004)

LUBOR, NIZEM

Lubor (***Civitas Luborn***, 965)
Luboraz (***Civitas Lubraz***, 1302)
Liubsi (***Liubsi***, 1004)
Lubusa (***Civitat Liubusa***, 1012)
Lucin (***Civitas Lucin***, 1269)
Lutin (***Civitas Liutinburch***, 979; Lutyn, 1217)
Mesibor (***Mersiburc Civitas***, 1150)
Misin (***Civitate Misin***, 968)
Mroscina (***Civitas Mroscina***, 1004)
Nizem (***Civitat Nizem***, 948)

OLESNICA, SKUDICI

Olesnica (***Civitas Olsnik***, 992)
Ostrog (***Antiqua Civitate Ostros***, 1326)
Pec (***Civitat Pechoui***, 946)
Plisna (***Aldenburch, Que Alio Nomine Plisne Nuncupatur***, 976)
Plot (***Civitat Plot***, 948)
Radobyl (***Civitas Rodobile***, 973)
Rusavin (***Civitas Russewyn***, 1286)
Sirtava (***Civitas Sirtavua***, 946)
Skolin (***Civitat Zcolm***, 1017)
Skudici (***Scudici Civitas***, 981)

SRBICI, TREBUS

Srbici (***Civitat Curbici***, 1015)
Srbiste (***Civitas Zirwisti***, 1007)
Srtava (***Civitat Surtavua***, 940)
Stobi (***in Stuwi Civitate***, 1012)
Storkov (***in Marchia, Quie Dicitur Luzist ... Urbis et Civitatis Sturkuowe***, 1200)

Stosin (*de Civitate Stosen*, 1300)
Strela (*Civitatem Ztrele*, 1210)
Sulpiza (*Civitas Sulpize*, 968)
Trebin (*Civitas Trebeni*, 1430)
Trebus (*Civitat Triebus*, 1004)

TRNOV, ZVENKOV

Trnov (*Civitat Trnov*, 800)
Tuchovici (*Civitas Quae Tuchamuzi Vocatur*, 1046)
Visoka (*Civitat Wizoka*, 948)
Vitin (*Civitas Vitin*, 961)
Vran (*Civitat Vuronoizi*, 993)
Vrbin (*Civitas et Castellum Uuirbin*, 979)
Vresa (*Civitat Frohse*, 1025)
Vurcin (*Vurcini civitas*, 961)
Zitava (*Civitatis Sittaw*, 1283)
Zlopisti (*Civitas Zloupisti*, 1004)
Zulbica (*Civitat Zulbiza*, 995)
Zvenkov (*Civitas Zuenkouua*, 974)

SLAVORUM CASTELLIS

There are also numerous references to castles in **Slavia** (*Slavorum castellis*) and castles with integral Slavic names. The following series is from **White Serbia** (original name followed by Latin citation and year).

BARUTH, GODIVO

Baruth (*Castrum Baruth et Bona*, 1319)
Budisko (*Castello ... Budisko Nominato*, 979)
Budysin (*Castrum Budesin*, 1144)
Chojno (*Castrum in Koyne*, 1320)
Cerin (*Castellum Cirin*, 1012)
Difnosedlo (*Castrum Tyfenowe*, 1082)
Doblin (*Castellum Doblin*, 1350)
Domic (*Castellum Domuki*, 981)
Drevsk (*Castrum in Dreyzic*, 1297)
Godivo (*Castellum Godibi*, 1007)

GOLISIN, KAMBOR

Golisin (*Castrum Golsin*, 1301)
Gomila (*Castella Gummere*, 973)
Grabov (*Castrum Grabow Cum Terris et Villis Adiacentibus*, 1306)
Gradista (*Castellum Grodista*, 962)
Grobsk (*Castrum Gropceke*, 1291)
Grodc (*Castrum Goriz*, 1225)
Gvozdec (*Castrum Nomine Gvozdec Propre Urbem Misen*, 1123)
Gvozno (*Castellum et Hwoznie Nuncupata in Pago Dalminze*, 981)
Jarchov (*Castrum et Villa Jericho*, 1148)

Kambor (***Castro meo Kamburch***, 1166)

LESAN, MOYBIN

Lesan (***Castrum in Lesna***, 1247)
Lisinik (***Castrum Lisnik***, 1188)
Loztov (***Castella Loztoue***, 973)
Lubnjov (***Castrum Lubenow***, 1315)
Lubus (***Castrum Lubus***, 1226)
Lucin (***Castrum Lutzin***, 1330)
Lutin (***Castellum Lutin***, 1217)
Medebor (***Castellum Quod Medeburu Vocatur***, 1012)
Milov (***Castrum Milow***, 1145)
Moybin (***Castrum Oywin***, 1315)

NIVETRY, PRISLAV

Nivetry (*Nyweter*, 1327; ***Castrum Netro***, 1452)
Ostrog/Ostrozin (***Castellum Ostrusna***, 1007)
Pec (***Castellum Pechouue***, 965)
Polznica (***Castrum Polsnicz***, 1350)
Prislav (***Castro Quod Prizlava Dicitur***, 1056)
Ratin (***Castro Ratny***, 1361)
Ravno (***in Castro Ronaw***, 1268)
Rogodez (***Castellum Rochedez***, 1074)
Stolpin (***Castro Stolpen***, 1405)
Sedlo (***Castrum de Sydlo***, 1243)

SKOLANI, VRAN

Skolani (***Castrum Schalon***, 1018)
Svetic (***Castellum Zuetie***, 981)
Todic (***Castrum Teuditz***, 1321; *Thoiditz*, 1436)
Trebista (***Castellum Trebista***, 1006)
Trnov (***Castrum Trnov***, 800)
Tuchorin (***Castello Tuchern***, 1150)
Vran, Vranes (***Castrum Wraneschen***, 1144)
Vrbin (***Castro Wirben***, 1135)
Zadel (***in pago Castri Zadil***, 1074)
Zatim (***Castrum Sathim***, 1140)
Zavis (***Castellum Zavviza***, 1046)
Zitici (***Castrum in Cicze***, 1228)

GRADS

In addition to a good number of **Bel-grads, Novi-grads Stari-grads, Vise-grads** and **Vel-grads** and other such **grads** (e.g. *Cuninggarod, Gramaningorod, Kerlingorod,* and *Nubgrad*), a large number of fortified settlements are identified simply as **grads**. The same is true of **grad** 'suburbs' or **podgrads** that sprang up beneath the castle walls.

WHITE SERBIA

The following series of **grads** and **podgrads** is limited to *White Serbia* (original name followed by Latin or German citation, year, and location in terms of a nearby modern town or city).

GRADEC, GRODCANE

Gradec (Johannes De Gardiz, 1259, Zerbst)
Gradec (*Allodium* Grocz, 1360, Eisenberg)
Gradec (Groten Gardes, 1364; *Propre Soltwedel)*
Gradic (*Villa* Grautitz, 1240, Torgau)
Grodc (Grotz, 1506, Schonebeck)
Grodc (Groiz, 1225, Plauen)
Grodc (Bym Groitzsch, 1530, Otterwisch)
Grodc (Groicz, 1217, Eilenberg)
Grodc (Grocz, 1560, Eisenberg)
Grodc (*Grousch Antiqua*, Aldingroycz, 1378, Leipzig)
Grodc (Groyczs, 1378, Nossen)
Grodcane (*Villam Quondam Groutsene Dicta*, 1264, Graitschen)
Grodcane (Groyczen, 1377, Jena)
Grodcane (Grodzane, 1040, Camburg)

GRODCANE, GRODNO

Grodcane (*Villa Quondam Groutsene Dicta*, 1264, Dorndorf)
Grodcane (in Groczene, 1366, Calbe)
Grodcane (de Groyschen, 952, Gera)
Grodcane (Grozene, 1211, Halle)
Grodice (Im Burgward Woz, 1071, Gau Nisane)
Grodiscane (*in Villa Grodizan*, 1154, Zeitz)
Grodisce (Grodisti, 991, Naumberg)
Grodisce (Grodisti, 965, Gau Nizizi)
Grodisce (de Gorthizte, 1162, Lubben)
Grodisce (de Grodiz, 1217, Riesa)
Grodisce (*Czaslav de Grodis*, 1381, Weissenberg)
Grodisce (Grodisch, 1623, Forst)
Grodisce (Crupa, Zebechuri, Crodesti, 880, Halle)
Grodno (Groden, 1346, Elsterwerd)

PODGRADS

The **grad** suburbs or **podgrads** were generally surrounded by a wall or earth and timber like the castle-town itself.

Podgrodici (*villa Podegrodici*, 976; *Villa Podegrodiz in Pede Montis Puzowe*, 1151, Bosau)
Podgrodici (Podegrodici, 976, Altenberg)
Podgrodici (Podegradiz, 1313; Podgradicz, 1378, Dobeln)
Podgrodici (*Poppo de Podgrodis*, 1221; Podgraditz, 1243, Oschatz)
Podgrodici (Pogeritz, 1347, Halle)

Podgrodici (Pothegrodice, 1157; Podegruz, 1288, Wettin)
Podgrodici (Podegroitz, 976, Zeitz)
Podgrodze (Podegros, 1521; Poderosche, 1721, Rothenberg)
Podgrodici (Padegricz, 1378; Wusten Podegriczsch, 1411, Dresden)

SLAVIA, GERMANIA

In addition, in Germania east and west of the Elbe, outside the historic borders of **White Serbia,** many more *Grads, Podgrads, Prigrads,* and *Zagrads* are recorded (e.g. Gradac, Gradcik, Gradcin, Gradec, Gradisce, Gradisko, Gradno, Gradovo, Gradzov).

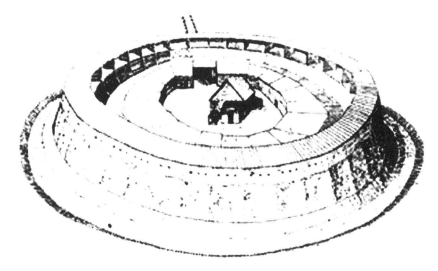

Grad (Regnum Soraborum)

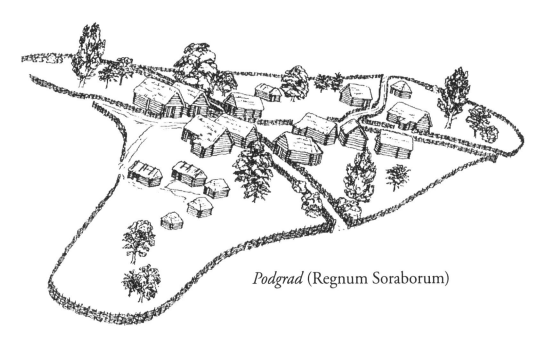

Podgrad (Regnum Soraborum)

6. SRBIN-DORF

There are many direct ethnonymic references to **Slavia's** Slavic communities in medieval German sources, many with apparent or real German names (e.g. *Suabehusa slavica*).

VICO SLAVONICORUM, SLAVANICAS CALUO

Ascolveswenden (*vico Slavonicorum*)
Baudisin (*villa sclavica*)
Byere (*Slavicum Byere*)
Blekede (*Slavicum Blekede*)
Boetze (*Slavico Boetze*)
Boor (*Boor Slavonicum*)
Borswicz (*Borswicz Slavica*)
Burchstede (*Sclavica Burchstede*)
Butstat (*Butstat Schlavorum*)
Caluo (*Slavanicas Caluo*)

SLAVICA CHUDEN, SLAVICALIS DOLSLEBEN

Ceten (*Slavicalia ...Cetene*)
Chuden (*Slavica Chuden*)
Clenobie (*Sclavonice Clenobie*)
Crimpelsdorf (*Slavica villa*)
Doberan (*villa Slavica*)
Cowal (*Cowal Slavicalis*)
Dolen (*Slavicalia ... Dolene*)
Donstede (*Slavica Donstede*)
Dorfern (*Slavicalis Dorfern*)
Dosleben (*Slavicalis Dolsleben*)

SLAVICUM DUSNIK, SLAVICALI GYSCHOWE

Dusnik (*Slavicum Dusnik*)
Ganzov (*Slavicalia Ganzove*)
Gene (*in Slavico Gene*)
Glusinge (*Sclavicis Glusinge*)
Goretin (*Slavos Gorentin*)
Gromazle (*Sclavicalia Gromaszle*)
Gumthouwe (*nova vlla Slavicalis*)
Guriz (*Slavos in Guriz*)
Gutzin (*ville Slavicalis*)
Gyschowe (*Slavicali Gyschowe*)

INSULA VILLA SLAVICA, SLAVICALIS KUSTRINKIN

Insula (*in Insula villa Slavica*)
Jevenitze (*Slavicalem Jevenitze*)
Jezne (*Slavi de Jezne*)
Kardestorpe (*Slavicalia Kardestorpe*)

Khyz (*vicus Slavicalis*)
Kolov (*Slavicalia Kolove*)
Konov (*Slavicalia Konove*)
Kroditze (*Slavicalia Kroditze*)
Kummerviz (*villam Slavicalem*)
Kustrinkin (*Slavicalis Kustrinkin*)

SCLAVOS LOCHOWO, SLAVICALIA IN MULTZENE

Lochowo (*Sclavos Lochowo*)
Lypa (*villae Slavicales Lypa Inferior et Lypa Superior*)
Malotin (*in Sclavonice Malacin in Teutonica Egisvilla*)
Marbech (*Sclavorum de Marbeche*)
Metniz (*Slavicum Metniz*)
Morungen (*Morungen Propre Stendal Slavitica villa*)
Mose (*Mose Sclavorum*)
Motzov (*Slavicalis Motzov*)
Mulinge (*in Villa Mulinge Slavorum*)
Multzene (*Slavicalia in Multzene*)

VICO SLAVONICORUM, SLAVICUM POGATZ

Nazenrad (*vico Slavonicorum*)
Niendorp (*ville Slavicalis*)
Noide (*villa Slavica*)
Novente (*Slavicalia in Novente*)
Nuthilikesvelde (*Slavica Villa*)
Oberhaid (*Slavuis in Haida*)
Otliva (*Slavonice Otlivva*)
Pazelicz (*Pazelicz Slavicum*)
Plot (*Slavi de Polthe*)
Pogatz (*Slavicum Pogatz*)

SLAVICALI POKLENTZE, SLAVICA SAARINGEN

Poklentze (*Sclavicali Poklentze*)
Prester (*Slavicis Prestere*)
Priessnitz (*in Vulgari Nomine Dictam Presnize*)
Rammershorn (*Sclavis Rammershorn*)
Rashuwicz (*Slavica Rashuwicz*)
Redemutzle (*Slavos in Redemutzle*)
Ricze (*Slavicalis Ricze*)
Rodenvort (*Slavica Rodenvort*)
Rustenbek (*Slavicalem Rustenbeke*)
Saaringen (*Slavica Saaringen*)

SCLAVICO SALBEKE, STENDAL SLAVITICA

Salbek (*Sclavico Salbeke*)
Scheldorp (*Slavicalemque Scheldorp*)
Schiltbach (*Slavicam Vocatam*)

Scholene (*Sclavi in Scholene*)
Scorstorpe (*Slavicalia Scorstrope*)
Sethorp (*Slavicum Sethorp*)
Sinov (*Slavicam Sinow*)
Slikov (*Slavicalia in Slikove*)
Steinbruch (*Steinbruche Sclavorum*)
Stendal (*Stendal Slavitica*)

SUABEHUSA SLAVICA, SLAVICALI IN ZACHEUE

Suabehus (*Suabehusa Slavica*)
Surznic (*Sclavica Surznic*)
Tzibelin (*Slavicalia Tzibelin*)
Uraso (*Sclavanicas in Uraso*)
Wiriben (*Sclavis Wiribeni*)
Wolimirstaedt (*in Slavischen Sprache Ustiure*)
Wulcow (*Wulcow villam Quoque Que Slavica Wulcow Eademque et Minor Vulsow Dicitur*)
Zarentin (*Slavicalis Zarenthin*)
Zacheu (*Slavicalia in Zacheue*)

SLAV

One finds the ethnonym ***Slav*** in the root-name of numerous towns and villages, including, among many others:

SLAV, SLAVOMIRICI, SLAVUTOV

Slava	Slavno
Slavanka	Slavoborici
Slavatic	Slavokoty
Slavek	Slavomir
Slavetin	Slavomirici
Slavia	Slavonia
Slavibor	Slavoroty
Slavici	Slavosic
Slavin	Slavotic
Slavkojce	Slavotin
Slavkotici	Slavovic
Slavkov	Slavsici
Slavkovici	Slavtici
Slavlici	Slavutov

BRATOSLAV

One also finds the ethnonym ***Slav*** in the suffix of villages with personal and family names.

BUDISLAV, GOSTISLAV, MIROSLAV

Badeslav	Budislav
Berislav	Bogislav

Bojslav
Branislav
Bratislav
Caslav
Chotislav
Domaslav
Drzislav
Goreslav
Goslav

Gostislav
Krasislav
Ludislav
Maloslav
Mecislav
Metislav
Miloslav
Miroslav
Mislav

PAKOSLAV, RADOSLAV, STOJSLAV

Pakoslav
Paslav
Prebislav
Predislav
Premislav
Preslav
Pribislav
Radoslav
Rostislav
Rostislav
Sulislav

Stojslav
Sveslav
Sybislav
Ubislav
Velislav
Virchoslav
Vislav
Zaloslav
Zdislav
Zelislav

SRBIN, ZERBERSDORF

In some instances one finds a mixed name, the **_Slav-Serb_** ethnonym modified by a German ending (e.g. -dorf):

Caslav is Caslavdorf
Slavin is Slavendorph
Slavobor is Schlabendorf

Slavkot is Schlagsdorf
Sybslav is Sybislavdorf
Srbin is Zerbersdorf

7. VIND, WEND, WIND
WENDISCH DREHNA, SERBSKI DRENOV

In addition to the ethnonym Slav, the Serbs and other Slavs of medieval *Slavia* were known by other names.

SCYTHIANS, SARMATIANS, VANDALS

Inspired by early historians, some medieval sources refer to the Slavs as:

- **Scythians** (*Scytharus gentes*)
- **Sarmatians** (*Sclavi Sarmati*)
- **Vandals** (*Wandali; in Wandalos; Contra Liutizi, Wandali*)

HUNS, ALANS

In some instances, Slavs are recorded as Huns and Alans:

- *Alanos, Quo Dicunt Sclavos*
- *Hanc Sclavi Inhabitant Qui Huni Vocabantur*
- *Cum Nostris Huninidis Qui Appellantur Semeldinc*
- *Ludouicus Cum Saxonibus Contra Hunnos*

PAGANS, BARBARIANS

Other sources, enlightened by the Christian spirit, refer to the Slavs as pagans, pseudo-Christians and barbarians.

- *Inter Paganos*
- *Paganisimus Sclavorum*
- *Slavi Pagani*
- *Winidos, Gentem Paganissimam*
- *Contra Liutizi ... Pagani, Slaui*
- *Dux Nomina Svantopolcus Desperatus Tyrannus et Pseudocristianus*
- *Barbari*
- *Barbarici Ritus*
- *Regiones Barbaroum*

BARBAROS ET MALOS CHRISTIANOS

In his work *(Rerum Gestarum Saxonicarum)*, Widukind, for example, acting on Christian principles, refers to the Slavs (*Christi adversarios*) as barbarians.

- *Adversus Barbaros*
- *De Expeditione Regia in Barbaras Nationes*
- *Degentes Barbaros*
- *Duos Subregulos Barbarorum*
- *Omnes Barbarae Nationes Usque in Oderam Fluvium*
- *Omnes Christi Adversarios, Barbaros et Malos Christianos*
- *Principem Barbarorum*
- *Stoineffo Barbarorum Rege et Milite Qui Eum Occidit*

RUSTICS

In some instances, Slavs are simply identified as rustics:

- *Rustici*
- *Rusitici, Qui Dicuntur Witessen*
- *Rustica Gens Hominum Sclavorum*

VULGARITER

In others, as speakers of the native or vulgar tongue:

- *Grebenize Vulgariter Nuncupatur*
- *Lesten Vulgariter Nominata*
- *Vulgari Nomine Dictam Presnize*
- *Punteme Vulgariter Dicitur*

MAGNUS NUMERUS WINIDORUM

In most instances, however, the Slavs *(Sclavi Cognomento Winidi; Sclavos, quos nos Vionudos dicimus)* and *Slavia* (*Winidorum* as in *Magnus Numerus Winidorum*) are called by cognates of **Wend**, including such cognates as *Guandali* and *Guinidi* (*Guandali dicuntur Sclavi in Latino, in lingua vero Theotonica vocantur Guinidi; Sclavi, qui in lingua Teutonica vocantur Guinidi, in Latina autem Guandali*).

WINIDI

Winidi ... eum super se eligunt regem, 623-24
Sclavos coinomento Winedos perrexit, 623-24
Wallacus ducem Winedorum, 630-31
Contra Samonem et Winidis, 631-32
Sclavi coinomento Winidi, 631-32
Winidorum gentem, 631-32
Wenedos in Toringiam, 632-33
Insolentia Winidorum, 633
Quos nunc appellant Guenedos, 680
Windos in Sclavia, 696
Vinidorum, 741
Uuinedi, 746
Widochindis rebellis, 777
Magnus numerus winidorum, 780
Gentilium Winethorum hominum, 780
Widochinidis, 782
Winidos gentem paganissimam, 788

WINIDORUM

Reges Winidorum, 789
Sclavos, quos nos Vionudos dicimus, 790
In Wenedum, 797
In finem Winidis, 798
In Wihmuodi, 804

In Wenendonia, 805
Ad Beuwinides, 805
In regione Winidum, 806
Nostris Hwinidis, 809
Nostris Guinidinis, 809
Wenedi, 810
Winidorum advenerat in Alsatiam, 837
In Winithos, 844
Contra Winidos ultra Albiam, 846
Beuwinitha vocamus, 846
Guinedes contra Ludowicum, 853
Winidorum regulo, 861

VUINEDOS

Vuinedos, 862
Winidorum marcam, 864
Winidorum regulo foederatur, 864
Principatum Vuinidorum, 864
Vinidos, qui e regione Saxonum habitant, 869
Winidorum regulum, 870
Principatum Winidorum, 870
Per missos suos Winidos, 873
Wenedi, 955
Gens que Guinula vocabantur, 961
Princeps Winulorum, 982
Rex Winidorum, 990
Gentem Winulorum, 1013
Principes Winulorum, 1014
Inimicis Dei Winulis, 1028
Gentem Winithorum, 1028
Gente Winulorum, 1035
Winuli venientes, 1043

SERBIS, VENEDORUM, WENDEN

The interchangeable terms are nicely illustrated by the title of a late 17th century study: *Disputation Historica De Serbis. Venedorum Natione Vulgo Dictis De Wenden*, 1675. From the Oder to the Rhine a great number of place names are derived from local variations of **Wend**, including; **Vind, Vinidi, Vuinidi, Wandal, Wend, Wendeschen, Wendischen, Wind, Windisch, Windischen, Windehusen, Winedi, Winethi, Winidi, Wyndishenn, and Wynethusun.**

RUOTSUUINDENHUSEN • WENDISCHEN DONSTEDE

Ruotsuuindenhusen, 906
Vualahrammesuvuinida, 908
Vuinidiscunburg, 937
Vuinedehusuno marco, 941
Vuinidon, 953

Winidsazin, 953
Wendischen Jena, 1012
Wynethusun, 1021
Dalewinethum, 1055
Abbetes-Winethen, 1128
Ernestewiniden, 1150
Rotherwindehusen, 1151
Winederoth, 1167
Windiskin Rugerit, 1186
Windischen Marke, 1306
Wendeschen Vlechtinge, 1311
Whyndishenn Lutera, 1318
Schlawendorf, 1329
Windischen Sula, 1330
Roslawendorf, 1350
Wenden et iterum Wenden, 1350
Windisch Hohberg, 1351
Wendischen Donstede, 1380

-VIND, -WIND, -WEND

The following series represents some of the better known place names derived from local cognates of Wend, featuring the suffixes -vind, -wind, and -wend.

ABSTWENDEN • HEBARTSWIND

Abstwenden	Eitenwiniden
Almerswind	Elmutwinden
Altwenden	Engmarswinden
Ascherwenden	Ernesteswiniden
Atzelnschwende	Erpswenden
Bernardswinden	Etterwinden
Bischwenden	Ferchwind
Branchewinda	Gerbrechstwinden
Brechtwende	Gniwendorf
Brodswinden	Gotzwinden
Burgwenden	Gundelswind
Burgwindheim	Haubinda
Diezenwinden	Hagenwinden
Ditterswind	Herbartswind
Dittwenden	

HERRNSCHWENDE • WOLFERSCHWENDE

Hohenwenden	Offenwinden
Hohwenden	Ottowind
Meerwinden	Polenwinden
Nahwinden	Poppenvinden
Neumanswind	Puckenwinden
Oberwind	Regenharteswineden

Reinhardswinden
Rosperwende
Ruckerswind
Rudenschwinden
Schwienswende
Sinswinden

Thalwinden
Tutchwende
Untriwindbach
Valdsvind
Wickerswinden
Wolferschwenda

WEND-

The following series feature the prefix Wend-.

Wendelbuttle
Wendelmaresburg
Wendelstroff
Wendhausen Mark
Wendilburgoroth
Wenden (Westphalia)
Wenden (Rrunswick)
Wenden (Drubeck)
Wenden (Hornburg)
Wenden, Gross- (Lohra)

Wendenkirchof
Wendhausen (Treffurt)
Wendhausen (Vippach)
Wendhausen (Thale)
Wendesse
Wendewisch
Wendenturm
Wendishain
Wendlingen

WENDESCHEN-

The following series feature the prefix Wendeschen-.

Wendeschen Apenburg
Wendeschen Borstle
Wendeschen Everinge
Wendeschen Gravenstede
Wendeschen Panchow

Wendeschen Tornow
Wendeschen Tune
Wendeschen Vlechtinge
Wendeschen Wantzewer

WENDISCH-

The following series feature the prefix Wendisch-.

WENDISCH BAGGENDORF • WENDISCH KREUTZ

Wendisch Baggendorf
Wendisch Baselitz
Wendisch Berkentin
Wendisch Biere
Wendisch Bierstadt
Wendisch Bodenstede
Wendisch Bor
Wendisch Borgitz
Wendisch Bork
Wendisch Borschutz
Wendisch Briest
Wendisch Brome

Wendisch Buch
Wendisch Bucholz
Wendisch Cunnersdorf
Wendisch Dorfern
Wendisch Drehna
Wendisch Gercho
Wendisch Grabenstadt
Wendisch Heiligen
Wendisch Kalbu
Wendisch Kiesdorf
Wendisch Kochberg
Wendisch Kreutz

WENDISCH KUNZENDORF • WENDISCH ZUSATZ

Wendisch Kunzendorf
Wendisch Langenbeck
Wendisch Lobbese
Wendisch Luppa
Wendisch Muhlingen
Wendisch Mutz
Wendisch Ossig
Wendisch-Ossnig
Wendisch Paretz
Wendisch Paulsdorf
Wendisch Pogeez
Wendisch Salbke

Wendisch Schwabhausen
Wendisch Segrahn
Wendisch Sohland
Wendisch Sornow
Wendisch Steimke
Wendisch Wehningen
Wendisch Wildau
Wendisch Wilmersdorf
Wendisch Wubiser
Wendisch Wustreue
Wendisch Zella
Wendisch Zusatz

WENDISCHEN-

The following series feature the prefix Wendischen-: Wendischen Bele; Wendischen Bugkow; Wendischen Donstede; Wendischyn Gerinchin; Wendischen Gositz.

WIND-

The following series feature the prefix Wind-/Wint-.

WINDEBY • WINTPOZZINGEN

Windeby
Windehausen
Windenhof
Windelberode
Windham
Windehausen (Nordhausen)
Windhausen (Carsdorf)
Windhausen (Meinigen)
Windishain
Windelsbach
Windberge
Winddorf (Osterhausen)

Windorf
Windorf (Lommatzsch)
Windorff (Leipzig)
Windsbach
Windsfeld
Windsheim, Bad-
Windshub
Winne
Wintdorf (Rudolstadt)
Wintdorf (Cottbus)
Wintpozzingen

WINDISCH-

The following series feature the prefix Windisch-.

WINDISCH BALLHAUSEN • WINDISCH SOLENDE

Windisch Ballhausen
Windisch Bruchter
Windisch Einberg
Windisch Gasse (Allstedt)
Windisch Gasse (Breitungen)
Windisch Gasse (Weimar)
Windisch Geich

Windisch Gerrin
Windysche Heide
Windisch Hohberg
Windisch Holzhausen
Windisch Leuba
Windisch Lutter
Windischmarke

Windisch Racswicz
Windisch Reureith

Windisch Sletten
Windisch Solende

WINDISCHEN

The following series feature the prefix Windischen-.

Windischenbach
Windischendorf
Windischen Gostiz
Windischen Horka
Windischen Jhene

Windischen Raczwiczsch
Windischen Riez
Windischen Storkow
Windischen Sula
Windischen Weissbach

WENDISCH DREHNA • SRBSKI DRENOV

In some cases, the Slav villages are also recorded by native ethnonyms, as well as the German *Wend:* Wendisch Baselitz is **Serbske Pazlicy;** Wendisch Drehna is **Serbski Drenov;** Windisch Kamnitz is **Serbska Kamenice;** Wendisch Kunnersdorf is **Serbske Kundracicy;** Wendisch Paulsdorf is **Serbske Pawlecy;** Wendisch Sohland is **Serbski Zalom.**

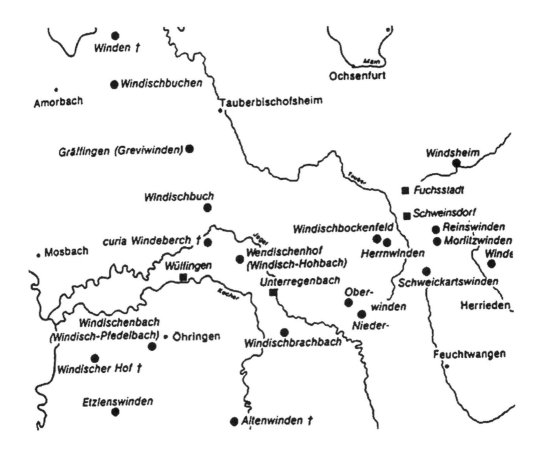

WIND place names in Franconia

189

PART VII

1. VILLA KUSENTI IN PAGO QUI VOCATUR SURBA

In medieval Europe, ***villa***, from the Latin ***vicus*** (village, hamlet, country-seat), connotes a rural community. The following series of ***villas*** is mainly from core lands of historic ***White Serbia***.

BRODICI, CRNICIN, DOLICA

Borkovici (*duos mansos in Borkeuuize*, 1150)
Brec, Brechov (*Brewschau villa deserta*, 1378)
Breznica (*conventus sanctimonalisum in Brisenize*, 1300)
Breznicani (*villa Bresnizani in utroque litore ripe*, 976)
Brodici (*in pago Puonzouua dicta Brodici*, 976)
Bukovani (*villa Bocmani in pago Puonzouua dicto*, 976)
Crnicin (*ville dicte Czernicin*, 1393)
Dobic (*villa que vulgari nomine Dobic vocatur*, 1298)
Dolica (*villa Dolicz circa ... que Ridelbagh dicitur*, 1223)
Dragobudovici (*Dragobudowice in burchwardo Godiwo*, 1071)
Dragos (*Drogis in burgwardo Chvine*, 1069)

GLINA, GOLISA, GOSPODIC

Glina (*villa que Glina dicitur*, 1160)
Glusina (*villa Glussi in pago Dalaminci*, 1013)
Golisa (*villas ... Golsowa ... sitas in burgwardo Chvine*, 1069)
Gorisin (*in campo ville dicte Weynegen-Gorsne*, 1330)
Gorsk (*villas quae dicitur Gors*, 1273)
Gorskovic (*una curia in Gorskewicz*, 1395)
Gospodic (*Gospedicz districtus Misnensis*, 1386)
Gostov (*in campis ville dicte Goztowe*, 1332)
Grislav (*ecclesia sancte Marie in Grizlaw*, 1234)
Gvizda (*in villa Quiz dicte*, 1080)

HRABRAN, LAZ, LESCINA

Hraban (*in villa que dicitur Rabensberch*)
Ilov (*villam quandam Hyla dictam*, 1090; *Ylow*, 1416)
Kremen (*laifodia in Krymmen*, 1399)
Krolup (*in villa que dicitur Chrolpae*, 1045)
Krstic (*Rodichen propre Kerschsticz*, 1378)
Krupin (*villa inferior Kroppin*, 1360)
Kurovic (*Churuuiz in pago Uueta vocato*, 976)
Kusat (*villa Kusenti in pago qui vocatur Zurba*, 1040)
Laz (*in pago ville dicte Lasan*, 1270)
Lepic (*in villa que dicitur Lipicz*, 1157)
Lescina (*villa quae Lesten dicitur*, 1157)

LESKA, LUG, MASLA

Leska (*fratres de Lizezeke*, 1151; *villa Letzka*, 1190)
Lisnja (*villa que dicitur Lyzenlo*, 1230)
Lomsko (*Lomsgo in pago Puonzouua*, 976)
Lubanovic (*Frankendorp, qui et Liubanuwiz vocatur*, 1184)
Luben (*villa que dicitur Luben*, 1399)
Lubesici (*Sybotone archiprebytero ... in Lobeschitz*, 1299)
Lubotici (*villa Liubatici in pago Mrozini*, 975)
Lubici (*Lubbicz villa deserta*, 1495)
Lucin (*in villa dicta Luzen*, 1377)
Lug (*in villa Lughe*, 1350)
Lusov (*in pago villae Luschowe*, 1311)
Masla (*in villa Mazlowe*, 1307)
Misici (*Misici in pago Scudizi*, 1030)

MYSLIBOZ, ROGAC, SCAVNICA

Mysliboz (*in villa Mizleboze*, 1139)
Niprodavici (*villa olim Niprodewiz ... nunc Hagendorf dicta*, 1219)
Otliv (*villa que diciture Otlivuua*, 979)
Ovca (*in villa dque dicitur Owe*, 1148)
Ozda (*in villa que Ozde vocantur*, 1154)
Ponikvica (*usque ad villam Bounkouuize*, 1030)
Potim (*villae Puntyme, villa que Punteme vulgariter dicitur*, 1300)
Rasnic (*villam que Rosneci dicitur*, 1015)
Rodicin (*villa Rodedhen propr Styz*, 1300)
Rogac (*Rogacz in pago Susilin*, 1043)
Roznetici (*villam quandam Rosnetici dictam in burchwardo Trebeni*, 1062)
Scavnica (*in pago ville Schebenyz*, 1430)

SLAVIN, SOKOLIC, TISIN

Slavin (*in campis ville dicte Slawendorf*, 1335)
Slavkot (*in villa Slaukat desolata*, 1350)
Slavokot (*villa que dicitur Zlacoboth*, 1185; *Slaukot*, 1485)
Sokolic (*in villa et pago ville Tzokliz*, 1350)
Stasovici (*villa Tawize*, 1145; *Stawice*, 1154)
Stub (*in villa Stobe*, 1350)
Studenica (*Lvkardis domina de Studeniz*, 1300)
Svec (*in villa et pago Zwezesdorph*, 1296)
Svesovici (*in campis ville Zwezwitz*, 1345)
Svetici (*Zwitich villa in pago Dalminza*, 1159)
Tisin (*in pago ville nostre Tysene*, 1320)

TREBUN, ZELEZNA

Trebun (*villa que dicitur Tribun*, 1217)
Tuchin (*villa Tuchin in burcwardo Treben in pago Zcudici*, 1041)
Tusovici (*in villa que vocatur Thysewiz*, 1236)
Viserob (*tres agros in Wuischraben*, 1230)

Vuic (*Wucz propr Cipzlawendorf,* 1300)
Zelezna (*in villa Silezen nuncupata,* 1157)

SELO, SEDLO

In some instances, the recorded place name is derived from old Slavic words for rural settlements, namely cognates of **selo** and **sedlo**.

Sedlo, Sedelic— Sedelicz, 1359 (Nieder Sedlicz)
Sedlo, Sedlisce— Klein Zcedelicz, 1510 (Klein Sedlitz)
Sedlisce— Czedlicz, 1412 (Gross Sedlitz)
Sedlisce— Sedelist, 1410 (Sedlitz)
Sedlisce— Czettlist, 1521 (Zeitlitz)
Sedliscani— Cedlisciani, 992
Susedlo— Susedelicz, 1359 (Sausedlitz)

BOR SEDLO

Some *sedlo* place names reveal personal names (Brochotin), physical features (bor/pine) and use (kozle/goat).

Bor Sedlo/Sedlibor— *Setlesboresdorf in burchwardo Boruz,* 983
Brochotin Sedlo— Brochotinacethla, 1013 (Brockwitz)
Divno Sedlo— Difnoouccthla, 1013
Dubrava Sedlo— Dubraviensis, 1293; *sedis Dubravis,* 1318
Golenica Sedlo— *Golenciza sethla, villa in pago Gudici,* 983; Golencizacethla, 1013
Kozle Sedlo— Kosseln, 1428 (Kahsel)

NOVO SEDLO, STARO SEDLO

There are numerous references to new (*novo sedlo*) and old settlements (*staro sedlo*) in medieval sources.

NOVO SEDLO

Novosedel— Nouzedel, 1266 (Nussedel)
Novosedel— Novzedel, 1285 (Nausedel)
Novosedel— Nouzedel, 1395 (Nussedel)
Novosedel— Nauzedele, 1159 (Nausedel)
Novosedlici— Noussedlicz, 1374 (Nausslitz)
Novosedlici— Nouzedelicz, 1292 (Gross Neusslitz)
Novosedlici— Nusedlicz, 1350 (Nauslitz)
Novosedlici— Nuzedlicz, 1334 (Nosslitz)
Novoselici— Nuzzelicz, 1378 (Nauslitz)
Novoselici— Neusellicz, 1404 (Nosselwitz)

STARO SEDLO

Staro Sedlo— Ztarcedele, 1277 (Starsiedel)
Staro Sedlo— Sczarczedel, 1268 (Starseddel)
Staro Sedlo— Altersattel (Rudolstadt)
Stare Sedlo— Starzelt (Rudolstadt)

Stare Sedlo— Starzedel (Neuzelle)

CRVEN SEDLO, CRNO SEDLO
In some instances, new settlements or ***novo sedlos*** are identified by color as well as age.

> **Novosedlic**— Noussedelicz, 1374; Czerwene Nosslitze, 1700 (Roth-Nausslitz)
> **Novosedlic**— Nowazodliz, 1228; Swarczen Nesselicz, 1430 (Schwarz Nasslitz)

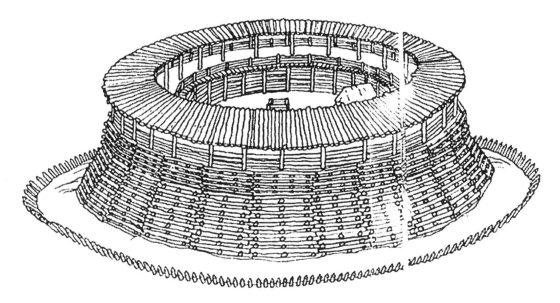

Grad Trnov/Tornow (Luzica)

Grad Radus/Raddusch (Luzica)

2. VILLA DOBRICIN, VILLA MILORAD

Many medieval villages feature prototypical Slavic personal names. The following in-depth series features personal names beginning with the letter **D** (original name followed by medieval citation followed, in parentheses, by later name and nearby town or city).

DOBCIN, DOBRA, DOBRIC
Dobcin— Dobeczen, 1395 (Dobitzschen, Zeitz)
Dobra— Dobra, 1501 (Dobra, Radeburg)
Dobra— Dobra, 1422 (Dobra, Liebenwerda)
Dobra— Dobra, 1528 (Dobra, Schmolln)
Dobra— Doberaw, 1336 (Dobra, Stolpen)
Dobra— Dober, 1441 (Dobra, Glashutte)
Dobra— Dobre, 1432 (Dobra, Kamenz)
Dobra— Brunn Dobra, 1768 (Kligenthal)
Dobran— Dobran, 1501 (Dabern, Finsterwalde)
Dobric— Dobrbichau, 1571 (Dobrichau, Zerbst)

DOBRICIN, DOBRUN, DOBRUS
Dobricin— Dobruzschin, 1445 (Dobitschen, Altenburg)
Dobricin— Dobritzschen, 1540 (Dobritschen, Camburg)
Dobricin— Dobritzen, 1460 (Dobritschen, Jena)
Dobrin— *magna Dobryn,* 1495 (Gross Dobbern, Cottbus)
Dobrin— Dobibrn (Dobern, Bitterfeld)
Dobrin— Dobbryn, 1200 (Dobien, Wittenberg)
Dobrobud— Dobribusch. 1557 (Dobberbus, Lieberose)
Dobrogost— Dobergost, 1300 (Dobergast)
Dobrun— Dobrun, 1353 (Dabrun, Wittenberg)
Dobrus— Dobrusch, 1363 (Doberschau, Bautzen)

DRAGAN, DRAGOBYL, DRAGOS
Dobrusk— Dobrusken, 1419 (Drebusken, Luckau)
Dosin— Dosin, 1350 (Dosen, Leipzig)
Dosin— Dozzen, 1378 (Dossen, Delitzsch)
Dragan, Drogan— Drogan, 1214 (Drogen, Altenburg)
Dragan— Dragansdorff, 1365 (Dragensdorf, Schleiz)
Drago— Dragaw, 1350 (Drogen, Altenburg)
Dragos, Drogos— Drogscowe, 1214 (Droschau, Meuselwitz)
Dragobyl— Drogobuli, 965 (Drobel, Bernburg)
Drasko— Draschka, 1557 (Draschke, Rochlitz)
Drasko— Drozka, 1350 (Droschka, Eisenberg)

DRASKO, DRAZIMIR, DRAZUL
Drasko— Drosskaw, 1492 (Drosskau, Groitzsch)
Draz, Droz— Droze, 1370 (Drosa, Kothen)
Draze— Drosege, 964 (Drosege, Anhalt)

Drazimir, Drozimir— Drosemicz, 1455 (Drossnitz, Kahla)
Drazin, Drozin— Drosene, 1376 (Drosehne, Bernburg)
Drazin, Drozin— Drosin, 1336 (Drossen, Ronnenburg)
Drazul, Drozul— Drosule, 1350 (Dreisel, Duben)
Drzislav— Dissernitz, 1456 (Dorschnitz, Lommatzsch)
Drozavin— Droswin, 1378 (Droswien, Zeulenroda)

PERSONAL NAMES

The following representative in-breadth series features personal names beginning with letters other than **D** (original name followed by medieval citation).

BADOGOST, BLOGOS, BOZKO

Badogost— *magna Badegast,* 1370
Belosin— Beloschin, 1761
Blagos— Blagusche, 1318
Bolibor— Boleboris, 1012
Borisa— Borist, 1331
Boyan— Boian, 1012
Boyan— Boyan, 1583
Boyim— Boym, 1313
Bozetin— Bozetyndorf, 1371
Bozko— Boskaw, 1350

BUDIGOST, GRUBISIN, HOSTIMIR

Budigost— Budegosth, 1330
Budin— Budin, 1404
Budisin— Budisin, 1440
Goremir— Gormir, 1336 (Gorma)
Gorisin— *minori Gorzene,* 1351
Gorislav— Gorselwittz, 1464
Gostirad— alde Gostrasze, 1382
Grubisin— Grubschene, 1378
Gvozden— Gesden, 1381
Hostimir— Hosterwicz, 1515

LUBOBYL, MILORAD, MIRAN

Lubobyl— Leubobel, 1332
Lubogost— Lubegast, 1408
Luborad— Luboratz, 1295
Milin— Mylen, 1140)
Milisa— Milsin, 1150)
Milobud— Melpuz, 1359
Milorad— Melraqsza, 1441
Milsin— Milsin, 1150
Milus— Melis, 1010; Mehlis, 1548
Miran— *utrumque Meran,* 1205; Miran, 1206

MIRKO, PRIBIL, RADOBYL

Mirko— Merko, 1524
Muzigost— Musegost, 1288
Nebysa— Nebysin, 1439
Paslav— Pazleve, 1334
Pribil— Priebel, 1518
Radibor— Radbor, 1382
Radis— Radis, 1528
Radisin— Raczen, 1378
Rado— Radow, 1406
Radobyl— Radebol, 1500

RADOGOST, RADOVID, STOSIN

Radogost— Radegast, 1408
Radomysl— Radamischil, 1394
Radosul— Radesul, 1378
Radovid— Radoweiss, 1545
Razvod— Rozvaz, 1214
Rusavin— Russeweyn, 1286
Slavin— Slowin, 1197
Stanov— Stanowe, 1074; Stanow, 1378
Stosin— Stosen, 1378

SUILIMIR, VELKO, VISEMIR

Strosin— Strossin, 1205
Sulimir, Sulisa— Zulistorf, 1274)
Temysl— Themuzlerus, 1294
Tesimir— Tesemer, 1421
Velko— Welkau, 1091
Velkos— Welcosch, 1316; Welkos, 1327
Vidogost— Widogost, 979
Vidorad— Wederoz, 1350
Vidov— Widowe, 1226; Widow, 1234
Viselub— Wiselob, 1378
Visemir— Wiesmar, 1564

VJELKO, VOLIGOST, ZELKO

Vjelko— Wjelkow, 1225
Volibor— Volbor, 1291
Voligost— Wolgast, 1355
Volimir— Wolmeriz, 1239
Vudin— Wudin, 1326)
Vulko— Wulcow, 1144
Vusin— Wussin, 1336
Zaligost— Saligast, 1285
Zelidrag— Selderoysen, 1334
Zelko— Zelechow, 1291; Selkow, 1335

3. VILLA DOBRANOVIC, VILLA SRBOVIC

Many medieval villages feature prototypical Slavic family names ending in -IC. The following in-depth series features villages with family names beginning with the letter **D** (original name followed by medieval citation followed, in parenthesis, by later name and nearby town or city).

DANOVIC, DOBIC, DOBROMIRIC
Danovic— Danewicz, 1495 (Dahnitz, Wurzen)
Dedic— Deditz, 1529 (Deditz, Grimm)
Dedisovic— Didiswitz, 1205 (Doschutz, Grossenhain)
Desic— Deziz, 1332 (Deetz, Lindau)
Dobic— Dobich, 1446 (Dobichau, Naumberg)
Dobisovic— Dobschwitz, 1534 (Debschwitz, Gera)
Dobromiric— Dobermaricz, 1335 (Dobernitz, Leisnig)
Dobranovic— Dobranwicz, 1334 (Dobernitz, Lommatzsch)

DOBRANOVIC, DOBRODANOVIC, DOBROVIC
Dobranovic— Dobranowiz, 1245 (Dobranitz, Bischofserda)
Dobravic— Dobrawiz, 1221 (Dobritz, Meissen)
Dobravic— Dobrawicz, 1071 (Dobritz, Possneck)
Dobravic— Dobberitz, 1572 (Dobritz, Zeitz)
Dobrodanovic— Doberdanuwiz, 1236 (Dobernitz, Riesa)
Dobrkovic— Dobirkewicz, 1359 (Doberquitz, Leisnig)
Dobrovic— *minori Doberwitz,* 1378 (Klein Dobritz, Dresden)
Dobrovic— *magna Dobrowicz,* (Gross Dobritz, Radeburg)

DOMASLAVIC, DRAGASAVIC, DRAGOVIC
Dobrsic— Dobierschicz, 1378 (Doberzeit, Pirna)
Dobrsovic— Doberschwicz, 1350 (Dobershutz, Eilenburg)
Domaslavic— Domezlawiz, 1218 (Domselwitz)
Draganic— Drackenitz, 1464 (Dragnitz, Torgau)
Dragasavic— Dragaswicz, 1251 (Draschwitz, Zeitz)
Dragovic— Drogowice, 1157 (Drobitz, Zorbig)
Dragolic— Drogolisci, 992 (Dorlitz, Hettstedt)
Draskovic— Droskewitz, 1286 (Draschwitz, Leisnig)

DRASKOVIC, DROGOVIC, DROZOVIC
Draskovic— Drawsskewicz, 1453 (Drauschkowitz, Bautzen)
Droganic— Droganic, 1136 (Drognitz, Saalfeld)
Droganic— Drogenize, 1142 (Drognitz, Torgau)
Drogovic— Drogewitz, 1395 (Drognitz, Konnern)
Drogovic— Drogouwize, 1179 (Drogwitz, Kothen)
Droskovic— Droschkowicz, 1433 (Droschkewitz, Meissen)
Drozovic— Drosewiz, 1328 (Drosewitz, Calbe)

FAMILY NAMES ENDING IN -IC— CASLAVIC, SRBOVIC

The following representative series features villages with family names beginning with letters other than **D** (original name followed by medieval citation.

BEDOSIC, BELKOVIC, BOGISLAVIC

Bedosic— Bedosiki, 979
Beganovic— Begenowiz, 1251
Belkovic— Belkewitz, 1378
Bodanic— Bodenitz, 1458
Bogislavic— Bosslawicz, 1446
Bojnic— Boyniz, 1251
Bolesovic— Bolschwitz, 1673
Boliboric— Bolberitz, 1301

BORISLAVIC, BOZANKOVIC, BOZOVIC

Boranovic— Borenwiz, 1280
Borislavic— Bursluwicz, 1277
Borkovic— Borkewiz, 1300
Borsic— Borschiz, 1160
Boslavic— Basslewicz, 1433
Bozankovic— Bosankewitz, 1519
Bozenic— Boscnitz, 1571
Bozovic— Buzewicz, 1271

BUDOSTOVIC, CASLAVIC, DOLGANOVIC

Brchovic— Burchewitz, 1486
Budostovic— Bustewicz, 1331
Bukelic— *Magnum Buchlicz*, 1378
Caslavic— Czazluwicz, 1349
Dobranovic— Dobranowitz, 1245
Dobrovic— *Magna Dobrowicz*, 1369
Dolganovic— Dolganewiz, 1242
Gostovic— Gostewitz, 1440

GRUBOSIC, KOLISOVIC, KRALOVIC

Grubosic— Grubschitz, 1590
Grubotic— Gruptitcz, 1445
Jarotic— Gertewitz, 1486
Kokanic— Kokenicz, 1350
Kolisovic— Kulschewicz, 1350
Konovic— Kunewitz, 1264
Kozlovic— Koseilwitcz, 1421
Kralovic— Krolewicz, 1341

LUBORODIC, LUSKOVIC, LUTOBORIC

Kusovic— Kuschwicz, 1397
Luborodic— Liuborodici, 1014

Luskovic— Luzkewiz. 1154
Lutetic— Luteticz, 1323
Lutoboric— Luthoboritz, 1273
Lutolic— Lutelitz, 1441
Lutovic— Lutewicz, 1334
Malkovic— Malkewicz, 1311

MALESOVIC, MIRASOVIC, MYSLAVIC

Malesovic— Maleswicz, 1261
Mecislavic— Meczlawicz, 1378
Mirasovic— Meraschwitz, 1326
Modlovic— Modelwitz, 1136
Mozgovic— Moskewicz, 1409
Munsovic— Munschwitz, 1518
Myslovic— Misselquuiz, 1311
Myslavic— Myzlawic, 1239

NASIBORIC, PASLAVIC, POMIROVIC

Nasiboric— Nasseboritz, 1165
Nedelcic— Nedelczicz, 1350
Nikrasic— Nicracis, 1206
Nisulovic— Nitculbitz, 1412
Oraskovic— Oraschwicz, 1378
Paslavic— Paclewizze, 1205
Peskovic— Peskewicz, 1374
Pomirovic— Pomerwicz, 1441

PRELOVIC, PREMILOVIC, ROGOVIC

Prelovic— Preluwicz, 1350
Premilovic— Prymillwitz, 1495
Premyslovic— Premselwitz, 1358
Pribyslavic— Pribislawiz, 1184
Rodlovic— Rodelwicz, 1378
Ranisovic— Rancschewicz, 1378
Rogovic— Rogewicz, 1446
Rozvadic— Roswadewicz, 1400

RATIBORIC, RATOVIC, RUSOVIC

Ratiboric— Borthebariz, 1311
Ratiboric— Rothebariz, 1311
Ratovic— Ratewiz, 1300
Rodkovic— Rodeghewiz, 1333
Rogovic— Rogewiz, 1377
Roslavic— Rosslawicz, 1346
Rostovic— Rostwiz, 1138
Rusovic— Ruschewitz, 1378

SIBYSLAVIC, SLAVKOVIC, SRBOVIC

Sibyslavic— Zibislawic, 1215
Slavkovic— Schlagwitz, 1498
Slavomiric— Zlamerize, 1159
Slavotic— Slauticz, 1441
Slavsic— Zlaweschiz, 1241
Srbovic— Zcorbewicz, 1350
Stasovic— Staswice, 1154
Strazevic— Struzewyz, 1332

SULATIC, SVETOMIRIC, TESKOVIC

Strezevic— Stresewicz, 1350
Sulatic— Sulaticz, 1334
Sulkovic— Sulkewicz, 1362
Svetomiric— Zuetmariz, 1251
Svotic— Zvotiz, 1185
Svosovic— Zwoswicz, 1313
Teskovic— Theeschutz, 1250
Tolisic— Tollschutz, 1532

TREBASOVIC, VLODAROVIC, ZALOSIC

Trebasovic— Trebaczschewlcz, 1471
Ubyslavic— Obzlawiz, 1285
Uglic— Uglici, 993
Uskovic— Uskewicz, 1365
Utesovic— Usteskwicz, 1252
Vicazic— Wicaswicz, 1320
Vlodarovic— Loderwyz, 1330
Vunusic— Aldenwunschicz, 1350
Zalisici— Salczicz, 1330
Zalosic— Salczicz, 1320

4. VILLA PO-BREZE

The following representative series features villages beginning with the prepositions **po-** (along, by, near, nearby), **pod-** (below, beneath, under, lower), **pre-/pred-** (before, in front of) **pri-** (at, about, near, nearby) and **za-** (behind, in back of, on the other side).

PO-

Po-breze— Pobrese, 1288 (Bobersen, Riesa)
Po-caply— Postschapel, 1206 (Potschappel, Dresden)
Po-dole— Podel, 1476 (Podel, Pirna)
Po-dolovic— Podelwicz, 1156 (Podelitz, Zorbig)
Po-dolic— Podelicz, 1299 (Podelist, Naumberg)
Po-dolsic— Bodelschitz, 1457 (Podelsatz, Jena)
Po-lipa— Poleb, 1195 (Poleb, Jena)
Po-mjeza— Pomezin, 1255 (Pomssen, Grimm)
Po-nize— Ponezze, 1378 (Ponsen, Borna)
Po-reka— Poritsch, 1141 (Poritzsch, Saalburg)
Po-zdren— Posidirn, 1161 (Poserna, Weissenfels)

POD-

Pod-breze— Podebriz, 1274 (Boderitz, Altenburg)
Pod-breze— Podebrese, 1350 (Boderitz, Dresden)
Pod-caplici— Poczaplicz, 1376 (Pottschapplitz, Bischofswerda)
Pod-celo— Podizchli, 1298 (Podeschil, Zeitz)
Pod-lese— Polesyn, 1371 (Podelsem, Wettin)
Pod-lese— Poclessen, 1400
Pod-luzic— Podlusic, 1268 (Podelwitz, Colditz)
Pod-mose— Podemuz, 1405 (Podemus, Dresden)
Pod-meke— Podmeke, 1387 (Podemeke, Stassfurt)
Pod-modlic— Pothmodelize, 1142 (Pothmodelize, Torgau)
Pod-mokla— Pademok, 1463 (Pademagk, Calau)
Pod-moklic— Podmarlicz, 1377 (Podmoklitz, Coblenz)
Pod-ploz— Podenpulz, 1378 (Podenbuls Zeitz)

PRE-

Pre-del— Predel, 1461 (Sanserderf)
Pre-del— (Preddel, Bitterfeld)
Pre-delica— (Predalitz, Blumenberg)
Pre-drete— Prederten, 1354 (Prederitz)
Pre-laz— Prelicz, 1464 (Prelitz, Meuselwitz)
Pre-sek— Prezez, 1300 (Pretsch, Merseburg)
Pre-sir— Presser, 1346 (Pressel, Torgau)
Pre-trnik— Pretrnig, 1020 (Pretrnick, Wettin)

PRI-

Pri-buz— Paribiz, 1552 (Klein-Priebus)

Pri-dub— Pridob, 1240 (Predau, Meuselwitz)
Pri-lep— Prelepe, 1289 (Perlipp, Calbe)
Pri-luk— Prelag, 1614 (Prielack)
Pri-rov— Prerow, 1265 (Prierow, Luckau)
Pri-sec— Prissitz, 1371 (Priesitz, Wittenburg)
Pri-sek— Pricizke, 1206 (Priesig, Weissenfels)
Pri-vel— Priwil, 1181 (Priefel, Altenburg)

ZA-

Za-borov— Sabrowe, 1174 (Sabrau, Bernburg)
Za-brod— Zabrod, 1380 (Sabrodt, Hoyerswerda)
Za-gor— Zagar, 1409 (Sagar, Muskau)
Za-goric— Sageritz, 1552 (Sageritz, Riesa)
Za-gost— Salegost, 1208 (Sallgast, Finsterwalde)
Za-krov— Sacrowe, 1300 (Sacro, Forst)
Za-lesno— Salesyn, 1378 (Saalhausen, Oschatz)
Za-lom— Zalom, 1241 (Sohland, Rotstein)
Za-luz— Salhusen, 1290 (Saalhusen, Senftenberg)
Za-morsk— Zamursk, 1204 (Sommeritz, Schmolln)
Za-reka— Sarecz, 1416 (Saritsch, Bautzen)
Za-slom— Sasslem, 1346 (Sassleben, Calau)
Za-thym— Sathim, 1140 (Saathain, Bad Liebenwerd)
Za-vlok— Zaulop, 1295; Sawleke, 1480 (Sauleck, Barby)

NE-, NI-

Numerous villages have archaic Slavic names and archaic forms, including, for example, village names featuring the negative prepositions **ne-** and **ni-** (e.g. nebil or ne-bil or non-white).

Ne-bil— *Nible antiquitus nunc alde Groisch dicto,* 1190 (Altengroitzsch, Leipzig)
Ne-bil— Nebildow, 1378 (Nobeln, Rochlitz)
Ne-belsic— Nebilczicz, 1445 (Nebelschutz, Pirna)
Ne-belsic— Nebilschicz, 1304 (Nebelshcutz, Kamenz)
Ne-budic— Nebudiz, 1143 (Nobdenitz, Schmolln)
Ne-budic— Niubudice, 1156 (Nehlitz, Halle)
Ne-budic— Nobedicz, 1350 (Nobeditz, Weissenfels)
Ne-budim— Nebedim 1140 (Noben, Schmolln)
Ne-chorin— Necherin, 1421 (Nechern, Bautzen)
Ne-dan— Nydan, 1402 (Neiden, Torgau)
Ne-da-mir— Nedemer, 1400 (Diemer, Rothenberg)
Ne-dasin— Nidazne, 1256 (Neissen, Zeitz)
Ne-kaznic— Nekaznitz, 1274 (Neckanitz, Lommatzsch)
Ne-lub— Neleben, 1484 (Nelben, Asleben)
Ne-porovic— Nipperwicz, 1421 (Nepperwitz, Wurzen)
Ne-radovic— Neradwitz, 1473 (Neraditz, Kamenz)
Ne-radkovici— Niredecauuiz, 1044 (Nerkewitz, Jena)
Ne-svacil— Nizuuazil, 1160; Nizwasele, 1197 (Nissmitz, Naumberg)

Ni-bel— Nibeldowe, 1350, Nybildow, 1378 (Nobeln, Rochlitz)
Ni-dan— Niden 1260 (Neiden, Torgau)
Ni-dobudovic— Nidabudowiz, 1234 (Leisnig)
Ni-gradov— Nigradow, 1286 (Niegeroda, Grossenhain)
Ni-mirkovic— Nymerkitz, 1477 (Limmritz, Dobeln)
Ni-prodavici— Niprodewiz, 1219
Ni-sulovic— Nitzculbitz, 1412
Ni-vetro— Nyweter, 1327

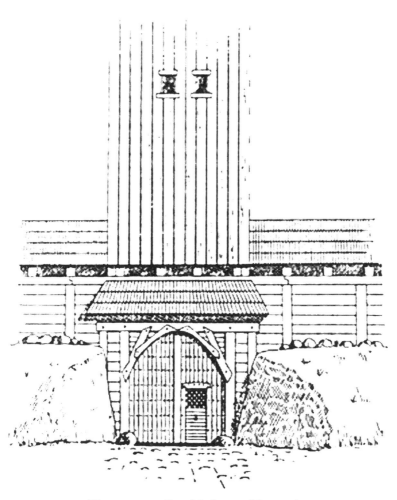

Town gate *Grad* Arkona (Rugen)

5. ALLODIUM BUKOVINA, MOLENDINUM KOSMATICA

As the following representative series from **_White Serbia_** indicates, throughout the medieval-feudal period the names of basic rural entities, **_allodiums, grangrias, molendinums, and prediums,_** retained their Slavic character.

ALLODIUM

In medieval Germania, the Latin term **_allodium_** generally refers to land freely held, without obligation of service to any overlord.

BABIN, CAJETIN, DOBRUSA

Babin— _allodium Babindorf,_ 1333
Bukovina— _allodium Bukewen,_ 1227
Cajetin— _allod Zschaiten,_ 1350
Cavic— _allod Schawicz,_ 1350
Cerin— _allod Cerin,_ 1316
Chotovici— _Kothewicz cum allodiis,_ 1349
Dobravic— _allod Dubravic,_ 1220
Dobrusa— _allodis Dobrucz,_ 1407
Dragolic— _allodium Drogelicz,_ 1256

DRAZIN, KOSOVIC, LUBISIC

Drazin— _allodium Drozendorf,_ 1369
Grodec— _allodium Grocz,_ 1360
Gusarov— _allodium Gosseraw,_ 1528
Korsobuk— _allod Korzeburg,_ 1350
Kosovic— _allod Koczwicz,_ 1350
Kovrotic— _allod Cowertiz,_ 1245
Krusnica— _allodium Krusnicz,_ 1350
Lechov— _allod Lechowe,_ 1234
Lubisic— _allodium Lubeschicz,_ 1350

LUBOSC, MILENKOVIC, OSTROBUD

Lubosc— _allod Lubocz,_ 1350
Lysov— _allod Lysow,_ 1350
Malesovici— _allodium Malswiz,_ 1225; Maleswicz, 1261
Milenkovic— _allodium Mylenkwiz,_ 1314
Mysliboz— _allodium Muszelbuz,_ 1350
Nedalkovic— _allod in Kelkewicz,_ 1350
Nosakovic— _allod in Nussewicz,_ 1350
Ostrobud— _allodium in Ostresbude,_ 1286
Petici— _villa dictam Petytz ... sitam apud allodium sanctimonalium in Mollebergh dictum Cothyn,_ 1376

PRISTANOVIC, SELO, TEMIRICI

Picici— *allodio suo Pictzwicz*, 1225
Presek— *allodium in Prizzez*, 1230
Pristanovic— *allod in Priestanwicz*, 1350
Ratsovic— *allodium Ratzewicz*, 1335
Repetici— *allodium Repticz*, 1314
Selo— *allodium Selowe*, 1169
Strogov— *allod Stragow*, 1399
Svoyim— *allodium Zweym*, 1430
Temirici— *allodium Tymericz*, 1225

VRENTINA, VUDIN, ZRNOVICA

Tunc— *allodium Tunsch*, 1360
Veznica— *allod Wesnicz*, 1350
Vrentina— *allodium Wrentin*, 1283
Vulcic— *allodium Wiltschiz*, 1254
Vudin— *allod Vden*, 1220
Zelov— *allodium Zelowe*, 1169
Zicani— *allodium novum in Sycene*, 1225
Zrnovica— *allodium Sornewicz*, 1402

GRANGRIA

Grangria, from the Latin *granum*, plant or seed, generally refers to a granary.

Kusat— *grangria in Kusenze*, 1145
Kusan— *grangria Cusene*, 1140
Lepici— *grangria in Leipicz*, 1300
Lokovic— *grangria Lochwitz*, 1517
Pozelici— *Poseliz grangia*, 1215
Skoblov— *grangria Scopecou*, 1209
Tribun— *grangria de Tribun*, 1206
Visov— *grangria Wicouge*, 1142

MOLENDINUM

Molendinum, from the Latin *moldendin-um* (mill), gerund of *molere* (to grind), refers to a grinding-mill.

CHOTEBUZ, KOSMATICA, PELES

Brosin— *molendinum in Brossen*, 1296
Chotebuz— *molendinum Kothebuz*, 1336
Dalovici— *molendinum Talewicz*, 1314
Kosmatica— *molendinum Cosmatice*, 1253
Krusevica— *molendinum Crussewicz*, 1314
Lescina— *molendina Lesten vulgariter nominata*, 1350
Lukonov— *molendinum Lukenowe*, 1258
Peles— *molendinum in Peles*, 1332

PODOLICA, SEDLORAZ, ZETZE

Pestovici— *de molendino Martini Pestewicz,* 1370
Podolica— *molendinum Podelicz situm in Sala,* 1307
Polcic— *molendinum Pulschitz,* 1369
Rostovic— *molendinum in Rostewice,* 1138
Sedloraz— *molendinum Selderoz,* 1336
Viserobi— *mondinum in Wisseraben,* 1144
Vulkin— *molendinum in Volquin,* 1360
Zetze— *molendino in Zetze,* 1360
Zrnosek— *molendium in Surnezsc,* 1350

PREDIUM

From the Latin *praes, predium* is a farm, a landed estate.

BEGOV, KON, KRANOVICI

Begov— *predium Bigowia,* 1106
Chotenic— *predio in Cehotennewiz,* 1203
Chotovic— *predium in Kotewicz,* 1300
Grotovic— *praedium Grothowizi,* 1030
Kon— *predium Cone infra novam et antiquam albim situm,* 1208
Kotovic— *predium in Cotewize,* 1300
Kranovici— *predium in Cranewiz,* 1216

POZELIC, RADUN, SKOLANE

Nizalin— *predium Nizalin,* 1052
Pozelic— *praedium Posliz,* 1206
Pretrnik— *Preternig predium,* 1020
Radun— *predium Rodonsleba,* 1043
Rogalic— *predium Rogalici,* 1017
Rogaz— *predium Rogaz,* 1043
Rub— *predium Rube,* 1207
Skolane— *predium in loco Ihholani,* 1046

Radlo, Plug

6. AQUA (REKA)
RIVUS BISTRICA, FLUVIUS RIBNICA,
STAGNUM RADOMIR, MONS CRNOVIC

Colorful and compelling evidence of the depth and breadth of medieval *Slavia's* Slavic foundations is found in the quintessential Slavic names of its hydronyms and toponyms, of *Slavia's* waterways, highlands, fields, and forests, its *aquas, rivuses, fluvius, stagnums, blotos, mons*, **goras**, *campos, locuses*, and *silvas.* The following series is mainly from *White Serbia* (original name followed by recorded Latin or German version).

AQUA— BELI POTOK, JEZERCE, REKA

> **Beli Potok** (*Belipotoch,* 1241)
> **Bloto** (*acqua Plota,* 1264)
> **Golica** (*aqua Golz,* 1266)
> **Gornica** (*acqua Gornicz,* 1378)
> **Grob** (*aqua Grob,* 1009)
> **Jezerce** (*aqua Zehorzerce,* 1241)
> **Loznica** (*aqua Loznic,* 1331)
> **Luzica** (*Lusicz aqua,* 1315)
> **Luznica** (*aqua Lusenize,* 1181)
> **Pakov** (*acqua Poka,* 1352)
> **Reka** (*aqua Riczk,* 1298)
> **Vichov, from Vitoslav** (*ad acquam que dicitur Wilchaw,* 1299)

RIVUS— BISTRICA, HODZIVICA, JESENICA,

> **Bistrica** (*rivulum Bysterize,* 1316)
> **Groznica** (*rivulus Crosenicz,* 1298)
> **Gus, Guska** (*rivulus Gusc,* 1241)
> **Hodzivica** (*rivulus Hodziwice,* 1413)
> **Jesenica** (*rivulus Jesnicz,* 1298)
> **Klusnica** (*rivulus Clesniz,* 1174)
> **Kokotov** (*rivus Cocotwia,* 1122)
> **Kreba, Krebac** (*rivulo dicto Crebazbach,* 1317)

LOZNICA, ZLATOVINA, VOLOVICA

> **Loznica** (*rivulus Losnicz,* 1352)
> **Luznica** (*rivulus Lusnitz,* 1143)
> **Pest, Pestov** (*rivulus Peztau,* 1228)
> **Ponikva** (*circum rivulum Poniqua,* 1239)
> **Strigus** (*rivulus Strigus,* 1185)
> **Tusin** (*rivum Tussin,* 1241)
> **Zlatovina** (*rivus Zalatwina,* 1241)
> **Vira** (*rivus Wira,* 1105; Wyrawe, 1143)
> **Volovica** (*rivus Welewiz,* 1241)

FLUMEN, FLUVIUS— CRNICA, JASENICA, KAMENICA

Bloto (*Blote*, 1278)
Crna (*Schirna*, 1143)
Crnica (*Scurnice*, 1118)
Drenov (*Threne*, 1447)
Jasenica (*usque ad fluvium que dicitur Iesniz*, 1244)
Kamenica (*in Kamnizam fluvium*, 1174)
Kobyla (*Kubelitze*, 1358)
Linov (*ad fluvium Lynaw*, 1185)

LOMNICA, OSTROZNICA, RADIN

Lomnica (*Lomniza*, 1122)
Luben (*fluvius Loben*, 1159)
Nitlava (*fluvius Nitlawe*, 1149)
Olesnica (*fluvius Olsnitz*, 1250)
Orla (*Orla*, 1071)
Ostroznica (*Oztrosniza*, 1241)
Paklica (*cuius fons supram villam Lubenov*, 1300)
Radin (*qui a Radinzca fluvio*, 1025)

RIBNICA, SNEZNICA, TREBELIN

Ribnica (*Ribnica*, 977)
Slubc (*ad fluvium Slube*, 1301)
Sneznica (*Snesniza*, 1122)
Strumma (*Stremme fluss*, 1145; *Strumma*, 1150)
Trebelin (*Trebelyn maior et minor*, 1316)
Vedro (*Wydera*, 1509)
Vodrica (*Wudritz*, 1548)
Vrsnica (*Wurschnitz*, 1226)
Zirava (*fluvius Sirouve*, 1122)

STAGNUM: CERVENSK, MURIZ, RADOMIR

Cervensk (*stagno Zcerwencyk*, 1329)
Muriz (*Muriz stagnum*, 1273)
Nizki (*stagnum dicto Nyze*, 1250)
Pinov (*stagnum Pynnow dicti*, 1331)
Polica (*stagnum Palitz*, 1316)
Radomir (*stagnum Radomer*, 1244)
Vrchov (*stagnum Virchowe*, 1290)

BLATO, BLOTO

In the case of certain waterways, the original Slavic name, *bloto-blato*, a generic Slavic term for waterways (e.g. Baltic, Balaton), especially marshlands, has survived with varying degrees of distortion. In the following series, the original Slavic name is followed by an early Latin/German version, followed by a later or modern version with reference to a nearby town or city.

Bloto— Blota (Ploth, Torgau)
Bloto— Pladeck, 1619 (Platek, Borna)
Bloto— Blotko/Platko, 1527 (Plattkow, Beeskow)
Bloto— Plote, 1350 (Plothen, Schleiz)
Bloto— Bloda, 1161 (Plotha, Weissenfels)
Bloto, Blocani— Bloczin, 1398 (Plotzen, Lobau)
Bloto, Blotic— Bloizice, 1147 (Loitzschutz, Zeitz)
Bloto, Blotic— Blotitz, 1327 (Plotitz, Riesa)
Bloto, Blotic— Blocz, 1403 (Plotz, Halle)
Bloto, Blotov— Plotte, 1233 (Plottwitz/Eilenburg)
Kosovo Blato— Kosenblot, 1307 (Kossenblatt/Beeskow)
Luto Bloto— Lutenblat, 1419 (Luttenblatt, Bitterfeld)
Po Bloto— Pobloz, 1350 (Pobles, Hohenmolsen)
Pod Bloto— Bodblozi, 945 (Bodblozi/Bernburg)
Vrh Blato— Wirchenblatt
Za Blato— Sablath, Zablath
Za Blatovici— Zablatwitz, 1210

CAMPO, CAMPUS— DRAGOBYL, LYSINA, PRILUK

Bolin— *campo Bolin*, 1288
Borovici— *campus Borewicz*, 1400
Doben— *campo Dobene*, 1319
Dragobyl— *campis Drobele*, 1240
Drva— *campo qui dicitur Drvest*, 1472
Jezero— *campo Jezere*, 1365
Krivica— *campis Criwitz*, 1363
Krupica— *campo Crupiske*, 1290
Kyrc— *campus Kirtzs*, 1143
Lubogost— *campis Lubegastis*, 1310
Lysina— *campo Lizzene*, 1267
Mrocin— *campo Mertzin*, 1357
Muskov— *campo Muscowe*, 1311
Podgrad— *Potgrot, campus desertus*, 1300
Priluk— *campus Prilok*, 1356
Slavia— *campo Slavicali*, 1274
Vidogost— *in campo Wedegist*, 1322
Zacinic— *campis Zcynsch*, 1430

LOCUS— DOBRIGLUG, PODLUG, VISEBOR

Chvojin— *in loco Quina*, 945
Crnicin— *in loco dicte Czerniczin*, 1393
Dobrilugk— *locum qui Dobraluk dicitur*, 1012
Mokrina— *locus Mucherini*, 1012
Mychyl— *locus Muchele*, 1213
Pinov— *locum qui pynnow dicitur*, 1281
Podlug— *in loco Putlandes*, 1329
Praskov— *in loco qui vulgariter Prazkowe*, 1304

Smolin— *locus Zmolensis,* 1138
Stena— *in loco Stene,* 945
Visebor— *in locis Vuuzboro,* 937

MONS— POZOV, HUM, JAVOR

Baba— *mons Babe,* 1223
Bozov— *mons Buzowe,* 1121
Chotemir— *mons Khotsmerberg,* 1311
Chrostovica— *mons Chrostwitze,* 1143
Crnovic— *Schirnwicz,* 1350; *monte Scherwist,* 1357
Hum— *monte Kulme,* 1324
Hum— *bona sita in monte qui Chuylmen vulgariter nominatur,* 1297
Jansk— *in monte qui dicitur Jentzike,* 1244
Javor— *mons Jawor,* 1241
Jazvinka— *mons Yezwinche,* 1241
Kal— *in sereno Monte Kal,* 1161
Olesnic— *mons Olsnich,* 1228
Opcin— *mons Obizsenen,* 1350
Radobyl— *in pedem montis Radbize,* 1228
Skutkov— *montem Scutkowe,* 1241
Tisov— *mons Tizov,* 1228
Zid— *mons in Zagozd qui Syden vocatur,* 1188

GORA— BELAGORA, DOBRAGORA, LISAGORA

Babiagora, 1220
Belagora, 1360
Besovagora, 1459
Bukovagora, 1229
Dobragora, 952
Jelenagora, 1228
Kamenagora, 995
Lipovagora, 1228
Lisagora, 1573
Smogora, 1474
Soblagora, 1442
Trebelgora, 1314

SILVA— LIPA, MEDENICA, PO REKA

Bojan— *Boyan silva,* 1583
Dobrici— *silva Dubreze,* 1209
Dragobyl— *silva cui nomen Drogbul,* 1159
Gornica— *silva Gornicz,* 1378
Granica— *silva quae Greneize vulgariter,* 1304
Grebenica— *silva quad Grebenize vulgariter nuncuatur,* 1304
Gruz— *silva Gruz,* 1269
Humec— *per silvan ad Hlmec,* 1057
Lipa— *silva Lipe,* 1290

Luc— *silva Luch,* 1200
Lug— *quandam siluam, que Luk vulgari nomine nuncupatur,* 1280; *silva Luk,* 1301
Medenica— *silva dicta Medenicz,* 1350
Mrtvica— *silva Mortewicz,* 1378
Nebuz— *silva Nobuz,* 1236
Osa— *silva Ozzen,* 1378
Po reka— *silva Poregi,* 946
Pustenica— *sylva Pustenitze,* 1319
Sokol— *Sokola dambroa,* 1239
Veliki— *silva Willekin,* 1378
Vukov, Vulkov— *silva dicta Volchow,* 1378
Zelezna— *silva Silazne,* 1176

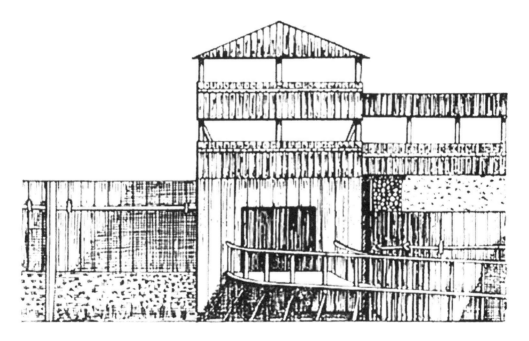

Town gate *Grad* Behren-Lubchin

PART VIII

1. CURIA BOR, MUNICIO DOBRISIN,
URBS DOBRA GORA,
OPID OSTROG, BURGWARD SRBICI

In medieval Germania the names of many basic administrative entities, *curias*, *municios*, *urbs*, *oppids,* and **burgwards**, retained their Slavic character.

CURIA

In Rome, *curia* refers to an ancient division of the Roman people. In medieval Europe, the term refers to a court, a local judicial-administrative entity.

BOR, DOBROVIC, KON

Bor— *curia Bore dicta,* 1278
Bukelic— *curia Buchelicz,* 1350
Budoraz— *curia Buerz,* 1309
Bysenovic— *curia Buschenewitz,* 1325
Cilov— *curia Zscilowe,* 1225
Chojno— *curia Chojno,* 1146
Dobrovic— *curia Doberwicz,* 1350
Glusin— *curia nostra Glusinghe,* 1313
Gorskovic— *curia in Gorskovic,* 1395
Kanica— *curia in Kanytz,* 1350
Kon— *curiam Kuene,* 1157; *Cone,* 1205

MALINA, PODGRIM, STUDENC

Malentic— *curia in Malentesch,* 1350
Malina— *curia dicta Melin,* 1350
Morica— *curia Muritze,* 1352
Nisici— *curia in Nyzicz,* 1348
Penkov— *curia et campo Penkow,* 1400
Podgrim— *Podagrym curia,* 1319
Sirica— *curia in Schiricz,* 1350
Sosna— *curia Zossen,* 1252
Studenc— *curia in Studowe,* 1274
Styc— *curia in Sticz,* 1350
Tesnica— *curia in Thesniz,* 1300

CURIA WICHMANESBURG

Curias with German names were often made up of Slavic villages. In the case of mid-12th century *curia Wichmanesburg,* for example, some of the villages were *villas Slavica* (e.g. *In curia Wicmanesburg ... dedid insuper 20 villas Slavica ad eandem curiam pertinentes, 1140*).

MUNICIO DOBRISIN

In Roman times, a *municio* was a community incorporated into the Roman state. In medieval Europe, a political subdivision with limited financial and judicial powers.

Chojno— *municio Chojno,* 1200
Dobrisin— *municio quoque Dobreschen,* 1190
Kuna— *municio Kaune,* 1288
Luznica— *municio Lusenycz,* 1289
Milsin— *munitionem Milsin,* 1040
Ploncovic— *munitionem Plonswicz,* 1327
Strbil— *munitionem Tirbil,* 1327
Suselic— *munitio Susliz,* 1226
Zpitno— *municipium Zpuitno,* 979

URBS

In Roman times and in medieval Europe the term *urbs* generally refers to a walled city or town.

BELA GORA, BROD, JARINA

Bela Gora— *urbs Belegori,* 1017
Bezun— *urbs magna Businc,* 1012
Bichin— *urbs Bigni,* 979
Brod— *urbibus Broth,* 966
Budusin— *Budusin urbem,* 1004.
Dobra Gora— *urbs Throbragora,* 966
Dubin— *urbs Dibni,* 979
Gana— *urbs quae dictur Gana,* 929
Jarina— *urbs Jarina,* 1010
Jena— *urbe quae Genium dicitur,* 1012

KOBYLICA, LIPA, LUBISIC

Jezeriska— *urbs Gezerisca,* 979
Klodno— *urbs Clotna,* 1004
Kobylica— *Marienburg urbem que et cobelitze dicitur,* 1150
Krana— *urbem Crana dictam,* 1003
Lipa— *urbs Lipzi,* 1040
Liubanici— *urbs Liubanici,* 979
Lubin— *urbs Lubin,* 1150
Lubisic— *urbs Lubizici,* 1004
Lunkin— *urbs Lunkini,* 929
Misin— *urbs Misin,* 1090

MOGILNO, SVETIM, USTI

Mogilno— *urbs Mogilna,* 1003
Pauk— *urbs Pouch,* 979
Pretim— *urbs Pretim,* 1004
Rocholenzi— *urbs Rocholenzi,* 1009

Sciciani— *urbs Ciani,* 1015
Scudizi— *urbs Scudizi,* 1004
Siusli— *urbs Siusli,* 1004
Svetin— *urbs Suetna,* 1004
Svircov— *urbem Schworz nomine construxit,* 1150
Usti— *urbs Ustiure,* 1003
Vozgrina— *urbs Uuazgrini,* 1004

OPPIDUM

In Roman times, the term *opid* refers to the town center of a Roman community. In medieval Europe, *opid* is a smaller, provincial town.

DOLINA, GORISIN, LUBANICI

Dolina— *oppidum Dollen,* 1258
Drevsk— *oppidum Droyssig,* 1483
Gorisin— *oppido Goresin,* 1012
Grmin— *Grimmi oppidum,* 1065
Gubin— *oppidum Gubin,* 1235
Kalovica— *oppidum Kalewicz,* 1350
Kamjenc— *Kamenz oppidum,* 1225
Lipsk— *oppidum Libziki,* 1021
Lubanici— *oppidum Liubanici,* 1240
Lubnjov— *Lebenow cum opido,* 1315
Lubov— *oppidum Lubaw,* 1221
Lucin— *oppidum Lutzin,* 1330

MEDZIREKA, OSTROG, STRELA

Medzireka— *oppidum Miedzyrec,* 1300
Milisa— *oppidin in Milsin,* 1210
Nosin— *oppidum Nossin,* 1376
Osek— *Ozzek oppidum,* 1212
Ostrog— *oppidum Oztrosen,* 1241
Plotce— *oppidum Plotzka,* 1221
Polznica— *opidum Polsnitz,* 1318
Stojsin— *iuxta oppidum Stosene,* 1285
Strela— *oppidum in Strela,* 1228
Tuchorin— *oppidi Thvchirn,* 1315
Zitici— *oppicum Cicze,* 1228
Velin— *Welen oppidum,* 1495

BURGWARD

Burgwards, from *burg*, connoting castle, citadel, stronghold, fortress, and ward, connoting observation, watchtower, were basic administrative units formed in Slavic territories.

BELICI, BISTRICA, BUDIGOST

Barbogi— *burchward Barabogi,* 999

Belici— *burguuwardium Belizi,* 997
Bidrici— *burgwardus Bidrizi,* 932
Bistrica— *burcuuardo Bvistrizi,* 1068
Bolechin— *burchwardo Bolechin,* 1046
Borus— *burgwardo Boruz,* 983
Budigost— *burgwardo Budegast,* 1017
Buzin— *burgward Busin,* 1090
Chojno— *burgwardo Chvine,* 1069
Chojin— *burgward Kayna,* 1069

DOBRUS, GROB, KLUC

Colodic— *burchwardo Cholidistcha,* 1046
Dobrus— *burguardus Dobrus,* 1241
Dolgovic— *burquardus Dolgawiz,* 1241
Godivo— *burchwardo Godiwo,* 1071
Grob— *burchwardo Grobi,* 1046
Gvozdec— *burchwardo Guozdezi,* 1045
Klec— *Clitze cum burchwardo,* 1145
Kluc— *burchwardium Cluzi,* 1149
Lagov— *burgwardo Lagowe,* 1226
Lesnik— *burchwardo Lesnic,* 1040

LIUBUSA, MOKREN, NEREKOV

Liubusa— *burgward Liubusua,* 1012
Lubin— *burguuwardo Luuine,* 1069
Milisa— *burgwardo Militzin,* 1556
Mokren— *burgward Mokernik,* 992
Nemocov— *burchwardo Nimucowa,* 1090
Nerekov— *burguuardium Nirechouua,* 997
Niempsi— *civitatem Niempsi dictam in ripa fluminis Niza sitam atque illud burgwardum,* 1000
Rochelinzi— *burgward Rochelinti,* 1017
Skolin— *burgwardo Szholin,* 1031
Sputin— *burgward Spuitene,* 961

SRBICI, TREBEN, ZADEL

Srbici— *burgward Zurbizi,* 1075
Suselzi— *burhwardio Suselzi,* 997
Svojim— *burgwardo Zwegene,* 1091
Tetibuzin— *burwardo Titibutziem,* 1018
Treben— *burcwardo Treben,* 1062
Treskov— *burchwardo Trescowo,* 1130
Zadel— *burgwardo Zadil,* 1074
Zicani— *burgwardo Schizani,* 1001
Zcolm— *burgward Zcolm,* 1017
Zrebec— *burgwardus Serebez,* 1064

2. PAGO SRBA, PROVINCIA SERBIA, REGIO SRBI, REGIO SORABOS, TERRA SORABI, TERRITORIO SRBISTE

In the Middle Ages the terms *pago, provincia, regio, regione, terra,* and *territorio* were often used for a territorial polity representing the historical center of a distinct Slavic community. In the following series all territorial entities are from *White Serbia* and bordering areas.

BELO ZEMLYA, BROD, DALMATIA
Belo Zemlya— ***pago Beleseim,*** 983
Brod— ***pago Broto,*** 1004
Butzin— ***pago Butzin,*** 1150
Cabnici— ***pago Schebeniz,*** 1349
Chutici— ***pagus Chuntizi,*** 1030
Coldici— ***pago Colidiki,*** 981
Dalmatia— ***pago Dalmatia,*** 1046
Delcic— ***pago Delsche,*** 1386
Dobna— ***pago Dobna,*** 1122
Gorsin— ***pago Gorsene,*** 1316

LOKAVICA, LUSICI, MORACA
Ilov— ***pago Ylowe,*** 1268
Jena— ***pago Giinnaha,*** 1044
Krimov— ***pago Cremowe,*** 1265
Kusici— ***pagus Kuschez,*** 1289
Lanevici— ***pago Lanewizi,*** 1108
Lokavica— ***pago Langguizza,*** 932
Lusici— ***pago Lusici,*** 1005
Milzani— ***pago Milzani,*** 1007
Moraca— ***pago Moroszanorum,*** 965
Muzkov— ***pago Muschowe,*** 1314
Neletici— ***pago Neletici,*** 965

NOVIGRAD, ORLA, REKA
Nizizi— ***pago Nikiki,*** 981
Novigrad— ***pago Novigroda,*** 1028
Nudzici— ***pagus Nudzici,*** 965
Orla— ***pago Orla,*** 1169
Plisna— ***pago Plisina,*** 976
Pozowa— ***pago Puonozowa,*** 976
Quezici— ***pago Quezici,*** 1000
Reka— ***pago Rekken,*** 1242
Scitici— ***pago Scitici,*** 992
Sermunti— ***pago Sermunti,*** 945
Sibrovic— ***pago Spiliberch,*** 1053
Skorlup— ***pago Zcurlup,*** 1212

SRBA, SRBISTI, STRUPANICE

Skudici— *pago Scudizi,* 1030
Srba— *pago Zurba,* 1040
Srbisti— *pago Zervisti,* 973
Strupanice— *pago Strupanice,* 1136
Susilin— *pago Susilin,* 1043
Tuchorin— *pago Tuchorin,* 1040
Velez— *pago Weliz,* 1240
Vulki— *Uolaki,* 973
Zlomici— *pagus Zlomizi,* 1003
Veta— *pago Uueta,* 976
Vetrosit— *pago Witerschit,* 1292
Zitici— *pago Zitici,* 945

VILLA ET PAGO BUKOVICA, VILLA ET PAGO SVEC

Bukovica— *villa et pago Buckowicz,* 1251
Gorskovic— *villa et pago Gorscuwiz,* 1264
Laz— *in pago ville dicte Lasan,* 1270
Luben— *in villa et pago wenygen Luben,* 1399
Luskov— *in pago villae Luschowe,* 1311
Sokolic— *villa et pago ville Tzokliz,* 1359
Svec— *villa et pago Zwezesdorph,* 1296

DUB, GLOMACI, MILIN

Bozevici— *in provincia Buzewicz,* 1210
Chuntici— *provincia Chuntici,* 973
Domici— *provincia Domitz,* 1223
Dub— *provincia Dahme,* 1166
Glomaci— *provintiam Glomacia,* 1012
Heveli— *provincia Heveldon*
Milin— *provincia Milin,* 1212
Nizizi— *provintia Nizizi,* 983
Plisni— *provincia Plisni,* 974
Roglezi— *provincia Rochelenzi,* 1100

SERBIA, STODOR, ZAGOST

Scudici— *provincia Zcudici,* 1004
Serbia— *provincia quae Suurbia dicitur,* 1124.
Siusli— *provincia Siusili,* 973
Stodor— *provincia Stodor,* 906
Zagost— *provintia Zagost,* 1144
Zarov— *provinciolam Sarowe,* 859
Zcudici— *provincia Zcudici,* 1004
Zluvini— *provintia Zliuvini,* 973
Ztrele— *provincia Ztrele,* 1210

REGIO QUAE VOCATUR SURBI

Belo Zemlya— ***Balsamorum regio,*** 1025
Chutici— ***regio Chutici,*** 974
Neletici— ***regio Neletice,*** 965
Neletici— ***altera regio Neletici,*** 961
Nisan— ***regio Nisene,*** 948
Serimunt— ***regio Serimunt,*** 951
Srbi— ***regio quae vocatur Surbi,*** 850

REGIO COLODICI-SORABOS

Colodici— ***regio Koledizi,*** 973
Colodici— ***Sorabos, qui Colodici vocantur,*** 839

REGIONE CHUTICI

Regione Chutizi, 974
Regione Liudizi, 1002
Regione Miltizieni, 1002
Regione Neletici, 973
Regione Schutizi, 1004

TERRA SORABI

Chozimi— ***terra Chozimi,*** 961
Dobni— ***terra Dobene,*** 1267
Lusici— ***terra Lusici,*** 953
Milzani— ***terra Milze,*** 992
Selpoli— ***terra Selpoli,*** 961
Sorabi— ***in terram ... qui dincuntur Sorabi,*** 806

TERRITORIO SRBISTE

Srbiste— ***territorio Zerbiste,*** 1003
Tuchorin— ***teritorio Tucherin,*** 1004

3. NEMANIC MARK, BERLINISCHE WENDE MARCKEN

In medieval and post-medieval Germania the term mark refers to a basic political-administrative unit, initially a frontier territorial entity administered by a *markgraf*. The names of most German marks established in the territory of *Slavia* have obvious Slavic roots. The following series is from *White Serbia.*

NEMANIC MARK
Numerous marks are derived from Slavic family names ending in **-IC**.

BERISLAVIC, BLAZIC, DRAGANIC
Beri-slav, Beric— Berze, 1265; Beridorfer M
Belko, Belkovic— Belkewitz, 1378; Belkewitz M, 1404
Blazic— Blasiz, 1246; Blossitzer M, 1564
Bozen, Bozenic— Bosenitz, 1571; Bosenitz M, 1536
Dal, Dalovic— Delewiz, 1251; Delbitz M
Dan, Danovic— Danewicz, 1495; Danitz M
Dragan, Draganic— Drockenitz, 1428; Drackenitz M, 1464
Drogo, Drogolici— Drogolisci, 992; Dorgelitz M, 1542
Drogo, Drogovic— Trognitz M, 1755
Gos, Gosovic— Geschewitz M, 1474

GOSTIC, LUBANOVIC, MIRKOVIC
Gost, Gostlic (Gost)— Gostewitz M, 1754
Gost, Gostovic— Gostewitz, 1440; Gostitz M, 1420
Kolek, Kolekovic— Kolkewitz, 1360; Kolkewitz M, 1499
Lesa, Lesovic— Leschwitz, 1350; Leschwitz M, 1501
Luban, Lubanovic— Lobenicz, 1288; Lobenutz M, 1755
Lubos, Lubosici— Lubschitz M, 1481
Luto, Lutotici— Latzetz M, 1568
Mirko, Mirkovic— Erkecwitz, 1501; Ekewitz M, 1551
Mysl, Myslovic— Muselicz M, 1445

NEMANIC, PRIBISLAVIC, RADAKOVIC
Nemanic— Nemenitz, 1481; Nemptitz M, 1481
Nerad, Neradic— Neritz, 1549; Neritz M
Nikur, Nikurovic— Niquirbicze, 1156; Neckewitz M
Premysl-ovic— Premselwitz, 1358; Premeslicz M
Pribislav-ic— Pribizlawiz, 1184; Prestelwitz M, 1485
Radak, Radakovic— Radekewicz, 1349, Rackewitz M
Radko, Radkovici— Rachewiz M, 1495
Rod, Rodic— Rodiz, 1538; Reitz M, 1538
Rodok, Rodokovic— Redeghewitz, 1333; Rachewitz M
Vulkmir-ic— Volkmeritz, 1498; Volkmar M, 1498

BOCHUTIC MARK
From less common Slavic family names ending in **-IC**.

BEZDEVIC, CEPELIC, CHOTIC

Bezdevic— Bestewitz, 1394; Besswitzer M, 1529
Bochut, Bochutic— Bochutize, 1043; Pechlitz M, 1650
Bol, Bolic— Bolitz, 1160; Bolitz M
Bras, Brasovic— Braschewicz, 1421; Broschwitz M, 1576
Cab, Cabin, Cabnic— Schebenyz, 1349; Schobnitz M, 1858
Celin— Czelinic, 1404; Zellen M, 1404
Cepel, Cepelic— Zsepeliz, 1285; Zschepels M, 1557
Chlud— Cludenic, 1225; Cleuden M, 1542
Chotel, Chotelic— Gotliz, 1549; Goltiz M
Chotimir, Chotic— Hotsitz, 1224; Gotz M

LUPOSIC, SKOBLIC, TUSOVIC

Chotimir, Chotovic— Kottwitz M, 1858
Lobz, Lobzic— Lobesiz, 1286; Lobitz M, 1755
Lubis, Lubisa— Lobesicz, 1288; Lobitz M, 1755
Lupos, Luposic— Lupschicz, 1378; Luptcztit M, 1460
Mas, Maskovici— Maschwitz M, 1858
Nis, Nisul, Nisovic— Nischwitz, 1600; Nichtewiz M, 1549
Pret, Pretovic— Pritewiz, 1207; Preitcz M, 1516
Skobl, Skoblic— Schobelitz, 1450; Schobnit M
Tichor, Tichoric— Tickeritz, 1182; Dekeriz M, 1386
Ustim, Ustimic— Ucztemicz, 1350; Ustemiczer M, 1399
Tus, Tusovic— Thyshewiz, 1236; Tauschwitz M, 1824

BOYAN MARK

From common Slavic personal names.

BORETA, DRAZ, GRUBISIN

Boreta, Boretin— Bortin, 1350, Parthin M
Borko— Borkow, 1440; Burckau M, 1555
Boyan— Boyan, 1583; Bougen M
Dosin— Dosen, 1442; Dossen M, 1486
Draz, Drozin— Drosen M, 1549
Drazul/Drozule— Dreyseul M, 1592
Dusov— Dussow, 1400; Dussu M
Gnev— Gnewe, 1268; Gnebe M, 1485
Gost— Goste, 1413; Gassitz M
Grubisin (Grubscene, 1424), Gruppschen M
Hrabar, Chrobr— Krober, 1468; Crebern M, 1600

LUBUN, SLAVKO, VLOD

Jaksa— Jaxowe, 1321); Jaxo M
Lesa, Lesin— Leischen, 1243; Lesch M, 1796
Luben— Luben M, 1499
Lubun— Labun, 1713; Labaun M, 1768
Luto, Lutota— Luitatczie, 978; Latzetz M, 1563

Premislav— Premslawitz, 1376; Premitz M, 1570
Radobyl— Radegall M, 1450
Slava— Schlaevendorf M, 1858
Slavko— Schlocken, 1530; Schlikau M, 1858
Stas— Staczschow, 1378; Statz M, 1600
Velisin— Welsin, 1491; Welssen M, 1492
Vlod— Vlochow, 14494; Flochau M, 1610

KRAK MARK

From less common Slavic personal names.

BROSUCH, CHOTUL, GODISLAV

Brosuch— Broschuck, 1575; Proschuk M, 1671
Can— Schans-dorf, 1160; Zambsdorf M, 1534
Chodra, Chodrin— Gross-Godderische M, 1800
Chotensk (Chotin)— Gotenzke, 1334), Gottentz M
Choter, Choterad— Gothere, 1378; Gotter M, 1537
Chotul— Gotule, 1280; Gattul M, 1566
Dika, Dikov— Dieko, 1600; Dicker M, 1600
Domaluz (Domalud)— Domlutz M, 1494
Don, Donis, Donisin— Donicz, 1382; Donitz M, 1755
Godislav— Gozlic, 1417; Gebschelitz M, 1660

KOLISA, MILCHIN, NEDAMIR

Kludim— Kludeme, 1350; Cleudene M, 1542
Kol, Kolisa— Colsow, 1158; Kulsch M
Krak— Krackow, 1497; Krakau M, 1563
Krek— Krekow, 1378; Krik M, 1569
Levota, Levotic— Lewtitz, 1400l; Lewitz M, 1560
Lichan— Lychen, 1333; Leychen M, 1499
Loch, Lochov— Lochow, 1383, Lochau M, 1455
Milchin— Miltschen, 1350; Melscher M, 1517
Nedamir— Nedemer, 1400; Diem M, 1467
Pomysl, Pomila— Pomelyn, 1263; Pomleynn M

PLONI, PLONIKOLSA

From Slavic words beginning with the letter **P** relating to flora and fauna, to waterways, to land features, location, use, activities, structures.

Pasek (*clearing*)— Paskaw, 1434; Posaw M, 1497
Pasin (*meadow*)— Paszini, 1012; Pozzen M, 1710
Pic, Picin (*fodder*)— Picz, 1350; Pitz M
Ples, Plesovica (*waterway*)— Plezwiz, 1271), Plotzk M
Plon (*flatland*)— Plons, 1184; Plons M
Plonikolsa (*infertile flatland*)— Plonkolsaw, 1350; Plonekulsch M
Pluc (*plow*)— Plucz, 1398; Plutig M
Podol, Podolovica (*along the valley*)— Podelwice, 1156; Podelicz M

Podmeke (*under the moss*)— Pomeke, 1387; Pode M
Polica (*field*)— Politz, 1465; Politz M
Potok, Potocic (*brook, stream*)— Potzsch M, 1534
Potok, Potocek— Potzsher M, 1534
Predel (*border land*)— Predel, 1496; Preddel M, 1549
Predrete (*arable land*)— Prederten 1354; Proderitz M, 1641
Prelaz (*crossing*)— Prelicz, 1464; Proytzsch M, 1562
Priluk (*near the meadow*)— Prilok, 1356; Prolick M, 1566
Put, Putnic (*fetter, harness*)— Putenize, 1182; Peutnutz M, 1472

BEZ (ELDERBERRY)
From Slavic words for common flora.

Bez, Bezdevica (*edelberry*)— Bestwitz, 1394; Besswitzer M
Jablan (*apple*)— Jablence, 1222; Gebelentz M, 1466
Jemel (*misletoe*)— Gemelsch, 1466; Memmel M, 1460
Klip (*corn cob*)— Klipczene, 1445; Klipczen M, 1461
Lin (*flax*)— Linss, 1517; Linster M
Loz, Lozovic (*vine*)— Lozewicz, 1383; Lossewitz M, 1456
Malina (*rasberry*)— Malin M, 1566
Vres, Vresin (*heather*)— Wrezsen, 1350; Press M

DUB (OAK)
From Slavic words for common species of trees.

Brez, Brezovica (*birch*)— Bresewitz, 1419; Presterwitz, M, 1419
Brest (*elm*)— Presten, 1500; Prest M, 1589
Buk, Bukovica (*beech*)— Bockwitz, 1791; Bockwitz M, 1814
Dub, Dubic (*oak*)— Deubitzsch M, 1592
Dub, Dubsk (*oak*)— Dubisc, 1330; Dupsch M, 1568
Grab, Grabovica (*hornbeam*)— Grabowice, 1156; Grabitz M
Lipa (*lime tree*)— Lippe, 1520; Leipen M, 1800
Lipa (*lime tree*)— Lipzick, 1350; Leipzigk M 1520
Oles, Olesin (*alder*)— Olczney, 1527; Oltzneyhe M, 1539
Trn, Trnovica (*hawthorn*)— Tornewitz, 1200; Dornewitz M, 1555
Vrba Vrbin (*willow*)— marcquwirbene, 1231

DREZ (WOODLAND)
From Slavic words relating to wood, woodlands.

Drez, Drezga (*woodland*)— Dresse, 1520; Dress M, 1556
Drv, Drevo, Drevnica (*woods*)— Drebenitz, 1486; Drebitz M, 1800
Kloda (*log*)— Cloden, 1461; Kloden M, 1500
Kolc, Kolcov (*tree stump*)— Kelczaw, 1376; Koltczschaw M 1486
Komol, Komolic (*stump*)— Komelicz, 1509; Kummeltz M, 1555
Posek (*forest clearing*)— Boseck, 1541 Boseck M, 1536

BYK (OX)

From Slavic words for domestic and wild animals.

Byk, Bykov (*ox*)— Bitzkow, 1513; Pitzsch M
Kobyla (*mare*)— Kobelicz, 1376; Gebeltz M, 1600
Kon, Konov (*horse*)— Konow, 1457; Conische M, 1500
Gus, Gusic (*goose*)— Gusicz M, 1463
Kos, Kosovka (*blackbird*)— Kossowke, 1394; Cossack M, 1592
Kuna (*marten*)— Kunitz M, 1800
Jez, Jezkov (*sea urchin*)— Jeschkau, 1531, Geetsch M
Kolp (*swan*)— Culpin, 1382; Culpyn M, 1539)
Lis, Lisov (*fox*)— Lizowe, 1264; Litzau M, 1571
Los, Losnica (*elk*)— Lossnicz, 1466; Losnitz, M, 1518
Ovce, Ovcane (*sheep*)— Zscehen M, 1460
Riba, Rybisin (*fish, fishing ground*)— Rebeschin M, 1436
Svin, Svinica (*swine*)— Swinitz, 1457; Schweinitz M, 1549
Vulk, Vulkovic (*wolf*)— Vulqwitz, 1949; Volkwitz M, 1498
Zeruz, Zeruzin (*crow's feet*)— Seresin, 1421; Gross Seerhaus M, 1800

BLOTO (MARSH)

From Slavic words for bog, moor and marsh.

Bloto (*marsh*)— Blotowe, 1233; Plote M, 1529)
Kal (*marshland*)— Kalewiz, 1251, Kolbitz M
Lug (*marsh*)— Lughe, 1350; Lucke M
Luz (*marsh*)— Lusitz M, 1504
Luzica (*marsh*)— Lausitz, 1555; Lausig M, 1791
Luzk (*marshy grassland*)— Lusk, 1445; Laussick M, 1549

BROD (FORD)

From Slavic words relating to water and waterways.

Brod, Brodici (*ford*)— Proytzsch M, 1562
Guben (*estuary*)— Gubbin, 1575; Gubien M, 1671
Jezer (*lake*)— Jezer, 1303; Jheser M, 1442
Malovoda (*small water*)— Molweid M, 1589
Stekl (*stream, river juncture*)— Steklig, 1480; Steblick M, 1755
Tek, Tekl, Teklovica (*flowing water*)— Teklewytz, 1334; Diklasberg M, 1300
Vretin (*foaming, gushing water*)— Brentin, 1288; Brantin M, 1755

ROSA (DEW)

From Slavic words relating to wetness— Rosa (*dew*).

Rosnicza— Rosenicz, 1370; Rosnitz M, 1466
Vlozno (*damp land*)— Wollozze, 1378; Lossen M, 1477

CHOLM (HILL)

From Slavic words relating to land features or qualities.

Cholm (*hill*)— Golm, 1376; Gom M
Dobragora (*Good Mountain*)— Throbagora marca, 952
Dol, Dolany (*valley*)— Dolenigk M, 1512
Gola, Golina (*barren land*)— Gollun, 1377; Gallinisch M, 1555
Golka (*moor*)— Golkwitz, 1578; Kolkewitz M, 1499
Gorb (*hill*)— Gorbuz, 1305; Korbitz M, 1542
Gorica (*mountain*)— Ghorycz, 1340; Goritz M, 1600
Jal, Jalov (*infertile land*)— Jalaw, 1350; Gahla M, 1529
Kremenica (*stone, flintstone*)— Kremitze, 1360; Kremitz M, 1446
Laz, Lazic (*clearing*)— Lasicz, 1350; Lositz M, 1443
Slep (*bluff*)— Schlepkaw, 1587; Schlepek M, 1541
Sval (*wavy, rolling land*)— Svaliz, 1189; Schwolitz M, 1681
Svetc (*forest clearing*)— Switz, 1404; Sweetz M, 1486

ZABOR (BEHIND THE PINE TREES)
From Slavic words relating to shape and location of land.

Krivica (*on the curve*)— Criwize, 1205; Crewitz M, 1563
Krn, Krnal (*cut-off*)— Carnal/M, 1472
Kut, Kutc (*corner*)— Kucz, 1476; Leutz M, 1500
Predel (*near the boundary*)— Predele, 1156; Prelre M
Ugal, Uglic (*on the corner*)— Uglici, 993; Oeglitzsch M, 1858
Ustim, Utimic (*opening*)— Ucztemicz, 1350; Ustenitz M, 1660
Vysoke (*high*)— Wysigk, 1500; Weissig M, 1620
Zabor, Zaborov (*behind the pine trees*)— Sabrowe, 1195; Zabro M, 1600

BEL (WHITE)
From Slavic words relating to color.

Bel (*white*), Bela— Behla M, 1553
Bel, Belkovic— Belkewitz, 1378; Belkewitz M, 1404
Kras, Krasna, Krasin (*red*)— Krassen, 1480; Trossin M, 1600
Nebelic, Ne-belic— (*not white*)— Neblitz, 1539; Neblitz M, 1541

STOLP (PALISADE)
From Slavic words relating to structures and residents.

Cheza, Chyza (*house*)— Keysig, 1323; Keytzen M, 1486
Chlev (*stall*)— Glewitz, 1419; Gerewitz M, 1423
Kol (*fence, palisade*)— (Kolitz, 1575; Kolitz M 1555
Stolp, Stolpen (*fenced enclosure, palisade*)— Stolpen M, 1900)
Vlodar, Vlodarovic (*headman, ruler*)— Loderwyz, 1330; Lodderitz M, 1494

BERLINISCHE WENDE MARCKEN
Several names are derived from *brla*, a Slavic word connoting dirt, mud, twigs, branches, leaves and combinations of same, including fishtraps of mud, twigs, and leaves.

Brla, Brlin Brljaga— Berlin; Berlinischen, 1585; Berlinische Wende Marcken, 1603

Brla, Brloz— Berlos, 1376; Barlowische M, 1566

ALMOST, NEARLY, HAD TO FART

As befits a rural and agricultural time and place, many names are derived from Slavic words connoting manure, smell, and stink. None, however, have the comical vibes of Mark *Skoropurdi* (Almost, Nearly, Had to Fart/Stink) and Feldmark *Priperde* (Before the Fart/Stink), names second only to *Velepurdi* (the Big or Great Fart/Stink).

Feldmark Priperdi— Pripdere, 1516; Pripert, 1600

Mark Skoropurdi— Skorporde, 1378; Schererperde M, 1465

BLATO, DOBRAGORA

Some names have especially strong Serb-Yugoslav overtones.

DUBICA, GOSTILICA, JESENICA

Dubica (Daubitz M, 1508)

Duga (Dugow M, 1442)

Glav (Glaw M, 1600)

Glina (Glein M, 1592)

Gorane (Gorene, 1174, Gren M)

Gostilica (Gostilize, 850; Gestewitz M)

Grabov (Grabov, 1299; Grabo M)

Grobica (Grobicz, 1443; Groptc M)

Greben (Grebene, 1140; Kryben M)

Jesen (Jesen, 1381; Gesen M)

Jesenica (Gerschnitz M, 1600)

TREBIN, PODGRAD, VISEGRAD

Kamen (Caminisch M, 1575)

Kljuc (Clutzow M, 1523)

Koren (Kuren M, 1495)

Krupa (Krupe, 1400; Grubl M)

Lesin (Lesch M, 1796)

Meden (Meden M, 1532)

Podgrad (Pothegrodice, 1157; Pogeritz M, 1755)

Trebin (Trebeni, 1430; Treben M, 1858)

Visegrad (Wischerod M, 1622)

Vrbica (Werbiz, 1796; Werbitzer M, 1894)

Vranov (Wranow, 1371; Granow M, 1446)

STADT, STETTLEIN

The term stadt generally refers to a municipally centered commune. Some marks are also recorded as stadts and others as mark-stadts.

Dobric— Markstatte Dobberitz, 1496

Donin— Donin stadt, 1272

Drevsk— Droesigk Stedel, 1600
Grab— Grabenstadt, 1458
Gumnica— statt Huwicz, 1378
Lobisic— Lobeschitz, 1299; Lob Stadt, 1748
Lokov— Lochow, 1339; Lochow M, 1382; Lochau Stetlein, 1528
Lubogostic— Lubegostiz, 1253; Lobe Stedt, 1506
Mysliboz— Mizleboze, 1139; Muselbicz Stadt, 1399
Podlese— statt Poclessn, 1400
Skolane— Scholen Stadt, 1446
Skudici— Stadt Schkeuditz, 1300
Trgov— Turquo stadt, 1102
Tuchor— Stettlein Tuchor, 1530
Tuchovic— Alden stad Tauchlitz, 1406

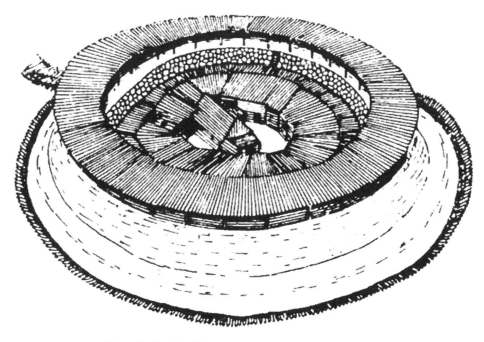

Fortified *Grad*/town (Regnum Soraborum)

PART IX

1. MILES ZOLUNTA, VOGT PRIBISLAV

In spite of determined efforts to replace traditional, pagan Slavic personal names with Christian names, one often finds references to Slavic names in medieval German church and state registers.

BORISLAV DE DOBLIN

The following series is a random sample of Slavic names found in various German sources in the 10th, 11th, and 12th centuries.

BELESTA, ZRUBO

Belesta, 900

Bezeko, 1002

Bolibor, 1071

Bor, 1140

Boris, 1197

Boris, 1005

Borislav, 1071

Bronislav, 1161

Luzicho, 1136

Mistivoi, 1012

Mizborus, 1071

Prebislav, 983

Sveslav, 1071

Tugost, 973

Wilico, 1031

Zrubo, 1011

IN THE 13TH CENTURY (BOHUSE, PRIBISLAV)

Bohuse, 1234

Boranta, 1249

Borasch, 1283

Boreslaus, 1220

Borezlaus, 1203

Boyzlaus, 1265

Bozh, 1250

Branislav, 1242

Bratrisin, 1231

Chotebor, 1239

Chotemir, 1238

Czakan, 1271

Dobromysl, 1296

Domamir, 1290

Drzislav, 1236

Janiko, 1299

Luboslav, 1276

Moyko, 1222

Predborus, 1234

Pribislav, 1216

IN THE 13TH CENTURY (PRIBISLAV, ZTOAIN)

Pribislav, 1277

Primuzil, 1223

Radegozin, 1281

Radoslav, 1216

Rodoslav, 1233

Radovan, 1269

Rotzlav, 1223

Slavko, 1234

Sulimir, 1296

Sulimir Tesimeric, 1219

Trebimir, 1228

Wrisco, 1298

Woiz, 1297

Zdislav, 1234

Zelimir, 1298

Ztenco, 1290

Ztoain, 1231

IN THE 14TH CENTURY (APECZCO, VOLIGOST)

Apeczco, 1350	Jenchin, 1340
Apeczko, 1320	Jenchin, 1374
Bohusius, 1351	Jenichinus, 1350
Blagusch, 1381	Jenik, 1374
Czakan, 1371	Jentsco, 1350
Czaslav, 1357	Jeroslav, 1328
Czaslaw, 1381	Jerusch, 1359)
Czernic, 1378	Kunzko, 1326
Czeschan, 1342	Pawil Peskovic, 1374
Czeschanin, 1390	Pribor, 1310
Drohost, 1374	Sdyslav, 1329
Droysek, 1311	Seldrog, 1330
Drozko, 1311	Slavko, 1324
Gerchko, 1339	Slotekin, 1311
Grodel, 1324	Krizan, 1374
Jan, 1339	Thyczo, 1313
Jaros, 1359	Volcko, 1348
Jenchin, 1309	Voligost, 1372
Jenchin, 1324	

IN THE 15TH AND 16TH CENTURIES (BOG, YEROCH)

Bog, 1485	Krotk, 1541
Czenko, 1423	Pawil Cakovic, 1400
Hrotczk, 1444	Pawil, 1421
Jan, 1442	Vrban, 1599
Jaros, 1486	Wokun, 1423
Jeresch, 1486	Wron, 1428
Jersczhe, 1446	Wustan, 1439
Jherek, 1455	Yenisch, 1405
Krol, 1484	Yeroch, 1524

COMES, MILES, VOGT

In some cases, nobles, high-ranking officials, and clergy in imperial service are recorded with Slavic personal names, including:

Miles Zolunta (**qui Szlavonice Zolunta vocatur**), a Serb knight serving in Otto II's personal bodyguard during his 982 Italian campaign; *Miles Bolilut,* commander of Brandenburg province (**Quae post a Brennebrugiensis iniusto provisore civitatis Boliluto capta in tantum constricta,** 994);

Miles Isich, commander of Lebusa (**et eiusdem custom Scih, vulneratus,** 1012); *Dirzislav,* **Dirzislau castellanus de Schidelow,** 1236; *Bozata,* son of **kastellan** Johannes, 1259; ***Vogt** Pribislav,* governor of Meissen province in the mid-12th century; ***Jentsco, miles de Lucenicz,*** 1293 (Licenici (Lysczenicz, 1317, now Lutzschnitz, near Lommatzsch);

Pronotar Zlatek (Slotekini), 1306; *Luscevic,* **Miles Luschewitz**, 1315; **Miles Petzko de Lossow**, 1317; **Zabel castellanus de Pyzene**, 1317; **Slavkinus Miles ac Pribeslavs fratres germani dicti Slavkovitz**, 1332; **dominus Slawekinus de Podemin Miles**, 1334; **Miles Caslav** (Zschaslau), 1356.

BOLILIUT, ZOLUNTA

Boliliut, 994
Budislav, 1017
Dragebodo, 1201
Isich, 1012
Jaromir, 1045
Kos, 1071

Lubo, 982
Misicho, 992
Pribislav (Meissen, 1156)
Sulimir, 1257
Zolunta (*qui Szlavonice Zolunta vocatur*, 982)

FIDELIS, SENIOR, VIRO, DOMINUS

Numerous men of rank and officials with Slavic personal names are identified as **Fidelis** (e.g. **fidelis Sveslav**); **Senior** (e.g. a **Sclavis in Zuencua sub Cuchavico senior sibi multum dilecto haberi**); **Viro** (e.g. **viro Moic**); **Dominus** (e.g. **dominus Bozh**).

BORAN, VECEMYSL

Boran, 1249
Bozh, 1250
Branislav, 1161
Budislav, 1378
Cuchavicus, 955
Drzik, 1028
Drzislav, 1236
Isich, 1012

Jaczo, 1295
Jeroslav Lyblicz, 1387
Luboslav, 1276
Moic, 1042
Nezan, 974
Radoslav, 1176
Sveslav, 1031
Vecemysl, 1005

PRIESTER, KLERIKER

One even finds Slavic personal names among the Christian clergy: **Bratislav,** 1000; **Lubor** 1211; **Popel,** 1207; **Prebor,** 1000; **Venceslav,** 1000; **Slavos,** 1207; **Stodor,** 1000.

PLACE NAMES, FAMILY NAMES

In addition, of course, throughout Germania, in varying degrees of adaptation, thousands of Slavic personal names are preserved in place names, and many more in family names.

Bedro, Bedrovic—Bederwicz, 1370
Bodan, Bodenic—Bodenicz, 1365
Boran, Boranovic—Baranewicz, 1370
Boso, Bosovic—Boschewicz, 1363
Bozan, Bozankovic—Bosenkewicz, 1365
Buk, Buko—Buko, 1325

2. HERBORDUS DE SRBOV
SIFFIRED DE SRBOVIC

It is clear from diverse sources that conversion of the Slavs of Germania was followed by the adoption of Christian names at all social levels, namely local adaptations of Greek-Latin names favored by the church.

HEINRICUS, PRIZZLAVIS

Two of the four Slavic nobles recorded in Havelberg in 1228 have Christian names, two have Slavic names: *Slawi noblies Heinricus, Prizzlavis, Pribbeslau, Andreas.*

Heinrich and Boriz are the names of two brothers granting hereditary lands to a local convent in 1243: *Heinrici et Boriz ... villas omnes, que per provinciam Tolenze ad eas spectant hereditaria nost assignavant conviventia.*

MISTIVOI

There is good reason to believe that Christian Slavic nobles had two names, one, a native Slavic name, another, a Christian name. This duality appears to be the case in one of *Terra Abodritorum's* great ruling houses, beginning with *Duke Mistivoi* in the late 10th century. With fire and sword, *Mistivoi* had rid *Slavia,* up to and including Hamburg, of an avaricious, corrupt, and oppressive Christianity. In his last years, *Mistivoi* accepted Christianity, an act that forced him to flee *Slavia.*

PRIBIGNEV (UDO)

Pribignev (d. 1031), *Duke Mistivoi's* son and successor, seems to have had a second name. In contrast to Saxo Grammaticus and other sources, Helmold calls him Udo. In the words of Helmold, a bad Christian, nevertheless, *Pribignev's* son, Gottschalk, was given to God in deed as well as name, to the study of theology and learned disciplines in St. Michael's monastery at Luneburg. Gottschalk had two sons, both Christians. One named *Budivoi.* Another named Henry, the issue of his marriage to the daughter of Denmark's king Canute.

WLODIMIR, SVETOPOLK, CANUTE, PRIBISLAV

Henry had three sons. One son, Canute, carried the name of his maternal grandfather. Two sons had Slavic names, *Wlodimir* and *Svetopolk,* the latter Henry's successor. *Svetopolk* was succeeded by a son, *Zvinislav,* whose death ended the *Mistivoi* line in *Slavia. Zvinislav* was succeeded by *Pribislav,* the issue of one of Henry's cousins.

PRIBISLAV / HEINRICAS

The early 11th century ruler of Branibor/Brandenburg was well known by both his native Slavic name, *Pribislav,* and his Christian name, Heinricas: *Heinricas, qui slavonice Pribesclaus, christiani nominis cultor, ex legitima parentele successione huius urbia ac tocius terre.*

MEINFRIED, MOJMIR

The name of *Pribislav's* contemporary, *comes Slavorum* Meinfried of Branibor/ Brandenburg, is believed to be a German equivalent of the native Slavic *Mojmir.* Another contemporary, Duke Widukind, the powerful Slavic ruler of Haveland, seated at Havelberg, is known only by his Christian name.

HERTWICUS SUPANUS

The 'zupan of Batic' is Hertwig is: *Hertwicus supanus* (1248).

MAGISTER HEINRICUS

'Heinricus the Slav' is magister of a village near Brandenburg: *Heinricus Slavus, magister civium dicte ville* (1226).

COMMONERS

Only one of four non-titled Slavs named in a 1136 document is recorded with a traditional Slavic name, *Luzicho;* the three others have Christian names: *Quatour Slavi de sepe nominata villula ... Herold, Odalrih i Kuno.*

WERNHERUS, PRIBIZLAUS

In some instances one finds a mixture of personal and place names: *Wernherus et Pribizlaus de Tanninberch*, 1227; *Nycolaus, Albertus, Branislaus de Borsiz*, 1242; *Pawil et Hanczeman Czakewicz*, 1400.

BARTOLDUS, HENRICUS

In a number of 13th century documents all the Slavs have Christian names: *Bartoldus slavus; Borchardus dictus slavus; Conrado sclavo; Henricus sclavio; Hildebrandus sclavus; Johannes et Burchardus slavi; Sifridus Slavus; Magester civium Henricus Slavus.*

THIDERICUS, LAURENTZ

A century later we have a Slav named Thidericus: *In bonis meis inquibus nunc sedet Slavus nomine Thidericus'* (1307). Also a Wend named Laurentz: **Komen mit rechte van Laurentze den Wende vmme dt penninge** (1385).

SLAVOS DICTOS DE JAZEKE

In early 14th century Neu-Brandenburg a number of Slavs are recorded with essentially Latin or Latinized names: *Slavos dictos de Jazeke, videlicet Janekinum longum, Nyclolaum longum, Lemmekinum et Hincekinum, Thiedericum Cunradum de Lypa, Thydericum Jermiz ... et Tessekinum Kucker* (1330).

PRIBISLAV KOSEN, KOSENSON

In 14th century Rugen a number of interesting combinations of Slavic-German/ Danish personal and family names are recorded. In some instances, one finds family members with Slavic and non-Slavic personal names and Slavic family names: *Ralic and Godeschalk Ralekevitz; Sum, Razlaf and Johan Sumovitz.* In other instances, while the Slavic personal name is retained, the patronymic family name has a non-Slavic ending. Kosen's son *Pribislav,* for example, is recorded as *Prybbeslaf* Kosen and *Prybeslav* Kosenson.

GOTTHELF, POMGAJBOG

The personal and family names of Serbs students from *Luzica/Lusatia* at the University of Halle in the 18th century offers some insight into the personal and family name situation in the medieval period. It appears that the Serb students had two sets of names, unofficial, native, personal and family names, and official, often equivalent, German personal and family names.

Bogumil Fabricius, Gottlieb Fabricius
Jan Bedrich Fryco, Johann Friedrich Fritze
Jan Bogumer Rychtar, Johann Gottfried Ohnefalsch Richter
Jan Fryco, Johann Fritze
Jan Juro Rezak, Johann Georg Resag
Jan Rychtar, Johann Richter
Jan Zygmunt Bjedrich Syndlar, Johann Siegismund Friedrich Schindler
Karlo Boguchwal Korn, Carl Gottlob Korn
Pomgajbog Kristalub Fryco, Gotthelf Christlieb Fritze

HERBORD OF SRBOV, SIFFIRED OF SRBOVIC

In the following series, Christian Slav residents of villages with typical Slavic or ethnonymic names (e.g. Srbov, Srbovic) are recorded with typical Christian names (e.g. Herbord, Siffired).

PETRUS DE BELA, PETRUS DE CRNOGLAV

Bela (Petrus de Bele, 1309)
Bolebor (Gerhardus de Bolberitz, 1301)
Borlin (Petrus de Borlin, 1200)
Brezna (Burchardus de Brezne, 1208)
Cholm (Stephanus de Chulme, 1222)
Cremensica (Kyrstina de Shremsenicz, 1290)
Crnicin (Henricus de Schyrnyschyn, 1305)
Crnoglav (Petrus de Schorneglowe, 1248)
Dobra (Anoldus de Dobora, 1298)
Dobros (Johannes de Dobros, 1196)
Dol (Johannes plebanus in Dolen, 1275)
Gora (Tizco von Gor, 1429)
Gornica (Heynricus de Gorenz, 1282)

HERMAN DE GOSTILICA, MARTIN DE KOBYLA

Gostilica (Hermannus de Gostilice, 1135)
Jablan (Albertus de Gabla, 1330)
Javorno (Conradus de Javorno)
Jezero (Ludgerus de Jezere, 1202)
Jezersk (Thieofoldus de Iserike, 1182)
Kamenica (Henricus de Kemenytz, 1297)
Klekovica (Radolphus de Clekewitz, 1220)
Kobyla (Martinus de Kobelowe, 1233)
Kolisin (Johannes von Kollisene, 1359)

Kom (Petris de Chulme, 1206)
Koprica (Otto de Kopericz, 1225)
Krivica (Hugo de Criwitz, 1216)
Krusovica (Anroldus de Crusewicz, 1281)

JOHAN DE MALOVODA, ULRIC DE MIRKOVIC

Lubosevici (Gerhardus de Lubosevic, 1209)
Malovoda (Johannes de Milvede, 1351)
Medevic (Petrus de Medewicz, 1332)
Milobuz (Hermannus de Melebuz, 1230)
Mirkovic (Ulricus de Merkwitz, 1266)
Nisic (Ramvoldus de Nyschicz, 1350)
Ostrosin (Georg von Ostrosichin 1429)
Peles (Conradus de Peles, 1200)
Plav (Reinhard de Plawe, 1222)
Plavnica (Ludewicus de Plaunitze, 1192)
Pluskovic (Petrus et Nycolaus de Pluskewicz, 1375)
Podcapli (Tidericus de Postshapel, 1206)
Podluzi (Wernherus de Podeluz, 1217)
Pravovic (Petrus de Pravitz, 1225)

CONRAD DE RADOSUL, JOHAN DE VRSIN

Radosul (Conradus de Rodesul, 1350)
Roglica (Volradus de Roglitz, 1248)
Rudenica (Kunlin von Reudenicz, 1355)
Rupica (Johann von Rupitz, 1265)
Slavin (Heinricus de Slawin, 1350)
Srbov (Herbordus de Zurbowe, 1216)
Srbovici (Siffired de Zcorbewicz, 1350)
Strumen (Theordericus de Ztrumene, 1261)
Stupica (Nycolaus de Stupicz, 1333)
Velez (Adelbero de Welez, 1133)
Velkov (Everhardus de Wilchow, 1225)
Vrsin (Johannes de Versen, 1196)

ALBRECTIC

In some instances, the change manifests itself in the partial 'Slavization' of Christian-German names. Near Lommatzsch, for example, are several villages with such adaptations as: Albrecht, Albrechticz, 1279; Arnolt, Arnoltitz, 1320; Bernhart, Bernharticz, 1336. Near Delitzsch: Elber, Elberitz, 1442; Eginhart, Einovic, 1270; Etil, Etilovic, 1495.

PART X

1. REGIO SURBI, REGIO DOCLEA: BUDIM, KOSOVO, LUBOTIN, PEC, PLAVNICA, RAS, RUDINA, VIR, ZATON

Many place names in Germania's ***regio Surbi*** are identical with historic place names recorded in ***regio Doclea*** or ***Dukljanska Drzava*** (*Prevalis, Duklja, Zeta, Crna Gora*), the first Serb state and kingdom established in the former Roman province of Dalmatia.

REGIS SCLAVORUM GLORIOSISSIMII

At different times, up to the late 11th century, and the rule of Bodin, ***filli nostri Bodini, regis Sclavorum gloriosissimi*** (Pope Clement III, 1089), ***regio Doclea*** incorporated all historic Serb lands, namely *Travunia, Zahumlya-Neretva, Serbia-Bosnia and Serbia-Raska.*

SERBIA-RASKA

Throughout *regio Doclea*, including *Serbia-Raska*, one finds many parallels with place names in Germania's ***regio Surbi***.

RAS, KOSOVO, PEC

For dramatic example, three historic place names in medieval Serbia-Raska, namely **Ras**, **Kosovo** and **Pec**, have numerous parallels in ***regio Surbi*** (*A. Urosevic, Toponimi Kosova, 1975*).

RAS

In addition to a Ras (Rassau) near Bleckede, a Ras-Rasov (Raschau) near Forcheim, a good number of Ras place names are recorded in medieval Germania. The following series is limited to the core lands of Germania's **regio Surbi**.

> **Ras, Rasenici**— Raszenitz, 1091 (Rassnitz, Merseburg)
> **Ras, Rasin**— Raschini, 1761; Rasyn, 1843 (Ressen Calau)
> **Ras, Rasin**— Rasyn, 1886 (Riessen, Guben)
> **Ras, Raskovic**— Raskewicz, 1350 (Raschutz, Colditz)
> **Ras, Rasov**— Raschov, 1404; Rasov, 1843 (Rascha Bautzen)
> **Ras, Rasov**— Raschowe, 1281; Raschow, 1378 (Raschau, Oelsnitz)
> **Ras, Rasov**— Raschowe, 1240 (Raschau, Schwarzenberg)
> **Ras, Rasovic**— Raschicz, 1368; Raschwitz,1500 (Raschutz,Grossenhain)
> **Ras, Rasovic**— *slavica Rashuwitz*, 1320; Windischen Raczwiczsch, 1378; *maior Raczwchewicz*, 1408; Grossen Raschewitz, 1493 (Gross Raschutz, Grossenhain)
> **Ras, Rasovic**— Klein Raschitz, 1551 (Klein Raschutz, Grossenhain)
> **Ras, Rasovic**— Raschwitz, 1562 (Raschwitz, Merseburg)
> **Ras, Rasovici**— Raschewitz, 1285 (Raschutz, Grossenhaim)
> **Ras, Rasovici**— Raschwitz, 1562 (Raschwitz, Merseburg)

KOSOVO

Kos, Kosin— Kosyn, 1900 (Coschen, Guben)
Kos, Kosin— Kosyn, 1446 (Koscen, Senftenberg)
Kosovo— Kozovo, 1105 (Cossa, Borna)
Kosovo— Kossov, 1336 (Ober Kossa, Alterburg)
Kosovo Bloto— Cossinblath, 1346 (Kossenblatt, Beeskow)
Kosovic— Cossewiz, 1268 (Gaschutz, Mugeln)
Kosovic— Kosswitz, 1518 (Chossewitz, Friedland)
Kosovic— Koschwicz, 1350 (Coschutz, Dresden)
Kosovic— Koschwitz, 1541 (Coschutz, Elsterberg)
Kosovica— Cossewiz, 1215; Kozzewik, 1305 (Coswig, Dessau)
Kosovica— Koswik, 1350 (Coswig, Meissen)
Kosovica— Cozwig, 1301 (Coswig, Torgau)
Kosovica— Koczwig, 1350 (Coswig, Worblitz)
Kosovica— Cossauuiki, 979 (Coswig, Wedegast)
Kosovik— Koswig, 1420 (Kosswig, Calau)
Kosovka— Kossowke, 1394 (Kossacke, Bad Duben)

PEC

Pec— Pecz, 1290 (Peetz, Zerbst)
Pec/Pecic— Peczicz, 1397 (Pietsch, Torgau)
Pec/Pecic— Peczicz, 1377 (Pietschwitz, Bautzen)
Pec/Pecin— Peczicz, 1397 (Pietsch, Belgern)
Pec/Pecin— Peschen, 1292 (Pieschen, Dresden)
Pec/Pechov— Pechoui, 948 (Pechau, Schonebeck)

ZUPAS

Many place names in Germania's *regio Surbi* have parallels in the names of *zupas* recorded in *regio Doclea*. In the following series, *regio Doclea zupas* are followed by place names in and near *regio Surbi* (*G. A. Skrivanic, Imenik. Geografskih Naziva Srednjovekovne Zete, 1959*).

BISTRICA, CRNICA, KRAYINA

Breznica— Breznica
Bistrica— Bistrica
Budim— Budim
Crnica— Crnica
Drenica— Dreznica

Drenov— Serbski Drenov
Gacko— Gac
Gorska— Gorska
Komarnica— Komarno
Krayina— Krayina

LUBUSKO, PLAV, ZAGORE

Krican— Kricin
Lubusko— Lubusko
Luska— Luska
Moraca— Moracia
Papratna— Papratna
Plav— Plav

Podluzi— Podluzi
Rudina— Rudina
Trebin-ye— Trebin
Vrsin-ye— Vrsin
Zagore— Zagore

GRADS

The same is true of place names in *regio Surbi* and historic *grads* in and near *regio Doclea*.

BAR, GRADAC, KLOBUK

Bar— Bar	Dubrovnik— Dubravnik
Borac— Borac	Gradac— Gradac
Brodar— Brod	Kljuc— Kluc
Budim— Budim	Klobuk— Klobuk
Budos— Budov	Oblik— Obla, Obli

OSTROG, SOKOL, VISEGRAD

Onogost— Nongost	Susjed— Susedlic
Ostrog— Ostrog	Svac— Svac
Rijeka— Reka	Starigrad— Starigrad
Samobor— Samobor	Visegrad— Visegrad
Sokol— Sokolic	Zabes— Zabes

BLATO, BOYANA

In and along the borders of Germania's *regio Surbi* one finds a number of interesting parallels with common and uncommon names of hydronyms, toponyms, settlements, and fraternal-communities or *plemes* in *regio Doclea*.

BOLJEVIC, CEKLIN, DROBNJAK

Bes— Bes	Ceklin— Caklin; Cechlin,
Blato— Blato	Cetin-je— Ceten,
Boljevic— Bolevici	Crno Glav— Crno Glav
Boyana— Boyan	Crnovic— Crnovic
Bratonic— Bratrnosic	Decani— Delcani
Brnisce— Brnisce	Drezga— Drezga
Cajetin— Cajetin	Drobnjak— Drobnik

GOLIYA, KOLASIN, KOMARNO

Goliya— Golica	Gruda— Gruda
Glogovac— Glogov	Gruza— Gruza
Godin-ye— Godin	Gusin-je— Gusin
Gomilya— Gomilya	Kolasin— Kolsin
Gorane— Gorane	Kom— Kolm
Gorica— Gorica	Komane— Koman
Gostilye— Gostilica	Komarno— Komarno

KOMARNICA, KRIVOSIJA, LUBOTINJ

Komarnica— Komarnica	Lesan— Lesan
Kopaonik— Kopanick	Lesko-polye— Lesko
Kosier-evo— Kosir	Lisinj— Lisin
Krivosija— Krivosic	Lubotinj— Lubotin
Krnjica— Krnica	Lukavica— Lukavica

Luzani— Luzani
Medjurecje— Medzireka

Mozur— Mozeri
Moykovac— Moykovic

PLAVNICA, PODGORICA, SAMOBOR

Nivice— Nivice
Plavnica— Plavnica
Poljica— Polica
Podgorica— Potgorize
Radogost— Radogost
Radomir— Radomir
Radun-je— Radun

Recane— Recane
Ribnica— Ribnica
Rogozno— Rogozin
Samobor— Samobor
Senica— Senica
Slatina— Slatina
Sopot— Szopot

VRAN, VRBA, ZAVAL

Sozina— Sozene
Stena— Stena
Strelac— Strela
Studenica— Studenica
Velez— Velez
Vir— Vir

Vran— Vranov
Vransko— Vransko
Vrba— Vrba
Zaton— Zaton
Zaval— Zaval

PREVAL, DUKLJA, ZETA

Mention should also be made of interesting and perhaps coincidental parallels such as **Preval** (Preval or ***Prewal magnum***, 1378); **Doclea-Duklja** (Dukelwica, 1157, Doklewiz, 1238, and Doclewicz, 1381); Zeta (Zetaw, 1466; Zetta 1590).

POPOVIC

In Germania's ***regio Surbi*** many place names are derived from personal and family names that are common in historic Serb lands (e.g. Popovic— Popouuizie/978, Popuwize/1179, and Poppewizze/1205).

BANOVIC, BOJANIC, BRATISIC

Banovic— Banewicz, 1469
Blazovic— Blasewicz, 1569
Bogutic— Bochutize, 1043
Bojanic— Boynitz, 1298

Bojetic— Beytitz, 1271
Borovic— Borewicz, 1400
Bozovic— Bozewicz, 1467
Bratisic— Bratzitz, 1388

BRATRONIC, CRNOVIC, GOLUBIC

Bratrisic— Braterwsitz, 1268
Bratronic— Breternitzi, 1074
Budisic— Budeschicz, 1378
Crnovic— Schernewicz, 1389

Draskovic— Drawsskewicz, 1453
Kosovic— Cossewiz, 1268
Gojnic— Goynicz, 1350
Golubic— Golbicz, 1381

GRUBANOVIC, KRIVOSIC, LEKOVIC

Grubanovic— Grubanewicz, 1348
Grubisic— Grubschicz, 1350
Jankovic— Jankewicz, 1460
Jerkovic— Jecherwitz, 1579

Krivosic— Crischwicz, 1303
Lekovic— Lekewicz, 1501
Lelic— Lelicz, 1378
Lesovic— Leshewicz, 1305

LUBANIC, LUBISIC, LUBOTIC

Lubanic— Lubanicz, 1254
Lubanovic— Lubanitz, 1225
Lubic— Lubitz, 1421
Lubisic— Lubsiz, 1186

Lubsic— Lubscic, 1186
Luboric— Luberitz, 1424
Lubosovic— Lubosovic, 1209
Lubotic— Liubatici, 975

MEDENICA, MEDVEDIC, MILANOVIC

Lubovic— Liubisici, 961
Malovici— Maluwiz, 1214
Medenica— Medenicz, 1350
Medovic— Medewitz, 1443

Medvedic— Midewedics, 1303
Milanovic— Mylanuwitz, 1283
Milenkovic— Mylenkwiz, 1264
Miletic— Miletiz, 1218

MILORADIC, MILOTIC, MILOSEVIC

Milic— Milicz, 1378
Miloradic— Mulraditz, 1267
Milosic— Alte Meilschnitz, 1557
Milotic— Mylutuytz, 1284

Milovic— Milwicz, 1414
Mirkovic— Merkewicz, 1350
Milosevic— Milschewicz, 1466
Neshovic— Neschewycz, 1366

PETROVIC, POPOVIC, RADANOVIC

Niksic— Nikschitz, 1565
Petrovic— Peterwicz, 1350
Popovic— Popewiz, 1322
Prelovic— Preluwicz, 1349

Pristanovic— Prestanewicz, 1350
Radakovic— Radekewicz, 1400
Radanovic— Radanwicz, 1378
Radisic— Radeschitz, 1401

RADOGOST, RADOMIRIC, RADUSIN

Radogost— Radegast, 1408
Radoman— Rademin, 1344
Radomiric— Radmericz, 1345
Radosevic— Rodeswicz, 1378

Radoslav— Razlawesstorph, 1316
Radovic— Radewitz, 1523
Radusin— Raduuassendorf, 1040
Rakovic— Rakewicz, 1404

SOKOLIC, STANOVIC, TOMIC

Ratovic— Ratewicz, 1386
Sokolic— Zokelicz, 1375
Sokolic— Zokelicz, 1375
Skokovic— Schochewicz, 1182

Stanovic— Stanewicz, 1358
Stojsovic— Stoyschewicz, 1180
Strahotic— Strachtiz, 1190
Tomic— Thomicz, 1374

VELKOVIC, VOJNIC, VUCKOVIC

Tuchovic— Tuchewiz, 1281
Velkanovic— Welkanewiz, 1241
Velkovic— Welkewitz, 1497
Vojanovic— Woganewicz, 1334
Vojetici— Woiticz, 1446
Vojnic— Woynitz, 1296

Vojnovic— Waynewicz, 1486
Volimiric— Wolmeriz, 1239
Vranovic— Vuronovici, 993
Vuckovic— Wuschewitz, 1486
Vudesic— Woodeschiz, 1441
Vuskovic— Wuschkewitz, 1470

BODIN, NEMAN, NEGOS

In Germania's *regio Surbi* one also finds place names derived from uncommon personal and family names that are historically significant in medieval and modern Serb lands.

BODIN

In *regio Surbi* and bordering *Terra Slavorum* we have such relatively uncommon personal names as *Bod, Bodin, Bodimir* and *Bodisa;* and such place names as *Bodin* (e.g. villis Bodin/1252). In *regio Doclea* we have the personal name *Bodin,* from the root *bod,* as in *Bodin* (***Bodini ... regis Sclavorum gloriosissimi***), the late 11th century ruler of greater Duklja (including Raska and Bosnia) and briefly *Tsar of Bulgaria* (1072),

NEMAN

In *regio Surbi* we have numerous place names derived from cognates of *Neman,* as in *Nemanya,* the legendary founder of the *Nemanyic* dynasty in medieval Serbia.

Neman, Nemota, Nemotic— Nimotitz, 1205 (Nimtitz, Lommatzsch)
Neman— Nymene, 1375 (Niemen, Torgau)
Neman— Nymen, 1378 (Nimen, Womirstedt)
Neman, Nemanic— Nemenitz, 1356 (Nemitz, Delitzsch)
Neman, Nemanic— Nemenitz, 1356 (Nemitz, Doberstau)
Neman, Nemanic— Nemptitz 1474
Nemas, Nemas— Nehmitzsch, 1551 (Niemtsch, Senftenberg)
Neman, Nemochov— Nimucowa, 1090 (Mochau, Dobeln)
Neman, Nemota— Nemot, 1354 (Nempt, Wurzen)

NEGOS, NJEGOS

In another case, in *regio Surbi* and throughout *Terra Slavorum* we have place names derived from cognates of *Negos* or *Njegos* as in *Mt. Negos* in western Montenegro and the *Negos-Njegos* dynasty of Montenegro, which ruled until the first decades of the 20th century.

Negos, Negost— Negast, near Stralsund
Negos— Nygas, 1333; Wenigen Negaz, 1364; Nygas, 1364 (Negis,Gera)
Negos— Negos, Negojce (Nexdorf, Finsterwald)
Negos— Negos, Negoluz— Negoludz, 1761 (Lubben)
Njegos— Njaglos, 1761 (Njagluz, Lubben)

MISLJEN

One also finds in *regio Surbi* place names derived from such uncommon personal and family names as **Misljen** (e.g. Mislenwiz, 1336; Mysselenwycz, 1369), a name by and large limited to medieval Bosnia and Montenegro. In Bosnia, for example, one finds *gost Misljen*, an elder and deputy of the Church of Bosnia (1404). The following inscription is found on his tombstone— *A se lezi dobri gospodin gost Misljen komu bise priredio po uredbi Avram svoje veliko gostoljubstvo. Gospodine dobri, kada prides prid gospodina nasega Isusa Hrista jednoga, spojmeni i nas svojih rabov. Pisa gramatik.*

Ꙗ СЄ ЛЕЖН ДОБРН ГАНЬ ГОСТЬ МНШЛЕНЬ КОМУ
  БНШЕ ПРН РЕДНО
ПО ХРЕДБН ДВРꙖМЬ СВОЕ ВЕЛНКО ГОСТОЛУБСТВО
  ГОСПОДН
NЄ ДОБР Н КꙖДꙖ ПРНДЕЩЬ ПРНДЬ Г̅Д̅Ꙗ NꙖШЕГꙖ
  НСУ ХꙖ ЄДNO ГꙖ СПО
МЕNН Н NꙖСЬ СВОНХЬ РꙖБОВ ПНСꙖ

Also *Knez* Djuro **Misljenovic** of Bosnia (1434). In Montenegro, the **Misljen** branch of of the Ivcevic **brastvo**/brotherhood of *pleme* (fraternal-territorial community) **Gluhi Do, Crmnica, Old Montenegro** (*J. Vukmanovic, Crmnica. Antropogeografska i Etnoloska Ispitivanja, 1988*).

House of Nemanjic

Djurdja Crnojevic, Gospodara Crne Gore

2. REGIO SURBI, REGIO DOCLEA
DEDIC, KMET, KNEZ, SMERD, VITEZ, ZUPAN

In **White Serbia** and throughout **Slavia** numerous place names are derived from ancient Slavic social-political institutions and titles, from institutions and titles found in medieval **Doclea** *(J. Rozwadkowski, Studia nad nazwami wod slowianskich, 1948. G. Labuda, Pierwsze panstwo slowianskie, 1949. O.N. Trubacev, Istorija slavjanskih terminov rodstva, 1959. Z. Suslowski, Slowianskie organizajce polityczne nad Baltykiem, RoH 25, 1960. J. Brankack, Studien zur Wirtschafts- und Socialstruktur der Westslaven zwischen Elbe, Saale und Oder aus der Zeit vom 9. bis 12. Jh, SpL 33, 1964. A. Hejna, Zu den Anfangen der Fursten- und Herrensitze im westslawischen Raum VpS 7, 1972. W. Prochazka, Die patriarchale Stadt als Entiwcklungsstufe des alteste politischen Organisation bei den Slawen, VpS 3, 1972. H. Brachmann, Zur Socialstruktur der slawischen Stammes des Elbe-Saale-Gebietes im 6. bis 10. Jh., BeR II, 1973. L. Dralle, Slavische Herrschaft zwischen mittlere Elbe und Oder vom 8. bis 10. Jh, SlA 27, 1980. L.E. Havlik, Moravska spolecnost a stat v 9. stoleti: Moravsky stat a jeho vladni organizace v 9. stoleti, SlA 28, 1981-82. J. Rajman, Dominus – Comes – Princeps. Studium od Jaksach w XII wieku, Studia Historiczne 33, 1990).*

DEDIC

From **ded**, a Slavic word for grandfather, elder, the title dedic, connoting community elder, advisor and guardian of ancient laws and traditions. In diverse administrative-legal contexts medieval German sources identify and recognize the title and role of **ded**:

- *Dedina*
- *Dedin ius*
- *Qui vulgariter didicin dicuntur*
- *Qui vulgariter didiczen nuncupantur*
- *Qui vulgo dedici appellantur*

From **ded** the place names: Dedic— Detitz, 1314 (Deetz, Zerbst); Dedic— Deditz, 1529 (Deditz, Grimma); Dedisovici— Didiswitz, Didiscuitz, 1205 (Doschutz, Grossehnhain); Dedelov— Dedlow/1320 (Dedelow, Prenzlau). Also medieval Dedic, Dedic Grad and Dedisce Grad.

DVORNIK

From **dvor**, a Slavic word for palace, court, and **dvornik**, a member of the court, the place names Dvor, Dvorany, Dvornica, Dvornik and Dvory *(L. Gornicki, Dworzanin polski, 1954. H.H. Bielfeldt, Slav. *dvornica, wohnraum?, ZtS 9, 1969).*

DRUZINA

Druzina is a Slavic term for a group of warriors in the service of a ruler, generally cited as ***slavonici milites*** in medieval German sources and contexts— ***Slavonici milites … unum equum, cum quo serviat domino*** *(V. Vanecek, Les "druziny" (gardes) princieres dans les debuts de l'Etat tcheque,Czasopismo Prawno-Historyczne 2, 1949. F. Graus, Ranestredoveke druziny a jejich vyznam pro vzniku stat ve stredni Evrope, CcH 13, 1965).* In addition to a number of place names derived from **druzina** (e.g. Druzevici, Druzkov, Druzno), one also finds place names derived from other Slavic words for warrior, e.g., cognates of **rat** and **boj** and combinations of **rat** and **boj**: **Ratovici**— Ratewiz, 1171 (Ratehwitz, Naumberg); **Bojetici**—

Beytiz, 1271 (Beuditz, Merseburg); **Ratiborici**— Rothebariz, 1311 (Rottewitz, Meissen).

GOSPODAR

From **gospodar**, a Slavic word for lord, ruler, one finds a Gospodic (Gozpodicz, 1334; Gospedicz, 1414), now Gastewitz, near Mugeln *(E. Fraenkel, Slavisch gospod, lit. viespat, preuss, waispatting und Zubehor, ZsP 20, 1948. H. Lowmianski, Podstawy gospodarcze formowania sie panstwa Slowianskich, 1953. L. Leciejwicz, Glowne linie gospodarszego rozwoju w VI-XI, Historia Pomorz 1, 1969. K. Modzelewski, Organizajca gospodarcza panstwa piastowskiego X-XII. Wiek, 1975).*

KMET

The more important farmers, Herrmann writes, **were known as Kmetz or Kmets; smaller, more or less independent farmers were called Smirdz. These are the Smerds or Smurds encountered in medieval manuscripts from the Elbe-Saale region and Mecklenburg.** Also in medieval manuscripts from neighboring Bohemia and Poland— *honorabilis kmethlo noster et miles; kmetho noster comes; fidelis kmetho noster; universis kmetonibus, baronibus seu nobilibus regni Bohemiae (N. van Wijk, O proishozdenii obshe-slavjanskago slova kmet, Slavia 4, 1925. J. Birkenmajer, Kmiec i starosta, JeZ 21, 1935. J. Otrebski, O pochodzeniu wyrazu kmiec, SlA 1, 1948. M. Budimir, O dardanskim kmetovima, Glasnik SaN 1, 1949. N. Klaic, Sto su kmetovi Vindolskog zakona, Radovi Filozofskog fakulteta u Zagrebu 4, 1962. R. Schuster-Sewc, Die Beziechnung der Bauern im Slawischen: Cholp, smrd, kmet, ZtS 2, 1964.).*

KNEZ

There are numerous references to the title of **knez**, a Slavic word for prince, duke, or ruler, in medieval German sources *(V.D. Koroljuk, Gosudarstvo Bodricieii v pravlenie knjazi Gotsalka, SlO 22, 1962. M. Holban, Varations historiques sur le probleme des cnezes de Transylvania, Revue Roumaine d'Historie 4, 1965).*

- *Homines in quinque iustitiis ut edelsten, knechte*
- *Iure knesitz*
- *Knesitzen*
- *Sclavia ... Usuali quidem loucuciones causa dignitatis vel reverencie knese quemlibet vocare consuevit*

KNEZ PLACE NAMES

The following are some of the numerous place names derived from **knez:**

- *In eodem comitatu iuxta aguam, qui dicitur Knesaha*
- *In loco Chnezziseo*
- *Knegyn*
- *Ad rivulum qui dicitur Knegena*
- *Knegyna Reka*
- *Knegyna Prales*
- *Kneza Dabrova*
- *Knetzgau*
- *Knetzburg*
- *Kneza Granica*
- *Knez*
- *Kneze*

- *Knetzingen*
- *Polostrov Knez*

KROL, KRAL

In ***White Serbia*** one finds several place names derived from **krol** or **kral**, a Slavic word for king *(G. Labuda, Rozprzestrzenienie sie tytulu "krolu" wsrod Slowian, Wieki Srednie, 1962. L.E. Havlik, Slovanska "barbarska" kralovsti 6. stoleti na uzemi Rumunska, Slovansky prehled 60, 1974),* namely: Krolovic— Krollewitz, 1382 (Krollwitz, Apolda); Krolovic— Krolewitz, 1381 (Krollwitz, Halle); Krolovic— Krolewicz, 1341 (Krollwitz, Merseburg).

SMERD

The following are some of the many references to **smerds**, from **smerd**, a Slavic word connoting, smell, stink *(G. Ilinski, K voprosy o smerdah, SlO 11, 1932. W. Kuraszkiewicz, Rad bywa smard, gdzie rajtarka, JeZ 34, 1954. K. Tymienicki, Uwagi o smerdach Slowianskich, Studia Historica H. Lomianskiego, 1958. A.A. Zimin, O smerdah drevnei Rusi XI - nacala XII v., Istoriko-arheologiceski sbornik, 1962. J. Bardach, Zmierzsch smerdow na ziemiach ruskich Korony i Litwy, Polskie Studiea Slawistyczne 3, 1968).*

- ***Aldionibus vel smurdis***
- ***Area cum zmurdis***
- ***Colonis, qui vulgo vocantur Smurdi***
- ***Cum tribus zmurdis***
- ***De mansis smurdorum***
- ***In iure smurdorum***
- ***Ius smurdonum***
- ***Liberi vel smurdi***
- ***Mancipia zmurdi scilicet proprique homines***
- ***Mansi, qui dicitur smorthove***
- ***Quatuor zmurdi***
- ***Schmordt hufen***
- ***Servi, qui smardi vulgariter appelantur***
- ***Zmurdi, qui cottidiano servicio imperata faciunt***
- ***Zmurdones***

SMURDA, SMURDEVIC

In ***White Serbia*** and bordering lands many place names are derived from **Smerd**:

Smorda, 1425— later Schmorda, Possneck
Smurdewitz, 1244— later Schmorditz, Grimma
Smordin, 1313— later Schmorren, Mugeln
Zmirdica im burgwardo kabeliz quet et marienburgh dicitur, 1150

SLUGA

Sluga, from a Slavic word for servant, is the root of several place names in Germania, including Sluzkov, modern Schleuskau, near Camburg, and Sluzkov, modern Schluschow, near Lauenburg.

STAR, STAROTSA

From cognates of **star**, a Slavic word for elder, the **starik, staritsa, starotsi**, the community elder served a role similar to that of the **dedic**, namely an authoritative advisor on community traditions and values. In medieval Poland, the traditional **starotsa** evolved into royal governors, appointed and removed at the royal will *(J. Birkenmajer, Kmiec i starosta, JeZ 21, 1936).*

In medieval Germania one finds the root **star/staritsa** in family names (e.g. Jors Staritsa; Petrus Staritsa) and many place names (e.g. Starely, insula Starin, Starkov, Starkovici, Starsov, Starsovici). In the latter case, however, in some instances the root **star** may refer to age rather than title.

VITEZ

Vitez, a Slavic word for knight, is recorded in medieval German sources *(M. Rudnicki, Sufiksy -man, -tuch-, -van, vit-, SlO 5, 1926. A. Stender-Petersen, Zur Geschichte des altslavischen *viteg, ZsP 4, 1927. A. Bruckner, Preussen, Polen, Witingen, ZsP 6, 1929. H.F. Schmid, Die Meissener 'vethenici' bei Thietmar von Merseburg, ZsP 7, 1930. R. Ekblom, Zur Etymologie von slav. vitedz, ZsP 16, 1939. R. Ekblom, Zur Etymologie von slav. vitedz, ZsP 16, 1939. V. Machek, Quelques mots slavy-germaniques, sl. Vitedz, Slavia 22, 1953).*

- *In equis servientes id est Withasii*
- *Mansi qui dicitur Witsax*
- *Mansi Wischacaz*
- *Rusticis, qui dicuntur Witessen*
- *Satellites dicti Sclavonici vethenici*

Vitez (e.g. Vitedze, Vitenici, Vitez, Vitezovic) is the root of a number of place names in Germania (e.g. Durr-Wicknitz, near Kamenz, formerly Witeniz, 1224; Witenicz, 1263 and Vetenicz, 1374 Wiednitz, near Ruhland, formerly Wittnitz, 1536; Witnitz, 1668 Witessen, near Weitzahueffen).

VLADAR, VLASTELIM

Vladar or **Vlodar**, a Slavic word for ruler, is the root of several and perhaps more place names in Germania, namely the town and mark of Vlodarovici— Loderwyz, 1330; Lodderitz Mark, 1494 (Lodderitz, Barby) and Vlodkov, northeast of Berlin. **Vlast**, a related Slavic word connoting power, authority, government, is the root of a town (Vlastejovsko) and lake Vlastojsko near Quedlinburg *(J. Mijuskovic, Humska vlasteoska porodica Sankovici, Istorijski Casopis XI, 1960. M. Dinic, Humsko-trebinjska vlastela, 1967).*

VOIVODA

Voivoda, a Slavic word for commander, is the root of several places names in medieval Germania, namely Voidar Grad, Voidarze, and Voivoda. As late as the 17th century the native Slavs of *Hanover Wendland* referred to their area as **Voivodstvo** or **Voidarstvo Hanover** *(E. Mucke, Slovane ve vojvodstvi Luneburskem, SlP 6, 1904. I. Belu, S. Dragomir, Voievozi, cnezi si crainici la romanii din Muntii Apuseni si din regiunea Bihorului in evul medie, Acta Musei Napocensis 3, 1966. A. Gieysztor, Urzad wojewodzinski we wczesnych panstwach slowianskich s IX-XI, PoL 16, 1971. S. Colombeanu, Cnezate si voievodata romanesti, 1973).*

ZUPAN

Zupan, is a Slavic word for the head of a **zupa** (county) or some smaller or greater political-administrative division. In Germania, the title is easily recognizable in medieval sources *(A. Lippert, Uber den historischen Wert der Bezeichungen "zupan" und "zupa" in bohmischen Geschichtsschreibung, Mitteilungen des Veriendes fur Geschichte der Deutschen in Bohmen 20, 1892. J. Gruden, Slovenski zupani v preteklosti, 1916. R. Becker, Supanie, Burgward und Pfarrspengel in Daleminze, NeU 38, 1917. N. Zupanic, Zupan i zupa, VI Kongres Slovenskih Geografa, 1936. M. Budimir, Klasicno poreklo izraza zupan I stopan, III Medjurnarodni Kongres Slavista, 1939. R. Buttner, Die Supane der osterreichischen Donaulander, Archaeologia Austriaca 27, 1955. V.P. Gracev, Termin "zupan" i "zupa" v serbskih istocniah XII-XIV, Istocniki i Istoriografii slavinskogo srednevekovi, 1967. S. Walter, Suppan und Dorfrichter in der Steiermark, Alpes Orientales 5, 1969. T. Wasilewski, Les zupy et les zupanie des Slaves meridonaux et leur place dans l'organisation des Etats medievaux, Int Congress of Slavic Archaeology 3, 1970. D. Dragojlovic, La Zupa chez les Slaves balkaniques au Moyen Age, Balcanica 2, 1971. P. Malingoudis, Die Institution des Zupans als Problem der fruhslawischen Geschichte, CyM 2, 1972-73. J. Kalousek, Novy dukaz za v davnych Cechach dekanaty shodovaly se s zupami, Casopis Narodniho Musea 48, 1974. V. Prochazka, Zupa a Zupan, SlA 15, 1968. M. Hardt, Der Supan, ZoS 39, 1990).*

- *Alter villa in monte suppani*
- *Baroun et suppanorum*
- *Crafto, filius Suppani*
- *Hertwicus supanus in Baticz*
- *Iopan, qui vocatur Physso*
- *Seniores villarum, quos lingua supanos vocant*
- *Supani*
- *Supanus de Techobudici*
- *Sex mansos in villa Iauren ... que supen vulgariter nuncupatur*
- *Duos mansos ipsi Schibanos hos mansos contulimus rite et iuste iure hereditario possidendos*
- *Supanus miles*

Zupan is the root of a number of place names (e.g. Seupahn, near Colditz; Suppen, modern Suppo, near Bautzen; Suptitz, seat of the Torgau district zupan) and family names (e.g. Supans of Golnicz in *pago Plisni*) in medieval Germania.

ZUPAN/PAN

Pan, a cognate of **zupan**, is the root of a number of Germania place names *(J. Widajewicz, Panstwo Wislan, 1947. G. Labuda, Organizajce panstwowe Slowian w okresie kszaltowani sie panstwa polskiego, Poczatki Panstwa Polskiego, 1962. J. Bardach, Historia panstwa i prawa Polski, 1965. W. Hensel, Poczatki Panstwa Polskiego i jego kultury, 1971).* In one early instance, 'the nobles of Panovich,' title and place name are one and the same— *Nobiles de Panewicz, 1240 (Panovici/Pannewitz, near Bischofswerda).* Also, among others:**Panic** (Panitz, 1279; Panitz, Riesa); **Panovic** (Panewycz, 1311; Bannewitz, Dresden); **Panovic** (Panwicz, 1336; Pahnitz, Atenburg); **Pancic** (Panczicz, 1382; Panschitz, Elstra).

PART XI

1. OD BRLINA DO BRANIBORA

In the case of many towns and cities, mixed Slav-German constructions have evolved over the many centuries. The following series telescopes the evolutionary process with regard to some of Germany's better-known cities.

BERLIN, DRESDEN, MEISSEN

Berlin—	**Brla, Brlin**	Kulmbach—	**Cholm**
Bohlen—	**Belina**	Havelberg—	**Obla, Habola**
Brandenberg—	**Branibor**	Kopenick—	**Kopjenick**
Chemnitz—	**Kamenica**	Leipzig—	**Lipa, Lipsk**
Colditz—	**Coldici**	Leisnig—	**Lisnik**
Delitzsch—	**Del'c**	Lubeck—	**Lubice**
Dresden—	**Dregza**	Mecklenburg—	**Velgrad**
Erfurt—	**Brod**	Meissen—	**Misin**
Groitsch—	**Grodisko**	Merseburg—	**Mesibor**

POTSDAM, SPANDAU, ZEITZ

Naumberg—	**Novigrad**	Spandau—	**Spadov**
Oldenburg—	**Starigrad**	Torgau—	**Trgov**
Olsnitz—	**Olesnica**	Werben—	**Vrbin**
Oschatz—	**Osec**	Wettin—	**Vetin**
Potsdam—	**Podstupi**	Wismar—	**Visimir**
Prenzlau—	**Premyslav**	Wittstock—	**Visok**
Rathenow—	**Rat, Ratin**	Zeitz—	**Zitice**
Rostock—	**Roztok**	Zittau—	**Zitava**
Schwerin—	**Zverin**	Zwickau—	**Zvikov**

BERLIN-BRANDENBURG

Every change in place name has its own interesting history and insight into Slavic-German relations. The following examples are from the Berlin-Brandenburg area.

BRLIN-BERLIN

Medieval sources record a number of hydronyms, toponyms, and place names derived from the Slav root-word *brla*, connoting straw, leaves, mud, marsh, and swamp, connoting fish-traps made from straw, leaves, twigs, branches, and mud.

Brlin— Arnoldus Berlin (1243); Berlinische wende marcken (1603); Berlinichen (1618), near Zerbst

Brlin— Berlinchin (1463), Berlinchen (1623), near Calau

Brlos— Johannes Berlos, 1243, near Dessau

Brlin— de Burlin, 1200, near Wurzen

Brlin— Brlin, near Delitzsch

Brlin— Berlein, near Bitterfeld

Brloz— Borloz (1378), near Dresden

Local Serbs still refer to modern Berlin as **Brlin**, the name of an ancient Serb fishing village on the right bank of the Spree River.

BRLIN-COLIN

A twin settlement, **Colin**, was located on an island in the middle of the Spree, opposite **Brlin**. Such islands were a favored location for Slavic forts. It is not surprising therefore that **Colin**, also **Kolin**, was one of many place names derived from the Slavic root **col** or **kol** connoting palisades, that is, stakes set firmly in ground in a close row to form a defensive enclosure. Place names with the same root and connotations are recorded throughout **White Serbia.**

Kol— Koltzschke, near Zorbig		**Kol**— Collnitz, near Leipzig	
Kol— Colln, near Bautzen		**Kolic**— Kolzig, near Forst	
Kol— Kohlen, near Bernburg		**Kol**— Kollau, near Eilenburg	
Kolin— Colln, near Meissen		**Kol**— Kolkau, near Rochlitz	
Kol— Kolbitz, near Leipzig		**Kol**— Kolka, near Gethain	

ALT-KOLN

Medieval Kolin is modern Alt-Koln, the island part of modern Berlin where today one finds a fish market near the ancient church of St. Peter, the patron saint of fishermen. It is interesting and significant that a number of Slavic words are alive and well in the speech of the Berlin area, that Slavic words relating to fish and fishing are well represented in the jargon of local fishermen *(B. Peesche, Der Wortschatz der Fischer im Kietz von Berlin-Kopenick, 1955. J. Wiese, Slawische Worter im Berlinischen, ZtS 32, 1987).*

JACZA OF BERLIN

Regarding Berlin's status in the mid-12th century, J. Herrmann writes:

> **Knez Jacza of Kopenick, as he styles himself on his coins, owned Berlin-Kopenick about 1150** *('The Northern Slavs,' The Northern World, 1980).*

FROM MILITARY DEMOCRACY TO ARISTOCRACY

At another point, regarding the changing political order, Professor Herrmann writes:

> **As society stabilized, the old 'military democracy' that seems to have characterized the early Slavs was replaced by a class system headed by an aristocracy. About 1150, the area round Berlin was ruled by a feudal prince called Jacza of Kopenick, some of whose coins survive.**

JACZA OF KOPENICK

According to historical sources, Kopenick was the primary seat of the legendary **Jaksa of Kopenick** (that Jaxa should be read Jaksa is clear from many sources, including, for example, the one time village of Jaxo near Zorbig, recorded as Jhacsaw in 1459). Place names with the same or related roots connoting pile, mound, burial ground are recorded throughout **White Serbia.**

Kopan— Coppan/1295, Kappan, near Juterbog
Kopic— Kopicz/1417, Copitz, near Pirna
Kopic— Koppiczsch/1465, Kopitzsch, near Possneck
Kopanik— Kopenic/1361, Kopnick, near Wittenburg
Kopanc— Copanz/1304, Coppanz, near Jena
Kopac— Koppatz/1581, Koppatz, near Cottbus

Knez Jaksa had a secondary capital and residence/stronghold at *Brla* (Berlin). According to tradition, it was there, on the Havel River, that *Jaksa* led the Serbs in the last great battle against imperial forces 1157. Defeated, *Knez Jaksa,* it is said, escaped capture by fleeing across the Havel River on the back of his gallant steed. The historical *Knez Jaksa* is a lively figure in past and present scholarship *(M. F. Rabe, Jaczo von Copnic, 1856. M.S. Vlahovic, Luzicki Srbi i Njihova Domovina, 1930. H. Ludat, Legenden um Jaxa von Kopenick, Slaven und Deutsche im Mittelalter, 1982).*

BERLIN'S SLAVIC FOUNDATIONS

Some measure of the breadth, depth, and intensity of Berlin's Slavic foundations is found in the great number of ancient and modern place names derived from Slavic roots. In the following short citations from the greater Berlin area, the Slavic root is followed by its German version.

BARNIM, MEDOVIC

Barnim— Altbarnim
Breza— Briese
Brod— Broddin
Bukov— Buckow
Danovici— Danewitz
Grad— Garzau
Grob— Groben
Ilov— Ihlow

Kas/Kasov— Kasow
Kopr— Karpow
Laka— Lanke
Loknica— Locknitzinsel
Medovic—Altmadewitz
Mal— Malchow
Mal— Malz
Milkov— Melchow

MILOV, TRNOV

Milov— Milow
Mir— Mehrow
Modr— Mudrow
Mogilin— Moglin
Mur— Murow
Nesov— Netzow
Pak— Pankow
Pec— Pechteich

Predel— Priedel
Sedlo— Zehlendorf
Stolpe— Stolpdorf
Stolpe—Wannsee
Strela— Stralau
Trnov— Tornow
Tuch— Tuchen
Visevir— Wuschewier

In the following longer citations from the greater Berlin area, the Slavic root is followed by its German version.

BATIN, CHYZA

Batin— Batyn, 1316, Battin
Bezmir— Byssemarowe/1292, Biesenbrow
Bogoslav— Bogslov/1375, Batzlow

Bogov— *in maiori villa Bochow*/1386, Bochow
Bogumil— de Boghemyl/1298, Bagemuhl
Brod— Brodewin/1258, Brodowin
Brod— Brodeze/1174, Broitz
Ceprnik— Heinricus de Cepernick/1289, Zepernick
Chyza— Kyzmul/1375, Kietz
Chyza— Kycze/1343, Altkietz

DEDELOV, KLADOV
Dedelov— *in Dedelow*/1320, Dedelow
Dobri— Dobrichov, Dobbrickow/1480, Dabrikow
Dobrisin— Doberzin/1485, Dobberzin
Dol— Dolovica, *molendinum, quod vulgariter nominatur Dolewitz*/1370, Dahlwitz
Glav— Glaw/1434, Glau
Gostov— *apud Gustow*/1304, Gustow
Jagov— *oppidum Jagow*/1375, Jagow
Jazor— Jasorcz/1579, Hohenseefeld
Kladov— Cladow/1375, Kladow

KLOBUK, LUBAS
Klobuk— Klobik/1375, Klobbicke
Kopan— *silvam dictam Coppan et Warzum, sitam iuxta ipsamcivitatem*/1295, Kappan
Kot, Kotin — *in villa Koten*/1334, Cothen
Koze Rogy— Kuzeroggey/1588, Kutzerow
Kriv— Krywen/1354, Criewen
Krusov— Krussow/1540, Crussow
Lipa— *Jordanis de Lipe*/1229, Liepe
Lis— Lysen/1446, Liessen
Lom— Lomen/1375, Lohme
Lubas— Lubas/1375, Lubars

LUBEC, POPELICA
Lubec— *cum villis Lubetz*/1285, Liebatz
Lubis— Lubistorff/1446, Liebsdorf
Lubuski— Lebbusigke/1328, Lebuske
Ludislav— *villa Ludzlau*/1240, Lutzlow
Malosin— Maloschyne/1579, Melnitz
Milobrat— Milderbratsdorp, 1325, Milmersdof
Milsov— Melsow/1540, Melzow
Pecula— *supper villa Pechule*/1225, Pechule
Petko— Petkow/1500, Petkus
Popelica— Popelicz/1363, Paplitz

PREDKOV, SLAVIN
Pred, Predkov— *in precaria villarum predicowe sita*/1340, Pradikow
Presel— Pressel/1375, Protzel

Radik, Radikov— Radikow/1707, Radekow
Radomir— *stagnum Rademer*/1244, Rahmersee
Raden— Radenstorf/1375, Rahnsdorf
Rud, Rudov— Rudow/1373, Rudow
Rudenica— Rudenitzs/1527, Rudnitz
Rudnica— Rutenica/1174, Ruthenitz
Sedlo— Sedlo/1579, Wentdorff.
Slavin— *villam Slawe*/1300, Schlandorf

SLAVKO, TREBKOV

Slavko— Zlaukendorp/1318, Schowickendorf
Slavobor— Schlaberstorff/1527, Schlagsdorf
Slavtici— Slautitz/1384, Slautitz
Strezov— Strezow/1354, Stresow
Studenica— *villa Studenitz*/1225, Studenitz
Svet— *civitatem Scwet*/1265, Schwedt
Trgov— Torgow/1422, Torgelow
Trebenic— Trebenitz/1244, Trebnitz
Trebin— Trebin/1375, Alttrebbin
Trebkov— Trebkow/1568, Treptow

TREBLIN, ZATON

Treblin— Trepelin/1345, Treplin
Trebus— *Johanni Trebuz*/1333, Trebus
Trebus— Tribustorp/1242, Triebelsdorf
Tuchobad— *ville dicte Tuchebant*/1336, Alt Tucheband
Varnov— *Johannes de Warnowe*/1247, Werneuchen
Vinov— *in Vinowe*/1258, Hohenfinow
Vodov— Woddow/1437, Woddow
Volilub— Wollub/1496, Wollup
Volin— Wolyn/1354, Wollin
Vresna— *opidanos in Wrizna*/1320, Wriezen
Zabel— *Johannes de Zabelstrop*/1284, Zabelsdorf
Zaton— Sathan/1258, Hohensaaten

BEESKOW-STORKOW

In a recent article, K. Muller examines the Slavic roots of numerous place names in the Beeskow-Storkow area southeast of Berlin. In the following series, the original Slavic place name is followed by medieval and modern versions *(K. Muller, Zur Schichtenspezifik der slawischen Namen im Lande um Beeskow-Storkow, Beitrage zu Namenforschung 29/30, 1994-1995).*

BUKOV, GLINA

Bezkov— Beskowe, 1272, Beeskow
Bloz, Blozin— Blossen/1492, Blossin
Brest, Bresce— Brist/1490, Briescht
Buk— Bugk/1416, Bugk
Buk, Bukov— Buchaw/1141, Buckow
Cholm— Golm/1418, Golm

Cholm— Gollmitz/1752, Gollmitz
Dlugibrod— Dolgenbrod/1321, Dolgenbrodt
Glina, Glinik— Glinig/1421, Glienicke
Glov, Glova— Glo/1415, Glowe

GORSKO, KOBYLOV
Glub, Glubik— Glubick/1744, Glubig
Gor, Gorsko— Jortzck/1393, Gorzig
Ker, Kerik— Kyrigk/1493, Kehrigk
Kobyla, Kobylov— Cabelow/1445, Kablow
Kol, Kolnica— Kelnize/1209, Kollnitz
Komor, Komorov— Kummerow/1418, Kummerow
Kolp, Kolpin— Colpyneken/1448, Kolpin
Kopati, Kopalin— Coplin/1745, Koplin
Koz, Kozolica— Kaselitz/1861, Kaselitz
Krus, Krusnik— Krusenigk/1376, Krausnick

LUBICIN, PRERAD
Kupka— Kupke/1537, Kupka
Lom, Lomac— Lamaczsch/1490, Lamitzsch
Lom, Lomin— Lomen/1375, Niederlehme
Lub, Lubicin— Lubinchen/1493, Lebbin
Mir, Mirici— *J. de Mertz*/1341, Merz
Pes, Pesak, Peske— *Marggrefen pysk*/1435, Margrafpieskie
Pes, Pesak, Peskov— Pieske/1495, Pieskow
Prerad, Preradz— Preroz/1319, Prieros
Rad, Radlo— Radelow/1445, Radlow

RECICA, TREBAC
Recica— Windiszschen Riecz/1376, Rietz
Rog, Rogov— Rogow/1344, Ragow
Rov, Rovno— *vulgo Ruwen*/1285, Rauen
Scav, Scavin— Schwaen/1495, Schauen
Sova, Sovin— Sawen/1495, Sauen
Str, Strmen— Stremen/1495, Stremmen
Stregan, Streganici— Stregantz/1321, Streganz
Treb, Trebac— Trebetsch/1324. Trebatsch
Treb, Trebic— Tripsch/1797, Triebsch
Tuchov— Twchow/1495, Tauche
Ugl, Uglina— Ogelyn/1344, Oegeln
Vran, Vransk— Wrantzck/1393, Ranzig
Vrh, Vrchnov— Werchnow/1366, Werchenow
Vochov— Woches/1321, Wochowsee
Zabrod— Sabrot/1490, Sabrodt
Zar, Zarov— Soraw/1463, Saarow
Zaval— Sawoll/1503, Sawall
Zelichov— Selcho/1321, Selchow
Zverin— Swerin/1321, Schwerin

2. BRANIBOR-BRANDENBURG

An ancient Slav stronghold, *Branibor* is believed to be derived from two related Slavic roots, *bran/bron,* connoting defense, and *bor,* connoting war.

Bran— Branitz, near Cottbus
Bran— Barnena, near Konnern
Bron— Branitz, near Eilenburg
Bran— Brohna, near Bautzen
Bran— Brankow, near Calau
Bor— Bolibor, near Bautzen
Bor— Bolibor, near Merseburg
Bor— Bahren, near Finsterwalde
Bor— Bornitz, near Zeitz
Bor— Bornewitz, near Rathenow
Lutobor— Leuterwitz, near Leisnig
Ratibor, 1221— near Bautzen

TERRA SLAVORUM

In *Terra Slavorum* Branibor was the central town of the Slavs known as *Hevelli*:

> *Terra Sclavorum in pago Heueldun in civitate Brandenburg.*

G. Fehring traces Branibor's origin to:

> **A 7th century fortified site on an island in the Havel, which after repeated rebuilding developed into the tribal center of the Heveldi, with its princely seat, dependent settlements, cemeteries, and the tribal sanctuary of Triglav ... In the 11th and 12th centuries this place was again the seat of a Slavic prince, probably with a trading settlement on either side of the river.**

TRIGLAV

Branibor/Brandenburg was the site of an important pre-Christian temple dedicated to an aspect of *Svar*, namely Svar's trinity called *Triglav*, the three-headed lord of past, present, and future, of all on, above, and below the Earth.

PRIBISLAV OF BRANIBOR

Branibor's ruler, *Prince Pribislav* (1127-1150), a convert to Christianity, found it politic to tolerate the temple on the Harlungerberg in full view of his own castle and chapel on an island in the Havel River.

BROTHER-IN-CHRIST

When *Prince Pribislav* died without Christian heirs in 1150, he left his territory by bequest to his German brother-in-Christ, Albrecht the Bear, who occupied the city.

The occupation was brief. In the same year the city was seized by ***Knez Jaksa of Kopenick,*** who held it until 1157.

PERMIXTA SLAVONICA ET SAXONICA

Given its history, it is not surprising that 14th century sources refers to Brandenburg's 'mixed' Slav-Saxon population: ***Gens permixta Slavonica et Saxonica; Gens illa Saxonica Slavica.***

DO BRANIBORA

Local Serbs still refer to Brandenburg as Branibor as in: **Do Branibora; V Braniborje; Braniborski; Branborski Serbsi Casnik.**

BRANDENBURG'S SLAVIC FOUNDATIONS

In the following short citations from the greater Brandenburg area, the Slavic root is followed by its German version *(W. Vogel, Der Verbleib der wendischen Bevolkerung in der Mark Brandeburg, 1960. U. Bentzien, Regelitz—ein brandenburgisches Mundartwort aus der slawischen Pflugnomenklatur, ZtS 11,1966. H.H. Bielfedlt, Deutsch Radlitz, Redelitz, Regelitz, Pflugschar, ZtS 11, 1966. G. Schlimpert, Dies Ortsnamen des Teltow, Brandenburgisches Namenbuch, 1984. S. Wauer, Die mit de Suffix -ov gebildeten Ortsnamen in Brandenburg. Ein Beitrag zum Slawischen Onomastischen Atlas, ZtS 26, 1981; Zur Problematik der Eindeutschung slawischer Ortsnamentypen in Brandenburg, Linguistische Studien, 1981. E. Foster, S. Wauer, Die slawischen Kulturnamen in Brandenburg, ZtS 28, 1983).*

BRATOVICI, KAMENICA

Brat/Bratovici— Brachwitz	**Dabolag**— Damelang
Brez/Brezina— Gross Briesen	**Gol/Golovica**— Gollwitz
Brilov— Brielow	**Gor/Gorica**— Goritz
Brod— Degebrod	**Grabov**— Grabow
Bus/Busov— Butzow	**Dobrov**— Doberow
Cholm— Golm	**Grab**— Grabow
Chot/Chotin— Gottin	**Kamenica**— Kemnitz

KOLPIN, ZIVAN

Kolpin— Kolpin	**Slony Lug**— Schlalach
Mokosov— Motzow	**Stol/Stolin**— Stolln
Nesimir— Nietzmar	**Viserab**— Klein Weseram
Predmici— Premnitz	**Volovica**— Wallitz
Prezimir— Prietzen	**Vosty**— Wust
Pyrnica— Pernitz	**Vuk/Wulk**— Wulkow
Reka— Reekahn	**Zivan/Zivanov**— Schwanow
Roskov— Roskow	

In the following longer citations from the greater Brandenburg area, the Slavic root is followed by its German version.

BELOTICI, CRNSK

Belotici— *burgwardis Beltitz*/1161, Belzig
Bobr— Bubrow/1590, Boberow

Bogutici— Boghetiz/1313, Baitz
Bozkov— Buszkow/1496, Buschow
Chleboloky— Clebeloc/1197, Knoblauch
Chot, Chotic— *ville Gotiz*/1193, Gotz
Cisty Kal— *villam Cistecal*/1193, Cistecal
Crnic— Czernstorph/1383, Zehnsdorf
Crnikov— Schernekow/1365, Zernikow
Crnsk— Czernstorph/1383, Zehrensdorf

DETIC, JEZER

Detic— *ville Detiz*/1193, Deetz
Dobrogost— Dobergotz/1540, Dabergotz
Gradc, Gardc— *villam Garditz*/1334, Gortz
Gol, Golsov— *usque bruch seu golsowe*/1219, Golzow
Gorne— *curie Gorne*/1307, Gorden
Greb, Grebsk— Grebtzik/1375, Grebs
Grob— *inter villam Grobene et villam Derentin*/1381, Gorisgraben
Gomenik— *molendinum Gomenik*/1251, Gumno
Jalova Gora— Jaleberge/1421, Gahlberg
Jezer— Jezerick/1450, Jeserig

KADLUB, LOKET

Kadlub— Cadleb/1500, Kardeleben
Kocur— Kotzure/1375, Ketzur
Kora, Korane— *Albertus plebanus de Korane*/1230, Krahne
Krak— *curiam Krakowe*/1209, Krakau
Krusevica— Crucewitz/1320, Klein Kreutz
Kulbac— Kulebacz/1385, Kuhlowitz
Len, Lenin— *claustro Lenin*/1204, Lehnin
Leskov— Lessekouw/1491, Lasikow
Lobuz— Lobze/1380, Lobbese
Loket— Lokede/1303, Locktow

LOZK, NIVICA

Lozk— Loczk/1381, Lotzschke
Lubanic— *hinrico, plebano in Lubenitz*/1314, Lubnitz
Lug— Lugow/1423, Logow
Lun— Lunowe/1335, Lunow
Medovic— Medewitz/1487, Medewitz
Mokos— Moczow/1550, Moltzow
Myslotici— Muselitz/1365, Mutzlitz
Myslotin— Misseltin/1540, Metzelthin
Nedesim— *in stagno Nedesin*/1282, Netzen
Nivica— *in curia Newitz*/1413, Niewitz

NOVOMICI, RADOVID

Novomici— Novmitz/1280, Nahmitz
Pavesin— Pevesin/1775, Pawesin

Plan, Plon— *villam nostram Planowe*/1297, Planow

Plav— *Henricus de Plawe*/1197, Plaue

Plusin— *villam Plusetsin, que alio nomine Reinoldesdorf*/1197, Reinoldsdorf

Pribic— Pribitz/1557, Prebitz

Rad— *stagnum adjacens Radel*/1181, Radel

Radan— Raden/1557, Radansleben

Radoslav— Radensleue/1422, Radensleben

Radovid— Radewede/1413, Radewege

RATIN, SMERK

Rat, Ratin— Ratenow/1244, Rathenow

Redica— *partem stagni Retitz*/1273, Rietz

Rok, Rokyta— Rotscherlinde

Roztok— Rostok/1251, Rottstock

Rudnik— Rudenick/1540, Ruthnick

Rup— *antiqua Rupin*/1291, Alt Ruppin

Sedlici— *curiam in Cedelitz*/1273, Cedelitz

Slavobor— Slavbuer/1533, Schlabom

Sliva— Sliven/1489, Schleuen

Smerk— *in ville Smerzich*/1286, Schmerzke

SMOLIN, TRNOV

Smolin— Smolne/1365, Schmollen

Spadic— *tydericus de Spadiz*/1245, Spaatz

Suchydub— Zuchedam/1258, Zauchdam

Svin— *villam Zvine*/1193, Schwina

Tik— Tikow/1317, Tieckow

Trebogost— *villam Trebegoz*/1251, Trebitz

Trebsin— Trebbesinn/1571, Trebzin

Trebun— *die Trebun*/1609, Tribun

Trechovici— *Arnoldus decanus de Trecwiz*/1303, Trechwitz

Trnov— *villam Tornowe*/1247, Tornow

VELIVAS, VRENTIN

Veli-vas, Velivas— *des Velewanz*/1249, Vehlefanz

Velici— *Johann Vilitz*/1542, Vielitz

Ver-jezer, Verchjezer— Vercheyser/1450; Ferchgezer/1496, Ferchesar

Veslin— Wesselin/1578, Wetzlin

Visnica— Vysenytz/1365, Vietznitz

Vostrov— *de Wozstrow*/1288, Wustrau

Votin— Wotenowe/1319, Wuthenow

Vrentin— Wrenthien/1598, Warenthin

3. PODSTUPI-POTSDAM

Potsdam or **Pod-stubi** is derived from two Slavic words, **Po** or **Pod**, connoting by, near, and along, and **Stub**, **Stob**, connoting wall, brick wall, palisade *(T. Witkowski, Der Name Potsdam, Brandenburgischen neueste Nachrichten, 1967; G. Schlimpert, Der Name Potsdam, ZtS 15, 1970)*.

Thus **Pod-stubi** is a settlement by, near or under the wall or palisade, thus **Stolpъ** as in the *Primary Chronicle's* Tower of Babel: **Zdati stolpъ de nebese i gradъ okoli i-ego BABILONъ.**

Medieval sources record numerous place name in **White Serbia** with the same root and connotations.

> **Staupitz** near Doblen, *Hermannus de Stupiz,* 1241; de Stupicz, 1333
> **Staupitz** near Finsterwalde, Stupiz/1243; Stupisch/1456
> **Staupitz** near Torgau, Stupwiez/1251, Stuypytz/ 1253; Stupcyz/1342
> **Stolpchen** near Grossenhain, Stolpen/1406; Stolpichen/1463
> **Stolpen** near Borna, *villa Stulpen*/1166; *villa Stulpe*/1188
> **Stolpen** near Pirna, *Moyko de Stulpen*/1222
> **Stulpe** near Luckenwalde, Stolpe/1499

Also Gross Stobnitz near Altenburg (Stubenicz, 1291; Gross Stobenicz, 1378); Gross Stolpen near Borna (Grosse Stolpe, 1405); Stoben near Camburg (Stubi, 1088; in Stube, 1300); Stobnig near Rochlitz ((Stoben, 1350; Stobenig, 1378); Stolpen near Wurzen (Stulpen, 1431; Stolpen,1555).

CHOTEMYSL'S ISLAND

As with many other medieval Slavic strongholds, **Hevelli Po-stubi** was situated on an island, on **Chotemysl's** island *(H. Schall, Der Name Potsdam und die "Insel des Chotemysl", JbR 9, 1958)*.

> • **Dua loca Geliti et Poztupimi vocata in provincia Hevellun et in insula Chotiemuizles sita,** *993*
> • **Oppidi Postam,** *1317*
> • **Oppidi Pozstamp,** *1323*

JELITI

Geliti, from the Slav Jeliti/Jelitov, is modern Geltow, and *Chotemysl,* from the popular Slav personal name *Chotemysl,* is the ancient name for the isle of Potsdam. Geliti, 993; -Jelt, 1242; -Ghelt, 1355; -Gelt, 1375. Recent excavations confirm that the lower strata of Potsdam **(Pod-stubi),** Spandau **(Spadov)** and neighboring towns are of early Slav construction. Regarding the strong and enduring Slavic foundations of this general area, J.F. Thompson writes:

> **Even after the conversion, vestiges of Slavonic paganism**
> **persisted for many years around Spandau in the heart of**

the marshes of the Havel and in the Spreewald *(Feudal Germany, 1928)*.

POTSDAM'S SLAVIC FOUNDATIONS
In the following short citations from the greater Potsdam area, the Slavic root is followed by its German variation.

BLIZ, KOPYTO, PLUSIN

Bliz— Bliesendorf
Bog/Bogov— Bochow
Bucin— Petzin
Der/Derbica— Derwitz
Glin— Glindow
Grez— Grentzel
Kamenica— Kemnitz
Kles/Klescov— Klaistow
Kopyto— Capputh
Kana/Kanin— Kanin

Krapa— Krampnitz
Kycin— Korzin
Les/Lescje— Leest
Lin/Linovica— Lienewitz
Lok/Loknica— Locknitz
Michin— Michendorf
Novin— Nauen
Plon/Plonica— Planitz
Plusin— Plotzin
Priscirje— Priscere

RADICH, TOPLA, ZAKROV

Radich— Reesdorf
Rez/Rezov— Resau
Ribin— Rieben
Sedlisce— Zedlitz
Slunk— Schlunkendorf
Suchovica— Zauchwitz
Sulisa/Sulichov— Zolchow
Tesik— Tesekendorf
Topla/Toplin— Templin

Tur— Thur
Ubyslav— Oberzlaw
Visok— Witzke
Vr/Vrch— Ferch
Vres/Vresov— Fretzow
Za-krov/Zakrov— Sacrow
Za-skorin/Zaskorin—Satzkorn
Zid/Zidin— Seddin

In the following longer citations from the greater Potsdam area, the Slavic root is followed by its German variation.

BELICA, CRNOV, GROB

Bel, Belica— (*oppido Belitz*/1252), Beelitz
Bobrov— Buberow/1422, Babelsberg
Dol/Dolovica— *in villa Dolwiz*/1305, Dahlewitz
Drevic— *miricam que dicitur Drewicz*/1284, Drewitz
Glas— Glaszow/1450, Glasow
Glin— Glinicke/1267, Gross Glienicke
Golin— *pratum Golyn*/1339, Gallin
Cholm— Golm/1289, Golm
Crnov— Zernower/1528, Zernow
Grob— *Henricus, dictus de Grobene*/1284, Groben

JUTROGOST, NEDELIC, PLUSIN

Jutrogost— *rusticis de Jutergotz*/1284, Guterfelde

Karc/Karcov— Cartzow/1375, Kartzow
Klescov— Cleistow/1420, Klaistow
Kycin— Ketzin/1375, Korzin
Machnov— *Machnow parva*/1375, Kleinmachnow
Nedelic— *ad passagium Nedliz*/1323, Nedlitz
Pec/Pecov— Petzow/1437, Petzow
Perva/Pervenic— *Johannes de Perwenitz*/1275, Perwenitz
Plesov— Plesowe/1287, Plessow
Plusin— *in villa Plusin*/1179, Plotzin

RATIN, STARY JEZER, TREBOGOST
Rat, Ratin— Ratenow/1244, Rathenow
Rib, Ribin— *in villa riben*/1362, Rieben
Skorin— Scoryn/1313, Schorin
Slunk— Schlunkendorf
Smerz— *villam Smergowe*, Schmergow
Stary Jezer— *villa Staregesere*/1287, Strajesar
Sulchov— Zolgowe/1290, Zolchow
Topelica— *insula Topeliz*/1318, Alt Toplitz
Trebin— Trebinstorf/1375, Tremsdorf
Trebogost— *et curiam Trebegoz*/1305, Trebegotz

TREBUN, TRNOV, VRBA
Trebun— *die Trebun*/1609, Tribun
Trnov— Tornow/1683, Tornow
Usici— Uzzytz/1313, Uetz
Veselin— Wesselin/1578, Wetzlin
Vr, Vrch— *Verch superior et inferior*/1375, Ferch
Vrba— Verbicz/1441, Ferbitz

4. HYDRONYMS: QUE VOCANTUR TREBOW

Another measure of the breadth, depth, and intensity of greater Berlin-Brandenburg's Slavic foundations is the great number of ancient and modern hydronyms derived from Slavic roots (e.g. Daba/Dahme; Dosov/Dosse; Mura/Muhre; Nudov/Nuthe; Sana/Suhne; Spreva/Spree; Sprevica/Spreewitz; Vinov/Finow).

HABOLA-HAVEL

Havelberg (*in Hawelbergium*/983), Haveland and the Slavs called *Hevelli* (**Sclavos, qui dicuntur Hevelli**/928) take their name from the Havel River **(Heveldi, qui iuxta Habolam fluvium sunt).**

OBLA

More correctly, the Obla River from the Slav root **obla** connoting round, curve, and bend, words descriptive of the lower Havel's course *(J. Nalepa, Obla, Oblica, Oblisko. Pierwotna naz rzeki Havel i jej derywatov, Sprakliga Bidrag 2/9, 1957).*

- *Abola/789*
- *Iuxta Habolam/1075*
- *In Obula/1204*
- *Aqua Obula/1205*
- *Renus influat in Obulam/1238*
- *Obulam/1288*
- *Ad Obula/1378*

Recent excavations have uncovered the remains of a number of ancient triangular forts built by the native Slavs on strategic peninsulas or bends in the Havel River.

v'OBL/OBLICA

The names of more than several area waterways have the same **Obla** or **v'Obla** root:

v'Oblica or Wublitze/1358, near Potsdam
v'Obl or Wobelitz/1491 near Rathenow
v'Obl or Woblitz/1861 near Teltow
v'Obla or *stagnum* Woblesko/1170, near Wesenburg

WHITE SERBIA

Place names derived from the same root are recorded throughout Germania (e.g. Oblic, near Atlmersleben; Oblisko, near Malchow; Obli, near Parchim) including the following from **White Serbia:**

Obli, Obelicz/1278, Oblitz, Naumberg
Oblovica, Obluviz/1300, Oebles, Merseburg
Okolo, Ocul/1453, Gross Ockrilla, Dresden
Okolo, Ocul/1400, Ogkeln, Wittenberg
Okrul, Ogkrul/1378, Ockrilla, Meissen

Okrul, Ockrul/1448, Ockrill, Muhlberg

TERRAM BRIZANORUM, STODERANUM

The *Haveli/Hevelli* were also known as the *Brezani* (also known as the *Neletici*) and *Stodorani*.

- *Omnem enim terram Brizanorum, Stoderanum multarumque gentium habitantium iuxta Habelam et Albiam misit sum iugum.*
- *Brizanorum et Stodoranorum populi, hii videlicet qui Havelbert et Brandenberg habitant.*
- *Brizanorum populus.*

HEVELLUN, STODERANIUM HAVELAND

Haveland was also known by its native name, *Stoderanium*, after the *Stoderani* (K. Myslinski, Zachodnioslowianskie ksiestwo Stodoran w XII wieku i jego stosunek do Polski, Europa-Slowianszczyzna-Polska, 1970).

- *Stoderanium, que Hevellun dicitur*
- *Ztoderaniam, quam vulgo Heveldum vocant*
- *Ex provincia nomine Stodor*
- *Provincia nomine Stodor*

TERRE DE HAVELANT

The lands along the the *Haveli/Hevelli* (*pago Heuellon, pago Heveldun, provincia Heuellon, provincia Hevellun, terre de Havela, terre de Havelant*) were long centers of fierce resistance to Christianization. Indeed, until the mid-12th century Havelberg was the site of an important temple dedicated to a manifestation of *Svar* called *Jar*.

HYDRONYMS

In the following series of hydronyms from the greater Berlin-Brandenburg area, the Slavic root is followed by its German version.

TREB, TREBUS

The first series covers some of the many recorded hydronyms derived from the omnipresent Slavic root *treb,* connoting offering, sacrifice: **Das Wort kann am ehesten als slaw. treba angehesen werden und bedeutete offenbar 'Opfer,' das einem Gotzen (also einer heidnischen Gottheit) dargebracht wurde (werden musste). Wir finden es Altrussischen reich belegty: altruss. treba "zertva", aber auch "zertvoprinosenie" und "ispolnenie svjascennogo obrjada", auch "molitva, poklonenie"; daneben stand di Polnoglasie-Form tereba, die die Dabringung eines Opfers bezeichnete. Naturlich is treba such im Altbulgarischen gut vertreten. Inwiewit es nun auch anderen slawischen Sprachen, vor allem den westslawischen, bekannt war, ist noch nicht hinreichend untersucht ... Fur die Toponomastik ist ubrigens der Nachweis eines Wortes treba 'Opfer' (urslaw. *terba) insofern von Bedeutung, als dann eine Reihe von Toponymen, die auf urslaw. *terb- und dessen Ableitungen beruhen, als mythologisch aussagefahige Namen in Betracht kamen. Der Nachweis des slawischen Wortes fur Opferstatte im Gebiet der Main- und Rednitzwenden, die den Westslawen zuzuordnen sind und bekanntlich sprachlich den Sorben**

nahestanden *(E. Eichler, Zum slaswischen mythologischen Wortschatz, AnP 22, 1994).*

Treb— Trebowersee/1351, Trebelsee
Trebica— der Triebitsch See/1734, Triebsch See
Trebin— *stagnum nomine Trebenyke*/1375, Trebehnsee
Trebin— den Trebin/1436, Truber See
Trebkov— der Trepkow/1745, Treptowsee
Treblin— Trepelin *magnum et parvum*/1373, Trebliner See
Trebnica— die Trebnitz/1668, Trebnitz
Trebov— Trebelsee, 1305
Trebus— *de lacu Trybuss*/1285, Trebuser See

The following series list some of the many hydronyms derived from different Slavic roots.

BABIN, BUKOVICA, GLAVA

Babin— Babinsee
Babic— Babitzer Bach
Bel— Behlenseehlen
Bobr— Boberow-See
Bogosin— Buginsee
Brenica— Brenitz-See
Brus/Brusnica— Breutzen See
Bukovica— Buckwitzer See
Caplov— Schaplowsee
Cepr— Zepernicksee

Crn/Crnov— Zernow-See
Divnica— Dievenitz Bach
Dosov— Dosse
Dol/Dolc— Dolschsee
Glovac— Glabatzsee
Glava/Glova— Glawkesee
Golina— Golingsee
Grab/Grabov— Grabowsee
Grib— Griepensee
Chud/Chudel— Gudelacksee

JABLO, KOPANICA, PALIC

Jablo— Gabelsee
Jaroch— Jerchsee
Kolpin— Kolpinsee
Konotop— Kohntopp Fluss
Kopanica— Kuhpansee
Krepin— Kreppinsee
Kvet/Kvetnica— Quenzsee
Kvil/Kvilov— Quillow Bach
Labuz— Labuske-See
Lub/Lubelov— Lubelowsee

Lub/Lubica— Lubitzsee
Modla— Madlitzer See
Mura— Muhre
Nudov— Nuthe
Olsin— Olse
Palic— Palitz-See
Plon— Plunzsee
Plot— Plotzsee
Polnica— Polenzsee
Prek— Pritschingsee

RUDOV, STARE JEZERO, STRUGA

Prickov— Pritzkower See
Pri-rov/Prirov— Prierowsee
Rakov— Raacksee
Reka/Recica— Rietzer See
Rog/Rogolin— Ragollinsee
Rep/Repisce— Riepischzsee
Rudov— Rudower See

Rupin— Ruppiner See
San— Saan
Scepin— Stiepensee
Slon/Slonica— Schlanitzsee
Smrd— Schmartensee
Somin— Zemminsee
Sosnik— Zutzenicksee

Sprev— Spree	**Steklin**— Stechlin-See
Sprevica— Spreewitz	**Strega**— Streganzer See
Stare Jezero— Starjesar	**Struga**— Tschugga

UKLEI, VOSTROV, ZAGOST

Trnica— Tarnitz Bach	**Vosin/Vosinac**— Wussnatzsee
Tymen— Thymen-Bach	**Vostrov**— Wustrowsee
Uklei— Ukleisee	**Vostrovica**— Wosteritz See
Vadolica— Wandlitz-See	**Vupac**— Wupatzsee
Vinov— Finow	**Vyplav**— Wopachsee
Vokol— Wokuhlsee	**Zagost**— Sagast Bach
Vokun— Wukensee	**Za-krov/Zakrov**— Sacrower See
Vokunica— Wocknitz	**Zalikov**— Salchowersee
Volcina— Volzine Bach	**Zelub**— Seelubber See

The following series includes the dates of early citations of some of the many recorded hydronyms derived from different Slavic roots.

BISTRICA, BROD, CRN

Bistrica— *in rivulum Bysteritze*/1316, Bistritz
Boleglav/Boleglov— Buleglove/1301, Bullow-See
Breznica— dis Brissnitz/1684, Briessensee
Brod— *stagnis Brodewinschee*/1258, Brodowin-See
Buc, Bucov— die Buz/1525, Butzsee
Bukov— der Bukowen/1441, Buckow
Chor, Chorin— *stagnis Chorin majus et minus*/1258, Choriner See
Cicen, Cicenov— der Zizenow/1590, Zietzenow
Cist— Tzist/1333, Ziestsee
Crn, Crnica— Zernitze/1744, Zernitz
Devin— Dewien-see/1772, Dovinsee

DOBRA, DUBRAVA, GOLICA

Dobra— *aqua dicta Dobera*/1274, Daber
Dolgin— *stagnum nomine Dolghen*/1375, Dolgensee
Dol, Dolin— *stanum nomine Dollyn*/1375, Dollinsee
Dollgowsee— der Dolgow/1799, Dolgow
Drob— der Drobsch See/1847, Drobschsee
Dubrava— der Dubraitz/1800, Dubreitze
Glin— *stagnum Glyndersee*/1317, Glindow
Godim— *stanum, quod dicitur Godemo*/1375, Gamensee
Golica— der Golitzsche/1663, Gohlitzsee
Glubok— Klein Glubike/1748, Glubigsee
Gogol, Gogolica— *aquam, que Gugelitz vocatur*/1259, Jaglitz

GORINA, JEZER, KNEZ

Gorina— Gorin/1591, Gorinsee
Govno— *stagno Gouenow*/1348, Huwenowsee

Grim— der Grimmische, 1591, Grimme-See
Jezer— *stagni Jeserik*/1367, Jeseriger See
Karus— *in stagno, quod dicitur Caruthz*/1315, Karutzsee
Knez, Kengyna— *ad rivulum qui dicitur Knegena*/1263, Kneeden
Kostrin— *in nostro stagno dicto kosterin*/1328, Kustrinchener Bach
Kostrnica— *in fluvio Costernitz*/1248, Kosternitz Bach
Koval— *stanum nomine Kuwal*/1375, Kuwal See
Krap— *stanig, quod Kremp dicitur*/1335, Krempfliess
Krinica— Krienitz/1826, Kirenitzsee

KRUP, MALOGOST, PEC

Krup— Crupe/1375, Krupelsee
Lesnica— *villa lesniz ... que apud lesniciam sita est*/1244, Lesnitz
Lichen— *stagnum Lychen*, 1299
Lub, Lubinov— *duo stagna, unum dicitur Lubnoweche*/1375, Lubeenower See
Lub, Lubotov— *cum stagno Lubetow*/1249, Lubetowsee
Lub, Lubov— in den Lubow/1649, Lubowsee
Lubinic— Lubenitz/1375, Lipenitzsee
Lupanica— *in rivulum Lupaniz*/1258, Limnitzgraben
Malogost— *stagnum nomine Malgast*/1375, Mahlgastsee
Mel, Melica— die Melitz/1530, Mehlitzsee
Mogyla— *ad fluvium Moegelitz*/1299, Meglitz
Nehmic— der Neimitz/1530, Nehmitz-See
Parst, Parstin— *stanum Parsten*/1258, Parsteiner See
Pec— die Petsche, 1780, Petschee

PLANA, PLAVA, RADOMIR

Plana, Plona— *ad rivum Plane*/1205, Plahne
Platkov— *stagnum Platekouv*/1299, Platkowsee
Plav— die Plawe/1525, Plagge
Ples— Plesov, *stagum Pleso*/1317, Plessower See
Poradz— *stagnum Poratz*/1300, Poratzsee
Premislav— Prinzlow/ 1335, Prentzlauersee
Prezimir— *stanum dicta Pretzimar*/1333, Prietzen
Psibor, Pribor— Pschiburg/1772
Radel, Radlica— Redelitz/1287, Redlitz
Raden— die Radensseen/1751, Rathsee
Radomir— die Rademer/1476, Rahmersee
Radov— *que dicitur Randowa*/1250, Randow

REKA, RYBIN, SREM

Reka, Recica— Rietziza/1745, Rietzitza Bach
Rod, Rodan— *silva nostra Rodana*, 1240, Roddansee
Rog, Rogosin— *rivulum Rogosene*/1277, Ragose See
Ryba, Rybin— de Ryben/1335, Riebener See
Scepnica— der Stepenitze/1337, Stepenitz

Scina— an der Tschinicka/1736, Tschinkasee
Slavobor— Schlagenbornsche See/1772, Sclabornsee
Slub, Sluba— daz wazzer Slube/1336, Schlaube
Somit— der Sammetkow/1655, Schumkesee
Sosny— Zozen/1575, Zootzen-See
Srem— *per silve et rivi, qui vulgariter Schremmedicitur*/1274,Schremme
Staganica— Stengenitz/1525, Stendenitzer See

STARICA, STRUM, STUDENICA

Stan, Stanica— der grossen und kleinen Stanitz/1696, Stanitzsee
Star— Starensee/1844, Starsee
Starica— *silvam Stariz*/1232, Storitzsee
Stob, Stoborov— *fluvium qui Stoborov nuncupatur*/1245/Stobber
Stolec— der Stollentze/1541, Stollense
Straz— *rivulam Strazzovva*/1233, Strassow
Strel, Strelov— die Strelow/1598, Strehlsee
Strum, Strumen— *Strumma fluvius*/946, Stremme
Studenica— Studenitz/1247, Stienitz
Svar— Swartenze/1375, Schwarzensee
Svat— Swantyke/1375, Schwanter See
Svet— *in ... alio stagno, quod zuwet vulgariter appellatur*/1225, Zwet

TISIN, VISEGOST, VOLOVICA

Svekov— *in stagno Zevecow*/1400, Sewekow-See
Svilov— *in stagno Zwilov*/1205, Schielowsee
Tesin, Tesimir— Tessmar See/1654, Tetzensee
Tis, Tisin— *stagnum Tytzen dictum*/1285, Tietzen See
Tymenica— *super Timanize fluvium*/1232, Temnitzbach
Varblin— Werblin/1525, Werbellinsee
Visegost— Wicegast/1275, Wicegast See
Vesel— der Weselitz/1592, Weselitz-See
Vircovica— Verketz/1375, Fergitz
Voblica— der Wobelitz/1556, Woblitz Bach
Volcica— der Woltzitze/1748, Wolzitze
Volova Struga— *rivulus Wolowastruga*/1299
Volovica— der Wolwitz/1799, Wulwitzsee
Volk— *stagnum Wolke*/1288, Volz
Volksa— *lacus et paludes Voltscha*/1313, Wolkau
Vomaz, Vomazov— *stagnum Womazowe*/1274, Wummsee
Zaba, Zabin— Sabinsee/1788, Sabinensee
Zakanica— an der Zakenitze/1528, Zakenitz See
Zarnov— *cum aqua Sernow*, Sarnow
Zelchov— *stangnis Selchow*/1348, Salchowsee
Zukov— *stagna nomine Sukow*/1375, Suchowsee

5. BORK SLAVICA, WINDISCHEN BUCK

As the following series indicates, medieval and later sources identify numerous villages, towns, and toponyms in the greater Berlin-Brandenburg area as *Slav/Wend* villages, towns, and toponyms.

ALSTORP SLAVICA, MOSTIZ SLAVICALI

Alstorp *Slavica*

Bork *Slavica*

Buck *Slavica*

Buten *Slavica*

Cowal *Slavicali*

Kummerviz *Slavicalem*

Linde *Slavica*

Moczow *Slavicali*

Mostiz *Slavicalis*

Slavicali Bucholt

Slavicali Porats

Slavicali Slatadorf

SLAVICAM STOLP, SLAVICUM TORNOW

Slavicalis Grezowe

Slavicam Crucewitz

Slavicam Stolp

Slavica ville Stulp

Slavicum Tornow

Slavos sue ville dicte Repente

Stanstorpp *Slavica*

Walterstorf *Slavica*

Wusterhuse *Slavica*

WENDESCEMUSTIZ, WENDESCHEN BUTEN

*Wend*dorf

*Wend*dorf-Stucken

*Wend*escemustiz

*Wend*efeld

*Wend*emarck

*Wend*enberg

*Wend*enfriedhof

*Wend*enkirchenhof

*Wend*enschloss

*Wend*eschen Bockholz

*Wend*eschen Buten

*Wend*eschen Garsedow

WENDESCHEN ROCHOW, WENDESCHEN TORNOW

*Wend*eschen Gotzkow

*Wend*eschen Panchowe

*Wend*eschen Rochow

*Wend*eschen Stanstorff

*Wend*eschen Tornow

*Wend*eschen Warnow

*Wend*esteig

*Wend*ewasser

*Wend*land

*Wend*orfer

WENDISCH GRABEN, WENDISCH WOTZ

*Wend*orpen

*Wend*isch Bucholz

*Wend*isch Caweln

*Wend*isch Graben

*Wend*isch Linde

*Wend*isch Spree

*Wend*isch Wotz

*Wend*ische Kirchhofe

*Wend*ische Kirchhofstucken

*Wend*ische Krampitz

*Wend*ischen Alsdorff

*Wend*ischen Borgk

WENDOCHOW, WINDISCHEN BRIST

*Wend*ischen Woltersdorff
*Wend*ischen Wusterhausen
*Wend*lobbese
*Wend*ochow
*Wend*pfuhl
*Wend*tdorf

*Wend*thof
*Wend*tsee
*Wend*tshof
*Wind*ische Wiltaw
*Wind*ischen Brist
*Wind*ischen Buck

SER(B), SAR(B)

As is to be expected, the ethnonym *Sar(b)/Ser(b)* is also present in the greater Berlin-Brandenburg area. *Sarmstorf*, for example, is originally *Serbin/Sarbin*, and secondarily *Serb's dorf* or *Sarbenzdorf* and *Sarbensdorp*. Similarly, *Zorndorf* is originally *Sarbin*, secondarily *Sarbinovo*.

SAR-MUNTI

The root *Sar* is found in the Saar River, a branch of the Nuthe River near Potsdam, where one finds the village of Saar-mund, originally Sar, secondarily Sar-munt (1349), Sar-emunt (1349), and Sar-munt (1359).

The suffix -munt is a German add-on: **Der Name wurde als deutsche bildung des 12. Jahrhunderts "Ort and der Mundung der Saar" gedeutet. Die Form -mund statt des im nd. Sprachgebiet sonst ublichen -munde (vgl. Ueckermunde, Swinemunde) wurd auf den Einfluss niederlandischer Siedler zuruckgefuhrt** *(R. Fischer, G. Schlimpert, Vorslawische Namen in Brandenburg, ZtS 16, 1971).* Thus *zupa Ser*, later *Ser-munti* (*pago Serimunti*, 951), modern Sermuth, near Grimma, in the heartland of historic *White Serbia.*

SARNOV, SERNOV

Other possible onomastic references to the Serbs are found in names with the prefixes *Cer-, Sar-, Ser-, Zar-, Zor-* (e.g. *aqua Sernow*/1303, Nieplitz tributary; Sarnow/Bernau, *duo molendina superiora in Sarnowe*/1267; Sarnow/Pritzwalk, Sarnowe/1309; Sernow/Juterbog, *ville Sarnowe*/1227, *plebanus in Sernow*/1241; Sernow/Juterbog, Serrnow/1300; Sornow/Luckau, Sernowschen/1472, Sernischen/1546).

GOPLO

It is both interesting and suggestive that near Brandenburg one finds the village of Goplo and master 'Heinrich the Slav' (*villam Gople ... Heinricus Slavus, magister civium dicte ville*, 1226; *villa Gopel*, 1375). The name Goplo has its counterpart in Lake Goplo, near Gniezno, an ancient center of Serb settlement in *Vielkopolska.*

6. TREBOGOST, RADOBYL, CHOTEMIR

Modern Germany remains a treasure trove of archaic Slavic personal names preserved in varying degrees in German place names.

BOR, BUD, LUB, MIR, PAK, RAD, SUL, ZAL

The long list of archaic Slavic-German place names includes, for example, names beginning or ending with *Bor, Bud, Lub, Mir, Pak, Rad, Sul,* and *Zal*.

Bor (Bolibor, Lutobor, Ratibor, Sedlobor)
Bud (Budorad, Chotebud, Prebud)
Dra (Dragobud, Dragovid, Zelidrag)
Lub (Luborad, Velelub)
Mir (Chotemir, Gnevomir, Unemir)
Pak (Pakobud, Pakomir, Pakoslav)
Rad (Radovid, Sedlorad, Tuchorad)
Sul (Nisul, Radosul, Sulimir)
Zal (Zaligost, Zalimir, Zalislav)

GOST

The following series of *White Serbia* place names features archaic Slavic personal names with **gost** as prefix or suffix.

UDOGOST, BUDIGOST

Audigast (Groitzsch)— **Udogost**
Badegast (Kothen)— **Badogost**
Bietegast (Wittenberg)— **Bytogost**
Budigast (Leipzig)— **Budigost**
Dobertast (Zeitz)—**Dobrogost**
Gadegast (Seyda)— **Chotegost**
Gastewitz (Grimm)— **Gostanovic**
Gastrose (Guben)— **Gostirad**

GOSTIMIR, GOSTILOVICI

Gestewitz (S. Naumberg)— **Gostici**
Gestewitz (N. Naumberg)— **Gostici**
Gestewitz, Klein- (Camburg)— **Gostovici**
Goschwitz (Bautzen)— **Gostici**
Goseln, Ober- (Dobeln)— **Gostnic**
Gossmar (Finsterwalde)— **Gostimir**
Gossnitz (Eckartsberg)— **Gostanovici**
Gosswitz (Gorlitz)— **Gostilovici**

GOSTOV, GOSTIRADICI

Gostau (Weissenfels)— **Gostov**
Gostelitz (Naumberg)— **Gostilice**
Gostemitz (Eilenburg)— **Gostilici**

Gostewitz (Riesa)— **Gostavici**
Gostitz (Naundorf)— **Gostici**
Gostritz (Dresden)— **Gostiradici**
Gottschdorf (Konigsbruck)— **Gostin**
Grosswitz (Reichenbach)— **Gostolovic**

LUBOGOST, MILOGOST

Kordigast (Lichtenfels)— **Cotogost**
Laubegast (Dresden)— **Lubogost**
Leugas (Tirschenreuth)— **Lubogost**
Leugast (Kulmbach)— **Lubogost**
Liebegast (Wittichenau)— **Lubogost**
Lobstedt (Jena)— **Lubogostic**
Mellies (Ludwigslust)— **Milogost**
Meusegast (Pirna)— **Muzigost**

ONOGOST, ZIVOGOST

Nunkas (Eschenbach)— **Onogost**
Radegast (Zorbig)— **Radogost**
Rodias (Kahla)— **Rodogost**
Rodigast (Jena)— **Radogost**
Saalegast (Bitterfeld)— **Zalgost**
Sallgast (Finsterwalde)— **Zalgost**
Schorgoast (Kulmbach)— **Skorogost**
Seugast (Amberg)— **Zivogost**

TREBOGOST, VOLIGOST

Trebast (Kulmbach)— **Trebogost**
Trebgast, Alten- (Bayreuth)— **Trebogost**
Weddegast (Bernburg)— **Vidogost**
Wolgast (Bayern)— **Voligost**
Wulst (Neuhaus)—**Voligost**
Zegast (Stadtsteinach)— **Zagost**
Zetegast (Cumlmitz)— **Cetogost**
Zschagast (Borna)— **Cagost**

SL, YL

The following series, mainly from *White Serbia,* features archaic Slavic personal names with **SL** and **YL** as prefix or suffix.

DRAGOMYSL, VELEMYSL

Bademeusel (Forst)— **Badomysl**
Demeusel (Plauen)— **Temysl**
Dramissle (Grafenrod)— **Dragomysl**
Drobel (Bernburg)— **Drogobyl**
Duchumuzlidorf— **Duchomysl**
Liebon (Bautzen)— **Lubobyl**

Mehlmeisel (Wunseidel)— **Velemysl**
Meuschlitz (Zeitz)— **Myslici**

MYSLOTICI, MYSKLEOVICI
Meuselko (Schweinitz)— **Mysliko**
Meuselwitz (Altenberg)— **Myslibuz**
Meuselwitz (Colditz)— **Myslotici**
Meuselwitz (Reichenbach)— **Myslovici**
Meusslitz (Dresden)— **Myslic**
Michelwitz (Groitzsch)— **Myslovici**
Michlitz (Lutzen)— **Myskleovici**
Miesitz (Triptis)— **Mysici**

MYSOVICI, MYSLANOVICI
Mischutz (Dobeln)— **Mysovici**
Mischwitz (Neissen)— **Mysovici**
Mischwitz (Wurzen)— **Mysovici**
Mischwitz (Weimar)— **Mysovici**
Misselquitz (Zeitz)— **Myslekovici**
Misselwitz (Altenburg)— **Myslanovici**
Misselwitz (Kothen)— **Myslovici**
Moschlitz (Schleiz)— **Myslici**

PREMYSL, RADOBYL
Muschelwitz (Bautzen)— **Myslesovic**
Nissmitz (Freyburg)— **Nesvacyl**
Pomsel (Bitterfeld)— **Pomysl**
Premeusel (Stadtsteinach)— **Premysl**
Premeischl (Oberpfalz)— **Premysl**
Priemausel (Meningen)— **Premysl**
Radebol (Dahlen)— **Radobyl**
Radewell (Halle)— **Radobyl**

RADOMYSL, DRAGOMYSL
Rodameuschel (Camburg)— **Radomysl**
Rodameuschel (Schmollin)— **Rozmysl**
Rodebille (Dessau)— **Radobyl**
Rotheul (Sonnenberg)— **Radobyl**
Rottelmisch (Kahle)— **Radomysl**
Scheibelau (Jena)— **Skobyl**
Schwemsal (Duben)— **Svemysl**
Trainmeusel (Ebermannstadt)— **Dragomysl**

TUCHOMYSL, CETOMYSL
Tuchamuzi (Zeitz)— **Tuchomysl**
Zettmeisel (Kulmbach)— **Cetomysl**
Zettmeisel (Harsdorf)— **Cetomysl**

Zidimuslesdorpf— **Sdemysl**
Zothen (Camburg)— **Cetobyl**

CHO-, CHU-, CHY-

The following series features Slavic-German place names derived from archaic Slavic personal names beginning with the prefixes **CHO-**, **CHU-** and **CHY-**.

CHOTOVICI, CHOTICI

Godewitz (Zorbig)— **Chotovici**
Godnitz (Barby)— **Chotenici**
Gothewitz (Weissenfels)— **Chotovici**
Gottitz (Brehna)— **Chotici**
Gottlitz (Landsberg)— **Chotelici**
Gottnitz (Zorbig)— **Chotenici**
Gottwitz (Mutzschen)— **Chotici**
Gotzitz (Barby)— **Chotici**

CHODISIN, CHOTENOVICI

Kadischen (Zeitz)— **Chodisin**
Kathewitz (Naumberg)— **Chotovici**
Kathewitz (Torgau)— **Chot, Chotovici**
Kattnitz (Dobeln)— **Chocovici**
Kettewitz (Meissen)— **Chotenovici**
Kittlitz (Calau)— **Chytlici**
Kauscha (Dresden)— **Chudosov**
Kautzsch (Dresden)— **Chudosov**

CHOJNO, CHOROVID

Kayna (Zeitz)— **Chojno**
Kayna (Lobitz)— **Chojno**
Keune (Forst)— **Chojno**
Kodderitz (Kothen)— **Chotrici**
Kodderitzsch (Apolda)— **Chodrici**
Koditz (Rudolstadt)— **Chodici**
Koitzsch (Kamenz)— **Chojica**
Korbussen (Ronneburg)— **Chorovid**

CHOCEMIR, CHOTEMIR

Kosmirsdorf (Niesk)— **Chocemir**
Kottenewitz (Lommatzsch)— **Chotenovici**
Kothenitz (Schmolln)— **Chotimici**
Kothensdorf (Rochlitz)— **Chotemir**
Kotschau (Jena)— **Chotsov**
Kotschlitz (Markranstadt)— **Chocelici**
Kotsschen (Jena)— **Chotsin**
Kotten (Wittichenau)— **Chotin**

CHOTERAD, CHOTEBUD

Kotten (Torgau)— **Chotin**
Kotteritz (Altenburg)— **Choterad**
Kotteritzsch (Colditz)— **Choterici**
Kottewitz (Grossenhain)— **Chotacovici**
Kottewitz (Meissen)— **Chotebud**
Kottewitz (Pirna)— **Chotenici**
Kottichau (Hohenmolsen)— **Chotechov**
Kottlitz (Torgau)— **Chotelici**

CHOTOVICI, CHOJNICA

Kottmarsdorf (Lobau)— **Chotemir**
Kottmerode (Naumberg)— **Chotemir**
Kottwitz (Merseburg)— **Chotovici**
Kottwitzsch (Rochlitz)— **Chotovici**
Kotzschau (Merseburg)— **Chocov**
Kotzschwitz (Magdeborn)— **Chocovic**
Koyne (Kleinleipisch)— **Chojna**
Kuhnau (Dessau)— **Chojin**
Kunitz (Bautzen)— **Chojnica**

RADOVAN'S DORF

In the case of many villages it is common for Slavic-German place names derived from Slavic personal names to be 'Germanized' by the addition of German suffixes connoting rural settlements, namely 'dorf' and 'schutz.' In the following series, all the 'dorfs' are from the Zeitz area in *White Serbia.*

DOBRIGOST'S DORF

Blochsdorf is **Mloch's/Mlodota's dorf**—Molochosdorf (1152); Molochestorf (1160)
Doberstorf is **Dobri's/Dobrigost's dorf**—Dobristorf (1049)
Dragsdorf is **Dragan's dorf**––*Drogis in burgwardo Chvine* (1069) and Dragendorf (1121)
Droszdorf is **Droz's dorf**— Droissforff (1256); Drosdorf (1694)
Gniebendorf is **Gnevin's dorf**— Gniwendorf (1300); Gnywindorff (1378)

BUDSIN'S DORF

Niscinsdorf is **Niscin's dorf**—Niscinsdorf, (1121)
Pitzschendorf (Osterfeld) is **Budsin's dorf**—Buczkindorf (1300); Buckindorff (1349)
Puschendorf is **Puscin's dorf**— Puschendorf (1583)
Rossendorf is **Roslav's dorf**—Rosslavindorf (1336)
Rumsdorf is **Radovan's dorf**— Rodowvanstorf (1160)

SLAVIN'S DORF

Schlawendorf is **Slavin's dorf**— Slawendorff (1329); Slawendorf (1335)
Tessendorf is **Tesim's/Tesimir's dorf**— Tesmendorf (1214)

Zamilsdorf is **Zamysl's dorf**— *Zamyvzlesdorf in burgwardo Chvine* (1069)

Zaschendorf is **Czas/ Czasin's dorf**— Czaschindorff (1378); Czassindorff (1458)

Zeundorf is **Cuncin's dorf**— Czunczin (1443)

SERB'S DORF

Zerbersdorf is **Serb's dorf**— Zerbstorff (1558), Zerbisdorf (1640)

Zetzschendorf is **Czes's dorf**— Czesdorff (1452)

Zipsendorf is **Sybislav's dorf**— *Herbo de Cybezalundorf* (1168) and Cypzlawendorf (1295)

Zschansdorf is **Skanov's dorf**— Scandorf (1160)

Zulistorf is **Sulisa's dorf**— Zulistorf (1274)

Zweimilsdorf is **Svemysl's dorf** as in —***nova milla quam Zvemuzi quidam primus incoluit*** (1146)

LUBO'S SCHUTZ

In the following 'schutz' series, a nearby reference town is given in parentheses.

DOBROS' SCHUTZ

Bloaschutz (Bautzen) is **Blos/Blosovici**— *Heinemannus de Bloschwicz* (1296) and Bloeschicz (1515)

Burtshcutz (Zeitz) is **Boris/Borsici**— Borsiz (1145); Borschicz (1256)

Delmsuchutz (Mugeln) is **Tolmas/Tolmasici**— Talmaschiz (1311); Telmaschwitz, (1319)

Dennschutz (Lommatzsch) is **Tencin/Tencici**—Tenschicz (1334); Tencschicz (1378); Denczschicz (1445)

Doberschutz (Bautzen) is **Dobros/Dobrosici**—Doberswicz (1280); Dobirschwicz (1374)

DOBROSIC'S SCHUTZ

Doberschutz (Eilenburg) is **Dobros/Dobrosici**— Doberwicz (1314); Doberschwicz (1350)

Doberschutz (Konigswartha) is **Dobros/Dobrosici**— Doberswicz (1350); Dobirswicz (1447)

Dobraschutz (Altenburg) is **Dobros/Dobrasici**— Dobirschicz (1336)

Dollschutz (Eisenberg) is **Delsin/Delsici**— Delsize (1145); Delschicz (1378)

Doschutz (Dobeln) is **Dedis/Dedisovici**— Didiswitz, Didiscuitz (1205)

LUBOSIC'S SCHUTZ

Doschutz (Dobeln) is **Tesin/ Tesic**— Tesice (1071); Tesciz (1217); Teschicz (1428)

Liebschutz (Oschatz) is **Lubos/Lubosici**— Lubezic (1233); Lubeschwicz (1307)

Liebschutz (Possneck) is **Lubos/Lubosici**— Lobesiz (1258)

Lobschutz (Bad Kosen) is **Lubis/Lubisici**— *plebanus de Lubiz* (1264)

Lobschutz (Jena) is **Lubis/Lubisici**— Lobeschniz, 1365

MORASIN'S SCHUTZ

Lobschutz (Lommatzsch) is **Lubis/Lubisic**— Lubiziz (1216); Lubueschwiz, 1311

Lobshchutz (Meissen) is **Levos/Levsici**— Leustitz (1205); Leuschicz (1334)

Lubschutz (Wurzen) is **Lubos/Lubosici**— Liubizici (1004); Luebschicz (1570)

Marcshutz (Lommatzsch) is **Morasin/Morasovici**—Marocswicz, (1334); Maracswicz (1378)

Merschutz (Muegeln) is **Miras/Mirasovici**— Meraschwitz (1326); Merschuwitz (1350)

MUZKO'S SCHUTZ

Minschutz (Dobeln) is **Miso/Misovici**— Misechewicz (1321); Mischwicz (1334)

Mollschutz (Camburg) is **Modlisa/Modlisici**— *Thime de Modelsicz* (1350)

Muschutz (Lommatzsch) is **Muzko/Muzkovici**— *Matheus de Muscuitz* (1205)

Nedaschutz (Bautzen) is **Nedasin/Nedasovici**—*Johannes de Nedaswicz* (1317)

Nellschutz (Weissenfels) is **Nedelk/Nedelsic**— Nedelschitz (1311); Nedelczicz (1350)

BUDISIN'S SCHUTZ

Neidschutz (Naumberg) is **Niksin/Niksici**— *Petrus de Nitschiz* (1265)

Pauschutz (Meissen) is **Budisin/Budisici**— Budesitz (1205), Budeschicz (1334) and Budeschitz (1445)

Plennschutz is **Plenk/Plencic**— Plentschitz (1458); Plentzschitz (1501)

Pratschutz (Schkolen) is **Pras/Prasici**— Praschitz (1299)

Ranschutz (Dobeln) is **Ranis/Ranisovici**— Ranschewicz (1378); Ranczschkewicz (1501)

Raschutz (Colditz) is **Rasin/Rasovici**— Raskewicz (1350), *Clare de Raczschicz* (1411) and Rasswitz (1473)

Remschutz (Saalfeld) is **Remis/Remsici**— Remischzi (1074); Remschicz (1378)

Robschutz (Rudolstadt) is **Robis/Robisici**— Robesiz (1083); Robeschicz (1378)

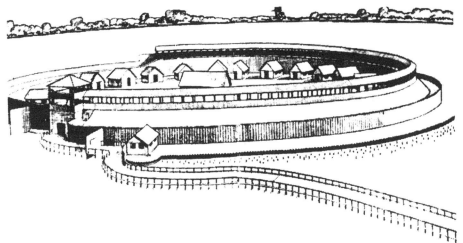

Fortified *Grad*/town with causeway (Slavia)

7. KAMEN, KLOBUK, KON, KOBYLA

Many original Slavic place names in modern Germany have survived with minor changes. In many instances the changes are more apparent in terms of awkward spelling or contractions than real in terms of Slavic roots, sounds, and rhythms.

The following series is from ***White Serbia*** (the modern name and location in terms of nearby town or city follows the original Slavic name).

KAMEN, KLOBUK

The following comprehensive series of modern Slavic-German place names, limited to names beginning with the letter **K,** is characterized by relatively minor changes in spelling and sound.

KAK, KISELOVIC

Kak— Kaka (Osterfeld)
Kakov— Kakau (Dessau)
Kala— Kahla (Jena)
Kamen— Kamenz (Dresden)
Kaskov— Kaschka (Meissen)
Kerm— Kermen (Zerbst)
Kiselovic— Kieselwitz (Liesnig)

Klekovic— Kleckewitz (Dessau)
Klen— Clennen (Leisnig)
Klepac— Kleppisch (Pirna)
Klesc— Kletzen (Delitzsch)
Klik— Klicken (Dessau)
Klicin— Klitzschen (Torgau)
Klin— Kleina (Orla)

KLOBUK, KOMOR, KOPANIK

Klobuk— Klobikau Dessau)
Kloda— Kloden (Jessen)
Kokul—Kukulau(Naumberg)
Kolk— Kolka (Gethain)
Komor Commerau (Bautzen)
Kopac— Koppatz (Cottbus)
Kopanik— Kopnick (Wittenberg)
Kopic— Copitz (Pirna)

Korb— Corba (Rochlitz)
Kosmatic— Kosmatitz (Torgau)
Koza— Cosa (Kothen)
Kozica— Cositz (Kothen)
Kozlic— Koselitz (Naumberg)
Kotel— Kothel (Altenburg)

KRAI, KRUG, KUPA

Krai— Krei (Dobeln)
Krak— Krackau (Weimar)
Kras— Krassa (Altenburg)
Krim— Krimla (Gera)
Krinica— Kreinitz (Strehla)
Krot— Crotta (Pirna)

Krug— Krugen (Schonebeck)
Krolup— Kralapp (Rochlitz)
Kuklic— Kaucklitz (Torgau)
Kupa— Kauppa (Bautzen)
Kurbica— Kurbitz(Altenburg)
Kutin— Kutten (Halle)

KON, KOBYLA

As diverse sources testify to the fact that the ***White Serbs*** were renowned horsemen who lived and often died with their steeds, it is not surprising that many modern place names in historic ***White Serbia*** are derived from the Old Slavic words relating to horse **(kon)** and mare **(kobyla).**

KOBYLA

Kobyla— Cabel (Calau)
Kobyla— Kobbeln (Guben)
Kobyla— Kobel (Riesa)
Kobyla— Koblenz (Altenburg)
Kobyla— Koblenz (Wittichenau)
Kobyla— Kebeliz (BadDuben)
Kobyla— Kugel (Halle)
Kobylani—Koblen (Merseburg)
Kobylani— Kofeln (Gera)
Kobylica— Kobelitz (Zorbig)

KOBYLICA

Kobylica— Coblenz (Bautzen)
Kobylica— Kolbitz (Grafenhainichen)
Kobylov— Kablow (Storkow)
Kon— Kone (Schonebeck)
Kon— Kone (Pretzien)
Konane— Kanena (Halle)
Konar— Konnern (Halle)
Konar— Konrick (Gerbstedt)
Konarovic— Kunnerwitz (Gorlitz)
Konebudi— Kanebude (Wittenberg)

KONENOVIC

Konenovic— Canitz (Meissen)
Konica— Konitz (Saalfeld)
Konotop— Constappel (Meissen)
Konov— Konow (Dessau)
Konovic— Canitz (Bautzen)
Konovic— Cunnewitz (Wittichenau)
Konovic—Cannewitz(Grimma)
Konovic—Connewitz (Wurzen)

The following series is representative of the minor changes in spelling and sound in a greater range of modern Slavic-German place names, namely place names beginning with the letters **B** through **S.**

BABIZNA, BOR, BUDA

Babizna— Babisnau (Dresden)
Bara— Bahra (Gottleuba)
Bela— Biehla (Kamenz)
Bledin— Bleddin (Kemberg)
Blosin— Blossin (Storkow)
Bobric— Bobritzsch (Freiberg)
Bodrin— Badrina (Delitzsch)
Bor— Bohra (Schmolln)
Branic— Branitz (Cottbus)
Bren— Brehna (Halle)
Brodkovic— Brodkowitz (Cottbus)
Brosin— Brossin (Zeitz)
Buda— Bauda (Grossenhain)
Buk— Bugk (Storkow)

BUKOV, DOBRILUG, DOLINA

Bukov— Buckow (Beeskow)
Chleb— Kleba (Dresden)
Chlebno— Kleben (Weissenfels)
Chmeln— Kmehlen (Elsterwerda)
Cholm— Collmen (Wurzen)
Chrost— Krostau (Plauen)
Dobra— Dobra (Radeburg)
Dobrik— Dobbrick (Cottbus)
Dobrilug— Doberlug (Finsterwalde)
Dobricin— Dobritschen (Camburg)
Dolina— Dohlen (Dresden)
Dolnica— Dollnitz (Halle)
Dub— Daube (Pirna)
Dubin— Duben (Bitterfeld)

DUBRAVA, GLINA, JABLAN

Dubrava— Dubrau (Calau)
Dubrov— Dubro (Herzberg)
Duga— Dugau (Halle)
Glava— Glowe (Beeskow)
Glina— Gleina (Zeitz)
Graba— Graba (Saalfeld)
Greben— Grebehna (Delitzsch)
Groba— Groba (Riesa)

Jablan— Gablenz (Crimmitschau)
Jama— Jahmo (Zahna)
Jasenica— Jessenitz (Bautzen)
Javor— Jauer (Elstra)
Javornik— Jauernik (Lobau)
Jesen— Jessen (Lommatzsch)

JEZER, LUG, MALINA

Jezer— Jehzer (Calau)
Laz— Laas (Oschatz)
Lipa— Leipa (Torgau)
Lisnik— Leisnig (Dobeln)
Luba— Leuba (Ostritz)
Liga— Liega (Grossenhain)
Lisin— Lissen (Naumberg)

Loma— Lohma (Altenberg)
Lug— Lug (Cottbuss)
Luka— Lucka (Jena)
Lupa— Luppa (Dahlen)
Mala— Mahla (Torgau)
Malina— Mahlen (Zeitz)
Malis— Mahlis (Mugeln)

MEDEN, MIR, MOST

Malsin— Malsen (Oschatz)
Maslo— Masslau (Leipzig)
Maznic— Massnitz (Zeitz)
Meden— Meden (Altenburg)
Meran— Mehren (Meissen)
Mesto— Miest (Halle)
Mir/Mirov— Miera (Doblen)

Mis/Misov— Meuscha (Pirna)
Mlod— Mlode (Calau)
Mokric— Mockritz (Torgau)
Moric— Moritz (Zerbst)
Most— Most (Zorbig)
Most— Most (Bitterfeld)
Mostic— Mosticz (Torgau)

MUR, NAPADZ, OLSA

Mostin— Masten (Dobeln)
Moz/Mozin— Mosen (Gera)
Mur/Murov— Meuro (Wittenberg)
Mur/Murov— Muhro (Zerbst)
Musov— Meuschau (Merseburg)
Muzin— Meusen (Rochlitz)

Napadz— Nappatsch (Niesky)
Nechan— Nechen (Lobau)
Nicka— Nitzschka (Grimma)
Nidan— Neiden (Torgau)
Nivisce— Niewisch (Beeskow)
Nivica— Niewitz (Lubben)
Olsa— Oelshau (Torgau)
Olsin— Olsen (Beeskow)

ORLA, OSTROV, PEC

Orla— Orla (Kahla)
Osa— Ossa (Gethain)
Osec— Oschatz (Leipzig)
Osek— Ossig (Zeitz)
Ostrov— Ostra (Dresden)
Ozd— Osida (Zeitz)
Pec— Pechau (Schonebeck)

Penik— Penig (Rochlitz)
Pesnik— Possneck (Jena)
Pasek— Paska (Saalfeld)
Pec— Pietsch (Torgau)
Pena— Penna (Rochlitz)
Penik— Penig (Rochlitz)
Peric— Pehritzsch (Eilenburg)

PLON, PONIKVA, PREDEL

Pesin— Peissen (Halle)
Peskov— Pieskow (Beeskow)
Pleso— Plessa (Elsterwerda)
Plon— Plohn (Reichenbach)
Polensk— Polenz (Meissen)
Ponikva— Ponickau (Grossenhaim)
Popel— Popelln (Gera)

Posek— Posseck (Oelsnitz)
Predel— Predel (Zeitz)
Prerov— Prierow (Luckau)
Puscin— Peuschen (Possneck)
Radan— Radden (Calau)
Raden— Raden (Grossenhain)
Radis— Radis (Wittenberg)

RADO, RIBICA, ROGOV

Radlov— Radlow (Storkow)
Rado— Roda (Riesa)
Radus— Raddusch (Calau)
Rakov— Raackow (Cottbus)
Repin— Reppen (Riesa)
Repov— Repau (Zorbig)
Ribica— Reibitz (Delitzsch)

Ripin— Rippien (Dresden)
Robin— Roben (Gera)
Roblic— Roblitz (Saalfeld)
Rodin— Roden (Zeitz)
Rodun— Rodden (Merseburg)
Rogalin— Rugeln (Riesa)
Rogov— Ragow (Beeskow)

ROGUN, RUDA, SLAMEN

Rogun— Raguhn (Dessau)
Ronis— Ranis (Possneck)
Rub— Rauba (Lommatzsch)
Rubin— Ruben (Cottbus)
Ruda— Rauda (Eisenberg)
Rudno— Reuden (Bitterfeld)
Rusic— Rusitz (Gera)

Rusin— Russen (Borna)
Sanic— Schanitz (Nossen)
Sedlic— Sedlitz (Dresden)
Skolane— Schkolen (Eisenberg)
Skorlup— Schkorlopp (Leipzig)
Skudic— Schkeuditz (Leipzig)
Slamen— Slamen (Spremberg)

SMERD, STRUMEN, STUDEN

Smerd— Schmorda (Possneck)
Sosne— Sossen (Lutzen)
Spal— Spaal (Rudolstadt)
Spor— Spora (Zeitz)
Stana— Stahna (Dobeln)
Staric— Staritz (Torgau)
Stob— Stoben (Camburg)
Stolpin— Stolpen (Pirna)
Stolpin—Stolpchen (Grossenhain)
Storkov— Storkau (Weissenfels)

Stosin— Stoszen (Weissenfels)
Strela— Strehla (Riesa)
Strela— Strelln (Torgau)
Strog— Stroga (Grossenhaim)
Strumen— Streumen (Riesa)
Stud— Stauda (Meissen)
Stud— Steutz (Zerbst)
Studen— Steudten (Lommatzsch)
Studen— Steuden (Halle)

MOST, BROD

In addition to the several **mosts** (an Old Slavic word for bridge) cited in the above series (e.g. Most, Motic, Mostin), a number of interesting and rather colorful Slavic-German names derived from **brod,** an Old Slavic word for a river-crossing or ford (e.g. Slavonski Brod, Bosanski Brod), have survived with varying degrees of change.

BROD, GOLIBROD, ZABROD

Brod— Brodau (Delitzsch)
Brod— Prosa (Liebenwerd)
Brodic— Broditz (Bautzen)
Brodic— Broditz (Zeitz)
Brodic— Broitz (Halle)
Brodic— Pretzsch (Merseburg)
Brodkovic— Brodtkowitz (Cottbus)
Daniborowebrod (*trans Sprewam*)
Dubibrod— Dolgenbrodt (Storkow)

Golibrod— Goberode (Dresden)
Kozibrod— Casabra (Oschatz)
Skocibrod— Kotzschenbrod (Dresden)
Skocibrod— Schosebrode (Merseburg)
Zabrod— Sabrodt (Beeskow)
Zabrod— Sabrodt (Hoyerswerda)

BREG, GNEZDO

The following series is representative of Slavic-German names with relatively greater changes in spelling and sound.

BREG, GORA, GRANICA

Breg— Briesen (Calau)
Breza— Brasen (Rosslau)
Celkov— Schelkau (Teuchern)
Ciplic— Scheiplitz (Naumberg)
Crmna— Schirma (Freiberg)
Delcane— Dolzschen (Dresden)
Glusina— Glossen (Lobau)
Gnezdo— Gniest (Kemberg)

Golica— Golenz (Bautzen)
Gora— Gera (Reichenbach)
Gornica— Gohrenz (Leipzig)
Granica— Grantiz (Brand-Erbisdorf)
Greda— Greithen (Grimm)
Gumno— Gimritz (Halle)

KAMENICA, KOBYLA, KOKOTA

Jale— Gale (Delitzsch)
Jata— Jethe (Forst)
Jutro— Eutrich (Konigswartha)
Kamenica— Kemnitz (Dresden)
Kobyla— Koblenz (Altenberg)
Kokota— Jocketa (Elsterberg)
Kopriva— Kopschin (Elstra)

Koren— Kahren (Cottbus)
Kosovik— Kosswig (Calau)
Kosovo— Kossa (Altenberg)
Kremen— Kremitz (Halle)
Krivic— Krewitz (Kriebitzsch)
Krs— Krosigk (Halle)
Krupa— Graupa (Pirna)

LUG, MODRIC, MOKRA

Lozin— Lossen (Merseburg)
Lucno— Lutzen (Merseburg)
Lug— Laue (Delitzsch)
Malotes— Maltis (Altenburg)
Maltic— Maltitz (Borna)
Milsin— Molsen (Weissenfels)
Modric— Moderau (Halle)
Mokra— Muckrow (Spremberg)

Nedasin— Nedissen (Zeitz)
Nemci/Nemic— Nehmitz (Borna)
Netin— Niethen (Weissenberg)
Nismen— Nissma (Zeitz)
Nizan— Neussen (Torgau)
Nizko— Nieska (Riesa)

ORLICA, PELES, PLAVNO

Nos/Nosin— Nossen (Meissen)
Nunic— Neunitz (Grimma)
Okolo— Ogkeln (Wittenberg)
Okrug— Ockrill (Muhlberg)
Oploz— Ablass (Oschatz)
Orlica— Horlitz (Senftenberg)
Ovca— Otc (Calbe)
Ovcic— Eutzsch (Wittenberg)
Ovna— Oehna (Bautzen)
Parez— Peres (Borna)
Peles— Pohlitz (Naumberg)
Pitin— Piethen (Kothen)
Plavno— Plauen (Dresden)
Podole— Podel (Pirna)

POREKA, PRIDUB, RECICA

Poreka— Poritzsch (Saalburg)
Pozarin— Paserin (Luckau)
Prelaz— Prehlitz (Zeitz)
Presec— Pretzsch (Naumberg)
Pretim— Prettin (Torgau)
Pridub— Predau (Meuselwitz)
Prilug— Preilack (Cottbus)
Privel— Priefel (Altenburg)
Proloz— Prohliz (Dresden)
Pupic— Paupitzsch (Delitzsch)
Rasov— Raschau (Oelsnitz)
Recica— Rietchen (Rothenberg)
Semsin— Zembschen (Teuchern)
Svetov— Zwietow (Calau)

SVOJIM, TREBIN, TRGOV

Svojim— Zweimen(Merseburg)
Skopov— Schkopau (Merseburg)
Takov— Tackau (Deuben)
Tersnik— Thierschneck (Camburg)
Tisin— Theiszen (Zeitz)
Trebac— Trebatsch (Beeskow)
Trebin— Treben (Lutzen)
Trebnic— Trebnitz (Teuchern)
Trebnic— Trebnitz (Krossen)
Trebnic— Trebnitz (Merseburg)
Trebusa— Trebbus (Sonnenwalde)
Trgov— Torgau (Torgau/Elbe)
Trnov—Tornau (Hohenmolsen)
Trupica— Traupitz (Zeitz)

UGLIC, USTA, VRBA

Tuchin— Taucha (Rippach)
Tuchorin— Teuchern (NW Zeitz)
Ubic— Aubitz (Eisenberg)
Uglic— Oglitzsch (Weissenfels)
Ulog— Auligk (Groitzsch)
Upaz— Aupitz (Weissenfels)
Upin— Oppin (Halle)
Uraz— Auras (Cottbus)
Usta— Maust (Cottbus)
Velez— Wahlitz (Hohenmolsen)
Velic— Wahlitz (Hohenmolsen)
Virsin— Werschen (Teuchern)
Vrba— Werben (Weissenfels)
Vrbin— Werben(Werben/Elbe)

VISOKA, ZAGORIC, ZAVAL

Visoka— Weissig (Hoyerswerda)
Vrlic— Worlitz (Dessau)
Vulkov— Wolkau (Bad Durrenberg)
Vusoka— Weissagk(Forst)
Zagoric— Sageritz (Riesa)
Zara— Sohra (Freiberg)
Zarec— Saritz (Calau)
Zaspa— Saspow (Cottbus)
Zaval— Sawall (Beeskow)
Zelezin— Schleesen (Wittenberg)
Zestin— Sohesten (Lutzen)
Zucane— Sautzschen (Zeitz)

BISTRICA, BUKOVICA

The following series is representatives of the greater changes in sound and spelling characteristic of longer and complex Slavic-German names.

BISTRICA, BUKOVICA, GOLUBIN

Bistrica— Beutersitz (Liebenwalda)
Bukovica— Bockwitz (Zeitz)
Cirnovic— Schirnewitz (Jena)
Dobryn— Dabern (Finsterwalde)
Dobrobuz— Doberburg (Beeskow)
Dobrodanovic— Dobernitz (Riesa)
Dubrava— Dubrau (Forst)

Dulovici—Deulowitz (Gueben)
Golubin— Golben (Torgau)
Gusteric— Gaustritz (Dresden)
Kal, Kalov— Calau (Calau)
Kokanic— Kockenitzsch (Schkolen)
Kolovoz— Kohlwesa (Weissenberg)
Krusovica—Krauschitz (Eslterwerda)

MEZIREKA, MEZIVODA, OSTROVICA

Krynica— Crinitz (Finsterwalde)
Medebor— Magdeborn (Leipizig)
Mezireka— Mehderitzsch (Belgern)
Mezivoda— Medewitz (Bischofswerda)
Nadelovic— Nadelwitz (Bautzen)
Nedelic— Nedlitz (Zerbst)
Nelubin— Nelben (Alsleben)

Nigradov— Niegeroda (Grossenhain)
Ocholic— Ochlitz (Querfurt)
Ocholmic— Ochelmitz (Filenburg)
Ogrozno— Ogrosen (Calau)
Ostrovica—Osteritz (Wittenberg)
Ovcarin— Owtzarin (Lutzen)
Rakovica—Rackwitz (Delitzsch)

SEKIR, STUDENICA, VIROVICA

Rogovic— Ragewitz (Grimma)
Scenovic— Steinwitz (Altenburg)
Sekir— Zeckerin (Finsterwalde)
Skorolub— Schkortleben (Weissenfels)
Skorotic— Schkortitz (Grimma)
Starsedlo— Starsiedel (Merseburg)
Studenica— Staudnitz (Grimm)
Studenica— Steudnitz (Jena)
Techobudici— Techwitz (Zeitz)
Travorad— Tragarth (Merseburg)
Vecerad— Witzscherdorf (Markranstadt)

Vetrosibe— Wetterzeube (Zeitz)
Virovica— Wurchwitz (Zeitz)
Visebor— Weiszeborn (Zeitz)
Viselub— Wuschlaub (Lutzen)
Visepic— Wispitz (Wispitz/ Saale)
Visemir— Weszmar (Schkeuditz)
Vran— Ranzig (Beeskow)
Vrbinici— Wormlitz (Mockern)
Zitovic— Seidewitz (Schkolen)
Zrnovic— Sornewitz (Meissen)

BELA

The preceding series only scratches the surface of Slavic-German names in central and eastern Germany. Some idea of its true scope and density is found in the many past and present place names in *White Serbia* derived from Slavic words for basic colors, for example, from **bel** or white.

BELA, BELA GORA, BELANOVICI

Bela (Behlau, Wurzen)
Bela (Biehla, Elsterwerd)
Bela (Bohla, Grossenhain)
Bela (Bohla, Prettin)
Bela (Bohla, Riesa)
Bela (Bohla, Seerhausen)
Bela (Gross Bohla, Oschatz)
Bela (Nasse-Bohla, Grossenhain)
Bela (Pohl, Plauen)
Bela (Pohla, Altenberg)
Bela (Pohla, Schwarzenberg)
Bela (Pohlau, Zwickau)

Bela (Wein-Bohla, Meissen)
Bela (Buhlau, Dresden)
Bela (Buhlau, Stolpen)
Bela Gora (Alt-Belgern, Muhlberg)
Bela Gora (Belgern, Bautzen)
Bela Gora (Belgern, Torgau)
Belanovici (Pillnitz, Dresden)
Belavici (Belwicz, Lobau)
Belica (Belitz, Bernburg)
Belica (Bohlitz, Ehrenberg)

BELICA, BELOSIN, BELOVIC

Belica (Bohlitz, Mutzschen)
Belica (Bohlitz, Grimm)
Belica (Bohlitz, Wurzen)
Belica (Bohlitz, Osterfeld)
Belica (Bohlitz, Leipzig)
Belica (Belitz, Peisen)
Belin (Byhlen, Lubben)
Belina (Alt-Biehlen, Calau)
Belina (Biehlen, Ruhland)
Belina (Bohlen, Grimm)
Belina (Bohlen, Ilmenau)
Belina (Bohlen, Leipzig)
Belina (Bohlen, Leisnig)
Belisovic (Belsechwicz, 1365, later Ebendorfer, near Bautzen)

Belkov (Bielecke, Eilenberg)
Belosici (Biewoschitz, Hoyerswerda)
Belosin (Bohlscheiben, Rudolstadt)
Belotici (Piltitz, Halle)
Belotin (Belten, Calau)
Belov (Behlow, Lubben)
Belov (Pelsen, Oschatz)
Belov (Pulbitz, Zwickau)
Belovic (Polbitz, Zwickau)
Belovic (Bellwitz, Lobau)
Belsin (Gross Pelsen, Oschatz)
Belsko (Polzig, Gera)

SCHIRN, TSCHERN, ZSCHERN

An equal or greater number of past and present toponyms, hydronyms, and place names are perhaps derived from the Slavic word for black (**crn**)— e.g. Schirnewitz; Schirnwicz; Schyrne; Scurnice; Tschernitz; Tschernsdorf; Tschirne; Tschirtenbach; Tschornau; Tzschernitz; Tschernowitz; Tschirna; Zerna; Zernikal; Zscharnitz; Zscherben; Zscherne; Zscherneddel; Zschernitz; Zschernitzsch; Zaschernitzschen; Zscherntnitz; Zschirnitz; Zschorgula; Zschorn; Zschorna; Zaschornau; Zschorne; Zschorneck; Zschornegosda; Zschornewitz.

8. COMMON SLAVIC ENDINGS

German villages, towns, cities, toponyms, and hydronyms with certain endings tend to be derived from Slavic place names. The following series of place names is representative of Slavic-German names in *White Serbia* beginning with the letter **B** and ending in -**ITZ**.

BORENOVICI, BOBICI, BOJETICI

Baditz— **Bodatic**

Balditz— **Palotic**

Bannewitz— **Panovici**

Barmentiz— **Bormic**

Barnitz— **Borenovici**

Basankwitz— **Bozankovici**

Baseritz— **Bozerovici**

Bebitz— **Bobici**

Beckwitz— **Bekovici**

Bederwitz— **Bedrovici**

Bennewitz— **Penovici**

Berwitz— **Berovici**

Beuchlitz— **Pycholici**

Beuditz— **Bojetici**

BYSTRICA, BLAZEVICI, BUKOVICA

Beulwitz— **Bylovica**

Beutersitz— **Bystrica**

Beutnitz— **Bytonici**

Birmenitz— **Birmica**

Blasewitz— **Blazevici**

Blochwitz— **Blogovici**

Boblitz— **Bobolica**

Bobritz— **Bobrovica**

Bockelwitz— **Bukolovici**

Bockwitz— **Bukovica**

Bodelwitz— **Podolovici**

Boderitz— **Podbreze**

Bodnitz— **Bodanici**

Bolbritz— **Boleborici**

BOJANICI, BORICI, BOZOVICI

Bolitz— **Bolici**

Bolschwitz— **Bolesovici**

Bonitz— **Bojanici**

Boritz— **Borici**

Bornitz— **Boranovici**

Bortewitz— **Boretovica**

Bosenitz— **Bozenich**

Bosewitz— **Bozovici**

Braschwitz— **Brasovici**

Brenitz— **Brenica**

Bresewitz— **Brezovica**

Breternitz— **Bratronici**

Briesnitz— **Breznica**

Brochwitz— **Brochotici**

Brodewitz— **Brodovica**

Burgwitz— **Borkovici**

Buschewitz— **Byserici**

TREBULA TO TREBEN

In order to appreciate the great density of place names ending in -**itz**, the following place names are recorded in a narrow and short corridor running from *Trebula,* north of Altenberg, to *Treben,* south of Altenberg.

CROLOWITZ, NENEWITZ

Crolowitz

Kaimnitz

Kothenitz

Kraschwitz

Kursuwiz

Lehnitsch

Lopitz

Molbitz

Nenewitz

Nobitz

Paditz	Pahnitz

ZSCHCASELWITZ, ZSCHERNITZSCH

Poschwitz	Tauschwitz
Rothenwitz	Wilchwitz
Schlauditz	Zschcaselwitz
Schelchwitz	Zschernitzsch
Schlopitz	Zschewitz
Steinwitz	Zschopperitz

BOCKA, ZWESC

In the same *Trebula-Treben* area one also finds many **non-itz** place names which also appear to be derived from Slavic roots:

CHOZBUDE, GROBA, ZEHMA

Bocka	Mecka
Bohra	Mizow
Buchow	Rodnetow
Chozbude	Skura
Dogscow	Wolowe
Drogen	Zehma
Gieba	Zebecur
Gohren	Zschaiga
Groba	Zwesc

-CH, -CHEN, -CHKA ENDINGS

The following series is representative of Slavic-German place names beginning with the letter **L** and ending in **-ch, -chen,** and **-chka.**

LOMICA, LUBUS, LESIN

Lamitsch— **Lomnica**	Lietzsch— **Lysici**
Laubusch— **Lubus**	Lippitsch— **Lipic**
Laucha— **Luchov**	Litschen— **Zlycin**
Lauschka— **Luskov**	Lobitzsch— **Lubisic**
Lautzschen— **Lucane**	Loitsch— **Lucic**
Lehnitzsch— **Vlenc**	Loschen— **Lezina**
Leibsch— **Lubus**	Lotschen— **Lucane**
Leischen—**Lesin**	Lubbinchen— **Lubinik**
Leschen— **Lesin**	Lutzschena— **Lucane**
Leutzsch— **Luce**	

SCH-, TSCH-, ZSCH-

The following series of Slavic-German place names in *White Serbia* is representative of place names with **sch-, tsch-,** and **-zsch** prefixes or suffixes.

SLIVNICA, SLATINA, CEPELICI

Schleinitz—**Slivnica**	Schleuskau— **Sluskov**

Schlottweh— **Slatina**
Schortau— **Cortov**
Schwoditz— **Svotici**
Tschernitz— **Crnic**

Tschernsdorf— **Crnov**
Tschirna— **Crna**
Zscarnitz— **Crnici**
Zscheplitzi— **Cepelici**

CRNA, CRNOGLAV, CRNOVIC

Zscerhnik— **Crnik**
Zschernitzschen— **Crnicin**
Zschernsdorf— **Crnov's Dorf**
Zschernske— **Crnsk**
Zschirna— **Crna**

Zschochergen— **Cachor**
Zschorgula— **Crnoglav**
Zschornau— **Crnov**
Zschornegosda— **Crna Gvozd**
Zschornewitz— **Crnovic**

-IG ENDINGS

USTIK, DUB, GLINICA

Aussig— **Ustik**
Barzig— **Bartsk**
Bosewig— **Bezovik**
Coswig— **Kosovik**
Diebzig— **Dub**
Dolzig— **Dolsk**
Droyzig— **Draskovich**
Elsnig— **Olesnik**
Gamig— **Kamen**

Glinzig— **Glinica**
Gorzig— **Gorsk**
Grabig— **Grabik**
Graupzig— **Grubica**
Greussnig— **Grusnik**
Grosswig— **Grozovik**
Gurig— **Gorica**
Kleipzig— **Klepica**
Klessig— **Klesovik**

KOSOVIK, LISNIK, SRBICI

Kosswig— **Kosovik**
Kreupzig— **Krupica**
Leisnig— **Lisnik**
Lossnig— **Lesnik**
Losswig— **Losovik**
Lonzig— **Lomsko**
Lunzig— **Lunsk**
Mockzig— **Mokrosuky**
Oelsnig— **Olesnik**

Ossig— **Olesnik**
Ossnig— **Osnik**
Pozig— **Pesk**
Sornzig— **Zrnovici**
Stobnig— **Stobnik**
Wednig— **Vednik**
Wessnig— **Veznik**
Zorbig— **Srbici**

-GK, -IGK, -IK ENDINGS

ULOG, DREZGA, GLUSINA

Augligk— **Ulog**
Bugk— **Buk**
Burgk— **Bork**
Drossigk— **Drezga**
Elsnigk— **Olesnik**
Glausigk— **Glusina**

Jessnigk— **Jesenik**
Josigk— **Gozd**
Krausnik— **Krusnik**
Krosigk— **Krsik**
Thierschneck— **Tersnik**

-K, -KA, -KE, -KO ENDINGS

BUKOV, BOR, DRASKO

Bocka— **Bukov**
Barneck— **Parnik**
Brieschko— **Brezko**
Bucko— **Bukov**
Burk— **Bor**
Dobbrick— **Dobrik**

Dobschke— **Debiskov**
Doschko— **Daskov**
Draschke— **Drasko**
Dreska— **Drezga**
Dubraucke— **Dubravka**
Gohrick— **Gorka**

GVOZD, GRANICA, JAVORNIK

Goseck— **Gvozd**
Granick— **Granica**
Jauernick— **Javornik**
Jehserik— **Jezersk**
Jerischek— **Jarezk**
Krausnick— **Krusnik**

Lausick— **Luzk**
Mucka— **Mikov**
Nieska— **Neskov**
Possneck— **Pesnik**
Zemnick— **Cemnik**

-OW ENDINGS

BELOV, BUKOV, GLAVA

Babow— **Bobov**
Bathow— **Batov**
Beeskow— **Bezkov**
Behlow— **Belov**
Bronkow— **Bronkov**

Buckow— **Bukov**
Gaglow— **Gogolov**
Glowe— **Glava**
Golschow— **Goles**
Grabow— **Grabov**

GORA, MOKROV, OSTROV

Guhrow— **Gora**
Kablow— **Kobylov**
Kackrow— **Kokor**
Laasow— **Lazov**
Leeskow— **Leskov**

Muckrow— **Mokrov**
Ostrow— **Ostrov**
Pinnow— **Penov**
Pieskow— **Peskov**
Plattkow— **Blotkov**

-AU ENDINGS

BOROV, DRENOV, DRASKOV

Bohrau— **Borov**
Brokau— **Brekov**
Buckau— **Bukov**
Doberstau— **Dobrostrov**
Dobrichau— **Dobrichov**

Drobischau— **Trebisov**
Drehnau— **Drenov**
Drochaus— **Drogov**
Drosskau— **Draskov**
Druschkau— **Treskov**

DUBRAV, RASOV, SRBOV

Dubrau— **Dubrav**
Gesau— **Jezov**
Glassau— **Glazov**

Krieschau— **Krikov**
Leckau— **Lekov**
Letzkau— **Leskov**

Ostrau— **Ostrov**
Raschau— **Rasov**

Tornau— **Trnov**
Zorbau— **Srbov**

-IN, -LN, -UN ENDINGS

BODRIN, BELOSIN, DOBRUN
Badrin— **Bodrin**
Battin— **Batun**
Beedeln— **Bedlin**
Beltin— **Belosin**
Bleddin— **Bledin**
Blossin— **Blosin**

Borgishain— **Borkjane**
Borln— **Borlin**
Dabrun— **Dobrun**
Dobeln— **Doblin**
Gallin— **Golina**
Gallun— **Goliya**

-EN ENDINGS

BABIN, BUZANE, PODBREZE
Babben— **Babin**
Bassen— **Buzane**
Badersen— **Podbreze**
Bahren— **Boren**
Berlinchen— **Brlicin**

Betten— **Butin**
Bobbersen— **Pobreze**
Borten— **Boretin**
Brasen— **Breza**
Breesen— **Brezina**

BREG, DOLANE, DLUGY
Brehmen— **Breme**
Briesen— **Breg**
Brossen— **Brosin**
Butzen— **Budsin**
Dahlen— **Dolane**

Deuben— **Dubin**
Doben— **Dobna**
Dohlen— **Dolina**
Dollingen— **Dlugy**
Dosen— **Dosin**

-ENA, -ENZ, -ERN ENDINGS

DOLANE, DOBRANICI, GOLICA
Bagenz— **Bagenc**
Dabern— **Dobran**
Dalena— **Dolane**
Dobbern— **Dobrina**
Doberenz— **Dobranici**
Durchena— **Strahovane**

Gablenz— **Jablan**
Gasern— **Kozarin**
Gauern— **Javorno**
Golenz— **Golica**
Gommern— **Komoran**
Gorenz— **Gorensk**

-A, -O, -S ENDINGS

BARA, BOROV, PORAD
Ablass— **Oploz**
Auras— **Uraz**
Bahra— **Bara**
Bahro— **Barov**
Beucha— **Pychov**

Bias— **Vjez**
Blosa— **Blezov**
Boblas— **Bobolusky**
Bocka— **Bukov**
Bockedra— **Bukodrov**

Bohra— **Borov**	Borda— **Porad**

BREZA, DOBRA, DUBRAV

Borlas— **Brloz**	Dohna— **Donin**
Brohna— **Brana**	Dorna— **Trnov**
Brosa— **Breza**	Drasdo— **Drazan**
Buro— **Burov**	Drehsa— **Droza**
Diehsa— **Deza**	Drogis— **Dragis**
Dobra— **Dobra**	Drosa— **Drag**
Dohma— **Domin**	Dubro— **Dubrav**

HYDRONYMS

The following series is representative of a great number of hydronyms ending in **-itz** and a greater number of other endings that appear to be derived from Slavic roots.

BISTRITZ, DOLLNITZ, KEMNITZ

Aupitz	Jasnitz
Bistritz	Kemnitz
Boritz	Kirnitzsch
Colmnitz	Locknitz
Dollnitz	Muglitz
Dommitz	Murscnitz
Geygeritz	Nieplitz
Gimmlitz	Pegnitz
Itz	Pesterwitz
Jaglitz	Prebnitz

ROGNITZ, WOBLITZ, WUDRITZ

Pressnitz	Weiseritz
Pulsnitz	Weisseritz
Recknitz	Wesenitz
Rednitz	Wilsch
Regnitz	Woblitz
Rognitz	Wollnitz
Sebnitz	Wornitz
Sornewitz	Wudritz
Stepnitz	Wurschnitz
Triebisch	Wyritz
Wakenitz	

PART XII

1. NOT OF THE FRANKS, BUT SLAVIA

The borders of *Slavia* did not end at the western borders of the former German Democratic Republic. The *racial* borders of *Slavorum populi* ran west of the Elbe and deep into the territory of the former Federal Republic of Germany.

SLAVIA

With regard to the borders of *Slavorum populi* in the West, in the early 1800s, German historian D. Popp advanced the idea of early Slav settlement in the Upper Palatinate. Decades later, C. Robert, an eminent French scholar, will extend the borders farther north and west: **Even in the time of Charles the Great, all that was on the other side of the Rhine, was not of the Franks, but Slavia.**

BALTIC SEA

No area on the other side of the Rhine was more thoroughly Slavic than the Baltic coast and interior. Some scholars find evidence of early Slavic settlement in Roman sources. In *Chorographia III* (c. 45 AD), Pomponius Mela refers to *Indi* seamen from the *Indic* ocean cited in an incident noted by an earlier Roman official: **Cornelius Nepos reports the testimony of Q. Metellus Celer ... that when he was proconsul in Gaul, the king of the Boti presented him with several Indi [seamen] ... when he inquired whence they had arrived in his land, he was told they had sailed from the Indicus Ocean ... that a violent storm had thrown them out on the shores of Germania.**

OVENEDIKOS KOLPOS/SINUS VENEDICUS

If one assumes thats the *Indi* and *Indicus* should be read as *Vindi* and *Vindicus*, that the *Indicus* Ocean is the Baltic Sea (Ptolemy's *Ovenedikos kolpos*, Mela's *Sinus Venedicus*), then the *Indi* are actually *Vindi* from the Baltic Sea, that is, Baltic Slavs.

SETTLED BY SERB-WENDS

In the past, German historians have not hesitated to stress the deep Slavic foundations of lands on the Baltic Sea. In a 16th century study of German lands, German historian W. Pirckheimer writes: **The entire Baltic coast, to the Vistula, with the interior, was settled by Serb-Wends** *(Germaniae Tam Superioris Quam Inferioris, Description Norimbegae).*

CIVITATES NOVAE A SORABI SCLAVIA

Rostock, Lubeck, Stargard, and other cities on and near the coast, Pirckheimer writes, were established by the ancient Serbs: **Rostock was a Serb-Slav city, *civitates novae a Sorabi Sclavia,* as were the other cities on the Baltic from Rostock to the Vistula.**

WENDISCH STAEDTE

A century later, in a study of Helmold *(Observationes ad Helmoldi Chronicon Slavorum),* and other such sources, German historian J. Micraeli writes: **Early German sources refers** to cities along the Baltic, to Lubeck, Rostock and others, as Wendische Staedte.

SERB-WEND WORDS

Centuries later, in a history of Saxony *(Rerum Germanicarum Historici Clariss Saxonia)*, A. Krantz writes: **Oldenburg or Stargard is actually Stari Grad from the Serb-Wend words for old/stari and city/grad** *(H. Sauer, Hansestadte und Landesfurten: Die Wendisch Hansestadte in der Auseinandersetzung mit den Furtsenhausen Oldenburg und Mecklenburg wahren der zweiten halftes des 15. Jahrhunderts, 1971. I. Gabriel, Burg, Siedlung und Graberfeld im fruhmittelalterlichen "Starigrad (Oldenburg in Holstein), AkO 5, 1975; Strukturwandelk in Starigard/Oldenburg warhendder zweiten Halfte des 10l Jahrhunderts auf Grund archaologischer Befunde, ZtA 18, 1984. W. Prummel, Starigard/Oldenburg. Hauptburg der Slawen in Wagrien, IV, 1993).*

FROM THE SERB WENDS

Occasional 'patriotic' attempts to Germanize the Baltic were often ridiculed by German scholars. Thus the words of German historian S. Shurzfleisch: **Some believe that Rostock is the same as Rosenstock, but that is complete nonsense, because Rostock is a Wendic word. Nor is Wittenberg the same as Weissenberg ... These are Wendic words from the Serb-Wends who settled there after expelling the Saxons** *(Germaniae Principes, Sive Discursis Historico-Politicus De Germaniae Principum Nonulorum Originibus).*

A WENDIC WORD

In fact, *Rostock* is a *Wendic* word: from the Slavic word for a place where waterways are divided *(roztok)*. In addition to a *Grad Rostock* on the Baltic (*Urbs Rostock*, 1160; *Urbs Roztoc*, 1171; *Castrum Rostock*, 1182), numerous Slavic settlements called *Roztok* are recorded throughout medieval Germania, including, among others: Rostok, 1381 (Rodstock, Sorau); Rodstok, 1326 (Rostack, Dresden); Rostok, 1306 (Rossdach, Bamberg); Rodstok, 1326 (Rostig, Grossenhain); Roztok (Rottstock, Belzig).

GREAT SLAV CITIES OF THE NORTH

It is important to remember that the great Slav cities of the north were important and leading centers of industry, commerce, trade, and in many ways ahead of their time. We know from diverse sources, for example, that ancient *Wolin* was at one time, in Helmold's words: **Truly the largest of all cities in Europe, that the natives surpass all other northern peoples in the practice of agriculture and the manufacture ... of useful objects** *(T. Lehr-Splawinski, O nazwie promoskiego grodu Wolin-Julin ny wysiciu Odry, Rocznik Gdanski 7-8, 1935. O. Kunkel, K.A. Wilde, Jumne, "Wineta", Jomsburg, Wollin, 1941. R. Kiersnowski, Kamien i Wolin, ZaC 1, 1945; Plemiona Pomorz Zachodniego w swietle naj starsych zrodel pisanych, SlA 3, 1951-52).*

NORTHERN RIVERS

We also know that a number of important cities were located along northern rivers. Excavations, for example, have confirmed the existence of an important manufacturing and trading center of the *Wilti* on the Peene river near Menzlin *(U. Schorknecht, Wikingische Graber bei Menzlin, Kr. Anklam, AuF 13, 1968. Menzlin. Ein frugeschichtlicher Handelsplatz an der Peene, 1977; Handelsbeziehungen der fruhmittelalterlichen Siedlung Menzlin bein Anklam, ZtA 12, 1978).*

CIVITAS MAGNA SCLAVORUM

Adam of Bremen calls Aldinburg *civitas magna Sclavorum*. Regarding the great scope of *civitas magna Sclavorum's* commercial activities, Adam writes: ***Per mare navim*** *ingrederis as Sliaswig vel Aldinburg, ut pervenias ad Iumne [Wolin]. Ab ispa urbe vela tendens XIIIIcimmo die ascendes ad Ostrogard [Novgorod]; cuius metropolis civitas est Chive [Kiev], aemula sceptri Constantinopolitani.*

SLAVICA LINGUA STARIGARD

In the same century, decades later, Helmold cites *civitas magna Sclavorum's* importance in the following terms: *Est autem Aldenburg, ea quae Slavica lingua Starigard ... Haec autem vivitas sive provincia fortissimis quondam incolebatur viris, eo quod in fronte tocius Slaviaeposit contiguos haberet Danorum sive Saxonum populos.*

CIVITATEM SCLAVORUM, QUAE DICITUR LIUBICEN

Recent excavations confirm historical sources that characterize *Lubeck* as one of the great Slavic cities of the north. Regarding *Old Lubeck,* the German archaeologist G.P. Fehring writes: **A tripartite topographical and functional division can be recognized as this place, so excellently sited geopolitically and for travel and communication: 1. The princely seat is a fortified enclosure; a military centre offering protection to the exercise of lordship, administration and the practice of the Christian cult. 2. Settlement of relatively well-to-do artisans in the suburbs. 3. Anchorage for the transhipment of goods and, on either side of the Trave, a settlement with its own church for long-distance merchants, who were probably organized in a guild** *(G.P. Fehring, Alt Lubeck und Lubeck, LsK, 7, 1983; Besiedlungsstrukturen des Lubecker Beckens und ihre Voraussetzungen in slawischer Zeit, ZtA 18, 1984. Der slawische Burgwall Alt-Lubeck, LsK, 1988; Archaeological Evidence from Lubeck for Changing material Culture and Socio-economic Conditions from the 13th to the 16th Century, Medieval Archaeology 33, 1989. Die Entstehung von Lubeck, ZtA, 25, 1991).*

AMONG THE LEADING CITIES OF ITS TIME

In an essay on the *Origins and Development of Slavic and German Lubeck*, Fehring writes: **Old Lubeck is righly reckoned among the leading cities of its time, for here was to be found a city divided up into three in accordance with its topographical and functional features: first, a princely residence in a fortified stronghold that constituted a political, military, and cultural centre; second, a 'suburbium', with a craftsmen's settlement; and, third, a port with a merchant's settlement. The position of the merchant's quarter, to one side of the town and over the river, clearly reflects the special constitutional position of the merchants, who were organized in their companies, as opposed to the fortified residence, where the population was directly dependent on the ruler** *(From the Baltic to the Black Sea, 1990).*

EXPANSION

In the 11th and 12th centuries successive Slavic princes extended and strengthened the city's fortifications: **A large-scale expansion of the early Slavic fortifications with massive timber works took place as early as c. 1058, during the reign of the Obotrite prince Gottschalk (1043-1066) ... After an interlude when the stronghold was ruled by the Wagrian Cruto (1066-1093), there followed another extension of Old Lubeck by Gottschalk's son, King Henry (1093-1127), as the prince's permanent residence and home for his family. King Henry had extended the fortifications yet again by c. 1087 and erected a stone church in the middle of the castle. It** served, among other things, as a court chapel and royal burial place. This is borne out by the fact that the bodies were buried with gold bowrings and fingerrings of both Slavic and West European origin and also by a recently discovered gem of the Alsen type.

GERMAN LUBECK

For Lubeck, Fehring writes, **former ideas about the founding of a prototype for the modern western 12th century town on the basis of a deliberate act of planning need to be revised. After the long-distance trade functions and the name had been shifted from the Old City on the city hill, Bucu, German Lubeck in the second half of the 12th century represents the extension of a Slavic settlement complex ... which had been in existence for hundreds of years. The first founding of a German city in 1143 is, therefore, not a new beginning. It is far more likely, as was the case for other German foundations in what had previously been areas of Slavic occupation, that a late Slavic settlement complex was expanded and reworked by German city founders to develop into a market settlement belonging to an early stage of urban development.**

GREAT OBOTRITE STATE

Fehring sums up the rise and fall of *Old Lubeck, **locus capitalis slavie***, in the following terms: **It has been established that the late Slavic Old Lubeck under King Henry was the fortified settlement and royal residence of the great Obotrite state ... Old Lubeck had Gottschalk and Henry to thank for its expansion; they wanted to create a Slavic state within the framework of a Christian and eastern culture. Their ultimate failure was due to disputes between the various groups of Slavs, and in 1138 Race, a relative of Cruto, destroyed Old Lubeck.**

11TH CENTURY: DUKE KRUTO

From 1066 until his death in 1093 pagan ***Duke Kruto*** was the absolute lord of North Germania. Regarding this dark, anti-Christian period, when ***Kruto ... obtinuitque dominium in universa terra Slavorum,*** Helmold sums it up in the following words: **And Kruto prevailed and the work prospered in his hands and the strength of the Saxons was worn down and they served Kruto under tribute ... All the territory of the Nordalbingians, which is divided into three peoples, the Holsteiners, Sturmarians and those who lived in Ditmarsch—these bore the heavy yoke of servitude during the whole life of Kruto, and the land was filled with robbers, who visited rapine and death upon the people of God.**

BUKU

A bitter enemy of the 'renegade' Christian house of ***Gottschalk, Kruto*** had a residence at an older stronghold, *Buku,* situated on a hill above *Lubeck,* expanded and strengthened by the 'lord of the north.' Fehr writes: **Here we find a late Slavic extension of an older circular ditched fortification, which dominated the shipping and long-distance trade routes. Next to the settlement of the stronghold itself there was an extended *suburbium*. To the south of the city hill, around the cathedral, numerous finds point to a settlement dating from the Middle to late Slavic period ... In addition numerous pieces of building timber, reused mainly in the**

13th century, were found in various parts of the town, in particular those near the Trave river. Dendrochronology establishes that they had been used for building, some precisely in the year 1095 and others in the period (c. 1097) up to or shortly after 1109. They point to a wide-scale extension of the settlement on the city hill during the reign of King Henry. It should be noted that the Lubeck city hill, Bucu, in the 11th and more particularly in the 12th centuries, was far from being an an unsettled wooded area. It was, on the contrary, likely to have been a cultivated landscape, characterized by a fortified stronghold on the north, by areas of settlement on the cathedral hill to the south, and by a well-sited harbour area to the west, on an important long-distance trade route and with land given over to **arable farming** *(G.P. Fehring, Der slawische Burgwall Buku im Bereich des ehemaligen Burgklosters zu Lubeck, LsK 17, 1988).*

NORTH GERMAN LEGEND

According to a modern study, ***Kruto*** lives on in modern German legend and song: **The memory of Kruto is still preserved in North German legend as a terrible ogre. I have heard German children singing jingles about him in the street** *(Feudal Germany, 1928).*

12TH CENTURY: DUKE NIKLOT

In the second half of the 12th century *Rostock* was the residence of the great Slav lord of the North, ***Duke Niklot,*** whose fleets and horsemen fiercely resisted the 'great Wendish Crusade' of 1147, and who remained a political force to be reckoned with for years to come.

12TH CENTURY: DUKE PRIBISLAV

Lubeck was the residence of ***Niklot's*** cousin, ***Duke Pribislav,*** who, after the 1147 Crusade, worked hard to rebuild the great Slav cities of the north. According to Helmold: **Duke Pribislav ... sate quietly and content with the portion of territory allotted him ... and rebuilt the towns of Mecklenberg, Ilow and Rostock, and collected his people therein.**

GREAT RESPECT

Helmold makes it clear that the native Slav rulers fared rather well in the new order and maintained good relations with both Crown and Church. **The bishops of Oldenburg ... held the rulers of the Slavs in great respect because, through the munificence of the great prince Otto, they had been provided with an abundance of wordly goods from which they could dispense generously and win for themselves the good will of the people** *(F. Lotter, Bemerkungen zur Christianiserung der Abodriten, FsT W. Schlesinger, II, 1974).*

HANSEATIC LEAGUE

On the Trave and Wakenitz rivers, close to the Baltic Sea, *Lubeck,* a free city after 1226, was the center of the Hanseatic League, an association of more than one hundred cities that dominated commercial activity in northern Europe from the 13th to the 15th centuries.

SLAVIC LAWS OF LUBECK

Not surprisingly, the League was governed by time-honored rules established by the *Slavic Laws of Lubeck*. Throughout this period **the richest and oldest families in Hanseatic cities proudly proclaimed their Wendisch origin.** In fact, pride in Slavic rather than German ancestry was strong throughout the upper classes. In the 20th century, for example, the ruling family of Mecklenburg proudly traced its roots to Slavic rulers of *Slavonia* (*H. Sauer, Hansestadte und Landesfurtsens: Die wendischen Hansestadte Ausenandersetzung mit den Furstenhausen Oldenburg und Mecklenburg in der zweiten halftes des 15 jahrhunderts, 1971*).

WENDENTALER

One of the larger coins of the Hanseatic realm in the 16th century was the *Wendentaler*. Inscribed ***MONET-CIVITAT-WANDAL***, the *Wendentaler* was popular throughout the northland, in Luneburg, Hamburg, Wismar, Lubeck, Rostock, Stralsund.

13TH, 14TH, 15TH CENTURIES

Pirate fleets recruited from the Baltic Slavs played an important and decisive role in the defense of the Hanseatic League throughout the 13th, 14th, and 15th centuries.

ROZTOK, VISEMIR, V'MORE

In 1389, for example, after a German army suffered a crushing defeat at the hands of allied Danish and Swedish forces on land, the Hanseatic League turned to more reliable forces, to pirates from Roztok/Rostock and Visemir/Wismar (***Aqua, quae Wissemara dicitur***, 1167; ***portus, qui dicitur Wissemer***, 1211; *Wyssemaria*, 1229; ***Wismaria***, 1253; ***antiqua Wissmaria***, 1272); to pirates from ancient centers of Slavic piracy such as the island of ***V'more*** or Fehmarn: ***insulae ... quarum una Vemere vocatur***, 1200; de Vemeren, 1289; *Vhemern*, 1550. (*H. Kunstmann, 'Mecklenburg und Wismar und Fehmarn,' Beitrage zur Geschichte der Besiedlung Nord- und Mitteldeutschland mit Balkanslaven, 1987*).

VITALIANS

Taking full advantage of the situation, the pirates succeeded in establishing an independent maritime sphere of power and interests. Regarding their range of operations, M. Klinge writes, **the pirates organized a kind of sea state called the Vitalians, which briefly held Stockholm and, for a longer period, some of the Finnish coast, including Korsholm, Turku, and Viborg** (*The Baltic World, 1994*)**.**

The situation was much the same in the 15th century. According to Klinge, **pirates continued to hold sway on the Baltic Sea throughout the 15th century, partly because they supported the Hansa and German interests against Sweden and Denmark.**

15TH CENTURY: SLAVONIA

There is certain evidence that the North was known as *Slavonia* as late as the 15th century, that Slavic was the language of the natives. Laskaris Kanasos, a Greek merchant traveling along the Baltic, after stopping at Danzig writes: **I travelled west to Slavonia, and its main city, Lubeck.** As the language of the Slavs of *Slavonia* sounds the same as the language of the Slavs of the Peloponessus, Kanassos believes that **Slavonia is the ancestral home of the Peleponessian Zigiotes since they speak the same language.**

293

ZIGIOTES, JEZERITI

Zigiotes, from *Jezeriti/Jezeriotes*, the name of a large Slavic tribe centered in the rugged heights of the Taegetus range, is a generic Greek name for the Slavs of the Peloponessus. There is good evidence that the local spirit of independence survived relatively intact throughout the Ottoman period.

PALPABLY SCLAVONIAN NAMES

Regarding its ethnic and political character in the mid-19ᵗʰ century, an English traveler writes: **Thanks to their almost impregnable position, these people contrived to maintain themselves in a state of qualified independence of the Mussulmans ... they were sufficiently strong to make terms with the oppressors, and paid a tribute on condition of being left alone. They plume themselves much, we were told, even to this day, on their invincibility ... The palpably Sclavonian names which the villages bear, prove the inhabitants to have as much claim to Hellenic descent as the citizens of Warsaw** *(W.A. Clarke, Peloponnesus: Notes of Study and Travel, 1858).*

GRANITSA, TZERNITSA, VISOKA

It is interesting that in this area one finds a number of villages with names that are common to Serb lands in both *Germania* and *Illyria* (e.g. **Banitza, Granitsa, Lukavitza, Mostitza, Polovitza, Strabova, Strezova, Tzernitsa, Visoka and Zatun**).

LUBIS I A, KAMENITZA

One also finds a good number of toponyms (e.g. **Mts. Elenitza, Khelmos, Klinitza, Lubista, Malevo, Nerovitza, Stremnitza, Varnevo, Zakuka, Zarukla, Zavitza**) and hydronyms (e.g. **Czernota, Kamenitza, Lestenitza, Nimnitza, Zaraka**), common to *Germania* and *Illyria*.

VELIGOSTI

It should also be mentioned that in this general area one also finds the ruins of the once important medieval mini-state of **Veligosti**, an archaic Slavic name also common to *Balkania* (e.g. **Velogoshte**/1491, modern Belogoshte, near medieval **episopatum Belogradensem**/878; **De Belgrado**/1281, modern Berat, and medieval **Novi Grad**/1466, modern Elbasan, central Albania) and *Germania* (**Urbs Woligost**/1123, modern Wolgast, near medieval **Ostrozno**/1166, modern Wusterhusen, and medieval **civitas Uznoim**, modern Usedom, northeast Germany).

2. SCHLESWIG-HOLSTEIN

West of the Elbe, along the Baltic, history and archaeology speak loud and clear of the Slavic settlement in Germania's Schleswig-Holstein, a historic region occupying the southern half of the Jutland Peninsula.

Schleswig, the area north of the Eider river, is bounded by the North Sea in the west, the Baltic Sea in the east, and Denmark in the north. Holstein, the area beween the Eider and Elbe rivers, is bounded by Kiel in the north, Lubeck in the east, Hamburg in the south and the North Sea in the west. Slavic settlements in Schleswig were especially dense along the *Schles River* and the towns and districts of *Cosel, Olrenitz, Warnitz,* and *Wendish Bucholz,* where one finds the survival of a number of Slavic words and sounds in the local dialect. In Holstein, Slav settlements were especially dense in a line that ran from *Borkau, Varnou, Loptin, Stolpe,* and *Belau* in the north to *Mozen, Kukels, Trglau, Grbau, Meritz,* and *Folitz* in the south, to *Grove, Kolov, Gulzov, Cucliz, Krukov,* and *Kruzen* in the east.

NUMEROUS STUDIES

Numerous past and recent studies document the antiquity, character, scope, and density of Slavic settlements in Schleswig-Holstein:

- *Die slawischen Ortsnamen Holstein und im furstentum Lubeck, I-III, 1901-03*
- *Zu den slawischen Ortsnamen in Holstein, 1903*
- *Zur frage nach ausdehnung und verleib der slawischen Bevolerkerung von Holstein und Lauenburg, 1929*
- *Zur deutschlands slawischen Siedlungsgeschichte Mecklenburgs und Ostholsteins im mittelalter, 1933*
- *Das Ostseeslawische Sprachgebiet und seine Ortsnamen, 1947*
- *Zu den slawischen Ortsnamen Holsteins, 1947*
- *The Influence of Slavonic Languages in Schleswig-Holstein, 1949*
- *Die slavischen Ortsnamen Mecklenburgs und Holsteins, 1950*
- *Die wendischen Ortsnamen Ostholsteins, Lubekcs, Lauenbergs und Mecklenburgs, 1950*
- *Die slawischen Ortsnamen Mecklenburgs und Holsteins, 1950*
- *Geschichte Schleswig-Holsteins, 1955*
- *Der slawischen Ortsnamen in Schleswig-Holstein, 1957*
- *Die slawischen Ortsnamen in Holstein, 1957*
- *Die wenden in Ostholstein, 1957*
- *Wendische hugelgraber im ostlichen Holstein, 1957*
- *Die slavischen burgen in Wagrien, 1959-61*
- *Die Ortsnamen in Schleswig-Holstein. Mit einschluss der nordselbische teile von Gross-Hamburg und der Vierland, 1960*
- *Historisches Ortsnamenlexikon von Schleswig-Holstein, 1967*

- *Fruhe slawische burgwallkeramik aus Ostholstein, 1968*
- *Sachsische und slawische burgen in Holstein, 1968*
- *Deutsche und slawen in der Besiedlung Ostholsteins und Lauenburgs, 1971*
- *Burg, Siedlung und Graberfeld im fruhmitteralterlichen "Starigard" (Oldenburg in Holstein), 1975*
- *Die chronologie der slawischen Keramik Ostholsteins nach den Ausgrabungen in Warder, Kr. Segesberg, 1975*
- *Oldenburg-slawischer Ringwall, 1981*
- *Die slawen in Ostholstein. Studien zu Siedlung, Wirtschaft und Gesellschaft der Wagrier, 1983*
- *Zur einwanderung der slaven in Ostholstein und auf den Suddanischen inseln, 1990*
- *Die slawisch-deutschen mischnamen im Ost- und Sudholsteinischen Siedlungsgebiet, 1990*
- *Ortsnamen in Schleswig-Holstein in Starigrad/Oldenburg. Ein slawischer herssersitz des fruhen mittelalters in Ostholstein, 1991*

PLACE NAMES

Medieval German sources record numerous Slavic place names in Schleswig-Holstein. In the following series the original Slavic place name is followed by its later, Germanized version.

SER, SERBIN

Place names indicating **Serb** settlement.

Serbin (Cerben, 1341, *in villis Cerben*, 1351), Zarpen
Sers (*in villa Sursdorpe*, 1303), Sursdorf

SLAVICO BROCHOV

Place names indicating **Slavic** settlement.

Brochov (*de Slavico Brocov*, 1289), Barkau
Botele (*slavica villa Botele*), Fehrenbotel
Cachor (*in Slavico Tsachere*, 1230), Zecher
Groby (*Groue als Slavica villa*, 1526), Grove
Medzirece (*ad rivulum, quem Sclavi Mescenreiza vocant*, 1100), Mascenreiza
Papov (*in Slavico Pampowe*, 1299), Pampau
Parin (*villam suam slavicam Poryn*, 1334)
Pustin (*Pustin Slauvicum*, 1426), Hobsti
Tumin (*Tymendorpe slavicum*, 1426), Timmendorf

BERISLAV, SLAVOMIR

Place names with **Slav** as a prefix or suffix.

Berislav (*villam Berizla*, 1263), Gross Barnitz
Slavisa (*Slawaesthorp*, 1329), Schlagsdorf

Slavomir (*ville Slamersekede*, 1288), Eichede
Slavomir (*Slamerstorp*, 1307), Schlamersdorf
Slavomir (*de Slamerstorp*, 1325), Schlamersdorf
Teslav (*in villam Tezlauesthorp*, 1287), Testorf

WEND, WIND, WINT
Place names with the prefix *Wend.*

IN WENDESCHEN BERKOWE
Brochov (*in Wendeschen Berkowe*, 1328)
Parin (*villa dictam Wendeschen Poryn*, 1334)
Parsov (Wendesche Partzowe, 1426), Rastorferpassau
Wend (Wentorpe, 1460), Wendtorf
Wend (Wentorp, 1528), Wentorf
Wend (Wenttorpen 1423), Wentorf
Wend (Wentorppe, 1493), Wentorf

VILLAM WENDESCHEN NUCHELE
Wend (Hoghewentorp, 1476), Wentorf
Wend (Wendeby, 1554), Windeby
Wenden (Wendembuttel, 1546), Wennbuttel
Wenden (Windemark, 1509), Winnemark
Wendesche (Tralouwe, 1426), Traluerholz
Wendisch-Nuchel (*villam Wendeschen Nuchele*, 1352), Wendisch-Nuchel
Wendischen-Alversdorf (*villam Wendeschen Alversdorf*, 1301)

MIRKOVIC, TRIBIMIR
Place names with *Mir* as prefix or suffix.

Cicimir (*villa que Sycima nuncupatur*, 1253), Cismar
Dumimir (*villam que Dummerstrop dicitur*, 1268), Dummersdorf
Mirkovici (*in Merkevitze*, 1426), Markwitz
Moyslimir (*in villis Moysmerstorpe*, 1382), Meischenstrof
Ratimir (*in Rataemaersthorp*, 1231), Rataemaersthorp
Ratimir (Ratmerstorpe, 1426), Rathjensdorf
Ratimir (*ville Ratmerstorpe*, 1469), Rathmannsdorf
Tagomir (*pro villis Tangmer*, 1377), Tangmer
Tesimir (*villas Tesmerthorpe*, 1231), Tesmersdorf
Tribimir (*villam Tribemersthorp*, 1199), Tribemestorp

GOSTIRAD, LUBORAD
Place names with *Rad* as prefix or suffix.

Gostirad (Gutzrade, 1345), Guster
Luborad (Lybrade, 1300), Lebrade
Rade, Rades (Redesthorp, 1327), Rastorf
Radek (*per provinciam Radekowe*, 1235), Ratekau

Radek (*in villa Radechestorpe*, 1294), Reesdorf
Radomysl (*cum villa Rodemozle*, 1194), Romnitz
Turad (Toradestorp, 1230), Toradesdorf

BORISCE, RATIBOR
Place names with *Bor* as prefix or suffix.

Borisce (*villam Borist*, 1186), Borse
Krsibor (Kerseborch, 1230), Kasseburg
Ratibor (*castellum Razesburg*, 1062), Ratzeburg
Ratibor (*ad stagnum Racesburgense*, 1188), Ratzeburger

LUB, LUBOTIN
Place names with the prefix *Lub.*

Lubas (*in villa que dicitur Lubbasce*, 1263), Lebatz
Lubin (Lybeuen, 1429), Lebeben-See
Lubotin (Lubodne, 1300), 1346
Lubotin (Libetine, 1232), Luptin

PRODAN
Place names with the prefix *Prodan.*

Prodan (Prodanistorp, 1316), Brodau
Prodan (*in Prodenowe*, 1426), Pronau
Prodan (*villam Prodenstorp*, 1423), Projensdorf

PRIBICI, MYSLICI
Place names ending in *IC.*

BOBICI, PRIBICI, MALKOVICI
Bobici (*villam dictam Bobitze*, 1348), Bobs
Goldonici (Guldenize, 1313), Goledenitz
Gnevici (*de Geninghe*, 1504), Gneningen
Kitlici (Kitlist, 1230), Kittlitz
Kuklici (Kukelitze, 1343), Kukels
Pribici (Pryvisse, 1506), Pries
Macevic (*villam Matzevitz*, 1214), Matzwitz
Malkovici (Malkeviz, 1251), Malkwitz

MALKOVICI, SADKOVICI, ZEMICI
Maslovici (Mazleviz, 1230), Matzlewitz
Myslici (*super villis Moscelinge*, 1265), Moisling
Plesovici (Liezcevitz, 1259), Plessewitz
Sadkovici (*in Zadekevitze*, 1426), Satjewitz
Techelovic (Techelwitzendorf,1286), Techelwitz
Vardolici (Wanderlitze, 1501), Wandelwitz
Zemici (*apud Cimezen*, 1307), Siems

BOJAN, DRAGAN, DRAZEVO
Place names derived from uncommon and common personal names.

Bliz (Bliesendorpe, 1302), Bliesdorpf
Bojan (Boyaenthorp, 1329), Bojendorp
Boyko (Boyke, 1426), Boyke
Chocolin (*villam, que Cuculune dicitur*, 1214), Kukeluhn
Chvalik (*in villa Qualizke*, 1375), Quals
Dargan, Dragan (Darganthorp, 1321), Darganthorp
Dirzov (Dersow, 14701), Dersau
Drazevo (Dransov, 1289)
Druzen (Drvsen, 1444), Drusen
Makar (Mankre, 1325), Gross Anker

MALEK, NEMAN, VOLIGOST
Malek (*villam Malkendorp*, 1340), Malkendorf
Malusa (Mallusendorpe, 1304), Malussendorf
Malyta (Malugestorpe, 1289), Malugestorp
Maruta (Maruthendorpe, 1289), Marutendorf
Milety (*in parochia Malente*, 1345), Malente
Miliko (Milekenthorpe, 1434), Mielkendorf
Neman, Nemota (*villarum et Nemete*, 1244), Nehmten
Never (*villas Niversthorpe*, 1460), Neversdorf
Purek (*villam Purekestrope*, 1344), Prusdorf
Sadek (Sattekendorpe, 1426), Stajendorf
Voligost (Walegosta, 1194), Walksfelde

BOZ, CRKVICA, PERUN
Place names with religious roots or connotations.

Boz, Bozov (*in Bozowe*, 1216), Bosau
Crkvica (*in villa Cerkuvitze*, 1356), Sarkwitz
Djavao (*villam Dyauele*, 1323), Jagel
Dusnik (Dusniz, 1252), Disnack
Jarochov (Jarchowe, 1316), 1316
Jarovec (*in villa Ghervitze*, 1400), Gerwitz
Perun (*in Perone*, 1216), Pronstorf
Svar, Svartov (*fluvius Swartow*, 1200), Schwartau

SVAR, SVETINA, VYSEBOGY
Svar, Svartov (*in Swartow*, 1422), Schwartau
Svartopuk (Swartepuk, 1426), Schwartbuck
Svetina (*in ipsum flumen Zuentinam*, 1100), Schwentine
Svetina (Schwentinemunde, 1224), Schwentinemunde
Svetina Pol (*ad campum Zuentifeld*, 1100), Schwentinefeld
Triglav (Trglau)
Vysebogy (*villam dictam Waschebuch*, 1375), Wasbuck

Zarno (Saren, 1251), Sohren
Zarov (Sarowe, 1230), Sarau

DVORNIK, GARDEC, KNEGENA
Place names relating to or indicating strongholds and titles.

Dvornik (Dorneke, 1495), Dornick
Gardec (Gartze, 1462), Gaarz
Gardno (*de villa Ghardin*, 1390), Gaarden
Gardov (*villam Gadoze*, 1373), Gardensee
Knegena (*ad rivulum qui dicitur Knegena*, 1263), Kneeden
Kotel (*que Cotel vocabatur*, 1345), Kothel
Linov (*in castro Lynow*, 1349), Linau

OSTRO, POSADA, STOLPE
Ostro (Ostro, 1561), Ostrohe
Pan (Panstorpe, 1464), Pansdorf
Plon (*in castro Plune*, 1189), Plon
Posada (*villam Potzade*, 1373), Passade
Podgarde (Potgarde, 1231), Puttgarden
Stolpe (*in Ztolpe*, 1316), Stolpe
Stolpe (Stolpe, 1316), Stolpe

BARNICA, DRUZEN, GRMEC
Place names indicating waterways.

Barnica (*in aquas Bernize*), Barnitz
Bisnica (*ad rivum qui dicitur Bizneze*), Bisnitz
Druzen (*stagni Drusene*, 1383), Drusensee
Grinov (*in aquas Grinawe*, 1263), Grinau
Grmec (*cum medietate aque Gremenze*, 1215)
Grobenica (*ad rivum qui Grobenize dicitur*, 1238), Gromitz
Karcnica (*ad fluvium qui Carzniz appelatur*, 1226), Karzeniz
Kosirin (*iuxta fontem Cuserin*, 1200), Cuserin

KRAPINA, PODLUGE, STEKNICA
Krapina (*apud Krempinum fluvium*, 1200), Kremper Au
Lovec (*in aquas Lovenze*, 1300), Lowenitz
Lutesov (*a fluvio Lutesov*, 1139), Lutzbek
Moizin (*plaga rivi Moyzen, cum villis Mozene*, 1137), Mozen
Plon (*iuxta magnum stagnum Plone*, 1288), Ploner See
Podluge (*a rivo Padeluche*, 1247), Padelugge
Skala (*in stagno, quod Scale dicitur*, 1376), Schaalsee
Steknica (*iuxta rivum Stekenitze*, 1377), Steknitz

STRUMEN, TRAVA, VOKENICA
Stregnica (*in aquam Streciniziam*, 1194), Strecknitz
Strumen (*fluvii dicti Stremmine*, 1353), Stremmin

Trava (*fluui Travene*, 1188), Trave
Vadrava (*in aqua que Wandrawe nuncupatur*, 1220), Wanderau
Vokenica (*in flumine Wakenize*, 1199), Wakenitz
Volsa (*rivum eciam qui Wilsov dicitur*, 1225), Wilsau

POMORE, POREKA

Place names relating to water, waterways.

Bela Loky (Bolunke, 1249), Blunk
Penice (*villa Penze*, 1308), Ponitz
Pesak (Pezeke, 1230), Pezeke
Pomore (*in villa Pomerbul*, 1450), Pommerby
Poreka (Poretze, 1222), Preetz
Prevloke (*insulam que Priwole nominatur*, 1343), Priwall
Reka (Reke, 1570), Reecke
Uklei (Vkele, 1429), Uklei See

BROD, MOST

Place names relating to water-crossings.

Brod (Brodesende, 1400), Brodesende
Brod, Brodno (Brotne, 1315), Brodten
Brod (Brotne, 1525), Brothen
Brod (*vocatur Brode*, 1397), Grossenbrode
Most, Mostina (*in parrochia Mustian*, 1194), Mustin

BEL, CRN

Place names with the prefix **Bel** (white) or **Crn** (black).

Bel (Bele, 1278), Behl
Bel, Belin (Belendorpe, 1224), Behlendorf
Bel, Belin (Bellin 1426), Bellin
Bel, Belota (Boltyn, 1426), Beutinerhof
Bel, Belov (Belowe, 1433), Belau
Bel, Belov (Belowe, 1194), Balau
Crn, Carn (*de Zyarnestorp*, 1329), Sahrensdorf
Crn, Carnkov (Scarnekowe, 1194), Sarnekow

GOL, GOLICA

Place names with the prefix **Gol.**

Gol, Gola (Gol, 1231), Gold
Gol, Gola (*in Ghole*, 1426), Goh
Gol, Goles (Goleskendorp, 1356), Gleschendorf
Gol, Golovici (Golewiz, 1350), Gols
Golcev (*de Gultzowe*, 1343), Gulzow
Golica (*villam Gulze* 1262) Gulze

GOR, ZAGOR

Place names with the prefix *Gor, Zagor.*

Gor, Gorica (*Novum et antiquum Gyritz*, 1249), Gors
Gor, Gornica (*in Gorense*, 1340), Gornitz
Gor, Gorska (*in villa Gorceke*, 1310), Gortz
Zagor, Zagorane (Zageran, 1194), Segrahn

PODLUZE, PRIDOLE

Place names with the prefixes *Pod, Pri* and *Za.*

Podluge (*in villa Padeluche*, 1322), Plugge
Podluze (Putluse, 1426), Pettluis
Podluze (*in Putlose*, 1555), Putlos
Pridole (*de Pridole*, 1221), Perdol
Pridole (Pridelo, 1199), Preidelo
Zadel (*in Zadelbandia*, 1191), Sadelbande

BUK, DAB, JAVOR

From Slavic words relating to *flora* and *fauna:*

Buk, Bukov (Bucu, 1200), Bucu
Dab Laz (*ville Damclozc*, 1373), Damlos
Dabky (Dahmke, 1799), Dahmker
Golabici (Golenbitze, 1302), Goldenbeck
Grabov (*villas Grabowe*, 1259), Grabau
Javorno (*de Jaworn*, 1264), Neuwuhren
Kolpin (Colpin, 1262), Kulpin
Kozlov (*de Kozelav*, 1238), Koselau

KOZEL, MEDVEDY, ROGY

Kozel (Koselstrope, 1449), Kahlstorf
Kosov (Cosowe, 1426), Koselau
Lipa (Lippan, 1480), Lephan
Malin (Malinesuelde, 1215), Liensfeld
Medvedy (Medewade, 1640), Meddewade
Pinov (*villam Pinnowe*, 1263), Pinnau
Rogy (*villae Rogae*, 1312), Roge
Trava (*Travena silvam*, 1100), Travena Silva

VIRBA, VULK, ZABNICA

Trut (Trutauen, 1304), Trittau
Varnov (Warnow, 1542), Warnau
Varnov (*que Warnow vocatur*, 1460), Fahren
Virba (*in villis Verwe*, 1340), Farve
Virbica (Farwitz)
Vulk (Wolkenweh, 1448), Wolkenwehe

Volsa (*de villa Wilse*, 1390), Wellsee
Zabnica (*exceptis villia Sabeniz*, 1315), Sahms

SLAVIC PLACE NAMES

From Slavic place names generally, including all the above categories.

BARAC, BAZ, BLIZ

Badov (Bandowe, 1194), Bannau
Barac (Barac, 1300), Barac
Bardin (Bardin, 1426), Bardin
Baz, Bazdov (Basdowe, 1339), Basedow
Berov (*in villa que Berowe nuncupatur*, 1263), Burau
Bliz (Blystorpe, 1400), Bliestorf
Bliz, Blizek (Blisekindorp, 1329), Blieschendorf
Bolkov (Bolckow, 1744), Bolkau

BRALIN, BREZNIK, BYSKY LUGY

Bones (Bonessendorpe, 1426), Nessendorf
Bralin (Braline, 1426), Berlin
Brana (*apud Bramnensem provinciam*, 1200), Bramnes
Brezane (Brisan, 1250), Bresahn
Breznik (Birnzig, 1100), Birnzig
Bychel (Bichele, 1318), Bichel
Bysky Lugy (Boyzekeloughe, 1334), Beusloe
Bysov (Bussowe, 1197), Bussau

CHLEVEC, CHOROV, CHYNIN

Cemer (Cemerstorp, 1230), Cemersdorf
Chlevec (Klevetze, 1460), Kleveez
Chochol (*villam Kukole*, 1287), Kakhol
Chorov (Corrowe, 1307), Curau
Chorose (*in Corosse*, 1426), Kross
Chotov (Guttowe, 1301), Guttau
Chvaly (*de Quale*, 1226), Quaal
Chynin (*in villa Genin*, 1249), Genin

CHYCE, DALUG, DARGANOV

Chyce (*que Kys dicuntur*, 1440), Kietz
Chorlein (*curiam meam Korlyn*, 1139), Korlyn
Dadov (*in villis Dodow*, 1345), Dodau
Dalug (*villam dictam Dalugenrode*, 1383), Dalungenrode
Dalugin (Dalugendorp, 1300), Luhndorf
Danov (*villam dictam Dannowe*, 1375), Dannau
Darce (Dertzendorp, 1365), Dvinn
Darganov (Dargenowe, 1230), Dargenow

DARGUN, DOBER, DOLZNICA

Dargov (Dargowe, 1230), Dargow
Dargun (*in pago Dargune*, 1200), Dargune
Devetica (*villam Deventze*, 1361)
Dirzikin (Derzekendorpe, 1365), Dassendorf
Dober (Doberstorp, 15113), Dobersdorf
Dolgy (*a palude que Dolge dicitur*, 1263), Dolgen
Dolznica (Dulzanica, 1200), Dulzanica
Durmin (*apud locum, qui dicitur Dormin*, 1230), Dermin

GLABOK, GLAZOV, GNESOV

Dysov (Dyzzouwe, 1368), Dissau
Gal, Galin (*Antiquo Galendorpe*, 1365), Altgalendorf
Gal, Galin (Galenthorp, 1329), Gahlendorf
Glabok (Glameke, 1365), Glambek
Glazov (Glasowe, 1514 (Glasau)
Gnesov (Gnessow, 1216), Gnissau
Gnevin (*villam nostram Gneverstorpe*, 1349), Gneversdorf
Godov (*de Godowe*, 1349), Godau

GOMOLE, GRABOV, GREBEN

Godov (*parrochia Godowe*, 1194), Gudow
Gomole (*ville Gumalic*, 1216), Gumale
Gorkov (*in villa Gorcowe*, 1361), Garkau
Govno (*in Gowense*, 1470), Gowens
Graboky (Grambeke, 1230), Grambeck
Grabov (*villa Grabowe*, 1259), Grabau
Greben (Grebyn, 1652), Grebin
Groby (*de Grobe*, 1352), Grube

GUMNO, KADLUB, KAPA

Gronov (Gronowe, 1299), Gronau
Grmec (*molendinum Gremetze*, 1376), Gremsmuhlen
Gumno (Gummese, 1316), Gomnitz
Jelitkin (Gletkendorpe, 1426), Gleschendorf
Kadlub (*de Karlybbe*, 1341), Kalubbe
Kakolov (Kankelow, 1434), Kankelau
Kapa (Dudesche Kampe, 1426), Kamp
Kapica (*in villa Kempiz*, 1267), Kembs

KLECOV, KLENOV, KOLOV

Karp (*in antiqua Karbe*, 1460), Karpe
Karsov (*de Karzowe*, 1321), Kassau
Klecov (Clentzouwe, 1426), Klanzau
Klenov (*in Klennow*, 1462), Klenau
Klepov (*de Clempowe*, 1330), Klempau

Klucin (*in villa Clutzin*, 1271), Klotzin
Kokor (*iuxta Kokore*, 1286), Kokor
Kolov (Coledowe, 1230), Kollow

KOSIOR, KOVALI, KRAPICA

Korniy (Kornig, 1325), Kornick
Kosior (*villam Chuserestorp*, 1229), Kasseedorf
Koslin (Cuzalina, 1200), Cuzalina
Kovali (*villarum et Cowale*, 1323), Kogel
Krapica (*palude Crampesze*, 1226), Crampesze
Krapica (Krempetzel, 1306), Krems
Krapov (Crampowe, 1300), Campowe
Krempina (Crempene, 1222), Altenkrempe

KROMESA, KRUKOW, LACICA

Krokov (Krukowe, 1460), Krokau
Kromesa (Crummesce, 1299), Krummesse
Kromesa (Crummeseem 1429), Krummsee
Krukow (Crukowe, 1319), Krukow
Kurno (*de Kuren*, 1220), Kuhren
Kusek (*villam Kusekestorpe*, 1293), Kustorf
Kusno (Kucen, 1344), Kuhsen
Lacica (Lantsatze, 1525), Lanze

LAKA, LEDZANI, LESKA

Laka (Lanken, 1226), Lanke
Laka (Lancken, 1470), Lanken
Lakov (Lancowe, 1263), Lancow
Lakov (*in villa, que Lankowe dicitur*, 1294), Lankau
Ledzani (Lensane, 1316), Lensahn
Lelekov (*villam nostre Lelekowe*, 1306)
Lepelka (*in villa Lepelkendorpe*, 1500), Lepelkendorf
Leska (*in villam Letzeke*, 1345), Letzeke

LINOV, LOVIN, LUTIKIN

Linov (Linouwe, 1513), Linow
Lojen (Logen, 1400), Loyen
Lojevo (*de Loyowe*, 1324), Loja
Lovin (Lowen, 1401), Altlauerhof
Luchov (Lychowe, 1374), Luchow
Lutikin (*de Lutikinborg*, 1221), Lutjenburg
Lutov (*exceptis villis Lutowe*, 1315), Lutau
Lutov (Lytowe, 1230), Lutau

MASLOV, MORICA, NEZENA

Maslov (*novale, quod Mazelowe dicitur*), Maselow
Mechov (Mechowe, 1230), Mechow

Moras (*villam dictamn Moresse*, 1400), Morest
Morica (*in agris qui dicuntur Westermoritszervele*, 1333), Westermorterfeld
Mucholy (*total villam Bugghele*, 1342), Mucheln
Nezena (*in loco, qui dicituyr Nezenna*, 1200), Nezena
Nuchele (*in parrochia Nugele*, 1346), Kirchnuchel
Nuckov (Nutzicowe, 1343), Nutschau

PLON, POGATE, POLICA

Pachor (Pankuren, 1476), Panker
Parchotin (Parketin, 1299), Berkenthin
Pinov (*villam Pinnowe*, 1263), Pinnau
Plon (*de Luncowe*, 1316 (Plunkau)
Pogate (*due Pogaz*, 1252), Pogeez
Polica (*in villis Politze*, 1352), Pohls
Polica (*in villis Politze*, 1352), Politz
Pomen (Pemen, 1382), Pehmen

RATLOV, ROKYTA, SEDLIN

Prisov (*in Pryzouwe*, 1426), Prisow
Ransov (*de Ranzow*, 1376) Rantzau
Ratlov (*de Ratlowe*, 1426), Rathlau
Rokyta (Raketin, 1312), Rettin
Ronov (Ronnow, 1426), Ronnau
Rycerov (*in molendino Rithserove*, 1377), Ritzerau.
Sedlin (Tzedelin, 1470), Sellin
Sedlin (*pro villis et Cetelin*, 1304), Siblin

SITNO, SMOLY, STRALY

Sitno (*cum villa Cithene*, 1194), Ziethen
Skorobys (*de total villa Scorbuce*, 1271), Scharbeutz
Smilov (*in campum Zmilowe*, 1219), Schmilau
Smoly (Smole, 1571), Schmoel
Stavec (Stovetz, 1426), Stofs
Straly (*in parrochia Stralige*, 1194), Sterley
Strezov (Stresouwe, 1546), Stresow
Svisle (*cum villis Zvizle*, 1216), Schwissel

SVOCHELE, TRESOV, VELEN

Svochele (Swchele, 1335), Schwochel
Sypin (Cypppin, 1426), Cyppin
Telkov (*villam que Telecowe dicitur*, 1241), Talkau
Tesik (Tessikaenthorp, 1231), Teschendorf
Tralov (*de Traloe*, 1221), Tralau
Tresov (Tresstorpe, 1426), Tresdorf
Utin (*in Uthine*, 1200), Eutin
Velen (Wylen, 1329), Wielen

VELIN, VISOK, VODOLE

Velin (*in curia Vellyn*, 1398), Vellin
Verchomily (*in villa Verchemile*, 1258) Fargemiel
Verchov (Verchowe, 1309), Farchau
Verchov (Verchouwe, 1426), Fargau
Visok (Wizoc, 1230), Wizok
Vitcin (Vistin, 1313), Fitzen
Vodole (Wudole, 1465), Widole
Vosec (Totzeze, 1399), Witzee

VYSOV, ZALIM, ZIRAVA

Vosek (*in villa nostra Voceke*, 1302), Wessek
Vysov (Viszowe, 1244), Fissau
Zachov (Saghow, 1479), Sagau
Zalim (Salem, 1221), Salem
Zelety (*in parrochia Zelente*, 1342), Selent
Zelichov (Sellekowe, 1426), Selkau
Zirava (Syrave, 1426), Sierhagen
Zuzely (*in parochia Susele*, 1351), Susel

Moneta Wandal

3. TERRA HAMBURGENSIS, WESTPHALIA, ON THE RHINE

West of Schleswig-Holstein, there is abundant evidence of Slavic settlement and activity in ***Terra Hamburgensis***. Indeed, the evidence suggests that as late as the early 12ᵗʰ century, Hamburg itself was a tenuous imperial-Christian stronghold in ***Terra Slavorum***.

It is a matter of record that in times of conflict, Slavic rulers of ***Regnum Obotritorum*** had little trouble in routing imperial forces and imposing their authority and will in the Hamburg region.

983

In 983, for example, ***Mistivoi, rex Obodritorum,*** sent Hamburg up in flames. Regarding this moment, Helmold writes: **The Slavs embraced the opportunity to collect an army and wasted first the whole of Nordalbingia, with fire and sword. Then ... they burned all the churches and destroyed them even to the ground. They murdered the priests and the other ministers of the churches with diverse tortures and left not a vestige of Christianity beyond the Elbe. At Hamburg, then and later, many clerics were put to death through the hatred of Christianity.**

1066

In the year 1066, once again Slav forces from ***Regnum Obotritorum,*** this time led by ***Prince Blusso,*** destroyed all pretensions of imperial rule in ***Terra Hamburgensis***. Helmold writes: **When the Slavs had achieved victory they ravaged the whole region of Hamburg with fire and sword. Nearly all of the Sturmarians were killed or led into captivity. The stronghold of Hamburg was razed to the ground and even crosses were mutilated by pagans in derision of our Saviour.**

1137

The situation was not much improved in the first half of the 12ᵗʰ century. Circa 1137, Helmold records a Slav uprising that made the land unsafe for Saxon or Christian: *a Slavicus furor propter occupationes Saxonum.*

WESTPHALIA

The very well informed and authoritative 10ᵗʰ century source, Ibrahim ibn Jakub, places the Slavs in numbers and strength in lands west and south of ***Terra Hamburgensis***, including Westphalia. Ibn Jakub locates two towns in Westphalia, one near Dortmund, the other near Bielefeld, as towns in ***Terra Slavorum:*** **Sodest and Paderborn are fortified towns in the Slav lands.**

Medieval records confirm the existence of numerous Slavic settlements in Brunswick and Westphalia, including among others, *Goren* and *Sabrow.* Today one finds traces of early Slav settlements in several place names derived from the ethnonym ***Wend*** (e.g. *Wenden* near Brunswick; *Wenden,* near Olpe in Westphalia).

ON THE RHINE

Citing ancient chronicles, an important 16th century German historian, C.M. Spangenberg speaks of great battles fought against the *Serb-Wends* along the Rhine in the period 101-106 A.D. In his highly regarded multi-volume study, Karl Lamprecht identifies Slavic place names on both sides of the Rhine, including Lorraine *(Deutsche Geschited, 1909-1914).*

SLAV COLONISTS

There is clear evidence that some Slavs settlements near and along the Rhine are of a later date. According to Francis Dvornik, the Church played an important role in expanding the area of Slav settlement along the Rhine in the medieval period *(The Making of Cental Europe, 1974).*

Diverse sources make it clear that Slav prisoners captured in **wars/crusades** against the pagans of *Slavia* were an important source of labor for Church lands throughout Germany, including lands west of the Rhine.

WORMS, METZ

In the early 10th century, for example, Henry II gave Slav prisoners in servitude to the Bishop of Worms, an ancient city on the west bank of the Rhine River and 5th century capital of Burgundy.

In 1009 Henry's generosity reached the Moselle River in northeastern France: large numbers of captured *Lyutichs,* the notorious and fiercely pagan *Lyutichs,* were given in servitude to the Bishop of Metz

PART XIII

1. FOREIGN INTRODUCTIONS

Abrief review of the Baltic Slav imprint beyond the borders of *Slavia, Terra Slavorum*, and *Germania,* specifically the Baltic Slav role in the development of Scandinavia's early trading settlements and market towns, offers considerable insight into the scope, depth, and dynamics of Slavic expansion and settlement west and north of the Elbe. In the present context the term Scandinavia excludes Norway and refers exclusively to the peoples and lands of the 'West Norse' speakers, the Swedes, Gotars, and Danes, the medieval kingdoms of Denmark and Sweden. In the 9th century the whole of modern Denmark, together with the west coast of Sweden and southeast Norway, were considered Danish territory.

FOREIGN INTRODUCTIONS

Authoritative native and foreign historians and archaeologists agree that Scandinavia's first towns were foreign introductions *(H. Arbman, Birka I: Die Graber, 1943; Svear i Osterviking, 1955. S. Bolin, 'Muhammed, Karl Den Store Och Rurik', Scandia XII, 1939. M. Klinge, Itameren Maailma, 1994; H. Pirenne, Mahomet and Charlemagne, 1939. A. Schuck, Studier Rorande det Svenska Stadsvasendets Uppkomst och Aldsta Utveckling, 1926).* Historic, archaeologic, and linguistic evidence points to the Baltic, to *Mare Slavorum*, to the Baltic coast, to *Slavia*, as the primary source of foreign introductions[1]

TRG

One linguistic fact alone speaks volumes. *Trg* is an Old Slavic root for words connoting marketplace, market town, trading place, trading fairgrounds *(D. Kovacevic, Trgovina u srednjovjekovnoj Bosni, 1961. H. Ziolkowska, The Market before the Borough Charter Granting, Ergon 3, 1962. K. Buczek, Targi i miasta na prawie polskim, 1964. T. Lalik, Regale targowe ksiazat wxchodnio pomorskich x XII-XIII wieku, PrZ 56, 1965. A. Gieysztyor, Local Markets and Foreign Exchanges in Central and East Europe before 1200, Ergon 5, 1966. D. Trestik, Trh Moravanu, CcH 21, 1973).* Thus, for example, the modern Serb words *trg, trgovac, trgovacki, trgovati, trgovina,* and *trziste* connoting marketplace, merchant, commerce, trade, trading center. Thus the medieval *White Serbia* town of *Trg,* now Torgau on the Elbe. Also three *trgs* in three countries separated by distance and spelling: *Tirgoviste* in Romania, *Trgoviste* in Yugoslavia and *Turgoviste* in Bulgaria. Thus, the dozens of *trgs/trzs* in Slavic and other countries throughout medieval and contemporary central and eastern Europe: e.g. *Trz*cianka, *Trz*ciel, *Trz*cinno, *Trz*cinsko Zdroj, *Trz*ebiatow, *Trz*ebiel, *Trz*ebinia, *Trz*ebnica, *Trz*epowo in Poland; *Tir*gu Bujor, *Tir*gu Carbunesti, *Tir*gu Frumos, *Tir*gu Jiu; *Tir*gu Lapus, *Tir*gu Mures, *Tir*gu Neamt, *Tir*gu Ocna, *Tir*gu Secuiesc, *Tir*gusor in Romania. As the notion of marketplace, market town was beyond the reach of early medieval Scandinavian civilization, it was necessary to turn to the neighboring Baltic Slavs for an appropriate word. Thus the Slavic root *trg* passed to the Scandinavians as the Swedish *torg*, tbe Danish *torv*, and the Finnish *turku*.

SEA OF THE SLAVS

As early as the 1st century A.D, Ptolemy identified the Baltic as the *Sea of the Slavs.* Historians and archaeologists agree that dense Slavic settlements were established between the mouth of the Vistula and the Bay of Kiel in the early medieval period, an area **rich in resources and foodstuffs**, settled by: **Slavs who surpass all other northern peoples in the practice agriculture and the manufacture of many useful objects.**

MEISSEN OF THE MIDDLE AGES

On the ***Sea of the Slavs*** one finds an unbroken chain of Slavic cities, of leading centers of agriculture, industry, and commerce, including, in the early medieval period: ***civitas Sclavorum Volin,* truly the largest of all cities of Europe.**

FELBERG, FRESENDORF POTTERY

A good measure of the technical and aesthetic standards is the Felberg and Fresendorf pottery produced by the ***Wilti***, an especially prized object of trade. On this point, Herrmann writes: **Carl Schuchhardt, one of the first scholar to identify it, called this pottery the 'Meissen of the Middle Ages' on account of its fine finish and high technical standard** (*L. Schuchhardt, Arkona, Rethra, Vineta, 1926. E. Schuldt, Die slawische Keramik von Sukow und das Porblem der Feldberger Gruppe, JbM 1963. W. Losinski, Einige Bemerkungen zur fruhmittlealterlichen Keramik des Feldberger Typus, PoL 9, 1966).*

SLAVIC MANUFACTURE

Pottery of Slavic manufacture was the pottery of choice throughout the Baltic area. So much so that Slavic pottery appears to be have been copied in eastern Sweden by Slavic potters imported for that purpose.

WEAPONS

The same high standards were maintained in other areas, including the manufacture of weapons, of swords, spears, and battleaxes.

POTENT MARTIAL INFLUENCE

With regards to military technology generally, a highly respected authority on Northern Europe and Director of the the British Museum (London), David M. Wilson writes: **The Slavs were one of the most potent martial influences in northern Europe. Their state of almost constant warfare internally and externally may well have had considerable influence, for example, in the field of military engineering, on the Danish state** (*The Northern World, 1980*).

SHIP BUILDING

It appears the Slavs were first and foremost in the in the construction of ships. Several historical-linguistic studies indicate that the Scandinavians learned their first lessons about ships and shipbuilding from neighboring Slavs. Among the basic maritime terms that appear to be derived from Slavic roots are the Scandinavian words for *boat, ship,* and *ferryboat.*

FORTIFICATIONS

The timberwork of the impregnable ramparts that enclosed Slavic cities on the Baltic and the interior was characterized by high construction craftsmanship, including a specifically Slavic jointing technique of anchor balks. Indeed, the impregnable walls of Stetin gave rise to a Baltic proverb: **As safe as Stetin wall.**

DRESS

Scandinavian dress and fashion, too, had a certain Slavic flavor. Caftans, tunics, and patterned linen shirts worn in Scandinavian towns were imported from neighboring Slavic lands. Finely crafted gold, silver, and bronze jewelry, metal earrings, pendants, female fertility symbols, and other such ornaments were also imported from neighboring Slavic lands. Furs from Slavic lands were so great that it influenced speech as well as dress and introduced a number of Slavic words into the languages of northwestern Europe. *Kuna,* the Slavic word for marten and marten-skin, for example, is probably the basis for a number of medieval cognates, namely the Latin *crusna,* the German *kursinna* and the Frisian *kersua.*

LOCATION

For commercial reasons, Slavic cities were generally located near waterways, often estuaries of major river systems; for strategic reasons, often on islands in rivers, lakes, bays, and lagoons. Ralswiek, for example, was located on an island in a system of inlets that dissect the northern coast of Rugen island; Menzlin, on a ridge in the wetlands around the Peene River; Stettin, Uznoim, and Volin on islands in the Oder river system.

RALSWIEK

Ralswiek, an important center of shipbuilding, illustrates the importance of industry, trade, and shipping to even the most warlike and piratical Slavic communities. Excavations reveal that it was made up of a number of settlement sites, each with a number of homes and workshops, with several landing places. Excavations also reveal the rather extraordinary measures taken by the natives to establish nearly instant access to their ships: **Anchorages for ships were constructed on the lakeside by digging channels from the lakes to individuals house plots and building jetties of piles and planks, some of which supported buildings.**

HEDEBY

In some cases the Slavic roots of Scandinavian trading settlements, of coastal centers of industry and commerce, are direct and dramatic. This is certainly true of Hedeby, the largest and most important town in Scandinavia during the Viking Age.

RERIC

Medieval sources record *Reric* as an important emporium in the lands of the Slavic *Obodriti*. In fact so important that Adam of Bremen calls the *Obodriti* and *Polabian* Slavs generally: *Rericites* or *Reregi: Obodriti, qui nunc Reregi vocantur; Obodriti vel Reregi vel Polabingi*. In the early 9th century *Reric* was known as an emporium in that part of *Obodritorum* ruled by *duke Drasko: Trasco, dux Abodritorum in emporio Reric.*

RERIC, HEDEBY

In the year 808, Godfred, king of Denmark, invaded *terra Obodritorum* and seized *Reric (distructo emporio, quod in oceani litore constitutum lingua Danorum Reric dicebatur).* Instead of attempting to occupy and defend *Reric,* Godfred razed the town and relocated its Slavic craftsmen and merchants to nearby Danish territory, to a place on the inner part of the Schlei fjord, south and opposite the town of Schleswig.

The Royal Frankish Annals give the following details of Godfrid's less than triumphant campaign: **Then, he [Godfrid] withdrew, suffering severe casualties ... But he lost his best and most battle-tested of his soldiers. With them he lost Reginold, his brother's son, who was killed at the siege of a town with a great number of Danish nobles.** Transplanted on Danish soil, Reric was now Hedeby (also called *Haithabu*), soon to be the largest and most important emporium in all Scandinavia until 1066 when it was overun and destroyed. According to Helmold, Reric was **utterly demolished by Slav raiders,** by the *Obodriti* (*H. Steuer, Neues zum Befestigungswesen von Haithabu, PhZ 46, 1971. H. Jankuhn, Eing Handelsplatz derWikingerzeit, 1972. H. Steuer, Die Sudseidlung von Haithabu, 1974).*

ENDNOTES

(O. Eggert, Danisch-wendische Kampfe in Pommern und Mecklenburg 1157-1200, BaL 30, 1928. M. Vasmer, Wikingerspuren bei den Westslaven, ZoG 6, 1932; Beitrage zur slavischen Alterkumskunde. Spuren von Westslaven aus den danischen Inseln, ZsP 19, 1942. B. Nerman, Die Verbindungen zwischen Skandinavien und dem Ostbaltikum in der Jungeren Eiszeit, 1929. S. Sawicki, Uber die lechitischen Ortsnamen in Suddanemark, Acta Philologia Scandinavica XII, 1938. O. Klindt-Jensen, Foreign Influences in Denmark's Early Iron Age, Acta Archaeologica 29, 1949. E. Assmann, Die Schauplatze der danisch-wendisch Kampfe in den Gewassern von Ruggen, BaL 43, 1955. J. Kalima, Die slavischne Lehnworter im Ostseefinnischen, Slavistische Veroffenlichungen 8, 1956. V. Kiparsky, O hronologii slavjano-finskih leksiceskih otnosenii, Scando-Slavica 4, 1958. J. Zak, Problem pochodzenia mieczow tzw. "wikinisch" na ziemiach zachodnioslowianskich, glownie polskich, Archeologia Polski 4, 1959; Ceramika typu zachodnioslowinaskiego w Lilleborgu na Bornholmie, SlA 8, 1961; Studia nad kontaktami handlowymi spoleczenstw zachodnioslowianskich za skandynawskimi od VI do VIII w. n. ery, 1962; "Importy" Skandynawskie na Ziemiach Zachodnioslowianskich od IX do XI wieku, 1963; Die Beziehungen zwischen Skandinavien und den slawischen Stammen, ZtA 1, 1967. G. Labuda, Slavs in Eearly Medieval Pomerania and their Relations with the Scandinavians in the 9th and 10th Centuries, 1960; Zrodla skandynawskie i anglosaskie do dziejow Slowianszczyzny, 1961. Polska i Skandynaiwa w IX-X wieku, Poczatki Panstwa Polskiego I, 1961; Norwegia Stosunki za Slowianami, SsS 3, 1967. Slowianie w Danii, SsS 5, 1975. Zrodla Skandynawskie (pisane) Do Dziejow Slowian, SsS 7, 1982. J. Kostrzewski, Dania. Stosunki za Slowianami, SsS 1, 1961. H. Priedel, Die slawisch Keramik im wikingischen Skandinavien, DwS 7, 1962. M. Thorndahl, Slavische Ortsnamen in Danemark, 1963. S. Rospond, Skandynawpwoe na Pomorzu w swietle nazewnictwa miejscowego, Rocznik Olsztynski 7, 1968. M. Stenberger, Slawische Funde auf Oland, Studien zur europaischen Vor-und Fruhgeschichte, 1968. H. Helbaek, Da Rugen kom til Danmark, 1970. E. Hoffman, Kurt der Heilige und die Wende der danischen Geschichte im 11. Jh, HtZ 218, 1974. J. Herrmann,Nordwestslawische Seehandelspatz de9.-10. Jr. und Spuren ihrer Verbindungen zum Nordseegebiet, EtH 16, 1975. H.J. Eggers, Funde der wendisch-wikingischen Zeit in Pommern, 1978. K.W. Struve, Bestanden verwandtschaftliche Beziehungen der Wagrierfursten nach Skandinavien?, DiE 85, 1978. L. Leciejewicz, Die Anfange des Staatswesens bie den Westslawen und in Skandinavien—einiger Parallelen und Unterschiede, RaP I, 1979. D. Warnke, Skandinavische Einflusse im nordwestslawischen Siedlungsgebiet vor dem 10. Jh, Das Altertum 33, 1987. T. Damgaard-Sorensen, Danes and Wends, Peoples and Places, 1991. H. Machajewski, Skandinawskie elementy kulturowe na Pomorzu zachodnim z okresu wecrowek ludow, PrG 40, 1992. M. Roslund, Baltic Ware—A Black Hole in the Cultural History of Early Medieval Scandinavia, Contacts Across the Baltic Sea During the Late Iron-Ages, 1992. M. Andersen, Westslawischer Import in Danemark etwa 950- bis 1220—Eine Ubersicht, ZtA, 1994. U. Schoknecht, Wikinger und Slawen. Ein Jahrtausend Mecklenburg-Vorpommern, 1995.

2. RUGIANS, NOT SWEDES?

In order to better understand the role of the ***Baltic Slavs*** in the formation and growth of Scandinavia's towns, industry, and commerce in the 9th and 10th centuries, it is important to remember that Scandinavia's early history and civilization has an Eastern orientation, that the runic alphabet is Greek in origin, that scenes depicted on large limestones relate to Greek rather than Nordic mythology.

M. Klinge, a leading Finnish authority on the Baltic writes: **Contrary to early belief, the fascinating large pictorial stones that have been preserved in Gotland do not seem to to reflect the mythical-historical world immortalized by Norwegian and Icelandic sagas and runes. Strange to say, they actually depict scenes from the epics of Homer** *(M. Klinge, The Baltic World, 1994).*

BALTIC ISLANDS

The early history of industry, trade, and commerce in Scandinavia is essentially the history of the Baltic islands, Bornhom, Oland, and Gotland, that run northeast from ***Slavia's*** coast, from the lands of the ***Wilti (Velichi, Lyutici),*** from the island of ***Rugen: in Slaviam, Rugian vocitatam,*** 844.

BALTIC SPRINGBOARD: WILTI

The deep roots of the ***Wilti*** in the Baltic springboard opposite the Baltic Islands are a matter of record. Ptolemy mentions the ***Wilti (Viltaei)*** in the 1st century A.D.

TOWN OF THE WILTS

In his magnum opus, *Historia Ecclesiastica gentis Anglorum,* published in 731, the Venerable Bede (672-735), the *Father of English Scholarship,* establishes the great age and range of ***Wilti*** maritime operations in the following terms. Following Wilibord's consecration in 696, Bede writes: **Pepin gave him a place for his episcopal see, in his famous castle, called by an ancient of those countries Wiltaburg, as you would say Town of the Wilts; but, in the Gallic tongue it is called Trajectum:** *Donavit autem ei Pippin locum cathedrale episcopalis in castello suo inlustri, quod antiquo gentium illarum verbo Viltaburg, id est, Oppidum Viltorum, lingua autem Gallica Traiectum vocatur* *(W.H. Fritze, Beda uber die Ostseeslaven, ZtS 8, 1974).*

The ***Wilti*** mainland is a chain of fortified cities, of important centers of industry and commerce: e.g. *Bardo, Bukov, Bialograd, Dimin, Chozgov, Dimin, Grozvin, Grubno, Kamenc, Kolobreg, Kujavice, Lubin, Lubochin, Malachov, Menzlin, Ostrozno, Pozdevolk, Stetin, Trebotin, Trebuz, Uradz, Uznoim, Volin, Voligost* (W. Kowalenko, Staroslowianski grody portowe na Baltyku, ZaC 6, 1950. Z. Sulowski, Slowianskie organizacje polityczne nad Baltykiem, RoH 26, 1960. L. Leciejewicz, Grod i podgrodzie u Slowian zachodnich, Pocztaki zamkow w Polsce, 1978).

BALTIC SPRINGBOARD: RUGINI

A distinct and independent element of the ***Wilti*** federation, the ***Rugenites,*** native of island of ***Rugen,*** were known far and wide as *lords of the Baltic Sea.* As were the ***Wilti,*** the ***Rugenites*** were also known to the Venerable Bede who mentions them in the year 689: **Such now are the Frisons, Rugins, Danes, Huns, Old Saxons, and**

Boructuars: *Sunt autem Fresones, Rugini, Danai, Hunni, Antiqui Saxones, Boructuarii* (W. H. Fritze, Bedas Rygini und Willibords Danenmission, ZtS 32, 1965).

MARE RUGIANORUM

That the Baltic Sea was known as **Mare Rugianorum,** that at one **Rugen** site modern excavations have revealed a great silver hoard of some 2,270 Arab coins, the largest number of pre-850 coins discovered in the Baltic, tells a great deal about the bounce in the **Rugen** springboard (J.G.L. Kosegarten, Arabische Munzen auf der Insel Rugen, BaL 19, 1861).

LAPLAND OR RUIA

A great deal, but not all. It seems that the **Rugen** sphere of influence ran as far north as **Lapland** or **Ruia,** where they established pirate settlements. Noting that **Rugen** was the German name for Norwegian Finnmark, originally called **Ruia** or **Rugia** in Latin, **Ruija** in modern Finnish, Professor Klinge writes: **The people of Rugen had evidently gained control of the Lapland fur trade. It seems that the trade route that ran along the eastern coast of the Baltic, then via Saarema to southwestern Finland the Bothnian Bay marked Rugen's trading area.**

ANCIENT RUS

Certainly one of the more impartial as well as informed authorities on the subject, Professor Klinge believes that the ancient **Rus** originated in Baltic **Slavia** (H. Lowmianski, O znaczeniu nazwy Rus w X-XIV wieku, KwA 1, 1957. J. Otrebski, Rus, LpS 8, 1960. S. Rospond, Pochodzenie nazwy Rus, RoC 38, 1977. G. Schramm, Die Herkunft des Namens Rus, FoG 30, 1982. G.F. Kovalev, Esce raz o proischozdenii etnonima Rus, Acta Balto-Slavica XVII, 1987). More precisely, Professor Klinge believes that the ancient **Rus** originated that part of Baltic **Slavia** dominated by the **Rugians:** **A nation famed for their travels and warlike expeditions.** An interesting fact in favor of Klinge's thesis is the fact that in some medieval documents the **Rugians** are identified as **Ruscis:** *Qui primitus Ruscis ad praedicandum directus vix evasit, 969.*

SWEDEN

The notion that the **Rus** originated in Sweden, Klinge writes, is untenable on both historic and linguistic grounds: **It is in many more ways more likely that the West Slavic Rugians founded Novogorod as an extension of their 'sea power' to the east** (The Baltic World, 1994).

OTHER RUSSIAN PRINCIPALITIES

It is also Professor Klinge's thesis that there is substantial evidence, cultic and otherwise, that the **Rugenites/Rusi** played a leading role in the founding of other Russian principalities (A. Haas, Slawische Kultstaetten aus der Inseln Ruegen, Pommersche Jb 19, 1918; J. Oseiglowski, Wyspa slowianskich bogov, 1971).

3. BALTIC ISLANDS

Some measure of the early and leading role of the Baltic islands in Scandinavia's trade is found in the fact that over half of the silver coins so far discovered in Scandinavia have been found in the Baltic islands, mainly Gotland.

BORNHOLM, GOTLAND, OLAND

As late as 890 the island of Bornholm was not part of Denmark or Sweden. Gotland was also an independent entity in the early Middle Ages. The artifacts, structures, and burial customs on the islands differ from those found on mainland Scandinavia. Large quantities of Slavonic pottery are found on the islands. On the Gotland stones one sees warriors wearing helmets crowned with a pike, a Slavic fashion. In addition to numerous finds of Slavic origin, Marten Stenberge, a leading Swedish archaeologist and excavator of Ekestorp on Oland, finds evidence **that Oland was occupied by Slavs from the southern coast of the Baltic as is indicated by Saxo and the *Knytlinga Saga.*** Regarding Bornholm, Gotland, Oland, and southern Sweden generally, Herrmann writes, not only have many finds of Slavic origin been found in this area, but, from the mid-10th century onwards, he finds evidence of **earlier Slavic strongholds being re-fortified.**

PAVIK, VISBY, BOGEVIK

On the Gotland coast several harbors and trading settlements in the Slavic manner have been revealed by excavations. One at Pavik, on the mouth of a river that flows into the Pavik lagoon, one at Visby, where a shallow lagoon harbor is sheltered by steep limestone cliffs, and a third harbor of the same type at Bogevik.

BALTIC MAINLAND

It is important to keep in mind that Sweden's first centuries were almost wholly east-facing, that it had no western coastline until the 13th century, that its greatest mainland settlement and development takes place in the Lake Malar region bordering on the Baltic.

HELGO, BIRKA, SIGTUNA

The earliest mainland trading settlements are found on islands near the Baltic coast, namely Helgo, on the island of Helgo in Lake Malaren (where the largest hoard of Byzantine gold coins of 6th century date has been discovered). Birka *(**portum regni ipsorum qui Birca dicitur),*** Helgo's successor, on the neighboring island of Bjorko in Lake Malaren, is one of the earliest true urban centres of the Swedish mainland: ***Ad quam stationem, qui tutissima eest in maritimis Suevoniae regionibus, solent omnes Danorum vel Normannorum itemque Sclavorum ac Semborum naves aliique Scithiae populi pro diversis commerciorum necessitatibus sollempniter convenire.***

On a rocky and wooded peninsula, running deep into Lake Malaren, between the islands of Helgo and Birka, excavations have also revealed a small trading settlement in the Slavic manner at Sigtuna. Here and throughout southeastern Sweden the local dress was similar to that of the Baltic Slavs. Tunics and patterned linen shirts in the Slavic fashion were very much in vogue.

AHUS, RIBE

In the modern Swedish province of Scania, on an estuary near the Baltic shore-line, excavations at Ahus, an early medieval trading settlement, have uncovered pottery that indicates close contacts with the Slavonic region across the Baltic to the south. In west Jutland, on marshland beside the Ribe river, near the North Sea coast, Ribe was an important settlement for trade with western Europe, with roots in the 8th century, when it appears to have been a seasonal trading center with several workshops, similar in name, location, and structure to other Slav maritime trading outposts.

JUTLAND

There is solid evidence that the Slavs were a serious challenge to Scandinavian rule in Jutland north of Hedeby prior to its destruction in 1066. Some time during the reign of Magnus Olafsson, King of Norway (1042-1047): **A great battle against the Wends was fought at the Konge River a little to the north of Hedeby on Lyrskov Heath** *(Knytlinga Saga)*.

ZEALAND, FYN

There is also solid evidence that as late as the mid-12th century the Slavs were a force in the affairs of the large and important islands off Sweden's west coast, namely Zealand and Fyn. Svein Ericksson *the Scorcher,* King of Denmark (1146-1157), it is said, **fought the Wends at Kalvslunde [on Zealand] where he won the victory and killed a great number of men** *(Knytlinga Saga)*.

PAID THE WENDS

Some time later, the Slavs are important and decisive allies in Svein's struggle with a dynastic rival and successor (Valdimar *the Great*, King of Denmark (1157-1182). The *Knytlinga Saga* is perhaps a bit discreet regarding Svein's reliance on his Slav allies: **After King Svein had been in Saxony a short while, he got tired of it and went over there to Wendland, where he paid the Wends to ferry him over to Fyn.**

SIX HUNDRED WENDISH SHIPS

That the Slavs were a decisive a factor in the struggle is indicated that immediately after a fierce storm wrecked **six hundred Wendish ships off the Jolu Islands [islands off the southwestern coast of Sweden], Svein was defeated and killed (caught hiding in a bush where he was rushed up and killed by Gvenmar Ketilsson).**

4. WENDENINSEL

There is some evidence that suggests permanent Slavic settlement in Scandinavia, namely place names and toponyms with the prefix **Vend-** or **Wend-** : e.g. *Vend*al, Sweden; *Vend*elsby, Sweden; *Vend*esund, Norway; *Vend*syssel, Denmark; *Vind*eby, Sweden; *Vind*elalven, Sweden; *Vind*erup, Sweden; *Wend*eninsel, Sweden; *Wend*enmeerenge, Norway; *Wind*eby, Sweden.

WILTORUM OPPIDUM

Other and later sources confirm the Venerable Bede's account of *Wilti* settlements along the North Sea coast, including Wiltaburg/Utrecht. The *Chronicon Hollandiae* (1617), for example, traces Utrecht's roots: **To Slavs called Wilts, the founders of Wiltorum oppidum, Wiltraetcum and Wiltaburg.**

Numerous scholars including an 18th century authority, T. Segerum *(De Slavis et Lecho, 1772)* are certain that a number of place names in northeastern Netherlands are derived from Slavic roots originating in early Slavic trading settlements.

WILTI SETTLEMENTS

With regards to *Wilti/Velici* settlements in Batavia, J.P. Safarik writes: **Ze Veleti v Nizozemi, mezi odnozemi Renu, jmenovite v podkraji reky Wahalis (Wahl), blize mesta Utrechtu, tez dale na pomori Frislandskem ... Procez v pozedjsich casich jen podridku a nedosti znale slepeje slovanskych Veletuv v Nizozemsku se namitaji. Sem prinalezeji predevsim mistni jmena budto k Veletum obzvlaste, budto ke Slovanum vubec se vztahujici, np. Wiltswee v Holandsku, Wiltenburg blizko Utrechtu, Wilta, Walsum un Dinslakna 1. 1144, Kamen, Sueta, Wideniz (Vodenica), Hudnin, Zwola, Wise, cz. Wespe (Vyspa?), Slota atd. Podbone v jazyku starohollandskem nektere sledy slovanciny znamenati lze na. skatt (skot), leth-slachta (genus litorum), o nichz snad jindy mistneji promluvime** *('Veleti v Batavii a Britannii,' Sebrany Spisy, II, 1862).*

WILTA AD MOSAM

According to the *Chronici Zelandiae* (1634) the *Wilti* also gave their name to *Wilta*, an important city on the Meuse River *(Wilta ad Mosam)*, modeled after *Wineta* [Volin/Wolin], the great Slav city on the Baltic: **Wiltam eandem fuisse cum Wineta, amplissimo Slavorum oppido.**

Medieval sources relating to the *Wilti* in Hollandia and Britannia are cited and discussed in Safarik's chapter on the *Wilti/Velici* *('O Slovanech polabskych. Popis vetvi a sidel,' Sebrany Spisy, II, 1862).* The following brief excerpts from medieval sources cited by Safarik confirm the presence and important role played by the *Wilti* in northwestern Europe.

> • *Slavi in Frisia seu Hollandia ... quidam pforecti sunt ... ad partem inferiorem Gelriae, qui populos tunc vocatus est de Wilten*
> • *Ad isto Slavos et Wilten ... pugnavit cum Slavis et Wilten*
> • *Slavi et Wilti ... Wilti illi de aquilonari Hollandia et Slavi ... Frisones*
> • *Wiltones et Saxones ... castrum Wiltenburg*

- *Saxones cum Slavis profecti sunt in Britanniam*
- *Frisones et Saxones et Wilti*
- *Slavi vel Hollandini et Wilci*
- *Frisones et Slavos et Wiltos*
- *Slavoniam et Hollandiam*
- *Antiqum Slavenburch, quae nucn Vlaerdingen est*
- *Frisiem et Slaviam Descenderunt per Slaviam*
- *Adducit laudatque versiculos de Wiltis ex chronico rhythmico annos, ut ai, antea quam ipse scribebat fere trecents hollandica lingua composito, quibus Saxones in Wiltorum nomen transiisse innuerit.*

ENGLAND

The year 1010 finds Svein I Forkbeard, King of Denmark (986-1014), near Canterbury, **at the head of an army of Danes and Slavs,** defeating an English-Norwegian army led by England's Ethelred and Norway's Olaf Harald. There is direct and substantial evidence that Slav armies were involved in prior and successive invasions of England, including the campaigns of 1013 and 1015 that brought England to its knees and placed the English crown on the head of King Canute in 1016, as well as other Viking campaigns in northern Europe.

ANGLES, SAXONS, JUTES, WILTAE

The *Bodrici* were not the first Baltic Slavs to take part in the invasions and conquest of Britannia. That honor belongs to the *Wilti* who took part in the Anglo-Saxon (Angles, Saxons, Jutes, *Wiltae*) invasion and conquest of Britannia. Safarik finds evidence of *Wilti* settlement in English place names: **K vire podobno jest, ze tymz casem i v Britanii nektere celedi Veletuv se osadily, kdez neco pozdeji mesto Wiltun, krajina Wiltsaeten cz. Wilts (nyni Wiltshire) a lide Wiltunisci se pripominaji. Oboji osadnici, nizozemsti i britansti nezjevivse se nikde v dosti jasnem svetle v histori, brzo a obsoru jejiho se trati ... Mnohem temnejsi a nejistejsi jsou zpravy o nekdejsim prebyvani Veletuv v Anglicanech, jmenovite v te krajine, kteraz po osazeni se Anglosasuv v Britannii Wiltsaeten Wilts sloula, a z niz nynejsi hrabstvi Wiltunshire povstalo. Tamze i mesto Wiltun (nynyi Wilton), obyvatele Wiltuni, Wiltunisci, dosti casne se pripominjali** *(Sebrany Spisy, II, 1862).*

WAR

As in peace, so in war the Baltic Slavs were superior to the Scandinavians. Indeed, the record is clear that the Slavs had little regard for the martial prowess of the *fierce* and *terrible* Vikings. With regard to the Danes, the mighty lords of Scandinavia, Helmold writes: **They think nothing of the attacks of the Danes; in fact, they esteem it play to measure arms with them.** Indeed, according to Helmold, the Danes were so easy to defeat that wars against them tended to soften the Slavs: **Filled with the riches of the Danes; they grew fat. I say, thick, gross!**

PIRATE RAIDS

Perhaps the most authoritative and graphic account of the consequences of Slav domination and command of Scandinavian waters, islands, and coastal lands in the mid-

12th century, of continuous raids by Slav pirates, namely the **Obodrites, Lutici** and **Rugians,** is found in Saxo's *Gesta Danorum:* **Piracy was so unchecked that all the villages along the eastern coast, from Vendsyssel to the Eider, were empty of inhabitants, and the countryside was untilled. Zealand was barren to the east and south, and languished in desolation ... Pirate raids had left nothing of Funen, except for a few inhabitants. Falster ... kept the enemy away either by treaty or by force. But Lolland ... sued for peace and paid tribute. Other places were desolated. Thus there was no confidence either in arms or in forts; and the inlets of the sea were obstructed by long pales and stakes, so as not to let the pirates in.**

TAKE VENGEANCE ON THE DANES

When the Danes fell out of favor with the Saxons in the 1170s, the **Rugenites**, Helmold writes, were called on 'to take vengeance on the Danes.' **The bars and doors with which the sea had been closed were moved away; and it burst forth, surged, poured over, and threatened with destruction the many islands and coastal regions of the Danes. The Slavs restored their pirate ships and seized opulent islands in the land of the Danes. They were, after their long abstinence, filled with the riches of the Danes.**

ALPHA AND OMEGA

According to Helmold, piracy, an ancient and deeply engrained pirate impulse, was the alpha and omega of the Baltic Slavs: **The Slavs are exceedingly skilled in making clandestine attacks. Hence, also, predatory habits have until this present age been so strong among them that they have always turned their hands to the fitting out of naval expeditions to the utter neglect of the advantages of agriculture. The ships are their only hope and the sum total of their wealth.**

JOMSVIKINGS

It is not surprising therefore that the great Icelandic saga, *The Saga of the Jomsvikings,* a highly fictionalized account of the greatest Viking community of all times, a highly idealized pirate community centered at **Volin** in the 9th and 10th centuries, appears to be based not on Scandinavian Vikings, but on the exploits of Baltic Slav *Vikings.* All attempts to give this heroic community of Slavic *Vikings* a Scandinavian dimension have wilted under the hard facts of history, archaeology, linguistics, and logic. According to the *Saga,* the Joms or **Volin** Vikings were a one-for-all and all-for-one heroic brotherhood of warriors/pirates. More than everything else, however, what distinguished this fiercely independent, self-governing entity from other pirate-warrior communities was its strict set of rules: **The first section of their laws was that no man should become a member who was older than fifty or younger than eighteen ... Kinship was not to be taken into consideration when those who were not members wished to be enrolled. No man must run from anyone who was as doughty and well-armed as himself. Each must avenge the other as his own brother. No one must speak a word of fear or be frightened in any situation however black things looked. Anything of value, however big or small it was, which they won on their expeditions was to be taken to the banner, and anyone who failed to do this was to be expelled. No one was to stir up contention there. If there was any news, no one must be so rash as to repeat to all and sundry.**

There is good reason to believe, Safarik writes, that the Volsung Vikings celebrated in *The Saga of the Volsungs* are actually Slavic *Vikings (Sebrany Spisy, II, 1862):* **Mezi skandinavskymi povestmi neposledni misto zaujima Volsungasaga, tak nazvana podle hrdinskeho kmene Volsungar, jehoz praotec Vosungr cz. Volsung (zdef uzita otecne forma misto puvodniho jmena Valsi cz. Velsi) i v povesti Sverrissaga a v nekterych jinych se pripomina. Tyz hrdina slove v anglosaske basni Beowulf Valse, syn jeho Valsin, v nemecke pak povesti Wilkinasaga onen Wali, Welsi, tento Walsing, Welsing, kmen Welisunga, a coz najpamatnejsiho jest, v teto a v jine povesti, recene Blomsturvallasaga, les Walslonguwald, jinak i Latiwald. V pozdejsich pamatkach divotvorny mec hrdiny nos cestne jmeno Walsung, Welsung, Wilsung. Zdaliz toto preneseni hrdinskeho jmeno Walsi, Welsi, do baje na severu u Skandinavcuv, cili na zapadu u Frankuv se zapocalo, nemecti zpytatele nechaf rozhodnou: ze jmeno to od hrdinskeho narodu Veletuv na smyslene reky nemecke preslo, zda se byti nepochybne V jinych povestech a basnech panuje form Wilz, mn. cz . Wilzi. Tak v baji recene Dietrichsflucht zeme jinde Wilkinaland jmenovana slove "der Wilzen Land" u basnika Marnera narod Veletuv "der Wilzen diet" tyz u Reinmara Zweterskeho a Tanhusera "Wilzen."**

PART XIV

1. VOJVODSTVI LUNEBURSKEM

According to a late 8th century source, **Hliuni**/Luneburg (**in locum qui dicitur Hluini**) was considered part of the great Slav confederation centered in northeast Germania, the renowned **Lutici** of **Luticiorum**:

> **Liunniburc quoque oppidum maximum Ottonis ducis Saxonici, situm in confinio Saxonum et Luticiorum, 795.**

Numerous sources testify to early and dense Slavic settlement **in locum qui dicitur Hliuni**. Evidence relating to the Slavic foundations of the *Duchy of Luneburg* (**vojvodstvi Luneburskem**) the constituent districts of Bleckede, Bodenteich, Clenze, Dannenberg, Fallersleben, Gartow, Grifhorn, Hitzacker, Isenhagen, Knesebeck, Luchow, Medingen, Meinersen, Oldenstadt, and Wustrow, is especially strong and well-documented in German and European scholarship *(E. Mucke, Slovane ve vojvodstvi Luneburskem, SlP 6, 1904).*

SLAVIC SETTLEMENT

One source of evidence is the many modern place names obviously derived from Slavic roots. Hundreds of villages, towns, toponyms, and hydronyms with Slavic names are detailed in numerous studies.

- *Uber die Sitten und Gebrauche der heutigen Wenden im Luneburgischen, 1817*
- *Die Slaven in Luneburgischen, 1845*
- *Die sprachlichen Denkmaler der Drevjaner und Glinianer Elbslawen im Luneburger Wendlande, 1857*
- *Die slavischen Orts- und Flurnamen im Luneburgischen, 1901*
- *Slawische Familiennamen in der Stadt Hannover, 1907*
- *Orts und Flurnamen in Luneburg, 1914*
- *Zur Mundart des Luneburger Wendlandes, 1924*
- *Slawische Orts- und Flurnamen in dem Lauenburgischen Winkel zwischen Elbe und Bille, 1939*
- *Die Slawischen Funde aus dem hannoverschen Wendland, 1961*
- *Z nowszych badan nad dziejami Drzewian polabskich i hannoverskiego Wendlandu, 1976*
- *Slawische Siedlungsspuren im Raum um Uelzen, Bad Bevensen und Luneburg, 1978*
- *Das Dravanopolabische des 17. und 18. Jahrhunderts als Zeugnis eines untergehenden Slawenstammes, 1987*
- *Zum Zeugnis der altpolabischen Ortsname im Luneburger Wendland furdie Sprachgeschichte, 1993*
- *Die Ortsnamen des Landkreises und der Stadt Hannover, 1998*

SLAVIC SPEECH

Numerous studies also document the survival of Slavic speech in the 16th and 17th centuries and traces of Slavic speech in modern times:

- *Uber die slawische Sprache, sonders uber die Luneburgisch-Wendische, 1814*
- *Szczatki jezyka polabskiego Wendow Luneburskich, 1904*
- *Die Luneburger Wenden in Geschichte Volkstum und Sprache, 1908*
- *Sprachstudien im Luneburger Wendland, 1918*
- *Zur Volkssprache des Luneburger Landes, 1927*
- *Jeszcze o etymologiach slowiansko-niemieckich jezyka Wendow lunebruskich, 1961*
- *Zur christlichen Terminologie in der Sprache der Dravafnopolaben, 1975*
- *Deutsch und nicht Wendish, 1977*
- *Zum Dialektologie des Wendlandes, 1993*

BONA SLAVICALIA

There are numerous references to Slavs and Slavic institutions in medieval Germania sources. The following are some of the **bona Slavicalias** recorded in 1189.

IN CETENE, IN DOLANE

bona ***Slavicalia*** in Cetene

bona ***Slavicalia*** in Dolane

bona ***Slavicalia*** in Ganzowe

bona ***Slavicalia*** in Gromaszle

bona ***Slavicalia*** in Honcethen

bona ***Slavicalia*** in Kardestorpe

bona ***Slavicalia*** in Poklentze

bona ***Slavicalia*** in Kolove

bona ***Slavicalia*** in Konove

bona ***Slavicalia*** in Kroditze

bona ***Slavicalia*** in Moylen

bona ***Slavicalia*** in Multzene

bona ***Slavicalia*** in Nendorpe

bona ***Slavicalia*** in Novente

bona ***Slavicalia*** in Saltendike

bona ***Slavicalia*** in Scorstorpe

bona ***Slavicalia*** in Slikove

bona ***Slavicalia*** in Zuliendorpe

VILLA SLAVICOS

The following are some of the **Slavicums** and **villa Slavicos** recorded in the 13th and 14th centuries.

*Ad **Slavicum** Sarowa, 1230*

*Usque ad **Slavicum** Blekede, 1209*

*Villa **Slavico** Boitze, 1316*

*Villis **Slavicis** Glusinge, 1244*

*Villa **Slavica** Nuthlikesvelde, 1288*

*Villa **Slavico** Sedorpe, 1316*

*Villa **Sclavicis** Windelmerbutle, 244*

WENDISCH STEIMKE

Some Slav settlements are recorded as **Wend/Wendish** villages and towns.

Wendekoten, 1190
Wendeschen Borstle, 1325
Wendeschen Everinge, 1450
Wendeschen Gravenstede, 1320

Wendewisch, 1373
Wendisch Steimke, 1366
Wendeschen Tune, 1491

TRES SLAVOS IN GURIZ

The following are some of the references to Slavs, Slav institutions and Slav officials in 13th and 14th century sources.

- *Gromaszle: Quattuor **Slavorum** advocaciam in Gormaszle, 1329*
- *Chinowe: in villa Chinowe in curia qua nunc sedet **Slavus**, Wernerus nomine, magister civium, 1321*
- *Guriz: tres **Slavos** in Guriz, 1290*
- *Muchelinge: **Slavi** in villa Muchelinge, 1320*
- *Redemuzle: **Slavos** in Redemuzle, 1295*
- *Robbelstorff cum molendino et cum iure **Slavico** quod Dedenick vocatur, 1354*
- *Scerembeke: **Slavi** monarchorum in Scerembeke, 1450*
- *Sterle: duos **Slavos** in villa Sterle*
- *Swendale: cum curia in villa Swendale propre Dalenborch, quam quidam **Slavus** nomine Arneke nunc inhabitant, 1357*
- *Thidericus: **Slavus** nomine Thidericus, 1307*

MYSL

In this area one finds place names derived from Slavic personal names. The following place names feature the prefix/suffix *mysl.*

Malomysl—Malemoyssell, 1451 (Mammoissel)
Myslici— Moyzliz, 1297 (Meussliessen)
Pomysl— Pomoysele, 1360 (Pommoissel)
Radomysl— Redemuzle, 1295 (Redemoissel)
Svemysl— Svemelitze, 1360 (Schwemmlitz)

RAD

The following place names are derived from Slavic personal names featuring the prefix/suffix *rad.*

Badirad— Banderatze, 1397 (Banratz)
Radin— Reddyn, 1451 (Reddien)
Radibor— Redhebere, 13522 (Raber)
Radoboric— Ridderetze, 1368 (Reddereitz)
Radobyt— Redebutze, 1360 (Reddebeitz)
Radogost— *mansum in Radegast*, 1326 (Radegast)
Zalorad— Salderatze, 1352 (Salderratzen)

BOZEN, MALISIN, SLAVOKOT

As the following series illustrates, in many instances the Slavic personal names have survived more or less intact and recognizable.

Belan— Bellan, 1352 (Bellahn)
Bozen— Bozene, 1352 (Bosen)
Lubel— Lubelen, 1363 (Lubeln)
Lubov— Lubbowe, 1352 (Lubbow)
Lutetin— Lutentin, 1352 (Lutenthien)
Malisin— Mallesen, 1240 (Molzen)
Pribin— Probin, 1330 (Probien)
Sul, Sulkov— Zolcowe, 1352 (Solkau)
Tus, Tuskov— Tuschowe, 1352 (Tuschau)
Slavokot— Slowkoten, 1368 (Schlagte)
Sves, Sveskov— Sweskowe, 1372 (Scheskau)
Tus, Tuskov— Tucschowe, 1382 (Tuschau)

BELICA, BELITZ

As the following series illustrates, the same is true of many other 'Germanized' place names in the former *Duchy of Luneburg.*

BELICA, DOLANE, KOKOT

Belica— Belitze, 1352 (Belitz)
Belov— Beleve, 1451 (Belau)
Breze— Breze, 1360 (Breese)
Dalim— Dalme, 1380 (Dahlem)
Dolane— Dolan, 1352 (Dallahn)
Glinica— Glinitze, 1361 (Glienitz)
Gol— Golau, 1760 (Gollau)
Gor— Gorisse, 1112 (Gohr)
Grabov— Grabow, 1330 (Grabau)

JABLY, KONOV, LAZ

Jably— Jabele, 1320 (Jabel)
Jemel— Jamel, 1395 (Jameln)
Kokot— Kokote, 1451 (Kukate)
Konov— Konove, 1289 (Konau)
Koval— Kovall, 1499 (Kovahl)
Kremlin— Kremelyn, 1450 (Kremlin)
Laz— Laze, 1360 (Laase)
Lipa— Lipe, 1389 (Liepa)
Lomica— Lomiz, 1342 (Lomitz)

LUBEN, PODREP, POSAD

Luben— Luben, 1451 (Luben)
Lugov— Lugheve, 1360 (Luggau)
Lukov— Lukow, 1451 (Luckau)

Orla— Orle, 1360 (Orrel)
Plote— Plote, 1369 (Plate)
Podrep— Poderepe, 1360 (Pudripp)
Polov— Polow, 1614 (Polau)
Popelov— Popelow, 1391 (Pop
Presek— Preseke, 1352 (Priesseck)
Prilip— Prilip, 1614 (Prielipp)
Smardov—Smardow, 1365 (Schmardau)
Sneg— Snege, 1304 (Schnega)
Solane— Sollan, 1451 (Sallahn)
Studen— Stude, 1701 (Stude)
Trebel— Trebel, 1613
Trebun— Trebun, 1349 (Trabuhn)
Vila— Vile, 1563 (Viele)
Vrecha— Wrechau, 1650 (Wrechau)

GREATER CHANGE

In the following series the Slavic root and character of the place names have undergone greater change and the Slavic roots are often less obvious or certain.

BORAC, BREZNA, CHERNIN

Borac— *molendinum in Borech,* 1273 (Borg)
Brestani— Breystian, 1451 (Breustian)
Brezna— Brezne, 1329 (Breetze)
Brezolado— Breselenze, 1352 (Breselenz)
Budin— Budinsola, 1006 (Gross Bollensen)
Chernin— Schernyn, 1360 (Zernien)
Chernytin— Cernytyn, 1360 (Zarenthien)
Chmelin— Gymelen, 1360 (Gamehlen)

CHOTEMIN, DRAGISIN, GOLOBRDA

Chotemin— Chatemyn, 1503 (Katemin)
Chvarstov— Quartzow, 1614 (Quartzau)
Chylov— Chileve, 1352 (Gielau)
Dalin— Dallin, 1764 (Dellien)
Dikovici— Dykvitze, 1451 (Dickfeitzen)
Dragisin— Dargessen, 1352 (Darzau)
Dreza— Drezdem, 1322 (Drethem)
Golobrda— Kolbarde, 1360 (Kolbarde)

GORETIN, JASLA, KLANAC

Golovasy— Gulevantz, 1450 (Gohlefanz)
Goretin— Gorenthin, 1296 (Granthein)
Goric— Guriz, 1296 (Guhreitzen)
Jasla— Jasle, 1360 (Jassel)
Kijev— Kyve, 1451 (Kiefen)
Klanac— Poklentze, 1352 (Clenz)

Klevici— Clewicz, 1378 (Klebitz)
Kluc— Kloutzeke, 1384 (Klautze)

KOBYLIN, MEDOVICA, NIVICA

Kobylin— Govelin, 1360 (Govelin)
Kol— Colne, 1352 (Kohlen)
Kolopot— Kulepand, 1322 (Kolepant)
Kopr— Koperen, 1360 (Kapern)
Kosobod— Cozebode, 1296 (Kussebode)
Kotin— Kotyn, 1360 (Kattien)
Konsk— Cuntzke, 1564 (Kunsche)
Medovica — Middevetze, 1364 (Middefeitz)

MOJKOVICI, NA RECE, RIBAROVO

Mojkovici— Moicheviz, 1490 (Meuchefeiz)
Moskovasy— Mussekevanz, 1352 (Moschefanz)
Na Rece— Neretze, 1450 (Neritz)
Nivica— Nivelitz, 1614 (Nievelitz)
Podluze— Putlose, 1600 (Putlosen)
Podbydlo— Pottbuttle, 1352 (Puttball)
Pomoy— Pomoyge, 1400 (Pommau)
Ribarovo— Ryberauw, 1450 (Riebrau)

RECICA, SEKYRA, SVEPET

Recica— Reyze, 1336 (Reitz)
Sece— Zetze, 1360 (Zeetze)
Sekyra— Zecherie, 1800 (Zicherie)
Sirica— Siritze, 1614 (Zieritz)
Strez— Stretze, 1360 (Steetz)
Svepet— Szweput, 1296 (Schiepke)
Techel— Techelhusen, 1450 (Teichlosen)
Tolstovasy— Tolstevance, 1296 (Tolstefanz)

VULKOVIN, VIR, VISOCE

Tupadly— Tupatell, 1451 (Thunpadel)
Vadisin— Wedessem, 1295 (Vadessen)
Vadovici— Waddevitze, 1451 (Waddeweitz)
Vulkovin— Volkevin, 1670 (Volkfine).
Vedrin— Wederin, 1360 (Wedderien)
Vikla— Wichle, 1303 (Wiecheln)
Vir— Wiren, 1540 (Vieren)
Visoce— Wyyzetze, 1352 (Wietzetze)

ZA GORANE, ZA MOCE, ZA RECE

Vitovici— Vitevzen, 1360 (Wittfeitzen)
Vsezegly— Wuzzezegkele, 1352 (Wussegel)
Za Gorane— Zagharan, 1330 (Saggrian)

Za Moce— Sammatze, 1564 (Sammatz)
Za Rece— Sareitze, 1636 (Sareitz)
Zarnoseky— Sartzeke, 1564 (Sarenseck)
Zelen— Zelen, 1330 (Sellien)
Zilov— Zileve, 1352 (Seelwig)
Zirava— Serave, 1451 (Seerau)

BONA SLAVICALIA IN SUWELDORPE

In the case of some mixed names, of Slav-German hybrids, in addition to other changes over time, the Slavic root name is modified by a German ending, namely *dorf*, a German word for village.

BABIN'S DORF, DOMAMIR'S DORF

Bavendorpe (Luneburg)— **Babin's dorf**
Boytelsdorpe (Luneburg)— **Bytila's dorf**
Dalsdorf— **Dal's dorf**
Darrigstorf (Knesebeck)— **Dargo's dorf**
Dumsdorf (Dahlenburg)— **Domamir's dorf**
Gulsdorf (Neuhaus)— **Golisa's dorf**
Jastorf (Medingen)— **Jares's dorf**
Kuhstorf (Knesebeck)— **Kozar's dorf**

RADIS' DORF, TESIMIR'S DORF

Pevestorf (Gartow)— **Pives's dorf**
Prabstorf (Dannenberg)— **Prava's dorf**
Restorf (Gartow)— **Radis' dorf**
Schostorf (Bodenteich)— **Skor's dorf**
Solchsdorf (Medingen)— **Solek's dorf**
Suhlendorf (Bodenteich)— **Sulisa's dorf**
Suschendorf (Dahlenburg)— **Susek's dorf**
Teschendorf (Knesebeck)— **Tesin's dorf**
Tesdorf (Medingen)— **Tes, Tesimir's dorf**

BANZAU

As is more often than not the case in Germania, in the *Duchy of Luneburg* the Slavic origin and character of place names is indicated by certain endings (e.g. place names roots ending in *-au*).

BELAU, GRABAU, KONAU

Banzau, Belau, Bielau, Buckau, Bussau, Darzau, Gaddau, Gielau, Gohlau, Gollau, Grabau, Gustau, Kakau, Kassau, Kolau, Konau, Luckau, Luggau, Maddau, Nestau, Witzeetze, Zeetze

2. HANOVER WENDLAND, VENEDICA GENS

As late as the 18th one could still hear **Slav** or **Wend-Polab** speech (*die polabischer sprache*) or **Wend Drevani** speech (*wendischer sprache Drawey*) in the *Duchy of Luneburg* (*in den luneburgischen Amtern Dannenburg, Lucho und Wustro*), and in the **Wendland** known as **Hanover Wendland** or *das Hannoversche Wendland* (*J.H. Schulze, Etwas uber den Bezirk und namen des wendischen Pagus Drawn, 1795. O. Koch, Das Hannoverschen Wenderland der de Gau Drawehn, 1898. B. Wachter, Zur politischen Organization der Wendlandischen Slawen vom 8. bis 12. Jahrhundert, 1989).*[1]

NICHT WORT DIE DEUTSCHEN SPRACHE

Numerous 17th and early 18th century sources note that in some rural areas the sounds of German speech were seldom heard or understood: **Die alten Leutte, weil sie Wendisch, verstehen nicht Wort die deutschen Sprache, will geschweigen den Catehchisimum, 1669.**

WENDEN, GOTTLOSEN

As some Church officials tended to equate German speech with God's presence, there were even doubts as to God's existence in *Hannoversche Wendland:* **Von der in Wustrow, Luchow und anderer in orten gesessenen Wenden unvernunfftigen gewohnheiten und gottlosen Leben,** 1671.

HABITANTS GENUS DICENDI SLAVONICUM

The linguistic situation in the early 18th century was stated in the following terms by an early authority on the subject, Johannes Freidrich Pffefinger, *Professor der Luneburger Ritterakdademie:* **Habet tandem Venedica gens in Ducatus Luneburgici Praefecturis Luchoviensi et Dannenbergensi habitants genus dicendi Slavonicum, quod considerationem nostram meretur. Derisi quidem homines hujus gentis quondam cum sua lingua a nostyris Saxonibus habiti sunt, act usu illius a Praefectis gravi sub poena interdicto, plerumque ejus se gnaros esse negarunt, quo factum, ut ea inter serniores duntaxat ruricolas vigeat. Et brevi habuissemus gentem vernaculae suae ignaram, nisi sub Georgii Ludovici Serenissimi Electoris nostri clementi regimine ad conservationem atque usum illius iterum excitati fuissent nostri hi Slavi** (*Johannes Freidrich Pffefinger, Vocaubularum Venedicum, 1711*).

DE ORIGINIBUS LINGUAE SORABICAE

Serious interest in the study of the Slavic language in *Hanover Wendland* and Germany's Slavic languages generally was stimulated by Abraham Frencel's pioneering encyclopedic study of the Serbian language or *Srbska rec*, a work that affirmed its antiquity and historical-cultural merit (*M. Abraham Frenceli, De Originibus linguae Sorabicae. Liber primus, 1692; Liber secundus, 1694-96*).

WENDISH OR SARMATIAN LANGUAGE

Dedicating his work with a note of welcome in Serbian to **the great Tsar and Grand Duke Peter I**, expected to visit Dresden, **who with many millions of subjects speaks in our Wendish or Sarmatian language**, Frencel did not hesitate to hail *Linguae Sorabicae's* great political potential.

LIEBNIZ, SERBSKA VOTCHINA

The next important step was taken by a native of the ancient Serb *civitas* of *Lipsk* in the historic *Srbska Votchina*, namely G. W. Liebnitz, the great philosopher, mathematician, and scholar who emerged as a leading patron of efforts to record and preserve the Slavic languages and of Germany. According to the *Slavonic Encyclopaedia*: **William von Liebnitz (1646-1716) was of Slavic descent ... His true name was Labienicz, derived from the river Laba/Elbe**

POLABIAN STUDIES

It is important to note that Liebnitz took a personal, active, and hands-on interest in **Polabian Studies** *(K. Bittner, Slavica bei G.W. von Liebniz, Die polabische Frage, Germanoslavica, 1, 1931)*. One of the first **Polabian** texts (1691), for example, originated in a letter from Liebnitz to Privy Councillor Christian Schrader in Celle, who, in turn, wrote to Georg Friedrich Mithoff, the magistrate in Luchow, regarding Polabian antiquities and language *(G.F. Mithoff, De lingua Winidorum Luneburgensium, 1691)*.

LINGUA WINIDORUM LUNEBURGENSIUM

Thus it is not surprising that the first important collection of texts, vocabulary, and commentary on **lingua Winidorum Luneburgensium** appeared in 1711, namely a study by one of Liebnitz's research assistants, Georgi Eccardi's **Historia Studii Etymologici**.

VOCABULAIRE VANDALE

A sub-section on the Slavic languages of Germany *(De Slavonicae Linguae Dialectiis In Germania Superstitibus, Et De Scriptoribus Huc Spectantibus)* included Professor Pfeffinger's French-Polabian glossary, **Vocabulaire Vandale**, an important source of **Polabian** words and phrases.

VOCABULARIUM VENEDICUM

More importantly, Eccardi's work included excerpts from Christian Hennig von Jessen's German-Wendisch dictionary of some 5,000 words, the most important source of **Polabian** texts and words *(Christian Henning von Jessen, Vocabularium Venedicum, oder Wendisches Worter-Buch, von der Sprache, Welche unter den Wenden in den Chur-Braunschweig-Luneburgischen Amtern Luchow und Wustrow annoch im Schwange gebet, 1711. R. Olesch, Vocabularium von Christian Hennig von Jessen, 1959)*.

SERBSKI KRAJ

Though German by birth, language, and culture, Pastor Hennig's efforts were aided by the fact that he was born in **Serbski kraj**, in Jessen near Cottbus, where he developed an interest in the Serb language and culture of **Serbska Luzica** or Lusatia.

LIEBNIZ, COLLECTANEA ETYMOLOGICA

In 1717 Liebnitz published **Collectanea Etymologica**, a collection that featured a number of Polabian texts and glossaries published for the first time, including an *Anonymous Glossary (Designatio Vocabulorum Aliquot, Winidis Luneburgensibus)*, considered to be the oldest text of its kind, and G.F. Mithoff's **De Lingua Winidorum Luneburgensium**, 1691.

IN LUSATIA ET IN LUNEBURGICO

Slightly more than a decade later, a ***Polab-Serb*** connection will appear in linguistic terms, namely an authoritative study by a member of the *Brandenburg Society of Sciences,* Johann Leonhard Frisch, who finds the Slavic dialects of *Luzica/Lusatia* and the *Duchy of Luneburg* to be closely related *(Johann Leonhard Frisch, De Dialectis Vendorum in Lusatia et in ducatu Luneburgico, 1730. J. Koblischke, Altsorbisches und Drawehnnisches, Slavia 2, 1923).*

ENDNOTES

[1] J.H. Schulze, Etwas uber den Bezirk und namen des wendischen Pagus Drawan, 1795. K. Hennings, Das hannoversche Wendland, 1862; Sagen und Erzahlungen aus dem hannoverschen Wendlande, 1864. H. Steinvorth, Das hannoverske Wendland, 1886. Burgemeister Koch, Das Hannoversche Wendlande oder der gau Drawhen, 1898. F. Tetzner, Polaben im hannoverschen Wendland, 1900. P. Rost, Die Sprachreste der Dravano-Polaben im Hannoverschen, 1907. P. Kuhnel, Interessante slawische Sprachuberrest im hannoverschen Wendlande, 1909. G. Schwantes, Zur Urgeschichte der Slawen in hannoverschen Wendlande, 1914. J. Strelczyk, Z nowszych badean nad dziejmi Drzewian polabskich i hanowerskiego Wendlandu, Studiea historica slavo-germanica, 5, 1976. R. Grenze, Die slawischen Funde aus dem hannoverschen Wendland, 1961. B. Wachter, Deutsche und Slawen in hannoverschen Wendland, Niedersachsisches Jb fur Landesgeschichte, 44, 1972; Die wirtschaflichen und politischen Verhalnisse des 10. Jahrhunderts im Hannoverschen Wendland und angrenzenden Gebieten, ZtA 18, 1984.

Hanover Wendland

3. WENDLANDSICHEN BAUERCHRONIK

It is interesting that a number of local Wendish peasants took an active role in Wendish studies and German efforts to record and preserve the Wendish language and other surviving elements of local Wendish culture.

JAN JANISCHKE

Hennig's research owes much to his collaboration with informant-mentor Jan Janischke, a peasant from Klennow. Indeed, Janischke's contributions were such that Hennig refers to him as his teacher or *Lehr-Meister*.

WENDLANDISCHEN BAUERCHRONIK

The only one to directly leave information about the language and customs of *Hanover Wendland* was Johan Parvum-Schulz (1667-1740), a largely self-educated native of Suthen, a village near Luchow.

PERFECT WENDISH

In his 310-page German language autobiography, *1725)*, Parvum-Schultz writes that his grandfather and father were fluent in both **Wendish** and German: **Meine Grossvater redete zu das Zeit viel auf Wendisch und mein Vater, der wuste die Wendische Sprache auch profect, wie sie beide auch gud Dautsch redeten** *(Wendlandischen Bauerchronik)*. Like his father before him, Johann was mayor or *schultz* of Suthen, thus the adopted family name Schultz. Johan was the son of Jurgen Niebur, and his actual family name was Niebur (Ni-bor, Nibor?). The official record of birth *(Catalogus bapticatorum, 1677)* reads: **Suthen ... Jurgen Nibuers Gattin Suthen sein Sohnlein Johan Parum tauffen lassen** *(R. Olesch, J.P. Schultzii, StF 7, 1967)*.

HALF-WENDISH, HALF-GERMAN

Most others, however, he writes, spoke less than perfect **Wendisch** or good German. Instead, they spoke a mixed language, half-**Wendish**, half-German, which, he explains, had become widespread during the Thirty Year's War: **jn der 30 jahrige Krieg ist die Dautsch Sprache alhier geredet worden. man kann so eben nicht wissen, wo weit diese Sprache in Umkreys ist gebraucht worden, dess es stehet in der Welt Beschreibung, dasz das Mecklenburger Land ist Wendishch gewesenk, denn ihr Konig ist auch Wendisch gewesen. seen ich aber allda im Lande gewesen bis an Wismar, Schwerin, Boitzenburg, Lubeck, Hamberg, und kann ich doch I nicht erforschen, dasz da Wenden gewohnet haben; oder wenn sie gewohnet haben, so muste das Volck ganz ausgerottet worden seyn; denn Ursach dieser, wenn ich nach ihrer Felder Namen oder Wiesen Namen haben gefraget, die haben sie mir alle auf Dautsch hergerecht; denn wenn die felder wendische Namen worin hatten gehabt, so blieb es noch bey dieselbe. ihr auf dieser Umkreysz bis Ueltzen, Ahrendsee, Salzwedel, bey fosfel im Dorf rum haben sie Ziede leiswt, Triep Neist, Tola, Landes Namen; dieses ist auf Wendisch; haben wor diesen reden kunt, und die Elbe Bleckede sin mit wendischen Namen die felder bis auf diesen Tag** *(W. Wedemeyer, Die Chronike des Bauern J.P. Schulze, Hannoverland 8, 1914. R. Olesch, Fontes Lingvae Davaeno-Polabicae Minores et Chronica Venedica J.P. Schlutzii, 1967. W. Schulz, Johann Parum Schultze (1677-1740) -ein wendlandischer Bauer und Chronist, 1978)*.

WENDISH WORDS

Thanks to Schulze, Liebnitz, Henning, A. Hilferding, and others, basic ***Polabian*** words and expressions were preserved *(R. Olesch, Thesarus Linguae Draveanopolabicae, I-IV, 1983-87. D. Gerhardt, Polabische nachlese IV: Parum Schultzes Glossar, FsT H. Kunstmann, 1988).* In spite of the often mangled attempts to capture the language's sounds and grammar, failure to notice and distinguish dialects, and other inaccuracies (e.g. through a field-worker's confusion of gold with cold, Pfeffinger records 'zima' or 'cold' as the ***Wendish*** word for 'gold'), most recorded ***Wendish*** words of all sorts are easily understood by speakers of modern Serbian.

BRADA, DRAVA

In the following series the recorded ***Wendish*** word is followed by its Serbian equivalent and English equivalent.

Broda, Brada— Chin
Bub, Bob— Bean
Bug, Bog— God
Bukva, Bukva— Beech
Carven, Crven— Red
Cesat, Cesat— Brush
Corna, Crno— Black
Criv, Crev– Shoe

Daim, Dim— Smoke
Dan, Dan— Day
Dausa, Dusa— Soul
Deiva, Div— Wild
Deta, Deta— Child
Dirzet, Drzat— To Hold
Dol, Dol— Valley
Drava, Drvo— Wood

GLAVA, KLOBUK

Dumb, Dub— Oak
Glad, Glad— Hunger
Glava, Glava— Head
Gnuj, Gnoj— Manure
Grob, Grob— Grave
Gruzno, Grozno— Ugly
Jautra, Utro— Morning
Jede, Jedi— Eat
Klesda, Klesta— Tongs

Klobuk, Klobuk— Hat
Kreuska, Kruska— Pear
Led, Led— Ice
Leht, Leto— Summer
Leiseitzja, Lisica— Fox
Leva Runka, Leva Ruka— Left Hand
Lostoweitzia, Lastavica— Swallow

MEDA, PIVO

Meda, Meda— Honey
Metlam Metla— Broom
Mlauka, Mleko— Milk
Molareka, Malareka— Small River
Molavoda, Malavoda— Stream
Muckra, Mokra— Wet
Nebuy, Nebo— Sky
Nidiglia, Nedelja— Sunday

Nigga, Noga— Leg, Foot
Pehre, Peri— Wash
Pero, Pero— Feather
Perundan, Cetvrtak— Thursday
Peyje, Pije— Drink
Pnediglia, Ponedelja— Monday
Pas, Pas— Dog
Pivo, Pivo— Beer

PLUG, POSTEL

Piosak, Pesak— Sand
Pic, Pec— Oven
Plauca, Pluca— Lungs
Plauck, Plug— Plough
Plokat, Plakati— To Cry
Plone, Pljosni— Flat land
Plosat, Plesat— Dance
Porstin, Prsten— Ring

Postil, Postel— Bed
Puhje, Poja— Sing
Punct, Put— Path
Pupeel, Pepel— Ash
Rado, Rado— Gladly
Ramang, Rama— Shoulder
Rana, Rano— Early
Rebra, Rebra— Rib

REC, SLAMA

Rec, Rec— Speech
Reibo, Riba— Fish
Reka, Reka— River
Runka, Ruka— Hand
Ryk, Rog— Horn
Sehna, Zena— Woman
Setiar, Sekir— Ax
Schlepe, Slep— Blind

Schwetza, Svetlo— Light
Seyma, Zima— Winter
Sestra, Sestra— Sister
Siewat, Zivot— Life
Slamu, Slama— Straw
Sleisat, Slusat— Listen
Sluvo, Slovo— Word
Skokne, Skok— Jump

SREBRO, SVETI

Schmarde, Smurd— Stink
Sobo, Zabo— Frog
Srebru, Srebro— Silver
Sreeda, Sreda— Wednesday
Sriv, Crev— Shoe
Staudinac, Studenac— Well
Stohr, Star— Old
Stoyje, Stoj— To Stand
Strajah, Stric/Striko— Uncle
Suboida, Subota— Saturday

Svate, Sveti— Holy
Sveca, Sveca— Candle
Sveinya, Svinja— Pig
Svetet, Svetao— Bright
Tama, Tama— Dark
Tila, Tela— Calf
Tilca, Ptica— Bird
Tjord, Tverd— Hard
Toplu, Toplo— Warm
Trase, Trese— Shakes

VAN, CREVU

Vana, Van— Outside
Vilkavoda, Velkavoda— Ocean
Vlassa, Kosa— Hair
Voda, Voda— Water
Vohl, Vol— Ox
Voska, Vosak/Voska— Wax
Vovoda, Voivoda— Prince
Vuhk, Vuk— Wolf
Watorna, Zatvor— Prison
Vuhu, Uho— Ear

Vauja, Ujak— Mother's brother
Zal, Zal— Sorrow
Zat, Zet— Son-in-Law
Zena, Zena— Woman
Zeyve, Sivo— Grey
Zlata, Zlata— Gold
Zohrne, Crne— Black
Zori, Zore— Dawn
Zornu, Zrno— Kernel
Zrevu, Crevu— Intestine

PERUNDAN, POREIN

One cannot help but notice that the **Polabian** word for *Thursday*, **Perendan/Perundan** or **Perun's Day**, and lighting a fire, recorded as **Porein**, are obviously derived from the ancient Slavic deity **Perun**, the lord of thunder, lightning, and fire.

PHRASES

Even the most cursory review of common phrases reveals the strongest ties with the modern Serb.

Good-bye— **Sabuggom (Zbogom)**
Good morning— **Dibbre jautra (Dobro utro)**
Good evening— **Dibbre vjtzeer (Dobro vecer)**
Good night— **Dibbre noc (Dobro noc)**
Can't eat— **Ni muse jest (Ne moze jest)**
Can't chew— **Ni muse sawat (Ne moze zvakat)**
The child is crying— **Deta plohtze (Deta place)**
The child is shouting— **Deta vuhtze (Deta vice)**

FINIS LINGVAE DRAVAENOPOLABICAE

A recent article by the foremost modern authority on the **Polab/Hanover/Dravani Wends**, Professor Olesch traces the languages's last moments in the mid-late 18th century *(R. Olesch, Finis Lingvae Dravaneopolabicae, FsT F. von Zahn, MdF 50/1, 1968).*[1] It is clear from the sources cited by Olesch that the Wendish language did not die entirely from natural causes, but in great part from repressive official policies and prohibitions. Regarding the impact of such policies on the **Wends** of the Luchow district, in the early 18th century, citing a sympathetic observer, Olesch writes: **Dass die Wenden solch ihr wesen, so viel muglich, heimlich halten, da es ihnen verboten ist, dies berichet aus Luchow, in gegenwart der geistl. und beampten kein wendisch zureden.** That such public policies encouraged private hostilities against the **Wends** and **Wendish** is clear from many sources. Regarding one such moment, Henning writes: **Und wenn die Teutschen einen horen Wendisch sprechen, haben sie mit Fingern auf Ihn gewiesen und ihren Spott mit ihm getriebe: Wesswegen ein steter Hass unter ihnen entsprungen, duer sich auch noch nicht gantzlich gelegt: obgleich dieses Orts kein gross Wunder mehr draus gemacht wird, wenn beyderley Nationen, Teutsche und Wende, sich untereinander verheyrathen.**

ENDNOTES

[1] R. Olesch, Dravenopolabica I, 1989; Cetera Slavica II, 1992. Also: J.B. Maly, Ponemcili Slovane lunebursti a jejich vlasnosti, CmC, Prague, 1857. A.J. Parczewski, Potomkowie Slowian v Hannoverskim, Wisla, 13, 1899. F. Tetzner, Die Drawehner im hannoverschen Wendlande um das Jahr 1700, Globus, 81, 1902. P. Kuhnel, Slawische Familiennamen in der Stadt Hannover, Hannoverland, 1907. B. Syzdglowska-Ceglowa, Dras Dravanopolabische des 17. und 18. Jahrhunderts als Zeugnis eines untergehenden Slawenstammes, SfS 32. 1987.

PART XV

1. THURINGIA: RESPUBLICA SORABICI

Onomastic and other evidence make it clear that Slavic settlement in Germania did not end or dissipate south and west of the Elbe and Saale rivers. In fact, *Serb-Wend* settlement in this area was equally intense and wide-ranging and long the subject of informed inquiry. Regarding the circumstances of the *Slavs called Serbs* occupation and settlement, a German historian writes: **Attacking and expelling the ancient Teutons, they moved across the Elbe and Saale and settled the lands there.**

THURINGIA

In eastern Thuringia, the same historian writes, they displaced the resident German nation: **Attacking and expelling the Hermenduri, the Slavs also called Serbs, then occupied the mines near Halle.**[1]

DOBRI SOL

According M.C. Spangenberg's 16th century study, *Quernfurtische Chronicka*: **The Serbs established a town, Dobrisol (Good Salt) near the salt mines at Halle and established strong fortifications at Meteriz and Podegrodici, near Mt. Premysl [now Mt. Priemauselm 625m].**

SALTUS SCLAVORUM

Early medieval sources refer to the Thuringian highlands as ***saltus Sclavorum***, while the dense Thuringian Forest was known as *Lovia,* a Slavic word connoting hunting ground *(L. Gerbin, Die Verbreitung der Loiba-Namens im Thuringerwald, MvH 1904. P. Mitzschke, Der Waldname Loiba, MvH, 1908. W. Schindhelm, Slawisch-deutsche Beziehungen auf dem Thuringer Wald und in seinem sudlichen Vorland im Lichte der Ortsnamen, OsG 4, 1968).*

SORABICI LIMITIS, RESPUBLICA SORABICI

Some 9th century German sources refer to Thuringia as *Sorabici limitis*. Other German sources refer to Thuringia as *respublica Sorabici: Interea nuntiatum est ei in oriente respublica Sorabici limitis, esse turbatam, eq quod Sorabi duce eius Zistiboro nomine sibi fidelissimo perempto defectionem meditarentur (858).*

DUX SORABICI LIMITIS

In the mid-9th century German authority in Thuringia was represented by Takulf: *dux Sorabici limitis: Thachulf scienti leges et consuetudines Sclavicae gentis; erat quippe dux Sorabici limitis (849).*

COMES ET DUX

Poppo, Takulf's successor, had a similar title: ***Poppo, comes et dux Sorabici limitis.*** At this time, writes a noted Polish historian, the evidence suggests that Thuringia was a Serb borderland under German march administration: **A wiec rowniez i w wypadku limesu serbskiego odnosna marchia miescila sie w obrebie owczesnego terytorium turyngskiego, a przylegajace do Turyngii ksiestwa slowianskie byly jednie** poddane nadzorowi frankonskiego margrabiego. Wynika z tego, ze godnosc: "dux Sorabici limitis" byla w istocie rzeczy tym samym co godnosc: "marchio Thoringorum" *(J. Strzelczyk, Djiejow Slowianzsczyzny zachodniej, 1975; Turyngia-Slowianie w Turyngii, SsS 6, 1977).*

PATRIA SCLAVORUM

One finds the term *patria Sclavorum* in a 953 grant from Otto I's vassal, Bilingus (e.g. *in pago Neletici in comitatu Bilingi comitis, 965*) to St. Maurice's monastery (*sanctum Mauritium*): *Bilingus ... nobis tradidit pro prorietare nostra, qual illi donavimus in patria Sclavorum et in Thuringia.*

ULTRA SLAVONICA VILLA

A 1068 document records Henry IV's grant of a number of Slavic villages in north Thuringia to the Bishop of Halberstadt in the following terms: *Villis Bredenstidi et in alio Bredanstidi, Lamseli Stimpeli, Nagorit et ultra Ara slavonica villa in potestate Udonis marchionis sitos.*

FAMILIAS SCLAVORUM

In 10th, 11th, and 12th century registers relating to north Thuringia and bordering areas one finds numerous references to the number of Slav families or homes in a village, and in mixed German-Slav communities, the number of German colonists.

- Balgestat (*hube III de Sclavis manentibus*)
- Biscofeshusun (*villam qu dicitur Biscofeshusun et sunt ibi hube XXXa et manent Sclavi*)
- Bucow (*XII familias sclavorum in buchow [in pago northuringa]*)
- Butesstat (*in Bubesstat et Dungede et Suabehusun hubas XII, et Sclavi habitant ibi*)
- Byere (*in byere IX mansos slavicum byere totum X scilicet mansos*)
- Drummaresdorf (*huba I Sclavis manentibus*)
- Friedemaresleba (*in friedemaresleba in pago nordduringa LVI familias sclavorum*)
- Grimhereslebu (*in grimhereslebu [in pago norturinga] XV familias sclavorum*)
- Lizichesdorf (*hube III de Sclavis manentibus*)
- Miluhesdorf (*hube II Sclavis manentibus*)
- Mulnhusun, Remmidi, Rudolfestat (*hubas VII, et Sclavi manent in illis*)
- Pamuchesdorf (*hube IIII Sclavis manentibus*)
- Pizzenitse (*VII familias sclavorum in pizzenitse*)
- Pretulitse (*VIII familias sclavorum in pretulise*)
- Rodenstein (*In Rodestein humas XIIII et Sclavi manent ibi*)
- Rundunestorf (*In Rundunestorf hube II de Sclavi menentibus*)
- Trumpsitse (*XX familias sclavorum in trumpsitse [in pago nordthuringa]*)
- Vmisa (*hube III Sclavis manentibus*)

- Vraso (*in vraso familias sclavanicas XV et totidem in Calvo*)
- Vuiterihhesdorp (*in vuiterihhesdorp [in pago nordduringa] XXIII familias sclavorum*)
- Wenninge (*hube XXX, et ibi Sclavi manent*)
- Zatesdorf (*in Zastesdorf hube IIII de Sclavis manentibus*).[2]

VITEZI, VULCI

Among the Slavic villages (e.g. Cudenicze, Gline, Stubene) recorded in an 1121 document relating to a monastery near Halle, two names are especially interesting, namely *Uvitazewice*, a *Vitaz/Vitez* settlement, and *Uvilce*, a *Vulci* (?) settlement, the former connoting *knights*, the latter, settlers from the *Vulci/Lyutic* (?) lands.

KIEV RUS, POLAND

A comprehensive and systematic anthropological-archaeological analysis of the 11th to 12th century graveyard of Epsenfeld, a Slavic village near Arnstadt, reveals strong commercial ties with other Slavic lands: **The economic base of the Slavonic inhabitants of Epsenfeld was the commerce. Imported objects reveal far reaching commercial connections with the district of the 'Kiev Rus'. From there the pearls of semiprecious stones made of carnelian and rock-crystal have spread on the trade-routes known in the Middle Ages along the Volga and Dnieper, across the Baltic Sea-communications and along the trade-route directing across Poland, Saxony, and Thuringia, which connected Kiev with the Rhine district. Other imported goods, e.g. ornaments and some types of finger rings, refer to Polish origin** *(S. Dusek, Das spatslawische Graberfeld von Epsenfeld, Kr. Arnstadt, EzT 12, 1971).*[3]

ENDNOTES

[1] R. Schottin, Die Slave n in Thuringen, 1884. W. Carmesin, Thuringen in der Slawenpolitik der Merowinger, 1925. C. Albrecht, Die Slawen in Thuringen, Jahresschrift fur die Vorgeschichte der sachsisch-thuringischen Lander 12, 1925. M. Waehler, Die einstigen slavischen Nebensiedelungen in Thuringen, Beitrage zur Thuringischen und sachsischen Geshichte, 1929. B. Schmidt, Die spate Volkerwanderungszeit in Ostthuringen und das Einzugsbebiet der Slawen in Mitteldeutschland, WmL 3,1954. K. Steinbruck, Slawensiedlungen um Aschersleben, Harz-Zeitschrift 8, 1956. R. Schmidt, Zur Entstehung und Kontinuitat des Thuringerstammes, Germanen-Slawen-Deutsche, Forschungen zu ihrer Ethnogenese, 1969.

[2] H. Rempel, Die sorbische Keramik in Thuringen, PzT 37, 1959. E. Eichler, Zur germanoslawistischen Namenforschung in Sachsen und Thuringen, FuF 34, 1960. S. Dusek, Deutsch-slawische Kontakte im westsaalischen Thuringen des 10. bis 12. Jh, BeR, 1973. S. Dusek, Geschichte und Kultur der Slawen in Thuringen, 1983.

[3] S. Dusek, Deutsch-slawische Kontakte im westsaalischen Thuringen den 10. bis 12. Jh, BeR, 1973. E. Eichler, Zur gemanoslawistischen Namenforschung in Sachsen und Thuringen, FuF 34, 1960. W. Schlesinger, Geschichte Thuringen, 1967.

2. MYSI, VOITLAND, FRANCONIA: HELVETI SERBS

Early **Serb-Wend** settlement of *Mysi, Voitland,* and *Franconia* is a matter of massive onomastic fact and positive historical record. A 16th century compilation of sources, *Chronicon Saxionar,* identifies the settlers of *Mysi et Vogtland* as **Helveti Serbs: Voitland and Mysi were settled by the Helveti Serbs.**[1]

UPPER MAIN AND FULDA

From *Mysi* and *Voitland,* according to W. Schlesinger, a distinguished postwar historian: **The Serbs, moving south and southwest, settled along the Upper Main and the Fulda.**

FRANCONIA

An early 19th century German historian, N. Haas, is impressed with the antiquity, scope, and density of **Serb-Wend** settlements in Franconia. The fact that Frankish sources document the existence of **Windogau** county as early as 418, Haas writes, strongly suggests Slav settlement a century or centuries earlier. In fact, Hass writes: **The existence of Slav counties in the Windsheim area as early as 418 is the reason that scholars believe that the Winds or Wends were the ancient and original settlers of Franconia** *(N. Haas, Geschichte des Slaven-landes and der Aisch und den Erbrach-Fluchen, 1819).* In *East Franconia,* Hass notes: **The Bamberg bishopric was called 'Slavenland' in the 9th century.**

MAIN WENDEN, REGNITZ WENDEN

It is also a matter of record that lands along the Main and Regnitz rivers were settled by Slavs. Medieval documents, Hass writes, refer to the land between the Main and Regnitz rivers as *Main Wenden* and *Regnitz Wenden:* ***Qui sedent inter Moinum et Radantiam fluuios, qui vocantur Moinuvinidi et Radanzuvinidi.***

SLAVS, MAINLY SLAVS

Haas' examination of the historical record leads him to believe that: **Slavs, mainly Slavs, settled along the Regnitz, Main, Aurax, Wiesent, Aisch, Itz, and Bauhnah rivers; that the Slavs founded the towns and cities of Erlangen, Forheim, Halstaat, Bamberg, Oberheid, Baunau, and Eltman.**

WIND TOWNS AND CITIES

Haas points to the number of towns and cities obviously derived from the **Wind** ethnikon, including, among others: **Burgvindheim, Ferchwin, Meschelvind, Neumanswind, Obervind, Popenvind, Untervindbach, Valdsvind, Vind, and Vindek.**

SOLIDLY SLAV

Regarding the Slav settlement of eastern Franconia, a noted 20th century German authority observes: **The greater portion of eastern Franconia, the Upper Main, around Bayreuth, Bamberg, Wurzberg, and Nuremberg was solidly Slav before the year 1000.**

REGIO I TERRA SLAVORUM

In all of *Upper Franconia* and *Lower Franconia* to *Stiegerwald*, writes E.O. Schulz, a late 19th century German scholar, the **Serb-Wend** settlements were called **Moinwinidima and Ratanzwinidima and the land between the Main, Regnitz and Aisch rivers was known as 'Regio i terra Slavorum'** *(E.O. Schulz, Die Klonisierung und Germanisierung der Gebeite Zwischen Saale und Elbe, 1896).*

SERB-WEND NAMES

Thus, Schulz writes, the great number of towns originating in **Serb-Wend** settlements and derived from **Serb-Wend** names, among others: **Colmberg, Hummelstein, Kulmbach, Mogelndorf, Mugendorf, Muggenhof, Pegnitz, and Rezat.**

MOUNT DOBRA

It is perhaps not without interest or significance that the highest point in the Franconian Forest, **Mount Dobra**, has retained its ancient Slavic name.

ENDNOTES

[1] G. Hey, Die slavischen Siedlungen im alten Vogtland, Unser Vogtland 3, 1896-97.J. Richter, Eine neue slawische Fundstelle im Vogtland, AuF 1, 1956.E. Eichler, J. Leipoldt, Zur Deutung und Verbreitung der slawischen Flurnamen des Vogtlandes, Jb des Msuseum Hohenleuben-Reichenfels 11, 1962. V. Hellfritzsch, Zum Problem der slawischen Personennamen im Vogtland, OsG 2, 1966 E. Eichler, Die slawischen Ortsnamen des Vogtlandes, Le1 A/14, 1967. V. Hellfritsch, Vogtlandische Personennamen. Untersuchungen am Material der Kreise Plauen und Oelsnitz, 1969. J. Strzelczyk, Vogtland, SsS 6, 1977. V. Hellfritsch, J. Richter, Die Ortsnamen des sachsischen Vogtlandes, 1-2, 1983.

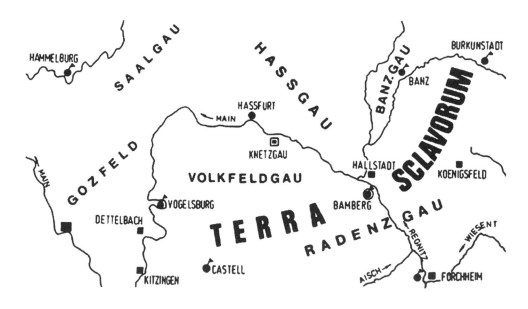

Terra Sclavorum

3. MOINUVINIDI, SERBORUM

From the Bamberg woodlands to deep into the Thuringian forest, to Erfurt and Eichsfeld, the countryside, according to Edward Otto Schulz, was settled almost exclusively by Slavs/Serb-Wends.

TERRA I REGIO SLAVORUM

Schultz's words are well documented by medieval monastery-convent registers and related documents. In 741-742, St. Boniface founded several historic sees in *Terra i Regio Slavorum*: *In terra Sclavorum, qui sedent inter Moinum et Radantium fluvios, qui vocantur Moinuuinidi et Ratanzuuinidi una cum comitibus qui super eosdem Sclavos constituti erant, procurassent, ut inibi sicut in ceteris Christianorum loci ecclesias construerentur, qutenus ille populus noviter ad Christianitatem conversus habere potuisset, ubi et baptismum perciperet, 864.*

SEE OF WURZBURG

One see at Wurzburg, the See of Wurzburg *in Slavorum* (*iuxta ripam Moin in regione sclavorum*), on the Moin/Main River in that part of *Slavorum* known as *Moinuvinidi* or *Main Wenden*, is granted: *Ecclesias in confinus Francorum et Saxonum atque Sclavorum suo officio deputavit.*

All 9th century and later sources confirm the mission of the see: to convert the native Slav pagans of *Terra Slavorum*: *Wolfgerius, Wirciburgensis ecclesie episcopu ... praecepisset, ut in terra Sclavorum, qui sedent inter Moinum et Radanziam fluvios, qui vocantur Moiwinidi et Radanzwinidi, una cum comitibus, qui super eosdem Sclavos constituti erant, procurassent, ut inibi sicut in ceteris christianorum locis ecclesie construerentur ... in terra praedictorum Sclavorum a memoratis episcopis constructae sunt, 826-830; Ut in terra Sclavorum, qui sedent inter Moinum et Radantiam fluvios, qui vocantur Moiuvinidi et Ratanzuvinidi ... qui super eosdem Sclavos constituti erant, procurassent, ut inibi sicut in ceteris crisitianorum locis ecclesiae construerentur...in terra praedictorum Sclavorum, 845; Arn Uirziburcensis aeclesiae episcopus nobis unum obtulit praceptum ... ut in terra Sclavorum, qui sedent inter Moinum et Radantiam fluvios, qui vocantur Moinuvinida et Radanzvuinida, una cum comitibus, qui super eosdem Sclauos constituti erant, procurassent, ut ibi sicut in ceteris christianorum locis aecclessiae construerentur, 889.*

SERBORUM

The *Wurzburg Privileges* refers to the See's subjects in the following terms: *In Privilegiis enim Virceburgensibus aliquibus mentio fit Vinidorum, Slavorum, Serborum, Mainvinidorum ac Radenvinidorum.*

SLAVS OCCUPYING CHURCH LANDS

In the 8th century the Bishop of Wurzberg seeks the Pope's permission to **Levy a tax on the Slavs occupying Church lands.** Such tax is both proper and necessary, Pope Zacharias answers: **For if they are made to pay tithes they will know who is the lord of the land.**

ABBEYS OF FULDA

On the Fulda River, St. Boniface's disciple Sturm founded the great Benedictine abbey of Fulda in 744. The abbey is soon the great Christianizing-Germanizing center of *Terra i Regio Slavorum*. By 822 there were 134 monks at Fulda, 600 men and women in orders, and some 4,000 more involved in the abbey's affairs. Their services were well rewarded. Grants of land and immunities gave the abbey great wealth: abbots became princes of the Holy Roman Empire and each monk became lord of an estate.

IN REGIONE SLAVIORUM

From its founding onward, the abbey's wealth was increased by numerous endowments of Slav villages by royal and noble patrons.

> • *In Sclavis in Heidu et in Truosnasteti,* 796
>
> • *In villa, quae vocatur Turphilun iuxta ripam fluminis Moin, in regione Slaviorum,* 824
>
> • *Vuinidsazin et in tribus villis Sclavorum et Vuinidon in pago Salagouue Steinbach et Leibolfes, Vuillimundesheim,* 953
>
> • *Quicquid in Frekenleba et Scekenstedt et Arnei et Lembeki et Faeresrod et Kerlingorod et Mannesfeld et Duddondorp et Rodonnuusalii et Nienstedt, et Purtin et Elesleba aliisve villis vel billarum partibus quas Sclavanicae familiae inhabitant, ad haec lo-cal pertinentibus,* 973
>
> • *Ezzilo comes tradidit s. Boanifation in eadem Slavorum regione villas has: Tutenstet, Lonrestat, Wachenrode, Sampach et Stetebach simul cum inhabitantibus Slavis, qui singulis annis censum reddere debent Fuldensi monasterio,* 1150

IN SUMERDI ... SCLAVI 13

The abbey's records and bookkeeping give detailed information regarding the duties and obligations of its Slavic subjects (*Sclavi nostri*). The following information, from a compilation known as *Codex Eberhardi* (1155-1165), relates to typical villages, most with German names.

DRAGENENFELDEN, LIUBCHENDORF

Abettesrode • Agecella • Bezzingen • Biberha • Breitenbach • Cruciburc • Dewinesdorf • Dragenenfelden • Drewichesdorf • Engelmarestat • Esgenebach • Fliedena • Folmaresdorf • Gerstungen • Geysaha • Goltbach • Hagen • Hamphestat • Haselo • Heringen • Hunifelt • Liubchendorf

RADISTORF, SUMERDE

Ludera • Luturenbach • Lypenszo • Nitharthusen • Nuenburc • Otricheshusen • Radistorf • Richenbach • Rora • Salzaha • Salzungen • Sconerstete • Spanelho • Steinbach • Stetifelt • Sulaha • Sumerde • Sulzbach • Varegelaha • Vgesberge • Westera

SCLAVI

In the following series, the typical duties and obligations in kind and coin of dependent Slavs in a number of villages are listed in varying degrees of detail.

- *In Abbertesrode ... Sclavi XXIII cum lino et avena reddentes. Insuper sunt VI hube quarum V siclos X et denarios XXX debent. Sclavi XXX ex his ad LXX camisiales debent.*

- *In Agecelia ... Insuper XII coloni singuli victimam i ouem uel capram et I gallinam cum X ouis Sclavi XXXVII quorum quisque ad duas camisiales linum dat et I paltenam et V modios auene. Adhec sunt XV coloni qui reddunt denarios.*

- *In Bezzingen ... Sclavi XXVIII quorum quisque I lodicem duplicem exceptis VI qui dant XII lodices et lini ad IIII et dimidium pannum XX modios frumenti et XX oues et XX arietes et bracium ad V ceruisias. Beneficii sunt XIII et dimidia huba. Due ecclesie cum duabus hubis.*

- *In Biberaha ... lidi VI Sclavi XXXVI servitores XXXVII tributarii XII qui unam uitimam soluunt. Limares villa XI sunt tributarii. Piscatores II cum suo beneficio.*

- *In Breitenbach ... XVIIII mansionarii totidem porcos et totidem arietes persolunt. De Sclavis ibidem commorabntibus XIIII libre lini et totidem modiide Sclavis ibidem commorantibus 8 libre lini et totidem modii auene et paltene totidem soluuntur. Et sinsuper V sicli pro hiemali opere mulierum redduntur.*

- *In Curciburc ... Insuper VIII uiri quorum unusqisque cutem caprinam et certam XII. taltentorum. Sclavi V linum et lanam reddunt*

- *In Engelmarestat ... Quidam liberorum id est Sclavorum cum libra lini.*

- *In Gerstungen ... Insuper 55 Sclavi singulos porcos ... Ad hec 23 Sclavi singulos porcos. Insuper 95 Sclavi, ex quibus 95 libri lini debentur singulesque paltene.*

- *In Geysaha ... Sclavi LV ex quibus XLIII cum lino XII librarum aut cum phalta reddunt. Omnes autem simul CCCC. XC modios bracii uel auene cum singulis modiis tritici uel siguli. Omnes hi habent CC. XV mansos. molend. X Insuper beneficium V hube et I molend ad villam respic.*

- *In Goltbach et circumiacentibus locis II territoria XXXIX hube singule singulas oues cum triduano servicio Sclavi V cum suo debito.*

- *In Gestungen ... Insuper LV Sclavi singulos porcos singulasque phaltas et III gallinas cum ovis. Adhec XXIII Sclavi singulos porcos. Insuper XCV Sclavi ex quibus CL libre lini debentur singuleque paltene.*

- *Ad Hagen ... Sclavi CXX singulas libras lini singulosque lodices duplices et unum modium auene ... Adhec predicti Sclavi primo anno decem porcos et VIIII lodices in secundo anno X lodices et VIIII porcos et totidem arietes in mense maio.120 singulas libras ... Ad hoc predicti Sclavi primo anno.*

- *In Heringen ... Sclavi L. unuwqisque linum ad II pannos et uname victimam por et avene ad VII ceruisie carradas. Insuper XXIII Sclavi singuli linum ad unum pannum et IIII modios avene et dimidiam paltenam. Adhec in novalibus XXX beneficia denarios reddunt.*

- *In Hunifelt ... Sclavi XXXV cum suo debito solvunt libras totidem lini*

- *In Ludera ... Sclavi cum pleno beneficio XI cum dimidio beneficio IIII Insuper sunt novem singulos boues persoluentes. Alie hube XII cume melle reddunt. Preterea cetere hube IIII talenta reddunt et X uncias set novem vaccas.*

- *In Lupenzo ... VI territoria lidi V singuli porcos saginatos et singuli pannos debent. Insuper alii decem singulos porcos saginatos singulosque pannos ... Sclavi uero L cum suo debito. Insuper XXVIII Sclavi kozzos reddunt. 66 camisiales debent Sclavi vero 50...Insuper 28 Sclavi Kossos reddunt.*

- *In Otriceshusen Sclavi sunt XI unusquisque persoslit siclos II.*

- *In Radisdorf ... in Fomaresdorf et Haselaho ... Sclavorum unusquique XL liberoum quisque XX meldatorum quisque XIII sunt molendine IIII.40.*

- *In Richenbach ... lidi X olim erant ... Sclavi XXX servitores XVIII tributarii XL singuli cum suo debito censu ut supra.*

- *In Salzungen ... Sclavi XXIIII cum lino reddunt. Omnes uero Slavi respic ... Omnes vero Sclavi singuli gallinam unam et X ova debent*

- *In Spanelo ... Et insupre V singulas oues singulasque carradas frument Sclavi LXXXVI singuli ad pannum linum et XXVII paltenas et auene ad XXVII carradas ceruisie. Adhec X linum et denarium reddunt. t avene at 27 carradas cervisiae.*

- *In Sulaha ... Sclavi XVI, quorum XVIII plenam libram lini et 1 phaltum et I gallinam et II modios avene ... Insuper XVIII Sclavi qui reddunt dum denar.*

- *In Sumerde ... Sclavi XIII quorum unusqiusque unam libram lini debet et duas phlatenas. In noualisbus sunt XL et I colonii qui CC libras reddunt lini et aune totidem modios.*

- *In Ugesberga ... Sclavi 9 singuli ... Sunt alli Sclavi coloni, singulos porcoes singulasques oves debentes, exceptis tribus, quorum quisque duos porcos et 2 oves debent*

- *In Vargelaha ... Sclavi XIII singulos lodices debent. Et septem ecclesie cum duabus hubis singule ... Sclavi sunt VIII qui singulos lodices duplices debent. Molendinae XVIII uinee due Beneficii seunt XI hube.*

- *In Vgesberge ... Sclavi VIIII singuli I libram lini et unam paltenam unam gallinam cuym V ouvis. Sunt alii Sclavi coloni singulos sporcos singulas oues debentes exceptis tribus quorum quisque duo porcos et II oues debent. Decem uiri singuli singulas situlas mellis debent et II. XXX denarios.*

- *In Weitaha lidi VI servitores XX Sclavi XIII Iuniores eorum V servitores XX.*

- *In Westera ... Sclavi II linum et avenam, gallinam et ova debent.*

ERFURT

In the year 742 Boniface founded a second see in **Terra i Regio Slavorum** at Erfurt/Brod, on the Gera (Gora?) River, an area, according to a 16th century German chronicle, occupied by the **Serb-Wends** in the mid-5th century. By 805 Erfurt was an important military-administrative center on the eastern border of the Frankish empire. By the mid-12th century the See gained ducal authority over almost all of eastern Franconia.

IN SARBUNEN

As with Fulda, this See's records document the area's deep Slavic roots and character: ***In villa Doubeke XI manses ... in Sarbunen I mansum.***

IURA SLAVORUM

In 12th and 13th century Latin documents relating to Church estates in ***regione Sclavorum*** one finds references *to* ***iura Slavorum*** and ***schlavico iure:*** *Hoc etiam propter predictam oblationem ab abbate impetrarunt, quod advocato nullum placitum persolvunt, cetera vero legitima iura Slavorum, quae constituta sunt pro cedibus vel furto aliisque culpis quae suboriri poterunt, tempore vel loco, quo abbati placuerit, persolvere debebunt, 1136;* ***In Deusne schlavico iure possident bona et homines, qui antiquo iuro suo innitentes, decimam dari nondum consentiunt, ita et eodem iure et eadem consuetudine,*** *1189.*

ZMURDI, ZMURDORUM

In the same period one finds numerous Latin documents using the Slavic word ***smurdi*** (Latin, *plebanus*) in defining the status of ***Sclavi nostri*** *(J. Schutz, Frankens Mainwendische Namen. Geschichte und Gegenwart, 1994; Strukturelemente des Mainwendischen, ZsP 56, 1997).*

> • ***In Matheliz*** *VIII mansi sunt et totidem aree, quorum IIIIor sunt* ***smurdorum*** *... idem* ***zmurdi*** *arare, emundare et metere debent curie aut dabunt IIII modios so; ogomos et trotocvo ... Item quilibet* ***zmurdorum*** *dabit XXX tegetes ad tegendum oreum*

> • ***In Cozede*** *XV manse et tot aree, quorum X sunt* ***zmurdorum*** *... Quintus decimus et* ***zmurdicus,*** *pertinent ad jus villicale*

> • ***In Colend*** *VIII manse et totidem aree, quorum IIII sunt* ***zmurdorum***

> • ***In Zenplicen*** *IX mansi et tot aree, quorum IIII sunt* ***zmurdorum***

> • ***In Frosa*** *mansi servicii seu* ***smurdonum*** *homines in quinque iustitiis ut edelsten, knechte,* ***zmurde***

Knez/Knetz Gau

4. RADANZUVINIDI, SERBORUM

On the *Radantian* or Regnitz River, in *Radanzuvinidi* or *Regnitz Wenden*, in the year 1007 Holy Roman Emperor Henry II founded the See of Bamberg, a missionary base among the *pagan* Slavs/Serb-Wends of the Upper Main region.

IN VICINAS SCLAVORUM

The imperial cathedral contains the tomb of Henry II, who is remembered in the following missionary terms: *Ut et paganimus sclavorum destrueretur et christiani nominis memoria perpeualiter inibi cerebris haberetur ... Per quam ecclesiam et de inimico humani generis in vicinas Sclavorum gentes Deo opitulante, truimphabit.*

EX MAXIMA PARTE SCLAVONICA

In the Synod of Bamberg proceedings of 1058 one reads: *Erat einim plebs hujus episcopi utprote ex maxima parte Sclavonica.*

DE SCLAVIS

In 1059 the Synod declares that an increase in tithes is a just motivation for the forcible conversion of Slavs: *Decimam tributi quae de partibus orientalium Franchorum, vel de Sclavis ad fiscum dominicum annuatim persolvere solebant quae secundum illorum linguam steora vel ostastuopha vocant.*

ABHORRENS A RELIGIONE CHRISTIANA

The same Synod confirms the fact that most Slavs remained firm in their opposition to the predatory Christian order: *Maxima parte Sclavonica ... abhorrens a religione Christiana.*

SCLAVOS IBI HABITARE

In 1111, Arnold, Bishop of Halberstadt, informs Otto of Bamberg, that the countryside is filled with Slavs: *Totam illam terram paene silvam esse, Sclavos ibi habitare.*

90% SLAVISCHER PROVENIENZ

Recent excavations relating to the late 6th and 7th centuries tend to confirm the Slavic character of the land. In a recent article H. Jakob cites the results of the 'Domgasse' excavation: **Diese Anschauung hat nun die 1987 begonnene Grossgrabund in der Domgasse und vor allem in der Alten Hofhaltung nicht nur voll bestatigt, sondern daruber hinaus die erstaunliche Erkenntnis vermittelt, dass hier unter dem reichlich gehobenen Keramikmaterial bisher ca. 90% slavischer Provenienz sind und nur 10% germanisch, wahren es bei der Grabung von 1969-72 genau umgekehrt war**

(H. Jakob, Beitrage zum paganismus der Main- und Regnitzwenden, Ars Philologica Slavica, FsT H. Kunstmann, 1988).

KNEZ ZUPA, KNETZ GAU

Medieval sources reveal an ancient *Serb-Wend zupa,* in *partibus Sclaviniensibus* northwest of Bamberg, centered in an area bound by Hassfurt in the north and Eltmann in the south, namely *Knez-zupa*, later **Knetz-gau**. Also *Kencegowe*, 800; *Chenezogewe*, 815; *Knezgowe*, 900; *in loco Chnzziseo et in villa Chenizzgowa*, 911; *Knetzgau*, 1200; *Knetzburg*, 1575: *Ego Ilbinc trado sancto Bonifacio in Folcfelden predia mea in villis subscriptis: Knezcegewe ... et in Winideheim; In partibus Sclaviniensibus vero in comitatu Dudleipa vocato in loco Ruginesfeld, sicut Chocil dux ... in eodem comitatu iuxta aquam, que dicitur Knesaha, in benficium habetat.*

MILTZE

In this same area one finds a settlement recorded as *Miltze: Item Wolfinus de Gynesdorf recepit ... decimam in Miltze, item feudum in Damphah, item in Hutesmur curiam et feudum,* 1304. H. Jakob notes that the name may be a reference to the *Milcane Serbs* of *Luzica:* **Wenn fur die Obermaingegend von sorbischen Stammessplittern die Rede ist, warum nicht auch von solchen der Miltschaner im Raum Knetzgau?** *(H. Jakob, Slavische Wustungen im Raum Knetzgau-Hassfurt A.M., DwS 32, 1987).* Another possible reference to *Milcani Serbs* in this area is found centuries earlier in a Fulda Monastery register that records a place called *Milezi:* *Que cum in proprio domate sibi monasterium fecisset ... in loco, qui Milezi nuncupatur, cunctaque predia sua eidem loco in id opus attitulasset, ab incursu paganorum, Sclavorum videlicet* (799-800). On this same suject, H. Kunstmann writes: **Ea es auch die Schreibungen Milsche (1322) und Miltsch (1436) gibt, braucht nicht nur an den slavischen PN Milos, Milsec, Milek gedacht zu werden, da vielleicht auch Relikte des Stammesnamen der westslavischen Miltschaner (Milcane) vorliegen konnten** *(H. Kunstmann, Wo lag das Zentrum von Samos Reich, DwS, 1981).*

MYSL, STARC, TASIMIR

In this area one finds a number of names derived from Slavic words. For example: **Myslov**/Meusselau, Starc: *Item desolatum dictum Startz redactum est per totum in prata,* 1348; **Tasova** as in **Tas, Tasimir**: *id est in Bunahu et in Tasu/804; et insuper Praedium apud Dahsovva,* 1143, north of the Main River; **Winden** and others south of the Main River: *Item Hartmanus Zink recepit III jugera vineti in monte Keller et in Winden unum lehen, item in Diepach advocatiam super duabus hubis et unum lehen in Winden,* 1303.

CHASA ZUPA, HASS GAU

North and northeast of *Knetzgau,* Hassgau occupied an area on the left bank of the Rennweg River between Hassfurt, Hofheim and Koenigshofen. H. Kunstmann speculates that the name Hass is derived from the Slavic *chasa*, a term connoting a warrior/military entity, a war zone. Thus Hass Gau was originally *Chasa Zupa*, a western *Serb-Wend* border/war zone occupied and guarded by military communities: **Bedeutung von Kriegs-volk transparent ist: chasa vojskova. Uberraschend gut passt dazu das Vorkommen von chasa im mahrischen Dialekt, in den sich ebenfalls der kriegerische Aspekt wenigstens bis ins 19. Jahrhundert erhalten has: Bude vojna bude, bude verbovana, pujde na nu chasa vybirana. Es spricht in der Tat einiges dafur, dass die ursprungliche Bedeutung von chasa eben Kriegs-volk war.**

BANZ ZUPA, BANZ GAU

Due north of Bamberg, *Banz* Gau occupied an area between Hallstadt in the south and Coburg in the north. H. Kunstmann concurs with J. Schutz, a leading authority on the formation of Slavic *ortsnamen* in Bavaria, that **Banz** Gau was originally **Banz Zupa**, a name derived from a Slavic personal name ending in **-banz,** e.g. **Darghebanz, Ghorebanz, Chotibanz** (*J. Schutz, Ortsnamentypen und slawische Siedlungszeit in Nordostbayern, FrA 28, 1968*).

LARGE SLAV ADMIXTURE

With regard to modern Bamberg and surrounding territory, a contemporary observer writes, the Slav imprint is strong in modern body and speech: **The appearance and dialect of the people yet attest to a large Slavonic admixture.**

BAVARIA

Farther south and west, diverse sources document **Serb-Wend** settlements in northeastern Bavaria and southeastern Franconia, a fact confirmed by numerous place names derived from Slavic roots Serb in character (*O. Kronsteiner, Die slawischen Ortsnamen in Oberosterreich Baiern und Slawen in Oberosterreich, Problemee der Landnahme und Besiedlung, 1980*).

CETOMYSL, DRAGOMYSL

Cetomysl (Zetmeswel, 1398), now Zettmeisel (Harsdorf)
Chojno (Keyna, 1357), now Kainach (Ebermannstadt)
Chosten (Kosten, 1333), now Kostenberg (Stadtsteinach)
Crn (Tschirn, 1388), now Tschirn (Teuschnitz)
Crnidlo (Schirneitel, 1400), now Schirnaidel (Forcheim)
Crnovic (Schirnwiz, 1297), now Schirnitz (Neustadt)
Dragomysl (Dremeszzels, 1350), now Trainmeusel

GODIGOST, LUBOGOST

Drzenici (Durssniz, 1511), now Durschnitz (Bayreuth)
Godigost (Kotgast, 1376) now Kordigast (Lichtenfels)
Mt. Godigost, 535m (berg Gadegast, 1422), now Mt. Kordigast
Kloda (Kloden, 1071), now Wasserknoden (Kulmbach)
Lubogost (Leubgast, 1224), new Leugast (Tirschenreuth)
Lubogost (*Lubegast minori*, 1240), now Klein Leugast (Lichtenfels)
Luboraz (Leuberoz, 1310), now Leibaros (Ebermannstadt)

PREMYSL, SKOROGOST

Polst (Polst, 1348), now Pulst (Berneck)
Polz (Pulsnitz, 1402), now Pulschnitz (Munchberg)
Preymsyl (Premiscel, 1261), now Premeischel (Waldmunchen)
Premysl (Premeusel, 1520), now Premeusel (Stadtsteinach)
Roslav (Roslavs, 1393), now Reislas (Bayreuth)
Skorogost (Scoregast, 1109), now Markt-Schorgast (Kulmbach)
Sloma (Slomen, 1398), now Schlomen (Kulmbach)

TREBOGOST, ZIVOGOST

Trebogost (Trebegast, 1028), now Trebgast (Kulmbach)
Trebogost (Altenbregast, 1576), now Alten-Trebast (Bayreuth)

Velemysl (Welmyzels, 1280), now Mehimeisel (Wunseidel)
Voligost (Wolgast, 1366), now Wolgast (Bayern)
Vrbotin (Wurbotin, 1317), Wunseidel (Bayreuth)
Zagost (Cegast, 1369), now Zegast (Statsteinach)
Zivogost (Sugast, 1139) now Seugast (Amberg)

SCLAVOS, QUORUM VOCABULA SUNT SWRBI

Given the documentary fact that the Serbs were sometimes called *Svurbi* and *Swrbi* (*e.g. **Sclavos, quorum vocabula sunt Swrbi***), the following village names are believed to be derived from the ethnonym Serb and concrete evidence of Serb settlement in this area.

Svrb (Swubrz, 1303), now Schwurbitz (Lichtenfels)
Svrb (Swurbz, 1317), now Schwarz-hof (Kulmbach)
Svrb (Swurbz, 1419), now Schurz (Pegnitz)
Svrb (Swurbs, 1303), now Schwurbitz (Bamberg)

WINDISCH, WINDEN IN BAVARIA

Further evidence of the scope and density of Slavic settlement in this area is found in a recent study that identifies some 200 ***Windisch/Winden*** villages in Bavaria *(W.A. von Reitzenstein, Ortsnamen mit Windisch/Winden in Bayern, Deutsch-slawischer Sprachkontak im Lichte der Ortsnamen, 1993).*

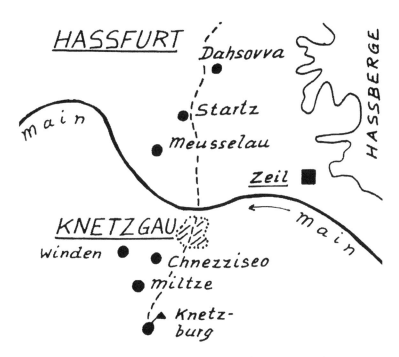

Knez/Knetz Gau: Miltze, Myslov, Starc, Tasimir

5. NABWINIDI, BADEN-WURTTEMBERG WINIDI

Slav/Serb-Wend setttlement in the Naab River region or *Nabwinidi* is the subject of a number of studies and articles by leading German scholars. In a recent article regarding *Nabwinidi,* H. Kunstmann writes: **Die Lehrmeinung is davon uberzeugt, dass sich die sogenannte Sorbenmark-dieser ungluckliche, da pauschale, ja ungenaue Begriff ist leider sehr verbreitet-von Norden nach Suden, also von Thuringen her in das Gebiet an Heidenaab, Waldnaab, Pfreimd und die "Sorbenmark" nur bis Hof ging, ist laut Gagel damit zu rechnen, "dass sich das Gebiet des Sorbenfursten uber die Pfreimd bis zum Regen erstreckte** *(Die Bedeutung der Cham-Further Senkd fur die Einwanderung von Slaven in die Oberpfalz im Spiegel der Namen Cham/Kamp, Osser, Domazlice, Tugast/Taust u.a., DwS 33, 1994).*

Onomastic evidence indicates that the Naab River region in the Upper Palatinate (Oberpfalz) was also a center of *Serb-Wend* settlements. In this area medieval documents record such names as *Nabawinida, Nahwinden, Nabenwiden,* and *Nahwenden.* In this general area numerous place names, toponyms, and hydronyms (e.g. *Trebinam* as in *id est villam que vocatur Nabavuinida iuxta rivula Trebinam,* 863) either refer to Slavs (e.g. *winden*) or are Slavic in origin (e.g. *Malisa's* dorf, later Mausdorf; *Vencenslav's* lake, later Vecenbach).

BADEN-WURTTEMBERG

Extensive lands north and west of *Nabawinidi* were also within the borders of *Slavorum/Serborum.* Some measure of the scope and density of Slav settlement is found in the onomastic evidence in a broad area between Heidelberg on the Neckar River (northwest Baden-Wurttemberg) in the west and Nuremberg on the Pegnitz River (Middle Franconia) in the east. More precisely, an area crossed by the Tauber, Jagst, Kocher, and Neckar rivers, bounded by Holzkirchen and Wurzburg in the north, Amorack and Mosbach in the west, Obstenfeld and Ellwangen in the south and Ansbach in the east.

ALTENWINDEN

In addition to numerous names with Slavic roots, medieval sources record an unusual concentration of names with *Wind* as prefix or suffix in this area.

- Altenwinden
- *curia Winderberch*
- Etzlenswinden
- Greviwinden
- Herrnwinden
- Morlitzwinden
- Niederwinden
- Oberwinden
- Reinswindern
- Schwickartswinden

- Winden
- Windischbockenfeld
- Windischbrachbach
- Windischbuch
- Windischbuchen
- Windisichenbach
- Windischer Hof
- Windisch Hohbach
- Windsheim

HESSE

North of Baden-Wurttemberg, there is evidence of ancient Slavic settlement in Hesse. In southern Hesse, for example, the highest elevation of the Odenwald range is **Mt. Malchen**. The prefix **Mal-** and the suffixes **-chin** (e.g. Malchin) and **-ow** (e.g. Malchow) are the Slavic roots of many names in Germania, including the following:

Malech, later Mahlis (Mugeln)
Malenc, later Mahlitzsch (Dobeln)
Malenc, later Mahlitzsch (Dommitzsch)
Malenc, later Mahlitzsch (Nossen)
Malina, later Malden (Zeitz)
Malov, later Mahlow (Torgau)
Malov, later Mahlow (Zossen)
Malchov, later Malche (Freinwalde)
Malchov, later Malchow (Berlin)
Malocin, later Malacin (Zwenkau)
Malecic, later Maltitz (Weissenberg)
Malsin, later Malsen (Oschatz)
Melkov, later Melchow (Eberswalde)

PORADNICI

With regard to Slav settlements in eastern Franconia, H.H. Howorth writes: **It would seem that the greater part of eastern Franconia and the districts of Wunsiedel, Waldsassen, Tirschenreut, and Bernau, as well as the greater part of the land on the Naab, Rednitz and the Upper Main about Baireuth, Bamberg, Wurtzburgh, and Nurnberg was in the ninth and tenth centuries occupied by Slavs. A large number of these settlements belonged to the Poradnitzi or inhabitants of the Rednitz, of whom we read in the life of St. Emmamarus:** *Tradidit cuidam Thuringo in finibus Parathanorum, ad is temporis crudelium paganaroum.*

SWISS SERBS

Howorth's examination of the historical record leads him to extends the scope of Serb settlement to lands farther south and west, to Switzerland. He suspects that the Slav colonies in Switzerland (***homines qui vocantur Wiinde)***, located in settlements with such names as Khunitz, Bumplitz, Czernec, Gradetz, Krimentz, Luc, Visoye, Grona, where, he writes, the natives **still use a corrupt Slavic dialect**, are mainly Serb in origin: **There can be small doubt that the greater part of them were emigrants from the country east of the Elbe, where the nearest Slavic settlements were, and which, as I have shown, were Serbian.**

ORTSNAMEN IN WENDENLANDS

Evidence relating to the density and character of Serb settlement in lands west and south of medieval Serbia/Germania, in the ***Main**, **Regnitz**,* and ***Nab Wendenlands***, is found numerous articles on the subject by German scholars, including, for example, the following two articles. In *Eine deutsche-slawische Symbiose in der Ellernbach-Talschaft nordostlich von Bamberg (OsG, XIX, 1990),* H. Jakob identifies a number of Germanized place names in an area northeast of Bamberg, an area where one often finds family name derived from Slavic place names (e.g. from **slap** as in Fritz Schlapan, Bamberg, 1363; Otto Slapan, Staffelstein, 1418). In the following series, the original Slavic place name is followed by later Germanizations.

BUDISIN, DRAZ, GROD

Bud, Budisin's dorf— Budesendorf/1158
Cek, Cekin's dorf— Czekendorf/1382; Zeckendorf
Cesic— Schehesilze/800; *civitas Schezliz*/1255; Schesslitz
Chotan, Chotan's dorf— Kotduanisdorf/1172; Kottendorf
Draz, Droz. Drozin's dorf— Drosendorf/1116; Drosendorf
Grod, Grodc— Grotze/1298; Burglein
Kremen— Cremelendorf/1248; Kremmeldorf

LES, LUBAN, LUBOMYSL

Lan— Landorf/1322; Lohndorf
Les— Lesen/1290; Burglesau
Lizo, Lizo's dorf— *Otgoz de Licendorf et frater eius Pillunc*/1136; Litzendorf
Lub, Luban— Lubende/1078; Laubendt
Lub, Luban's dorf— Leubendorf/1243; Leubendorf
Lubomysl, Lubomysl's dorf— Lumutzelsdorf/1237; Lomerstorf
Milek, Milkin's dorf— Meilkendorfff/1279; Melkendorf

MIRKIN, PODOLE, PUST

Mirk, Mirkin's dorf— Mirkendorf/1174; Merkendorf
Podole— Podelendorf/1096; Podeldorf
Pole, Polica— Polnitz/1417; Polnitz
Pust, Pustin— Pauster/1312; Pauster
Rostilub— Roslaub/1290; Roschlaub
Roztok— Roztoch/1250; Rossdach
Slap, Slapan— Slapansgereute/1299; Schlappenreuth

STUB, SVOJEK, VOJEK

Smir, Smir's dorf— Smireldorf/1341; Schmerldorf
Stan, Stanislav— Stanberg/1305; Stamberg
Stub— Stubeg/1157; Stubig
Svoj, Svojek's dorf— Sweicdorf/1341; Schweissdorf
Tas, Tasin's dorf— Taschendorf/1551; Doschendorf
Vojek, Vojkin's dorf— Weikendorf/1136; Weichendorf
Wind— Windisch Slatina/1125; Windissinleten
Wind— Starkolfswinden/1407, Starkenschwind
Wind— Windischen Gyech/1299; Wiesengiech

OBEREN MAIN

In *Die Stammeszugehorigkeit der Slawen am oberen Main im Lichte der Ortsnamen* (Sybaris, FsT Hans Krahe, 1958), E. Schwarz identifies a number of Germanized Slavic place names on the Upper Main River area derived mainly from several common Slavic roots. In the following series the original Slavic place name is followed by later Germanizations.

DRAG, DRAGOMIR, DRAGOMYSL

Berz, Berzjani— Perssin/1122; Perschen
Drag, Dragalov— Dragelaue/1363; Trogau
Drag, Drog, Drogenov— Drogenawe/1234; Trogenau
Drag, Dragin's dorf— Tragendorf/1151; Traindorf
Drag, Dragol, Drogol's dorf— Trogelsdorf/1399; Trogelsdorf
Drag, Dragomir's dorf— Tragemarsdorf/1231
Drag, Dragomysl— Tragamuetzel; 1137; Trainmeusel
Drag, Dragomysl— *mola Dragomysl*/1028

DRAGOS, DRAGOTIN, DROZIN

Drag, Dragonici— Drogunzei/1185; Treunitz
Drag, Dragos, Drogosin— Drogessangeruit/1062; Troschenreuth
Drag, Dragos, Dragosin's dorf— Tragesindorf/1043; Trauschendorf
Drag, Dragotin— Dragetin/1062; Tragweis
Drag, Dragov— Tragaw/1395; Trogau
Draz, Drazevici— Dreswitz/1233; H ohentreswitz
Draz, Droz, Drozin's dorf— Drosendorf/1116; Drosendorf
Draz, Droz, Drozin's dorf: Drosendorf/1139; Trosendorf

DRAZEN, DRAZENICI, GRADIC

Draz— Drosenfelt/1285; Neudrossenfeld
Draz— Drosenvelt/ Altdrossenfeld
Draz, Drazen's dorf— Dressendorf/1348; Draisendorf
Draz— Drasenfelt/1396; Untertresenfeld
Draz— Dressenvelt/1396; Tressenfeld
Draz, Drazenici— Dresnitz/1316
Gradic— Grodez/1071; Markgraitz
Kloden— Kloden/1071; Wasserknoden

MLODENEC, PODGRAD, SLATINA

Kloden— Cloden/1144; Hohenknoden
Kloden— di wasser die Knoden/1536; Knodenbache
Mlodenec— Lodencenreuth/1304; Lorenzreuth
Podgrad— Podgrat/1287; Pograth
Predroz— Prudus/1390; Bruderes
Slatina— Slattin/1261; Schlattein
Slop— Slopice/1065; Schlopp
Slop— Sloppin/1135; Gross and Kleinschloppen
Slop— Slopan/1133; Schloppach
Slop— Sloppe/1323; Lopp
Slop— Slopan/1395; Schloppenhof

6. SORABIA, QUI & SUNT BOHEMI ANTIQUITUS

The earliest recorded sources and modern scholarship agree that Bohemia was settled by Serbs, that Bohemia was a Serb land. Early medieval sources refer to Bohemia (also *Bechem, Beheim, Beheimare, Boemannia, Peehaimm, Peoma*) as **Slavonia** as in *de Sclavania onmes duces Boemannorum* (895), as **Slavonia terra** as in **terra Sclavorum, qui vocantur Beheimi** (805), as *Slavonia region* as in *Sclavos in regione Peehaim* (800), as *Slavonia regna* as in **regna Sclavorum Behmensium** (896).

SIRFISCHE SLAVEN

That the ***Bohemians*** were ***Serbs*** in the 6th century is clear from a German historian's account of Bavaria's conflict with Bohemia, with the ***Sirfische Slaven*** in 596. ***Also lessen wir dass Thabilo der Bayer Konig ih Jahr DXCV wider die Sirfische Slaven in Bohmen einen grossen Sieg erhalten haben.***

SORABIA, BOHEMI ANTIQUITUS

In his exhaustive study of the Franks, Johannes Thritmus records the ancient Bohemians as Serbs *(De Origine Gentis Francorum Compendium, 1514)*. ***Serbs, the Bohemians of antiquity, who are called Slavs: Sorabia, qui & sunt Bohemia antiquitus, under Schlavi nuncipati.***

GUARANTORS OF LEGITIMACY

The *Annals of Fulda* offer interesting evidence relating to ***White Serbia's*** relations with Bohemia and intervention in its affairs in the mid-9th century. Apparently acting as guarantors of legitimacy, in 856 the ***White Serbs*** take an active role in putting down a rebellion of a number of Bohemian tribes. The next year, 857, following ejection by his brother **(Slavitah)**, the rightful ruler of Bohemia takes refuge with a Serb prince, ***Zistibor***. The ***White Serbs*** respond by taking part in an expedition against the insurgents. With ***Slavitah*** defeated, the ***White Serbs*** withdraw, and the aggrieved party returns to his rightful place in Bohemia.

SERBS ARE CZECHS ARE SERBS

The Serbs are Czechs are Serbs thesis is supported by authoritative Czech and foreign scholarship. Dalimil's early 14th century Czech chronicle clearly places the Czechs as well as the Croats within the ***Serb Volkstamm***.

> *V srbskem jazyku jest zeme*
> *Jiez Charvatci jest jme*
> *V tej zemi liese lech*
> *Jemuz jme biese Cech*

SETTLED BY SERBS FROM LUZICA

Regarding the Serb settlement of Bohemia, F. Pubicka writes that: **Bohemia was settled by Serbs from Luzica, that the settlement probably took place in the late fifth century, that over time the original name, Serb, was gradually replaced by the local name, Czech** *(Slavorum in Bohemiam Adventu ad Baptizmum Borzivoi, 1779)*.

MAINLY FROM LUZICA

Noting that unlike the omnipresent Serbs, there is no record of a Czech nation in Germania, J. Jablonowski is certain that: **Czechia was settled by Serbs (Serbos, Srbos, Sorabos), mainly Serbs from Luzica, who themselves originated in the Volga region** *(Lechi et Czechi, 1771)*.

CZECHS WERE SERBS

A leading authority on the Slavs of Germania and Bohemia, M. Pelzel writes: **The Czechs were Serbs before they were Czechs ... Over time, however, the general name, Serb, gave way to the specific name, Czech** *(Geschichte der Bohmen, 1817)*. With regards to the ethnonym ***Czech*** it is perhaps significant that there is no record of a ***Czech natio*** in early medieval German sources. Instead, there are numerous references to: ***Boemiorum gentem; Boemorum gens; gens Boemica; gens Bohemie; gens Bohemorum: gente Bohemica; gentis Bohemice.***

ORIGINATED IN WHITE SERBIA

The contemporary Czech historian, Francis Dvornik, commenting on the *national tradition that the Czechs originated in **White Serbia***, writes: **If we remember that the occupation of Bohemia, especially its western half, started from Lusatia which became the centre of a State controlled by the Serbs, the occupation of central and western Bohemia could be regarded as the normal expansion of White Serbia** *(The Making of Central and Eastern Europe, 1974)*.

BEHEIMARE, IN QUA SUNT CIVITATES XV

A good measure of the relative size and strength of the Serb lands relative to Bohemia in the early 9th century is found in the *Descriptio Civitatum* where many more *civitates* are found in a single component of the Serb community than all of Bohemia. More than 60 *civitates* are recorded in the ***Upper Luzica*** and ***Lower Luzica Serb*** tribal-territorial complex east of Meissen, for example, compared to only fifteen in all Bohemia: ***Beheimare, in qua sunt civitates XV.***

PSOV (MELNIK)

In the last decade of the 9th century, a Serb prince, ***Slavibor***, father of Ludmila, patroness of Bohemia (***srbskeho knizete dcera***), is at the head of the historic town and province of *Psov*, later *Melnik*, some 18 miles north of Prague: ***Zlaviboris, comitis ex provincia Sclavorum, que Psou antiquitus nuncupatur, nunc a modernis ex civitate noviter constructa Mielnik vociatur.***

LEMUZI

There is evidence of a Serb presence in several provinces north of Psov. Czech sources identify a Serb nation, the ***Lemuzi*** (***Lemuzi, srbske knizectvi na sever od Litomericu***), as occupants of an area north of Litomerice, a historic town and province (***provincia Lutomerici***) northwest of Psov.

BELINA ET LUTOMERICI

There is also evidence suggesting a possible Serb presence in the 9th century in the northwest provinces of *Litomerice*, *Belina* (***duarum provinciarum Belina et***

Lutmerici), *Decane* (**Dechinensis provincia**), modern *Decin*, and other northern and western lands, including those occupied by the *Lucane*, *Sedlicane*, and *Zlicane*.

LUZICA GORA, KRKONOSE GORA

The record is clear that present Czech borderlands south of the **Luzica Gora** and **Krkonose Gora**, running from *Decin* in the west to *Jablonec* in the east, were historic **Serb Luzica** lands.

SRBSKO, SRBY, SRBICE

Historical evidence and scholarship relating to Serb settlement are supported by hard onomastic facts on the ground, namely the numerous place names in Bohemia/ Czechia derived from the Serb ethnonyms. It is significant that the Serb ethnonyms are not concentrated in one area or along medieval Bohemia's northern border with medieval **White Serbia** *(E. Eichler, Tschechisch-sorbischen Parallelen in der Toponomastik, Zur Herkunft der Slawen im Elbe-Saale-Gebiet, 1964. G. Labuda, Serbowie w Czechnach, SsS 5, 1975. H. Brachmann, Historische und kulturelle Beziehungen der Sorben zu Bohmen und Mahren, RaP 1, 1979. A. Sedlacek, O ustaleni hranica mezi Cechami a Luzici, CmM 66, 1982).* Instead, the Serb ethnonyms range far and wide through the greater part of north, central, and southwest Bohemia: From *Vysoke Myto* (eastern Bohemia) to *Podebrad* (central Bohemia), near Kutna Hora, the birthplace and residence of Hussite King George of Podebrad, to *Slani* (west central Bohemia, northwest of Prague) to *Kdyne* (southwest Bohemia, southwest of Pilsen) to *Klatov* (foothills of Cesky Les, southwest Bohemia) to *Teplice-Sanov* (foothills of Erzebirge, northwest Bohemia) to *Kostelec nad Labem* (central Bohemia, northeast of Prague) to *Polica nad Metuji* (Sudetes foothills, northeast Bohemia) to *Beroun* (central Bohemia, southwest of Prague) to *Mnichovo Hradiste* (northern Bohemia, between Liberec and Mlada Boleslav) to *Nove Straseci* (central Bohemia, northwest of Prague) to *Slany* (northwest of Prague) to *Hostoun*, southwest Bohemia, southwest of Pilsen *(A. Profous, J. Svoboda, Mistni Jmena v Cechach. Jejich Vznik Puvodni Vyznam z Zmeny, IV, 1957).*

- **Srbce, v Srbcich, do Srbcu, za Srbec, srbecekej** (Vys. Myto)
- **Srbce, v Srbcich, do Srbec, Srbecak i Srbak** (Podebrady)
- **Srbec, v Srbci, do Srbce, Srbecak** (Nov. Straseci)
- **Srbec** (Slany)
- **Srbice, v Srbicich, do Srbic, Srbickej** (Kdyne)
- **Srbice, Srbiczi**, Jan Horcice z **Srbic**/1449 (Klatov)
- **Srbice, Stara Srbice** (Teplice-Sanova)
- **Srbice, Nove Srbice** (Teplice-Sanova)
- **Srbice, *in villa Srbicz*/1405** (Otic)
- **Srbin, v Srbine, do Srbina** (Kostelce)
- **Srbska, Nizka Srbska, Nizkosrbska, v Nizke Srbske, do Nizke Srbske** (Police)
- **Srbska, Vysoka Srbska, ve Vysoka Srbske, do Vysoka Srbska** (Nizka Srbska)
- **Srbsko, v Srbsku, do Srbska** (Beroun)
- **Srbsko, v Srbsku, srbsky, vsi Srbsko cele**/1534 (Mnich. Hrad)

- **Srby, v Srbech, do Srb,** *molendinum sub villa Tuchlowicz Srbij,* 1330 (Nove Straseci)

- **Srby, v Srbech, do Srb, zamek Zelenu horu ... ves Srby,** 1558 (Nepomuku)

- **Srby, Vaclav z Srb**/1452; **vsi Srby**/1539 (Hostoune)

CES, CZES, CZECH, CZECHOV

There is evidence that the ethnonym **Czech** is derived from the personal names such as **Ces, Cech,** and concomitant place names such as **Cecholin, Cechov, Cechyn** found throughout German Slavia. The evidence is especially strong in **White Serbia,** the ancestral homeland of the Czechs. In **White Serbia** one finds a a number of recorded place names derived from the personal name **Czech,** including, among others:

- **Cesici** (*Cesice in pago Uueta vocato,* 976), near Naumberg.

- **Czech** (Cech, 1495; Czechsdorf, 1507), near Forst.

- **Czechov** (Zechowe, 1214), near Altenburg.

- **Czesevic** (Sescuize, 1105), near Borna.

- **Czesevic** (Schezvwiz, 1290; Czessewicz, 1378), near Leisnig.

- **Czesevic** (Czeschewicz, 1368; Czeczeewitz, 1445; Czscheczewicz, 1501).

- **Czeczh** (Schez, 1447; Czecsch, 1378; Czetzsch, 1458), near Hohenmolsen.

- **Czes-** or Czech-dorf (Czesdorff, 1452; Czeschdorff, 1600), near Zeitz.

- **Czesov** (Zaschesschow, 1357; Scheschow, 1374; Czeschaw, 1440; Czessow, 1482), near Konigswartha.

- **Czesko** (Czeskecy, 1360), near Bautzen.

— • —

There are numerous direct references to **Serbs, Serbia, Serb** notables, **Serb** cities in the first Czech chronicles, namely *Chronicon Bohemorum* (circa 1125) or *Kronika Ceska* by the Bohemian Herodotus, **Cosmas** (c. 1045-1125), Canon of Prague; and *Staroceska Kronica* (circa 1308-1316), by **Dalimil,** the first historical work written in the national language.

— • —

COSMAS, KRONIKA CESKA

Book I, Chapter 13

(890) ... Vystavev na rovine novy hrad Drahus ne brehu reky Ohre u vsi Postoloprt ... odevzdal jeje i hocha vychovateli, jemuz ho jiz vlastni otec sveril, jmenem Durynkovi; byl to rod ze **Srbska,** clovek az nelidsky zlocinny, nad nejhorsiho horsi a nad kazdou selmu ukrutnejsi ... Zatim ten neslechetny **Srbin,** horsi nez pohan, spase ukrutny zlocin.

Book Two, Chapter 9

Roku od narozeni Pane 1040 ... A ihned rozeslav listy po cele risi, sebral velmi silne vojsko. Jednou cestou, kudy se choi pres *Srbsko* a kde je vychod z pomezniho hvozdu do nasi zeme pres hrad Chlumec, kazel Sasum vtrhnouti do Cech.

Book Two, Chapter 39

Roku od narozeni Pane 1087. Kral Vratislav sebrav vojsko tahl do *Srbska*, jez mu kdysi cisar Jindrich navzdy udelil v drzeni.

Book Two, Chapter 40

Roku od pane narozeni Pane 1088 ... Mezitim se stalo, ze kral Vratislav ope pritah se svym vojskem do *Srbska*, aby receny hrad Hvozdec prolozil ne jine pevnejsi misto. Dovedev se, ze je Beneda nad hrad Misni, poslal pro nej, aby k nemu prisel pod zarukou bezpecnosti.

Book Three, Chapter 4

Roku od narozeni Pane 1095 ... I byl Bozej jat, jak znel orzkaz, vsazen ihned na lod i s manzelkou a dvema syny a vypovedem do *Srbska*; odtud odjel to Polska, kde nalezi sveho pribuzneho Mutinu, a knize polsky je velmi vlidne prijal.

Book Three, Chapter 28

Roku od narozeni Pane 1109 ... Jakmile vsak uslysel Borivoj, ze se jeho mladsi bratr po smrti Svatoplukove zmocnil knizeciho stolce, ihned odesel z Poslka a odebral se do *Srbska* k sveme svargru Viprechtovi.

Book Three, Chapter 39

I vydal se Sobeslav, vrativ se k svym lidem, ihned na cestu, chte se pres *Srbsko* odebrati do Polsko, nebot se velmi bal pritomnosti sveho bratra. A kdyz presel pres pomezni hvozd, prijel mu naproti Ekembert, purkrabi hradi Donina, z uskocneho *Srbska*, plyn lsti, a predstiraje mu pratelsky mnohe veci, sliboval mu, ze by mohl milosti cisarovou dojiti ve vsem sveho prava, kdyby se k cisari osobrne dostavil.

—————— • ——————

DALEMIL, STAROCESKA KRONIKA

Chapter 50

Po tom kral pro kneze moravskeho
pobi Lipolt, vevodu rakuskeho.
Pak jide na kneze *srbskeho*,
tocis na markrabi misenskeho.
Hvozdec hrad kral bliz Misne postavi
a voje pred Minsem zsatvi.
Na Misni Beneda udatny biese
ten kralovy milisti nemejiese.

Chapter 50

Tepruv se i jechu zeme hubiti

a Sasice i s detmi biti
Tehdy kral i Sasice i **Srby** pobi
a jich zeme mnogo doby.

Chapter 58

Vece knez Vladislav: "Nu vzvezte ku boji!"
Lide, ze **Srbov** mnoho, se vzhrozichu
a kneze na to namluvichu,
ze pred **Srby** do Prahy pojjide.
Ale kde mesta dojide,
do mest jeho nepustichu.
Vrativse se, s **Srby** se vzbichu
Tu se Cechy dobre jmiechu,
slechetne boj na **Srbiech** obdrzechu.
Ktoz v tom boji i malo ranen byl,
Kako malo odren, vask inhed zivota zbyl.

Chapter 59

Ciesar kneze **srbskeho** Valcava je
a kneze Borivoje.
Mnogo kaza hlava stieti
a mnoghu kaza oci vynieti/
aby kniezatom svym verni byli
a v hromadu jech nevadili.

Chapter 74

Tehdy kneze Otty bra, Brecislav,
po Danieli biskupem biese
a ten kneze miesto zemi vladiese
Ten knez **Srby** hrdinsky pobi
a mnogo him tvrzi a mest doby.

SLAVIBOR, KMETA Z HRADKU PSOVA

There are also a number of interesting indirect references to Serbs, including Serbs active in Bohemia's affairs (e.g. **Slavibor, kmeta z hradku Psova; Vaclav, knize srbsky, syn Viprechta Grojcsekho**), to Serb provinces (e.g. **hranice Milcanu**) and Serb cities (e.g. **hrad Donin**, near Drazdan/Dresden; **hrad Hvozdec**/Gvozdec; **hradu Misne**/Meissen).

Part XVI

I. REGIO QUAE VOCATUR SRBI

Numerous sources agree that the ancient Serb name was retained and preserved by the Slavs who settled lands between the Sudet mountains, the Elbe, and the Saale, namely the *White Serbs* of *White Serbia.*

SLAVONICE DICTI SRBI AB ALBI

White Serbs and *White* Serbia are not native terms. The Serbs of Germania or Sarmatia never called themselves *White Serbs* or their lands *White Serbia.* The terms were also unknown to contemporaneous German chroniclers and later commentators who refer to native Serbs as *Srbi* (e.g. *Srbi, aut Sorabi, Slavonice dicti Srbi ab Albi*) and many other names (e.g. *Rorabi, Soavi, Sorabi, Sorbi, Suburbi, Suirbi, Surabi, Suurbi, Swrbi, Zrbii, Zurbi, Zurvi*). The Serb lands are recorded as *Regio quae vocatur Surbi, Serborum, Soraborum, Suirbia, Suurbia, Universum Sorabi,* and many other names.

With the exception of *Cosmas Chronicle's Zribi* (*fui fuit de Zribia genere*) medieval Czech sources, *Dalimil's Chronicle,* for example, record the Serbs as *Srbs: Srbiech, Srbov, Srbskeho, Srbove, Srby.* Medieval Polish sources favor *Sarb, Sorab, Sarbia, Sorabia: Terre autem predictorum principum fuerunt hoc: Boleslai Pomorania inferiori ... Jaxe Sorabia, Worcislai Rania, Prizibislai et Odonois Drewina, Prezemisali Szgorzelic, que nunc Brandeborg appellatur* (Chronica Poloniae maioris); *Habuit [Wandalus] quoque multos filios ... Sarbiam qua nunc Saxonia dicitur* (*Mierzwy Kronika*). *Chronica Poloniae maioris* explains the origin of the Serb name in the then popular patronymic terms: *Verius autem creditur, quod Sorabe a Sarb, quod et Sarban nomen accepit, sicuti a Juda Judei a Lech Lechite et ceteri nominantur.* The same source also identifies a Balkan Serb *regnum* called Rascia: *Item regnum Rascie a Racz quod vestigium equorum multiudinis exercitum in unum congregatorum dicitur nominatam. Nam ex hoc Slawi multitudinem equitancium dicunt Raci ... Nam Gallici appellantillam regionem Seruiam violentes dicere* (Chronica Poloniae maioris).

ALSO CALLED WHITE

The name *White Serbs* and *White Serbia* for the Serbs and Serb lands north of the Danube originates with Constantine's mid-10th century *De Administrando Imperio*: **The Serbs are descended from the unbaptized Serbs, also called *White,* who lived beyond Turkey [Hungary] in a place called by them Boiki.** The terms *White Serbs* and *White Serbia* owe their use and legitimacy to their service as simple and effective means of distinguishing Serbs and Serb lands of *Germania* and *Sarmatia* from the Serbs and Serb lands of *Illyria, Dalmatia, Pannonia, Moesia, Dacia.*

PREHISTORIC WHITE SERBIA

The greater part of *(Bel) White Serbia's* history prior to the 9th century falls within an essentially prehistoric period, with few written records regarding territory or organization.

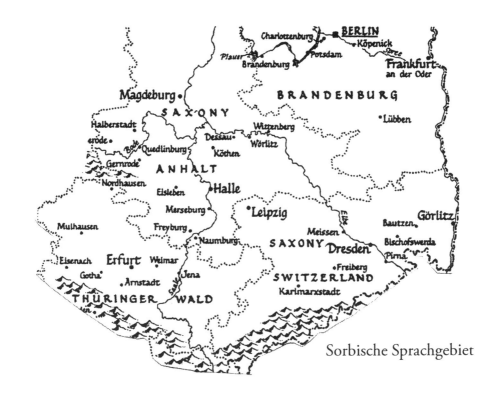

Sorbische Sprachgebiet

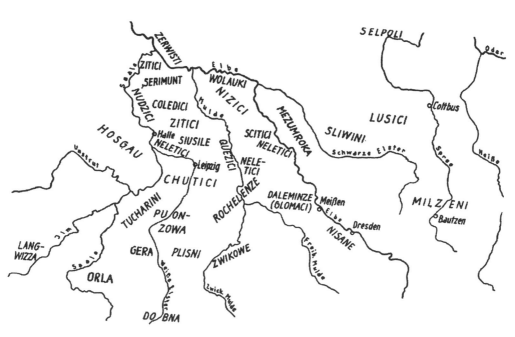

Serb Natios/Provincias

HISTORIC WHITE SERBIA

Historic **White Serbia** is a far lesser **White Serbia** in time and space. It is a relatively short history, mainly the 9th, 10th, and 11th centuries, of a relatively diminished land, recording little of its former glory and all of its retreat, decline, and, ultimately, loss of independence.

ENTER HISTORICAL RECORD

It is not surprising that Germania's **Slavs** first enter the written historical record as **Serbs**. In the first decades of the 6th century, Vibius Sequester registers the following fact: **The Elbe divides the Suebi from the Serbs.** Historians suspect that Sequester's Serbs are not Serbs in a particular or **White Serb** sense, but Serbs in a *generic*, **all-Slavic sense** (e.g. **Serb as the ancient, common name of all or most Slavs**).

AMICITIAS WINIDIS

In the year 630 there is an indirect reference to the Serbs (**Winidis**) in *Fredegarius' Chronicle*, an original source for events in the Frankish kingdom from 548 to 642:

> *Amicitias cum Winidis firmans ceterasque gentes, quas vicinas habetat, cultu amicitiae obligabat, 630.*

SCLAVI SARMATAE

Later references to the Serbs are often concealed by such terms as *Sarmatians, Scythians, Slavs, pagans,* etc. A 921 account of Heinrich's wars with Serbs between the White Elster, Mulde, and Middle Elbe refers to the Serbs as **Sclavi Sarmatae**.

DUX GENTE SURBIORUM

The following year the same source introduces the Serbs in a more specific sense, namely in the person of **Drvan**, a Serb duke.

> *Dervanus dux gente Surbiorum, que ex genere Sclavinorum erant, 631.*

> *Ito ut Dervanus dux, qui urbibus praeret Sclavorum, 631.*

SALAM ET ALBAM

Ten years later the same source informs us that the land between the Saale and Elbe is settled by **Wendic** Slavs called Serbs.

> *Quidquid inter Salam et Albam terrarum jacet, a Venedis Slavis qui et alio nomine Sorabi dicti, inhabitatum videbimus, 641.*

SORABI SCLAVI, PROVINCIA SORABIE

As the following series indicates there are numerous references to Serbs and Serb lands in later centuries.

GENS SURBI

• *Gens **Surbi**, 631*

- *Super **Sorabos**, qui campos inter Albiam et Salam iacentes incolebant, eo quod fines Thuringorum ac Saxonum sibi confines praedandi causa fuiseent ingressi, 782*

- *Regi, quod **Sorabi** Sclavi. qui campos inter Albiam et Salam iacentes incolunt, in fines Thuringorum ac Saxonum sibi confines depredandi causa fuiseent ingressi, 782*

- *Gens quoque Sclavorum **Sorabi** cognomine dicta, 782*

- *Qui medias **Sorabi** terras, 782*

- ***Sorabos** et Abodritos, 789*

- *Sclavi **Surbi** et Abotridi, 789*

- *Sclavos cum eo, quorum vocabula sunt **Swrbi**, 789*

- *Sclavi cum eo **Suburbi**, 789*

- ***Suurbi**, 789*

- *Etiam Sclavi cum eo, quorum vocabula sunt **Surbi**, 789*

- *Contra **Sorabos** sclavos, 789*

REGEM EOREM [SURBI] NOMINE SEMELA

- *Regem eorem [**Surbi**] nomine Semela, 805*

- *In Sclaviniam qui dicitur **Sorbi**, 806*

- *In terram Sclavorum qui dicuntur **Sorabi**, qui sedent super Albium fluvium, 806*

- *Terram Sclavorum qui **Suurbi** dicuntur direxit et super Albiam fluvium, 806*

- *In terram Sclavorum, qui dicitur **Rorabi**, super Albiam fluvium ... in qua congressione Miliduoch, 806*

- *In terra Sclavanorum qui **Suurbi** dicuntur, 806*

- *In **Siurbis**, 806*

- *In **Sarabos**, 806*

- *Karolus iunior **Sorabos**, 806*

- *Circa **Surabis** patria, 806*

- *In **Sorabos** super Albim fluvium, 806*

- ***Surabi**, 807*

WELETABI, SORABI, ABODRITI

- *Omnes barbaras ac feras nationes ... Welatabi, **Sorabi**, Abodriti, 808*

- *Omnes barbaras nationes ... Veletabos, **Sorabos**, Abodritos, 814*

- *In **Sorabos** Sclavos, 816*

- *Contra **Sorabos** Sclavos, 816*

- *Legat i ... **Soraborum**, 822*

- *In quo conventu, omnium orientalium Sclavorum ... **Soraborum**, 822*

- *In parte orientali Saxoniae, quae **Soraborum** finibus contigus est, 822*

- *Sorabos*, 833
- *Sorabici* limitis, 839
- *Contra* **Sorabos**, qui Colodici vocantur, 839
- *Regio quae vocatur* **Surbi**, 839
- *In* **Sorabos**, 855

PER SORABOS TRANSIENS

- *Per* **Sorabos** transiens, 856
- *Per* **Sorabos** iter faciens, 856
- *Zistiboron* **Sorabum**, 857
- *Respublica* **Sorabici** limitis, 858
- *Per Thachulfum in* **Sorabos** dictos, 858
- **Sorabos**, Susos et ceteros Sclavorum populos, 864
- **Sorabi** et Siusli iunctis sibi Behemis circumcirca vicinis antiquos terminos Thuringorum transgredientes plurima loca devastant et quosdam sibi incaute congredientes interficiunt, 869
- **Sorabi** et Siusli itemque Boemani Thuringian vastan t ... **Sorabos**, 869
- *Comes et dux* **Sorabici** limitis, 873
- *Boemi,* **Surabi**, *Susi et ceteri Slavi,* 876
- *Slavi, Dalmatae,* **Soavi [Sorabi]**, *Bohemi idem sunt,* 878

DUX SORABICI LIMITIS

- *Quibus Boppo comes et dux* **Sorabici** limitis, 880
- *Sclavi qui vocantur Dalmatii et Behemii atque* **Sorabi** caeterique circumcirca vicini audientes stragam Saxonum a Nordmannus factam pariter conglobati Thuringios invadere nitunter et in Sclavis circa Salam fluvium Thurungiis fidelibus praedas et incendia exercent, 880
- **Sorabi**, Dalamatae et Boemani Sclavi collecto exercitu Thuringiam, 890
- *Ab expeditione Boemica reversus occiditur a* **Sorabis**, 892
- **Soraborum** provintiam, 932
- *In* **Suirbia**, 933
- *In* **Syrbia**, 933
- *Territorio* **Zerbiste**, 948
- *In pago* **Zervisti**, 973
- **Sorabos**, qui Colodici vocantur, 973
- *Sclavi insuper omnes exceptis* **Sorabis** a Saxonibus defercerunt, 994
- *In privilegiis enim Virceburgensibus aliquibus mentio fit Venidorum, Slavorum,* **Serborum**, *Mainvinidorum,* 1000

IN TERITORIO ZERBISTE

- *In teritorio **Zerbiste**, 1003*
- *Civitas **Zirwisti**, 1007*
- ***Zurbice**, 1009*
- *Civitate **Curbici**, 1015*
- *In pago qui vocatur **Zurba**, 1040*
- ***Sorabos**, 1076*
- *Provincia quue **Suurbia** dicitur, 1124*
- *In provincia que dicitur **Swurbelant**, 1136*
- *In provincia **Surbia**, 1180*
- *Pagus Strupenice in provincia **Swurbeland**, 1136*
- ***Surabi, Sorabie**, 1172*

VILLAGES, TOWNS, CITIES

In and along the borders of **White Serbia** medieval sources record numerous toponyms, hydronyms, villages, towns, cities, and regions with names derived from the Serb ethnonym.

Sarbin— Sarbindorf (Malchin)
Sarbin— Sarbinovo (Brandenburg)
Serbica— (Weningen Serwicz)
Serbici— (Bitterfeld)
Serbin— (Calbe)
Serbin— (Forderstadt)
Serbin— (Magdeburg)
Serbin— (Stendal)
Serbin— (Zerbersdorf)
Serbov— (Merseburg)
Serbska Krayina– Border (Upper Saale)
Serbska Blota—Marshes (Lusatia)
Serbska Hola–Heath (Spreewald)
Serbst— (Dessau)
Srbovici— (Merseburg)

REX CZIMISLAV

Beginning with **Dervanus, dux gente Surbiorum**, the names of Serb rulers, kings, dukes, and princes, are recorded in diverse medieval sources.

- ***Dervanus**, dux gente **Surbiorum**, 631*
- *Rex **Semela**; Et ibi pugnaverunt contra regem eorum nomine **Semela**, et vincebant sum, 805*
- ***Milito**, rex superbus, qui regnabat in **Siurbis** … et mandavit eis regibus **Siurborum**, 806*
- ***Melito**, rex superbus, qui regnabat in **Siurbis**, 806*

- *Miliduch*, rex superbus, qui regnabat **Surbi**, 806
- *Miliduch* ducem eorum occidit, 806
- *Miliduoch* dux **Soraborum**, 806
- *Tunglo*, unus de **Soraborum** primoribus, 826
- *Nam et duos duces, Ceadragum Abotritorum et **Tunglonem Soraborum**, 826*
- *Rex **Czimislav**, 839*
- *Regeque ipsorum **Cimusclo** interfecto, 839*
- *Zistibor, 858*
- *Zistiboron Sorabum, 858*
- *Quod Sorabi duci eius **Zistiboro** nomine, 858*
- *Comes **Slavibor**; zemi Luzickych **Srbu**, kde vladl **Slavibor**, 894*
- *Dobromir, 987*
- *Tercia fuit Emnildis, edita a venerabili senior **Dobremiro**, 987*

ALBIM ET SALAM

Medieval sources consistently center the Serbs on the rivers Elbe and Saale.

- *Sorabi Sclavi*, qui compas **inter Albim et Salam** interiacentes incolunt, 782
- *Sorabi*, qui sedent super **Albim** fluvium, 806
- *Salam* fluvium, qui Turingos et **Sorabos** dividit, 833

FEARED BY ALL

As late as the 9th century medieval sources place the Serbs of a greatly diminished *White Serbia* west of the Elbe, and as late as the mid-10th century, according to al-Mas'udi, **the Serbs were a nation feared by all Slavs and others.**

LIMES SORABICUS

The construction of a defensive *limes Sorabicus* in the early 9th century, running from the mouth of the Elbe in the north to the middle Danube, with important frontier stations at Barodwiek, Schesel, Magdeburg, Erfurt, Halstadt, Pfreimt, Forcheim, Lorch, and Regensburg, establishes the Serbs as a force to be reckoned with west of the Elbe *(P. Honigsheim, Der "limes Sorabicus", ZvT 24, 1908. G. Labuda, Limes Sorbica, Fragmenty dziejow Slowianszczyzny Zachodniej I, 1960. O. Dobenecker, DerSturz des Markgrafen Poppo von der Sorbenmark, ZvT 9, 1985).*

ARENDSEE

An 822 entry in the *Royal Frankish Annals (RFA)* suggests that additional defensive efforts were necessary to cope with Serbs west of the Elbe: **Likewise in eastern Saxony toward the Serbian border in the wilderness near Arendsee, the ground was raised into a dam** *(in parte orientali saxoniae, quae Soraborum finibus contigua est).*

THURINGIA

Mid-9th century sources confirm a strong Serb presence in Thuringia as indicated by the terms ***respublica Sorabici limitis*** and ***Sorabici limitis***. It is interesting and perhaps significant that in Cosmas' *Chronica Beomorum, Duringo* is the name of a Serb advisor at the court, a name that appears to be derived from the Serb's native land, *Duringia* or *Thuringia:* **[dux Boemorum] tradidit eam [urbem nomine Dragus] et puerum [filium Wlatizlavis ducis Luczanorum] pedagogo, cui antea pater suus eum commiserat, nomine Duringo, fui fuit de Zribia genere.**

SARBUNUMS, SERBORUMS

Tenth and 11th century sources suggests that the Slavs of Franconia remained Serbs, that the **Wends** of **Terra Slavorum** were Serbs as in the recorded **Sarbunums** and **Serborums**.

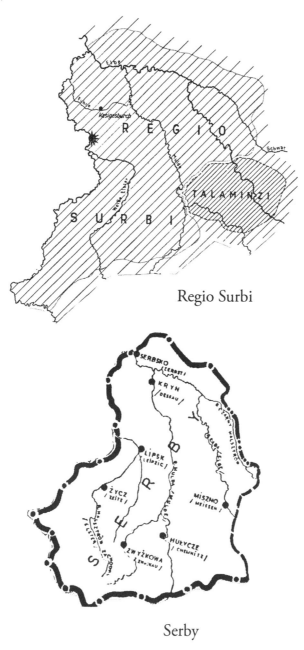

Regio Surbi

Serby

2. SRBI, ABORIGINES POPULOS

A number of German and other historians suspect that the Germans and Slavs were neighbors in Germania from the earliest times. An equal number suspect that numerous German nations recorded in Germania were actually Slavic nations.

SUEBI

Some believe, for example, that Tacitus' **Suebi** were in some part Slavs: **We must now speak of the Suebi, who do not ... constitute a single nation. They occupy more than half Germany, and are divided into a number of separate tribes under different names, though all are called by the generic title of Suebi.**[1] In a very interesting work, August Wersebe advances the radical thesis that Tacitus's **Svevi** (also **Suebi**) are actually Slavs, who, on organizing a strong Slavic state in Germania, gave their name, **Svevi** (also **Svovi, Svoven, Sloven**) to the **Slovens** or Slavs east of the Elbe[2] *(Ueber die Volker-Budnisse des Alten Teutshlands, 1826. K. Tymieniecki, Ze tudiow nad starozynosciami slowianskimi. Lugowie i Swevovie, PrZ 41, 1950).*

SVEVI, SUEBI, SIRBI, SERBI

In this connection it should be noted that some scholars believe that the ethnikons **Svevi, Suebi**, **Sirbi, and Serbi,** share a common linguistic ancestry. On this point, Z. Golab writes: **It [an underlying pronominal adjective *svobu/*svebu which represents PIE *sue/o-bho-] is indirectly attested by the ethnikon Suebi (a latinized form), OHG Swaba ... and has the following correspondence in IE languages: OI sabha 'Versammlung, Gemeindehaus', Goth. Sibja, OHG sipp(e)a 'Sippe, Gesamtheit der eigenen Leute; the two formations presupposed a PIE *sebho- ... Against this background, Proto-Germanic *sueba- = Schwabe could represent a vrddhi formation derived from a nominalized (collective?) *sueba with the meaning...'frei zum eigenen Volke gehorig' ... If we accept the existence of a PIE adjectival form *s(u)e/obho- then we will have a striking suffixal parallel to the PSL *sirbu, i.e. IE *krHbho- ... If the above semantic interpretation of the PIE *s(u)ebho- is correct, then we can define our word into something like 'von anderer' "Halfte", i.e. 'a person being an actual or potential spouse or affine of a given "ego". Of course, the collective formations like *s(u)ebha- etc., or *suebhoda (=Slavic svebhoda/svoboda, etc.) would simply mean 'all the members of an exogamic moiety'—'actual or potenital affines'. In view of these semantic reconstructions based upon the derivational analysis of the PIE *s(u)ebho-, the continuation of the latter in various IE ethnica seems to be self-explanatory: they simply denote groups of affines as do other old IE ethnica which denote groups of blood relatives, e.g. Slav. *Sirbi, etc** *(Z. Golab, About the Connection Between Kinship Terms and some Ethnica in Slavic. The Case of *Sirbi and Slovene, International Journal of Slavic Linguistics and Poetics, XXV/XXVI, 1982).*

APPEAR TO BE SLAVIC

German and other historians note that a number of *German* tribes cited by Tacitus, Strabo *(Geographia, 7 B.C.),* and Ptolemy *(Geographike Hyphegesis, 127-45 A.D.),* among others, appear to be Slavic in name and character.

CELMANTICI, DALEMINCI

For example, some historians suspect: 1) Ptolemy's *Celmantici* and *Calucones* are the Serb *Daleminci* and *Glomaci*; 2) Tacticus' *Coldui* are Strabo's *Coldulos* are the Serb *Colodici*; 3) Tacitus' *Dulgubs* are (**the Angrivarii and Chamavi have a common frontier on one side with the Dulgubnii**) Slav *Dulebs*; 4) Tacitus' *Lugs/Lugii* (**Suebia, in fact, is cut in two down the middle by an unbroken range of mountains, beyond which live a multitude of tribes, of whom the Lugii are the most widely spread, being divided into a number of smaller units**) are Strabo's *Lugi* are Ptolemy's *Lugi* are the Slav *Lugs*, plural *Luzani*; 5) Strabo's *Mugils/Mugilons* are the Slav *Mogils*; 6) Tacitus's *Sems/Semnones* (**The oldest and most famous of the Suebi, it is said, are the Semnones, and their antiquity is confirmed by a religious observance ... The grove is the centre of their whole religion**) are the Slav *Zems*; 7) Strabo's *Sibs* (*Sibins*) are Sequester's *Cers* (*Cervets*) are the *Sers/Serbs*; 8) Tacitcus' *Svarins, Rudins* and *Varins* are Slavs; 9) Tacitus's *Vuithones/Vulti*, actually *Vilthones/Vilti*, are Ptolemy's *Veltae* are the Slav *Velti/Velici/Lutici*; 10) the *Zuma* are the Slav *S(h)uma*.[3]

LUGS

Numerous scholars have little doubt that the *Lugs* and *Mugilons* were Slavs, not Germans. An early source offers interesting information on the identity and locations of the *Lugs: Itamque multarum civitatum inter Lygios appelationes extructae sunt, propter Henetorum, quos et Vuinidos et Vandalos nuncupamus incursionem et ocupationem. Nam eo loco veteres Germanos eosque Lygios habitasse non est obscurum, et cum horum nominum neque allusiones habeantur, necque certi situa in tabulis Ptolomeii inveniantur, haud facile quis recentes nationes Polonicas, cum vetustis Lygiorum Suevorum apposite conferret. Ita Venedi sunt quoque in Sarmatia, sed Germania adnumerati juxta Ptolomaeum videntur esse.*[4]

MUGILONS

The *Mugilons*, Jacob Grimm writes, are almost certainly a Slavic tribe, an ethnonym derived from *mogila*, an Old Slavic word for mound or hill, located in an area where one finds the medieval *Serb-Wend* town of *Mogilno*, the modern German Mugeln (Mogelini984; Mogilina/1003; Moglin/1185; Mugelin/1198, now Muglen, near Oschatz). In addition, a number of other *Mogils/Mogilnos* are recorded in the same general area, including, among others: **Mugelin**/1347, Mogelin/1350, later Muglen, near Pirna; **Mogele**/143, Mogil/1506, later Muglen, near Schweinitz; **Mogelentcz**/1446, Mogelentz/1469, later Muglenz, near Wurzen.

RUDINS

Rud, connoting ore, mineral, mine, mining, miner, is the Slavic root of a number of ancient Slav settlements in *White Serbia* and Germania east and west of the Elbe: Rudenica (Rudeniz/1248), near Leipzig; Rudin (*villa Rudin*, 1235), near Zeitz; Rudin (Ruden, 1245), near Zerbst; Rudina (Rudene, 1323), near Bitterfeld; Rudov (Rudow, 1375), near Templin; Rudovina (Ruthewyn, 1316), near Lebus; Rudnica (Rutnizze, 1174), near Juterbog; Rudnica (Reudnitz, 1683), near Beeskow.

GERMANS OR SARMATIANS

Tacitus admits to considerable confusion as to where *Suebia-Germania* ends and *Sarmatia* begins: **Here Suebia ends, I do not know whether to class the tribes ... with the Germans or with the Sarmatians.** Thus Tacitus' *Venedi*, though *Sarmatian* in appearance and habits, are, he writes, to be classed as *Germans*.

WHITE SERBIA

A number of early German historians are certain that the *White Serbs* were the first to settle Germania's *White Serbia*. More precisely, they are certain that **the Serbs were the first to settle the area between the Elbe and Saale rivers, with especially strong concentrations on and along the waterways: the Bode, Unstrut and Ilm west of the Saale; the Orla, Nuthe, Fuhne, Weisse Elster, Pleisse, Mulde, Zwickauer Mulde, Schopau, and Freiburg Mulde east of the Saale.**

ABORIGINES POPULOS

Erasmus Stella, a 16th century German historian, is certain that the Serbs are the ancient and original inhabitants of the lands between the Elbe and Saale rivers *(De Rebus ac Populis Orae Inter Albim et Salam Germaniae Flumina)*. In this vital, historic area, Stella writes: **The Serbs are the *aborigines populos*.**

ABORIGINIES

Two centuries later, a rigorous examination of the historical record of this area *(Allgemeine Nordische Geschichte)*, centered on the the principality of Anhalt-Serbst, leads the historian August Ludwig Schlozer to the same conclusion: **The Serbs are the aboriginies.**

ALBIM ET NISA

Stella, Schlozer and numerous other historians have little doubt that: **The Serbs are the ancient and original inhabitants of the land east of the Elbe, the area between the Elbe and Luzicka Nisa or Neisse rivers, with especially strong concentrations on and along the the major and minor waterways, the Elster, Roder, Schwarze Elster, and Spree rivers.** Among other historians, one finds essentially the same views in the writing of C. Manlius, an early 18th century authority on Lusatia/Luzica *(Lusaticarum Deigma, Scriptores Rerum Lusaticarum Antiqui et Recentiores, 1719)*.

URBES ET CASTELLA

They are also certain that the *White Serbs* built and established the first castles, towns, and cities in this area: *Primrose urbes et castella in has regione condisse.* All sources agree that *White Serbia* was a land of many towns, opulent cities, and strong castles: *In Sorabi Alba ea multae sunt opulentissima civitates, munitissimaque castella.*

SERB FOUNDATIONS

In the past, German historians noted and often stressed the *White Serb* foundations of major cities, of Dresden, Leipzig, Meissen and others. In the past, German historians were especially attentive to the fact that the Serbs were the ancient and original settlers of the principality of Meissen.

EVERYONE KNOWS

Indeed, it was long common for German scholars and commentators to consider the so-called Germans of Meissen to be Serbs. Regarding the ethnic origin and character of Meissen, Stella writes:

> **Everyone knows that the natives of Meissen are Serbs.**

SORABIA, SERBIA

Regarding this same area, the principality of Meissen, Stella's contemporary, Peter Albinum writes *(Commentarius Novus de Mysnia oder Newe Meynische Chronica):*

> **For seven hundred years this land was known as Sorabia or Serbia**

MISIN, MEISSEN

As for its main city, Albinum writes:

> **For seven hundred years the city of Meissen was known by its Serb name, Misin.**

SERBS, SERBIA

In *Alten Slawen Ursprung, Sitten, Gebrauche, Meinungen und Kenntnisse* (1783), Karl Gottlob von Anton, one of the most important scholars of the German enlightenment, reminds his readers that:

> **In the Middle Ages Meissen was called Serbia.**

In fact, he writes:

> **It was not too long ago that the natives of Meissen called themselves Serbs and their land Serbia.**

Moreover, von Anton adds:

> **We still have one Serb realm: the Wends of Upper and Lower Lusatia who still call themselves Serbs and their homeland Serbia.**

ENDNOTES

[1] R. Much, Die Germania des Tacitus, 1937.

[2] For a comprehensive discussion of the Slavic roots and character of nations cited by ancient writers and geographers: W. Ketrzynski, Die Lygier. Ein Beitrag zu Urgeschichtge der Westslawen und Germanen, 1868. Also: T. Lehr-Splawinski, O starozytnych Lugiach, SlA 1, 1948. K. Tymieniecki, Lugiowie w Czechach, PrZ 7, 1951. M. Vasmer, Lugii und Mugilones, Sybaris, 1958.

[3] In a very interesting and authoritative study on the subject, R. Much advances the thesis that the once populous and powerful Lugs disappeared from the historical record in name only, that they survived under different names, including, Slavs called Vandals (Lugier, Reallexicon der germanischen Altertumskunde, 1916).

Part XVII

1. IN RETREAT

Onomastic and other evidence indicates that at its height *White Serbia's* historic lands west and south of the Saxonian Saale, in terms of occupation and settlement, ran deep into Thuringia, Mysi-Voitland, Franconia-Bavaria, Baden-Wurttemberg, and Hesse, into *Terra Slavorum's Respublica Sorabici, Moinvinidi, Radanzvinidi,* and *Nabvinidi.*

On greater *White Serbia's* central and southwest borders, a leading authority on the subject, Adolf Cerny, writes: **Jihu horami ceskymi az do okoli Brodu** [*Brod* is the Slavic name for Furth in Middle Franconia, a city on the Rednitz River, where it joins the Pegnitz to form the Regnitz River] **a Chamu na Reznu v Horni Falc** *(Luzice a Luzicti Srbove, 1911).*

IN RETREAT

In the 9th century *Regnum Sorabia* was a lesser *regnum,* one in full retreat before an advancing *Regnum Francorum*, a Holy Roman Empire in progress. In the early 9th century the area between *Regnum Francorum's* **limes Sorabicus** border stations in Thuringia and Franconia, from Magdeburg in the north to Erfurt to Forcheim in the south, and *White Serbia's* provinces along the Saale, was already a diminishing borderland *(S.A. Wolf, Die slawische Westgrenze in Nord- und Mitteldeutschland im Jahre 805, DwS 2, 1957. H. Brachmann, Der Limes Sorabicus-Geschicte und Wirkung, ZtA 25, 1991).*

KRAJINA SRBSKO

It appears that one part of the borderland, between the upper Saxonian Saale and the Erzgebirge, was organized and administered as a *krajina Srbsko* or Serb borderland consisting of eight *zupas*. Cerny writes: **Mezi Horni Salou a horami Krusnymi [Krusne Hory is the Slavic name for the Ezgebirge Mountains] byla krajina Srbsko s 8 zupami.** In other words, *krajina Srbsko* was located in a borderland area between Weimar, Rudolstadt, Saalfeld, and Hof in the north and west, and the Bohemian borderlands in the south and east *(H. Walther, Slawische Name im Erzgebirge in ihrer Bedeutung fur die Siedlungsgeschichte, in BnF 11, 1960. K.Gebhardt, Die Ortsnamen des mitteleren Erzgebirges, 1967).*

LOKAVICA, SALA, VISICI

Though the exact location of *krajina Srbsko* or the identity and location of any of its *zupas* is unknown, several 'unattached' border *zupas/pagos* are recorded in this general area, namely *pagos Lokavica, Salagov,* and *Visici:* **pago Lokavica** (**pago Launuuizza**, 932; **pago Lanewizi**, 1108), centered on the Ilm River; **pago Sala** (as in *Sclavorum et Vuinidon in pago Salagouue*, 953), on Thuringian Saale, centered near modern Saalfeld; **pago Visichi** (**Wisichgaw**, 974; **pago Visichgoven**, 1051), centered on the Unstrut River *(R. Fischer, Slawisches Sprachgut westlich der Saale. Der Name Langwitz, Wissenschaftliche Annalen 2, 1952).* A late 10th century source places the villages of *Zidici, Vuidri,* and *Zuchibuli* on the Unstrut, near Sommerda and Kolleda.s

SERB SETTLEMENT

There is no room for doubt about the borderland's ethnic foundations and character in the area running from Orla to Saalfeld (on the northeastern slope of the Thuringian forest) in the southwest, to Ilmenau (on the Ilm River) and Rudolstadt (on the northeastern foot of the Thuringian forest), to Weimar, Apolda, Kolleda, and Sommerda (on the Unstrut) in the northwest *(C. Albrecht, BeT zur Kenntnis der slawischen Keramik auf Grund der Burgwallforschung im mittleren Saalegebiet, 1923. R.Fischer, Ortsnamen der Kr. Arnstadt und Ilmenau, 1955; W. Bastian, Eine slaswische Furstenburg der Kolonisationszeit von Neuburg, Kr. Weimar, AuF 2, 1957. R. Fischer, K. Elbracht, Ortsnamen der Kr. Rudolstadt, 1959. E. Eichler, H. Deubler, Slawische Flurname im Kr. Rudolstadt, RuD 7, 1961. W. Fuhrmann, Die Ortsnamen des Stadt-und Landkreises Weimar, 1962; Linguistische Studien zu den slawischen Toponymen des Bereiches der Ilm-Saale-Platte und des mittleren Saale-gebietes. M. Reiser, Slawische Flurnamen der Kr. Greiz und Zeulenroad, Jb des Museums Hohenleuben-Richenfels 15/16, 1967-68. G. Mobes, Deutsche und Slawen vom 10. bis 16. Jh in Grossbrembach, Kr. Weimar, AuF 22, 1977).*

SERB SETTLEMENT

The Serb settlement of this area is clear and documented by the names of the numerous communities recorded throughout the medieval period (e.g. *Cunbici, Dachiza, Unschi, Vulchistedin, Vunschi*, 899), from the names in the following representative series.

BELIN, BELOSIN, BREZOVICA

Belin— Belin, 1416 (Bohlen)
Bezgoz— Bysegacz, 1373 (Piesigitz)
Bodanici— Bodenitz, 1458 (Bodnitz)
Belosin— Belschiben, 1411 (Bohlscheiben)
Bratronici— Bretternitz, 1417 (Breternitz)
Brchovici— Burchewitz, 1486 (Burgwitz)
Brezovica— Brisewitz, 1125 (Presswitz)
Bukodry— Buckedrowe, 1367 (Bockedra)
Chodic— Codiz, 1336 (Koditz)
Chodric— Codrice, 1216 (Kodderitzsch)
Cholm— Kolm, 1497 (Kulm)
Chotici— Chotizi, 1074 (Koditz)
Chrostin— Krostin, 1402 (Crosten)
Dobjar— Dobyar, 1394 (Dobia)
Dobrovici— Dobrawicz, 1071 (Dobritz)
Dolina— Dolene, 1215 (Dohlen)

DROGANICI, GNUS, GORSICI

Droganici— Droganic, 1136 (Drognitz)
Gabrovica— Gaberwicz, 1450 (Gabritz)
Glina— Gline, 1309 (Gleina)
Gnus— Gnus, 1516 (Gneus)
Godavin— Godawini, 1074 (Judewin)
Gojnici— Goynicz, 1350 (Geunitz)
Golus— Goles, 1414 (Golitz)
Gorsici— Garschiz, 1289 (Garsitz)

Gosovici— Gossewitz, 1529 (Gosswitz)
Grab— Graba, 1370 (Graba)
Greben— Greben, 1288 (Groben)
Grob— Crop, 1136 (Krobitz)
Gruda— Gruda, 1350 (Greuda)
Jugov— Jugowe, 1450 (Gauga)
Jarotici— Gertewiz, 1486 (Gertewitz)
Klinov— Clinowa, 1074 (Kleina)

KOSOBODY, KRAK, LAZANE
Kloskovic— Kloskewicz, 1378 (Closwitz)
Klukov— Clukowe, 1133 (Clukow)
Kolkovici— Culcawitzi, 1074 (Kolkwitz)
Kosobody— Kossebode, 1447 (Kospoda)
Koznic— Kosenitz, 1312 (Kosnitz)
Krak— Krockau, 1541; Krakau, 1718 (Krakau)
Krsic— Curstiz, 1133 (Kursitz)
Lazane— Lazan, 1372 (Laasen)
Lescina— Lestini, 1074 (Lehesten)
Lom— Lomen, 1417 (Lohma)
Lozica— Losit, 1410 (Losits)
Lubis— Lubis, 1414 (Leibis)
Lubosici— Lobesiz, 1258 (Leibschutz)
Lucin— Lutzscha, 1366 (Lauscha)
Lukavica— Longawitzi, 1074 (Loquitz)
Lutinic— Lutnitz, 1495 (Leutnitz)

LUZNICA, MILICI, NEDAMIR
Luznica— Lusenitz, 1271 (Lausnitz)
Mez, Meza— Mesitz, 1472 (Miesitz)
Milici— Milicz, 1378 (Melitz)
Modlovici— Modelwitz, 1136 (Moderwitz)
Mokos, Mokosov— Mogzow, 1378 (Moxa)
Munsovici— Munschwitz, 1518 (Munschwitz)
Nedamir— Nedemer, 1400 (Diemer)
Paseka— Pasecke, 1378 (Paska)
Parno— Parn, 1378 (Pahren)
Penovici— Penewicz, 1338 (Pennewitz)
Podolovici— Bodelwicz, 1358 (Bodelwitz)
Premsnica— Bremsenitz, 1431 (Bremsnitz)
Prilep— Prilep, 1074 (Prelipp)
Radogost— Radegast, 1427 (Rodias)
Radomysl— Roidemusle, 1083 (Rottelmisch)
Ramen— Romen, 1496 (Rehmen)

RATOVICI, RODILOVICI, RUDA
Ranis— Ranis, 1185 (Ranis)

Ratovici— Rettwitz, 1549 (Rettwitz)
Remisici— Remischzi, 1074 (Remschutz)
Robolici— Robelitz, 1279 (Roblitz)
Robsici— Robeschicz, 1378 (Robschutz)
Robus— Robuz, 1252 (Rabis)
Rodilovici— Rodelwicz, 1378 (Rodelwitz)
Ruda— Ruda, 1219 (Rauda)
Rusovici— Ruschwitz, 1378 (Rauschwitz)
Skala— Schala, 1071 (Schaala)
Skatin— Schetin, 1317 (Schoten)
Skoblov— Schobelaw, 1448 (Schiebelau)
Skomici— Schomlitz, 1621 (Schomlitz)
Skopsk— Schopcz, 1435 (Schops)
Skorov— Schoraw, 1400 (Schorau)
Slavin— Slowin, 1197 (Schloben)

SMIRICI, SMOLIN, SMORDA

Smirici— Smiricz, 1319 (Sehmieritz)
Smirim— Smirme, 1350 (Schirma)
Smolin— Smollin, 1365 (Schmolln)
Smorda— Smorda, 1425 (Schmorda)
Spal— Spal, 1450 (Spaal)
Stanov— Stanow, 1378 (Stanau)
Stebrica— Stebrize, 1156 (Stiebritz)
Stobor— Stober, 1450 (Stobra)
Storkus— Storkus, 1354 (Storkus)
Strezovici— Stresewicz, 1350 (Strosswitz)
Sulkovici— Sulkewicz, 1362 (Solkwitz)
Svinica— Sweinitz, 1498 (Schweinitz)
Tesici— Teschitz, 1422 (Doschnitz)
Tisov— Tissouwe, 1450 (Dissau)
Trnov— Tyrnowe, 1324 (Dorna)

Row Houses, Serbski Misin (Old Meissen)

375

2. NORTHWEST FRONTIER

Our review of **White Serbia's** north and northwest borderlands covers the following *natios* and *provincias*. From north to south: 1) *provincia Neletici;* 2) *regio Belzem;* 3) *teritorio Serbiste;* 3a) *provintia Ploni;* 3b) *pago Spreva;* 4) *provincia Moraciani;* 4a) *provincia Zemzici;* 4b) *provincia Liezizi.*

ARENDSEE

The *RFA* render certain evidence that, one, the area around Arendsee was situated on a contested borderland, and, two, the lands east of the Arendsee were within **White Serbia's** political borders in the early 9th century: **In eastern Saxony toward the Sorbian border in the wilderness near Arendsee, the ground was raised into a dam … it formed a rampart-like embankment one Gallic mile in length,** 822. Equally certain sources place the lands east and opposite Arendsee, centered at Havelberg, within the borders of one of the larger **White Serb** sub-nations, the **Neletici.**

1. NELETICI

The *Descriptio Civitatem* records 74 *civitats* in **Neletici**, a number that may not take into account all the *civitats* in **Neletici** territories in western and central **White Serbia. Znetalici haben civitates LXXIIII.**[1] Numerous sources place Havelberg, an ancient stronghold located on an island in the Havel, near its mouth on the Elbe, *in provincia Neletici.*

- *Castri et civitatis Havelberg in provincia Nieletizi, 948*
- *Havelburg castrum et civitas sitas est in provincia Nieletitzi, 964*
- *Provincia Nielietizi, 1150*
- *Nieleitizi, 1179*

CIVITAS NIZEM

It is also clear that **provincia Neletic** included lands north of *civitas* Havelburg, including **civitas Nizem** (from the Slavic *nize zemlje* or lower land), modern Nitzow, a town north of Havelburg.

- *In eadem provincia Nizem civitatem, 948*
- *In provinicia Nieletizi Niziem civitas cum toto burgwardo, 1150*
- *In villa Nizzowe, 1282*
- *Nizowe civitatem, 1179*
- *In villa Nizzow, 1310*
- *Terra Nitzezim qui Nitczow dicitur, 1337*
- *Nytzowe, 1344*
- *Nitczow, 1431*

NELETICI-BREZANI

The size, strength, and importance of the **Neletici** in the Havelberg area is even greater if, as medieval sources suggest and modern scholarship confirms, the **Brezhani** were a branch of the *Neletici*. J. Herrmann refers to the *Nielitizi-Brizani* (Siedung, Wirtschaft der Slawischen Stamme Zwischen Oder/Niesse und Elbe, 1968).

NELETICI-BREZANI, STODERANI

The *Neletici-Brezhani* occupied a large area between Havelberg in the northwest and Brandenburg in the southeast, where they bordered and intermingled with the *Stoderani* (Z.Sulowski, Brezanie, SsS 1, 1961).

- *Brizanorum et Stoderanorum populi, qui Havelberg et Brandenburg habitant.*
- *Omnem enim terram Brizanorum, Stoderanum mutarumque gentium habitantium iuxta Habelam et Albiam misit sub iugum.*

In this general area today one finds, from north to south, the following towns and cities: Havelberg, Sandau, Rhinow, Schollene, Rathenow, Premitz, Milow, Pritzerbe, Plaue, Brandenberg (W. Seelman, Die Alte Sorbisch-Lutizische Grenze, ZoN 13, 1937).

2. REGIO BELZEM

Medieval sources locate *regio Belozem* (from the Slavic *Belo Zemlya* or *White Land*) in the Altmark, a historic region between and below the Arendsee frontier in the west and *provincia Neletici* in the east (J. Schultze, Der Balsamgau in den Pegauer Annalen, JbG 13-14, 1965. M. Bathe, Belxem, ein Gau- und Flussname?, WzH 16, 1967. H. Schonfeld, Zu slavischen Flurnamen in der Altmark, WzH 16, 1967. J. Schneider, Neue altslawische Siedlungsfunde aus der sutostlichen Altmark, JmV 57, 1973. H.K. Schulze, Die Besiedlung der Altmark, FsT W. Schlesinger, 1973).[2]

- *Om Belxam, 938*
- *Arnaburch (Arenburg on the Elbe, north of Stendal) in pago belcseim, 981*
- *Arneburg in pago Beleseim, 983*
- *In loco qui Belcsem dicitur, 983*
- *In Balsamis iuxta civitatem Nienburch* (Nienburch or Newburg is believed to be another name for Arneburg), *993*
- *Civitas Arenburg in pago Belcsem, 1006*
- *Bremezhe (Briest, east of Tangerhutte), Eilerdesthor (Elversdorf, southwest of Tangerhutte) ... in pago Belsheim, 1013*
- *Diozese ... Belkishem, 1022*
- *In pago Belshem, 1022*
- *Bremezhe, Eilerdestorp, Steinedal* (Stendal, northwest of Tangermunde) *... in pago Belshem, 1022*
- *Slavischen fursten Wilk in Balsamorum, 1023*
- *Balsamorum possidens fines, 1050*
- *Belchesheim, 1052*
- *Belzem, in pago belcsem in comitatu wrizonis, 1096*
- *Balsamorum regio, 1150*

- *Balsamerland ... quae dicitur, 1160*
- *Balsamorum in terra palustri, 1161*

The same sources center **Belzem** in an area between the Elbe in the west, Milde in the east, Biese in the north, Tanger in the south, and along the Uchte in the center, an area that includes modern Arneburg, Stendal, Tangerhuttethe, Briest, and Elversdorf *(P.L.B. Kupka, Slavische Skelettgraber von Tangermunde, Jahresschrift fur die Vorgesch der sachsisch-thuringischen Lander 14, 1926. W. Hoffman, Slawische Funde aus Korpergrabern in Tanergumende, Kr. Stendal, Altmarksiches Museum Stendal 13, 1959).*

BELZEM, NIZEM
It is perhaps significant and evidence of a **Neletici** connection that **pago Belzem** is opposite **provincia Nielietizi's** *Nizezem* (**terra Nizezin que Nitczow dicitur**), north of Havelberg.

WILHELMUS SLAVUS
Various sources indicate that as early as the 13th century, a number of Slavs of **Belzem** were already German in name and Christian in faith.

- *In Stendal consules ... wilhelmus sclauus, 1233*
- *In Stendal ... jacobus sclauus, 1251*
- *In Stendal ... adam sclauus, 1251*

SORBISCHE STAMME AM FLAMINGRAND
Midway between **provincia Neletici** in the north and **regio Neletici** in the south, Herrmann locates two Serb nations, the **Moraciani** and **Zerbisti**, in the Flamingrand east and southeast of Magdeburg *(Sorbische stamme am Flamingrand).*

3. SERBISTI-ZERBISTE
In addition to the obvious facts of time, place, and historical circumstance, there are compelling linguistic reasons to read **Zerbiste** as **Serbiste**. Regarding this matter, H. Kunstmann's rejection of *Zirbiste* as *Cirvisce* and definitive affirmation of **Zerbiste** as **Serbiste** deserves detailed attention.[3]

SRBISTI
South of **provincia Moraciani**, Hermann centers **Serbiste** at Zerbst on the Nuthe, the Zerbster Nuthe. There are references to **civitas, pago, teritorio** and **urbs Serbiste** in 10th and 11th century sources.

- *Teritorio Zerbiste, 948*
- *In pago Zervisti, 973*
- *Teritorio Zerbiste, 1003*
- *Civitas Zirwisti, 1007*
- *Urbs Zirwisti, 1007*

TERITORIO SERBISTE
Medieval sources indicate that **teritorio Serbisti** was centered in a densely settled

area around and between modern Zerbst, Rosslau, Dessau, Mosigkau, Osternienburg, Kothen, Baalberge, Bernburg, Nienburg, Aken, Calbe, and *Barby* *(S. Wauer, Zum Problem der polabisch-sorbischen Grenze in den Kreises Schonebeck und Zerbst, Slavische Namenforschung, 1961. B. Schmidt, W. Nitzschke, Untersuchungen in slawischen Burgen zwischen Saale und Flaming, AuF 20, 1975. J. Schultheis, Zur Geographie slawischer Ortsnamentypen im Gebiet des Sudwesflamings, OsG 11, 1976).* Regarding **Serbisti's** core area and general boundaries, Herrmann writes: **Die Beschreibung der Diozese Brandenburg nach Gauen (948) macht deulich, dass sich der Gau Serbiste zwischen den Territorien der slavischen Moraciani and Ploni befunden haben muss. Nach einer modernen Beschreibung erstreckte sich das Siedlungsgebiet sudlich von Moraciani an der Zerbster Nuthe und an der Elbaue (Nuthgebiet). Seine grenzen waren im Norden und Osten die Flamingwalder, im Suden die Elbe. Im Nordwesten grentze das Siedlungsgebiet an das Ehle-Ihlegebiet. Das zentrale Gebiet dieses Gaues muss demnach der Raum zwischen Elbe and Nuthe gewesen sein.** The following place names are typical of the communities recorded in and near **teritorio Serbiste** in the medieval period.

BOZENICI, DOBRIC, DUB

Bodec, Bodeta— Bodetz, 1307 (Badetz)
Bozenici— Bozenitz, 1571 (Bosenitz)
Brla, Brlin— Berlin, 1324 (Berlin)
Bulsk— Bulzk, 1335 (Bulzig)
Cholm, Cholmen— Golmeglin, 1524 (Golmenglin)
Dobric— Doberiz, 1285 (Dobritz)
Dobrichov— Dobbrischau, 1571 (Dobrichau)
Dub, Dubsk— Dubz, 1307 (Diebzig)
Gradec— Gardiz, 1259 (Garitz)
Grdin— Gherden, 1332 (Gehrden)
Godnici— Gotheniz, 1182, (Godnitz)
Grm, Grom— Grymmene, 1326 (Grimme)
Jablan— Jablinze, 1150 (Gablenz)
Jutrochov— Juterchowe, 1273 (Jutrichau)
Jutrokliky— Juterklik, 1319 (Gutterluck)
Kol, Kolsov— Culszhowe, 1161 (Kulso)
Krupica— Crupiz, 1280 (Kreupzig)

LESKA, LUZOV, MORICANI

Kurno— Curni, 939 (Kuhren)
Leska— Liezeca, 995 (Leitzkau)
Lepotici— Leptiz, 1393 (Leps)
Lepotov— Lebethowe, 1213 (Lepte)
Luzov— Lusow, 1307 (Luso)
Morica— Mordiz, 1259 (Moritz)
Moricani— Morzahn, 1354 (Zahna)
Murov— Murow, 1307 (Muhro)
Nedelica— Nedelitzinne, 1329 (Nedlitz)
Okun— Ankun, 1214 (Ankuhn)
Pec— Pecz, 1290 (Peetz)

Pomelica— Pameliz, 1187 (Pamelitz)
Pol, Polica, Polensk— Polenzk, 1365 (Polenzko)
Roslav— Roslowe, 1315 (Rosslau)
Rudno— Rudin, 1235 (Reuden)
Skor— Shore, 1325 (Schora)
Stud, Studica— Studiz, 1265 (Steutz)
Streg, Stregota— Stregut, 1307 (Straguth)

CZERNIG

Hans Czernig is one of many Germans with obvious Slavic family names recorded in Zerbst in the late 14th century.

ANHALT-ZERBST

Zerbst was long the capital city of the Duchy of Anhalt-Zerbst. Sophia August of Anhalt-Zerbst, later Catherine the Great, Empress of Russia (1762-96), spent her youth and formative years here. One of the leading French authorities on ancient Slavic civilization, Louis Leger, liked to remind his students: **If the famous empress had known the history of her native country better she might have told her new Russian subjects that she was giving them a princess of Slavic origin.**

SORBISCHE SPRACHGEBIET

According to one postwar study north central Serb settlements ran south of a line marked by the villages of Furstenwalde-Kopenick in the east and Zerbst-Juterbog in the west *(S. Wauer, Zum Problem der polabisch-sorbischen Grenze in den Kreises Schonebeck und Zerbst, Slavische Namenforschung, 1961)*. A more recent and exhaustive study places Serb settlements and *das Sorbische Sprachgebiet* farther north and just south of the Berlin-Brandenburg line in the 16th century. *(Die Slawen in Deutschand, 1970)*.

3A. PROVINTIA PLONI

Situated within the *Sorbische Sprachgebiet*, **provintia Ploni** takes its name from the Serb word *plon* connoting flat, level, treeless land *(Herrmann:* **Der Name Ploni geht auf ein dem niedersorbischen plony entsprechendes Adjektiv zuruk und bedeutet 'eben')**. The are several brief references to *provincia* and *pago* in 10th and 12th century sources.

- *Provintiae Moraciani ... Ploni, 948*
- *In pagos Ploni, Niccici, 965*
- *In pagis qui dicuntur Siusili et Plonim, 965*
- *In provincia et pagis ... Lusice, Ploni, 973*
- *Burguuardium Belizi ... in provincia Bloni, 997*
- *Provincias ... Ploni, 1161*
- *Ploni, 1188*

Ploni's center was midway between Juterbog in the southeast and Brandenburg in the northwest, perhaps centered at Belzig (Belici), centered by Glienicke, Golzow, Bruck, Niemegk, Wiesenburg, and Gorzke *(A. Wedzki, Ploni, SsS 4, 1970)*. The one burgward recorded in ***Ploni*** is in this area, *Belizi* (Belici), modern Beelitz, on the Nieplitz river, indicates that its borders were farther north and east *(A. Wedzki, Belizi, SsS 1, 1961)*.

Regarding its general boundaries, Herrmann writes: **Die Sudgrenze bildete der Flaming, im Norden lag das Zaucheplateau, im Westen das Sanderbebiet des Brandenburg-Neustadtischen Forstes, die Ostgrenze lag auf der Teltowhochflache und im Ostteil der Luckenwalder Heide.**

3B. PROVINCIA SPREVA

Clearly within *Sorbische Sprachegebeit*, and on the northern edge of the great *Luzica* Serb confederation with sixty-plus *civitats*, **provincia Sprewa** takes its name from the *Spreva* (a Serb word connoting a rushing, fizzy, spraying waterway) or Spree river, by and large a Serbian waterway from beginning to end.

> • *Provintiae Moraciani, Cieruisti (Serbisti) ... Zpriauuani, 948*
> • *In pagis Niccici et Sprewa ex utraque fluminis parte, quod dicitur Sprewa, nen noc iiet in Lusyciz atque Mrocini, 965*
> • *Tria milia mansorum et amplius in Sprewe et Niemze, 1180*
> • *Provincia Zpriavani, 1188*

Rising in the *Luzicka Gory* (Lusatian Mountains), the Spreva flows north past Budusin (Bautzen), where it temporarily splits into two branches, *Velka Spreva* (Grosse Spree) and *Mala Spreva* (Kleine Spree), that come together at Sprev (Spremberg), where it passes from **Luzica Gorni** (Upper Luzica) to **Luzica Dolni** (Lower Luzica), north past Chosebuz (Cottbus), west to Lubnov, north past Lubin, and northwest to Kopenick/Berlin.

> • *Sprewa, 965*   • *In Sprewa, 1373*
> • *In Sprewa, 1004*   • *Sprew, 1431*
> • *Ultra Szpream, 1238* • *Die Sprewitz, 1591*
> • *Zprewa, 1268*

Above **urbs Lubin**, a chain of Serb settlements dot the Spreva's course to Berlin, including, among others, Peski (Peskow); Zarov (Bad Saarow); Storkov (Windischen Storkow/Storkow). The same is true of the Dahme, a Spree tributary that rises in **Luzica Dolni** and flows north past **castrum Golisin** to the Spree at Kopenick/Berlin *(F. Metsk, Zur sorbischen Siedlungs- und Namenkunde der Umgegend von Dahme, Orbis Scriptus, 1966; P. Redlich, Begenungen slawischer Stamme an der Dahme im Spiegel von Orts und Flurnamen, GgC 1974).*

PAGO SPREV

Scholars locate **pago Sprev** east and slightly northeast of **provincia Ploni**, centered on the Spreva, east and south of Berlin-Kopenick, the twin residences of **Spreva's** legendary **Knez Jaksa**, said to be the last independent Serb ruler.

4. MORACIANI

It is clear from diverse sources that north of **Serbiste**, the **Moraciani** occupied a broad area running from the Elbe near Magdeburg in the west, along the Ihle and Ehle rivers, to the Buchau near Tucheim in the northeast *(G. Labuda, Morzyczanie, SsS 3, 1967).*

ET MORIZANI

The *Descriptio Civitatem* identifies the **Moraciani** as one of three nations, **Bethenici, Smeldingi** and **Morizani**, with eleven *civitats* and locates them east of the **Linaa** and west of the **Hehfeldi** [Haveli]: *Linaa est populus, qui habet civitates VII. Propre illis resident, quos vocant Bethenici et Smeldingon et Morizani, qui habent civitates XI. Iuxta illos sunt, qui vocantur Hehfeldi.*

PROVINCIA MORACIANI

Medieval references to *provincia Moraciani's* villas, civitats, oppids, and burgwards in 10th and 11th century sources reveal important information relating to its size and location.

- *In Mortsani, Ligzice et Heveldun, 937*

- *Civitates Sirtavua [Schortau], Grabauua [Grabow], Buchoe [Buckaw] in pago Moraciani, 946. X Provincia Moraciani, 948*

- *Marienborch (north of Jerichow, on the southeastern border of provincia Belzem) civitas in morician, 949*

- *Merianburg urbem que et coblitze dicitur, 1150*

- *Curtem de burwardo kobelitz que et marienburgk dicitur, 1159*

- *In pago Moriziani ... Preszici [Brietzke], Moseri [Moser], Nedialesci[Nedlitz], Puciani [Pothen], 961*

- *Civitates Luborn [Loburg] et Tuchime [Tucheim] in pago Moroszanorum, 965*

- *Urbs Tuchime in pago Moresceni, 965*

- *Villa Liubatici [Lubs] in pago Mrozini, 975*

- *In pago Morazena: Budim [Buden], Curozuzi, Frabonizi, Grabonizi, Grobizi, Liuzeuua, Netruzina, Neuplizi, Nezesouua, Neziuni, Ozimi, Rozmuzl, Senatina [Klein-Seeden], Sipli [Ziepel], Soliteso, Tribeni [Treben], Tropeni, Uuiplizili, Uissoilizi, Uirbinizi [Wormlitz], Ziazinauizi [Luttgenziatz], Zobemeh, 992*

- *Burgwardium Bitrizi [Biederitz] in pago Moraciani, 995*

- *Villa senotina in pago morozini, 995*

- *Pagum, qui Morezini dicitur, iuxta Magadaburch, 1007*

- *Burguuaridium Dreizele [Dretzel] in pago Mrozani, 1011*

- *Comes cummultis aliis a morasciensibus occisus, 1092*

- *Pago Morschoni, 1114*

- *Mozeri in pago Morizani, 1188*

According to the above sources, ***provincia Moraciani's*** territory included an area that now includes Biederitz in the west, Hohenseeden in the north, Tucheim and Ziesar in the east, and Gommern and Lietzkau in the south.

ZEMSICI, LISICI

On the right bank of the Elbe, north of ***provincia Moraciani,*** their were two small, twin provinces, ***provincia Zemzizi*** (*Zemsici*, from the Serb root *zem* or earth) and to its north, ***provincia Liezizi*** (*Lisici*, from the Serb root *Lis* or fox), in an area bound by the Elbe, Havel, and Stremme rivers *(H. Schall, Der Volksname 948 Zemcici, MaR 4, 1960; J. Herrmann, Zamcici-Zemcici. Ein Beitrag zum Problem der Wohnsitze der slawischen Stammer zwischen Elbe und Oder, MaR 4, 1960).*

4A. PROVINCIA ZEMSICI

Ninth and 10th century references to ***Zemsici*** confirm its provincial status and general location.

- ***Vuccri, Riaciani, Zamcici, Dassia,*** *948*
- ***Droganizi in pago Zemzizi,*** *948*
- ***In provincia Zemzizi … Malinga [sub-pago of Zemzizi], Buni et Orogaviz [Drogaviz], in Malinga [Zemzizi sub-province],*** *948*
- ***In provincia Zemzici … in Malinga [Mellingen, near Schelldorf, SE of Tangermunde], Buni, Droganitzi, Poregi [originally Poreka, now Parey on the Elbe, southwest of Genthin],*** *1003*
- ***Sacerdotis de luburch sacerdotis de drogewiz [Orogaviz],*** *1211*

ZEMSICI PLACE NAMES

The following are typical place names and toponyms in ***provincia Zemsici***: Brskov; Chotelin; Dabcina; Jarochov; Jezerica; Kobylica; Ostica; Ploty; Radkyna; Trebesin; Slavotin; Vostrovec; Zemlin.

ZEMZIZI (ZEMSICI), ZEMSICI (ZAMCICI)

Some scholars have good reason to believe that the ***Zamcici*** recorded west of Brandenburg in the 9th and 10th centuries and the ***Zemzizi*** recorded near Havelberg in the 12th century are two names for the one and same nation. On this question, J. Herrmann writes: **Nicht sicher zu beantworten erscheint die Frage, ob Zamcici der Brandenburger Urkunde identisch is mit Zemzici des Havelberger Privilegs. Die Lage von Zamcici im Ruppiner Gebiet erscheint nach den vorhergehenden Ausfuhrungen wahrscheinlich. Zur Lokalisierung von Zemzici fuhrt in erster Linie die Stellung an der Spitze der Gaureihe im Havelberger Privileg. Diese Tatsache allein wurde bein der spaten Ausstellungszeit der Urkunde (2.H. 12. Jh.) und der von K. Bruns-Wusterfeld angenommenen Moglichkeit der Interpolation vom Zemzici bei der Falschung dieser Urkunde nicht gegen seine Lokalisierung in der Ruppiner Gegend sprechen, solange man an der Identitat Zemzici=Zamcici festhalt. Unwahrscheinlich hingegen wird diese Lage un damit die Identitat durch die Erwahnung von drei Orten Buni, Orogaviz und Malinga in diesem Gau. Unter der Voraussetzung, dass die Havelberger Rechte an diesen drei Orten auf eine Schenkung Heinrichs II. Zuruckgehen, ware die Moglichkeit der Lage Zemzicis ostlich von Desseri an den Ruppiner Seen auszuschliessen; den diese Schenkung setzte wohl einen tatsachlichen Besitz an den drei Orten voraus, der im 11. Jahrhundert in der Ruppiner Gegen sicher nicht bestand. Damit aber kamen wir** zu dem Ergebnis: es gab im 9. und 10. Jahrhundert einen Gau Zemzici, er wahrscheinlich zwischen Elbe und Streem zu suchen ist. Und einen Gau Zamcici im Ruppiner Gebiet. Als im 12. Jahrhundert wahrend der deutshcen Ostexpansion und Kolonisation die Bistumer Havelburg und Brandenburg wieder erneuert wurden, erfolgte die Neuabrenzung der Sprengel nicht ausschliesslich mehr auf Grund er Urkunden des 10. Jarhrhunderts, sondern entsprechend den neu enstandenen Machtverhaltnissen. Dassia kam als Desseri zu Havelberg, ebenso wurde auch das Ruppiner Gebiet Teil des Havelberger Sprengels *(J. Herrmann, Zamcici-Zemzici. Ein Beitrag zum Problem der Wohnsitze der slavischen Stamme zwischen Elbe und Oder, Wege Zur Geschichte, 1985).*

4B. PROVINCIA LISICI

Several early references to *Lisici* confirm its provincial status and general location *(G. Labuda, Lesici/Lisici, SsS 3, 1967).*

> • *In Morstani et Ligzice et Hueldon, 937*
>
> • *Marienborch castrum (the same Marienborch, north of Jerichow, on the southeastern border of provincia Belzem, is also recorded in provincia Moraciani) in provincia Liezizi, 946*
>
> • *In provincia Liezizi castrum Marienborch et villas Priecipini (Briest), Rozmoc, Cotini, Virskroiz, Niecurim, Milcuni (Melkow), Malizi, Rabbuni, Podesal et Ludini, 948*
>
> • *Lisici, 1008*
>
> • *At liesca curtem quondam wigonie episcopi et tunc feris innumerabilibus inhabitatam venit, 1017*
>
> • *In local capitali liezecho, 1114*
>
> • *In liezecka, 1114*
>
> • *Lizzizi, 1150*
>
> • *Lytze, 1233*
>
> • *Terre dicte Liza, 1274*
>
> • *Litze, 1445*

LISICI PLACE NAMES

The following series is typical of place names and toponyms in *provincia Lisici*: Chyce, Dalechov, Gorne, Gradec, Klic, Lubas, Malici, Morica, Pretocno, Skolany, Skorolube, Varnov, Vrchlic.

MORACIANI, ZEMSICI, LISICI

It is clear from ecclesiastic sources that there were no Germans and few Christians to speak of in *provincias Moraciani, Zemsici,* and *Lisici* in the first half of the 12th century.

> • *Qualiter ritun sume persecutus paganorum una cum familiaribus meis admodum paucis scilicet monacho cuidam adalberone prout potuimus multa atque innumerabilia destruximus ideola et in loco capitali lizecho in*

provincia morschene inter albiam et hauelam (bishop of Brandenburg, 1114).

• *Ultra albiam in urbe luburch...adhuc pene fuerat paganus eo quod ultra albiam illis temporibus rarus inveniebatur christianus, 1114.*

• *In villae liezeka inter male fidei christianos et sclauos ... constituti name sclaui taum iuxta ritum paganorum ad oclenda ideola adhuc erant inclinati, 1137.*

ENDNOTES

[1] H. Lowmianski, O pochodzeniu Geografa bawarskiego, RoH 20, 1951-52; O identifikaciji nazw Geograf bawarskiego, ZrO 3, 1958.

[2] A. Bruckner, Die slavischen Ansiedlungen in der Altmark und im Magdeburgischen, 1879. S. K. Papierkowski, Szczatki jezyka slowianskich mieszkancow Starej Marchii okolic Magdeburga, SlO 9, 1930. P.L. Kupka, Die Altslawen in der Nord-d.h. spateren Altmark, Saschsen und Anhalt, 1936. J. Schultze, Nordmark und Altmark, JbG, 1957. J. Schneider, Neue altslawische Siedlungsfunde aus der Altmark, BeR, 1970; Neue altslawischen Siedlungsfunde aus der sudostlichen Altmark, JmV 1973; Beitrage zur Besiedlung der Altmark im fruhen Mittelalter, RaP, 1979.

[3] Ein Teil der Forscher wie etwa Niederle sieht in Cieru- einen Reflex von Serb- oder Srb-, also des Serben-/Sorbennamens, so dass *Serb-iste bzw. *Srb-iste ein alter Name fur das Sorbenland sei. Doch schon mit Hey bahnte sich eine vollig andere Deutung dieses Namens an. Hey, der seine Ansicht spater mit K. Schulze wiederholte, interpretierte Zerbst als *cerviste 'Heustelle, Schoberfleck'. Doch diese Ansicht setze sich gegenuber der folgenden, von Trautmann initiierten nicht durch. Trautmann gelangte namlich zu dem Ergebnis, dass Zerbst nichts mit dem Sorbennamen zu tun habe, sondern aus dem alterm *cirvisce hervorgegangen sei, das seinerseits auf polab.-pommoranisches *cirv (nso. cerw) zuruckgehe. Trautmanns Deutung schloss sich in der Folge mit besonderem Nachdruck E. Eichler an. der in Cieruisti ein auf asorb. cirv gestutztes *cirvisce zu erkennen glaubt, wobel cirv das Insekt Cochenille bezeichne, eine spezielle "Schildlaus, aus der ein roter Farbstoff gewonnen wurde". Diese Schildlaus-Etymologie wird auch von anderen Gelehrten gutgeheissen. Doch es fallt schwer, dieser Etymologie zu folgen, da es gegen sie nicht allein linguistische, sondern mehr noch sachliche Vorgenhalte gibt. Die Schidlaus-Version (<*cirv) unterscheidet sich lautlich von der Sorben-Komponente (<*srb(b) im Grunde nur in der Beurteilung des anlautenden Konsonanten C- (Cieruisti), hinter dem die einen ein c-, die anderen ein s- vermuten. Dies ist der Kern des Prolbems, das nachfolgend erneut uberpruft werden soll. Zunachst ist zu sagen, dass die Mehrzahl der Belege das fragliche Toponym mit C- oder aber Z- schreibt; die Versionen mit K- und Sc- sind die Ausnahme, wie gezeigt wird. Eichler halt das C- (ts) der Urkunden fur fruhe Widegrabe von slav. c, welcher Meinung auch Schultheis ist, der C- als mittelniederdeutschen Ersatz fur die slavische Affrikata begreift. Die Richtigkeit dieser beiden Ansichten lasst sich bezweifeln, da, wie gut bekannt, deutsches c und z ja ebenfalls Vertretungen von slav. s sein konnen. Die Beispiele dafur sind keineswegs so "wenige", wie Schultheis meint, im Gegenteil, sie sind gerade im Anlaut ausgesprochen zahlreich, und zwar sowohl in Nord- und Mitteldeutschland als auch in Nordostbayern. Schultheis selbst zieht fur eine Vertretung von s durch z folgende Belege an: 961 Zurbici < *Srbici = Zorbig; 1176 Zuche < *Sucha = Zauche; 1317 de Zuchwiz < *Suchovec = Zauchwitz; 1290 Zolgowe, 1375 Czolchov = Zolchow. Allein diese Bespiele bestatigen, dass fur Zerbiste, Zierwisti oder Zirwisti ebensogut Serbiste oder Sirvisti gelesen werden kann. Nicht weniger gut lasst sich aber auch die Vertretung von s durch c belegen: 1290/1305 Cyngst < *Senisce = Zingst; 1324, 1325 Cyrowe < *Sirov = Zierov; 1312 Cyrsowe, 1354 Zyrsowe, 1342 Cyreszowe, 1345 Cyrrezowe < *Sirosov = Zierzow ... Es liegt somit kein zwingender Grund vor, anlautendes c- bzw z- als Ersatz fur slav. c- zu halten. Ein anderes Problem stellt das graphisch als –u- aufscheinende –v- in Cieruisti dar, das bei nur einer Ausnahme – 1003 Zerbiste – in der Tat sehr konsequent verwendet wird. Darin spiegelt sich m.E. genau wie in dem Ethnonym Zeriu-ani ursprungliches *serv- wider, wahrend es beim Serben-/Sorbennamen zu einem systematischen Betazismus gekommen ist.

Part XVIII

1. SURBI INTER SALAM

In the following chapters our review of **White Serbia's** main nations/provinces follows the major river systems from west to east (e.g. Saale, Elster, Mulde, middle Elbe, Spree, Niesse). We begin with the westernmost Serb nations and provinces, with *regios, teritorios, provincias, pagos* and *terras* centered on the Saale River and its western and southwestern tributaries: 1) Serbia (*regio Surbi*); 2) Nudzici (*pago Nudzici*); 3) Neletici (*regio Neletici*); 4) Chutici (*provincia Chutici*); 5) Veta (*pago Weta*); 6) Orla (*pago Orla*).

1. REGIO SURBI

The *Descriptio Civitatem* records 50 *civitats* in **White Serbia's** heartland, in *regio Surbi. Iuxta illos (Hehfeldi) est regio, quae vocatur Surbi, in qua regione plurest sunt, que habent civitates L.*

Some idea of *regio Surbi's* inner core area or *gniezdo* is suggested by a concentration of ethnonymic place names radiating from an area bound by the Saale, Bode, Fuhne, Nuthe, Ihle, Ehle, Elbe, and White Elster rivers, from Stendal in the north to Zeitz in the south:

Srba—	Zerba (Naumberg)	**Srbin**—	Zerbersdorf (Zeitz)
Srbi—	Cerbez (Weissenfels)	**Srbin**—	Servitz (Calbe)
Srbi—	Syrbuis (Gera)	**Srbov**—	Zurbovo (Weissenfels)
Srbic—	Zurbici (Bitterfeld)	**Srbov**—	Zurbau (Merseburg)
Srbic—	Serbitz (Delitzsch)	**Srbov**—	Zorbau (Mucheln)
Srbic—	Serbitz (Altenburg)	**Srbovic**—	Zurbewiz (Merseburg)
Srbin—	Cirbe (Griefenberg)	**Srbst**—	Zerbst (Anhalt-Zerbst)
Srbin—	Zerwist (Stendal)	**Srbst**—	Klein-Zerbst (Nienburg)

2. PAGO NUDZICI

The *Nudzici* were centered along and between the Saale and Fuhne rivers: *Pagus Nudzici, Nudici, 961; In pago Nudhici, Nudzici, 965 (J. Nalepa, Nudzicy, SsS 3, 1967).*

From Laublingen in the north to Konnern to Lobejun to Wettin to Rothenburge in the south, the following communities are specifically recorded in *pago Nudzici* in the year 961: **Brandanburg**— (Konnern, near Saale); **Trebonizi**— (Trebnitz, Konnern); **Libuhun**— (Lobejuhn, NW Halle/Saale); **Loponoh**— (Laublingen, N Alsleben/Saale); **Vitin**— (Wettin/Saale, NW Halle; **Zputineburg**— (Rothenburg/Saale).

Spytin, later Zpuitneburg, appears to have been an old and important town and stronghold: *Municipium vel burgwardum urbs Zpuitneburg in pago Nudzici sitam, 970.* Further evidence of the core territory of the *Nudzici* is found in a place name derived from the ethnonym *Nudzic,* namely the village of Nudzici, later Neutz, north of Halle.

3. REGIO NELETICI (SAALE)

On the Saale, near Halle, one finds a second **Neletici** territory, *regio Neletici*, sometimes referred to as *pago Neletici*:

- *Regio Neletici, 961*
- *In pago Neletici, 965*

CIVITATS, URBS

Early medieval sources reveal important information regarding the location of *civitats* and other communities in Saale centered *regio Neletici*:

- *In Neletic I ... civitas que Giuicansten nuncupatur, 961*
- *In omnem regionem pagumque Neletici ... urbs Giebichenstein et Saline, 965*
- *In omnem regionem pagumque Neletice ... urbs Giuiconsten et St aline, 965*
- *In pagum igitur seu regionem Neletici ... civitates Gibikonstein, Dobragora et Robobile ... et Saline, 973*

Guiscansten, Giebichenstein, Giuiconsten, and Gibikonstein are Giebichenstein, north of Halle. Dobragora is Gutenberg, north of Halle; Rodobile is Radewell, south of Halle. Saline refers to the important salt fields or salt mines found in **Neletic** lands near and around Halle, an important source of medieval wealth *(H.J. Mrusek, Die Funktion und gaugeschichtliche Entwicklung der Burg Giebichenstein in Haale (Saale) und ihre Stellung im früh- und hoch-feudalen Burgenbau, 1970)*.

4. PROVINCIA CHUTICI

The **Chutici** were also a great Serb nation *(L. Bonhoff, Chutizi Orientalis, NeU 31, 1910. R. Holtzmann, Der Slavengau Chutizi und der Ort Schkeuditz, Zur Geschichte und Kultur des Elb-Saale-Raumes, 1939. E. Muller, Die Ausdehnung des Gaues Chutizi und seine spatere Entwicklung, Leipziger Studien 1957)*. There are numerous references to *pago, provintia, regio,* and *regione Chutici* in western and central **White Serbia** in 10th and 11th century sources:

- *Pagus Chutizi, 892*
- *In pago Cutizi, 892*
- *In pago Chutizi dicto, 908*
- *Pago Chutizi. 970*
- *Provintia Chuntici, 973*
- *Regione Chutizi, 974*
- *Pago Chutizi, 974*
- *Regione Chutizi, 974*
- *Ad Gutizi orientalem, 981*
- *Pago qui dicitur Scuntiza, 982*
- *Provincia Chutizi, 997*
- *Regio Schutizi, 1004*
- *Pago Chutizi, 1012*
- *Pago Gudici, 1013*
- *Comitatus Chuontiza, 1028*
- *Pago Chuntizi, 1030*
- *Pago Scudizi, 1031*
- *Pago Zhudici, 1031*
- *Pago Zcudici, 1040*
- *Pago Zcudici, 1041*
- *Pago Chutizi, 1046*
- *Pago Szudici, 1050*

CHUTICI (SAALE)

South of the Saale *Neletici*, the *Chutici* occupied a large area along the Saale, Mulde, and Pleisse rivers. The following are some of the earliest communities recorded on or near the Saale in *pago Chutici* in the 10th and 11th centuries: **Bresniza**— (Priesnitz, S Camburg/Saale); **Misic**— (Meisitz, S Weissenfels/Saale); **Ouszarin**— (Eutschern, S Merseburg/Saale); **Szholin**— (Schkolen, S Naumberg/Saale); **Trebeni**— (Treben, N Weissenfels).

5. PAGO VETA

This province runs along a river of the same name, the **Weta**: *Ubi confluunt Sala et Wetaa; In ripa fluminis Wetha; Ad aquam, que dicitur Wythawe.*

ILM, SAALE, WETA

Centered at *Weta*, a stronghold on the river *Weta*, near Naumberg, the *Weta* occupied lands along the Ilm, Saale, and *Weta* rivers *(A. Wedzki, Weta, SsS 6, 1977)*. A 9th century reference to *civitas Weta* is followed by more references to *pago Veta* in 10th and 11th century sources:

- *Civitas Vitin, 861*
- *Pago Ueta (Chaca in pago Ueta), 976*
- *Pago Uueta (in pago Uueta vocuto basilicam in Gruza cum dote Golobina), 976*
- *Pago Uueta, 977*
- *Pagus Vedu, 981*
- *Pago Vedu, 1012*
- *Pago Vueitate, 1039*
- *Pago Vueitao (villam Kizerin in pago Vueitao), 1039*
- *Pago Weitaa, 1039*
- *Pago Weita, 1040*
- *Pago Weytaha (in loco Ihholani dicto in pago Weytaha), 1046*

NAUMBERG, JENA

From Weissenfels in the north to Naumburg to Camburg to Jena in the south, the following communities are recorded in *pago Veta* in 10th and 11th centuries. It is interesting and perhaps significant that the name of one of the communities, *Cesice*, is derived from the ethnonymic name *Czech* (e.g. Czes, Czescz, Czech).

Cesice— (Zeschitz, SSE Naumberg/Saale)
Chaca et Chaca— (Ober-, Unter-Kaka, W Zeitz/White Elster)
Churuuiz— (Cauerwitz, N Jena/Saale)
Golobina— (Golben, SSW Weissenfels/Saale)
Gruze— (Gorschen, SW Weissenfels)
Izzolani— (Schkolen, S Naumberg)
Kizerin— (Kitzern, S Wettaburg)
Nivedecavi/Niradkovici— (Nerkewtiz, Jena)
Suseliz— (Seiselitz, E Camburg/Saale)
Weta— (Wethau/Wetha, S Naumberg)
Wetaburc— (Wetta-burg/Wetha, SSE Naumberg)

VETS, VETINS, VETINICI

The **Vetins** are cited in medieval and historical sources under different names:

- *Dicti Sclavonici Vethenici*
- *Bitni, Vets, Vetins, Vintons, Vinithi, Winthhones, Widenzi*
- *Vuitingi et Albi*

WINTTHONES

According to E. Stella, the **Vets** were far from newcomers to Germania. They were known to Tacitus by the name **Wintthones**, from the name of their territory, **Wittonum** *(E. Stellla, Derebus ac populis orae inter Albim et Salam Germaniae flumina)*. The name of both the province and river are believed to be related to the **Vets**, one of the more powerful, belligerent Serb nations occupying the western borderlands of **Universum Sorabi**. According to Z. Golab, the name **Vet** has the deepest roots in Proto-Slavic and Slavic history, including one of the oldest recorded names of the Slavs. The name appears to be derived from the Proto-Slavic root *vet-*, connoting great size, power, victory. The **Vets, Vetins, then, are warriors, a warrior class, members of a powerful, belligerent and conquering nation** *(Z. Golab, Veneti/Venedi: The Oldest Name of the Slavs, InD 3, 1975)*. The scarce historical record certainly tends to confirm Golab's etymology: *Vet, Vetins from old Slavic term for a ruling class of warriors > *Uenetes*. The **Vets** or **Vetins**, according to historian A. Vienensis, were always encouraging the Saxons to revolt against their Frankish overlords. At some point in the Frank-Serb wars, P. Albin writes, the Franks gained control of two important Serb strongholds established by the **Vetins**, namely **Vetin** on the Saale and **Wittenberg** on the Elbe *(Commentarius novus de Mysnia oder Newe Meysnische Chronica, MDLX)*.

WEIDAHABURG, WETTABURG

Likewise, the name of medieval **Weidahaburg**, where the Serbs were defeated in 766, is believed to be derived from the **Vets/Vetins**. **Weidahaburg**, P. Grimm writes, is actually **Wettaburg**, an old **Serb-Vetin** stronghold on the Elbe *(Die Vor- und Fruhgeschichlichen Burgwalle der Berzirke Hall und Magdeburg, 1958)*. Evidence of their once great range is perhaps found in numerous place names along the Elbe, Saale and Main rivers that may be derived from the ethnonym **Vet,** namely those featuring the prefix **Wet**, **Wettin**, **Witt**en (**Wet**ha, **Wet**tin, **Wint**enboren, **Witt**enbert, **Witt**enburg, **Witt**endorf, **Witt**enforden, **Witt**ensee, **Witt**enweir, **Witt**inga, **Witt**ingen, **Witt**onus).

VET / WET, WETIN

J.C. Dreyhaupt, a mid-18th century German historian and authority on *pagus Neletici et Nudzici,* believes that the renowned house of Wetin is of *Vet/Wet* ancestry, possibly of the princely **Budesecz** lineage *(Pagus Neletici et Nudzici, 1749. J. Strzelczyk, Wettynowie, SsS 6, 1977)*.

BETS, BETINS, BETINICI

Some scholars believe that the **Bets, Betins, Betinici** cited in 9th century sources (**Bethenzr, Bechelenzi, Bethenici**) are actually **Vets, Vetins, Vetinici**, a northern branch of the **Vet/Vetins** centered in *pago Veta/Weta* in **White Serbia's** heartland. All evidence indicates that the **Bets/Betins/Betinici** were centered in the Prignitz region, in *provincia Prignicz,* in an area northwest of and bordering on Havelberg's *provincia Nielitizi.*

VETS, VETONS

Some historians believe that the Germania *Vets* took an active role in the **Serb-Wend** settlement of *Dalmatia,* namely the medieval Serb principalities of *Zahumlya* and *Travunia.* Apparent evidence in support of this thesis is found in Anna Komnena's (1083-1155) reference to **the Vetons, barbarians on the Adriatic coast opposite Apulia.** Further onomastic evidence of *Vetin/Veton* settlement in *Illyria* is found in several place names near Belgrade, namely *Vetenicka Bara,* near Krnjace; *Vedenicarska Greda, Vetina Bara,* and *Vetin Predok,* further east *(R. Novakovic, Balticki Sloveni u Beogradu i Srbiji, 1985).*

6. PAGO ORLA

There are a number of references to *flus Orla,* **pago Orla** and **Orla region** (e.g. *in Orla*) in the 11th and 12th centuries:

- *In Orla, 1002*
- *In Orla, 1057*
- *Pagum Omen, qui dicitur Horla, 1083*
- *In pago Orlan, 1120*
- *In pago Orla, 1179*

Pago Orla was centered in an area between the Saale and Orla rivers where, in addition to Orla, a town on the Orla River, several other communities reflect the provincial name: Orlamunde, 1071 (on Thuringian Saale at mouth of river Orla); Frienorla, 1350 (Freyen Orla, 1497, later Frien-Orla, southwest of Kahla); Langenorla, 1401 (langen Orla, 1486, later Lange-Orla), south of Kahla. A *Salalueldon castellum* is recorded in Orla in 1057 *(H. Rempel, Zur Stellung des Orlagaues in frühgeschichtlicher Zeit, AuF 4, 1959; Saalfeld und der Orlagaues in frugeshichtlicher Zeit, Saalfelder Kulturblatter 3/4, 1963).*

DENSE SERB SETTLEMENT

As in Serb lands beyond the borders of *White Serbia,* in borderlands to its west, northwest and southwest, *pago Orla* was an area of dense Serb settlement.

SUB-PROVINCES

In *White Serbia* along the Saale River, from Schonebeck in the north to Jena in the south, a number of sub-provinces are recorded in medieval sources.

IN PAGO GORSCUWIZ

Del, Delc— Delicz, 1200 (Bitterfeld); *in pago Delsche,* 1368
Bukov— *provintia et pagus Buchuue,* 973 (Ziesar)
Dobra Gora— *Dobragora marca,* 952 (Halle)
Gorskovic— *pago Gorscuwiz,* 1261 (Weissenfels)
Jena— (Niradkovici) *in pago Ginnaha,* 1044
Laz— *pago Lasan,* 1270 (Naumberg)
Luben— *pago wenygen Luben* (Altenburg)
Lusov— *pago Luschowe,* 1311 (Camburg)

Mrozin— *pago Mrozini* (Zerbst)
Musov— *pago Muschowe*, 1214 (Merseburg)
Sibrovic— *pago Sibrovici*, 1053 (Naumberg)
Srba— *in pago qui vocatur Zurba*, 1040

IN PAGO STRUPANICA

Srbia— *in pago qui vocatur Swurbeland*, 1136
Srbia— *in provincia Sorabie*, 1180
Srbiste— *pago Zerviste*, 973
— *territorio Zerbist*, 1003
— *provincia Ciervisti*, 1161
— *terra Scerwist*, 1264
Strupanica—*In pago Strupanice*, 1136 (Jena)
Svetic— *pago Zwezesdorph*, 1134 (Merseburg)
Treben— *pagus Trebani*, 1066 (Weissenfels)
Upin— *Vpina marca*, 952 (Halle)
Vetrosity— **Wittershitz supra Wetam**, 1290; **pago Witerschit**, 1292
Zizov— *provincia et pagus Zizouua*, 973 (Barby)

BURGWARDS, CIVITATS

The following are some of the Saale River *burgwards, castellos, civitats, municios, oppids,* and *urbs* recorded in medieval sources.

CIVITAS LISNIK

Barbogi— *barbogi civitatem*, 964 (Barby)
Dobra Gora— *civitas Dobragora*, 973
Dretze— *civitat Driezele*, 1011 (Dretzel)
Gvozdec— *Gozacha civitas*, 979
Hum— *civitas Holm*, 962 (Halle)
Lisnik— *civitas Lisnik*, 1278
Lopjeno— *civitas Loponoh*, 961 (Bernburg)
Lubocin— *civitas Liubuhun*, 961 (Halle)
Lubor— *civitas Luborn*, 965
Lutin— *civitas Lutinburch*, 979

CIVITAS DRIBANI

Radobyl— *civitas Rodebile*, 973 (Halle)
Srbici— *civitas Curbici*, 1015
Stobi— *Stuwi civitate*, 1012 (Camburg)
Stosin— *civitate Stosen*, 1300
Treben— *civitas Dribani*, 993
Tuchomir— *civitas Tucheim* (965)
Tuchovic— *civitas quae Tuchamuzi vocatur*, 1004 (Weissenfels)
Budisko— *castello Budizco,* 979 (Bernburg)
Grodista— *castellum Grodista*, 952 (Halle)
Gvozdec— *castellum Gozcoburch*, 1135

CASTRO WIRBEN

Lisnik— ***castrum Lisnik***, 1188 (Weissenfels)
Lutin— ***castellum Liutinburch***, 979 (Halle)
Pec— ***castellum Pechouue***, 965 (Schonbeck)
Skolani— ***castrum et oppidum Schalon***, 1350 (Camburg)
Todic— ***castrum Teuditz***, 1321 (Bad Durrenberg)
Vran— ***castrum Wraneschenstein***, 1144 (Halle)
Vrbin— ***castellum Uuirinburch***, 979 (Halle)
Vrbin—***castro Wirben***, 1135
Buzin— ***burgward Busin***, 1090 (Naumberg)
Dobra Gora— ***urbs Throbragora***, 966 (Halle)
Dobricin— ***municio Dobreschen***, 1298 (Camburg)
Jena— ***urbe nomine Gene ... in Slauico Jenae***, 1197

BURCHWARDO TREBENI

Nemota, Nemocov— ***burchwardo Nimuucowa***, 1090 (Merseburg)
Srbici— ***burgward Zurbizi***, 992 (Zorbig)
Sputin— ***burgward Zpuitene***, 961 (Rothenberg)
Stosin— ***oppidum Stosene***, 1285 (Weissenfels);
Svirc— ***urbem Schworz***, 1150; Swercshow, 1378 (Zerbst)
Svojim— ***burgwardo Zwegene***, 1091 (Merseburg)
Treben— ***burchwardo Trebeni***, 1041 (Weissenfels)
Tuchovici— ***burchuuardo Tuchvviza***, 1046 (Tauchlitz)
Veta— ***Wetta-burc***, 1300; Wetterburgk, 1532 (Naumberg)

Descriptio civitatum et regionum ad septentrionalem plagam Danubii.

Isti sunt, qui propinquiores resident finibus Danaorum, quos vocant Nortabtrezi, ubi regio, in qua sunt civitates LIII, per duces suos partitae. Vuilci, in qua civitates XCV et regiones IIII. Linaa est populos, qui habet civitates VII. Propre illis resident, quos vocant Bethenici et Smeldingon et Morizani, qui habent civitates XI. Iuxta illos sunt, qui vocantur Hehfeldi, qui habent civitates VIII. Iuxta illos est regio, quae vocatur Surbi, in qua regione plures sunt, quae habent civitates L. Iuxta illos sunt, quos vocant Talaminzi, qui habent civitates XIIII. Beheimare, in qua sunt civitates XV. Marharii habent civitates XI. Vulgarii regio est immensa et populus multus, habens civitates V, eo quod multitudo magna ex eis sit et non sit eis opus civitates habere. Est populus, quem vocant Merehanos, ipsi habent civitates XXX. Istae sunt regiones, quae terminant in finibus nostris.

Isti sunt, qui iuxta istorum fines resident. Osterabtrezi, in qua civitates plus quam C sunt. Miloxi, in qua civitates LXVII. Phesnuzi habent civitates LXX. Thadesi plus quam CC urbes habent. Glopeani, in qua civitates CCCC aut eo amplius. Zuireani habent civitates CCCXXV. Busani habent civitates CCXXXI. Sittici, regio immensa populis et urbibus munitissimus. Stadici, in qua civitates DXVI populusque infinitus. Sebbirozi habent civitates XC. Unlizi, populus multus, civitates CCCXVIII. Neruiani habent civitates LXXVIII. Attorozi habent CXLVIII, populos ferocissimus. Eptaradici habent civitates CCLXIII. Vuillerozi habent civitates CLXXX. Zabrozi habent civitates CCXII. Znetalici habent civitates LXXIIII. Aturezani habent civitates CIIII. Chozirozi habent civitates CCL. Lendizi habent civitates XCVIII. Thafnezi habent civitates CCLVII. Zeruiani, quod tantum est regnum, ut ex eo cunctae gentes Sclavorum exortae sint et originem, sicut affirmant, ducant. Prissani, civitates LXX. Velunzani civitates LXX. Bruzi plus est undique, quam de Enisa ad Rhenum. Vuizunbeire, Caziri civitates C. Ruzzi, Forsderen liudi, Fresiti, Serauici, Lucolane, Ungare, Vuislane, Sleenzane civitates XV. Lunsizi, civitates XXX, Dadosesani, civitates XX. Milzane, civitates XXX. Besunzane, civitates II. Verizane, civitates X. Fraganeo, civitates XL. Lupiglaa, civitates XXX. Opolini, civitates XX. Golensizi, civitates V.

2. SRBI IUXTA SALA ET MULDE

All sources confirm the fact that the area between the Saale and Mulde rivers was densely populated, heavily fortified, and played an important role in the history of **White Serbia**. From north to south, the following Serb nations/provinces were centered in lands between the Saale and Mulde rivers: 1) Sittici (**Regio Sittici**); 2) Sermunt, Ser-munt (**Pago Sermunt**); 3) Colodici (**Regio Koledici**); 4) Siusili (**Pago Siusili**).

1. REGIO SITTICI

The *Descriptio Civitatem* records **regio Sittici** in the following terms: **Sittici, regio immensa populis et urbibus munitissimis.** The words **regio immensa populis et urbibus munitissimis** confirm characterizations of **regio Surbi** as a densely populated and heavily fortified Serb land. Some scholars believe that the *Descriptio's* **Sittici** are the **Citici** (**Citice iuxta Albam**), **Scitici** (**in pago Scitici**) and **Zitici** cited in other and later sources, a name apparently derived from a Fuhne River tributary, the Zit, Zitov: *Zitowe*, 986; *Cythowe*, 1361; *Tzitowe*, 1372 *(A. Wedzki, Sittice, SsS 5, 1975; H. Blackmann, Serimunt-Zitice: Rekonstruction einer fruhgeschichtlichen altlandschaft, OsG 12, 1979. S. Strzelczyk, Ztycy, SsS 7, 1982).*

CIVITAT SRBICI

Medieval sources place the **Sittici/Zitici** on the Fuhne, midway between the Saale and Mulde rivers, centered at **Srbici** (**Zurbici**), modern Zorbig, near Jessnitz (**Jesenica**) and Radegast (**Radogost**), midway between Kothen (**Kotin**) in the north and Halle (**Hola/Gola**) in the south, an area still rich in see-through Serb place names (e.g. Zscherndorf/*Crn's* dorf; Zschornewitz/*Crnovici*).

- ***Zitici que habet civitatem Zurbici (Zorbig), 961***

2. PAGO SERMUNT, SER-MUNT

There are numerous references to the ***pago Sermunt*** in 10th century sources *(H. Naumann, Serimunth-Sermut. Ein Beitrag zur Namenkunde, WiS 5, 1961).*

- *pago **Seromunti**, 945*
- *pago **Serimunitlante**, 945*
- *pago **Serimunt**, 951*
- *regionem **Sermunt**, 964*
- *pago **Serimunti**, 985*
- *pago **Serimode**, 973*
- *pago **Serimunit**, 974*

- *pago **Serimunt**, 974*
- *pago **Zirmute**, 978*
- *pago **Sirmuti**, 980*
- *pago **Serimunt**, 980*
- *pago **Zirimudis**, 986*
- *pago **Sirimunti**, 992*

IN PAGO, REGIONE SER

Without the common German add-on *mundi/munti* (e.g. Sar-mund, Swinemunde, Ueckermunde), the name is actually ***pago Ser***, ***regione Ser***, one more of many territorial entities derived from the ethnonym ***Serb/Sar/Ser/Serb***. Tenth century sources record the following communities in ***pago*** and ***regione Ser***.

Near Bernburg on the Saale: **Bog, Bogovici**— Bogouuiki (E Bernburg); **Drogobyl**— Drogubulesthorp (Drobel, E Bernburg); **Kosovici**— Cossauuiki (Coswig, NE Bernburg); **Podblato**— Bodplozi (S Bernburg); **Predriti**— Prederiti (Prederitz, S Bernburg); **Ruskovici**— Rusocouuiki (Roschwitz, SW Bernburg); **Vidogost**— Uuidogost (Weddegast, E Bernburg); **Vuizekiani**— (S Bernburg); **Zachliandorp**— Zechelitz (E Bernburg). Near Dessau on the Mulde: **Chojno**— Qiuna (Kuhnau, NW Dessau); **Stena**— Steno (Stene, S Dessau). Near Kothen, midway between the Saale and Mulde: **Bedos, Bedosici**— Bedosiki (W Kothen); **Gorsk, Gorsko**— Gorizka (Gorzig, S Kothen); **Malovoda**— Malouuodi (Molweide, NW Kothen); **Neozodici** — (*in Burgward Budizco*, W Kothen); **Zito, Zitov**— Zitowe (Wohlsdorf, W Kothen). Near Magdeburg, at confluence of Saale and Elbe: **Biendorp**— Biendorf (S Magdeburg); **Calbe**— Calbe/Saale (SSE Magdeburg). Near Wispitz on the Saale: **Sublici**—(E Wispitz); **Visepici**—Vuissepici (Wispitz); ***civitat Bulzina***— (N Edderitz); **Pezodulba**— (Wispitz); **Rosburg**—(Klein Rosenburg/Saale); **Scrobouueki** (Schwarwegk, N Gross-Paschleiben); **Trebukovici**— Trebucouuici (Trebbichau, Wolfen/Saale); **Vuitouulici**— (Wedlitz/Saale).

SKADAR, SCHEUDER

In this area, in the name of a small village, Scheuder (Scudere/1314; Scudere/1320; Skudere/1335), near Dessau (southwest of Dessau) and Kothen (east of Kothen), H. Kunstmann finds a Balkan connection, one that suggests the time, place and origin of Slav settlements in Germania. Kunstmann believes the name can be traced to Illyrian-Slav roots, to Skadar of the Illyrian Labeates, to Skadar of the Serb Dukljans.[1]

SER, ZITICI

One part of *Ser* territory is recorded as a separate pago, ***pago Zitici*** *(W. Schulz, Probleme der Burgenforschung im Kreis Zeitz, Geschichte der Zeitzer Heimat I, 1955).* Some idea of this *pago's* location and extent is provided by two *marks* recorded in ***Sermunti Zitici***: *Tribunica* and *Zucha*.

> • *In paganos ... in pago lingua Sclavorum Zitice nominato ... marca Tribunica, 945 (Tribunica* is modern Trabitz, east of Calbe, and *Zucha*, modern Zaucha, east of Wedlitz).
> • *In pago Zitici ... in villa et in marca Zucha, 979*

SERMUNTI, SERMENDE

Some scholars, including Ludwig Albrecht Gebhard, suspect that the ***regionem Ser-munt*** Serbs of medieval German sources, are descended from *King Alfred's Sers* or *Ser-mende* or *Sermende,* i.e., the Serbs of Pomerania and lands farther east, and, further, that Germania's Serbs originated in *Sermende,* an older and greater Serb homeland *(Geschichte Aller Wendisch-Slavischen Staaten, 1790).*

SERMENDE

King Alfred's **Sermende** are located with reference to an uncertain entity, *Maegtha land,* and the *Riffen mountains,* an apparent reference to a western branch of the Ural Mountains *(L. Havlik, Slovane v anglosaska chorografii Alfreda Velikeho, VpS 5, 1964).* A second reference places the ***Sermende*** east of the *Burgendan,* who are north of the ***Surfe Serbs***: **East of** them (Danes) are the tribe the Osti [almost certainly the *Slavi Haisti* as in *Ad litus austriale Slavi Haisti, aliaquediverse incolunt nationes, inter quos praecipui sunt Weletabi qui Wilzi dicuntur*] and to the south the Afdrede (*Bodrici*). The Osti have to the north of them the same area of the sea and the Wends and the Burgendan. South of them are the Haefeldan (the *Haveli* of Haveland). The Burgendan have the arm of the sea to their west and the Swedes to the north. East of them are the Sermende and to their south the Surfe (*Surfe Serbs*).

BURGENDAN

If one reads *Burgendan* as (*Regnum Francorum*) Burgundy, the credibility of Alfred's location of northeastern lands is undermined. However, if one reads *Bergendan* as *Bornholm* or *Borgundholm*, the Baltic island said to be the original homeland of the Burgundians, then Alfred's location of nations-lands holds together. The same is also true if one reads *Burgendan* as *Burg-land* or *land of burgs*, as an Old English equivalent of the Scandinavian *Gardarike* (*the land of gards/grads, of fortified towns and cities*), a generic term for the northern Slav lands. Both readings place the **Sermende** on the Baltic and in lands said to be an ancient Serb heartland.

GROSS-, KLEIN SERMUTH

The ethnonym *Ser/Sermunti* is preserved in the modern German towns of Gross- and Klein Sermuth north of Colditz on the Mulde: Sermut/1386; Wenigen Sermut/1331; *parvum-, magnum Czeremut*/1368; Grossen, Cleinen Sermath/1490; Sermuth/1800 *(S. Strzelczyk, Serimunt, SsS 5, 1975)*.

3. COLODICI: SORABI QUI COLODICI VOCATUR

The name *Colodici* appears to be derived from the Serb word *kol*, connoting palisades, timbered fortifications *(T. Lehr-Splawinski, Koledzicy, SsS 2, 1964)*. Thus *regio Koledizi* is a land of many fortifications, of many castles. One measure of the size and strength of the *Serbs called Colodici* in the first half of the 9th century is found in a brief 838 account of a battle with the Saxons recorded in the *Annals of St. Bertin*: **Meanwhile the Saxons fought a battle at Kesiegesburg against those Serbs who are called the Colodici and thanks to heavenly help won the victory. The Serbian king Czimislav was killed at Kesiegesburg and eleven forts were captured.** Unfortunately, the location of Kesiegesburg and the 11 captured forts remains a guessing game *(H. Brachmann, Cositz-Kesiegesburch. Zur Geshichte der Hauptburg des sorbischen Stammes der Colodici, Symbolae Praehistoricae, 1975)*.

REGIO COLEDICI

In spite of its former size and power, there are few references to *regio Koledizi* in the 10th century: *Regio Koledizi, 973; Provintia and pago Chlodiki, 973; In pago Colidiki, 981*.

JEZERI

The few communities recorded in 10th century *regio Koledizi* are all located on or near the Fuhne, near Lobejun and Zorbig: *Jezeri, Ezeri* (Edderitz, N Kattau); *Kotov, Koteeuui* (Kattau/Fuhne, N Lobejun); *Pitin, Biten* (Piethen, N Kattau).

MARCA GUMIETE

There is one sub-province or mark recorded in *regio Koledizi*, namely Gumnisce or *marca Gumiete: Marca que vocatur Gumiete ... in pago Colidiki.*

BURCHWARDO

In the 11th century the former *regio Koledizi* is recorded as a *locum* and, perhaps, a *burgward*: *Ut ad locum Colidici dictum, 1015; Burchwardo Cholidistcha, 1046.*

It appears that *burchwardo Cholidistcha*, modern Colditz (Cullidiz, 1103; Colidiz, 1158; Coledize, 1161), south of Grimma on the Mulde, is related to *regio Koledizi*. If such is the case, then, perhaps, at one time, *Koledizi territory* or settlements extended eastward as far as the Mulde.

4. PROVINCIA SIUSLI

The name *Siusli* appears to be derived from the Slavic *Susel* or *Suselci*, terms connoting settlements, neighboring settlements *(E. Eichler, Der Name der terra Sclavinica Siuseli, WiS 4, 1954-55; J. Nalepa, Suslowie 3, 1975).*

OROSIUS

The *Siusli* are another once great Serb nation with deep roots in the past and one of several Serb nations recorded in King Alfred's *Orosius*: **East of them [the Wilte known as Afdrede], is the land of the Wends called Sysyle, and southeast the Maroara who extend over a wide territory ... To the north east of the Maroara are the Dalamenstan ... North of the Dalamenstan are the Surpe and west of them the Sysyle.** According to Alfred, in the 9th or earlier centuries the *Siusli Serbs* occupied a wide territory east and south of the *Obodrites/Afdrede* and west of the *Surpe Serbs*.

PROVINCIA LINAGGA

Some indication of the extent of *Siusli* settlement is found in a late 9th century source that places the *Siusli* near the *Linones/ Linjani* in an area between Lenzen in the north and Havelberg in the south: *Sclavi, qui vocantur Linones et Siusli eroumque vicini.*

MARCA LIPANI

This location is confirmed by a late 10th century source that places the *Siusli* in number and strength in an area near *Marca Lipani*, along the western borders of *Hanover Wendland* *(R. Steinberg, Die Mark Lipani, JbG 11, 1962. G. Lipianie, SsS 3, 1967):* *Unam terram Sclauinicam Siuseli nuncupatam, cum urbibus ac vicis ad illam terram iure pertinentibus, 992.*

PROVINTIA SIUSLI

Siusli territory in the 10th and 11th centuries is not nearly as great. Scholars place the geographical center of later *Siusli* lands between Leipzig and Wittenberg, and, further, *Siusli* territory in an area bound by the Saale, White Elster, Partha, and Mulde rivers. There are numerous references to *pago, provintia,* and *terra Siusili* in 10th and 11th century sources.

- *In pago Siusile*, 961
- *Pago Siusili*, 965
- *In Provintia et pagus Siusli*, 973
- *Provinciae Siusil*, 974
- *Terram Slavinicam Siuseli*, 999
- *Pago Susilin*, 1005
- *Et super Siusili pagum*, 1016
- *Pago Siusili*, 1017
- *Inter Salam et Mildam fluvios et Siusili ac Plisni pagos*, 1018
- *Pagus Sausuli*, 1018
- *Pago Susali*, 1031
- *Pago Susilin*, 1043
- *Pago Siusli*, 1050
- *Susos*, 1076
- *Susi*, 1172

IN PAGO SUSELCI

Except for *Holm civitat*, the few communities recorded in **pago Suselci** are limited to the 11th century.

> **Hum**— *Siusile in qua est civitat Holm nominata Holm civitat*, 961; *in ecclesia Cholmensi*, 1326 (Gollma, E. Halle/Saale)
> **Nezalin**— Nizalin, 1052 (Nesseln, Nesselburg, SSW Torgau/Elbe)
> **Rogac**— Rogaz, 1043 (Roitzsch, SW Bitterfeld/Mulde)
> **Vetovici**— Vetovvizi, 1031 (Wedelwitz, SE Eilenburg/Mulde)

DIELIZ IN PLACITO PROVINCIALI

The area around Delitzsch (Delicz, 1200; Dieliz, 1207; **civitatem Deltz**, 1322; *in pago Delsche*, 1368), from the Serb *del* or hill, was an area of heavy settlement, mainly **Siusile**, but also **Neletici** and **Quezici**. The following are representative of the Serb settlements in **placito provinciali** (E. Eichler, *Die Orts- und Flussnamen der Kreise Delitzsch und Eilenburg. Studien zur Namenkunde und Siedlungsgeschichte im Saale-Mulde-Gebiet, 1958*).

BELIC, BUDIN, BROD

> **Bel, Belic**— Belicz, 1378 (Behlitz)
> **Bel, Belotici**— Biltcz, 1442 (Piltitz)
> **Bloto**—Blotowe, 1233 (Plottwitz)
> **Bud, Budin**— Budein, 1404 (Beuden)
> **Boj, Bojeta**— Boyden, 1400 (Boyda)
> **Brn, Brnisce**— Brynis, 1349 (Brinnis)
> **Brod**— Brod, 1404 (Brodau)

CRNIC, CRNOV, DOBRNICA

> **Brod**— Broden in Nuwendorf, 1378 (Brodenaundorf)
> **Crn, Crnic**— Cherniz, 1263 (Zschernitz)
> **Crn, Crnkov**— Czernkov, 1347 (Zschorneck)
> **Crn, Crnov**— Schornkow, 1361 (Zschornau)

Crn, Crny— Czirne, 1404 (Zscherne)
Dob, Dobrn— Dobirn, 1404 (Dobern)
Dob, Dobrnica— Dobernitcz, 1349 (Dobernitz)

DROZKOVICI, GRUBOSICI, LUG

Dob, Dobrostov— Doberstow, 1349 (Doberstau)
Drozkovici—Droskewicz, 1378 (Droyssig)
Glazin— Glesin, 1349 (Glesien)
Grabosici— Grabschicz, 1378 (Grabschutz)
Greben— Grebene, 1251 (Grebehna)
Grubosici— Grubschicz, 1340 (Grubschitz)
Lug— Luge, 1378 (Laue)

LISOV, PORECE, RYBICA

Lis, Lisov— Lisszov, 1158 (Gross Lissa)
Lubanici— Liubanici, 981 (Lobnitz)
Lukovany— Luckowene, 1308 (Luckowehna)
Plony Kolsa— Plonokolsa, 1349 (Plonakolsa)
Polica— Politz, 1465 (Polis)
Pomil, Pomilin— Pomelyn, 1263 (Pomelin)
Po-rece— Poracz, 1349; Poritzsch, 1570 (Pohritzsch)
Rybica— Ribitz, 1495 (Reibitz)

SLAVETICI, SVEC, VELISIN

Slavetici— Slauweticz, 1401 (Schladitz)
Smrod— Smorode, 1350 (Sproda)
Susedlici— Susedelicz, 1349 (Sausedlitz)
Svec, Svet— Swette, 1497 (Schwetzsch)
Svec, Svetec— Swetz. 1404; Swetcz, 1442 (Schwatz)
Vel, Velisin— Welsin, 1491 (Wolls)
Vel, Velkos— Welzcowe, 1347 (Welksow)

VELKOV, VERBA, VYSOKY

Vel, Velkov— Welkow, 1349 (Gross-Wolkau)
Verba— Werbin, 1404 (Werben)
Verba, Verbelin— Werblin, 1349 (Werbelin)
Vetrov— Wethrowe, 1289 (Wiederau)
V'orlica— Werlicz, 1349 (Werlitzsch)
Vysoky— Wysigk, 1500 (Weissig)

OTHER SUSELCI?

If the *Siusli* are indeed *Suselci*, it is possible that the *Suselci* recorded in other areas suggest past *Suselci* territories. It is also possible that they share nothing more than a common or similar name.

SUSELCI IN PROVINTIA NIZIZI

There are several references to *urbs/burgward Suselci* in *provintia Nizizi* (centered on the Elbe near Belgern).

- *De provintia Sclavorum Nizizi ... urbibus Susili*, 961
- *In pago Nizizi in burhwardio Suselzi ... villas Gohtzizi, Uissirobi*, 997
- *Burhwardio Suselzi*, 997

SEUSELITZ

Burhwardio Suselzi is Seuselitz on the Elb*e (Suselzi, 997; Susili, 1004; Suseliz, 1194; Suselitz, 1147),* north of Dessau on Mulde, where *villas* **Gohtziz** and **Uissirobi** are also recorded. There is also an apparent reference to the **Suselci** in *pago Uueta*: *In pago Uueta ... villa Suseliz, 976;* **Suseliz (Suselicz, 1228; Suselicz, 1378; Sewsselitz, 1532) is Seiselitz, south of Naumberg.** An apparent reference to the **Suselci** is *Siuselingun*, a settlement in the *Slavenkirchen* of **Terra Sclavorum** near Bamberg recorded in 1013.

ENDNOTES

[1] Scheuder erklart sich als die uberraschend gut erhaltene Vertretung von slav. *Skъdr-, das aus romanischen Scodra, entstanden und als alban. Shkoder, serbokroat. Skadar, ital. Scutari bekannt ist. Weil die Slaven in der ersten Silbe ein –b- substituierten, lasst sich vermuten dass sie, wie Schramm es ausdruckt, eine regionalbarbarische Form ubernommen haben, die, ahnlich wie Doclea > Duklja oder *Tocla > Tuklaca, von romanisch Scodra > *Sku dr- > *Skъdr- und Skadar fuhrte. Im Grunde geht es hier also um eine Form der Romanisation, die gerade in der Gegend um Lissus und Doclea, also zu beiden Seiten der heutigen Nortwestgrenze Albaniens festen Fuss gefasst hat ... Zur Entstehung des ON Scheuder gibt es nun eigentlich kaum mehr etwas zu sagen. Dass anlautendes sk- von Scodar im Deutschen uber sk- zu sch- (s) wurde, ist hinlanglich bekannt. Der dipthong –eu- ist mit grosser Wahrscheinlichkeit Einfluss des Polabeslavischen, das u in aller Regel zu eu dipthongiert, vgl. Gleupe, cheude, meucho, l'eudi usf.

Scodra, am Sudostufer des Skutarisees gelegen, war in vorromischer Zeit Zentrum des illyrischen Stammes der Labeaten, danach Haupstadt des illyrischen Konigreiches. Durch die Teilung Dalmatiens unter Diokletian wurde Scodra Haupstadt der provincia Praevalitana, spater gehorte es zur byzantinischen Provinz Dyrrachion. Scodra war somit eine bedeutende und wichtige Stadt, das ergab sich allein aus deren Lage an der altesten, von den Romern angelegten Kustenstrasse, die Salona mit Tragurium, Scardona und Jadera einerseits...

Die letzte Nachricht uber den in Scodra seit dem 4. Jhd. bestehenden Bischofsitz stammt von 602. danach herrscht Schweigen, was gewiss mit der Zerstorung der Stadt wahrend des grossen Anstrums von Awaren un Slaven in Verbindung steht. DieAnwesenheit von Slaven in der naheren Umgebung von Scodra ist angeblich seit dem 6. Jhd. bezeugt, auch nimmt man slavische Siedlungskontinuitat bis ins 11. Jhd. an. In anhaltischen Scheuder spiegeit sich somit der Name einer bedeutenden illyrisch-romischen Balkanstadt wider.

3. SRBI IUXTA SALA, ELSTRA ET PLISA

A number of Serb nations/provinces are recorded in an area bound by the Saale, White Elster, and Pleisse rivers: 1) *Chutici;* 2) *Tuchorini;* 3) *Puonzowa;* 4) *Gera;* 5) *Plisni;* 6) *Dobna;* 7) *Plav* (H.J. Vogt, Zur Kenntnis der materiellen Kultur der Sorben im Elster-Pleisse-Gebiet, ZtA 2, 1968).

1. CHUTICI

The *Chutici* straddled the White Elster and Pleisse, an area that included an important stronghold at *Slavorum civitatem Lipsk*, modern Leipzig.

- *In urbe Libzi vocata, 1005*
- *In Libzi, 1017*
- *In burcvardo Libizken, 1050*
- *Usque Libiz, 1080*
- *Usque Liptzk Slavorum civitatem pervenit, 1193*
- *Lipzenses, civitas Lipzensium, 1216*
- *Miles de Lipzc, 1216*

LESNIK BURCHWARDO

The following are some of the fortified communities recorded near *Liptzk Slavorum civitatem* in the 10th and 11th centuries (E. Eichler, Slawischer namen im Bereich der Stadt Leipzig, ZtS 4, 1959. E. Eichler, E. Lea, H. Walther, Die Ortsnamen des Kreises Leipzig, 1960). Lesnik—*Lesnic burchwardo*, 1040 (Lossnig, S. Leipzig); Medubor—*castellum quod Medeburu vocatur*, 979 (Magdeborn, SSE Leipzig); Skolin—*burgvardo Szholin*, 1031 (Schkolen, SW Leipzig); Skudici—*Scudici urbs*, 981 (Schkeuditz/White Elster, NW Leipzig); Zvenkov—*Zuenkouua, 1031* (Zwenkau/White Elster, SE Leipzig).

BUDIGOST VILLA

The following are typical of the communities recorded near Leipzig in the medieval period.

BUDIGOST, CASLAVICI, DOLICA

Budigost— Budegast, 1017 (Bugigast)
Caslavic— Zcazluwicz, 1349 (Zaschwitz)
Dobseici— Dobeschitz, 1275 (Dobschitz)
Dolica— Dolicz, 1350 (Dolitz)
Glazov— Glasowe, 1215 (Glasau)
Golusa— Golusch, 1359 (Gohlis)
Gornica— Gorentz, 1443 (Gohrenz)
Kocvary— Koetzschewer, 1548 (Kotzschbar)

KOLISIN, LUZA, MIRKOVIC

Kolis, Kolisin— Kollynschen, 1335 (Goltzschen)
Krosnovic— Kroznewitz, 1285 (Crostewitz)
Lucin— Lusene, 1221 (Lutschen)
Lugorady— Ludgrede, 1378 (Lauer)

Luza— Luszh, 1295 (Leutzsch)
Milkov— Mylkowe, 1324 (Molkow)
Milotic— Mileticz, 1215 (Miltitz)
Mirkovic— Mirkiwicz, 1438 (Merkwitz)

MOKRANE, REPOVICA, RUDENICA

Mokov— Mochowe, 1287 (Mockau)
Mokrane— Mokeren, 1335 (Mockern)
Pesna— de Pesna, 1306 (Gross-Posna)
Plachtovici— Plachtewitz, 1466 (Plagwitz)
Repovica— Repewyz, 1334 (Rapitz)
Rodsovic— Rodeswicz, 1378 (Raschwitz)
Rudenica— *Rudeniz juxta Lipcz*, 1248 (Reudnitz)
Slizk— Slisk, 1397 (Schleussig)

STODORICA, VIDORAD, ZAGORICI

Stodorica— Sthodericz, 1325 (Stotteritz)
Sukolazy— Zcukelosin, 1378 (Zuchelhausen)
Varin— Warin, 1232 (Wahren)
Vidorad— Wederaz, 1285 (Gross Wiederitzsch)
Zabnica— Zcabencz, 1350 (Seebenisch)
Zagorici— Segericz, 1350 (Segeritz)
Zelici— Selicz, 1350 (Sehlis)

2. TERITORIO TUCHORINI

Teritorio Tuchorini was centered in an area between the Saale and White Elster. The name appears to be derived from the personal name *Tucho* as in *Tuchomir* or *Tugumir*, *Tuchomysl*, and *Tuchorad* (H. Popowska-Taborska, Tuchurini, SsS 6, 1977). There are several references to *burgward, castello, opid, pago teritorio, marckt, and **stadt Tuchorin*** in medieval and later sources.

- *Pago Ducharin, 976*
- *Pagus Tuchurini, 981*
- *Territorium Tucherin, 1004*
- *Thuchrin, 1135*
- *Pago ... qui vocatur Tuchorin, 1040*
- *Thucheren, 1197*
- *Pago et oppidi Thvchirn, 1317*
- *Stettlein Teuchern, 1530*
- *Birgwardis Thvchorin, 1042*
- *Suburbanium Thvcherin, 1068*
- *Castello Tuchern, 1150*
- *Tewchern marckt, 1487*
- *Stettlein Teuchern, 1530*

BREZNICA VILLA

The following are some of the villages and towns recorded within the borders of *teritorio Tuchorin* in the 10th and 11th centuries.

BREZNICA, PONIKVICA, GLADOV

Bisilouua— (Weidau, NW Zeitz, White Elster)
Breznica— Breznizani (Priesen, S Weissenfels/Saale)
Ponikvica— Bucinauuiz (Punkewitz, S Naumberg/Saale)
Butici— (Beuditz, S Naumberg/Saale)
Krocov— Chroiziuua (Kretschau, W Zeitz)
Kroslin— Crozlino (Ober-, Nieder Krossuln, W Teuchern)
Gladov— Gladovsi (Gladitz, Teuchern)

GRIBNO, GRODCANE, TUCHORIN

Gostici— (Gross Gestewitz, S. Naumberg)
Gribno— Gribna (Griefen, W Zeitz)
Grodcane— (Graitschen, W Schkolen)
Grodiscani— (Groitschen, WNW Zeitz)
Lokonosy— Longonosi (Lagnitz, S. Teuchern)
Strekov— Strecouua (Streckau, NW Zeitz)
Tuchorin—*uburbanio Tvcheri*; *villa Tucherin*; *castello Tuchern* (Teuchern, NW Zeitz)

3. PONZOUUA

Scholars are uncertain about the correct reading of the name. Some assistance in this matter is perhaps found in names relating to local terrain and structures *(E. Eichler, Aus der slawischen Toponomastik der Landschaft Puonzowa, Studia Linguistica T. Lehr-Splawinski, 1963)*. The name of a nearby dominant height, a favored place of pagan Slav religious ceremonies, is **Bozowe** or God's Mountain, from *boz*, a Slavic word for god: **Mons Buzowe, 1121; Mons Bozowe, 1151; Mons Pozowa, 1154.**

ABBAS DE BOZOWE

The name's sacred origin and pagan character is confirmed by the establishment of a Christian monastery in the early 12th century, a common practice in medieval times *(K. Hengst, Die Ortsnamen des Bosauer Zehntverziechnisses, OsG 4, 1968).*

- *Monasterium Bosov, 1119*
- *Abbatiam construxi in monte, qui dicitur Buzowe, 1121*
- *Abbas Bozauiensis, 1140*
- *Gerungus abbas de Bozowe, 1150*

PROVINCIA PONZOUUA

Provincia Ponzouua appears to be centered in an area that ran across and along the White Elster, below its juncture with the Pleisse.

- *Pago Puonzouua, 976*
- *Provincia Ponzouua, 995*
- *In Puzowe, 1192*
- *In Bozowie, 1195*
- *Iudicium in provincia Buzewiz, 1210*
- *Comitatus Buzewitz, 1271*
- *Iudicium Buzewicz, 1528*

CIVITAS ITACA

In the late 10th century *civitas Zeitz* is recorded in *Puonzouua*: **In pago Puonzouua civitas Itaca, 976.**

CITICI, SITICI, ZITICI

There are numerous references to *loco, castro, urbs, civitas,* and **aecclessia Citici,** Zitici, medieval Serb forerunners of the town and district of modern Zeitz.

- *Citice, 968*
- *Citice aecclesia Citicensis,996*
- *In loco Zitizi dicto, 995*
- *Citicensis urbs, 1000*
- *Siticensis ecclesia, 1028*
- *In Ziticensis loco, 1032*
- *Castrum et oppidum in Cicze, 1228*
- *Zceitz, 1480*
- *Czeitze, 1521*
- *Zeitz, 1541*

BUKOVANI

The communities recorded in **Puonzouua** in the 10th and 11th centuries leave little doubt as to the province's political center.

BRODICI, BUKOVANI, CRNOGLAV

Bukovani— Bocmani (Bockwen, E Zeitz)
Buosenrod— (*beneficium Citicensis aecclesiae*)
Brekov— Brkeouew (Brockau, SSE Zeitz)
Brodici— (Broditz, S Weissenfels/Saale)
Cetobyl— Zcetebul (Zettweil, S Zeitz)
Crnoglav— Zschoningolowe (Zschorgula, W Zeitz)
Dobros— Dobros (Dobris, N Zeitz)

DRAGASOVIC, GOLUBIN, GRANOV

Dragasovic— Dragaswicz (Draschwitz, ENE Zeitz)
Dubno— Duben (Deuben, NW Zeitz)
Glina— Glina (Gleina, E Zeitz)
Golubin— Golobina (Golben, SSW Zeitz)
Granov— Granowe (Grana, W Zeitz)
Grobec— Grobeze (Grobitz,
Kolcov— Kultschow (Goldschau)

KROSNO, MYSLIBOZ, NIKASOVICI

Kube— Chube (Kube, N Zeitz)
Krosno— Crozna (Krossen, SW Zeitz)
Lomoseky— Lonisgo (Lonzig, SSW Zeitz)
Lokonosy— Luongonosi (N Zeitz) *(H. Schall, Zangenberg ist Luongonosi, Zeitzer Heimat 6, 1959).*

Mysliboz— Mizleboze, 1139 (Meuselwitz, E Zeitz)
Nikasovici— Nicasaauiuz (Nixditz, N Zeitz)
Nunavici— Neunaiz (Nonnewitz, N Zeitz)

OSEK, PODGROD, PREDEL

Osek— Ozzek (Ossig, SSW Zeitz)
Owa— (*in villa que dicitur Owa*, 1147)
Gruonouua— (Aue/Zwickauer Mulde, SE Zwickau)
Podgrod— *Podegrodici in pede montis Puzove* (Bosau, Zeitz)
Predel— Predele (Predel, N Zeitz)
Tuchlica— Tuchelitz (Tauchlitz, S Zeitz)
Trebesici— Trebesciz (Trebnitz, SW Zeitz)

PAGO BUKOVICA

A number of sub-provinces or **zupas** are recorded in the **Chutici**, **Tuchorin**, and **Puonzouua** provinces, an area bound by the Saale, White Elster, and Pleisse rivers, especially near ancient Serb strongholds at Leipzig and Zeitz.

BUKOVICA, DOSENE, GORSIN

Bukovica— pago Buckowicz, 1241 (Bockwitz, ESE Zeitz)
Cabnici— *pago Schebenyz*, 1349 (Schebnitz, S Lutzen)
Dosene— *in pago villae Dosene*, 1325 (Dosen, Leipzig)
Gorbuz— *in villa et pago Gorbuz*, 1305 (Gorbitz, Leipzig)
Gorsin— *pago Gorsene*, 1012 (S Lutzen)
Krimov— *pago Crimowe*, 1240 (Grimma, ENE Hohenmolsen)

REKA, SKUDICI, TISIN

Kucas— *pagus Kuschez*, 1289 (Gautzsch, S Leipzig)
Pizelow— *pago Pizelowe*, 1251 (NW Zeitz)
Reka— *pago Rekken*, 1242 (Rocken, SW Lutzen)
Skorlup— *pago Zcurlup*, 1242 (Schkorlopp, SW Leipzig)
Skudici— *in pago Zcudici*, 1040; Nuwindorph ... *in pago Szcudici in burcvardo Libizken*, 1050 (*R. Holtzmann, Der Slavengau Chutizi und der ort Schkeuditz, Zur Geschichte und Kultur des Elb-Saale—Raumen, 1939.*)
Tisin— *pago Tysene*, 1320 (Theisen, NNW Zeitz)

BURGWARD CHOJNO

In addition to those already cited, the following *burgwards, castrums, munitios, oppids,* and *urbs* are recorded in this area.

CHOJNO, MEDUBOR, MILSIN

Chojno— *burwardo Chvine*, 1069 (Kayna, SSE Zeitz); *castrum* Koyno, 1320
Drevsk— *castrum in Dreyzic*, 1297 (Droyssig, WSW Zeitz)
Gorsin— *oppido in Gorsin*, 998 (S Lutzen)
Lesnic— *burchwardo Lesnic*, 1040
Lucina— *civitas Lucin*, 1269 (Lutzen, SW Leipzig)
Medubor— *castellum, quod Medeburu vocatur*

Milsin— *munitionem nomine Milsin*, 1080 (Hohen-Molsen, NW Zeitz)

NIVETRY, SCUDICI, ZVENKOV

Nivetry— *castrum Netro*, 1452 (Nathern, W Zeitz)
Skolin— *burgwardo Szholin*, 1031 (Schkolen, SW Leipzig)
Scudicz— *oppidum Scudicz*, 1346 (Schkeuditz, Leipzig)
Skudici— *urbs Scudici*, 981 (Schkedutiz, Leipzig)
Svirc— *urbem Schworz*, 1150 (Schwerzau, NNE Zeitz)
Zvenkov— *civitas Suemcua*, 974 (Zwenkau); *civitas Zuenkouusa*, 1004; Zcwengonia, 1021; *in Zwencowe*, 1195; Czwenkowe, 1316.

SENIOR CUCHAVICUS

Circa 970 a Slav notable named **Cuchavicus** (also *Euchavico, Suchavico*) is the recorded commander of *civitas Suencua*: **Sclavis in Zuencua sub Cuchavico senior**.

ZUPAN, TECHOBUDICI

Evidence suggesting that old Serb political-administrative titles, namely *zupa* and *zupan*, were still in use in this area in the late 13th century is found in the *Zupan of Techobudici* (Techebudiz, 1121; Techebodiz, 1145; Techebodiz, 1151; modern Techwitz), a settlement north of Zeitz: **Supanus de Techewiz, 1287**.

4. PROVINCIA GERA

This province takes its name from the river **Gera**, a name of uncertain origin *(J. Nalepa, Gera, SsS 2, 1964)*. The province was centered at **Gorin** (Gorem, 1421; Goryn, 1436; Goren, 1462), modern Gera, a stronghold on the west bank of the White Elster, southeast of Jena. There are several references to *pago, provintiam*, and river **Gera** in medieval sources.

- *Terminus Gera, 993*
- *Ad terminum Gera, 995*
- *Provintiam Gera dictam, 999*
- *In pago Geraha, 1152*
- *In pago Gera, 1160*
- *In pago Gera, 1171*
- *Geraha, 1222*

BORUS VILLA

The following are typical of the villages near **Gera** in the medieval period *(R. Fischer, Ortsnamen and der Gera, WzJ 3, 1952-53; B.H. Rosenkranz, Ortsnamen des Bezirkes Gera, 1982)*.

BELSKO, BORUS, KOBYLANE

Belsko— Belcz, 1196 (Polzig)
Bezgoz— Byzegacz, 1373 (Piesgitz)
Borus— Porres, 1526 (Poris)
Cholm— Kulmen, 1333 (Culm)
Chronsovici— Cronschwitz, 1305 (Cronschwitz)
Dobsovici— Dobschwitz, 1534 (Debschwitz)
Gusin— Guzen, 1358 (Gessen)

        Kobylane— Kobelnn, 1209 (Kofeln)

KOKORICA, KOLIS, LUBOSICI
        Kokorica— Kokeritz, 1209 (Kockritz)
        Kolis— Collis, 1534 (Collis)
        Kostrica— Kostricz, 1364 (Bad Kostritz)
        Kresovici— Gresewiz, 1121 (Cretzschwitz)
        Lozin— Lozen, 1284 (Lusan)
        Luben— Lubene, 1257 (Hohen-Leuben)
        Lubosici— Lubschwicz, 1359 (Liebschwitz)
        Lunsk— Luntzk, 1503 (Lunzig)

MILICI, MILOVICI, NEGOZ
        Lusov— Lussowe, 1364 (Lessen)
        Lutolici— Lutelitz, 1441 (Letilitz)
        Milici— Militz, 1279 (Meilitz)
        Milovici— Milwitz, 1322 (Milbitz)
        Mosin— Mosyn, 1388 (Mosen)
        Myslici— Muslitz, 1366 (Moschlitz)
        Negoz— Negaz, 1364 (Negis)
        Nibor— Nybern, 1529 (Niebra)

PALICA, POLCANE, POLNICA
        Palica— Palicz, 1364 (Pohlitz)
        Parno— Parn, 1387 (Parhen)
        Penik— Pessnig, 1430 (Posneck)
        Polcane— Poltschen, 1348 (Poltschen)
        Pole— Polen, 1311 (Pohlen)
        Polnica— Polnicz, 1300 (Pollnitz)
        Robin— Robin, 1364 (Roben)
        Robsici— Roptschicz, 1322 (Roppisch)

SLAVICI, SRBIS, TRNOV
        Rupicane— Ropizane, 1121 (Ropsen)
        Slavici— Slowicz, 1314 (Schleiz)
        Spytovici— Speutwitz, 1506 (Speutewitz)
        Srbis— Syrbis, 1351 (Sirbis)
        Trnov— Tornowe, 1324 (Dorna)
        Utechov— Ottichaw, 1359 (Ottich)
        Zar, Zarov— Sara, 1533 (Saara)
        Zelim— Selmiz, 1121 (Sommnitz)

5. PROVINCIA PLISNA
        Consistent with its name, from the Slavic *pleso (*connoting water, waterway, lake, sea) ***provincia Plisina*** occupied both banks of the river ***Plisa***: Plisnam, 1021; ***Schirna Blisna id est Swarzpach***, 1143; das wasser dy Plyssen, 1402. ***Provincia Plisna*** was centered in the area around the ancient Serb stronghold of ***Plisna***, later Altenburg: ***Aldenburch, que alio nomine Plisne nuncupatur, Altenburg civita***.

IN PLISNI

The following are typical references to ***provincia Plisna*** found in 10th, 11th, and 12th century sources, including one that records ***Plisna*** as one of three *pagos* between the Saale, Elstra, and Mulde rivers *(H. Schall, Der Sorbengau Plisni als Siedlungseinheit und Sprachdenkmat, ZtS 3, 1958; A. Wedzki, Plisni, SsS 4, 1970).*

> • *Pagus Plisina, 976*
> • *Pars episcopatus nostri, quae iacebat inter Salam et Elstram ac Mildam fluvios et Plisni, Vedu et Tuchurini pagos, 981*
> • *Pagus Plisni, 1018*
> • *In pago Blisina, 1066*
> • *De pago Plisna, 1145*
> • *In terra Plyssne, 1173*
> • *Provincia Pliesna, 1218*

LINGUA VERO PATRIA ZTARECOZTOL VOCATUR

A mid-12th century ecclesiastical source originating in *Altenkirch*, relating to some forty villages under its jurisdiction, suggests that the Serb language was alive and well in ***provincia Pliesna***: *In terminis antique ecclesi, que lingua rustica Aldenkirkin, lingua vero patria Ztarecoztol vocatur.* ***Ztarecoztol***, of course, is the Serb ***Stary Kostol*** or Old Church or Old Castle (early churches were alien and hostile castles/ fortresses in *terra pagania*).

QUE SUPEN VULGARITER

In late 13th century ***provincia Pliesna*** there are several references to local land-holders with the title of ***zupan***. In the village of ***Javor*** (Jauern), southwest of Altenburg: ***Sex mansos in villa Iauren, quatus, que supen vulgariter nuncupantur, 1280***. In the same village eleven years later, a local ***zupan/supan*** is recorded as ***Schiban***: ***Duos mansos, ipsi, Schibano hos mansos contulimus rite et iuste iure hereditario possidendos, 1291.*** In the 15th century ***zupan*** as ***supan*** is recorded as a family name in the village of Golnica/Gollnitz, southwest of Altenburg, later ***Supan***.

COMMUNITIES

The following are typical of the communities recorded near Altenburg in ***provincia Pliesna*** in the medieval period *(L. Fahlbusch, Die slavischen Ortsnamen dem Altenburgen Ostkreises, 1952; K. Hengst, Soziologische Aspekte der slawischen Toponymie und Antrhroponymie. Sociologische-siedlungskundliche Analyse altsorbischer Ortsnamen im Raum Plisni, SlO 2, 1981).*

BREZNA, DOBRICIN, GLUM

Brezna— Bresen, 1181 (Breesen)
Cakovici— Zcakewicz, 1336, (Zagkwitz)
Caslavici— Scazlawicz, 1214 (Zschaschelwitz)
Cvik, Cvicin— Czwotzschen, 1445 (Zweitschen)
Dobricin— Dobruczschin, 1445 (Dobitschen)
Godsov— Godessouua, 976 (Godissa)
Glum— villa Glumin, 1283

GORA, HRABR, JASENICA

Gora— Goren, 1181 (Gohren)
Hrabr, Chrobri— Chrobrin, 1214 (Krobern)
Jarsic— Jarschicz, 1350 (Gardschutz)
Jasenica— Jessenicz, 1336. (Gassnitz)
Komor, Komory— Cumere, 1291 (Kummer)
Krasov— Craazowe, 1181 (Krassa)
Loka, Locica— Luczicz, 1418 (Lutschutz)

LOM, LYSINA, MALOVIC

Lom— Lom, 1222 (Lohma)
Lom, Lomicin— Lomichin, 1336 (Lohmigen)
Lom, Lomsko— Lomzke, 1140 (Lumpzig)
Lubovic— Lubuwiz, 1229 (Lopitz)
Lukov— Lukowe, 1320 (Lucka)
Lysina— Lysina, 976 (Leesen)
Malovic— Maluwiz, 1181 (Molbitz)

MALOTES, MEKOV, MYSLINOVIC

Malotes— Maltes, 1188 (Maltes)
Maslotop— Mascelthorp, 976 (Monstab)
Mekov— *Makow magnum*, 1378 (Gross Mecka)
Minov— Minowe, 1204 (Mehna)
Myslinovic— Mislenwiz, 1136 (Misselwitz)
Nasiboric— Nassoberitz, 1165 (Nasperitz)
Nikrasovic— Nicrazwicz, 1296 (Kraschwitz)

PODBREZE, PODEGRODICI, SMOLIN

Podbreze— Podebriz, 1274 (Boderitz)
Podegrodici— Pauritz, part of Altenburg
Rodov— Rodiuue, 976 (Gross-Roda)
Sedloraz— Selderoz, 1336 (Selleris)
Serbici— Serewicz, 1336 (Serbitz)
Smolin— Smollna, 1132 (Schmolln)
Strbly Glowy— Ztribeglowe, 1140

STUDENICA, TRESKOV, ZAROV

Studenica— Studincsen, 1181 (Stunzhain)
Svec— Zwentz, 1260 (Schwanditz)
Treskov— Trescouua, 976 (Dresche)
Vlozno— Wlozne, 1191 (Lossen)
Zarov— Zarowe, 1214 (Saara)
Zetsce, Zetscov— *villa Scescowe superiori*, 1244; *villa Schezouwe minor*, 1290 (Ober- and Unter-Zetscha)

RADOVAN'S DORF

In the early 13th century a number of villages have *mixed names*, Serb roots with

German dorf/torf endings: ***Bloto***, Plotin-dorf; ***Boras***, Borascazs-torf; ***Boris***, Borchistorf; ***Dobr***, Doburmans-torf; ***Grab***, Grobos-dorf; ***Lucin***, Lucins-dorf; ***Lug***, Lugindorf; ***Nerad***, Nirakin-dorf; **Plichta**, Phlichtin-dorf; ***Radovan***, Rodwanis-torf; ***Rozenc***, Rosinez-dorf; ***Tesimir***, Tesmen-dorf. In addition to the communities cited, further evidence of the very high density of Serb settlement in the Altenburg region is found in the many communities recorded in the year 1200 *(K-H. Hengst, Die Orstnamen des Bosauer Zehntverzeichnisses, OsG, IV, 1968)*. In the following series the original Slavic name is followed by Germanized versions.

BLIZ, BORAC, BOSOVICI
Batici— Baticz/1378; Paditz
Besovici— Bessuwiz/1227; Poschwicz
Bliz— Bliz/1200
Blchovica— Bluchwiz/1200
Borac— Borascazstorf/1200
Boretin— Boretin/1140; Borthen/1445
Borov— Borowe/1445; Bohra
Bosovici— Bossuwiz/1200; Poschwitz

BREZ BUKOV CELADICI
Brez— Brezen/1308; Breesen
Budovlici— Budowliz/1200; Podelwitz
Bukov— Buchowe/1200
Bukov— *in secundo Buchowe*/1200; Bocka
Cajov— Sceiowe/1270; Zschaiga
Cechov— Scescowe1273; Cechow/1378
Celadici— Sceldiz/1210; Scheldiz
Ceporici— Stchoperiz/1200; Zschopperitz

CESOVICI, CHOTIRADICI, CRNISCE
Cesovici— Sechezewitz/1288; Zschechwitz
Cetkov— Cetetchowe/1200; Zcetkow/1336
Chotimici— Chotmiz/1200; Kottemicz/1278; Kothenitz
Chotiradici— Cotirdiz/1200; Koterdiz/1274; Kotteritz
Churdera, Chuderin— Gudrin/1200; Guderin/1174; Godern
Chyn, Chynici— Kynicz/1337; Kaimnitz
Circov— Circhowe/1222; Zurchau
Crnisce— Schirniz/1205; Zschernitzsch

DREN, GOLNICA, GOREMIR
Dolsko— Dolzke/1154; Dolzig
Dren, Drenov— Drenowe/1271; Thrana
Drogan— Drogane/1140; Drogen
Drogosov— Droczchow/1391
Gnas, Gnasovici— Gnaschwiz/1256; Gnadschutz
Golnica— Golniz/1140; Gollnitz
Gorbus— Gorbucz; 127; Garbus

Goremir— Gormir/1200; Gormar/1378; Gorma

GRABISICI, GRUBOS, KOBYLA

Grabis, Grabisici— Grabsciz/1200
Grabisici— Grabisiz/1200; Greipzig
Griva— Griwe/1200; Grev/1277; Groba
Grubos, Grubosov— Grubschowe/1200
Gruzim— Grusim/1200
Jimel— Gymel/1349; Gimmel
Knev— Chewe/1200; Knev/1280; Knau
Kobyla— Kobelicz/1378

KRB, KOSOBODY, KOTEL

Kolc, Kolcov— Kulschouwe/1290; Goldschau
Korb, Krb, Krbica— Kvrbize/1275; Corbitz
Korsovici— Kursuwiz/1200
Kosmin— Kosmin/1378; Kosma
Kosobody— Kossebode/1336
Kotel, Kotelcane— Kodelczen/1327; Goldschen
Kovarovici— Chowaruwiz/1200; Kauritz
Krac— Craz/1140; Crahz/1291; Kratschutz

KRC, LUB, LUBEN

Krc, Krcic— Kirsiz/1140; Kertschutz
Kricin— Cricin/1378; Kryczen/1378; Kreutzen
Krolovici— Croluwiz/1140; Kralawicz/1336
Kur— Curindorf/1200, Kauerndorf
Kyov— Chiowe/1200; Chyovve/1210; Kyowe/1254; Gieba
Lipa— *Lypen inferior*/1290; Niederleupten
Lipa— *In alio Lipen*/1227; Oberleupten
Lub, Luben— *In villa Luben minori*/1269; Windischleuba

LUG, MED, MOKRANE

Lug— Lugiendorf/1378; Lehndorf
Malos— Malus/1140; Mohlis
Med, Medin— Medene/1378
Micho, Michov— Michowe/1140; Meucha
Mysov— Mizowe/1200
Mokrane— Mocren/1200; Mogkran/1214; Mockern
Mokrosoky— Mocurzoch/1200; Mogczok/1378; Mockzig
Nacebor, Naceborici— Nazibriz/1200

NEZABUD, OLSINA, PLOT

Nenovici— Nenewiz/1200; Nenuwiz/1289
Nezabud, Nezabudici— Nubodiz/1200; Nobdenitz
Nipaskov— Nizpasscowe/1200
Niradek— Nirodichow/122; Nirakindorf/1336

Olsa, Olsina— Holcinas/ 1200
Pan, Panovici— Panewitz/1344; Pahnitz
Platecici— Platicizci/1140; Platshcutz
Plot— Plotendorf/1280; Plottendorf

PREN, PYSKOVICI, RODETA

Ponik, Ponikovici— Poniczewicz/1378; Pontewitz
Pren— Prene/1378; Prehna
Prestavilky— Pristaulic/1336; Prisselburg
Privil— Priwil/1290; Priefel
Putes, Putesov— Putesowe/1200; Petsa
Pyskosici— Piskasicz/1378; Piskenicz
Rodeta, Rodetov— Rodnetowe/1200
Rola, Rolek— Roluch/1200

RODEMYSL, SCENOVICI, SLEP

Rodesici— Rodesicz/1215; Rositz
Rot, Rotin— Rotin/1200; Rothin/1279
Rot, Rotnica— Rotenize/1291; Rothenitz
Rodemysl— Rodemuschil/1336; Rodameuschel
Rozvaz— Rozwaz, 1200; Rasephas
Rudas— Rudaz/1200; Raudenitz
Scenovici— Steniwiz/1217; Steinwitz
Sebekury— Zebecuri/976; Cebecur/1216
Slep, Slepica— Slepiz/1297; Schlopitz
Sluc— Slucz/1285; Schlauditz

STUDENC, VOL, ZELIDROZ

Smec— Smecz/1336
Studenc— Studenschen/1263; Stunzhain
Techovici— Techewitz/1170; Tegkwitz
Tetov— Thetow/1237; Tettau
Trebeglov— Ztribeglowe/1140; Trebula
Trebin— Trebine/ 1290; Treben
Tusovici— Tussuwiz/1140; Grosstauschwitz
Uncin— Untzhin/1418; Untschen
Vol, Volov— Wolowe/1200
Zelidroz— Zeldros/1200; Selderoz/1378; Selleris
Zem— Zemov/1200; Zehma

6. PAGO DOBNA

Pago Dobna was centered at **Dobna**, later *Dobenau,* a stronghold northwest of Plauen. The name is derived from either one of two Slavic roots, namely *dub* (oak) or *dob* (arable land).

- *In pago Dobna, 1222*
- *Pagi Dobnensis, 1244*

- *Terra que Dobene nominatur, 1267*
- *In terminus Dobene, 1278*
- *In terra Dobnensi, 1280*
- *Terra Dobene, 1328*

7. IN STADT PLAUEN

Pago Dobna's early importance owes much to its location, to its relation to **Plav** or **Plauen** or **Plauen im Vogtland**, from the Slavic *plav*, connoting water lands (Plawe, 1122; Plawe, 1244; Plawen, 1267). An early Serb stronghold on the White Elster, at the northwest foot of the Erzgebirge range, **Plauen** secured an important trade route with Bohemia. The thoroughly Serb character of this well-settled area is evident in the names of social and natural entities: provinces (**Milin**— *provinciam que Milin dicitur*, 1212); strongholds (**Drevno**— *castrum Drewen*, 1329; **Grodc**— *castrum Groiz*, 1225); waterways (**Breza**— Friesen-bach; **Groznica**— *rivulus Crosenicz;* **Jesenica**— *usque at fluvium, que dicitur Iezniz;* **Kamenica**— *Kamenizam fluvium;* **Kokot**— *rivus Cocotwia;* **Milin**— *in ascensu ripe Mylen;* **Stribog**— *Striboz-bach;* **Trebes**— *Triebes-bach;* **Virsnica**— *Wurschnitz-bach;* **Zir, Zirova**— *inter ripam ripam Sirowe*).

BELA, GORNICA

The names of the many villages in this area are often derived from common Serbian names and terms.

BELA, GRADAC, JABLAN

    Bel, Bela— Bele, 1292 (Pohl, Plauen)
    Buzin— Buzin, 1263 (Pausa, Plauen)
    Delc— Dalch, 1421 (Dehles, Plauen)
    Gornica— Gornicz, 1378 (Gornitz, Oelsnitz)
    Gradac— Groytz, 1209 (Greiz, Plauen)
    Grob, Grobla— Grobowe, 1313 (Grobau, Plauen
    Groznia— Rosnicz, 1297 (Rossnitz, Plauen)
    Jablan— Iabelon, 1290 (Gablau, Elsterberg)

JESENICA, KAMENICA, LUBOTIN

    Jesenica— Jezenicz, 1263 (Jossnitz, Plauen)
    Kamenica— Kemeniz, 1298 (Kemnitz, Plauen)
    Kurovici— Kurwicz, 1294 (Kurbitz, Plauen)
    Laz, Lazane— Lazan, 1400 (Losa, Elsterberg)
    Les, Lesov— Lezowe, 1335 (Lossau, Zeulenroda)
    Lubanovici— Lubenwitz, 1300 (Leubnitz, Muhltroff)
    Lubotin— Lubotin, 1378 (Leubetha, Adorf)
    Mesovici— Meschwitz, 1370 (Moschwitz, Plauen)
    Milan— Meilan, 1462) (Mehla, Triebes)

POSEK, RUDNICA, SLAVOTICI

    Olesnica— Olsniz, 1359 (Oelsnitz, Plauen)
    Posek— Possegk, 1506 (Possig, Plauen)
    Rasov— Raschowe, 1281 (Raschau, Oelsnitz)

Rudnica— Rudnicz, 1333 (Reudnitz, Greiz)
Rusa, Rusin— Rusen, 1438 (Reusa, Plauen)
Sdenc— Stens, 1303 (Steins, Plauen)
Sikor— Cykorauwe, 1307 (Zickra, Berga)
Slavotici— Zlautiz, 1267 (Schloditz, Oelsnitz)

SLEME, TREBANICI, VRSNICA

Sleme, Slemen— Slemen, 1499 (Schlemen, Oelsnitz)
Svosovic— Zwoskwicz, 1282 (Zwoschwitz, Plauen)
Temysl— Temuzler, 1301 (Demeusel, Plauen)
Trebanici— Trebenitz, 1366 (Tremnitz, Greiz)
Trebes— Triebes, 1512 (Triebes, Zeulenroda)
Tusovic— Touschewicz, 1438 (Tauschwitz (Plauen)
Visek— Vuizekiani, 945 (Wisegk, Plauen)
Vrsnica— Wirseniz, 1328 (Wurschnitz, Oelsnitz)
Zornov— Sornow, 1378 (Sorna, Auma)

DOBROTA'S DORF

As elsewhere in Germania, here too, many communities with German sounding names, often with the suffix *dorf*, are often, in fact, cognates derived from common Serb personal names.

Dortendorf (Hohenleuben) is **Dobrota's dorf**— Doberenndorf, 1293; Dobertendorf, 1356
Drossdorf (Oelsnitz) is **Drozan's dorf**— Drosansdorf, 1267; Drosindorff, 1378
Fassendorf (Plauen) is **Bozeta's dorf**— Vozetendorf, 1328
Merkendorf (Auma) is **Mirek's dorf**— Myrkindorf, 1324
Pansdorf (Elsterberg) is **(zu)Pan's dorf**— Pansdorff, 1422
Raasdorf (Oelsnitz) is **Radan's dorf**— Radiansdorf, 1328
Steinsdorf (Plauen) is **Stan's dorf**— Stanstorff, 1438
Tirschendorf (Auma) is **Tesin's dorf**— Teschendorf, 1378
Untendorf (Auma) is **Uneta's dorf**— Onetendorf, 1378
Zaulsdorf (Oelsnitz) is **Sulen's dorf**— Zculenstorf, 1378

4. SRBI IUXTA MULDE

The following are some of the Serb nations/provinces recorded along the Mulde: 1) Quezici (*Kvasici*); 2) Rochelenze (*Rogolenzi*); 3) *Altera Regio Neletici;* 4) *Chutici Orientalis;* 5) *Zvikov.*

1. QUEZICI (KVASICI)

The recorded name *Quezici* appears to be derived from the Slavic *kvas*, a word connoting leavening, fermentation, yeast *(A. Wedzki, Quesizi, SsS 4, 1970).* Scholars tend to classify *pago Quezici* as a *Siusili sub-province*, located on the west bank of the Mulde, centered at Ilburg/Eilenberg. There are few direct references to *pago Quezici* in medieval sources: *In regionibus ... Quezici, in qua est civitas Ilburg, 961; Villa Gubici dicta ... in pago autem Quezici dicto in burgwardio Ilburg sitam, 1000.*

CIVITAS ILBURG

In the 11th century the area of *pago Quezici* is known as *civitas Ilburg*, after its capital city *(J. Nalepa, Ilburg, SsS2, 1964).* The name Ilburg is believed to be derived from the Slavic root *Il, Ilov,* connoting clay, clayland, a rather common root of place names throughout *Slavia* (e.g.Eulau/Naumberg: Ilauua, 850, Ylawe, 1061, Ylowe, 1268; Eula/Borna: Ylow, 1416; Eula/Geithain: Yle, 1350; Eula/Greiz: Eyle, 1454, Ylawe, 1466; Eulau/Groitsch: Ylowe, 1268, Ylo, 1482). The following are some of the references to *civitas Ilburg* in 10th and 11th century sources:

- *Civitas Ilburg, 961*
- *Urbes Ilburg, 981*
- *Burgwardio Ilburg, 1000*
- *De Eilenburg, 1015*
- *Civitas Ilburg, 1015*
- *Civitas Eilenburg, 1017*

Later sources simply refer to the town: Hilburch, 1181; Ilburc, 1233; Ileborch, 1314; Eilenburgk, 1545. The following are typical of the place names found near *civitas Ilburg.*

GOSPODA, GOSTILICA, GRODISCE

Batun— Batun, 1314 (Battaune)
Bucina— Boczin, 1404 (Botzen)
Cepelin— Schepelin, 1242 (Zschepplin)
Cholmenc— Kolmencz, 1378 (Gollmenz)
Dobrasovici— Doberschwicz, 1349 (Dobershutz)
Gospoda— Kospoda, 1359 (Kospa)
Gostilica— *Gostelize villa*, 1161 (Gostemitz)
Grdanovici— Gurdunewice, 1156 (Gordemitz)
Grodisce— Groitz, 1184 (Groitzsch)

MILANOVICI, VELIMIN, VRESIN

Jezovici— Jhesewitz, 1495 (Jesewitz)

Luzk— Lusczk, 1464 (Laussig)
Lomany— Lumene, 1238 (Liemehna)
Milanovici— Mylanuwitz, 1288 (Molbitz)
Vel, Velenov— Welnov, 1314 (Wollnau)
Vel, Velimin— Welmyn (1363)
Vel, Velun— Welin, 1340 (Wellaune)
Vetovici— Vetovizzi, 1021 (Wedelwitz)
Vresin— Wressen, 1340 (Pressen)

VILLAS QUES

Medieval sources record a number of villages derived from the root *Kvas/Ques*. Whether some share a common provincial ancestry or simply a common name is pure speculation.

- Quasitz/Schkolen (Quasicz, 1285; Quaschicz, 1321; Quasitz, 1506)
- Quasnitz/Leipzig (Quazniz, 1271; Quasnicz, 1383)
- Quesitz/Markrandstadt (Qvesiz, 1226)
- Quetz/Zorbig (Queschiz, Quessiz, 1254)
- Queis/Halle (Quecz, 1350)
- Quesitz/Leipzig (Qvesiz, 1226; Queschiz, 1254)
- Quesnitz/Zeitz (Quesiz, 1267; Quezyz, 1300; Quesitz, 1486))

2. ROCHELENZI

One of the smaller provinces, ***provincia Rochelenze*** (from the Serb *Rog-* or *Rok-lezi*) was centered in an area bound by the Zwickauer Mulde, Zschopau, and Freiberger Mulde rivers, and traversed by *ripa Rochelinze (A. Wedzki, Rocholenzi, SsS 4, 1970)*. There are almost as many variations of the name as their are references to ***urbs, burgwardo,*** and ***provincia Rochelenzi*** in 10th and 11th century sources.

- *In Rochilenze, 959*
- *Urbs Rocholenz, 1009*
- *Burgward Rochlitz, 1017*
- *Urbs Rocholenz, 1012*
- *Burgwardo Rochelinti, 1017*
- *Ad Rochelinzi, 1018*
- *In Rochidez, 1046*
- *Provincia Rochelez, 1100*
- *D comitis de Rochelez, 1156*

MILES BUDIZLAV

It should be noted that the year 1017 finds ***miles Budizlav*** in command of ***burgward Rochlitz.***

ROCHLITZ

Urbs and ***burgward Rocholenzi*** (also Rochidez, Rochidaz, Rochlezi, Rogheliz, Rochelez, Rocheliz, Rochilez, Rogeliz, Rochelich) are modern Rochlitz on the Zwickauer Mulde, south of Colditz. As elsewhere in central and eastern Germania, many modern communities in this area have Slavic foundations and Slavic-German names *(H. Walther,*

Die Orts- und Flurnamen des Kreises Rochlitz. Ein Beitrag zur Sprach- und Siedslungegeschichte Westsachsens, 1957; Ort- und Flurnamen des Rochlitzer Landes in namengeographischer Sicht, 1957; E. Benedict, Das Rochlitzer Land, Sachsische HmB 7-8, 1961-62).

DELCIC, DOBRANICI, DOLINA

Bezgrim— (Besegrim/1350), Biesern
Delcic— (Delcz/1350), Dolitzsch
Devcin— (Devzin, 1283), Seebitzschen
Dobranici— (Dobranicz/1445), Doberenz
Dolina— (Dolen, 1291), Dohlen
Katovici— (Kethewiczs, 1378), Kottwitzsc
Korbov— (Korba, 1580), Corba

LUBIN, MILKOV, NIBEL

Kosin— (Kossin, 1280), Cossen
Kutrin— (Kutterin, 1378), Kottern
Lubin— (Luben, 1290), Leuba
Milkov— (Milkow, 1378), Milkau
Mocedrady— (Mutzschenroda, 1433), Mutzshcenroda
Muzin— (Musyn, 1329), Meusen
Nibel— (Nibel, 1540), Nobeln

PENIK, POPOVIC, SELICI

Penik— (Penic, 1264), Penig
Penov— (Penaw, 1496), Penna
Popovic— (Popewicz, 1368), Poppitz
Scitin— (Scytan, 1445), Steudten
Selici— (Seliz, 1174), Seelitz
Stobnik— (Stobenick, 1325), Stobnig
Zrnoseky— (Zorneske, 1208), Sornzig

CHYTAN, GBELSK, GORA, GROB, GRABISIN

The following five communities with names beginning with the letter **G** represent typical etymologies.

• **Geithain**, west of Rochlitz, originally ***Chytan*** (Chiten/1186, Gitan/1205, Gytan/1365), an old Serb personal name connoting trapper, hunts-man *(J. Goschel, Die Ort-, Flur- und Flussnamen der Kreise Borna und Gethain, 1964).*

• **Gepulzig**, south of Rochlitz, originally ***Gbelsk*** (Gepulczk/ 1350, Gebulcz/ 1378, Gebuluczk/1451) is derived from the Serb/Slav root *gbel*, connoting bend, curve, turn.

• **Gohren**, southwest of Rochlitz, originally ***Gora, Gorane*** (Goren/1282, Gorin 1448), from the Serb/Slav root *gor* root, connoting highland, mountain.

• **Groblitz**, east of Rochlitz, originally ***Groblica*** (Grobelicz/1350, Grabelicz/ 1378, Groblicz/ 1445), from the Serb/Slav root *grob* connoting graveyard, burial ground;

- **Grobschutz**, east of Rochlitz, originally *Grabisici* (Grabeschicz/ 1378,Grebeschitz/1498), from the Serb/Slav personal name *Grabis, Grabisin*.

3. ALTERA REGIO NELETICI

Two 10th century sources place the ***Neletici*** on the Mulde. One places ***civitas Vurcine***, modern Wurzen on the Mulde, in *altera regio Neletici ... civitas Vurcine, 961*. A second source places ***provintia et pago Neletiki*** next to the Mulde: ***Provintia et pago Neletiki iuxta Mildam flumen, 973***.

4. CHUTICI ORIENTALIS

Numerous sources also place the ***Chutici*** on the Mulde. The following communities are recorded in ***Chutici Orientalis*** (*villis Wissepuig et Lostatawa, quae ad Gutizi orientalem pertinet ad fluviis Caminici, Albique distinguitur*, 981) in the late 10th century *(L. Bonhoff, Chutizi Orientalis, NeU 31, 1910)*.

> **Bigni**— (Puchau/Mulde)
> **Dybin**— Dibni (Bad Duben/Mulde)
> **Jezero, Jezeriska**— Gerzerisca (Teifensee, W Duben/Mulde)
> **Grotmici**— Grothomizi (Grottewitz, S Nerchau/Mulde)
> **Il-burg**— Ilburg (Eilenburg/Mulde)
> **Lubanici**— (Lobnitz, N Bitterfeld/Mulde)
> **Vlastov**— Lostatuua (Lastau, N Rochlitz/Zwickauer Mulde)
> **Nerchov**— *Nirechouua burguuardium* (Nerchau/Mulde)
> **Po-uchat**— Pauch (Pouch, E. Bitterfeld/Mulde)
> **Vrcin**— *Vurcin civitas* (Wurzen/Mulde)
> **Wissepuig**— (Rochlitz)

CHUTICI, LUZICA

Apparent evidence of ***Chutici*** settlement farther east is found in *Chutici* (Chutiz, 1278, now Gutz), the name of a village near Landsberg/Finsterwalde in ***Lower Luzica***.

ZWIKOWE

This region takes its name from the river ***Zvik***, later Zwikauer Mulde. It was centered at ***Zwikov*** (modern Zwickau), a Serb stronghold on the west bank of the ***Zvik*** *(W. Schenck, Die Ortsnamen des Kreise Werdau und Zwickau, 1959)*. The following are typical of the Serb communities recorded in this general area.

BELOVICI, BREZOVANE, BUKOVANE

> **Bela**— Bele, 1358 (Pohlau)
> **Belovici**— Belwiz, 1219 (Polbiz)
> **Brezovica**— Bresewicz, 1423 (Bresewitz)
> **Bukovane**— Buckawen, 1436 (Bockwa)
> **Dalsk**— Daltzak, 1395 (Dalzig)
> **Cetovici**— Czethewitz, 1322 (Schedewitz)
> **Glusov**— Glouchouwe, 1372 (Glachau)

GORNOVIC, GORSK, KRAKOV

Goris, Gorisin— Goris, 1488 (Garnitz)
Gornovic— Gernewitz, 1421 (Gornewitz)
Gorsk— Gorck, 1346 (Gurigk)
Gorskovici— Gorscuwiz, 1261 (Groschwitz)
Imanici— Imeniz, 1182 (Imnitz)
Krakov— Krakowe, 1350 (Krakau)
Krinici— Crinicz, 1445 (Crinitz)

MILISA, PLAVNICA, RADLO

Lubenici— Lewbenitz, 1484 (Leubnitz)
Milisa— Milsin, 1328 (Mulsen)
Plavnica— Plauwuniz, 1216 (Planitz)
Radlo, Radlic— Rodlitz, 1493 (Rodlitz)
Radsov— Ratscha, 1140 (Rotschau)
Sedlov— Schedelowe, 1307 (Schiedel)
Sleme— Sleme, 1487 (Schlema)
Slunsk—- Sluntzk, 1418 (Schlunzig)

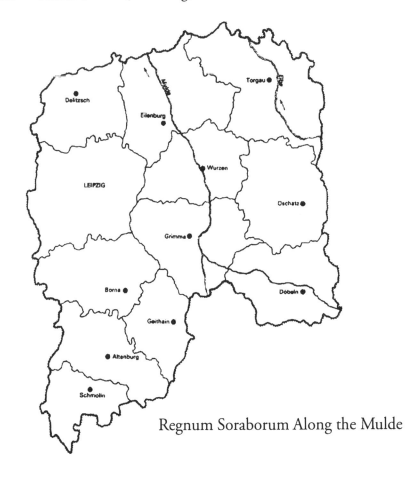

Regnum Soraborum Along the Mulde

5. SRBI IUXTA ALBA

This chapter covers a number of Serb nations/provinces, except the ***Dalminze-Glomaci,*** situated along the Elbe: 1) ***Woulauki***; 2) ***Zluvini***; 3) ***Nizizi***; 3A) ***Nisici vel Mezumroka***; 4) ***Scitici***; 5) ***Chutici***; 6) ***Nisane/Nizane.***

1. WOULAUKI

A subnation of the ***Nizici,*** the ***Woulauki*** occupied an area that straddled the Elbe between its juncture with the Schwarze Elster in the east and the Mulde in the west, essentially the area around Wittenberg. There is only a single direct reference to the ***Woulauki*** in 10th century sources: ***Uuolauki in quo Broto, 973. Broto*** (Broth, 966; Brot, 1004; Brote, 1200), from the Serb *brod* (ford, a place to cross a river or stream) is modern Pratau on the Elbe, opposite Wittenberg on the north bank.

IN NIZIZI

Two sources place the ***Uuolauki*** centered at Wittenberg/Pratau in ***provintia Nizizi*** *(J. Nalepa, Nizycy, SsS 3, 1975).* One, a 10th century source: ***De provintia Sclavorum Nizizi ... urbibus Broth, 966.*** The other, an early 11th century source: ***De Sclavorum provintia Nizizi ... urbes ... Brot, 1004.*** The following place names are typical of the Serb communities found near Wittenberg in the medieval period *(R. Willnow, Die Ortsnamen des Kreises Wittenberg, 1971).*

BADOMIR, BISTRICA, BOZ
> **Brkov**— Berkow, 1371 (Berkau)
> **Badomir**— Bodemer, 1396 (Bodemar)
> **Bistrica**— Bisteritcz, 1361 (Peisteritz)
> **Boz**— Boza, 1388 (Boos)
> **Brezka**— Breczke, 1419 (Breske)
> **Bukovica**— Buckewitz, 1703 (Buchwitz)
> **Bulsk**— Bulzk, 1335 (Bulzig)

BYTOGOST, DOBRUN, GORA
> **Bytogost**— Bitegast, 1375 (Bitetegast)
> **Dobrin**— Dobbryn, 1200 (Dobien)
> **Dobrun**— Dobrun, 1353 (Dabrun)
> **Dusov**— Dussow, 1400 (Dusso)
> **Golina**— Gollyn, 1377 (Gallin)
> **Gora**— Gore, 1200 (Gohrau)
> **Grab, Grabov**— Grabow, 1378 (Grabo)

JABLAN, KONEBUDY, LUBEC
> **Grob, Grobsk**— Groptzk, 1460 (Gropzig)
> **Jablan**— Jablinze, 1150 (Gablenz)
> **Jama**— Jame 1419 (Jahmo)
> **Konebudy**— Kanebudy, 1464
> **Lec, Ledce**— Letze, 1400 (Leetza)
> **Lubas**— Lubaas, 1356 (Lubast)

Lubec— Lubetz, 1331 (Labetz)

LUBICHOV, NESKOV, OKOLO
Lubichov— Lobbechow, 1410 (Lobichau)
Mirkovici— Merkewicz, 1350 (Merkwitz)
Murov— Murow, 1410 (Meuro)
Nadkov— Nadekaw, 1200 (Naderkau)
Nenotici— Neyntitz, 1575 (Nentitz)
Neskov— Nessko, 1442 (Nieska)
Okolo— Ocul, 1400 (Ogkeln)
Osnica— Ossenitze, 1423 (Ossnitz)

OSTROVICA, PRISEC, RUDNO
Ostrovica— Ostirwicz, 1440 (Osteritz)
Pankov— Panekaw, 1367 (Pannigkau)
Parez— Parys, 1323 (Paris)
Pretocno— Prietozina, 1004 (Pretzsch)
Prisec— Prizcez, 1290 (Priesitz)
Rodis— Rodiss, 1383 (Radis)
Rokyta— Rogkit, 1324 (Rackith)
Rudno— Ruden, 1385 (Reuden)

STRAH, UPOR, ZAGORANE
Splav— Slaw, 1388 (Splau)
Strah, Strasni— Strach, 1390 (Straach)
Upor— Uper, 1376 (Euper)
Usici— Usizi, 965 (Eutsch)
Zachov— Sachow, 1406 (Sachau)
Zagorane— Segrene, 1390 (Seegrehna)
Zelezin— Zelezne, 1179 (Schleesen)
Zelovici— Selewitz, 1388 (Selbitz)

PROVINTIA ZLIUVINI
South of **Wolauki, provintia Zliuvini**, centered near modern Schlieben, occupied an area east of the Elbe, along the right bank of the Schwarze Elster, as far north and east as near Luckau, where it bordered with **Luzica:**

- *In provinciis vel pagis subnominatis ... Zliuvini, 973*
- *In loco Zliwin, 1269*
- *Datum et actum Zliwen, 1285*

Later sources indicate that **Zliuvini** is derived froms the Serb root *sliv* as in Zliv, 1181; Sliwne, 1228; Zliwene, 1238; Zliwin, 1242; Sliwen. Scholars believe that the name is derived from either *sliv* (river basin) or *sljiva* (plum).

DE PROVINTIA SCLAVORUM NIZIZI
Centered on the Elbe, the **Nizizi** occupied a wide area between the Mulde, Elbe, and Schwarze Elster rivers. There are numerous references to **provintia Sclavorum**

Nizizi in 10th and 11th century sources.

- *De provintia Sclavorum Nizizi nominata, 965*
- *Pago Nizizi, 965*
- *In pagus Nicici et Sprewa, 965*
- *Provintia Sclavorum Niziz, 966*
- *Ultra Provinciam Nizizi ad ipsum terminum sine dubio nec non in altera parte Luzice et Selpoli, 968*
- *Nidkiki, 973*
- *Et ultra provinciam Nizizi ad eundem terminum sine dubio nec non in altera parte Lusizi et Selboli, et sic usque ad civitatem Zulpiza, 995*
- *Niziz, 996*
- *In pago Nizizi, 997*
- *Sclavorum provintia Nizizi, 1004*
- *Pago Nicici, 1018*
- *In pago Niciza, 1069*
- *In Nithsice, 1073*
- *In pago regioneque Nietci, 1073*

BELGORA IN NIDKIKE

The above sources record the following Serb communities in *provintia Sclavorum Nizizi.*

BELGORA, BROD, GRODISTI

Belgora— (Belgern/Elbe, S Torgau)
Brod, Broth— (Pratau/Elbe, S Wittenberg/Elbe)
Clotna— (Kloden, N Pretzsch/Elbe)
Dumoz— (Dommitzsch, near Elbe, NW Torgau)
Gohtzizi— (Gotthiz, N Dessau on Mulde/Elbe confluence)
Grodisti— (SW Wittenberg/Elbe)
Nessuzi— (Neszve)

OLSNICH, PRETOKINA, SUSELIZ

Olsnich— (Elsnig, S Dommitzsch)
Pretimi— (Prettin, near Elbe, N Dommitzsch)
Pretokina— (Pretzsch/Elbe, S Wittenberg/Elbe)
Prietozini— (Pretzsch/Elbe, NW Dommitzsch)
Rochutini— (Rackwitz, S. Wittenberg/Elbe)
Sipnizi— (Suptitz, W of Torgau/Elbe)
Suseliz burhwardio— (Seuselitz/Elbe, N Dessau)

TORGUA, VISSIROBI, ZUETNA

Torgua— (Torgau/Elbe)
Triebaz— (Trebitz, NW Pretzsch/Elbe)
Uerliazi— (Worlitz, E of Dessau)
Usizi— (Eutzsch, S Wittenberg/Elbe)
Vissirobi— (by Seuselitz/Elbe)
Zuetna— (Zwethau, E Torgau/Elbe)

Wozgrinie— (Axien, E Pretzsch/Elbe)

PAGO BELA GORA

In the 10th and 11th centuries ***Nidkike's Belegora*** is recorded as a *civitate, urbs* and *pago*:

- ***Civitate quae dicitur Belegora, 983***
- ***Urbem Belegori dictam, 1017***
- ***In pago Belgor, 1130***

CONVENTUS BELA GORA

In the 11th century ***Bela Gora*** emerges as a favored place for regional assemblies:

- ***Fit conventus in Belegori, quod pulcher mons dicitur, 1009***
- ***Iuxta locum, qui dicitur Zribenz, convenimus et six sursum usque propre Belegori dcendimus, 1012***

PROVINCIA DOMMITZSCH

Nikiki's Dommitzsch, ***civitat Domuki*** in 981 is ***provincia Domitz*** as in ***ville Rodhewiz et Bnewetiz dicte, site in provincia Domitz, 1223.***

NIKIKI VEL MEZUMROKA

As the following references indicate, ***provintia Nisisi*** or ***Nikiki*** was sometimes called ***Mezumroka,*** from the Serb words *mezu* and *mroka* or between the marshlands (*E. Eichler, Eine westslawische Bezeichnung fur "Sumpf, Feuchtikeit": altsorbisch *mroka. ZtS 1, 1956*). Scholars suspect that ***Mezumroka*** refers to the eastern part of the province, the area between the Elbe and Schwarze Elster rivers:

- ***In partibus Sclavonie ... in pago Nikiki vel Mezumorka, 979***
- ***In pago Nikiki vel Mezumroka dicto, 981***

SCITICI

The ***Scitici*** occupied the west bank of the Elbe, south of **Nizizi** proper and west of ***provintia Mezumroka*** (*S. Strzelcyzk, Scitizi, SsS 5, 1975*). There are several references to ***pago Scitici*** in 10th century sources: ***In partibus Sclavonie castella Olsnic, Domkui et Zuetie in pago Scitici, 979; Civitates Olsnik, Dommitz in pago Scitizi, 992.***

SUB-NATION/PROVINCE

It is clear from the following communities recorded in ***pago Scitici*** that the ***Scitici*** were a sub-nation or province of the **Nizizi.**

- ***Domuki civitat*** (Dumoz, 965; Domuki, 981; Domuiz, 992; Domitz, 1223; Dommiczsch, 1434; modern Dommitzsch), from Serb *dumuci,* connoting windstorms.

- ***Olsnik civitat*** (Olsnich, 965; Olsnic, 981; Olsnik, 992; Elsnick, 1495, modern Elsnig), from *Olsa, Oles,* Serb cognates connoting shrub or tree growing in moist places.

- *Zuetie* (979), modern Zwethau, east of Torgau, is almost certainly derived from the Serb *Svet, Svetc, Svetic* connoting light, sanctity, holy. More than several settlements have similar onomastic roots (e.g. Zvenz/1140, now Schwanditz; Swetz/1404, now Schwatz; Zvetiz/1251, now Schweditz).

NELETICI

On the Elbe, the **Neletici** were centered in an area around Torgau on the Elbe: *Parvum Neletiki ubi Turquo stat, 973.*

NIZIZI, NELETICI

The following place names are typical of the medieval Serb communities recorded in the sometimes overlapping provinces of **Nizizi** and **Neletici** centered on the Elbe *(H.B. Wieber, Die Ortsnamen des Kreises Torgau, 1968).*

BEGANOVICI, BUKOVICA, CHOTIMYSL

Bagno, Bagenc— Pagenz, 1821 (Bahnitz)
Bekovici— Bekewicz, 1314 (Beckwitz)
Beganvoci— Begenowiz, 1251 (Beinewitz)
Bezovik— Besewig, 1394 (Besswig)
Bukovica— Bucuwiz, 1241 (Bockwitz)
Chotelici— Chothelitz, 1253 (Kottlitz)
Chotimysl— Chotimesdorf, 992
Cremesnica— Shremsenicz, 1290 (Schirmenitz)

DEBLICI, GOLUBIN, KOSMATICI

Deblici— Debilicz, 1415 (Doberlitz
Droganici— Drockenicz, 1428 (Dragnitz)
Gnusin— Chnussin, 1233 (Knessen)
Golubin— Goplbyn, 1380 (Golben)
Gubin— Gubin, 1394 (Guben)
Kosmatici— Kosmaticz, 1373 (Kosmatitz)
Lesnik— Lesnick, 1275 (Lossnig)
Lesno— Lesne, 1442 (Lohsten)

LIPA, LOZNICA, LUBORAZ

Lipa— Lipe, 1376 (Leipa)
Lochov— Lochow, 1339 (Lochau)
Loskovici— Loskewiz, 1251 (Losswig)
Loznica —Lossnicz, 1589 (Lossnig)
Lubin— Lubin, 1330 (Lebien)
Luboraz— Luberaz, 1287, (Liebersee)
Lubovici— Lobewicz, 1314 (Lobewitz)
Lukov— Lichowe, 1230 (Lucke)

MEZIREKA, MOKROVICA, MOSTIC

Luzno— Lusene, 1251 (Lausa)
Mezireka, Mezirec— Meseriz, 1251 (Mehderitzsch)

Mokrina— Mokrene, 1445 (Mockrehna)
Mokrovica— Mokerwicz, 1350 (Mockritz)
Milobuz— Melpuz, 1251 (Melpitz)
Mostic— Mosticz, 1243 (Mostitz)
Niploc— Niplock, 1399 (Leiploch)
Odolovici— Odilwicz, 1314 (Adelwitz)

OSTROBICI, PAKOBUZ, POLOVICA

Olesnik— Olsnich, 965 (Elsnig)
Ostrobici— Ostrobicesdorf, 992
Pakobuz— Pokkubus, 1240 (Packisch)
Plosk— Plosk, 1495 (Plossig)
Plot— Plote, 1251 (Plotha)
Pec, Pecica— Peczica, 1397 (Pietsch)
Polovica— Pollewycz, 1289 (Polbitz)
Pretim— Pretimi, 965 (Prettin)

PRUGA, RADOTAVICI, STARICI

Pruga— Pruz, 1251 (Prausitz)
Rochovici— Rachewicz, 1314 (Rochlitz)
Rocici— Rocschicz, 1378 (Roitzsch)
Radotavici— Rodotewicz, 1291 (Runditz)
Rudno— Rudin, 1428 (Reuden)
Sobasovici— Sobaswicz, 1291 (Sobaswitz)
Starici— Staricz, 1314 (Staritz)
Strahovane— Strochwene, 1385 (Durchwehna)

STRELA, SVETOMIRICI, ZUPANICI

Strela, Strelica— Strelitz, 1378 (Strehlitz)
Strela, Strelin— Strelen, 1494 (Strellin)
Stupovici— Stupuwicz, 1291 (Staupitz)
Svetomiric— Zuetmariz, 1251
Treblgora— Trebilgor, 1380 (Drebligar)
Vresov— Wrisow, 1350 (Briesau)
Vretin— Wrentin, 1283 (Brenten)
Zupanici— Sipnizi, 965 (Suptitz)

CHUTICI

On the Elbe, the ***Chutici*** appear to be centered in the area around Groba, north west of Riesa on the Elbe: ***Burchwardo Grobi ... in pago Chutizi***, *1046*

NISANE (NIZANI), BEHEM

One source places the ***Nisani*** along the border with Bohemia: **Duarum regionum Behem et Nisenen**, 948. A second source indicates that ***pago Niseni*** ran alongside ***pago Dalamenci*** as far as ***urbs Mogelini***, modern Mugeln, northwest of Meissen: ***Per Niseni et Deleminci pagos usque ad Mogelini ducitur***, *984*. A third source places ***provinciam Nice*** near the Spree River bordering on ***Budusin*** in ***Luzica***: ***Terra Budusin inde provinciam Nice vocatam intinere attingens, iuxta Sprewam metatus est***, *1006*

According to sources, the *Nisani* were located in small part west and northwest of Meissen, in great part east and southeast of Dresden to the border with Bohemia *(L. Bonhoff, Der Gau Nisan in politischer und kirchliche Beziehung, NeU 36, 1915).* The following are some of the references to the *Nisani* recorded in the 10th and 11th centuries.

- *Regio Nisenen, 948*
- *Nisinen, 968*
- *In Talemence, Nisanen, Lucize, Milczane, Diedesa, 968*
- *Nisane, 971*
- *Provincia Dalminza, Nisane, Diedesa et Milzane et Lusica, 971*
- *Pago Nisen, 984*
- *Regiones Nisenin, 995*
- *Nisenin, 996*
- *Inde provinciam Nice vocatam itinere attingens, iuxta Sprewam fluvium castra, 1005*
- *In Niseni, 1013*
- *In pago Niseni, 1013*
- *In pago Nisani, 1068*
- *In Nisen, 1083*

PAGO NISENI

Brochotinacethla or *Brochota's sedlo* (settlement) is one of the earliest communities recorded in *Nisane*: *Brochotinacethla in pago Niseni, 1013*. An important stronghold appropriately named *Rat*, connoting war, battle, was located east of Pirna: Ratin (1261*), castra Ratny* (1361), modern Rathen.

SERB COMMUNITIES

The following place names are typical of the Serb communities recorded either in or near the borders of medieval *provincia Nisane* *(W. Coblenz, Zu den slawischen Wallanlegend des Gaues Nisan, Fruhe Burgen und Stadte, 1954; Bemerkungen zum Slavengau Nisane AgT, 1977. E. Beckmann, Ortsnamen in der ehemaligen slawischen Landschaft Nisane, 1965).*

BLAZENOVICI, CHLEBA, GOLOBROD

Blazenovici— (Blazenwicz, 1384), Blasewitz
Chleba, Hleba— (Clebe, 1288), Kleba
Chudosov— (Cudeschowe, 1288), Kauscha
Domin— (Domyn, 1316), Dohma
Dub— (Dube, 1378), Daube
Golobrod— (Gollebrode, 1425), Golberode
Gorus— (Gorusch, 1437), Gohrisch

HOSTIMIRICI, KAMEN, KRAVA

Gosov— (Goszow, 1350), Goes
Hostimirici— (Hostenbricz, 1406), Hosterwitz
Kamen— (Camen, 1463), Gamig
Korkonos— (Korkanus, 1378), Gornitz
Krava— (Crawas, 1288), Krebs

Krup— (Krub, 1378), Graupa
Lubanici— (Lubanitz, 1227), Leubnitz

LUKANICA, MUZIGOST, PREMYSLOVIC

Lukanica— (Lucawitz, 1288)
Misov— (Mischow, 1378), Meuscha
Muzigost— (Musegost, 1288), Meusegast
Ploskovici— (Ploskewicz, 1347), Ploschwitz
Pravcici— (Prautschicz, 1350), Pratzschwitz
Premyslovic— (Prymselwicz, 1412), Primselwitz
Pyrno— (Pyrne, 1239), Pirna
Ratin— (Raten, 1261), Rathen

RYPIN, STOLPIN, ZABNICI

Rypin— (Rypin, 1295), Rippien
Sobijar— (Sebegar, 1445), Sobrigen
Scirce— (Stircze, 1435), Sturza
Sporovici— (Sporwicz, 1400), Sporbitz
Srsen— (Sursen, 1309), Surssen
Stolpin— (Stulpen, 1122, Stolpen
Strupin— (Struppin, 1361), Struppen
Zabnici— (Sabnize, 1228), Sebnitz

6. SURBI IN SURBIA

The ***Dalminci-Glomaci*** are another once great ***White Serb*** nation with deep and intriguing historical roots *(H. Kunstmann, Kamen die westslawischen Daleminci aus Dalmatien, DwS 28, 1983)*. Alfred's *Orosius* locates the ***Dalminze*** in the following terms: **To the east of the Maroara [Moravia] is the land of the Vistula ... To the north east of the Maroara are the Dalamenstan ... North of the Dalamenstan are the Surpe and west of them the Sysyle.** The *Descriptio Civitatem* places the ***Dalminze*** after the Serbs: ***Iuxta illos [Surbi] sunt quos vocant Talaminzi.*** The ***Dalminzi*** are said to have 14 *civitates*: ***Talaminzi, qui habent civitates XIIII.*** The ***Dalminzi*** are followed by the ***Beheimari*** (***In terram Sclavorum, qui vocantur Beheimari***) *or* the Bohemians who are greater by only one *civitat*: ***Beheimare, in qua sunt civitates XV.***

DALMINZI, GLOMACI

Medieval sources note that the ***Dalminzi*** are also called ***Glomaci***; also *Glomaci, Glomize, Glomuzi, Glomuci, Glumici, Zlomizi (G. Labuda, O nazwie plemenia: Glomacza, Studia linguistica slavica Baltica 53, 1964; E. Eichler, Zur altsorbischen Ethnonymi Daleminzi und Glomaci, Let B/22, 1975)*.

> • ***In partibus Sclavonie ... in pago Dalminze vel Zlomekia,*** *979*
> • ***In pago Dalminze seu Zlomekia vocato,*** *981*
> • ***In provintiam, quam nos Teutonice Deleminci vocamus, Sclavi autem Glomaci appelant,*** *1012*

PAGO GLOMACI

Occasionally one finds reference simply to ***pago Glomaci: Hic pagus, qui Zlomici dicitur,*** *1003*. Several sources, including an early 11th century source, relate the name *Glomuzi* to a local waterway, to a 'sacred' waterway, to a 'holy' water. ***Glomuzi est fons, non plus ab Albi quam duo miliaria positus,*** *1012*. There are indications, etymological and otherwise, that link the 'holy water,' ***Glomuzi,*** to an Old Slavic word connoting a rocky height, where, it was said, pagan 'dancing rituals' were performed.

SCLAVI QUI VOCANTUR DALAMATII

There are numerous references to the ***Dalminzi/Glomaci*** in medieval sources.

SUPER HWERENOFELDE ET DELMELCION

> • ***Super Hwerenofelde et Delmelcion,*** *805*
> • ***Dalmatas,*** *856*
> • ***Sclavi qui vocantur Dalamatii, et Behemi atque Sorabi,*** *880*
> • ***Dalamenstan,*** *890*
> • ***Daleminzien,*** *906*
> • ***Dalminzien,*** *929*
> • ***Daleminzier,*** *929*
> • ***Daleminzier,*** *933*

DALMATIA, DALAMANCI, DALAMANTIA

> • ***Dalmatia, Dalamanci, Dalamantia,*** *940*

- *Provincia quae dicitur Talemence, 968*
- *In provincia Talemence, 968*
- *Provincia Dalaminza, 971*
- *Provincia Dalaminza, 971*
- *Adversus Dalamantiam, 973*
- *Dalamanci vero inpetum illius fere, 973*
- *Dalamantiam reversi, 973*

IN DALAMANTIA

- *In Dalamantia, 973*
- *Contra Dalamantiam, 973*
- *Et iter agentes per Dalamantiam ab antiquis opem petunt amicis, 973*
- *In pago Dalaminza, 983*
- *Pago Deleminci, 984*
- *Pagus Zlomizi, 1003*
- *Regio Deleminci, 1012*

DALMATIAE TERMINOS OCCUPAVIT, URBE COLOCI

- *Dalmatiae terminos occupavit, urbe Coloci, 1012*
- *Terminos Dalmantiae, 1013*
- *In pago Dalaminci, 1013*
- *In pago Dalaminci, 1021*
- *In pago Dalmatia, 1046*
- *In pago Dalmatia dicto, 1046*
- *In pago Deleminze, Talmence, 1046*
- *In pago, qui dicitur Talmence, 1065*
- *In pago Dalminca, 1069*

IN PAGO THALEMENCE

- *In pago Thalemence, 1074*
- *In regione Thaleminci, 1090*
- *In Daleminziergau, 1091*
- *In regione Thaleminci, 1095*
- *In pago Dalminza, 1159*
- *In provincia, que dicitur Dalminze, 1162*
- *In pago Dalaminza, 1168*
- *In pago Daleminza, 1170*

LESSER DALMINCI-GLOMACI

Tenth and 11th century sources center a lesser **Dalminci-Glomaci**, from west to east, along the Mulde, Zwickauer Mulde, Zschopau, Freiburger Mulde, Elbe, and Grosse Roder rivers, centered at Meissen, including such historic communities as Grimma, Lommatzsch, Pulsnitz, Riesa, Strehla *(K. Hertz, Das Lommatzscher Land. Wissenschaftliche Veroffentlichungen des Deutschen Institutes fur Landerkunde, 17/18, 1960).*

CASTELLA, BURCWARDO

The following are some of the earliest recorded strongholds in ***provincia Dalmatia*** *(D. Freydank, Ortsnamen der Kreises Grimma und Wurzen, 1962. E. Eichler, Nochmals zum Ortsnamen*

BOLECHIN, DOBLIN, DOLANE

- Bolechin— *in burchwardo Bolechina*, 1046 (Polkenberg, Leisnig)

- Boruz— *villa Setlesboresdorf ... in burcwardo Boruz*, 983; *burchwardus Boruz*, 1065 (Boritz, Riesa)

- Ceren— *Cirin castellum in pago Zlomizi*, 1003 (Zehren, Meissen)

- Difnosedlo— *Tyfenowe castrum*, 1082 (Riesa)

- Doblin— *Doblin castellum ... in partibus Sclavonie ... in pago Dalminze*, 979; *castella eudeam et loca ... Dobelin ... nuncupata in pago Dalminze*, 981 (Doblen/Freiberger Mulde)

- Dolane— *oppidum in Dolen*, 1228; *Zciscyn apud oppidum Dolen*, 1308 (Dahlen, Oschatz)

- Gana— *urbs quae dicitur Gana*, 929; *burgwardus ad Ganam*, 1150 (Jahna, Mugeln)

- Groba— *Grobe ... burcwardo sito in pago Talmence*, 1064 (Groba, Riesa)

- Grobi— *in burchwardo Grobi*, 1046

- Grodisce— *Grodiz*, 1229 (Groditz, Riesa)

GRODISCE, LESNIK, MOGYLA

- Grodisce— *Groydzs*, 1378 (Groitzsch, Nossen)

- Gvosdec— *burchwardo Guozdezi* (1045); *castrum nomine Gvozdec propre urben Misen, castra ultra oppidum Guozdec* (1123); *burgwardo Woz*, 1140 (Meissen)

- Gvozdno— *castella quedam et loca ... et Hwoznie nuncupata in pago Dalminze*, 981; *Hwoznie castella ... in partibus Sclavonie ... in pago Dalminze* (979); *in burcwardo Gozne*, 1214 (Gozne/Dobeln)

- Kalovica— *oppidum Kalewicz*, 1350 (Calbitz, Dahlen)

- Lesnik— *castrum Lesnik*, 1168; *oppidum Lesnik*, 1215, Leisnig *(H. Walther, Der Ortsnamen Leisnig. Alteste Uberlieferung, Deutung und Lokalisierung, OsG 21, 1994).*

- Lubin—*Sanice in burgwardo Lvvine* (Schanitz, Lommatzsch); *duas villas quidem uno nomine Domcice dictas ... in pago Dalminca et in burguuardo Lvvine*, 1069 (Leuben, Lommatzsch)

- Mogyla— *Mogilina urbs*, 1003; *Mogilina castrum*, 1261; *Mogilina civitas*, 1288 (Mugeln, Oschatz)

- Nemochov— *in burcwardo Nimucowa*, 1090; *in burcwardo Mochowe*, 1162 (Mochau, Dobeln)

- Nosno— *castrum Nosno*, 1289; *oppidum Nosno*, 1376 (Nossen)

NOVIGRAD, SUSELIC, ZAVIS

- Novigrad— *in pago Novvuigroda in comitatu Chuontiz*, 1028 (Nauberg, Leisnig)

- Osec— ***Oszechs oppidum***, 1065; ***civitas Oschez***, 1350 (Oschatz, Riesa)
- Rusavin—***civitas sue oppidum Rusavin***, 1286 (Rosswein)
- Strela— ***ad Strela urbem***, 1002; ***civitas Strehla***, 1012 (Strehla, NW Riesa)
- Suselic— ***munitio Susliz***, 1226; ***oppidum sive castrum Suselitz***, 1273 (Seusslitz, Riesa)
- Zadel— ***in burgwardo Zadili***, 1074; ***in pago castri Zalin***, 1079; ***Bronislav de Zhadele***, 1203 (Zadel, Meissen)
- Zrebe— ***burgwardus Serebez***, 1064 (Schrebitz, Mugeln)
- Zavis— ***Zavissa castellum in pago Dalmatia in marcha Missenensi***, 1046; ***in burcwardo Ziauzo***, 1071 (Zschaitz, Dobeln)

CASTRUM LESNIK

The following place names are typical of the Serb settlements recorded near ***castrum Lesnik***, modern Leisnig, in the medieval period.

BUDIRAZ, DOBRAKOVICI, GORNICA

Breza— Bresan, 1390 (Brosen)
Budiraz— Buderaz, 1309 (Paudritzsch)
Bukolovici— Bukelwicz, 1215 (Bockelwitz)
Chropotovici— Croputwitz, 1306 (Kroptewitz)
Dobrakovici— Dobraquitz, 1308 (Doberquitz)
Dobromirici— Dobermaricz, 1335 (Dobernitz)
Dolina— Dolan, 1390 (Dohlen)
Gornica— Gornycz, 1289 (Gornitz)
Grusovic— Grusewicz, 1308 (Grauschwitz)

KISELOVICA, LIPNICA, MUZKOV

Kiselovica— Kiselwitz, 1340 (Kieselwitz)
Klen— Klee, 1215 (Cleen)
Korcmic— Gorczchemicz, 1378 (Gorschmitz)
Lipnica— Lipniz, 1277 (Leipnitz)
Luskov— Luskow, 1378 (Lauschka)
Masovici— Maschewitcz, 1449 (Maschwitz)
Mokrici— Mockerwitz, 1340 (Motterwitz)
Morasovici— Moraswitz, 1284 (Marschwitz)
Muzkov— Muscowe, 1244 (Muschau)

OSTROV, PODOLSICI, POSELICI

Nidabudovici— Nidabudowiz, 1234 (Nidabudowitz)
Nikrasovici— Nyrkracwicz, 1378 (Nicollschwitz)
Ostrov— Osztrowe, 1274 (Ostrau)
Poselici— Poseliz, 1215 (Poselitz)
Posovici— Poschewicz, 1421 (Poischwitz)
Podolsici— Podolozicz, 1360 (Polditz)
Rodov— Rocow, 1378 (Roda)
Zidovici— Sydewicz, 1350 (Seidewitz)

Zitin— Syttin, 1213 (Sitten)

VILLAS

The following are some of the earliest villages recorded in ***provincia Dalmatia***
(E. Eichler, H. Walther, Die Ortsnamen in Gau Daleminze.Studien zur Toponymie der Kreise Doblen, Grossenhain, Meissen, Oschatz und Riesa, 1/11, 1966).

BOR, CHOLM, DREZNICI
Bukovane— Bukewen, 1180 (Bockwen)
Bor— Bor, 1183 (Bohrigen)
Brochotin Sedlo— Brochotinacethla, 1013 (Brockwitz)
Cavic— Csawiz, 1180 (Zschauitz)
Cholm— Chulmice, 1185 (Colln)
Chotanovici— Chotanewiz, 1190 (Kottenewitz)
Cilov— Schilow, 1180 (Zscheila)
Drzenici— Dersniz, 1190 (Dorschnitz)
Dubnica— Duueniz, 1180 (Daubnitz)

GLUSINA, LUTANOVICI, MILOBUZ
Gluchy— Gluch, 1197 (Glaucha)
Glusina— Glussi, 1013 (Glossen)
Gola, Golisa— Goliz, 1186 (Gohlis)
Kregus— Creuz, 1186; Kryguz, 1336 (Krogis)
Kyjovica— Chewiz, 1190; Kywizsch 1291 (Kiebitz)
Lutanovici— Lutunewiz, 1186 (Leutewitz)
Machotici— Machtice, 1140 (Machtitz)
Malis— Mals, 1198; Malis, 1551 (Mahlis)
Marus— Marus, 1183 (Mahris)
Milobuz— Milbuz, 1185 (Mulbitz)

MOKRUS, OSTROV, RATIBOR
Miratin Sedlo— Miratincethla, 1013 (Mertitz)
Mokrus— Mocruz, 1198 (Gross-Mockritz)
Nutnica— Nutnize, 1190 (Nutnitz)
Olesnik— Ulsnic, 1198; *Olsnich mons*, 1228 (Ossig)
Ostrov— Ostrow, 1190 (Ostrau)
Parnica— Parniz, 1190 (Pahrenz)
Promnica— Prominiz, 1186 (Gross Promnitz)
Ratibor— Ratiborici, 1074 (Rottewitz)
Repa, Repin— Repin, 1198 (Reppen)

SEDLOBOR, VISOCANI, VOJNICI
Sanic— Sanici, 1069 (Schanitz)
Sedlobor— Sedlobor, 983 (Setlesboresdorf)
Senica— Zenizi, 1013; Senicz, 1428 (Sonitz)
Slavin— Slowin, 1186 (Schleben)
Ulica— Uliz, 1190 (Eulitz)

Visocani— Visocani, 1090 (Weitzschenhain)
Vojnici— Woiniz, 1185 (Wuhnitz)
Vystud— Wistud, 1180 (Wistauda)
Zalovici— Zcelewiz, 1150; Sallwewitz, 1445 (Salbitz)

MISIN, MISNIA

Misin or *Misni*, later Meissen on the Elbe, an area long known as **Serbia**, was the center of **Misnia**, later **Meissen mark**, in **provincia Dalmatia**. There are numerous references to *urbs, civitas, marca,* and *rivulus* **Misin** throughout the medieval period *(W. Radig, Der Burgberg meissen unde der Slawengau Daleminzie, 1929. W. Colbenz, Burg Meissen und Burgward Zehren. Zur Frage der "slawischen Burgen" in Sachsen, BeR 1961. E. Eichler, K. Rosel, Slawische Flurnamen im Kreise Meissen, Sachsische HmB 11, 1965. W. Coblenz, Grabungen am Burgwall Zadel, Kr. Meissen, AuF 29, 1984).*

- *Daleminzier, urbs Misni, 929*
- *Civitas Misna in provincia Talemence, 968*
- *Et urben ... de rivo quodam qui in septentrionali parte eiusdem fluit, nomen eidem Misni imposuit, 1012*
- *In pago Dalmatia in marcha Missenensi, 1046*
- *Urbs Missin, 1090*
- *Urbs Misen, 1123*
- *Rivulus que dicitur Misne, 1150*
- *Pribislav de Misne, 1156*
- *Marchiam in Misnie, 1185*
- *Misin ... in Zribia, 1200*
- *Marchio Misnensis, 1210*
- *Ad partes Misnenses ... Misnensem et Lusicz, 1221*
- *Burcgravius de Mysena, 1295*
- *Stadt Meissen, 1485*

VITEZI

Settlements of Serb knights or *vitezi/vethenici* are recorded in the year 1002: **Misnens ... in ear parte, qua satellites habitant dicti Sclavonice Vethenici.** In 1045 **miles Jarmir** is granted several properties in *villa Scutropei* in **burgward Gvozdeci**, near Meissen. In the 13th century a village of the 'brave, heroic' (*hrabri*) is recorded: Chrobry; Chrobere, 1233, later Grobern, north of Meissen.

SERB COMMUNITIES

The following place names are typical of the Serb communities recorded in *Misnia* in medieval times (e.g. **Conradus de Boruz dem Hospital in Misna/Meissen decimam solventem ... sitam iuxta Drezga/Dresden in villis ... Gniwalitz, 1288**).

BUDISICI, DRASKOVICI, JAVORNICA

Beganov— Begenaw, 1428 (Pegenau)
Budisici— Budesitz, 1205 (Pauschutz)
Doblin— Doblin, 982 (Dobeln)

Dobravici— Dobrawiz, 1221 (Dobritz)
Draskovici— Drosechkowicz, 1433 (Droschkewitz)
Jarez— Jerez, 1378 (Gohrisch)
Javornica— Jauwirnicz, 1347 (Gauernitz)

JESEN, KONOTOP, KOZARIN

Jesen— Yessen, 1311 (Jessen)
Jezeric— Yesseriz, 1311 (Jesseritz)
Konotop— Kuntopel (Constappel)
Korsobuk— Korsebugk, 1445 (Garsebach)
Kovaci— Kowacz, 1428 (Kobitzsch)
Kozarin— Kozerin, 1252 (Gasern)
Lubisov— Lubesowe, 1277 (Lobsal)

LUG, MILOTICI, NESOVICI

Lug— Luge, 1334 (Luga)
Miran— Miran, 1206 (Mehren)
Milotici— Milticz, 1334 (Miltitz)
Mirotici— Mereticz, 1360 (Mertitz)
Misovici— Mischewitz, 1268 (Mischwitz)
Nesovici— Nischwicz, 1438 (Nieschutz)
Penkovici— Penkuwicz, 1350 (Pinkowitz)

PRAVDA, RADANOVICI, REKA

Polensk— Polenzke, 1180 (Polenz)
Pravda— Prewda, 1373 (Proda)
Prosovici— Proschewitz, 1371 (Proschwitz)
Radanovici— Radanwicz, 1378 (Radewitz)
Ratovici— Ratsuwitz, 1205 (Radewitz)
Reka, Recny— Recschen, 1378 (Roitzschen)
Repnica— Repnicza, 1366 (Reppnitz)

ROSLAVICI, SENICA, ZRNOVICI

Roslavici— Rozalwicz, 1334 (Rasslitz)
Sebesici— Sebeschicz, 1427 (Seebschutz)
Senica— Senicz, 1428 (Sonitz)
Strosin— Stroschin, 1402 (Stroischen)
Stud, Studov— Studow, 1378 (Stauda)
Zletov— Zletowe, 1205 (Schletta)
Zrnovici— Sornewicz, 1378 (Sornewitz)

DREZGA, DRESDEN

Southeast of *urbs Misni*, *Drezga* was the Serb antecedent of modern Dresden (*in civitate nostra Dreseden, 1216*). The following place names are typical of the Serb communities recorded near Dresden in medieval times.

BABIZNA, BELANOVICI, BOLESICI

Babizna— Babisnow, 1378 (Babinsau)
Belanovici— Belenewitz, 1335 (Pillnitz)
Bely— Bele, 1351 (Buhlau)
Bistrica— Bvistrizi, 1068 (Pesterwitz)
Blozenici— Blosenicz, 1350 (Blasewitz)
Bolesici— Bulsize, 1140 (Bulsize)
Boretin— Borrenthin, 1286 (Borthen)
Borloz— Borloz, 1378 (Borlas)

BOZKOV, BOZOVICI, BREZNICA

Bozkov— Boschowe, 1316 (Boschkau)
Bozovici— Bozewicz, 1467 (Bosewitz)
Brezna— Bresen, 1362 (Brosegn)
Breznica— Bresnice, 1071; *Luciwice et Worncitine in burcwardo Bresnice*, 1071 (Briesnitz)
Lucovici— Lucewice, 1071 (Leutewitz)
Panovici— Panewycz, 1311 (Baewitz)
Pestovici— Pestewicz, 1370 (Pestitz)

PLAVNO, POCAPLY, PROLOG

Plavno— Plawen, 1206 (Plauen)
Pocaply— Potschapel, 1206 (Postchappel)
Podbreze— Poderbrese, 1350 (Boderitz)
Podgrodici— Podegriczsch, 1414 (Poyritz)
Podmos— Poedemiz, 1350 (Podemus)
Popovici— Popuwicz, 1350 (Poppitz)
Pravcici— Prawczicz, 1470 (Brabschutz)
Prolog— Prolos, 1288 (Prohlis)

GANA, (G)LOMMATZSCH

Two important and historic strongholds were northwest of ***urbs Misni***. One, ***urbs Gana (Dalminzien, urbs Gana***, 929; ***urbs quae dicitur Gana***, 960), is modern Jahna, on the river Gana as in ***ad fluvium Ganam*** *(R. Becker, Supanie, Burgward und Pfarrsprengen in Daleminze, NeU 38, 1917; W. Coblenz, Archaologisches Betrachtungen zur Gana-Frage im Rahmen alterslawischen Besiedlung des Gaues Daleminzi, Beitrage zur Archivwissenschaft und Geschichtforschung, 1966; Bemerkungen zur "urbs" Gana, EtH 16, 1975)*. A second ***urbs***, *Glomac*, is modern (G)Lommatzsch, recorded as Lomacz, 1190; Lomaz, 1230; Lomatz, 1283; Lomatsch, 1308 *(K. Herz, Das Lommatzscher Land. Eine historische-geographisce Untersuchunt, Wissenschaftliche Veroffentlichungen des Deutschen Instituts fur Landerkunde 17/18, 1960. W. Coblenz, Slawisches Skelettgraberfeld von Altlommatzsch, Kr. Meissen, AuF 3, 1959; Archaologisches Bemerkungen zur Herkunft der altessten Slawen in Sachsen, ArB 13, 1965; Das slawische Skelettgraberfeld von Alt-Lommatzsch,1 ArB 16/17, 1967)*.

SERB COMMUNITIES

The following place names are typical of the Serb communities recorded in ***Glomac/Lommatzsch*** in medieval times.

BOJTICI, DOMASLAVICI, JESEN

Becic— Beschiccz, 1378 (Pezschewitz)
Bojtici— Boititz, 1445 (Poititz)
Bratrosovici— Braterswicz, 1268 (Praterschutz)
Brmici— Birmiz, 1202 (Birmenitz)
Domaslavici— Domezlawiz, 1218 (Domselwitz)
Drznici, Drzislav— Dirseniz, 1206 (Dorschnitz)
Glina— Glyn, 1428 (Gleina)
Jesen— Yessen, 1311 (Jessen)

LESCINA, LUBSICI, MUZKOVICI

Lescina— Lestin, 1334 (Losten)
Lipane— Lypene, 1334 (Leippen)
Losin—Lossen, 1334 (Lossen)
Lucane— Lutsene, 1221 (Lautzschen)
Lubsici— Lubizizi, 1216 (Lubshutz)
Lutetici— Luteticz, 1323 (Leutewitz)
Mecislavici— Meczlawicz, 1378 (Mettelwitz)
Muzkovici— Muscuitz, 1205 (Muschutz)

PLAVNOVICI, PODBREZE, PROBOSTOVICI

Picovici— Picswicz, 1334 (Pittschutz)
Plavnovici— Plawenuwiz, 1311 (Planitz)
Pnovici— Pynewicz, 1334 (Piewitz)
Podbreze— Podbrese, 1334) Badersen)
Polcane— Polzen, 1255 (Paltzschen)
Polst— Polst, 1378 (Pulsitz)
Pravda— Prewda, 1350 (Proda)
Probostovici— Probistwicz, 1445 (Prositz)

PRV, SLIVNICA, STUDEN

Pruga— Pruz, 1356 (Prausitz)
Prv, Prvy— Perbe, 1501 (Perba)
Roslavic— Rozalwicz, 1334 (Rosslitz)
Rub— Rube, 1207 (Rauba)
Slivnica— Slynicz, 1334 (Schleinitz)
Streganovici— Stregnewicz, 1261 (Striegnitz)
Studen— Ztudene, 1243 (Steudten)
Svochov— Swochow, 1378 (Schwochau)
Tryskov— Trizcow, 1334 (Dreissig)

7. LUZICE DOLNI, LUZICE GORNI

R egarding *Luzica's* historic lands, a leading authority writes: **Once the Lusatian Serbs were to be found in the whole southern area of the German Democratic Republic between the Oder, the Elbe, and the Saale. Their villages even lay to the west of the Saale in north-eastern Bavaria and in northern Bohemia. They left behind a large number of settlements, cemeteries, and fortified centres.**

Our survey of *Luzica* is limited to areas within later and lesser century boundaries, namely lands bound by the Dahme, Schwarze Elster, Pulsnitz, Grosse Roder rivers in the west, the Spree and Neisse or Luzicka Neisse in the center, the Pleiske, Oder, Bober, and Queis rivers in the east. A 1301 document defines the lands and borders of *Luzica* in the following terms: ***Predicta enim terra seu marchia Lusacie incipit ab illa parte aque Damis et continet in se terram Sarowe et terminatur, ubi terra Sarowe terminatur. Item distinguiter, quia predicta terra incipit ab Elstra nigra et protenditur usque ad Oderam et ab Odera usque ad fluvium Slube et a fluvio Sluve usque ad fluvium Bobere et specialiter in se continet terram Sarowe, que extenditur usque ad terminos Polonie et usque ad terminos terre Budesinensis. Item continent in se curiam Prebuz et opidum Trebule, item castrum Golsin et opidum et castrum Lukowe, opidum Gubyn, opidum et castrum Lubrasz, castrum Schedlowe, opidum et castrum Schedlowe, opidum et castrum Sprewenberch, Pizna, opidum et castrum Sunnenwalde, opidum et castrum Dinsterwalde, opidum et castrum Semftenberch, curiam Dannenrode, opidum Kalow et novum castrum apud Kotebuz cum opido et castro Kotebuz, castrum Lubenowe, item castrum et opidum Vredeburch, castrum et opidum Schenkendorp, castrum et opidum Trebezt, curiam Zcinnitz, castrum Richenwalde, curiam Reinoldeswalde.***

SERBSKA VOTCHINA, SERBSKA REC

Until recently, the Slavic natives of *Luzica* called this area *Serbska Votchina* (*Serb Fatherland*) and *Serbski Kraj* (*Serb land*), where *Serbska Rec* (*Serbian*) was spoken *(L.A. Tyszkiewicz, Luzye; Lucyczanie, SsS 3, 1967. J. Herrmann, Die Lusici im Fruhen Mittelalter, LeT B/22, 1975).*

LUZANI, LUZICE DOLNI

The name *Luzica*, after the Serbs called *Luzani*, was originally applied only to what is today known as *Luzice Dolni* or *Lower Luzica*, an area centered along the lower reaches of the Spree River.[1] Above the town *Chotebuz* (Cottbus), the historic capital of *Luzice Dolni*, the Spree divides into a network of channels that form a marshy region known as the *Serbska Bloto* or Spreewald.

MILCANI, LUZICE GORNI

In earliest times, *Luzice Gorni* or *Upper Luzica*, the area centered along the upper reaches of the Spree, was known as *regio, terra, provincia, pago Milzani*, after the Serbs known as *Milcani* or *Milzani* *(S. Urbanczyk, Mlczanie; Milsko, SsS 3, 1967).*[2]

SERBSKA HOLA

In the center, where *Luzice Gorni* and *Luzice Dolni* meet, is the *Serbska Gola*

Hola or Serbian Heath, an area of sandy soil and coniferous forests.

LUNZISI

The *Descriptio Civitatem* records 30 *civitats* in **Luzica** or **Luzice Dolni** (M. Rudnicki, *Nazwy Slowian Polabskich i Luzyckich u Geograf Bawarskiego z IX wieku, Opuscula Casimiro Tymieniecki, 1959*): **Lunzisi, civitates XXX.**

SCLAVOS, QUI DICUNTUR LUSIKI

There are numerous references to the **Luzani** and their lands in medieval sources, including *Chronicon Cosmas* (**Nec superfluum esse iudicavimus ... consertum est inter Boemos et Luczanos; Et Luczanos, qui nunc a modernis ab urbe Sate vocitantur Satcense**).

IN LONSICIN
- *In Lonsicin, 932*
- *Luzizi, 948*
- *In terrae Lusici, 961*
- *Lusici, 963*
- *Sclavos, qui dicuntur Lusiki, 963*
- *Pagos Luzici, 965*
- *Liuzici nostris pridie, quam ad Oderam fluvium venirent Luzici, 1007*

IN PAGO LUSICI
- *In pago Lusici, 1010*
- *Inde ad Luzici pagum, 1010*
- *Inde ad pagum Lusici, 1015*
- *Regionem Lusizi, 1031*
- *In Lusatia, 1032*
- *Luzice, 968*
- *Luzic , 968*

LUSICA
- *Lusica, 971*
- *Lusice, 973*
- *Venerabilis senior Dobromir, rex Luzica, 987*
- *Tercia fuit Eminildis, edita a veneabili seniore Dobremiro, 992*
- *Lusizi, 995*
- *Regiones Luidizi, 1002*
- *In pago Lusici, 1004*

IN PAGO LUSICI
- *In pago Lusici, 1005*
- *Liuzici: Post haec Luzensi, 1005*
- *Et ut marchia ... In Lusyciz, 1117*
- *Marchione in Lusiz, 1181*
- *Marchiam vero eius Lusicensem, que nunc Orientalis dicitur, 1136*
- *Provincia, que Lusitze nuncupatur, 1137*
- *Terra Lusice, 1179*

REGIONEM LUSIZ

- *Sclavi, Litwitici et Pomerani regionem Lusiz trans Albiam*, 1180
- *Marchiam in Lusnich*, 1185
- *Provinciae Lusici*, 1188
- *In marchia Lusitz*, 1198
- *Lacum in marchia, que dicitur Luzist*, 1209
- *In Lusazia*, 1225
- *In terra Lusaciase*, 1252
- *Terras Lusaciae*, 1283

MILZANE

In one instance, the *Descriptio Civitatem* records 30 *civitats* in **Luzice Gorne** or **Milzane**: **Milzane civitates XXX.** If, as numerous scholars believe, the **Miloxi** are the **Milzi** (*Milzane, Milcani*), in a second instance, the *Descriptio Civitatem* records 67 in **Luzice Gorne**: **Miloxi, in qua civitates LXVII.**

SCLAVOS MILKIANOS

There are numerous references to the **Milcani** in medieval sources.

MILZANE

- *Milzane*, 850
- *Milzener*, 932
- *In Milczsane*, 968
- *Provincia Milzsane*, 971
- *Milzientos*, 987
- *In terram Milze et a fine Milze recte intra Oddere*, 992
- *Descursis tunc Milcini terminis huic ad Diedesisi pagum*, 997

MILCINI PAGO DIEDESA

- *Milcini pago Diedesa*, 1000
- *In Milzaniam*, 1000
- *Redditis sibi Ludizi et Miltizieni regionibus*, 1002
- *Ad Milzieni* expeditionem, 1003
- *Duco novo Milzienos*, 1004
- *Sclavos Milkianos*, 1004
- *Milzienos*, 1004
- *In pago Milzani*, 1007
- *Nostri autem per Milzienos fines laeti ad Albim remeabant*, 1010

IN MILZANIAM

- *In Milzaniam*, 1012
- *In pago Milsca*, 1071
- *Milcianorum*, 1086
- *In regione Milce*, 1091
- *Milcianorum*, 1125
- *Partibus Milesko*, 1131
- *In pago Milzana*, 1165

URBS, CIVITATS

The following are some of the *grads* and *podgrads, urbs, opids, municios, civitats,* and *burgwards* recorded in **Luzica**, a land known to be densely scattered with hill-forts of a circular ground-plan (*A. Meiche, Die Oberlausitzer Grenzkunde vom Jahre 1241 und die Burgwarde Ostrusna, Trebista und Godobi, MaG 84, 1908. W. Coblenz, Zu den slawischen Burgwallen der Oberlausitz, Kongres 1968, III, 1970*).

CASTRUM BARUTH

- Barut (NW Weissenberg)— *castrum Baruth et bona*, 1319; *castrum Baruth*, 1353.

- Besicow— *civitas Besicow*, 1272 (Beeskow).[3]

- Bezun— *urbs magna Businc*, 1012; *civitat Businc*, 1015 (Biesnitz).

- Budusin on the Spree (historic capital of Lower Luzica)— *Budusin civitatem cum omnibus appertinenciis comprehendes*, 1002; *Budusin urbem possedit*, 1004; *Budusin civitas*, 1007; *in quadam urbe Budusin dicta*, 1018; *castrum Budesin*, 1144; *pagus Budessin*, 1160; *terra Budshyn*, 1226 (Bautzen).

- Chotebuz on the Spree (historic capital of Upper Luzica)— *H. castellanus de Chotebuz*, 1156; Godebuz, 1199; *Et novum castrum apud Kotebuz cum opido et castro Kotebuz*, 1301 (Cottbus).

- Dabna on the Dabna— *Dahme usque ad Dame*, 1266 (Dahme, W Luckau); *provincia Dame*, 1166; *provincia Dame*, 1171.

- Dobrusa— *burgwardo Dobrus: De burquardo Dobrus: Ab antiquo campo trans Sprewam Daniborowobrod; abinde in antiqum semitam, qua iturm Weletin, et sic per eam usque in Sebnizam in locum, ubi mansit antiquitus heremita. Item ex alio latere a cumulo, qui est inter Kossciz et Nowozodliz, in aquam, que dicitur Zehohzere usque in Dimin, inde in maiorem stratem contra Niwenkyrchin usque in Ratolfis siffen et per decursum eius in Wazowenizam, abinde in Tyzowe et in montem Buckowagora, abinde ad summitatem montis, unde oritur rivus Welewiza et Zlatwina, abinde in Sebnizam et per ascensum eius usque ad locum heremite predicti. Ad Misnensem episcopatum pertinent, qui hiis terminis includuntur*, 1228. Doberschau, 1228

DOBRALUH DICITUR

- Dobry Lug— *Exercitum autem nostrum cum prosperitate ad locum, qui Dobraluh dicitur in pago Lusici*, 1005; *Lusizensis marchio Dobrelugensem*, 1124; *Fratres de Dobroloc ... vel locabunt in nemore, a quod Socola dambrova vulgariter nuncupatur*, 1269; *In Dobirlug*, 1297. Doberlug (*W. Lippert, Die Dobrilukschen Klosterdorfer Nussedil und Dobristoh, NiE 6, 1900*).

- Dolgavic— *burquardus Dolgawiz, Item de burquardo Dolgawitz: Ab eo loco, ubi influit Lubotna et Oztsniza, ad defluentem in Oztsnizam rivum Peztyow et ortum eius; abinde in semitam Betokaziza et in montem Jelenihora; abinde in ortum Camenize et per decursum eius usque ad distinctionem Zagost et Budissin; abinde in rivum, qui Sprewa dicitur et defluit per Gerhartsdorf, et decursum eius usque ad antiquam stratem con-*

tra Jawornik; ab ispa strata contra Budissin in Sprewam, que defluit per villam Zalom, et per decursum eius in rivum Jedle et quendam cumulum ex directo; inde in simitam, qua itur de Glussina in vallam et per eandem vallem in Lubotnam. Omnis fundus terminis hiis inclusus ad Misnensem episcopatum, 1241. Dolgowitz.

• Godivo— *castellum Godibi ... in pago Milzani*, 1007; *un burcwardo Godiwo, villa Drogobudowice*, 1071; *Pribizlaus sacerdos de Godowe*, 1216. *Item hii sunt limites, qui distinguunt Godowe et terram regis: a loco, ubi a semita de Syzen per limites Radel, Camenahora, Belipotoch et decursum Lozine in Sebnizam pervenitur, inde in ortum Lozine; abinde in ortum Lezsne sicce et per decursum eius, donec defluat in Wazowenizam; per decursum Weszonize ad rubum Erlinum; abinde super montem Scutkowe usque in Vischpach usque in Rederam, qui fluit per Saeliginstate et usque ad ortum eius; abinde in rivum, qui fluit inter Frankintal et Harte; exinde in mediuam paludem, que est inter Ramnowe et Gisilbrehtisdorf; exinde in Album Lapidem et usque in fontem propre Tutizk; abinde in veram Zrebernizam. Omnia infra hos limites contenta ad Misnensem pertinent ecclesiam*, 1216. Goda.

• Golsin— *Golsyn*, 1276; *Castrum Golsin*, 1301. Golssen.

• Gradista— *Gradis*, 1222 (Grodtiz, Weissenberg); *Czaslaw de Grodis*, 1331. Groditsch.

• Gubin— *oppidum Gubin*, 1235; *Opidum Gubyn*, 1305. Gubben.

• Izgorjelc— *Yzhorelik i partibus Milesko iuxta fluma Niza, quod antea et Drenow vocabatur*, 1131 (Gorlitz): *Domino ... judice tunc provinciali terrae Gorlicensis*, 1285; *Fideli nostro J. de Sunnenwalde, tunc judice provinciae Gorlicensis. Izgorjelc, civitas nostra Gorlicz*, 1322. Gorlitz.

URBS JARINA

• Jarin— *urbs Jarina in pago Lusici* (Gehren, SW Luckau); *in Jarina per Milzienos fines*, 1010; *Inde ad Luzici pagum, in cuius fronte urbs quaedam Jarina stat*, 1010. Gehren.

• Kalow— *civitas Calowe*, 1279; *opidum Kalow*, 1301. Calau.

• Kamenc— *civitas Kamenz*, 1248. Kamenz.

• Lagov— *burcwardo Lagowe in terra Budessin*, 1226. Loga.

• Lesan— *castrum in Lesan*, 1247; *castrum Lesne*, 1268. Lauban.

• Lubenov— *castrum Lubennowe*, 1301. Lubbenau.

• Lubin— *urbs Lubin*, 1150; *stadt Lubin*, 1288. Lubben.

CASTELLUM LIUBOGOLI

• Lubochol (Leibchel, N Lubben)— *duas nostri iuris civitates ... et Liubocholi ... in pago Lusici*, 1004; *duas nostris iuris civitates ... et Liubocholi*, 1004; *castellum Liubogoli*, 1024; *castellum Liubogoli*, 1145; *dua civitates ... et Lubicholi dictas*, 1171; *Burgward Liuodholi*, 1179. Liebchel.

• Lubov— *Lubaw oppidum*, 1221. Lobau.

• Lubraz— *civitas Luberas*, 1295; *opidum et castrum Lubraz*, 1301. Lieberose.

• Lubusa— *civitat Liubusua; Ex ea Milzenos suae subactos dicioni censum persolvere coegit. Urbem quoque Liubusuam de qua in posterum lacius disputaturus sum ...* 932 (Lebusa, N Schleiben); A Slav named 'Isich' is Burgkommandant of Lebusa in 1012.

• Lukow— *magister Lubeslaus de Lukkowe*, 1276; *opidum et castrum Lukowe*, 1301. Luckau.

• Luznica— *municio Lusenycz*, 1289. Laussnitz.

• Moybin— *castrum Oywins*, 1315 (Oybin, Zittau); *Ztenco de Moibin*, 1290; *castrum Oywins*, 1319; *castrum Moywyn*, 1346.

CIVITATEM NIEMPSI DICTAM

• Niempsi— *civitatem Niempsi dictam ... in ripa fluminis Niza nominati sitam atque illud burgwardium cum omnibus villulis ad illus pertinentis Pozdietin, Gotheiuuva, Zepi, Tamarini villula*, 1000; *Iterum castellm Niemszi, Pozdiatin, Bezdiez, Gotheiuua, Gozeuua*, 1024; *ad illud pertinentibus castellum Niemszi, Pozdiatin, Bezdiez, Gotheiuua, Gozuua*, 1145; *Civitatem Niemeze vocatam cum omni provincia ei attinente, que habet septem milia mansorum*, 1171; *Burgward Niemptz*, 1179; *de provinciis Nemiz*, 1225. Niemitzsch.

• Ostrog— *castellum Ostrusna ... in pago Milzani*, 1007; *oppidum Oztrosen*, 1241; *in novo Ostros*, 1326. Ostritz.

• Podgrad— *Podegros*, 1421; *Podogros*, 1442. Podrosche.

• Polznica— *castrum Polsenitz*, 1318; *opidum Polsnitz*, 1318; *castrum Polsnicz*, 1350, Pulsnitz.

• Prebuz— *curia Prebuz*, 1301. Priebus.

• Ronov— *castro Ronaw*, 1268. Rohnau.

• Sedelov— *Peregrinus, kastellan von Sidlou*, 1232; *Dirzislaus, kastellan von Schiedlo*, 1236; *Sydlo castrum*, 1243; *castrum Schedlowe*, 1301. Schiedlow.

URBS CIANI

• Sciciani (NW Cottbus)— *urbs Ciani*, 1015.

• Spreva, an old stronhold on an island in the Spree River, near the juncture of the Mala Spreva and Velka Spreva near Nove Mesto and south of Grodk— *Sprewitz*, 1568; *Spreetza*, 1845; Sprejcy, 1886. Spemberg.

• Sturkov— *civitas Sturkowe*, 1209. Storkow.

• Sulpiza (near Lubben)— *civitas Sulpize*, 968; *civitas Zulbiza, in Selpoli*, 995.

• Trebec— *castrum et opidum Trebetz*, 1301.

• Trebista— *castellum Trebista ... in pago Milzani*, 1007 (in Milce); *in burgwardo Trebiste*, 1071.

• Trebul— *opidum Trebule*, 1301. Triebel.

CIVITATEM TRIEBUS

• Trebus— *civitatem Triebus ... in pago Lusici*, 1004; *castellum Treibus*, 1024; *castellum Triebus*, 1145; *civitas Triebus*, 11150; *civitat Trebus*, 1171; *Burgward Treibus*, 1179. Trebbus.

• Zicani— *burgwardus Schizani in regione Milce*, 1001; *burgwardo Schilani in regione Milce*, 1091; *burguardus Sizen*, 1241; *Heynko de Ziczan*, 1371; *Petir Syczhen*, 1381. *Itemde burquardo Sizen: Per simitam de Sizen in Godowizam; inde in cumulum Cossow; ab illo in cumulum prope viam, qua itur de Budissin Zocowe; ab eadem via donec prope viam Gunthersdorf; inde in rivum Guzk et in maiorem rivulum de Guzk in Radel; de Radel in Camenahora; abinde in summitatem montis inter Poren et Lipowahora; abinde in Belipotoch et sic usque in Wazownizam; abinde in Isenberch; abinde ubi Lawan et Poliza confluuntm, per decursum Polize, usque dum confluat cum Lozna; a Lozna in Sebnizam et usque ad locum, ubi limites Tyzowe, Bucowahora, Welewiza in Sebnizam protenduntur.* Gross Seitschen.

• Zinic— Cinnicz, 1255; *curia Zcinnitz*, 1301. Zinnitz.

• Zitava, an important Serb stronghold in the Lusatian Mountains, near the modern Czechoslovak-Polish borders— *Et Luczanos, qui nunc a modernis ab urbe Sate vocitantur Satcense; civitatis Sittaw*, 1283; *Chastoslaus ... de Situviu*, 1283; Sittaw, 1250; Zyttavla, 1350. Zittau.

CASLAV

Of course, one cannot help but note the undiluted Slavic personal names found above and below (e.g. *Caslav, Castislav, Drzislav, Luboslav, Pribislav, Tyzko Vigrad, Stanko).*

TRNOV, TORNOW

Archaeological excavations confirm an important fact: not all *Luzica's* urbs and *civitats* are a matter of record. Recent (*in the years 1961 to 1962 and in 1965 to 1967*) and thorough excavations (**not only of the hill-fort itself but of the settlements in its surroundings so that a picture was built of of the development of the whole settled area**), for example, have uncovered the important hill-fort of *Tornow* in the Calau district of **Lower Luzica** (*J. Herrmann, Die Germanischen Und Slawischen Siedlungen und das Mittelalterliche Dorf von Tornow, Kr. Calau, 1973*). Radioactive C 14 carbon analysis dates the older castle at *Tornow* to the 7th and 8th centuries, the later castle to the end of the 9th century. Excavations reveal that the hill-fort's central area was taken up by the residence of the lord of the castle and his retinue, who occupied dwellings set into the fortifications. The remaining area was taken up mainly by storage facilities for food, mainly grain, levied from the population around the castle. Also cattle, honey, linen, furs, textiles, and other products made up by village craftsmen, such as pottery, iron tools and weapons, as well as articles made by coopers and carpenters. Similar excavations have also revealed an early and impressive hill-fort at *Radus* (Radisch, 1294; Radisch, 1312; Radusch, 1761), modern Raddusch, also in the Calau district of *Lower Luzica* (*M. Ullrich. Sondage am slawischen Burgwall "Schanze" bei Raddusch, Kr. Calau, AuF 31, 1986*).

Given its size, it is not surprising that some of **Luzica's** sub-nations or sub-provinces or **zupas** are recorded as distinct territorial-political entities: 1) **Besunzan**, 2) **Golesin**, 3) **Lupiglav**, 4) **Lubus**, 5) **Nisa**, 6) **Selpol**, 7) **Slube**, 8) **Trebovan**, 9) **Zagozd**, 10) **Zar**.

1. BEZUNI, BEZUNZANI

The *Descriptio Civitatem* records two *civitats* in **provincia Besunzane**: **Besunzane, civitates II.** One *civitat* is its capital city, **Bezun: urbs magna Businc**, 1012; **civitat Businc**, 1015; **major villa dicta Bysint**, 1315; Grossen Besenicz, 1448; Wulka Biesniza, 1719; Gross-Biesnitz. A second *civitat* is perhaps **Bezun minor** or Klein Biesnitz, kleyne Besenitcz in 1471 *(R. Jecht, Erste Erwahnung der Oberlausitz. Der Gau Besunzane und die urbs Busine sind gleich dem Orte Biesnitz a.d. Landeskrone, MaG 97, 1928. J. Nalepa, Biezuncznie. Nazwa i polozenie, PaM 4. 1964; Biezunczanie, SsS 1, 1961).*

2. GOLENSINI, GOLENSIZI

The *Descriptio Civitatem* records five *civitats* in **provincia Golensizi**, centered on and along the river Goles/Golesin *(J. Tyszkiewicz, Z badan nad wczesnosredniowiecznym osadnictwem gornego dorzecza Odry. Pierwotne brzmienie i umiejscowienie Lupigaa i Golensizi tzw. Geografa Bawarskiego, Studia z dziejow osadnictwa 1, 1963):* **Golensizi, civitates V.**

3. LUBIGLAV, LUPIGLAA

Thirty *civitats* are recorded in **provincia Lubiglav** or **Lupiglaa**, centered at Lubsko on the river Lube: **Lupiglaa, civitates.**

4. LUBUS, LUBUSANI

There is a difference of informed opinion regarding the affiliation of **terra Lubus** or **Lubusani**, centered at **grad Lubus** on the Oder. Some scholars, A. Muka among others, consider it a **Luzica zupa**, others a **regio Lyutic zupa** *(J. Knebel, K problemej staroserbskeho "mesto" Liubusa, LeT B/2/1, 1956).*

5. NISA

Cerny locates **zupa Nisa** east of **zupa Golesin**, between the rivers Spree and Neisse, centered in an area between the towns of Lubin and Luboraz.

6. SELPOLI

Scholars locate the oft-cited **Selpoli** on the Oder and Spree rivers below Lebus. In this area a chain of some 20 strongholds have been discovered. There are numerous references to the **Selpoli** in the latter half of the 10th century *(M. Polandt, Selpoli, NiE 16, 1924. G. Labuda, Studia z dziejow Slowianszczny zachodnici. Pagus Selpuli, SlO 19, 1948; Selpuli, SsS 5, 1975. M. Rudnicki, Slupia, Slupa, OnO 1, 1955. P. Grunitz, Siedlungsweise und- verhaltnisse beim sorbischen Stamm der Selpoli, Gubener HmK 1976-78).*

CIVITAS SULPIZE
- **Selpoli**, *948*
- **Selpoli**, *961*
- **In terrae Lusici, Selpoli et Chozimi**, *961*

- *Marchio Lusici et Selpoli,* 963
- *In altera parte Luzice et Selpoli, et sic usque ad civitate Sulpize illam videlicet infra eundem terminum et inde in aquam, que dicitur Odera,* 968

(S. Strzelczyk, Sulpize, SsS 5, 1975).

- *Luzice, Selpoli ... civitas Sulpize ... Milczsane,* 968
- *Luzice, Selpoli, civitas Sulpize,* 968
- *Civitas Sulpize,* 968

PAGO SELPULI
- *Pago Selpuli,* 990
- *Ad pagum Selpuli dictum venerunt ac iuxta unam paludem,* 990
- *Lusizi, Selboli, civitas Zulbiza,* 993
- *In altera parte Lusizi et Selboli, et sic usque ad civitatem Zulpiza,* 995
- *Rochilinze, Lusizi, Selpoli ... civitas Zulbiza,* 995
- *Selboli,* 996
- *Luzici, Zara et Selpoli ... civitas Budusin,* 1007
- *Selpuli,* 1008

7. SLUBE, SLUBANE

Zupa Slube occupied an area on the river Slube, a tributary to the Oder, centered near the town of Slube: *Ab Odera usque ad fluvium Slube et a fluvio Slube usque ad fluvium Bobere,* 1301.

8. TREBOVANI

Cerny locates *zupa Trebovan* south of *provincia Zarovan*, centered at *Trebel*.

9. ZAGOZD

Cerny and others locate the *Milcani* (*Milcansko*) *zupa Zagozd* on the *Luzicka Nisa*, south of Zittau (the ancient Serb stronghold, *civitatis Sittaw*), in northern Bohemia, along the Loucna River to Liberec to *Serbska Kamenica* in northern Bohemia (*E. Schwarz, Wendische Ortsnamen im Lande Zittau, Nieder Lausitzer Magazin, 103. 1927. J. Heinrich, Die Ortsnamen der Kreise Gorlitz und Zittau, 1965. A. Wedzki, Zagost, SsS 7, 1982*). Regarding the medieval territory of *zupa Zagozd*, it is important to note that the *Luzicke Gory* or *Luzica Mountains* extend into bordering areas of Poland and Bohemia, including its highest peaks, namely *Mts. Jested* and *Kozakov* (*R. Wenisch, Die Grentzen zwischen Bohmen und Oberlausitz, 1929. A. Sedlacek, O ustaleni hranice mezi cechami a Luzici, CmM 66, 1982*).

- *Provincia Zagost,* 1144
- *Mons in Zagozd qui Syden* (*Zid, Zidin*) *vocatur,* 1188
- *Sagost,* 1228
- *Zagost,* 1228

10. ZAR, ZAROVANI

Cerny locates *provincia Zarov* in the area around Zarov between the Neisse and Bober rivers, centered near German Sorau, Polish Zary (*E. Rzetelska-Feleszko, Zara, Zary, SsS 7, 1982*).

- *Luzici, Zara et Selpoli*, 1007
- *Zara*, 1008
- *In marcia Lusicensi vel in Zarowe*, 1249
- *Sorawia*, 1273
- *In se continet terram Sarowe, que extenditur usque ad terminos Polonie et usque ad terre Budesinensis*, 1031
- *Soravie. Tizko de Ympnitz, Apezko de Lucko, Tyzko Schoneeysche, vasalli nostri; et Conradus Melod magister civium Seyfridus de Benym, Tyzko Wygrad et Renytz dictus Slycher cives Soraviae et alii quam plurimi fide digni*, 1329
- *In castro nostro Soraw*, 1329
- *Terra Sorau*, 1350

ENDNOTES

[1] R. Lehmann, Urkundinventar zur Geschichte der Niederlausitz bis 1400, 1968; Quellen Zur Geschichte der Niederlausitz, I-III, 1972-79; Historisches Ortsleksikon fur die Niederlausitz, 2, 1979. E. Eichler, Die Ortsnamen der Niederlausitz, 1975. G.E. Schrage, Slaven und Deutsche in der Niederlaustiz, 1990. S. Korner, Ortsnamenbuch der Niederlausitz, 1993. H. Schuster-Sewc, Ortsnamen der Niederlausitz und sorbische Sprachgeschichte, ZfS 39, 1994.

[2] K. Blaschke, Die Entwidklung des sorbischen Siedelgebietes in der Oberlausitz, Siedlung und Verfassung, 1960. J. Meschang, Die Ortsnamen der Oberlausitz, 1973. E. Eichler, Ortsnamenbuch der Oberlausitz: Studien zur Toponymie der Kreise Bautzen, Bischofswerda, Gorlitz, Hoyerswerda, Kamnez, Lobau, Niesky, Senftenburg, Weisswasser und Zittau, 1975-78. J. Huth, Die Burgwarde der Oberlausitz, Let B/28, 1981.

[3] K. Muller, Zur Schichtenspezifik der slawischen Namen im Lande um Beeskow-Storkow, Beitrage zur Namenforschung 29/30, 1994-95.

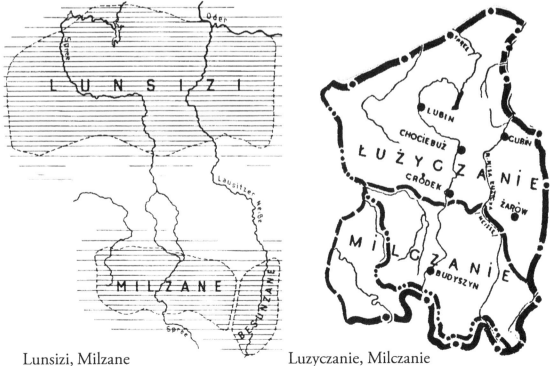

Lunsizi, Milzane   Luzyczanie, Milczanie

PART XIX

1. SERBS, NOT SORBS; SERBIA, NOT SORBIA

SERB VOSTANU (FOREVER SERB)

Serb chu ja bys a vostas rady,
Chu Serbstvo vieczne lubo miec;
Niech przindzeja tez vszelkie pady
Mi zivjenske, Serb chu ja rady,
Za Serbstvo chu ja vojovas,
Ma naszich votcov czas chu zady!
Ze zrudnym vokom zahladovac
Njech njebjesa so posmievkuja
Nad tobu, droga Luzica
A tebi czasy vubudzuja
Hdzez Serbov slava plody ma.[1]

It was once common for German scholars to call the **German Serbs** by their true and native name, **Serbs**, a name that vibrated with vital evidence relating to the origin and history of the Serbs (e.g. **Der Serbe in der Lausitz**). Later, in order to distinguish the **German Serbs** from the **Balkan Serbs**, German writers began using a German word for Serbs, **Sorben** (e.g. **Die Sorben und die Lausitz**). In order to avoid the national and historical distortions that flow from the exclusive use of **Sorben**, some German writers will use both terms, the native **Serb** and the German **Sorben** (e.g. **Die Wenden, Serben oder Sorben**). However, it soon became standard for non-German writers to confuse fiction with fact, to call the *German Serbs Sorbs* and only **Sorbs**, period, thereby obscuring critical elements of the historical record.

SERBS, SERBIA, SERBSKA REC

From the earliest times to the present the **Serbs** of *Germania* have called themselves **Serbs** and only **Serbs**. From the earliest times to the present the **Serbs** of *Germania* have called their land **Serbia**. From the earliest times to the present the **Serbs** of *Germania* have called their language **Serb** or **Serbska Rec**.

EVANGELISKICH SERBOV

The **Serb** name is found in the earliest religious works.

- *Spevarske Knihi za Evangeliskich* **Serbov**, *mid-15th century*
- *Tehn Psalter* **Serbskey** *Rhetzy, mid-16th century*
- **Serbske** *Katolse Kerluse, late 17th century*

SCHOLARSHIP

The Serb name is also found in early 'scientific' works, even one dealing with mathematics: *De Mathesi* **Serborum**, 1750.

SERBSKA NOVINA

The **Serb** name is featured in the first and later newspapers:

- **Serbski** Povedar a Kurier, Jene Mjesaczne Pismo, Schitkim Serbam k Trjebnoszi, 1809
- **Serbow** Kurier a Povedar, Mjesacne Pismo, K … **Serbovstva,** 1810
- **Serbov** Jedinici Novinynscer, 1811
- **Serbska** Jutrnicka, 1842
- **Serbski** Novinikar, 1840s
- **Serbska** Novina, 1846
- **Serbski** Dzenik, 1919

MACICA SERBSKA

Following the example of Serbia's *Matica Srpska* (1826), the first Slav *Matica*, *German Serbs* founded a society for the promotion of literature, culture, and science: *Macica Serbska* in 1845.

WILLIAM RICHARD MORFILL

The society had a number of distinguished foreign members, including Professor William Richard Morfill, who dominated Slavonic studies at Oxford in the late 19th century.[2] **Morfill's publications range over virtually all the Slavonic literatures**, writes J. D. Naughton, **and include several substantial items on Czech topics, most notably his 'Grammar of the Bohemian or Cech language' and the section on 'The Early Literature of Bohemia' in his Slavonic Literature** *(J.D. Naughton, Morfill and the Czechs, OsP 17, 1984).*

Morfill was well-informed on the Serbs and impressed with their considerable literary achievements under the most adverse circumstances. So much so that his insightful and eloquent remarks on the subject bear repeating. In an 1881 review of a history of Slavonic literatures, Morfill writes: **This complete and well-written work concludes with an account of the scanty literature of the Lusatian Wends, who form a small island, as it were, in a Teutonic ocean. It is indeed astonishing and may console any depressed nationality, when we reflect what this courageous little people has done, cut in two as they are, and divided between Saxony and Prussia. In spite of vexatious laws and the affected contempt of their German masters, they still publish a variety of useful books and their Casopis or journal appears twice a year. The dictionary of this language, published by Dr. Pfuh in 1886, is of considerable value, not merely to the Slavonic scholar, but to the student of comparative philology generally** *(G. Stone, Morfill and the Sorbs, OsP 4, 1971).*

Morfill, Stone writes, was not only aware of the Serb's political plight, but he was also highly sympathetic to their determination to preserve language and culture in the face of official oppression. **The little Slavonic island … in a German sea … has attracted scarce any attention in the rest of Europe. The German affects to treat the Wend of Lusatia with somewhat of the contempt assumed by the Englishman for the Celt, and hopes for his speedy amalgamation with the Teutonic race.** At the present time, Morfill writes: **We find almost the same struggles going on between the English and the Welsh. Everything which ridicule and other agencies can bring about has been done: the language has been driven from the schools, and German pastors, where possible, have been forced upon their congregations. It is just the** same talk which we constantly hear from the English Philistines, whose object is to stamp out the Welsh language. In spite of all these efforts at Germanisation, the Sorbs still maintain their nationality, though Herr Andree, in his 'Wendische Wanderstudien' (Stuttgart. 1874), would have us think otherwise. In this case, however, the wish is probably father to the thought *(W.R. Morfill, Slavonic Literature, 1899).*

CASOPIS MACICY SERBSKEJE

Shortly thereafter, again following the Serbian example *(Casopis Matica Srpska)*, **Macica Serbska** published a journal: **Casopis Macicy Serbskeje.** In 1866 **Macica Serbska** approved a plan for the construction of the **Serbski Dom** or Serbian House to serve as the society's headquarters.

SERBSKI STUDENT

The **Serb** name is featured in most student organizations.

- **Serbske** Predarske Tovarstvo, 1716
- Tovaristvo **Serbskich** Studujucich, 1846
- **Serbski** Student, 1919

JOURNALS

The **Serb** name is prominently featured in almost all social, literary, and cultural journals.

LUZISKICH SERBOV

- Luziskich **Serbov**, 1841
- **Serbovka**, 1846
- **Serbske** Noviny, 1854
- Lipa Serbska, sub-titled Casopis Mlodych **Serbov**, 1876
- **Serbski** Hospodar, 1881
- Kolo **Serbskich** Spisovacelov, 1900
- **Srbska** Ludova Knijhovna, 1901
- **Serbska** Dzivadlovna Zberka, 1921

ZVJAZK SERBSKICH SPEVNSKICH TOVARSTVOV

- Zvjazk **Serbskich** Spevnskich Tovarstvov, 1923
- Kolo **Serbskich** Spisovacelov, 1925
- Skovronck za **Serbskich** Honov, 1926
- Kolo **Serbskich** Tvorjacych Vumelcov, 1948
- Institut za **Serbski** Ludospyt, 1951
- Kolo **Serbskich** Tvorjacych, 1956
- Dom za **Serbske** Ludove Vumelstvo, 1956
- Kruza Mlodych **Serbskich** Avtorov, 1957
- Za **Serbov** Myzki, 1959

SOCIAL, POLITICAL ORGANIZATIONS

The **Serb** name is stressed in almost all 19th and 20th century social and political organizations.

- **Serbska** Narodny Vuberk, 1918
- **Serbske** Hospodarsko Tovarstvo, 1919
- **Serbska** Ludova Strona, 1924
- **Serbska** Ludova Rada, 1924
- **Serbo**-Luzyckiego Komitetu Narodna, 1942
- Luzisko-**Serbska** Narodna Rada, 1945
- Nemsko-**Serbske** Ludowve Dzivadlo, 1963

LITERATURE AND FINE ARTS

The *Serb* name is featured in many important literary works, musical compositions, and songs, including the 10th century epic, **Serbsky Dobyca**.

• Serbske Dobyca

Serbjo so do Njemcow hotowachu,
Slowcka pak Njemski nemozachu.
Swoje sej koniki sedowachu,
Swoje sej wotrobi psipinachu.
Swoje sej meciki psipasachu,
Do runoh pola so zjezdzowachu.
Prjeni kroc na woynu ce nichu,
Wul'ke tam dobycje scinichu
Dyz bje to z'onil tam kral a fjersta
Dal je jich wsitkich won psed so psinc,
Dal je jim wsitkim won nowu drasta,
Dal je jich wsitkich won do wojakow.
Druhi kroc na wojnu ce'nichu,
Wulke tam dobycje scinichu.
Dyz bje to z'onil tam kral a fjersta,
Dal je jich wsitkich won psed so psine.
Dal je jich wsitkich won zwobl'ekac,
Do lutoh cerw 'enoh corlacha.
Tseci kroc na wojnu cenichu,
Wulke tam dobycje scinichu.
Dyz bje to z'onil tam kral a fjersta
Dal je jich wsitkich won psed so psine,
Dal je won kojzdemu ryzy konja.
Hisce ton swjetly mec zejrawanju.

In the 19th and 20th centuries the Serb name is often found in the titles of poems and is often the central theme of poems by prominent Serb poets.

• Bozemje Serbam

Serby, kotrez kolebale mje sce,
Zdobnych pocciwoscow blysc was debi!
Pychu swery, sprawnosce a cesce
Na wasich sym honach scipal sebi! —
Boz'mje. Serby! Boz'mje, lozko zboza!

Sylzy zacemnic mi woci hroza.

- **Bitva V Serbskej Jorcmje**

- **Hlosy Ze Serbov Do Serbov**

- **Ja Sym Serb**

- **Kajke Rostliny Znaja Serbjov**

- **Kak Som Serbski Nawuknul**
  Ja som nemski narozony,
  Cuzeg kraja syn ja som,
  Som pak k serbskem psiwucony,
  Serbske slowo lubujom.
  Ja mam serbsku wutsobu,
  Serby moje bratsi su.

- **Lecce Zynki Do Serbow!**
  Lecce, zynki, do serbskeho kraja!
  Jako mjetele so w kwetkach honja,
  Jako do lipow so pcoly saja,
  Kaz so rosy krjepje rano ronja:
  Plencce mojim Serbam so do wusi
  Budzce horilwosc we kozdej dusi!

- **Na Drogu Do Serbow**
  Zi, moj postrow, do tych chromow,
  do tych lubych serbskich domow,
  wuzywaj tu dobru gozbu,
  witaj cytarjowu swojzbu,
  podaj wsyknym moju ruku,
  zyc jim wjasele a gluku!

- **Na Serbsku Luzicu**
  Rjana Luzica,
  sprawna precelna,
  mojich serbskich wotcowkraj,
  mojich zboznych sonow raj,
  swjate su mi twoje hona!

- **Nowa Serbska**
  Leci sokol z poldnja dele
  prez tej serbskej Luzicy,
  naleci sej Serbow wjele,
  wola mocnje z Prasicy:
  "Stan a wojuj, mloda Serbska,
  mesta njedaj cuzbnikam!
  Stan a wojuj, mloda Serbska,
  Narodnosc zdzerz krajnikam!"
  Hdzez su Serbja z knjezom byli,
  dyrbja Serbja kralowac.

Hdzez su Serbja knjejstwo meli,
dyrbi Nemc so zdalowac.
Stan a wojuj, mloda Serbska
Mesta njedaj cuzbnikam!
Stan a wojuj, mloda Serbska,
narodnosc zdzerz krajnikam!

• O Serbska Zemja

• Pojz Sobu Do Serbow?

Pojz sobu do Serbow,
tam se me zda,
tam jo tak rednje, tam se me zednje
njewostuza!
Pojz sobu do Serbow,
tam jo moj dom,
tam jo tak ksasnje,
lubje a jasnje:
A rad tam som!

• Pozytnosc Serbstwo Stama

Byl serbski mlozene, co jo z nim se stalo?
Jo wbogi narod spuscil pjenjez dla!
A weto to jom psecej brachowalo…
Dokulaz njej wo wjetse dary prosyl,
jo nimjernje dla kroskow starosc nosyl…
a chuduski se lagnul do rowa.

• Prjedy Serb

Nihdy! Twjerdy Serb nop nosy z cescu;
—Ani sudnik z mocu, ani z lescu
Pop jon njerozmechi—runu siju
Nosi, njech ju majkaju, njech biju.

• Rov V Serbskej Holi

• Serbam

O lubuj, Serbo, serbski kraj,
Tu lubosc cylu jemu daj!
W srjedz duse swec so jako hwezda
Hrej k woporam a k skutkam krej,
Ce jimaj z kuzlom, z kajkimz sej
Holb kurci holbicu do hnezda!
Kaz twjerde serbske hory su,
Kaz wesce zita do zni ktu,
Tak k Serbam dzerz we krutej swerje!
Ce cesila je serbska mac,
Tuz k jeje mas so krewi znac
A zanc mec rec a wotcow cerje!

- **Serbam**

  Najkruciso so netk mi spinaj, truna zlota!
  Akordy z njej najmocnise wab, porsto mlody!
  Spew spewac chcu, kiz mojim Serbam do swobo
  Ze sumom dobycerskim wulamal by wrota.

- **Serbow Kral**

- **Serbow Zni**

- **Serbska Mac**

  Hdyz tajke njewjedra su w Serbach prale,
  Su zony w lubosci a swerje stale
  A serbski su wam starok dodzerzale.
  A net, hdyz spurane najhorse djasy
  Su, net, hdyz w lepsich kolijach du casy,
  Net w Serbach prestac mele serbske kwasy?

- **Serbska Rec**

  Hdyz maly nas je ludzik, rec je nasa
  Cim wulkotnisa; pjasc hdzy Serbow slava,
  Rec brinci z mjecom a kaz wichor hraba;
  Lud nizki njech, rec za tronom so prasa

- **Serbska Svajzba V Blotach**

- **Serbska Wjeska**

- **Serbska Zemja**

  Wusoke su serbske te gory,
  kwiesca ta nizyna,
  Smejuce gumna a dwory,
  gola jo zelena,
  Sprjewja se zwali a gluskoco
  wolsa psi brjoze tak borkoco:
  Redna sy zemja, ty luzyska,
  ksasna a jasna, ty serbojska!

- **Serbske Basnje**

- **Serbske Jatzy**

- **Serbske Pravo**

- **Serbske Zyniki**

- **Serbskeg Luda Skjarzba**

  Daj tez tym to du wutsoby
  Kenz ak Serby k Nemcam du:
  Az smu psez nich Nemcow sklony,
  Gaz se k nam njwrosiju.

- **Serbske Podtykowanje**

  Rec kozdy, jako jemu rosce z pyskja!

Serb serbski njech a neme njech nemski reci!
Skorc hwizda, skowronck spewa, sorka skreci…
A prez hono a holu krasnje wyska. —

• Serbske Preswedcenje

Ze preswedcenja Serbej zelo rosce,
Kiz kryte we wutrobje jemu kceje;
Kiz w lece dawa chlodk a w zymje hreje
A towars pri kwasu je z nim a w posce.

Serb narodzil so sy, Serb swernje ziwy
Tuz budz, a serbsce wumrec so ci slusa
A tak, zo serbska w dzecoch tez je dusa.

• Serbskej Recy

Rec serbska jo tak redna, zuk meki ma,
az kuzde jeje slowcko nam dusu wogrewa.
Kaz knezna wupysnjona, tak wona ksasna jo,
a drosego nic nad nju mysli serbska njeznajo.
Ga kline me psecej mocnjej, ty droga serbska rec,
ty njedejs zachysona bys neto zednje wec:
Ab moglo Serbstwo naso how tras a zawostas,
kaz kralowna dejs gjarda se serbskim dusam stas!

• Serbskej Zemi

Zemja ksasna serbojska,
tebje dusa lubo ma!
Gaz na tebje spomnjeju.
k tuznosci wse mysli du.
Modre twoje gory su,
zwernje tebje scitaju,
Lubin knezy nad nimi,
Serbow gluka we njom spi.

• Serbskemu Ludoju

Moj serbski narod, lud moj lubodrogi,
jan tebje z luboscu cu w dusy gres,
jan twojom mjenju dawas w pesnjach znes,
az zmas jo budu wsulme sweta rogi!

• Serbski Kraj

Co jo toge serbskeg luda kraj?
Jo Bajerska, jo Swajc? —Godaj!
Jo Spaniska, jo Grichiska?
Ab jo daloka Aziska?
Ach ne, tam Serbow njepytaj,
tam njejo serbskeg luda kraj.
Ten serbski kraj drje wjetsy jo,
Gaz jaden wsykno rachnujo,
Kenz Slowjanstwo net wopsima

A coz tud k njomu psislusa.
Nam Serbam pak ta Luzyca
Jo ksasny kraj tog Serbojstwa.

• Serbski Kvas

• Serbski Rekviem

• Serbski Wucer

Serb wuknje rad a lubsoc tuz ma k suli,
A do njej swoju krej, swoj poklad preni
Rad dawa. Jako mac a dusna knjeni
Pak, sula, cin tez w Serbach wsudzezkuli!

• Serbskim Hospodarjam

Hospodarjo, wam do rukow data
Dzelo wazne je! wy dzelac mace
Serbsku rolu — podlozk za wobstace
Serbowstwa – o powolanje swjate,
Wulkotne! Tuz mejce tole dzelo
Zanc a cince, zo by rostlo, kcelo!

• Serbstwo Njezajzo

Winik groni: Serbstwo mrejo,
dlujko wecej njetrajo
smjertny zwonk juz jomu znejo,
sledny gerc jom zejgrajo.—
Sami na psichod pak werimy,
sami se na se pak spuscimy:
My zajzis njebzomy, njocomy, njebuzomy,
se zywis buzomy a corny a buzomy;
my Serby wostanjomu,
do nimjernosci!
Serbska mysi jo hysci zywa,
serbska drastwa chwalona,
serbska rec nam hysci kiwa,
serbska radosc zakwita.
Luzyca redna wuchwalona
Serbam wot Boga psizelona,
My zajzis njebzomy, njocomy, njebuzony,
Se zywis buzomy a corny a buzomy;
my Serby wostanjomy
do nimjernocsi!

• Skjarzba Na Zachadanje Serbskego Spewanja

Serbstwo! Ty sy tak bogate,
A ty samo to njewes!
Cuzym su te stucki znate,
Kenz ty samo njocos mes!
W cuzych serbske proznicki,

Serbski glos se lubi wsuzi,
Jano doma wam njezni.

- **Sesc Srbskisch Spevov**

- **Srbskim Holocam**

- **Styskanje Serbskego Zowca W Cuzem Mesce**
  Nent som tud stworty tyzen juz
  po scenach, zurjach zo moj pus.
  Njeslysym rec how serbojsku,
  njewizim rolu zelenu
  We malej kolni nanowej
  by ksela bys nent nejrazej.

- **Sym Serbov Serbske Holico**

- **Vsem Serbam K Novem Letu**

- **Wuchowajce Zemju Serbsku!**
  Hdyz wjecorna, hdyz jurtrna sweci hwezka,
  Serb na starosci mej, sto Serbam tyje,
  Sto rad a rolu jim najlejpje kryje,
  Kak skodam do Serbskow so haci sczezka!
  Nic horsc nam zhubic njesme so, nie kroma!
  O dzerzce ze wsej mocu na to tola,
  Zo Serb by wostal knjez sam w Serbach doma!

- **Za Serbskeje Zemje**

- **Zderz Serbski Lud!**
  Slys, Knjeze, hdyz swoj pacer praju:
  Zdzerz serbski lud!
  We worcrnym mojim lubym kraju
  Zdzerz serbski lud!
  Kiz modre hory nam a hona nam zelene
  A prackow spewy skitas w haju,
  Zdzerz serbski lud!

- **Zo Hysci Serby Bydle?**
  Zo hysci Serby bydle
  we swese wjelikem?
  We Blotach, tam se znaju,
  we rednem serskem kraju
  zelnmem, lubosnem.
  Zo hysci Serby bydle
  we swese sjelikem?
  We Luzycoma: Dolnej
  a Gornej, wobej polnej
  stej z ludom serbojskim.

455

- **Zwernosc K Serbojstwu**

  A stare serbske cesne nalogi
  se zachowajso pod serbskeju stsechu!
  Coz nega cescil jo nan njabogi,
  bys zednje njedej jogo zesam k smechu.
  Z tej mocu Serbstwo derbi dobywas,
  z njej kone se scyni wsomu podlocenju,
  z tej wolu buzo Serbstwo nimjer tras
  a z njeju cesc dej wurosc serbskem mjenju!

DICTIONARIES

The *Serb* name is found in all phrase books and dictionaries.

- *Vocabularium Latino-**Serbicum***, 1721
- Maly **Serb,** 1841
- Nemsko-**Serbsko** Slovnik, 1843
- Mala **Serbska** Recnica, 1850
- **Serbski** Vsovedny Slovnik Horjoluziskeje Rece, 1910

SERBSKA REC

Of course, the name *Serb* is found in all serious studies of Serb history, culture and language:

- Prehlad Pismovstva Katholskih **Serbov**, 1867
- Historija **Serbskeho** Naroda, 1884
- **Staroserbske** Slova v Lacanskej Liscinje z Leta 1241, 1894
- **Serbska** Bibliografija, 1952
- **Serbske** Pesen, 1953
- Stravizny **Serbskeho** Pismonovstva, 1954
- Casova Dokumantacija k Najnovsim **Srbskim** Staviznam, 1965
- Listovy Studij za Vucerjov **Serbscina**, 1956
- Stravizny Horjeje a Delnjeje **Serbsciny**, 1956
- Nasa **Serbska** Rec, 1962
- **Serbske** Vumelstvo Vcera d Dzensa, 1962
- Gramatika **Hornjoserbskeje Rece**, 1968

SER, SERSKI, SZAR, SZARSKI

In spite of the fact that in *Luzica* alone there are several distinct Serb dialects, some scholars say separate languages, through the centuries there are infrequent and minor variations of the Serb name.[3] Several are found in 18th century religious works. *Ser* or *Serskeje* instead of *Serb* or *Serbskeje* (*Serskeje* Reczje Samozenja a Kvalba v Reczerskim Kyrilischu, 1757; To Boze Pismo Starego Testamenta, Kotarez Do Teje *Serskeje* Rezi, 1796). Also in a 1782 poem by Michal Hilbjenc (Vopomnjene Vubernych *Serskich* Vucerjov). In a 1769 Serb hymnbook one finds *Szarski* instead of *Serbski* (Lubnovski *Szarski* Sambuch). In the 19th century one finds the *Ser* variation in the names of three newspapers (*Serska* Novina, 1826; Tydzenska Novina, Aby *Serske* Poveszje Sa Hornych Luzicanov, 1842; Bramborski *Serski* Casnik, 1848).

That *Ser* and *Serska* are informal ***Lower Luzica*** variations on the ***Serb*** name is indicated by the fact that ***Serska*** Novina was founded by members of the ***Serbske*** Predarske Tovarstvo, who, after the admission of German students from *Lusatia*, organized a separate Serbian section, ***Sorabija*** or ***Sorabicum***, an ancient name for the once great Serb lands cited in medieval Latin texts.[4] Moreover, the founders and other contributors to ***Serska*** Novina always use ***Serb*** or ***Serbska*** in their writing. The same is true for the Tydzenska Novina and the Bramborski ***Serski*** Casnik, which, was later revived and renamed Bramborski ***Serbski*** Casnik.

ENDNOTES

[1] Jan Smoler (1816-1884), leader of the mid-19th century Serb cultural and national renaissance.

[2] J.S.G. Simmons, Slavonic Studies at Oxford, 1844-1899, OsP XIII, 1980.

[3] Some scholars find four basic Serb dialects in Lusatia while others insist that Upper and Lower Serbian form two separate and independent languages

[4] The name *Sorabija* is not without romantic precedent. In 1766 the composer Jurij Rak composed an ode in *gallant style* to mark the 50th anniversary of *Sorabia*, a Serbian student society in Leipzig.

The Budisin/Bautzen Burgher's Oath (1532)

**Ja pschisaham Bohu a naschemu
Neygnadneyschemu Knyezu Knyezu
Kraly Czeskom a geho gnadie diediczuom
A vschiczknym potomnym kraluom Czeskym
Burgermaistru a Radyie thoho Miesta
Budissina vierny posluzny a podany
beyczsch vedne a vnotzy, kdysch ja vodnich
napomenam budav a pschy raddie staysch
vschicznich veczich, kotare vony zalepschy
poznayu, gych lepsche peytaczsch. A gych
Horsche vobvarnovaysch tack jacko my
Buoh pomuoz a geho Svate Slovo.**

Ein Ewigwe-
render Kirchen Calender/
wie man den Sontags Buchsta-
ben/ die zeit zwischen dem Christtage.
vnd Fastnacht gründtlichen
erfinden möge.

Auch ein Wendisches Ge-
sangbuch/ darinnen auff die Hohe Fest/die
Introitus. Kyrie, & præfationes, in Lateinischer
vnd Wendischer Sprache/ vnd die Geistliche
Lieder/ auch etliche Psalmen Reimweise
begriffen/neben den Gebetlein.

Auch der Kleine Catechis=
mus/ mit dem Tauff vnd Tråwbuchlein/
Wendisch vertiret. Alles zu Gemeinem Christ-
lichem Gebrauch vnd Nutz zusammen gebracht
geordnet/ vnd proprijs expensis
publiciret, durch

Magistrum Albinum Mollerum Strau-
picensem, Lusatiæ inferioris, Astronomiæ Culto-
rem, & Ecclesiæ Christi Pastorem.

A N N O.

M. D. LXXIIII.

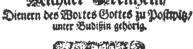

BIBLIA,

To je,
Syte
Szwjate Pißmo

Stareho a Noweho Sakona,
predy do njemskeje,
wot
D. **Mertena Luthera,**

njetko pak
do horneje Ludiskeje serskeje recje
se wschitkej swjernostzu a preju
wot
Njekotrych Evangeliskich Prjedarjow
pschelozena.

✝

Wincza Nezußowa

to yo
Ponizne stare Waschno
Kaz su pobozni Kjesczineno
zandzenem w starem Tlaku pooukhalt
tu Winczu t ho Kneza
dziwacz
habe
Kaz su worni pzi Boiepi LNschi zawschicz
-kich Ludji Boha protheli
Na Sersku Retz
pzewozena, ha tem dzenczuschin Kjesczi-
nyanam k Pjißwadey hakpobojnomu
Sczehuwahu won duta,
ztemi
XV. Poboinemi Modlitwami
Brigitte wot tere hortkeyaMatti
Kristußoweye
Ha
Paczekami
Za Neschpore, za Khorech, ha zakozde
druhi Tlat.

Czizcziana wo tem Letu tohoKneza
1737

Derer
Oberlausitzer Sorberwenden
umständliche
Kirchengeschichte,

darinnen

derselben Heidenthum, Bezwingung zur
chriülichen Religion, derselben erste Beschaffen-
heit, evangelische Reformation und folgender Zu-
stand des Christenthums, imgleichen die wendischen Kirchspiele, und dann der wendischen
Sprache Geschichte und Bücher,

so zum Theil einen großen Einfluß
in

die Kirchengeschichte

der Oberlausitzer Deutschen
hat,

ordentlich und deutlich beschrieben
von

Christian Knauthen
Pfarrer zu Frickersdorf bey der Landeskrone.

Zu finden bey dem Autore in Frickersdorf; bey Herr
Matth. Schultzen, Diac. en Kittlitz; und bey Herr
Lahoden in Kitz.

Görlitz, gedruckt bey Joh. Friedr. Fickelscherer. 1767.

Luvnowski
Szärski
Sambuch

wo kotaremz
se namakaju
240.
Karlischow

kenz
s keje-bauerskeze Rejs
su pschrstawörte wordowali
wot
Mag. **Jana Gottlieba Hauptmanna**
Duschego Farrara Lubnowa
a
schischczane Lübine
wot
Jana Michala Driemels
Lische 1769

Wohleingerichtetes
wendisches
Gesangbuch
in welchem
442 der geistreichsten Gesange.

Nebst einem
Neuen Anhange
von 124 der neusten ausgesuchten und
erbaulichsten Lieder zu finden,
welche bishero nur geschrieben sind gesungen
worden,
nunmehro aber, von mehrerer Uebereinstimmung
und Ordnung willen
zum Gebrauch bey dem öffentli=
chen Gottesdienste auf Verlangen
dem Druck übergeben.

Cottbus, im Rühnischen Verlage
zu bekommen. 1786.

Spěwawa
Jězußowa Wincza
to je
duchowne ha powne
Kherluschowe
Knihi
Bohu k Wescźi, ha tém hornowuzliskim Chorokoscźi
Serbam k Wobojnoscźi, ha kschědnomu Wužiteku,
Nawschitke wrocźne, ha druhe Plaß,
na te Siwate Dnè, ha nawschitke
Potrébnoscźie,

Kuře, kak te kroks pčědè wondate Modslerwow Knihi
teje Jězußoweje Wincźi, ha po tém Rladže
toho cźěwoho lèta
do schtérjoch Dźélow zwořenez
Dlež ku tém předarschim staréim, nět znowa přespi=
šaném, teji nowe Kherlusche plidate, ha z dwojim
Registérom habè Pokazuwarom wosżarnoz,
romadu zbérane
wot
Michawa Wawdě,
Kanonikuša pola S. Pětra w Budischilè,
w lètu toho Kncźa 1787.
Superiorum permissu, et Voluntate.

w Budischilè z Winklerowémi Pißmikami ßtischkane

Sserskeje Reczje
Samozenje a Kwalbu
we
reczerskim Kyrlischu

spjewasche
Juri Möhn
zwojim Claßu prjenschi Duchowny w Nesiwachišich.

Poredzi a wohnda
Augaust Theodor Rudolph Möhn
Duchowny w Kotejach.

w Budyschini
z Monsowymi Pißmkami.
1806

Persté
Spiwarsté Knigli
Wš kotarich netkeische nakajdi Zaß tog
zeleg Lèta richtowane, A woßebše pak
radam Lizba tich rédaeischich
Sakopowarskich = Spiwañow
gromadu
dwa hundert šedim a zeweschjaßet
ako teke
šedim rèdnich Bätowañow natz hußoke
zwezèše še ngmákaju,

Choschobußu saß na nowe schischejane,
a šu néekatare Spiwañ pschištawdne hordowali
wdtom Lèsche 1806,

Te na pošeje dane schešči Spiwaña šu šlèßi tich Bato=
wañow šatzni fort dužimi Numerami knamákaju.

A šu ku kridhéäu podla tog Knighschischejara
Žůhua.

PRINCI-
PIA

LINGUÆ
WENDICÆ,

Quam
ALIQUI WANDA-
LICAM VOCANT.

Cum licentia Superiorum.

PRAGÆ, Typis Universitat: Carolo-
Ferdinand: in Collegio Societ: JESU ad
S. Clementem, Anno 1679.

VOCABULA-
RIUM
LATINO-SERBICUM,

To je/

Wßaczenskich Hwowow,
na Serbsku Retz Pße-
woженo/

wośebie

Tech tak mnohich / schelakich/ ha po-
ezemnech SS. Pißma Tertißkow dla/
woM. Juriia Hauztena Swótßka/ SS.
Theologiä Bakkalaureußa; Jenoho
hußoto dostoinoho / ha Swo-
bodnoho Kapitula podla
S. Pétra w Budéschne
Seniora

Romadu zbicane,

Za nétßo k Pospolnom Krapownicżom Wa-
ßißkej, tuh na te Waßchno hwon dahte.

w Budeschne s Pißmikami, Gottfrida Gottloba
Richtera,
Kaihownoho Ckißcheia
pßimaha Kneża, 1721.

✠
VOCABULARIUM
Latino-Serbicum,

potissimum ob difficiliores S. Scripturæ
textus rite vertendos, (conformiter libello Evan-
geliorum nec non Canticorum Serbicorum,) col-
lectam, & in ordinem Alphabethicum,
congestum

Litteræ n, a, e, vocabulis Serbicis præposita, deno-
tant articulos, nempé n. Ton. generis masculini
ä, Ta, gen fem. ei Tei gen. neutrius,

A.

A. Ab. Abs. Wot.
Abacus, ci. Abax.cis. ocu. co. m. g. Rhucharsce,
vel Schenkarsce, item Rachnarsce Blido.
Abalieno. Woczuzobñam.
Abamita. a Djedowoho Djeda Cjeta.
Abavunculus. n Wówczkneje Worki Bratr.
Abbas, m. g. n Woсj.
Abbas, m. g. n Abt. Abbatissa a Abtißa. Abbatis,
w. je Abstwo.
Abavus, Djedjowoho Djeda Djed.
Abbrevio, as, Pßkrotjam.
Abdico, as, pen. cor. Wotrekñu ßo. Wahwam ßo.
Abdomen, pen. prod. inis. g. m. e Kutwo.
Aberceo, Wotwobaram.
Aberro, Wotbuhbjam. Zabuhbjam.
Abfore, Podla ñeboсj. Nepßitomne bóсj. Idem
quod Abesse.
Abhinc, Stuhde ßem.

A 2   Ab-

HISTORIJA
SERBSKEHO NARODA.

SPISAŠTAJ

WILHELM BOGUSŁAWSKI

MICHAŁ HÓRNIK.

———

BUDYŠIN.
Z NAKŁADOM MICHAŁA HÓRNIKA.
1884.

Droběnje
je
Serbskeje historije.

———

K 25 lětnemu
falojeńskemu żwejeńu

Maschize Sserbskeje
w Dolnej Łužyzy
napißał
H. Jordan
z psichipomozu někotarych zejejonych żłonkow M. S.

———

Towaŕstwownych knigłow zhbuł 45.

Worcijach 1905.
Schjchejane pla A. Łapftidja.

PROF. DR. ERNST MUKA:

SŁOWNIK
DOLNOSERBSKEJE RĚCY
A JEJE NARĚCOW

———

PROF. DR. ARNOŠT MUKA

SLOVNIK
DOLNOLUZICKEHO JAZYKA
A JEHO NAREĆI.

I.

A N.

NAKŁADEM RUSKÉ AKADEMIE VĚD A ČESKÉ AKADEMIE VĚD A UMĚNÍ.
PETROHRAD.   PRAHA.
1911—1915.   1926.

HISTORISCHE UND VERGLEICHENDE

LAUT- UND FORMENLEHRE

DER

NIEDERSORBISCHEN (NIEDERLAUSITZISCH-WENDISCHEN)
SPRACHE.

MIT BESONDERER BERÜCKSICHTIGUNG

DER GRENZDIALECTE UND DES OBERSORBISCHEN.

VON

DR. KARL ERNST MUCKE,
OBERLEHRER AM GYMNASIUM ALBERTINUM ZU FREIBERG I. S.

Motto: Lingua non habet osorem nisi ignorantem.

GEKRÖNTE PREISSCHRIFT.

463

Pschi tym Wotendźeniu
tcho
Wobozydźeri Wobźebneho a Wobozydźeri
Wučeneho Kneśa
KNESA
Jana Wencka
sWonej we hor. Wuj.
iaϟ
TONSSANY
iϟ
Wobϟoku Schulu we Wittenberku
we hapurleiϟkim Mieϟazu 1759
Kwałdu worschcʒi
a ϟo do Jenu poda
TEMUSSAMEMU
sWoju Sauwernoϟʒ a Wbʒherϟichϟwo wćhre tu te Seuszϟi wopoϟoloei
ćʒi ϟami ϟiʒ ϟo we Serʒkim priedarϟtim Towarϟtwi namuΙ:
Michaw Schmoler, sWoriʒhi pola Budeϟchina.
Juri J. Kalϟchmiedt, sMeϟhwaʒiϟtwa we horn. Wuj.
Dieter J. Fuhrmann, sWejeru we horn. Wuj.
L. G. Reim, sWujeϟda pschi Tucherju we Michaałϟkim.
J. L. Beer, sWojeru we horn. Wuj.
Matthei Dan, sKlorurch: Noϟϟlu we Mrihonϟkim.
L. H. Sehlisch, sKublanda we horn. Wuj.
H. H. Kauderbach, sWojeru we horn. Wuj.

Wittenberku ćiϟhrϟiane pola Jana Dori.

Serbski
Kurier.
a
Powedar
Mieϟaʒnepiϟmo,
kHohrieϟbiehanju Serbowϟtwa.

Druhim kϟeʒi pϟeni Kruh.
Wuiti Roϟchl (Januarius.)
1810.

Budϟchini, ϟalaj a woηubole:
Jan Gottlob Deuka.

Lubiϟu riϟϟeli:
Jan Kriϟtijan Schlenkan

Serbski
Powedar
a
Kurier.
Mieϟaʒnepiϟmo,
schirkim Serbam kTrjebnoϟti.

Serdmy Kruh.
Prjenje Ljeto 1809.
Julius, abo ϟyzowy Mieϟaz.

Nuzwedźenje,
kbruħemu pot ϟjetej.

Sa wobiaruju, ϟo je tu te Piϟmo ħlϟchʒien tak
maϟo we Serbowϟwi ϟeϟnate. Pϟchi ħlϟchʒien, pϟches po-
tojju ħerʒkich Woϟϟadow ħiϟhʒien kliϟho wo niϟϟ
nawje, doϟelϟ ϟz ħiϟhʒien ħimor nejϟhym Kwilje
mjet, ħam ϟchudjora kojncʒ; a bes nami ϟiebi je-
dyn druħemu tak maϟo ϟuħoϟije wopoϟaje, ϟo ħym
ja ϟϟoro twungowany, ϟchudjom ħam kici, we ko-
kotreϟi Woϟiadʒi ʒu, ϟo by Nuzkhod doϟtaly. Σ
ħiϟchʒien je ϟo temu Piϟmej na pwor Blakach (na-
ich najwetϟchich) deʒi ħym ħam rodny, tak ϟeϟichia,
ϟo nijjena newotter vbje. Tak woϟϟoko tam Serbjo
ħerʒku Rycʒ waja! — Njekotre maϟe Woϟiaou
paϟ ϟu ϟo na te Mjeϟto wuʒichowałe, ϟchtej wot
G   tej

Tym
Woϟϟebnje ćheϟzenym
njedy Ssobustawam
Prjedarskeho Towarstwa Lipsku,
jako sso teheϟsameho
na 13tym inenskeho M. 1828
psches woϟϟebnu Sawedżen dopomnichu,
podate
wot tych njetsiϟchich Ssobustawow.

Lipsku

СЕРБСКЕ
ЛѢТОПИСИ
ЗА ГОД. 1825.
ПЕРВА ЧАСТИЦА,

изданa
ГЕОРГІЕМ МАГАРАШЕВИЋЕМ,
ПРОФ. У ГИМНАЗІИ НОВОС.

Иждивеніем Господара КОНСТАНТИНА КАУ
ЛИЦЫ Књигопродавца Новосадскога.

Serbische Monatschrift auf das Jahr 1825.
У БУДИМУ
Писмены Крал: Всеучилища Пештанскогъ.
1824.

ČASOPIS
TOWAŘSTWA
MAĆICY SERBSKEJE
1861.

Redaktor
Jakub Buk.

Hornjołužiska
SERBSKA RYČNICA
na přirunowacym stejišću.
Spisał
Dr. Pful.

XIV. Lětnik. — III. Zwjazk. 7. 8.

W Budyšinje.
Z nakładom Maćicy Serbskeje.

ČASOPIS
TOWAŘSTWA
MAĆICY SERBSKEJE
1864.

Redaktor
Jakub Buk.

XVII. lětnik. — IV. zwjazk. 3. 4.

W Budyšinje.
Z nakładom Maćicy Serbskeje

ČASOPIS
TOWAŘSTWA
MAĆICY SERBSKEJE
1866.

Redaktor
Jakub Buk.

XIX. lětnik. — IV. zwjazk. 7. 8.

W Budyšinje.
Z nakładom Maćicy Serbskeja.

Tydźeńska Nowina

aby

serske Powesyje za hornych Łużičanow.

1. Cisło.   2. Dźeń Brajnika.   1842.

Najlubšchi Serbja,
woli cjeŝeni Rwěŝje Bratŝja a Ŝŝodulcajnjŝi

Bes Zensurv.   25. Klerza.

Serbſki

Nowinkar.

Tydźenſki Ĉjaßopiß
wot tych najwažniſchich Podawkow njetŝiſcheho
Ĉjaßa.

1. Liſtno.   Redaktor a Sakojer: 1848.
             F. A. Reichel we Budyŝchini.

Bramborſki ŝerſki Ĉaſſnik.

Herausgegeben von Nowka.

№ 7.   Mittwoch, den 16. Auguſt   1848.

LIPA SERBSKA.

Časopis młodych Serbow.

Wudawar: Jurij Nowak w Budyŝinje. — Zamołwity redaktor: Arnošt Muka w Lipsku.

Čo. 1.   Oktober 1877.   2. lětnik.

Čisło 15. — 13. haperleje. — 1878

Serbske Nowiny.

Zamołwity redaktor a wudawar
J. R. Smoleŕ

Čisło 5. — Meja 1879. — 19. lětnik.

Łužičan.

Měsačnik za pismowstwo, ryčespyt a narodopis

a polobiznami slowjanskich časorunikow, kaž tež z hudźbnymi a belletristiskimi přiłohami po ajewobmjezowanych časach.

Zamołwity redaktor a wudawar: J. R. Smoleŕ w Budyšinje.

ŁUŽICA.

Měsačnik za zabawu a powučenje.

Zhromadny organ serbskich towaŕstwow.

Zamołwity redaktor a wudawar: Dr. phil. Ernst Muka w Budyšinje.

Čisło 1. — Januar 1882. — Lětnik 1.

ŁUŽISKI SERB.

Časopis za serbski lud a studentow.

Samostatna přiłoha „Serbskich Nowin"

Nakhwilny redaktor: Mikławš Žur.

Čisło 1. — Julij 1885. — Lětnik 1.

Serbski Hospodař.

Časopis za serbskich ratarjow.

Samostatna přiłoha k „Serbskim Nowinam".

Wukhadźa w Budyšinje
prěnju a třeću sobotu
kóždeho měsaca.

Płaći na lěto 76 p. Po
pósće do domu z při-
raškom porta.

Redaktor: G. Kubaš w Njebjelčicach.

„Wćł k njebju, ruoy k dźěłu, dowěru k sebi!"

Čisło 3.　　　　7. februara 1891.　　　　Lětnik 11.

SERBSKE SŁOWO

Listy za Serbstwo. — Blätter für das Wendentum.

Přenumer. ...	Wuchnyol a zamołwity redaktor: A. Strynpa w Drjéždźanach.	Inserata pro ↓ prąeałisen Klekszla 15 Pfg. Auf Wiederholungen Rabatt.

Čisło 1.　　　Sobotu 25. januara 1919.　　　I. lětnik.

Lubi Serbja!

Hnurje mjez serbski, kotrež je swětowy rozpławřót porobil, zctykniż so pola Němcow z dospołnym sjedorozo-mjenjem. Jim je Serbstwo dźiwnostka, na kotruž so při

Liebe Wenden!

Ne aus der Weltrevolution hervorgegangene Wendenbewegung begegnet bei den Deutschen vollkommen Unverständlichkeit. Das Wendentum ist ihnen ein Kuriosum, dessen sie sich bei besonderen

---

SRBSKA LUŽICA

ČASOPIS PRIJATELJA LUŽIČKIH SRBA U JUGOSLAVIJI

GOD I.　　　　　　　　　　　　　　LJUBLJANA
BROJ I.　　　　　　　　　　　　　　JULIJ 1934

Sadržaj: Naš časopis »Srbska Lužica« (Uredništvo). Posublijena prošnja. — Lužičko-srpski kompositor Bjer-nat krone a jugoslaviji. Lužiškoserbske narodne prjomyslov i tinakow hik in ovias. 2. Porodni mol. — Bjernat Krawc: K. A. Kocor. — Dr. Jan. Pětr: Iz kulturnego življenja Lužišikh Srbov po svetovni vojni. — V. Cuo-Kuio: Dr. Arnošt Muka i htro. — V. Ra Votramejer lužiško-srbski niv not. — Vrni iz srbske Lužev. Iz slovanskega sveta a tojega porta. — Tiskovni pregled.

Howiny za serbski lud

	W dźensnišim čisle:

Čisło 20 (54)　　　　Budyšin / Bautzen, 24. septembra 1949　　　　2. lětnik

Dobyće demokratiskeho ducha w Sakskej nastupaće njonémske naruody

Sakski sejm zawěsći serbskemu ludej swobodne wuwiće!

2. SERBS, ONLY SERBS

The evidence suggests that from the 'beginning' the sense of nationhood was stronger among the **Luzica Serbs** than among the Germans. From Fredegar's mid-7th century four-book history of the Franks, the *Chronicle of Fredegar*, to Johannes Trithemius's early 16th century history of the Franks, *De Origine Gentis Francorum Compendium*, the Franks claimed descent not from a Germanic people, but from the Trojans, from Greek-speaking *Trojans* called *Sicambers:* **The Sicambers, who were descended from the survivors of Troy and were settled near the mouth of the Danube.** According to Trithemius' detailed account, circa 430 B.C the Sicambers entered Germania and settled lands along the Rhine: **It is certain that the Sicambers received their first home where Geldern, Westphalia, Munster, and Cleves are now located.** Sometime after **acquiring Weteranum and everything up to the territory of the Saxons**, the Sicambers, out of love for one of their greatest kings, *King Frank,* called themselves *Franks* (**Sicambri amore sui regis se vocari statuerunt**). During the reign of King Priam: **The Sicambers ... began to forget their noble language and ancient homeland and gradually began to use the Germanic language as well, until finally none of them knew any language except the Teutonic. Many words remained with them which seem to have a Greek rather than a Germanic origin, as anyone well knows who understands both Greek and Teutonic. It is still the same today.**[1]

ROMANS

At the same time, the Franks and their successors pretended to be the greatest Romans and the greatest Christians. Charles the Great and successors were: *A deo Coronato ... hristianisimus ... Caesar ... Imperium Romanorum ... magnifico et pacifico imperatori ... felicitor Octaviano, melior Traino ... totius mundi dominus ... caput orbus.* For the learned Alcuin (730-804), the most famous scholar of the day, Charles the Great, a noble son of Troy, had legitimate rights to titles greater than *rex Francorum* or *imperator Romanorum*, to nothing less than *caput mundi*.

MACEDONIANS

Other German nations also claimed non-Germanic roots. The Saxons traced their origin to Macedonia and Alexander the Great, survivors of Alexander the Great's army who fled the conquered lands after the death of their leader. By a different genealogical route, the Swabians also claimed a Macedonian origin. The Bavarians, the sons of Bavarus, migrated from Armenia after the great flood.

BARBARIANS

In spite of such claims, in the eyes of their peers, the Germans remained barbarians, **uncouth, rude, uncivilized barbarians.** Using religion as a defense, in the early 16th century, a German scholar and theologian pleads for an end to the steady stream of insults and contempt that attend the German name: **Many writers have calumniated the Germans by labeling them barbarians ... Today the word should not be used at all except except to describe the enemies of the Christian faith. It ought never to be applied to Germans, for ... the Christian religion has utterly extinguished all traces of barbarism in Germany** *(Franciscus Irenicus, Exegesis Germaniae, 1518).*

HOUSTON STEWART CHAMBERLAIN

According to Houston Stewart Chamberlain, the 20ᵗʰ century's greatest champion of *Germanism*, from the 'beginning' the ancient Slavs had a stronger sense of self, language, and culture than the other nations of Europe, including the Germans: **The extreme trouble experienced in converting the Slavs to Christianity is a testimony to their deeply religious nature: Italians and Gauls were the easiest to convert, Saxons could be won only by the power of the sword, but it took long years and fearful cruelties to make the Slavs give up the faith of their fathers. The notorious persecution of the heathen lasted, in fact, to the century of Gutenberg** *(Die Grundlagen des Neunzehten Jahrhunderts, 1899)*. In the Christian era, Chamberlain writes, the Slavs alone had the national strength and will to resist Rome and Latinity, to resist **divine service in any language but their own!** Chamberlain traces the roots of 'Reformation' in continental Europe to reformist and patriotic tendencies in Slavic lands.

SLAVOGERMANEN

Chamberlain sees a direct and positive correlation between the Slavic component and German civilization; the greater the Slavic component, the greater the German or 'Slavogermanen' achievement: **The Franks grow to their full strength and give the world a new type of humanity where they mingle ... as in Franconia, from the exact point of union of the most German Slavonic elements. Saxony, which has given Germany so many of its greatest men, contains a population quickened almost throughout by a mixture of Slavonic blood. And has not Europe seen within the last three centuries how a nation of recent origin-Prussia-in which the mixture of blood was still more thorough, has raised itself by its preeminent power to become the leader of the German empire?**

LUZICA SERBS

Unlike the Germans, the *Serbs* of *Luzica* were never ashamed of their ancestry, native language, and culture. They never pretended to be Trojans, Greeks, or Romans. In spite of an often oppressive religious-political environment, the history of *Luzica's Serbs* is the history of a heroic struggle for national, linguistic, and cultural survival and affirmation.[2]

SAINTS CYRIL, METOD

In eastern Germany, reformist and patriotic tendencies were perhaps inherent in a popular Christianity cleansed in part by the residual humanity and decency of pre-Christian Slavic civilization. Thus perhaps the *instinctive* support for the mission of *Saints Cyril* and *Metod,* for the Slavic language, letter, and liturgy in Christian services (e.g. the **Old Slavic** manuscript from **Gosmarja** in **Lower Luzica**, possibly dating from the late 9ᵗʰ century; local sympathy for the great Czech religious reformer Jan Hus (1372-1415) in historic Serb lands; and numerous Serbs who played an important role in the propagation and defense of Hus' reforms, including *Petr of Prisec* and *Nikolas of Dresden*).

MARTIN LUTHER

Martin Luther and Lutheranism open up a special chapter in the history of Germania's Serbs. It seems that Luther himself was of **Serb-Wend** ancestry. According to a standard reference work: **Martin Luther (1483-1546***)* **was descended from the Slavonic stock of the tribe of Lutici. His ancestral name was Luyt (meaning strong, harsh, tough). Predecessors were forced to Germanize the name to Lutyr, then Luthyr, and finally to Luther. Born in Lower Saxony in a place which is today called Einsleben, earlier known by its Slavic name, Sebenica, which is retained even today in the name of the 'old town' district called Siebenhitze.**[3] There is also circumstantial evidence that Luther's wife had **Serb-Wend** antecedents. The village of **Lipa**, later Lippendorf, near **Serb civitas Lipsk**, modern Leipzig, is the ancestral home of the von Bors and the birthplace of Luther's wife, Katherine von Bora. **Bor** as in *liber homo Bor vocitatus natione Slavus* is a singularly Serb name. **Bor, Bolibor, Mesibor** and **Borislav** are four of the nine Serb names recorded in Meissen in 1071.

BOHEMIAN VIRUS

The historical record reflects sympathy and support for Luther's *Bohemian virus* in historic Serb lands, (e.g. the numerous Serbs who will play an important role in the Protestant Reformation: *Jan Bogac, Jan Brezan, Pawol Bosak, Miklaws Jakubica, Jakub Jan,* and others). The record also suggests Luther's singular sense of freedom and security in Wittenberg, an early center of learning in **Sorabia, Vandalia, Sarmatia** (***Nostra haec Vandalia est mera Sarmatia***).[4]

AT LUTHER'S SIDE

At Luther's side, a number of distinguished Serbs (e.g. professor *Jan Rak, poeta laureatus,* respected scholar at many European universities, and *Kaspar Peuker,* scholar, theologian, physician, and university professor) worked closely with Luther and P. Melanchthon in Wittenberg *(H. Kuhne, Kaspar Peuker. Leben und Werk einen grossen Gelehrten and der Wittenberger Universitat im 16 Jahrundert, LeT B/30, 1983).*

PEUKER, MELANCHTHON

As their 1,200 page revision of the *Chronicon Carionis* demonstrates, *Peuker* and Melanchthon, his father-in-law, shared a deep and passionate interest in the history of the Slavs, especially the **Serb Wends**, in *Peuker's* words, the **Sorabi Serbs**, the original, **true Sarmatians**.[7]

TRUEST CHRISTIANS

In certain reformist circles, the Serb Christians were seen as the truest Christians in substance and in form, in their individual and collective adherence to basic Christian values, and in the democratic letter and spirit of their church organization.

PERFECT MODEL FOR REFORM

This notion finds it strongest expression in the writings of a Swiss German, Pamphilus Gegenbach. In *Von Drien Christen* (Basle, 1523), Gegenbach outlines in great detail the reasons why he believes the Christian Serb community is a perfect model for reform. Similar ideas are also found in Melanchton's writings. Great respect for the authentic faith and piety of the Orthodox Serbs is also found in Benedikt Kuripesic's account of his passage through Ottoman lands *(Putopis Kroz Bosnu, Srbiju, Bugarsku i Rumeliju, 1530).* A member of Emperor Ferdinand's mission to Sultan Suleiman, Kuripesic took great interest in the condition and sympathies of Bosnia's Christians. Though the lot of Bosnia's Christian Serbs was a hard one, their faith, Kuripesic stressed, was strong, vital and consistent with basic Roman Catholic doctrine. In fact, he noted, the Christian Serbs hoped that their simple and pure faith would inspire other Christians to remain true and strong.

GERMANIA SERBS, ILLYRIA SERBS

It is not surprising, therefore, that Germania's reformers, including Germania Serbs, saw the Serbs of *Illyria*, Europe's '**truest Christians**', as natural allies in the Lutheran quest for a more perfect Christian order in Europe.

ORTHODOX SERB CLERIC

In 1559, a trusted confidant, a learned Orthodox Serb cleric, **uceni Srb, Demetrij Srb,** will carry Melanchthon's letter to the ecumenical Patriarch of Constantinople, calling for a Lutheran-Orthodox rapproachement, for the 'unity of all true Christian communities.' Two years later, two Orthodox Serb monks, one from **Bosnia, Matija Popovic**, the other from **Serbia, dijak Jovan Malesevac,** will assist in the Serb language and letter translation of the New Testament, the foundation of Lutheran plans to bring the evangelical message to the South Slavs.

THOMAS MUNTZER

It is perhaps more than coincidence that deep in the Serb heartland, at Zwickau, home of the *Zwickau prophets* (**true authority lay in the inner light given by God to his own, rather than in the Bible**), near the border with Bohemia, the revolutionary German reformer, Thomas Muntzer (1490 1525), founds the Anabaptist movement.

NOWY ZAKON SERPSKY IMPRIMO

Taking full and complete advantage of the Reformation's emphasis on the vernacular, Germania's Serb scholars, ecclesiastic and lay, set about translating religious literature into Serb.

- M. Jakubica, Lower Serb translation of New Testament (**Nowy Zakon Serpsky Imprimo**), based on a Lower Serb dialect spoken east of the Neisse, 1548

- A. Moller, **Lower Serb hymnal and catechism**, 1574

- Pastor Wjaclaw Warich, **Upper Serb translation of Luther's Catechism**, 1597

- H. Tara, *Enchiridion Vandalicum* (Lower Serb translation of Luther's Catechism), 1610

- G. Martin, **Upper Serb collection of psalms**, 1627

- M. Frencel, **Upper Serb translation of the gospels of SS Matthew and Mark**, 1670

- J. Swetlik, **Swjate scenja** (The Holy Gospels, an Upper Serb book ofreadings from the scriptures), 1690

- M. Frencel, **Upper Serb translation of New Testament**, 1706

- J. Swetlik, **Serbske katolske cherluse** (first Upper Serb Catholichymnbook), 1695

- Bogumil Francius, **Lower Serbian translation of New Testament**, 1709

- **Printed hymnal for Upper Serb Protestants**, containing 202 hymns, 1710
- **Duchomne kyrlisowe knihi** (Printed hymnal containing 529 hymns), 1741
- J. Swetlik: translated from the Vulgate, an **Upper Serbian bible for Catholics**, 1711
- **Upper Serb translation of the Bible**, 1728
- P. Kowar, **Jezusowa winica** (Upper Serb prayers for Catholics), 1737
- M. Walda, **Jezusowa winica haby wucby ha modlitwow knihi** (Upper Serb prayers for Catholics), 1783
- M. Walda, **Sprewawa Jezusowa winica** (Upper Serb hymnal containing 659 hymns for Catholics), 1787
- F. Fryco, **Lower Serb translation of Old Testament**, 1796

PRINCIPIA LINGUAE WENDICAE

The religious literature was accompanied by numerous Serb grammars, dictionaries, and orthographies.

- Z. Bierling, *Didascalia seu Orthographia Vandalica, 1619*
- J. Chojnan, *Linguae Vandalicae ad dialectum districtus Cotbusiani, 1650*
- J. Ticin, *Principia Linguae Wendicae, 1670*
- *Lexicon harmonico-etymologicum Slavicum, 1694*
- J. Swetlik, *Vocabularium Latino-Serbicum, 1721*
- J. Matej, **Wendische Grammatica**, *1721*
- J. Bogumil Hauptmann: *Lexicon Vandalicum, 1731*
- J. Bogumil Hauptmann: **Niederlausitzische Wendische Grammatica**, 1761
- J. Hancka, *Gramatica serbicae linguae composite et conscripta, 1768*
- J. Hancka, *Vocabularium Germano-Serbicum combinatum, 1782*

EFFICACY, RICHNESS, SUBTLETY

In 1757 Jurij Mjen translated parts of Klopstock's *Messias,* 'the most majestic and sublime poem in German,' in order to demonstrate the **efficacy, richness of vocabulary and subtlety** of the Serb language.

DE ORIGINIBUS LINGUAE SORABORUM

In the 17th and 18th centuries Serb scholars, writing in Latin and German, authored numerous studies relating to the origin, history, language, and culture of the Serbs.[6] The following titles give some idea of the subject, scope, and depth of intellectual inquiry.

- *De conversione Soraborum*
- *De Diis Slavorum et Soraborum in specie*
- *De idolis Soraborum*
- *De mathesi Serborum*

- *De Originibus Linguae Sorabicae* [7]
- *De Originibus Slavicis, opus chronologico-geographico-historicum*
- *De poesi Serborum*
- *De Serbis, Venedorum natione, vulgo dictis 'Die Wenden'*
- **Gedanken eines Oberlausitzer Wenden uber das Schicksal seiner Nation Origines Lusaticae**
- *Origine Lusatiae complexae historiam Geronis*
- **Philologisch-kritische Abhandlung von der Wendischen Sprache und ihrem Nutzen in den Wissenschaften**
- **Schutzschrift fur die Alten Slaven unde Wenden**
- **Uber die Musikinstrumente der slawischen Volker**

LIPSKE NOWIZNY A WSTIIZNY

In the second half of the 18th century a Serb journal, a Serb-German society, and a Serb newspaper made their appearance. In 1766 the Serb student society at the University of Leipzig published the first issue of **Lipske nowizny a wstiizny.**

UPPER LUZICA SOCIETY OF SCIENCES

In 1779 Jan Horcanski was co-founder of the Serb-German *Upper Luzica Society of Sciences*, an important center of Serbian studies. A number of journals connected with the society published numerous articles relating to Serbian studies (e.g. *Lausitzisches Magazin*; *Lausitzer Provinzialblatter*; *Lausitzische Monastsschrift*).

MESACNE PISMO

In 1790 Korla Serach, from Budusin, and Jan Janka, from Bukecy, published the first Serb newspaper *(Mesacne Pismo K Rozwucenju A K Wokrewjenju: A Monthly Paper for Information and Entertainment).* The fact that the newspaper was banned after the first issue speaks volumes of the repressive political environment.

GERMAN SCHOLARSHIP

The Serbs were not alone in the promotion and defense of national, linguistic, and cultural rights in Germany in the 18th century. Their efforts were vastly strengthened and reinforced by the authoritative studies of outstanding German scholars. A member of the *Brandenburg Society of Sciences*, Johann Leonard Frisch *(Historia Linguae Sclavonicae, 1730)* was an early authority on Slavic languages generally and the Serb language in Luzica specifically. Johann Gottlieb Hauptmann *(Nieder-lausitzsche Wendische Grammatica, 1761)*, an early student and authority on the structure and grammar of the Serb language in *Lower Luzica*, established Serbian as **an ancient and venerable language.** Georg Korner's objective and scholarly inquiry into the history and language of the Serbs led him to defend it existence and encourage its further development *(Philologische-kritische Abhandlung von der Wendischen Sprache und ihrem Nutzen in den Wissenschaften, 1766).* In his veritable encyclopedia of Serb studies,Christian Knauth insisted on recognition and respect for the history, language, and culture of the Serbs *(Derer Oberlausitzer Sorberwenden umstandliche Kirchengeschichte, 1767).* August Ludwig Schlozer, an authority on *Serbian* and its relation to other Slavic languages, urged German support for the development of Slavic language and culture *(Allgemeine Nordische Geschichte, 1771)*. One of the founders of Slavic studies in Germany, Karl Gottlob von Anton, was the author of a brilliant study on the origin, history, language, and culture of the German and Balkan Serbs *(Erste Linien eines Versuches uber der alten Slawen Ursprung, Sitten, Gebrauche, Meinungen und Kenntnisse, 1783)*. Several specifically linguistic studies related to the Serbian language in *Upper* and *Lower Luzica* *(Kleines Niederlausitzisch Wendisches Worterbuch, 1788; Etwas uber die Oberlausitzische Wendische Sprache, 1797)*.

AUTHENTIC NATION, LEGITIMATE RIGHTS

The history of the Serb struggle for national rights in Germany is the history of an authentic nation and legitimate rights with the deepest roots in history, territory, language, and culture. In fact, the Serbs were never a spurious nation, a 'state of mind' spawned by alien ambitions and interventionist-expansionist schemes. Equally important, the Serb struggle was always principled, open and above-board, never a matter of deception and treachery. Nor was it ever a matter of tribal theater: onstage, flamboyant, hysterical, belligerent, jingoistic German superpatriots; offstage, ruthless, and rabid 'Serb-uber-alles' genocidal racists.

KING FRIEDRICH AUGUST

Thanks to the loyalty, protection, and assistance of his Serb troops, King Friedrich August of Saxony managed to escape from a revolt in Dresden in 1849. In recognition of the role played by Serb troops in defense of the royal family, Friedrich August directed that Crown Prince Albert, who was then about to rejoin his regiment in Bautzen, should study the Serb language. The Serb writer, poet, and patriot J.E. Smoler was appointed to be his teacher.

LOYAL SAXONS, PRUSSIANS

It is also important to keep in mind that high proportions of young Serbs served in Prussian and Saxon armies, that the Serbs were often the first to enter and the last to leave the battlefield. In World War I, for example, the number of Serb soldiers killed was high and out of all proportion to their number in the total population. In other words, in matters of war and peace, in spite of oppressive conditions and policies, the Serbs were never in any way 'lesser' Germans, but in every decent, honorable, and truly patriotic way, perhaps 'greater' Germans.

ENDNOTES

[1] Regarding the *real* time and circumstance of Frank settlement on the Rhine, R. Katicic writes: **Treba podsjetiti na to da se i Franci javljaju tek u 3. stoljecu na istocnoj obali Rajne, dakle takodjer na pogranicnog rijeci, a da im je glavna aktivnost bila pljackasko zalijtetanje na teritorij oslabljenoga Carstva. Medju starim germanskim plemenima nema im traga. Ime im je novo, a etimologija toga imena nejasna i sporna ... Franci su u medjusobnom ophodjenju preuzeli zapadnogermanski jezik onoga sireg Porajnaja is kojega su pritjecali njihovi borci** *(Uz pocetke hrvatskih pocetaka, 1993)*.

[2] In Anhalt it was ordained in 1293 that the trials of Slavs should be held in German only. In 1327 similar laws were passed in the law-courts of Altenburg, Leipzig, and Zwickau. In 1424 similar laws were adopted in Meissen.

[3] James S. Roucek (ed), Slavonic Encyclopaedia, 1949.

[4] J. Malink, Die Beziehungen Martin Luthers zu den Sorben, LeT B/30-1, 1983. Frido Metsk, "Die Bezichungen Martin Luthers zu den Sorben" in neuer Sicht?, LeT B/30-2, 1983.

[5] *Chronicon Carionis, expositum, et auctum multis, et veteribus, et recentibus historiis in discriptionibus regnorum & gentium antiquarum, & narrationibus rerum Ecclesisticarum & Politicarum Graecarum, Romanorum, Germanicorum & aliarum, ab exordio mundi usque ad Carolum Quintum Imperatorum; a Philippo Melanchtone & Casparo Peucero* (Bern, 1601).

[6] As Serbian students and scholars were active at leading universities, it is not surprising that Serbian student associations promoting Serbian language and culture were established at universities in Germany and Bohemia, at Leipzig, Wittenburg, and Prague, in the 18th century. Earlier, in the mid-16th century, a Serbian gymnasium (***Viadrina, Universitas Serborum***) was established at Frankobrod (Frankfurt/Oder).

[7] One of the most important Slavists of his time, the vast creative work of Abraham Frencel (1656-1706) fills 34 volumes that deal mainly with the origin of the Serbian language, history, and customs of the Serbs.

WOJNSKI KJARLIŽ

Naše golcy z wojny jĕdu,
   hyj! z wojny jĕdu;
našog pana konja wjedu,
   hyj! konja wjedu.
Glĕdaj, kak ten ryśaŕ sejźi,
kak se jogo woko swĕśi!
Witaj, pan, witaj k nam,
   hyj, hyj, witaj, pan!

Wojnarje k tej rĕce pśidu,
   hyj, k rĕce pśidu;
našog pana konja myju,
   hyj, konja myju.
Glĕdaj, kak ten koń se swĕši,
kak se jogo sedło błyśći!
Glĕdaj jan, zwjercha pan!
   Hyj, hyj, witaj, pan!

Kogo slĕzy pana wjedu?
   hyj, pana wjedu?
mjazy kšawnem wojnskem rĕdu?
   hyj, wojnskem rĕdu?
Glĕdaj, kak won k zemi glĕda,
kak se jomu droga njezda!
Nĕmski kral, pana chwal!
   Hyj, našog pana chwal!

Knĕni, coš wot bitwy słyšaś,
   hyj, bitwy słyšaś,
dejš ty toś tych golcow pšašaś,
   hyj, golcow pšašaś.
Kaž ten pogrim dołoj grima,
tak tog knĕza śĕžka heja.
Jo, naš pan, witaj k nam!
   Hyj, hyj, witaj k nam!

PART XX

1. SERBJA, ZACHOVAJCE SVERCU, SVOJICH VOTCOV REC A VERU

Dramatic evidence of the great strength and vitality of the Serb idea in *Luzica* is found in the Serb settlements in Texas established in the mid-19th century. Centered at Serbin, in Lee County, the Serbs soon established related communities in neighboring areas (e.g. Giddings, Lincoln, Mannheim, Loebau, Dime Box, Fedor, Lexington in Lee County; Warda, Winchester, La Grange, Swiss Alp, and Green's Creek in Fayette County; Hochkirch, Walburg, Thorndale in Williamson county; The Grove, Copperas Cove, Aleman, Cisco, Albany, Vernon, Kingsville, and Bishop in other counties)[1].

SERBJA, ZACHOVAJCE SVERCU

What distinguished the Serbs from other immigrants was the uncommon determination to preserve the language and culture of their ancestors.[2] In the beginning the Texas Serbs made every effort to live the words of their favorite hymn:

> *SERBJA, ZACHOVAJCE SVERCU, SVOJICH VOTCOV REC A VERU* (Serbs, maintain faithfully the language and religion of your forefathers); *SRBI, SACUVAJTE VERNO SVOJIH OCEVA REC I VERU* (the same idea and syntax in modern Serbian).[3]

REC

In their communities the Serbs, some of whom knew only Serbian, spoke Serbian, sang Serbian songs, wrote letters in Serbian, read the Bible and religious books in Serbian, listened to sermons in Serbian, and subscribed to Serbian-language newspapers *(Serbske Noviny)* and almanacs *(Predzenak,* the almanac of Upper Luzica).

VERU

True to the faith of their ancestors, to deep and sincere religious values, the Texas Serbs were also determined to **worship God according to the dictates of their own minds.** Regarding their opposition to **the dictates of others**, namely the king of Prussia and state decrees uniting the Lutheran and Reformed churches, Pastor Jan Kilian writes: **What the decrees and bulls of the Roman Pope are, namely statutes of men intended to enslave souls, such are also the cabinet orders of the pope of Berlin, the king of Prussia, according to which Evangelical Lutheran Church, since the year 1830, has been violated with regard to the society rights guaranteed by the Peace of Westphalia and robbed of its earthly goods. By these regal cabinet orders, by which, arbitrarily and violently, a new church or a church of confusion has been made, the faithful Lutherans in Prussia have been placed in such distress that they are seriously suffering, no matter whether they leave the Church of the King or remain in it.**

THE FIRST SERBIAN LUTHERAN CHURCH

Soon after their arrival the Serbin Serbs built a larger house that served as church, school and parsonage. In 1859 a new church was built to take care of the growing spiritual needs of the community. Construction of a bigger church was started in 1866 and completed in 1871. Still in service, **the First Serbian Lutheran Church in Texas, later St. Paul's Lutheran Church in Serbin, is one of the oldest churches in America in continual use since its construction.**

REVEREND JAN KILIAN (1811-1884)

From 1854 to his death in 1884, the Reverend Jan Kilian was the spiritual leader of the Texas Serbs. A man of 'noble form,' of high intelligence and character, of education, culture, and accomplishment, Kilian was an exceptionally gifted, strong, principled and dedicated leader, in every way a true representative of his congregation's best interests. Jan Kilian was born in *Dolina*/Dohlen, a village in Upper Luzica. In Germany, following graduation from the University of Leipzig, in addition to ministering to several parishes in Upper Luzica, Kilian did his best to serve the needs of the faithful in some eighteen other communities. In Texas, his ministerial duties included visits on horseback to communities some forty miles distant from Serbin. In spite of his arduous and exhaustive duties, Kilian, a composer of some note, found time to publish a hymn book, *Spevarske Vjesel*, with twenty-eight of his hymns, including the popular *Serbja, zachovajce sveru, svojich votcow rec a veru*, translations of the *Augsburg Confession* and Luther's *Large Cathechism* as well as original prayer books, numerous sermons, and tracts.

Regarding the man and his mission, Professor Engerrand writes: **Evidently he was a scholar, quite at ease in these two languages, able to preach in English after a few years in Texas, and so familiar with Latin that he could not only read Cicero in the text, but he could even talk and write verse in that language. Evidently he belonged to the noble lineage of those who expatriate themselves, if they need to, in order to follow their own religious convictions, and that is a type of man, frequently represented in early history of America, before which we bow deeply whatever our own faith may be. In Kilian's case expatriation meant not only breaking away for always his ties with his dear old country ... but also assuming the terrific responsibility of the inrooting, materially and spiritually, of several hundred human beings on a foreign soil ... I find still another proof of his strong personality in the fact that although he was living in something like a wilderness for thirty years, he nevertheless retained his energy and talents while giving himself entirely to others. However, what a change from the library of the University of Leipzig to a log hut in Serbin, without the slightest hope of any reward but the joy coming from the accomplishment of a duty! ... Today there is a Kilian Hall in the Lutheran Concordia College, at Austin, where the bell he brought from Germany is piously exhibited on a pedestal, but nothing could be more inspiring about him than his modest tomb in the uninspiring little cemetery of Serbin.**[4]

TEXAS WENDISH HERITAGE SOCIETY AND MUSEUM

The Serb past in Texas is present in many ways. Thanks to the **Texas Wendish Heritage Society and Museum** of Serbin, Texas, the local history of Luzica's Serb settlers is a matter or detailed record and continuous study.[5] Moreover, the Society also sponsors events such as the *Annual Wendish Fest,* that welcome (**Witajce k nam!**) one and all to eat, sing, dance, and have an old-fashioned good time in the **Serbja** manner.

UPPER LUZICA

The first Serb settlers were Lutherans from Upper Luzica, from an area centered on the Spree River, between Budusin/Bautzen in the south and Sprevica/Spreewitz in the north, from villages and towns with the deepest roots in the Serb past.

BELA VODA, BLOTO, BREZOVICA

Bela Voda— (Bjelawoda, 1800), Weisswasser
Belovici— (Merten von Belwicz), Bellwitz
Blezov— (Blesaw, 1436), Blosa
Bloto Blocany—(Blote, 1278), Plothen
Bosovichi— (Boschewicz, 1364), Baschutz
Brezovica— (Bresewicz, 1413), Briessnitz
Bukojna— (Bokownia, 1719), Buchwalde
Brusk— (Brausk, 1545; Hornje Brusy, 1886), Ober-Prauske

BUDOSTOVICI, CAKOVICI, CHVATICI

Budostovici— (Bustewicz, 1331; Budesteze, 1700), Gross-Postwitz
Bynovici— (*Svichercus de Binuiza*, 1280), Binnewitz
Cakovici— (Pawil Czakekwicz, 1400), Scheckwitz
Chelcov— (Czelchow, 1360), Zschillicau
Chortnica— (Cortenicz, 1407; Kortnica, 1866), Cortnitz
Chotovici— (Cothewicz, 1315), Kotitz
Chrost— (Croste, 1461; Khrost, 1843), Crosta
Chvatici— (Kwaczicz, 1684), Quatitz

CRNOVICI, DOLANE, DUBRAVA MALA

Crnovici— (*Petrus de Czornewitz*, 1361), Zscharnitz
Deza, Dezin— (Dyzin, 1241; Wulki Dazen 1700), Gross-Dehsa
Dobrosovici— (de Doberswizc, 1280), Doberschutz
Dolane— (de Dolen, 1206; Dolan, 1396), Dohlen
Drenov— (Drehno, 1400), Drehnow
Drozov— (Drosaw, 1400; Drozdze, 1767), Drehsa
Dub, Duban— (Duban, 1377), Dauban
Dubrava Mala— (*Dubra parva*, 1419; Mala Dubrawa, 1800), Klein Dubrau

DUBRAVKA, GRADISCE, JABLON

Dubravka— (*Mertin Dubrawca,* 1472; Dubrawka, 1700), Dubrauke
Gbelsk— (Gebelczk, 1365), Gebelzig
Glina— (Glyn, 1447), Gleina
Gradisce— (Gradis, 1222; *Czaslaw de Grodis,* 1381), Groditz
Gutina— (Guttin, 1222), Guttau
Hoznica— (Hosniza, 1767), Petershain
Jablon— (Gablonz, 1613; Jablon, 1761), Gablenz

Jamno— (Jamen, 1390), Jahmen

JAVORNIK, KOMOROV, KOLOVOZ

Jastreb— (Jatrzebie, 1419; Jastrob, 1866), Jetscheba
Javornik— (Jawornik, 1241), Jauernick
Kobylici— (Kobelicz, 1350), Coblenz
Komorov— (Komeraw, 1399; Dobry Komorow, 1719), Commerau
Kosla— (Koschele, 1419; Koschla, 1800), Kaschel
Kletno— (de Cleten, 1396), Klitten
Kluks— (Jenchin von Clux, 1324), Klix
Kolovoz— (Kolewasine, 1363), Kohlwesa

KRAKOVICI, KYSELICA, LIPA

Koprica— (Kopericz, 1224), Kuppritz
Kotovici— (*Vitgo et Cunradus de Kotwitz*, 1280), Kotitz
Krakovici— (de Krekewicz, 1352), Kreckwitz
Kupsici— (Cupcici, 1088), Kubschutz
Kyselica— (Kyseliz, 1400), Geisslitz
Lemisov— (Lemeschaw, 1410), Lomischau
Leske— (Leske, 1360), Lauske
Lipa, Lipchin— (Lipchen, 1419), Leipgen

LUBOV, MALISICI, MILAN KAL

Lubov— (Lubaw, 1221), Lobau
Lutolin— (Leutten, 1564; veliki Lutol, 1761), Leuthen
Luzica— (Lusicz, 1391; Luschitz, 1505), Lauske
Luzka— (Lussk, 1445), Lauske
Malisici— (Malssicz, 1407), Maltitz
Malisovici— (Maleswicz, 1224), Malschwitz
Mikov— (Michow, 1408), Mucka
Milan Kal— (Milekal, 1322; Mylekal, 1430), Milkel

MUZAKOV, NOWA WES, PAKOSNICA

Mulkovici— (Mulkwiz, 1597), Mulkwitz
Muzakov— (*Theodericus de Muschowe*, 1251), Muskau
Nechorin— (*Hannus de Necherin*, 1421), Nechern
Netin— (Nyten, 1370; Netin, 1413), Niethen
Nosatici— (*Petrus de Noztize*, 1280), Nostitz
Nowa Wes— (Nowa Wes, 1843), Neudorf
Pakosnica— (Paskosnitz, 1625), Schadendorf
Polovici— (Polowiczy, 1471), Halbendorf

PRILUG, RADIBOR, RODOVICI

Plusinkovici— (Plussinkeicz, 1399), Pliesskowitz
Prilug— (Preylag, 1614), Preilack
Privitici— (Priwiticz, 1250; *Petrus de Priwiticz*, 1364), Preititz
Rachlov— (Rachelow, 1359), Rachlau

Radibor— (Radebor, 1359), Radibor
Radisovici— (Radischwicz, 1419; Wulki Radzischow, 1767), Gross-Radisch
Rakol— (Rakil, 1331), Rackel
Rodovici— (G. de Rodewicz, 1364), Rodewitz

ROVNO, SERBSKI ZALOM, TREBENC

Rovno— (Rowno, 1866), Rohne
Serbske Kundracicy— (Serbske Kundraczizy, 1848), Wendisch Cunnersdorf
Serbski Zalom— (Zalom, 1241), Sohland
Slepe— (Slep, 1272), Schleife
Sprevica— (Sprewitz, 1568), Spreewitz
Stajnica— (Steynicz, 1469), Steinitz
Stroza— (Stroza, 1700), Wartha
Trebenc— (Trebnitz, 1520), Steindorfer

TREBIN, UJEZD, VURSIN

Trebin— (Treben, 1597), Trebendorf
Truskovic— (Trusskowic, 1345), Trauschwitz
Tur— (Thure, 1447), Tauer
Ujezd— (Wujezd, 1719), Uhyst
Vavici— (Wawiz, 1228), Wawitz
Vichov— (Wichowe, 1241), Weicha
Vunesov— (Wunyschaw, 1533), Wunscha
Vursin— (*Petir de Wursin*, 1359), Wurschen

VYSOKA, ZABROD, ZARECE

Vysoka— (Wisok, 1374), Weissig
Wolesnica— (Olsenicz, 1452; Kleinolssa, 1792), Klein Oelsa
Wujezk— (Pavil von Ugyst, 1400), Wuischke
Wuskidz— (Wuskidz, 1800), Weisskeissel
Zabrod— (Zabrod, 1380), Sabrodt
Zagor— (Zagar, 1409), Sagar
Zarece— (Scharezk, 1413, Saritsch
Zarki— (Jan de Zarg, 1365), Sarka
Zidov— (Sydov, Zidow, 1360), Seidau
Zubrnica— (Zaubernitz, 1419), Kleinsaubernitz

SLAVIC ROOT

In spite of the official tendency to either 'Germanize' Serbian names or impose a German equivalent (e.g. Arnost Mjerwa/Ernst Moerbe; Korla Wicaz/Karl Lehmann; Jan Hola/Johann Hohle; Jan Hurban/Johann Urban; Kovar/Schmidt), the Slavic root is evident in the modified family names of many immigrants. In the following instances it is perhaps more evident than in others.

BENOWSKI, JURISCHK, KRAKOWSKY

Benowski • Blasig • Boback • Bohot • Doman • Dommaschk • Drosche • Dube • Hannusch • Hobratschk • Hola/Hohle • Hurban/Urban • Jannasch • Jentho • Jurak

• Jurischk • Knippa • Kokel/Kockel • Koslan • Kovar/Schmidt • Krakosy • Krakowsky • Kurio

MEDACK, NAGORSKA, WUKASCH

Leitko • Malke • Medack • Miertschin • Michalk • Mickan • Mjerawa/Moerbe • Mroske • Nagorska • Noack • Prelopp • Schoppa • Sprejitz • Swidom • Simank • Sucky • Tschatschula • Wicaz/Lehmann • Wukasch • Wunsche • Zieschank • Zosch • Zschech • Zwahr

REAL GERMAN NAMES

In other instances, owing in part to the Slavic roots or character of many 'real' German names (e.g. 'real' German names ending in -au, -ick, ig-, -in, -itz, -sch), the Slavic element is sometimes difficult to distinguish from either 'true' or 'common' German names.[6]

BAMSCH, KASPERICK, LORENSCHK

Bamsch • Bartsch • Blumech • Buscha • Falke • Fasslan • Goreschel • Greulich • Handrick • Hausch • Helas • Kasperick • Kieschnick • Kubitz • Kulke • Kunze • Kupitz • Lorenschk • Lowke • Mathiez

NERETTIG, PROSKE, SYNNATSCHK

Mertink • Mitschke • Mohle • Mooske • Nerettig • Niemtschk • Nietsche • Olbrich • Pantik • Patschke • Pietsch • Pillack • Proske • Schatte • Schautschick • Schellnick • Stephan • Synnatschk • Thun • Wenke • Wurm

GERMAN NAMES

A good number of Texas Serbs are recorded with common German names (e.g. Bernstein), apparent German (e.g. Kasper) or apparent non-Slavic names (e.g. Pallmer).

BERNSTEIN, BUCKHORN, MEISSNER

Arldt • Becker • Behrens • Beisert • Bernstein • Birnbaum • Boerger • Buchkhorn • Dressler • Dutschmann • Engelke • Farrack • Forster • Fritsche • Graf • Haken • Heintz • Hilscher • Iselt • Kasper • Kiesling • Lammert • Lehmann • Meissner

NEUMANN, SCHUBERT, WAGNER

Neumann • Oertel • Pallmer • Proft • Reidel • Ritter • Schmidt • Schramm • Schroeder • Schubert • Schulz • Schuster • Sedler • Teinert • Wacker • Wagner • Walther • Waschmann • Weise • Weiser • Werner • Winkler • Winter

ENDNOTES

[1] At roughly the same time that some *Luzica Serbs* saw immigration to the United States and Australia as the best way to preserve their language and faith, some *Luzica Serbs* felt a moral/patriotic duty to defend the Serbs in Serbia and the Balkans. This was true of the brothers Eugene and Pavle Jurisic, natives of Gorlitz on the Neisse in Upper Luzica (Izgorelc, *Yzhorelik in partibus Milesko*, 1131), who, resigning their commissions in Prussia's armed forces, immigrated to Serbia in 1876 and volunteered for service in Serbia's defense. Graduates of several

military academies, veterans of the Franco-Prussian war of 1870-71 (wherein Pavle was awarded the Iron Cross), the brothers served with great heroism and distinction in the Serb-Turkish war of 1877-78. Yugoslav sources summarize Pavle's service in the following words: **Na svim duznostima koje je vrsio, pokazao osobitu volju i hrabost. Kao hrabar, neustrasim staresina isticao se i bio je odlikovan.** At the war's end, Eugene, the older brother, returned to Germany, where he died in 1901. Pavle remained in Serbia, where hereafter, in tribute to the aggressive, storm-like assaults of infantry units under his command, 'Sturm' was added to the family-name. Serving with great distinction in the wars that followed, Pavle rose rapidly through the ranks, to the rank of general in 1912. In the Balkan Wars of 1912-13, armies under General Pavle Jurisic-Sturm's command played important roles in the great victories at Kumanovo and Bregalnica; in World War I (1914-18), in the even greater victories at Cer, Kolubara and Kaimakchalan. The great warrior and patriot's services came to an end with his death in 1922, a year after his retirement from active duty. Yugoslav biographical sources pay great tribute to Pavle's persona, intelligence, energy, character, and moral authority: **Visoka rasta, prav kao bor, dostojanstvena drzanja, ponosit, na koga ni teret ni godina, ni ratne teskoce, ni privatne nevolje nise mogle da uticu, on je ostajao vecito mlad i svez ... Imao je retku, neslamoljivu energiju ... Karaktera je bio crvstog i postojanog, iskren i posten ... Bio je vojnik u pravom smislom reci. Uz to odlican, pravedan staresinsa, pun takta, lepih manera; u drustvu ljubazan a na sluzbi strog, tacan i pedantan ... Nesto ga je narocito isticalo i pridobijao mu ljubav, privrzenost njegovih potcinjenih prema kojima je pokazivao pazne i takta ... Radio je i na strucnoj, vojnoj knizevnosti a narocito se zadrzalo na omiljenom mu rodu oruzja, u kome je skoro ceo svoj vek proziveo, na pesadiji. O njoj je napisao nekoliko rasprava, a njegove kritike manevarski radova smatraju se kao dela savrsenstva.** Pavle Jurisic-Sturm had three sons: Pavle, Momcilo and Pantelija. Fol-lowing their father's footsteps, all served with distinction in Yugoslavia's military forces; all were known and respected for their high personal and professional standards; for their positive Yugoslav patriotism in the best sense of the word. Born in Macva, Serbia, in 1881, Pavle's eldest son, Pantelija, serving with distinction in both Balkan Wars and World War I, also rose to the rank of General. As head of the Yugoslav government-in-exile's embassy at Berne during World War II, Momcilo Jurisic-Sturm occupied the most sensitive post in the Yugoslav diplomatic system, in New Order circumstances without precedent or parallel in European history.

[2] In sharp contrast to the Serbs, German settlers often went to great lengths to conceal their true identity. According to F. Roemer, while in Texas, he a German from Wittenberg who had been in our state for only a few years—who insisted that he had forgotten his mother tongue *(F. Roemer, Texas, mit Besonderer Rucksicht auf Deutsche Auswanderung)*. Roemer adds that this was often the case in America ... That it was also true of Germans in other parts of the World, especially in Latin America *(G.E. Engerrand, The So-Called Wends of Germany and their Colonies in Texas and in Australia, 1934)*.

[3] While *Srbi* is the modern name for the Serbs, in some medieval documents one finds variations similar to *Serbja*, to *Srbljem Bosne*. Serb rulers sometimes refer to the Serbs as *Srblye, Srblyi*. Ban Matei Ninoslav of Bosnia (1232-1252), always refers to his people as *Srbljima*. Later popular sources sometimes refer to the Serbs collectively as *Srbalj, Srbljah* as well as very many other variations.

[4] It is interesting and significant that Reverend Kilian's pastoral successors in Serbin, including his son, Reverend Hermann T. Kilian (1884-1920), were without exception men of true faith and high character, deeply committed to the spiritual and material welfare of their congregation, a simple fact is undoubtedly responsible for the number of Lutheran preachers from Serbin (i.e. J. Urban, H. Schmidt, B. Fritsch, L. Werner, B. Miertschin, G. Krause, W. Schulz, G. Blasig, G. Zoch, W. Urban, and T. Kilian.)

[5] **Texas Wendish Heritage Museum**, Route 2, Box 155, Giddings, Texas 78942-9769. Tel: 409-366-2441. Fax: 409-366-2805.

[6] Inasmuch as the greater number of organized *(Verein zum Schutze deutscher Einwanderer, 1844-47)* and unorganized *German* immigrants were from eastern Germany, from lands with the strongest Slavic element, where it is not uncommon for *German* surnames to have a certain Slavic tone and color, where one finds the personal name *Bogislav* favored by certain distinguished elements of the upper social strata, personal and family names are a less than certain way to distinguish *Germans* or *Germanized Slavs* from the *Serbja* of *Luzica*.

PART XXI

1. BEYOND REGNUM SORABORUM

The following chapters review important elements of the historical record relating to the size, location, cities, rulers, and policies of the better known Slavic nations of medieval Germania north and west of *regnum Soraborum.*

Some historians suspect that inasmuch as *Serb is the ancient name of all Slavs*, that the Slavs entered Germania as Serbs, that the distinct and different Slavic political-territorial entities were originally members of the great Serb family of nations.

Noting that *Serb is the ancient name of the Sarmatians*, an early 16th century German source describes the devolution process in the following terms. **The ancient Serb name was retained by the Slavs who settled between the Sudet mountains, the Elbe and the Saale rivers, while Slavs on the Wendic Gulf and the Baltic Sea were known as Wends and by many tribal names.**

In fact, far beyond the political borders of *White Serbia*, in all parts of Germania's *Terra Slavorum*, in parts east and south of Germania's *Terra Slavorum*, one finds evidence of an early Serb presence and settlement in the numerous place names derived from the Serb ethnikon.

Early evidence of a common Serb origin and name is found in a long chain of Serb settlements leading to Germania's eastern borders. Also in 6th and 7th century sources that refer to Germania's Slavs as *Serbs* and in medieval and later German sources that refer to the northern, Baltic Slavs as *Serb-Wends.*

On the basis of archaeological, historical, and linguistic evidence, some scholars also suspect that the great Slavic rulings-houses of Germania and Bohemia, namely *regnums Obotritorum, Luticiorum, Heveldun* and *Boemorum*, originated in *White Serbia*. On this subject, for example, B. Friedmann writes: **This kinship between the dynasties of the Abodrites and the Hevelli and their "southern origin" are substantiated by the fact, that the names of the princes of the Abodrites and the Hevelli show the component 'drag-' which is not usual in the dialects of the North-Western Slavs** *(Untersuchungen zur Geschichtye des Abodritschen Furstentums bis zum Ende des 10. Jahrhunderts, 1986).*

Two of Germania's greater Slav kingdoms, the *Bodrici* and the *Velici/Lutici* have deep and broad roots in the history of northern Europe.

The *Velici/Lutici*, also called *Wilti,* for example, founded one of Europe's first great cities as well as numerous trading stations along the Baltic and Atlantic coasts. It appears that the *Wilti* took part in the conquest and occupation of England in the 6th century by the Angles, Saxon, Jutes, and others.

The *Bodrici* were also a political and commercial power to be reckoned with in northern European affairs. In the early 11th century, for example, the historical record places the **Bodrici** alongside the Danes in the invasion and conquest of England.

One of the most intriguing chapters in northern Europe's early history was perhaps written by the mighty **Rugenites** or **Rani**. Some scholars, it bears repeating, notably Finland's Matti Klinge, suspect that the fierce, seafaring **Rani**, also known as **Ruthenians** and **Rusi**, not only played an early and important role in distant northern affairs, but they, not the Swedes, are the original **Rusi,** the earliest pioneers of trading settlements in northern Russia as well as the bearers of **Rugian** religious cults.

There is good evidence and reason to believe that the high moral-ethical content of traditional religion and the long, stubborn national-political resistance of Germania's Slavs to the more grotesque and inhuman elements of Judaeo-Christian civilization played an important role in preparing the ground in Central Europe for Hus, Luther, and the Reformation, in civilizing the predatory Roman version of Christian civilization. **Nowhere,** H.S. Chamberlain writes, **does the organic unity of Slavonic Germanicism manifest itself more convincingly than in this revolt against Rome.** Indeed, in the words of Chamberlain, the Germano-Slav population of Franconia, Saxony and Prussia is the most vital and dynamic part of the German nation.

Most historians believe that Germania's Slavic nations played an important role in the Slavic invasion and settlement of Balkan lands, of Danubian and Adriatic Serb lands. In addition to the Serbs, the historical record clearly and unmistakably documents the role of the **Bodrici.** The case can be made, however, that the recorded role of the **Bodrici** in Danubian affairs implies the presence of neighboring northern Slav nations, especially the **Velici/Lutici.**

A Byzantine source offers interesting and hard evidence of a Baltic Slav presence in *Greek* lands in the 6th century. Historian Theophylactus Simocatta records the following episode. In the year 592 three Slavs were captured in *Thrace.* The prisoners identified themselves as Slavs, *emissaries* from Slav lands bordering on the *Western Ocean* (i.e. from *westernmost Slavia*, from Slav lands bordering on the *Atlantic Ocean*). According to their account, the *[Avar?] Khagan,* soliciting support for a campaign against the Byzantines, had sent messengers laden with rich gifts to the Slav chieftains. The gifts were accepted. Later, however, given the great distance, the chieftains decided their armies could not take part in the campaign. The three bearers of bad tidings informed the *Khagan* of the change in plans. It took them, they said, **15 months to reach the Khagan's court,** a fact that tends to confirm the great distance of their *Slavia* homeland. Fearing that the less than pleased *Khagan* might not honor the law of emissaries, the right of safe return, they decided, at an opportune moment, to flee his court and take their chances in Byzantine territory.

2. BODRICI: GENS INDOMABILIS

The *Serb-Wends* on and near the Wendic Gulf and the Baltic Sea, centered in Schleswig, Holstein, and Mecklenberg were known as the ***Obotriti***, namely the ***Bodrici***. The following are some of the numerous renditions of the ***Bodrich*** name in medieval sources (e.g. ***congregati sunt Sclavi nostri qui dicuntur Abotridti***, *798).*

- *Abatrenis*
- *Abatarensis*
- *Abdriti*
- *Abitrices*
- *Abitriti*
- *Abodritae*
- *Abodrites*
- *Abodriti*
- *Abodritos*
- *Abotriti*
- *Abotridi*
- *Abotritae*
- *Abotriti*
- *Abroditae*
- *Abroditi*
- *Abrothidi*
- *Abrotidae*
- *Abrotides*
- *Abrotidi*
- *Apdrede*
- *Apodriti*
- *Habitriti*
- *Nortabtrezi*
- *Obodriti*
- *Obotriti*
- *Osterabtrezi*

ALFRED

Alfred the Great speaks of the ***Apdrede***: ***And be nord'an him is Apdrede, and eastnor', the man Aefeldan hact …*** A contemporaneous source, the *Descriptio Civitatem* records the ***Nortabtrezi***, with 53 civitates: ***Isti sunt, qui propinquiores resident finibus Danaorum, quos vocant Nortabtrezi, ubi regio, in qua sunt civitates LIII, per duces suo partitate.***

TERRA OBOTRITORUM

In medieval sources there are numerous references to ***Bodrich*** lands or *Obotritorum*:

- *Abodritorum*
- *Abodtritorum*
- *Legatos Obodritorum*
- *Maior Terra Obotritorum*
- *Provincia Obotritorum*
- *Terra Obotritorum*

Regarding the territory and ancient sites of the ***Bodrici***, Herrmann writes: **Von diesem Stamm war das Wismar-Schweriner Siedlungsgebiet, zwischen Wismarer Bucht im Norden und dem sudwestmecklenburgischen Sandergebiet sudlich der Schweriner Seen, bewohnt. Uber die Lewitz gewann es Anschluss an das untere Elde-Locknitzgebiet. Die Ostgrenze verlief in einem siedlungsfreien oder siedlungsarmen Streifen in der Richtung Bruel Schonlage-Julchendorf-Holzendorf, die Westgrenze gegen das Wakenitz-Schaalgebiet lag anscheinend in altslawischer Zeit in einem breiten Streifen von der Kuster uber Grevesmuhlen-Gadebusch-Hagenow. In jungslawischer Zeit wurde dieser breite Grenzstreifen wesentlich eingeengt bzw. in dem Bereich mit fruchtbaren Boden ganz beseitigt, und ein**

Ubergang des Wismar-Schweriner Siedlungsgebietes zum Wakenitz-Schaale-Siedlungsgebiet hergestellt. Das Siedlungsgebeit im Osten der Wismarer Bucht und des Salzhaffes mit den Zentren Ilow und Alt-Gaarz (Rerik) nahm einen 15-20 km tiefen Kustensaum bis in die Gegend von Heiligendamm ein, und war moglicherweise durch eine schmnale siedlungsfreie Zone vom Wismar-Schweriner Gebiet und durch einem breiten Grenzgurtel vom Warnowgebiet geschieden. In Wismar-Schweriner Siedlungsgebiet lagen die bedeutenden Burgen der Obodriten: Mecklenburg, Schwerin, Dobin. Zu diesem Stamm gehorte sicherlich auch das Gebiet am Salzhaff. Hier wurde in Alt-Gaarz wohl zu Unrecht das Kaufmannsemporium des 9 Jh., Reric, lokalisiert, und diese Lokalisierung sowie offenbar lockere Zusammenhang mit dem Wismar-Schweriner Gebiet war auch Anlass, hier die 'Rereger' anzusetzen.

REGNUM OBOTRITORUM
In medieval sources, there are numerous references to the **Bodrich** kingdom and crown: ***Corona Regni Obotritorum; Regnum Obotritorum.***

REX ABODRITORUM
Also to **Bodrich** kings (*reges Abodritorum*).

REX ABODRITORUM CEADRAG
- *Cedrag: Rex Abodritorum Ceadrag*
- *Ceadragus filius Thrasconis*
- *Dobemysl, rex Abodritorum*
- *Rex exorum Tabomuizlem*
- *Drasko: Rex Abodritorum Drasko*
- *Gostimysl, regem Sclavorum Gestimulum*
- *Obodritos ... rex eorum Goztomuizli*
- *Rege eorum ... Goztomuizli*
- *Unus ex regibus eorum interiit, Gestimus nomine*

GOTTSCHALK, REX ABODRITORUM
- *Gottschalk, rex Abodritorum*
- *Henry, Heinricus vocatusque est rex in omni Slavorum et Nordalbingorum provincia*
- *Niklot, rex Abodritorum*
- *Pribignev/Uto, rex Abodritorum*
- *Rastislav, Rex Abodritorum Rastislav*
- *Slavomir, Sclaomir Abodritorum rex et primores populi sui*
- *Sclaomirus rex Abodritorum*
- *Ceadrago Thrasconis filio datum*
- *Sclaomim ... in patriam remittitur*

SELOAMIR, REX ABODRITORUM
- *Seloamir, rex Abodritorum*
- *Svetipolk, Zuentepolco regio Sclavorum*
- *Zuentepolch ... direxit in provinciam Obotritorum obseditque urbem quae dicitur Werlo*

- *Stoinev, de Stoineffor barbaroum rege et mlite qui eum occidit*
- *Visan, Rex Abodritorum Visan*
- *Abodritorum rex Witzan*
- *Regis Wizzin, regem Abodtridarum*
- *Rex Abodritorum fuit is cognomine Witzin*

DUCES ABODRITORUM

In medieval sources, there are numerous reference to **Bodrich** dukes, to **Duces Abodritorum.**

BOLIZLOVO, DUX ABODRITORUM
- *Bolizlovo, dux Abodritorum*
- *Budivoj, dux Abodritorum*
- *Ceadragus Abodritorum dux, melioes ac praestantiores Abodritorum*
- *Dobemysl, Dux Abodritorum Dobemysl*
- *Ducem eorum Tabomuizlem rebellantem*
- *Drasko, Dux Abodritorum Drasko*
- *Drasco dux ex Dodelaibus alius dux Abodritorum*
- *Godoliub, dux Abodritorum*
- *Mistui, Abodritorum dux*

ABTRIDORUM DUX MITUI
- *Abtridorum dux Mitui*
- *Mstivoj, princeps Winulorum*
- *Dux Sclavanicus Mistiwoi*
- *Mistav Abdritis*
- *Nacocnis, dux Nacocnis*
- *Stoinev, dux Stoinnegui; occiso duce illorum nomine*
- *Ztoignavo, Duce illorum nomine Ztoignavo*
- *Witzan, Abotriti, quorum princeps fuit Witzan*
- *Abodritos, quorum princepts erat Witzan*

PRINCIPES SCLAVORUM

Also, to **Bodrich** princes, **to principes Sclavorum qui vocantur Abodriti.**

- *Ceadragus, Abodritorum princeps*
- *Gneus, principes Winulorum Gneus*
- *Mstislav, Obotritorum princeps Mstislav*
- *Pribislav*
- *Stoinef, Principem barbarorum, qui dicebatur Stoinef; duos subregulos barbarorum, Saxonibus ial olim infestos*
- *Naconem et fratrem eius (Ztoignav)*
- *Vratislav*
- *Witzan-Abotriti, quorum princeps fuit Witzan*
- *Witzen princeps Abotritorum*

NOTABLES

Also, to **Bodrich** notables (*meliores, praestantiores, primores, regules, sub-regules*) with unrecorded titles:

- **Boleslav** (married to Hodica, Mistislav's sister)
- **Blusso** (married to Gottschalk's sister)
- **Godoliub** (Drasko's brother)
- **Grin** (father of Kruto)
- **Lubomir** (Niklot's brother)
- **Slavinia** (wife of Kruto)
- **Svetibor** (father of Slavinia)
- **Zvinik** (Sventepolk's son)

VEL-GRAD, OBOTRITORUM CIVITAS

Numerous sources identify **Vel-Grad/Velgrad** (Great City), later **Magnapolis**, *Mecklenburg*, as a large and well fortified city and seat of ruling dynasts.

- *In Magnapoli ... quae est inclit Obotritorum civitas*
- *In Magnapolim, quae est civitas inclit Obodtritorum*
- *Magnapolis ipsa est Miklinburg*
- *Michilenburg, civitatem Obodtritorum*
- *Mikilenburg, civitas Slavorum*
- *Obodriti ... et civitas eorum Magnapolis*
- *Slavi de Miklinburg*

VELGRAD PLACE NAMES

Bobisce • Borisov • Brezno • Budisov • Bukov • Dobin • Gvozdy • Ilov • Jastrov • Javor • Jezerica • Lubenec • Lubesin • Lubimir • Lubov • Novetin • Ponat • Radogost • Radomir • Radotin • Rudnik • Scavno • Stitno • Tresno • Visemir • Visoka • Vitezde

ZVERIN

South of **Velgrad**, **Zverin** (Schwerin) was another important center of the **Bodrich**, strategically located, on the southern base of the Schweriner See, west of the **Polabi** and east of the **Warnavi**.

- *(Mstislav's) civitas Zuarina, 1018*
- *(Niklot's) castrum Zwerin, 1160*
- *(Guncelinus) de Zuerin, prefectus terrae Obotritorum, 1163*
- *Castrum Zuerin, 1164*
- *Oppidum Swerinum, 1164*
- *(Pribislav) urbs Zuerin, 1164*
- *(Pribislav) terram Obotritorum preter Zuerin et attinentia, 1167*

ZVERIN PLACE NAMES

Brusovici • Domamir • Gorica • Goreslav • Gorno • Kosobody • Krivec • Leso • Lubese • Lutosov • Mirov • Mostilin • Ovcin • Preseka • Pretocno • Radolube • Ratipole • Rogan • Sedlisce • Slava • Slavek • Trebov • Trstin • Vysoka • Zelezne

DUBIN

On the northern end of the Schwerin See, **Dubin** (*castrum Dubin; Dobinum; Dobin*) was an important stronghold and pirate base: *Dobinum, insigne piratica oppidum.*

ABODRITORUM, DUAS PARTES

Accordng to medieval sources, the **Bodrich** lands were divided into two distinct parts, each with its own territory and traditions, **Bodrich** proper and the lands of the **Wagiri** *(W. Sokolowski, Wagrowie, Slowinszczyzna Polabska, 1981).* Regarding historic **Wagiri** lands and sites, Herrmann writes: **Im Kustenbereich der Ostsee um Lutjenburg und Oldenburg erstreckte sich bis nach Fehmarn ein ausgedehntes Siedlungsgebiet, das im Suden durch einen breiten fundleeren Gurtel -die ehemaligen Walder Isarnhoe und Travena silva-von dem Siedlungsgebiet um Plon abgegrenzt war. Mittelpunkt der ostlichen Siedlungskammer ist seit altesten Zeiten Oldenburg gewesen, wahrend im Westen ein Zentrum um Giekau bestanden hat. Ein zweites Siedlungsgebiet lag um Plon bis zur oberen Trave, ein weiteres umfasste das westliche Kunstengebiet an der Lubecker Bucht von Neustadt im Norden mit Einschluss des unteren Travegebietes bis in den Kreis Grevesmuhlen, Bez. Rostock. Dieses Gebiet an der unteren Trave fand seine Fortsetzung Trave aufwarts. Bis zum Oberlauf des Flusses lagen die Burgen und Siedlungen in einem schmalen Streifen auf beiden Ufern dicht beieinander. Nach Suden ging das Gebiet ohne erkennbare Grenze in das Wakenitz-Schaalegebiet uber. Die genannten drei Siedlungsgebiete gehorten seit altesten Zeiten zum obodritschen Stamm der Wagrier. Als Sudgrenze der Wagrier nennt Helmold die Trave. Aus dem Gebiet der Wagrie sind im 12. Hf. die Untergaue Eutin, Susel und Dargun bekannt. Susel lag im Kustengebiet nordlich von Alt-Lubeck, Eutin war eine Siedlungskammer des Ploner Siedlungsgebietes. Dargun ist eventuell um Warder bei Segeburg zu suchen. Diese Bezirke des 12Jh. setzen, den Burgen nach zu urteilen, die Siedlungs-tradition der altslawischen Zeit fort ... Im Travegeiet ware dann, wie in zahlreichen anderen Fallen, der Fluss gleichermassen als Ruckgrat des Siedlungsgebietes auch namengebend fur die Siedlungseinheit an seinen Ufern gewesen.**

POPULUS ... QUI ABOTRI ET WARI VOCANTUR

Medieval sources sometimes refer to the **Bodrich** in the following dualities:

- *Populus istius, qui Abotri et Wari vocantur*
- *Waigiri et Obodriti; Warris et Abdritis*

TRAVA

Various sources identify the the *Trava River* with the **Wagiri: *Travenna flumen est, quod per Waigros currit in mare Barbarum.*** According to Helmold, the *Trava* seprates the **Wagiri** from the **Obodriti: On crossing the river Trave, then, one comes into our province of Wagria.**

REGIONE SLAVIAE WAGHERE

There are numerous references in medieval sources to the lands of the **Wagiri**, the lords and masters of East Holstein or **Terra Wagiorum.**

- *In partes Wagriae*
- *In Wagira*
- *In Wagiram*
- *In Wagirensi terra*
- *In Wagria*
- *Regione Slaviae Waghere*
- *Slavorum, qui olim Wagirensium terram*
- *Terra Wagiorum*
- *Wageren*
- *Wagirorum provinciam*
- *Wagirensium provincia*

STARIGRAD

It is clear from all sources that *Starigrad (antiqua urbs* or *Aldinburg)*, was the great city of the *Wagiri (eorum civitas Aldinburg maritima)*.

- *Aldinburg civitas magna Sclavorum, qui Waigri dicuntur, sit est iuxta mare, quod Balticum vel Barbarum dicitur* (Adam of Bremen)
- *Est autem Aldenburg, ea quae Slavica lingua Starigard hoc est antiqua civitas, dicitur, sita in terra Wagirorum, in occiduis partibus Balthici maris* (Helmold)

STARIGRAD PLACE NAMES

Belin • Brody • Crnobog • Devetica • Dobros • Drazevo • Gola • Grade • Greben • Jarovici • Javorno • Kapica • Klucina • Kozlov • Lesky • Malkovici • Milety • Mirkovici • Podluze • Polica • Posady • Prodanov • Ratimir • Rogalin • Slavno • Svartebok • Vrbica • Zalosov • Zelety

V'MORE (FEHMERN)

Regarding ancient *V'more*, Helmold writes: **There are also in the Baltic Sea, islands that are inhabited by Slavs, one of these islands is called Vemere (***insulae … quarum … Vemere vocatur***), is opposite the Wagiri and so near that it may be seen from Oldenburg.** *Vemere*, from the Slavic *V'more* (*in or on or by the sea*), known far and wide for its fierce pirates, was purely Slavic as late as the 12th century.

V'MORE PLACE NAMES

Badimir • Bojan • Carn • Dragan • Galin • Glaboka • Gol • Grad • Podgrade • Ratmir • Slava • Stopec • Tesimir

LIUBICEN, CIVITATEM SLAVORUM

It appears that the great *Bodrich* fotress of *Lubece* (*castro Lubece*) and city of *Liubice* (*civitas Liubice*) or *Liubicen* (*civitatem Slavorum, quae dicitur Liubicen*), later *Lubeck*, was in *Wagiria*: *In Lyubeba in Wagria villam, qui Cucline dicitur, 1203.*

LIUBICEN PLACE NAMES

Berislav • Brezno • Brodno • Bukovec • Crkvica • Domamir • Javor • Knegyna • Lokvica • Lutosici • Morina • Perun • Podlug • Pogate • Ponat • Radkov • Radogost •

Radost • Radovan • Reka • Slavomir • Sorbino • Sorby • Trebotov • Svartava • Vodnica • Zemici

KRUTO, BUKU

In the latter half of the 11th century, ***Kruto***, a ***Rugian,*** the leader of the great Slav rebellion of the 1066, and undisputed ruler of ***Universa Terra Slavorum***, will fix his capital on the island of ***Buku*** at the confluence of the Trave and Wochnitz rivers, a short distance from Lubeck *(W.G. Beyer, Konig Kruto und sein Geschlect, JbM 13, 1848).*

PRINCEPS SLAVORUM IN WAGRIA

There are occasional specific references to the rulers of ***Wagria***, to ***princeps Slavorum in Wagria*** (e.g. ***Zelibor*** in ***Wagria*** and ***Mstislav*** in ***Bodrich***).

- ***Selibur prereat Waaris, Mistav Abdritis***
- ***Alter vocabatur Selibur, alter Mistav***

TERRA POLABORUM

In the narrow sense, the ***Polabi***, also ***Polabingi***, derived from the Slavic ***po Labe*** or on the Elbe, refers to Slavs centered around the ancient city of ***Ratibor***, later Ratzeburg:

- ***Castellum Razeburg ... in pago Polabi***
- ***Comcs Polaborum***
- ***Pagus Polabi***
- ***Polabia***
- ***Polabingi, quorum civitas Razipurg***
- ***Racesburch cum terra Polaborum***
- ***Versus nos Polabi, civitas eorum Racisburg***

Regarding the territory and sites of the ***Polabi***, Herrmann writes: **Ein grosses Siedlungsgebiet bildete das Wakenitz-Schalle-Gebiet. Es reichte vom Travegebiet im Norden bis zur Elbe zwischen Boizenburg und Lauenburg im Suden. In jungslawischer Zeit erfuhr es eine betrachtliche Ausweitung nach Suden bis zur Elbe und nach Osten bis an die obere Sude. Es fand hier direkte Beruhrung mit dem Siedlungsgebiet um Schwerin. Dieses grosse, relativ einheitliche Gebiet war von dem obodritischen Stamm der Polaben mit dem Vorort Ratzeburg bewohnt.**

PIRATES

As with all the Slav nations on the Baltic coast, the ***Polabi*** were great and incorrigible pirates. Though there were numerous churches in the land of the ***Polabi***, Helmold writes: **Nonetheless, they were still not able to keep the Slavs from plundering. To this day, indeed, they cross the sea and despoil the land of the Danes; they have not yet departed from the sin of their fathers.**

RATIBOR, DUX SLAVORUM

Ratibor is one of the notables of ***terra Polaborum*** in the mid-12th century.

- ***Ratibor, dux Slavorum***

*   *Ratibor, illustri princeps dux Slavorum*
*   *Ratibor, tyranni Ratibor*

TERRA POLABORUM PLACE NAMES

Crnotin • Druzno • Duskov • Golica • Greben • Kneze • Kovali • Lesane • Loveca • Luchov • Lutov • Mostin • Murin • Radomysl • Rogoznica • Skala• Smilov • Velun • Visemir • Vojvoda • Voligost • Zalim

WARNAVI

Beyond the *Polabi*, writes Adam of Bremen, **are the Linguones and Warnavi**. Historians tend to center the *Warnavi* in an area between the Warnow and Mildenitz river, between but not including Schwerin in the west and Krakow in the east. Regarding the territory and sites of the *Warnavi*, Herrmann writes: **Das Mildenitz-Eldebebiet. Dieses Gebiet ist uneinheitlich. Wenigstens zwei grosse Teile lassen sich erkennen: eine Siedlungseinheit an der Mildenitz, vom Goldberger See und der Siedlungskammer um Dobbertin bis zur mittleren Warnow. Uber das Warnow-Quellgebiet einerseits und uber das obere Mildenitzgebiet anderseits hatte diese Siedlungskammer Verbindung mit dem mittleren Eldegebiet um Parchim. In jungslawischer Zeit wurde diese Siedlungskammer nach Osten erweitert und fand Anschluss an die Krakower Siedlungskammer und im Norden an das untere Warnowgebiet. Im Bereich des Mildenitz-Eldegebietes lag im 12. Jh. die terra Warnowe, und der Stamm der Warnaber wird hier anzusetzen sein. Weitere Moglichkeiten als diese Namensgleichheit bestehen zur Lokalisierung dieses obodritischen Teilstammes nicht.**

TERRA WARNORUM PLACE NAMES

Belov • Caple • Dobele • Golabov • Gorna • Grabov • Klodoraby • Kosobody • Krivec • Mostelin • Ovcin • Prisnotin • Ratipole • Sedlisce • Stolpe

TERRA WARNORUM

Archaeological excavations have revealed a number of important fortified *cities* in this area. In a recent study, in addition to *magna Radem* (1271) on *stagnum Radem* (1256), modern Gross Raden, E. Schuldt identifies the location of a number of cities in *terra Warnorum* (*In Gross Raden. Ein Slawischer Tempelort de 9./10. Jahrhunderts in Mecklenburg, 1985*).

1. Basthorst	6. Gaarz	11. Quetzin
2. Dabel	7. Goldenbow	12. Sternberger Burg
3. Dobbertin	8. Gross Gornow	13. Sternburg
4. Eickhof	9. Parchim	14. Wendorf
5. Friedrichsruhe	10. Plau	15. Woserin
		16. Woteno

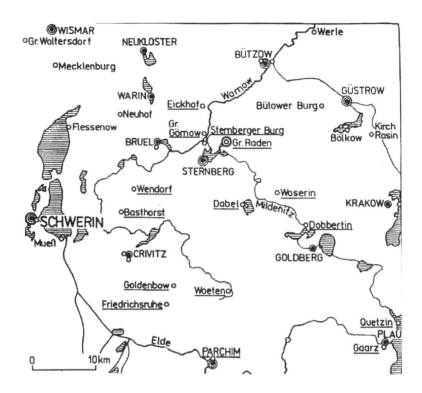

Fortified *Grads* in Terra Warnorum

Terra Abodritorum

3. DANUBIAN BODRICI:
QUI VULGO PRAEDENECENTI VOCANTUR

In 818 we find the envoys of the Danubian *Bodrici*, *Guduscani*, and *Timocani* at the court of Louis the Pious at Heristal, three nations that found it in their best interests to withdraw from an alliance with the Bulgars in favor of an alliance with the Franks:

> *Erant ibi et aliarum nationum legati, Abodritorum vidlicet ac Borne dusic Guduscanorum, Timocianorum, qui numper a Bulgarorum societate desciverant et ad fines nostros se contulerant.*

ABODRITORUM, PRAEDENECENTORUM

In 822 envoys of the *Bodrici* and *Praedenecenti* and other Slav nations are present at a general assembly held in Frankfurt:

> *In quo convento omnium orientalium Sclavorum. Id est Abodritorum, Soraborum, Wilzorum, Beheimorum, Marvanorum, Praedenecentorum, et in Pannonia residentium Avarum.*

QUI VULGO PRAEDENECENTI VOCANTUR

The *RFA* records that at Aachen in 824 the emperor received the envoys of the *Obodrites* who are commonly called *Praedenecenti*:

> *Caterum legatos Abodritorum, qui vulgo Praedenecenti vocantur.*

DACIAM DANUBIO

More important, we are told that the *Obodrites* called *Praedenecenti* live in Dacia on the Danube as neighbors of the Bulgars: *Et contermini Bulgaris Daciam Danubio adiacentem incolunt.* The *Descriptio Civitatem* appears to place the *Bodrich*, that is, the *Eastbodrici* or *Osterabtrezi*, in the same Danubia-Moravia area. In this area the *Vulgari* or *Bulgars* are followed by the *Merehanos* or *Moravians* of the Morava River valley: *Est populus, quem vocant Merehanos, ipsi habent civitates XXX. Istae sunt regiones, quae terminant in finibus nostris.* The *Bulgars* and *Moravians* are followed by the *Osterabtrezi*: *Isti sunt, qui iuxta istorum fines resident. Osterabtrezi, in qua civitates plus quam.*

BRANICABIN

More than a century later, al-Mas'udi at one point mentions the *Istabrana* and at another locates the *Gussanin* and *Branicabin* (*Guduscani* and *Branicevci*) in the Danube-Morava area, namely near Branicevo in northwestern Serbia. It is the opinion of a number of authorities on the subject that Einhard's *Abodriti-Praedenecenti* are the *Descriptio Civitatem's Osterabtrezi* are al-Mas'udi's *Abodriti-Istabrana* or *Istbrana-Branicabin* (*Branicevci*).

DANUBE, TISA, MURES

Later attempts to identify and locate the Danubian **Bodrich** suggest that the **Bodrich** were called **Praedenecenti** only in the Branicevo area. Elsewhere, namely along the Danube, Tisa and Mures rivers, the onomastic evidence suggests that they were known by their proper name. A 1730 study by two German historians, places the **Bodrich** in southern Hungary, between the Danube and Tisza rivers, an area where one finds traces of the **Bodrich** in place names, toponyms, and hydronyms *(C. Schottigen, G. Kreysig, Diplomatische und Curieuse Nachlese der Historie von Ober-Sachsen und Angrentzenden Landern).*

SERBULJANI, SERBLI, SERBLII

According to a slightly later source, over time the **Bodrich** were known as **Serbs** *(Topografia Magnil Regni Hungaraie, 1750):*

> **The Bodrich settled in Aurelian's Dacia, on the Danube and the Isker, and were neighbors of the Bulgars. It is said that the Bodrich were later known as Serbuljani, Serbli, and Serblii.**

THAFNEZI SERBS

It is interesting that in this same general Danubian-Moravian area (Moesia Inferior), according to H. Kunstmann, the *Descriptio Civitatem* identifies the territorial base of a great mass of Serbs *(257 civitats)* recorded as **Thafnezi: Thafnezi habent civitates CCLVII.** On this point Kunstmann writes: **Ubertritt und Ruckkehr der Slaven fandem it Gewissheit im Bereich der unteren Donau statt. Das aber konnte besagen, dass unter den Thafnezi des GB (Geographus Bavarus) eine Gruppe von Serb zu verstehen ist, dies es aus der Gegend der Donaukast ells Daphne in den Norden verschlug. Damit liessen sich die Thafnezi des GB als eine Art Synonym fur Serben befreifen, wofur auch die verhaltnismassig grosse Anzahl von 257 civitates sprache.**

PRISSANI SERBS

Kunstmann also notes that the *Descriptio Civitatem* appears to locate another Serb group in this area, next to the **Thafnezi**, namely the **Brezani** *(70 civitats)*, who are recorded as **Prissani: Prissani civitates LXX.**

OBODRITEN UND SMOLJANEN

As is always the case, J. Herrmann's general and specific remarks on this relatively obscure subject deserve close attention: **Unter den slawischen Stammen, die sich auf byzantinischem Boden niederliessen, tragen einige solche Namen, die im Norden wiederkehren. Ausser den schon genannten Serben/Sorben sind das die Obodriten und Smoljanen. Die Smoljanen waren im 6. Jh. in den Rhodopen am Fluss Mesta zwischen Plodiv und Saloniki ansassig geworden. Ein Stamm gleichen Namens, der in den lateinischen Urkunden und Chroniken des frankischen und deutschen Reiches set dem 9. Jh. als Smeldingi, Smeldinger usw. Erwahnt wird, sass ostlich der unteren Elbe. In den Kampfen zwischen frankischem Reich und bulgarischem Reich in der ersten Halfte des 9. Jh. werden die Obodriten qui vulgo Praedenecenti vocantur gennant. Um 850 erwahnt sie der Bayrische Geograph als**

Oster-Abtrezi. Ihre Wohnsitze sind zwischen Pannonien und dem Bulgarenreich des 9. Jh. in der Nahe der Donau und der unteren Sawa, also etwa in der Gegend Von Sirmium (Srem) und Sinigdunuum (Belgrad) zu suchen.Der nordliche Stamm oder richtiger Stammesverband der Obodriten wird seit dem Ende des 8. Jh. in frankischen Chroniken erwahnt. Seine Wohnsitze sind zwischen Unterelbe und Ostsee gut zu umgrenzen. Wahrend der Name der Smoljanen nach der Berufsbezeichnung sowohl auf dem Balkan als auch an der Untelelber selbstandig gebildet sein kann, scheidet eine solche mehrfache, voneinander unabhangige Bildung bei dem Namen der Obodriten mit grosster Wahrscheinlichkeit aus, d.h. der Name verweist unds auf eine Verwandtschaft zwischen Donauobodriten und Obodriten an der Unterelbe.

TRAVA, TRAVJANI, TRAVUNIA

Of special interest is Herrmann's mention of a possible connection between Germania's **Obodriten** on the **Trava** River, the **Travjani**, and Illyria's **Travunia**, a Serb principality located between modern Dubronik and Kotor: **Schliesslich finden sich an der adriatischen Kuste zwischen Raguga und Cattaro, d.h. 200 km sudlich der Obodriten, die Travunia (Travnjane, Trebinje u.a. uberlieferte Formen). Die Etymologie ist nicht klar, vermutet wird illyrische Herkunft unter Angleichung an das slawische trebiti roden. Auffallend ist, dass auch im Bereich des obodritischen Stammesverbandes an der Ostsee-kuste der Stammesname Travnanye uberlierfert wird** (*J. Herrmann, Byzanz und die Slawen "am austerten Ende des wetlischen Ozeans", Wege Zur Geschichte, 1986*).

PART XXII

1. VELICI, LUTICI:
GENS FORTISSIMA SCLAVORUM

The Slavs between the middle Elbe and the Baltic were known for their great ferocity in battle and recognized far and wide as the bravest of the brave.

- *De durissima gente Luticeni*
- *Ferocissima natio barbarorum*
- *Gens fortissima Sclavorum*
- *Populi fortitudine celebres*
- *Populus ferocissimus*

VEL, VULK, LUT

Evidence of their great power and prestige is found in their several names. In chronological order, they were the **Velici**, from the Slavic root *Vel*, the great, mighty, powerful; the **Vulkci/Vuilci**, from **Vulk**, the Wolves; **Lutici**, from **Lut**, the Fierce.

SCLAVOS, QUI DICUNTUR WILTI

Beginning with Ptolemy's **Viltae**, the earliest sources often refer to the **Velici**, to Slavs mainly called **Vilti/Wilti**.

- *Sclavos qui dicuntur Huvilti*
- *Sclavos, qui dicuntur Vuilti*
- *Sclavos, qui Vulti dicuntur*
- *Sclavos, qui dicuntur Uilti*
- *Sclavos, qui dicuntur Wilti*
- *Sclavos, qui dicuntur Wiltrei*
- *Sclavos, qui dicuntur Wulti*
- *Sclavos, qui dicuntur Wylti*
- *Wilti vel Vionudi*

TERRA WILTZORUM

The lands of the **Vilti/Wilti** are mainly known as **Wilcia**, **Wiltia**, and **Wiltzorum**.

ET IPSIUS WILTIAM

- *Et ipsius Wiltiam*
- *Gens est Slavorum Wilti cognomine dicta*
- *Gens Wiltzorum, quamvis bellicosa et in sua numerositate confidens*
- *In Winnete, pervenitque in Wilcia*
- *Natio Wiltzorum*
- *Populus Wiltzorum*
- *Regem Wilzorum*
- *Reges Wiltzorum*

REGIS WILTZORUM
- *Regis Wiltzorum*
- *Rex Wiltzorum*
- *Sclavos in Wilcia*
- *Soraborum et Vultzorum*
- *Terra Wiltzorum*
- *Wiltia consequit in partibus aquilonis usque ad mare*
- *Wiltorum terras*
- *Wiltzorum, Sclavorum primores*
- *Wiltzorum regulis et nobilitate*

ALFRED'S VYLTE/VELICI
King Alfred's *Orosius* records the **Velici** as **Vylte: And eastnord Vylte.**

SLAVI QUI DICUNTUR WILZI
Owing to their great ferocity in battle, the **Velici/Wilti** were also known as the *Wolves* or **Vulkci**, also **Vilci/Vuilci** and **Wilci/Wuilci**, and their land, **Vil/Vuil/Wilzorum**.

ABATARENIS ET VULCIS
- *Abatarenis et Vulcis*
- *Abodritos et Wilzos*
- *Contra Wulzis*
- *Et Vulcis*
- *Gentem Wilzorum*
- *Gentem Vulzorum*
- *Illis Wilzi*
- *Obodritos et Vuilzos*

PARTIBUS SCLAVANIAE, QUARUM VOCABULUM EST VULZE
- *Partibus Sclavaniae, quarum vocabulum est Vulze*
- *Populis Wilzorum*
- *Sclavorum gentem, qui dicuntur Wilzi*
- *Sclavos, qui dicuntur Villzi*
- *Sclavos, qui nostra consuetudine Wilzi vocantur*
- *Slavi qui dicuntur Wilzi*
- *Sclavos, qui Vulti dicuntur*
- *Slavos qui Vulzi vocantur*
- *Winidos, qui dicuntur Wilzi*

VUILCI, WILIZI, WILCI
The *Descriptio Civitatem* records the *Vuilci*: **Vuilci, in qua civitates XCV et regiones IIII.** Einhard records the *Wilzi*: **Sclavis, qui nostra consuetudine Wilzi.** Adam of Bremen records the *Wilzi*: **Itaque cum multi sunt Winulorum populi fortitudien celebres, soli quatuor sunt, qui ab illis Wilzi.** Helmold records the *Wilci*: **Quatuor autem sunt populi eorum qui ... Wilci dicuntur.**

WELETABI
Einhard and others note the **Vulci's** primary name by stating that they call them-

selves the **Weletabi** (an obvious cognate of the Slavic root *Vel, Veleti, Veletici*):

- *Wilzi, proprie vero, ie est sua locutione **Weletabi** dicuntur.*
- *Qui nostra consuetudine **Wilei**, id est, **Winidi**, sua loucutione **Welitabi** dicuntur.*
- *Sclavos qui dicuntur **Vulsi** ... id est sua locutione **Veletabu** dicuntur.*
- *Natio quaedam Sclavorum est in Germania sedens super litus oceani, quae propria lingua **Vvelatabi**, Francica autemn **Vvilzi** vocantur.*
- *Omnes barbaras ac feras nationes ... **Welatabi**.*
- *Omnes barbaras nationes ... **Veletabos**.*

WLOTABI, WLOTABARUM

In the mid-10th century *Quedlinburg Annals* one finds the **Weletabi** recorded as *Wlotabi*: **Congregati Wlotabi.** The same source records the **Weletabi** lands as *Wlotabarum*: **Terras Wlotabarum.**

WALITABA, THE GREATEST OF THEIR TRIBES

One of the most interesting tributes to the age and power of the **Velici** is found in al-Mas'udi's commentary on the Slavic world. According to al-Mas'udi: **The Slavs comprise many tribes and a vast number of types and often war among themselves. One of the tribes, in which the kingdom (al-mulk) was of old, appears to have been at the head of a great Slav confederation in times past. Their king was called Madjak and his tribe is called Walitaba. The tribes of the Slavs followed this tribe in other times past. The Walitaba,** he writes, **were the purest of Lineage ... the greatest of their tribes and the foremost among them. Then the authority between these tribes was disputed and their political organization came to an end. Their tribes formed different groups. Each tribe placed a king over itself.**

LUTITI SIVE WILCI

Most 9th century and later sources, including Einhard, Adam and Helmold, are careful to note that the **Vulci** are the **Lutici** are the **Vulci** (*Z. Sulowski, O synteze dziejow Wieletow-Lucicow, RoH 24, 1958; Geneze i upadek panstwa Wieletow-Lucicow, KwA 70, 1963; Sporne problemy dziejow zwiazku Wieletow-Lucicow. Slowianszczyzna polabska, 1981*).

- *Dicti sunt Wilzi vel Leutici a fortitudine*
- *Gentem Vulzorum ... qui Lutici vocantur*
- *Illis Wilzi a nobis dicuntur Leutici*
- *Inde Wilzi et Leuticii sedes habent usque ad Oddaram flumen*
- *Lutitii sive Wilci dicuntur*
- *Ultra Leuticos, qui alio nomine Wilzi dicuntur*
- *Wilzos appellant vel Leuticos*

SCLAVI, GENS LEUTICI

Over time, the name *Lutici* as **in gens Lutici pagani, Liutico suis, qui communiter Liutici vocantur; Sclavi Liutewici, Vindelici et Leutici** and **Sclavi, gens Leutici** took precedence over earlier names:

- *Leutici*
- *Leuticos*
- *Liutici*
- *Liutizi*
- *Liuzici*
- *Liudicii*
- *Liudizi*
- *Liuthici*

- *Liuticense*
- *Liutewici*
- *Liutici*
- *Loticiii*
- *Luidicii*
- *Luidizi*
- *Lutici*
- *Lutiti*

DANUBIAN ORIGINS

Some scholars believe that the **Luticihians** cited in the *Russian Primary Chronicle* (**When the Volokhs attacked the Danubian Slavs ... those Slavs went and settled on the Vistula and obtained the name of Lekhs. Of these same Lekhs some were called Polyanians, some Lutichians, some Mazovians, and still others Pomorians; Sloveni ... sedosa na Visle, a prozvasasja Ljachove, a ot tech Ljachov prozvasasja Poljane, Ljachove druzii Lutici, ini Mazovsane, ini Pomorjane**) is an obvious reference to the *Lutici* and evidence of their Danubian roots *(J. Nalepa, Ljutici a nie Lutici w Povesti Vremennych Let, Opuscula Slavica I, 1971).*

WANDALI

As was the case with other Slav nations, in some instances, the **Lutici** are additionally identified as *barbarae*, *pagani*, and *Wandali*. An account of a 1046 campaign against the **Lutici**, refers to the **Lutici** as **Lutici** and as **Wandali**.

REGIO LIUTIZIORUM

Similarly, the lands of the **Lutici** were more often than not called **Lutici-orum** as in **Leuticiorum episcopus** and **episcopis gentem Leuticorum**:

- *Dux Liuticorum*
- *Gentem Leuticorum*
- *Legati Liutiziorum*
- *Liuticiorum comitatu*
- *Liuticiorum provinciam*

- *Regio Liutiziorum*
- *Terra Luticiorum*
- *Turba Liuticorum*
- *Urbs Liuticiorum*

MORE LIUTICIO

Lutici primacy in shipping and piracy was such that the Baltic Sea was also known as the **Liutici** Sea or **More Liuticio** in the early medieval period.

REGES LIUTIZIORUM

There are many references to the nobles and rulers of **Lutiziorum**, to its *duces*, *primores*, *regulis*, and *reges*, to **Cealadrag**, **Dragovit** (**rex Slavorum**), **Liub** (**regis Wiltzorum**), **Mistislav** (**Mistizlavum seniorem**) **Milegost**, and others. The following are typical references to **Dragovit** and **Liub**.

- *Cum primum civitatem Dragawiti ventum est (nam is ceteris Wiltzorum regulis et nobilitate generis et auctoritate senectutis longe praeminebat), extemplo cum omnibus suis ad regem de civitate processit obsides qui imperabantur dedit, fidem se regi ac Francis servaturum jurejurando promisit. Quem ceteri Sclavorum primores ac reguli omnes secuti, se regis dicioni subdiderunt, 789*

- *Reges Sclavaniorum, Dragitus et filius eius, et alli reges Witsan et Drago cum reliquos reges Winidorum, 789*

- *Regem Sclavorum nomine Dragovit, ep ipsius Wiltiam, 789*

- *Rege eorum Tranuito, 789*

- *Rege nomine Tragovit, 789*

- *Sclavorum rex ad eum qui vocabatur Drogoviz, 789*

- *Liutwidun regem Wilzorum, 820*

- *Duo fratres, reges videlicet Wiltzorum, controversiam inter se de regno habentes, ad praesentiam imperatoris venerunt, quorum nomina sunt Milegastus et Cealadragus. Erant idem filii Liubii, regisnWiltzorum, qui licet cum fratribus suis regnum divisum teneret, tamepropterea, quod major natu erat, ad cum totius regni summa pertinebat, 823*

Also: *Dragavistus regulus Wiltazorum, primores ac reguli Sclavorum; Dragoidus rex Wilciorum; Drogoviz rex Sclavorum; Tragovwit rex Wilciorum; Tranvitus rex Vulsorum.*

DUX, PRINCEPS LIUTICIORUM

The Holy Roman Empire's eastward expansion in the late 12th century moved the political center of *Slavia* eastward to less exposed lands. In the case of *Luticicorum*, northeast to northwest *Pomeranorum*. Thus successive rulers of western *Pomerania* will title themselves dukes and princes of *Luticiorum*.

- *Bogislav I, Dei Gratia Princeps Liuticiorum, 1170*
- *Bogislav I, Pomeranorum et Liuticorum Dux, 1182*
- *Bogislav I, Dei Gratia Princeps Liuticiorum, 1183*
- *Bogislav I, Leuticie Dux, 1186*
- *Casimir II, Pomeranorum Dux, Leuticicorum Princeps, 1215*

IN CONFINIO SAXONUM ET LUTICIORUM

With regards to *Luticiorum's* western borders, it is interesting and significant that a late 8th century source suggests that at that time the *Luni* and their one time capital city of *Luniburc* (modern Luneburg) were within the borders of Saxony and *Luticiorum*: *In locum qui dicitur Hliuni ... Liuniburc quoque oppidum maximum Ottonis ducis Saxonici, situm in confinio Saxonum et Luticiorum, 795.*

WESTERN TERRITORY, BORDERS

Regarding *Luticiorum's* western territory and borders, Herrmann writes: **Die Grenze zwischen und Obodriten ist unklar und nicht genau zu bestimmen. Sie unterlag zudem im Verlauf der Jarhunderte verschiedenen Veranderungen. Die schriftlichen Quellen dazu sind erst im 12. Jh. entstanden, also in einer Zeit, in der der lutizische Stammersverband zerfallen und seine Gebiete teilweise von den Obodriten erobert worden waren. Durch Ausdehnung der Siedlungsgebiete in** jungslawischer Zeit sind alte Grenzzonen beseitigt und das Problem ist kompliziert worden. Sichen ist die Uberlieferung, dass Obodriten und Warnower die bieden ostlichen Obodritenstamme waren, wahrend Kessiner und Zirzipaner zu den Lutizen bzw. Wilzen gehorten. Ebenso sind die Muritzer sicher nicht obodritisch gewesen. Die Wilzen-Obodriten-Grenze muss folglich in den Grenzgebieten zwischen den genannten Stammen verlaufen sein.

REGIONES IIII

According to the *Descriptio Civitatem*, in the mid-9th century the **Vuilci's** 95 *civitates* were situated in four *regiones*. Helmold records the name and location of the four regions in the following terms: **Then, beyond the sluggish current of the Oder and the territory peopled by the Pomeranian tribes, there lies towards the west the country of the Winuli, of those, namely, who are called Tholenzi and Redarii. Their town is the very widely known Rethra ... Next one comes to the Circipani and Kicini whom the Peene River and the town of Demmin separate from the Tholenzi and Redarii. The Kicini, and Circipani live on this side of the Peene; the Tholenzi and Redarii, on the other. Because of their bravery these four peoples are called Wilzi, or Lutici.**

POTENTISSIMI OMNIUM SUNT RETHARII

There are numerous references to the **natio Redarii** in medieval sources:

- *Militavit contra Redarios*
- *Inter quos medii et potentissimi omnium sunt Retharii*
- *Redarii defecerunt a fide, et congregata multitudine*
- *Visum est pacem iam datam Redariis oportere stare*

The following are some of the more common renditions of the name.

- *Redarii*
- *Redarios*
- *Rederi*
- *Rederrarii*
- *Retharii*
- *Retheri*
- *Riaderi*
- *Riaduri*
- *Sclavorum nationibus Riederi*

REDARIORUM

There are also many reference to **Redarii** lands, to **terra Redarii** or **Redariorum** in medieval sources.

- *Est urbs quaedam in pago Riedirierun Riedegost nomine*
- *Inpetum fecerunt in urbem quae dicitur Wallislevo in Redariorum provincia*
- *In Raduir*
- *In Radur*
- *Nuncios quoque Rederariorum et horum, qui Liutici dicuntur*

- *Provinciis Sclavorum ... Riedere*
- *Provintia Sclavorum qui vocantur Riaderi*
- *Radwere*
- *Redariorum provincia*

PODULIN, TVARDULIN

A 1170 reference to *terra Raduir* confirms the thoroughly Slavic character of this area in the late 12th century: **In Raduir. Podulin. Tribinsowe. Wigon. Cussowe. Tvardulin. Dobre. Step. Sovene. Privlbiz. Nicakowe. Malke. Kamino. Lang. Ribike. Tsaple. Nimyrow. Malkowe. Stargard. et Lipiaz cum omnibus villis suites in stagnum Woblesko, et sursum Havelam usque Chotibanz, et desertas villas. quae a Vilim inter fines Chotibanz. Lipiz et Haveldam iacent.**

CONVOCATISQUE OMNIBUS SLAVIS

As *Rethra* was one of the foremost political-religious centers in all *Slavia,* a true *metropolis Sclavorum*, the seat of *Redigast, princeps Demonum*, it was feared and hated by medieval Christian commentators: *Civitas Rethra ... in terra Luticiorum ... convocatisque omnibus Slavis,* 982.

SEAT OF IDOLATRY

The very widely known *Rethra* is, Helmold writes: **A seat of idolatry, where a great temple had been erected to the demons, the chief of whom is Redigast. His image is ornamented with gold, his bed bedecked with purple. The fortified center of this town has nine gates and is safeguarded on all sides by a deep lake. A wooden bridge, over which the way is open only to those who would make sacrifices or seek oracular advice, affords a means of crossing.**

CONCILIUM PAGANORUM

Adam of Bremen records that two Bohemian monks in disguise penetrated the sanctuary in 1050 while a *concilium paganorum* was in session, and, once discovered, were put to death *(Z. Rajewski, Problem Radgoszczy i Swarozyca, ZaC 4/9, 1948. H.D. Schroeder, W. Hornemann, Die Sitze der Redarier und die Lage Rethras, GrL 10, 1972-73).*

REDARII PLACE NAMES

Bezirece • Bodreska • Brezovici • Gnevotici • Jezero • Kamenica • Kobylanky • Lukov • Lysovici • Milesov • Nemirov • Nikakovo • Prilubici • Radolin • Smord • Stargrad • Trebotov • Visetin • Vojutin • Vokun • Vrbno

TERRITORY, BORDERS

Regarding *Redarii* territory and borders, Herrmann writes: **Das sudlich an das Tollensegebiet angrenzendee Siedlungsgebiet umfasste die Neustrelitzer Seenplatte von der Seenrinne von der Seenrinne um Mirow im Westen uber das obere Havelgebiet bis an die Lychener und Felberger Seen im Osten. Die Nordgrenze zum Tollensegebiet ist fliessend, die Westabgrenzung zum Muritzgebiet kann nicht allzu betont gewesen sein, im jungslawischer Zeit ist sie sicherlich als Siedlungsscheide ganz verschwunden. Im osten trennten grosse siedlungsarme Zonen das Siedlungsgebiet der Neustrelitzer Seenplatte vom Uckergebiet; die**

Verbindung zwischen beiden wurde durch die Siedlungskammern um Feldberg und um Naugarten hergestellt. Die Sudgrenze lag in einer wasser- und siedlungsarmen Sanderzone am oberen Rhin, sudlich von Rheinsberg bis zur Havel zwischen Burgwall und Zootzen. Jenseits der Havel fand dieser siedlungsarme Grenzstreifen Anchluss and den Templiner und Lychener Forst und schliesslich an die Grenzzone zum Uckergebiet.

THOLENZI

Helmold places the **natio Tholenzi** (also Dolenz, Tholenzi, Tholosantes, Tolensa, Tolensane, Tolense, Tolentz, Tolenz, Tolonseni) west of the Peene. The name is believed to be derived from the Slavic *dol* or alley, thus the **Dolzani** or **Dolezani**, thus the name **Dolenz** recorded in 12th century sources. German scholarship centers **pago, provincia, terra Tholensani** (**pago Tholensani**, 995) in the land between the Tolensee and the Peene, south of Demmin and north of the Kleine Peene.

- *Provinciis Sclavorum Tolensani, 965*
- *In pago Tholensani, 995*
- *Cum terris et villis scilicet Tolenze, 1170*
- *Provinciam Tolenze cum omnibus insulis suis, 1186*
- *In terra Tolense, 1264*

According to Helmold, the **Tholenzi** and **Redarii** were closely related, one nation in peace and war. **The Redarii and Tholenzi desired to rule because of the high antiquity of their stronghold and the great reputation of the fane in which there is exhibited of Redigast. They claimed for themselves special preferment in respect of nobility because on account of the oracle and the annual offerings of sacrifices, they were frequently visited by all the Slavic people.**

THOLENZI PLACE NAMES

Gostislav • Grabov • Javorec • Klet • Lescno • Lukov • Mirkov • Pribignev • Pribislav • Radkovici • Ratenov • Roztok • Svete • Teslav • Trebotov • Volkov • Zaval

TERRITORY, BORDERS

Regarding **Tholenzi** territory and borders,Herrmann writes: **Im Sudosten des Recknitz-Trebel-Peenegebietes und nordostlich des Muritz-gebietes lag das Siedlungsgebiet an der Tollense und am Tollensesee. Eas nahm einnnnen breiten Streifen beiderseits von Fluss und See ein. Schon fur die altslawische Zeit macht es einen geschlossenen Eindruck. Wahrend die Grenzzonen im Wester und Osten verhaltnismassig gut sichtbar werden, lasst sich eine zuverlassige Sudabgrenzung bisher nicht erkennen. Vielmehr bestand ein fliessender Ubergang in das Siedlungsgebiet der Neustrelitzer Seenplatte. Das Tollensegebiet wurden von den Tollensern bewohnt. Die Tolensane wurden auf Grund schriflicher Quellen des apten 12. Jh. Nur auf dem westlichen Ufer der Tollense, ostlich der Linie Demmin—Peene—Kummerower See—Ostpeene angesetzt. Auf dem Ostufer der unteren Tollense wurde dad Land Ploth der Havelberger (gafalschten!) Urkunde von 946 lokalisiert, das zumindest zum grossen Teil auf jung-besiedeltem Gebiet zu liegen scheint und den Eindruck einer pommershcen Terra des 12. Jh. macht. Fur das** ubrige Siedlungsgebiet ostlich der Tollense fehlt ein Stammesname uberhaupt. Mit Rucksicht darauf, dass die Tolensane ein Hauptstamm des Liutizenbundes waren, erscheint das Tollensegebiet als ganzes eher ein dem Stamm angemessenes Siedlungsgebiet als nur seing westlicher Teil. Die Sudgrenze des Tollensgebietes ist zweifelhaft. Es grentze, wie die haufige Wiedekehr seiner Stellung in den Urkunden zeigt (Riaziani, Riedara, Tolensane, Zerezepani) an das Redarierland im Suden und an das Zirzipaneland im Norden bzw. Nordwesten. Die Nordgrenze des Redarierlandes gegen die Tolensane verlief im spaten 12. Jh. im Suden des Tollensesees, ohne dass die Urkundenforschung endgultige Ergebnisse erlangen konnte.

CIRCIPANI

It appears that Helmold's location of the **Circipani** on this side of the Peene' refers to the river's west bank, to the land between the Peene and Reka rivers, south of Lubecinca and north of Malchow. There are numerous references to the **natio Circipani** in medieval sources.

- *Chircepene*
- *Circipen*
- *Cirzipen*
- *Czirzipene*

- *Zcirzsipanis*
- *Zerezepani*
- *Zirzipani*

TERRA CIRCIPANIA

There are also numerous references to **Circipani** lands, to **terra Circipania,** in medieval sources.

- *Circipinensis provincia*
- *Cirpania*
- *Cyrspania*
- *Syricipensium Sclavorum*

- *Terra Circipene*
- *Terram Circipanorum*
- *Terris Cyspanie*
- *Zirzipa*

CIVITAS MAXIMA

At the juncture of the Trebel and Peene rivers, on **terra Circipene's** northeast border with **terra Tolense, Dimin** (e.g. **in ostio Peanis fluvii civitas maxima est, quae Dimine vocatur**) was an important and autonomous political entity often cited in medieval sources.

- *Civitas quae Dimine vocatur*
- *Demina urbs*
- *Dimin castrum*
- *Dimin urbs*
- *Dimine civitas*
- *Dimine urbs*
- *Dymin castrum*
- *Dymine urbs*

- *Diminium*
- *Dyminum*
- *Insigne et nobile castrum Dimin*
- *Timin*
- *Timina civitas*
- *Timina urbs*
- *Timine*

As the following references indicate, *Dimin* was also a distinct territorial entity within *terra Circipanie*: *Dargun ... in terra Circipanie*, 1238.

- *Duas villas propre Dimin et unam in Circipine, 1178*
- *Duas villas propre Demmyn Woteneke et aliam adiacentem, et locum Dargun dictam ... et duas villas in Circipen, 1189*
- *Duas villas propre Dimin, videlicet Vozthroze et Losiz dictas ... de duas villas in Cirzipen, 1197*

BISHOP OTTO

In Christian circles *Dimin* was notorious for its stubborn resistance to marauding Christian missionaries, including Bishop Otto in the early 12th century: **For the inhabitants of this town, being as yet ignorant of God, were fierce and ill disposed to Christians, and we had come as strangers to strangers.**

CIVITAT DRAGAVITUS

There is informed speculation that *Dimin* rather than *Brandenburg* is *civitas des Dragowit*, the residence of one of *Luticiorum's* greater kings, *Dragovit, rex Slavorum* (789), a fact, if true, that would explain in some part *civitas Dimin's* distinct political-territorial status.

SERS/SERBS ON THE PEENE

One of the foremost German authorities on ancient and medieval German *Slavia,* H. Kunstmann is certain that the so-called *Circipani* or *Cirs* on the Peene are actually the *Ser/Serbs* on the Peene. The *Cirs* are *Sers* thesis is consistent with the simple fact that *Ser* and *Serski* are the ethnonymic cognates of *Serb* sometimes favored by the ancient and modern Serbs around Brandenberg (e.g. *Serski Casnik, Serska Novina).*

TERRA CIRCIPENE PLACE NAMES

Bogutica • Dobromysl • Drenove • Golica • Gnojno • Klobucici • Knegyna • Kosorov • Lubechin • Poduskovici • Poglove • Radoscevici • Rakonica • Rokytnica • Sarbin • Slavek • Srbin • Svakovici • Svecin • Trebomir • Trigork • Vrcin • Zabik • Zalim

TERRITORY, BORDERS

Regarding the territory and borders of *Circipene,* Herrmann writes: **Das Zirzipaneland war Anfang des 12h. Jh. in drei Provinzen geteilt, von denen zwei nach spateren Quellen annahernd geographisch festzulegen sind. Die provincia Bisdede war die Umgebung von Gustrow, also das Gebiet am Augraben bzw. Der oberen Recknitz, das schon seit altester Zeit als Siedlungskammer bestand. Die provincia Tribeden war der nordostliche Teil Zircipaniens, etwa dat spatere Land Gnoien: eine enge siedlungsmassige Verbindung muss seit alters zu der Siedlungskammer an der mittleren Trebel um Tribsees bestanden haben. Moglicherweise handelt es sich hier um eine alte, spater verlorengegangene zirzipanische Siedlungskammer. Der breite Grenzsaum, der sich zwischen dieser und dem rugenischen Kustengebiet erstrckte spricht dafur. Die dritte provincia wird namentlich nicht aufgefuhrt, von F. Wigger (1860) wurde sim um Malchin,** von W. Bruske (1955) **um Teterow vermutet.**

KICINI

Helmold also places the ***Kicini*** (***Chizzini***) west of the Peene.

- *Kicini*— **urbs Kicinorum**
- *Kixini*— **villas in Kixin**
- *Kizzin*— **terra Kizin**
- *Kizini*— **urbs Kizin**
- *Kizuni*— **urbs Kizun**
- *Kycini*— **terra Kycinorum**
- *Kytini*— **terra Kytin**
- *Kyzini*— **terra Kyzin**
- *Kyzhini*— **castrum Khyzhin**

KICINI, CHYZA

The name ***Kizin/Chyzin*** is believed to be derived from *chyza,* an Old Slavic word for house. German scholarship places ***terra Kyzin*** northwest of the ***Circipani***, south and east of ***provincia Rodestoch*** along the Upper Warnow between Kessin (***castrum Kyzhin***) and Wrle: **Wurle,** *situm iuxta flumen Warnou propre terram Kicine; in conventu populi in loco qui dicitur Werla* (*G.C.F. Lisch, Uber die Wendische Furstenburg Werle, JbM 6, 1841*).

URBS, CASTRUM WRLE

There are several interesting references to ***castrum*** and **urbs *Wrle*** and the ***duke of Wrle*** in medieval sources. Retreating from the great army led by Duke Henry, Helmold writes: **Niklot ... set fire to all his strongholds, namely Ilow, Mecklenburg, Schwerin, and Dobin ... One fortress only did he save for himself, Werla, situated on the River Warnow near the Land Kicine. From it the Slavs went out day after day and reconnoitered the duke's army and struck down the unwary from ambushes.**

PRIBISLAV, DUX WRLE

Following ***Niklot's*** death and the end of resistance, one of **Niklot's** sons ***Pribislav*** emerges as ***dux Wurle:***

- ***Post haec redierunt filii Nicloti in gratiam ducis, et dedit eis dux Wurle et omnem terram***

- ***In Kixzin, que pertinere solebant ad Werle, quas idem quondam dux consensu Pribeslai contulit Botissiu***

According to Hemold, ***Niklot's*** sons were less than satisfied with dominion over ***Kycinorum*** and ***Circipanorum***: *****Filii enim ... non contenti terra Kycinorum et Circipanorum aspirabant ad requirendam terram Obotritorum.*****

TERRA KYCINORUM PLACE NAMES

Bysovici • Chyziny • Druzevici • Gnevici • Gribnica • Kneze • Kusevici • Lipa • Lubkovici • Lusovec • Marlov • Nekrinica • Nikac • Pec • Prag • Radola • Ratibor • Recica • Ribnica • Slava • Tesin • Trebom • Zivina • Zverovici

TERRITORY, BORDERS

Regarding the territory and borders of ***terra Kycinorum***, Herrmann writes: **Die Siedlungsgebiet an der unteren Warnow war Wohnsitz des lutizischen Stammes** der Kessiner. Die Grenze diese Stammes sind in altslawischer Zeit bestimmt worden durch die breiten fundleeren, d.h. siedlungsarmen Zonen beiderseits des unteren Warnowtales und um Butzow. W. Bruske konnte mit Hilfe der altslawische Grenzzone in Verlangerung der Rostock-Gelbensander Heide zur Recknitz nicht erfassen und liess daher das alter Kessinergebiet bereits biz zur Augraben-Rechnitzniederung reichen, als bis in das Peene-Recknitz-Trebelgebiet.

———————— • ————————

VELZETIA, VELEYZETIA

It is interesting that the names of one or more autonomous Slav kingdoms or *Sklavinias* recorded in 8th century Greece are derived from the root *Vel-*, namely *Velzetia* and *Veleyzetia*. If *Velzetia* and *Veleyzetia* are in fact two different political entities, Toynbee speculates that the former were probably located within striking distance of Athens, the latter, in the hinterland of the Gulf of Volos. He further speculates **that the name Veleyzetia may survive in the name of the modern town of Velestino.**

SIEGE OF THESSALONIKA

Circa 602, the *Veleyzetia* play an important role in a land and sea siege of Thessalonika carried out by a number of Slavic nations (e.g. *Dhragouvitai, Saghoudhatai, Vaionetai, Verzitai*), the same nations **that had devastated the whole of Thessaly, the islands adjacent to Thessaly and Elias, the Kykladhes Islands, the whole of Achia and Epirus.** According to Toynbee, the kingdom of *Velzetia* appears to have had enough substance and staying power to be an important factor in the region's political affairs in the late 8th and early 9th centuries. In one such instance, it seems that in the year 799, the chieftains of *Velzetia* were involved in a plot to liberate the sons of Byzantine Emperor Constantine V (741-775), interned at Athens, as well as an abortive putsch against Byzantine Empress Irene (797-802).

RHYNIKHINOI

Another possible connection with the *Vels/Luts* of Germania is found in the name of another Slavic kingdom in Greece in the mid-7th century. At that time, King *Pervound* (*Perun?*), the ruler of *Sklavinia Rhynikhinoi*, is recorded as living in Thessalonika, wearing Greek dress and speaking Greek.

According to Toynbee, **the Imperial Government's probably unjustified arrest and execution of the Romanophil Graecized Slav chieftain Pervound provoked Pervound's tribesmen and their Slav neighbors into besieging Thessalonika.** It should be mentioned that in this instance, the Slav siege was broken in large part by ships bringing food and supplies from the Slavic *Veleyzetai*.

RHYN

Rhyn- is the root if the *Rhin/Rin/Ryn* region of *Velici/Lutici* lands in Germania:

- *Rinowe, 1216*
- *Terra Rynowensis, 1281*
- *Land Rhynow, 1376*
- *Oppidum dictum Rynowe, 1333*

- *Land Rinow, 1541*
- *Die Rhinow, 1854*

Ryn is the name of a Havel River tributary (e.g. ***In Renum ... Renus influate in Obulam***, *1238;* ***Inter Renum***, *1315;* ***Rine***, *1336).* It is more likely than not that the name of the river, region, and state is derived from cognates of the Slavic root *rin, rinuti,* connoting a fast flowing waterway. Regarding this area, the *Brandenburgisches Namenburch (Teill 4, Die Ortsnamen das Havellandes, 1976)* gives the following information: **Zum Lanchen Rhinow gehorten die Stadt Rhinow, Kietz mit Muhlenburg, Stolin, Wolsier, Wassersruppe, Witzke, Spaatz, Prietzen, Gulpe, Strodehne, Parey, Semlin, Schonholz sowie die Wustungen Glewe, Wetzlin, Trepzin und Steppin ... Die alteste deutsche Siedlung der spateren Stadt Rhinow ist die Muhlenburg, so dass sich der Beleg von 1216 auf diese Befestigungsanlage beziehen kann.**

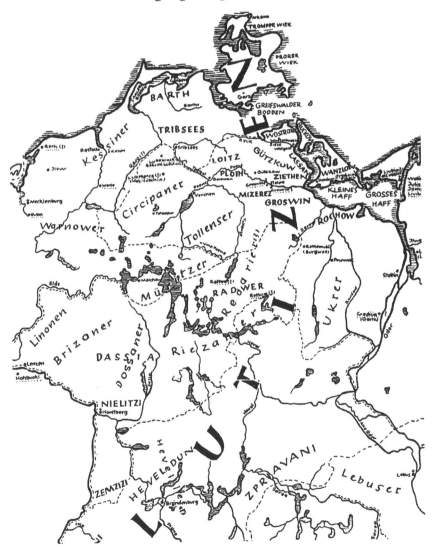

Regio Liutiziorum

510

2. REGIO LIUTIZIORUM

Following are some of the better known *castros, civitats, opids, urbs, provincias, natios, and terras* of **Regio Liutiziorum**, which, in some instances, are followed by typical village place names, by informative characterizations and commentaries from several biographies of *Otto, Apostle of Pomerania*.

BARTH
Provincia Barth, 1178

Blizno • Brezkovec • Chojnica • Carnkovici • Dababora • Glovica • Grabov • Plavnica • Ratiborici • Starkov • Svety Ostrov

——————— • ———————

BUKOV
Provinciis Buccua, 1193; Terra Buckowe et insula dicta Gniz et omnia, que infra; Penam fluvium sunt contenta, 1295; Patronatus ecclesie Cromin in ipsa terra Bucow site, 1302; Villam Cromyn, Tsys, Maltsow ... in terra Bukow et in terra Usenam, 1309

Gat • Jeromici • Knezde • Kozarevo • Kujavice • Lutkov • Malesov • Pole • Sekerin • Sinovica.

——————— • ———————

CHORICE
Provincia Chorize Plot civitatem, 948

——————— • ———————

CHOZKOV
Civitas Chozgov, 1128; Urbs Chozegowa, 1128; Villam Sclatkoviz ex burgwardio Gozcouensi ... Spasceviz, Dobol, Miriviz et Cossuz, 1175; In provincia Gozchowe villas Spaceviz, Dolpowe, Mireviz, Cossozuwe, Prossizovwe, Solathkeviz, 1178; In provincia Chozkowe villa Poluziz, villa Quilowe, villa Chabowe, 1183; In provincia Gutzekowe villas Bambic, Bubaliz, Dirscowe, Jerognev, Karbowe, Malescisce, Petzekowe, Vitense, campo Targossin sito, 1184-1233; Castro Cotscof, 1194; Territorio Gotzhowensi, 1228; Terra Guzzekowe, 1281.

TEMPLES OF GREAT BEAUTY
In this town there were temples of great beauty and marvellous design ... shrines of marvellous workmanship, images of great size and marvellously sculptured, covered too with most beautiful designs.

MIRACLE OF CHOZKOW
According to Christian sources, **Chozkow** was the site of one of the many miracles that accompanied the advance and triumph of *the one true faith*. At **Chozkow**, when the pagan shrines were being destroyed by the Christian faithful, **flies of unusual size,**

such as were never before seen … rushed from the ruins of the idols in such vast numbers that they darkened the whole of the district round the city and seemed to obscure the daylight by a hideous darkness … When, however, they were driven away by violent slaps of the hand, they kept coming and with no less insistence, till at length as the believers sung aloud the praises of God and carried round the standard of the Cross, a detestable monster fled out of the open doors and with the utmost speed made for the country of the barbarians who are called Ruthenians (natives of Rugen).

———————— • ————————

DARGUN

Castro de Dargon, 1173; Capellula in Dargon … quod et primum consecratum est in total Circipen, 1173; Dargun … in terra Circipanie … fundatum, 1238

———————— • ————————

GROZVIN / BROTVIN

Provincia Brotwin, 948; Groswin et Penen fluvium, 1178; Grotzuina, 1185; Terra Grozwinensis, 1233; Civitatis Tanclym et totius terra Groswyn, 1304;

———————— • ————————

LESAN

Provincias … Lesane, 1136; Terra Lassan cum opidis, 1295

Bogov • Crnotin • Gnevotin • Jarognev • Lubanov • Mokos • Prizir • Radesin • Sekerice • Slavoborici • Slavutov • Voligost • Vyblica • Zlatkov

———————— • ————————

LOSICA

Provinciis … Lositza, 1193; Racowe … majus et Racowe minus et tercium Pretuzhine, in terra … Losiz, 1232; Terre Lositz … civitalis Lositz … villas Rustowe, Rustowe, Mederowe… Drusdowe et Zarneglove, 1242; Ttres villas nostras … Gribenowe, Pansowe et Subbezowe … in terra nostra Losiz situata, 1248; Dersekowe cum molendino, in terra Losiz Gribenowe, Pansowe, Subbezowe, 1281.

———————— • ————————

LUBICHIN

Urbs Lubekinca, 982

———————— • ————————

LIUBIN

Liubin in littore maris sita, 1124; Castellum Lubinum, 1124; Lyubin, 1173.

———————— • ————————

MEDZURECANI, MEZIREC

Provincia Mezirech, 1183; Terra Myseritz, 1214; Provincia Mizeretz, 1222.

Blazovici • Bobolici • Budisov • Dirzkovici • Grabesov • Jelenina • Medova • Mokra • Mysetin • Nematovici • Parpatno • Peckov • Plotsk • Premcici • Radesin •

Sedlotici • Slup • Stolpe • Trstenici • Vosetin

———————— • ————————

MURIZ

Provincia Murizzi, 946; Provincia Morizi, 1150; Terra Moriz, 1185; Barbaroum natio que Moriz dicitur, 1200; Muriz stagnum, 1273; Muriz aqua, 1273; Curia Muritze, 1352.

Budkov • Chotun • Chvalisov • Crnov • Gnevy • Jamno • Morin • Palec • Popetin • Radochlin • Robole • Rokotina • Sulisov • Svecin • Vedrovo • Vysina • Zilov

RACE CALLED MORIZ

After five days spent in traversing it he came to a stagnant lake of great length ... There was there a race of barbarians called Moriz. When they had heard what the blessed bishop had to tell them, they sought of their own accord to be initiated by him into the sacraments of the faith ... They, however, declared that they would not follow the Bishop of Magdeburg, inasmuch as he strove to inflict upon them a yoke of cruel servitude.

———————— • ————————

OSTROZE

Ad locum, cui nomen Ostrozno, 1166; Wuztrowe castrum 1170; Ostrozna, 1178; In Ostrusim villam unam scilicet Mylziz, 1193; In Wostrozne: Darsim, Gubistiuviz, Gwisdoi, Merotiz et locum molendini in Caminiz, 1218; Villam Gwizdoy in provincia Wostrozn ... usque ad rivulum, qui Quezibrod appellatur ... usque in rivulum, qui Zroya dicitur ... usque in Puleznam, 1229; Woztrov, castrum cum villa in radur, 1244; In terra Woztrosnae ... Jarizin ... Inter Darsim et Beliz sive Lodizin rivulus, 1248; (In terra Woztrosane villas) Brusow, Budim, Cruselin, Cunirow, Gnuyentin, Golcow, Golletow, Gustebin, Latsow, Lodesin, Lubbenim, Malin, Nubo, Stevelin, Stilow, Trepelin, Virow, Warszin, flumine Tzise; gangriam Dersim (1250-1305).

———————— • ————————

PITINA

Terram Pytne vocatam, 1171; Terra Pitina, 1178

———————— • ————————

PLOT

Plot civitatem, 948; Terris et villis Plote, 1170; A Wolegost Penum fluuium sursum versus usque Mizerech usque Plote includens, et terram Plote totam usque Tolenze, ipsamm provinciam Tolenze cum omnibus insulis suis et terminis tota includens, 1186; Terra Plotae, 1249.

———————— • ————————

POZDEVOLK

Urbs Posduwlc, 1157; Castrum Pozdewolk, 1178; Villam etiam Sarnotino in provincia Pozdwolk, 1216.

POZLOV

Silvam, que laica lingua Vkersce wolt dicitur ... ad orientem versum oppidum, quod Pozlowe dicitur, 1239

PRISLAV

Castrum Prizlava, 1056

RECANE

Sclavorum nationibus Riezani, 965; Provinciis Sclavorum Receni, 973.

ROKOV

In provincia Rochov cum fluvio Klestniza et toto stangno Klestno ...usque Vccram fluvium versus villam Rochov terminum facit, fluvius etiam Lochnize usque ad locum, qui dicitur Nekloniza Mozt ... cum stangno Karpion usque ad silvam Komore, et inter duos fluvios Uccram et Locnizam nemus usque Liza Gora, et ab eodem loco videlicet Lopata... ad torrentem, qui dicitur Cemunicam, 1216; In provincia Rochow villa Sosnica ... Dambabora ... Lipegora, 1241

Dabagora • Gumenec • Karpin • Koblynica • Komorov • Kozlikov • Lukov • Pinov • Turaglova • Varsin • Vokunica • Zelechov

SITNE

Provincias ... Meserechs et Sitne, 1136; In provincia Schithene due ville: Rochoviz et Corine, et tercia pars villa Slavboriz, 1159; In provincia Scitene ... item villam Corene cum hereditate Nemanteviz, 1179; In provincia Scitene ... villa Corone ... ville Slavboriz, et super rivum Ribeniz, 1184; In provincia Cyten villa Mechomyrzk, 1214; In provincia Scytin sitos, Plachtina et Mancelin nominatos, 1231; In Sitine villa Chorene, villa Ribeniz, 1241; In terra Cyten, 1269.

STETIN

Civitas antiquissimas et nobilissima in terra Pomeranorum materqu civitatum, 1120; Gradiciam videlicet et Lubinum, que in confinio posita ad pagum pertinebant Stentinensum, 1120

Barnislav • Bogomil • Dobra • Goslav•Grabov • Jelen • Kamenc • Krekov • Myslitici • Plavno • Pomily • Pomorany • Preslav • Prilep • Rabin • Radkov • Radovec • Radsin • Repoglovy • Sadlo • Smoletin • Zalosov

WHICH FEARS NEITHER GOD NOR MAN

This people (Stetin) for whom you ask is a stiff-necked people, which fears neither God nor Man ... The bishop (Otto) proposed to go to Stetin with his assistants in order to convince its proud inhabitants of the wickedness of their apostasy. The clergy ... knowing that the people of Stetin were barbarous and cruel feared both for his safety and their own and urged him diligently not to go further.

POLAND'S CRUSADING BOLESLAV III

Situated on the west bank of the Oder, *civitas Stetinensi*, the first city of West Pomerania was also an integral part of Slavia, of *Regio Liutiziroum*. Stetin's capture by Poland's 'crusading' Boleslav III in 1121 and the imposition of Christianity immediately placed the city's fortunes in a downward cycle.

———— • ————

STOLPE

Locus Stolpe, 1164

———— • ————

TREBUSA

Terris et villis ... Tribuzes, 1170; Terram Circipanorum, que Tribuses contigua erat, 1182; Ad terram, que Tribeden vocatur, 1186; Tribuses autem et Wostroe ... sed a nobis habet in foedum dominus Jarimus, 1194; Nec terre Jeromari, quae Tribuses dicitur, 1198; In terra Tribuses, 1255; In terra nostra Tribuses, 1272; Civitatis et territori Trebetowe, 1304.

Bakovici • Borsin • Brdo • Brezkovec • Chojnica • Crnoglav • Dabec • Divici • Dve Gore • Glovica • Grubno • Gusterov • Jarosin • Kucin • Lobanici • Losica • Lubkovici • Morica • Negotin • Plavnica • Ratiborici • Sedlovici • Trebuz • Velegost • Vreskovici• Zale

———— • ————

UKRANI

Vucrani, 934; Sclavorum nationibus ... Ucranis, 965; Provinciis Sclavorum Ucrani, 973; Provincia quoque Vcra villa Gramsowe, 1178; Provincia Vkere, 1179; In provincia Ukra ville Bitcowe, Sarnotino, Caruviz, Mokle (1183-1216); Terram, que Vkera dicitur ... flumina Wilsna ... usque per medium paludis, que dicitur Randowa, a medio Randowe usque ... fluminis, quod dicitur Lokeniza ... usque ad flumen, quod dicitur Vkera ... usque in fluminem, quod dicitur Zarowa, 1250.

Bogomil • Budisina • Draze • Gostov • Gumenec • Jagov • Koblynica • Krasici • Lipa • Lipa Gora • Loknica • Lubenov • Milonici • Novograd • Plavno • Premislav • Recin • Smolno • Stolec • Trebeno• Veselic

BARBAROUS PEOPLE CALLED UCRANIANS

There were on the other side of the sea a barbarous people called Ucranians who were distinguished for their cruelty and savagery. When these heard news of the good bishop, they sent to him a number of messengers who assured him that if ever he should venture to come to their land he and all his companions would immediately be delivered over to a most cruel death ... The men of God then understood that the Ucranians were unworthy to receive the gift of the gospel ... judged the Ucranians unworthy to hear the world of salvation.

———————— • ————————

UZNOIM
*Civitas Uznoimi, 1125; **Oppidum Osnum**, 1166; **Urbs Ozna**, 1173.*

Divochov • Groby • Lipa • Lubomici • Lutobog • Miletin • Milotici • Morignevici • Parpatne • Pesky • Podglave • Radimici • Radostov • Rankovici • Sekerin • Slup • Stolpy • Struga • Zalotin

A PEOPLE CALLED UZNOIM
He (Otto) arranged to approach once more the territories of the barbarians ... of subjecting to the yoke of the faith another people called Uznoim which had not year heard the name of Christ.

———————— • ————————

VOLIN
The ancient and glorious city-state of the ***Volinyani (cum Sclavis qui dicuntur Vulini)***, centered on an island at the mouth of the Oder, was long considered an integral part of ***Regio Liutiziorum: De Luticis magna civitas Livilni*** (***Vulini, Wolin***), 1007.

Boguslav • Borutin • Crnoglovy • Dobropole • Domislav • Grad • Gradec • Gostin • Jarebovo • Kamen • Kosovo • Leska • Lubevo • Mezivode • Miroslav • Mokrica • Moravec • Poborov • Plusina • Radavka • Rakov • Rekovo • Sibin • Svatos • Svetoustje • Svetovec • Teslav • Trebenov • Trebesov • Visoka • Zagor • Zelislav

CRUEL AND BARBAROUS
We travelled by boat to Volin through lakes and lagoons made by the sea. This city is large and strongly built, but its inhabitants were cruel and barbarous. Approaching Volin, Otto's guide said: Father, we are afraid for you and your companions, for this people is fierce and unrestrained. If it be your pleasure, let us bring the boat to land land wait on the shore till dusk, so that we may not raise a tumult against us by entering the city in daylight. Shortly after finding shelter in a local safe-house or sanctuary, a very strong building made with beams and large planks which the people called 'stupa', the people, seized with a senseless rage, raised a great uproar and, armed with axes, swords, and other weapons, burst into the Duke's court, without showing any regard for it, and threatened us with instant death unless we fled from the court and the city with utmost speed ... It seemed for a moment as though the people would abandon their fury, but in their madness blazed forth all the more and, making a rush, they attacked the 'stupa' and overthrew it, dragging down and demolishing first the roof and then the beams... Desptached from Volin by boat, the missionaries were encouraged to take their

message elsewhere, to nature: "If you have a great desire to preach, preach to the fishes of the sea and the fowls of the air, and beware that you presume not to cross the boundary of our land."

POLAND'S CRUSADING PRINCE WARCISLAV

Volin's capture by 'crusading' Prince Warcislav and the imposition of Christianity in the early 1120s set in force the once great city's rapid decline and demise.

——————— • ———————

WANZLOV

Provinciam Wnzlov, 1128; Provincia Uanzlo, 1159; Provincia Wanloue, 1178.

Busino • Chelm • Crkvisce • Gradisce • Kluc • Leznica • Lutobog • Miletin • Milotici • Neradkovo • Radosov • Svinarovici • Tesetin • Vir • Zalotin • Zelenin

——————— • ———————

WOLIGOST

Urbs Woligost, 1123; Civitas Hologosta, 1125; Castrum Wolgost, 1184; Castro Waleguste, 1194; Terra Wolgast, 1236; Castri et terre Wolgast terram, que Vkera dicitur, 1250.

A VERY WEALTHY TOWN CALLED HOLOGOST

When Otto went to a very wealthy town called Hologost, he was informed by the wife of the town's prefect, that the magistrates and all the people of this town have decreed that if you should appear here you should be killed without hesitation. Later, after the missionaries were concealed, the enraged people burst in and searched everything and demanded with violence that the strangers who had entered should be put to death. A native priest stated the town's position in the following terms: What have we to do with a foreign god? What have we to do with the religion of the Christians? Our god is rightly disturbed and angered if, after all the benefits he has conferred, we turn in our folly and ingratitude to another god. But, lest he be angry with us, let us be angry with and kill those who are come hither to lead us astray.

EXCAVATIONS

Archaeological excavations have revealed a large number of hill-forts and other walled fortifications, often on or near waterways, often strategically situated on islands in *Terra Luticiorum*. In a recent article, in addition to Lieps in the Tollensesee, V. Schmidt identifies the location of some eighty excavations of old and young Slavic walled/fortified 'cities' within and along the borders of *Terra Luticiorum* (*Lieps. Eine Slawische Siedlungskammer am Sudende des Tollensesees, 1984*). In the following alphabetical series, in addition to map and numerical map references, in some instances the specific location is followed by county identification.

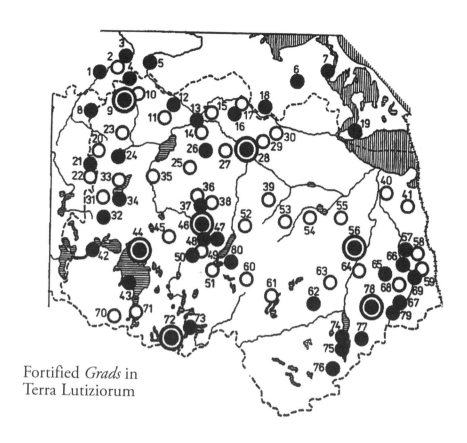

Fortified *Grads* in
Terra Lutiziorum

Northern Slavia

3. SCLAVOS, QUI DICUNTUR HEVELLI

According to the *Descriptio Civitatem*, next to the **Sclavi qui vocantur Linones** are those known as **Bethenici et Smeldini et Morizani**. Next to them, the **Hehfeldi** (Hevelli): **Iuxta illos sunt, qui vocantur Hehfeldi, qui habent civitates VIII.**

SCLAVOS QUI DICUNTUR HEVELLI

A central *natio* in **Slavia's** geography and history, there are many references to *natio* and *provincia* **Hevelli** in medieval sources: **Hehfeldi; Heveldi, qui iuxta Habolam fluvium sunt; Sclavos qui dicuntur Hevelli.**

IN PROVINCIA HEVELLON

- *In Mortsani, Ligzice et Heveldun, 937*
- *In terra Sclavorum in pago Heveldun in civitas Brendanburg, 948*
- *Terra Sclavorum in pago Heveldun, 948*
- *Castella et municipia in ... provintia Heuoldo, 973*
- *Provintia et pagus Heuoldo, 973*
- *Loca et castella in partibus Sclauonie ... Dubie et Briechouua in pago Heuellon, 979*
- *Loci Poztupimi et Geliti in pago Heuellon ... insula Chotiemuizles, 993*
- *In provincia Heveldon, 1010*
- *Urbs Brandenburg ... ex provincia Hevellun, 1010*

AQUA OBULA

Natio Hevelli and **provincia Hevellun** take their name from the hydronym **obla**, a name derived from an Old Slavic word connoting a twisting, curving waterway.

- *In Obula*
- *Aqua Obula*
- *Aqua Obulam*
- *Habola*
- *Iuxta Habolam*
- *Terra de Havela*
- *Inter Havelan*
- *In der Havele*

STODORANI

The **Hevelli** were also known as the **Stodori** or **Stodorani** (In the 10th century a cleric named **Stodor** (**Sztodorinu**) is recorded near Magedburg).

- *Ztodoraniam, quam vulgo Heveldum vocant*
- *Stodorania sive Heveldun*
- *Stoderaniam, quae Hevellun dicitur*

STODORANI, LUTICI

Medieval sources make it clear that the *Stodorani* were affiliated with the *Lutici* confederation. A 10th century source relates *Princess Dragomira* and *provincia Stodor* to the *Lutici* in the following terms: *Dragomira, de durissima gente Luticensi ... ex provincia Stodor.* A later source links the *Lutici* with *provincia Stodor* in similar terms: *gente Luticensi ... ex provincia nomine Stodor.*

On *provincia Stodor's* borders generally, Herrmann writes: **Das bedeutendste Siedlungsgebiet im sudlichen Lutizenraum war das mittlere und ein Teil des unteren Havelbebietes biz zur Rhinmundung. Dieser schon in alt-slawischer Zeit geschlossene Siedlungsraum hatte klare Grenzen im Osten (Barnim-Teltow-hochflache) und im Suden (Zaucherplateau-Sucha im 12. Jh., Brandenburg-Neustadtischer Forst under der 1009 erwahnte Fienerwald). Im Westen bildeten die Walder des Genthiner Landes und des Landes Schollene eine naturliche alte Grenzscheide. Im Norden sind die Verhaltnisse unklarer. Die Besiedlung ging in die des Rhingebietes uber. Es bleibt daher unentschieden, ob das Rhingebiet Teil des Havel-gebietes war oder ob es als eigenstandiges Siedlungsgebiet eines Klein- oder Unterstammes anzusehen ist.**

PRITZERBE, POTSDAM

According to Herrmann, two strongholds marked *provincia's Stodor's* borders in the west and east: *Pritzerbe* (*Pricervi, 948*) in the west and *Potsdam* (*Poztupimi, 993*) on *Chotemysl's isle* in the east.

BOGOLUBIC OF STODOR

One of the first recorded rulers of *Heveldun* is identified as *Bogolubic* of *Stodor: Bacqlabic of Octotrana*, 928.

BREZANI

The *Stodorani*, politically centered at Brandenburg, were linked with the *Brezani,* who were politically centered at Havelberg in west *Heveldun*: *Brizanorum et Stoderanorum populi, qui Habelberg et Brandenberg habitant; Omnem enim terram Brizanorum, Stoderanum multarumque gentium habitantium iuxta Habelam et Albiam misit sub iugum.*

BREZANI, NELETICI SERBS

Numerous sources indicate that the *Brezani* were Serbs, that *Brezani* was another or local name for the *Neletici Serbs* settled along *White Serbia's* northwest frontier. Indeed, Haveland's western capital, the city and and fortress of Havelberg was located in *Neletici province: Castrum et civitas sita est in provincia Nieletitzi.*

PREPARED TO DIE

The *Brezani* were long noted for their stubborn resistance to exploitative and repressive Christianity. Passing through the diocese of Havelberg, **which at that time had been so completely ruined by the incursions of the heathen that there remained in it hardly any who bore the Christian name,** Otto, Apostle of Pomerania, was informed that **the people had rebelled against their Archbishop Noribert because** he had tried to subject them to hard servitude, and confessed that they could not be compelled to accept teaching from him, but were prepared to die rather than submit to such a burdensome servitude ... They declared that if they were placed under another archbishop they would of their own free will gladly receive baptismal grace.

LUTICI NATIOS

In addition to the *Stoderani*, two other *Lutici* border *natios* are associated with Haveland, namely the *Dossani* and *Zamzizi*. The *natio Doksani* (*Desseri, Doxani*) takes its name from a hydronym, the Dosse River (*iuxta Doxam*). A mid-10th century source identifies two strongholds in provincia Desseri or *Dassia* (*Dosja zemja?*), namely *civitas Wizoka* and *civitas Pochlustim*. *Wizoka* is modern Wittstock, a town on the Dosse River, southwest of Mirow and northwest of Kopernitz and Lindow. *Pochlustim*, is Putlitz, a town on the Stepenitz River, northwest of Wittstock, near Milow, Grabow, Zierzow, and Marnitz. In the north, *provincia Desseri* appears to be bound by *silva Besut*, in the south, by *silva Roddana*.

Regarding *natio Dosane's* borders, Herrmann writes: **Ein weiteres eigenstandiges Siedlungsgebiet erstreckte sich am Dosselauf und an den Kyritzer Seen. Wahrend sich die West-, Nord-, und Nordostgrenzen deutlich zu erkennen geben, bestand nach Suden in das Rhingebiet ein fliessender Ubergang. Ebenso kann das Siedlungsgebiet vom Ruppiner Gebiet im Osten durch keinen allzu betrachtlichen Grenzsaum getrennt gewesen sein. Das Dossegebiet war von den Dosane behwont. In Desseri lag nach den Havelberger Diozesanurkunden Wizoca civitas. Der Name ist nach dem Fluss Dosse gebildet und das Stammesgebiet durfte beide Uferzonen nordlich von Wittstock bis sudlich Wusterhausen umfasst haben. Im Suden lag der Wald Rodane.**

DOSANI PLACE NAMES

Babice • Chorice • Drozdov • Jablan • Klepov • Lelechov • Leskov • Lugov • Myslotin • Plonica • Tesici • Vosece • Vostrozne • Zilovo

LUTICI ZAMZIZI

North and west of the Rhin River, *provintia Zamcici* occupied an area running along *provincia Desseri's* east central and south central borders in the west and *provincia Recane* borders in the east. Given the absence of solid documentary information regarding *natio Zamzizi's* borders, Herrmann's reading of the archaelogical-historical record is especially important: **Ostlich des Dossegebietes erstreckte sich das Ruppiner Siedlungsgebiet, das einen Scherpunkt am mittleren Rhin und an den Ruppiner Seen hatte. Die Abgrenzung durch weite siedlungsarme Zonen ist besonders im Norden und Osten deutlich. Uber das Gebiet von Lindow und Grunberg scheint eine Verbindung zum Havel-Finowgebiet vorhanden gewesen zu sein, uber den Rhin gelangte man in das langgezogene Siedlungsgebiet von Kremmen bis Rhinow. Der Zuzenwald schied beide Siedlungsraume voneinander. Das Ruppiner Gebiet wurde ... zum Gau Dassia gerechnet. Auf grund der schirftlichen Uberlieferung und der Stammesfolge in den Brandenburger und Havelberger Diozesanurkunden sind jedoch hier die Zamzizi zu lokalisieren.**

TUGUMIR

There is evidence that dynastic ties, namely the circa 930 *marriage* of King Heinrich's son Otto with a Havel princess and the birth of a male heir, led to early collaboration with imperial interests in *Slavia: Nobili tam erat genere procreata; de matre quamvis captiva et Sclaveronica tamen nobili.* It seems, that *Prince Tugumir* of Havel (*qui iure gentis paterna successione dominus esset eroum qui dicuntur Heveldi, dictus Tugumir*) had a role in Count Gero's monstrous treachery, namely the slaughter of some 30 Slavonic chieftains invited to a banquet in the name of peace and friendship around 939.

PRIBISLAV

In 983 Prince Pribislav's marriage to Mathilde (*cuidam Sclavo Prebislav*), daughter of Dietrich von Haldensleben, 'Markgraf' of Nordmark, in 983 is another sign of close dynastic ties with high-ranking imperial officials.

REX HENRY

In spite of such ties and collaborations, Haveland was Slavic in body, pagan in mind, and rebellious in spirit until well into the 12th century, a land notoriously unsafe for Germans and Christians. In the century's first years, the *Bodrichi*, headed by *rex Gottschalk's* son, *rex Henry*, ardent advocates of the Christian idea, served as defenders of state and church in Haveland. Helmold writes: **At one time when the Brizani and Stoderani, those, namely, who inhabit Havelberg and Brandenburg, were making ready to rebel, Henry deemed it necessary to take up arms against them for fear that the defiance of two peoples would bear a litter of rebellions in the whole east ... He went out ... with his very faithful warriors ... came to Havelberg to which he laid seige. And he ordered all the Abodrite folk to go to the siege of the stronghold.** In the end, Helmold writes, **the Brizani and the other rebels sued for peace and gave the hostages which Henry demanded.**

WIREKIND, PRIBISLAV

Later in the 12th century Christian beliefs and sympathies will compel two Christian Slav rulers, namely Prince Wirikind of Havelberg, where *Svarog* as *Jarovit* was worshiped, and Prince Pribislav of Brandenburg, where *Svarog* as *Triglav* was worshiped, to turn away from their 'pagan' brothers in blood, language, and history, and, instead, turn to their brothers in Christ, to Christian Crown and Church for temporal rule and divine redemption. In this peaceful and accomodating manner, dominion over the *Brezani* and *Stoderani* passed from native to imperial rulers.

GRADS

Medieval sources and archaeological excavations (e.g. at or near Brunne, Dyrotz, Golpe, Gulpe, Hohennamen, Klinke, Landin, Linum, Nedlitz, Plaue, Pritzerbe, Rhinow, Ribbeck, Stresow) combine to reveal a large number of *grads* or walled cities (e.g. *castrums Dub, Brekov, Novigrad, Prislav, Vrisak; castrum et oppidum Cosetsyn; civitats Bellin, Brandenburg, Cremmen, Havelberg, Kietz, Potsdam, Pritzerbe, Spandau, Ziesar*) surrounded by villages with quintessential Slavic names (e.g. Bogov, Bukov, Glin, Golyn, Gorna, Grabov, Krusevic, Lipa, Muzkov, Radovid, Sedlisce, Stolp) in Haveland.

BUKOV, KLADOV, MOGILA

Though situated in the center of nearly a thousand years of German history and culture, evidence of the Haveland's broad and deep Slavic foundations is found everywhere, in countless toponyms and hydronyms (e.g. Stepenitz). The same is true of Haveland's villages, towns, and cities. Today, as yesterday, a great number of Haveland's villages, towns, and cities carry names obviously derived from Slav names:

BAGOW, BUCKOW, GOLM

Bagow • Barnewitz • Betzin • Bochow • Boetzow • Bradikow • Bredow • Brielow • Briesen • Briest • Buckow • Buschow • Butzow • Dallgow • Doberitz • Etzin • Geltow • Gohlitz • Golm • Go

GRABOW, LUNOW, PINNOW

Grabow • Kartzow • Kladow • Leest • Lentzke • Liepe • Lietzow • Lochow • Lunow • Marzahn • Moegelin • Motzow • Muetzlitz • Niebede • Paretz • Pawesin • Perwenitz • Pessin • Pinnow • Plaue

RIBBECK, STOLP, ZEDLITZ

Plotzin • Prietzen • Radewege • Ribbeck • Riewend • Roskow • Sacrow • Schwante • Spaatz • Stechow • Stolp • Strodehne • Tieckow • Tietzow • Toeplitz • Tremmen • Wachow • Werni • Witzke • Zachow • Zedlitz • Zeestow

KREUTZ, CRUCEVIC

In a good number of instances apparently German sounding names are also actually Slavic in origin (e.g. Frisack from Vrisac; Ketzin from Cosetsyn; Kotzenband from Chocebad; Knoblauch from Chleboloky; Kreutz from Crucevic; Vehlefanz from Velevasy; Wassersuppe from Viatrosiby).

4. SCLAVOS, QUI VOCANTUR LINAI

The *Linjani* are one of several Slavic nations with uncertain political affiliations located in the borderlands south and southeast of the *Bodrici,* west, southwest of the *Lutici,* north, northwest of the *White Serbs*, and east of the *Dravani,* centered either in western *provincia Prigenicz* (Prygnitz/1349; Land di Prigniz/1373; *provincia Prignicz*/Prigenicz/1375; lande der Pregnetz/1388; in der Pregenitz/1416) or the province's southern and southwestern borderlands north of Havelberg, overlapping an area where two powerful Serb nations are recorded, the *Neletici* and *Siusli.* There are numerous references to the *Linjani* in medieval sources.

ULTRA ALBIA, AD ILLOS SCLAVOS, QUI VOCANTUR LINAI
- *Ultra Albia, ad illos Sclavos, qui vocantur Linai, 808*
- *Sunt Sclavi quidam Lini cognomine dicti, 808*
- *Linones et* Smeldingos, *808*
- *Trans Albiam in Linones, 810*
- *Unum trans Albiam, qui Hilinones debellavit, 810*
- *Unum trans Albiam, qui Hylviones debellavit, 810*

ULTRA ALBIAM AD ILLOS SCLAVOS QUI NOMINATUR LANAI
- *Ultra Albiam ad illos Sclavos qui nominatur Lanai,* 811
- *Trans Albin in Linones, 811*
- *Trans Albiam in Limones, 811*
- *Linones, 839*
- *Linaa, 850*
- *Linones, 858*

SCLAVI QUI VOCANTUR LINONES
- *Sclavi qui vocantur Linones, 877*
- *Linagga, 946*
- *Linoges, 1057*
- *Linagga, 1150*
- *Lini sive Linoges, 1168*
- *Lingnones, 1172*
- *In provinciis ... Linagga, 1179*

SEVEN CIVITATS
According to *Descriptio Civitatem* the *Linjani* were a relatively small *natio* with only 7 *civitats*: *Linaa est populus, qui habet civitates VII.*

BETINS, SMOLINS, MORACIANI
The same source locates the *Linjani* near the *Betins* and *Moraciani* (roughly speaking, an area bounded by the Havel, Stremme, Uchte, Milde, Dosse, and Stepenitz rivers): *Linaa ... Propre illis resident, quos vocant Bethenici et Smeldingon et Morizani.*

SIUSLI

A later 9th century source identifies the **Linjani** as neighbors of the **Siusli Serbs**: *Sclavi, qui vocantur Linones et Siusli eorumque vicini.* By placing elements of the **Siusli** near the **Linjani**, the statement tends to confirm the once great range of the **Siusli Serbs**, centered between the Mulde and Saale rivers in **White Serbia's** heartland, and suggests that some of the nations recorded south of the **Linjani** are **Siusli Serbs** called by other names.

NELETICI, DOKSANI

A mid-10th century source places *provincia Linagga* near the Havelberg **Neletici** and the **Dosani** centered on the Dosse River northeast of Havelberg: *Provinciae Nieletizi, Desseri, Linagga.*

WIZOKA CIVITATEM, SILVA NOSTRA RODANA

J. Herrmann centers the **Doksani** (*Desseri*/946; *Doxani*/1074; *Desseri*/1150; *Desseri*/1179) in an area between Wittstock (***Wizoka civitatem***) in the north and the Rodane forest (***silva nostra Rodana***/1240) in the south: **Nach Norden reichte es bis Wittstock, im Suden befand sich das Waldgebiet Rodane.**

DOSOV

In this area, south of ***Wizoka civitatem***, medieval sources record an important **Doksani** stronghold at Dosov, modern Dossow: *Dosse*/1273; ***opidi dicti Dossa***/1274; *in Dossov*/1295; ***Opidi Magna Dosse***/1316; ***Opidum quod dicitur Maior Dossa***/1325; **Stedlein Dosso**, *Dossow*/1541.

POLABINGI

A mid-11th century source locates the **Linjani** south of the **Bodrici** called **Polabingi**: *Populi Sclavorum Waigri, Obodriti vel Reregi vel Polabingi, Linoges.*

PROVINCIA LINAGGA

Scholars tend to center ***provincia Linagga*** between the Elbe and Elde rivers, between Lenzen (***urbs Lunkini***) in the south and Malchow in the north. Regarding the territory, borders, and neighbors of ***provincia Linagga***, Herrmann writes: **Im Westen und Osten wurde es durch grosse Grenzwalder von den Polaben und Wilzen geschieden; zweifehalft ist die Grenze im Bereich der Lewitzwanne und an der Mittelelde. Von den Nieletici (Brizanen) um Havelburg waren die Linonen durch Walder und Sumpfe getrennt, deren Bewaltigung fur eine Kriegstruppe zwei Tage dauerte ... Die relative weite Ausdehnung des Linnonenstammes uber ein dichtbesiedeltes Gebiet erklart ohne weiteres sine Starke, die sich in seiner wierdeholten politischen Aktivitat Zeigte. Im Westen der Elde um Menkendorf wurde ... der Stamm der Smeldinger lokalisiert. Das ist nicht sicher zu begrunden. Verschiedene Quellen scheinen hier sogar die Ansetzung der Smeldinger zu verbeiten. Die siedlungsmassigen Voraussetzungen sprechen gleichfalls nicht dafur. Es ist unwahrscheinlich, dass der starke Stamm der Linonen uber langere Zeit einen kleinen Stamm wie den der Smeldinger in seinem Siedlungsgebiet als politisch selbstandige Einheit bestehen liess.**

POLITICAL STATUS

There are several interesting and informative references relating to the political affiliations and status of the *Linjani* and their neighbors in 8th and 9th century sources. A late 8th century source appears to place the *provincia* within *Regnum Obotritorum's* sphere of influence: **[The king] entered Saxony with an army and reached the Elbe at Lune [modern Lentzen]. At that time, Witzin, the king of the Abodrites [allies of the Franks], was slain there by the Saxons [enemies of the Franks]**, 795.

LENZEN

East of *Hanover Wendland's Drevani*, **Lenzen** on the Elbe in northwestern *provincia Prigenicz,* is the site of an ancient Slav city/stronghold.

- *Urbem obsidere quae dicitur Lunkini, 929*
- *Castrum Lunzini, 929*
- *Lontio, in civitate Leontia, 1066*
- *In urbe Leontio, quae alio nomine Lenzin dicitur, 1163*
- *Lensyn terra, 1312*

LINJANI, SMOLINCI (SMELDINGI)

Two early 9th century references indicate that the *Linjani* and *Smolinci* (from the Slavic root *smol*, connoting pitch, tar) were neighbors and allies in wars against the Franks and their allies. **Charles, the son of the emperor, built a bridge across the Elbe, and moved the army under his command as far as he could against the Linones and Smeldingi. These tribes had also defected to Godofrid. Charles laid waste their fields far and wide and after crossing the river again returned to Saxony with his army unimpaired**, 808.

The following year, an old ally of the Franks, *duke Drasko of the Bodrici,* moved an army under his command against the *Smolinci.* **Supported by the Saxons, he (duke Drasko) attacked the neighboring Wilzi and laid waste their fields with fire and sword. Returning home with immense booty and with even more help from the Saxons, he conquered the largest city of the Smeldingi (*Smeldingorum maximam civitatem*). By these successes he forced all who had defected from him to join him again**, 809.

MAXIMAM CIVITATEM

The identity and location of *Smeldingorum maximum civitatem* remains less than certain. Some scholars believe it is *Smeldinc-connoburg*, modern Conow, near Mecklenburg.

- *Ultra Albiam et fregerung unam civitatem cum nostris Hwinidis, qua appellatur Smeldinc-connoburg, 809*
- *Nostris Huninidis qui appelantur Semeldinc, Connoburg, 809*
- *Nostris Guinidinis que appellatur Semeldinc-connoburg, 809*

Others are less certain. For example, Herrmann writes: **Bei Menkendorf glaubte er die 809 zerstorte Smeldingorum maximam civitatem gedunden zu haben. Danach** setze er die Smeldinger an "zwischen Sude un Elde" im wesentlichen die heutige Jabelheide bewohnend und daher das Obodritenland von der Elbe trennend.

LINJANI, BETINICI

Several years later the same source relates the *Linjani* to the *Betenici*, a nation bordering on the Havelberg *Neletici*, centered in an area bound by the Karthane, Elbe, Havel, and Dosse rivers *(Z. Sulowski, Bethenici et Smeldingon. Przyczinek do krytki Geografa Bawarskiego, Studia Historica H. Lowmanskiego, 1958).*

- *Ultra Albiam ad illos Sclavos qui nominatur Lane et Bethenzr, 811*
- *Sclavos qui nominantur Lanai et Bethenzr, 811*
- *Sclavos qui nominantur Lanai et Bechelenzi, 811*

LINJANI, WILZI

It appears that *castrum Hohbuoki* (scholars tend to place *castrum Hohbuoki* southwest of Lenzen on the opposite or left bank of the Elbe) was in *provincia Linaa* and well within the sphere of *Regnum Wiltzorum's* strategic interests and operations. **It was reported that ... the castle of Hohbuoki on the Elbe, with Odo, the emperor's envoy, and a garrison of East Saxons, had been captured by the Wilzi, 810; One army went beyond the Elbe against the Linones, which ravaged their territory nd restored the castle of Hohbuoki on the Elbe destroyed by the Wilzis in the previous year, 811.**

LINONES, ABODRITES

Several decades later an imperial campaign allies the *Linjani* with the *Abodrites*. **Two expeditions were mounted: a Saxon one against the attacks of the Serbs and Wilzis who have recently left several villages of the Saxon March in flames; and a combined Austraian-Thuringian one against the rebellious Abodrites and the people called the Linones, 839.**

DUKE MISTIVOI

In the early 12th century, circa 1112, there is an interesting reference to the *Linjani* in Helmold's *Chronica Slavorum*, namely the raid and plunder of *Linjani* lands by a *Bodrich* army under the command of *Duke Mistivoi*, son of King Henry. While the main *Bodrich* force under Henry laid siege to rebel Slavs (*Brezani*) at Havelberg, a siege that wore into days and months, Helmold writes: **Mistivoi was informed that there was a nearby folk rich in all kinds of wealth and that its people were peaceful and suspicious of no disturbance. These Slavs were called Lini or Linoges. Without consulting his father, Mistivoi, at the head of an army of picked men, attacked the Lini. Bursting upon the carefree and unsuspecting people, he took from them much spoil and made captive many of their men; and he went off heavily laden.**

It is also clear from Helmold's account that the *Slavs called Lini or Linoges* were not easy pickings, so to speak, that they fought the good fight to the very end: **But while they were making their way in hasty retreat through the more difficult parts of the marsh, behold, the inhabitants of the neighboring places came together and at once rushed forth to battle ... When those who were with Mistivoi saw that they** were beset on all sides by an immense multitude of enemies and that a way would have to be opened by them with the sword, they exhorted one another and with the exertion of all their strength annihilated the whole multitude of those who withstood them at the edge of the sword.

PROVINCIA PRIGENICZ

Medieval sources record a large number of Slavic strongholds (e.g. *castrum Preslav; civitat Visoka*) and villages (***villa Dobrisin, villa Kamenica***) in *Linjani* and bordering lands (e.g. ***Betenici, Doksani, Smolinci***) either centered in *provincia Prigenicz* or an area along the province's southern and southwestern borders.

BABICA, BELOV, BODIN

Babica— Babiz/1274 (Babitz).
Belov— *Nicolaus, miles de Below dicta*, 1318 (Balow)
Bodin— Boddin/1486 (Boddin)
Borentin— *Villa Borentin*/1337 (Barenthin)
Breza— Lutken Bresce/1441 (Breese)
Brezka— Breszk/1282 (Bresch)
Brla, Brlin— Berlin1277; *Maiorem Berlin*/1311 (Gross Berlin)
Brla, Brlin, Brlincin— *Ville minoris Berlin … cum duobus stagnis adiacentibus*/1274; Berlienchen/1649 (Berlinchen)

BUKOV, BOROV, CRNOTIN

Bukov— Bukow/1492 (Buckow)
Borov— Burow/1408 (Burow)
Caple— Stapel13412 (Zapel)
Cechlin— *In loco, qui Szechelyn dicitur*/1255 (Zechlin)
Cepov— *Ville Szempowe*/1274 (Zempow)
Crnica— Czernicze/1427 (Zernitz)
Crnkov— Tzernickow/1488 (Zernikow)
Crnotin— Zarenthin/1667 (Zarenthin)

CHOLM, DOBRA, DOLNI

Cholm— Gholme/1392 (Golm)
Dab-laka— Damlank/1275 (Damelank)
Dabrov— Dambrow/1250 (Damerow)
Dalemin— Dalemin/1239 (Dalemin)
Dobra— Dobere/1325 (Daber)
Dobrisin— *Curiam in ville Dobersin*/1322; *ante portam nostre civi tatis que dicitur Dobercynensis*/1354 (Dobberzin).
Dolni— Dolne/1344 (Dollen)
Dosov— *Opidi dicti Dossa*/1274; *opidi Magne Dosse*/1316

DRAZ, GARDEC, GLAVACIN

Draz— *Grangriam Drans*/1225; Dransz/1529 (Dranse)
Drenkov— Drenckow/1333 (Drenkow)
Drenov— Drehnow/1728 (Drehnow)

Drevin— Drewen/1338 (Drewen)
Dupov— *Wesselinus de Dupow*/1239 (Dupow)
Gardec— Garditz/1343 (Garz)
Glava— Glawe/1343 (Glawe)
Glavacin— Clawezin/1252 (Glovzin)

GOLICA, GORSKE, JEZERIC

Glina— Glinike/1652 (Glienicke)
Gol, Golov— *Plebanus de Gulow*/1299 (Gulow)
Golica— Gulitze/1542 (Gulitz)
Gornica— Gornitz/1581 (Gornitz)
Gorske— Gorcke/1344 (Gorike)
Jablo— Jabel /1418 (Jabel)
Jagla— Jaggell/1542 (Jagel)
Jezeric— Jeseritz/1652 (Jederitz)

KAMENICA, KOBYLA LAKA, KON

Kamenica— *Villa in Kemenitz*/1320 (Kemnitz)
Klesc— Klest/1541 (Kleeste)
Klic— Klietsche/1558 (Kletzke)
Klokov— Klokow/1395 (Klockow)
Kobyla-laka— Kobellancke/1571 (Kuhblank)
Klin, Klenov— Klenowe/1332 (Kleinow)
Kol-rib—Kolrip/1343 (Kolrep)
Kon, Konikov— Kohnickow/1762 (Konikow)

KOLIN, KOMARNICA, KRIV

Kon, Konov— Konow/1305 (Kunow)
Kol, Kolin— Colln/1780 (New Colln)
Komarnica— Kumernitz/1528 (Kummernitz)
Koselin— Kotzelin/1374 (Kotzlin)
Kovali— Cowale/1208 (Cowale)
Krinica— Krinitz/1362 (Krinitz)
Kriv— Criwe/1312 (Kribbe)
Krusov— Krussow/1558 (Alt Krussow)

KYRICA, LELECHOV, LUBIN

Kvicov— *Plebanus de Quitsow*/1299 (Quitzow)
Kyrica— Kiritze/1435 (Kyritz)
Lazk—Lasske/1492 (Laaske)
Lelechov— Lelechowe/1307 (Leelichow)
Lenovici— Lennewitz/1588 (Lennewitz)
Lepin— Lepin/1248 (Gross Leppin)
Lom— *Ville Lom*/1343 (Lohm)
Lubin— *In ville Luben*/1339 (Gross Luben)

LUBISOV, MILOV, MOKRA GOLA

Lubisov— Lubbezow/1319 (Lubzow)
Melin— Mellin/1480 (Mellen)
Meskov— Mescow/1356 (Mesekow)
Milov— Milow/1542 (Milow)
Mokra Gola— Muckerguhl/1542 (Muggerkuhl)
Motyla— Motelik/1377 (Modlich)
Nemir Laka— Nymerlank/1389 (Niemerland)
Nesov— Nezow/1329 (Netzow)

PORYBI, POSTOLIN, PREDOL

Pinov— Pinnow/1400 (Pinnow)
Pirov— Pyrowe/1370 (Pirow)
Podarze— *Molendini Podarse*/1274 (Podarft)
Po-nic, Po-nikva— Ponitze/1536 (Ponitz)
Po-rybi— Poribe/1295 (Poreb)
Po-stolin— Postelin/1542 (Postlin)
Pod-chlusti— Pochlustim/946 (Putlitz)
Pre-dol— Predole/1314 (Preddohl)

PRESLAV, PRIBIL, RADISIN

Premysl— Premyslin/1315 (Premslin)
Preslav— *Castrum Prizlava, quod situm est in litore Albis fluvii, in ostio ubi in se recipit Habolam* **fluvium**/1056 (Prinzlow)
Pribil, Pribilov—Prievelow/1707 (Prebelow)
Priperde— *Feldmark Priperde*/1516 (Pripert)
Pri-stavalc— Pristualka/1373 (Pritwalk)
Radis—*Ressie situm*/1344 (Reetz)
Radisin—Retzin/1388 (Retzin)
Radov—*Villam Randowe*/1274 (Randow)

RADOGNEV, RUDO, SCEPNICA

Radognev— Radgnew/1490 (Ratechow)
Rodlin— Rodelyn/1307 (Redlin)
Rokitin— Rokentyn/1424 (Reckenthin)
Rudo, Rudov— Rudo/1336 (Rudow)
Sarnov— *Sarnow, Civibus in Kyritz*/1328 (Sarnow)
Scepnica— *Stepenitz villam*/1246 (Stepenitz)
Scirbica— Sterbitzwe/1588 (Sterbitz)
Semil, Semilin— Zemelin/1399 (Semlin)

SKOK, STOLP, STRELA

Skok— Schok/1352 (Schook)
Skripkov— Screpkow/1373 (Schrepkow)
Smarzov— Smarssow/1492 (Schmarsow)
Sosn—Zotzen, Sotzen/1540 (Zootzen)
Stavinov— Stavenow/1703 (Stawenow)

Stezov— Stesowe/1355 (Steesow)
Stolp— Stolpe/1339 (Stolpe)
Strela— Strel/1344 (Strehlen)

STUDENICA, SULISLAV, TRI GOLICA

Studenica— Studeniz/1274 (Studenitz)
Sule, Sulislav— Solenthin/1667 (Sollenthin)
Techov— Thechow/1306 (Techow)
Topole— Toppell/1469 (Toppel)
Tis, Tis—Theecz/1438 (Teetz)
Tri Golica— Triggelitze/1422 (Triglitz)
Trnov— Tornow/1454 (Tornow)
Tucho, Tuchomir— Tuchem/1480 (Tuchen)

VELIN, VELOV, VETIN

Untici— Untiz/1339 (Uenze)
Varcin— Wartzin/1573 (Gross Werzin)
Varnov— Varnow/1373 (Vahrnow)
Vel, Vele— Velle/1401 (Gross Welle)
Vel, Velin— Velin/1560 (Vehlin)
Vel, Velov— Velow/1311 (Vehlow)
Velgost— Veleghast/1490 (Vehlgast)
Vet, Vctin— Vettin/1343 (Vettin)
Vilsin— Wilsnack/1300 (Bad Wilsnack)
Vis, Visin— Wyssen/1491 (Weisen)
Visok— *villam Vysagk*/1335 (Viessecke)

VISOKA, VOLOVICA, VRANA

Visoka— *Wizoka civitatem*/948 (Wittstock)
Volovica— Waleitz (Gross Walwitz)
Vostrov— Wustrow/1588 (Wustrow)
V'otok— Wustoch/1344 (Wutike)
Vrana— Vrene/1424 (Frehne)
Vrba, Vrbic— Verbetz/1424 (Ferbitz)
Vrh, Vrhcov— Verchow/1492 (Ferchow)
Vulkov— Wulkow/1666 (Wuklow)
Zagost— Czagest/1490 (Sagat)
Zasek— Saczeke/1390 (Zaatzke)
Zivkov— Zevekow/1490 (Sewekow)

TOPONYMS, HYDRONYMS

As the following brief series indicates, the same is true of *provincia Priegenitz's* hydronyms and toponyms.

BARNICA, CESLAV, WENDLANDER

- **Barnica**— (Barnitz)
- **Bykov**— (Biekow)
- **Ceslav**— (Zieslow)
- **Crnicin**— (Zernezin)

- **Dolnica** —(Duhlenz)
- **Domarad**— (Damradt)
- **Dragun**— (Dragun)
- **Drenov**— (Drehnow)
- **Drozdov**— (Drusedow)
- **Grib, Gribin**— (Griebsee)
- **Jama, Jamin**— (Jemenn)
- **Jec, Jecin**— (Jentzin)
- **Kolpin**—(Kolpin)
- **Laka**—(Lacke)
- **Lubkov**—(Lubkow)
- **Lutov**— (Lutow)
- **Malchov**— (Malchow)
- **Milan**— (Milan)
- **Potyrov**— (Potrow)
- **Radotin**— (Radenthin)
- **Sedlisce**— (Siedlitz)
- **Sedlisce**— (Zedlitz)
- **Sedlisce**— (Zielitz)
- **Sedlisce**— (Zielitzen)
- **Vostrov**— (Wastrow)
- **Wendenberg**— (*Ex monte schlauorum*)
- **Wendendorf**

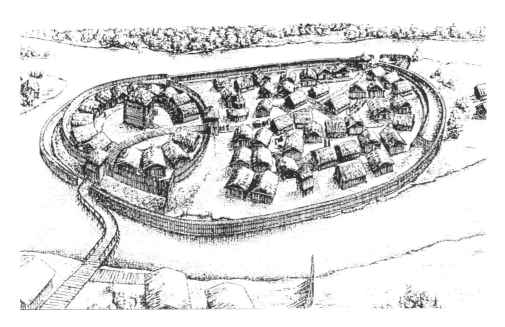

Old Spandau (10ᵗʰ century)

PART XXIII

1. ZVANTEVITH, DEUS TERRE RUGIANORUM

The great island-nation of *Rugen* (*insular parvam et populosam*) was both a leading member of the *Velici/Lutici* confederation and at the same time a separate and independent entity with its own history and culture. It is located in the Baltic Sea opposite Stralsund and separated from the mainland by the Strela Sound and Boden Strait. From north to south its length is 32 miles, from west to east its maximum width is 25 miles.

PRIMATAM PRAETER GENTES IN OMNI SLAVORUM NATIONE

Diverse medieval sources testify to *Rugen's* special and often dominant role in Baltic and Slavic affairs. Regarding the islands of the Slavs, Helmold writes: **Another and far greater island is situated opposite the Wilzi and is inhabited by the Rani, also known as the Rugians, the strongest of the Slavic peoples ... So much are the Rani feared on account of their familiarity with the gods, or rather demons, whom they honor with a greater devotion than do the other Slavs, that nothing can lawfully be done in public matters without their sanction.**

MAINTAIN A PRIMACY

At another point, Helmold writes: **Now the Rani, who are called Runi by others, are a fierce people who dwell in the heart of the sea ... They maintain a primacy over every Slavic tribe and have a king and a very celebrated fane. Wheretofore, too, on account of the special veneration paid this fane, they hold the first claim to respect. Although they impose their yoke on many, they themselves are subject to no one's yoke, since they are hard to reach by reason of the nature of their situation.**

JAROMIR/ARKONA

Jaromir, recorded as *Arkona*, **urbs principalis Rugianorum**, was the foremost cult center in all *Slavia*. Helmold writes: **Oracular responses are there sought by all the provinces of the Slavs and annual sacrifices duly performed.**

ZVANTEVITH, DEUS TERRE RUGIANORUM

All commentators agree that *Rugen* (*Zvantevith, deus terre Rugianorum*) was the religious and political center (*Zvantevith, quod colebatur ab omni natione Sclavorum*) of the cult of *Svar* as *Svarog* as *Svantevit*.

FOREIGN MERCHANTS

Foreign merchants were also required to pay their respects to *Svarog*. **Even merchants who happen to come into these parts are not given leave either to buy or sell until there has been laid before the god of the Rani whatever is most valuable in their merchandise.**

CHRISTIANITY

Regarding their fierce and stubborn resistance to Christianity, actually only aggressive, intrusive, and intolerant Christianity, Helmold writes that: **Not a barbaric** state under heaven abominates Christians and priests more.

OTTO, APOSTLE OF POMERANIA

Otto, Apostle of Pomerania, was immediately put on notice by the *Rani* called *Ruthenians* that his missionary activities would not be tolerated: **They (Ruthenians) declared that if any of his companions would presume to approach the borders of Ruthenia, for the sake of preaching the gospel, their heads would be cut off forthwith and they should be exposed to be torn by wild beasts ... For they (Ruthenians) said that he would find with them nothing but bitter punishment and certain death.**

STETIN

Indeed, far beyond the borders of *Ruthenia*, all who submitted in some part for whatever reason to the 'Christian law' had to fear the wrath of the *Ruthenians*. Even proud, strong city-states like Stetin. **The Ruthenians, who were still bound in heathen error, when they heard of the conversion of the people of Stetin, were exceedingly angry because they had renounced their idols and submitted to the Christian law without reference to, or consultation with them ... The Ruthenians began to offer open opposition to the people of Stetin. First of all they kept their ships from their own shores, and later on by a unanimous decision they resolved that they should be regarded as enemies ... On many occasions the Ruthenians had reviled the men of Stetin and had assailed their territory with armed ships.**

LUBECK

Lubeck also had to fear the *Ruthenians*. In the first decades of the 12th century, when there was neither church nor priest among all the people of the *Lutichi*, *Abodrites*, and *Wagiri*, except only in the stronghold of Lubeck. Henry, Christian king of the Slavs, **gave them (Vicelin and two other missionary priests) the church at Lubeck that they might live in a secure abode with him and carry on the work of God.** However, shortly after: **The Rugiani attacked the city ... and they demolished the town with its fortress. As the barbarians broke in one door of the church, the illustrious priests slipped out by another and saved themselves by taking refuge in the neighboring woods and then fled back to the haven of Faldera.**

MORAL ORDER

As with all Slavonians, the *Rani* were also guilty of the sins of rusticity, an authentic humanity, an integral and pervasive morality, and an uncompromising sense of personal and collective honor. Although Hemold and other commentators never tire of noting *Slav/Rani* opposition to Christianity in the most terrible and crazed terms, at the same time, they often concede their moral superiority. Helmold notes, strange as it may seem to members of the one true faith, that, unlike Christians, their word, oath, and pledge were inviolable: **They admit oaths with the greatest reluctance; for among the Slavs to swear is, as it were, to forswear oneself, because of the avenging wrath of the gods.**

SOCIAL ORDER

According to Helmold, the *Rani* social order was also to be admired: **For there prevails among them an abundance of hospitality, and they show due honor to** their parents. There is not a needy person or beggar to be found in their midst at any time. As soon as infirmity or age has made any of them frail or decrepit, he is committed to the charge of his heir to be cared for with the utmost kindness. Regard for hospitality and respect for parents stand as prime virtues among the Slavs.

SACRI VITI

At one point, the relatively open-minded and tolerant *Rugenites* accepted a form of Christianity consistent with their own beliefs, namely the cult of *St. Vitus* as *Svetovid* as *Svarog*. Regarding this accomodating moment Helmold writes: **Putting a creature above the Creator, they worship as God, Saint Vitus, whom we recognize as a marty and servant of Christ ... They glory only in the name of Saint Vitus, to whom they have with the most elaborate rites even dedicated a temple and image, attributing to him in particular a primacy of divinity.**

POLITICAL ORDER

Perhaps the greatest sins of the Slavonians generally and the *Rani* specifically related to their political values, a love for freedom and democratic institutions. All sources indicate that the *Rani* were a thoroughly democratic people, that their affairs were a matter of traditional law and popular consent.

MARE RUGIANORUM

From the earliest times, *Rugen* was a center of trade and commerce with lands near and far. Undisputed lords of the Baltic Sea or *Mare Rugianorum* and related waterways, *Rugen's* bold and enterprising merchant fleets were important sources of wealth and power. Impressive evidence of the importance of shipping in peace and war is found in the often energetic and creative attempts to link inland settlements with waterways. At Ralswiek, for example, in the center of the island, a settlement on an island-like hill between the bay of Jasmund (*terra Jasmundia*) and a lake, a German historian writes: **Anchorages for ships were constructed on the lakeside by digging channels from the lake to individual house-plots and by building jetties of piles and planks, some of which supported buildings.**

PIRATE FLEETS

The approach of *Rugen's* pirate fleets sent shivers through the German and Scandinavian coastlands. Piracy, Helmold writes, was from earliest times a way of life for the Baltic Slavs generally and the *Rani* specifically: **The Slavs are exceedingly skilled in making clandestine attacks. Hence, also, predatory habits have until this present age been so strong among them that they have always turned their hands to the fitting out of naval expeditions to the utter neglect of the advantages of agriculture. The ships are their only hope and the sum total of their wealth. They do not even take pain in the construction of their houses; nay rather, they make them of plaited withes, only taking counsel of necessity against storms and rains.**

12TH CENTURY

As late as the 12th century, *Rugen* raiders were a constant threat to one and all. In 1110, they invaded Holstein and penetrated nearly to Hamburg. When the Danes fell out of favor with the Saxons in the 1170s, Helmold writes: **The Rani were called on to take vengeance on the Danes: The bars and doors with which the sea had been closed were moved away; and it burst forth, surged, poured over, and threatened with destruction the many islands and the coastal regions of the Danes. The Slavs restored their pirate ships and seized opulent islands in the land of the Danes. They were, after their long abstinence, filled with the riches of the Danes.**

IUS SLAVICUM, IUS KNESITZ

Ius Slavicum appears to be a factor in determining obligations and rights on church lands in the late 12th and early 13th centuries (e.g. *omnis consuetudo, que ius Slavicum publice appellatur, 1249*). In the same period, *knesitzen or iure knesitz* appear to be the basis for determining fiscal obligations: *Dobermoizle (Dobromysl) ... de pensione laterum carnium, quam possidet iure knesitz (1296).*

RUGIANCENSES SLAVOS

There are many references to **Rugen** and **Rugenites** (*Rani ... gens Slavorum, Rhuni, Roiani, Royani, Ruani, Rugiancenses Slavos, Rugiani, Rugini, Rujani, Rusci, Rutheni, Ruyani, Slavos dictos Robos*) in medieval sources.

- *Dominium Ruie*
- *In Slaviam, Rugian vocitatam*
- *Insula Rugia*
- *Insula Ruiana*
- *Insula Rujacensia*
- *Insulam Rujanam*
- *Insulari terra Ruye*
- *Insulis Rive*
- *Regione quadam, quae a Theutonicus Ruiana, a Slavis autem Rana dicitur*
- *Reune insula*
- *Roiana insula*
- *Roijanorum*
- *Roja*
- *Ruanorum*
- *Rugacensis insulae Slavos*
- *Ruginaroum sive Ranorum*
- *Rugiam insulum cum tota circumiacente provincia Slavorum*
- *Rugis*
- *Rugorum*
- *Ruiam*
- *Ruiancensis insulae Slavos*
- *Ruianorum*
- *Ruja*
- *Rujam insulam*
- *Rujana*
- *Rujanorum*
- *Runoroum*
- *Ruya*
- *Ruyam*
- *Ruyiam*
- *Slavi insulae Rugiacensis*
- *Terra Rugianorum*
- *Terra Ruje*
- *Terra Ruya*
- *Terra Ruye*

TERRITORY, SITES, BORDERS

Regarding the territory, sites and borders of **Terra Ruya**, Herrmann writes: **Im Norden des Recknitz-Trebel-Peenegebietes lagen dreis kleinere Siedlungskammern auf dem Darss, an der unteren Barthe und am Niederungsgebiet der oberen Barthe. Sie standen offenbar in Zusammenhang mit den Siedlungskammern auf der Insel Rugen: um Bergen-Garz-Lancken, auf Jasmund, auf Wittow und um Gingst. In**

jungslawischer seit 1136 ise in den zuerst genannten Gebieten das Land Tribsees gelegen, das eventuell in die spateren Terrae Pitina, Gristow und Barth unterteilt war. Barth in der Siedlungskammer an der unteren Barthe und Pitina (Putte) am Niederungsgebiet der oberen Barthe sind offenbar, ebenso wie Tribsees selbst, auf der Grundlage altslawischer Siedlungskammern entstanden. Dagegen scheint Gristow (w. Greifswald, n. des Ryck) eine ausgesprochene Terra der landesausbauzeit zu sein. Die Siedlungskammern nordlich von Recknitz, Trebel und Ryckgraben, die nur eine unbedeutende Ausdehnung hatten und deshalb wohl in den schriftlichen Quellen erst so spat entgegentreten, waren im 10. bis 12. Jh. wahrscheinlich von Ranen besiedelt oder gehorten zumindest zum Einflussbereich dieses Stammes, der die Insel Rugen und deren Siedlungskammern seit altesten Zeit bewohnte.

REX RUGIANCENSES SLAVOS

In 11th, 12th, and 13th century sources one finds numerous references to *Rugen's* rulers (*rex Rugiancenses Slavos*) and princes (*principem Rugianorum; princeps Roianorum; Rujanorum princeps*).

- *Barnota filius domini Jaromari de Ruia*
- *Barnum I dux Slavorum in insulari terra Ruye*
- *Dominus Germarus, Dominus de Rugen*
- *Gestimulum (in slaviam Rugian vocitatam et eorum regem gestimulum); Rugiacenses sclavos … et rege ipsorum perempto Gestimulo*
- *Jaromarus dei gratia princeps Ruianorum*
- *Kruto, dominus de Universa Terra Slavorum*
- *Terra Ruie dominus Jaroslaus*
- *Wiceslavs Ruianorum dominus*
- *Wislai, principis Ruianorum*
- *Wissezlaus, Rujanorum princeps*
- *Wizeslaus, die gracia Rvianorum dominus*
- *Wizlaus, dei gracia princeps Ruianorum*
- *Worcislai Rania*
- *Wuslavus eadem gratia Ruyanorum princeps*
- *Wysseslauus quod … constructum est in ruya loco, qui dicitur Gora*

BABA, NEGOSC, ZAGRADE

The populous island's many place names, toponyms, and hydronyms recorded by H. Skalova are thoroughly Slavic and often identical with those found in Adriatic/Balkan Serb lands, including *Negosc*, midway between Preborov and Rabin in southwest *Rugen*.

GRANICA, JAVOR, KAMEN

Baba • Borovo • Brezno • Bukov • Dolane • Dolgomost • Gorica • Grabica •

Grabovici • Gradiste • Granica • Javor •Kamen • Kapa • Komorov • Koserov • Kot • Krivica • Lazy • Lopata • Luban • Medov • Mirkov • Mogylica

NEGOSC, PODGRADE, SRPCEVIT

Mokrani • Mostici • Negosc • Parez • Podgrade • Polica • Pozarica • Preseka • Pristavalac • Pustecov • Radovici • Recica • Sitno • Slavosici • Slavotici • Srbcevit • Strumen • Svetagora • Tvrdola •Virovice • Vrchoslavici • Zabesici • Zabnica • Zabrode • Zagrade • Zaloslavici

PERUN, ZALIKOV, MOKOSA, DEVIN

On mainland **Rugen**, opposite the island, across the Straslund or *Strela* strait, in addition to the standard Slavic place names (e.g. Batovici, Bory, Gosenici, Jelen, Komorov, Muskov, Polane, Porece, Stralovo), H. Skalova records a singular sequence of names relating to ancient Slavic beliefs and rituals: **Perun, Zalikov, Mokosa,** and **Devin**. It is also worth noting that at the end of this unique chain of pagan names, there is a second **Negosc**, southwest of **Devin**. Further evidence of the island's many parallels with Adriatic/ Balkan Serb lands is found in diverse medieval sources relating to village, personal, and family names ending in *–ic/-ich*.

BADISLAVICI, BORKOVICI, BOLEVICI

Badislavici— (Bandelslavitze/1314), Gross Banzelvitz
Barnekovici— (Barnutitze/1314), Barnkevitz
Basinovici— (Banseenevitze/1314)
Bezdomici— (Bisdomitze/1314), Bisdamitz
Bobkovici— (Bubkevitze/1318), Bubkevitz
Borkovici— (Borkevitze/1314), Burkvitz
Bolevici— (Bollevitze/1314), Boldevitz
Bornici— (Burenitz/1314), Burnitze

BOZKOVICI, CHOTICI, CICERADICI

Bortici— (Buretitze/1314), Borchtitz
Bozkovici— (Buskevitze/1318), Buschvitz
Busovici— (Bussevitze/1318), Bussvitz
Chotici— (Ghuttise/1318)
Chotici— (Gutitz/1232)
Chotmici—(Ghotemitze/1314), Goetmitz
Chudrici— (Chuderitze/1314), Gudderitz
Ciceradici— (Cyceradicz/1306)

DALIMIRICI, DARGOLICI, DOBRICHOVICI

Dalimirici— (Dalmeritz/1318)
Dalkovici— (Dalkevitze/1318), Dalvitz
Dargolici— (Dargoliz/1318), Zargelitz
Dargosovici— (Dargucevitze/1314)
Darzici— (Darsitze/1318), Darz
Desici— (Decitze/1314)
Dobrichovici— (Dubrechovitze/1346), Dubkevitz

Domagnevici— (Dummagnevitze/1318), Dumgenevitz

DOMASOVICI, DUSICI, GOLSICI

Domasovici— (Domassevitze/1314), Dumsevitz
Doncici— (Dunecitze/1314), Dumsevitz
Drevsici— (Drewsitz/1314)
Dubnici— (Dubenitze/1314), Dubnitz
Dusici— (Dusitze/1314), Dussvitz
Gaslici— (Gansilitze/1314)
Godimovici— (Gadymowysz/1249), Gademow
Golsici— (Golezyczs/1300)

GOROVICI, GOSTIRADICI, JARKOVICI

Gorovici— (Ghurevitze/1314), Gurvitz
Gortici— (Ghoretitze/1318), Gurtitz
Gostavici— (Ghustavitze/1318), Wostevitz
Gostiradici— (Gusteraditze/1314)
Gostlici— (Ghustelitze/1318)
Grabtici— (Grambetitze/1313), Gramtitz
Izmerici—(Iszmaritz/1477)
Jarkovici—(Jarkovici/1314)

KOTOVICI, LUBOVICI, LUBANOVICI

Karsinovici— (Karsenevitze/1318), Kasnevitz
Kotovici— (Cutevitze/1311)
Krepsici— (Crepasitze/1314), Kreptitz
Losetici— (Losentitze/1314), Losenitz
Lubovici— (Lubbevitze/1318), Lubitz
Lubanovici— (Lubanovitz/1242), Libnitz
Lubsici— (Lubbesityze/1381)
Lutkovici— (Lutkovitze/1314), Luttkevitz

LUTOSICI, MALOMIRICI, MYSLIBORICI

Lutosevici— (Lutyytusevitze/1314), Lussvitz
Lutosici— (Lutositze/1314), Lutzitz
Malkovici— (Malkevitze/1318), Malkvitz
Malmoirici— (Malmeritze/1318)
Morkovici— (Murkevitze/1318)
Mysici— (Moystize/1313)
Mysliborici— (Moyselboritze/1318), Moisselbritz
Myslidarzici— (Moyszeldarsitz/1171)

MYSLIKOVICI, NEDASICI, PLATKOVICI

Myslikovici— (Moyslekowe/1300)
Nacevici— (Natzvitze/1318), Natzevitz
Nedasici— (Nedasitze, 1318), Neddesitz
Nimpomerovici— (Nimpomervitze/1318), Nardevitz

Novelitici— (Novelitze/1318)
Platkovici— (Platekevitze/1314), Patvitz
Prisovici— (Prescevitze/1314), Prisvitz
Prosnici— (Prosnitze/1314), Prosnitz

RATINOVICI, SERSICI, SLAVISICI

Ratici— (Retelitze/1417), Reteliz
Ratinovici— (Ratnevitz/1320)
Rezici— (Rentize/1314), Renz
Ruskovici— (Ruskevitze/1313), Ruschvitz
Sersici— (Syrzycz/1300), Alt Sassistz
Sersovici— (Cyrosevitz/1300), Zirzewitz
Slavicici— (Slawesthorpe/1314; villa Slawice/1325
Slavisici— (Slavesitze/1314; Slawice/1325), Schlavitz

SLAVKOVICI, STARSEVICI, SULISLAVICI

Slavkovici— (Slawkewiz/1307)
Smatovici— (Smantevitze/1318)
Starsevici— (Starsevitze/1318), Sarritz
Strachotici— (Strachutitze/1314), Strachtitz
Stolnikovici—(Stulnekevitze/1318), Stonkvitz
Sulici— (Sulitze/1353), Zuhlitz
Sulislavici— (Syalleslvitze/1318), Sullitz
Sulkovici— (Solkevitze/1314)

SVECHOVICI, TAGOMIRICI, TREBOVICI

Svechenovici— (Swetzenevitze/1321)
Svechovici— (Swechevitze/1318), Schweikvitz
Tagomirici— (Tangomicz/1314), Tangnitz
Techodarzici— (Techodarsize/1304)
Tesici— (Thesitze/1314), Tetzitz
Tesinovici— (Tessenevitze/1314), Thesenitz
Teskovici— (Teskevitze/1314), Teschvitz
Tolkomici— (Tolkemitze/1314), Tolkmitz
Trebkovici— (Tripkevitze/1314), Tribkevitz
Trebovici— (Tribbevitze/1314), Tribbevitz

VOJKOVICI, VULCEVICI, VUSICI

Ubychlovici— (Ubechlevitze/1314)
Uzdarzici— (Udarsitze/1314), Udars
Varskovici— (Varskevitze/1313), Vaschvitz
Vojkovici— (Wojkewitz/1314), Veikvitz
Volksici— (Volkasitze/1313), Volksitz
Vulcevici— (Vultzevitze/1313), Volsvitz
Volsekovici— (Wolsekevitze/1320)
Vusici— (Wutzetz/1314), Wussitz
Zabsici— (Zabucitze/1314), Sabitz

Zalosici— (Zalositze/1318), Salsitz
Zelatici— (Silladutze/1318)

SLAVKOVICI, SLAVOSICI, SERSICI

In addition to the numerous place names with **_Slav_** as a prefix- or suffix (e.g. Badi*slavi*ci, Slavkovici, *Slav*osici, Suli*slav*ici, Vrcho*slav*ici, Zalo*slav*ici), several feature the Ser/Serb ethnonym (e.g. *Ser*sici, *Ser*sovici, *Srb*cevit).

PERSONAL NAMES

Medieval sources record the survival of traditional Slavic personal names on the island, including the personal names of titled notables.

BLIZIMIR, LUBOMIR, MYSLIMIR

- Blizimir Vojkovic, 1310
- Bolen, 1293
- Borjanta (*dominus Borjanta*, 1300)
- Dobimir (1335)
- Dobrislav Smatovic (Dubbeslaf Smantevitze), 1396
- Dobromysl, 1296
- Jaromir, 1185
- Lubomir (*Lubemarus*), 1173)
- Myslimir, 1240
- Myslimir Dubbertitze, 1322
- Myslibor (*Mysliborius*, 1291)

PRIBISLAV, RATISLAV, SIROSLAV

- Goslav, 1325
- Pribislav, 1355
- Pribislav Tesimiric (*Pribislaws Tessimeritz*), 1360
- Pridbor, 1300
- Radovin, 1285
- Ratislav, 1316
- Slavek Dubbertitze, 1329
- **_Slavek miles_**, 1332
- Slavush (*Ritter Slavus*, 1221)
- Sirsici (*Ritter Sirich*, 1300)
- Siroslav (Sirislav, 1189)

STOISLAV, RATISLAV, VOISLAV

- Siroslav (*Siroslaus*, 1180)
- Stoislav, 1300
- Sulislav (*Ritter Syalleslav*, 1294)
- Sumislav (*Ritter dominus Sumislav*, 1325)
- Svar Slavek, 1335
- Ratislav, 1325
- Teslav Slavkovic (Thezlaf Zlawcovitz, 1316)
- Teslav Zabesic, 1319

- Viseslav (*Ritter Wiceslaus Wotmitz*, 1233; Wizlaus Wotmityz, 1242)
- Voislav (Wojzlaus, 1296)
- Zelimir, 1325

14TH CENTURY

In 14th century **Rugen** one often finds mixed personal and family names. In some cases, though the traditional family name is retained, one member of the family will have a Christian personal name, the other, a traditional name, and vice versa: Hinrik Smentevitze, Dubbeslaf Smantevitze, 1396; Goslav, Zelimir, Ratislav and Johannes Sumovic/1325;Hennek Zabesic, 1358; Zlawek Dubbertitze, Claus Wosceke, 1371; Vicko Moteke, Sclaweke Dubbertitze, 1375; Hennek Slaweke, 1382; Vicke Slaweke, 1396.

In some cases the family name's Slavic root is modified by a Danish ending: e.g. **Zlawsson** instead of **Slavkovic** (*Razalav Zlawsson*, 1316). In the case of the brothers Werner, Willek, Hennek, Nicolaus, and Pavel Bolenson, for example, one brother has a Slavic name and the family name is **Bolen(son)** instead of **Bolenovich**.

16TH, 17TH CENTURIES

It is both interesting and compelling evidence of the depth, breadth, and strength of the island's Slav foundations that in the late 16th and early 17th centuries, a great number of family names recorded in church registers appear to be Slavic in origin. The following series of family names is typical of the more obvious Slavic family names recorded throughout the island. Here too, one cannot help but note the persistence of **Svar** and **Jar**, two names with powerful pre-Christian religious conntations.

BLASICH, DOBBRAN, RADDEVAN

Blasich • Boj • Bor • Bregatz • Dallemer • Dargemer • Darguntz • Dergemer • Doblick • Dobbran • Dran • Drob •Dubbran • Glovate • Gutzkow • Gutzslaff • Jarandt • Jarmer • Jarnavitz • Jawern • Jurrevitz • Klentze • Klukow • Kon • Koppatz • Kruse • Kussow • Labban • Lubbe • Lubbekesche • Niemoy • Millatz • Miltze • Moislich • Moykow • Pamereske • Pluggentin • Pottesche • Pribe • Pribber • Pudbrese • Pussesche • Pusichel • Radas • Raddevan • Radeleff • Raleke • Ratenow • Ristich • Roggelin • Slavke • Staneke • Stanekesche • Stanick • Stare •Subglave •Swarte • Techmer • Trebesche • Turow • Urkewitz • Utesche • Vossesche • Witmuss • Woytke • Woye • Wusseck • Wosswode • Zarnek • Zavit • Zitegorre

PRIB, JAROSLAV, PAWEL

Church registers record relatively few traditional Slavic personal names. In addition to **Prib** (e.g. **Pribe** Cholste, **Pribe** Horn, **Pribe** Meyer, **Pribe** Moller, **Pribe** Trebesche, **Pribe** Zume), one also finds such traditional names as **Dubschlaff** Riske, **Labban** Plate, **Jarschlaf** Bernekow, **Radeleff** Heket. On the other hand, **Pawel**, a Slavic version of the Christian name Paul, is one of the more common personal names (e.g. **Pawel** Cholste, **Pawel** Drantzke, **Pawel** Klatte, **Pawel** Koldewitz, **Pawel** Lokenvitz, **Pawel** Nehels, **Pawel** Puschesche, **Pawel** Urkewitz, **Pawel** Zeket, **Pawel** Zore, **Pawel** Wiese, **Pawel** Woite).

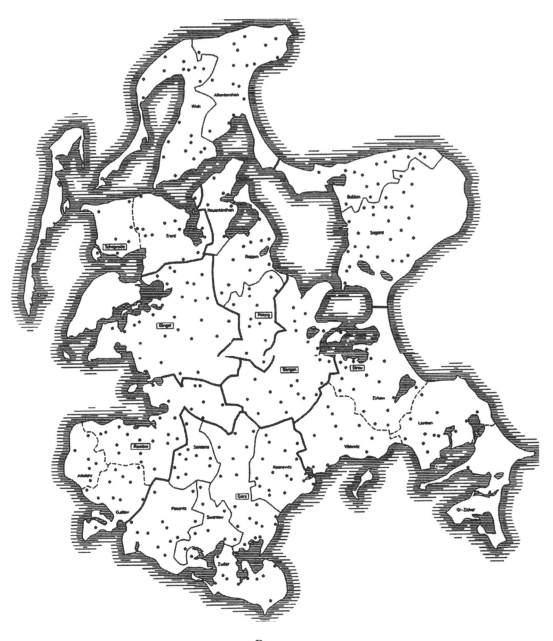

Rugen

PART XXIV

1. FOEDERATI, AMICI

The so-called German-Slav wars, the medieval *Drang nach Osten,* wars that began after the Franks had smashed the Bavarians and, after a long and bloody struggle, crushed the Saxons, are only half of the story. The other half is a story of Slav-German alliances, 'alliance de convenance' and otherwise, of Slav *foederati* and *amici.*

DEEP ROOTS

This half has deep roots in Slav-German relations. Slav mercenaries, for example, served in the armies of Odoacer (434-493), the leader of the insurrection that caused the fall of the Western Roman Empire in 476, and in the armies of other Gothic chieftains.

FOEDERATI

Centuries later, Slavs will serve as esteemed allies or *foederati* in the armies of Charles the Great and successive emperors. As allies of the Franks, the **Bodrici (Sclavi nostri qui dicuntur Abodritos)** will play an important role in the conquest of the Saxons.

ALWAYS AIDED THE FRANKS

Conversely, Saxon wars against the Franks were also wars against the **Bodrici.** In the year 798 when Charles the Great took up arms against the rebels ... and laid waste the whole of Saxony between the Elbe and the Weser ... Saxons from the far side of the Elbe attacked the *Obodrites:* **They took up arms and set out against the Obodrites. The Obodrites have always aided the Franks, ever since the Franks accepted them as their allies (Abodritos, qui cum Francis olim foedera ti erant).**

FOUR THOUSAND SLAIN

The same source goes on to say that the rebels **were defeated in battle when they engaged Thrasco, duke of the Obodrites ... Four thousand of them were slain on the battlefield; the rest fled, escaped, and entered into peace negotiations; but many of them also perished.**

GIVEN SAXON LANDS

When the Saxons living north of the Elbe were deported to Franconia in 804, their lands were given to the *Obodrites* by Charles the Great: **The emperor spent the winter at Aachen. But in the summer he led an army into Saxony and deported all Saxons living beyond the Elbe and in Wihmuodi [east of the Weser near Verden] with wives and children into Francia and gave the districts beyond the Elbe to the Obodrites.**

FOES DOMESTIC AND FOREIGN

Not long thereafter, Slav and Saxon will serve together in imperial armies and carry out devastating campaigns against foes domestic and foreign. In the year 815, for example: **The emperor commanded Saxons and Obodrites to prepare to march** against the Norsemen. Then all Saxon counts and all troops of the Obodrites ... marched ... across the River Eider into the land of the Norsemen called Silendi ... But the sons of Godofrid, who had raised against a large army and a fleet of two hundred ships, remained on an island three miles off the shore and did not dare engage them. Therefore, after everywhere laying waste the neighboring districts and receiving hostages from the people, they returned to the emperor in Saxony.

CONTRA REBELS

Slav armies sometimes serve as imperial enforcers of *legitimacy* in neighboring lands. In 856, Serb troops take part in an imperial expedition against rebel forces in Bohemia. In 857, when rebels force **Svetipolk**, the *legitimate* ruler, to flee to **regio Soraborum**, to the court of *duke Zistibor* (**dux Zistiboro**), Serb forces join a second imperial expedition that restores **Svetipolk** to his rightful rule.

IMPERIAL RIGHTS, PRIVILEGES

Slavs armies also served as enforcers of imperial rights and privileges in neighboring lands. When the king of Denmark refuses demands for tribute and hostages in the mid-12ᵗʰ century, the Slavs are called on to bring the Danes to their senses: **He summoned the princes of the Slavs and bade them take vengeance on the Danes. They were called and they said: "Here we are." With joy they obeyed him who sent them.**

WITH TENFOLD VENGEANCE

With joy and without fear they plundered the width and length of the Danish lands. Danish attempts to take the war to the Slavs were few and futile. In one such instance, Helmold writes: **The king of Denmark collected an army and smote a small part of the Circipanian region. A son of the king, named Christopher, also came with a thousand mailed men to Oldenburg and ravaged along its coast ... As the Danes withdrew, the Slavs followed upon their heels, making good their losses with tenfold vengeance.**

CONTRA MAGYARS

In the year 955, Slav troops under the command of **duke Bolislav** of Bohemia (**milites, Burislao Sarmaturum principe**), take part in the annihilation of a great Magyar host on the Lechfeld Plain by imperial forces led by **King of the Slavs**, Emperor Otto I (936-973), thereby ending once and forever the so-called Magyar threat to European civilization.

ITALY

When Otto's son, Otto II (973-983), following his marriage to Byzantine princess Theophano, adopts the title *Emperor Augustus of the Romans,* and tries to extend his control to southern Italy, Serb troops join his 982 Calabrian campaign and Serb knights serve in his bodyguard. Another important contribution to imperial ambitions in Italy was made by **Duke Mstislav** of the **Obodrites** who served at the head of a thousand **Obodrite** horsemen, nearly all of whom died in battle.

TREATIES

Fear of Germania's northern Slavs gave the empire great leverage in its relations with northern neighbors. In the mid-12th century, when Duke Henry the Lion concludes a treaty of friendship with Denmark, Waldemar, king of the Danes, asks him: **To procure peace for him from the Slavs, who without intermission were devastating his kingdom ... The count, therefore, solicited Niclot through the medium of the elders of Wagria, Marchad and Horno, and asked him of his own good will to keep inviolate faith with respect to his territory. With this request Niclot complied with becoming fidelity.**

DYNASTIC WARS

Slavs also took active and important roles in dynastic wars and rebellions in the 9th century and later. In 861, for example, ***Rastiz the Wend (Rastislav, 861-873) of Megale Moravia (Great Moravia)*** took sides with Karlmann: **Karlmann, son of Louis king of Germany, made an alliance with Rastiz, petty king of the Wends, and defected from his father. With Rastiz's help he usurped a considerable part of his father's realm.** In 866, ***Rastiz the Wend*** sided with another son, Louis: **Louis, son of King Louis of Germany, started a rebellion against his father. Young Louis also roused Rastiz the Wend to come plundering right up to Bavaria, so that while his father and his faithful men were fully engaged in the region, he himself might be freer to continue with what he had begun.**

CONTRA COUNTER-KING

In the late 11th century, at the battle of Flarcheim, ***Duke Bretislav*** of Bohemia, fighting under the banner of the Emperor, captured the golden lance of the papal counter-king, Rudolph of Swabia.

REBELLIONS

In the mid-9th century, a number of rebellious Saxon barons fled to safety in Serb lands, where they played an active role in Serb resistance to imperial expansion.

CONQUEST OF SLAVIC LANDS

By far the greatest Slavic contribution to imperial expansion was made in Germania, in imperial wars against the Slavs, in the conquest of Slavic lands east of the Elbe. The dissolution of a common Slavic front against imperial expansion was by and large a consequence of Christian expansion. From the beginning, Christianity was a relentless and escalating source of dissension and conflict at all levels.

UNREST, CIVIL WAR

Time after time the *conversion* of ruling Slav princes and dukes led to unrest and civil war in trans-Elbean lands, where as late as the 12th century Christians were few and far between (***ultra Albiam illis temporibus rarus inveniebatur Christianus***): **There was neither church nor priest among all the people of the Lutici, Abodrites, and Wagiri, except only in the stronghold of Lubeck.**

DUKE GOTTSCHALK

In the mid-11th century, ***Duke Gottschalk's*** attempt to spread Christianity in *terra **Obotritorum*** triggered a popular uprising that led to his murder and the ascendance of ***Kruto***, who championed the *old religion* and *old freedoms,* **who bore deadly hatred toward the Christian name.**

OLD FREEDOMS

The *old freedoms* included the freedom to work the land without *God's* interference, death threats, and worse, including capital punishment. In one typical instance, surely one of the sources of the 'deadly hatred,' when a passing priest **spied peasants reaping in their fields during the feast of St. Lawrence, he warned them that their profanation of the birthday of the blessed martyr Lawrence would bring God's wrath upon them. He had scarcely uttered these words when the fire of God fell from heaven ... and reduced to ashes the harvest they had gathered.** Many other peasants were not so fortunate. In another instance, when a peasant and his wife had gone out to reap during the festival of Mary, a passing priest ordered them: **Abandon your work. It is altogether wrong to attend on this renowned festival of the most holy mother of God. When they refused to listen and continued to work, the priest said: As you do not believe my words your blood shall be upon your head, and ye shall know by manifest proofs understand what is the punishment of this transgression. He had hardly finished speaking when the unbelieving peasant fell backwards and expired.**

DUKE HENRY

In the early 12th century Christian ***duke Henry's*** missionary activities were so contrary and offensive that his sons, who succeeded to his dominion, were so much troubled by domestic wars that they lost the peaceful times and the tribute of the lands which their father had procured by the vigor of his arms. In fact, ***Henry's*** sons were soon succeeded by princes ***Pribislav*** and ***Niklot*, who divided the principiate into two parts so that one governed the country of the Wagiri and the Polabi, the other, that of the Abodrites.** Helmold writes: **These two men were truculent beasts, intensely hostile to the Christian. In those days a variety of idolatrous cults and superstitious aberrations grew strong again throughout all Slavia.**

DUKE VRATISLAV

In the early 12th century, Pomerania's ***Duke Vratislav's*** secret conversion soon led to war and his death in battle against his *pagan* brothers (in Otto's kind words: **animals who with unbridled neck spurned the yoke of Christ's universal church**). More often than not, such conversions were secret. In the case of ***Duke*** Vratislav's conversion, one of Bishop Otto's biographers writes that, owing to his fear of pagans, his Christianity was perforce a secret matter.

NATION AGAINST NATION

Even more destructive, time after time the conversion of Slav princes, duke and kings led to active and energetic collaboration with imperial interest and bloody conflict with Slav nations resisting *Christian law.*

CONTRA SERBS, LUTICI

When Germania's pagan Slavs along the Elbe rebelled in 994, a joint Christian

Polish-Bohemian army came to the assistance of Otto III and took an active role in the fighting against the **Serbs** and **Lutici.**

CONTRA RANI

Following years of raids and plunder that carried the pagan **Rani** to the walls of Hamburg, the **Bodrici,** led by **duke Henry,** an early convert to *Christian law*, rose to the defense of their Christian and German neighbors in Nordalbingia and Holstein: *Pagani victores totam Nordalbingiam deinceps habuerunt in sua ditione, bellatoribusque occisis aut in captivitatem ductis, provincia in solitudinem redacta est.*

SAVED NORDALBINGIA, HOLSTEIN

Regarding the decisive role of the Christian wing of the **Bodrici**, J.W. Thompson writes*:* **Probably nothing but the loyalty of these Christian Wends to the faith ... saved Nordalbingia and Holstein from a second eclipse of the church there this time.**

RANIBERG

On one occasion in the year 1111 not only were the **Bodrici** victorious, but the slaughter was so great that out of the bodies of the fallen **Rani, a huge mound was erected called Raniberg, which was long pointed out to the curious.**

GREAT SLAVIC ARMY

Several years later, following defeat and the death of a son at the hands of the **Rani**, **duke Henry** led a great Slavic army against the **Rani**. Regarding this moment, Helmold writes: **He sent messengers to all the Slavic lands to bring together auxiliaries, and all who were assembled were alike willing and of the same mind that they should obey the king's commands and make war on the Rani. And they were "many, as the sand which is by the sea."** If not exactly as many *as the sand which is by the sea,* by all accounts it was an *exceedingly great army.* **Hosts of Slavs from every province had spread over the face of the sea, set off in companies and battalions, awaiting the command of the king.** It seems, however, that after a long and arduous march, much tramping over ice and deep snow, the great army lost some of its warlike spirit. After setting on fire a number of border villages, it settled for the payment of money and rendering of hostages. The following year, **Henry** mobilized another great army of Slavs and Saxons against the **Rani.** This time, on reaching the **Rani** borderland, perhaps once again realizing the great risk of their undertaking, they turned back without taking any action.

CONTRA PAGAN POMERANIA

The Polish champion of Christendom, Duke Boleslav III, carried one of the more savage crusades against Pomerania out in 1121: **It was said that he slaughtered eighteen thousand armed men and that he led away as captives to his own country eight thousand men together with their wives and little children, and placed them in positions exposed to danger as well as in cities and camps, that they might serve as a guard to his country and might help him to wage war with his foreign enemies. An additional condition was that they should abandon their idols and conform in** all aspects to the Christian religion.

CONTRA CHRISTIAN STETIN

In 1147, when a crusading army laid siege to Christian Stetin, defended by Christian Slavs, including **Christian Prince Ratibor** and **Adalbert, Bishop of Pomerania,** Bishop Zdik of Olomouc, at the head of a crusading Bohemian contigent, was among the more zealous prelates in opposition.

CONTRA LUTICI

Several years later, **Obodrite Duke Niklot**, with assistance from his close friend and frequent ally, Count Adolf of Holstein, will launch an aggressive and expansionist campaign against bordering **Lutici**, namely the **Kessins** and **Sircipans**.

CONTRA RUGEN

When the island of **Rugen** was finally taken in 1168, the invading forces included great numbers of Christian Slavs, including, among others, **Bodrici** led by **Prince Pribislav** and **Pomeranians** led by **Princes Casimir** and **Bogislav**. In this instance, fortunately, the more calamitous consequences of *Christian law* were muted by the persona and tact of *Jaromir*, prince of the **Rani,** who, on accepting **the true God and the Catholic faith, led his people down a safe path: Acting in the capacity of an apostle, partly by assiduous preaching, partly by threats, he [Prince Jaromir] converted the folk, rude and savage with bestial madness, from their natural wildness to the religion of a new life.**

RETALIATION

Of course, the pagan Slavs took advantage of every opportunity to retaliate against Slavs, Christians and others, who collaborated with foreign kings and emperors. From the beginning, from the late 8th century forward, the mighty **Wilzi/Lutici** were first and foremost in avenging campaigns against renegade and collaborating Slavs. Thus the following words from the *Royal Frankish Annals of 789*: **The Wilzi have always been hostile to the Franks and used to hate and harass their neighbors who were either subject to the Franks or allied with them and provoke them into war.**

PRO GODOFRID

When the Danes and others invaded the northern borderlands, the **Wilzi** were natural allies in campaigns against the Franks, Saxons, and **Obodrites.** This was certainly the case in 808: **On this expedition Godofrid has as his allies the Slavs called Wilzi, who joined his forces voluntarily because of their ancient conflicts with the Obodrites. When Godofrid returned home, they also went home with the booty which they had been able to capture from the Obodrites.**

PRO EMPEROR HENRY

In order to take advantage of every opportunity to retaliate against Christian Slav adversaries, it was sometimes necessary to collaborate with imperial interests. Thus the **Lutici** served as shock troops in an imperial campaign, assisted by Bohemian forces, against Christian Poles in Silesia, under siege in the castle of Nimptsch near mount Zobten, a rugged mountain southwest of Vratislava. Thietmar writes: **After another assault by the Lutici was repulsed, the emperor (Henry II, 1002-1024) realised** that his forces could never take the castle defended by the Christian Poles in the name of and under the standard of the Cross.

TWELVE POUNDS OF GOLD

Finding discretion the better part of valor, **the emperor returned in a most troublesome retreat, to Bohemia.** At this point, the *Lutici* in the pay of the emperor, seek and receive, on pagan principles, additional pay: **The infuriated Lyutichi dispersed to their homes and raged over the humiliation to their goddess. For one of the Margrave Hermann's companions had hurled a stone at her image on the standard and made a hole in it. The pagan priests reported the incident, with great indignation, to the emperor, who presented them with twelve pounds of gold by way of compensation.**

IMPOSSIBLE TO OVERESTIMATE

Given the basic and compelling facts of the matter it is almost impossible to overestimate the role of collaborating and allied native and Christian Slavs in the conquest of pagan Slav lands east of the Elbe.

MARTIAL PROWESS

In one way or another medieval sources consistently concede the individual and collective superior martial prowess of the Slav over the German and Scandinavian. Thus it is not surprising that in disputes with the Germans, the Slavs favored trial by combat. A 1031 border dispute between Slavs and Saxons illustrates the point. Since each side blamed the other, J.W. Thompson writes, the Slavs requested and were granted trial by combat. Each side chose a champion. The result was perhaps predictable: **The Slav champion won to the great elation of his compatriots and chagrin of the Saxons, especially the clergy, whose prestige as dispensers of the will of the Almighty was somewhat injured.**

MANY TIMES BEATEN BY THE PAGANS

It is clear from the historical record that the Slavs gave as good as they got and more in the wars with the Germans. Helmold's comments on the 11th century efforts of one of Germania's more active and determined crusaders, Ordulf, Duke of Saxony, tell much of the story: **Thereafter until the end of his life, Duke Ordulf vainly fought against the Slavs, but was never able to win a victory. Many times he was beaten by the pagans and was an object of his derision unto his own people.**

NO SUCCESS AT ALL

The same fate often befell other Germania commanders before and after Ordulf, not to mention King Louis of Germany. In 866, for example, it is recorded that Louis had *no success at all*: **Louis ... attacked the Wends. Having lost some of his leading men, he had no success at all, so that he took hostages and returned to his palace at Frankfurt on the Main.**

VERY HEAVY LOSSES

In 869 matters went from bad to worse: **They asked Charles to stay where he was ... until his brother King Louis of Germany had returned from his campaign** against the Wends. He had been threatened by them often during this year and the previous year, and though his men had fought against them, they had achieved virtually no success, but had in fact suffered very heavy losses.

EXTREMELY HEAVY LOSSES

Matters went from worse to disastrous in 871, when Louis suffered extremely heavy losses in men and disastrous losses of territory: **Louis made for Regensburg, because he had suffered extremely heavy losses at the hand of the nephew of Rastiz who had succeeded him in the Wendish chieftaincy. Wendish attacks had been so severe that Louis had lost his markiones with a large force of his men, and also suffered disastrous losses of the territory he had gained in the years preceding.**

LIBERTY ABOVE COMFORT

A German chronicler was close to the essential truth when he characterized the Slav resistance to imperial authority in the following terms: **The Slavs preferred war to peace, valuing dear liberty above comfort ... That kind of people is tough, perservering and abstemious.**

PITIABLE RESULTS

In spite of near unlimited access to Christendom's human and technical resources (e.g. the *military technology,* the *engines of war* and *instruments to cast fire, the siege tactics and war engines* imported from Italy) in spite of the collaboration of Germania's Christian Slavs and the assistance of neighboring Slav kingdoms, after centuries of intrigue, warfare and crusades, the great Holy Roman Empire had little to show for its efforts.

SEIGE TACTICS

Duke Henry the Lion, writes a modern German historian, **learned certain siege tactics in Italy which enabled him to reduce even the strongest of Slav fortresses.** Regarding the application of this technology to the siege of *Werla*, Helmold writes: **He [Henry] immediately ordered wood to be fetched from the dense forest and war engines to be constructed, such as he had seen at Cremona and Milan. They proved highly effective. One consisting of several tiers, was designed to breach the walls of the castle. The others, even higher, towered above them, so that arrows could be discharged downwards upon the defenders.**

IN 1066

A modern authority on medieval Germany succinctly sums up the matter in the following words. With regard to the situation following the great Slav rising in 1066, J. W. Thompson writes: **The entire achievement of German civilization and Germanic Christianity, save around Bremen and in Holstein, was wiped out.**

IN 1125

With regards to the situation in the first half of the 12th century, a time when several Christian-Slav princes were murdered or otherwise removed from authority (e.g. **Henry** of Lubeck, **Meinfried/Mojmir** of Brandenburg, **Witikind** of Havelberg), Thompson writes: **For 142 years, from the great Wendish rebellion in 983 to the** accession of Lothar II in 1125—the eastward expansion of the Germans across the Elbe was halted by the Slavs. After two hundred years of effort the Franconian period with pitiably insignificant results, so far as east German colonization was concerned. In 1125 the linguistic frontier was still there where it had been in the reign of Charlemagne.

GREAT WENDISH CRUSADE, 1147

There was little or no change in the situation after the *great Wendish Crusade* of 1147. Though the crusading host, the flower of Saxon and Danish Christendom, including two Danish fleets, reinforced by contigents from Burgundy, Moravia and Poland, envenomed and fanaticized by numerous bishops and a papal legate, under the command of experienced and able dukes, margraves, counts, as well as two kings of Denmark, the great army failed to gain a single foot of ground.

TWO DANISH KINGS SENT PACKING

While each side had minor victories and defeats, the Slavs scored the greatest victories: **Allied Rugians destroyed a Danish fleet in the Bay of Wismar and the Obodrites annihilated a Danish army near Dobin, devastating blows that sent the two Danish kings, Canute V and Sweyn III, packing back to Denmark.**

KNEZ JAKSA, 1150

Another sign of the times was the events following the death of **Duke Pribislav** of Brandenburg in 1150. Shortly after **Pribislav's** friend, brother-in-Christ, heir, and successor, Albrecht the Bear, occupied Brandenburg, it was seized by **Knez Jaksa of Kopenick**, and not recovered until 1157.

DUKE PRIBISLAV, 1164

In defense of his patrimony, the **Abodrite** lands ruled by his father, **Niklot, duke Pribislav** destroyed a Saxon army near Demmin in 1164.

MODERN GERMANIA, GERMANS

With regard to the situation in later centuries up to and including the 20th century, Professor F. Lotter writes: **Even if in some cases Slav peasants had to give way to German ones, the Slav population not only survived as a massive ethnic substratum, but also continued in existence, beside the Germans, in the higher strata of society right up to the ruling classes. At the end of the 12th century there was little difference between princes of Slavonic or German origin with regard to politics, interests, and cultural efforts ... First the Wendish dukes and nobles became Germans, and then the middle and lower layer of society followed. Even if only in the eastern part of the Serb marches, which had been incorporated already in the 10th century, did the Slav language and folklore survive in the country up to the present day, there are good reasons for supposing that within the entire German population east of the Elbe the Slavonic heritage preponderates. Thus besides Teutons and Romanized Celts [in the west], Slavs are to be considered ancestors of the modern Germans too.**

PART XXV

1. ASHKENAZIC JEWS

It seems that one of the consequences of medieval Crusades in Germania/Slavia was the racial transformation of the European Jewish community, one that transformed the Ashkenazic Jews into a predominantly Slavic community, more Serb/Sorb (*Serbja*) than Semitic.

In *The Ashkenazic Jews: A Slavo-Turkic People in Search of a Jewish Identity* (1993), Professor P. Wexler renders a comprehensive and commanding study of the historical, religious, and social dynamics of the racial transformation: **I will motivate the hypothesis that the Ashkenazic Jews are predominantly of Slavic, and secondarily of other Indo-European, Turkic and Palestinian, origins—on the basis of linguistic evidence and on the basis of Ashkenazic religious and folk practices.**

According to Wexler, **the Jewish migration to northern Europe occurred at a time when the eastern reaches of present-day Germany and southern Austria were thickly populated by Slavs.**

The first Jewish settlers in the mixed Germano-Slavic lands, Wexler writes, **were probably speakers of South Slavic; thus, the little difficulty in acquiring Sorbian, the only Slavic language to survive to the present in Germany ... In the 9ᵗʰ-12ᵗʰ centuries the differences among the Slavic languages were marginal, but since Sorbian is the only surviving Slavic language in Germany today, I take the liberty of defining the Judeo-West Slavic speech as (Judeo-) Sorbian. My choice of the latter term does not mean that the Jews were settled in, or that Slavic slaves converted to Judaism uniquely or predominantly from, Lausitz/*Luzica* (the area with the highest concentration of Sorbs/*Serbja* today), since the primeval Slavic settlements in German were far more extensive a millennium ago.**

In addition to a Slavic language, Wexler writes, **the ethnic origins, folkways and religion of the Ashkenazic Jews are also largely of Slavic origin** (e.g. Western Yiddish *kowlec*, Eastern Yiddish *kojlec* 'braided festive bread'— from the Slavic *kolac, kojlec*; Eastern Yiddish *praven* 'conduct a religious ceremony' — from the Slavic *pravic, spravit*; Eastern and Northeast German Yiddish *trejbern* 'render meat kosher by removing forbidden fat and veins'— from the Slavic *triebiti, trjebic, treba, trebiti, trebiste*; Yiddish *gojlem*, Yiddish Hebrew *golem* 'supernatural servant made out of clay'—from the Slavic *holemek, holomek, holemy, golem*; Eastern Yiddish *pare(e)ve* 'food that can be eaten with milk or meat meals'—from Upper Sorbian *parowac*'; Eastern Yiddish *dezje* 'kneading trough'—from the Slavic *diz, dizva*). Not only original Slavic terms and practices, Wexler writes, but also Slavicized German terms and practices as well. Moreover, the Germans may have actually passed on originally Slavic customs to the Jews.

With regard to *voluntary* transformation dynamics, Wexler writes: **In the mixed Germano-Slavic lands, the pagan Slavs were under pressure to accept the German language, along with the German religion, Christianity ... Sorbs could have considerably improved their chances of surviving as Slavs if they joined the Jewish**

554

community, since most or all the Jews were presumably Sorbian speaking, and since as Jews the Sorbs/*Serbja* would not have constituted the main object of Christian missionary activity.

At another point, Wexler writes: **association with the Sorbian Jews would have enabled the Slavs to avoid 'denationalization' at a time when German settlers were imposing their Christian religion, their German language and culture … Conversion to Judaism would have protected the Sorbs/*Serbja* from German Christian persecution, since the independent status of the Jews was recognized by the Christian Authorities … The Sorbian speaking Jews were one of the few elements of the Slavic population in the Middle Ages to maintain a separate identity during the Germanization of the territory … I theorize that conversion to Judaism was most likely wherever the Slavs felt their ethnic identity was in danger, e.g. in the Sorb/*Serbja* lands.**

With regard to the *involuntary* transformation dynamics, Wexler writes: **By steadfastly rejecting Christianity, the West Slavs living among the Germans provided the German missionaries and colonists with an excuse to expand into their territories … Hence the West Slavs came to form the bulk of the slave population in a German dominated society … The Jews were also active in the international slave trade, most of which centered in the Slavic lands; Jewish practice called for the conversion of non-Jewish slaves employed by Jewish households.**

Yiddish, Wexler writes, **is a Slavic language, a form of the West Slavic Sorbian and the Ashkenazic Jews are predominantly of Slavic origins. As I have demonstrated elsewhere, Yiddish in contrast to its massive German vocabulary—has a native Slavic syntax and phonology since it was a form of the West Slavic language Sorbian which became re-lexified to High German. A massive German lexicon cannot make Yiddish German, just as the massive Franco-Latin component of modern English gives no grounds for declaring that English has ceased to be a Germanic language, and has moved over to the Roman camp.**

It appears that in terms of race and history, Zionist Ashkenazic Jews are on the wrong track. Instead of attempting to return and reclaim a fictive ancestral homeland in the Middle East, race, history and logic point to Germania, to an authentic ancestral homeland centered between the Elbe and Oder rivers, and a restoration of *Regnum Sorabia*, a *Greater Regnum Sorabia* stretching from a Main/Regnitz line in the west to the Vistula in the east.

As fate would have it, instead of a re-Slavicization of Germania/Slavia, Zionism, Wexler writes, has resulted in the mass Slavicization of Semitic Jews and others in Israel: **After the creation of the State of Israel in 1948, most of the Jewish communities Africa and Asia were liquidated when hundreds of thousands of their members immigrated to Israel. There they gradually became "assimilated" to Ashkenazic religious, cultural and linguistic patterns. The assimilation of the non-Ashkenazic Jews to Ashkenazic culture is certainly one of the more grandiose instances of Slavicization in modern history.**

REGNUM SLAVORUM CONTINUATIO

All who wish to know more about **Svetopelek**, Dukljanin writes, **the most holy king, who ruled forty years and forty days should read the Slavic book, Methodius.** *Svetopelek,* Dukljanin writes, was buried at the Church of St. Mary in the city of *Duklja,* where his son, **Svetolik,** is installed by bishops and archbishops. From that **day forward it was the custom to crown all kings of the land in the same church.**[1]

SUCCESSORS

Good and bad kings follow *Svetopelek.* Dukljanin mentions son **Svetolik, Vladislav, Tomislav, Sebeslav, Razbivoj, Vladimir, Hranimir, Tvrdoslav, Ostrivoj, Tolimir, Pridislav, Krepimir, Svetozar, Radoslav,** a man of great virtue (**omni bonitate fuit ornatus**), and **Caslav.**

INVASIONS

In this period several invasions are recorded. German advances into Istria and *Croatia* are turned back by **Krepimir.** After learning a bitter lesson, the German commander, a cousin of the Emperor, offers his daughter in marriage to **Krepimir's** son, **Svetozar.** As intended, the marriage improves relations and secures peace between the two parties. An able and popular ruler, after 25 years, **Krepimir** is succeeded by son **Svetozar** and grandson **Radoslav,** one and the other able and just rulers. Hungarian advances into *Bosnia* and *Srem* are halted by **Caslav, Radoslav's** son. At a great battle near the *Drina River, Caslav's* forces inflicts a defeat so great **that the battleground is even today known as Cvilino, or The Place of Screams, from the screams and moans of the Hungarians cut to pieces.** Prince Kis, the Hungarian commander, is killed by one of Caslav's favorites, **Tihomir. A powerful young lad, Tihomir,** son of **Budislav, from the village of Rabike in the district of Sraga**, is rewarded with the *Drina Zupania* and marriage to the daughter of the *Ban of Raska.*

ROYAL CASUALTIES

Several kings are killed in defense of the kingdom. At the head of a large army raised in *Rascia* and *Bosnia* (**congregans gentem ex Rasaa et Bosna**), **Hranimir** is killed in battle with rebels on the plain of *Livno.* In battle with rebels in *Bosnia* (**baroni de Bosnia**), **Pridislav** is killed. **Caslav** is killed in battle with Hungarians in *Srem.*

BELO PAVLIMIR

As **Caslav** is without a successor, the crown reverts to his exiled father, **Radoslav,** to grandson, **Pavlimir,** better known as **Belo Pavlimir**, on account of his bellicose nature (**eo quod bellum facere valde delectabatur**). From *Dubrovnik,* **Pavlimir** advances into *Travunia,* where he receives the crown from an assembled and united nation, with one exception, the *Zupan of Raska.* **Pavlimir** marches into *Raska* and near the *Lim River* engages and destroys rebel forces, after which he marks the victory by building the Church of St. Peter at Ras and building a fortress, called Belo, on a nearby height. **Pavlimir** is quick to respond to all foreign threats to the kingdom. In *Srem* he meets and annihilates the Hungarians. In his memory and honor the site of that battle is called the *Belina Plain*. **From that time to the present, the Hungarians never once dared cross the Sava River, from its source, along its channel, to where it empties into the Danube.** *Pavlimir* dies from natural causes in a town in *Travunia*, where he is buried in the Church of St. Michael.

TJESIMIR

His son and successor, *Tjesimir*, marries a daughter of the *Ban of Croatia*, *Cudomir*, a union that begets two sons, *Prelimir* and *Kresimir*.

PRELIMIR, KRESIMIR

When fighting in *Prevalitania* claims *Tjesimir's* life, after defeating the rebels *Prelimir* takes the crown, and *Kresimir* takes *Serbia-Bosnia*, and, following *Cudomir's* death, *Croatia*.

CROATIA

Kresmir's son, *Stefan*, succeeds him as *Ban of Bosnia* **and establishes a dynastic line in Croatia that rules there from that time to the present.**

PRELIMIR REGAINS SERBIA-RASCIA

Internal order restored, the kingdom is faced with a serious foreign threat, a Byzantine offensive that ends in the annexation of *Serbia-Rascia*. Over time, *Prelimir* succeeds in organizing a rebellion and expelling the Byzantines from *Serbia-Rascia*, where he installs brother-in-law *Radigrad* as *Veliki Zupan*. Well into his reign, *Prelimir* establishes a tetrarchy, the system of government proclaimed by Diocletian at the end of the 3rd century, literally the rule of four. In this instance the rule of *Prelimir's* four sons: *Duklja* goes to *Hvalimir*, *Travunia* to *Boleslav*, *Zahumlja* to *Dragoslav*, *Podgorje* to *Prevlad*. Just as Constantine's tetrarchy failed to outlive its originator, *Prelimir's* experiment fails to survive his passing. Instead of unity and harmony, it is a source of anarchy and conflict until *Hvalimir* reunites the kingdom.

REX VLADIMIRUS, ST. VLADIMIR

From *Hvalimir* the crown passes to *Petrislav* to his son, *rex Vladimirus*, perhaps the most illustrious and enduring figure in Serb and South Slav history and the first Serb to gain sainthood. The cult of *St. Vladimir* will reach lands near and far and cross national and confessional lines. Renowned for his piety, virtue, wisdom, stature and manly beauty, *Vladimir's* just rule (990-1016) could not resist the powerful forces unleashed by a Bulgar rebellion against Byzantine rule.

TSAR SAMUILO

In less than a decade the Bulgars, led by Samuilo, later Tsar Samuilo, take Bulgaria, Macedonia, western Thrace, Thessaly, Epirus, most of Albania, including *Drac*, from the Byzantines. From *Drac* the Bulgars move against *Duklja*, lay siege to two strongholds, *Oblik*, defended by *Vladimir*, and *Ulcinj*. Repulsed at *Ulcinj*, the invaders concentrate their forces against *Oblik*. Samuilo offers *Oblik's* defenders their freedom if *Vladimir* will meet with him. Hoping to spare his kingdom further bloodshed and devastation, *Vladimir* enters into negotiations with Samuilo. Betrayed by his negotiator, the *Zupan of Oblik*, **Vladimir** is captured and sent in chains to Samuilo's capital at Prespa. Continuing his conquest of *Dalmatia*, Samuilo's powerful armies burn *Kotor* and *Dubrovnik*, reach *Zadar*, and return home through the twin provinces of *Bosnia-Rascia*.

KOSARA

At Samuilo's court dungeon, according to the custom of the time, **Vladimir** and other noble prisoners are tended to by the Emperor's daughter, Kosara, and her ladies. **Vladimir's** noble bearing, piety and virtue gain **Kosara's** profound love: *Inter haec cernens Vladimirum et videns quot esset pulcher in aspect, humilis, mansuetus atque modestum et quod esset repletus sapientia et preudentia domini, morata locuta est cum illo. Videbatur namque ei loquella illius dulcis super mel et favum. Igitur non causa libidinis, sed quia condoluit iuventuti ext pulchritudini illius, et quoniam audiret eum esse regem et ex regali prosapia ortum, dilexit eum et salutato eo recessit.*

MARRIAGE

Given **Vladimir's** royal blood and noble character, Samuilo approves the marriage: *Quia valde diligebat filiam suam et quia sciebat, Vladimirum ex regali progenie ortum, laetus effectus est, annuit fieri petitionem illus.*

RETURN TO DUKLJA

With Samuilo's blessing, **Vladimir** and **Kosara** return to a greater *Duklja*, enlarged by Samuilo's grant of the theme of *Drac* (**terra Duracenorum**), without the city of Drac.

TSAR VLADISLAV

A crushing defeat at the hands of Emperor Basil I leads to Samuilo's death in 914. He is succeeded by an able son, Gavrilo Radomir, who, the following year, is assassinated by a dynastic rival, Vladislav. Three times Vladislav's emissaries summon **Vladimir** to **Prespa**. Suspecting treachery, **Kosara** answers the first summons and is received with appropriate honors and gifts. A second mission offers **Vladimir** a golden cross and a sacred oath of safe passage and return. Citing Christ's example, **Vladimir** asks them to return with a wooden cross and leaders of the church. Two bishops and a monk bring a wooden cross to **Vladimir** and swear to Tsar Vladislav's oath of safe passage and return. His conditions met, **Vladimir**, the two bishops, monk, and escort set out for *Prespa*.

ASSASSINATION

The Tsar's plans call for **Vladimir's** ambush and murder by *unknown* assailants on the way to *Prespa*. At each ambush along the way, however, the assassins are driven off. When **Vladimir** arrives safe and whole at *Prespa*, Vladislav orders his immediate execution. Assassins rush to the church where **Vladimir** is praying, order him to leave, and murder him on the church steps (1016).

MIRACLES, PILGRIMAGES

The night of **Vladimir's** burial, a holy light, like that of many bright, radiant candles, appears over his grave: *Nocte vero vidabatur ibi ad omnibus lumen divinum* *at quai plurimas ardere candelas. Vladimir's* grave is soon the sight of many miracles. Pilgrims arrive from many Balkan lands. Many are healed and made whole.

RETURN TO DUKLJA

Eager to rid himself of **Vladimir's** sacred remains, Vladislav permits **Kosara** to return to *Duklja* with **Vladimir's** remains, where next to his residence in *Krajina* (*in loco qui Craini dicitur*), in the Church of St. Mary's (*ubi curia eius fuit et ecclesia sanctae Mariae*), his body, whole fresh and fragrant (*lacet corpus eius integrum et redolt quai pluribus conditum aromatibus*), is reburied. The Church of St. Mary or the Church of Our Lady of Krajina (*Precista Krajinska*) was a large, beautiful church situated on the northern edge of *Lake Skadar,* with an open and stunning view of the *Duklja* heartland all the way to the city of *Skadar* on the opposite end. It is here that **Kosara** dedicates her life to good works, preserving her husband's memory, and establishing a woman's monastery (*collegius sacarum Virginium*). Since then, to this day, Dukljanin writes, the day of **Vladimir's** death is marked by services in his honor. In a second statement that suggests an early and vital literacy in *Duklja*, Dukljanin writes: **Who wishes to know more of the number and nature of the many good deeds and miracles of St. Vladimir, let them read the book about his deeds and miracles, and he will learn that this saintly man was at one with god.**

BYZANTINE AND OTHER SOURCES

It is interesting that the basic moments of the life and death of **St. Vladimir** are confirmed by Bzantine and other sources. *The Chronicle of John Scilitzes*, for example, records that: **Vladimir was a man of peace, justice and many virtues ... That while he ruled in Duklja there was peace in the Serb lands, including Drac ... That Vladimir was deceived ... That he trusted a pledge of safe-conduct delivered by David, the archbishop of Bulgaria ... That he was killed, after which the situation in the Drac district went from bad to worse.**

PRINCIPALITY OF EPIRUS

Perhaps the greatest historical testimony to **St. Vladimir's** status in the Christian hierarchy in the Balkans is found in the events that took place in the early 13th century, following the formation of a powerful Byzantine state between the Gulf of Corinth in the south and *Drac* in the north, the principality of Epirus founded by Michael Angelus (1204-1215). In the year 1215, the Epirotes seized and occupied the city of *Skadar*. In a raid along the shores of Lake Skadar, the Epirotes succeed in capturing the remains of **St. Vladimir.** After a brief stay at *Drac,* the Epirotes place the remains to rest at St. John's Monastery (thereafter **St. John Vladimir's** Monastery) near Elbasan in central Albania.

ST. VLADIMIR'S DAY

St. Vladimir's fame attracts pilgrims of all faiths from Greece, Macedonia, and Albania. Each year on **St. Vladimir's** day, the stone sarcophagus is opened and the wooden coffin is carried to the courtyard for observation and worship by pilgrim processions. In 1380 the monastery is renovated by Karlo Thopi, the leading figure in Albania between the Mat and Skhumb rivers. The epitaph is in three languages: Greek, Latin, and Serbian.

MT. RUMIJA

St. Vladimir's wooden cross remains in *Duklja,* where each year a great procession of pilgrims of all faiths climbs the rugged slopes of *Mt. Rumija.* At the top, **St. Vladimir's** cross is raised and celebrated in a small chapel built from stones carried by worshipers, where candles are lit and services are held.

SUCCESSORS

Vladimir was succeeded by his uncle, **Dragimir,** whose efforts to restore the kingdom are cut short by his treacherous murder in a church in *Kotor.* N.W. Ingham summarizes this moment in the following words: **Dragimir is enticed to an island (Prevlak) by an invitation to a feast; the people want to attack him at the meal, but he takes refuge in a church. They kill him by throwing rocks and other objects through an opening in the roof** (*N.W. Ingham, The Martyrdom of Saint John Vladimir of Dioclea, International Journal of Slavic Linguistics and Poetics 35-36, 1987*).

STEFAN VOJISLAV

Dragimir's son and successor, **Stefan Vojislav** (1035-1050), born and raised in *Bosnia,* educated in *Dubrovnik,* is faced with with a new cycle of Byzantine aggression. Following the collapse of the Second Bulgarian Empire, the Byzantines seize Bulgaria, *Serbia (Bosnia and Rascia)* and most of *Upper Dalmatia* **(Basilius ... obtinuit totam Bulgariam, Rassam et Bosnem totamque Dalmatiam omnesque maritimas regiones usque in finibus inferioris Dalmatiae).** Byzantine interventions in *Duklja's* affairs alert *Vojislav* to the dangers inherent in maintaining friendly relations with a neighboring empire. At an opportune time, with his five grown sons, **able and tough fighters one and all, Vojislav attacks and expels the Greeks and takes all the land up to Toplica** *(c. 1040).* Matters are further aggravated by *Vojislav's* seizure of ten *kenetars* of gold from a Byzantine ship forced ashore and broken up on the Adriatic coast. A punitive expedition against *Duklja,* commanded by George Probat, is met and destroyed.

VICTORY AT VRANJ

Eager to destroy this **wise and clever barbarian**, Emperor Michael (1034-1041) sends one of his top commanders against **Vojislav Dukljanin.** A large army of infantry and cavalry enters *Duklja* by way of the *Zeta Plain* **(usque ad planotiem Zentae)** and advances with fire and sword. Near *Vranj* **(in locum, qui Vurania dicitur)**, the Byzantine army is met and destroyed. Dukljanin gives the following information regarding the victor's strategy and tactics. Placing one part of his army under the comand of his five sons, **King Vojislav has them take a position at a place called Vranj, on the east side, where they are to await the outcome of the main battle.** Attacking from the west, the army under *Vojislav's* command **overcomes and destroys all resistance.** Son *Radoslav* plays an important role in the victory. **Cutting his way through the Greek ranks, Radoslav reaches and fells their commander. Seeing this, the Greeks panic and retreat in disorder. So many were killed it was impossible to count their losses.** The most terrible fate was perhaps suffered by those who fled. **Many who fled, who appeared to escape the slaughter, were attacked and killed by the king's sons waiting in ambush.**

BYZANTINE SOURCES

Byzantine sources not only confirm Dukljanin's account of the battle, but also offer a more vivid and complete account of the disaster. Indeed, compared to Byzantine sources, Dukljanin's words are an understatement. **Stefan Vojislav ... occupied the Illyrian mountains ... attacked and plundered the Serbs and other nations subject to the Romans ... The Emperor Monomah ordered the arhont of Drac to defeat Stefan ... A large army, some sixty thousand strong invaded Duklja and plundered the lowlands ... The Serbs held the highlands and controlled the passes ... The Serb attack was horrible ... Some forty thousand were killed ... The hollows, ravines, and river-beds were filled with our dead ... The rest fled and hid in the forests and mountains, where, later, under the cover of night, they returned home, naked and barefoot, a tragic sight for all to behold.**

DIVIDE AND CONQUER

Determined to avenge the catastrophic defeat, the Byzantines, up to their old divide-and-conquer tricks, send emissaries laden with gifts of gold and silver to **the Zupan of Rascia, the Ban of Bosnia, and Knez of Zahumlja, so that they will send their armies against the king. After assembling a mighty force, Ban and Zupan, call on Ljutovid, Knez of Zahumlja, to serve as commander of a united army.**

Emperor Constantine (1042-55) takes every step and measure to ensure a definitive victory. **The Emperor raised an army greater than the first one. He ordered the governor of Drac, Kursilija, to mobilize all available manpower and take command. So many were called to arms in Drac and neighboring themes that it was difficult to assemble the army in one place. The assembled forces were so great in number that the two armies, imperial and provincial, were barely contained by the Skadar plain.**

VICTORY IN CRMNICA (1042-43)

Gathering his sons to his side, *Vojislav* outlines his battle plan: **My dear sons see how great in number is the Greek army, how few in number is our army ... This is what we must do: Gojslav and Radoslav, stay with me. The others take swift men with bugles and horns, climb to the top of surrounding heights, move around in a way that will cause the Greeks to think we are many and they are surrounded. With my forces I will attack their camp at dawn. When you hear our bugles and horns, you do the same, moving from place to place, blowing and shouting as loud as you can. Descend slowly and advance toward their camp. When you are close, be without fear. Attack in a manly manner and God will grant us victory.**

To reinforce the illusion, the king sends a friend from *Bar* to the nearby Greek camp. Pretending to be an informer, he gives warning to Kursulija: **Be careful, my Lord. Make no mistake, you are surrounded on all sides by large and powerful armies. You must take prudent steps if you are to escape with your great army.** The warning spreads like wildfire through the Greek camp and gives rise to new fears, intensified by attacks on and liquidation of all guard and observation posts. In a decisive battle in *Crmnica,* the Byzantines suffer an even greater defeat. According to plan, at a critical moment, **when the king and his commanders saw signs that the Greeks** were beginning to waver and panic, they attacked their camp at dawn, wounding or killing all in their path. Attacking from all sides, the king's sons drove the survivors back to the Drim River, where many were wounded, killed or captured.

BYZANTINE SOURCES

According to Byzantine sources, the imperial army alone **numbered some sixty thousand, of which some forty thousand were killed, including seven strategs.**

KNEZ LJUTOVID

The battle with the Greeks settled, *Vojislav* sends son *Gojslav* against *Ljutovid.* Crossing the *Bay of Kotor*, then *Konavli, Gojslav* routs *Knez Lyutovid's* forces near a height called *Klobuk.* **No one daring to oppose them, Stefan Vojislav and his sons rule in peace.**

VOJUSHA RIVER

Taking territorial advantage of his victories, *Vojislav* annexes the theme of *Drac* and expands the kingdom's southern border to the *Vojusha River* in Albania, **where a strong fortress is built and stationed with brave men, who raid and plunder the Byzantine lands and each day capture many Byzantines.** After twenty-five years of distinguished service to his people, *Stefan Vojislav* dies at his residence at *Papratin* and is buried at the nearby Church of St. Sergius.

THE CASE OF VOJISLAV DUKLJANIN

More subtle measures were also used against *Vojislav.* One measure is recorded in a Byzantine casebook. The case of *Vojislav Dukljanin* is a warning to all strategs dealing with barbarians. **An important lesson is found in the experience of Katalon, the strateg in Dubrovnik. He attempted to use false friendship as a means to capture Vojislav Dukljanin. Here's what he did. He made friends with Vojislav and often sent him gifts, hoping thereby to conceal his true intentions. Although a barbarian, by nature and experience Vojislav was wise and clever. He accepted the gifts and also pretended to be a friend and ally. Moving forward with his plan, the strateg offered to be god-father to Vojislav's recent born son. The strateg hesitated when Vojislav replied,** *If such is your wish, come to us.* **Instead, they agreed to meet at a halfway point on the coast. In well-placed and concealed offshore boats the strateg positioned his forces, which, on signal, were to land and capture Vojislav. As planned, they met, exchanged warm greetings and sat down. However, no sooner were they seated, a signal was given by Vojislav, the strateg was seized, so too his son and all others. In this way, to the great shame of the Romans, the strateg fell into the very traps and nets he set for the other. We must be very careful that our clever ideas are not the means of our enemy's victory, that our disgrace and misfortune do not add to his fame and glory. Therefore it is important that we proceed with great caution, that we not repeat this same and very recent mistake.**

REX SCLAVORUM

Following a transition period involving the Queen and his brothers, *Mihailo* (1050-1082), called *Rex Sclavorum* by Pope Gregory VII, assumes the throne of a united and powerful kingdom.

ZAHUMLJA

In *Zahumlja,* at *Statania,* the old city of *Ston,* on the *Peljesac* peninsula, **Mihailo** establishes a royal residence and founds the Church of St. Mihailo. A surviving fresco portrays **Mihailo** with a crown on his head and a church in his hands. In all things energetic, with his first wife **Mihailo** fathers seven sons; with a second wife, a cousin of the Byzantine emperor (**consobrianem imperatoris**), he fathers four sons.

RASCIA

After his sons secure *Rascia,* son **Petrislav** is left to govern there.

TRAVUNIA, ZAHUMLJA

Mihailo's brother, **Radoslav,** liquidates opposition in *Travunia* and re-unites *Travunia* and *Zahumlja* to the kingdom.

BULGARIA

Next, **rex Mihailo** is asked to accept an imperial crown from the Bulgarians. Instead, **Mihailo** sends his sons, led by **Bodin,** to Bulgaria (**quam provincial dedit rex Michala Bodino filio ad regendum**), to lead the rebels against the Byzantines.

BODIN, EMPEROR OF BULGARIA

After successive victories over the Byzantines, **Bodin** is crowned emperor of Bulgaria. Dukljanin's account of **Bodin's** accession to the throne is confirmed by Byzantine sources. **In the first years of our Emperor's rule, the Serbs invaded and conquered Bulgaria ... Let me tell you how this happened ... The rebel leaders of Bulgaria pleaded with Mihailo, ruler of Duklja, to assist them, to join forces, to allow a son to be crowned Emperor of Bulgaria ... In response, Mihailo sent an army led by his son, Bodin ... At Prizren the assembled Bulgars crowned him Peter, Emperor of Bulgaria ... After destroying a large Byzantine army near Prizren, Bodin moved against the Nish district, where he destroyed everything in his path, while Petrilo (another commander from Duklja), moved against the Romans in the district of Kastoria.**

REX RADOSLAV

After 35 years of distinguished rule, **Mihailo** dies and is buried at the Church of St. Sergius. **Mihailo** is succeeded by his brother, **Radoslav,** who rules for sixteen years.

BODINI, REGIS SCLAVORUM GLORIOSISSIMI

Pushing **Radoslav** aside, **Bodin** (1081-1116), called **filii Nostri Bodini, regis Sclavorum gloriosissimi** by Pope Clement II, assumes the throne and moves against all opposition in *Duklja.*

SERBIA-RASCIA

After quelling opposition in *Duklja,* **Bodin** secures *Serbia-Rascia* and appoints two members of his court, **Zupans Vukan** and **Marko,** to rule there.

SERBIA-BOSNIA

Next, **Bodin** secures *Serbia-Bosnia* and appoints **Knez Stefan** to rule there.

DRAC

The situation in *Dalmatia* under control, **Bodin** moves against the Normans in the *Drac* theme. Expelling the Normans, **Bodin** gives the city to the Byzantines and anexes the rest of the theme to his kingdom (1085).

CIVIL WAR

Bodin is more than equal to all tasks but one—healing the dynastic wounds inflicted by his treatment of his uncle, **King Radoslav. Radoslav's** eight sons are determined to recover the kingship, especially Branislav and his six sons. **Bodin's** arrest of **Branislav** leads to civil war.

BODIN CAPTURES DUBROVNIK

When the rebels take a stand at *Dubrovnik,* **Bodin** responds by executing **Branislav** before the city's walls and capturing the city, but not before the rebels flee by ship (1104). According to *Dubrovnik* sources, **Bodin's** *Bosnian* vassal, **Stephanus dux Bossinae**, plays an important role in the siege and capture of *Dubrovnik.* He **also builds a castle near the Church of St. Nicholas at Prijeki.** Before leaving Dubrovnik, **Bodin** builds a fortress in the city and places a certain **Utvigo Gradiense** in command, the ancestor of the noble *Ragusan* house of **Gradich.**

BEGINNING OF THE END

After 26 years of rule, **Bodin** is buried at the Church of St. Sergius. He is succeeded by brother **Dobroslav,** an unpopular and harsh ruler, who is hard put to cope with the fierce and resolute resistance of the brothers, sons, and supporters of the **Branislav** line. In the period that follows it is rather standard practice for one or more of the contesting parties to retreat to *Serbia,* raise an army there and re-enter the dynastic fray in *Duklja.*

KOCAPAR

One of **Branislav's** brothers, **Kocapar,** retreats to **Serbia-Rascia** and gains the support of **Zupan Vukan. Kocapar** and **Vukan** invade *Duklja,* defeat and capture **Dobroslav** at a battle on the *Moraca River* (**in Dioclia supra fluvium, qui Moracia dicitur**). In a struggle over the spoils, in fear of **Vukan, Kocapar** flees to *Bosnia,* marries the daughter of the *Ban of Bosnia.* Shortly thereafter he is killed in battle in *Zahumlja.*

VLADIMIR

Dobroslav is succeeded by **Vladimir,** one of **King Mihailo's** many grandsons, who marries **Zupan Vukan's** daughter.

DJURO

An able, just, and popular ruler, **Vladimir** is poisoned by **Bodin's** wife and succeeded by her son, **Djuro,** who invades **Serbia-Rascia,** frees **Vukan's** successor, **Urosh,** and reinstalls him as *Zupan of Rascia,* the last effective *Dukljan* intervention in *Rascia's* affairs.

GRUBISHA

Shortly, **Djuro** is ousted in favor of one of **Branislav's** sons, **Grubisha,** who is crowned with imperial and popular support (**iussu imperatoris constitutus est rex a** *populo*).

DJURO RETURNS

Djuro returns with an army raised in *Serbia-Rascia*. At a battle near *Bar*, *Grubisha* is killed and *Djuro* recovers the crown, if not the land. *Gradinja* and *Dragilo,* two of *Grubisha's* sons, retain control over a number of important and strategic *zupas.*

REX GRADINJA

Following a definitive defeat of *Djuro, Gradinja,* the last *Oistrolovic* to rule over *Duklja-Dalmatia,* is crowned king with popular approval and support. **In spite of the intrigues of numerous evildoers, Gradinja's eleven year reign is marked by peace, justice and compassion. His death is mourned by the nation and he is buried with honors at the Church of St. Sergius.**

DESA, ZUPAN OF RASCIA

Radoslav's efforts to succeed his father are frustrated by rivals who turn parts of the kingdom over to *Urosh's* son and successor, *Desa,* Zupan of Rascia.

KNEZ RADOSLAV

Never a king, only a prince, *Knez Radoslav's* (*knesius Radoslavus*) rule is reduced to a principality that is little more than a narrow strip on the coast between and including *Kotor* and *Skadar* (*remansit maritimia regio et civitas Decatarum usque Scodarim*).

ENDNOTES

[1] S. Novakovic, Prvi osnovi slovenske knjizevnosti medju balkanskim Slovenima: Legenda o Vladimiru i Kosari, 1893. I. Markovic, Dukljansko-Barska Mitropolija, 1902. K. Jirecek, Geschichte der Serben, I-II, 1918. F. Sisic, Letopis Popa Dukljanina, 1928. P. Skok, Ortsnamenstudien zu De Administrando imperio des Kaisers Constantin Porphyrogennetos ZfO 4, 1929. N. Radojicic, Drustveno i drzavno uredjenje kod Srba u ranom Srednjem veku— prema Barskom rodoslovy, Glasnik Skopskog naucnog drustva, XV-XVI, 1936; O najtamnijem odeljky Barskog rodoslova, 1951. M. Budimir, Porfirgent i nasa narodna tradicija, GIA 1, 1949. V. Mosin, Ljetopis Popa Dukljanina, 1950. S. Cirkovic, Srednjevekovna srpska drzave, 1959; Stari srpski zapisi i natpisi, 1982; Bar, grad pod Rumijom; R. Mihaljcic, Enciklopedija srpske istoriografije, 1997. T. Wasilewski, Administraja bizantyska na ziemiach slowianskich i je polityka wobec Slowian w XI-XII w, KwA 70, 1963. S. Mijuskovic, Ljetopis Popa Dukljanina, 1967. B. Ferjancic, Vizantija i Juzni Sloveni, 1966. M. Dinic, Serbski zemlje u srednjem veku, 1978. N. Banasevic, Letopis Popa Dukljanina i Narodna Predanja, 1971. J. Ferluga, Byzantium on the Balkans: studies on the Byzantine administration and the Southern Slavs from the 7th to the 12th centuries, 1976; Vizantijski uprava u Dalmaciji, 1978. L. Steindorff, Die Synode auf der Planities Dalmae. Reichseinteilung und Kirchenorganisation im Bild der Chronik des Priesters von Diocela, Mitteilungen des Instituts fur Osterreichische Geschichtsforschung 93, 1985. J. Udolph, Zu Deutung und Verbreitung des Namens Dukla, BnF 23, 1988.

BIBLIOGRAPHY

1. Ernst Eichler
2. Joachim Herrmann
3. Heinrich Kunstmann
4. Ethnonym Serb
5. Slav and German in Germania
6. Slavs in Germania
7. Slavs in Germania: Main, Regnitz, Naab Wendenlands.
8. Slavs in Germania: Borders, Borderlands
9. Slavs in Germania: Languages, Dialects, Speech
10. Slavs in Germania: Archaeological Sites
11. Slavs in Germania: Burgs, Burgwalls
12. Slavs in Germania: Ortsnamen
13. Slavs in Germania: Hydronyms, Toponyms
14. Slavs in Germania: Names, Name Formation
15. Slavs in Germania: Mixed Names, Name Integration
16. Slavs in Germania: Serbs
17. Slavs in Germania: Serb Provinces, Borderlands
18. Slavs in Germania: Serb Language
19. Slavs in Germania: Luzica Serbs
20. Slavs in Germania: Obodritorum
21. Slavs in Germania: Luticiorum
22. Slavs in Germania: Rugianorum
23. Slavs in Germania: Polaborum, Wendorum
24. Slavs in Germania: Hanover Wendland
25. Slavs in Germania: West, Northwest, Baltic Slavs
26. Slavs in Germania/Polonia: Volin, Stetin
27. Slavs in Germania/Polonia: Pomoranorum
28. Germania Serbs in Texas: Serbin, Texas

1. ERNST EICHLER

Der Name der terra Sclavinica Siuseli, WiS 4, 1954-55.

Eine westslawische Bezeichnung fur "Sumpf, Feuchtikeit": altsorbisch *mroka, ZtS 1, 1956.

Beitrage zur Erforschung altsorbischer Stammes- und Gaunamen, BnF 7, 1956.

Zu einigen slawische Flussnamen des Saale- und Muldesystem, Leipziger Studien, 1957.

Die Orts- und Flussnamen der Kreise Delitzsch und Eilenburg; Studien zur Namenkunde und Siedlungsgeschichte im Saale-Mulde-Gebiet, 1958.

Slawisch Wald und Rodungsnamen an Elbe und Salle, Benennung und Sprachkontakt bei Eigennamen, BnF 9, 1958.

O. Kieser, Zur Geographie slawischer Lehnworter im nordl. Obersach, FuF 33, 1959.

Slawischer namen im Bereich der Stadt Leipzig, ZtS 4, 1959.

Zur gemanoslawistischen Namenforschung in Sachsen und Thuringen, FuF 34, 1960.

E. Lea, Hans Walther, Die Ortsnamen des Kreises Leipzig, 1960.

Probleme der Analyse slawischer Ortsnamen in Deutschland, Leipziger namenkundliche Beitrage, 1961.

H. Deubler, Slawische Flurname im Kreise Rudolstadt, RuD 7, 1961.

Daleminze und Dalmatien, Balkansko ezikoznaie 5, 1962.

Grundzate beim Ansatz altsorbischer Namenformen, ZtS 7, 1962.

Drevneluzickaja jazykovaja oblast po dannym toponimiki, VjZ 11, 1962.

Zur Deutung und Verbreitung der altsorbischen Bewohnernamen auf -jane, Slavia 31, 1962.

Zur Etymologie und Struktur der slawischen Orts- und Flurnamen in Nordostbayern, Leipziger Abhandlungen zu Namenforschung und Siedlungsgeschichte, 1962.

H. Jakob, Slawische Forst- und Flurnamen im Obermaingebiet, Leipzizer Abhandlungen zu Namenforschung und Siedlungsgeschichte, 1962.

R. Fischer, H. Naumann, H. Walther, Beitrage zum Slawischen Onomastischen Atlas aus der DDR, ZtS 8, 1963.

Zur Geographie und Chronologie der slawischen Namen in Nordostbayern, Slawische Namenforschung, 1963.

Aus der slawischen Toponomastik der Landschaft Puonzowa, Studia Linguistica in Honorem T. Lehr-Splawinski, 1963.

Die altsorbische Namengeographie im Dienste der Sprachgeschichte, WiS 12, 1963.

H. Naumann, H. Walther, Materialen zum Slawischen Onomastischen Atlas, 1964.

Ergebnisse der Namensgeographie im altsorbischen Sprachgebiet, Materialen zum Slawischen Onomastischen Atlas, 1964.

Einige kulturgeschichtlich aufschlussreiche Namen aus dem altsorbischen Sprachgebiet, LeT C/6-7, 1964.

Tschechisch-sorbische Parallelen in der Toponamastik, Zur Herkunft der Slawen im Elbe-Saale-Gebiet, 1964.

K. Rosel, Slawische Flurnamen im Kreise Meissen, Sachsische Heimatblatter 11, 1965.

Aus dem altsorbischen Namenwortschatz, ArB 14/15, 1965.

Studien zur Fruhgeschichte slawischer Mundarten zwischen Saale und Neisse, 1965.

Etymologisches Worterbuch der slawischen Elemente in Ostmitteldeutschen, SpL 29, 1965.

Zur Methodik der Namenforschung im deutsch-slawischen Beruhrungsgebiet. WiS 14, 1965.

Volker- und Landschaftsnamen im altsorbischen Sprachgebiet, LeT A/13, 1966.

Zur Rekonstruction der altsorbischen possessivischen Ortsnamen vom Typ L'uban uws. Eing Beigrag zum Slawischen Onomastischen Atlas, Studia jezykoznawcze poswiecone S. Rospondowi, 1966.

Hans Walther, Dies Ortsnamen im Gau Daleminze. Studien zur Toponymie der Kreise Dobeln, Grossenhain, Meissen, Oschatz, und Riesa, I, II (1966-67).

Die slawisches Ortsnamen des Vogtlandes, JiS 14, 1967.

Die slawistischen Studien des Johann Leonhard Frisch. Ein Beitrag Geschichte der Deutschen Slawistik, 1967.

J. Schulteis, H. Walther, Beitrage zum Slawischen Onomastischen Atlas aus dem altsorbischen Sprachgebiet, ZtS 12, 1967.

Zur Ortsnamen-Forschung in der Niederlausitz, NiS 1, 1967.

Zur Struktur und Chronologie slawischer Namentypen, OsG 3, 1967.

Die slawischen Ortsnamen des Vogtlandes, LeT A/14, 1967.

R. Fischer, Slawische Ortsnamen am Bohmischen Mittelgebirge II, OsG 4, 1968.

Grundzatzliche Bemerkungen zur Erforschung des vorslawischen Substrats in der alt-sorbischen Onomastik, ZsP 2, 1968.

H. Walther, Zur altsorbischen Sozioctoponomie, Siedlung, Burg und Stadt, 1969.

Die niedersorbischen Namen fur die Stadte in der Niederlausitz, Regionalgeschichte und Namenkunde, 1969.

T. Witkowski, Namen der Stamme und Landschaften, Die Slawen in Detuschland, 1970.

K voprosu o rekonstrukcii drevneluzickogo slovarnogo sostava, Issledovanija po serboluzickim jazykam, 1970.

J. Schultheis, Zur Rekonstucktion slawischer Otsnamen vom Typ Radogosc, Luban (Possessiva auf -j-). Ein Beitrag zum Slawischen Onomastischen Atlas, OsG 5, 1970.

Zur sprachgeschichtlichen Auswertung der slawischen Ortsnamen im nordwestlichen Waldviertel, Studien der Namenkunde und Sprachgeographie, 1971.

R. Willnow, Probleme namenkundlicher Etymologie in altsorbischen Ortsnamen, OsG 6, 1971.

H.D. Krausch, Die Sudgrenze des Landes Lebus im Lichte der Topographie und Namenkunde, LeT A/21, 1974.

Die sorbischen Flurnamen im Bereich des fruheren Stiftes Neuzelle, GgC 1974.

Hans Walther, Ortsnamen der Oberlausitz, 1974.

Die Bedeutung der Onomastik fur die historische Erforschung des Wortschatzes, Slawische Wortstudien, 1975.

H. Walther, Die Ortsnamen der Niederlausitz, 1975.

Die slawische Landnahme: Daleminze und Glomaci, LeT A/22, 1975.

Zur altsorbischen Ethnonymi: Daleminze und Glomaci, LeT A/22, 1975.

Ortsnamenbuch der Oberlausitz: Studien zur Toponymie der Kreise Bautzen, Bischofswerda, Gorlitz, Hoyerswerda, Kamenz, Lobau, Niesky, Senftenberg, Weisswasser und Zittau, 1975-78.

Die Slawische Landnahme, OsG 10, 1976.

Beitrage zur konfrontierenden Sprachwissenschaft, 1976.

Beitrage zur Theorie und Geschichte der Eigennamen, 1976.

Die slawische Landnahmen im Elbe/Saale- und Oder-Raum und ihre Widerspiegelung in den Siedlungs- und Landschaftsnamen, OsG 10, 1976.

Zur Siedlungsgeschicte und zum sorbisch-deutschen Sprachkontakt im Lichte der Flurnamen des fruhen Stiftes Neuzelle, LeT A/23, 1976.

Slawisch Forst- und Flurnamen im Obermaingebiet, 1976.

Beitrage zum deutsch-slawischen Sprachkontakt, 1977.

Onomastik und historische Lexikologie des Westslawischen, ZtS 24, 1979.

Slawistische Palaolinguistik und Fruhgeschichte. Mythologisches in Ortsnamen, SlG 7-8, 1980-81.

Alte Gewassernmane zwischen Ostsee und Erzgeberge, BnF 16, 1981.

H. Walther, Studien zur historischen Toponymie des Mittelsaale-/Weisse Elster-Gebiets, ZtS 26, 1981.

Zur altesten (vorslawischen) Schicht der Gewassernamen im altsorbischen und altpolabischen Sprachgebiet, LeT A/28, 1981.

Zur Erforschung des westslawischen toponymischen Wortschatzes, LeT A/29, 1982.

H. Walther, Studient zu Suffix -ov gebildeten Ortsnamen in Brandenburg, ZtS 26, 1981.

Ergebnisse der Namenforschung im deutsch-slawischen Beruhungsgebiet, 1982.

'Ostliche' Spuren im altsorbischen Namengut?, BuF II, 1982.

V. Hellfritzsch, J. Richter, Die Ortsnamen des saschsischen Vogtlandes, 1-2, 1983.

Sorben und Deutsche im Daleminzgau im Lichte der Toponomastik, OsG 14, 1984.

H. Walther, Untersuchungen zur Ortsnamenkunde und Sprach- und Siedlungsgeschichte des Gebietes zwischen mittlerer Saale und Weisser Elster, 1984.

Reinhold Trautmann und die Deutsche Slawistik, 1984.

Probleme der Deutung altpolabischer Stammesnamen, ZtA, 1984.

Beitrage zur Deutsch-Slawischen Namenforschung (1955-1981): mit Vorwort und Namenregister, 1985.

Nochmals zum Ortsnamen Grimma, OnO IV, 1985.

Slawische Ortsnamen zwischen Saale und Neisse: ein Kompendium, 1985-1993.

Zur Typologie der slawishen Ortsnamen Niederosterreichs, OsG 15, 1986.

Probleme namenkundlicher Etymologie in slawischen Ortsnamen, Teil IV, OsG 15, 1986.

K. Hengst, W. Wenzel, Zur Entwicklung der deutsch-slawischen onomastischen Sprachkontaktforschung, OsG 15, 1986.

H. Walther, Stadtenamenbuch der DDR, 1986.

Probleme namenkundlicher Etymologie in altsorbischen Ortsnamen, Teil V. Nochmal zum Ortsnamen Grimma, OsG 16, 1987.

Die sprachliche Stellung der slawischen Dialekte im heutigen deutschen Sprachraum im Lichte der Onomastik, ZtS 32, 1987.

Zur deutschen Lautgestalt von Ortsnamen slawischer Herkunft in Nordostbayern, FsT H. Kunstmann, 1988.

Zwei Beitrage zur Geschichte der slawischen Sprachwissenschaft, 1988.

Probleme namenkundlicher Etymologie in altsorbischen Ortsnamen: Teil V. Nochmals zum Ortsnamen Grimma, OsG 16, 1988.

Das integrierte (slawisch-deutsch) Toponym in der lexikographischen Bearbeitung, OsG 16, 1988.

Probleme namenkundlicher Etymologie in slawischen Ortsnamen. V. Zum Gotternamen Mokos im Altsorbischen, OsG 17, 1988.

F. Debus, H. Walther, Bennenung und Sprachkontakt bei Eigennamen, 1988.

Zwei Beitrage zur Geschicte der Slawistik, 1988.

W. Sperber, K. Krueger, A. Thiels, Wort und Text: Slawistische Beitrage zum 65, 1988.

G. Wiemers, Zwei Beitrage zur Geschichte der Slawistik, 1988.

G. Schlimpert, Die slawistische Namenforschung in der DDR, ZtS 34, 1989.

Kontinuat und Diskontinuitat im deutsch-slawischen Sprachbereich, Dialetkgeographie und Dialektologie, 1989.

Probleme namenkundlicher Etymologie in slawischen Ortsnamen. VI. Wissepuig bei Thietmar, OsG 19, 1990.

Zur deutsche-polnischen Symbiose im Lichte der Toponymie, Sprache in der Slavia und auf dem Balkan, 1992.

R. Schmidt, Wendland und Altmark, 1992.

D. Krueger, Slawische Ortsnamen in der ostlichen Oberlausitz, Teil !, OsG 21, 1994.

Zum Zeugnis der altpolabischen Ortsnamen im Luneburger Wendland fur die Sprachgeschichte in Deutsch-slawischer Sprachkontakt im Lichte der Ortsnamen, 1993.

Zum slawischen mythologischen Wortschatz, AnP 22, 1994.

Namenforschung: ein internationales Handbuch zu Onomastik, 1995.

Zur Deutung slawischer Ortsnamen in der Frankischen Schweiz, Studia Onomastica et Indogermanica, 1995.

Sorbische Sprachgebiete und Onomastik, Symbolae Slavisticae, 1996.

Die westlichste Peripherie des slavischen Sprachgebietes, ZtS 57, 1998.

2. JOACHIM HERRMANN

W. Unverzagt, Das slawische Brandgraberfeld von Prutzke, Kr. Brandenburg, 1958.

Die wor-und fruhgeschictlichen Burgwalle Gross-Berlin und des Bezirkes Potsdam, 1960.

Zamcici—Zemcici. Ein Beitrag zum Problem der Wohnsitze der slawischen Stammer zwischen Elbe und Oder, MaR 4, 1960.

Kopenick. Ein Beitrag zur Fruhgeschichte Gross Berlin, 1962.

Burgbezirk und Rundwall in slawischer Zeit im mittleren Gebiet zwischen Elbe und Oder, Aus Ur- und Fruhgeschichte, 1962.

Einige Frager der slawischen Burgenentwicklung zwischen mittlerer Elbe under Oder, SlA 10, 1963.

Das Land Lebus und seine Burgen westlich der Oder, Varia archaeologia, 1964.

Kultur und Kunst der Slawen in Deutschland vom 7.—13. Jahrhundert, 1965.

Tornow und Vorberg. Ein Beitrag zur Fruhgeschichte der Lausitz, 1966.

Anfange und Grundlagen der Staatsbildung bie den slawischen Stammen westlich der Oder, ZtG 15, 1967.

Gemeinsamkeiten und Unterschiede im Burgenbau der slawischen Stamme westlich der Oder, ZtA 1, 1967.

Siedlung, Wirtschaft und gesellschaftliche Verhaltnisse der slawischen Stamme zwischen Oder/Niesse und Elben. Studien auf der Grandlage archaologischen Materials, 1968.

Siedlung, Burg und Stadt, 1969.

Die Schanze vom Vorwerk bei Demmin - die Civitas des wilzischen Oberkonigs Dragowit?, AuF 14, 1969.

Feldberg, Rethra und das Problem der wilzischen Hohenburgen, SlA 16, 1969.

Geistige und kultisch-religiose Vorstellungen der Nordwest-Slaven und ihre Widerspiegelungen in den archaologischen Quellen, Das heidnische und christliche Slaventum, AiS II/1, 1969.

Die Slaven in Deutschland, 1970.

E. Lange, Einige Probleme der archaologischen Erforschung der fruhmitteralalterlichen Agrargeschichte der Nordwestslawen, SlV 18, 1970.

Zur Einwanderungszeit und Herkunft der nordwestslawischen Stamme, Actes du VIIe Congres InT des sciences prehistoriques et protohistoriques/1966, 1971.

Zwischen Hradschin und Vineta; fruhe Kulturen der Westslawen, 1971.

Einige Bemerkungen zu Tempelstatten und Kultbildern im nordwestslawischen Gebiet, PoL 16, 1971.

Byzanz und die Slawen am ausseren Endes des westlichen Ozeans, Klio 54, 1972.

Die Nortwestslawen und ihr Anteil an der Geschichte des deutschen Volkes, 1972.

Der germanischen und slawischen Siedlungen und das mittelalterliche Dorf von Tornow, Kr. Calau, 1973.

Das Zusammentreffen von Germanen und Slawen in Mitteleurope im 6. Jh, Actes du VIIIe Congres InT des sciences prehistorique et protohistorique, 1973.

Die Nordwestslawen und ihr Anteil and der Geschichte des deutschen Volkes, 1973.

Arkona auf Ruegen - Tempelburg und politisches Zentrum der Ranen vom 9. - 12. Jh, ZtA 8, 1974.

Probleme der Herausbildung der archaologischen Kulturen slawischer Stamme des 6.-9. Jh, Rapports du III Congres InT d'Archeologie Slave, 1975.

Nordwestslawische Seehandelsplatz des 9.-10.Jh. und Spuren ihrer Verbindung zu Norseegebiet, EaZ 16, 1975.

Die Spuren des Prometheus. Der Aufstieg der Menscheit zwischen Naturgeschichte und Weltgeschichte, 1975.

Die Lusici im Fruhen Mittelalter, Let B/22, 1975.

Die fruhmittelalterliche slawische Siedlungsperiode, AuF 21, 1976.

Archaologie als Geschichtswissenschaft, 1977.

Hinterland, Handel und Handwerk der fruhen Seehandelsplatze im norwestslawischen Siedlungsgebiet, La formation et le developpement des metiers au moyen age, 1977.

Archaologische Denkmale und Umweltgestaltung, 1978.

Polabskie i il'menske slavjane v rannesrednovekovoj baltijskoj torgovie, Drevnaja Rus i slavjane, 1978.

Ralswiek auf Rugen - ein Handelsplatz des 9. Jh und die Fernhandelsbeziehungen im Ostseegebiet, ZtA 12, 1978.

Zu den kulturgeschichtlichen Wurzeln und zur historischen Rolle nordwestslawischer Tempel des fruehen Mittelalters, SlV 26, 1978.

Okonomie und Gesdellschaft and der Wende von der Atnike zum Mittelalter, 1979.

The Northern Slavs in the Northern World, The Northern World, 1980.

Edifices et objets sculptes a destination culturelle chez les tribus slaves due nor-ouest entre le VII et le XII siecles, SlG 7-8, 1980-81.

Staatsbidlung in Sudoesteuropa und in Mitteleuropea, Jb fur Geschichte des Feudalismus, 1981.

Fruhe Kulturen der Westslawen. Zwischen Hradschin und Vineta, 1981.

Ein neuer Bootsfund im Seehandelsplatz Ralswiek auf Rugen, AuF 26, 1981.

Die Pferde von Arkona, Beitrage zur Ur- und Fruhgeschichte, 1982.

Wikinger und Slawen. Zur Fruhgeschichte der Ostseevolker, 1982.

Wanderungen und Landnahme im westslawischen Gebiet, Gli Slavi Occidentali e meridonali 30, 1983.

Lexikon fruher Kulturen, 1984.

Reric-Ralswiek—Gross Raden. Seehandelsplatze und Burgen an der sudlichen Ostseekuste, LsK 9, 1984.

Germanen und Slawen in Mitteleurope: zu Neugestaltung der ethnischen Verhaltnisse zu Beginn des Mittelalters, 1984.

Westslawen und Germanen im Spannungsfeld von Assimilation, Konfrontation und kulturellem Austausch (interationen der mitelleuropaischen Slawen und anderen Ethnika im 6.-10. Jh, 1984.

Der Liutizenaufstand 983, ZtA 18, 1984.

Die Slawen in Deutschland. Geschichte und Kultur der slawischen Stamme weslich von oder und Neisse vom 6. bis 12. Jh., 1985.

Griechenland - Byzanz - Europa, 1985

Ralswiek. Maritime Trading Station and Harbour Development from the 8th to the 10th century along the southern Baltic Sea, Conference on Waterfront Archaeology in North European Towns 2, 1985.

Germanen und Slawen in Mitteleuropa, Wege zur Geschichte, 1986.

Die Welt der Slawen: Geschichte, Gesselschaft, Kultur, 1986.

Slavjane i Skandinavy, 1986.

Wege zur Geschichte, 1986.

Ruzzi, Forderen liudi, Fresiti. Zu historischen und siedlungsgeschichtlichen Grundlagen des "Bayrisches Geographen" aus der ertsten Halfte des 9. Jh, Wege Zur Geschichte, 1986.

Der Liutizenaufstand 983—Ursachen, politische-militarische Vorlaufer, Verlaud und Wirkungen, Wege Zur Geschichte, 1986.

Die Verterritorialisierung - ein methodisches und historisches Problem slawischer Wanderung, Landnahme und Ethnogenese, Studia nad Etnogeneza slowian i kultura europy wczesnosredniowiecznej, 1987.

Burgen und Befestigungen des 12. und 13. Jh in landesherrlicher Territorialpolitik und bauerlicher Siedlung in der weiteren von Berlin, ZtA 20, 1987.

Archaologische Feldforschungen und Ausgrabungen des Zentralinstituts fur Alte Geschichte und Archaologie in der Mitte und zweiten Halfte der 80er Jahre, AuF 33, 1988.

Das Ende der Volkerwanderungszeit: Slavische Wanderungen und die germanisch-slavischen Siedlungsgrenzen in Mitteleuropa, FsT H. Kunstmann, 1988.

Die Slawen in der Fruhgeschichte des deutschen Volkes, 1989.

Archaologie in der Deutschen Demokratischen Republik, 1989.

Wilte—Haefeldan/Aefeldan und Osti. Zu Namen und Wohnsitzen slawischer Stamme in der angelsachsischen Volkerliste Konig Alfreds aus dem Ende des 9. Jh, OsG 19, 1990.

Griechische und lateinische Quellen zur Fruhgeschichte Mitteleuropas bis zur Mitte des 1. Jahrtausends, 1990.

Inventaria archaeologica: corpus des ensembles archeologiques, 1990.

U. Heussner, Dendrochronologie, Archaologie und Fruhgeschichte vom bis 6. 12. Jh in den Gebieten zwischen Saale, Elbe und Oder, AuF 35, 1991.

Wikinger, Warager, Normannen. Die Skandinavier und Europe 800-1200, 1992.

Ein Versuch zu Arkona Tempel und Tempelrekonstruktionen nach schriftlicher Uberlieferung und nach Ausgrabungsbefunden im nordwestslawischen Gebiet, AuF 38, 1993.

Probleme und Fragestellungen zur Westausbreitung slawischer Stamme und deren Burgenbau vom ende 6. bis zum ende des 8. Jh in Mitteleurope, SlA 27, 1996.

3. HEINRICH KUNSTMANN

Dagobert I. und Samo in der Sage, ZsP 38, 1975.

Was Besagt der Name Samo und wo liegt Wogastiburg?, DwS 24, 1979.

Samo, Dervanus und der Slovenenfurst Wallucus, DwS 25, 1980.

Uber die Herkunft Samos, DwS 25, 1980.

Spuren polnischen Zwangsansiedlung in Nordostbayern?, SlA 27, 1980.

Zweit Beitrage zu Geschichte Der Ostsseslaven. 1. Der Name der Abodriten; 2. Rethra, die Redarier und Arkona, DwS 26, 1981.

Die oberfrankische Ortsname Banz, DwS 26, 1981.

Wo lag das Zentrum von Samos Reich, DwS 26, 1981.

Ein neuer Bootsfund im Seehandelsplatz Ralswiek auf Rugen, AuF 26, 1981.

Vorlaufige Untersuchungen uber dan Bairischen Bulgarenmore von 631-632, 1982.

Der anhaltische Landschaftsname Serimunt, FsT J. Holthusen, 1983.

Zwei Beitrage zur Geschichte der Ostseeslaven. 1. Der Name der Abodriten. 2. Rethra, die Redarier u. Arkona, DwS 26, 1983.

Samo, Dervanus und der Slovenenfurst Wallucus, DwS 28, 1983.

Noch einmal Samo und Wogastiburc, DwS 28, 1983.

Der anhaltische Lanschaftsname Serimunt, FsT J. Holthusen, 1983.

Kamen die westslawischen Daleminci aus Dalmatien, DwS 28, 1983.

Wie die Slovene an den Ilmensee kamen, DwS 29, 1984.

Uber die Herkunft der Polen vom Balkan, DwS 29, 1984.

Woher die Kaschuben ihren Namen haben, DwS 29, 1984.

Mecklenburgs Zirzipanen und der name der Peene, DwS 29, 1984.

Derevljane, Polocane und Volynjane, DwS 29, 1984.

Die Landschaftsnamen Masowien und Masuren, DwS 29, 1984.

Die oberfrankischen Raumnamen Hummelgau und Ahorntal, Aspekte der Slavistik, FsT J. Schrenk, 1984.

Der anhaltische Landschaftsname Serimunt, Text-Symbol-Weltmodell, Johannes Holthusen zum 60. Geburtstag, 1984.

Woher die Kaschuben ihren namen haben, DwS 30, 1985.

Wie die Slovene an den Ilmensee kamne, DwS 30, 1985.

Die Namen der ostslavischen Derevljane, Polocane und Volynjane, DwS 30, 1985.

Der Name "Piast" und andere Probleme der polnischen Dynasten-Mythologie, Suche die Meinung, 1986.

Woher die Russen ihren Namen haben, DwS 31, 1986.

Woher die Huzulen ihren Namen haben, DwS 31, 1986.

Der Wawel und die Sage von der Grundung Krakaus, DwS 31, 1986.

Beitrage zur Geschichte der Besiedlung Nord- und Mitteldeutschlands mit Balkanslaven, 1987.

Gniezno und Warta, DwS 32, 1987.

Waren die ersten Premysliden Balkanslaven?, DwS 32, 1987.

Der alte Polennname Lach, Lech und die Lendizi des Geographus Bavarus, DwS 32, 1987.

Gniezno und Warta, DwS 32, 1987.

Die slovakischen Hydronyme Nitra, Cetinka, Zitava un Ipel—Zeugen der slavischen Sud-Nord Wanderung, DwS 33, 1988.

Die balksnsprachlichen Grundlagen einiger polnischer Toponymie und Hydronymie, DwS 33, 1988.

W Sprawie Rodowodu Mieszka, SlA 31, 1988.

Der Dukla-Name und seing Weg von Montenegro uber die Karpaten nach Nordwesrussland, DwS 34, 1989.

Bojan und Trojan. Einige dunkle Stellen de Igorliedes in neuer Sicht, DwS 35, 1990.

Kretanje Slavena u srednju i istocnu Europu, Kolo 5-6, 1991.

Die Bedeutung der Cham-Further Senkd fur die Einwanderung von Slaven in die Oberpfalz im Spiegel der Namen Cham/Kamp, Osser, Domazlice, Tugast/Taust u.a., DwS 33, 1994.

Der toponymische Typ Naklo als Terminus der fruhen slavischen Schiffahrt, FsT M. Kucera, 1994.

Die Slaven. Ihr Name. Ihre Wanderung nach Europa und die Anfange der russischen Geschichte in historisch-onomastischer Sicht, 1996.

4. ETHNONYM SERB

M. Budimir, Anadol i anticka Serbija, Glasnik I, 1949.

——Protosloveni i Staroanadolski Indoevropljani, Zbornik filozofskog fauklteta, 1952.

——Quaestio de Neuris Cimmeriisque, Glas SaN CCVII, 1954.

——Pelasto-slavica, Rad Jugoslavenske akademije znanosti i umjetnosti, 9, 1956.

——Dva drustvena termina dubrovacka. 1. Lada, II. Sebar, Anali Historijskog instituta u Dubrovniku 4-5, 1956.

——Protoslavica, Slavjanska filogija 2, 1958.

——O starijim pomenima srpskog imena, Glas SaN CCXXXVI, 1959.

——De nominis serbici vestigis classicis, Zbornik za filologiju i lingvistiku Matice srpske, 3, 1960.

——Mariani, OsJ 5, 1975.

Z. Golab, Nazwa etniczna Serbowie (sch. Srbi gluz. Serbja) na tle ethnonimi slowianskie, Zbornik Radova povodom 70. godisnjice zivota akademika Jovana Vukovica, 1977.

——About the Connection between Kinship Terms and Some Ethnica in Slavic (the Case of *Sirbi and Slovene), InT Journal of Slavic Linguistics and Poetics 25, 1982.

H. Gregorie, L'origine et le nome des Croates et Serbes, BzT 17, 1944-45.

G. Ilinskij, K etymologii imeni serb, JuZ 12, 1933.

R. Novakovic, Odakle su Srbi dosli na Balkansko poluostrvo, 1977.

——Gde se nalazila Srbija od VII do XII veka, 1981.

——Balticki Sloveni u Beogradu I Srbiji, 1985.

——On the Hitherto Unused Sources of Information on the Origin of the Serbs, BaP 4, 1989.

——Jos o poreklu Srba, 1992.

——Srbi, ime Srbi kroz vreme I prostor, 1993.

——Karpatski i Likijski Srbi, 1997.

H. Popowska-Taborska, Rdzen *srb- w dialektach kaszubskich, Zbornik Radova ... Jovana Vukovica, 1977.

——Serb i sobaka-dva slowa sluzace jako argumenty w dociekaniach nad etnogeneza Slowian, Studia z Filologii Polskie i Slowianskiej 27, 1985.

S. Rospond, Baza onomastyczna pie. *ser-, *sar-, *sreu- (Sarmaci i Serbowie), LpS 10, 1965.

H. Schuster-Sewc, Sprache und ethnische Formation in der Entwicklung des Sorbischen, ZtS 4, 1954.

——Zur Geschichte und Etymologie des ethnischen Namens Sorb/Serb/Sarb/Srb, LeT A/30-32, 1983.

——Dva zapazanja o srpskohrvatskoj etimologiji (Srbin, Jug, Jugovic), VuK 13, 1983.

——O istoriji i geografiji ethnickog imena Sorb/Serb/Sarb/Srb(in), Zbornik matice srpske za filologiju i lingvistiku 27-28, 1984-85.

O.N. Trubacev, O praslavjanskich leksiceskich dialektizmach serbo-luzickich jazykov, Serbo-Luzicki lingvisticeskij sbornik, 1963.

N. Zupanic, O poreklu imena Srbin, Novi Zivot 9, 1922.

——Srbi Plinija i Ptolemeja. Pitanje prve pojave Srba na svetskoj pozornici sa historijskog, geografskog i etnoloskog stanovista,

Zbornik Radova Posvecen Jovanu Cvijicu, 1924.

——Izvor Srbov, Ljubjanski Zvon XLV, 1925.

——Prvi nosioci ethnikih imen Srb, Hrvat, Ceh i Ant, Etnolog II, 1928.

5. SLAV AND GERMAN IN GERMANIA

G. Bellmann, Slavoteutonica Lexikalische Untersuchungen zum slawisch-deutschen Sprachkontakt im Ostmitteldeutschen, 1971.

S. Brather, Hochmittelalterliche Siedlungsentwicklung um Kloster Lehnin. Slawen und Deutsche in der Zauche, VbL 27, 1993.

S. Brather, "Germanische", "slawische" und "deutsche" Sachkultur des Mittelalters - Probleme ethnischer Interpretation, EaZ 37, 1996.

E. Donnert, Zur Entwicklung der deutschen Slawenkunde im fruhen Mittelalter, ZtS 18, 1973.

L. Dralle, Wilzen, Sachsen und Franken um das Jahr 800. Nationes, Historische und Philologische Untersuchungen zur Ensthehung der europaischen Nationen im Mittelalter 1, 1978.

S. Dusek, Deutsche-slawische Kontakte im West-Saalischen Thuringen des 10. bis 2. Jh, 1973.

K. Elbracht, Deutsche und Slawische Siedlungen and der oberen Ilm in fruhen Mittelalter, Leipziger Studien, 1954.

F. Engel, Deutsche und slavische Einfluss in der Dobbertiner Kulturlandschaft, 1934.

R. Fischer, Slavisch-deutsches Zusammen lebe im Lichte der Ortsnamen, 1955.

W.H. Fritze, Untersuchungen zur fruhslavischen und fruhfrankischen Geschichte bis ins. 7. Jh, 1952.

——Germania Slavia I, 1980.

——Germania Slavia II, 1981.

——Die Begegnung von deutschen und slawischen Ethnikum im Beriech der hoch mittelalterlichen deutschen Ostsiedlung, Siedlungsforschung, Archaologie-Geschichte-Geographie 2, 1984.

——Villae slavicae in der Mark Brandenburg, JbR 41, 1990.

F. Graus, Deutsche und Slawische Verfassungsgeschicte, HtZ 197, 1963.

——Slavs and Germans, Eastern and Western Europe in the Middle Ages, 1970.

K. Grebe, Die Ergebnisse der Ausgrabungen in Brandenburg, Germanen- Slawen-Deutsche. Forschungen zu ihrer Ethnogenese, 1968.

P. Grimm, Zum Verhaltnis von Slawen und Germanen/Deutschen im Elbe-Saale-Gebiet vom 8. bis 13. Jh, BeR, 1970.

E. Gringmuth-Dallmer, Siedlungsarchaologische Beobachtungen zur Namengebung im slawische-deutschen Kontaktgebiet zwischen Elbe und Oder/Niesse, OsG 17, 1988.

B. Guttmann, Die Germanisierung der Slawen in der Mark, FbP 9, 1897.

H.B. Harder, Slawen und Balten in Deutschland, Deutsche, Slawen und Balten, 1989.

H. Hecker, S. Spieler, Deutsche, Slawen und Balten, 1989.

J. Henning, Berlin-Hellersdorf "Schleipfuhl" -Siedlungsgrabung zum Problem germanisch-slawischer Kontakte in der Mittel des !. Jahrtausends, AuF 32, 1987.

——Germanen-Slawen-Deutsche. Neue Untersuchungen zum fruhgeschichtlichen Siedlungswesen ostlich der Elbe, PzT 66, 1991.

K. Holter, Baiern und Slawen in Oberosterreich: Probleme der Landnahme und Besiedlung, 1980.

W. Hulle, Westausbreitung und Wehranlagen der Slawen in Mitteldeutschland, 1940.

H. Jakob, Slavisch-deutsch benannte Wehranlange in Oberfranken, OsG 3, 1967.

——Eine deutsch-slawische Symbiose in der Ellernbach-Talschaft nordostlich von Bamberg, Fst H. Kunstmann, 1988.

H.J. Kaack, Slawen und Deutsche im Lande Lauenburg, Ratzeburg, 1983.

H.D. Kahl, Slawen und Deutsche in der brandenburgischen Geschichte des 12 Jh, Die letzen Jahrzehnte des landes Stodor, 1964.

J. Kostrzewski, Slowanie i Germanie na Ziemiach na Wschod od Laby w. 6. - 8. w. po Chr, PrG 7, 1946.

R. Kotzschke, Deutsche und Slaven im mitteldeutschen Osten, 1961.

W. Lammers, Germanen und Slawen in Nordablingien, ZsH 79, 1955.

——Probleme der Germania Slavica zwischen Elbe und Oder, Germania Slavica II, 1981.

K. Lamprecht, Deutsche Geschichte, 1909-1914.

K. Leube, Germanische Volkerwanderung und ihr archaologischen Fundniederschlag. Slawische-germanische Kontakte in nordlichen Elb-Oder-Gebiet, EaZ 36, 1995.

F. Lotter, The Crusading Idea and the Conquest of the Region East of the Elbe, Medieval Frontier Societies, 1989.

H. Ludat, Die altesten geschictlichen Grundlagen fur das deutsch-slawische Verhaltnis, Das ostliche Deutschland, 1959.

——An Elbe und Oder um das Jahr 1000. Skizzen aur Politik des Ottonenreiches und der slavischen Machte in Mitteleuropa, 1971.

——Slaven und Deutsche im Mittelalter. 1982.

A. Lubos, Deutsche und Slawen: Beispiele aus Schlesien und anderen Ostgebieten, 1984.

G. Mobes, Deutsche und Slawen vom 10. bis 16. Jh in Grossbrembach, Kr. Weimar, AuF 22, 1977.

M. Muller-Wille, D. Meier, H. Unverhau, Slawen und Deutsche in sudlichen Ostseeraum vom 11. bis zum 16. Jh, 1995.

B. Neveux, Slaves et Germains sur l'Elbe et la Vistule, Etudes Germainiques 21, 1966.

E. Nickel, Deutsch-slawisches Zusammenleben im Mittleren Elbegebiet, ZtA 2, 1968.

J. Prinz, Betrachtungen zum Verhaltnis des slawischen und deutschen Elements zur Zeit der deutschen Kolonisation Brandenburgs anhand des Namenmaterials, JbG 20, 1971.

M. Reiser, Deutsche-slawische Beruhrungen im ehemaligen thuringischen Vogtland im Spiegel der Ortsnamen, JhR 17, 1969.

H.F. Schmid, Die slavische Altertumskunde und die Erforschung der Germanisation des deutschen Nordosten, ZsP 1, 1925.

B. Schmidt, Zur Enstehung und Kontinuuitat des Thuringerstammes, Germanen-Slawen-Deutsche, Forschungen zu ihrer Ethnogenese, 1969.

——F. Rossler, Kelbra-Kyffhauser-Lindeschu. Deutsche und Slawische Siedlungen in der goldener Aue, AuF 24, 1979.

E. Schmidt-Thielbeer, Germanische und slawische Siedlungen bei Micheln, Kr. Kothen, AuF 28, 1983.

M.B. Schukin, Roman and the Barbarians in Central and Eastern Europe, 1st Century BC-1st Century AD, 1989.

H. Seyer, Germanische und slawische Brunnenfunde in der Siedlung von Berlin-Marzahn, ZtA 14, 1980.

P. Siebert, Deutsch-westslawische Beziehungen zu Fruhlingsbrauchen, 1968.

J. Strzelczyk, Slowiane i Germanie w Niemczech srodkowych we wczesnym sredniowieczu, 1976.

J.W. Thompson, Feudal Germany, II, 1928.

M. Vasmer, Germanen und Slaven in Ostdeutschland in alter Zeit, Namn och bygd 21, 1933.

B. Wachter, Deutsche und Slawen im hannoverschen Wendland, SaC 44, 1972.

K. Zernack, Die Frage der kontinuitat zwischen dem deutschen und slavischen Stadtwesen in der mark Brandenburg, Grundlagen der Geschichtlichen Beziehungen zwischen Deutschen, Polaben und Polen, 1976.

6. SLAVS IN GERMANIA

C. Albrecht, Die Slawen in Thuringen; ein Beitrag zur Festlegung der westlichen slawischen Kulturgrenze des fruhen Mittelalters, 1925.

H. Bach, S. Dusek, Baiern und Slawen in Oberosterreich, 1980.

R. Beltz, Zur altesten Geschichte Mecklenburg. I: Die Wenden in Mecklenburg, 1893.

——Germanen und Slawen in Mecklenburg, Der Ostdeutsche Volksboden. Aufsatze zu den Fragen des Ostens, 1926.

U. Bentzien, Slawische Pfluggerate und ihre jungeren Traditionen in ostlichen Deutschland, LeT C/15, 1972.

E. Bohm, Teltow und Barnim, 1978.

H. Birnbaum, Slavisches Namengut aus dem fruhmittelalterlichen bayerischen Raum, WsJ 21, 1975.

H. J. Brachmann, Zur Geschichte der Slawen des Mittelb-Saale-Gebietes im 6. bis 10. Jh, EaZ 1955.

——Zur spatslawischen Zeit im Mittelb-Saale-Gebiet, ZtA 2, 1968.

——Zur Geschichte der Slawen des Mittelb-Saale-Gebietes im 6. bis 10. Jh auf Grund archaologischer Quellen, 1969.

——Slawische Stamme an Elbe und Saale. Zu ihrer Geschichte u Kultur im 6.-10. Jh auf Grund archaologischer Quellen, 1978.

J. Brankack, Zur Fruhgeschichte der feudalen Staaten auf westslawischen Boden, WiS 7, 1957-58.

——Einige Betrachtungen uber Handwerk, Handel und Stadtentwicklung der westslawen an der Ostseekuste vom 9. bis 12. Jh, Hansische Studien, 1961.

——Betrachtungen zur politischen Geschichte der elbslawischen Stammerverbande im 9. Jh, L'Europe auz IXe-XIe siecles, 1968.

K. Bruns-Wustfeld, Die Uckermark in slavischer Zeit, 1919.

B. Bukowski, Slowiane nad Dolna Laba w XX wieku, Problemy, 1951.

W. Coblenz, Archaologische Bermerkungen zur Herkunft der altesten Slawen in Sachsen, ArB 13, 1964.

——Zur Herkunft der Slawen im Elbe-Saale-Gebiet, ArB 13, 1964.

E. Donnert, Das Heidentum der Slawen in der schriftlichen Uberlieferung der franksichen Fruhzeit im 7. und 8. Jh, SlG 7-8, 1980-81.

R. Drogereit, Bremen, Barowick-Verden. Frugeschichte und Wendenmission, Bremisches Jb 51, 1969.

L. Dralle, Slavische Herrschaft zwischen mittlerer Elbe und Oder vom 8. bis 10. Jh, SlA 27, 1980.

S. Dusek, Geschichte und Kultur der Slawen in Thuringen, 1983.

——Die materielle Kultur der slawischen Dorfbewohner im deutschen Feudalstaat, ZtA 2, 1968.

H. Eidam, Die Slawen in Nordbayern, ZtB 4, 1931.

F. Escher, Zur politischen Geschichte der Slawen zwischen Elbe und Oder, 1983.

R. Fischer, Zur Geschichte Slawischer Stamme und Stammesnamen, ZtS 4, 1959.

R. E. Fischer, G. Schlimpert, Vorslawisches Namen in Brandenburg, ZtS 16, 1971.

H. Friesinger, Studien zur Archologie der Slawen in Niederosterreich, 1971-77.

W.H. Fritze, Untersuchungen zur fruhslawischen und fruh Frankischen Geschichte bis ins 7. Jh, 1994.

M. Glaser, Die Slawen im Ostholstein, 1983.

H. Glass, Bayern – Egerland – Vogtland, MzB 7-8, 1991.

W. Gley, Die Besiedlung der Mittelmark von der slavischen Einwanderung bis 1624, 1926.

J. Godlowski, Die Frage der slawischen Einwanderung ins ostliche Mitteleuropa, ZoS 28, 1979

K. Grebe, Slawische Bestattungen von Marquardt, Kr. Potsdam-Land, AuF 7, 1962.

U. Gross, Slavische und slavisch beeinflusste Funde zwischen Altmuhl unde Oberrhein, DwS 35, 1990.

W. Hensel, Die Slawen im fruhen Mittelalter, 1965.

M. Hellman, Grundfragen slavischer Verfassungsgeschichte des fruhen Mittelalters, JgO 2, 1954.

B. Herrmann, Die Herrschaft der Hochstifts Naumburg and der mittleren Elbe, 1970.

W. Hessler, Mitteldeutsche Gaues des fruhen und hohen Mittelalter, 1957.

W. Hoppe, Die Prignitz und Wittstock, Brandenburgia 34, 1925.

——Lenzen 929-1929, 1929.

H. Jakob, War Burk das Historische Wogastiburc, und wo lag das Oppidum Berleich. Eine historische-geographische Standort-Analyse, DwS 24, 1979.

R. Kotzschke Die deutschen Marken im Sorbenland, Deutsch und Slaven im mitteldeutschen Osten, 1961.

E. Kranzmeyer, Slavische Ortsnamen in der Karolingischen Ostmark, AiS 1/2 , 1966.

F. Kruger, Der Bardengau und die Slaven, Die Kunde, 1936.

P.L. Kupka, Die Altslawen in der Nord- d.h. der spateren Altmark, Sachsen und Anhalt 12, 1936.

W. Lammers, Germanen und Slaven im Nordalbingien, ZsH 79, 1955

T. Lehr-Spalwinski, Plemiona slowianskie nad Laba i Odra w wiekach sredenich, 1947.

L. Libert, Die Slawen in der Uckermark, Hk Kr. Prenzlau 16, 1973.

K. Lubeck, Die Slawen des Klosters Fulda, FgB 24, 1931.

H. Ludat, Die Slawen und das Mittelalter, Welt als Geschichte, 1952.

——An Elbe und Oder um das Jahr 1000; Skizzen zur Politik des Ottonenreiches und der slavischen Machte in Mitteleuropa, 1971.

——Wik im Slavischen, FsT W. Schlesinger I, 1973.

K.H. Marschalleck, Aus der Vor- und Frugeschichte des Kr. Lubben, Lubbener Hk, 1939.

W. Meibeyer, Slaven in Niedersachsen, DwS 11, 1966.

C. Menke, Das Amt Wolgast, PjB 26, 1931.

H. Naumann, Mischnamen in Nord-Bayern u. agrenzdenden Gebieten, Slavische Namenforschung, 1963.

V. Nekuda, Die altslawische Dorf in Berlin-Mahlsdorf, AiB 6, 1982.

W. Neumann, Die Entwicklung slawischer Flurnamensuffixe im sudwestlichen Mecklenburg, ZtS 11, 1966.

H. Priedel, Slawische Alterumskunde des Ostlichen Mitteleuropas im 9. und 10. Jh, 1961-66.

P. Reinecke, Die Slawen in Nordostbayern, ByV 7, 1927-28.

——Zur Geschichte der Slawen in Nordostbayern, ByV 8, 1929.

A. Rudloff, Geschichte Mecklenburgs vom tode Niclots bis zur Schlacty bei Bornhoved, 1901.

M. Rudnicki, Nazwy Slowian zachodnich w dokumentach niemieckich, SlO 7, 1928.

W. Sage, Slawen in Oberfranken, Oberfranken in vor- und frugeschichtelicher Zeit, 1986.

H. Schall, Der Pristavel und die Stadenamen Pritzwalk und Pasewlak, JbR 10, 1959.

W. Schlesinger, Egerland, Vogtland, Pleissenland, in Sachsen und Bomen, Forschungen zur Geschichte Sachsens und Bohmens, 1937

——Die Anfange der Stadt Chemnitz und anderer mitteldeutscher Stadte, 1952.

——Mitteldeutsche Beitrage zur deutschen Verfassungsgeschichte des Mittalters, 1961.

H.F. Schmid, Beitrage zur Social- und Rechsgescicte der fruheren slawischen Bevolkerung des heutingen nordostlichen Deutschlande, ZsP 7, 1930.

B. Schmidt, Die spate Volkerwanderungszeit in Ostthuringen und das Einzugsgebiet der Slaven in Mitteldeutschland, WuL 3, 1954.,

E. Schmidt, Die Mark Brandenburg unter den Askaniern (1134-1320), 1973.

H. Schroke, Zur Frage Sclavi-Slawen in Deutschland, Geschichte und Gegenwart, 1988.

J. Schultze, Die Prignitz, 1956.

E. Schwarz, Wenden beim Landesaubau in Deutschland, ZoS 7, 1958.

U. Schonknecht, Menzlin. Ein Frugeschichtlicher Handelsplatz an der Peene, 1977.

E. Schuldt, Slawische Topferei in Mecklenburg, 1964.

E. Schwarz, Wenden beim Landesausbau in Deutschland, ZoS 7, 1958.

——Die slavische Einwanderung in Ostdeutschland, FrA 34/35, 1975.

J. Scultze, Die Prignitz, MdF 8, 1956.

R. Steinberg, Die Mark Lipani, JbG 11, 1962.

H. Steiner, Slaven und Deutsche in Hannoverschen Wendland, RaP, 1979.

L. Stern, H.J. Bartmuss, Deutschland in der Feudalepoche von der Wende des 5.-6. Jh bis zur Mitte des 11. Jh, 1970.

J. Strzelczyk, Z nowszych prac nad historia osadnictwa na dawnych terenach slowianskich w Sasksonii Dolnej, Kwartalnik Historii Kultury Materialnej, 15/3, 1967.

——Der Slawische Faktor im Lichte Schriftlicher Quellen der Geschichte Mitteldeutsch lands vom 6-8 Jh, LeT B/27, 1980.

F. Tetzner, Die Slawen in Deutschland, 1902.

K. Tymieniecki Podgrodzia w polnocno-zachodniej slowianszczyznie i perwsze lokajce miast na prawie niemieckim, SlO 2, 1922.

J. Udolph, Prignitz-Pregynja, OnO 7-8, 1991.

M. Vasmer, Slavenspuren auf der Insel Hiddensee, ZsP 9, 1932.

Z. Vana, Die Slawen in Bayern im Lichte der Bodenfunde, VpS 2, 1958.

M. Vasmer, Slavische Refestigungen an der deutschen Ostseekuste, ZsP 10, 1933.

——Slavische Spuren auf Fehmarn, ZsP 11, 1934.

—— Spuren von Westslaven auf den danischen Inseln, ZsP 18, 1942.

V. Vogel, Slawische Funde in Wargien, 1972.

H. Walther, Die Ausbrietung der slawischen Besiedlung westlich von Elbe/Saale und Bohmerwald, Die Slawen in Deutschland, 1985.

S. Wauer, Die Wiedergrabe slawischer Stammes- und Landschaftsnamen im Deutschen, OsG 19, 1990.

H. Witte, Slavische Reste in Mecklenburg und an der Niederelbe, Der Ostdeutsche Volksboden, 1926.

H. Witz, Die Slavenin Nordbayern , ZtB 7, 1934.

H. Wolfram, Uberlegungen zur politischen Situation der Slawen im heutigen Oberosterreich, Baiern und Slawen in Oberosterreich, 1980.

F. Zagiba, Das Geistesleben der Slaven im fruhen Mittelalter. Die Anfange des slavischen Schrifttums auf dem Gebeite des Ostl. Mitteleuropa vom 8. bis 10. Jh, 1971.

——Din Anfange des slawischen Schrittums auf den Gebeite des Ost- Mittel Europe von 8. bis 10. Jh, 1971.

H. Zettel, Deutschland und die Elbslawen im 10. Jh, 1986.

7. SLAVS IN GERMANIA: MAIN, REGNITZ, NAAB WENDENLANDS

N. Haas, Geschichte der Slavenlandes an der Aisch und den Elbrach-Flusschen, 1819.

M. Hellman, Bemerkungen zum Aussageweit der Fuldauer Annalen und anderer Quellen uber slawische Verfassungszustande, FsT W. Schlesinger, 1973.

E. Herrmann, Zur Assimilierung der Slawen in Ostfranken im Hochmittelalter, AgO 48, 1968.

R. Holinka, Moinwinidi et Radanzwinidi, Zpravy Anthropologicke spolecnosti 4, 1951.

H. Jakob, Abegegangene Siedlungen der Main- und Regnitz-Wenden um Bamberg, FuF 32, 1958.

——Siedlungsarchaologie und Slavenfrage im Main-Regnitz-Gebiet, BaM 96, 1959.

——E. Eichler, Slawische Forst- und Flurnamen im Obermaingebiet, WiS 11, 1962.

——Die "Burg" in der Maintal-Aue bei Kemmern. Refugium und Kultstate der Mainwenden, DwS 24, 1979.

——Zur Gentilaristokratie der Main- und Regnitzwenden, AgO 62, 1982.

——Der Klotzgau-ein slavische Kleingau am Rande der Frankischen Alb, ZtA 16, 1982.

——Die Wustungen der Obermain-Regnitz Furche und ihrer Randhohen vom Staffelberg bis zur Ehrenburg, ZtM 12, 1984.

——E. Eichler, Nachlese slawischer Flurnamen im Obermaingebiet, OsG XV, 1986.

——Slavische Wustungen im Raum Knetzgau-Hassfurt an Main, DwS 32, 1987.

——Beitrage zum Paganismus der Main- und Regnitzwenden, Ars Philologica Slavica, FsT H. Kunstmann, 1988.

——Eine deutsch-slawische Symbiose in der Ellernbach-Talschaft nordostlich von Bamberg, OsG 21, 1994.

K. Lubeck, Die Slawen des Klosters Fulda, FgB 24, 1931.

W. Merkert, Studien zum oberfrankischen Slawen-problem. Die -gast -Orte, ein Altstrassen-Kriterium. "Terra Slaworum" - Slawenland, Frankische Blatter 8, 1965.

W. Sage, Zur Bedeutung des Bamberger Domberges fur die Geschichte der Obermaingebietes im fruhen Mittelalter, OsG 19, 1990.

J. Schutz, Frankens Mainwendische Namen, Geschichte und Gegenwart, 1994.

——Strukturelemente des Mainwendischen, ZsP 56, 1997.

E. Schwarz, Die Stammeszugehorigkeit der Slawen am oberen Main im Lichte der Ortsnamen, Sybaris, FsT Hans Krahe, 1958.

——Die Stammeszugehorigkeit der Mainwenden, FuF 32, 1958.

——Die Mainwenden und Wogastiburg, ZoS 16, 1976.

H. Walther, Deutsche und slawische Siedlung im oberen Maingebiet, Slawische Namenforschung, 1963.

F. Weisser, Zu den slawischen Spuren im Land- und Stadtkreis Erfurt, OsG 12, 1979.

J. Will, Die Ortsnamen des Kreises Neustadt an der Waldnaab, Heimatblatter fur den oberen Naabgau 17, 1939.

8. SLAVS IN GERMANIA: BORDERS, BORDERLANDS

H. Aubin, Die Ostgrenze des alten deutschen Reiches, Historische Vierteljahrschrift 28, 1933.

H. Brachmann, Slawen an der ostlichen Peripherie des Frankischen Reiches, Institut des recherches scientifiques de la culture des ancients Slaves, 1986.

W. Budesheim, Der "limes Saxonia". Grenze des Reichs nordlich der Elbe vom 9. -12. Jt gegen die Slawen, Tumult-Schriften zur Verkehrswissenschaft, 1992.

W. Filipowiak, Das wilzisch-pommersche und polnische Grenzgebiet im 10. und 11. Jt, ZtA 19, 1984.

M. Hardt, Das Hannoversche Wendland - eine Grenzregion im fruhen mittealter, Beitrage zur Archaologie und Geschichte Nordostniedersachsens, 1991.

L. Havlik, Slovane vd Vychodni marce v 9.-11. stoleti, SlA 11, 1964.

P. Honigsheim, Der limes Sorabicus, ZtG 24, 1924.

K. Hucke, Die sachsisch-slavische Stammesgrenze in Holstein zur Frugeschichtlichen Zeit, NdV 12, 1936.

H. Jankuhn, Bergan am Limes Saxoniae, DiE 57, 1950.

——Zur slawischen Westgrenze in Norddeutschland im fruhen Mittelalter, HuN 17, 1965.

W. Ketrzynski, O Slowianch mieszkajacych niegdys miedzy Renem a Laba, Sala i czeska granica, Rozprawy Akademii Umietjenosci 2/15, 1901.

E. Klebel, Die Ostgrenze des Karolingischen Reiches, Jb fur Landeskunde von Nieder Osterreich 21, 1928.

J. Kostrzewski, W sprawie zachodniej granicy Slowian w Niemczech srodkowych, PrG 22, 1946.

A.L. Kuhar, The Conversion of the Slovenes and the German-Slav Ethnic Boundary in the Eastern Alps, 1959.

W. Lammers, Die germanisch-slawische Volksgrenze in Nordalbingen, Bericht uber die Tagung fur Fruhgeschichte Lubeck, 18/19, 1955.

——Die germanisch-slawische Volksgrenze in Noralbingien, BeR, 1961.

K. Maleczynski, Najstarsza zachodnia granica Polski nas Podstawie Zrodel X wieku , Poczatki Panstwa Polskiego I, 1962.

T. Milewski, Zachodnia granica pormoskiego obszaru Jezykowego w wiekach srednich, SlO 10, 1931.

H. Osterun, Der Limes Saxonia zwischen Trave undSchwentine, ZsH 92, 1967.

A. Sedlacek, O ustaleni hranice mezi Cechami a Luzici, CmM 66, 1982.

Z. Sulowski, Najstarza Granica Zachodnia Polski, ZaC 8, 1952.

W. Timpel, Neue archaologische Untersuchungen im westsaalischen Thuringen zum Umfrang und zur Grenze der slawischen Besiedlung im mittealterlichen deutschen Feudalstaat, RaP I, 1979.

R. Wensch, Die Grenzen zwischen Bohmen und Oberlausitz, 1929.

S.A. Wolf, Die Slawische Westgrenze in Nord- und Mitteldeutschland im Jahre 805, DwS 2, 1957.

9. SLAVS IN GERMANIA: LANGUAGES, DIALECTS, SPEECH

G. Bellman, Slavoteutonica. Lexikalische Untersuchungen zum slawisch-deutschen Sprachkontakt im Ostmitteldeutschen, 1971.

U. Bentzien, Regelizt—ein Brandenburgisches Mundarwort aus der slawischen Pflugnomenklatur, ZtS 11, 1966.

H.H. Bielfeldt, Slavisches im deutschen Wortschatz, ZtS 3, 1958.

——Did slavischen Worter in der deutschen Sprache, Forschen und Wirken, 1960.

——Slawische Worter im Deutschen Vorpommerns, ZtS 5, 1960.

——Die historische Gliederung der slawischen Worter im Deutschen, 1963.

——Die slawischen eigenlichen Reliktworter in den deutschen Mundarten, ZtS 8, 1963.

——Neue Arbeiter uber slavische Worter im Deutschen, ZtS 9, 1964.

——Die slawische worter in Deutschen Brandenburgs, ZtS 15, 1970.

——Die slawischen Worter im Deutschen: Ausgewahte Schriften 1950-78, 1982.

H.M. Brinjen, On the Phonology of the Sorbian Dialect of Slepe [German Schliefe], Dutch Contributions to the 11th International Congress of Slavists, 1994.

C.C. Burmeister, Uber die Sprache der fruher in Mecklenburg wohnenden Obodriten-Wenden, 1840.

J. Dobrovsky, Uber die slawische Sprache, sonder uber id Luneburgischen, Slovanka 1, 1814.

L. Fahlbusch, Slawisches as Daubes Worterbuch der Altenburger Mundart, ZtS 1, 1956.

R. Fischer, Slawisches Sprachgut westlich der Saale. Der Name Langwitz, WaN 2, 1953.

——Die slawischen Sprachdenkmaler Deutschlands, SpL A/2, 1954.

R. E. Fischer, Die slawische-deutschen Mischnamen im altpolabischen Sprachgebiet, NaM 20, 1972.

G. Gerhardt, Slavische Restworter in Saschen, ZsP 15, 1938.

J. Hanus, Zur Literatur und Geschichte der slavischen Sprachen in Deutschland, namentlich der Sprache der ehemaligen Elbeslaven oder Polaben, Slavische Bibliotek oder Beitrage zur slavischen Philologie und Geschichte 2, 1858.

K. Hengst, Zur Intergration slawischer Toponyme in Deutsch, OsG 13, 1981.

——Beginn, Verlauf und Dauer des slawisch-deutschen Sprachkontakts an mittlerer Saale und Weisser Elster, OsG 17, 1988.

——Namenforschung, slawisch-deutscher Sprachkontakt und fruhe slawische Sprachstudien im Elbe-Saale-Grenzraum, OsG 19, 1990.

A. Hilferding, Die sprachlichen Denkmaler der Drevjaner und Glinianer Elb-slawen im Luneburger Wendlande, 1857.

F. Hinze, Slawische Lehn- und Reliktworter im vopommersch-mecklenburischen, ZtS 35, 1990.

G. Holzer, Die Einheitlichkeit des Slavischen um 600 n. Chr. und ihr Zerfall, WsJ 41, 1995.

——Zu Lautgeschichte und Dialekten des mittelalterlichen slavischen in Osterreich, WsJ 42, 1996.

M. Jezowa, O Dawnych slowianskie dialktach miedzy dolna Odra i Laba, Szczechin 6/7, 1960.

——Dawne slowianskie dialekty Meklemburgii w swietle nazw miejscowych i osobowych, I. Fonetika, 1961.

——Dawne slowianskie dialekty Meklemburgii w swietle nazw miejscowych i osobowych, II. Slowotworstwo, 1962

A. Keseburg, Der Wilzenbund und die Prignitz. Eine quellenkkkritische Linguistische Studie Zur Brandenburgischen Landesgeschichte, JbR 24, 1973.

A. Kleczkowski, Slowianskie wplywy jezykowe w Szleswiku i Holsztynie, Biuletyn Polskiego Towarzystwa Jezykoznawcgego 8, 1948.

——Influence of Slavonic Languages in Schleswig and Holstein, LgP, 1949.

J. Knobloch, Jazykovy odraz merovejsko-slovanskych stykss, StU 12, 1966.

H. Krahe, Vorgeschichtliche Sprachbezichungen von den baltischen Ostseelandem bis zu den Gebieten um den Nordteil der Adria, 1957.

E. Kuck, Zur Volkssprache des Luneburger Landes, Luneburger HmB 2, 1927.

R. Lotzsch, Slawisches Elemente in der grammatischen Struktur des Jiddischen, ZtS 19, 1974.

V.V. Martynov, Slavjano-germanskoe leksiceskoe vzeimodejstvie drevensej pory, 1963.

——Tipologija i vzaimodejstvie slavjanskih i germanskih jazykov, 1969.

K. Muller, Plotze. Die Geschichte eines slawischen Wortes im Deutschen. Beitrage zum deutsch-slawischen Sprachkontakt, 1977.

R. Olesch, Finis Lingvae Dravaneopolabicae, MdF 50/1, 1968.

——Zur christlichen Terminologie in der Sprache der Dravanoplaben, FsT B. Stasieski, 1975.

S.K. Papierkowski, Szczatki jezyka slowinaskich mieszkancow Starej Marchii i okolic Magdeburga, SlO 9, 1930.

R. Peesch, Der Wortschatz der Fischer im Kietz von Berlin-Kopenick, 1955.

P. Rost, Die Sprachreste der Dravano-Polaben im Hannoverschen, 1907.

E. Schwarz, Sprache und Siedlung in Nordostbayern, 1960.

D. Stellmacher, Zur Dialektologie des Wendlandes in Deutsch-slawischer Sprachkontakt im Lichte der Ortsnamen, 1993.

B. Syzdglowska-Ceglowa, Jeszcze o etymologiach slowiansko-niemieckich jezyka Wendow luneburskich, SlO 21, 1961.

R. Trautmann, Die slawischer Volker und Sprachen, 1946.

E. W. Selmer, Sprachstudien im Luneburger Wendland, 1918.

H. Walther, Die historischen Grundlagen fur slawisches Sprachgut im Deutschen, NaM 11, 1987.

S. Wauer, Sprachkontakte in der Prignitz in Nachbarschaft zum Hannoverschen Wendland, Deutsch-slawischer Sprachkontakt im Lichte der Ortsnamen, 1993.

P. Wexler, Explorations in Judeo-Slavic Linguistics, 1987.

J. Wiese, Slawische Worter im Berlinischen, ZtS 32, 1987.

E. Winter, Die Pflege der west- und sudslawischen Sprachen in Halle im 18. Jh, 1954.

T. Witkowski, Strela-Stralow-Stralsund-Schadergard sprachlich, GsJ 1964.

——Urslaw. y und seine spaters Aussprache in den ehemaligen slawischen Dialekten Mecklenburgs und Vorpommers, ZtS 10, 1965.

——Slawische Namenforschung im niederdeutschen Sprachgebiet, Niederdeutschen Jb, 1966.

H. Wurms, Sprachliche Anmerkungen zu den slawischen Ortsnamen des kreises Herzogturm Lauenburg, LbH 82, 1975.

10. SLAVS IN GERMANIA: ARCHAEOLOGICAL SITES

M. Agthe, Mesolithische, neolithische und slawische Funde von Uhyst, Kr. Hoyerswerda, AuF 30, 1985.

S. Albert, W. Timpel, Slawisches Grabersfeld bei Epsenfeld, Kr. Arnstadt, AuF 5, 1960.

K. Andree, Die Wustungen der Ostprignitz, 1957.

H.H. Andersen, Das Ur-Altlubeck, Die Heimat 85, 1978.

A. Bach, W. Timpel, Ein slawisches Graberfeld von Wichmar, Kr. Jena, AuF 28, 1983.

H. Bach, S. Dusek, Slawen in Thuringen. Geschichte, Kultur und Anthropologie im 10. bis 12 Jh Nach den Ausgrabungen bei Espenfeld, 1971.

H. Bartels, E. Schmidt-Thielbeer, Slawische Siedlungen mit eingetieften Hausern bei Michlen, Kr. Kothen, AuF 28, 1982.

——Lobitz, eine slawische Wustung bei Micheln, Kr. Kothen, AuF 31, 1986.

W. Baumann, Slawische Siedlungsreste in den Trofschiten des Gottwitzer Sees bei Mutzschen, AuF 6, 1961.

——R. Dunkel, Weitere Ausgrabungen im Stadtkern von Taucha, Kr. Leipzig, AuF 10, 1965.

A. Beck, Die windischen Grabfunde aus Pommern, BaL 59, 1969.

D. Becker, Slawische Brunnen von Redentin und Gross Stromkendorf, Kr. Wismar, AuF 22, 1977.

——Die slawische Inselsiedlung im Trenntsee, Gemarkung Patin, Kr. Sternberg, JbM 1980.

——Neue Funde zur fruhslawischen Besiedlung Westmecklenburgs, AuF 31, 1986.

——Zur Befestigung der slawischen Siedlung Scarzyn, Gemarkung Parchim, JbM 1990.

G. Behm, Eine spatslawische Siedlung bein Berlin-Kaulsdorf, PzT 32/33, 1941-42.

P. Berghaus, H.G. Peters, G. Osten, Das wendische Reihengraberfeld von Noventhien, Kr. Uelzen, AuN 3, 1966.

M. Bernatzky-Goetze, Die slawisch-deutsche Burganlage von Meetschow und die slawische Siedlung von Brunkendor, NeU 19, 1991.

G. Billig, Burgenarchaologische und sielungskundliche Betrachtungen zum Flussgebiet der Zschopau und der Freiberger Mulde, ZtA 15, 1981.

I. Borkovsky, Die altslavische Keramik in Mitteleuropa, 1940.

J. Brandt, Neue slawische Siedlungsfunde aus der Stadt Schwerin, Informationen des Bezirksarbeitkreises fur Ur- und Fruhgeschichte Schwerin, 1985.

S. Brather, Altslawische Keramik in Mecklenburg und Vorpommern Probleme der Typenverbreitung, ZtA 27, 1993.

——Feldberger Keramik and fruhe Slawenb. Studien zur nordwestslawischen Keramik der Karolingzeit, 1994.

——Nordwestslawische Siedlungskeramik der Karolingerzeit - Frankische Waren als Vorbild?, Germania 73, 1995.

——Feldberger Keramik und fruhe Slawen. Studien zur nordwestslawischen Keramik der Karolingerzeit, Praehist. Arch 34, 1996.

——Merowinger und karolingerzeitliches "Fremdgut" bein den Nordwestslawen. Gebrauchsgut und Elitenkultur im sudwestliche Ostseeraum, PzT 71, 1966.

R. Breddin, Eine spatslawische Siedlung in Frankfurt (Oder)-Birnbaumsmuhle, AuF 4, 1959.

——Ein spatslawisches Gefass von Bad Saarow-Pieskow, Kr. Furstenwalde, AuF 6, 1961.

A. Bruckner, Die slavischen Ansiedelungen in der Altmark und im Magdeburgishcen, 1879.

——Die Slavischen Ansiedlungen im Hassengau, Archiv fur slavische Philologie 5, 1881.

W. Budesheim, Die Entwicklung der mittelalterlichen Kulturlandschaft des heutigen Kreises Herzogtum Lauenburg und bedonserer Berucksichigung der slawischen Besiedlung, 1983.

——Zur slawischen Besiedlung zwischen Elbe und Oder, 1994.

W. Bunnig, K. Grebe, Ausgrabungen auf einem slawischen Fundplatz in Hohennauen, Kr. Rathenow, AuF 32, 1987.

——Eine fruhslawische Befestlgung von Butzer, Kr. Rathenow, AuF 33, 1988.

H. Burhow, G. Kohn, Ein spatslawische Korpergraberfeld bei Ropersdorf, Kreis Prenzlau, Mitteilungen des Bezirksfachauschusses fur Ur- und Fruhgeschichte, Bezirk Neubrandenburg, 1984.

B. Buschendorf, Zwei spatslawische Grabfunde aus Sachsen-Anhalt, JsH 34, 1950.

P. Butzmann, Ein slawischer Topferofen an der Schwarzen Elster bien Kremitz, Kr. Jessen, AuF 4, 1959.

A. Christal, Eine spatslawische Flachsrostgrube aus der Cottbuser Alstadt, AuF 32, 1987.

——G. Christl, Neue spatslawische Funde aus der Cottbuser Alstadt, AuF 33, 1988.

W. Coblenz, Dis slawische Sumpfschanze von Brohna, Kr. Bautzen, Germania 30, 1952.

——Slawisches Skelettgraberfeld von Altlommatzsch, Kr. Meissen, AuF 3, 1959.

——Zur Situation der archaologischen Slawenforschung in Sachsen, Siedlung und Verfassung, 1960.

——Archaologische Bemerkungen zur Herkunft der altesten Slawen in Sachsen, ArB 13, 1964.

——Archaologisches Bermerkungen zur Herkunft der altesten Slawen in Sachsen, ArB 13, 1965.

——Das slawische Skelettgraberfeld von Alt-Lommatzsch. ArB 16/17, 1967.

——Bemerkungen zur slawischen Besiedlung nordlich von Erzgebirge und Lausitzer Bergland, BeR, 1970.

——Bemerkungen zur Chronologie in den slawischen Gauen Daleminzien und Nisan, PoL 16, 1971.

——Bemerkungen zum Slawengau Nisane, Archaologie als Geschichtwissenschaft, 1977.

——Archaologische Betrachtungen zur Gana-Frage im Rahmen der alterslawischen Besiedlung des Gaues Daleminzien, Beitrage zu Archivwissenschaft und Geschichtsforschung, 1977.

——Bemerkungen zur slawischen Archaologie der sorbischen Gau, RaP, 1979

P. Donat, Zur Nordausbreitung der slawischen Grubenhauser, ZtA 4, 1970.

——Die unregelmassigen Gruben und der Hausbau bei den Nortwestslawen, SlA 24, 1977.

——Zur zeitlichen und regionalen Gliederung der altslawischen Keramik zwischen Oder und Elbe/Saale, Studia nad etnogeneza Slowian, FsT W. Hensel, 1987.

M. Dulinicz, Die fruheste slawische Besiedelung in Ostholstein, Offa 48, 1991.

——Von Mecklenburg bis zur Weichsel Befunde und Funde von ausgewahlten fruhslawischen Fundstellen, EaZ 34, 1993

R. Dunkel, Fruhslawische Siedlungsfunde bei Dewitz, Ort von Taucha, Kr. Leipzig, BuF 2, 1982.

S. Dusek, Das Spatslawisch Graberfeld, EzT 12, 1971

W. Erdmann, Der Lubecker Stadthugel in slawischer Zeit (8.-12. Jh), Archaologie in Lubeck, 1980.

I. Ericsson, Futterkamp. Untersuchungen mittelalterlicher befestigter Siedlungen im Kreis Plon, Holstein, 1981.

——Kontinuitat und Diskontinuitat im slawisch-deutschen Siedlungsraum, LbH 103, 1982.

G.P. Fehring, Archaologisch-gaugeschichtliche Erkenntnisse zu Topographie und Besiedlung, Bau, Wirtschafts- und Sozialstruktur des mittelalterlichen Lubeck, DiE 85, 1978.

——Die Entstehung von Lubeck, ZtA 25, 1991.

——The Archaeology of Medieval Germany: An Introduction, 1992.

B. Fischer, Zwei neue altslawische Siedlungen sudlich von Berlin, Auf 16, 1971.

——Fruhe Slawen in der Notte-Niederung bei Konigs Wusterhausen, Hk Kreis Zossen 28, 1971.

——Die Slawen und ihre geschichtliche Bedeutung beim Landesebau im Teltow, Hk fur den Kreis Zossen, 1974.

——H. Seyer, Neue altslawische Siedlung von Berlin-Wartenberg und Berlin-Marzahn, Jb des Markischen Meuseum 1, 1975.

——E. Kirsch, Die fruhslawische Siedlung von Waltersdorf, Kr. Konigs Wusterhausen, AuF 31, 1986.

——M. Hofmann, Eine fruhslawische Siedlung von Waltersdorf, Kr. Konigs Wusterhausen, AuF 31, 1986.

——S. Gustavs, Volkerwanderungszeitliche und fruhslawische Siedlungspuren bei Kiekebusch, Kr. Konigs-Wusterhausen, VmU 27, 1993.

H. Friesinger, Studien zur Archaologie der Slawen in Niederosterreich, 1971-77.

W.H. Fritze, Eine Karte zum Verhaltnis der fruhmittelalterlich-slawischen zur hochmittelalterlichen Siedlung in der Ost-prignitz, Germania Slavica II, 1981.

C. Fritzsche, M. Gutsche, H.J. Vogt, Slawische Siedlung und Graberfeld bei Liswsa, Kr. Delitzsch, AuF 31, 1985.

O. Gehl, U. Lehmkuhl, Das Knochenfundut einer jungslawischen Siedlung am ehemaligen Loddigsee bei Parchim, JbM 1980.

W. Gley, Die Besiedlung der Mittelmark von der slawischen Einwanderung bis 1624, 1926.

C. Goehrke, Furhzeit des Ostslaventums, 1992.

K.D. Gralow, H. Strange, Ein slawisches Hugelgrab von Locknitz, Kr. Pasewalk, AuF 17, 1972.

——Mittelslawische Siedlungsgruben von Sulten, Kr. Sternberg, AuF 28, 1983.

K. Grebe, Slawische Bestattungen von Marquardt Kr. Potsdam-Land, AuF 7, 1962.

——R. Hoffman, Slawische Grabfunde von Fahrlans, Ketzin Und Phosen. Ein Beitrag zur Kenntnis der slawischen Bestattungssiten im Havelland, VmU 3, 1964.

——Die Slawische Siedlung von Brandenburg (Havel)/Neuendorf, AuF 12, 1967.

——Neuentdeckte slawische Befestigungsanlagen im Bezirk Potsdam, AuF 20, 1975.

——Zur fruhslawischen Besiedlung im Havelgebietes, VmU 10, 1976.

——Die Slawenzeit im Havelland, das 6. bis Jh, RaT 28, 1983.

——Archaologische-kulturelle Gruppen und die Stufengliederung der fruhslawischen Zeit im Havelgebiet, VbL 28, 1994.

R. Grenz, Die slawischen Funde aus dem hannoverschen Wendland, 1961.

——Das Opfer des menschlichen Hauptes bei den Westslawen in Ost- und Mitteldeutschland, ZfO 12, 1963.

——Die Munzdatierung der slawischen Grabfunde im westslawischen Siedlungsgebiet, Studien zur europaischen Vor- und Fruhgeschichte, 1968.

E. Gringmuth-Dallmer, Die mittelalterliche Siedlungsentwicklung im Gereich des Klosters Dobrilug, GgC 22, 1958.

——A. Hoonagel, Jungslawische Siedlung mit Kultfiguren auf der Fischerinsel bei Neubrandenburg, ZtA 5, 1971.

——Siedlungsarchaologische Beobachtungen zur Namengebung in slawische-deutschen Kontaktgebiet zwischen Elbe und Oder/ Neisse, OsG 27, 1988.

——Deutsche und Wendisch — Gross und Klein. Zur siedlungsgeschithlichen Aussage von Ortsnamen im unterscheidenden Zusatzen in der Mark Brandenburg, OsG 29, 1990.

U. Gross, Slawische Keramkifund in Unterregenbach. Denkmalpflege in Baden-Wurttenberg, 1990.

——Slavische und slavisch beeinflusste Funde zwischen Altmuhl unde Oberrhein, DwS 35, 1990.

S. Gustavs, Fruhslawisches Gefassfragment mit Darstellung einer kultischen Szene von Schulzendorf, Kr. Konigs Wusterhausen, ZtA 13, 1979.

——Eine spatslawische Siedlung von Schmergow, Kr. Potsdam-Land, AuF 28, 1983.

O. Harck, Spatslawische Grabfunde in Norddeutschland, 1976.

——Zur spatslawisch-fruhmittelalterlichen Besiedlung auf den Ostseeinseln Rugen und Fehmarn, Offa 45, 1989.

I. Heindel, Axted des 8. bis 14. Jh im westslawischen Siedlungsgebiet zwischen Elbe/Saale und Oder/Neisse, ZtA 26, 1992.

P. Herfert, Slawische Schalengfasse von der Insel Rugen, GsJ 4, 1964.

——Ein mittelslawischer Hausgrundriss von Varbelvitz, Kr. Rugen, AuF 9, 1964.

——Slawische Hugelgraber mit Steinsetzungen von der Insel Pulitz, Kr. Rugen, AuF 10, 1965.

L. Herklotz, D. Stuckly, Fruhslawischer Kastenbrunnen mit Holzfunden aus Eythra, Kr. Leipzig Land. ArB 31, 1987.

J. Henning, Berlin-Hellersdorf "Schleipfuhl": Siedlungsgrabung zum Problem germanisch-slawischer Kontakte in der Mittel des 1. Jh, AuF 32, 1987.

G. Hey, Die slawischen Ansiedelungen im Konigreich Saschsen: mit Erklarung ihrer Namen, 1893.

——Die slawischen Siedlungen im alten Vogtland, Under Vogtland 3, 1896-7.

M. Hofmann, H. Seyer, Eine fruhslawische Siedlung im Zentrum von Berlin, AuF 32, 1987.

——Die fruhslawische Siedlung bei Berlin-Hellersdorf, VmU 22, 1988.

R. Hoffman, J. Herrmann, Zolchow, eine slawische un fruhdeutsche Wehranlage im Kreise Potsdam-Land, AuF 2, 1957.

A. Hollnagel, Kulturreliktpflanzen auf slawischen Inselsiedlung im Kr. Neustrelitz, JbM 1953.

——Die jungslawische inseliedlung im Trennt See bein Pastin, Kr. Sternberg, AuF 14, 1969.

K. Holter, Baiern und Slawen in Oberosterreich: Probleme der Landnahme und Besiedlung, 1980.

K. Hucke, Wendische Hugelgraber im ostlichen Holstein, DiE 64, 1957.

——Porez - eine slawische Siedlung an der Schwentine, DiE 68, 1961.

W. Hulle, Westausbreitung und Wehranlagen der Slawen in Mitteldeutschland, 1940.

J. Huth, Slawischen Siedlungen und Burgen im Eigenschen Kreise, ArB 11/12, 1963.

M. Jahrig, E. Gringmuth-Dallmer, Zur dendrochronologischen Absolutdatierung der jungslawischen Siedlung auf der Fischerinsel bei Neubrandenburg, ZtA 7, 1973.

——Die Ergebnisse der dendrochronologsichen Untersuchung der Holzproben vom slawischen Burgwall "Grodisch" bei Wiesenau, Kr. Eisenhuttenstadt, ZtA 11, 1977.

H. Jakob, Fruhslavische Keramikfunde in Oberfranken, DwS 26, 1981.

P. Janesch, Die slawische Besiedlung im Gebiet von Plane, Nuthe, Nieplitz und unterer Spree vom 7. bis 12. Jh. auf archaologischer Grundlage, 1985.

H. Jankuhn, Die slawische Besiedlung des Hannoverschen Wendlandes im fruhen Mittelalter, SlV 18, 1970.

——Die archaologische Erforschung der slawischen Siedlungsgebiete des fruhen und hohen Mittelalters im Bereich der Bundesrepublik Deutschland seit 1945, RaP 1979.

H.G. Kaack, Von der slawischen Landhahme biz zur deutschen Besiedlung, LbH 99, 1980.

W. Kasbohm, Das slawische Korpergraberfeld von Damm, Kr. Rostock, JbM 1953.

H. Keiling, Keramikfunde aus einer fruhslawischen Siedlung von Cramonshagen, Kr. Schwerin, AuF 10, 1965,

——Zur Besiedlung der Flur Zapel, Stadt Hagenow, und das Problem der alterslawischen Keramik in Mecklenburg, JbM 1974.

——Ein jungslawischer Siedlungsplat am ehemaligen Lodigsee bein Parchim, JbM 1980.

——Ein jungslawisches Dorf an einem Eldeubergang bei Parchim, AuF 27, 1982.

——Ein jungslawischer Siedlungsplat mit Flussubergang und Kultbau bei Parchim im Bezirk Schwerin, Acta Visbyensia VII, 1983.

——Ein jungslawisches Bauwerk aus Spaltbohlen von Parchim, ZtA 29, 1984.

——Ein jungslawischer Siedlungsplatz mit Flussubergang und Kultbau bei Parchim, ZtA 19, 1985.

——Slawische Hausgrundrisse aus Mecklenburg und die Blockhauser vom jungslawischen Siedlungsplatz Parchim, ZtA 19, 1985.

——Slawische Burgwallreste auf der Schweriner Schlossinsel, AuF 33, 1988.

——Forschungsergebnisse von einer slawischen Marksiedlung zwischen Elbe und Oder, Beitrage fur Wissenschaft und Kultur, 1994.

E. Kirsch, Neue Grabfund aus spatslawischer Zeit im Bezirk Cottbus, VmU 12, 1979.

G. Kohn, Slawische Gruben bei Blindow, Kr. Prenzlau, AuF 27, 1982.

H.A. Knorr, Die slawische Keramik zwischen Elbe und Oder, 1937.

——Der Steigbugel von Pritzerbe, Kr. Brandenburg, AuF 2, 1958.

A. Krenzlin, Deutsche und slawische Siedlung in innere Havelland, AuF 1, 1956.

——Siedlungsformen und Siedlungsstrukturen in deutsch-slawischen Kontaktzonen, GsL 1, 1980.

B. Kruger, Zur Nordwestausbreitung der fruhslawischen Keramik im weiteren Elbe-Saale-Gebiet, Varia archaeologia 1964.

——Fruhslawische Grabfunde aus Sausedlitz, Kr. Delitzsch, AuF 11, 1966.

——Dessau-Mosigkau. Ein fruhslawischer Siedlungspatz im mittleren Elbe-gebiet, 1967.

——Eine altslawische Siedlung von Schulzendorf, Kr. Konigs Wusterhausen, AuF 14, 1969.

——Germanisch-slawische Siedlungsbeziehungen in der spaten Volkerwanderunszeit, EzT 13, 1972.

P.L.B. Kupka, Slawische Skelettgraber von Tangermunde, Jb fur die Vorgeschichte der sachsisch-thuringischen Lander 14, 1920.

W. Lampe, Neue slawisches Siedlungsfunde aus dem Westteil des Bezirkes Rostock, AuF 1, 1973.

——Eine jungslawische Siedlung bei Wendelstorf, Kreis Bad Doberan, JbM 1974.

——Die oberidischen Bodendenkmaler der Stubnitz, Kr. Rugen, AuF 19, 1974.

——Eine neue slawische Fundstelle am Petridamm in Rostock, AuF 24, 1979.

——Jungslawische Siedlungsfunde aus Morgenitz, Kr. Wolgast, AuF 27, 1982.

——Der siedlungsaubau auf der Insel Usedom un jungslawischer Zeit, Mensch und Umwelt, 1992.

E. Lange, Einige Ergebnisse der pollenanalytischen Untersuchungen bei Demmin, ZtA 4, 1970.

L. Leciejewicz, Die wirschaftliche Gliederung der elbslawischen Stamme im Lichte der Schatzfunde, ZtA 1, 1967.

——Zur Entwicklung von Fruhstadten an der sudlichen Ostseekuste, ZtA 3, 1969.

——Sachsen in den slawischen Ostseestadten im 10.—12. Jt, ZtA 21, 1987.

E. Lehmann, Plan einer mittelslawischen Siedlung in Berlin-Mahlsdorf, AuF 2, 1981.

A. Leube, Slawische Siedlungsfunde von Garftitz, Kr. Rugen, AuF 9, 1964.

——Ausgrabungen auf einer spatslawischen Siedlung bei Usedom, AuF 9, 1964.

——Zur slawischen Besiedlung der terra Wanzlow (Usedom), ZtA 4, 1970.

——Ein mittelslawischer Siedlungsaufschluss von Waltersdorf, Kr. Konigs Wusterhausen, ZtA 16, 1982.

H. Ludat, Siedlung und Verfassung der Slawen zwischen Elbe, Saale, und Oder, 1960.

T. Malinowski, Uber die Pommersche Kultur, ZtA 20, 1986.

G. Mangelsdorf, Ein furhslawisches Brandgrab des 6./7. Jt aus dem Havelgebiet, ZtA 10, 1976.

——Lage und Alter mittelalterlicher Ortswustungen im Elbhavelland, ZtA 11, 1977.

——Eine altslawische Siedlung von Mothlitz, Kr. Rathenow, AuF 22, 1977.

——Zur Verbreitung mittelalterlicher Ortswustungen im Bezirk Potsdam, ZtA 17, 1983.

K.H. Marschalleck, Fruhslawische Grabhugel bei Saaringen und Gotz, Kr. Brandenburg, AuF 1, 1956.

W. Mastaller, Fruhslawische Siedlungen im Kreis Gustrow, Informationen des Bezirksarbeitskreises fur Ur- und Fruhgeschichte Schwerin, 18, 1978.

W. Meibeyer, Die Rundlingsdorfer im ostlichen Niedersachsen. Ihre Verbreitung, Entstehung und Beziehung zur slawischen Siedlung in Niedersachsen, 1964.

A. Mirtschin, Das slawische Kindergrab von Strehal, Riesaer Heimat 3, 1958.

——Slawische Funde auf dem Schlossufer von Strehla, ArB 9, 1961.

R. Moschkau, Beispiele ungewohnlicher Musterung slawischer Keramik aus Nordwestsachsen, Alt-Thuringen 6, 1962-63.

H.H. Muller, Die Tierknochenfunde aus der slawischen Burganlage von Cositz, Kr. Kothen, ZtA 19, 1985.

R. Mulsow, Stadtkernforschung aus der Rotstocker Altstadt, AkO 22, 1992.

——Altslawische Siedlungsbefunde aus der Rostocker Altstadt, AuF 39, 1994.

H.E. Nellissen, Archaologische Forschungen zur slawisch-fruhdeutschen Geschichte in Ostholstein, KoR 1, 1971.

V. Nekuda, Die slawische Dorfsiedlung in Berlin-Kaulsdorf, AiB 6, 1982.

I. Nilius, Zwei neu entdeckte slawische Fundstellen im Bezirk Rostock, AuF 3 1958.

G. Osten, Slawische Siedlungsspuren im Raum um Uelzen, Bad Bevensen und Luneberg, 1978.

C. Plate, Slawische Graberfelder im Potsdamer Havelland, VmP 10, 1976.

——Ein altslawischer Hausgrundriss von Wustermark, Ot. Dyrotz, Kr. Nauen, AuF 22, 1977.

W. Prange, Die slawische Siedlungen im Kr. Herzogtum Lauenburg, Siedlung und Verfassung, 1960.

——Siedlungsgeschichte des Landes Lauenburg im Mittelalter, 1960.

R.J. Prilof, Lieps. Archaologische Untersuchungen an slawischen Tierknochen vom Sudende des Tollensesees, BuF 30, 1994.

A. Pudelko, Zur slawischen Besiedlung des westlichen Elbufers zwischen Schnackenburg und Langendorf, Kr. Luchow-Dannenburg, NaC 41, 1971.

K. Quilitzsch, Aus der Geschichte Ploddas (Sorben um 600), Bitterfelder Kulturkalender 1955.

P. Reichwaldt, Ein neuer altslawischer Fundplatz bei Dahlewitz, Kr. Zossen, AuF 24, 1979.

H. Rempel, Die sorbische Keramik in Thuringen, PtZ 37, 1959.

J. Richter, Eine neue slawische Fundstelle im Vogtland, AuF 1, 1956.

H. Schafer, Zur jungslawischen Keramik aus der 2. Halftes des 13. Jh in Greifswald, Archaologische Beritchte aus Mecklenburg-Vorpommer 3, 1996.

W. Schich, Zum Verhaltnis von slawischer und hochmittelalterlicher Siedlung in den brandenburgischen Landschaften Zauche und Teltow, JbG 26, 1977.

——Das Verhaltnis der fruhmittelalterlich-slawischen zur hochmittelalterlichen Siedlung im Havelland, Das Havelland im Mittelalter, 1987.

R. Schindler, Die Datierungsgrundlagen der slawischen Keramik in Hamburg, PzT 37, 1959.

E. Schmidt, W. Nitzschke, Neue slawische Graberfelder zwischen Saale und Weiser Elster, AuF 21, 1976.

——Lieps. Eine slawische Siedlungskammer am Sudende des Tollensesees, 1984.

E. Schmidt-Thielbeer, H. Bartels, Slawische Siedlungen mit eingetieften Hausern bei Micheln, Kr. Kothen, AuF 27, 1982.

——Lobitz, eine slawische Wustung bei Micheln, Kr. Kothen, AuF 31, 1986.

V. Schmidt, Eine Neue Slawische Siedlung bei Neubrandenburg, MbU 19, 1972.

——Slawische urnenlose Brandbestattungen in Flachgrabern aus dem Bezirk Neubrandenburg, ZtA 5, 1981.

——Ein slawisches Graberfeld an der Lieps bei Usadel, Kr. Neustrelitz, AuF 34, 1989.

——Die Gusstechnik im Schmukhandwerk bei den Westslawen, ZtA 28, 1994.

K.J. Schmidt, Neue Ausgrabunden in der slawischen Vorburgsiedlung in Wildberg, Kr. Neuruppin, AuF 34, 1989.

J. Schneider, Altslawische Siedlungsfunde von Grieben, Kr. Tangerhutte, MiT 51, 1967.

——Neue altslawische Siedlungsfunde aus der Altmark, BeR, 1970.

——Neue altslawischen Siedlungsfunde aus der sudostlichen Altmark, JmV 1973.

——Beitrage zur Besiedlung der Altmark im fruhen Mittelalter, RaP, 1979.

U. Schoknecht, Neue slawische Graber aus dem Bezirk Neubrandburg, AuF 8, 1963.

——Ofen in slawischen Siedlungen, AuF 16, 1971.

——Eine slawische Siedlung bei Neubrandenburg-Fritscheshof, AuF 17, 1972.

——Neue slawische Funde aus dem Bezirk Neubrandenburg, JbM 1974.

——Rettungsgrabungen in der kaiserzeitlichen und slawischen Siedlung von Neubrandenburg-Fritscheshof, JbM 1975.

——Eine munzdatierte jungslawische Grube aus Gielow, Kr. Malchin, AuF 20, 1975.

——Menzlin. Ein frugeschichtlicher Handelsplatz an der Peene, Beitrage Ur und Fruhgeschichte der Bezirke Rostock 10, 1977.

——Slawische Siedlungen bei Zirzow, Kr. Neubrandenburg, AuF 22, 1977.

——Handelsbeziehungen der fruhmittelalterlichen Siedlung Menzlin bei Anklam, ZtA 12, 1978.

——Altslawische Siedlungsgruben von Wetzenow, Kr. Pasewalk, JbM, 1981.

——Munzdatierte jungslawische Gruben aus Malkwitz, Kr. Waren, und Torgelow, Kr. Ueckermunde, AuF 29, 1984.

——Mittelalterliche Funde aus dem Klostersee bei Dargun, Kr. Malchin, JbM 1989.

L. Schott, Zur Anthropologie des slawischen Graberfeldes von Gustavel, Kr. Sternberg, JbM 1960.

E. Schuldt, Die slawische Keramik vom Fresendorfer Typ, JbM 1953.

——Eine slawisch Siedlung von Gross Stromkendorf, Kr. Wismar, JbM 1955.

——Die slawische Keramik in Mecklenburg, 1956.

——Die slawische Keramik von Sukow und das Problem der Feldberger Gruppe, JbM 1963.

——Bemerkenswerte Keramik aus der slawischen Siedlung des 9./10. Jt von Gross Raden, Kr. Sternberg, AuF 27, 1982.

E. Schultze, Die slawische Siedlung bei Brandenburg-Neuendorf, 1977.

H.K. Schulze, Die Besiedlung der Altmark, FsT W. Schlesinger, 1973.

——Der Anteil der Slawen and der mittelalterlichen Siedlung nach deutschem Rech im Ostmitteldeutschland, ZoS 31, 1982.

J. Schutz, Ortsnamentypen und slawische Siedlungszeit in Nordostbayern, FrA 28, 1968.

W. Seidel, Kaiserzeitliche und slawische Siedlungen in Gera-Tinz, AuF 9, 1964.

G. Sommer, Slawische Ansiedlungsfunde von Fahrland, Kr. Potsdam-Land, AuF 11, 1966.

——Altslawische Funde von Murow, Kr. Angermunde, AuF 16, 1971.

R. Spehr, Fruhslawische Funde aus Gohlis un Paussnitz, Kr. Riesa, AuF 12, 1967.

K. Steinbruck, Slawensiedlungen um Aschersleben, HaR 9, 1957.

H. Steuer, Slawische Siedlungen und Befestigungen im Hohbeck-Gebiet, Hannoversches Wendland 4, 1973.

K.W. Struve, Slawische Funde westlich des Limes Saxoniae, Offa 28, 1971.

H. Ullrich, Das spatslawische Graberfeld von Sanzkow, Kr. Demmin, AuF 14, 1969.

Z. Vana, Die Keramik der slawischen Stamme in Ostdeutschland, VpS 3, 1960.

H.J. Vogt, Die Grabungen auf der Wiprechtsburg in Groitzsch, Kr. Borna, AuF 9, 1964.

——Die Untersuchungen auf der Wiprechtsburg in Groitzsch, Kr. Borna, AuF 10, 1965.

——Fruhslawische Bodenfunde aus Westsachsen, ArB 19, 1970.

——Zur fruhslawischen Besiedlung des Elbe-Saalegebietes, BeR 1970.

——Archaologische Beitrage zur Kenntnis der landwirtschaftlichen Produktionsinstrumente der Slawen in den brandenburgischen Bezirken, EaZ 16, 1975.

T. Voigt, Neue fruhsorbische Brandgraber und Siedlungsreste aus dem Elb-Saalebebiet, NdV 18, 1942.

——Zur Herkunftsfrage der Brandgraber mit slawischem Kulturgut vom 6. bis 8. Jt im Elbe-Saale Gebiet, PzD 37, 1959.

B. Wachter, Das Verhaltnis von deutscher und slawischer Keramik im 11./12. Jahrhundert auf dem Weinberg in Hitzacker (Elbe) als chronologisches Problem, NnU 44, 1975.

——Das Abschluss der Ausgrabung auf dem Weinberg in Hitzacker (Elbe) im Jahre 1975, NnU 45, 1976.

H. Walther, Namenkundliche Beitrage zur Siedlungsgeschichte des Saale-und Mittelelbgebietes bis zum Ende des 9. Jh, 1971.

——Die Ausbreitung der slawischen Besiedlung westlich von Elbe/Saale und Bohmerwald, Die Slawen in Deutschland, 1985.

——Zur Chronologie und Stratigraphie der fruhmittelalterlichen Siedlungsnamentypen im Unteren Pleissenland, OsG 15, 1986.

D. Warnke, Das frugeschichtliche Hugelgraberfeld in den "Schwarzen Bergen" bei Ralswiek, Kr. Rugen, ZtA 9, 1975.

——Funde und Grabsitten des Graberfeldes in den "Schwarzen Bergen" bei Ralwiek im Rahmen der kulturellen Beziehungen im Ostseegebiet, ZtA 12, 1978.

——Slawische Bestattungssitten auf der Insel Rugen, ZtA 13, 1979.

——Eine "Vampir-Bestattung" aus dem frugeschichtlichenRU Hugelgraberfeld in den "Schwarzen Bergen" bei

Ralswiek auf Rugen, AuF 27, 1982.

——Bestattungssitten der slawischen Bevolkerung im Norden der DDR, ZtA 16, 1982.

W. Wenzel, Die slavische Besiedlung des Schweidnitzer Landes im Lichte der Ortsnamen, Slawische Namenforschung, 1963.

G. Wetzel, Slawische Hugelgraber bei Gahro, Kr. Finsterwalde, VmU 12, 1979.

F. Wietrzichowski, Bildliche Darstellungen auf fruhslawischem Keramik-material aus Mecklenburg, AuF 33, 1988.

——Eine fruhslawische Siedlungsgrube mit Bernsteinproduktion von Gross Stormkendorf, Kr. Wismar, JbM 1991.

——Untersuchungen auf einem fruhmittelalterlichen Seehandelsplatz von Gross Stromkendorf, Kr. Wismar, Inf. Bodendenkmalpfleger in Westmecklenburg 33, 1993.

H. Zoll-Adamikowa, Dei Grabsitten zwischen Elbe und Weitchsel im 6. bis 10. Jh als Quelle zur Religion der Westslawen, SlG 7-8, 1980-81.

——Die Einfuhrung der Korperbestattung bei den Slawen an der Ostsee, KoR 24, 1994.

H. Wusterman Slawische Bestattungen vom Fahrberg in Rostock-Geshisdorf, JbM 1981.

J. Zeman, Zur Problematik der fruhslawischen Kultur in Mitteleuropa, Pamatky Arch 70, 1979.

11. SLAVS IN GERMANIA: BURGS, BURGWALLS

A. Alvensleben, Ein slawischer Burgwall bei Rathenow, Correspondenblatte, 1879.

H.H. Andersen, Neue Grabungsergebnisse 1977 zur Besiedlung und Bebauung im Innern des slawischen Burgwalles Alt Lubeck, LsK 3, 1977.

——Das Ur-Altlubeck, Die Heimat 85, 1978.

——Der alteste Wall von Alt Lubeck, LsK 5, 1981.

M. Bastian, Mittelslawische Hohenburgen mid Hang- und Boschungsanlagen in Mecklenburg, JbM 1955.

W. Baumann, W. Coblenz, Der fruhgeschichtliche Wall von Hofgen, Kr. Meissen, AuF 10, 1965.

R. Becker, Wo lagen das catellum und der Burgward Hwoznie (Gozne)?, NeU 34, 1913.

A. Beltz, Der Burgwall von Alt-Gaarz, VoR 11, 1935.

H. Berlekamp, Die Funde aus den Grabungen in dem Burgwall von Arkona auf Rugen in den Jahren 1969-71, ZtA 8, 1974.

G. Billig, Burgenarchaologische und Siedlungskundliche Betrachtungen zum Flussgebiet der Zschopau und der Freiberger Mulde, ZtA 15, 1981.

W. Binder, Slawische Bodenfunde am Ringwall bei Arensdorf, Hk Kr. Furstenwalde, 1960.

E. Bohm, Slawische Burgbezirke und deutsche Vogteien. Zur Kontinuitat der Landesliederung in Ostholstein und Lauenburg im Hohen Mittelalter, Germania Slavica I, 1980.

——Spandau in slawischer Zeit, Slawenburg, Landesfestung, Industriezentrum, 1983.

H. Bollnow, Die Burgwalle des Kr. Anklam, Ht fur Stadt und Kr. Anklam 28, 1933.

H. Brachmann, Die Wallburg "Der Kessel" bei Kretzschau-Groitzschen, Kr. Zeitz, Siedlung, Burg und Stadt, 1969.

——Als aber die Austrasier das castrum Wogastiburc belagerten, OsG XIX, 1990.

——Westslawische Bergerschaft im Ubergang von der Stammes zur Staatsgesellschaft, Berliner Jb fur osteuropaische Geschichte, 1996.

D.W. Buck, H. Geisler, Ausgrabungen auf dem alterslawischen Burgwall "Grodisch" bei Wiesenau, Kr. Eisenhuttenstadt, im Jahre 1970, AuF 16, 1971.

W. Bunning, K. Grebe, Ein spatslawischer Abschnitswall von Milow, Kr. Rathenow. AuF 22, 1977.

W. Coblenz, Zu den slawischen Wallanlagen des Gaues Nisan, Fruhe Burgen und Stadte, 1954.

——Wallgrabung auf dem Burgberg Zahren, AuF 2, 1957.

——Die Grabungen auf dem Zehrener Burgberg, AuF 3, 1958.

——Burg Meissen und Burgward Zehren. Zur Frage der "slawischen Burgen" in Sachsen, 1961.

——Zu den slawischen Burgwallen der Oberlausitz, KoN 1968.

——Bemerkungen zur "urbs Gana", EtH 16, 1975.

——Grabungen am Burgwall Zadel, Kr. Meissen, AuF 29, 1984.

P. Donat, Vorbericht uber die Untersuchungen am Burgwall Mecklenburg, AuF 15, 1970.

——Die Mecklenburg—Stammeszentrum und Furstenburg der Obotriten, AuF 21, 1976.

——Zur Gliederung der altslawischen Keramik im westlichen Mecklenburg Ergebnissen der Grabung am Burgwall Mecklenburg, ZtA 16, 1982.

——Mecklenburg und Oldenburg im 8. bis 10. Jh, Mecklenburgische Jahresberichte 110, 1995.

F. Engel, Grenzwalder und slawische Burgwardbezirke in Nordmecklenburg, Siedlung und Verfassung, 1960.

I. Ericsson, Mittelalterliche Burgen um Futterkamp, Kreis Plon, Die Heimat 84, 1977.

G.P. Fehring, Der slawische Burgwall Alt-Lubeck, Archaologie in Lubeck, 1980.

——Der slawische Burgwall Buku im Bereich des ehemaligen Burgklosters zu Lubeck, Archaologie in Lubeck, 1980.

——Slawische und deutsche Burganlage an der Landbrucke zum Stadthugel von Lubeck, Liber Castellum, 1981.

——Ein neuetdeckter slawischer Burgwall bei Klempau, Kr. Herzogtum Lauenburg, und seine Funde, 1981.

——Alt Lubeck und Lubeck, LsK 7, 1983.

——Der slawische Burgwall Alt-Lubeck, LsK 17, 1988.

——Origins and Developments of Slavic and German Lubeck, From the Baltic to the Black Sea, 1990.

A. Frinta, Wogastiburg, Slavia 32, 1963

W.H. Fritze, Ostrogard bei Adam von Bremen, BnF 1, 1949-50.

I. Gabriel, Burg, Siedlung und Graberfeld im fruhmittelalterlichen "Starigrad" (Oldenburg in Holstein),' KoR 5, 1975.

——Das Graberfeld auf dem slawischen Burgwall von Oldenburg in Holstein, Die Heimat 83, 1976.

——Strukturwandel in Starigard/Oldenburg wahrend der zweiten Halfte des 10. Jt auf Grund archaologischer Befunde, ZtA 18, 1984.

——Starigard/Oldenburg im 1. und 12. Jt. Neue Strukturelement in Gesellschaft und Kultur, Miasto zachodnoslowianskie w X-XII wieku, 1991.

W. Gebers, Ausgrabungen in der Siedlungskammer Bosau. Die fruhslawische Burg auf dem Bischofswarder, KoR 3, 1973.

——Ausgrabunegen in der Siedlungskammer Bosau. Die fruhslawische Burg auf dem Bischofswarder, KoR 7, 1974.

——Untersuchung einer Siedlungskammer in Ostholstein. V: Der slawische Burgwall auf dem Bischofswarder, 1981.

H. Geisler, Ausgrabungen auf dem slawischer Burgwall "Grodisch" bei Wiesenau, Kr. Eisenhuttenstadt, AuF 15, 1970.

E. Gohbrandt, Die alte Wendenburg Dirlow, UrP 9, 1924.

K.D. Gralow, Eine Zellemailfibel von der slawischen Burg "Dope" bei Flessenow, Landkreis Parchim AuF 40, 1995.

K. Grebe, Ein fruher slawischer Burgwall von Leegesbruch, Kr. Oranienburg, AuF 9, 1964.

——Die altslawische Vorburgsiedlung von Wildberg, Kr. Neuruppin, AuF 15, 1970.

——Ein fruhslawischer Burgwall von Dyrotz, Kr. Nauen, AuF 19, 1974.

——Die Brandenburg (Havel)—Stammeszentrum und Furstenburg der Heveller, AuF 21, 1976.

——U. Heussner, Die Hohenburg von Waldsieversdorf, Kr. Strausberg, AuF 23, 1978.

——R. Schulz, Beobachtungen am Burgwall von Reitwein, Kr. Seelow, AuF 25, 1980.

——R. Kirsch, Zur Datierung des Burgwalls von Berge, Kr. Nauen, AuF 26, 1981.

——L. Heine, Ausgrabungen auf der Burg von Baruth, Kr. Zossen, AuF 35, 1990.

P. Grimm, Die vor- und fruhgeschichtlichen Burgwalle der Bezirke Halle und Magdeburg, 1958.

——Zu Burgenprolemen des 8.—10. Jh westlich der mittleren Saale, ZtA 16, 1982.

R. Grunwald, Wogastiburg, VpS 2, 1958.

M. Gumowski, Sprawa Baniborska XI wieku, SlO 7, 1928.

H.G. Hackbarth, Ausgrabung auf dem Burgwall von Zislow, Kr. Robel, AuF 6, 1961.

D. Heinrich, Scharstorf. Eine slawische Burg in Ostholstein, 1985.

J. Henning, Die altslawische Burganlange von Presenchen, Ortsteil von Schlabendorf, Kr. Luckau, AuF 25, 1980.

H. Hingst, Slawischer Burgwall bei Giekau, Kr. Plon, Germania 31, 1953

K. Hinz, Der slawische Burgwall "Hochborre" in Ostholstein, KoR 3, 1973.

A. Hofmeister, Der Burgwall auf der Insel im Teterower See und die Danenzuge nach Circipanien 1171 und 1184, Fruhe Burgen und Stadte, 1954.

A. Hollnagel, K. Schoknecht, Die Burgwallinsel bei Vipperow, Kr. Robel, JbM, 1954.

——Die altslawische Burg von Schaberow, Kr. Hagenow, JbM, 1974.

J. Huth, Slawische Siedlungen und Burgen im Eigenschen Kreise, AfB 11/12, 1963.

H. Jakob, War Burk Wogastiburc, unde wo lag oppidum Berleich, DwS 24, 1979.

H.D. Kahl, Schwerin, Svaringhaug und die Sclavorum civitas des Prudentius von Troyes, Beitrage zur Stadt- und Regionalgeschichte Ost- und Nordeuropas, 1971.

H. Keiling, Slawische Burgwallreste auf der Schweriner Schlossinsel, AuF 33, 1988.

T. Kempke, Die slawische Burg Poppendorf, Hansestadt Lubeck, LsK 1, 1978.

——Starigard/Oldenburg. Hauptburg der Slawen in Wagrien II, 1984.

E. Kirsch, Ein neuetdeckter alterslawischer Burgwall in Lubbenau, Kr. Calau, AuF 20, 1975.

H. Klare, Die Burg Gorzke und der Bugwall, Hk Kr. Belzig, 1963.

G. Labuda, Wogastisburg, SlA 2, 1949-50.

P. Laux, Der slawische Burgwall bei Hollenstedt, Hamburgs Meussen 11/5, 1987.

G.S. Lebedev, Der slawische Burgwall Gorodec bei Luga, BuF 2, 1982.

G.C.F. Lisch, Die Burg Dobin und die Dope bei Hohen Viechein, MgA 5, 1840.

——Uber die wendische Furstenburg Werle, MgA 6, 1841.

——Uber die bischofliche Burg zu Butzow, MgA 20, 1855.

H. Ludat, Branibor, havolanska dynastie a Premyslovci, CcH 17, 1969.

G. Mangelsdorf, Das Burgwardium Pritzerbe, RaT 16, 1972.

H.V. Mechelk, Erneute Grabungen am "castellum" Medeburu, AuF 25, 1980.

A. Meiche, Die Oberlausitzer Grenzurkunde vom Jahre 1241 und die Burgwarde Ostrusna, Trebista und Godobi, MaG 84, 1908.

D. Meier, Die slawische Burg Scharstorf, 700 Jahre Schellhorn. Chronik einer Gemeinde in Kr. Plon, 1986.

——Scharstorff, eine slawische Burg in Ostholstein und ihr Umland: archaologische Funde, 1990.

H.J. Mrusek, Die Funktion und baugeschichtliche Entwicklung der Burg Giebichenstein in Halle (Saale) und ihre Stellung im fruh- und hoch-feudalen Burgenbau, 1970.

——Thesen zur Geschichte der Burg Giebichenstein, Burgen und Schlosser 13. 1972.

A. Muller, Die slawischen Burgen von Spandau, AiB 2, 1971.

A. Muller-Muci, Die Ausgrabungen auf dem Burgwall in Berlin-Spandau, 1983.

H.H. Muller, Die Terreste der slawischen Burg Behren-Lubchin, 1965.

——Die Terreste aus der slawischen Burganlage von Arkona auf der Insel Rugen, AuF 19, 1974.

K. Myslinski, Slowian Brenna-Brandenburg i jej przejscie pod rzady margrabiow w polowie XII wieku, Rocznik Lubelski 10, 1969.

V. Nekuda, Die Keramikfunde vom Spandauer Burgwall, AiB 2, 1971.

——Die altslawische Dorf in Berlin-Mahlsdorf, AiB 13, 1982.

W. Neugebauer, Der Burgwall Alt-Lubeck, Offa, 21/22, 1964-65

G. Neumann, Der Burgwall auf dem Johannisberg bei Jena-Lobeda, AuF 4, 1959.

W. Nitzschke, Neue Untersuchungen auf dem Gelande der slawischen Burg in Landsberg, Saalkreis, AuF 10, 1965.

W. Petzsch, Ein spatslawisches Haus am Fusse des Burgwalles von Gutzkow in Vorpommern, Altschlesien 5, 1934.

W. Prummel, Starigard/Oldenburg. Hauptburg der Slawen in Wagrien, IV, 1993.

W. Radig, Der Burgberg meissen und der Slawengau Daleminzien, 1929.

——Die sorbischen Burgwalle Westsachsens und Ostthuringens, Die Westausbreitung und Wehranlagen der Slawen in Mitteldeutschland, 1940.

H. Reimer, A. Trager, Der slawische Burgwall von Repten, Kr. Calau, AuF 31, 1986.

H. Rosler, Ein altslawischer Burgwall mit fruhdeutscher Beobaung von Gross Lubbenau, Kr. Calau, AuF 28, 1983.

W. Schich, Die slawische Burgstadt und die fruhe Ausbreitung des Magdeburger Rechts ostwarts der mittleren Elbe, Studien zur Geschichte des sachsisch-magdeburgischen Rechts in Deutschland und Polen, 1980.

——Spandau als slawische Burgstadt, Die Ausgrabungen auf dem Burgwall in Berlin-Spandau, 1983.

G. Schlimpert, Der Name Potsdam unde die "Insel des Chotemysl", JbR 9, 1958.

——Der Name Potsdam, ZtS 15, 1970.

——Die alterslawische Besiedlung Brandenburgs im Lichte der Toponymie, MaK XL-XLI, 1989-90.

H.F. Schmid, Die Burgbezirksverfassung

U. Schoknecht, Krien und Gruttow, zwei altslawische Burgwalle im Kreise Anklam, AuF 17, 1972.

H.F. Schmid, Die Burgbezirkverfassung bei den slawischen Volkern in ihrer Bedeutung fur die Geschichte ihrer Siedlung und ihrer staatlichen Organisation, JbK 2, 1926.

E. Schmidt, W. Nitzschke, Untersuchungen in Slawischen Burgen zwischen Saale und Flaming, AuF 21, 1976.

V. Schmidt, Untersuchungen am slawischen Burgwall in Drense, Kr. Prenzlau, AuF 28, 1983.

J. Schneider, Die burg Plote und andere Burgen des Elbe-Havel-Gebietes vom 7. bis 12. Jh, Zur Geschichte der stadt und des Kr. Genthin 7, 1979.

——Ausgrabungen auf dem Burgwall Genthin-Altenplathow 1976-77, AuF 25, 1980.

C. Schuchhardt, Eine slawische Burg in Potsdam, PzT 3, 1911.

——Witzen und Starzeddel, zwei Burgen der Lausitzer Kultur, UnG 18, 1927.

E. Schuldt, Der slawische Burgwall von Liepen und die Burgen im Stammesgebiet der Circipaner, JbM 1960.

——Der slawische Burgwall von Liepen, Kr. Rostock und die Burgen im Stammesgebiet der Circipaner, JbM 1962.

—— Slawische Burgen in Mecklenburg, 1962.

——Die Ausgrabungen im Gebiet der "Alten Burg" von Sukow, Kr. Teterow,' JbM 1963.

——W. Unverzagt, Teterow. Ein slawischer Burgwall in Mecklenburg, 1963.

——Behren-Lubchin. Eine spatslawische Burganlage in Mecklenburg, 1965.

——Die slawischen Burgen von Neu-Niekohr/Walkendorf, Kr. Teterow, 1967.

——Der slawische Burgwall von Gross Raden, AuF 21, 1976.

——Burg und Siedlungen von Gross Raden, 1978.

——Burg und Siedlungen von Gross Raden, ZtA 12, 1978.

——Der Burgwall von Gross Gornow und die fruhen slawischen Befestigungen im Gebiet der oberen Warnow, JbM 1984.

——Gross Raden. Ein slawischer Tempelort des 9/10. Jh in Mecklenburg, 1985.

R. Schulze, Ausgrabungen auf der Siedlung dem slawischen Burgwall "Grodisch" bei Weisenau, Kr. Eisenhuttenstadt, AuF 20, 1975.

H. Seyer, Die Burg in Berlin-Blankenburg und die altslawische Besiedlung des Niederen Barnim, Archaologie als Geschichtswissenschaft, 1977.

——Die altslawische Burg bei Berlin-Blankenburg und ihr Verhaltnis zur slawischen Besiedlung auf der Barnimhochflache, RaP, 1979.

M. Solle, Zur gesellschaftlich- geschichtlichen Entwicklung der westslawischen Burgwalle nach archaologischer Forschung, VpS 6, 1966.

H. Steuer, Slawische Siedlungen und Befestigungen im Hohbeck-Gebiet, Hannoversches Wendland 4, 1973.

——Die slawische und deutsche Burganlage bei Meetschow, Kreis Luchow-Dannenberg, KoR 6, 1976.

K.W. Struve, Voruntersuchungen in der slawischen Burgwallanlage von Oldenburg in Holstein, Germania 33, 1955.

——Die slawischen Burgen in Wagrien, Offa 17-18, 1959-61.

——Die Burgwall von Hitzhusen, Kr. Segeberg, Offa 20, 1963.

——Grabungen auf slawischen und hochmittelalterlichen Burganlagen im Rahmen eines Burgenforschungsprogramms, Germania 42, 1964.

——Die Holzkastenkonstruktion in der slawischen Burganlage von Scharstrof, Kr. Plon, Studien aus Alt-Europa III, 1965.

——Fruhe slawische Burgwallkeramik aus Ostholstein, ZtA 2, 1968.

——Lag Reric and der schleswig-holsteinischen Ostseekuste?, Die Heimat 78, 1971.

——Die slawischen Wehranlangen des Kreises Plon unter besonderer Berucksichtung der Scharstorfer Burg, JbP 2, 1972.

——Ausgrabungen auf den slawischen Burgen von Warder, Kr. Segeberg und Scharstorf, Kreis Plon-Holstein, KoR 2, 1972.

——Die Ausgrabungen auf der befestigten slawischen Inselburg von Warder, Gemeinde Rohlstorf, Kr. Segeberg, Hk Jb Kr. Segeberg 20, 1974.

——Ziel und Ergebnisse von Untersuchungen auf drei slawischen Burgwallen Ostholsteins, Ausgrabungen in Deutschland 3, 1975.

——Die Burgen der Slawen in ihrem nordwestlichsten Siedlungsraum, Burgen aus Holz und Stein, 1979.

——Die Burgen in Schleswig-Holstein. 1. Die slawischen Burgen, Offa 35, 1981.

M. Ullrich, Sondage am slawischen Burgwall "Schanze" bei Raddusche, Kr. Calau, AuF 31, 1986.

W. Unverzagt, Der Burgwall von Kliestow, Kr. Lebus, Studien zur Vor- und Frugeshichte, 1970.

B. Wachter, Eine slawische Wallanlage, NnU 43, 1974.

——Die Burg auf dem Weinberg in Hitzacker-eine slawische Furstenburg, Die Kunde, 1974-75.

——Frugeschichtliche Burgen und fruhe Stadte im Hannoverschen Wendland, RaP, 1979.

D. Warnke, Rostock-Dierkow - ein Wirschaftzentrum des 8./9. Jahrhunderts an der Unterwarnow, ZtM 20, 1993.

——Rostock-Petrbileiche. Eine slawische Furstenburg des 12. Jh, Schriften des Kulturhistorischen Museums in Rostock, 1993.

G. Wetzel, Die erste slawische Burgwall des Kr. Bad Liebenwerda in Fichtenberg bei Muhlberg, AuF 22, 1977.

——Der Burgwall von Ragow, Kr. Calau, ZtA 7, 1985.

——Zwei neuentdeckte Burgwalle im Bezirk Cottbus, AuF 32, 1987.

G. Witkowski, R. Schulz, Norbergungen auf dem Gelande des Burgwalles von Neutrebbin, Kr. Seelow, AuF 19, 1974.

J. Zak, Najstarsze ostrogi zachodnioslowianskie, 1959.

K. Zernack, Die burgstadtischen Volksversammlungen bie den Ost- und Westslaven, 1967.

12. SLAVS IN GERMANIA: ORTSNAMEN

E. Beckman, Ortsnamen in der ehemaligen slawischen Landschaft Nisane, 1965.

H. Beckmann, Sind all Orte mid der Namensendung -in slawischen Ursprungs?, PjB XI, 1926.

J. Bilek, Die slawischen Ortsnamen des Kr. Neustrelitz, Hb des Kreises Neustrelitz, 1954.

——H. Schall, Slavische Ortsnamen aus Mecklenburg, ZtS 2, 1956.

I. Bily, Probleme der Namendeutung im Mittelelbischen Ortsnamenbuch, OsG 15, 1986.

——Zu den altsorbischen Ortsnamen mit den Suffixen -isce, -nik und -ik (Ein Beitrag zum Slawischen Onomastischen Atlas), OsG 21, 1994.

——Ortsnamen mit dem Suffix -ina im ehemaligen altsorbischen Sprachgebiet, Studia Onomastica et Indogermanica, 1995.

H. Bosse, Die Ortsnamen des Kreises Griefenberg, Unsere Heimat 11, 1935.

P. Bronisch, Die slawischen Ortsnamen in Holstein und im Furstentum Lubeck, 1901.

E. Crome, Die Ortsnamen des Kr. Bad Liebenwerda, 1968.

L. Fahlbusch, Die slawischen Ortsnamen dem Altenburger Ostkreises, 1952.

R. Fischer, Zur Namenkunde des Egerlandes. Die slawischen Ortsnamen des Egerlands und ihre Auswertung fur die Lautlehre und Siedlunsgeschichte, 1940.

——Ortsnamen an der Gera, WzJ 3, 1953/54.

——Die Auswertung der slawischen Ortsnamen in Deutschland; Vortrage auf der Berliner Slawistentagung, 1954.

——Slawisch-deutsch Zusammenleben im Lichte der Ortsnamen, 1955.

——Ortsnamen der Kr. Arnstadt und Ilmenau, 1956.

——K. Elbracht, Die Ortsnamen des Kr. Rudolstadt, 1959.

——Schwieriege Ortsnamen Thuringens, ZtS 6, 1961.

——Die Ortsnamen der Zauche, 1967.

——Die Ortsnamen des Kr. Belzig, 1970.

——Die Ortsnamen des Havellandes, 1976.

W. Fleischer, Namen und Mundart im Raum von Dresden. Toponymie und Dialektologie der Kr. Dresden-Alstadt und Freital als Beitrag zur Sprach- und Siedlungsgeschicte: Orts- und Ortsteilnamen, 1961.

E. Foster, Einige Bemerkungen uber die Zuordnung altpolabischer Ortsnamen den westslawischen Strukturtypen, OsG 21, 1994.

D. Freydank, Ortsnamen der Kr. Grimma und Wurzen, 1962.

——Ortsnamen der Kr. Bitterfeld und Grafenhainichen, 1962.

——Die Ortsnamen des Bernburger Landes, 1966.

W. Fuhrmann, Die Ortsnamen des Stadt- und Landkreises Weimar, 1962.

K. Gebhardt, Die Ortsnamen des mittleren Erzegebirges, 1967.

A. Graf, Die Ortsnamen des Kr. Pritzwalk, 1957.

——Die Ortsnamen des Kr. Kyritz, 1959.

E. Gringmuth-Dallmer, Deutsch und Wendish - Gross und Klein. Zur siedlungsgeschictlichen Aussage von Ortsnamen mit unterschiedlichen Zusatzen in der Mark Brandenburg, OsG 19, 1990.

F. Grucza, Die Ortsnamen des Kr. Kamenz, 1961.

——Die oxytonische Akzenstruktur der Ortsnamen slawischer Herkunft auf -in im Deutschen, OsG 4, 1968.

J. Heinrich, Die Ortsnamen der Kr. Gorlitz und Zittau, 1965.

K. Hengst, Die Ortsnamen der Kr. Glauchau, Hohenstein-Ernstthal und Stollberg, 1964.

——Die Ortsnamen des Bosauer Zehntverzeichnisses, OsG 4, 1968.

——Soziologische Aspekte der slawischen Toponymie und Anthroponymie. Sociologische-siedlunskundliche –Analyse altsorbischer Ortsnamen im Raum Plisni, Namenkundliche Informationen, Studia Onomastica 2, 1981.

——Ortsnamenbucher zu deutsch-slawischen Kontaktgebieten, OsG 18, 1993.

——Urkunde und Ortsname. Zum Typ der Ortsnamen auf -tzsch. Der Name Culitzsch, OsG 21, 1994.

G. Hey, Die slavischen Ortsnamen von Lauenburg, AhL 2, 1888.

F. Hinze, Dei Endbeutonung deutscher Ortsnamen slawischer Herkunft auf -, ZtS 8, 1963.

W. Kaestner, Zu den slawischen Ortsnamen des hannoverschen Wendlandes, Hannoverschen Wendland II, 1986.

H.D. Kahl, Der Ortsnamen Lubeck, ZtL 42, 1962.

G. Keller, Die Ortsnamen des Kr. Dresden-Stadt, 1956.

C. Klemz, Ortsnamen des Kr. Belgard, Aus Dem Lande Belgard, I, 1921.

——Ortsnamen des Kr. Belgard, Aus Dem Lande Belgard, II, 1923.

O. Knoops, Slavische Ortsnamenforschung in Pommern und der Name Stubbenkammer, PoM VI, 1921.

M. Kobuch, H. Walther, Die Ortsnamen Leisnig. Alteste Uberlieferung, Deutung, Lokalisierung, OsG 21, 1994.

S. Korner, Die Patronymischen Ortsnamen im Altsorbischen, 1972.

——Augeswahlte Ortsnamen der Niederlausitz mit schwierigen bzw. nicht eindeutigen Etymologien, OsG 17, 1988.

E. Korth, Die Ortsnamen mit den Suffixen -ov und -im Altsorbischen, 1974.

——Zur Integration der mit den altsorbischen Suffixen -ov und -in (-yn) gebildeten Ortsnamen in das deutsche Namensystem, OsG 11, 1976.

H. Krawarik, Studien zu Orts- und Bevolkerungsgeschichte von Windischgarten und dem Stodergebiet, 1967.

O. Kronsteiner, Die slawischen Ortsnamen in Oberosterrriech, 1980.

P. Kuhnel, Die slavischen Ortsnamen in Mecklenburg, JbM 46, 1881.

——Die slavischen Ortsnamen in Mecklenburg-Strelitz, 1881.

W. Laur, Historisches Ortsnamenlexikon von Schleswig-Holstein, 1967.

——Die Ortsnamen im Kr. Pinneberg, 1978.

R. Lehmann, Historisches Ortslexikon fur die Niederlausitz, I-II, 1979.

J. Meskank, Die Ortsnamen der Oberlausitz, 1981.

P.F. Miest, Die Ortschafter des Kreises Luchow-Dannenberg, Das Hannoverschen Wendland, 1985.

E. Mucke (A Muka), Die slawischen Ortsnamen in Neumark, Mitteilunger der Veriens fur die Geschichte Neumark 7, 1898.

——Die wendischen Ortsnamen der Niederlausitz nach Estehung und Bedeutung, NiE 17, 1925.

U. Ohainski, J. Udolph, Die Ortsnamen des Landkreises und der stadt Hannover, 1998.

S. Pirchegger, Die slavischer Ortsnamen im Murzgebiet, 1927.

B. Rachel, Sorbisch-deutsches und deutsch-sorbisches Ortsnamenverzeichnis der zweichnis der zweisprachigen Kreise der Bezirke Dresden und Cottbus, 1969.

G. Rauter, Slavische Ortsnamen im Brandburgischen, Die Grenzbloten 85, 1916.

M. Reiser, Deutsche-slawische Beruhrungen im ehemaligen thuringischen Vogtland im spiegel der Ortsnamen, JhR 17, 1969.

——Die slawischen und hybriden Ortsnamen der Kr. Greiz und Zeulenroda, OsG 6, 1971.

A. Richter, Die Ortsnamen der Saalkreises, 1962.

O. Ripecka, Zur semantischen Struktur der slawisch-deutschen Ortsnamen, OsG3, 1967.

B. H. Rosenkranz, Ortsnamen des Bezirkes Gera, 1982.

E. Sass, Ortsnamen mid den Suffixen -ov und -in im Altsorbischen, NaM 5/6, 1983.

——Deappellativische Ortsnamen mit dem Suffix -ov, OsG 17, 1988.

——Schriftsprachliche und mundartliche Ortsnamenformen auf -we (-weh) im Raum um Zeitz/Weissenfels, OsG 19, 1990.

W. Schenck, Die Ortsnamen des Kr. Werdau und Zwickau, 1958.

B. Schier, Ortsnamen und Hausformen der deutsch-slawischen kontaktzone in wechselseitiger Erhellung, FrA 21, 1961.

W. Schindheim, Slawisch-deutsche Beziehungen auf dem Thuringer Wald und in seinem sudlichen Vorland im Licthe der Ortsnamen, OsG 4, 1968.

H. Schlifkowitz, Typische Ortsnamen zwischen Elbe und Wischel, Ortsnamen auf au-, -ow, -witz, -schutz und -in, 1989.

G. Schlimpert, Teltow —Landschafts — und Ortsnamen, OsG 5, 1970.

——Die Ortsnamen des Teltow, 1976.

——Die Ortsnamen des Barnim, 1984.

——Die Ortsnamen des Kr. Juterbog-Luckenwalde, 1991.

A. Schmitz, Die Ortsnamen des Kr. Herzogtum Lauenburg und der Stadt Lubeck, 1990.

J. Schultheis, Umstrittene Deutungen von Ortsnamen des rechtselbischen Anhalt, OsG 4, 1968.

——Zu den Ortsnamen auf -itzsch/-itsch, Leipziger Namenkundlich Beitrage II, 1968.

——Zur Geographie slawischen Ortsnamentypen in Gebiet des sudwestflamings, OsG 11, 1976.

J. Schultz, Ortsnamentypen und slawische Siedlungszeit in Nordostbayern, FrA 28, 1968.

——Das sogenannte Banzer Reichsurbar als Quelle slawischer Ortsnamen in Oberfranken, FrA 46, 1986.

H. Schuster-Sewc, Zur Etymologie des Ortsnamens Baruth, LeT B/36, 1989.

E. Schwarz, Wendische Ortsnamen im Lande Zittau, MaG 103, 1927.

E. Schwarz, Die slawischen Ortsnamen in Nordbayern und ihr Verhaltnis zum deutschen Landesausbau, ZoS 5, 1956.

R. Trautmann, Die Elbe- und Ostseeslavischen Ortsnamen, I-III, 1947-48.

——Zur Lautlehre der Ostseeslavischen Ortsnamen, ZsP 20, 1948.

——Die slavischen Ortsnamen Mecklenburgs und Holsteins, 1950.

——Die wendischen Ortsnamen Ostholsteins, Lubecks, Lauenburgs und Mecklenburgs, Quellen und Forschungen zur Geschichte Schleswig-Holsteins 21, 1950.

M. Vasmer, Zur Oberlausitzer Ortsnamenforschung: 1. Bautzen. W. Zittau, Oberlausitzer Heimatzeitung, 5, 1924.

——Die slavische Ortsnamenforschung in Ostdeutschland, ZsP 6, 1929.

O. Vogel, Slavische Ortsnamen der Prignitz, 1904.

H. Walther, Ortsnamenchronologie und Besiedlungsgang in der Altlandschaft Daleminzi, OsG 3, 1967.

——M. Kobuch, Der Ortsnamen Leisnig. Alteste Uberlieferung, Deutung und Lokalisierung, OsG 21, 1993.

S. Wauer, Die Ortsnamen "Krakov" im polabo-pomoranischen und altsorbischen Gebiet, NaM 33, 1978.

—— Zur Problematik der Eindeutschung slawischer Ortsnamentypen, Brandenburg, Linguistische Studien, 1981.

——Die mit dem Suffix -ov gebildeten Ortsnamen in Brandenburg. Ein Beitrag zum Slawischen Onomastischen Atlas, ZtS 26, 1981.

——Einige Ergebnisse der Untersuchung der Ortsnamen in der Prignitz, OsG 17, 1988.

——Die Ortsnamen der Prignitz, 1989.

——Sprachkontakte in der Prignitz in Nachbarschaft zum Hannoverschen Wendland, Deutsch-Slavischer Sprachkontakt im Lichte der Ortsnamen, 1993.

——Die Ortsnamen der Uckermark, 1996.

W. Wenzel, Die Ortsnamen des Schweinitzer Landes, 1964.

B. Wieber, Die Ortsnamen des Kr. Torgau, 1968.

C. Willich, Untersuchungen zu Ortsnamen des Landes Lebus, OsG 21, 1994.

——Die Ortsnamen des Landes Lebus, 1994.

R. Willnow, Die Ortsnamen des Kr. Wittenberg, 1971.

T. Witkowski, Zu einigen problematischen Ortsnamen des Kr. Stralsund, ZtS 6, 1961.

——Die Ortsnamen des Kr. Stralsund, 1965

—— Zu einigen slawischen Ortsnamentypen im Polabischen (-ov, -ovici/evici), Slavica Pragensia 8, 1966.

——Die Ortsnamen des Kr. Greifswald, 1978.

H. Wurms, Sprachliche Anmerkungen zu den slavischen Ortsnamen des Kr. Herzogtum Lauenburg, LbH 1975.

13. SLAVS IN GERMANIA: HYDRONYMS, TOPONYMS

G. Alexander, Die Sorbischen Flurnamen des Kr. Bautzen (westlich der Spree), 1965.

M. Bathe, Belxem, ein Flussname? WzH 16, 1967.

J. Bilek, Slawische Sprachdenkmaler im Spiegel Nordbrandenburger Seenamen, MaR 3, 1959.

I. Bily, Zum altsorbischen appellativischen Wortschatz in Toponymen, OsG 17, 1988.

——Zum altsorbischen appellativischen Wortschatz in Toponymen, OsG 19, 1990.

H. Bosse, Die Forst-, Flur und Gewassernamen der Ueckermunde Heide, 1962.

W. Burghardt, Die Flurnamen Magdeburgs und des Kr. Wanzleben, 1967.

E. Foster, Gie Gewassernamen des Landes Ruppin, 1989.

——Zur Problematik der Gewassernamen, die im Zusammenhang mit anderen Toponymen

slawischer Herkunft Stehen, NaM 15/16, 1991.

B.W. Fuhrmann, Linguistische Studien zu den slawischen Toponymen des Bereiches der Ilm-Saale-Platte und des mittleren Saalegebietes, 1972.

K.-D. Gansleweit, Flurnamen und Siedlungsgeschichte in der nordostlichen Niederlausitz, OsG 13, 1981.

J. Goschel, Die Orts-, Flur- und Gewassernamen der Kr. Borna und Gethain, 1964.

G. Hanse, Die Flurnamen des Stadt- und Landkreises Weimar, 1970.

W. Hein, Die sorbischen Flurnamen des Kr. Bautzen (ostlich der Spree), 1963.

K. Hengst, Slawische Berg- und Talbezeichnungen im Namenschatz an Elbe und Saale. Untersuchungen zur Struktur der altsorbischen Toponymie, OsG 5, 1970.

——Soziologische Aspekte der slawischen Toponymie und Anthroponomie, OnO 2, 1981

——Zur Integration slawischer Toponyme ins Deutsche, OsG 13, 1981.

——Integrationsprozess und toponymische Varianten. Namenvarienten bie der Integration slawischer Toponymie ins Deutsche, OsG 15, 1981.

F. Hinze, Die etymologische Klarung von Namen im Leba-See in Hinterpommern, ZtS 15, 1970.

E. Hoffman, Ein Manuskript von Paul Kuhnel uber die slawischen Orts- und Flurnamen der Insel Rugen, OsG 21, 1994.

L. Hoffman, Die slawischen Flurnamen des Kr. Lobau, 1959.

J. Jejkal, Der Bergname Kotine, Deutsch-slawische Forschugen zur Namenkunde und Siedlungsgeschichte 5, 1957.

E. Kaiser, Appellativische Topolexeme in der dravanopolabischen Toponymie, ZtS 30, 1985.

P. Kuhnel, Die slavischen Orts- und Flurnamen im Luneburgishcen, 1901.

——Die slavischen Orts- und Flurnamen der Oberlausitz, 1982.

W. Lippert, Die Flurnamen der Uckermark, 1972.

W. Luhrs, Slawische Orts- unde Flurnamen in dem Lauenburgischen Winkel zwischen Elbe und Bille, DiE 49, 1939.

E. Mucke (A. Muka), Flurnamen aus dem sudostlichen Teile des Gubener Kr. sowie den angr enzenden Dorfern des Kr. Crossen nebst einigen Ortsnamen, NiE 10, 1908/08.

——Slavische Orts- und Flurnamen as den Kr. Lebus, Krossen und Zullichau, Scriften des Vereins fur Geshichte d. Neumark 22, 1908.

——Wustungen, Gewasser und Holzungen der Neumark mit slavischen Ortsnamen, Schriften des Veriens fur Geschichte d. Neumark 22, 1908.

——Slavische (altsorbische) Flurnamen in den Kreisen Bitterfeld und Delitzsch und ihren Nachbaaarbezirken, Archiv f. Landes- und Volkskunde d. Provinz Sachsen, 21, 1911.

——Flurnamen aus dem Kr. Sorau, NiE 15, 1920-21.

——Zupy a strozisca, reki a recki w stare, serbskem kraju, CmS 78, 1925.

——Serbske lezownostne mjena a jich woznam, SlO 6, 1927.

——Die sorbischen Flurnamen und idhre Bedeutung, SlO 6, 1926.

H. Naumann, Slawische Flurnamen in den Kr. Grimma und Wurzen, ZtS 4, 1959.

——Dies Orts- and Flurnamen der Kr. Grimma und Wurzen, 1962.

W. Neumann, Die Entwicklung slawischer Flurnamensuffixe im sudwestlichen Mecklenburg, ZtS 11, 1966.

H. Petzold, Hydronymische Untersuchung der slawischen Gewassernamen im Flusssystem der Elbe in Sachsen, OsG 6, 1971.

F. Redlich, Begegnungen slawischer Stamme and der Dahme im Spiegel von Orts- und Flurnamen, GgC 1974.

——Gewasser-, Fischerei-, und Flurnamen rund um den Schwieloschsee (Niederlausitz), OsG 4, 1986.

M. Reiser, Slawische Flurnamen der Kr. Greiz und Zeulenroda, JhR 15/16, 1967-68.

O. Ripecka, Begriffsinhalt und Formativstruktur der toponymischen Wortzeichen (Am Material der deutsch-slavischen Oikonymie), OsG 21, 1995.

M. Rudnicki, Studia nad nazwami rzek Lechickiej, SlO 14, 1935.

A. Rosenbrock, Uber die Flurnamen des Kr. Demmin, PjB XII, 1927.

G. Schlimpert, Slawische Gewassernamen im Raum von Berlin, Cetvrto zasedanie an Medunarodnata Komisja za Slovenska Onomastika, 1971.

——Zur Struktur und Semantik altpolabischer Gewassernamen in Brandenburg, ZtS 17, 1972.

——Die Gewassernamen Brandenburges, OnO 5, 1987.

A. Schmitz, Die Orts- und Gewassernamen des Kreises Ostholstein. 1981.

——Die Orts und Gewassernamen des Kr. Plon, 1986.

H. Schonfeld, Zu slawischen Flurnamen in der Altmark, WzH 16, 1967.

H. Schuster-Sewc, Noch einmal zur Herkunft und zur Bedeutung des Brandenburgischen Fluss- und Ortsnamen Dahme, ZtS 41, 1996.

E. Schwarz, Die slawischen Ortsnamen in Nordbayern und ihr Verhalnis zum deutschen Landesausbau, ZoS 5, 1956.

C.G. Schwela, Die Flurname des Kr. Cottbus, 1958.

G. Sperber, Die sorbischen Flurnamen des Kr. Kamenz, DsF 18, 1967.

W. Sperber, Die Bedeutung des Plurals bei sorbischen Flurnamen, ZtS 3, 1958.

F. Steingraber, Orts- und Flurnamen von Podewils, Aus dem Lande Belgard, III, 1924.

D. Stellmacher, Die Flurnamen des brandenburgischen Kr. Zauch-Belzig, BnF 12, 1977.

J. Udolph, Slavische Etymologien und ihre Uberprufund and Hand von Gewasser- Orts- und Flurnamen, Lautgeschichte und Etymologie, 1980.

E. Ulbricht, Die Gewassernamen der Thuringischen Saale, DsF 2, 1957.

P. Vauk, Deutungen slavischer Orts- und Flurnamen in der Umgegend von Everswalde, Daselbst, 1919.

H. Walther, Die Orts- und Flussnamen der Kr. Delitzsch und Eilenburg, 1958.

——Die Orts- und Flurnamen des Kr. Rochlitz, 1958.

S. Wauer, Problematische Namen unter den alteren Gewassernamen Brandenburgs, OnO VI, 1991.

W. Wenzel, Sorbische Flur- und Gewassernamen aus der Lausitz (Nach Quellen des 14. bis 18. Jh), OsG 17, 1988.

C. Willich, Die slawischen Ort- Gewasser- und Flurnamen des Landes Lebus, 1988.

W. Zuhlsdorff, Flurnamenatlas von Sudwestmecklenburg, 1988.

14. SLAVS IN GERMANIA: NAMES, NAME FORMATION

I. Bily, Zum altsorbischen appellativischen Wortschatz in Toponymen. II, OsG 17, 1988.

—— Zum altsorbischen appellativischen Wortschatz in Toponymen, III, OsG 18, 1989.

H. Birnbaum, Slavisches Namengut aus dem fruh-mittealterlichen bayerischen Raum, WsJ 21, 1975.

H. Brokmuller, Die Rostocker Personennamen bis 1304, 1993.

R. Fischer, Slawische Namen an der Ilm, ZtS 2, 1957.

——Resultate germanoslawistischer Namenforschung, OsG 3, 1967.

R.E. Fischer, G. Schlimpert, Vorslawische Namen in Brandenburg, ZtS 16, 1971.

——Vorslawische Namen in Brandenburg, OsG 21, 1994.

W. Fleischer, Namen und Mundart im Raum von Dresden. Toponymie und Dialektologie der kreise Dresden-Alstadt und Freital als Beitrag zur Sprach- und Siedlungsgeschicte, 1961.

——Namend und Mundart im Raum von Dresen: Flurnamen, 1973.

E. Foster, S. Wauer, Die slawischen Kulturnamen in Brandenburg, ZtS 28, 1983.

B.W. Fuhrmann, Linguistische Studien zu den slawischen Toponymen des Bereiches der Ilm-Saale-Platte und des mittleren Saalegebietes, 1972.

H. Gornowicz, Slawische zweigliedrige Beewohnernamen in ihrer Beziehung zu Appellativen und Personennamen, OsG 5, 1970.

E. Gringmuth-Dallmer, Siedlungsarchologische Beobachtungen zur Namengebung im slawisch-deutschen Kontaktgebiet zwischen Elbe und Oder/Neisse, OsG 17, 1988.

V. Hellfritzsch, Vogtlandische Personenamen. Untersuchungen am Material der Kr. Plauen und Oeslnitz, 1969.

K. Hengst, Strukturelle Betrachtungen slawischer Namen in der Uberlieferung des 11./12. Jh, Leipziger namenkundliche Beitrage II, 1968.

——Namenforschung, slawische-deutscher Sprachkontakt und fruhe slawische Sprachstudien im Elbe-Saale-Grenzraum, OsG 19, 1990.

M. Hornung, Beobachtungen uber die kategorienbildende Funktion slawischer Suffixe bei deutschen Namenmaterial in Sprachberuhrungszonen, OsG 13, 1981.

O. Kronsteiner, Die alpenslawischen Personennamen, 1981.

P. Kuhnel, Slawische Falmiliennamen in der Stadt Hannover, Hannoverland, 1907.

F. Linemann, Slawische Familiennamen im Territorium Thale/Harz, OsG 15, 1986.

F. Miklosic, Die Bildung der slavischen Personen- und Ortsnamen, 1927.

E. Mucke (A. Muka), Serbske swojbne mjena mesta Budysina z leta 1416, CmS 53, 1900.

——Ein Beitrag zu den sorbischen Familiennamen, CmS 57, 1904.

——Die Wendischen Familiennanmen des Kreises Lukau und ihrer Bedeutung, Bausteine zur Heimatkunde des Luckauer Kr., 1918.

——Uber die sorbischen Famlien- und Personennamen, CmS 77, 1924.

——Serbske mestnostne mjena a lich woznam, SlO 5, 1926.

——Wendische Familien- und Ortsnamen der Niederlausitz, 1928.

I. Neumann, Slawische Personennamen im Oschatzer Land, OsG 3, 1967.

Z. Pavlovic, Onomasticki derivati izvedeni iz lekseme "gost" u slovenskim jezicima, Prva Jugoslovenska onomasticka konferencija, 1976.

F. Redlich, Zur Personnenamenforschung im zweisprachigen Gebiet der Niederlausitz, OsG 5, 1970.

S. Rospond, Archetypiczne imiona slowianskie z czlonem Se- (Serad, Sesalv, Segost i inne), OsG 5, 1970.

—— Stratygrafia slowianskich nazw miejscowych na -jb, OsG 12, 1979.

H. Schall, Der Namen Berlin, Berliner Heimat, 1957.

——Der Name Potsdam und die "Insel des Chotemysl", JbR 9, 1958.

G. Schlimpert, Slawische Personennamen in mittelalterlichen Quellen Deutschlands, 1964.

——Slawische Personennamen in Mittelalterlichen Quellen zur deutschen Geschichte, 1978.

——Zur uberlieferung vorslawischer Namen in der DDR, 1988.

——Altpolabische-sudslawische Entsprechungen im Namenmaterial zwischen Elbe und Oder, ZtS 33, 1988.

——Problematische Namen in Brandenburg, der Name Peene, StO 4, 1990.

——Slawische Namen in Brandenburg und Umgebung, Beitrage zur Enstehung und Entwicklung der Stadt Brandenburg im Mittelalter, 1993.

B. Schubert, Die Familiennamen der Oschatzer Pflege, 1921.

E. Schwarz, Deutsch-slawische Namensbeziehungen von der Ostsee bis zur Adria, Studia Onomastica Monacensis 2, 1960.

W. Seibickie, Schichten slawischer Vornamen im Deutschen, OsG 19, 1990

B. Sicinski, Nazwiska niemieckie pochodzenia slowianskiego z formantem -k- na obszarze Brandenburgii i Pomorza Zachodniego w XV-XVI wieku, OsG 6, 1971.

Z. Steiber, Die slawischen Namen in der Chronik Thietmars von Merseburg, OsG 3, 1967.

H. Strobe, Toponymische Studien zum Erzegebirge und seinem Vorland, 1974.

R. Trautmann, Die altpreussischen personennamen, 1925.

J. Udolph, Das Dravanopolabische as namenkundlicher sich, Wendland und Altmark in historischer und sprachwisschatlicher Sicht, 1992.

H. Walther, Slawische Namen im Erzgebirge in ihrer Bedeutung fur die Siedlungsgeschichte, BuF 11, 1960.

S. Wauer, Zur Erschliessung des in brandenburgischen Namen enthaltenen Wortschatzes, OsG 21, 1994.

W. Wenzel, Die Familiennamen des Amtes Schlieben in ihrer Bedeutung fur die sorbische Sprach- und Siedlungsgeschichte, Sorabitiske Prinoski, 1968.

——Verifizierung und Prazisierung von Ortsnamendeutungen mit Holfe slawischer Familiennamen, OsG 7, 1972.

——Deutsche Lehnworter im Sorbischen in der Funktion von Familiennamen, Beitrage zum deutsch-slawischen Sprachkontakt, 1977.

——Deappellativische sorbisch Personennamen ohne Entsprechungen im niedersorbischen und obersorbischen Wortschatz, OsG 13, 1981.

——Studien zur sorbischen Personennamen, Systematische Darstellung, I, 1987.

——Areale Konstellaionen sorbischer Personennamen und ihre Bedutung fur die Siedlungsgeschichte, Slavistische Studien zum XI InT Slavistenkongress in Bratislava, 1993.

——Personennamengeographie und Personennamenstratigraphie. Dargestalt an sorbischen material, OsG 21, 1994.

T. Witkowski, Slawische Namenforschung im niederdeutschen Sprachgebiet, Niederdeutschen Jb 1966.

——Der Name Potsdam, Bradenburgische Neueste Nachrichten, 1967.

B. Wyderka, Zachodnioslowianskie nazwy miejscowe z formantem -iszcze, OsG 20, 1996.

15. SLAVS IN GERMANIA: MIXED NAMES, NAME INTEGRATION

A. Bruckner, Zur Slawisch-deutschen Namenskunde ZfO 9, 1933.

F. Debus, A. Schmitz, Die slawische-deutschen Mischnamen im ost- und sudholsteinischen Siedlungsgebiet, OsG 19, 1990.

R. E. Fischer, Zur Integration der "Mischnamen", StU 12, 1966.

——Die slawisch-deutschen Mischnamen im altpolabischen Sprachgebiet, NaM 20, 1972.

K. Hengst, Zur Integration slawischer Toponyme ins Deutsche, OsG 13, 1981.

——Integrationsprozess und toponymische Varianten, Namenvarienten bie der Integration slawischer Toponymie ins Deutsche, OsG 15, 1986.

H. Naumann, Die "Mischnamen", Materialen zum Slawischen Onomastischen Atlas, 1964.

M. Reiser, Die slawischen und hybriden Ortsnamen der Kreise Greiz und Zeulenroda, OsG 6, 1971.

E. Sass, Zu sogenannten Mischnamen im slawische-deutschen Beruhrungsgebiet unter besonderer Berucksichtigung des Wendlandes, Deutsch-slawischer Sprachkontakt im Lichte der Ortsnamen, 1993.

G. Schlimpert, Zu den sogenannten Mischnamen in Brandenburg, OsG 19, 1990.

R. Sramek, Die Stellung des onymischen Benennungsmodells in der Namenintegration, OsG 15, 1986.

H. Walther, Zur Typologie der sogenannten "Mischnamen" (onymischen Hybride), NaM 33, 1978.

W. Wenzel, Veranderungen sorbischer Personennamen auf der morphematischen Ebene wahrend und nach ihrer Integration in das deutsche Sprachsystem, OsG 15, 1986.

——Interessante sorbische Personennamen II, OsG 20, 1996.

16. SLAVS IN GERMANIA: SERBS

R. Andree, Wendische Wanderstudien. Zur Kunde der Lausitz und der Sorbenwenden, 1874.

H.H. Bielfeldt, Sudostbrandenburgisch Bris "Fischnetz" aus sorb. "mreza", ZtS 7, 1962.

——Sorbische Entlehnungen aus dem Deutschen in der Zeit des frankisch-karolingischen Reiches, SlO 2, 1978.

I. Bily, Zu den altsorbischen Ortsnamen mit den Suffixen -isce, -nik, -ik, OsG 21, 1993.

——Zum Atlas altsorbischer Ortsnamentypen, ZtS 41, 1996.

——Ortsnamen mit dem Suffix -ina im eheml altsorbischen Sprachgebiet, 1997.

K. Blaschke, Die Entwicklung des sorbischen Siedelgebietes in der Oberlaustiz, Siedlung und Verfassung, 1960.

Z. Bohac, Die Matrikel der Zoglinge des "Wendisches Seminars" in Prage 1728-1922, LeT B/13, 1966.

H. Brachmann, Serimunt-Zitice: Rekonstruktion einer frugeschichtlichen Altlandschaft, OsG 12, 1979.

——Historische und kulturelle Beziehungen der Sorben zu Bohmen und Mahren, RaP, 1979.

——Einige Bemerkungen zum Befestigungsbau der sorbischen Stamme, Slovane 6.-10. stoleti, 1980.

—— Zur religion Vorstellungswelt der sorabischen Stamme en Elbe und Saale, Namenkundliche Informationen, Studia Onomastica 5, 1987.

——Der Limes Sorabicus—Geschichte und Wirkung, ZtA 25, 1991.

J. Brankack, J. Knebel, Hrozisca serbskich kmjenov, pomniki nasich prjedownikow, 1958.

——Politisce Entwicklung und Militarische Aktivitat der Sorbischen Stammesgruppe im fruhen Mittelalter, LeT B/28, 1981.

——M. Unger, Politische und kulturelle Entwicklung der slawisch-sorbischen Stamme im Gebiet von Saale-Elbe-Neisse im 6. bis 10. Jh, Sachsische Ht 28, 1982.

W. Coblenz, Bemerkungen zur Slawischen Archaologie der Sorbischen Gaue, RaP, 1979.

——Das Sorbengebiet zur Zeit Liutizenaufstandes, ZtA 18, 1984.

A. Frinta, Slawny C. Peucer bese Serb, LeT A/1, 1952.

D.F. Gandert, Die obersorbischen- niedersorbischen Grenze in der Lausitz auf Grund der Bodenfunde, NiE 22, 1934.

W. Gesemann, "Serbow Dobyca", DwS 6, 1961.

H. Helbig, Die slawische Siedlung im sorbischen Gebiet, Siedlung und Verfassung, 1960.

G. Heyder, Sorbische Studenten an den Universitaten Prag, Leipzig, Halle und Wittenberg im 18 Jh, LeT B/38, 1991.

J. Irmscher, Der sorbische humanist Jan Rak, LeT A/30, 1983.

C. Knauthe, Derer Oberlausitzer Sorbenwenden umstandliche Kirchengeschichte, 1767.

J. Knebel, K problemej staroserbskeho "mesta" Liubusa, LeT B/2, 1956.

S. Korner, Die patronymischen Ortsnamen im Altsorbischen, DsF 31, 1972.

E. Korth, Zur integration der mit dem altsorbischen Suffix -0v und in (-yn) gebildeten Ortsnamen in das deutsche Namensystem, OsG 10, 1976.

R. Kotzschke, Die deutschen Marken im Sorbenland, Festgabe G. Seeliger, 1920.

H. Kuhne, Kaspar Peuker, Leben und Werk eines grossen Gelehrten and der Wittenberger universitat im 16 Jh, LeT B/30, 1983.

——Neues uber die Wendische Predigergesellschaft in Wittenberg, LeT B/30, 1983.

G. Labuda, Serbowie s Czechnach, SsS 5, 1975.

T. Lehr-Splawinski, Z onomastyki Slowian lechickich, Chutizi-Scudici, OnO 4, 1958.

T. Lewicki, Les Litzike de Constantin Porphyrogenitus — genete et les Serbes Blancs dan le nord de la Pologne, RoH 22, 1955-56.

R. Lotzsch, Einheit und Gliederung des Sorbischen, 1965.

C. Lubke, Vethenici und Wettiner, BnF 21, 1986.

H. Ludat, Das Lebuser Stiftregister von 1405. Studien zu den Sozial- und Wirtschaftsverhalnissen im mittleren Oderaum zu Beginn des 15 Jh, 1965.

——Legenden um Jaxa von Kopenick, Slaven und Deutsche im Mittelalter, 1982.

F. Metsk, Zur Frage der ethnischen Bevolkerrungstruktur im Gebiet der ehemaligen Stiftsherrschaft Dobrilugk, WiS, 1961.

——Die brandenburgisch-preussische Sorbenpolitik im Kr. Cottbus vom 16 Jts bis zum Posense Frieden, Veroffentlichungen des Instituts fur Slawistik 25, 1962.

——Die Sorben und die Universitat Wittenberg, WsJ 9, 1962.

——Uber den Hinteren Wendlischen Zirkel des sachsischen Kurkreises, DwS 7, 1962.

——Der Beitrag Abrahem Frencels (1656-1740) zur sorbischen Demographie in de Zeit des Spatfeudalismus, ZtS 8, 1963.

——Der Kurmarkisch-wendische Distrikt. Ein Beitrag zur Geschichte der Territorien Barwalde, Beeskow, Storkow, Teupitz und Zossen, 1965.

——F. Metsk, Zur sorbischen Siedlungs und Namenkunde der Umgegend von Dahme, Orbis scriptus, 1966.

——Die Stellung der Sorben in der territorialen Verwaltungsgliederung des deutschen Feudalismus, Schriftenreihe des Instituts fur sorbische Volksforschung 43, 1968.

——Studien zur Geschichte sorbisch-deutscher Kulturbeziehungen, 1981.

——Viadrina und Sorben, Die Oder-Universitat Frankfurt, 1983.

A. Mietzschke, Zur sorbischen Siedlungs- und Namenkunde der Umgebung von Dahme, Orbis Scriptus, 1966.

W.R. Morfill, Slavonic Literature, 1899.

A. Muka (E. Mucke), Luziskoserbske sydlisca w Cechach, Luzica, 1923.

——Serbske mestnostne mjena a jich woznam, SlO 3/4, 1923-24.

——Die wendischen Ortsnamen der Niederlausitz nach Entsehung und Bedeutung, NiE 17, 1925.

——Serbske lezownostne mjena a jich woznam, SlO 5, 1926.

——Serbske mestnostne mjena a jich woznam, SlO 6, 1927.

——Pucowanja po Serbach, 1957.

——Abhandlungen und Beitrage zur sorbischen Namenkunde, 1984.

A.J. Parczewski, Serbja w Pruskej po licenju luda z leta, CmS 52, 1899.

W. Radig, Die sorbischen Burgen Westsachsens und Ostthuringens, Die Westausbreitung und Wehranlangen der Slawen in Mitteldeutschland, 1940.

H. Rempel, Die Mittelslawische Zeit im Suden der DDR (Sorben). AuF 3,1958.

——Die sorbische Keramik in Thuringen, PzT 37, 1959.

W. Schlesinger, Die deutsche Kirche im Sorbenland und die Kirchenverfassung auf westslawichen Boden, ZoS 1, 1952.

——Die Verfassung der Sorben, Siedlung und Verfassung, 1960.

J. Schultheis, S. Korner, U. Wenzel, Onomastische Beitrage zur altsorbischen Lexikologie, ZtS 17, 1972.

——Die Ortsnamen mit Ne-/Ni- im ehemaligen altsorbischen Sprachgebiet: Ein Beitrag zum Slawischen Onomastischen Atlas, ZtS 37, 1992.

H. Schuster-Sewc, Die sorabistische sprachwissenschraftlichen Forschung, DwS 35, 1990.

——Dor sorbischen volkstumlichen Monatsnamen, ZtS 37, 1992.

J.S.G. Simmons, Slavonic Studies at Oxford, 1844-1899, OsP XIII, 1980.

J. Solta, Geschichte der Sorben, I-IV, 1974-79.

——Sorbische Studenten an den Universitaten Leipzig, Prag und Breslau (Wroclau) 1750-1850, Wegenetz europaisches Geistes II, 1987.

——Wirtschaft, Kultur und Nationalitat: ein Studienbund zur Sorbischen Geschichte, 1990.

W. Sperber, Die Bedeutung des Plurals bei sorbischen Flurnamen, ZtS 3, 1958.

G. Stone, Morfill and the Sorbs, OsP 4, 1971.

——Die katholischen Sorben und die Anfange ihrer Schriftsprache, Deutsch, Slawen und Balten, 1986.

J. Strzelczyk, Legenda o slowianskim-pochodzeniu rodu Wiprechta z Grojca, Slowianie w dziejach Europe, 1974.

E. Tschernik, Die Entwicklung der sorbischen Bevolkerung von 1832 bis 1945, 1954.

L.A. Tyszkiewicz, Podzialy plemienne i problem jednosci Slowian serboluzyckich, Slowianszczyzna polabska miedzy Niemcami a Polska, 1989.

H. J. Vogt, Zur Kenntnis der materiellen Kultur der Sorben im Elster-Pleisse-Gebiet, ZtA 2, 1968.

T. Voigt, Neue fruhsorbische Brandgraben und Siedlungsreste aus dem Elb-Saalegebiet, NdV 18, 1942.

H. Walther, Zur Wirtschaft der Altsorben im Bereiche der Altsiedel-Landschaft Daleminze, Regionalgeschichte und Namenkunde, 1970.

T. Wasilewski, L'origine d'Emnilda troisieme femme de Boleslas le Vaillant et la genese de la souverainete polonaise sur la Moravie, ApH 61, 1990.

W. Wenzel, Die sorbische-deutschen siedlungsverhaltnisse zwischen mittlerer Elbe und oberer Spree im spiregel der Personnennamen,

ZtS 39, 1985.

——Studien zu Sorbischen Personennamen, I-II, 1987-92.

——Sorbische anthroponymische Lexik in sprachgeographischer Sicht, NaM 58, 1990.

C. Widajewicz, Serbowie nadlabscy, 1948.

W. Zeil, Bolzano und die Sorben. Ein Beitrag zur Geschichte des "Wendischen Seminars" in Prag zur Zeit der josefinischen Aufklarung und der Romantik, 1967.

17. SLAVS IN GERMANIA: SERB PROVINCES, SERB BORDERLANDS

L. Bonhoff, Der Gau Nisan in politischer und kirchlicher Beziehung, SaC 36, 1915.

——Chutizi Orientalis, SaC 31, 1919.

H. Brachmann, Cositz-Kesiegesburch. Zur Geschichte der Hauptburg des sorbischen Stammes der Colodici, Symbolae Praehistoricae, 1975.

——Serimunt-Ziticem, OsG 12, 1979.

W. Coblenz, Zu den slawischen Wallanlagen des Gaues Nisan, Fruhe Burgen und Stadte, 1954.

——Slawen und Deutsche im Gau Daleminzien, AuS 1962.

——Bemerkungen zur Chronologie in den slawischen Gauen Daleminzen und Nisan, PoL 16, 1971.

——Bemerkungen zum Slawengau Nisane, Archaologie als Geschichtwissenschaft. Studien und Untersuchungen, 1977.

——Archaologische Betrachtungen zur Gana-Frage im Rahmen der alterslawischen Besiedlung des Gaues Daleminzien, Beitrage zur Archivwissenschaft und Geschichtforschung, 1977.

P. Grunitz, Siedlungsweise und- verhaltnisse beim sorbischen Stamm der Selpoli, Gubener Hk 1975-76.

R. Holtzmann, Der Slavengau Chutizi und der Ort Schkeuditz. Zur Geschichte und Kultur des Elbe-Saale-Raumen, 1939.

J. Huth, Versuch einer siedlungs- und landschafsgeschichtlichen Deutung possessivisch gebildeter Ortsnamen in dan Stammesgebieten der Milzener, Daleminzer, Lusizer and Nisane, LeT B/28, 1981.

G. Labuda, O nazwie plemieneia Glomacze, Studia linguistica slavica baltica, 1966.

T. Lehr-Splawinski, Z onomastyki Slowian lechichkich. Chutizi-Scudici, OnO 4, 1958.

E. Muller, Die Ausdehnung des Gaues Chutizi und seine spatere Entwicklung, Leipziger Studien, 1957.

H. Naumann, Serimunth-Sermuth. Ein Beitrag zur Namenkunde, WiS 5, 1961.

W. Radig, Der Burgberg Meissen und der Slavengau Daleminzien, Fuhrer zur Urgeshichte, 1929.

H. Schall, Der Sorbengau Plisni als Siedlungseinheit und Sprachedenkmal, ZtS 3, 1958.

E. Schwarz, Daleminze und Lommatzsch, ZoS 18, 1965.

J. Strzelczyk, Slowianie na poludnicwyn Pogorzu Harzu i na Zlotej Niwie, PrZ 65, 1974.

——Slowianie kolo Erfurtu, SlA 23, 1976.

——Turyngia-Slowianie w Turyngii, SsS 6, 1977.

Z. Sulowski, Bethenici et Smeldingon, Studia Historica...H. Lowmianskiego, 1958.

——Brezanie, SsS 1, 1961.

W. Wenzel, Die Familiennamen des Amtes Schlieben [Zliuvini] in ihrer Bedeutung fur die sorbische-Sprach- und Siedlungsgeschichte,

J. Zernack, Kopenick und das Land Zpriuuani in voraskanischer Zeit, JbG 9/10, 1961.

18. SLAVS IN GERMANIA: SERB LANGUAGE

M. Bathe, R.E. Fischer, G. Schlimpert, Zur sorbisch-polabischen Sprachgrenze zwischen Elbe und Spree, Beitrage zum Slawischen Onotmastischen Atlas, 1970.

H. Fasske, Vuk Karadzic und Handrij Zejler: Parallelism in ihren Sprachausffassungen, ZtS 33, 1988.

A. Frinta, Lexikalni a jine shody jazyku srbskochrvatskeho a luzickoserbskeho, Zbornik za filologiju i lingvistiku, 1957.

P. Ivic, Znacaj lingvisticke geografije za uporedno i istorisko proucavanje juznoslovenskih jezika i njihovog odnosa prema ostalim slovenskim jezicima, FiL 22, 1958.

J. Koblischke, Altsorbisches und Drawehnnisches, Slavia 2, 1923.

F. Metsk, Verschiebungen der deutsch-sorbischen Sprachgenze in den meissnischen Amtern Grossenhain und Muhlberg von 1500 bis zum Erloschen der sorbische Sprache, DwS 2, 1960.

E. Mucke (A. Muka), Die Grenzen des sorbischen Sprachgebietes in alter Zeit, ArC 26, 1904.

——Die Grenzen des sorbischen Sprachgebietes in alter Zeit, ArC 26, 1904.

C. T. Pfuhl, Luziski - Serbski slownik, 1866.

H. Popowska-Taborska, Dawne pogranicze jezykowe polsko-dolnoluzyckie, 1965.

P. Rezak, Deutsch-sorbisches enzyklopadisches Worterbuch der Oberlausitzer sorbischen Sprache,

D. Rzymmska, Czy dolnoluzicki dialetyzm praslowianski?, Studia z Filologii Polskiej i Slowianskie XXIV, 1987.

H. Schuster-Sewc, Status luzickosrpskog jezika i njegovo mesto u okviru drugih zapadnoslovenskih jezika, Zbornik za filologiju i lingvistiku 12, 1972.

——Das Altsorbische Dialektgebiet und Seine Sprachliche Stellung im Rahmen des Westslavischen, LeT B/19, 1972.

——Mesto serbloluzickog jazyka sredi drugich slavjanskich jazykov, VoP 2, 1976.

——Postoje li jezike veze izmedju srpskohrvatskog i srpskoluzickih jezika VuK 6, 1976.

——Historisch-etymologisches Worterbuch der ober- und niedersorbischen Sprache, 1978-79.

——Zur Bedeutung der sorbischen Lexik fur die slawische historisch-etymologische Wortforschung, ZtS 24, 1979.

——Die Ausgliederung der westslawischen Sprachen aus dem Urslawischen mit besonderer Berucksichtigung des Sorbischen, LeT A/29, 1982.

——Historisch-Etymologisches Worterbuch der ober und niedersorbischen Sprache I-II, 1981-84.

W. Seelman, Die Alte Sorbisch-Lutizische Grenze, ZfO 13, 1937.

J.H. Swetlik, Vocabularium latino-serbicum, 1721.

S. Wauer, Zum Problem der polabisch-sorbischen Grenze in den Kr. Schonebeck und Zerbst, Slavische Namenforschung, 1961.

19. SLAVS IN GERMANIA: LUZICA SERBS

K. Blaschke, Die Entwicklung des sorbischen Siedelgebietes in der Oberlausitz, Siedlung und Verfassung, 1960.

J. Bluthgen, Die Lausitzer Wenden im geographischen und historischen Kraftefeld, FrA 21, 1961.

W. Boelcke, Bauer und Gutsherr in der Oberlausitz, 1957.

B. Budar, Przewodnik: Luzyce, Drezno, Misnia, Saska Szwajcaria, Gory Zytawskie, Spreewald, 1975.

A. Cerny, Luzice a Luzicti Srbove, 1911.

J. David, Luziti Srbove, 1946.

F. Domanski, Luzyce, 1944.

B. Falinska, A. Kowalska, Leksykalne zwiazki jezykow Luzyckich z innymi jezykami slowianskimi, Prace Slawistyczne 99, 1992.

W. Frenzel, Beitrage zur Geschichte der Burg zu Ostro, Bautzener Geschichthefte 5, 1927-28.

—— Vorgeschichte der Lausitzen. Land und Volk, inbesonders die Wenden, Die Lausitzer Wenden, 1932.

O-F. Gandert, Die obersorbisch-niedersorbische Grenze in der Lausitz auf Grund der Bodenfunde, NiE 22, 1934.

K-D. Gansleweit, Untersuchungen zur Namenkunde und Siedlungsgeschichte der nordostlichen Niederlausitz: die Flur und Ortsnamen im Bereich des fruheren Stiftes Neuzelle, 1982.

M. Gruchmanowa, Luzycko-Wieklopolska Izomorfa nom. -acc.-vo. pl. dny, Z polskich studiow slawistycz 5, 1978.

J. Horvat, Luzica in njeni Srbi, 1988.

H. Houben, Die materielle Kultur der Lusizi, 1990.

J. Huth, Die Burgwarde der Oberlausitz, LeT B/27, 1980.

——Die Burgwarde der Oberlausitz, LeT B/28, 1981.

R. Jecht, Die Besitzverhaltnisse und die Besitzer der Oberlausitz von 1067-1158, MaG 97, 1921.

——Die Geschichte der Stadt Gorlitz, 1922.

J. Kapitan, Srbska Luzice, severozapadni hlidka slovanska, 1945.

M. Kasper, Language and Culture of the Lusatian Serbs throughout their History, 1987.

J. Knebel, Betrachtungen zum landschaftsbild u. zur Herausbildung frugeschichtlicher Sedlungskomplexe in der Oberlausitz, LeT B/12, 1965.

——Bemerkungen zur politischen und sozialekonomischen Stellung der Lusizer und Milzener zur Zeit des Lutizenaufstandes im Jahre 983, ZtA 1994.

W. Kochanski, Dole i niedole Serboluzyczan, 1962.

S. Korner, Ortsnamen mit schwierigen Etymologien in der Niederlausitz, ZtS 30, 1985.

——Ortsnamenbuch der Niederlausitz, 1993.

J. Kudela, Les Sorabes ou Serbes de Lusace, 1985.

W. Lippert, Die Dobrilukschen Klosterdorfer Nussedil und Dobristoh, NiE 6, 1900.

G. Labuda, Pagus Selpuli, SlO 19, 1948.

K.H. Marschallek, Lubben im Spreewald das Alte Liubusa, MaR 1/4, 1956.

M. Mehlow, Lausitzer Studenten die Universitat Halle im 18. Jh, ZoS 42, 1993.

B. Miskiewicz, Les Combats pour la defense des frontieres sur l'Odra et al Nysa Lusacienne aux Xe et XIe Siecles, Revue Internationale de l'historie militaire, 28, 1969.

R. Moderhack, Die Lausitz vom 10. bis zum 12. Jh, Brandenburgisches Jb 4, 1936.

E. Mueller, Das Wendentum in der Niederlausitz, 1922.

J. Nalepa, Biezuncznie, Nazwa i polozenie, PaM 4, 1954.

——Biezunczanie, SsS 1, 1961.

J. Nestupny, Praveke Dejiny Luzice, 1946.

J. Pata, Luzica, 1920.

——Josef Dobrovsky a Luzice, 1929.

J. Petr, Stan badan nad luzyckimi nazwami miejscowymi i osobowymi, OnO IV, 1958.

M. Pohlandt, Selpoli, NiE 16, 1924.

H. Popowska-Taborska, Dawne pogranicze jezykow polsko-dolnolyzyckie, 1965.

F. Redlich, Beitrage zur Siedlungsgeshichte der Niederlausitz in namenkundlicher Sicht, 1983.

M. Rudnicki, Slupa, Sluba, OnO 1, 1955.

G.E. Schrage, Slaven und Deutsche in der Niederlausitz, 1990.

—— Quellen und Historiographie zur Geschichte der Niederlausitz, JbG39, 1990.

C. Schuchhardt, Witzen und Starzeddel, zwei Burgen der Lausitzer Kultur, NiE 18, 1927.

H. Schuster-Sewc, Ortsnamen der Niederlausitz und sorbische Sprachgeschichte, ZtS 39, 1994.

M.I. Semiryaga, Luzhichanye, 1955

H. Sohnel, Die Rundwalle der Niederlausitz, 1886.

G. Stone, The Smallest Slavonic Nation: The Serbs of Lusatia, 1972.

L.A. Tyszkiewicz, Luzyce, Lucyzenie, SsS 3, 1967.

——Zur Prolematik der fruhmittelalterlichen Stammesgebiete und Burgbezirke in der Nieder- und Oberlausitz, Let B/15, 1968.

——Organizajca plemienno-grodowa a panstwowo-grodowa na przykladzie Luzyc i Slaska, Lokalne osrodki wladzy pamstwowej w XI-XII wieku w Europie Srodkowo-Wschodniej, 1993.

M. Vlahovic, Luzici Srbi i njihova domovina, 1930.

M. Zeiller, Topographia Superioris Saxoniae, Thuringiae, Misniae, Lusatiae etc, 1650.

V. Zmeskal, Luzicti Srbove, 1962.

20. SLAVS IN GERMANIA: OBODRITORUM

W.G. Beyer, Die wendischen Schwerine, MgA 32, 1867.

I. Boba, Abodriti qui vulgo Paredenecenti vocantur or "Marvani praedenecenti"?, Palaeobulgarica 8, 1984.

H. Bulin, Pocatky statu obodritskeho, Pravnehistoricke studie 4, 1958.

——Podunajsti "Abodriti", Slovanske historicke studie 3, 1960.

C.C. Burmeister, Uber die Sprache der fruher in Meklenburg wohnenden Obodriten-Wenden, 1840.

P. Donat, Die Mecklenburg—Stammerszentrum und Furstenburg der Obodriten, AuF 21, 1976.

——Die Mecklenburg—eine Hauptburg der Obodriten, 1984.

B. Friedmann, Untersuchungen zur Geschichte des abodritischen Furstentums bis zum Ende des 10. Jh, 1986.

W.H. Fritze, Die Datierung des Geographus Bavarus und die Stammesverfassung der Abodriten, ZtS 21, 1952.

——Probleme der Abodritischen Stammes- und Reichsverfassung und ihrer Entwicklung vom Stammesstaat zum Herrschaftsstaat, Siedlung und Verfassung, 1960.

M. Glaser, Die Slawen in Ostholstein. Studien zu Siedlung, Wirtschaft und Gesellschaft der Wagrier, 1983.

V.D. Koroljuk, Gosudarstva Gostsalka XI v., Slavjanski Sbornik, 1947.

——Gosudarstvo Bodricej i pravlenie knjaza Gotsalka (1031-1066), SlO 22, 1962.

——Gosudarstvo Bodricej v pravlenii knjazja, SlO 22 1962.

G. Labuda, Dynastia obodrzycka, SsS 1, 1961.

——Feudalizam u Slowian polabskich, dynastia obodrycka, SsS 2, 1964.

W. Lammers, Formen der Mission bei sachsen, schweden und Abodriten, Bll f. Dt. Landesgeschichte 106, 1970.

T. Lehr-Splawinski, Obodriti- Obodrzyce, SlO 18, 1947.

G.C. F. Lisch, Das Kloster Alt-Doberan zu Althof und Woizlava, des Obodriten-Konigs Pribislav Gemahlin, MgA 2, 1837.

——Uber die Wendisch Furstenburg Werle, MgA 6, 1841.

F. Lotter, Bemerkungen zur Christianiserung der Abodriten, FsT W. Schlesinger, Vol II, 1974.

J. Machal, O narodni pisni polabskych Bodricuv, SbO 5, 1886.

R. Marciniak, Ustroj polityczny zliaszku obodrychiego do polowy XI wieku, Materialy zachodniopomorske 12, 1966.

E. Mosko, Ubiedrza Obodrowo i Obodryci, JeZ 49, 1969.

J. Otrebski, Oder, Obodriten, Studia linguistica slavica baltica, 1966.

A.J. Parczewski, Wo casu wurmreca Meklenburskich Slowjanow, CmS, 1889.

J. Pfitzner, Zur deutschlandslavischen Siedlungsgeschichte Mecklenburgs und Ostholsteins im Mittealter, Jb fur Kultur und Geschichte der Slaven, 1933.

V. Prochazka, Pad rise Gostaklovy a osduy polabsko-pobaltskych Slovanu, Slovansky prehled 52, 1966.

W. Prummel, Starigard/Oldenburg. Hauptburg der Slawen in Wargrien IV, 1993.

S. Rudnicki, O nazwie Obodriti i innych nazwach, JeZ 50, 1970.

Starigrad/Oldenburg: Hauptburg der Slawen in Wagrien, 1993.

A.N. Salivon, Obodrity, SoV 4, 1981.

K. W. Struve, Die slawischen Burgen in Wagrien, 1959-61.

W. Swoboda, Obodryzce naddunajscy, SsS IV, 1967.

S. Urbanczyk, O pochodzeniu nazy Obodrytow, Studia linguistica Slavica Baltica, 1966.

M. Vasmer, P. Wiepert, Slavische Spuren auf Fehmarn, ZsP 11 1934.

——Die Wagrier, ZsP 11, 1934.

——Der name der Obodriten, ZsP 16, 1939.

——Nochmals der Name Wagrien, ZsP 23, 1954.

V. Vogel, Slawische Funde in Wagrien, 1972.

W. Vogel, Das Emporium Reric, FsT H. Koht, 1933.

R. Wagner, Das Bundniss Karls des Grossen mit den Obodriten, MgA 63, 1898.

R. Werner, Chronik der Stadt Rostock, 1911.

H. Witte, Wendische Bevolkerungsreste in Mecklenburg, Forschungen zur deutschen Landes- und Volkskunde, 1905.

——Slawische Reste in Mecklenburg und and der Niederelbe, Der ostdeutsche Volksboden, 1926.

21. SLAVS IN GERMANIA: LUTICIORUM

P. Beckmann, Die Rethra-Sagen in Mecklenburh, Deutsches Jb fur Volksunde, 5, 1959.

R.G. Beyer, Konig Kruto und sein Geschlecht, MgA 13, 1848.

W. Bruske, Untersuchungen zur Geschichte des Lutizenbundes, 1955.

H. Bulin, Pocatky statu veletskeho, Pravne historicke studie 5, 1959.

——Cesko-Veletske a polsko-veletske vztahy druhe polovine 10. stoleti, Studia z Dziejow Polskich i Czechoslowackich, 1960.

J. Dowiat, Ekspansja Pomorza Zachodniego na Ziemie Wielecko-Obodrzyckie w drugiej polowie XII weku, PrZ 50, 1959.

L. Dralle, Slaven an Havel und Spree: Studien zur Geschichte des hevellisch-wilzischen Furstentums (6. bis 10. Jt), 1981.

H. Dralle, Wilzen, Sachsen und Franken um das Jahr 800, Aspekte der Nationenbildung im Mittelalter, 1978.

W. Filipowiak, Das wilzisch-pommersche und polnische Grenzgebiet im 10. und 11. Jh, ZtA 18, 1984.

W.H. Fritze, Beogachtungen zu Entstehung und Wesen des Lutizenbundes, JbG 7, 1958.

L. Gisebrecht, Luitizische Landwehre, BaL 11/2, 1845.

——Die Landwehre der Luitizer und der Pommern auf beiden Seiten der Oder, BaL 11/2, 1845.

K. Grebe, Die Brandenburg (Havel)—Stammezentrum und Furstenburg der Heveller, AuF 21, 1976.

——Brandenburg, die Haveller und der Lutizenaufstand, Das Altertum 29, 1983.

T. Grudzinski, Stosunki Polsko-Wieleckie w drugiej polowie XI wieku, ZaC 8, 1952.

M. Hellman, Grundzuge der Verfassungsstruktur der Liutizen, Siedlung und Verfassung, 1960.

W. Hornemann, H.D. Schroeder, Die Sitze der Redarier und die Lage Rethra, GsJ 10, 1972-73.

A. Keseburg, Der Wilzenbund und die Prignitz, JbR 24, 1973.

Z. Lasocki, Dolezanie, SlO 17, 1938.

M. Last, Vom Liutizenaufstand zum deutsch-liutizschen Bundnis, ZtA 18, 1994.

L. Leciejewicz, Sepulcra antiquorum w okolicy Dargunia w ziemi Czrzepienskiej, Folia praehistorica Posnaniensia, 1984.

G.C.F. Lisch, Die Stiftung des Klosters Broda und das Land der Redarier, MgA 3, 1838.

——Uber die Lander Bisdede und Tribedne, MgA 12, 1847.

——Uber Chotibanz und Chutun, MgA 23, 1858.

——Urgeschichte des Ortes Malchow, MgA 32, 1867.

H. Ludat, Branibor, Havolanska dynastie a Premyslovci, CcH 17, 1969.

K. Myslinski, Zachodnioslowianskie ksiestwo Stodoran w XII wieku i jego stosunek do Polski, Europa-Slowianszczyzna-Polska, 1970.

J. Nalepa, Wyprawa Frankow na Wieletow s 789 r. SlA 4, 1953.

——Obla, Oblica, Oblicko. Pierwotna nazwa rzeki Havel i jej derywatov, Spraliga Bidrag, 2/9, 1957.

——Doszanie, SsS 1, 1963.

A.N. Salivon, Vilcy-Ljutici, SoV 2, 1983.

R. Schmidt, Rethra. Das Heiligtum der Lutzien als Heiden-Metropole, FsT W. Schlesinger, II, 1974.

V. Schmidt, Der Landsesaubau bein den slawischen Stammen der Wilzen/Lutizen zwischen dem 9. bis 11. Jh, Mensch und Umwelt, 1992.

H.D. Schroeder, W. Hornemann, Die sitze der Redarier und die lage Rethras, GsJ 10, 1972-73.

E. Schuldt, Der Landesbau bei den slawischen Stammen der Wilzen/Lutizen zwischen dem 9. bis 11. Jt, Mensch und Umwelt, 1992.

J. Strzelczyk, Rewizja dziejow Wieletow-Lucicow?, Studia historica slavo-germanica 11, 1982.

Z. Sulowski, O synteze dziejow Wieletow-Luzicow, RoH 24, 1958.

——Geneza i upadek panstwa Wieletow-Lusicow, KwA 70, 1963.

J. Widajewicz, Weleci, Instytut Slaski 2, 1946.

T. Witkowski, Der Name der Redarier und ihres zentralen Heiligtums, ZtS 13, 1968.

Z. Wojciechowski, Poczatki chrzesijanstwa w Polsce na tle stosunkow niemecko-wieleckich, Zycie i Misli 3/4, 1950.

22. SLAVS IN GERMANIA: RUGIANORUM

H. Batowski, Przyczynski do narzecza lechichko-rugijskiego, SlO VI, 1926.

J. Bilek, H. Schall, Slavische Siedlungstatigkeit im 14. Jh auf Rugen im Spiegel der Ortsnamen, ZtS 4, 1959.

H. Berlekamp, Die Funde aus den Grabungen im Burgwall von Arkona, ZtA 8, 1974.

L. Ellis, Reinterpretations of the West Slavic cult site in Arkona, InD 6, 1978.

C.G. Fabricius, Urkunden zur Geschichte des Furstenthums Rugen unter dem eingeborenen Fursten, 1841.

W.H. Fritze, Beda uber die Ostseeslaven, ZtS 21, 1952.

——Bedas Ryugini und Willibrords Danenmission, ZtS 32, 1965.

A. Haas, Die Insel Hiddensee, 1896.

——Die Granitz auf Rugen, BaL 20, 1917.

——Slawische Kultstaetten aud der Inseln Ruegen, PjB 19, 1918.

——Arkona in Jahre 1146, 1925.

P. Herfert, Slawische Schalengeffase von der Insel Rugen, GsJ 4, 1964.

——Slawische Hugelgraben mit Steinsezrung von der Insel Rugen, Kr. Putlitz, AuF 10, 1965.

——Die fruhmittelalterliche Grosssiedlung mit Hugelgraberfeld in Ralswiek, Kr. Rugen, AuF 12, 1967.

——Ralswiek-einfruhgeschichtlicher Seehandelspatz auf der Insel Rugen, GsJ 10, 1972-73.

G. Jakob, Das wendische Rugen in seinen Ortsnamen dargestellt, BaL 44, 1894.

P. Jakovenko, Selskoe naselenie v rujanskom kjnazestve vo vremja paravlenija mestnych knjazej, ZmN 1910.

K.A. Jenc, Rhetra a Radegast, Luzican 1, 1864.

W. Karbe, Arkona-Rethra-Vineta, ZtS 2, 1925.

M. Klinge, The Baltic World, 1994.

J. Knebel, Arkona, PrA 1970.

J.G.L. Kosegarten, Arabische Munzen auf der Insel Rugen, BaL 19, 1861.

T. Lehr-Splawinski, Szcatki jezyka dawnych slowianskich mieszkancow wyspy Rugji, SlO 2, 1922.

J. Matuszewski, Studia nad prawem rugijskim, 1947.

T. Milewski, Pierwotne nazwy wyspy Rugji i slowianskich jej mieszkancow, SlO 9, 1930.

H.H. Muller, Die Tierreste aus der slawischen Burganlage von Arkona au der Insel Rugen, ZtA 8, 1974.

——Tieropfer fuer Swantewit in der slawischen Tempelburg von Arkona auf Ruegen, Alterturm 22, 1976.

L. Niederle, Arkona, Rhetra, Redigast, Slavia 2, 1923-24.

J. Osieglowski, Poczatki slowianskiej Rugii do r. 1168, Materialy zachodnio-pomorskie 13, 1967.

——Slowianska Rugia w historiografii, Materialy zachodnio-pomorskie 15, 1969.

——Wyspa slowianskich bogov, 1971.

——Polityka zewnetrzna ksiestwa Rugii (1168-1328), 1975.

W. Petzsch, Rugens Burgwalle und die slawische Kultur der Insel, 1927.

H. Schall, Slavische Siedlungsstatigkeit im 14. Jh auf Rugen im Spiegel der Ortsnamen, ZtS 4, 1959.

H.D. Schroeder, Kampfe um Rugen in Mittelalter, GsJ 8, 1968-69.

W. Steinhauser, Rugen und die Rugier, ZsP 16, 1939.

M. Vasmer, Zur Orts- und Flussnamenforschung: Arkona, ZsP 19, 1944-47.

D. Warnke, Slawische Bestattungsstetten auf der Insel Rugen, ZtA 10, 1979.

23. SLAVS IN GERMANIA: POLABORUM, WENDORUM

R. Belz, Wendisch Alterthumer, MgA 58, 1983.

J. Brankack, Betrachtungen zur politischen Geschichte der elb-slawischen Stammesverbande im 9. Jh, L'Europe, 1968.

C.C. Buelow, Ueber die wendischen Schwerine, Mecklenburgische Jb 34 (1869).

H. Bulin, Povstani polabskych Slovanu na sklonku 10. stoleti, Slovanske historicke studie 2. 1957

——Nemecky prinos k dejinam Polabskych Slovanu, VpS 2, 1958.

——Safarik a polabske Slovanstvo, Casopis pro slovanskou filologii, 1961.

——Polsky prinos k dejinam Polabskych Slovanu, VpS 4, 1962

D. Cyzevski, Zwei polabische Texte, ZsP 17, 1941.

A. Fischer, Etnografja Slowianska. Zeszyt !: Polabianie, 1932.

R.E. Fischer, T. Witkowski, Zur Geographie altpolabischer Namentypen I, ZtS 12, 1967.

——T. Witkowski, Zur Geographie altpolabischer Namentypen II, Atlas onomastyzny Slowianszczyny, 1972.

L. Giesebrecht, Wendische Geschichten aus den Jahren 780-1182, 1843.

K. Godlowski, Problem chronologii poczatkow osadnictwa slowianskiego na ziemiach polabskich w swietle archeologii, Slowianszczyzna polabska, 1981.

P. Graff, Wendische Spuren im Knesebecker Lande, Niedersachsen, 1908-09.

M. Hamann, Mecklenburg zur Wendenzeit — im Lichte der neueren Forschung, Carolinum, 1970.

J. Hamm, Draeveno-Polabica. International Journal of Slavic Linguistics and Poetics XIII, 1970.

R. Kiersnowski, Kilka uwag o zanleziskach monet wczesnosredniowiecznych z Polabia, SlA 8, 1961.

——Wczesnosredniowieczne skarby srebrne z Polabia, 1964.

A. Krantz, Wandalia oder: Beschreibung Wendischer Geschichte, 1600.

Z. Kurnatowska, Glowne kierunki rozwoju osadnictwa i kultury Slowian polabskich, Sloiwanszczyzna polabska midezy Niemcami a Polska, 1981.

G. Labuda, Powstania Slowian polabskich u schylku X wieku, SlO 18, 1947.

L. Leciejewicz, Miasta Slowian polnocnopolabskich, 1968.

T. Lehr-Splawinski, Gramtyka polabska, 1929.

——— T. Polanski, Slownik Etymogiczny Jezyka Drzewian Polabskich, 1962.

E. Linnenkohl, Die Wend und die "Slawen" gennanten Volker, 1993.

H. Lowmianski, Geneza politeizmu polabskiego, PrZ 69, 1978.

J. Marvan, Polabstina na prahu novych cest, Slavia 66, 1997.

A.J. Pavinski, Polabskie Slavjane, 1871.

K. Polanski, J.A. Sehnert, Polabian-English Dictionary, 1967.

J. Posvar, Pocatky mince u polabskych a pobaltyskych Slovanu, VpS 5, 1964.

V. Prochazka, K otazce vzniku statu u polabskych i pobaltyskych Slovanu, Pravnehistoricke studie 3, 1957.

——Organisace kultu a kmenove zrizeni polabsko-pobaltskych Slovanu, VpS 2, 1958.

——Politicke zrizeni polabsko-pobaltskych Slovana, VpS 3, 1960.

——Politicki zrizeni polabsko-pobaltyskych Slovanu u zaverecnem udobi rodove spolecnosti, SlO 22, 1962.

——Vlastnictvi pudy u polabsko-pobaltskych Slovanu, VpS 4, 1963.

——Die Stammesverfassung der Elbslawen, ZtA 3, 1969.

L. Quandt, Herkunft der baltischen Wenden, BaL 24, 1872.

H. Sauer, Hansestadte und Landesfursten: Die Wendisch Hansestadte in der Auseinandersetzung mit den Furstenhausen Oldenburg und Mecklenburg wahren der zweiten halftes des 15. Jh, 1971.

G. Schlimpert, Altpolabische-sudslawische Entspreuchungen im Namenmaterial zwischen Elbe und Oder, ZtA 33, 1988.

E. Schwarz, Wendeim beim Landesausbau in Deutschland, ZoS 7, 1958.

L. Steinberger, Wandalen = Wenden. AsP 37, 1918/20.

W. Steller, Name und Begriff der Wenden (Sclavi), 1959.

G. Stimming, Die wendische Zeit in der Markj Brandenbur und ihrer Umgebung, Mannus 7, 1955.

J. Strzelczyk, Po tamtej stronie Odry; dzieje i upadek slowian polabskich, 1968.

——Slowianszczyzna Polabska miedzy Niemcami a Polska, 1980.

B. Szydlowska-Ceglowa, Materialna kultura ludowa Drzewian Polabskich w Swietle Poszukiwan Slownikowych, Lud 48, 1963.

T. Trebaczkiewicz-Oziemka, Role kaplanov poganskich v syciu plemiom polabskich, Na granicah archeologii, 1968.

N. Trubetzkoy, Polabische Studien, 1929.

H-J, Vogel, Der Verleib der wendischen Bevolkerung in der Mark Brandenburg, 1960.

R. Wagner, Die Wendenzeit, 1899.

H. Wesche, "Wendisches" im Wendland, Slawisch-deutsche Wechselbeziehungen in Sprache, Literatur und Kultur, 1969.

J. Widajewicz, Niemcy wobec Slowian polabskich, 1946.

T. Witkowski, Mythologisch motivierte altpolabische Ortsnamen, ZtS 15, 1970.

H. Witte, Wendische Bevolkerungreste in Mecklenburg, Forschungen zur deutschen Landes und Volkskunde, 1905.

F. Wrede, Uber die Sprache der Wandalen, 1886.

E. Ziehen, Geschichte und Bilder aus dem wendischen Volksleben, 1874.

24. SLAVS IN GERMANIA: HANOVER WENDLAND

D. Brosius, Wendlandische Regesten, Schriftenreihe des heimatkundlichen Arbeitskreises Luchow-Dannanberg 7, 1988.

A. Bruckner, Dravenisches, ZsP 7, 1930.

L. Buckmann, Orts und Flurnamen, Luneburger Hb 2, 1914.

J. Dobrowsky, Uber die slawische Sprache, sonder uber id Luneburgischen, Slovanka 1, 1814.

J.G. Domeier, Von dem Wendischen Pago Drawan gennant, 1752.

O. Felsberg, Das Havelland zur Wendenzeit, Jahresbericht d. Hist Vereins zu Brandenburg 32/33, 1901.

D, Gebhardt, W. Schulz, Johann Parum Schultze (1677-1740), ein wendlandischer Bauer und Chronist, 1978.

——Polabische nachlese IV: Parum Schultzes Glossar, FsT H. Kunstmann, 1988.

L. Giesebrecht, Wendischen Geschichte aus den Jahren 780 bis 1182, 1843.

R. Grenz, Die slawischen Funde aus dem hannoverschen Wendland, Gottingen Schriften zur Vor- und Fruhgeschichte, 1961.

K. Hennings, Das hannoversche Wendland, 1862.

——Sagen und Erzahlungen aus dem hannoverschen Wendlande, 1864.

A.G. Hilferding, Die sprachlichen Denkmaler der Drevjaner und Glinianer Elb-slawen im Luneburger Wendlande, 1857.

J.P. Jordan, Die Slaven in Luneburgischen, 1845.

W. Kaestner, Zum Alter der slawischen Siedlung im Wendland, Hannoversches Wendland 7, 1978/79.

E. Kaiser, Bildungstypen slavischer Ortsnamen im Hannoverschen Wendland, Slavistischen Studien zum 6. InT Slavistenkongress in Prag, 1968.

J. Koblischke, Drawano-Polalbisches, AsP 28, 1906

O. Koch, Das Hannoversche Wendland oder der Gau Drawehn, 1898.

E. Kohring, Chronik der Stadt Luchow, 1949.

E. Kuck, Zur Volkssprache des Luneburger Landes, Luneburger HmB 2, 1927.

P. Kuhnel, Die slavischen Orts- und Flurnamen im Luneburgischen, 1902-3.

——Slawische Familiennamen in der Stadt Hannover, Hannoverland, 1907.

——Finden sich noch Spuren der Slawen im mittleren und westlichen Hannover, Forschungen zur Geschichte Nierdersaschsens 1, 1907.

——Interessante slawische Sprachuberreste im hannoverschen Wendlande, Hannoverland, 1909.

T. Lehr-Splawinski, K. Polanski, Slownik etymologiczny jezyka Drzewian polabskich, 1962.

J.B. Maly, Ponemcili Slovane lunebursti a jejich zvlastnosti, CmC, 1857.

E. Mucke, Szczatki jezyka polabskiego Wendow Luneburskich, 1904.

——Slovane ve vojvodstvi Luneburskem, SiP 6, 1904

——Die Luneburger Wenden, Geschichte, Volkstum und Sprache, 1908.

J. Nalepa, Drzewianie, SsS 1, 1961.

R. Olesch, Ein Nachtrag zur Quellenlage des Dravanopolabischen, ZsP 32, 1952.

——Vocabularium von Christian Hennig von Jessen, 1959.

——Juglers Luneburgisch-Wendisches Worterbuch, StF 1 1962.

——Zur Forschungsgeschichte des Dravanopolabischen, ZtS 33, 1966.

——Fontes Lingvae Dravaeno-Polabicae Minores et Chronica Venedica et Chronica Vendica J.P. Schultzii, StF 7, 1967.

——Finis Lingvae Dravaneopolabicae, FsT Friedrich von Zahn, MdF 50/1, 1968.

——Zur Frage der ostfriesischen und dravanopolabischen Vokabulaire, Zetischrift fur Mundartforschung 35, 1968.

——Zur geographischen Verbreitung des Dravanopolabischen, Zur Sprache und Literatur Mitteldeutschlands II, 1971.

——Die mundartliche Gliederung des Dravanopolabischen, WsJ 21, 1975.

——Thesarus Linguae Draveanopolabicae, I-IV, 1983-87.

——Dravenopolabica, I, 1989.

——Cetera Slavica II, 1992.

G. Osten, Slawische Siedlungsspuren im Raum um Uelzen, Bad Bevensen und Luneburg, 1978.

A.J. Parczewski, Potomkowie Slowian v Hannoverskim, Wisla 13, 1899.

W. Pasche, Das Hannoversche Wendland. Beitrage zur Beschreibung der Landkreises Luchow-Dannenberg, 1977.

K. Polanski, T. Lehr-Splawinski, Slownik etymologiczny jezyka Drzewian polabskich, 1962.

——Slownik ethmologiczny jezyka Drzewian-polabskich 2-4, 1973-76.

W. Prange, Siedlungsgeschichte des Landes Lauenburg im Mittelalter, 1960.

W. Ribbe, Das Havelland im Mittelalter, 1987.

P. Rost, Die Sprachreste der Dravano-Polaben im Hannoverschen, 1907.

W. Schulz, Name, Gebiet und Gliederung des Hannoverschen Wendlandes, Luneburger Blatter 18, 1967.

——Der Drawehn, eine historische und naturliche Landschaft, Jahreshefte Hk 1969.

J.H. Schulze, Etwas uber den Bezirk und namen des wendischen Pagus Drawan, Neues Hannoverisches Magazin, 1795.

G. Schwantes, Zur Urgeschichte der Slawen in hannoverschen Wendlande, Luneburger Hb 2, 1914.

J. Schwebe, Volksgalube und Volksbrauch im Hannoverschen Wendland, 1960.

E.W. Selmer, Sprachstudien im Luneburger Wendland, 1918.

—— Zur Mundart des Luneburger Wendlandes, Nieder-deutsches Jb, 1924.

H. Steinvorth, Das Hannoverschen Wendland, Deutsch Geographisch Blatter, 1886.

J. Strzelczyk, Drzewianie polabscy, SlA 15, 1968.

——Z nowszych badan nad dziejmai Drzewian polabskich i haonowerskiego Wendlandu. Studia historica slavo-germanica 5, 1976.

B. Szydlowski-Ceglowa, Materialna kultura ludowa Drzewian polabskich w swietel poszukiwan slownikowych, Lud 48, 1962.

——Das Dravanopolabische des 17. und 18. Jh als Zeugnis eines untergehenden Slawenstammes, ZtS 32, 1987.

F. Tetzner, Die Polaben im hannoverschen Wendland, Globus 77, 1900

——Die Drawehner im hannoverschen Wendlande um das Jahr 1700, Globus 81, 1902.

B. Wachter, Die unverzierte slawische Keramik aus dem hannoverschen Wendland, Neue Augrabungen und Forschungen in Niedersachsen 4, 1960.

——Stadtkernuntersuchungen in Dannenberg (Elbe), Die Kunde 20, 1962.

——Die wirtschaflichen und politischen Verhalnisse des 10. Jh im Hannoverschen Wendland und angrenzenden Gebieten, ZtA 18, 1984.

——Hannoversches Wendland, 1986.

——Zur politischen Organisation der Wendlandsichen Slawen vom 8. bis 12. Jh Hammaburg, FsT fur W. Hubener, 1989.

W. Wedemeyer, Die Chronike des Bauern J.P. Schulze, Hannoverland 8, 1914.

H. Wesche, "Wendisches" im Wendland, in Slawische-deutsche Wechselbeziehungen, Sprache, Literatur und Kultur, 1969.

S.A. Wolf, Uber die "Gaue" des hannoverschen Wendlandes, ZtG 4, 1956.

25. SLAVS IN GERMANIA: WEST, NORTHWEST, BALTIC SLAVS

J. Brankack, Studien zur Wirtschaft und Sozialstruktur der Westslawen zwischen Elbe, Saale un Oder aus der Zeit vom 9. bis zum 12. Jh, 1964.

R. Ernst, Die Nordwestslaven und das frankische Reich, 1976.

A. Gilferding, Istorija baltijskich Slavjan, 1855.

F. Graus, Die Nationenbildung der Westslawen in Mittelalter, 1980.

W. Hensel, Anfange der Stadte bei den Ost- und Westslawen, 1967.

A. Hilferding, Borba slavjan i nemcami na Baltijskom pomore v sredne veka, 1861.

V.D. Koroljuk, Zapadnye slavjane i Kievskaja Rus v X-XI vv, 1964.

R. Kotzschke, Zur Sozialgeschichte der Westslawen, Beobachtungen aus dem Mittelgebiet, JbK 8, 1932.

W. Kowalenko, Staroslowianskie Grody Portowe na Baltyku, ZaC 6, 1950.

S. Kozierowski, Altz Nazw Geograficznych Slowianszczyzny Zachodnie, 1934.

I.A. Lebedev, Poslednjaja borba baltijskich slavjan protiv onemecenija, 1876.

L. Leciejewicz, Grod i Podgrodzie u Slowian Zachodnich, Poczatki Zamkow w Polsce, 1978.

——Die Differenzirungs- und Integrationprozesse in der westslawischen Kultur zur Zeit der Staatsbildung, LeT B/26, 1979.

——Slowianie Zachodni, 1989

J. Legowski, Die Sprache der baltischen Slawen.

W. Losinski, W sprawie genezy osiedli sczesnomiejskich u Slowian nadbaltyckich, SlA 35, 1995.

J. Nalepa, Powstanie i Rozpad jednosci Jezykowej Slowian Polnocno-Zachodnich, Opuscula Slavica, 1971.

H. Pieradzka, Walki Slowian na Baltyku w X-XI wieku, 1953.

E. Schuldt, Der Holzbau bein den nordwestslawischen Stammen vom 8. bis 12. Jh, 1988.

K. Slaski, Uzdial slowian w zyciu gospodarczym Baltyku na poczatku epoiki feudalnej (VII-XII w.), PaM 4, 1954.

——Slowianie zachodni na Balltyku w VII-XIII wieku, 1969.

J. Strzelczyk, Z nowszych badan nad dziejami Drzewian Polabskich i Hannoverskiego Wendlandu, Studia Historia Slavo-Germanica 5, 1976.

Z. Sulowski, Slowianskie organizajce polityczne nad Baltykiem, RoH 26, 1960.

K. Tymienecki, Podgrodzia w Polnocno-Zachodniej Slowianszczynie i Pierwsze Lokajce miast na Prawie Niemieckim, SlO 2, 1922.

K. Wachowski, Slowianszczyzna zachodnia, 1950.

K. Zernack, Die burgstadtischen Volksversammlungen bie den Ost- und Westslaven. 1967.

26. VOLIN, STETIN

H. Chlopocka, Poczatki Szczecina, RoC 17, 1948.

E. Cnotliwy, L. Leciejewicz, L. Losinski, Szczezin we wczesnym sredniowieczu, 1983.

——W. Losinski, Szczecin/Stettin. Vom fruhstadtischen Zentrum zur Lokationsstadt, SlA 36, 1995.

W. Filipowiak, Wolin - najwieksze miasto Slowianszczyzny zachodniej, Szkice z dziejow Pomorza, 1958.

——Wolinianie, 1962.

——Die Kulturproblematik in Wolin, Vor- und Fruhformen 2, 1974.

——Die Entwicklung der Stadt Wolin vom 9. bis zum 12. Jh, Rapports 1, 1979.

——H. Grundlach, Wolin, Vineta. Die tataschliche Legende vom Untergang und Aufstieg der Stadt, 1992.

O. Kunkel, K.A. Wilde, Jumne, "Vineta", Jomsburg, Wollin, 1941.

R. Kiersnowski, Kamien i Wolin, PrZ 1, 1945.

——Legenda Winety, 1950.

T. Lehr-Splawinski, O nazwie pomorskiego grodu Wolin-Julin ny wyjsicu Odry, Rocznik Gdanski, 7-8, 1935.

R. Rogosz, Zaplecze osadmiocze wczesnosredniowiecznego Szczecina, SlA 33, 1993.

E. Rzeteslka-Feleszko, Dawne slowianskie nazwy miejscowe Pomorz Szczecinskiego, 1991.

27. SLAVS IN GERMANIA/POLONIA: POMORANORUM

E. Bahr, Pommersch Geschichte in Polnischer Sicht, ZoF 11, 1962.

H. Bollnow, Studien zur Geschichte der pommerschen Burgen und Stadte im 12. und 12. Jh, 1969.

J. Dowiat, Ewolucja panstwa wczesnofeudalnego na Pomorzu zachodnim, PrZ 47, 1956.

J. Duma, E. Rzetelska-Felszko, Dawne slowianskie nazwy miejscowe Pomorza srodkowego, 1985.

O. Eggert, Wendische Kampfe in Pommern und Mecklenburg, BaL 29, 1927.

—— Die Wendenkreuzzuge Waldemars I und Knuts VI von Danemark nach Pommern und Mecklenburg, BaL 29, 1927.

——Danische-wendische Kampfe in Pommern und Mecklenburg (1157-1200), BaL 30, 1928.

W. Filipowiak, Najstarszy trakt Pomorza, Munera archeologica Iosepho Kostrzewski, 1963.

——Slawische Kultstatten Westpommerns im Lichte archaologisch-toponomastischer Untersuchungen, Das heidnische und christliche Slaventum I, 1969.

——Z badan nad wczesnosredniowieczna wsia zachodniopomorska, Arch Pol 17, 1972.

A. Hofmeister, Genealogische Untersuchungen zur Geschichte des pommerschen Herzoghauses, 1938.

R. Kiersnowski, Plemiona Pomorza Zachodniego w swietle naj starsych zrodel pisanych, SlA 3, 1951-2.

——W sprawie poczatkow organizacji panstwowej na Pomorzu Zachodnim. KwA 61, 1954.

K.O. Konow, Herzog Bogislaw X, von Pommern und Landgraf Wilhelm I, von Hessen, BaL 73, 1986.

L. Leciejewicz, Poczatiki nadmorskich mieast na Pomorzu Zachodnim, 1962.

——Die Pomoranen und der Piastenstaat im 10.-11. Jh, ZtA 18, 1984.

W. Losinski, Osadnictwo plemienne Pomorza (VI-X wiek), 1982.

L. Quandt, Zur Urgeschichte der Pomoranen, BaL 22, 1868.

K. Slaski, Podzialy terytorialne Pomorza s XII-XIII wieku, 1960.

——Ethnic Changes in Western Pomerania, ApH 7, 1962.

28. GERMANIA SERBS IN TEXAS: SERBIN, TEXAS

R. Biesele, History of the German Settlements in Texas, 1831-61.*

A. Blasig, The Wends of Texas, 1981.*

R.G. Burger, The Burger Family in Australia, 1983.

G. C. Engerrand, The So-Called Wends of Germany and their Colonies in Texas and Australia, 1934.

D.D. Garrett, Giddings Deutsches Volksblatt, 1899-1949; A History of the Newspaper and Print Shop of the Texas Wends, 1998.*

A. Grider, The Wendish Texans, 1982.

Rev. J. Kilian, Baptismal Records of St. Paul Lutheran Church, Serbin, Texas, 1854-1883, 1985.*

L. Moerbe-Caldwell, Texas Wends - The First Half Century, 1961.

G. Nielsen, In Search of a Home, Nineteenth-Century Wendish Immigration, 1989.*

J. Ritterhouse, Wendish Language Printing in Texas, 1962.

H.-D. Sennf, Australia's Forgotten Migrants, 1984.

*All books can be ordered from: Texas Wendish Heritage Museum, Route 2, Box 155, Giddings, TX 78942. Tel: 409-366-2441. Fax: 409-366-2805.